Land Transfer and Finance

Editorial Advisory Board

Little, Brown and Company

Law Book Division

Francis A. Allen
Edson R. Sunderland Professor of Law
University of Michigan

Thomas Ehrlich
Provost and Professor of Law
University of Pennsylvania

Richard A. Epstein
James Parker Hall Professor of Law
University of Chicago

E. Allan Farnsworth
Alfred McCormack Professor of Law
Columbia University

Geoffrey C. Hazard, Jr.
Nathan Baker Professor of Law
Yale University

Bernard Wolfman
Fessenden Professor of Law
Harvard University

EMERITUS

A. James Casner
Austin Wakeman Scott Professor of Law, Emeritus
Harvard University

Clark Byse
Byrne Professor of Administrative Law, Emeritus
Harvard University

Land Transfer and Finance

Cases and Materials

Third Edition

Allan Axelrod
William J. Brennan, Jr. Professor of Law
Rutgers Law School in Newark

Curtis J. Berger
Lawrence A. Wien Professor of Real Estate Law
Columbia University School of Law

Quintin Johnstone
Justus S. Hotchkiss Professor of Law, Emeritus
Yale Law School

Little, Brown and Company
Boston   Toronto

Copyright © 1986 by
Allan Axelrod, Curtis J. Berger, and Quintin Johnstone
All rights reserved. No part of this book may be reproduced in any form or by any electronic or mechanical means including information storage and retrieval systems without permission in writing from the publisher, except by a reviewer who may quote brief passages in a review.

Library of Congress Catalog Card No. 85-81851

ISBN 0-316-06035-6

MV

Published simultaneously in Canada
by Little, Brown & Company (Canada) Limited
Printed in the United States of America

Summary of Contents

Table of Contents   vii
Preface   xxvii
Acknowledgments   xxix

Chapter One	The Professional and the Land Transaction: Brokers and Lawyers	1
Chapter Two	Basic Financing Considerations of the Real Estate Transaction	111
Chapter Three	Basic Tax Considerations of the Real Estate Transaction	351
Chapter Four	The Contract of Sale: Duties and Remedies	437
Chapter Five	Title Protection	637
Chapter Six	Shared Facilities Ownership: Co-ops, Condos, & Homes Associations	931
Chapter Seven	Complex Forms of Land Finance	1029
Appendix A	Glossary of Real Estate Terms	1197
Appendix B	Exclusive Listing Agreement	1205
Appendix C	Contract of Sale	1207
Appendix D	Mortgage Note (Family Home)	1211
Appendix E	Mortgage (Family Home)	1215
Appendix F	Warranty Deed	1224
Appendix G	Settlement Statement	1226
Appendix H	Mortgage Commitment (Construction Loan)	1230
Appendix I	Purchase Agreement (Investment Property)	1235
Appendix J	Mortgage (Investment Property)	1248

Table of Cases   1265
Index   1271

Table of Contents

Preface   xxvii
Acknowledgments   xxix

Chapter One
The Professional and the Land Transaction: Brokers and Lawyers   1

A. Why So Much Litigation?   1
       Friedman, Contract Law in America   2
B. Broker's Duties to Buyer and Seller   5
       Currier, Finding the Broker's Place in the Typical Residential Real Estate Transaction   5
       Stambler and Stein, The Real Estate Broker — Schizophrenia or Conflict of Interest   15
       Federal Trade Commission, FTC Staff Report, The Residential Real Estate Brokerage Industry   17
       Real Estate Listing Service v. Connecticut Real Estate Commission   21
       Notes   27
       Haymes v. Rogers   29
       Notes   33
       Sanders v. Stevens   34
       Zichlin v. Dill   37
       Notes   38
C. Earning the Broker's Commission   38
       Blank v. Borden   38
       Notes   45
       McCue v. Deppert   46
       Notes   48
       Dworak v. Michals   49

				Notes	53
				Mellos v. Silverman	*54*
				Notes	60
				Wilbur Smith and Associates v. National Bank of South Carolina	*61*
D.	The Role of the Lawyer				64
				American Bar Association, Special Committee on Residential Real Estate Transactions, Residential Real Estate Transactions: The Lawyer's Proper Role	65
E.	Occupational Regulation				72
	1.	Regulating Competition			73
		a.	Unauthorized Practice		73
				Cultum v. Heritage House Realtors	*73*
				Notes	82
		b.	Antitrust		84
				Federal Trade Commission, FTC Staff Report, The Residential Real Estate Brokerage Industry	86
	2.	Advertising and Solicitation			87
				Koffler v. Joint Bar Association	*88*
				Notes	95
	3.	Conflict of Interest			95
				In the Matter of Dolan	*96*
				Notes	108

Chapter Two

Basic Financing Considerations of the Real Estate Transaction — 111

A.	The Mortgage Market			111
	1.	Primary and Secondary Markets		112
	2.	Conventional and Insured or Guaranteed Mortgages		112
	3.	Mortgage Lenders		113
		a.	Mutual Savings Banks	113
		b.	Savings and Loan Associations (Building and Loan Associations)	115
		c.	Commercial Banks	116
		d.	Life Insurance Companies	117
		e.	Mortgage Companies (Mortgage Bankers)	117
		f.	Real Estate Investment Trusts (REITs)	118

Table of Contents ix

		4.	Federally Chartered Secondary Market Lenders	121
			a. Federal National Mortgage Association (Fannie Mae)	122
			b. Federal Home Loan Mortgage Corporation (Freddie Mac)	123
			c. Government National Mortgage Association (Ginnie Mae)	124
			(1) The Tandem Programs	125
			(2) GNMA-Guaranteed Mortgage-backed Securities Programs	125
		5.	Redlining	127

                                Duncan, Hood and Neet, Redlining Practices, Racial Resegregation and Urban Decay: Neighborhood Housing Services as a Viable Alternative   127

                                Notes and Questions   128

B. The Credit Quartet   131
    1. Down Payment and the Loan-to-Value Ratio   131
    2. Length of Mortgage   135
        a. Mortgage Prepayment   137

                        Peter Fuller Enterprises, Inc. v. Manchester Savings Bank   *137*

                        Notes and Questions   140

        b. "Due-on" Clauses   143

                        Notes and Questions   145

    3. Rate of Interest   146
        a. Introduction   146
        b. Variable-rate Mortgages   146
        c. Limitations on the Lender's Return   149
            (1) State Usury Laws — Historical Antecedents   149

                        Salin, Usury   149
                        Note   152

            (2) Selected Usury Issues   152
                (a) When Is a Transaction "Usurious"?   152

                        Moran v. Kenai Towing and Salvage, Inc.   *152*

                        Notes and Questions   155

                        Continental Mortgage Investors v. Sailboat Key, Inc.   *156*

                        Notes and Questions   159

                (b) Choice of Laws   161

                        Continental Mortgage Investors v. Sailboat Key, Inc.   *161*

			(c)	Exempt Transactions	166
				(i) The Corporate-borrower Exemption	167
				Feller v. Architects Display Building, Inc.	*167*
				(ii) The Seller-financed Transaction	171
				Mandelino v. Fribourg	*171*
				Notes and Questions	174
			(d)	The Penalties for Usury	175
		(3)	The Financial Institutions Deregulation and Monetary Control Act of 1980		176
				The Financial Institutions Deregulation and Monetary Control Act of 1980	176
				Notes and Questions	178
	4.	Method of Amortization			178
C.	Alternative Mortgage Instruments				181
				Levin and Roberts, Future Forms of Financing — Lending Devices Addressed to Inflation and Tight Money	181
D.	Basic Security Transactions				188
	1.	Forms of Security Devices			188
		a.	The Mortgage		188
		b.	The Trust Deed Mortgage (Deed of Trust)		190
		c.	The Deed Absolute		192
				Cunningham and Tischler, Disguised Real Estate Security Transactions as Mortgages in Substance	192
		d.	The Installment Land Contract		197
				Warren, California Instalment Land Sales Contracts: A Time for Reform	197
				Notes and Questions	202
				Harris and Hines, Installment Land Contracts in Iowa	204
				Mixon, Installment Land Contracts: A Study of Low Income Transactions, with Proposals for Reform and a New Program to Provide Home Ownership in the Inner City	205
				Problem	213
		e.	Miscellaneous Security Devices		214

Table of Contents

2.	Junior (or Secondary) Financing		214
	a. Conventional Second Mortgages		214
		Spellman, A Banker's Tour Through the Second Mortgage Market	214
	b. The Wrap-around Mortgage		219
		Lifton, Practical Real Estate in the 80's: Legal, Tax and Business Strategies	219
		Notes and Questions	221
	c. Risks of a Junior Encumbrancer: The Open-ended Mortgage		226
		Kemp v. Thurmond	*226*
		Notes and Questions	229
3.	Transfers of Encumbered Property		233
	a. Has the Mortgage Been Assumed?		234
		Daugharthy v. Monritt Associates	*234*
		Notes and Questions	239
	b. Mortgage Takeover: The Rights of the Grantor as Against the Grantee		239
	c. Mortgage Takeover: The Rights of the Mortgagee as Against the Assuming Grantee		240
		Osborne, Nelson and Whitman, Real Estate Finance Law	240
		Note	243
		Schneider v. Ferrigno	*243*
		Notes and Questions	245
	d. Mortgage Takeover: Defenses to the Mortgagee's Suit on the Debt		246
	(1) Discharge of Grantor as Surety — Grantor's Defense I		246
		First Federal Savings and Loan Association of Gary v. Arena	*246*
		Notes and Questions	251
	(2) Failure to Exhaust Other Remedies — Grantor's Defense II		252
	(3) Subsequent Change of the Contract of Assumption — Grantee's Defense I		252
	(4) Usury in the Original Transaction — Grantee's Defense II		253
4.	Remedies of Secured Creditors		253
	a. Preforeclosure Rights		253
		Lifton, Real Estate in Trouble: Lender's Remedies Need an Overhaul	253

			(1)	Mortgagee in Possession	256

       (1) Mortgagee in Possession — 256
Myers-Macomber Engineers v. M.L.W. Construction Corp. — 256
Note on Mortgagee in Possession — 259
       (2) Appointment of a Receiver — 259
Wingfoot California Homes Co. v. Valley National Bank of Phoenix — 259
Notes on the Appointment of a Receiver — 261
       (3) Transfer in Lieu of Foreclosure — 262
Harbel Oil v. Steele — 262
Note on "Deed" in Lieu of Mortgage Foreclosure — 264
  b. Foreclosure — 265
       (1) Types of Foreclosure — 266
Prather, Foreclosure of the Security Interest — 266
Lifton, Real Estate in Trouble: Lender's Remedies Need an Overhaul — 268
Notes — 270
       (2) Selected Foreclosure Problems — 271
          (a) Foreclosure Sale Terms and Conditions: Price Adequacy and Chilled Bidding — 271
Manoog v. Miele — 271
Notes on Foreclosure of the Equity of Redemption — 275
          (b) Constitutionality of Power of Sale Procedures — 276
Warren v. Government National Mortgage Assn. — 276
Notes — 281
          (c) Omitted Parties — 282
Springer Corporation v. Kirkeby-Natus — 282
Notes — 285
          (d) Effect of Foreclosure on Tenant's Rights — 286
Conference Center Ltd. v. TRC — 286
Notes — 293
          (e) Risks of a Junior Encumbrancer: Senior Lien Default — 293
          (f) Foreclosure of a Wrap-around Mortgage — 295
J. M. Realty Investment Corp. v. Stern — 295

Table of Contents xiii

c.	Postforeclosure Redemption Rights	296
	(1) Effect of Redemption	297
	First Vermont Bank & Trust Company v. Kalomiris	297
	Notes	298
	(2) Federal Preemption	299
	United States v. Stadium Apartments, Inc.	299
	Notes	314
d.	Deficiency Judgments	316
	New York Real Property Actions Law	316
	Notes	317
	Ross Realty Company v. First Citizens Bank & Trust Company	*319*
	Notes	324
e.	Bankruptcy Considerations	324
	Johnson v. First National Bank of Montevideo, Minnesota	*325*
	Note	333
	Comment, Mortgage Foreclosure as Fraudulent Conveyance: Is Judicial Foreclosure an Answer to the *Durrett* Problem?	334
	Note	339
f.	Some Suggested Changes in Mortgage Lenders' Remedies	340
	Lifton, Real Estate in Trouble: Lender's Remedies Need an Overhaul	340
	Madway and Perlman, A Mortgage Foreclosure Primer: Part III, Proposals for Change	342
g.	Remedies of the Installment Land Contract Vendor	345
	Note, Reforming the Vendor's Remedies for Breach of Installment Land Sale Contracts	345
	Notes on the Recovery of Possession by Self-help	346
	Carlson v. Hamilton	*347*
	Notes on Forefeiture of Equity	349

Chapter Three
Basic Tax Considerations of the Real Estate Transaction   351

A. Classification of Real Property   351
  1. Property Held Solely as a Personal Residence   352
  2. Property Held for the Production of Income (Investment Property)   355
  3. Property Held for Use in a Trade or Business   358
  4. Property Held Primarily for Sale to Customers   360
     Malat v. Riddell   362
     Byram v. Commissioner   364
     Notes and Questions   370
B. Cost Recovery (Depreciation) and Other Investment Incentives   372
  1. ACRS: Cost Recovery for Property Acquired after 1980   373
     a. Eligible Property   373
     b. Cost Recovery Periods   374
     c. Cost Recovery Methods   374
     d. Prorating First and Last Year Allowances   375
     e. Anti-churning Rules   375
  2. Depreciation of Property Acquired Prior to 1981   376
     a. Useful Life   376
     b. Salvage Value   377
     c. Depreciation Methods   377
     d. Component Depreciation   378
  3. Depreciation Recapture   378
     a. Recapture for Realty Placed in Service after 1980   379
     b. Recapture for Realty Placed in Service before 1981   380
  4. Minimum Tax   381
     a. The Add-on Minimum Tax   381
     b. The Alternative Minimum Tax   381
  5. Tax Credits   382
     a. The Investment Tax Credit   382
     b. The Rehabilitation Tax Credit   383
  6. Election to Expense Assets in Lieu of Depreciation   384
C. A First Look at Tax Shelter   385
D. Tax Strategy: How to Postpone Taxes on the Sale of Real Property   388
  1. The Installment Sale   388
     a. Definitions   389
     b. Illustrations   390
     Commissioner v. Stuart   392
     Notes and Questions   396

Table of Contents

	2.	The Deferred Payment Method		397
	3.	Tax-free Exchanges Under Section 1031		398
		a. The Mechanics of Section 1031		399
			Biggs v. Commissioner	*401*
			Notes and Questions	409
			Magneson v. Commissioner	*410*
E.	Original Issue Discount (OID)			417
			Smith, Tax Shelter Topics	417
			Note	432

Chapter Four
The Contract of Sale: Duties and Remedies — 437

A.	The Buyer Fails to Close: Planning for Default or Cleaning Up the Mess			437
	1.	Is There an Enforceable Contract?		437
		a. Financing and Other Conditions		437
			Kovarik v. Vesely	*437*
			Gerruth Realty Co. v. Pire	*442*
			Notes	445
			Indoe v. Dwyer	*448*
			Note	453
		b. The Subordination Agreement		453
			Stenehjem v. Kyn Jin Cho	*454*
			Notes and Questions	466
	2.	Seller's Damages		468
		a. Fixing Damages by Resale		469
		b. Expenses of Resale, of Initial Sale		470
			Royer v. Carter	*470*
		c. The Middleman Seller		471
	3.	Retention of Deposit		472
			Farrand, Conveyancing Contracts	472
			Kraft v. Michael	*474*
			Notes	476
			Freedman v. Rector, Wardens & Vestrymen of St. Mathias Parish	*477*
			Hetland, The California Land Contract	480
			Smith v. Mady	*488*
			Notes and Questions	491
	4.	Rescission		492
		a. Time and the Essence		492

				Kasten Construction Co. v. Maple Ridge Construction Co.	492

                         Kasten Construction Co. v. Maple Ridge Construction Co.   492
                         Doering v. Fields   495
                         Notes on Time and the Essence   498
                         Cohen v. A. F. A. Realty Corp.   501
      b. The Buyer Ties Up the Property   502
                         Rogers Carl Corp. v. Moran   505
    5. Specific Performance   508
                         Centex Homes Corp. v. Boag   508
                         Notes   510
                         Aiken, "Subject to Financing Clauses" in Interim Contracts for Sale of Realty   513
                         Note: Vendor's Lien   516
B. Straws, Speculators, and Sharpies   518
    1. Liability Limitation   518
                         Houtz v. Hellman   *518*
                         Notes to Houtz v. Hellman   521
    2. Overreaching by Buyer   523
                         Storthz v. Arnold   *523*
                         Notes to Storthz v. Arnold   526
                         Bron v. Weintraub   *528*
C. Seller's Obligations   535
    1. Destruction of Premises During the Executory Interval   535
                         Bixby, The Vendor-Vendee Problem: How Do We Slice the Insurance Pie?   535
                         Skelly Oil Co. v. Ashmore   *537*
                         Notes   545
                         Vogel v. Northern Assurance Co.   *547*
                         Notes to Skelly and Vogel   550
                         Bixby, The Vendor-Vendee Problem: How Do We Slice the Insurance Pie?   552
                         Note   553
    2. Boundary Description and the Binding Effect of Writings   553
      a. Boundary Description Methods   555
          (1) Metes and Bounds Descriptions   555
          (2) Description by Fractional Part   556
          (3) Description by Government Survey   557
          (4) Description by Plat Reference   559
          (5) Multiple Description — "Being" Clauses   559
          (6) Plane Coordinates   560
      b. Professionals and Boundary Description   560

Table of Contents

		(1)	The Lawyer	560
		(2)	The Surveyor	561
			Bibliography	561
	c.	Informal Descriptions		562
			Martin v. Seigel	*562*
			Notes	566
	d.	Error and Ambiguity in Metes and Bounds Descriptions		570
			Cribbet, Principles of the Law of Property	572
			Cities Service Oil Co. v. Dunlap	*574*
			Notes	581
	e.	Errors Affecting Many Parcels		583
			Van Deven v. Harvey	*583*
3.	Quality			588
	a.	Introduction: Caveat Emptor		588
			Note: Caveat Emptor as a System of Propositions	588
	b.	Implied Warranty		590
			Richards v. Powercraft Homes, Inc.	*590*
			Notes	594
			G-W-L, Inc. v. Robichaux	*596*
			Notes	600
	c.	Express Warranty		600
			Garriffa v. Taylor	*601*
			P. B. R. Enterprises v. Perren	*604*
			Notes	607
4.	Seller's Title Obligation			608
	a.	Introduction		608
	b.	Marketable Title		612
			Melcer v. Zuck	*612*
			Notes	617
	c.	Title Standards		621
			Simes and Taylor, Model Title Standards	621
			Note	623
	d.	Remedies		624
			Mokar Properties Corp. v. Hall	*624*
			Note	626
			Valley Associates Corp. v. Rogers	*627*
			Notes on Specific Performance with Abatement	629
	e.	The Installment Buyer		630
			Warren, California Instalment Land Sales Contracts	630

				Luette v. Bank of Italy National Trust & Savings Assn.	*631*
				Notes	633

Chapter Five
Title Protection 637

				Note	639
A.	The Recording Acts				639
				Washington Revised Code Annotated	642
				Florida Statutes Annotated	642
				Arkansas Statutes Annotated	643
				Indiana Code Annotated	643
				Notes	643
	1.	Administration			644
				Notes	647
	2.	Protection Provided			650
		a.	Recordable Instruments		650
				Notes	651
		b.	Purchasers and Creditors		652
				Horton v. Kyburz	*652*
				Notes	660
				Osin v. Johnson	*661*
				Notes	666
		c.	Notice from Recording		667
				Kiser v. Clinchfield Coal Corp.	*667*
				Notes	670
				Cross, The Record "Chain of Title Hypocrisy"	673
				Note	679
				Note, The Tract and Grantor-Grantee Indices	680
				Notes	683
		d.	Notice from Other Public Records		686
				Lane and Edson, Land Title Recordation Systems: Legal Constraints and Reforms	687
				Whitehurst v. Abbott	*688*
				Notes	693
				First Federal Savings & Loan Assn. of Miami v. Fisher	*695*
				Notes	698

Table of Contents

			United States v. Union Central Life Insurance Co.	*700*
			Notes	703
		e. Off-record Risks		705
			Miller v. Green	*705*
			Notes	710
			Martinique Realty Co. v. Hull	*711*
			Notes	716
			Hadrup v. Sale	*716*
			Notes	719
	3. Eliminating Title Defects			723
		a. Statutes of Limitations, Adverse Possession, and Curative Acts		724
			Weeks v. Rumbaugh	*724*
			Notes	729
			Dennen v. Searle	*731*
			Notes	734
		b. Suits to Quiet Title		735
			Berry v. Howard	*735*
			American Land Co. v. Zeiss	*741*
			Comment, Enhancing the Marketability of Land: The Suit to Quiet Title	751
			Notes	752
	4. Liability of Title Searchers and Examiners			754
			Williams v. Polgar	*754*
			Notes	762
B. Title Insurance				764
	1. Administration			765
			Zerwick, Creation and Maintenance of a Title Plant	767
			Robinson, The Organization and Operation of Title Plants	768
			Note	772
	2. Protection Provided			773
			American Land Title Association, Loan Policy and Owner's Policy	774
			Note	794
			Smith and Lubell, Real Estate Financing: Protecting the Lender with Title Insurance	794
			Notes	798
			Note, Iowa's Prohibition of Title Insurance — Leadership or Folly?	799

			Sattler v. Philadelphia Title Insurance Co.	803
			Notes	806
			First National Bank & Trust Co. of Port Chester v. New York Title Insurance Co.	807
			Notes	815
			L. Smirlock Realty Corp. v. Title Guarantee Company	816
			Note	823
			Anderson v. Title Insurance Co.	823
			Notes	828
			Jarchow v. Transamerica Title Insurance Company	829
			Notes	843
	3.	Regulation of Title Insurers		845
			Quiner, Title Insurance and the Title Insurance Industry	846
			Notes	848
			Christie, Antitrust Update	850
C.	Reforming the System			851
	1.	Marketable Title Acts		852
			Basye, Trends and Progress— The Marketable Title Acts	853
			The Model Marketable Title Act	858
			Notes	862
			Lane and Edson, Land Title Recordation Systems: Legal Restraints and Reforms	863
			Notes	867
			Wichelman v. Messner	868
			Notes	879
	2.	Torrens Registration		881
		a. Administration		882
			Patton, Evolution of Legislation on Proof of Title to Land	883
			Barnett, Marketable Title Acts—Panacea or Pandemonium	889
			American Land Title Association, The Title Industry: White Papers	891
			Note	897
			Anderson v. Shepard	898
			Notes	902

Table of Contents　　　　　　　　　　　　　　　　　　　　xxi

		b.	Protection Provided	902
			Notes	903
			Eliason v. Wilborn	*904*
			Notes	906
			Lane and Edson, Improving Land Title Registration Systems	909
	3.	Other Reforms and Reform Proposals		911
			Booz, Allen and Hamilton, State-of-the-Art Report	911
			Lane and Edson, Land Title Recordation Systems: Legal Constraints and Reforms	916
			Bruce, An Overview of the Uniform Land Transactions Act and the Uniform Simplification of Land Transfers Act	919
			Notes	923
			Stoppello, Federal Regulation of Home Mortgage Settlement Costs: RESPA and Its Alternatives	924
			Notes	926
			Cotesworth, Mechanized Processing of Title Data	928
			Notes	929

Chapter Six

Shared Facilities Ownership: Co-ops, Condos, & Homes Associations   931

		Problem	932
A.	Choosing a Shared Facilities Arrangement		933
	1.	Introduction to the Stock-cooperative	933
		Berger, Land Ownership and Use	933
	2.	Introduction to the Condominium	934
		Berger, Condominium: Shelter on a Statutory Foundation	934
	3.	Introduction to the Homes Association	939
		Hyatt, Condominium and Home Owner Associations: Formation and Development	939
		Notes and Questions	942

B.	Selected Problems		943
	1. The Cooperative Apartment: Realty, Personalty, or Hybrid?		943
		State Tax Commission v. Shor	*943*
		Notes and Questions	947
	2. Liability in Tort		949
		White v. Cox	*949*
	3. The Delinquent Owner		955
		1915 16th St. Co-Operative Assn. v. Pinkett	*955*
		Notes and Questions	*959*
	4. Restraints on Alienation		960
		Penthouse Properties v. 1158 Fifth Ave., Inc.	*960*
		Chianese v. Culley	*964*
		Notes and Questions	967
	5. Protecting the Consumer		969
	a. Regulating the Offering Statement		969
		Securities Act of 1933 — Release No. 5347	969
		Notes and Questions	973
	b. Reaching the Overreaching Developer		977
		Point East Management Corporation v. Point East One Condominium Corporation	*977*
		Notes and Questions	982
	c. Regulating the Conversion of Rental Units		983
		Comment, The Condominium Conversion Problem: Causes and Solutions	983
		Flynn v. City of Cambridge	*998*
		Notes and Questions	1003
	6. Income Taxation		1004
	a. The Residential Owner		1004
		Notes and Questions	1006
	b. The Central Body		1006
	c. The Converter of Rental Apartments		1009
C.	Time-sharing Ownership		1012
		Vogel, The Tax Consequences of Time-Sharing	1012
		State v. Carriage House Associates	*1017*
		Cal-Am Corp. v. Department of Real Estate	*1019*
		In re Sombrero Reef Club	*1022*

Chapter Seven
Complex Forms of Land Finance   1029

A.	The Shopping Center Development			1029
	1.	Restrictive Covenants		1030
			Note, Restrictive Covenants in Shopping Center Leases	1030
			FTC and Shopping Centers— Dos and Don'ts for Major Tenants	1033
			Notes and Questions	1036
	2.	The Percentage Lease		1037
		a.	Definition of the Percentage Rental Base	1038
			Hempstead Theatre Corp. v. Metropolitan Playhouses	*1038*
			Mutual Life Insurance Co. of New York v. Tailored Woman, Inc.	*1043*
			Notes and Questions	1048
		b.	Percentage Tenant's Duties	1050
			Kauder, Klotz and Venitt v. Rose's Stores	*1050*
B.	The Ground Lease			1055
	1.	Introduction		1055
			Hecht, Long Term Lease Planning and Drafting	1055
			Problem	1057
	2.	Leasehold Revaluation		1058
			Hecht, Long Term Lease Planning and Drafting	1058
			Eltinge and Graziadio Development Co. v. Childs	*1058*
			Plaza Hotel Associates v. Wellington Associates	*1061*
			Notes and Questions	1064
	3.	Taxation of the Leasehold Interest		1066
			Internal Revenue Code of 1954	1067
			Notes and Questions	1068
	4.	The Leasehold Mortgage		1069
			Mark, Leasehold Mortgages— Some Practical Considerations	1069
			American Bar Association, Committee on Leases,	

			Ground Leases and Their Financing	1081

                Thomas, The Mortgaging of Long-Term Leases   1088

                Levitan, Leasehold Mortgage Financing: Reliance on the "New Lease" Provision   1092

    a. Real or Chattel Mortgage?   1098

        Harbel Oil Company v. Steele   *1098*

    b. Some Risks of the Leasehold Mortgage   1098

        Great Southern Aircraft Corp. v. Kraus   *1098*

        Jacob Hoffman Brewing Co. v. Wuttge   *1100*

        Williams v. Safe Deposit & Trust Co.   *1103*

        Ash v. Egar   *1107*

        Dugan v. First National Bank in Witchita   *1110*

        Ethical Consideration   1115

C. New Modes of Capital Assembly   1115

  1. The Sale and Leaseback   1115

    a. The Sale versus Mortgage Issue   1115

        Lifton, Practical Real Estate in the 80's   1115

        Del Cotto, Sale and Leaseback: A Hollow Sound When Tapped?   1117

        Frank Lyon Company v. United States   *1120*

        Notes and Questions   1131

    b. The Sale versus Exchange Issue   1140

        Leslie Co. v. Commissioner   *1141*

        Notes and Questions   1147

    c. The Issue of Genuineness   1149

        Estate of Franklin v. Commissioner   *1149*

        Notes on Sale and Leaseback Variants   1153

  2. The Real Estate Syndication   1155

        Berger, Real Estate Syndication: Property, Promotion, and the Need for Protection   1156

        Syndication Prospectus   1158

        Congressional Budget Office, Real Estate Tax Shelter

Table of Contents xxv

		Subsidies and Direct Subsidy Alternatives	1168
		Notes and Questions	1177
D.	Choice of Entity for Real Estate Ownership		1178
		Madden, Taxation of Real Estate Transactions — An Overview	1178
E.	How to Determine Real Estate Return on Investment		1190
		The Mortgage and Real Estate Executive's Report	1190

Appendix A	Glossary of Real Estate Terms	1197
Appendix B	Exclusive Listing Agreement	1205
Appendix C	Contract of Sale	1207
Appendix D	Mortgage Note (Family Home)	1211
Appendix E	Mortgage (Family Home)	1215
Appendix F	Warranty Deed	1224
Appendix G	Settlement Statement	1226
Appendix H	Mortgage Commitment (Construction Loan)	1230
Appendix I	Purchase Agreement (Investment Property)	1235
Appendix J	Mortgage (Investment Property)	1248

Table of Cases	1265
Index	1271

Preface

The scope and organization of the book reflect our belief that virtually every real estate transaction draws upon the lawyer's knowledge of relevant contract, financing, taxation, and titles doctrine and upon his familiarity with the institutional context of the real estate market. Thus, the book is both doctrinal and institutional—sometimes heavily one, sometimes heavily the other. The sections on finance and title insurance, for example, stress the descriptive, whereas the section on the "contract of sale" reinforces the doctrinal and analytical skills students have been gaining since the first day of law school. We have tried for a balance to suit our own tastes and, we hope, those of other instructors who elect this book.

We have written this book for a nationwide market, fully cognizant, however, of the land law's many local variations. We expect that a teacher may want to key into the text statutes, forms, and even court decisions to illustrate the practice of the community where his students are most likely to work. At the same time, we believe that real estate transactions, like commerce in goods, are undergoing a strong nationalizing influence, and we hope that the book reflects this trend. As an appendix to the book, we have included many sample forms both to indicate their contents and to give the instructor an incentive to work with forms, which can often be extremely effective teaching devices.

In selecting materials for inclusion, we have played down several topics that the lawyer who handles real estate transactions will sometimes face. In failing to deal extensively with racial discrimination or the control of land use, for example, we believed that these topics are usually and usefully handled in other regular courses. In a few other instances, we decided that the topic was educationally unrewarding for an upper-class course.

As with many casebooks, we are certain that more than one way will be found in which to organize and teach the materials inside. Some teachers may want to stress only those sections of the book that most directly concern taxation and financing, to wit: Chapters I, the first half of II, III, VI, and VII, using them as the basis for an advanced course or seminar in real estate transactions. Other teachers may find that their needs are best met by concentrating on the contractual and title aspects of the real estate transaction, giving minimal attention to income taxation and nonresidential financing. For these teachers, Chapters I, II, IV, V, and VI should make a workable package.

April 1986

Acknowledgments

American Bar Association, Committee on Leases, Ground Leases and Their Financing, 4 Real Prop. Prob. and Tr. J. 437-499 (1969). Copyright © 1969 by the American Bar Association. Reprinted by permission of the American Bar Association from Real Property, Probate and Trust Journal, a publication of the Real Property, Probate and Trust Law Section.

American Bar Association, Model Rules of Professional Conduct, Rule 1.7 and Comment (1984). Excerpted from the Model Rules of Professional Conduct, copyright © 1984 by the American Bar Association. All rights reserved. Reprinted by permission.

American Bar Association, Special Committee on Residential Real Estate Transactions, Residential Real Estate Transactions: The Lawyer's Proper Role, 14 Real Prop. Prob. and Tr. J. 585-590 (Fall 1979). Reprinted by permission of the Section of Real Property, Probate and Trust Law. Copyright © 1979 by the American Bar Association, Chicago, Illinois.

American Bar Association, Subcommittee on Leasehold Encumbrances, of the Committee on Leasing, Model Leasehold Encumbrance Provisions, 15 Real Prop. Prob. and Tr. J. 395, 399, 406-408 (1980). Copyright © 1980 by the American Bar Association. Reprinted by permission of the American Bar Association from Real Property, Probate and Trust Journal, a publication of the Real Property, Probate and Trust Law Section.

Aiken, "Subject to Financing Clauses" in Interim Contracts for Sale of Realty, 43 Marq. L. Rev. 265, 295 (1960). Reprinted by permission.

American Land Title Association, Loan Policy 1970 (rev. 10-17-70 and 10-17-84) and Owner's Policy Form 13-1970 (rev. 10-17-70 and 10-17-84). Reprinted by permission.

American Land Title Association, The Title Industry: White Papers vol. 1, pt. 5, 5-20 (1976). Reprinted by permission.

Barnett, Marketable Title Acts—Panacea or Pandemonium, 53 Cornell L. Rev. 45, 92-94 (1967). Copyright © 1967 by Cornell University. All rights reserved. Reprinted by permission of Cornell University and Fred B. Rothman and Company.

Bayse, Trends and Progress—The Marketable Title Acts, 47 Iowa L. Rev. 261-267 (1962). Copyright © 1962 by the University of Iowa (Iowa Law Review). Reprinted by permission.

Berger, Condominium: Shelter on a Statutory Foundation, 63 Colum. L.

Rev. 987 (1963). Copyright © 1963 by the Directors of the Columbia Law Review Association. All rights reserved. This article originally appeared at 63 Colum. L. Rev. 987 (1963). Reprinted by permission.

Berger, Real Estate Syndication: Property, Promotion, and the Need for Protection, 69 Yale L.J. 725 (1960). Reprinted by permission of the Yale Law Journal Company and Fred B. Rothman and Company.

Bixby, The Vendor-Vendee Problem: How Do We Slice the Insurance Pie?, 19 The Forum 112-114, 127-128 (1983), a publication of the American Bar Association. Reprinted by permission.

Bruce, An Overview of the Uniform Land Transactions Act and the Uniform Simplification of Land Transfers Act, 10 Stetson L. Rev. 1-2, 13-19 (1980). First appeared in 10 Stetson L. Rev. 1 (1980). Reprinted by permission.

Christie, Antitrust Update, 62 Title News No. 7, at 21 (1983). Reprinted by permission.

Comment, The Condominium Conversion Problem: Causes and Solutions, 1980 Duke L.J. 306. Reprinted by permission of the Duke Law Journal.

Comment, Mortgage Foreclosure as Fraudulent Conveyance: Is Judicial Foreclosure an Answer to the *Durrett* Problem?, 1984 Wis. L. Rev. 195-197, 214-218, 234-235. Copyright © 1984 by the University of Wisconsin. Reprinted by permission of the Wisconsin Law Review.

Comment, Enhancing the Marketability of Land: The Suit to Quiet Title, 68 Yale L.J. 1245, 1265, 1277, 1283 (1959). Reprinted by permission of the Yale Law Journal Company and Fred B. Rothman and Company.

Cotesworth, Mechanized Processing of Title Data (1970). Copyright © 1970 by H. A. Cotesworth and the International Business Machines Corporation. Reprinted by permission.

Cribbet, Principles of the Law of Property 169-171 (2nd ed. 1975). Copyright © 1975 by Foundation Press. Reprinted by permission.

Cross, The Record "Chain of Title Hypocrisy," 57 Colum. L. Rev. 787-796 (1957). Copyright © 1957 by the Directors of the Columbia Law Review Association. All rights reserved. This article originally appeared at 57 Colum. L. Rev. 787 (1957). Reprinted by permission.

Cunningham and Tischler, Disguised Real Estate Security Transactions as Mortgages in Substance, 26 Rutgers L. Rev. 1 (1972). Reprinted by permission.

Currier, Finding the Broker's Place in the Typical Residential Real Estate Transaction, 33 U. Fla. L. Rev. 655-681 (1981). Copyright © 1981 by the University of Florida Law Review. Reprinted by permission of the University of Florida Law Review.

Del Cotto, Sale and Leaseback: A Hollow Sound When Tapped?, 37 Tax L. Rev. 1, 3-9 (1981). Reprinted by permission.

Duncan, Hood and Neet, Redlining Practices, Racial Resegregation and Urban Decay: Neighborhood Housing Services as a Viable Alterna-

Acknowledgments

tive, 7 Urb. Law. 510, 513-514, 517-518 (1975). Reprinted by permission of The Urban Lawyer, the national quarterly journal of the American Bar Association, Section of State and Local Government Law.

Farrand, Conveyancing Contracts 300-305 (1964). The text on pages 472-474 is reproduced from Conveyancing Contracts (1964), by Professor Julian Farrand, with the kind permission of the publishers, Longman Group Ltd., 21-27 Lamb's Conduit Street, London, WC1N 3NJ.

Friedman, Contracts and Conveyances of Real Property 169-171 (4th ed. 1984). Copyright © 1984 by Milton R. Friedman. All rights reserved. Reprinted by permission of Milton R. Friedman, Contracts and Conveyances of Real Property, Fourth Edition, 1984.

Friedman, Contract Law in America 46-50 (1964). Copyright © 1965 by The Board of Regents of The University of Wisconsin System, by permission of The University of Wisconsin Press.

FTC and Shopping Centers — Dos and Don'ts for Major Tenants, 3 Real Est. L. Rep. No. 11 (April 1974). Copyright © 1974 by Warren, Gorham and Lamont, 210 South Street, Boston, MA 02111. All rights reserved. Reprinted by permission.

Gunning, The Wrap Around Mortgage . . . Friend or U.F.O.?, 2 Real Est. Rev. No. 35, at 43 (Summer 1971). Copyright © 1971 by Warren, Gorham and Lamont, 210 South Street, Boston, MA 02111. All rights reserved. Reprinted by permission.

Harris and Hines, Installment Land Contracts in Iowa (1965). Reprinted by permission.

Hecht, Long Term Lease Planning and Drafting 1-2, 13-16, 19 (Anderson, 1974). Reprinted by permission of the Anderson Publishing Company.

Hetland, The California Land Contract, 48 Calif. L. Rev. 729, 736-745 (1960). Copyright © 1960 by the California Law Review. Reprinted by permission.

Hyatt, Condominium and Home Owner Associations: Formation and Development, 24 Emory L.J. 977, 980-983 (1975). Reprinted by permission.

Lascher, Subordination Clauses in Court: Is California Unfair to Unfairness?, 1 San. Fern. V.L. Rev. 1 (1967). Reprinted by permission of the San Fernando Valley College of Law.

Levin and Roberts, Future Forms of Financing — Lending Devices Addressed to Inflation and Tight Money, reprinted in American Bar Association, Real Property, Probate and Trust Law Section, Financing Real Estate During the Inflationary 80's, at 31 (1981). Reprinted by permission of the American Bar Association from Financing Real Estate During the Inflationary 80's, a publication of the Section of Real Property, Probate and Trust Law. For more information about the publication write to American Bar Association, Order Fulfillment, 750 N. Lake Shore Drive, Chicago, IL 60611.

Levitan, Leasehold Mortgage Financing: Reliance on the "New Lease" Provision, 15 Real Prop. Prob. and Tr. J. 413 (1980). Reprinted by permission of the American Bar Association from Real Property, Probate and Trust Journal, a publication of the Real Property, Probate and Trust Law Section.

Lifton, Practical Real Estate in the 80's: Legal, Tax and Business Strategies 390-398, 497-499 (2d ed. 1983). Reprinted by permission of Law and Business, Inc.

Lifton, Real Estate in Trouble: Lender's Remedies Need an Overhaul, 31 Bus. Law. 1927, 1931-1945 (1976). Copyright © 1976 by the American Bar Association. All rights reserved. Reproduced by permission of the American Bar Association and its Section of Corporation, Banking and Business Law.

Madden, Taxation of Real Estate Transactions—An Overview, Portfolio 480 Tax Mgmt. (BNA) A-101, A-134 to 140 (1984). Reprinted by permission of Tax Management, Inc., Washington, D.C.

Madway and Perlman, A Mortgage Foreclosure Primer: Part III, Proposals for Change, 8 Clearinghouse Rev. 473, 478-479 (November 1974). Reprinted by permission of the Clearinghouse Review.

Mark, Leasehold Mortgages—Some Practical Considerations, 14 Bus. Law. 609-620 (1959). Copyright © 1959 by the American Bar Association. All rights reserved. Reproduced by permission of the American Bar Association and its Section of Corporation, Banking and Business Law.

Mixon, Installment Land Contracts: A Study of Low Income Transactions, with Proposals for Reform and a New Program to Provide Home Ownership in the Inner City, 7 Hous. L. Rev. 523-535 (1970). Reprinted by permission.

The Mortgage and Real Estate Executive's Report 5-7 (June 16, 1985). Copyright © 1985 by Warren, Gorham and Lamont, 210 South Street, Boston, MA 02111. All rights reserved. Reprinted by permission.

Note, Iowa's Prohibition of Title Insurance—Leadership or Folly?, 33 Drake L. Rev. 683, 695-701 (1983-1984). Reprinted by permission.

Note, The Tract and Grantor-Grantee Indices, 47 Iowa L. Rev. 481-485 (1962). Copyright © 1962 by the University of Iowa (Iowa Law Review). Reprinted by permission.

Note, Restrictive Covenants in Shopping Center Leases, 34 N.Y.U. L. Rev. 940 (1959). Reprinted by permission of the New York University Law Review.

Note, Reforming the Vendor's Remedies for Breach of Installment Land Sale Contracts, 47 S. Cal. L. Rev. 191, 205-206 (1973). Reprinted by permission of the Southern California Law Review.

Osborne, Nelson and Whitman, Real Estate Finance Law 268-274 (1979). Copyright © 1979 by West Publishing Company. Reprinted by permission.

Acknowledgments

Patton, Evolution of Legislation on Proof of Title to Land, 30 Wash. L. Rev. 224, 228-235 (1955). Reprinted by permission of the Washington Law Review and Fred B. Rothman and Company.

Prather, Foreclosure of the Security Interest, 1957 Ill. L.F. 420, 427-430. Copyright © 1957 by the Board of Trustees of the University of Illinois. Reprinted by permission.

Quiner, Title Insurance and the Title Insurance Industry, 22 Drake L. Rev. 711, 723-725 (1973). Reprinted by permission.

Salin, Usury, reprinted in 15 Encyclopaedia of the Social Sciences 193-197 (1934). Copyright © 1934, 1962 by MacMillan Publishing Company. Reprinted by permission of MacMillan Publishing Company from Encyclopaedia of the Social Sciences, Edwin R. A. Seligman, Editor-in-Chief.

Simes and Taylor, Model Marketable Title Act, reprinted in The Improvement of Conveyancing by Legislation 6-16 (1960). Copyright © 1960 by the American Bar Association. Reprinted by permission of the American Bar Association Section of Real Property, Probate and Trust Law.

Simes and Taylor, Model Title Standards 1-3 (1960). Reprinted by permission.

Smith, Tax Shelter Topics, 14 Real Est. Rev. No. 4, at 14 (Winter 1985). Copyright © 1985 by Warren, Gorham and Lamont, 210 South Street, Boston, MA 02111. All rights reserved. Reprinted by permission.

Smith and Lubbell, Real Estate Financing: Protecting the Lender with Title Insurance, 5 Real Est. Rev. No. 1, at 14 (Winter 1975). Copyright © 1975 by Warren, Gorham and Lamont, 210 South Street, Boston, MA 02111. All rights reserved. Reprinted by permission.

Spellman, A Banker's Tour Through The Second Mortgage Market, 148 Bankers Mag. No. 2, at 19-20, 22, 23, 24-25 (Spring 1965). Copyright © 1965 by Warren, Gorham and Lamont, 210 South Street, Boston, MA 02111. All rights reserved. Reprinted by permission.

Stambler and Stein, The Real Estate Broker — Schizophrenia or Conflict of Interest, 28 D.C.B.A.J. 16 (1961). Copyright © 1961 by the District of Columbia Bar Association Journal. Reprinted by permission.

Stoppello, Federal Regulation of Home Mortgage Settlement Costs: RESPA and Its Alternatives, 63 Minn. L. Rev. 367, 368-369, 423, 425-426 (1979). Reprinted by permission.

Thomas, The Mortgaging of Long Term Leases, 39 Dicta 363, 379-382 (1962). Reprinted by permission of the Denver Bar Association.

Vogel, The Tax Consequences of Time-Sharing, 10 J. Real Est. Taxn. No. 3, at 323 (Spring 1983). Copyright © 1983 by Warren, Gorham and Lamont, 210 South Street, Boston, MA 02111. All rights reserved. Reprinted by permission.

Warren, California Instalment Land Sales Contracts: A Time for Reform, 9 U.C.L.A. L. Rev. 608, 609-619, 625-630 (1962). Originally published in 9 U.C.L.A. L. Rev. 608 (1962). Copyright © 1962 by The Regents of the University of California. All rights reserved. Reprinted by permission.

Zerwick, Creation and Maintenance of a Title Plant, 34 Natl. Capitol Area Realtor No. 1, at 11 (1966). Reprinted by permission from the January 1966 issue of Realtor Magazine.

Land Transfer and Finance

CHAPTER ONE

The Professional and the Land Transaction: Brokers and Lawyers

A. WHY SO MUCH LITIGATION?

It is usually with a light heart that one with property to sell goes to a "realtor" and seeks help in selling. Not always does the lightness of heart persist through the process of paying the commission; for the broker's compensation can run into serious money. The broker is well aware of the uncertainties of his business, the effort fruitlessly expended on one property after another, and the fact that his wife and children must eat. To the customer, these things are likely to seem fairly unimportant; his thought is directed at the slight effort that may have been involved in selling the particular property which he owned.

Thus it is not surprising that actions for brokers' commissions are among the most common on the dockets of our trial courts. [Casner and Leach, Cases and Text on Property 683 (2d ed. 1969).]

Perhaps because of the intense land speculations of recent California history, that state would appear to have the most extensive case law on the realty brokerage situations. . . . [Stambler and Stein, The Real Estate Broker—Schizophrenia or Conflict of Interests, 28 D.C.B.A.J. 16, 19 (1961).]

There has been an immense amount of litigation with respect to the commissions of land brokers and other agents. This is due in part to the character of the business itself, vendors and purchasers often feeling that the commission charged is disproportionate to the service rendered. In large part, however, it is due to the fact that the terms of agreement between principal and broker are often expressed in vague form with no clear provision as to matters that become subjects of dispute. Much must be supplied from usages of the business that are none too well known or too definitely proved. Gaps must be filled by that uncertain process called "implication," a mixture of determining the meanings of the parties by interpretation of their words and actions and of doing justice according to the mores and practices of the community. The legal relations of the parties must vary with the variation of the operative facts of the particular transactions, their complexity and variation being increased by the fact that at least three parties are always involved—a seller, a purchaser, and a broker. [Corbin on Contracts §50, at 194 (1963).]

Friedman, Contract Law in America
46–50 (1964)

[In major part, this book is a report on the author's study of the records and historical contexts of all appellate contracts cases in Wisconsin in the three periods, 1836 to 1861, 1905 to 1915, and 1955 to 1958. Cases are categorized by the type of business context from which they emerged.]

The most striking aspect of the labor and service [appellate cases in Wisconsin between 1905 and 1915] was the ubiquitousness of the real estate brokers. In eighteen cases brokers brought suit to collect their commissions. The use of real estate brokers was common during the period. Of the thousands of sales through brokers every year, only a handful were litigated; even fewer were appealed. Nonetheless, compared with other occupations, the brokers took up far more than their fair share of the court's time.

The basic reason can be found partly in the nature of the business, partly in consideration of the type of brokers who litigated. The brokerage business was relatively disorganized. Entry into this business specialty was free to all. Professional organizations had not assumed control and the state did not yet license brokers. The nature of the business, indeed, was not conducive to internal control. The potential customers were a fluid, constantly shifting group. Buying and selling were usually non-recurring acts; the stabilizing effect of a "course of dealing" was lacking. The business required little specialized knowledge, despite what the "professionals" said. Any layman could fill in printed forms for ordinary deeds and learn how to handle a land transfer with a little experience. Then, too, Wisconsin (and America in general) had a long tradition of part-timers dabbling in real estate.

The land marketing and brokerage business was rich and colorful. At one end of the scale the large land companies of the north were highly organized and rationalized. The Tomahawk Land Company, which flourished after 1910, selected settlers, financed them, even rented them stump clearing machines. J. L. Gates sold land through agents who received $1 an acre for their pains.[52] In the cities and small towns, there were dealers who operated regular brokerage businesses over the years, as well as part-time

---

52. On J. L. Gates and the Tomahawk Land Company, see Arlan C. Helgeson, "Promotion of Agricultural Settlement in Northern Wisconsin 1880-1925" (unpub. Ph.D. thesis, U. Wis., 1951), pp. 138-46, 162ff.

Why So Much Litigation?

dealers, some of whom sold a lot or two and then quit. In the palmy days of land speculation, the farmer was lightly attached to the soil; land to him was (relatively speaking) emotionally colorless; every man was a potential land dealer. Perhaps the great number of fly-by-night brokers was an inheritance from this by-gone age. At any rate, real estate was an attractive side-line, not only for complete amateurs, but also for insurance men, lawyers, and stockbrokers. Thus we meet in one case with William J. Willis of Fond du Lac, who began by plastering and calcimining houses and ended by selling them.[53] It is easy to see why brokers were harder to "organize" than doctors and lawyers.

Of these various types of brokers, our eighteen cases concern, primarily, only one: the part-time or marginal operator. These were litigants like one Zitske, who devoted "full time" to real estate. But his contract was oral; he had no office and no records. He lived "just inside . . . New London in Outagamia County. . . . I travel on foot, sometimes with a team, and sometimes on the cars." [54] The cases show great variations in the commissions charged, a situation which hints at that most dreaded of occupational diseases, price-cutting. Commissions seemed to range from 2 percent to 5 percent; the magnitude of the sale made a difference. In some cases the seller fixed a minimum sale price and the broker took everything he could get over that price, or split the excess fifty-fifty with the owner.[55] Undoubtedly, the part-time and marginal brokers had the most price flexibility; a man like Zitske had no overhead to worry about. Many of the part-timers were probably out only to earn fast, occasional dollars. But in a disorganized market the "regulars" had not much chance to maintain their own rates. A broker of Green Bay testified frankly, if ungrammatically: "We have not at all times regular ironclad rules which governs us all in our actions. It depends on the people I am dealing with, and the amount of property, etc." [56] Undoubtedly, another problem faced by the brokers was widespread public misunderstanding of the schedules of rates (indeed,

---

53. Willis figured in Bowe v. Gage, 127 Wis. 245, 106 N.W. 1074 (1906), Cases and Briefs, "Record," 67. A lawyer land-dealer was Salmon W. Dalberg, in Dalberg v. Jung Brewing Co., 155 Wis. 185, 144 N.W. 198 (1913), Cases and Briefs, "Record," 22, 45-6. Real estate and insurance: Rowland T. Burdon, in Burdon v. Briquelet, 125 Wis. 341, 104 N.W. 83 (1905); Wright's Directory of Green Bay, with DePere and Brown County (1901), p. 86.

54. Zitske v. Grohn, 128 Wis. 159, 107 N.W. 20 (1906), Cases and Briefs, "Record," 19-20.

55. E.g., flat sum as commission: Schultz v. Eberle, 124 Wis. 594, 102 N.W. 1055 (1905), Cases and Briefs, "Record," 26 ($100 for sale of a farm); 2 percent: Tasse v. Kindt, 125 Wis. 631, 104 N.W. 703 (1905), 2½ percent Hoskins v. O'Brien, 132 Wis. 453, 112 N.W. 466 (1907); 3 percent: Hensel v. Witt, 134 Wis. 55, 113 N.W. 1093 (1907); 5 percent on the first $1,000, 2½ on the next: Hoffman v. Steele, 152 Wis. 84, 139 N.W. 733 (1913), Cases and Briefs, "Record," 20; 5 percent: Burdon v. Briquelet, 125 Wis. 341, 104 N.W. 83 (1905), Cases and Briefs, "Record," 111, 123-4, 126; minimum sale price, broker to take one-half of anything received in addition, Helgeson, "Promotion of Agricultural Settlement," p. 31, or all additional, McCune v. Badger, 126 Wis. 186, 105 N.W. 667 (1905).

56. Testimony of J. A. Cusick, in Burdon v. Briquelet, 125 Wis. 341, 104 N.W. 83 (1905), Cases and Briefs, "Record," 124.

of the nature of the brokerage commission altogether). The occasional buyer and seller of a house might view the broker's commission as an unjust exaction, a large price paid for a trifling amount of work. Nor did the public readily accept the broker's claim — more or less agreed to by the courts — that the commission was earned if he brought a buyer to the seller, even if the broker did not actively negotiate, or if the seller backed out of the deal. These problems were most critical for the marginal operators, whose business methods were the loosest. Such a broker was not a member of a real estate "board," thus not sympathetic to the "gentlemen's agreements" of the trade; he haggled about rates and service, undercut the regulars, competed with them for available business, and brought the whole corps of brokers into disrepute through "unprofessional" conduct.[57] . . .

Interestingly enough, in the years 1955-1958 the brokers' cases continued to come before the court. Unlike the brokers of 1905-1915, the new crop of broker-plaintiffs were regularly licensed brokers, members of an active professional group, with established businesses and fairly standardized business practices. Regulation, licensing, and tighter internal control had driven away the marginal brokers; but the inherent problems of customer relations were not so easy to cure. In one 1958 case the broker claimed commissions on repeated renewals of a lease first executed in 1937.[64] Probably the client was thoroughly disgusted with these "unearned" commissions. In other cases, it is clear that to a certain extent the brokers had brought their troubles onto their own heads. In five of these cases the customer's defense was based on a special section of the Statute of Frauds, passed in 1917, and applying only to real estate brokers. The reputable brokers themselves had hatched the statute, as a weapon against the marginal and part-time brokers who so plagued them.[65] Forty years

---

57. Brokers "do not wish longer to be called land sharks," John A. McCormick, broker, quoted in Milwaukee Journal, Feb. 16, 1917, p. 18. The desire to become "professional" was one factor which lay behind the licensing movement. . . . George Howe, Memoirs of a Westchester Realtor (New York, 1959), p. 29; A. D. Theobald, "Real Estate License Laws in Theory and Practice," J. Land & Pub. Util. Econ., VII (1931), 13.

Exclusive agency agreements (or variants) were frequent in brokerage contracts in [1905-1915], e.g., Hoskin's v. O'Brien, 132 Wis. 453, 112 N.W. 466 (1907) ("Exclusive Sale Contract" for six months).

64. Karl M. Elbinger Co. v. Geo. J. Meyer Mfg. Co., 3 Wis. 2d 202, 87 N.W.2d 807 (1958).

65. The brokers' Statute of Frauds (Wis. Laws 1917, ch. 221) was introduced into the Assembly by V. V. Miller, Republican of Rusk and Sawyer counties (1917 Wis. Assembly Journal, 221) who also introduced at the same session a bill (No. 377A) to license brokers (1917 Wis. Assembly Journal, 290). The unmistakable inference is that the same interests were behind both bills. The established brokers strongly favored licensing. See "Licensing of Brokers," Natl. Real Est. J. XVI (1917), 226.

The first case arising under the Wisconsin law was Gifford v. Straub, 172 Wis. 396, 179 N.W. 600 (1920). A contract stating "I agree to give [Gifford] . . . all he gets for my place over $11,500. Sept. 20-1919 exclusive sale [sic]" violated the Statute and gave rise to no action for commission. Gifford, of Pierce County, was a man about 60 years old. He testified, "I have tried to sell a little real estate. I never went to school very much. . . . I have no

later, through a cruel irony, the licensed brokers themselves felt the major bite of the statute.[66]

B. BROKER'S DUTIES TO BUYER AND SELLER[1]

Currier, Finding the Broker's Place in the Typical Residential Real Estate Transaction
33 U. Fla. L. Rev. 655-681 (1981)

The real estate broker's place in the residential real estate conveyancing process is not well understood. The law most often casts the broker as the seller's legal agent. This does not always accord with the expectations of home sellers and buyers about the broker's function; indeed, brokers themselves frequently take a broader view of their role than the law of agency implies. A broker who disregards the law's proscriptions, however, and seeks to fulfill the parties' expectations risks sanction if a disappointed seller or buyer later complains. Should fear of penalty lead the broker to keep his conduct within the boundaries of agency law, the parties to a transaction, particularly the buyer, may be denied the aid and counsel they need and expect from the broker.

Disparity between the legal model imposed on brokers and the expectations of the parties creates a dilemma for brokers and prompts consumer uncertainty about the broker's role. The law governing the real estate broker's place in a residential real estate transaction and the expectations of sellers and buyers about the broker's role need reconciliation. . . .

A Perspective on the Role of the Real Estate Broker

Most persons initiate residential real estate transactions by contacting a real estate broker.[2] The broker generally knows the local housing market,

---

permanent office." Cases and Briefs, "Record," 17. This was precisely the kind of operator the Statute was meant to help drive out of business.
   66. See, e.g., Gilbert v. Ludtke, 1 Wis. 2d 228, 83 N.W.2d 669 (1957).
   1. On real estate brokers, in addition to the articles and report from which excerpts appear immediately hereafter, see also Comment, The Real Estate Broker's Fiduciary Duties: An Examination of Current Industry Standards and Practices, 12 Pepperdine L. Rev. 145 (1984); and Comment, A Real Estate Broker's Duty to His Purchaser: Washington State's Position and Some Projections for the Future, 17 Gonz. L. Rev. 79 (1981).
   2. "Broker" is used in this article as a generic term to describe both the real estate broker and the real estate salesperson. All fifty states require licensing as a condition to lawfully acting as either a real estate broker or real estate salesperson. P. Goldstein, Real Estate Transactions 29 (1980). Real estate brokering consists of a person acting for another for compensation in the negotiation or attempted negotiation of the sale, purchase, exchange or rental of any interest in real property. See, e.g., Fla. Stat. §475.01(3) (1981). Although qualifications for licensing vary, typically the broker's license is more difficult to obtain than a

is experienced in the conveyancing process, and can present a house to many potential buyers. Sellers may consequently seek local brokers in an effort to obtain the timely sale of their property at the maximum price, on favorable terms. Brokers may thus be able to help sellers achieve their objectives in the real estate market and guard the seller from having to exert great personal effort. . . .

Potential buyers may also be concerned about purchasing a home because of the high transactional costs associated with real estate transactions. Inspecting a house for defects is often financially impossible,[7] and the conveyancing process is becoming increasingly complex. In addition, individuals participate in this market relatively infrequently during their lifetimes[9] despite the mobility of the population[10] and the high volume of real estate transactions.[11] The unfamiliarity of the process thus contributes to the anxiety many potential home buyers feel when entering the real estate market. . . .

The broker and buyer spend a considerable amount of time together during the often lengthy home search period. Inevitably, as several houses are visited, comparisons will be made regarding floor plans, neighborhood character and the like. The shared experience of buyer and broker makes

---

salesperson's license. For example, in Florida a person must complete a 51-hour course and pass an examination to be licensed as a real estate salesperson. Id. §475.17(2). To qualify for a broker's license, a person must have twelve months experience as a licensed salesperson in the office of a registered broker, take an additional 48-hour course, and pass another examination. Id. Salespersons can perform most brokerage services, but they must be employed by, and act under the supervision of, a licensed broker. Id. §475.01(4). Nothing prohibits a person licensed as a broker from acting as a salesperson for another broker or for a business association acting as a broker. In a large real estate brokerage firm many persons may be licensed as brokers although the business may be registered only in the names of the partners or a few of the active members. It is difficult to generalize about what brokerage activities cannot be performed by salespersons. . . .

Realtors are brokers who belong to the National Association of Realtors, which is the largest brokers' trade group. It has been active through local boards of realtors in operating multiple listing services and other aspects of the real estate business. . . .

7. This has been recognized at least with respect to new homes: "An experienced builder who has erected and sold many houses is in a far better position to determine the structural condition of a house than most buyers. Even if a buyer is sufficiently knowledgeable to evaluate a home's condition, he rarely has access to make any inspection of the underlying structural work, as distinguished from the merely cosmetic features." Duncan v. Schuster-Graham Homes, Inc., 194 Colo. 441, 444, 578 P.2d 637, 638-39 (1978).

9. Mobility among owners of homes is significantly less than among renters. Despite a high rate of mobility within the general population and the fact that about 64 percent of all housing units are owner-occupied, U.S. Dept. of Commerce, Bureau of the Census, 1979 Statistical Abstract of the United States 782 (hereinafter cited as Statistical Abstract), a family is not likely to make more than a few home purchases during its existence. Id. at 122; Speare, Home Ownership, Life Cycle State and Residential Mobility, 7 Demography 449 (1970).

10. From 1975 to 1978 over one-third of the population of the United States changed housing units, Statistical Abstract at 40. A study of mobility in St. Louis found that 39.3 percent of households sampled had moved within the preceding three years.

11. Approximately 4.7 million new and used homes were sold in 1978. Statistical Abstract at 791-92.

the broker the logical buyer's advisor as alternative courses are weighed and sifted. The broker's advice is influential because of his expertise.

Current conveyancing practices involve the broker with the buyer beyond the search-and-locate stage. A buyer may reasonably continue to rely on the broker's assistance as the offer is formulated and the final contract negotiated. The broker aids the buyer in preparing the offer that forms the basis of the land sale contract between seller and buyer. Although the buyer can reject the broker's aid and consult an attorney, time pressure may militate against this. The buyer may also feel the broker is the best person to advise him.

Both sellers and buyers contact brokers to help them achieve their differing goals in a real estate transaction. Sellers' objectives are straightforward and not as dependent on the development of a personal relationship with the broker for their success. Buyers' special needs, on the other hand, create a reliance on brokers during the natural progression of the broker-buyer relationship. A broker, however, experiences difficulty in performing the tasks expressly or impliedly entrusted to him by the buyer while remaining within the legal rules currently governing his conduct.

REAL ESTATE BROKERS AND THE LAW OF AGENCY

In practice both home buyers and home sellers have legitimate claims to the broker's loyalty. An analysis of agency law, however, reveals that the legal system affords more favorable treatment and greater protection to the broker-seller relationship than to that of the broker-buyer. This greater protection is derived from the legal effect of the listing agreement between the seller and broker, in which the seller promises to pay a commission to the broker thus making the broker his agent. Regardless of both the amount of time the broker and buyer spend together and the personal relationship that may develop between them, the broker is seldom considered the buyer's agent.

In the majority of cases, a written, exclusive right-to-sell agreement establishes the agency relationship between seller and broker. Under this contract, the seller promises to pay an agreed commission to the broker if the house sells during the listing period. The commission must be paid whether the sale results from the efforts of the listing broker, another broker, or the seller. Other forms of listing property with a broker are possible, but brokers promote the exclusive right to sell model, arguing that it assures the broker's best attention and effort to sell the property. In theory, sellers *must* count on the listing broker's efforts under an exclusive right to sell agreement to avoid potential liability for more than one commission. In practice, however, the listing broker will agree to cooperate with another broker and share the commission unless the listing broker has another offer in hand; part of a certain commission is better than the chance of a whole commission.

Cooperation among brokers is so sensible that it has become formalized in the multiple listing services (MLS) that permeate real estate markets across the country. The MLS concept is simple—brokers agree to pool listings and split commissions. Multiple listing services mitigate the harshness of exclusive right-to-sell listing agreements. A seller's property is included in the inventory of all MLS members by listing it with one, and the brokers' advance agreement to cooperate effectively eliminates the potential double commission problem.

Buyers as well as sellers benefit from MLS operations. One MLS member can show a house listed by any other member without having to arrange that member's cooperation in advance. Given the substantial market share of many multiple listing services, the "one-stop shopping" method appears to be a very efficient way to canvass available housing opportunities. Another consequence of the MLS arrangement, however, is not so advantageous to buyers. The agreement to pool listings and share commissions creates ties among member brokers that make each a subagent of every other member broker.

Once the broker becomes the seller's agent,[29] the law imposes certain duties on the broker. Because of the agency relationship's fiduciary character, the broker is subject to the duties of loyalty, honesty and full disclosure to his principal. These duties bind the agent because of the nature of an agency arrangement and do not depend on the listing agreement's terms. Basic principles of agency law require the broker to disclose information to the seller that would help him in the bargaining process. The broker must further refrain from disclosing information to the buyer that would harm the seller, unless failure to make the revelation amounts to fraud or misrepresentation.

The standard agency model works well for most purposes in the conveyancing process. It regulates the broker's behavior vis-a-vis the seller. For example, the broker cannot secretly profit by buying property he has agreed to sell at a bargain price and then reselling it at a profit. Self-dealing is not prohibited, but the broker must disclose his intentions to deal personally in the property and not take advantage of his superior knowledge to gain from the trust the seller has reposed in him.

Although a broker may advise a seller of his opinions concerning offers received, the law clearly states that all such decisions are the seller's. Offers

---

29. Agency is a consensual relationship between two persons wherein one of them, the principal, empowers the other, the agent, to act and the agent assumes to so act. Restatement (Second) of Agency §1 (1958); Defosses v. Notis, 333 A.2d 83 (Me. 1975). Generally, the broker is a special agent, as opposed to a general one. A special agent represents the principal in a discrete number of transactions without involving a continuity of service. Restatement (Second) of Agency §3 (1958). Ingalls v. Rice, 511 S.W.2d 78, 80 (Tex. Civ. App. 1974); Stenson v. Thrush, 36 Wash. 2d 726, 728, 219 P.2d 977, 978 (1950). The authority of the broker is confined to selling a described piece of real property for a given price. In practice the broker does not sell the property but solicits offers and aids in negotiating a sale on terms acceptable to the seller.

must be communicated to the seller regardless of the broker's evaluation of whether they should be accepted, rejected, or countered. A high standard of care applies to the broker's conduct regarding the accuracy and sufficiency of the advice. Failing to meet it, the broker risks possible disciplinary proceedings and sanctions.[36]

In contrast to the seller's legal relationship with the broker, the home buyer's position is a perilous one. Reposing confidence and trust in the broker, the buyer is potentially exposed to manipulation and exploitation. Brokers can successfully meet a buyer's complaints about alleged mistreatment with a defense based upon the law of agency. Of course, actions in fraud and misrepresentation afford some protection to the buyer. The buyer may alternatively assert an express agency relationship exists between himself and the broker or that mistreatment by a broker, while not amounting to fraud or misrepresentation, breaches duties owed to him even though he is not the broker's principal.

Establishing a formal agency relationship with a real estate broker, however, will be difficult for the buyer. The seller's contractual arrangement with the broker, because of its formality and an assumption that it arose first, may preempt any relationship buyer claims with the broker. The mere fact that the listing agreement is in writing, however, should not elevate the broker-seller relationship to a superior position,[39] rather, the listing agreement should be considered only one of many material facts necessary to determine who the broker's principal was in a particular transaction.

The person whose relationship with the broker began first could assert a stronger claim to the agent's loyalty. There is an unarticulated presumption that the broker-seller relationship is the initial one. Buyers thus bear the burden of overcoming this presumption; however, the presumption itself is questionable. The home buyer and the broker may be working together prior to the time the seller's house is listed. In tight real estate markets, a land sale contract may be entered within hours or days of listing. It is unlikely that these sudden sales result from the home buyer just

---

36. A broker may be denied his commission for not performing in a satisfactory manner the duties owed to the seller-principal. See, e.g., Security Aluminum Window Mfg. Corp. v. Lehman Assocs., Inc., 108 N.J. Super. 137, 260 A.2d 248 (Super. Ct. App. Div. 1970) (compensatory and punitive damages assessed against broker who led principal to believe that an offer of only $25,000 had been made when in fact a $50,000 offer had been received). The broker's license may be suspended or revoked for violation of a duty imposed on the broker by law or contract, without regard to whether the victim of the misconduct sustained loss or damage. Fla. Stat. §475.25(1) (1981). Additionally, members of the National Association of Realtors can be penalized by their local board for violating that group's Code of Ethics. Sanctions range from a reprimand to expulsion from the local chapter.

39. The listing agreement does not come under the statute of frauds because it provides for the broker's services in connection with the sale of land, not for the actual transfer of any interest in property. E.g., Jefcoat v. Singer Hous. Co., 619 F.2d 539, 543 (5th Cir. 1980). Some states nonetheless insist that brokerage contracts be in writing. E.g., Idaho Code §9-508 (1979).

happening into a broker's office moments after the listing has been obtained.

A buyer's claim that the broker is his agent is weakened because the seller pays the broker's compensation. Although one can act as an agent gratuitously, most brokers sell real estate to earn a living. Work done in the normal transaction is expected to lead to a commission. It seems reasonable, therefore, to expect the broker to give his allegiance to the party who is paying him. While the listing agreement legally obligates the seller to pay the commission, the home buyer may be paying all or part of the commission indirectly. Sellers often increase the price if they employ a broker so that the sale's net proceeds equal what might have been obtained by selling privately. The buyer thus effectively pays the commission, despite the fact that liability for the commission rests on the seller. In practice, the broker collects his commission at closing from money provided by the buyer. If a transaction does not close, the buyer may pay some compensation to the broker as an element of the seller's damages in an action on the purchase and sale agreement.[45] If the superiority of the broker-seller relationship is based on the broker's compensation flowing from the seller, it is therefore undermined to the extent that the commission is buried in the sales price.

Although custom dictates that the seller pays the commission, the mere fact that the seller agrees to make this payment is not sufficient to create an agency relationship between seller and broker. Sometimes facts and circumstances demonstrate the broker was really acting for the buyer in the transaction. When such a case arises, the seller's agreement does nothing more than determine how the broker is to be compensated for his efforts.

Nothing theoretically prohibits a buyer from hiring a broker, agreeing to pay a fee for services, and thus creating a principal-agent relationship. In practice, however, this seldom occurs. The organization and operation of the residential brokerage business discourages such arrangements. Home buyers understand that brokers will receive compensation from sellers, and they know that brokers will work with them without additional charge. Formal contracts are not solicited by buyers and brokers do not insist on them. The broker ends up a seller's agent in law, and an extension of the seller in the transaction. Despite the hours spent together and closeness of their relationship, buyer and broker become, at least in theory, adversaries in the negotiation process.

---

45. Seller can recover incidental damages flowing from the buyer's breach of the land sale contract, including any commissions for which the seller becomes liable. See Uniform Land Transaction Act 2-507(a). Land sale contracts typically let the seller keep as liquidated damages any deposit the buyer has made in lieu of, or as part of, an action for damages against a breaching buyer. A Maryland court recently held that the seller must elect between forfeiture of the deposit or an action for damages. Blood v. Gibbons, 288 Md. 268, 418 A.2d 213 (Md. 1980). If the seller keeps the deposit and does not seek damages, the broker usually accepts one-half the deposit (up to the amount of the commission) as compensation for services.

One argument remains for a buyer who feels mistreated by a broker who is the seller's agent and whose conduct does not amount to fraud. A buyer can assert the breach of certain duties brokers owe even to non-principal parties in a real estate transaction. The foundation of these duties is somewhat obscure. One source is the National Association of Realtors' Code of Ethics. Under it member brokers must deal honestly and in good faith with all non-principals, including buyers. Another source is the notion that the broker's license is a privilege conferred by the state in exchange for which the broker must act in the public interest. Dealing honestly and fairly with all members of the public is part of the broker's duty of furthering the public interest.

The idea that the broker must deal straightforwardly with the public adds dimension to the simple picture that emerges from strict application of agency law to the relationships among the parties in residential real estate transactions. That the brokers' professional organization has a code of conduct recognizing the needs of buyers implies that brokers believe they serve both parties to a real estate transaction and that agency law inaccurately reflects their dual role in the market place. . . .

Given the reasonable expectations both sellers and buyers harbor concerning the broker's loyalty, alternative ways of handling the legal relationships among the parties must be evaluated. Legal theory must be brought closer to the operation of the residential real estate market. Perhaps the tangled web of conflicting rights and duties could be clarified by only slight changes in the law. The viability of any alteration must be assessed in the context of the present structure of the real estate market. An examination of the advantages and problems with a number of possible reforms is necessary.

DUAL AGENCY

Recognizing a principal-agent relationship between broker and buyer along with the broker's traditional duties to the seller would provide legal support for the buyer's expectations regarding the broker's role as an advisor and give the broker a solid foundation upon which to engage in counseling activity. The duality of fiduciary responsibilities to parties who are often adversaries, however, conflicts with the agent's duty to serve the principal's interests above all others. The inherent shortcomings of dual agency considerably undercut its usefulness in coping with the problems considered here. . . .

Before the broker can act as a dual agent, the knowledge and consent of both principals must be obtained. Achieving such consent in the current market structure might be difficult. . . .

Another approach, related to dual agency, would permit a broker to represent the buyer's interests if another broker listed the house. Throughout this article the assumption has been that only one broker works on a sale, dealing with both buyer and seller. In the context of multiple listing services, however, the most suitable homes are likely to have been listed by someone other than the broker working with the buyer. In such a situation, a natural division of labor may result, serving the legitimate needs of each party — the listing broker can act as seller's agent, and the broker, who has established a relationship with the buyer and who shows him the house (the selling broker) can act as the buyer's agent. The parties may be comfortable with this arrangement, but it does not square with the legal framework which applies to the typical transaction. Legally the selling broker is the seller's agent because of the multiple listing agreement signed by member brokers which provides for splitting the commission between the brokers who participate in a conveyance. Courts have not been reluctant to hold the selling broker responsible to the seller, even though the two have no express agreement. To work for the buyer under the current legal framework, therefore the selling broker would have to become a dual agent. . . .

DISCLOSURE

The confusion about the broker's role in the conveyancing process can be viewed as a consumer protection problem. Attention has been focused recently on the frequent abuses consumers suffer in the property conveyancing process. These abuses relate primarily to expenses for obtaining financing and transferring title. Mandatory disclosure has become a significant consumer protection method. The seller or creditor must disclose pertinent information, including statements about the consumer's legal rights and the concomitant duties of the retailers, lenders and others with whom they deal. . . .

The principle of disclosure could nevertheless be applied to the real estate brokerage industry. Brokers could be required by law or regulation to inform buyers of the agency relationship the broker has directly with some sellers, through listing agreements, and indirectly with others, through multiple listing arrangements. The broker would have to explain that he may not volunteer more information than the owner of the home would have to disclose nor give advice about the appropriate price or subjective qualities of the houses inspected. If a dual agency approach is adopted, statements could be formulated for presentation to both parties at the outset of the broker's dealings with each of them.

Disclosure would reveal to buyers the constraints agency law places on the broker's actions and disabuse them of the belief that the broker is working for them. In the absence of a viable comprehensive solution to the problems considered here, disclosure in some form would aid buyers. Brokers and those who regulate them should give serious attention to the best form of disclosure and the best time for it. Disclosure, however, cannot solve the more fundamental problem of providing counsel to buyers. Disclosure helps but it is no cure for the lack of advice and guidance buyers expect.

MIDDLEMAN

A broker may act as a middleman in a real estate[103] conveyance. This characterization emphasizes the broker's independent objective to earn a commission in the transaction. As a middleman, the broker is limited to bringing the parties together and may not take an active part in the negotiations for either party. The middleman posture limits the broker to doing less than either party expects. Such a constrained role makes the usual commission the broker receives seem exorbitant. Casting the broker as a middleman may cure the conflict of interest problems, but it is overkill, eliminating the substance of the broker's participation in the conveyancing process.

BUYER'S AGENT

If buyers require the services and counsel of agents with expertise in real estate, a direct and obvious way to meet the demand is for some brokers to work exclusively for buyers. Nothing in the law of agency or real estate brokerage bars such an activity. Indeed, many cases holding brokers responsible to buyers involve agents employed to find property for buyers rather than to sell for owners.

Because buyer's agents would be a new development in residential real estate transactions, changes in the manner of conducting business would be required. A major difficulty would be determining the compensation of the buyer's agent. To make this agent's duties of loyalty and disclosure clear, his compensation ought to come solely from the buyer-principal.

If buyers have to pay the same price for a house plus a fee to secure the loyalty of the broker, they might avoid entering into such agency agreements, despite the benefits such an arrangement might offer. Obviously, buyer reception of the idea depends on the fee. In the multiple broker situation the selling broker usually gets the larger share of the commission. For this new concept to work, therefore, more than an incidental amount

---

103. A broker may claim middleman status to avoid the charge that he acted as agent for both parties without their consent to a dual agency. Harry M. Fine Realty Co. v. Stiers, 326 S.W.2d 392, 398 (Mo. App. 1959). Because dual agencies can be created, the broker need not reduce his participation to that of middleman. Mallory v. Watt, 100 Idaho 119, 122, 594 P.2d 629, 632 (1979). An excellent conception of the middleman's role is provided by an early North Dakota case: "A broker is simply a middleman . . . when he has no duty to perform but to bring the parties together, leaving them to negotiate and to come to an agreement themselves without any aide from him. If he takes . . . any part in the negotiations, however, he cannot be regarded as a mere middleman, no matter how slight a part it may be." Jensen v. Bowen, 37 N.D. 352, 358, 164 N.W.4, 5 (1917).

will need to be paid by the buyer because the broker must forego the customary selling broker's percentage of the commission.

A buyer may pay less for a house if he employs an agent to negotiate directly with the seller and the listing broker, however. A commonly held assumption is that the commission is buried in the sale price and, practically speaking, paid by the purchaser when a broker is involved in a transaction. Some buyers explore "for sale by owner" listings expecting to pay less for a house.[106] If the selling broker's share of the commission were not subtracted from the proceeds the seller received at closing because the purchaser paid for these services directly, the seller should accept a lower price for his house. The price of the house would, therefore, be lower by an amount approaching or equal to the fee paid by the buyer to employ the broker at the outset of the search process. Costs, therefore, should not inhibit the introduction of a buyer's agent into the conveyancing process.

Another question to consider is whether enough brokers would undertake such an activity to make it viable. If a broker could somehow be a buyer's agent for some clients and continue to list property, the industry might not resist this change. Even if buyers' agents were prohibited from listing property the concept might still work. So many people hold real estate sales and brokerage licenses[108] that one could expect a significant number to become buyers' agents to capture revenues such activity would generate. Certainly, many details and questions would have to be carefully thought out before the implementing of such a radical change in the way residential real estate sales are presently transacted. Given a problem as pervasive as this one, however, imagination and experimentation are necessary.

CONCLUSION

Home buying and selling are important events in the personal lives of most Americans. Counsel and aid ought to be available for those who want it. Although most real estate brokers understand the significance of their responsibilities and treat both buyer and seller with consideration, the law defining the broker's role in the conveyancing process is vague and inconsistent with the understanding of the parties involved. For the sake of brokers, sellers, and buyers, brokers' duties should be clarified. If possible,

---

106. There is an apparent lack of empirical verification of whether buyers save all or part of the commission by purchasing directly from the seller without the aid of a broker. Brokers hint that the commission is buried in the price. The National Association of Realtors gives as a reason for owners to list their homes that: "[I]n a Sale by Owner, the Realtor's commission is always deducted by the buyer and the seller is left to do all the work for nothing." National Association of Realtors, Sales Handbook 71 (1975).

108. In California more than 178,000 persons were active in real estate brokerage in 1976 and another 71,000 persons on inactive status. In San Francisco there were a phenomenal 186 licensees per square mile.

the duties should be defined in a way that meets the reasonable expectations of the parties.

Stambler and Stein, The Real Estate Broker — Schizophrenia or Conflict of Interest
28 D.C.B.A.J. 16 (1961)

Perhaps the most problematic areas in realty brokerage law are the factual situations involving (1) the question of for whom the broker acts in the transaction, and (2) the precise outlines of his legal responsibilities to that principal. True, there is an ingrained general tenet that the broker "owes his principal the highest fidelity." . . . But while [this] is determinative and workable in clean-cut cases of gross breach of fiduciary duty . . . it is of less help in resolving the ambiguous problems in the more conventional brokerage relationship. . . .

A hard, realistic view of these give-and-take brokerage transactions would seem in order. It makes clear that the broker acts as intermediary negotiator between the contracting parties, doing so for a contingent fee payable only and if the realty is actually sold. Moreover, since the broker is the active go-between, the basic direction and the intangible details of the evolving transaction are generally locked within his personal and private knowledge. With the buyer he offers and bargains; for the seller he interprets and recommends.

Accordingly, in such situations it may be asked whether the broker's interest is not by its very nature somewhat adverse to his principal's. In other words, whether the broker in such circumstances inevitably tends toward securing some reasonable and certain sale — albeit one that may also satisfy the parties — that will assuredly earn his fee, rather than fully prosecuting the vendor's interest where that necessarily risks losing the entire sale. This is in no way to suggest that the broker here is a violator of his acknowledged responsibilities, or that he may have the conscious desire to subordinate his principal's interests to his own. It does no more than to recognize the realistic facts of life inherent in the brokerage system of our commercial community.

To illustrate the problem, let us now turn to the particular everyday situation where the broker returns to the vendor-principal with the counteroffer of the potential buyer who, in the ordinary course, has rejected the original asking price. Here it is quite customary that the broker express a position respecting the negotiations. Indeed he is expected to. Otherwise he is no more than a messenger carrying price quotations between the parties. This aspect of negotiation raises the basic questions.

In so doing, does the broker remain solely the vendor's agent; or is he now acting solely or partially for the buyer in perhaps urging a sale at the lower price; or is his status a jumbled hotchpot of all three interests? If the broker is to act in any dual capacity can he be expected to segregate and properly serve such often-conflicting interests? Or, as a practical matter, can he pursue more than one interest only at cost to his fundamental duty to his principal, the vendor? In short, is he capable of conscious and controlled schizophrenia, or must his actions inevitably involve some conflict of interests?

Broker statutes, the reported cases, and the general texts are of limited assistance in finding appropriate answers. Thus, the District of Columbia Code (Section 45-1408) inter alia forbids realty brokers from acting for more than one party to the transaction without the knowledge of all. This principle is echoed by the courts and writers. (Keith v. Berry, 64 A.2d 300, D.C. 1949) See also Grossman v. Herman, 270 N.Y. Supp. 669, aff. 194 N.E. 694 (N.Y. Ct. App., 1935); 12 Corpus Juris Secundum, "Brokers," Sec. 14. But these citations provide no solution. The very question at issue here is to determine the party or parties for whom the broker is acting and how he may do so. There are also decisions stating the proposition that the broker's fiduciary duties require his obtaining the highest price and best terms reasonably believed available for the principal. (Smith v. Fidelity & Columbia Trust Co., 12 S.W.2d 276 (Ky. Ct. App., 1928)). He must inform his principal of the known availability of more advantageous terms than offered (Whiting v. Delozier, 255 Pac. 861 (Cal. Ct. App., 1st Div., 1927), Pederson v. Johnson, 172 N.W. (Wisc. Supr. Ct. 1919)). Thus, the broker's concealment of a material fact is a breach of the fiduciary relationship of full disclosure that bars his recovery of his fee. (Rawlings v. Collins, 36 U.S. App. D.C. 72 (1910); Nat. Savings & Trust Co. v. Sands, 44 U.S. App. D.C. 20 (1915)). So is inducing the buyer to believe that the property may be available for less than asked. (Haymes v. Rogers, 219 P.2d 339, rev'd on rehearing, 222 P.2d 789 (Ariz. Supr. Ct., 1950)). . . . For a discussion of Haymes see the Annotation at 17 A.L.R.2d 904.

Yet it must be clear that the indicated ordinary situation does not involve any of these proscribed activities. Rather, it entails the psychological inducement to the broker to find the transaction that will serve his interest (and simultaneously, or collaterally, the parties'), with this being done in ways so unconsciously subtle that no judge or jury — nor even a psychoanalyst — could recognize and deal with them. The ordinary buyer needs no inducement toward a lower price; that is his built-in goal. Similarly, the conventional transaction seldom involves the availability of prefixed better terms. The best price is, of course, that hammered out in the unhampered give-and-take of negotiation. It is just that which the principal may not get. But, by and large, there can be no proof of this; without proof, no remedy; and then ultimately, no effective legal right. . . .

From the above it may be surmised that the difficulty in resolving this problem results from the attempted forcing of general agency principles upon the uniquely special brokerage situation. Such technique here, as in trying to force a common last on an uncommon foot, is sure to pinch, pain and cause (legal) bunions. For the critical question is not whether the vendor may on his limited knowledge be satisfied with the sale. It is whether he might have been *more* satisfied had the broker acted otherwise in the *fullest* pursuance of his duties. In transactions such as these, it seems somewhat strange and artificial that the law has wholly refused to recognize the seemingly obvious fact that the broker may also be acting, in primary or integral part, for himself in the matter.

The final sale/purchase decisions are, of course, for the transacting parties. But the broker brings a wide range of general and particular experience to bear on such decisional process. Included are his general background in the field, his evaluation of the potential buyer's status and attitude, and probably even his formal recommendations on the transaction. These undoubtedly have a *major,* if not often controlling, effect upon such ultimate decisions. . . . The potential conflict in the broker's role is both fully understandable and socially acceptable if the law as well as the business world recognize it as a practical fact of life. In doing so they would take it into consideration in all realty transactions. Its undesirability stems from the possibility that the law may continue to overlook it while voicing inoperative platitudes of duty and responsibility. And then the business world (i.e., the mass of individual sellers and buyers) may unfortunately follow suit, to its detriment. If this happens, our body of commercial law will be perpetuating legal fiction that will prevent its coming fully to grips with the proper needs of the business world which, in the ultimate analysis, it is intended to guide and protect.

Federal Trade Commission, The Residential Real Estate Brokerage Industry[2]

F.T.C. Staff Rep. 7, 16, 17, 63, 110-112, 145-146 (1983)

Listing brokers perform a number of tasks designed to facilitate the sale of a home. Commonly, one of the most important of these is listing the home with the local "multiple listing service" (or "MLS"). This service, generally owned and operated by a local association of brokers, is an information sharing or exchange mechanism, the use of which is reserved to its broker members. It is a means of informing the members, who are potentially "cooperating brokers," of the seller's desire to sell. The listing broker will describe the property, the asking price, any unusual features, outstanding mortgages, and so forth in the "MLS listing" and also indicate his or her willingness to "split" the commission with any cooperating broker who finds a suitable buyer, indicating the percent of the commission which will

---

2. Footnotes omitted.

be given as a split (typically, this may amount to half of the total commission due on sale of the property).

Buyers often work with brokers to find suitable homes to buy. While a broker commonly will inform a prospective buyer of the broker's own listings first, he or she will then turn to the local MLS to find additional listings which may meet the buyer's needs. If the buyer makes a selection, the buyer makes an "offer" to purchase the home. This offer typically will be at a price below that originally asked by the seller. A process of negotiation often follows with "counter-offers" relating to price and other terms (who will pay for a termite inspection, for example) changing hands through the intermediation of the broker. . . .

Most MLSs allow only exclusive right-to-sell listing contracts to be processed using their facilities. Only 18 percent of the MLSs which responded to an FTC survey of such institutions reported accepting exclusive agency listings [broker receives a commission if another broker sells the property during the listing period but not if the seller does], and only 11 percent would accept open listings. Most brokers presumably prefer exclusive right-to-sell listings [broker receives a commission if the property is sold during the listing period regardless of who sells it]. Such listings have two obvious effects. They prevent the seller from selling the property without paying the broker a commission when the broker has spent serious time and effort in trying to dispose of it. And they also prevent a seller from putting pressure on a dilatory broker during the listing period by threatening to find a buyer and sell the house him or herself. . . .

The growth of the MLSs during the last 60 years has been the most important development in the modern brokerage industry. The historical reasons for and effects of multiple listing give important insights into today's industry. Today, 92 percent of sellers using brokers have their homes listed on an MLS. A number of industry commentators have concluded that the MLS is essential for a broker to compete and effectively market homes in most areas.

All MLSs impose conditions of membership. These rules and regulations may have a substantial impact on the nature and degree of competition in the industry. Of the MLSs we surveyed for this Report, 94 percent were affiliated with a local Board of Realtors. Membership in the Board usually is required to obtain access to a Realtor MLS. However, even where Realtor membership is not a condition, 89 percent of the brokers who participate in the MLSs were, on average, Realtors. Realtor membership, in turn, means accepting a number of conditions, including compliance with the NAR's Code of Ethics and payment of its membership dues (which include dues for membership in all three levels of the NAR structure — local, state, and national). . . .

The concept of multiple listing was based upon the need to devise an efficient method for marketing exclusive listings. With an exclusive listing only one broker had direct rights and incentives to sell the house. By the 1920's, however, sellers had become aware of the advantages of obtaining exposure through many brokers. For this reason exclusive listings had become nearly impossible for brokers to obtain. The open listing was the general rule.

From the broker's point of view, open listings were associated with a number of problems. These problems related to competition among listing brokers, competition with sellers, and duplication of effort by brokers. . . .

The MLSs and exclusive listing agreements, when used together, reduced the problems presented by unfettered competition. With an exclusive listing, only one broker could claim the commission. Other brokers could not work directly with the seller. Cooperation of other brokers with the exclusive listing broker (someone with whom they could anticipate dealing cooperatively on many different future sales and therefore with whom they could establish an ongoing professional relationship) was the basis of the new marketing system. "They have replaced the old spirit of competition for one of cooperation, and it has brought peace where there was strife, and harmony where discord reigned." [H. Nightengale, California Real Estate at 12 (April 1924).] . . .

Open listings were also associated with competition with the seller. Substantial numbers of sellers at that time were making direct sales to buyers even after listing their homes with a broker who spent time and effort to sell it. The MLSs and the exclusive-right listing agreement helped to stop this. The MLSs would accept only exclusive-right listings, and the exclusive-right listings most brokers came to insist upon in most transactions guaranteed the broker a commission even if the seller procured the buyer. . . .

Open listings sometimes might be given to as many as 20 brokers. Many of these brokers might spend time trying to sell the property only to find that they could not deliver the property to a prospective buyer. Either the property had been sold, withdrawn from the market, or the price had gone up. Listings were considered the broker's inventory, the stock on his shelves. Open listings, however, were analogized to perishable goods. A broker had no certainty that they would remain viable, saleable listings.

This waste of time and the inability to deliver properties even if purchasers were found are problems which brokers still associate with open listings. The exclusive contracts required by most MLSs eliminated these perceived problems by binding the seller to a specific listing period and a specific price. Further, with an exclusive, the listing broker receives some protection from other brokers and from the seller. Even if another, cooperating broker or the owner sells the listing, the initial, listing broker will receive a substantial portion of the commission. . . .

When the rewards for any occupation are inflated, the occupational choices of individuals are distorted, and, in the absence of barriers to entry, people will enter that occupation in excess numbers—in essence bidding away those higher rewards by lowering the productive value of each worker in the industry. If there are in fact higher-than-competitive commissions in the brokerage industry, that can be expected to have had the effect of attracting excess entry into the business of selling real estate. The goods and services such individuals would have produced in alternative fields will have been lost to the economy and are a measure of resource misallocation. Fred Case estimates that in 1979, there were 819,000 brokers and 1,218,000 salespersons licensed in the U.S. . . .

In recent years it has been fashionable to predict that eight to ten large national corporations and franchises will soon dominate the residential brokerage market. These predictions have been caused by two relatively recent phenomena. First, the spectacular rise in home prices combined with a stable or rising commission rate has meant a corresponding rise in total industry revenues. These revenues have attracted the attention of large national corporations, several of which have investigated the field. A few, e.g., Coldwell Banker and Merrill Lynch, undertook the process of entry through purchases of local, traditional brokerage firms. Second, there has been very rapid growth in real estate franchising in recent years.

At present, the largest corporate chain of residential brokerage offices is Coldwell Banker. This national firm's total national market share of residential brokerage transactions, based on revenues generated from residential brokerage, was, however, estimated at less than .5 percent in 1977.

Coldwell Banker, Merrill Lynch, and other large corporations attempting to enter or expand rapidly in the residential brokerage industry have generally done so by purchasing existing businesses. Acquisitions are preferred because entry at the local market level requires knowledge of the local market conditions. However, entry through such purchases has been quite difficult for at least two reasons. Because the primary assets of the firm are local management and a sales force with a knowledge of local conditions, it is very difficult to assign a dollar value to such corporations. If the talented people leave, the prospective corporate owner may have nothing left but an empty shell. Second, the taxation consequences of an acquisition to the broker-owners of traditional firms appear to be such that they often prefer to remain independent.

While the picture of rapidly escalating corporate growth through acquisition of existing firms may be somewhat exaggerated, the growth of the franchise systems has indeed been spectacular. From a very small market share in 1970, such systems may now account for as much as 38 percent of industry transactions. In 1977 there were approximately 7,000 franchisees. In 1979 this number had increased to approximately 15,000 franchisees.

Century 21 has been, at least in terms of number of franchisees, the most successful franchise system. This system was founded in 1972. By 1979 there were over 7,000 Century 21 franchisees. Their total industry market share for that year has been estimated at between 8 percent and 14 percent of total industry transactions. It may now have reached 18 percent.

Real Estate Listing Service v. Connecticut Real Estate Commission
179 Conn. 128, 425 A.2d 581 (1979)

ARTHUR H. HEALEY, Associate Justice. The plaintiff, Real Estate Listing Service, Inc. (hereinafter RELS), is comprised of a group of real estate brokers and is itself a licensed broker. The defendant is the Connecticut real estate commission (hereinafter commission). Pursuant to General Statutes §4-176, RELS sought a declaratory ruling from the commission to determine whether, under certain circumstances, §20-328-3 of the regulations of the commission would prohibit the plaintiff and its real estate brokers from negotiating the sale of real property pursuant to a certain real estate listing agreement. Section 20-328-3 of the regulations provides: "No licensee shall negotiate or attempt to negotiate the sale, exchange or lease of any real property directly with an owner or lessor knowing that such owner or lessor has an outstanding exclusive listing contract with another licensee covering the same property." The plaintiff submitted a sample "Non-exclusive Listing Agreement"[1] (hereinafter RELS listing) to the commission with two questions. First, the plaintiff sought to know whether a broker who had executed a RELS listing with a property owner would be in violation of §20-328-3 if he were to attempt to negotiate the sale of the property where another broker has, subsequent to the RELS listing, entered into an exclusive listing agreement with the same

---

1. In pertinent part, the RELS listing provides as follows: "This agreement is subject to section 53-35 of the General Statutes as amended (Public Accommodations Act). This will remain in effect until _____ and the owners also agree(s) to pay a commission of _____ of the agreed listed selling price. This listing is given to _____ as listing agent, who will distribute and solicit the assistance of each member of R.E.L.S. Inc. to find a purchaser for the above described property. It is agreed that this listing agreement does not restrict the owner's right to sell the property directly and without obligation to the listing agent, or to grant non-exclusive (OPEN) listing agreement to any other real estate agents. However, in order to insure a fair opportunity to show and sell the property during the term of this listing agreement, the owners agree not to grant any exclusive listing during the term of this agreement. Such an act on the part of the owners will be deemed a breach of this agreement causing damage to the listing agent. As damages will be difficult or impossible to measure, all parties to this agreement agree that the listing agent will be entitled to damages equal to the commission specified above on this listing agreement. It shall be payable by the owners at the time of granting an exclusive to any real estate agent on the above described property. The owners also agree to notify the listing agent of any change in the status of the property as to price and in the event of its sale will advise the listing agent in writing as to the names of the buyers, the selling price and the selling real estate agent.

Owner's [Name] _____ Address _____
Tel. _____ Attorney _____ Date _____
Listing Broker _____ Address _____
Tel. _____
MEMBER REAL ESTATE LISTING SERVICE 816-1616

Listing information is as furnished by the Seller and is purported to be accurate but not guaranteed. This is a legally binding contract; if not understood, seek competent legal advice."

property owner. Second, the plaintiff requested the commission to declare whether, in the situation set forth above, the agent who entered into an exclusive listing agreement with a property owner while the RELS non-exclusive listing agreement was in effect would be violating any regulation of the commission or any statute. The commission answered the first question in the affirmative and the second in the negative. RELS appealed from the commission's rulings to the Court of Common Pleas and sought a judgment declaring §20-328-3 of the regulations invalid. The trial court concluded that the RELS listing is "mostly an open listing" cancellable by the owner at any time and that the regulation was a valid exercise of the state's power to restrict the right to contract. Accordingly, it entered judgment for the defendant commission.

From that judgment the plaintiff has appealed, claiming that the RELS listing is a valid contract and that the regulation impairs the obligation of contract, violates the plaintiff's right to due process and denies equal protection of the laws, and, therefore, is unconstitutional. Were we to adopt the interpretation accorded the regulation by the commission, we would conclude that the regulation as applied here is unconstitutional. We find it unnecessary to adopt the commission's interpretation of the regulation, however, and conclude that, properly interpreted and applied, the regulation is constitutionally sound.

I

The threshold question in this appeal is whether the RELS listing is an offer looking to a unilateral contract terminable by the property owner at any time before the agent's performance of a bilateral contract with fixed rights and liabilities.[2] This initial determination is essential inasmuch as the plaintiff argues that a property right, which derives from a valid bilateral contract, has been destroyed by the regulation as interpreted by the commission. Because only three types of real estate listing agreements have traditionally been used in this state, the trial court felt obliged to place the RELS listing in one of the three commonly recognized categories. Those categories are: the open listing, under which the property owner agrees to pay to the listing broker a commission if that broker effects the sale of the property but retains the right to sell the property himself as well as the right to procure the services of any other broker in the sale of the property; the exclusive agency listing, which is for a time certain and authorizes only

---

2. We recognize the trend of recent authorities, including the Restatement (Second) of Contracts and the Uniform Commercial Code, not to use the terms "bilateral" and "unilateral." See Reporter's Note, Restatement (Second) of Contracts §12 (Tent. Draft No. 1, 1964). We employ the terms, however, because they are particularly useful in the analysis of the real estate listings we discuss in this opinion and do not here generate the adverse consequences sometimes said to flow from their mechanical application. See Calamari & Perillo, Contracts §1-10.

one broker to sell the property but permits the property owner to sell the property himself without incurring a commission; Firszt v. Wdowiak, 104 Conn. 744, 745, 133 A. 586 (1926); Harris v. McPherson, 97 Conn. 164, 167, 115 A. 723 (1922); see 12 Am. Jur. 2d Brokers, §226; and the exclusive right to sell listing, under which the sale of the property during the contract period, no matter by whom negotiated, obligates the property owner to pay a commission to the listing broker. Harris v. McPherson, supra, 167, 171, 115 A. 723; see 12 Am. Jur. 2d, op. cit.; see also Gross, Illustrated Encyclopedic Dictionary of Real Estate Terms. The open listing, as described above, is an offer looking to a unilateral contract; that is, an offer that is accepted by performance. Although the property owner promises to pay the listing broker his commission when he produces a ready, willing and able buyer, he does not seek a promise in return from the broker, but only performance of the act requested. 1 Corbin, Contracts §§70, 71; 1 Williston, Contracts (3d Ed. Jaeger) §§13, 65. Although such offers are often referred to as "contracts," they do not obligate the broker to do anything; hence, they lack mutuality of obligation and are, therefore, unenforceable. See Hess v. Dumouchel Paper Co., 154 Conn. 343, 347, 225 A.2d 797 (1966); Thos. J. Sheehan Co. v. Crane Co., 418 F.2d 642, 646 (8th Cir. 1969); 1A Corbin, Contracts §152; 12 Am. Jur. 2d Brokers, §32. The traditional open listing merely gives a broker permission to sell real property within a specified time. Since it is unsupported by consideration, an open listing may, in the absence of part performance or action in reliance, be revoked at any time before the broker's performance without the property owner incurring any obligation. Ibid.[3] Both the exclusive agency and the exclusive right to sell listings, as distinguished from the open listing, constitute valid bilateral contracts. Under both, the property owner relinquishes to some extent the right, although not the power,[4] to alienate his real property. Likewise, the broker incurs an obligation to use his best efforts during the contract period to procure a buyer.[5] Thus, the obligations being mutual, an enforceable contract has been formed and rights and liabilities have vested. Where an exclusive listing contract has been entered into, the respective obligations of each party are enforceable by the other even if the object of the agreement (the sale of the property) is never achieved.

The trial court concluded that the RELS listing is "mostly an open listing." This equivocal language reflects the flaw in the trial court's reasoning. Because the RELS listing contains a provision characteristic only of

---

3. Historically, there have been differing views on whether part performance would constitute acceptance and prevent the promisor from revoking an offer looking to a unilateral contract. See Calamari & Perillo, Contracts §2-24; Restatement (Second) of Contracts §§52, 63, 35A, 45 (Tent. Draft No. 1, 1964); §90 (Tent. Draft No. 2, 1965).

4. See Harris v. McPherson, 97 Conn. 164, 169-171, 115 A. 723 (1922); 12 Am. Jur. 2d, Brokers, §55.

5. Even if the exclusive listing agreement fails to obligate the broker to use his best efforts to obtain a buyer, this condition is implied by law in §20-328-6 of the regulations.

an open listing (permitting the property owner to obtain the services of other real estate brokers to effect the sale of his property), the trial court concluded that the RELS listing is essentially an open listing. As a consequence, the trial court ascribed to the listing submitted by the plaintiff all the features of an offer looking to the formation of a unilateral contract, including the promisor's right to terminate it at will prior to performance.

This interpretation is contrary to the plain language of the contract, which we cannot ignore. Scribner v. O'Brien, Inc., 169 Conn. 389, 398, 363 A.2d 160 (1975); see Anderson v. Pension & Retirement Board, 167 Conn. 352, 355, 355 A.2d 283 (1974). The contract is for a term certain and provides for liquidated damages upon its breach.[6] The broker promises to "distribute [the listing] and solicit the assistance of each member of R.E.L.S. Inc. to find a purchaser for the above described property." The property owner promises to pay a set commission to the broker if the property is sold at the listed price, and also agrees "not to grant any exclusive listing during the term of [the] agreement." These mutual promises, which confer benefits and corresponding detriments on the respective parties, are sufficient consideration to support a bilateral contract. See Calamari & Perillo, Contracts §4-1; 1 Corbin, Contracts §142; 1 Williston, Contracts (3d Ed. Jaeger) §100; State National Bank v. Dick, 164 Conn. 523, 529, 325 A.2d 235 (1973); Finlay v. Swirsky, 103 Conn. 624, 631-632, 131 A. 420 (1925). There being no essential element of a contract missing from the RELS listing or for which it does not make some provision, we must conclude that the RELS listing agreement submitted to the commission constitutes a valid bilateral contract.

II

We must now determine whether §20-328-3 of the regulations as interpreted and applied by the real estate commission is constitutional.[7] The commission decided that §20-328-3 would be violated by Broker A where Broker A and a property owner execute the RELS listing, the property owner later enters into an exclusive listing agreement with Broker B, and Broker A thereafter continues to attempt to sell the property. The plaintiff claims that §20-328-3 of the regulations, so interpreted, impairs the obligation of contract and thereby violates article 1, §10 of the United States constitution. We need not explore this claim in great detail inasmuch as the impairment of contractual obligations clause has long been interpreted to apply to state legislation or regulations; Appleby v. Delaney, 271 U.S. 403, 46 S. Ct. 581, 70 L. Ed. 1009 (1926); which, operating retrospectively, adversely affect the vested rights of parties to an existing contract. See

---

6. We are not called upon to pass on the validity of the liquidated damages provision.
7. We have already decided that §20-328-3 of the regulations is not unconstitutional on its face. See Brazo v. Connecticut Real Estate Commission, 177 Conn. 515, 524-525, 418 A.2d 883 (1979).

Ogden v. Saunders, 25 U.S. (12 Wheat.) 213, 218, 6 L. Ed. 606 (1827); Oshkosh Waterworks Co. v. Oshkosh, 187 U.S. 437, 439, 23 S. Ct. 234, 47 L. Ed. 249 (1903); Congressional Research Service, The Constitution of the United States of America, Analysis and Interpretation (1973) pp. 406-407; 16 Am. Jur. 2d., Constitutional Law, §450. There being no actual contract with vested rights in existence in this case, the constitutional prohibition is inapplicable. Cf. Elida, Inc. v. Harmor Realty Corporation, 177 Conn. 218, 222, 223, 413 A.2d 1226 (1979).

We now address the plaintiff's argument that the regulation as interpreted deprives it of property without due process of law. It has long been recognized that the right to make contracts is embraced in the concept of liberty under the due process clause of the fourteenth amendment to the United States constitution. Morehead v. New York, 298 U.S. 587, 610, 56 S. Ct. 918, 80 L. Ed. 1347 (1936); West Coast Hotel Co. v. Parrish, 300 U.S. 379, 391-392, 57 S. Ct. 578, 81 L. Ed. 703 (1937). It is also well settled, however, that the state may, in the exercise of its police powers, limit the freedom to contract where the health, safety, morals and well being of those subject to its jurisdiction require. West Coast Hotel Co. v. Parrish, supra, 391, 57 S. Ct. 578; Cyphers v. Allyn, 142 Conn. 699, 705, 118 A.2d 318 (1955). "[N]either the 'contract' clause nor the 'due process' clause has the effect of overriding the power of the state to establish all regulations that are reasonably necessary to secure the . . . general welfare of the community." Atlantic Coast Line R. Co. v. Goldsboro, 232 U.S. 548, 558, 34 S. Ct. 364, 368, 58 L. Ed. 721 (1914); see Brazo v. Connecticut Real Estate Commission, 177 Conn. 515, 524-525, 418 A.2d 883 (1979). The plaintiff's claim requires us to examine the regulation as interpreted by the commission to determine whether it serves some need of the public health, convenience and welfare in a reasonable and impartial way. C & H Enterprises, Inc. v. Commissioner of Motor Vehicles, 167 Conn. 304, 308, 355 A.2d 247 (1974); Mott's Super Markets, Inc. v. Frassinelli, 148 Conn. 481, 487, 172 A.2d 381 (1961). The prohibition imposed must have some rational relationship to a legitimate state interest sought to be protected. Ibid. We are mindful of the fact that the legislature, which has chosen to speak through a regulatory agency in this case; General Statutes §20-328; see Hartford Electric Light Co. v. Sullivan, 161 Conn. 145, 154, 285 A.2d 352 (1971); has broad discretion in passing on the interest to be protected and the method to be employed. Mott's Super Markets, Inc. v. Frassinelli, supra.

We are unable to discern any rational basis for the commission's interpretation of the regulation. We are not confronted with an administrative determination that only certain types of real estate listings can be employed in Connecticut.[8] The regulations contain no such restriction and it

---

8. We do note, however, that a "net price listing" is prohibited in Connecticut. See Regs., Conn. State Agencies §20-328-2.

is not our duty to fashion one. In the absence of a specific prohibition, the broad right that individuals have to fashion their contractual relations must prevail. It is the "general rule . . . that competent persons shall have the utmost liberty of contracting and that their agreements voluntarily and fairly made shall be held valid and enforced in the courts." Twin City Pipe Line Co. v. Harding Glass Co., 283 U.S. 353, 356, 51 S. Ct. 476, 477, 75 L. Ed. 1112 (1931); see Collins v. Sears, Roebuck & Co., 164 Conn. 369, 376-377, 321 A.2d 444 (1973). There is no doubt that the commission's interpretation of §20-328-3 not only permits a real estate broker to obtain an exclusive listing and thereby violate an existing valid bilateral contract, but encourages him to do so. The commission's interpretation of §20-328-3 does not further a legitimate interest of the state, and, in this case, operates in an arbitrary manner to deprive the plaintiff of a property right without due process of law.[9]

III

We cannot adopt the interpretation accorded §20-328-3 by the commission, which was accepted by the trial court. Although the factual and discretionary determinations of administrative agencies are to be given considerable weight by the courts; see General Statutes §4-183(g); Board of Aldermen v. Bridgeport Community Antennae Television Co., 168 Conn. 294, 298-299, 362 A.2d 529 (1975); Westport v. Norwalk, 167 Conn. 151, 355 A.2d 25 (1974); 2 Am. Jur. 2d, Administrative Law, §§645, 675; it is for the courts, and not for administrative agencies, to expound and apply governing principles of law. N.L.R.B. v. Brown, 380 U.S. 278, 291, 85 S. Ct. 980, 13 L. Ed. 2d 839 (1965); International Brotherhood of Electrical Workers v. N.L.R.B., 159 U.S. App. D.C. 272, 299-300, 487 F.2d 1143, 1170-1171 (D.C. Cir. 1973), aff'd, sub nom. Florida Power & Light Co. v. International Brotherhood of Electrical Workers, 417 U.S. 790, 94 S. Ct. 2737, 41 L. Ed. 2d 477 (1974); 73 C.J.S. Public Administrative Bodies and Procedure §69. Because we have concluded that the commission's interpretation of the regulation would compel us to declare it unconstitutional, we must determine whether another interpretation of the regulation, which would result in sustaining its constitutionality, is reasonable.[10] Lublin v. Brown, 168 Conn. 212, 219, 362 A.2d 769 (1975); Adams v. Rubinow, 157 Conn. 150, 153, 251 A.2d 49 (1968).

We observe that the language of the regulation is plain and unambiguous. Simply stated, it enjoins a broker from negotiating or attempting to

---

9. Our conclusion on this portion of the plaintiff's argument makes it unnecessary for us to reach the plaintiff's claim that the regulation denies him equal protection of the laws.

10. We must presume that the body that promulgated §20-328-3 intended to comply with the constitution. See Whitfield v. Empire Mutual Ins. Co., 167 Conn. 499, 507-508, 356 A.2d 139 (1975).

negotiate the sale or rental of real property where that broker is aware of an outstanding exclusive listing contract that the owner has entered into with another broker. The regulation does not purport to apply to a situation in which the property owner has earlier executed a valid bilateral listing contract, such as the one submitted by the plaintiff in this case. Thus, in terms of our earlier hypothetical, Broker A may, without violating §20-328-3, continue to attempt to sell the property listed in the RELS listing despite a subsequent exclusive listing agreement with Broker B. The owner has breached his RELS listing contract by signing the exclusive listing agreement with Broker B. Broker B has not violated §20-328-3 by obtaining an exclusive listing, although Broker B may thereby incur liability under private law principles arising out of tortious interference with contractual relationships.

The proper application of §20-328-3 of the regulations is illustrated in Brazo v. Connecticut Real Estate Commission, 177 Conn. 515, 524-525, 418 A.2d 883 (1979). In *Brazo,* a real estate broker and a property owner had executed an exclusive real estate listing agreement for the sale of certain property. Thereafter, knowing of the existing listing agreement, another broker negotiated the sale of property included in that agreement. *Brazo* demonstrates the appropriate factual setting in which §20-328-3 should be applied.

There is error, the case is remanded to the Superior Court with direction to modify the declaratory judgment in a manner not inconsistent with this opinion.

In this opinion the other Judges concurred.

NOTES

1. *Nonexclusive listing: multiple commissions.* (a) Casner and Leach, Cases and Text on Property 700 (3d. ed. 1984): "O places his property in the hands of B_1, B_2 and B_3 for sale at $10,000. B_1 produces a customer at $10,000. Before a contract is signed B_2 produces a customer at $11,000, so O refuses to sign with B_1's customer and instead signs with B_2's customer. B_2's customer suffers losses and cannot go through with the sale. Thereupon B_3 shows up with a customer at $9500, and O, disgusted with the whole affair, signs with B_3's customer and goes through with the deal. O has to pay three commissions."

Does the hypothetical suggest that O, under a nonexclusive listing, is liable to each of as many brokers as show up with buyers before O contracts with any buyer? Does the hypothetical suggest that O is liable for more than one commission if, after O contracts with B_2's buyer, B_2 (unaware of the signing) continues efforts and then produces a buyer? On these problems see Seavey, Agency §171 (1964).

(b) About half of the real estate brokers in the United States are organized into local trade associations known as Real Estate Boards, and in turn are members of the National Association of Realtors (NAR). Only members are entitled to use the registered service mark "Realtor."

The National Association publishes a Code of Ethics to which the "Realtor" is expected to adhere. Article 6 of the Code provides: "To prevent dissension and misunderstanding and to assure better service to the owner, the realtor should urge the exclusive listing of property unless contrary to the best interest of the owner." In a hearing on a client complaint, the NAR Professional Standards Committee held that two realtors dealing with the same client had violated Article 6 by not urging the client to list his property on an exclusive basis, thereby subjecting the client to a possible obligation to pay two commissions, as each realtor had produced a willing and able buyer on the client's terms. National Association of Realtors, Interpretations of the Code of Ethics, Case 6-2 (1976).

2. *Exclusive listing: multiple listing.* Owners who eschew the exclusive in favor of nonexclusive or open listings presumably have their property shown more often (with some nuisance) by the several brokers, though perhaps each broker's enthusiasm is diminished by the risk of losing out to the others.

An exclusive can be keyed into a multiple-listing system under which members of a local real estate board file their listings with the board, and all member brokers are privileged to sell any property thus filed. When the property is sold, the listing and the selling broker (if they are not the same) divide the commission on a formula set by the board.

Under multiple listing, sometimes the extra brokers function formally as sub-agents of the "exclusive" broker, sometimes viz., "the owner gives brokers and all active Realtor members of the Board of Realtors of the Plainfield Area, Inc., the exclusive right etc. . . ."

The broker-prepared listing agreements may obligate a broker to use multiple listing, perhaps to help bilateralize the contract.

3. Seller has listed with broker under an arrangement whereby broker may retain everything obtained from buyer over an amount designated as net of commission and payable to seller. The secondary authorities, for example, 12 Am. Jur. 2d §92 (1964), do not suggest that the arrangement is "illegal," but it is a queasy device, particularly where it is discovered that broker, acting through a dummy, obtains the property from seller in a sales contract put through at a price modestly above seller's net, but later resells at a price returning far more to broker than the usual commission. 12 Am. Jur. 2d, Brokers §91 (1964).

Whether or not the net listing is, per se, or in usual operation, interdicted by the common law, the National Association of Realtors in its Interpretations of the Code of Ethics, 1964, has suggested that a Realtor who enters a net listing arrangement with a customer violates a professional obligation to serve clients as a fiduciary rather than an antagonist and is subject to disciplinary action.

To the extent that there are ethics committees of local "Realtors" boards which enforce the NAR Code of Ethics, a nonjudicial forum is offered for brokerage disputes, one in which the broker is purportedly held to standards of conduct more rigorous than those of the common law. No formal information is available on the extent of use of these standards in this forum; several experienced brokers in different parts of the country have told us that board settlement of broker-client disputes is, in their areas, rare.

Can the NAR Code and the Interpretations be used to define tort standards of conduct or contract obligations for purposes of ordinary civil litigation against brokers who are members of "Realtors" boards? "Realtor" is a service mark owned by the NAR and only the members of local boards are privileged to use the mark. The mark "Realtor" is extensively advertised by the NAR: the ads represent that a "Realtor" is an adherent to a Code of Ethics that sets the realtor apart from and above you and me. To some extent, this representation is believed by the general community. Thus an article in Changing Times, Jan. 1964, at 22, states that the best protection in dealing with a real estate salesperson is to determine whether he or she is a member of a real estate board and thus bound by the NAR Code of Ethics.

In Ward v. Taggart, 51 Cal. 2d 736, 325 P.2d 502 (1958), the court quoted but did not rely on the NAR Code in holding a broker liable for breach of duty to the client. See also Gear v. Webster, 258 Cal. App. 2d 57, 65 Cal. Rptr. 255 (1968).

Modern tort law expanding as it is, perhaps the NAR and/or local boards have sufficiently represented "Realtor" as a seal of approval so as to be liable for individual broker derelictions. See Note, Tort Liability of Independent Testing Agencies, 22 Rutgers L. Rev. 299 (1968).

Haymes v. Rogers
70 Ariz. 257, 219 P.2d 339 (1950)

DE CONCINI, Justice. Kelley Rogers, hereinafter called appellee, brought an action against L. F. Haymes, hereinafter referred to as appellant, seeking to recover a real estate commission in the sum of $425. The case was tried before a jury which returned a verdict in favor of appellee. The said appellant owned a piece of realty which he had listed for sale with the appellee, real estate broker, for the sum of $9,500. The listing card which appellant signed provided that the commission to be paid appellee for selling the property was to be five (5%) percent of the total selling price. Tom Kolouch was employed by the said appellee as a real estate salesman, and is hereafter referred to as "salesman."

On February 4, 1948, the said salesman contacted Mr. and Mrs. Louis Pour, prospective clients. He showed them various parcels of real estate, made an appointment with them for the following day in order to show them appellant's property. The salesman then drew a diagram of the said property in order to enable the Pours to locate and identify it the next day for their appointment. The Pours, however, proceeded to go to appellant's property that very day and encountering the appellant, negotiated directly with him and purchased the property for the price of $8,500. The transcript of evidence (testimony) reveals that the appellant knew the Pours had been sent to him through the efforts of appellee's salesman but he did not know it until they verbally agreed on a sale and appellant had accepted a $50 deposit. Upon learning that fact he told the Pours that he would take care of the salesman.

Appellant makes several assignments of error and propositions of law. However, we need only to consider whether the trial court was in error by refusing to grant a motion for an instructed verdict in favor of the defendant.

One of the propositions of law relied upon by the appellant is as follows: "The law requires that a real estate broker employed to sell land must act in entire good faith and in the interest of his employer, and if he induces the prospective buyer to believe that the property can be bought for less, he thereby fails to discharge that duty and forfeits all his rights to claim commission and compensation for his work."

There is no doubt that the above proposition of law is correct. . . .

The facts here are clear and undisputed. The salesman informed the purchasers that he had an offer at $8,250 for the property from another purchaser which he was about to submit to appellant. He further told them he thought appellant would not take $8,250 but would probably sell for a price between $8,250 and $9,500 and that they in all probability could get it for $8,500. The agent was entirely without justification in informing the purchasers that the property might be bought for $8,500, since that placed the purchasers at a distinct advantage in bargaining with the principal as to the purchase price of the realty. As a general rule an agent knows through his contacts with his principal, how anxious he is to sell and whether or not the principal will accept less than the listed price. To inform a third person of that fact is a clear breach of duty and loyalty owed by the fiduciary to his principal. Such misconduct and breach of duty results in the agent's losing his right to compensation for services to which he would otherwise be entitled. 2 Am. Jur. 235, Agency, section 299, Restatement of Agency, section 469. . . .

This determination makes a consideration of the other grounds for appeal unnecessary. Under the circumstances the court should have directed a verdict for the defendant, appellant.

Judgment reversed.

La Prade, C.J., and Stanford and Phelps, JJ., concur.

UDALL, Justice (dissenting). I dissent for the reason that as I construe the record in the instant case the facts do not disclose such bad faith or gross misconduct on the part of the broker as to disentitle him to compensation.

Broker's Duties to Buyer and Seller

There is no disagreement between us as to the high standard which the law prescribes must be maintained in dealings between an agent and his principal. . . . The difficulty comes in applying the law to the facts of this case.

The great majority of the reported cases denying a brokerage fee involve instances where (1) the agent acts adversely for the purpose of securing a secret profit for himself or otherwise advancing his own welfare at the expense of that of his employer; (2) an agent disclosing the necessitous circumstances of his principal; (3) the agent is guilty of fraud or dishonesty in the transaction of his agency; (4) his conduct is disobedient or constitutes a wilful and deliberate breach of his contract of service; or (5) where he withholds information from his principal which it is his duty to disclose. . . . I submit, however, that the facts before us do not place the conduct of this broker within any of the prohibitions above enumerated and I have been unable to find a single case where the courts have denied compensation under a factual situation comparable to that presented by this record. . . .

An analysis of the testimony before us, when taken as it must be in the light most favorable to a sustaining of the judgment, shows but four questionable matters. First, the agent advised his principal, before the Pours came onto the scene, that in his opinion the listed sales price of $9500 was excessive. This statement was made after repeated efforts to sell to others at the list price had failed. I can see nothing improper in this. Second, the agent advised Pour (the ultimate purchaser whom he had procured) that his principal, the owner, then had on his desk for acceptance or rejection an offer of $8,250 which offer, in his opinion, the seller would not accept. There may have been some impropriety in this disclosure of his principal's business but I cannot read into this slip such gross misconduct as to warrant denying him compensation. Third, complaint is made that the broker failed to exert his best efforts to effect a sale to the Pours at the list price of $9500. In my opinion there is no merit to this contention because it is clear that the broker did advise the prospective purchasers that the owner's asking price was $9500 and it further appears that appellant perfected the sale with the Pours the evening of the first day they were contacted and before the broker's salesman had an opportunity to keep an appointment for the following day at 1:00 P.M., when he was to show them the property in question. It is unthinkable to believe that any purchaser would buy property without first seeing it. The majority evidently do not base the reversal upon any of these derelictions so finally we consider what is urged as the broker's most serious breach of duty to act in good faith and for the interest of the appellant, to wit, his unauthorized statement that the owner might accept less than the list price. To keep the record straight I quote from the cross-examination of salesman Tom Kolouch:

"*Q.* And you also told them at that time that you were pretty sure if they would offer $8500 for the property that they would get it?

A. I told them they might try $8500. I didn't tell them for sure they would get it because I wasn't setting a price on the other man's property.
Q. And you told them if they would offer $8500 that they might get the property?
A. They might have, yes.
Q. And there wasn't anything said at that time about their offering $9500 for the property?
A. I told them the price was $9500 on our list."

And the following is Mr. Pour's version of the matter:

"Q. He told you to go out there and offer $8500 for the property?
A. No, he told me it was listed for more, but he didn't think this offer would go through, and if I met somewhere in between I might get it."

In effect, as I view it, all the appellee intended by his statements to the Pours was to hold their interest in the property until he could show it to them and the parties could be brought together. I understand it to be the law that the ultimate duty of the broker toward his principal is to procure a purchaser ready, willing and able to purchase upon terms agreed upon by the owner and the purchaser. How then can it be said that the effort of the broker in the instant case in attempting to interest a purchaser and bring the purchaser and owner together by stating that the property might possibly be purchased for less than the quoted price (something which every prospective purchaser would be justified in assuming and which is a hope in the mind of every buyer) amounted to a breach of his duty to act for his principal's best interest? Will not the court's opinion be construed as holding that if a broker states to a purchaser or even indicates in any manner that property might be acquired for less than the listed price his right to a commission is thereby forfeited? If such be the declared law of this state it will certainly give a wide avenue of escape to unscrupulous realty owners from paying what is justly owed to agents who have been the immediate and efficient cause of the sale of their property. . . .

I would affirm the judgment as entered by the learned trial court.

On Rehearing: 70 Ariz. 408, 222 P.2d 789 (1950)

DE CONCINI, Justice. In our former opinion . . . we held that as a matter of law there was bad faith shown on the broker's part which precluded him from recovery of his commission. In the light of the motion for rehearing and a reexamination of the evidence and instructions we are constrained to change our view. . . .

The defendant below requested an instruction on bad faith which the trial court refused to give. . . .

The evidence in this case presents a close question as to good or bad faith on the part of the broker. The trial court should have submitted that issue to the jury to decide. . . .

In this case the appellant sold the property to a purchaser whom he knew was sent to him by the appellee's salesman. Therefore, in the absence of bad faith the broker is entitled to his commission when he is the procuring cause of sale. . . .

Judgment is reversed and the case remanded for a new trial with directions to submit the question of bad faith on the part of the appellee to the jury. Judgment reversed.

La Prade, C.J. and Udall, Stanford and Phelps, JJ., concurring.

NOTES

1. As to broker's duties to seller, aside from the usual fiduciary obligation of honesty, broker has to reach some level of competence. Causing the principal to miss a good deal or enter a bad one may cost the broker the commission. In Schoenberg v. Benner, 251 Cal. App. 2d 154, 59 Cal. Rptr. 359 (1967), broker recommended that seller sell to an impecunious buyer. Buyer had given broker a false statement of the value of his assets. Broker could easily have tried to confirm buyer's statement but failed to do so. Seller conveyed outright to this buyer; seller received from buyer $20,000 cash (of which $7500 went to broker) and buyer's promise to pay an additional $117,500, a promise not secured by a mortgage on the transferred land. Buyer then mortgaged the unencumbered land to a bona fide purchaser bank and absented himself with the proceeds. Seller was awarded a $125,000 judgment against the broker. On broker's action over against buyer, the court held that the buyer's misbehavior fell short of legal fraud on the broker. Also, failure of broker to provide seller with adequate information on prospective buyer's financial condition can prevent broker from being entitled to a commission even though broker produced an ostensibly able and willing buyer on the seller's terms. Gatlinburg Real Estate Co. v. Booth, 651 S.W.2d 203 (Tenn. 1983).

See generally Annot., Liability of Real Estate Broker to Principal for Negligence in Carrying Out Agency, 94 A.L.R.2d 468 (1960).

2. Some states have funds from which those damaged by wrongful acts of real estate brokers may recover at least some of their losses. Illinois's statute provides in part:

> **Ill. Ann. Stat. ch. 111, §§5823, 5828**
> **(Smith-Hurd Supp. 1985)**
>
> *§5823.* The Department of Registration and Education shall establish and maintain a Real Estate Recovery Fund from which any person aggrieved by an act, representation, transaction or conduct of a duly licensed broker, associate broker, salesperson or unlicensed employee, which is in violation of

this Act or the regulations promulgated pursuant thereto, or which constitutes embezzlement of money or property or money or property unlawfully obtained from any person by false pretenses, artifice, trickery or forgery or by reason of any fraud, misrepresentation, discrimination or deceit by or on the part of any such licensee or the unlicensed employee of any such broker, and which results in a loss of actual cash money as opposed to losses in market value, may recover. Such aggrieved person may recover by order of the circuit court of the county where the violation occurred, an amount of not more than $10,000 from such Fund for damages sustained by the act, representation, transaction, or conduct, together with costs of suit and attorneys' fees incurred in connection therewith of not to exceed 15% of the amount of the recovery ordered paid from such Fund. However, no licensed broker, associate broker or salesperson may recover from the fund unless the court finds that the person suffered a loss resulting from intentional misconduct. Such court order shall not include interest on the judgment.

The maximum liability against such Fund arising out of any one act shall be as provided in this Section and the judgment order shall spread the award equitably among all co-owners or otherwise aggrieved persons, if any. The maximum liability against such Fund arising out of the activities of any single broker, any single associate broker, any single salesperson or any single unlicensed employee, since January 1, 1974, shall be the sum of $50,000. . . .

Any person who makes application for an original license to practice as a broker, associate broker, or salesperson shall pay, in addition to the original fee, a fee prescribed in Section 15 of this Act for deposit in the Real Estate Recovery Fund. If the Department does not issue the license, this fee shall be returned to the applicant.

§5828. When, upon the order of the court, the Department has paid from the Real Estate Recovery Fund any sum to the judgment creditor, the Department shall be subrogated to all of the rights of the judgment creditor and the judgment creditor shall assign all right, title, and interest in the judgment to the Department and any amount and interest so recovered by the Department on the judgment shall be deposited in the Real Estate Recovery Fund.

Many states have similar funds, called client security funds, for lawyers' defalcations. Most such lawyer funds are administered by a bar association and financed by assessments on all lawyers in the state. See Comment, Attorney Misappropriation of Clients' Funds: A Study in Professional Responsibility, 10 U. Mich. J.L. Ref. 415, 423-432 (1977).

Sanders v. Stevens
23 Ariz. 370, 203 P. 1083 (1922)

MCALISTER, J. This is an action by Albert Stevens against B. B. Sanders, in which it is sought to recover $500 alleged to have been paid by the former as the result of certain false and fraudulent representations of the latter regarding the purchase price of certain real estate. The plaintiff was given judgment for $200, and from this and the denial of his motion for a new trial defendant appeals.

One G. R. Finch was the owner of certain real property in Tempe, Ariz., known as the Butte Garage. In March, 1919, B. B. Sanders, appellant herein, as his agent, sold this property to plaintiff, Albert Stevens, for $6,500, a payment of $1,000 being made at the time of the sale. Plaintiff complains that Sanders represented to him that he was commissioned to sell this property for $6,500, with a payment of $1,000 down, and that he believing these representations to be true, was thereby induced to and did purchase it for the sum and pay appellant $1,000 thereon; that subsequently he ascertained that the owner had commissioned appellant to sell the property for $6,000, and not for $6,500, and had required a payment of only $500 down instead of $,1000; and that appellant had paid the owner $500 of said $1,000, and retained the other $500 for his own use and benefit. . . .

It is contended in behalf of appellant that even though he did represent to appellee that Mr. Finch "asked $6,500 for the property, and that he required a $1,000 payment down," when the actual fact was that he wanted only $6,000 net to himself, a recovery cannot be had, because such representation, if untrue, is not actionable for the reason that there is no duty devolving upon the agent to disclose to the purchaser the owner's lowest price. An examination of the record discloses the fact that the statement was not made in response to a direct question by Mr. Stevens regarding the lowest price the owner would take, but arose in this way: Appellant knew from some source that appellee was looking for a location for a garage and, meeting him in the Farmer's and Merchants' Bank in Tempe on March 7, 1919, asked him if the Butte Garage would suit him. He replied that he thought it would if he could get it right, whereupon appellant said: "You leave it to me, and I will get you a good price on it." A day or two later they met on the streets and appellant stated to him that he had seen Mr. Finch, and "he asked $6,500 for the property, and that he required $1,000 down." . . .

[The court decided that the representation was not untrue: Mr. Finch did want $6000 net for the property, but he also must have wanted Sanders to get some reasonable return for his selling effort.]

But, conceding that it conveyed to appellee the impression that Mr. Finch "asked $6,500" less the usual commission of 5 percent, still such representation would not be actionable, because it was a matter of no concern to the purchaser how the purchase price was divided between the owner and the agent, so long as there is no claim that by reason of such false representation the purchaser paid an excessive value for the property. After deciding that it suited him, appellee, as a prospective purchaser, naturally became interested in the amount the property could be bought for — what the cost to him would be — and when he had ascertained this and satisfied himself of the reasonableness of it there remained but one thing for him to do to complete the purchase, and that was to pay the amount required. It was no concern of his whether all he paid or merely a part went to the owner, so long as it secured for him the property. The extent of the agent's commission, which he must have known was something, could have been of no possible materiality to him. . . .

Some authorities hold, however, that where the agent falsely represents the owner's lowest price when questioned directly by the prospective purchaser regarding it, he is liable for the "surplus [of the price paid] over and above the [net price] and his reasonable commission." Kice v. Porter (Ky.) 53 S.W. 285; Estes v. Crosby, 171 Wis. 73, 175 N.W. 933, 177 N.W. 512, 8 A.L.R. 1377. In this case there was no inquiry by the purchaser as to the owner's lowest price, but merely a statement by him that the property would be suitable "if he could get it right." The weight of authority, however, is to the effect that a false representation as to the owner's lowest price is not actionable, because it is not a representation of a material fact. The following excerpt from McLennan v. Investment Exch. Co., 170 Mo. App. 389, 156 S.W. 730, gives the reasoning of the courts holding this view:

"It is idle to talk of the plaintiff having a right to buy the land at the lowest price the owner would take for it. . . . Neither has a legal right to the other's best price, and, therefore, the representation of either that he has made his best offer cannot be said to be a representation of a material fact. To say otherwise would be to impose a restriction on the right of persons to make their own bargains. . . ."

In order that false representations may form the basis of an action for deceit, it must appear, in addition to the other necessary facts, that the person to whom they were made acted upon them to his damage; otherwise no cause of action is established. 12 R.C.L. 240. Appellee has not shown that he was damaged by the alleged false representations because there is no evidence that he could have purchased the property from Mr. Finch direct for $6,000, or any other sum under $6,500, if appellant had disclosed to him the amount of his commission. The mere fact that the owner had listed it with appellant to be sold for a certain sum "net to him" does not prove that he himself would have sold it for this amount to a purchaser whom appellant had caused to approach him on the subject. For him to have done so knowingly would have been profiting from appellant's labors without paying for them, a thing that the law, to say nothing of square dealing, does not permit.

The judgment is reversed, and the cause remanded, with directions to the superior court to enter judgment for appellant.

Ross, C.J., and Flanigan, J., concur.

Zichlin v. Dill
157 Fla. 96, 25 So. 2d 4 (Sup. Ct. 1946) (en banc)

ADAMS, Justice. This appeal brings for review an order dismissing appellant's bill on motion. The bill discloses that George E. Dill was a licensed real estate broker in Hillsborough County and advertised a piece of real estate for sale. Appellant responded to the "ad" and was shown the property and quoted a selling price of $5,500 by the broker. Later appellant was shown the property by the owner, who mentioned a figure of $4,500, whereupon appellant said she understood from the broker the price was $5,500. Then the owner told appellant all arrangements, including the price, were in the control of the broker. Appellant returned to the broker and said she desired to purchase the property but would like to buy it for $4,500. The broker took $200 from appellant as earnest money and represented that he would ascertain whether the property could be bought for $4,500. Later the broker notified appellant that the property could not be purchased for less than $5,500. The broker induced appellant not to engage an attorney to represent her in closing the transaction saying he would attend to all details and record the deed. It was about two weeks later the deed was mailed to her from the office of the clerk of the court when she then first learned the deed was from the broker rather than from the owner; that the property was conveyed by the owner to the broker and by the broker to appellant at, or near, the same time; that both conveyances showed a consideration of $4,500 and the broker, in fact, used appellant's money to purchase the property for himself, making a profit of $1,000.

Appellant's question posed in the brief states: "Is a purchaser of property who buys for $5500.00 after being advised by the broker that it can not be bought for less than that sum, when as a matter of fact the broker uses the money of the purchaser to buy the property for himself for $4500.00, and then on that same day conveys it to the purchasers for $5500.00, entitled to the return of $1000.00 from said broker?" Ultimately we must determine just what duty the broker owed appellant. Did he owe a duty to any one except the owner who had listed the property? Evidently the chancellor was of the view that he owed no duty to the buyer. In this he was in error. Generally speaking an agent is responsible only to his principal. This, however, is different. The broker in Florida occupies a status under the law with recognized privileges and responsibilities. The broker in this state belongs to a privileged class and enjoys a monopoly to engage in a lucrative business. See Sec. 475.01 et seq., Fla. Stat., '41 F.S.A. The statute requires that (475.17): ". . . all applicants who are natural persons shall be competent, honest, truthful, trustworthy, of good character, and bear a reputation for fair dealing. . . ."

The state, therefore, has prescribed a high standard of qualifications and by the same law granted a form of monopoly and in so doing the old rule of caveat emptor is cast aside. Those dealing with a licensed broker may naturally assume that he possesses the requisites of an honest, ethical man.

On this question the authorities are not uniform, however, because of the statute supra we are inclined to the view heretofore stated which finds ample authority among our sister states. Collins v. Philadelphia Oil Co., 97 W. Va. 464, 125 S.E. 223; Stevens v. Reilly, 56 Okl. 455, 156 P. 157; Hokanson v. Oatman, 165 Mich. 512, 131 N.W. 111, 35 L.R.A., N.S., 423; Hack v. Crain, Mo. Sup., 177 S.W. 587. See also notes in 8 A.L.R., page 1383; 12 C.J.S., Brokers, §41, page 96.

This bill, if proven, would support a decree for relief. The order dismissing the bill is reversed.

So ordered.

Terrell, Brown, Buford and Sebring, JJ., concur.

Chapman, C.J., and Thomas, J., dissent.

NOTES

1. What legal concept justifies recovery by the buyer against the broker in the *Zichlin* case — contract, tort, what?

2. A broker owes a duty to prospective buyers to submit their bids to the seller. In Stevens v. Jayhawk Realty Co., 236 Kan. 90, 689 P.2d 786 (1984), plaintiff's willingness to offer a price higher than that of the successful bidder was never communicated by the broker to the seller; as a result, plaintiff asserted that he lost money by failing to acquire a parcel of land on which he could turn a profit. Plaintiff sued the broker, the trial court awarded plaintiff damages of $37,000, but the judgment was reversed on appeal because the broker's alleged misconduct caused no loss to plaintiff since seller was aware of plaintiff's willingness to pay a higher price but despite this chose to sell to a lower bidder.

C. EARNING THE BROKER'S COMMISSION

Blank v. Borden[3]
11 Cal. 3d 963, 524 P.2d 127
(Sup. Ct. 1974) (en banc)

SULLIVAN, Justice. In the instant case we confront the question whether the familiar withdrawal-from-sale provision in an exclusive-right-to-sell con-

---

3. Some of the court's citations and footnotes are omitted.

tract between an owner of real property and a real estate broker exacts an unlawful penalty within the meaning of sections 1670 and 1671 of the Civil Code. We conclude that it does not. . . .

On April 26, 1970, defendant Erica Borden and plaintiff Ben Blank, a real estate broker, entered into a written agreement for the purpose of securing a purchaser for defendant's weekend home in Palm Springs. The agreement, a printed form contract drafted by the California Real Estate Association, was entitled "Exclusive Authorization and Right to Sell" and by its terms granted Blank the exclusive and irrevocable right to sell the property for the seven-month period extending from the date of the agreement to November 25, 1970. It further provided that if the property were sold during the said period the agent would receive 6 percent of the selling price, and that "if said property is *withdrawn from sale*, transferred, conveyed, leased without the consent of Agent, or made unmarketable by [the owner's] voluntary act during the term hereof or any extension thereof," the agent would receive 6 percent of the "price for the property" stated elsewhere in the agreement. (Italics added.) Relevant portions of the agreement are set forth [below].

EXCLUSIVE AUTHORIZATION AND RIGHT TO SELL
California Real Estate Association
Standard Form

1. RIGHT TO SELL. I hereby employ and grant Ben Blank Company, hereinafter called "Agent," the exclusive and irrevocable right to sell or exchange [the described real property]. . . .
2. TERM. Agent's right to sell shall commence on April 26, 1970 and expire at midnight on November 25, 1970.
3. TERMS OF SALE. (a) The price for the property shall be the sum of $85,000.00. . . .
4. COMPENSATION TO AGENT. I hereby agree to compensate Agent as follows: (a) Six % of the selling price if the property is sold during the term hereof, or any extension thereof, by Agent, on the terms herein set forth or any other price and terms I may accept, or through any other person, or by me, or six % of the price shown in 3(a), if said property is withdrawn from sale, transferred, conveyed, leased without the consent of Agent, or made unmarketable by my voluntary act during the term hereof or any extension thereof. . . .
5. If action be instituted on this agreement to collect compensation or commissions, I agree to pay such sum as the Court may fix as reasonable attorney's fees. . . .

Dated April 26, 1970,   Palm Springs,
                                                          California

x [signature]
Erica Borden, Owner

12. In consideration of the execution of the foregoing, the undersigned Agent agrees to be diligent in endeavoring to obtain a purchaser.

California

BEN BLANK COMPANY
Agent

By [signature]
Ben Blank

The findings of the trial court describe subsequent events in the following terms:

"5. Plaintiff at once began a diligent effort to obtain a purchaser for said property, including but not limited to the expenditures of monies for advertisements in the newspaper, but on or about June 26, 1970, while said exclusive sales contract was still in effect and while plaintiff was making a diligent effort to obtain a purchaser, defendant, without reason or justification, orally notified plaintiff that the property was no longer for sale and that he had no further right to make efforts to sell same or collect a commission, all in direct violation of said exclusive sales contract."

Determining that the foregoing constituted a withdrawal from sale within the terms of the agreement,[2] the trial court concluded that plaintiff Blank was entitled to compensation according to the agreement's provisions. Accordingly it rendered judgment in favor of plaintiff Blank in the amount of $5,100 (6 percent of $85,000) plus interest. Defendant has appealed.

At the outset we quickly dispose of two contentions relating to the substantiality of the evidence in support of the findings of the trial court which we have quoted above.

First, it is contended that there was no support for the finding that plaintiff was making a diligent effort to find a purchaser for the property when it was withdrawn from the market; this, it is urged, resulted in a failure of consideration. . . . There is evidence in the record that plaintiff contacted several parties — members of the country club on whose golf course the property fronted as well as other persons — with respect to the property, and that he ran newspaper advertisements concerning the property during the two months which preceded defendant's withdrawal of the property. The fact that plaintiff had produced no *offers* prior to the withdrawal of the property from the market of course does not in itself compel a finding that he was not making diligent efforts to find a purchaser.

Second, it is contended that the finding concerning defendant's with-

---

2. Apparently the property had not been returned to the market or sold by the time of trial. Defendant testified that she and her husband were at that time using the house as their principal residence.

drawal of the property from the market lacks substantial support. Again, however, our examination of the record discloses ample evidence to support the finding. The withdrawal occurred in the course of an argument which took place at the property between plaintiff and defendant's then fiance, Dr. Archer Michael.[3] Defendant was also present at the time. When Dr. Michael, after making statements which might reasonably be construed as threats of physical violence, told plaintiff to take his sign off the property and leave because his services were no longer wanted, plaintiff asked defendant whether she concurred. She replied that she did, and plaintiff departed. It was only after receiving a letter from plaintiff's attorney demanding payment pursuant to the contract that she attempted to soften her position and requested that plaintiff continue his efforts to sell the property. It was wholly within the province of the trial court, as finder of fact, to determine that the withdrawal was complete and unequivocal when made and that defendant's subsequent efforts through counsel to recant were ineffective and irrelevant.

We are thus brought to the single significant issue in this case, namely, the extent of recovery to which plaintiff is entitled under the contract.

It has long been the law of this state that any right to compensation asserted by a real estate broker must be found within the four corners of his employment contract. . . . By the same token, however, "[t]he parties to a broker's contract for the sale of real property are at liberty to make the compensation depend upon any lawful conditions they see fit to place therein. [Citations.]" (Leonard v. Fallas (1959) 51 Cal. 2d 649, 652, 335 P.2d 665, 668.) In short it is the *contract* which governs the agent's compensation, and that contract is strictly enforced according to its lawful terms.

It is equally well settled in this state that a withdrawal-from-sale clause in an exclusive-right-to-sell contract is lawful and enforceable, a claim for compensation under such a clause being not a claim for damages for breach of that contract but a claim of indebtedness under its specific terms. . . .

Defendant contends, however, albeit somewhat obliquely, that such clauses should be denied enforcement as an unlawful penalty[4] under the terms of Civil Code sections 1670 and 1671. The same argument was urged upon the court in Baumgartner v. Meek, 126 Cal. App. 2d 505, 272 P.2d 552, and was rejected in the following language: "We think this contention cannot be sustained in view of the contrary holdings in the cases referred to [i.e., Kimmell v. Skelly, supra, 130 Cal. 555, 62 P. 1067; Walter v. Libby (1945) 72 Cal. App. 2d 138, 164 P.2d 21; Fleming v. Dolfin (1931) 214 Cal. 269, 4 P.2d 776; Mills v. Hunter (1951) 103 Cal.

---

3. Subsequent to the events here in question but prior to judgment Dr. Michael and defendant were married.

4. "The term 'penalty' has traditionally been utilized to designate, inter alia, a charge which is deemed to be void because it cannot qualify as proper liquidated damages. . . ."

App. 2d 352, 229 P.2d 456]. The distinction between an action for breach of the promise by the owner not to revoke or deal through others or sell himself during the stipulated term, wherein damages are sought for such breach, and a contractual provision whereby, in consideration of the services of the broker to be and being rendered, the owner directly promises that if he sells through others or by himself or revokes he will pay a sum certain, is made clear in the cited cases, particularly in the quotations we have taken from the opinion in Kimmell v. Skelly. The action is for money owed, an action in debt, and the only breach involved is the failure to pay the promised sum." (126 Cal. App. 2d at p. 512, 272, P.2d at p. 556.)

We agree with the *Baumgartner* court that the withdrawal-from-sale clause in an exclusive-right-to-sell contract does not constitute a void penalty provision. . . .

. . . Its terms in no sense contemplate a "default" or "breach" of an obligation by the owner upon whose occurrence payment is to be made.[5] On the contrary, the clause in question presents the owner with a true option or alternative: if, during the term of an exclusive-right-to-sell contract, the owner changes his mind and decides that he does not wish to sell the subject property after all, he retains the power to terminate the agent's otherwise exclusive right through the payment of a sum certain set forth in the contract.

We do not see in this arrangement the invidious qualities characteristic of a penalty or forfeiture. As indicated above, what distinguishes the instant case from other situations in which a form of alternative performance is used to mask what is in reality a penalty or forfeiture is the element of rational choice. . . .

In the instant case . . . the contract clearly reserves to the owner the power to make a realistic and rational choice in the future with respect to the subject matter of the contract. Rather than allowing the broker to proceed with his efforts to sell the property, the owner, in the event that at any time during the term of the contract he changes his mind and decides not to sell after all, may withdraw the property from the market upon payment of a sum certain. In these circumstances the contract is truly one which contemplates alternative performance, not one in which the formal alternative conceals a penalty for failure to perform the main promise.[7]

---

5. Although the trial court's findings of fact and conclusions of law speak in terms of "breach" of the exclusive-right-to-sell contract, the judgment must be sustained if correct. "No rule of decision is better or more firmly established by authority, nor one resting upon a sounder basis of reason and propriety, than that a ruling or decision, itself correct in law, will not be disturbed on appeal merely because given for a wrong reason." . . .

7. The distinction we make here is discussed by McCormick in the following terms: "[I]n . . . an alternative contract the promise to pay may be a penalty, and void as such. If a contract provides that A will either convey land then worth about $10,000 within six months at a price of $10,000 or will pay $250, it is quite clear that a reasonable man might look forward to either choice as a reasonable possibility and there is no reason for hesitating to enforce the promise to pay if the land is not conveyed. If, on the other hand, A's promise provides that he shall either pay $100 on January 1st or $200 on demand thereafter, a

Further considerations support our determination that the contractual provision here at issue should be enforced according to its terms. First, it is important to recognize that we are not here concerned with a situation wherein the party who seeks to enforce the clause enjoyed a vastly superior bargaining position at the time the contract was entered into. On the contrary, the contract before us was one which was freely negotiated by parties dealing at arm's length.[8] While contracts having characteristics of adhesion must be carefully scrutinized in order to insure that provisions therein which speak in terms of alternative performance but in fact exact a penalty are not enforced, . . . we believe that in circumstances such as those before us interference with party autonomy is less justified. . . .

Moreover, it must be emphasized that the basic contract before us shares with other purely "commission" contracts the quality of being essentially result-oriented. Regardless of the amount of effort expended by the broker under such a contract, he is entitled to no compensation at all unless a sale occurs. By the same token, when a sale *is* effected, the compensation received is a percentage of the sale price—and this is paid regardless of the amount of effort which has been expended by the broker. If in this context we view the owner's exercise of a withdrawal-from-sale clause as an anticipatory "breach" of the main contract, the "damage" sustained by the broker would not be measured in the amount of effort expended by him prior to the "breach" but rather would be measured in terms of the value of the lost *opportunity* to effect a sale and thereby receive compensation. . . . The determination of this value would clearly degenerate into an examination of fictional probabilities—e.g., whether the broker, if allowed to continue his efforts for the full term of the contract, would have been successful in locating a buyer and effecting a sale. This consideration further strengthens our conviction that in these circumstances the contract of the parties, entered into in a context of negotiation and at arm's length, should govern their rights and duties. . . .

For the foregoing reasons we hold that the withdrawal-from-sale clause in an exclusive-right-to-sell real estate contract, long a part of real estate marketing practice in this state and long held to be valid and enforceable according to its terms, does not exact an unlawful penalty in violation of

---

different situation is presented. No reasonable man would, when the contract was made, consider that there was any rational choice involved (conceding the ability to pay either sum) in determining which course to pursue. If he can do so, he will pay the lesser sum, and the agreement necessarily is founded on this assumption, and the only purpose and effect of the formal alternative is to hold over him the larger liability as a threat to induce prompt payment of the lesser sum. Consequently, while an alternative promise to pay money when it presents a conceivable choice is valid, yet, if a contract is made by which a party engages himself either to do a certain act or to pay some amount which at the time of the contract no one would have considered an eligible alternative, the alternative promise to pay is unenforceable as a penalty." (McCormick, Damages, §154, pp. 617-618.) (Fns. omitted.)

8. The owner of real property has a considerable range of choice as to the type of arrangement he wishes to enter into with the broker he selects to effect the sale. (See, 1 Miller & Starr, Current Law of Cal. Real Estate, pp. 212-219.)

sections 1670-1671 of the Civil Code. The judgment below, which enforced the clause before us upon a showing that the explicitly stated conditions for its enforcement were present, was fully supported by the evidence and correct in all respects.

The judgment is affirmed.

Wright, C.J., and McComb, Mosk and Clark, JJ., concur.

BURKE, Justice (dissenting). I dissent. The majority never reach the question whether the "commission-on-withdrawal" clause in the instant case was an invalid penalty clause or an enforceable liquidated damages clause. (See Civ. Code, §§1670, 1671.) Instead, the majority neatly sidestep this issue by labelling the brokerage contract as one contemplating an "alternative performance" by the owner in the event he exercises his "true option" to withdraw the property from sale. To the contrary, the issue in this case cannot be avoided by the facile use of labels — otherwise any illegal penalty could be disguised as a "true option" by the promisor to pay a substantial sum for the privilege of breaking his contract. When we examine the essential nature of the exclusive brokerage contract, it becomes patently obvious that defendant *promised* to afford plaintiff broker the exclusive and irrevocable right to sell the property during a specified period, that defendant *breached that promise* by withdrawing the property from sale, that the contract itself specifies the *damages* for the breach, and that accordingly we must determine whether or not the damage provision was a penalty or liquidated damages provision. . . .

Nowhere in the contract is any mention made of any "option" given to defendant to withdraw the property from sale. Instead, the language of the contract makes it apparent that a withdrawal of the property without the broker's consent would constitute a breach of the owner's promise to grant an irrevocable right to sell the property during the specified period.[1] Indeed, it seems wholly naive to assume, as the majority do, that a property owner would have bargained for the "option" of withdrawing the property from sale, given the consequences of exercising that option, namely, the payment of the *full* commission which would have been payable to the broker had he sold the property for the original $85,000 asking price.

The majority suggest that defendant was given a "realistic and rational choice" under the contract to withdraw the property from sale, and that the contract was "freely negotiated" at "arm's length." Yet as the majority acknowledge in the first sentence of their opinion, the "commission-on-withdrawal" provision is a "familiar" one; in fact, the provision probably is

---

1. The trial court found that plaintiff had made diligent efforts to sell the property and that defendant without justification withdrew the property from sale, "in direct *violation* of said exclusive sales contract." (Italics added.) Accordingly, the trial court awarded plaintiff as his "commission" the sum of $5,100, representing six percent of the proposed sales price of $85,000, "as provided for in said contract in the event of a *breach* of said exclusive sales contract. . . . As a result of the foregoing, plaintiff has been damaged in the sum of $5,100.00. . . ." (Italics added.)

contained in every exclusive brokerage contract in this state.[2] In other words, no "true option" or "rational choice" is involved in this case — owners seeking to sell their property under an exclusive contract have no practical alternative but to agree to the "commission-on-withdrawal" provision. . . .

The specified damages could, of course, approximate actual damages in a situation in which the broker had negotiated a sale of the property at the original asking price, for in that situation the broker's actual loss would be the commission he otherwise would have earned. But the "commission-upon-withdrawal" clause purports . . . to require payment of the full commission whether or not a sale had been arranged. In that regard, the clause seemingly could not represent a reasonable effort to estimate the fair *average* compensation as required in *Garrett*. Moreover, as indicated in prior cases, ordinarily valuation of a broker's services is not so impracticable or extremely difficult as to justify use of a specified damages provision. . . .

NOTES

1. *Withdrawal from sale: likelihood of sale.* In Wright v. Schutt Constr. Co., 262 Or. 619, 500 P.2d 1045 (1972), broker sued owner for $20,000 as commission under a provision in an exclusive listing agreement that in the event the owner of the listed property withdrew the authority of the broker to sell the property, the owner agreed "to pay you the said commission just the same as if a sale had actually been consummated by you." The trial court was affirmed in its decision and findings of fact and law that (1) owner had breached the agreement by withdrawing the broker's authority during the listing period; (2) evidence as to the value of the property, and offers obtained prior to withdrawal showed that there was no reasonable prospect that broker could have arranged a sale during the listing at the listing price of "$200,000 net"; (3) accordingly, the provision for owner's liability for $20,000 upon withdrawal from sale was an unenforceable penalty rather than an enforceable pre-estimate of damages likely to flow from the breach; (4) plaintiff broker having failed to introduce evidence of damages was entitled to a judgment for nominal damages of $1, plus attorney's fees of $4330 (the legal foundation of the attorney's fee award is not set forth in the opinion). The Oregon Supreme Court expressly refused to follow Baumgartner v. Meek (the foundation case for Blank v.

---

2. "*The standard forms* of exclusive right to sell listings *in common use provide* . . . that the seller's withdrawal of the property from the market entitles the broker to his full commission immediately, regardless of whether he has procured a buyer before the time of the removal." (Italics added: California Real Estate Transactions [C.E.B.], §5.18, p. 137.) As the majority herein point out, "The agreement [was] a printed form contract drafted by the California Real Estate Association. . . ." (p. 32.)

Borden). The court noted that whether or not there was equality of bargaining power between the parties, the contract provision was in fact boilerplate.

2. *Types of listing contracts.* The *Blank* court, at its n.8, indicates that there are a variety of arrangements under which brokers are hired. The "exclusive" listing of the *Blank* case is a relatively recent institution, and should be contrasted with (a) "open" listing, under which the broker's efforts go unrewarded if, before broker has brought to seller a willing and able buyer, a seller either withdraws the property, sells it without broker's help, or sells it through another broker, and (b) "exclusive agency" listings, where broker earns a commission if the sale is arranged through another broker, but not if seller finds the customer or withdraws the property from sale.

McCue v. Deppert
21 N.J. Super. 591, 91 A.2d 503 (App. Div. 1952)

PROCTOR, J.S.C. Plaintiff appeals from a judgment entered in favor of defendant Peter C. Deppert upon a determination by the trial court at the close of the entire case that plaintiff had failed to prove facts sufficient to constitute a cause of action. Rule 3:50.

The evidence offered by the plaintiff may be summarized as follows: On March 25, 1949, Leon Kramer listed his farm property for sale with the plaintiff, a real estate broker. The asking price was $35,000 and the commission was to be 5%. The listing was oral. The property was also listed by Kramer with other brokers and plaintiff and another broker placed their signs on the property offering it for sale. Plaintiff showed the property to a number of prospective purchasers but, when no sale was effected, the owner reduced the asking price to $30,000 in September, 1949. Thereafter, plaintiff continued his efforts to interest buyers in the property. In January 1950 defendant Peter C. Deppert, who lived in Hasbrouck Heights, visited plaintiff's office in Red Bank and conferred with plaintiff's salesman, Lang, concerning the purchase of a ranch type house "with a little acreage." He was taken in Lang's car on a two-hour trip during which they visited several properties, including the Kramer farm in Colts Neck. Lang showed Deppert through the Kramer house, which was unoccupied at the time, and informed him that the asking price was $30,000. Deppert said that he liked the house and he thought his wife would like it, but he did not wish to acquire all the acreage and outbuildings. This being the only house in which Deppert expressed any interest, Lang suggested that they then confer with the plaintiff who might be able to make an arrangement with the owner to sell the property with less acreage. Deppert replied he was not in a position to do anything that day but, on parting, told

Earning the Broker's Commission

Lang "he would definitely be down within five or six weeks time with his wife" to see the house, and "if they were interested we would go down at that time to Mr. McCue's office and work out any particulars." Deppert never again communicated with plaintiff's office, but in April 1950 went to the Kramer property, made inquiries in the neighborhood and learned that the owner lived in Lakewood. Thereupon, although McCue's office in Red Bank was only 3 miles away, he proceeded to Lakewood, a distance of over 15 miles, where he met Kramer and discussed the purchase of the property. At this meeting Kramer inquired of Deppert whether he was sent by a broker and Deppert replied in the negative. During the course of the conversation, Kramer offered to show the property to Deppert. Deppert replied that he had already seen it; that as the gate was open, he drove in and, finding a door unlocked, he went through the house. Kramer then suggested that Deppert arrange to have his wife see the property, but Deppert answered that she had already seen it.

The sale was later consummated between Kramer and Deppert for $25,000. Kramer testified that he sold for this amount because "there was no broker charge for this." When drawing up the contract of sale on May 8, 1950, at the office of his attorney, in reply to a question from Kramer's attorney, Deppert stated that no broker was involved, and a clause, "The purchaser warrants that there is no broker involved," was inserted in the contract. At this time the listing of the property with the plaintiff was still in effect.

The trial court's basis for removing the case from the consideration of the jury was that the plaintiff, not having acquired a right to receive a commission from the seller, could have no claim against the buyer. . . .

The case is predicated upon an unlawful interference with plaintiff's business resulting in a deprivation of prospective or potential economic advantage. The right to pursue the real estate brokerage business is a property right that the law protects against unlawful interference. Kamm, Inc., v. Flink, 113 N.J.L. 582, 175 A. 62, 99 A.L.R. 1 (E. & A. 1934). . . . A misrepresentation made by the defendant for the purpose of securing a benefit with knowledge that it will be detrimental to the plaintiff is an [unlawful] act.

The circumstance that Kramer's agreement to pay a commission was oral and did not satisfy the statute of frauds does not remove the present action in tort against Deppert from the application of the above principles. The statute of frauds was enacted for the protection of the party sought to be charged. It is personal and not available to strangers to the agreement. Weinstein v. Clementsen, 20 N.J. Super. 367, 90 A.2d 77 (App. Div. 1952). Nor is it essential that plaintiff prove that he actually earned his commission under the brokerage agreement. While it is true the procurement of a ready, willing and able purchaser is a condition precedent to the duty of an owner to pay a real estate broker's commission, if the conduct of the defendant prevented that condition from happening, he cannot rely on his own wrongful acts as a shield from liability. It is sufficient that plaintiff prove facts which, in themselves or by the inference which may be legitimately drawn therefrom, would support a finding that, except for the tortious interference by the defendant with the plaintiff's business relationship with the owner, plaintiff would have consummated the sale and made a profit. The action lies not only for interference with the fulfillment of an executed contract but also for malicious interference with the right to conduct negotiations which might culminate in such a contract. . . .

From the proofs it was open to the jury to find that the defendant Deppert became interested in the property through plaintiff's efforts, determined to buy it, and, but for Deppert's representation to the owner that no broker was involved, it was reasonably probable that plaintiff would have consummated the sale; it was also open to the jury to find that this representation was untrue and made with the intention of eliminating plaintiff from the transaction to the defendant's financial gain. Such a finding would constitute an unjustifiable interference with plaintiff's prospective economic advantage. . . .

Reversed and remanded. Costs to abide the event.

NOTES

1. *Brokers' statute of frauds.* Many states have statutes or regulations barring a broker's action for a commission in the absence of a writing signed by the customer. Such a provision, for example, was upheld as valid and the broker denied a commission in Milholin v. Vorhies, 320 N.W.2d 552 (Iowa 1982), noted in 32 Drake L. Rev. 845 (1982-83), with cases in support collected. Furthermore, unlike other statute of frauds situations, a broker whose commission agreement is unwritten may not obtain a quantum meruit recovery for the value of services performed. 2 Corbin on Contracts §321 (1950). Why deny a broker a quantum meruit recovery if the commission agreement is unwritten?

See the material on the origins of the Wisconsin brokers' statute of frauds in Friedman, Contract Law in America, reprinted at page 2 supra. Is this relevant to the quantum meruit question?

2. *Nonexclusive listing: warranties.* Seller's lawyer in the *McCue* case exacted of buyer a warranty in the contract of sale: "[T]here is no broker involved." Is this clause relevant to broker's rights against *buyer*?

Compare the following, used where seller has listed with more than one broker: "The brokers and purchasers jointly and severally agree that in the event there is a claim for sales commission by any other broker on account of this sale, the brokers and purchasers agree to defend any action in court or otherwise at no expense to seller, and pay any amount for which seller is held liable, including costs."

Dworak v. Michals
211 Neb. 716, 320 N.W.2d. 485 (1982)

BUCKLEY, District Judge. This is an action brought by plaintiff, Douglas J. Dworak, a licensed real estate broker, against defendants, F. R. Michals, Sr., and Nebraska Real Estate Corporation, for the sum of $5,376, the same representing the amount of commission plaintiff claimed he was entitled to for having produced ready, willing, and able buyers to purchase an apartment complex owned by Michals and listed for sale with defendant Nebraska Real Estate Corporation, of which he was president.

The action was tried to the court, which determined that plaintiff was not entitled to a commission but was entitled to $250, which was one-half of the earnest money deposit, and entered judgment for that amount against both defendants. From this judgment plaintiff appeals.

The material facts are not disputed. The listing contract between Michals and Nebraska Real Estate Corporation was executed on April 6, 1977. It provided for a 6 percent commission in the event a purchaser was found "who is ready, willing and able to purchase the property before the expiration of this listing." It was a Multiple Listing Service contract, which meant that the listing was promulgated to all member realtors of the Multiple Listing Service in the Lincoln, Nebraska, area. This was accomplished by distribution of a Multiple Listing "sheet" or "ticket" which contained a photograph of the building and information concerning the property, which included an "income estimate" and "expense estimate." The income estimate specified 12 five-room apartments at $215 per month rent and 10 garages renting for $15 monthly.

Plaintiff, at that time a self-employed realtor and a member of the Lincoln Multiple Listing Service, received the listing on April 12, 1977. He contacted Michael Johanns and A. J. Swanson, whom he knew were interested in buying an apartment building for investment purposes. He gave them a copy of the listing sheet and took them through the property. Johanns and Swanson used the income and expense information on the listing sheet to calculate the cash flow, i.e., whether or not the rental income would be sufficient to cover all expenses, including the projected mortgage payment. They relied on the information on the listing sheet in making their cash flow calculations, which they determined would meet their requirements.

They then submitted an offer to purchase the property for $256,000 on April 14, 1977, which offer was accepted by Michals on the same day. The offer was accompanied by a $500 deposit, which was held by defendant Nebraska Real Estate Corporation.

While the buyers were in the process of securing a mortgage loan, the appraiser for the mortgage lender called Johanns on May 3 and told him that while he was at the property many tenants expressed extreme concern over the increase in rents planned for June 1, and that many of them threatened to move. Johanns relayed this to Swanson. Since both buyers were totally unaware of any planned increase in rents, Swanson immediately called Michals, who admitted that at about the same time the property was listed for sale the tenants were sent notices of an increase in rent, averaging about $15 per unit, effective June 1. He also admitted that the rents as shown on the listing sheet were not the rents currently in effect but in fact were the rents to be charged on June 1. When Swanson demanded that some form of action be taken over the situation, Michals immediately agreed to release the buyers from the purchase contract, which they elected to do, and the release was executed on the following day, with the $500 deposit returned to the buyers. The plaintiff Dworak first learned of the release later and, after his demand for a commission was refused, brought this suit.

The parties agree that if plaintiff is entitled to a commission it would be in the sum of $5,376, which is 2.1 percent of the sales price and his share as a nonlisting broker of the total commission due. Plaintiff contends he is entitled to the commission because he produced buyers who were ready, willing, and able to purchase the property when the contract to purchase was signed, notwithstanding that the sale was never closed. Defendants contend that plaintiff's commission would not be earned until the sale is consummated, unless the failure to consummate is the fault of the seller. They then contend that in fact the sale did not close because the buyers became unwilling and backed out of the agreement.

As to the applicable law, the defendants are correct. In the case of Cornett v. Nathan, 196 Neb. 277, 242 N.W.2d 855 (1976), we analyzed the law in this area. First, we noted that "[t]his court has consistently held that a broker has not earned his commission unless he produces a buyer who is ready, able, and willing to buy on terms satisfactory to the seller." Id. at 279, 242 N.W.2d at 857. In Wisnieski v. Coufal, 188 Neb. 200, 204, 195 N.W.2d 750, 753 (1972), we said: "A broker earns his commission and becomes entitled thereto when he produces a purchaser who is ready, able, and willing to purchase at a price and upon terms specified by the principal or satisfactory to him." In Huston Co. v. Mooney, 190 Neb. 242, 245, 207 N.W.2d 525, 527 (1973), this court said: "Ordinarily a real estate broker, who for a commission undertakes to sell land on certain terms and within a specified period, is not entitled to compensation for his services unless he produces a purchaser within the time limited who is ready, able, and willing to buy upon the terms prescribed."

In *Cornett,* however, the buyer was financially unable to consummate the sale. It is not clear whether this condition existed when he signed the agreement to purchase. We recognized that the intent of the parties in the usual listing agreement is that the seller expects to pay a commission only if the sale is completed, because, in most cases, the only source capable of paying the commission is the proceeds from the sale of the property. We further recognized that the reason for the payment of substantial commission fees is the requirement placed upon the real estate broker that he produce not just a person who will sign an agreement to purchase on hopes and expectation, but one who is ready, willing, and able to pay.

We then went on in *Cornett* to disapprove any notion that the commission is earned as soon as the seller accepts an offer to purchase, noting that to do this would place an unreasonable and unrealistic burden on the seller to determine the buyer's readiness, willingness, and ability to complete the purchase at the time the offer to purchase is made. Rather, we placed this burden and the risk involved on the broker, since this would be his most important function in earning his commission.

We then concluded in *Cornett* that where the buyer is financially unable to close the sale, the broker has not earned his commission. In support of this conclusion, we cited the following language from Ellsworth Dobbs, Inc. v. Johnson, 50 N.J. 528, 551, 236 A.2d 843, 855 (1967): "When a broker is engaged by an owner of property to find a purchaser for it, the broker earns his commission when (a) he produces a purchaser ready, willing and able to buy on the terms fixed by the owner, (b) the purchaser enters into a binding contract with the owner to do so, and (c) the purchaser completes the transaction by closing the title in accordance with the provisions of the contract." This three-part test, as generally stated, would apply to the unwilling as well as the financially unable buyer. Since the rationale previously stated for requiring consummation of the sale for the broker to earn the commission would be just as applicable to the buyer who becomes unwilling as it would to the buyer who becomes unable, we adopt the three-part test set out in *Ellsworth Dobbs* as the general rule to determine when a real estate broker earns his commission.

The adoption of this rule, however, does not alter the obligation of the seller to pay a commission if the sale is not completed due to the fault or refusal of the seller. We have always held that, in such event, the broker has a right to the commission called for. See, Jones v. Stevens, 36 Neb. 849, 55 N.W. 251 (1893); Howell v. North, 93 Neb. 505, 140 N.W. 779 (1913); Lincoln Realty Co. v. Garden City Land & Immigration Co., 94 Neb. 346, 143 N.W. 230 (1913); Wisnieski v. Coufal, supra. This is also recognized in Ellsworth Dobbs, Inc. v. Johnson, supra, where the court, after setting out the three-part test, went on to say: "If the contract is not consummated because of lack of financial ability of the buyer to perform or because of any other default of his . . . there is no right to commission against the seller. On the other hand, if the failure of completion of the contract results from a wrongful act or interference of the seller, the broker's claim is valid and must be paid. In short, *in the absence of default by the seller,* the broker's right to commission against the seller comes into existence only when his buyer performs in accordance with the contract of sale." (Emphasis supplied.) Id. at 551, 236 A.2d at 855.

This case, then, turns on the question of whether the buyers Johanns and Swanson had a legal right to refuse to go further with the sale. If not, they become unwilling buyers and plaintiff is not entitled to a commission. If they did, the failure to close the sale is attributable to Michals and plaintiff has earned his commission.

The trial court found that the buyers backed out of a valid purchase contract. We feel the evidence is insufficient to support that finding. The decision of Johanns and Swanson not to complete the sale was based on the representation of the rents on the listing sheet and their discovery that those rents were not the current rents but new rent increases effective almost immediately after they would become the new landlord. They faced the risk of tenants leaving, with resultant vacant units and an insufficient cash flow, the very thing they relied on in their purchase offer. It would also lock them in from June 1 as to future rent adjustments. And, as Johanns put it, "there was a general pervasive fear of whether I could trust this seller."

The buyers could have defended an action by Michals for specific performance on the ground of misrepresentation. The facts support the essential elements, namely, a representation as a statement of fact, untrue when made, known to be untrue by the maker, with the intention that it be acted upon, and acted upon with resulting detriment. Moser v. Jeffrey, 194 Neb. 132, 231 N.W.2d 106 (1975); Buhrman v. International Harvester Co., 181 Neb. 633, 150 N.W.2d 220 (1967).

Defendants argue that the buyers were not entitled to rely on the rents shown on the listing sheet because the listing contract states: "MULTI-DWELLING LISTING. This information, although believed to be accurate, is not guaranteed." This statement does not appear on the listing sheet given to the buyers and containing the information the buyers relied on. There is no evidence that "this information" includes the statements on the listing sheet, but even it if did, neither plaintiff nor the buyers ever saw the listing contract between the defendants or otherwise were aware of it.

Defendants produced a Lincoln real estate broker who gave an expert opinion that it would be proper to list rents on the listing ticket in April that would not be effective until June, even though no notation such as "effective June 1" was made on the ticket. The expert further testified that the information is not adequate to form the basis of a purchase. But even if the listing sheet was acceptable by real estate standards, or more information is needed by the buyer, this does not alter the fact that the representations as to rents currently in effect were made and, considering the obvious purpose of the information on the sheet is to give a prospective buyer more knowledge about the property, including its investment potential, that the seller knows and intends that this information is likely to be disseminated to the prospective buyer.

It is, of course, the rule that the finding of the trial court in a jury-waived law action will not be disturbed on appeal unless clearly wrong. Henkle &

Joyce Hardware Co. v. Maco, Inc., 195 Neb. 565, 239 N.W.2d 772 (1976). Here, there is no evidence in conflict which is relevant to the determination of the right of the buyers to refuse to consummate the sale. It becomes a matter of law and we find that the buyers did have a lawful right to decide not to complete the purchase and that, therefore, the failure to complete the contract to sell is attributable to the conduct of Michals, which therefore entitles the plaintiff to his commission.

Plaintiff's entitlement to the commission is from the seller Michals, but not from defendant Nebraska Real Estate Corporation. The Multiple Listing Service contract obligates the parties to pay 2.1 percent of the sales price, or 35 percent of the 6 percent total commission, to a member broker, such as plaintiff, who procures the buyer. The plaintiff, then, is a third-party beneficiary of the listing contract. The beneficiaries of a contract may recover thereon, though not named as parties, when it appears by express stipulation, or by reasonable intendment, that the rights and interests of such beneficiaries were contemplated and being provided for therein. Fowler v. Doran, 123 Neb. 37, 241 N.W. 759 (1932). Since defendant Nebraska Real Estate Corporation did not receive the commission, the plaintiff's right to recover the commission due him is against defendant Michals.

The judgment of the District Court is reversed and the cause remanded with directions to enter judgment for the plaintiff against defendant Michals in the sum of $5,376 plus interest from May 15, 1977, that being the date of the scheduled closing of the sale, and to dismiss the action as to defendant Nebraska Real Estate Corporation.

Reversed and remanded with directions.

NOTES

1. It is often declared to be the prevailing American position that absent a contract between broker and seller expressly to the contrary, the broker who produces a buyer ready, able, and willing to buy on the seller's terms is entitled to a commission. Movement away from this position is apparent, with a growing number of courts approving the three-part test set forth in the New Jersey case of Ellsworth Dobbs, Inc. v. Johnson and discussed in Dworak v. Michals. The *Dobbs* test is protective of the seller and places added risks on the broker, including no commission if the buyer changes his or her mind after expressing willingness to buy on the seller's terms. Colorado, by statute, imposes restrictions on commissions similar to those in the *Dobbs* case. The Colorado statute provides:

> §*12-61-201. When entitled to commission.* No real estate agent or broker is entitled to a commission for finding a purchaser who is ready, willing, and

able to complete the purchase of real estate as proposed by the owner until the same is consummated or is defeated by the refusal or neglect of the owner to consummate the same as agreed upon.

§12-61-202. *Objections on account of title.* No real estate agent or broker is entitled to a commission when a proposed purchaser fails or refuses to complete his contract of purchase because of defects in the title of the owner, unless such owner, within a reasonable time, has said defects corrected by legal proceedings or otherwise.

Colo. Rev. Stat. §§12-61-201, 12-61-202 (1973).

Which is preferable: the prevailing American position, the *Dobbs* test, or the Colorado statute? Should most residential buyers' lack of familiarity with brokers' practices and laws governing brokerage agreements and real estate transactions be a significant consideration in determining which of the above three positions is preferable?

2. In Hecht v. Meller, 23 N.Y.2d 301, 244 N.E.2d 77 (1968), the seller's broker brought buyer and seller into a contract for sale of seller's residence and lot. After contract but before closing, the house was substantially destroyed by fire. Under a New York statute, this destruction excused buyer from the contract and entitled him to recover his down payment from seller, which he did. Broker sued seller for commission, obtaining a judgment from the trial court that was reversed by the Appellate Division. The Court of Appeals reinstated the judgment for broker. In doing so it did not quote or comment on the language of either listing agreement or contract of sale. The court rejected seller's argument that the statute, which, in terms, excused the buyer's duties to seller, somehow also excused the seller's duties to broker. It concluded that the seller, having failed to shift the fire loss either to the buyer or the broker, had to bear it all himself.

Mellos v. Silverman
367 So. 2d 1369 (Ala. 1979)

TORBERT, Chief Justice. Appellants, Thomas and Anthi Mellos, appeal the trial court's order awarding a broker's commission to appellees, Joel Silverman and Associates Realty, Inc., pursuant to an exclusive listing contract for the sale of certain realty and improvements owned by appellants.

On November 15, 1976, appellants entered into an agreement with appellee Associates Realty, Inc. (Associates) whereby Associates was given the exclusive right to sell the Embers Restaurant and Bamboo Lounge owned by appellants. The period covered by the agreement extended to March 1, 1977. The agreement gave Associates an exclusive right to sell the property and provided for a ten percent commission in the event the property was sold at the price authorized in the listing agreement or at any

Earning the Broker's Commission

other price agreed to by Mellos. The agreement authorized a sales price of $450,000 with $100,000 down and the balance at 9% simple interest over a 10-year term. The agreement also contained an extension clause which provided:

> In the event of said premises being sold or leased by me or any other person during the term of this agency or a sale or lease is later consummated with prospect introduced or interested in said property during such term by The Associates Realty, Inc., the commission above specified shall be considered earned.

During the term of the listing agreement, Nikola Nikolic became interested in purchasing the property. On Friday night, February 4, 1977, he went to the Embers and inquired of Thomas Mellos if the property was for sale and expressed an interest in purchasing the property. Mellos replied that he was too busy to discuss the matter at that time and to come back the next day. The following day Nikolic went instead to see Joel Silverman with whom the Embers had been listed prior to the agreement with Associates. Nikolic testified he had previously learned from Silverman that the property was for sale and consulted Silverman to get his opinion of the property and its value.

Silverman assisted Nikolic in preparing a written offer for the property, and since his listing had expired, obtained permission from Associates to present the offer to appellants. Silverman presented the offer to Mellos in the presence of his attorney at the Embers on February 9, 1977. The terms of the offer included a sales price of $300,000 with $100,000 down and the balance over a 20-year term at 7%. Appellants rejected the offer and made a counter-offer of $350,000 with $95,000 down and the balance over 20 years at 7%. The counter-offer was rejected. Nikolic then informed Silverman that he was no longer interested in the property. Both the offer and counter-offer provided that Silverman and Associates would split the commission.

The testimony is conflicting as to further contact between Nikolic and Silverman. Silverman asserts that he continued to contact Nikolic until the end of February, a period of about three weeks, hoping to convince him to talk to Mellos again. Silverman testified that he finally concluded that Nikolic was simply not a prospect and did not contact him further. Nikolic, however, testified that he only talked with Silverman once or twice and within a couple of days after his rejection of Mellos' counter-offer. Nikolic stated that he told Silverman he was no longer interested in the property and had made plans for a trip to Europe.

On March 1, 1977, the listing agreement with Associates expired, and Mellos listed the Embers with the Jim Broxton Agency. Nikolic and Mellos talked to each other again on March 22. At that time Nikolic's wife offered $275,000 for the Embers with $50,000 down and the balance over a

15-year term at 7½%. The offer was accepted. Mellos testified that he accepted less money than that originally offered by Nikolic because he was ill and tired and needed to immediately sell the property for health and financial reasons. Nikolic testified that Mellos called him explaining that he needed to sell the property and Nikolic's wife then got on the phone and offered $275,000 stating that he (Mellos) would never get $300,000.

Mellos called Jim Broxton advising him of the sale and inquiring whether he owed him any commission. Broxton replied that he did not. No commission was paid to either Silverman or Associates.

Silverman and Associates filed suit against appellants and Nikolic for the commission provided in the listing agreement and for punitive damages for fraud. The trial court, hearing the evidence ore tenus, granted a directed verdict in Nikolic's favor at the close of plaintiff's evidence and ruled that Silverman and Associates were entitled to the commission by virtue of the extension clause. The court further found that appellants were not guilty of any fraud.

Under an exclusive right to sell agreement, the parties contract that the broker is entitled to a commission if within the time specified in the agreement he produces a person ready, willing, and able to purchase the property on terms authorized or agreeable to the owner. Extension clauses provide that the broker is entitled to a commission notwithstanding the expiration of the term of the listing agreement if the property is sold to one with whom the broker, prior to such expiration, negotiated or had some other form of dealing described in the agreement. Shorten v. Mueller, 206 Okl. 62, 241 P.2d 187 (1952). The purpose of such a clause is to protect the broker by preventing the owner from postponing acceptance until the listing agreement has expired and thereby circumvent the broker's right to compensation for locating a purchaser. Harkey v. Gahagan, 338 So. 2d 133 (La. App. 1976). The validity and enforceability of extension clauses have been universally upheld. See, e.g., Beck v. Neal, 228 Ark. 186, 306 S.W.2d 875 (1957); Whiting v. Johnson, 64 Wash. 2d 135, 390 P.2d 985 (1964).

The owner and broker are free to frame their agreement as they see fit and may make the broker's commission dependent upon whatever conditions they agree upon so long as such conditions are not unlawful or contrary to public policy. Fischer v. Patterson, 97 N.H. 318, 86 A.2d 851 (1952). Under the language typically employed in extension clauses, it is not necessary that the actions of the broker be the "procuring" cause[1] of the sale although the broker must show some minimal causal connection between his efforts and the eventual sale. See, e.g., E. A. Strout Co. v. Hubbard, 104 Me. 366, 71 A. 1020 (1908); Kaye v. Coughlin, 443 S.W.2d

---

1. Procuring cause refers to a cause originating with a series of events which without break in their continuity result in procuring a purchaser ready, willing and able to buy on the owner's terms. Absent contractual provisions otherwise, the broker's activities must be the procuring cause of the sale. 12 Am. Jur. 2d Brokers §§189, 190.

612 (Tex. Civ. App. 1969); Lloyd Hammerstad, Inc. v. Saunders, 6 Wash. App. 633, 495 P.2d 349 (Wash. App. 1972). The courts have not formulated any precise rule or standard by which to determine the sufficiency of the broker's efforts. This result is largely attributable to the wide range of terms and expressions used in extension clauses to describe the obligation of the broker. Therefore, the nature and extent of the broker's efforts contemplated by the agreement must be determined in each case by a construction of the particular language involved. Englemann v. Auderer, 10 La. App. 136, 121 So. 194 (1929).

The expression used most frequently in extension clauses is that the broker must have "negotiated" with the buyer which has been construed as requiring that the broker interest the prospect to the extent that he becomes a likely purchaser, or, coming to terms or arranging the terms and conditions of a sale. See Clarke v. Blackfoot Water Works, 39 Idaho 304, 228 P. 326 (1942). Other expressions include to "offer," or "quote," or "submit" the property to the purchaser. These expressions have been construed to require less activity by the broker than the term "negotiate." Bullis & Thomas v. Calvert, 162 La. 378, 110 So. 621 (1926). Compare Werner v. Hendricks, 121 Pa. Super. 46, 182 A. 748 (1936) with Coppage v. Woodward, 105 So. 2d 306 (La. App. 1958) and Whiting v. Johnson, 64 Wash. 2d 135, 390 P.2d 985 (1964).

In the instant case, the extension clause provided for a sale consummated with a prospect "introduced or interested" in said property. This expression seems to require even less effort still by the broker. See Wachtel v. Harkless, 112 Ind. App. 279, 44 N.E.2d 510 (1942). In Wachtel, the court construed "introduced" as equivalent to "found" or "procured" and stated that the sale must be traced to the introduction of the purchaser to the owner. A face to face introduction is not contemplated, rather it is sufficient if the parties are brought into communication with each other. In that case, the broker's agent took the two prospective purchasers to the property, a tavern, and introduced them to the bartender. The owner was not present. They stated to the agent that they were interested in a place like this. Subsequently, without any further communication with the broker or the agent, they purchased the property. The court held the broker's efforts were sufficient to entitle him to the commission for there was no evidence that the prospect would have become a purchaser without the information from the broker.

The court in Carter v. Hayes, 337 So. 2d 295 (La. App. 1976), upheld the trial court's award of a commission to a broker under an extension clause requiring the broker to "interest" the ultimate purchaser in the property. At a gathering of farmers, the eventual purchaser inquired of the broker if he had any farms for sale. The broker replied that he did, but did not specify any particular farm. The purchaser unsuccessfully attempted to contact the broker during the next few days, but finally arranged a meeting after the listing had expired where he discussed in detail two farms, one of which he subsequently purchased. The broker contacted the owner to inform him that he had a purchaser, and since the listing had expired, to determine if the owner still wanted to sell the land. The owner replied that he did. Subsequently, the broker called the owner and sent the purchaser to see him. The parties then concluded a sale in the absence of the broker. The owner refused to pay the commission so the broker filed suit. The trial court held the broker was not entitled to a commission since, although the purchaser knew the broker had some property for sale, the purchaser did not know the owner, price, or location of the property prior to expiration of the listing agreement.

On appeal, the trial court's ruling was reversed. The court stated the contract only required the purchaser to be interested in the property during the term of the agency. The court noted that the purchaser would not have learned of the property but for the activities of the broker, the owner would not have known of the purchaser had the broker not called, and the sale was effected within a period of one month during which time there were no other prospective purchasers. The court concluded from these facts that the purchaser became interested in the property as a result of the efforts or advertising of the broker during the active term of the listing.

In the instant case, the activities of Silverman have gone beyond merely "introducing or interesting" the prospect in the property. Although Nikolic and Mellos were acquainted, Nikolic testified that he first learned the Embers was for sale from Silverman. Silverman met with Nikolic and discussed the value of the property, equipment, and going business and, in addition, prepared a written offer for Nikolic. Silverman also presented the offer to Mellos, and after the rejection of the counteroffer, attempted to get the parties back together although the extent of his efforts is disputed.

To constitute performance the broker's activities must be at least minimally connected with the sale. Here there was such a connection since Silverman sparked Nikolic's original interest in the property which, though temporarily dormant, was revived at the prospect of a more favorable price.

Appellants contend that a broker must uninterruptedly continue to make efforts to bring about the sale in order to earn a commission under an extension clause. The cases relied on by appellant, however, are not persuasive. In Dancy v. Baker, 206 Ala. 236, 89 So. 590 (1921), the broker was to receive a commission if he found a purchaser ready, willing, and able to buy the property for $150,000. Negotiations between the parties terminated unsuccessfully. Four months later, the owner negotiated with the purchaser himself and sold the property on different terms. Unbeknown to the owner, the broker had continued his efforts to effect a sale. The opinion does not disclose if the agreement was an exclusive listing or the time of duration of the agreement. The court denied the broker his commission noting that since the broker had not fulfilled his obligation of procuring a purchaser ready, willing, and able to buy for $150,000, the owner was free to negotiate with the purchaser himself. The court reasoned to allow the broker a commission upon a sale on different terms than those authorized, in the absence of notice to the owner of the broker's renewed activities, would not alert the owner as to the broker's expectation of a commission and would prejudice the owner in negotiating with the purchaser. Therefore, the only significance of a subsequent sale upon different terms was the notice it afforded the owner respecting his right to conduct independent negotiations without incurring the responsibility for a commission.

In the instant case, appellees had the exclusive right to negotiate the sale. If the property was sold during the listing period, Associates would be entitled to the commission regardless of who effected the sale whether it be another agent or Mellos himself. Furthermore, the agreement did not limit the commission to the sale of the property at one definite price as in *Dancy,* but provided for a commission if the property was sold on *any* terms agreeable to Mellos. The court in *Dancy* expressly recognized these distinct situations and the requirement of notice of the broker's activities in respect thereto:

> We do not overlook the rule recognized in Handley v. Shaffer, [177 Ala. 636, 59 So. 286] supra, that where a broker is employed merely to find a purchaser, with whom his principal is to negotiate a sale upon whatever terms may be agreed upon as satisfactory, the broker's right to a commission does not depend upon his principal's knowledge of the fact that a purchaser to whom he has thus sold was sent to him by the broker. That rule of liability seems to be well settled. But where the broker is authorized to find and produce a purchaser only at a specified price and on specified terms, his commission being expressly made dependent upon a sale at that price (as is here the case), that rule of liability cannot be justly applied, unless the purchaser who presents himself to the principal is able and ready and offers to buy at the price and on the terms specified. Such an offer would be sufficient notice of the source of the purchaser, if notice were required; and, in any event, the absence of notice or knowledge could not prejudice the principal.

Id. at 239, 89 So. at 593.

Appellants also rely upon First National Bank of Birmingham v. Chichester, 352 So. 2d 1371 (Ala. Civ. App. 1977), where the broker attempted to recover a commission for the leasing of the property by the owner after he revoked the broker's authority to sell. The court, citing *Dancy,* noted that whether revocation ended the obligation of the owner depended upon the owner's good faith and whether the broker's efforts were the procuring cause of the sale. Thus, since an entirely different contract was eventually executed by the owners, to constitute the procuring cause, the broker had to show that the owner continued uninterruptedly the negotiations initiated by the broker. Such a showing was not made and the broker was denied his commission. The instant case differs in that by virtue of the extension clause Silverman's efforts were not required to be the procuring cause of the sale.

Nikolic was "introduced or interested" in the property and that was all that was required to be done by the listing agreement to recover a commission. The parties are free to enter into whatever agreement they wish, and appellants cannot defeat the broker's recovery by attempting to impose a duty more stringent than that provided for in the agreement.

Appellants further contend that Associates did not introduce or interest Nikolic in the property since Silverman is not connected with or employed by Associates. However, Silverman obtained Associates' permission to present the offer and was acting on its behalf. A broker may employ a subagent to aid him in procuring a purchaser for property listed with him. Rawls v. Carlisle Baston, 18 Ala. App. 644, 93 So. 818 (1921); Alford v. Creagh, 7 Ala. App. 358, 62 So. 254 (1913). Therefore, introduction by Silverman was equivalent to introduction by Associates.

The extension clause in the instant case did not specify a time period in which it was to operate. In such a case, a reasonable time is presumed. Moore v. Holman Real Estate Co., 129 Ark. 465, 196 S.W. 479 (1917); Messick v. Powell, 314 Ky. 805, 236 S.W.2d 897 (1951). The trial court found the sale was consummated within a reasonable time, and we agree. Therefore, since the extension clause was valid and appellees fulfilled their obligation pursuant to the listing agreement, they are entitled to the commission.

Affirmed.

Maddox, Jones, Shores and Beatty, JJ., concur.

NOTES

1. The seller, as principal, owes an obligation of good faith to his broker, and whether or not there is an extension agreement, the seller may not terminate the brokerage contract or wait out its termination for the purpose of avoiding payment of the broker's commission and after termination sell to a buyer introduced or interested by the broker. Bartsas Realty, Inc. v. Nash, 81 Nev. 325, 402 P.2d 650 (1965); Snyder v. Schram, 274 Or. 539, 547 P.2d 102 (1976); and Lady v. Realty Associates, 31 A.2d 875 (D.C. 1943).

2. *Statute of frauds: termination and extension.* Written listing agreements typically have a limited duration, and a broker's statute of frauds typically requires a written duration.

Cal. Bus. & Prof. Code §10176(f) (West Supp. 1977): A licensed broker is subject to disciplinary action for the practice of claiming a commission under an exclusive listing that does not contain "a definite, specified date of final and complete termination."

Kraemer v. Smith, 179 Cal. App. 2d 52, 3 Cal. Rptr. 471 (1960): Brokers' statute of frauds does not preclude broker recovery upon a sale made during an oral extension of the listing.

Gilbert v. Ludtke, 1 Wis. 2d 228, 83 N.W.2d 669 (1957): Broker cannot recover under an oral extension under which seller specified terms of sale differing from original listing.

Wilbur Smith and Associates v. National Bank of South Carolina
274 S.C. 296, 263 S.E.2d 643 (1980)

LITTLEJOHN, Justice. This appeal is from the order of the circuit court directing that James Cuttino & Sons be paid a real estate commission from the sale of real property by the executor of the estate of J. Willcox DesChamps. The executor appeals. We affirm.

DesChamps owned approximately 650 acres of undeveloped land in Sumter County. In March of 1973, DesChamps, then 80 years of age, entered into a contract with Cuttino. The printed form contract was labeled an "Exclusive Listing Agreement" and provided that, in consideration of Cuttino agreeing to advertise and make all reasonable efforts to sell the property, DesChamps authorized Cuttino exclusively to sell the land. The listing was for 15 years and the sale price was "to be mutually agreed upon after Wilbur Smith & Associates Study and recommendations are completed." The printed contract included a typed-in provision: "Above contract binding on heirs and assigns."

In July of 1974, after the Wilbur Smith feasibility study was complete, DesChamps executed a second exclusive listing agreement,[1] using the same form. This set the sale price at $1.5 million and reduced the term to 60 months. While both instruments provided for a 10% commission to Cuttino upon the sale of the property, the second made no reference to "heirs and assigns."

Upon DesChamps' death in December of 1976, the National Bank of South Carolina qualified as executor of the estate. The property was sold by the executor in August of 1977, through another realtor, for $700,000. Cuttino consistently maintained he had an exclusive listing of the property, but he did not participate in this transaction in any manner.

Wilbur Smith and Associates brought this action against the executor and against Cuttino to recover for development work on the property, which included preparation of an elaborate brochure. In answering, Cuttino cross-claimed against the executor for the commission he claimed to be due because of the exclusive listing. The claim of Wilbur Smith was settled and the only remaining controversy was the matter of the commission as sought in the counterclaim against the Bank-Executor.

---

1. The first listing agreement was recorded; the second was not.

After a hearing, the trial judge, sitting without a jury, found that Cuttino had a valid exclusive listing and that since the property was sold during the period of the listing, a commission of $70,000 was due. We agree.

The executor contends that the second instrument is complete in its terms and replaced the first as the entire contract between the parties. However, a reading of the first instrument shows that a second instrument was contemplated and actually required before Cuttino could effect a sale. The sale price was "to be mutually agreed upon after Wilbur Smith & Associates Study and recommendations are completed." The second instrument was used to indicate the mutually agreed-upon sale price. Cuttino testified that this price was to be effective for a 60 month period, at which time the parties would reappraise the property.

The court is faced with two instruments which it must consider to determine the rights of the parties. The applicable rule of contract construction, as recently noted by this court, is:

> [W]here the instruments have not been executed simultaneously but relate to the same subject matter and have been entered into by the same parties, the transaction comprising the contract will be considered as a whole. This is true even though the transaction consumed more than one day; the date of the writings constituting such transaction is immaterial. Construing contemporaneous instruments together means simply that if there are any provisions in one instrument limiting, explaining, or otherwise affecting the provisions of another, they will be given effect between the parties so that the whole agreement as actually made may be effectuated. Klutts Resort Realty, Inc. v. Down 'Round Development Corp., 268 S.C. 80, 232 S.E.2d 20, 24 (1977).

The two instruments must be read together to determine the whole agreement and intent of the parties. The second was supplementary to and not in lieu of the first.

The executor next asserts that even when the instruments are read together Cuttino is not entitled to a commission since the property was sold after DesChamps' death. Citing the fundamental rule that an agency relationship terminates at the death of the principal, the executor argues that the listing agreement was no longer valid after DesChamps' death. The language purporting to bind heirs and assigns is argued to be mere surplusage, which can have no legal effect.

This court has said:

> The purpose of all rules of contract construction is to determine the parties' intentions. The courts, in attempting to ascertain this intention, will endeavor to determine the situation of the parties, as well as their purposes, at the time the contract was entered into. [Citation omitted.] The court should put itself, as best it can, in the same position occupied by the parties when they made the contract. In doing so, the court is able to avail itself of the same

light which the parties possessed when the agreement was entered into so that it may judge the meaning of the words and the correct application of the language. Klutts Resort Realty, Inc. v. Down 'Round Development Corp., supra.

Applying this rationale, we hold that the contract was valid and binding on DesChamps' heirs and assigns and the executor.

Counsel for the executor admits in oral argument that it is legally permissible to draw a listing contract which would bind the heirs and assigns of a property owner to carry out a sale procured by a realtor, but argues that the contract here involved simply did not accomplish that result. It is a cardinal rule of contract construction, as cited in *Klutts*, that the court strives to carry out the intent of the parties. In construing a contract, meaning must be attached to all of the verbiage. What significance should be given to the clause, "Above contract binding on heirs and assigns"? The executor argues that these words have no meaning and should be ignored. We think, however, that the purpose of these words, which were not a part of the printed form but were added with a typewriter, was to continue the listing for a period of 15 years, which was later reduced to 60 months by agreement.

An ordinary real estate listing agency agreement would normally end upon the death of the property owner, but this contract is not an ordinary listing agreement entered into under ordinary circumstances. The label given to the contract is not conclusive of its legal nature. This is a contract between an 80-year-old man, who desired to develop and promote the sale of an unusually large tract, and a realtor, who desired to protect his projected investment of time and money. DesChamps wanted to develop his property to its best use, but realized that such an undertaking would require a long period of time, possibly reaching beyond the life span of one 80 years old. Cuttino wanted to list the property, but could not risk an extensive investment of his resources under an ordinary listing agreement. The 24 page color brochure in evidence prepared by Wilbur Smith with the cooperation of Cuttino depicts the potential of this land for residences, golf course, equestrian center, etc. It is a development plan designed to attract investors. The approach to marketing this property was totally different from the ordinary listing of a house and lot or a farm for sale. The brochure completely negates any idea that the parties treated the contract for sale as an ordinary listing agreement. Each party supplied ample consideration for the contract. DesChamps promised an exclusive listing for a term of years; Cuttino promised to use his best efforts in the promotion and sale of the property. Accordingly, to effectuate their desires and intent, they agreed the contract would bind DesChamps' heirs and assigns. This was a valid contractual provision which should be given full force and effect.

During DesChamps' life and after his death, Cuttino fulfilled his responsibilities under the contract. He did extensive work from February 6, 1974, to February 22, 1977, toward the development and sale of the property, making numerous trips to Columbia to confer with Wilbur Smith & Associates, placing numerous advertisements concerning the property, and showing the property to several prospective purchasers. In fact, a proposed land option was presented to DesChamps prior to his death and resubmitted to the executor following his death. The executor was aware of Cuttino's exclusive contract with DesChamps but chose to ignore it and sell the land, using the services of another realtor.

The argument that DesChamps' heirs and assigns could not be bound because Cuttino's were not is not valid. There is no such thing as committing ones heirs and assigns to perform personal service. To bind ones heirs and assigns as relates to use and/or disposition of real property is routine. The executor took charge of the property subject to its burden and was bound the same as any "heirs and assigns."

Under the express terms of the contract, Cuttino was authorized "exclusively to sell" the property. Thus, this can be termed an "exclusive sales contract." Courts "have interpreted an exclusive sales contract to be an agreement that gives the realtor sole right to sell the property, and a commission must be paid even if the owner sells the land." Dorman Realty & Ins. Co., Inc. v. Stalvey, 264 S.C. 94, 212 S.E.2d 591 (1975).

Under the terms of the exclusive sale provision of the contract, Cuttino was entitled to a commission of 10% upon the sale. The judge was correct in finding that Cuttino should receive the $70,000 commission due under the contract.

This is an action at law, tried by the judge without a jury. Our scope of review is limited to a determination of whether there is any evidence to support his findings. Townes Associates, Ltd. v. City of Greenville, 266 S.C. 81, 221 S.E.2d 773 (1976). The judge's finding that Cuttino had a contract binding on the executor is supported by the evidence, and his order is affirmed.

D. THE ROLE OF THE LAWYER

Real estate transactions, including representation of buyers and sellers, historically have been a major source of lawyers' work and continue so today. In many real estate sales transactions, however, lawyers are not utilized by the parties, document preparation and other formalities of transfer being performed by the parties themselves or by other service intermediaries such as brokers, lenders, or title insurers. Utilization of lawyers by buyers and sellers of real property is more likely when large amounts of money are involved, in states where lawyers still largely monopolize land title searches and examinations, and in states where unauthorized practice laws as to brokers and other conveyancing intermediaries are relatively strict. Lawyers are almost always involved in real estate sales of commercial or industrial properties, multiunit residential properties, and more expensive single family residences. With escalating prices of single family residences, it appears that lawyers are representing buyers and sellers in an increasing percentage of sales transactions as to even moderately priced homes, although often not until after buyers have contracted to buy.

The excerpt from the ABA Special Committee report that follows describes the steps needed to consummate a routine home purchase and sale financed by a mortgage. Similar procedures are commonly involved in transfers of nonresidential properties, although added steps frequently may be taken in connection with sales of some kinds of nonresidential land parcels. The ABA report is a position paper on the need for lawyers in residential real estate transactions, as viewed by the practicing bar, and is a response to criticism of the amount of lawyers' fees as an item in overall land sale costs.

American Bar Association, Special Committee on Residential Real Estate Transactions, Residential Real Estate Transactions: The Lawyer's Proper Role

14 Real Prop. Prob. and Tr. J. 581, 585-90 (1979)

A. THE BROKERAGE CONTRACT

Initially a seller will enter into a brokerage contract with a real estate agent. In many jurisdictions this contract is not required to be in writing with all of the usual dangers of unwritten contracts. A special peril faced by sellers who have not had the advantage of legal counsel is that they may employ more than one broker and, in the absence of a clear understanding concerning the conditions under which the brokerage fee is earned, the seller may become liable to pay more than one fee.

In practice, a high percentage of brokerage contracts are in writing. A common assumption is that the contract is simple and standardized. In fact, a properly drawn contract will anticipate a number of legal problems of some complexity, such as the right of the seller to negotiate on the seller's own behalf, the effect of multiple listings, the disposition of earnest money if the buyer defaults, the rights of the broker if the seller is unable to proffer a marketable title, the duration of any exclusive listing and, as already brought out, the point at which the brokerage fee is earned. Most of the terms are negotiable and, in theory, a new contract should be drawn each time a broker is employed.

Standardized forms, where carefully drawn, have certain advantages.

There are no objections to form contracts per se, as used by either brokers or other participants in the land transfer transaction. The objections to form contracts are that they may be inappropriate to the particular transaction, badly drawn intially or incorrectly filled in.

Any seller signing such a contract should have it approved by the seller's lawyer before signing. The seller should have the lawyer explain its meaning and be on hand to see that it is properly executed. (It is presumed that if the seller consults a lawyer, the lawyer will advise against entering into any oral agreement.) In other words, the seller needs the traditional legal services embraced in the expression "advice, representation and drafting." The broker needs similar services at one time or another and receives them from the broker's own lawyer as needed. In routine transactions the broker is sufficiently familiar with the details to be able to handle the matter without resort to professional assistance.

B. The Preliminary Negotiations

When the broker has found a potential buyer, negotiations between the buyer and the seller will begin, with the broker acting in the role of intermediary. In some cases the seller will leave to the broker all the work of negotiation and will merely ratify the agreement reached with the buyer.

It is generally thought that neither the buyer nor the seller needs a lawyer in the course of the negotiations. In theory this assumption is correct because neither party is bound until a written sales contract is signed. In fact, a great deal of trouble can be avoided if both the buyer and the seller consult their own lawyers during the course of the negotiations. If they are to make a proper bargain, they must know what to bargain about.

Aside from the question of price, which seems paramount in the minds of both parties, they should consider such problems as the mode of paying the purchase price and the tax consequences resulting therefrom, the status of various articles as fixtures or personal property, the time set for occupancy and the effect of loss by casualty pending the closing.

They can make whatever agreement they want, but they should anticipate all important questions and be certain a complete understanding has been reached. Failure to do so in the preliminary negotiations may mean, at the time for signing a contract, that they will have to start negotiations all over again. Worse, they may enter into a contract highly disadvantageous to one or the other, so uncertain as to require litigation to determine its meaning, or so ambiguous as to be void for indefiniteness.

C. The Commitment for Financing

Before entering into a sales contract, it would be desirable for the buyer to obtain as much of a commitment as possible for necessary financing.

The Role of the Lawyer

Many lenders, however, refuse to make the necessary inspections, appraisals and credit investigations to make such a commitment until the buyer can exhibit a signed purchase and sale agreement, and many buyers are reluctant to risk losing the property to a higher offer by deferring the execution of the purchase and sale agreement. All of this leads to the common practice of including in the agreement a "subject to financing" clause which should be examined by the lawyers for the parties before the contract is signed.

Finding a willing lender is not part of a lawyer's professional duties. In practice a lawyer, being a person of affairs, may be able to render this service. Legal expertise is exercised when the lawyer advises the buyer about problems the buyer should anticipate in coming to terms with the lender. By way of illustration, the buyer will seldom have any understanding of the potential effect of an acceleration clause. The buyer should know what the legal and practical consequences of such a clause will be. The buyer should also obtain an estimate of the closing costs that will have to be paid and should obtain legal advice as to all items found in the estimate.

The commitment contract between the lender and buyer will normally be prepared by the lender's lawyer. Before it is accepted, the buyer's lawyer should ascertain that it properly anticipates all important contingencies, comports with the oral agreement previously reached and binds the lender.

Normally the lender has much greater financial expertise than the buyer. This advantage may not have been of as much importance formerly as it is today, because the financing of homes has in many instances become extremely complex. For this reason, when dealing with the lender the buyer is in need of legal assistance.

D. The Contract of Sale

Once an informal agreement has been reached, the buyer and the seller will enter into a formal contract of sale. The importance of this document cannot be overemphasized. Once it is signed, the rights and obligations of the parties are fixed. Each transaction is unique and, in theory, a contract should be specially drafted for each.

The interested parties are the broker, the buyer and the seller. The contract should contain an appropriate provision with regard to the broker's commission. The buyer and the seller want assurance that the writing reflects their understanding. If they have not received legal advice during the preliminary negotiations, they will need to know what questions should have been anticipated and whether firm and advantageous provisions are found in the document. When the instrument is executed, their lawyers should be present to assure that the proper formalities are observed to make it binding. Here again the parties need legal services in the form of drafting, advice, and representation.

This need is not avoided by the use of forms. Even if the form is properly drawn, the printed portion may not adequately express the particular agreement made between the parties, or the words used in filling in blanks may distort its effectiveness. As a matter of practice standardized forms are widely used, and it is recognized that this practice likely will continue. It is recommended that local bar associations draft standard forms of sales agreements, and that joint seminars with real estate brokers and others regarding residential real estate transactions be held regularly. Whenever forms are used, any insertion should be carefully checked by the buyer's and seller's lawyers, and the appropriateness of the form for the particular transaction should be determined by the buyer's and seller's lawyers. The buyer and the seller are often unaware of what the contract means, what they should anticipate, and what steps are needed to make the instrument binding. They should be advised by their own legal counsel.

Prior to the time the contract is signed, the buyer and the seller should have detailed advice about many legal aspects of the transaction. For example, they may not be aware of the need to anticipate the question of who bears the loss or damage to, or destruction of, buildings on the premises between the time the contract is signed and the time of closing. They also may be unaware of the existence of such problems as whether the contract so changes the interest of the seller as to affect insurance policies; whether either the buyer or seller, or both, should execute new wills; whether federal and state gift and death tax matters are involved; whether joint tenancies or tenancies by the entireties will be affected; and the like.

E. Determining the Status of the Title

After the contract of sale is executed, the state of the seller's title must be determined to the satisfaction of both the buyer and the lender. This is generally the most important legal work connected with the transaction. The initial examination will be made by the lawyer for the buyer, the seller, the lender, or the title insurer, relying upon the official land title records or an abstract thereof, or a title plant maintained by a title insurance company. Where a lawyer's certificate is relied upon, either the lender or the buyer, or both, may desire additional protection in the form of a title insurance policy.

Whoever makes the title examination, the buyer's lawyer should inform the buyer of the limitations, if any, which impair the title. The buyer should also receive formal protection by a written opinion from the lawyer, an owner's title insurance policy, or both. If the buyer applies for title insurance, the buyer's lawyer should negotiate the provisions to be included or excluded from the policy. The lawyer should also make clear to the buyer what the policy means. In particular, the exceptions to coverage contained in the policy should be explained.

The Role of the Lawyer

The use of standardized exceptions is common to title insurance. They are complex and restrictive and are frequently not understood by the layman.

Each title insurance policy is unique in that it may contain exceptions peculiar to that individual title. The buyer must first be made aware of the existence of these exceptions and must then be made to understand them. If the exception is to a $10,000 mortgage and the buyer sees the provision, the buyer will probably not mistake its meaning. But if the exception is to "all of the conditions and restrictions found in deed of X to Y, recorded in the office of the clerk of the court of Z County, in Deed Book 309 at page 873," the buyer will not, in the first place, realize that the exception is important, or, if the buyer does, will not understand its meaning without assistance from the lawyer.

F. THE SURVEY

Survey problems arise in many transactions, and the lawyers for all parties should inform their clients of such problems. At some time prior to the approval of title the buyer, the lender, or the title insurance company may demand a survey. The primary purpose of the survey will be to find whether the legal description of the land conforms to the lines laid down on the ground. An additional purpose may be to determine whether structures on the premises violate restrictive covenants or zoning ordinances or constitute an encroachment. When the survey has been completed, the parties should have their lawyers advise them about any legal implications of the surveyor's findings and the scope and extent of the surveyor's certification.

G. CURATIVE ACTION

In some cases curative action is needed to make titles marketable. Any such curative action should be carried out by a lawyer for the seller, the buyer, or the lender. If the curative action is carried out by the lawyer for the seller, it should be checked for sufficiency by the lawyers for the buyer and lender; if by the lawyer for the buyer, by the lawyer for the lender; and if by the lawyer for the lender, by the lawyer for the buyer.

H. TERMITE INSPECTION

In jurisdictions where a termite inspection must be made and a certificate given to the buyer, showing that the premises are free of infestation or damage by termites, the certificate may be ordered by the broker, lender or the lawyer for any of the parties.

In jurisdictions where such certificates are not required, a provision should be added to the contract requiring the seller to provide a current termite certificate by a licensed pest control agency. If there is infestation or damage, the cost of treatment and the cost of necessary repairs of termite-caused damage usually are borne by the seller. The contract should spell out the seller's obligation. A termite clause should be included in all standard form contracts.

I. Drafting Instruments

Before closing, a lawyer should draft the deed, mortgage and the bond or note secured by the mortgage. As a matter of convenience these papers are commonly drafted by the mortgagee's attorney, although the representative of either of the other parties is equally qualified. Whoever does the work, the product should be examined by lawyers for each of the other two parties and the title insurance company, and they should be advised whether the instruments are effective and create the interests intended.

The drafting of these instruments is sometimes considered merely routine work. This is not true. For example, the description of the parties must be so phrased as to prevent confusion, and the description of the land must be complete and accurate. The importance of the form of warranties is often overlooked. By way of illustration, if the title is encumbered by equitable covenants or utility easements, either or both may be acceptable to the buyer and lender, but they should be excepted from the warranty.

How title is to be taken should have been provided in the initial contract between the buyer and the seller, and the buyer should be advised as to the tax and other effects of the manner in which title is taken.

Of equal importance are other special agreements reached earlier in the transaction. The controlling law may provide that the deed supersedes prior understandings so that if they are not embraced in the deed they are nullified. Each deed must therefore be examined to determine whether it carries out what has been agreed upon.

J. Incidental Paper Work

The Real Estate Settlement Procedures Act requires the preparation of a settlement statement in virtually all residential real estate transactions. In addition, the Truth-In-Lending form must be filled in and executed. If the mortgage loan is to be insured by FHA, VA or by a private mortgage insurance company, more paper work is required. The required documents are standardized and can be completed without resort to legal expertise. They are part of the financing, rather than the legal aspects of the sale and mortgage. Nevertheless, lawyers are frequently called upon to do this work. With a few exceptions, the government has taken the position that whoever performs these services shall receive no compensation therefor.

K. Obtaining Title Insurance

Where a title insurance policy for the buyer is based on the certificate of a lawyer not employed by a title insurance company, the lawyer may make an application for the initial binder and, after closing, send in a final certificate and procure a policy. This is work for which the lawyer normally, and properly, should be paid by the client to the extent the lawyer is not paid for these services as the agent of the title company. The lawyer should not accept compensation from a title insurance company solely for referring business to that company. This is, of course, clearly improper and contrary to the recorded position of the American Bar Association. The Real Estate Settlement Procedures Act specifically prohibits the acceptance of any "kickbacks" from the title insurance company.

L. Closing

A closing statement is generally prepared prior to final closing. The statement may take various forms and is designed to indicate the allocation of debits and credits to the various parties. In some cases it is prepared by a layman, in others by a lawyer. The buyer's and seller's lawyers should make certain their clients understand the nature and amount of all closing costs. The American Bar Association supported the adoption of legislation requiring a uniform closing statement in all government-related mortgage transactions. In addition it is recommended that local bar associations draft uniform closing statement forms for use in all other real estate transactions. Even a standard closing form in itself is not sufficient, unless the parties are assured by their own lawyers of the appropriateness of each item.

Unless there is an escrow closing, a further check of title should be made immediately prior to closing. If this check is not made, it is possible that the parties will be unaware that the title has been impaired between the time of the original examination and the closing date. This further check will generally be carried out by the lawyer, abstracter or title insurance company certifying or insuring title.

The closing is the proceeding at which the parties exchange executed instruments, make required payments, and conclude the formal aspects of the transaction. At this point the buyer, the seller, and the lender should be represented by their own lawyers. They require advice and may need representation if a disagreement arises. They should be assured that the legal documents they exchange create the interests intended, that they receive the protection to which they are entitled and that correct payments have been made to those entitled to receive them.

As a part of the closing, arrangements must be made for insurance, taxes, and other incidents of ownership. Instruments must be recorded and a final check of title made. Disbursements must be made and documents distributed to the parties entitled to receive them. Title insurance policies, where called for, must be procured. If a lawyer handles the closing, the lawyer will attend to all or virtually all of these details.

E. OCCUPATIONAL REGULATION

Real estate brokers and lawyers are subject to substantial regulation by government and their own associations. In every state, both occupations require licenses issued by the state, which may be revoked for improper conduct. Real estate brokers and salespersons are separately licensed, but their licensing requirements are less demanding than those for lawyers. Also, lawyers and real estate brokers possess limited monopolies protected by the state, and competitors may be enjoined or otherwise sanctioned for encroaching on these monopolies. Somewhat anomalously, there are state and federal antitrust laws designed to weaken these and other monopolies. In addition to antitrust monopoly laws, there are state statutes and state agency regulations governing the conduct of licensed personnel in the lawyer and broker occupations. Lawyers and brokers have, moreover, codes of ethics adopted by their national associations that regulate the behavior of their members. The brokers' code is the National Association of Realtors Code of Ethics. The lawyers have two major codes, the American Bar Association Model Code of Professional Responsibility, and its recommended replacement, the Model Rules of Professional Conduct. In most jurisdictions, either the Model Code or the Model Rules have been adopted as statewide rules of court by the state judiciary. These respective ethical codes have more effect on occupational behavior and are enforced more rigorously than is characteristic of most such occupational codes. In the case of lawyers, the usual sanctioning bodies for code violations are the courts, typically state supreme courts.

Within the real estate brokerage and legal professions are organizational structures for revising, interpreting, and enforcing the codes, and often, as well, for initiating enforcement action against unauthorized practitioners. The material that follows focuses on three of the more important regulatory problems concerning real estate brokers and lawyers: regulating competition, advertising and solicitation, and conflict of interest.

1. Regulating Competition

a. Unauthorized Practice[4]

Cultum v. Heritage House Realtors, Inc.

103 Wash. 2d 623, 694 P.2d 630 (1985)

PEARSON, Justice. At issue in this appeal is whether the completion by a real estate salesperson of a form earnest money agreement containing a contingency clause constitutes the unauthorized practice of law in violation of RCW 2.48.170-.190.

In deciding this issue, the trial court found that this conduct did constitute the unauthorized practice of law and was a per se violation of the Consumer Protection Act, RCW 19.86, warranting damages, attorney fees and injunctive relief. As a consequence, the trial court permanently enjoined defendant, Heritage House Realtors, Inc. (Heritage), from completing, filling in the blanks, or otherwise preparing any clause with respect to any real estate purchase or sale agreement, earnest money agreement, addenda thereto, or any other document intended to create or define contractual rights or obligations in connection with any real estate transaction. In addition, plaintiff, Diane Cultum (Cultum), was awarded damages of $178.65, representing the interest lost during the time Heritage retained the earnest money. Cultum was also awarded attorney fees and costs in excess of $32,000 under the Consumer Protection Act. RCW 19.86.090. We now reverse the decision of the trial court that defendant's actions constituted the unauthorized practice of law, dissolve the injunction, and remand for a determination of contractual attorney fees.

The salient facts are as follows. In 1980 Cultum contacted Heritage in response to an advertisement in the Seattle Times and was put in touch with Yvonne Ramey (Ramey), a real estate agent for Heritage. After viewing several homes, Ramey showed Cultum the home of Arthur and Paula Smith. Cultum decided to make an offer on the Smith home but was concerned that there might be something wrong with the house. Cultum therefore told Ramey that she wanted to have the house inspected and be able to withdraw her offer on the basis of that inspection.

---

4. On unauthorized practice of law, see Michelman, Guiding the Invisible Hand: The Consumer Protection Function of Unauthorized Practice Regulation, 12 Pepperdine L. Rev. 1 (1984); Rhode, Policing the Professional Monopoly: A Constitutional and Empirical Analysis of Unauthorized Practice Prohibitions, 34 Stan. L. Rev. 1 (1981); Shedd, Real Estate Agents and the Unauthorized Practice of Law, 10 Real Est. L.J. 135 (1981); Christensen, The Unauthorized Practice of Law: Do Good Fences Really Make Good Neighbors—or Even Good Sense?, 1980 Am. B. Found. Research J. 159; and Hunter and Klonoff, A Dialogue on the Unauthorized Practice of Law, 25 Vill. L. Rev. 6 (1979-80). For unauthorized practice regulations in a somewhat earlier period, including restrictions as to real estate transactions, see Johnstone and Hopson, Lawyers and Their Work ch. 5 (1967).

Thereafter Ramey prepared a real estate purchase and sale agreement (earnest money agreement) setting forth Cultum's offer to purchase the Smith home. This agreement and all other subsequent agreements contained an attorney fee clause which provided that

> [i]n the event that either the Buyer, Seller, or Agent, shall institute suit to enforce any rights hereunder, the successful party shall be entitled to court costs and a reasonable attorney's fee.

All agreements were prepared on standardized forms drafted by attorneys. Cultum's offer and a subsequent offer were both rejected. About a month later, Ramey and Cultum resubmitted the earnest money agreement with an addendum which raised the purchase price. Cultum later discovered that the agreement did not contain a structural inspection contingency clause and asked Ramey to prepare a second addendum. This addendum provided: "This offer is contingent on a Satisfactory Structural Inspection, To be completed by Aug. 20, 1980." Both addendums were on forms drafted by an attorney. Ramey merely inserted the desired modifications in a blank space. Ramey did not select the form since her employer used a single standard form.

The Smiths accepted this last offer and Heritage deposited Cultum's $3,000 earnest money into a noninterest bearing trust account. Thereafter, Cultum received a report on the house from Northwest Inspection Engineers. The report noted missing siding and caulking on exterior portions of the home, damage to the siding along one corner of the north entry door, deterioration on the roof which probably caused some leakage, inadequate support on a sheet of plywood on the roof of the new addition causing some softness in the roof, rusted gutters, soft mortar on the chimney, and evidence of minor roof leakage along the living room entry. The inspector found no major problems in the plumbing, heating or electrical systems.

Cultum found the report unsatisfactory and demanded return of her earnest money. Ramey immediately prepared a rescission agreement but the Smiths refused to sign it. The Smiths claimed there was nothing structurally wrong with the house and Cultum was acting in bad faith. The Smiths argued that the language of the inspection contingency meant that the report had to be truly unsatisfactory and reveal real structural defects based upon an objective standard. They therefore threatened to sue Heritage if it returned Cultum's money.

Heritage initially gave Cultum three options: It could continue to hold the money in a noninterest bearing account pending an agreement between Cultum and the Smiths; it could pay the money into a registry of the court; or, it could refund the money to Cultum in exchange for her agreement to indemnify Heritage in an action brought by the Smiths. Subsequently, Heritage also offered to place the money in an interest bearing account pending resolution of the dispute.

Because these options were each substantially less than Cultum had believed the agreement would provide her, she refused to accept them and hired an attorney. Six months later Heritage refunded Cultum's earnest money.

Cultum then filed this action against Heritage seeking damages for loss of the use of her money during the period Heritage held it. She also requested a permanent injunction restraining Heritage from engaging in the unauthorized practice of law. In addition, she sought attorney fees under the Consumer Protection Act, RCW 19.86.090.

I

The holding of the trial court was not surprising. In a series of recent cases this court has broadly defined the practice of law to include

> the selection and completion of form legal documents, or the drafting of such documents, including deeds, mortgages, deeds of trust, promissory notes and agreements modifying these documents. . . .

Bowers v. Transamerica Title Ins. Co., 100 Wash. 2d 581, 586, 675 P.2d 193 (1983) (quoting Washington State Bar Assn. v. Great W. Union Fed. Sav. & Loan Assn., 91 Wash. 2d 48, 55, 586 P.2d 870 (1978)); Hagan & Van Camp, P.S. v. Kassler Escrow, Inc., 96 Wash. 2d 443, 635 P.2d 730 (1981).

The trial court's extension of these holdings to completion of form earnest money agreements by real estate sales persons is logical since such agreements fix the legal rights and duties of both buyers and sellers of residential real estate. It therefore fits within the broad definition of the practice of law as we have previously defined it.

Nevertheless, without retreating from our rulings in those three recent cases, we think there are sound and practical reasons why some activities which fall within the broad definition of "the practice of law" should not be unauthorized simply because they are done by laypersons.

As we have so often stated, it is the duty of this court to protect the public from the activity of those who, because of the lack of professional skills, may cause injury whether they are members of the bar or persons never qualified for or admitted to the bar. *Great Western,* 91 Wash. 2d at 60, 586 P.2d 870. We have also made it clear that the practice of law is within the sole province of the judiciary and encroachment by the Legislature may violate the separation of powers doctrine. *Hagan,* 96 Wash. 2d at 453, 635 P.2d 730. This does not mean, however, that the attorney hegemony over the practice of law must be absolute. Hence, although the completion of form earnest money agreements might be commonly understood as the practice of law, we believe it is in the public interest to permit licensed real estate brokers or licensed salespersons to complete such lawyer prepared standard form agreements; provided, that in doing so they comply with the standard of care demanded of an attorney.

For a long time suppression of the practice of law by nonlawyers has been proclaimed to be in the public interest, a necessary protection against incompetence, divided loyalties, and other evils. It is now clear, however, as several other courts have concluded, that there are other important interests involved. See Conway-Bogue Realty Inv. Co. v. Denver Bar Assn., 135 Colo. 398, 312 P.2d 998 (1957). These interests include:

(1) The ready availability of legal services.
(2) Using the full range of services that other professions and businesses can provide.
(3) Limiting costs.
(4) Public convenience.
(5) Allowing licensed brokers and salespersons to participate in an activity in which they have special training and expertise.
(6) The interest of brokers and salespersons in drafting form earnest money agreements which are incidental and necessary to the main business of brokers and salespersons.

We no longer believe that the supposed benefits to the public from the lawyers' monopoly on performing legal services justifies limiting the public's freedom of choice. The public has the right to use the full range of services that brokers and salespersons can provide. Christensen, The Unauthorized Practice of Law: Do Good Fences Really Make Good Neighbors—or Even Good Sense?, 1980 Am. B. Found. Research J. 159. The fact that brokers and salespersons will complete these forms at no extra charge, whereas attorneys would charge an additional fee, weighs heavily toward allowing this choice.

Another important consideration is the fact that the drafting of form earnest money agreements is incidental to the main business of real estate brokers and salespersons. WAC 308-124D-020. These individuals are specially trained to provide buyers and sellers with competent and efficient assistance in purchasing or selling a home. See WAC 308-124H. Because the selection and filling in of standard simple forms by brokers and salespersons is an incidental service, it normally must be rendered before such individuals can receive their commissions. Clearly the advantages, if any, to be derived by enjoining brokers and salespersons from completing earnest money agreements are outweighed by the fact that such conveyances are part of the everyday business of the realtor and necessary to the effective completion of such business. See Cowern v. Nelson, 207 Minn.

642, 290 N.W. 795 (1940). See also 53 A.L.R.2d 788 §3 (Supp. 1978).

The interest in protecting the public must also be balanced against the inconveniences caused by enjoining licensed brokers and salespersons from completing form earnest money agreements. State ex rel. Reynolds v. Dinger, 14 Wis. 2d 193, 109 N.W.2d 685 (1961). Although lawyers are also competent to handle these transactions, lawyers may not always be available at the odd hours that these transactions tend to take place. As noted by the Minnesota Supreme Court:

> It is the duty of this court so to regulate the practice of law and to restrain such practice by laymen in a common-sense way in order to protect primarily the interest of the public and not to hamper and burden such interest with impractical technical restraints no matter how well supported such restraint may be from the standpoint of pure logic. . . . We do not think the possible harm which might come to the public from the rare instances of defective conveyances in such transactions is sufficient to outweigh the great public inconvenience which would follow if it were necessary to call in a lawyer to draft these simple instruments.

Cowern, 207 Minn. at 647, 290 N.W. 795.

In a few instances earnest money agreements may be complicated and one or both parties may realize the need for a lawyer to prepare the contract rather than use a standardized form. In fact, if a broker or salesperson believes there may be complicated legal issues involved, he or she should persuade the parties to seek legal advice. More often, however, these transactions are simple enough so that standardized forms will suffice and the parties will wish to avoid further delay or expense by using them. See Comment, The Unauthorized Practice of Law by Laymen and Lay Associations, 54 Calif. L. Rev. 1331 (1966). See also New Jersey State Bar Assn. v. New Jersey Assn. of Realtor Bds., 186 N.J. Super. 391, 452 A.2d 1323 (1982).

It should be emphasized that the holding in this case is limited in scope. Our decision provides that a real estate broker or salesperson is permitted to complete simple printed standardized real estate forms, which forms must be approved by a lawyer, it being understood that these forms shall not be used for other than simple real estate transactions which arise in the usual course of the broker's business and that such forms will be used only in connection with real estate transactions actually handled by such broker or salesperson as a broker or salesperson and then without charge for the simple service of completing the forms.

This conclusion is not inconsistent with the State Bar Act, RCW 2.48. Among the inherent powers of the judicial branch is the power to admit to practice, and necessarily therefrom the power to disbar from practice, attorneys at law. State ex rel. Laughlin v. State Bar Assn., 26 Wash. 2d 914, 917, 176 P.2d 301 (1947). This court has repeatedly emphasized that this power to regulate the practice of law lies within the sole jurisdiction of the courts. Hagan & Van Camp, P.S. v. Kassler Escrow, Inc., 96 Wash. 2d 443, 635 P.2d 730 (1981); State ex rel. Schwab v. State Bar Assn., 80 Wash. 2d 266, 493 P.2d 1237 (1972); Washington State Bar Assn. v. Washington Assn. of Realtors, 41 Wash. 2d 697, 251 P.2d 619 (1952). RCW 2.48 was adopted in the interest of uniformity of standard and to remedy and prevent mischief in the profession. It did not restrict or take away any of the courts' power. State ex rel. Laughlin, 26 Wash. 2d at 917, 176 P.2d 301.

In light of the courts' inherent power to regulate the practice of law, we believe it is totally within our power to allow brokers and salespersons to practice law within the narrow confines that our holding allows, irrespective of what the statutory language in RCW 2.48 might suggest.

II

Our decision to allow licensed brokers and salespersons to complete form earnest money agreements is based on the practical needs and interests of the public. The completion of a form earnest money agreement is in most instances less technical and more straightforward than closing a real estate transaction. This is not to say, however, that there is no possibility of injurious consequences from the acts of laypersons. The public still needs protection against incompetence, divided loyalties and other evils. RCW 18.85 controls the licensing of real estate brokers and salespersons. The statute provides some preliminary protection by dictating certain conditions and qualifications with which a person must comply prior to being licensed. However, as the court stated in *Hagan*, the fact that laypersons must comply with licensing requirements does not offer sufficient protection to the public. *Hagan,* 96 Wash. 2d at 448-49, 635 P.2d 730. Therefore, we hold that licensed real estate brokers and salespersons, when completing form earnest money agreements, must comply with the standard of care of a practicing attorney. See Bowers v. Transamerica Title Ins. Co., 100 Wash. 2d 581, 675 P.2d 193 (1983); Mattieligh v. Poe, 57 Wash. 2d 203, 356 P.2d 328 (1960); Hecomovich v. Nielsen, 10 Wash. App. 563, 518 P.2d 1081 (1974); and Andersen v. Northwest Bonded Escrows, Inc., 4 Wash. App. 754, 484 P.2d 488 (1971).

The trial court awarded Cultum damages based on a finding that the contingency clause as written by Ramey violated the standard of care of a practicing attorney. Whether or not the contingency clause as written by Ramey meets an attorney's standard of care, Ramey is nonetheless liable because the problems in this case were caused by Ramey's failure to follow her client's explicit instructions. This dispute arose because Cultum and the Smiths disagreed on whether the defects noted in the inspection report were sufficient enough to cause the real estate contract to fail. Cultum had wanted her offer conditioned on her subjective approval of the inspection.

Ramey, contrary to Cultum's wishes, failed to include a subjective right in the contingency clause. If Ramey had complied with Cultum's request, the dispute with the Smiths could not have arisen and Cultum's earnest money would have been refunded to her immediately.

It is the duty of an agent to obey all reasonable instructions and directions given by the principal and to adhere faithfully to them in all cases where they ought properly to be applied and in which they can be obeyed by the exercise of reasonable and diligent care. 3 Am. Jur. 2d Agency §206 (1962).

An attorney is liable for all losses caused by his or her failure to follow the explicit instructions of the client. Olfe v. Gordon, 93 Wis. 2d 173, 286 N.W.2d 573 (1980); 7A C.J.S. Attorney & Client §236 (1980). When a broker undertakes to practice law and prepares a contract at variance with the client's instructions, he or she is liable for negligence. *Mattieligh*, 57 Wash. 2d at 204, 356 P.2d 328. Therefore, because Ramey was practicing law and failed to comply with Cultum's wishes she is liable for all damages proximately caused by her negligence. It is irrelevant whether the language in the contingency clause may have somehow been improper.

III

The trial court awarded Cultum damages of $178.65 representing the interest lost during the time that Heritage retained her earnest money. If a real estate broker fails to exercise reasonable care and skill, the real estate broker is liable to the client for damages resulting from such failure. *Mattlieligh*, 57 Wash. 2d at 205, 356 P.2d 328. Based on this rule and our conclusion that Ramey failed to exercise the reasonable care and skill of a practicing attorney, we affirm the trial court's award of damages, including the amount, because it is within the range of relevant testimony and therefore will not be disturbed on appeal.[1] Ferrell v. Cronrath, 67 Wash. 2d 642, 409 P.2d 472 (1965).

IV

The final issue before us is the award of attorney fees. The trial court determined that Heritage and its agent, Ramey, had violated the Consumer Protection Act, RCW 19.86, and that therefore Cultum was entitled to attorney fees pursuant to the formula articulated by this court in Bowers v. Transamerica Title Ins. Co., supra. Unlike the trial court, however, we have concluded that Ramey's conduct did not constitute the

---

1. Heritage argues that the rate of interest used by the trial judge should have been 6 percent as authorized at the time by RCW 19.52.010. This statute only applies to loans or forbearance of money, goods or things in action. The statute is inapplicable to earnest money agreements which are neither loans nor a forbearance of money, goods or things in action.

unauthorized practice of law. Hence, there is no violation of the Consumer Protection Act and Cultum is not entitled to the attorney fees awarded by the trial judge. However, the earnest money agreement drafted by Ramey specifies that:

> In the event that either the Buyer, Seller, or Agent, shall institute suit to enforce any rights hereunder, the successful party shall be entitled to court costs and a reasonable attorney's fee.

In light of this provision, we remand for further proceedings to determine whether Cultum is entitled to contractual attorney fees. We dissolve the injunction.

William H. Williams, C.J., and Dolliver and Dimmick, JJ., concur.

Brachtenbach, Justice (Concurrence).

While I concur in the result, I disagree with much of the majority's rationale.

My starting premises are: (1) there is no such thing as a "simple" earnest money agreement; (2) the fact that it is printed or "standardized" is not relevant; (3) the fact that the form has been approved by a lawyer is not relevant — it is the tailoring of the form to a particular transaction which is critical; (4) the fact that the form is completed incidental to other services of the broker offers no protection to the public; and (5) the fact that the agreement is completed without charge is irrelevant.

A binding earnest money agreement is the document which firmly fixes the rights and liabilities of the parties. A typical form establishes the nature of the title which the seller must convey and the type of conveyance to be made, both of which the buyer must accept. It provides for the respective liabilities of various items by proration at closing. It specifies the nature of the title insurance to be furnished, usually by the seller. I doubt that many buyers know what a preliminary commitment for a standard form purchaser's policy of title insurance is or what alternative types of coverage are available.

The earnest money agreement, if it is a sale on contract, designates the form of the contract including all the terms by which seller and buyer shall be bound. It may attempt to eliminate all representations about very material matters unless contained in the agreement. It sets conditions of default including alternative remedies therefor. It may impose attorney fee liability which might not otherwise exist. It establishes the date of possession, but not whether the date refers to legal or physical possession. This hardly appears to be a "simple" document. I fail to perceive how the complexity of this document is lessened because it is printed.

That the form was initially prepared or approved by a lawyer will hopefully minimize the potential for disputes, i.e., the competent lawyer should have anticipated and provided for those events which most frequently occur in real estate transactions.

However, despite lawyer preparation of the forms, there are two problems. First, the form itself may contain provisions which are inadequate or inappropriate *to a particular* transaction, or such terms may be omitted entirely. Second, "filling in the blanks" requires at least minimal skill in drafting language as part of a binding document set in the framework of a vast array of statutory law and common precedents.

The earnest money agreement in this case illustrates the hazards of "filling in" the "simple" form. One provided, in part, that the agreement was conditioned on "inspection of plumbing and electrical systems, paid for by purchaser and inspection of heating system." The questions are immediately apparent. Who pays for the inspection of the heating system in view of the way the condition is expressed? Inspection by whom? A qualified plumber, electrician, a general contractor, a city inspector? Is it merely the fact of inspection which satisfies the condition? Must the inspection disclose conditions which are satisfactory to this buyer or to a reasonable, objective buyer? If the inspection discloses a minor defect which can be quickly remedied, does the seller have the option to so remedy? If inspection discloses a major defect, can the seller remedy? Must the corrected system also be inspected to the satisfaction of the buyer?

That an earnest money agreement is prepared incidental to the licensed services of a broker is of little consolation to the parties if it is not properly prepared to reflect the intent of the parties. That it is prepared without separate charge has no bearing on whether its preparation constitutes the practice of law.

I am not naive enough to believe that it is feasible for every earnest money agreement to be drafted anew and tailored to fit a particular transaction. Residential transactions particularly would grind to a halt. Buying and selling real estate, especially residential real estate, realistically cannot be done at the convenience of lawyers' office hours.

I would reach the same result as the majority by forthrightly recognizing that requiring lawyer preparation of every earnest money agreement is not a practicable alternative to the broker/salesperson preparation which works reasonably well in most instances. I would accept the current practice as a fact of life in the real world. The ultimate protection to the public is the requirement that the broker/salesperson be held to the standard of care of a practicing lawyer. The competent broker/salesperson should recognize when special circumstances require more skilled and knowledgeable drafting. If that decision is made at their peril, hopefully it will be made carefully, keeping in mind the fiduciary relationship and the requirements of the licensing statute.

For the above reasons, I concur in the result but not the rationale of the majority.

NOTES

1. Will the court's decision in the *Cultum* case holding real estate brokers to the standard of care of practicing attorneys discourage most brokers from completing form earnest money agreements? Would malpractice insurance for brokers be an adequate solution?

2. Although quite universally in the United States real estate brokers are legally authorized to prepare some legal documents related to the transactions in which they are acting as brokers, states differ considerably as to the scope of this authorization. Common restrictions on brokers are that they may only complete standard form documents, may not charge for this service, and may not give legal advice in relation to the documents. An important lead case, Chicago Bar Assn. v. Quinlan and Tyson, Inc., 34 Ill. 2d 116, 214 N.E.2d 771 (1966), restricts real estate brokers to filling in the usual form of preliminary contract or offer to purchase, as these are incidental to the performance of brokerage services and earning brokerage commissions. In New Jersey State Bar Assn. v. New Jersey Assn. of Realtor Boards, 93 N.J. 470, 475, 461 A.2d 1112, 1115 (1983), a more recent major case, a proposed consent judgment that the parties agreed to was approved by the court with minor modifications. The judgment provides in part:

> 1. Real estate brokers and salespersons licensed by the New Jersey Real Estate Commission shall be permitted to prepare contracts for the sale of residential real estate containing one-to-four dwelling units and for the sale of vacant one-family lots in transactions in which they have a commission or fee interest, PROVIDED that every such contract shall contain conspicuously at the top of the first page the following language:
>
>> THIS IS A LEGALLY BINDING CONTRACT THAT WILL BECOME FINAL WITHIN THREE BUSINESS DAYS. DURING THIS PERIOD YOU MAY CHOOSE TO CONSULT AN ATTORNEY WHO CAN REVIEW AND CANCEL THE CONTRACT. SEE SECTION ON ATTORNEY REVIEW FOR DETAILS.
>
> and shall also contain the following language within the text of every such contract:
>
>> ATTORNEY REVIEW:
>> 1. Study by Attorney
>> The Buyer or the Seller may choose to have an attorney study this contract. If an attorney is consulted, the attorney must complete his or her review of the contract within a three-day period. This contract will be legally binding at the end of this three-day period unless an attorney for the Buyer or the Seller reviews and disapproves of the contract.

A similar provision of the judgment permits real estate brokers and salespersons to prepare leases for a term of one year or more for residential dwelling units in transactions in which these persons have a commission or fee interest.

In Arizona, by constitutional provision, real estate brokers may "draft or fill out and complete, without charge, any and all instruments incident thereto, including, but not limited to, preliminary purchase agreements and earnest money receipts, deeds, mortgages, leases, assignments, releases, contracts for sale of realty, and bills of sale." Ariz. Const. art. 26, §1. This constitutional provision was adopted in 1962 by popular referendum following an Arizona Supreme Court opinion highly restrictive as to what documents title companies and brokers could prepare. State Bar of Arizona v. Arizona Land Title & Trust Co., 90 Ariz. 76, 366 P.2d 1 (1961), on rehearing, 91 Ariz. 293, 371 P.2d 1020 (1962). The Arizona Association of Realtors campaigned vigorously for the constitutional amendment. On the Arizona constitutional provision and the case that preceded it, see Romero, Theories of Real Estate Broker Liability: Arizona's Emerging Malpractice Doctrine, 20 Ariz. L. Rev. 767, 785-786 (1978).

The courts in some states have authorized real estate brokers to prepare a wide range of standardized real estate transfer documents pertaining to transactions being handled by brokers in their capacity as brokers. E.g., Pope County Bar Assn. v. Suggs, 274 Ark. 250, 624 S.W.2d 828 (1981); State v. Dinger, 14 Wis. 2d 193, 109 N.W.2d 685 (1961); Conway-Bogue Realty Investment Co. v. Denver Bar Assn., 135 Colo. 398, 312 P.2d 998 (1957).

To what extent should real estate brokers be permitted to perform services that would be the practice of law if performed by lawyers? Which solution mentioned above in this note should be preferred?

3. The Supreme Court of Washington, on grounds of separation of powers, held as unconstitutional a statute that authorized escrow agents to prepare contracts of sale, deeds, mortgages, and other documents in relation to escrow transactions. Bennion, Van Camp, Hagen & Ruhl v. Kassler Escrow, Inc., 96 Wash. 2d 443, 635 P.2d 730 (1981). The court subsequently adopted a court rule proposed by the state bar, Washington Admission to Practice Rule 12, permitting certain lay persons to qualify as closing officers under court regulation and control. Closing officers are authorized to prepare and complete certain form documents, including deeds and contracts of sale. The court rule apparently avoided the possibility of a constitutional amendment permitting preparation of real estate transfer instruments by lay persons.

4. The real estate brokers' monopoly will be enforced against persons who are not licensed real estate brokers or salespersons. In Tobin v. Courshon, 155 So. 2d 785 (Fla. 1963), it was held that a real estate broker was not obligated to share his commission with attorneys who found a buyer for property listed with the broker, even though the broker had agreed to pay the attorneys. Attorneys, the court determined, may not perform what

are exclusively real estate brokers' functions unless licensed as brokers, and unless the activity undertaken has no relation to their duties as attorneys. However, in Garafano v. Wells, 142 Vt. 641, 458 A.2d 1122 (1983), a finder was permitted to share in a broker's commission as agreed to even though the finder was not a licensed real estate broker or salesperson. In Vermont, by statute, a real estate broker or salesperson is one who for a consideration negotiates the purchase, exchange, or sale of real estate. A finder does not negotiate within the meaning of the act and hence is not covered by the statutory proscription of unlicensed persons acting as real estate brokers or salespersons. Some states exempt attorneys from real estate broker and salesperson licensing requirements if sales arise in the usual course of law practice. E.g., Tex. Rev. Civ. Stat. Ann. art. 6573a, §3 (Vernon Supp. 1985); and N.D. Cent. Code §43-27-07(2) (1978).

5. The American Bar Association's (ABA) Model Rules of Professional Conduct provide: "Rule 5.5. A lawyer shall not: . . . (b) assist a person who is not a member of the bar in the performance of activity that constitutes the unauthorized practice of law." Substantially the same language appears in the ABA's Model Code of Professional Responsibility DR 3-101(A) (1980), which preceded the Model Rules.

The National Association of Realtors Code of Ethics also has a provision concerning unauthorized practice of law: "Art. 17. The realtor shall not engage in activities that constitute the unauthorized practice of law and shall recommend that legal counsel be obtained when the interest of any party to the transaction requires it."

b. Antitrust

Both lawyers and real estate brokers have encountered significant antitrust problems in recent years. In Goldfarb v. Virginia State Bar, 421 U.S. 773 (1975), bar association minimum fee schedules were held to violate the Sherman Act. These schedules, formerly issued by many state and local bar associations and "suggesting" lawyers' minimum charges for many relatively standard forms of legal work, have since been abandoned. The fees challenged in the *Goldfarb* case were for real estate title examinations. Concern over antitrust vulnerability is also one reason why the ABA Model Code or Model Rules have now been generally adopted by state courts as rules of court. Such adoption increases the likelihood that the code and rules and their implementation will fall within the state action exemption to the antitrust laws.

In the late 1970s, the Antitrust Division of the United States Department of Justice filed a complaint against the ABA charging illegal restraint of trade in connection with the advertising sections of the Model Code. These charges were later dropped. See Justice Department Charges Code

Advertising Provisions Violate Federal Antitrust Laws, 62 A.B.A.J. 979 (1976); and White, Why Did the Antitrust Division Dismiss the Case?, 64 A.B.A.J. 1667 (1978).

Real estate broker antitrust difficulties have pertained to fee schedules, uniformity in commission rates, and multiple listing services. Publicly issued fee schedules have generally been abandoned by real estate brokers' organizations, as judicial and administrative agency decisions, including Goldfarb v. Virginia State Bar, have shown the vulnerability of such schedules under antitrust laws. However, even without formal fee schedules, there is a high degree of uniformity among real estate brokers in the commissions they charge, a major concern of the Federal Trade Commission in its recent staff inquiry and report. Multiple listing services are particularly suspect as a means of broker price-fixing. As one commentator has observed: "The MLS structure has a built-in device for detecting secret price cutting. Each MLS member always knows what other members are charging because commissions are split between the listing and selling brokers. Furthermore, MLS organizations have a number of methods of enforcing adherence to uniform prices among their members. The most blatant method is to threaten members who depart from fixed prices with expulsion. More subtle influences also operate. For example, MLS members simply may be less anxious to sell homes listed by brokers who charge less than the fixed rate."[5]

In their policies and effects, as they apply both to real estate brokers and lawyers, are antitrust and unauthorized practice laws inconsistent? How should any inconsistency be resolved?

---

5. Owen, Kickbacks, Specialization, Price Fixing, and Efficiency in Residential Real Estate Markets, 29 Stan. L. Rev. 931, 948 (1977). On antitrust laws as they relate to real estate brokers, see also Epley and Banks, National Real Estate Firms and Antitrust: Avoiding Liability, 12 Real Est. L.J. 243 (1984); Phillips and Butler, The Law and Economics of Residential Real Estate Markets in Texas: Regulation and Antitrust Implications, 36 Baylor L. Rev. 623 (1984); and Miller and Shedd, Do Antitrust Laws Apply to the Real Estate Brokerage Industry?, 17 Am. Bus. L.J. 313 (1979); Austin, Real Estate Boards and Multiple Listing Systems as Restraints of Trade, 70 Colum. L. Rev. 1325 (1970). Examples of important antitrust cases decided against real estate brokers are McClain v. Real Estate Board of New Orleans, 444 U.S. 232 (1980), complaint alleged that brokers had an effect on interstate commerce sufficient to constitute a valid allegation of a Sherman Act violation; United States v. National Association of Real Estate Boards, 339 U.S. 485 (1950), business of a real estate broker is trade within the meaning of the Sherman Act and a local board's schedule of commissions violates the act; Penne v. Greater Minneapolis Area Board of Realtors, 604 F.2d 1143 (1979), record presents a genuine issue of material fact that local board, as well as some board members, violated the Sherman Act in connection with operation of a multiple listing service; and United States v. Foley, 598 F.2d 1323 (1979), criminal conviction of real estate brokers upheld for fixing commissions illegally in relation to a multiple listing service, *cert. denied*, 444 U.S. 1043 (1980).

Federal Trade Commission, The Residential Real Estate Brokerage Industry

F.T.C. Staff Rep. 24, 64, 100 (1983)

Until the early 1970s agreements among real estate brokers to fix or stabilize commission rates and the terms of trade upon which they would deal were commonplace, in large part because the industry was not believed to fall under either state or Federal antitrust laws. Published, mandatory schedules of fees—and later "suggested" schedules—were widely used. Formal recommended schedules apparently were abandoned in the late 1960s and early 1970s. A long record of investigations, antitrust settlements, and prosecutions for covert conspiracies suggests that informal local price-fixing remained common in the industry for some time, however.

The industry today appears more aware of the illegality and risks of price-fixing. Nonetheless, given the structure of the industry, localized attempts to raise or stabilize rates can be expected to occur from time to time.

Our conclusion is that price-fixing is not a primary cause of local uniformity in commission rates, although there probably are residual effects left over from the era of fee schedules. Commission rates prevalent in a local market often are the same as those which were recommended in the last formal schedule of fees in effect in that market. There may also be a residual stigma in many markets attached to offering prices or terms which vary significantly from the traditional norms. . . .

The evidence indicates that brokerage commission rates are quite uniform within local markets. In most markets, the prevailing rate is either 6 or 7 percent. Furthermore, the dollar value of commission fees per transaction has increased very substantially in recent years when compared to the general rate of inflation or the incomes of other white collar workers. At the same time, there is at least some evidence that brokerage industry productivity apparently has declined in recent years.

Available statistics, therefore, strongly suggest that forces other than free competition are affecting the level at which commission rates are set. . . .

The modern Realtor system operates as a complex support mechanism for cooperative brokerage and for the interests of member brokers. Policy in the Realtor system flows in two directions: from the local Boards upward, and from the NAR down. However, the basic needs of local brokers are the paramount element in Realtor policy. The MLS and cooperation are essential for most local Realtors and are the primary concerns of their Boards.

The National Association, and to a lesser extent, the state Associations, are, however, playing increasing leadership roles in the development of Realtor policy. This is apparent in Realtor policy on MLS operations, agency law, the independent contractor status of real estate salespersons, legal defense, and political activity. Today, more than ever before, it is accurate to speak of a unified brokerage industry.[212]

The Realtors face a dilemma in attempting to increase industry efficiency without limiting competitive freedom and innovation. They have developed a mechanism, the MLS, and an ethic, the norm of cooperation, in an attempt to make brokerage more efficient and more profitable. These innovations have helped to improve the efficiency of housing markets, but they have also fostered uniformity of brokerage practice at the expense of competition. This uniformity has occasionally led to such overt abuses as secret fee schedules and price-fixing conspiracies, and also to the subtle discouragement of innovation and alternative forms of practice.

This uniformity may in some instances have limited the competitive freedom of brokers without justification. Certain restrictions on MLS access and use, Board membership and rules, and on other aspects of the Realtor system can hamper alternative forms of practice and yet may not be conditions necessary for MLS or Board survival.

2. *Advertising and Solicitation*

Real estate brokers have always been permitted to generate business by advertising and solicitation, although the NAR Code of Ethics does require truthfulness in advertising.[6] By contrast, lawyers until recently were prohibited from advertising and lawyer in-person solicitation still is generally prohibited.[7] The turnaround in lawyer advertising authorization

---

212. Practices in different eras and at the different Realtor levels should, however, be distinguished. Certain of the Realtors' historical conduct—particularly the use of fee schedules—are clearly unlawful under current interdependence of antitrust laws, and we have found no current evidence of such schedules on the parts of the NAR or the several state Associations we have studied. However, recent antitrust prosecutions and lawsuits at the levels of the local Boards suggest that price-fixing activities continue to some extent on a local basis. See, e.g., United States v. Jack Foley Realty, Inc., 598 F.2d 1323 (4th Cir. 1979), cert. denied, 100 S. Ct. 727 (1980); United States v. Greater Syracuse Bd. of Realtors, 1978-1 Trade Cases 62,008 (N.D.N.Y. 1978). . . .

6. National Association of Realtors Code of Ethics art. 19:

> The Realtor shall be careful at all times to present a true picture in his advertising and representations to the public. He shall neither advertise without disclosing his name nor permit any person associated with him to use individual names or telephone numbers, unless such person's connection with the Realtor is obvious in the advertisement.

7. On lawyer advertising and solicitation, see Andrews, The Model Rules and Advertising, 68 A.B.A.J. 808 (1982); Devine, Letting the Market Control Advertising by Lawyers: A Suggested Remedy for the Misled Client, 31 Buffalo L. Rev. 351 (1982); Murdock and Linenberger, Legal Advertising and Solicitation, 16 Land and Water L. Rev. 627 (1981); Annot., Advertising as Ground for Disciplining Attorney, 30 A.L.R.4th 742 (1984); and Note, In-Person Solicitation by Public Interest Law Firms: A Look at the A.B.A. Code Provisions in Light of Primus and Ohralik, 49 Geo. Wash. L. Rev. 309 (1981).

came in 1977 with the United States Supreme Court case of Bates v. State Bar of Arizona, 433 U.S. 350, permitting lawyers, on First Amendment grounds, to engage in advertising that is not misleading. The ABA Model Rules of Professional Conduct and Model Code of Professional Responsibility, within perceived constitutional boundaries, set limits on permissible lawyer advertising.[8]

Lawyer solicitation by in-person contact with prospective clients is prohibited under most circumstances, and the Court has refused to extend First Amendment protection to this kind of lawyer self-promotion. Ohralik v. Ohio State Bar Assn., 436 U.S. 447 (1978).[9]

Koffler v. Joint Bar Association
51 N.Y.2d 140, 412 N.E.2d 927 (1980)

MEYER, Judge. Direct mail solicitation of potential clients by lawyers is constitutionally protected commercial speech which may be regulated but not proscribed. The Appellate Division's contrary holding, predicated upon an artificial distinction between solicitation and advertising, should, therefore, be reversed, without costs.

The appeal comes before us as of right, on constitutional grounds. It is from an order of the Appellate Division, made in a disciplinary proceeding, which confirmed the report of the referee that respondents-appellants Koffler and Harrison (hereafter respondents) had violated section 479 of the Judiciary Law and DR 2-103(A) of the Code of Professional Responsibility, but which, finding that respondents had apparently acted in good faith, imposed no sanction.

The proceeding, begun by the Joint Bar Association Grievance Committee, Tenth Judicial District (hereafter Committee), charged that respondents, in violation of section 479 of the Judiciary Law and the Code of Professional Responsibility, caused to be mailed between August 24, 1977 and October 24, 1977, to approximately 7,500 individual real property owners a letter on respondents' legal stationery which solicited the addressees to use respondents' services in connection with the sale of real property, and during the same period caused to be mailed to a number of real estate brokers a letter on respondents' legal stationery soliciting the brokers to refer clients to respondents in connection with the purchase or sale of real property. The texts of the two letters are set forth in the Appellate Division's opinion (70 A.D.2d 252, 254-255, 420 N.Y.S.2d 560) and need not be repeated here. The Appellate Division noted (id., at p. 256, 420 N.Y.S.2d 560) respondent Koffler's testimony that the results of

---

8. American Bar Association Model Rules of Professional Conduct Rule 7.2; and American Bar Association Model Code of Professional Responsibility DR 2-101, 102, and 105.

9. An exception is made for in-person solicitation of prospective litigants by lawyers representing nonprofit organizations that engage in litigation as a form of political expression and political association. In re Primus, 436 U.S. 412 (1978).

their *Newsday* advertisement, reproduced as part of their letter, "'were negligible'" and that respondents "'felt if we could direct our advertising specifically at the person who was interested in the sale of a house, — for example, instead of just advertising in a paper with a general circulation — we might be able to get better results and do the mass production idea that we had.'" He also testified that the firm did about 200 closings at the fee stated in the letter.

By their answer and by stipulation made before the referee respondents admitted sending the letters and the text of them. The answer, however, alleged as a defense that both facially and as applied the Judiciary Law and the code violate the First and Fourteenth Amendments to the United States Constitution, that respondents acted in good faith reliance on the decision of the Supreme Court in Bates v. State Bar of Ariz., 433 U.S. 350, 97 S. Ct. 2691, 53 L. Ed. 2d 810 decided June 27, 1977, and that they have acted and are continuing to act in compliance with the guidelines for advertising adopted by the New York State Bar Association and approved by the Appellate Division, Second Department.

Since overbreadth analysis is not applicable to commercial speech (Ohralik v. Ohio State Bar Assn., 436 U.S. 447, 462, n.20, 98 S. Ct. 1912, 1922, n.20, 56 L. Ed. 2d 444; People v. Mobil Oil Corp., 48 N.Y.2d 192, 199, 422 N.Y.S.2d 33, 397 N.E.2d 724), respondents are limited to contesting the invalidity of the statute and code provisions as applied to them. The referee concluded that respondents had violated the Judiciary Law and DR 2-103(A) of the code because their communications constituted constitutionally unprotected solicitation rather than advertising. In so finding he made no distinction between the letter to homeowners and the letter to brokers, nor had any distinction between them been suggested by the Committee's presentation at the hearing before the referee. Confirming, the Appellate Division, without reaching the question whether all mailing to nonclients is proscribed, held the statute and DR 2-103(A) "constitutional insofar as they ban solicitation of legal business by mail as well as in person" (70 A.D.2d 252, 274, 420 N.Y.S.2d 650) but, except for a passing footnote reference to the potential conflict of interest that could be involved in the solicitation of real estate brokers to refer clients to respondents, likewise did not differentiate between the two letters. For the reasons hereafter set forth we conclude that neither statute nor code provision can constitutionally prohibit advertising of attorneys' services by direct mail addressed to potential clients. We do not, however, pass upon direct mail solicitation of clients through materials addressed to third persons, preferring to leave determination of that question, distinguishable as it is in a number of ways from direct client solicitation by letter,[2] for

---

2. For example, third person mailings will, if their ends are to be achieved, almost always involve in-person solicitation by the intermediary, and are, therefore, much closer to speech of the type Ohralik v. Ohio State Bar Assn., 436 U.S. 447, 98 S. Ct. 1912, 56 L. Ed. 2d 444 has held can be proscribed (cf. Matter of State Bar Grievance Administrator v. Jacques, 407 Mich. 26, 51, 281 N.W.2d 469 [Coleman, Ch. J., dissenting]).

a matter in which a more complete record has been made and there has been more extensive consideration by the Appellate Division, in which is vested primary jurisdiction in matters of discipline.

While prohibitions against solicitation of legal business by or for attorneys have ancient roots (Note, Attorney Solicitation of Clients, 7 Hofstra L.R. 755, 757), their constitutionality has come into question only recently. The proscriptions the Committee seeks to enforce against respondents are contained in section 479 of the Judiciary Law, which read in 1977 and still reads: "It shall be unlawful for any person or his agent, employee or any person acting on his behalf, to solicit or procure through solicitation either directly or indirectly legal business, or to solicit or procure through solicitation a retainer, written or oral, or any agreement authorizing an attorney to perform or render legal services, or to make it a business so to solicit or procure such business, retainers or agreements," and section DR 2-103(A) of the Code of Professional Responsibility, which as it read at the time respondents' letter to homeowners was circulated, provided: "A lawyer shall not recommend employment, as a private practitioner, of himself, his partner, or associate to a non-lawyer who has not sought his advice regarding employment of a lawyer."[3] Since to recommend one's self for employment is to solicit employment, the two provisions are, at least in the context of the present proceeding, coextensive.

We disagree, however, with the Appellate Division's conclusion that the solicitation that those provisions condemn can be differentiated from constitutionally protected commercial speech simply by categorizing the former as solicitation and the latter as advertising. The Supreme Court has said so in so many words, overruling in N.A.A.C.P. v. Button, 371 U.S. 415, 429, 83 S. Ct. 328, 336, 9 L. Ed. 2d 405, the contention that "solicitation" is wholly outside the area of First Amendment protection, and declaring in Bigelow v. Virginia, 421 U.S. 809, 826, 95 S. Ct. 2222, 2235, 44 L. Ed. 2d 600 that: "Regardless of the particular label asserted by the

---

3. On April 29, 1978, DR 2-103 was amended. Subdivision (A) and (F) of the amended provision read as follows:

(A) A lawyer shall not solicit employment as a private practitioner of himself or herself, a partner or an associate to [sic] a person who has not sought advice regarding employment of a lawyer in violation of any statute or court rule. Actions permitted by DR 2-104 and advertising in accordance with DR 2-101 shall not be deemed solicitation in violation of this provision.

(F) Advertising permitted under DR 2-101 shall not be deemed in violation of any provision of this Disciplinary Rule.

On March 1, 1978, the Appellate Division, Second Department, implemented its rule 691.22, originally filed in 1976 (22 NYCRR 691.22). The rule is entitled "Advertising and publicity by attorneys" and, in pertinent part, permits public communications that are not false or deceptive and that do not include puffery or claims concerning quality of services that cannot be measured or verified, and requires that advertised fees be maintained for specified periods. DR 2-101, referred to in DR 2-103(A) and (F), is, except for the substitution of "lawyer" for "attorney," identical with rule 691.22. When respondents' letters were sent, however, the guidelines were not in effect.

State — whether it calls speech 'commercial' or 'commercial advertising' or 'solicitation' — a court may not escape the task of assessing the First Amendment interest at stake and weighing it against the public interest allegedly served by the regulation." (See, also, Matter of Madsen, 68 Ill. 2d 472, 478, 12 Ill. Dec. 576, 370 N.E.2d 199).

Semantically, of course, there is a difference. Not all solicitation is advertising, though all advertising either implicitly or explicitly involves solicitation. To "solicit" means to move to action, to endeavor to obtain by asking, and implies personal petition to a particular individual to do a particular thing (Webster's Third New International Dictionary, p. 2169; Black's Law Dictionary [5th ed], pp. 1248-1249), while "advertising" is the calling of information to the attention of the public, by whatever means (Webster's, p. 31; Black's, p. 50). To outlaw the use of letters, the content of which does not violate DR 2-101, addressed to those most likely to be in need of legal services, because in addition to "advertising" the nature of the service and its price the letters implicitly or explicitly suggest employment of the writer to perform those services, ignores the strong societal and individual interest in the free dissemination of truthful price information as a means of assuring informed and reliable decision making in our free enterprise system, about which both the Supreme Court (Bates v. State Bar of Ariz., 433 U.S. 350, 364, 97 S. Ct. 2691, 2699, 53 L. Ed. 2d 810 supra) and we (People v. Mobil Oil Corp., 48 N.Y.2d 192, 200, 422 N.Y.S.2d 33, 397 N.E.2d 724, supra) have had occasion to comment, and can only be productive of confusion for the profession (see Freedman, Lawyers' Ethics in an Adversary System, ch. 10). To do so, moreover, is to suggest that there is necessarily something improper about an attorney's desire to earn a fee, and that there is something different about the legal profession that makes direct mail advertising improper though it would not be for other businesses or professions and though indirect forms of advertising are not improper even for the legal profession, notwithstanding the contrary indications in the writings of both the Supreme Court (*Bates*, supra, at pp. 368-369, 371-372, 97 S. Ct. at pp. 2701, 2702-2703; Pittsburgh Press Co. v. Human Relations Comm., 413 U.S. 376, 385, 93 S. Ct. 2553, 2558, 37 L. Ed. 2d 669) and of our court (Matter of Gordon, 48 N.Y.2d 266, 272, 422 N.Y.S.2d 641, 397 N.E.2d 1309).

Turning, then, to consideration of the provisions in question in the context of the case law on commercial speech, we note that the Supreme Court of Kentucky has upheld letter solicitation of clients in real estate transactions (Kentucky Bar Assn. v. Stuart, 568 S.W.2d 933 [Ky.]; see, also, the reference to "mail circulations" in the concurring in-part opn. of Mr. Justice Powell in Bates v. State Bar of Ariz., 433 U.S. 350, 402, n.12, 97 S. Ct. 2691, 2718, n.12, 53 L. Ed. 2d 810 supra), but that none of the United States Supreme Court's pronouncements in cases concerned with lawyer-client speech is directly in point. Matter of Primus, 436 U.S. 412, 98 S. Ct. 1893, 56 L. Ed. 2d 417, dealt with lawyer-client speech but at the political and associational level, not here involved, and while it held protected letter solicitation of a prospective client, did so on the basis (see 436 U.S., at p. 431, 98 S. Ct. at p. 1904) of the more generous protection accorded such speech. Bates v. State Bar of Ariz., supra though it held protected price advertising by lawyers, did so with respect to the more indirect method of newspaper advertising. Ohralik v. Ohio State Bar Assn., 436 U.S. 447, 98 S. Ct. 1912, 56 L. Ed. 2d 444 supra, while it held constitutional a restriction on in-person solicitation of accident victims while in the hospital, did so on the possibility of overreaching inherent in such a person-to-person confrontation.

Those cases are nonetheless helpful in the determination of the instant appeal, as is the more structured analysis for commercial speech cases stated by the Supreme Court in its most recent opinion on the subject, Central Hudson Gas v. Public Serv. Comm., 447 U. S. —, 100 S. Ct. 2343, 65 L. Ed. 2d 341. In that case the court defined commercial speech as "expression related solely to the economic interest of the speaker and its audience" (447 U.S. at p. —, 100 S. Ct. at p. 2349), a definition within which respondents' letter to homeowners comfortably fits, and posited a four-part analysis (447 U.S. at p. —, 100 S. Ct. at p. 2351): (1) Is it misleading or related to unlawful activity? (2) Are the Government interests sought to be protected substantial? (3) How directly does the regulation advance those interests? (4) Is there a less restrictive alternative?

The Committee did not claim in its petition that respondents' letter was either misleading or related to unlawful activity. At the hearing before the referee, its counsel rested after putting on record the stipulation by which respondents' sending of the letters and the content of them was put in evidence and cross-examined respondents only to show that they were commercially motivated. The Appellate Division (70 A.D.2d, at p. 274, n.5, 420 N.Y.S.2d 560) characterized as a questionable tactic the statement in the letter that " 'We understand that you are selling your home,' " noting that the mailing of 7,500 such letters "would apparently indicate that they [respondents] had no such understanding at all," but made no finding that the letter was misleading, as, indeed, on the record it could not have, there being nothing in the record to indicate how the list of addressees was compiled by respondents. We conclude that the letter to homeowners was neither misleading nor did it relate to unlawful activity.[4]

The interests sought to be protected are identified in the Appellate Division opinion (70 A.D.2d, at p. 274, 420 N.Y.S.2d 560) and in the Committee's brief as the potentials[5] for deception, for invasion of privacy,

---

4. Of course, the Committee in seeking to have respondents disciplined for violating the Judiciary Law is, in one sense, urging that respondents acted unlawfully, but that is not the activity (sale of a house) to which the letter was related.

5. It is the potential that is to be considered in determining constitutionality (Ohralik v. Ohio State Bar Assn., 436 U.S. 447, 464, 98 S. Ct. 1912, 1923, 56 L. Ed. 2d 444 supra), although respondents could not be disciplined unless their "activity in fact involved the type of misconduct at which" the prohibitions in question are directed (Matter of Primus, 436 U.S. 412, 434, 98 S. Ct. 1893, 1906, 56 L. Ed. 2d 417, supra).

for overcommercialization of the profession and for conflict of interest. *Bates, Ohralik* and *Primus* establish that these are legitimate and important State interests.

There is, however, obvious tension between these interests and the societal interest, already noted, in the free dissemination of truthful price information in order to assure "informed and reliable decisionmaking" (*Bates*, 433 U.S. 350, 364, 97 S. Ct. 2691, 2699, 53 L. Ed. 2d 810 supra). It is in the light of that tension that the directness of relation of regulation to purpose is to be considered. So considered, the only interest concerning which it can be said that there is a sufficiently direct relationship is prevention of deception. The Committee does not suggest how conflict of interest can arise through direct mail client solicitation or how the proscription of such solicitation will "help to avoid situations where the lawyer's exercise of judgment on behalf of a client will be clouded by his own pecuniary self-interest," as its brief suggests, and no such possibility occurs to us (cf. Note, 81 Yale L.J. 1181, 1187).

The overcommercialization potential of direct mail advertising is now sufficiently controlled by the Appellate Division's rule 699.12 and DR 2-101, the constitutionality of which have not been questioned in this proceeding. Though those controls were not in effect when respondents mailed their letters, the connection between professional standards (as distinct from the traditions of the profession, cf. *Bates*, supra, at p. 371, 97 S. Ct. at p. 2702) and direct mail advertising of the nature and cost of legal services offered is too indirect to sustain proscription of such advertising (cf. *Central Hudson Gas*, supra, 447 U.S. at p. —, 100 S. Ct. at p. 2350; Terry v. California State Bd. of Pharmacy, D.C., 395 F. Supp. 94, 106, aff'd. 426 U.S. 913, 96 S. Ct. 2617, 49 L. Ed. 2d 368). The more so is this true in light of *Bates'* conclusions that "competition through advertising is ordinarily the desired norm" (at p. 378, n.35, 97 S. Ct. at p. 2706, n.35) and that restraints on advertising "are an ineffective way of deterring shoddy work" (at p. 378, 97 S. Ct. at p. 2706).

Invasion of privacy and the possibility of overbearing persuasion, both of which were condemned in *Ohralik* and which could conceivably be present in telephone solicitation as the Appellate Division suggests (70 A.D.2d, at p. 273, 420 N.Y.S.2d 560), are not sufficiently possible in mail solicitation to justify banning it. As the Supreme Court put it in Consolidated Edison Co. v. Public Serv. Comm., 447 U.S. —, —, 100 S. Ct. 2326, 2336, 65 L. Ed. 319, a recipient of a lawyer's letter "may escape exposure to objectionable material simply by transferring . . . [it] from envelope to wastebasket." It is not enough to justify a ban that in some situations (marital discord, a death in the family) a solicitation letter may be offensive to the recipient, or that some people may fear receiving a lawyer's letter, or to suggest that there may be some who by reason of frequent receipt of lawyers' solicitation letters may discard without opening a mailed summons.

The potential for deception is a different matter, for unlike newspaper, television or radio advertising, direct mail goes only to the addressee. The temptation for deception is, therefore, greater, and the probability of exposure less, than for those more public media. Enforcement of the State's strong interest that "the stream of commercial information flow cleanly as well as freely" (Virginia Pharmacy Bd. v. Virginia Consumer Council, 425 U.S. 748, 772, 96 S. Ct. 1817, 1831, 48 L. Ed. 2d 346) and that, to that end, there be effective oversight of members of the Bar is less probable, therefore, with respect to mail than to media advertising (see *Ohralik*, 436 U.S. 447, 466-467, 98 S. Ct. 1912, 1924-1925, 56 L. Ed. 2d 444, supra; Allison v. Louisiana State Bar Assn., 362 So. 2d 489, 496 [La.]).

That there is a substantial State interest to which the regulations are closely related does not end the inquiry, however, for complete suppression is not constitutional if the State's interest can be adequately protected by more limited regulation. That it can be seems hardly open to question, in view, for example, of the filing requirement for retainer statements now contained in the Appellate Division's rule 691.20 (22 NYCRR 691.20). That similar filing of a solicitation letter assures the public ample protection was the conclusion of the Supreme Court of Kentucky (Kentucky Bar Assn. v. Stuart, 568 S.W.2d 933, 934 [Ky.], supra).[6]

Our discussion so far assumes that the ban against solicitation is a restriction as to content or subject matter, rather than manner of communication. The Supreme Court has, however, differentiated between the two applying the criteria discussed above to content restriction but upholding a regulation of time, place or manner if reasonable, if it serves a significant governmental interest and if it leaves ample alternative channels for communication (Consolidated Edison Co. v. Public Serv. Comm., 447 U.S. —, —, 100 S. Ct. 2326, 2332, 65 L. Ed. 319 supra; Virginia Pharmacy Bd. v. Virginia Consumer Council, 425 U.S. 748, 771, 96 S. Ct. 1817, 1830, 48 L. Ed. 2d 346, supra).

Since that categorization gives rise to some problems in analysis (cf. Reich, Preventing Deception In Commercial Speech, 54 N.Y.U. L.R. 775), we note that the result would not differ were we to apply the manner rather than the content criteria. The Committee argues that "ample alternative channels" are left open because nothing in the letter, with the exception of the personal references, was unsuited to communication in a newspaper, magazine, advertising supplement, telephone directory, radio or television advertisement. There is, however, nothing to show what the comparative costs of the suggested alternatives is or whether the more direct and discursive letter form is not more effective, and thus no basis for concluding that the alternatives are "ample." There is, moreover, respondent Koffler's testimony that at least the newspaper advertising which they

---

6. Our discussion of a filing requirement is, of course, by way of example only and not by way of prescription.

tried first was ineffectual, the response being negligible, whereas they were retained for some 200 closings as a result of their letter to homeowners. Moreover, unless the reasonableness of regulation is to be considered in the abstract, a regulation which completely proscribes use of direct mail when the State's purpose can readily be achieved by a less restrictive alternative cannot be said to be reasonable.

Whether considered as a restriction on the content of, or a regulation of the manner of, commercial speech, the restrictions in question may not constitutionally proscribe direct mail advertising of the availability of particular legal services and the cost of those services.

For the foregoing reasons, the order of the Appellate Division should be reversed, without costs, and the proceeding dismissed.

NOTES

1. In Greene v. Grievance Committee, 54 N.Y.2d 118, 429 N.E.2d 390 (1981), *cert. denied,* 455 U.S. 1035 (1982), the New York Court of Appeals decided the direct mail to brokers issue that it refused to pass on in the *Koffler* case. Respondent in the *Green* case mailed approximately one thousand advertising fliers to real estate brokers in his area. In these fliers he sought referrals of clients from the brokers; offered to handle real estate sales transactions from contract through closing for $335, apparently a low price competitively; and promised to prepare a contract or other documents on two hour's notice. The court found respondent's conduct to be illegal solicitation. Accord In the Matter of Alessi, 60 N.Y.2d 229, 457 N.E.2d 682 (1983), *cert. denied,*—U.S.—, 104 S. Ct. 1599 (1984). If lawyers can send direct mail advertisements to prospective clients, why cannot they seek clients through brokers by sending to brokers direct mail advertisements seeking client referrals?

2. Should it be professionally proper conduct for a lawyer to seek real estate closing work by telephoning prospective clients?

3. If real estate brokers are permitted to seek customers by face to face solicitation, why are lawyers prohibited from doing so?

3. Conflict of Interest

Conflict of interest is a common professional responsibility problem facing lawyers.[10] It can arise in all kinds of law practices and in all kinds of

---

10. On conflict of interest involving lawyers, see Stoltenberg and Whitman, Direct Mail Advertising by Lawyers, 45 U. Pitt. L. Rev. 381 (1984); Moore, Conflicts of Interest in the Simultaneous Representation of Multiple Clients: A Proposed Solution to the Current Con-

law offices. Potential conflict may require a lawyer not to accept proffered representation, and if an actual conflict arises a lawyer may be disqualified from continuing to represent one or more clients. Under some circumstances, consent of affected parties, with adequate disclosure as to the nature of the conflict, may justify the lawyer in acting in a conflict of interest situation. In real estate transactions, lawyers often are asked to represent concurrently parties with differing interests, such as a buyer and seller or mortgagor and mortgagee. Almost invariably this poses a conflict of interest issue.

In the Matter of Dolan
76 N.J. 1, 384 A.2d 1076 (1978)

PER CURIAM. A complaint was filed with the Middlesex County Ethics Committee charging respondent with conflicts of interest in connection with certain real estate transactions. After receipt of the Committee's report the Court directed the Central Ethics Unit to file a petition for an Order to Show Cause, which issued in due course. That petition asserts that respondent's conduct constituted violations of DR 5-105, DR 8-101, and DR 9-101, dealing respectively with conflicts, abuse of public position, and the appearance of impropriety.

I

The public position which respondent held during the times pertinent hereto was that of municipal attorney for the Borough of Carteret, to which he was appointed at the beginning of 1971. For some time prior to the events in question the Borough had implemented a policy of urban renewal pursuant to Federal Housing Authority (FHA) procedures. By ordinance it created the Carteret Redevelopment Agency (Agency), consisting of six members, five of whom were appointed by the municipal governing body. The Agency's function was to solicit proposals from developers for utilization of certain tracts for low and moderate income multi-family dwelling units. Gulya Brothers, Inc., a developer, submitted a proposal for a townhouse project on one of the tracts, which the Agency accepted. Thereafter, on April 5, 1971, Gulya Bros. Redevelopment Corp. (Gulya) was established for the purpose of purchasing the land from

---

fusion and Controversy, 61 Tex. L. Rev. 211 (1982); Aronson, Conflict of Interest, 52 Wash. L. Rev. 807 (1977); and Note, Conflicts of Interest in the Legal Profession, 94 Harv. L. Rev. 1244 (1981).

the Agency and developing it, and marketing the townhouses which it erected thereon.

Upon acceptance of Gulya's proposal the Agency was required to obtain the necessary approvals from the municipal planning board, board of adjustment and governing body. Additionally, it was obliged to convey to the developer marketable title to the tracts involved. In due course the Agency, which was represented by its own counsel, successfully processed applications before the appropriate municipal bodies, and on November 15, 1971, the Borough gave final approval to the project.

Thereafter Gulya's attorney sought financing for the project on behalf of the developer but was unsuccessful. To aid in this endeavor the developer's attorney sought out the respondent, who had "handled matters for him in the past," was "familiar with mortgage financing," and had done "some extensive real estate work." In May or June of 1972 respondent, at the instance of Gulya's attorney, discussed the project with the principals of Gulya and at that point took over the representation of the developer, with the full consent of previous counsel. Prior to this respondent had not represented Gulya in any capacity whatsoever. Specifically, he had not appeared on the developer's behalf before the Agency; neither had he represented either the planning board or board of adjustment at the time of the Agency's applications to those bodies or at any other time. Respondent was, however, attorney for the Borough when the Council acted favorably on the board of adjustment's recommendation to grant the Agency's application for the necessary variances for this project.

Respondent's efforts on Gulya's behalf produced the required financing through a New Jersey mortgage company. The financing consisted of both the construction mortgage and permanent mortgages available to the buyers of the townhouses. Respondent's representation of the developer continued throughout the initial construction stage of the project, during which time he was, as has been indicated, attorney for the municipality in which the development was located, albeit that representation of the municipality was not in any wise in connection with any business of or application on behalf of the developer.

Respondent also represented the mortgage company in sales involving permanent mortgages used in the purchase of townhouses from Gulya. In those same transactions he came to act as well on behalf of purchasers-mortgagors of the housing units at their closings of mortage loan and title, under the following circumstances. In order to market the townhouses the developer engaged a real estate agent, whose function it was to attact buyers and assist those buyers in obtaining FHA approvals. It was the agent who led the buyers through whatever preliminary steps were required leading to execution of the contracts, and it was the agent who secured execution of those contracts. Respondent did not enter the picture until after the contracts had been signed by the buyer. The contract forms utilized by the agent, pursuant to these procedures, contained the following clauses:[1]

> Purchaser shall be responsible for paying the closing attorneys for the mortgage (sic) their legal fee for examination of title and recording of deed and mortgage and shall also be responsible for and shall pay for survey, mortgage title insurance, hazard insurance premium, escrow funds for taxes and insurance, appraisal and inspection fees and a one percent processing fee except as may be otherwise provided herein. . . .
>
> If purchaser uses seller's attorney, the seller will pay the legal fee for title examination, recording of deed and mortgage, survey, mortgage title insurance, appraisal and inspection fees.

By virtue of the arrangement last referred to either respondent or an associate in his office attended closings not only for the seller in sixteen instances, but also for the purchasers-mortgagors in at least fourteen of those closings.[2] At these closings purchasers were notified for the first time of the potential conflicts of interest arising out of respondent's multiple representations. They were presented with and executed two separate waiver and consent forms, one acknowledging and approving respondent's representation of purchaser and seller and the other acknowledging and approving his representation of mortgagor, mortgagee and seller.

As may be seen, then, there are two separate areas of potential conflict of interest called to our attention by the Committee report and the Central Ethics Unit's presentment.[3] The first centers about respondent's representation of the builder-developer while at the same time serving as attorney for the Borough of Carteret. The second focuses on his representation at the closing of the seller, the purchasers-mortgagors and the mortgagee under circumstances casting doubt on the informed nature of the consents given by the buyers to this multiple representation.

II

We address first the asserted conflict presented by respondent's representation of the developer while concurrently acting as borough attorney. Respondent points out that at no time did his representation of

---

1. These clauses have not been directly attacked in these proceedings and we do not pass on their propriety.

2. In a letter answer to the complaint, marked in evidence at the Committee's hearing, respondent indicated that "one or two of the people did bring their own attorney to the closing."

3. A third area emerges, although it was not touched upon in the complaint, testimony, report or presentment. It is the arrangement under which respondent represented both Gulya and the mortgage company with respect to the construction mortgage—again at a time when he was municipal attorney. Much of the thrust of this opinion can be directed with equal force to that relationship even though it has not been presented to us directly.

Gulya involve any dealings or transactions with the Borough. All applications to municipal boards necessary to permit the Agency to convey clear title to the developer had been completed before respondent's representation of the developer commenced. Throughout the course of negotiations with the Agency involving Borough-related matters, Gulya was represented by its own attorney who eventually called on respondent for assistance when financing loomed as an obstacle.

With all of this, however, the fact remains that respondent's conduct was directly contrary to the mandate of this Court in In re A. and B., 44 N.J. 331, 209 A.2d 101 (1965). There it was noted that while in some situations it may be proper (within the proscription of DR 5-105) for an attorney to engage in dual representation, nevertheless

> the subject of land development is one in which the likelihood of transactions with a municipality and the room for public misunderstanding are so great that a member of the bar should not represent a developer operating in a municipality in which the member of the bar is the municipal attorney or the holder of any other municipal office of apparent influence. We all know from practical experience that the very nature of the work of the developer involves a probability of some municipal action, such as zoning applications, land subdivisions, building permits, compliance with the building code, etc.
>
> It is accordingly our view that *such dual representation is forbidden even though the attorney does not advise either the municipality or the private client with respect to matters concerning them. The fact of such dual representation itself is contrary to the public interest.* [44 N.J. at 334-35, 209 A.2d at 103 (emphasis added).]

While in a sense this rule may be deemed somewhat harsh, particularly in a situation where, as here, the representation of both municipality and developer was at no time in connection with a transaction involving both clients, we are strongly of the view that the public interest demands strict adherence to the letter of In re A. and B., supra. A municipal attorney's public obligations are such that he must take particular pains to avoid the shadow of suspicion which inevitably is cast when he begins to entangle himself in a representative capacity in the legal affairs of a developer operating within the municipality. If the municipal attorney is not a full-fledged member of the "municipal family," he is least in such a close and confidential relationship with it as to warrant his not representing those who may benefit (or, as here, have already benefitted) from successful applications by others (here, the Agency) to the planning board and zoning board of adjustment.

In this case the affirmative action of those municipal boards, while made at the Agency's behest, inured to the benefit of Gulya. Those applications were, in a very real sense, in Gulya's interest, were made at a time when respondent represented the Borough, and were then followed by respondent's representation of Gulya in connection with the same development project. This representation ignored the clear admonition of In re A. and B., supra, and hence merits our disciplinary action.

III

We turn our attention to the conflict presented by respondent's multiple representation of seller, purchaser-mortgagor, and mortgagee.[4] At the outset we recognize the emphasis that our disciplinary rules place on the desirability of completely independent counsel. Specifically, DR 5-105 prohibits multiple representation except under certain severely circumscribed circumstances.[5] See In re A. and B., supra, 44 N.J. at 335, 209 A.2d 101 (Schettino, J., concurring). The sense of our rules is that an attorney owes complete and undivided loyalty to the client who has retained him. The attorney should be able to advise the client in such a way as to protect the client's interests, utilizing his professional training, ability and judgment to the utmost. Consequently, if any conflicting interest could arise which would stand in the way of that kind of unstinting zeal, then the client must be so informed and the attorney may continue his limited representation only with the client's informed consent.

In a real estate transaction, the positions of vendor and purchaser are inherently susceptible to conflict. In re Kamp, 40 N.J. 588, 595, 194 A.2d 236 (1963). This is likewise the case with a borrower-lender relationship. Id. at 596, 194 A.2d 236. The requirements of an attorney involved in

---

4. In an analogous context, the not uncommon practice by some lending institutions of requiring real estate mortgagors to be represented by the lender's attorney has not gone unnoticed by the Legislature. N.J.S.A. 46:10A-6 prohibits such a practice in a mortgage loan transaction where the mortgagee is a consumer. Senate Bill 35, an amendment to this statute which has passed the Senate and is now before the Assembly Banking and Insurance Committee, expands the scope of the statute to prohibit such a practice in all mortgage loan transactions, regardless of whether the mortgagee is a consumer or a commercial party.

5. DR 5-105. Refusing to Accept or Continue Employment if the Interests of Another Client May Impair the Independent Professional Judgment of the Lawyer

(A) A lawyer shall decline proffered employment if the exercise of his independent professional judgment in behalf of a client will be or is likely to be adversely affected by the acceptance of the proffered employment, except to the extent permitted under DR 5-105(C).

(B) A lawyer shall not continue multiple employment if the exercise of his independent professional judgment in behalf of a client will be or is likely to be adversely affected by his representation of another client, except to the extent permitted under DR 5-105(C).

(C) In situations covered by DR 5-105(A) and (B), except as prohibited by rule, opinion, directive or statute, a lawyer may represent multiple clients if he believes that he can adequately represent the interests of each and if each consents to the representation after full disclosure of the facts and of the possible effect of such representation on the exercise of his independent professional judgment on behalf of each.

(D) If a lawyer is required to decline employment or to withdraw from employment under DR 5-105, no partner or associate of his or his firm may accept or continue such employment.

such multiple representations of purchaser, vendor and mortgagee are set out in Justice Proctor's opinion in In re Kamp, supra, where he said:

> Full disclosure requires the attorney not only to inform the prospective client of the attorney's relationship to the seller, but also to explain in detail the pitfalls that may arise in the course of the transaction which would make it desirable that the buyer have independent counsel. The full significance of the representation of conflicting interests should be disclosed to the client so that he may make an intelligent decision before giving his consent. If the attorney cannot properly represent the buyer in all aspects of the transaction because of his relationship to the seller, full disclosure requires that he inform the buyer of the limited scope of his intended representation of the buyer's interest and point out the advantages of the buyer's retaining independent counsel. A similar situation may occur, for example, when the buyer of real estate utilizes the services of the attorney who represents a party financing the transaction. To the extent that both parties seek a marketable title, there would appear to be no conflict between their interest. Nevertheless, a possible conflict may arise concerning the terms of the financing, and therefore at the time of the retainer the attorney should make clear to the buyer the potential area of conflict. In addition, if the buyer's interests are protected only to the extent that they coincide with those of the party financing the transaction, the attorney should explain the limited scope of this protection so that the buyer may act intelligently with full knowledge of the facts. [40 N.J. at 595-96, 194 A.2d 240.]

See also N.J. Advisory Committee on Professional Ethics, Opinion 51, 87 N.J.L.J. 705 (1964).

In the application of these principles to the matter before us we are mindful of the circumstances surrounding this type of transaction, namely, the purchase of low and moderate income dwellings with federally guaranteed financing, which serve to distinguish it from the conventional transfer of real estate. There is less flexibility in the terms. Federal auspices in this context brings with it a certain rigidity which leaves little room for negotiation of price and such other commonly negotiable features as limits and rates on borrowed money. The prescribed forms for bond and mortgage contain fixed terms from which variance is rarely, if ever, permitted. Nevertheless, the severely strictured nature of the relationship between mortgagor and mortgagee in no wise serves to diminish the essential obligation of full and timely disclosure. The opportunity for conflict to arise — for instance, in terms of a condition of title acceptable to one party but not the other — while perhaps remote is by no means non-existent. More apparent is the possibility that as between buyer and developer-seller there may ripen some disagreement respecting the physical condition of the premises. Without presuming to suggest an exhaustive list of potential areas of conflict, we draw attention to these as the kinds of matters of which consenting purchasers-mortgagors should be made aware before they consent to the attorney representing another party to the transaction.

Here the consent forms executed by purchasers at the eleventh hour amounted to little more than a perfunctory effort formally to comply with *Kamp's* admonition. After the respondent was retained, he had an "immediate" duty to explain to the client the nature of his relationship with the seller and inform the client of the significance of any consent that the client may have given to dual representation. In re Kamp, supra, 40 N.J. at 596, 194 A.2d 236; see In re Lanza, 65 N.J. 347, 350-51, 322 A.2d 445 (1974).

The problems that can arise from the failure to heed that instructive warning are graphically demonstrated in the matter before us. The record reveals that a purchaser objected to signing one of the consent forms after the conflict of interest situation had been explained to him (because he believed it might place him in the position of approving a conflict which was "illegal"), but ultimately he executed the form as the result of persuasion from his wife and a desire to avoid the serious disruption of his moving plans resulting from any adjourned or cancelled closing. Although we agree with the Committee's conclusion that the consent form was signed voluntarily in the literal sense that neither respondent nor the seller exerted any over pressure on the client, nevertheless we are left with the impression, as was the Committee, that execution of the form was due more to the exigencies of the situation than to an unfettered will. And this need not and should not have been. The circumstances surrounding the execution of the consent form in this instance and in every other instance where the forms were executed in like fashion should not have been permitted to arise. The record before us reveals that respondent's office dealt with the purchasers "for several weeks before . . . the closing." Somewhere in that interval the time should have been taken and the opportunity created to explain to the purchasers the potential conflicts — the "pitfalls" — so as to allow for execution of the consent forms after due deliberation.

While the practicalities of this type of purchase may generate joint representation of low or middle income purchasers-mortgagors and their sellers and mortgagees by a single attorney, those practicalities in no sense justify any relaxation of the requirement of full, complete and timely explanation of the pitfalls and implications of such representation and the potential for conflict. Indeed, given the increased likelihood that this class of clients may be without the resources to obtain separate representation, the need for meticulous observance of the requirement of full disclosure and informed consent is underscored.

IV

While tenable arguments have been made in favor of a complete bar to any dual representation of buyer and seller in a real estate transaction, see e.g.,

In re Lanza, supra, 65 N.J. at 353, 322 A.2d 445 (Pashman, J., concurring); In re Rockoff, 66 N.J. 394, 397, 331 A.2d 609 (1975) (Pashman, J., concurring), on balance we decline to adopt an inflexible per se rule. Confining ourselves to the type of situation before us (assuredly there are others, entirely unrelated to financial pressures), the stark economic realities are such that were an unyielding requirement of individual representation to be declared, many prospective purchasers in marginal financial circumstances would be left without representation. That being so, the legal profession must be frank to recognize any element of economic compulsion attendant upon a client's consent to dual representation in a real estate purchase to be circumspect in avoiding any penalization or victimization of those who, by force of these economic facts of life, give such consent.

This opinion should serve as notice that henceforth where dual representation is sought to be justified on the basis of the parties' consents, this Court will not tolerate consents which are less than knowing, intelligent and voluntary. Consents must be obtained in such a way as to insure that the client has had adequate time — manifestly not provided in the matter under consideration — to reflect upon the choice, and must not be forced upon the client by the exigencies of the closing. This applies with equal force to the dual representation of mortgagor and mortgagee.

In view of respondent's impeccable record, including a history of significant public service and contributions to the legal profession, we conclude that appropriate discipline is exercised by the imposition of this public reprimand.

Pashman, J., concurring in the reprimand.*

For reprimand: Chief Justice Hughes, Justices Mountain, Sullivan, Pashman and Clifford and Judge Conford — 6.

Opposed: None.

PASHMAN, J., concurring and dissenting. While I applaud the Court's tightening of the rules governing multiple representation in real estate transactions by further narrowing its permissible circumstantial basis, I am afraid that its effort to provide an additional safeguard for consumers of legal services simply does not go far enough. The prophylactic rule announced herein will do little to enhance the likelihood that the quality of representation provided in such circumstances will duplicate that which would be provided by counsel with undivided loyalty. Similarly, the Court's admonition that attorneys must avoid "any penalization or victimization" of clients who, as a result of economic constraints, consent to dual representation will be far from effective to prevent the various abuses endemic in such situations.

On two previous occasions I have sought to enumerate the compelling reasons supporting adoption of a per se rule forbidding dual representation

---

* Only as to §II of the majority opinion.

in certain situations where an irreconcilable conflict of loyalty so inheres in the circumstances that adequate protection of the interests of each of the multiple clients is precluded. In re Lanza, 65 N.J. 347, 353, 322 A.2d 445 (1974) (Pashman, J., concurring); In re Rockoff, 66 N.J. 394, 397, 331 A.2d 609 (1975) (Pashman, J., concurring). I write now to reiterate my adherence to those principles and to note my continuing concern with the Court's present posture in this troublesome area of professional ethics. The result herein continues the Court's acceptance of dual representation in circumstances where, notwithstanding full disclosure and knowing consent by the derivative client,[1] the intrinsic degree of divided allegiance is so intolerable that the proscribed adverse effect on the exercise of the attorney's independent professional judgment on behalf of that client must ipso facto be conclusively presumed.[2] See D.R. 5-105(B). In so doing, the Court relies on the fiction that a lay client can effectively consent to dual representation and perpetuates the cruel myth that adequate representation can be provided in such cases by an attorney who supposedly can simultaneously protect the inevitably adverse interests of his two masters. The reality, of course, is that it is well-nigh impossible for the derivative client to be so well attuned to the numerous legal nuances of the transaction that his consent can be said to have been truly informed.[3] The propriety of according dispositive effect to consent so obtained is further undermined when it is frankly acknowledged that the consent is induced by the deriva-

---

1. The derivative client is the client whose representation by the attorney derives from his participation in a transaction with the party who is the primary client of the attorney. The derivative client is the client to whom disclosure is made and from whom consent to the dual representation is sought.
2. See New Jersey Supreme Court Advisory Committee on Professional Ethics, Opinion 212, 94 N.J.L.J. 553 (1971) (improper for attorney to continue to represent either party to real estate transaction after controversy has arisen between them).
3. The most frequent topics of controversy at closing are:

A) Difficulties with the quality of title deliverable by the seller.
B) Disputes over alleged structural defects.
C) Warranties.
D) Unfinished work.
E) Leaks.
F) Cellar problems.
G) Construction of roads and sidewalks in the development on schedule.
H) Drainage problems.
I) Problems as to utilities.
J) Defective masonry foundations.
K) Mortgage and tax escrows — amount and interest.
L) Escrows of a part of seller's money to assure compliance with above problems, including schedule for release of funds.
M) Appropriate remedies for compliance with any agreements concerning the above.

There are, of course, innumerable variations of such problems within the above general areas. These are in addition to the many subjects as to which intolerable conflicts of interest result if the attorney provides dual representation at the contract negotiation stage as well as at the closing of title.

tive client's reliance on a promise by the attorney which cannot be fulfilled — the promise of adequate representation of each of his two clients.

Surely the Court is not so naive as to the economic realities of such transactions as its utopian stance would indicate. Any conflicting interests which are potentially disruptive of the ultimate goal—the expeditious consummation of the sales transaction—must inevitably be resolved in favor of the primary client and for that same reason will probably not even be brought to the attention of the derivative client. This problem is even more aggravated in circumstances such as those of the instant case where the primary client of the attorney is a developer with whom the attorney has a potentially long-term and profitable relationship. Consequently, the attorney has a substantial economic stake in maintaining the continued goodwill of this primary client. As our Advisory Committee on Professional Ethics has observed, in such situations

> . . . the attorney, either consciously or unconsciously, will be influenced by a desire to maintain his economically profitable relationship with the seller. The developer has more homes to sell, hence more profitable professional employment for the attorney. The desire to maintain his relationship will make it difficult in any given case for the attorney to devote himself to the interests of a buyer with the same degree of vigor and undivided loyalty which would be the case were such desire not present. This motivation may very probably cause the attorney's representation of the buyer to be less searching, less demanding and in general less effective than would be the case were the attorney not reluctant to risk the loss of what for him has become a profitable monopoly.
>
> A second point, interrelated with the first, stems from the fact that the attorney acquires a very extensive intimate knowledge of the developer and of the tract in question as the result of the work he carries out for the owner. If the developer will not be able or willing to construct roads as rapidly as is represented, if a subcontractor is not doing his work well, if drainage problems exist and have not been solved, if there is a question as to when and how all utilities will be introduced, if, as an example only, the masonry foundations of various homes have proven defective, the attorney in each case will perforce possess this knowledge. These are only a few of the possibilities. Anyone who has had direct contact with projects of this sort will be able to add other examples from his own experience. Undertaking a dual representation, the attorney will find himself in an impossibly equivocal position. As representing the seller, he must use all reasonable and proper means to see that the proposed sale of his client's property is consummated; as representing the buyer, he has an obligation to reveal any information which would be of genuine interest or help to the buyer in determining whether to make the purchase and in protecting his rights after the contract has been signed. It is apparent that this twofold obligation cannot be met in circumstances where the attorney's knowledge embraces any fact, known to him as the result of his relationship with the seller, which, if known to the buyer, might influence him to reject the purchase or to insist upon terms or conditions less favorable to the seller.

As mentioned above, there is a very definite interrelationship between these two factors the existence of which we have sought to emphasize. In general they will not be present in the ordinary isolated transaction where an attorney represents both buyer and seller. On the other hand they would seem to be endemic in the kind of situation we are considering. Accordingly, it seems clear that unless in any given case these factors for some reason fail to exist or unless their influence can be minimized to the point of complete insignificance, they constitute an *insurmountable impediment* to the kind of dual representation here being considered. [New Jersey Supreme Court Advisory Committee on Professional Ethics, Opinion 51, 87 N.J.L.J. 705 (1964); (emphasis added).]

Even assuming that dual representation in an "ordinary isolated" real estate transaction should not be per se impermissible, the practice is wholly unsupportable where the attorney involved is the representative of a developer. The attorney's economic disincentive to be vigilant in safeguarding the buyer's interests in such a case is too strong, and a per se prohibition is absolutely imperative. Dual representation in these circumstances forces the derivative client to play with a stacked deck. I cannot countenance the Court's continued tolerance of such farcical and often duplicitous behavior by some members of the legal profession. The injustice of this is heightened by the fact that it occurs in what for most consumers is the transaction of greatest personal and financial moment in their lifetime in which their need for adequate representation is acute.

I am similarly distressed by this Court's continuing condonation of the concept of "limited" dual representation, first sanctioned in In re Kamp, 40 N.J. 588, 595-596, 194 A.2d 236 (1963). By securing the derivative client's consent to such a limitation on his duty, the attorney, in addition to his plenary representation of the primary client, "represents" the derivative client also as to some matters involved in the closing of title but not as to others. In practical terms what this arrangement means is that at the settlement table, moments after having purportedly acted on behalf of the derivative client's interest, the attorney will turn on his "former" client and act solely as the advocate for the primary client as to the matters reserved from dual representation. One can readily imagine the bewilderment of the derivative client as he sees the attorney transformed from ally to enemy in a matter of seconds. He didn't bargain for that result when he gave his "consent" to the limits of the dual representation he would receive. Agreeing to allow an attorney not to press certain matters on your behalf is not equatable with agreeing to have him press those very matters against you. This incongruous situation would be ludicrous were it not so tragic. Yet the Court sees fit to perpetuate such an arrangement, which in reality is nothing less than a travesty of the attorney-client relationship and mocks the very concept of the professionalism of lawyers. The impropriety of permitting an attorney to act as both the advocate and adversary of a client in a single transaction is too obvious even for statement.

The Court fails to make its position more palatable by noting that meaningful independent representation for the purchasers in the instant transactions would have been unlikely in any event because of the "rigidities" occasioned by the fact that the housing program involved was under "federal auspices." I am not persuaded that inadequate representation should be acceptable because on some occasions adequate representation might not bear any significant fruit.

Moreover, the Court's assumption that adoption of a per se prohibition of dual representation in a real estate transaction would somehow prevent persons of modest means from being represented at all is unwarranted. The more likely result of a per se rule will be to alert such persons to the gravity of the contemplated transaction and consequently impel them to secure their own counsel. In this regard it is not inappropriate for us to notice the greater access by consumers to information concerning the cost of legal services as a result of fee advertising in this post-*Bates*[4] era. Considering the more than adequate number of attorneys in this state, it is very likely that representation in such relatively uncomplicated matters as residential real estate settlements at moderate fees will be readily available. Furthermore, the cost of obtaining independent counsel is normally only an incremental addition to the cost of the entire transaction and is a cost that most purchasers would willingly bear if they were aware of its potentially significant benefit. The assumption that such persons will totally forego legal representation rather than spending a relatively insignificant additional amount for an attorney is dubious at best. Naturally, many purchasers will leap at the opportunity to avoid a purportedly unnecessary extra expense when they are misled into believing that the seller's attorney can and will give them equally effective representation for free or at a lesser cost than if they obtained their own representation.[5] However, it does not necessarily follow that prohibition of dual representation will deprive most purchasers of the services of an attorney.

Were these purchasers not induced to believe that the quality of the derivative representation they would receive from the seller's attorney is the equivalent of any representation they could receive from their own counsel, it is reasonable to assume that they would have obtained independent representation. In short, the Court allows dual representation to be a self-justifying practice by accepting the theory that its sine qua non role in the provision of housing to persons of limited means is proven by the fact

---

4. Bates v. Arizona State Bar Association, 433 U.S. 350, 97 S. Ct. 2691, 53 L. Ed. 2d 810 (1977).

5. In this regard it is noteworthy that in the instant case the developer's standardized agreement of sale contained the following specially inserted provision:

> If purchaser uses seller's attorney, the seller will pay the legal fee for title examination, recording of deed and mortgage, survey, mortgage title insurance, appraisal and inspection fees.

The substantial saving for the purchasers resulting from their utilization of the seller's attorney makes this offer quite persuasive, and vitiates the voluntariness of its acceptance. The Court fails to comment on the ethical implications of this clause although a functionally indistinct practice was condemned in In re Kamp, 40 N.J. 588, 598, 194 A.2d 236 (1963).

that so many persons consent to it. I am unable to concur in that assessment. The incidence of exploitation of unsophisticated purchasers as a result of the conflicting loyalties of an attorney with "two clients" counsels against our making such tenuous assumptions.

It is virtually impossible for an attorney to contend for that which duty to another client requires him to oppose. This impossible fact pattern prevents the fulfillment of that undivided loyalty owed by a lawyer to his client. We must decisionally or by Canons of Ethics discourage an attorney from taking any chances where such a highly charged potential for conflict exists. Misconduct may be found despite disclosure and consent.

Absent any explicit demarcation of the line beyond which attorneys tread at their peril in this murky area of ethical behavior, I believe it is inappropriate for the Court to broaden the concept of the type of consent required to avoid a finding of impropriety and then to apply it in an ex post facto manner to the conduct of the particular respondent before us. Is it fair to premise a finding of misconduct on a practice whose ethically violative nature has only this day been explicitly defined? I think not, and for that reason dissent from the disciplinary action taken against Mr. Dolan for conduct only technically improper under the present state of the law and which would in all likelihood not have occurred if this Court had provided attorneys with the needed guidance in the first place. By starkly dramatizing the plethora of pitfalls which await attorneys who are foolhardy enough to chance a misstep in this precipitous area of professional ethics, this case underscores the critical need for a per se prohibition of dual representation which will deter attorneys at the threshold of that hazardous journey.

While I concur in the reprimand of the respondent for the conduct described in Section II of the Court's opinion, I hasten to add that my comments herein on the issue of multiple representation are not addressed to Mr. Dolan's particular conduct. It is an unfortunate fact of life that respondent is not alone in treading at the razor's edge of ethical behavior. However, as he was in technical compliance with the disciplinary rules as presently formulated, there is no valid basis for imposing any sanction for the multiple representation disclosed in this record.

NOTES

1. The ABA Model Rules of Professional Conduct have several rules on conflict of interest, the most widely applicable of which is Rule 1.7:

RULE 1.7 Conflict of Interest: General Rule
   (a) A lawyer shall not represent a client if the representation of that client will be directly adverse to another client, unless:
   (1) the lawyer reasonably believes the representation will not adversely affect the relationship with the other client; and

(2) each client consents after consultation.

(b) A lawyer shall not represent a client if the representation of that client may be materially limited by the lawyer's responsibilities to another client or to a third person, or by the lawyer's own interests, unless:
- (1) the lawyer reasonably believes the representation will not be adversely affected; and
- (2) the client consents after consultation. When representation of multiple clients in a single matter is undertaken, the consultation shall include explanation of the implications of the common representation and the advantages and risks involved.

COMMENT

Loyalty to a Client

[1] Loyalty is an essential element in the lawyer's relationship to a client. An impermissible conflict of interest may exist before representation is undertaken, in which event the representation should be declined. If such a conflict arises after representation has been undertaken, the lawyer should withdraw from the representation. See Rule 1.16. Where more than one client is involved and the lawyer withdraws because a conflict arises after representation, whether the lawyer may continue to represent any of the clients is determined by Rule 1.9. See also Rule 2.2(c). . . .

2. How should this matter be decided? A lawyer represents a syndicate of several businessmen in the purchase and clearing of title to a large apartment building that the syndicate plans to convert to condominiums after the closing and after title defects are cleared, selling off apartments to individual condominium owners. The lawyer's fee is to be a share in the syndicate. After his work is completed and he acquires his interest in the syndicate, disciplinary proceedings are brought against the lawyer for unprofessional conduct.

3. Lawyers are subject to extensive conflict of interest restraints; real estate brokers are not. Why this disparity, and can and should it be changed by substantially increasing conflict of interest restraints on real estate brokers? Consider again the Currier and Stambler and Stein excerpts appearing at the beginning of this chapter.

CHAPTER TWO

Basic Financing Considerations of the Real Estate Transaction

At the heart of most real estate transactions lies the fact that a buyer seeks financing on terms as favorable as prevailing conditions and the buyer's own circumstances permit. Tax, business and investment-yield factors generally make it unwise to acquire the property "free and clear"—a choice that most buyers do not even have. From the young marrieds who are buying their first home to the hard-bitten professionals who are enlarging their empire, the questions (though hardly the answers) are the same: What are the sources of real estate loans? On what basis are loans available? If financing alternatives exist, how does one choose between them? In the pages that follow, we will examine in turn the mortgage market, the credit "quartet," and some of the more common methods of financing a real estate transaction.

A. THE MORTGAGE MARKET

Generally, the term "mortgage market" refers to those funds available to finance the acquisition, construction, or improvement of an interest in real property.[1] Until quite recently, the market suffered from recurring cycles in the availability of funds. At times the supply was so ample (relative to demand) that lenders pursued tract developers and other active borrowers with a lover's ardor and even paid finder's fees, as was done regularly in

---

1. Mortgage proceeds sometimes are applied to uses unrelated to property; tuition payments are a common example. Mortgages may also be written as collateral security for obligations other than in money, for the guaranty of the debts of another person, or for obtaining proceeds for use on property other than the mortgaged property.

the late 1940s. At other times the supply became so exhausted that even prime customers found it difficult and expensive to finance their ventures.

Today, extreme polar conditions of "easy money" and "tight money" no longer characterize the mortgage market. This has resulted from a vast influx of funds derived chiefly from an expanding national (and even international) secondary market in mortgage-backed securities. For example, between 1980 and 1983, the outstanding mortgage debt on one- to four-family homes rose from 987 to 1133 billion dollars. Virtually this entire growth stemmed from the increase in mortgage-backed securities. During the same interval, the portfolio of savings and loan associations, the chief source of home-mortgage financing, actually declined.[2]

The mortgage market, like the stock market, is not one market but many. The market for one-family homes differs from that for high-rise apartments, and separate markets exist for each major form of real estate improvement: one- to four-family residence; multiple dwelling; commercial (stores and office buildings); industrial. There are also separate markets for new structures and old; for well-maintained structures and run-down; for luxury housing and low-rent; for urban real estate and rural; for improved real estate and raw land; for segregated neighborhoods and interracial; for construction loans and "permanent" financing; for private ownership and public, and so on. Some of these markets cast a weak shadow, but in time one learns how and where to find them.

1. *Primary and Secondary Markets*

The market is also organized into primary and secondary markets. The term "secondary" causes some confusion, since it is used in two dissimilar ways. In one of its senses, secondary market refers to activity in junior liens (viz., the second mortgage), as distinguished (very!) from the market in first mortgages. But secondary also refers to a sequence of events whereby a mortgage (be it senior or junior) changes ownership, often by prearrangement even before the mortgage is placed; an originating or primary lender sells (assigns) the mortgage to a secondary lender. The presence of a "take-out" or secondary source of mortgage money is a major spur to new construction, brings money from capital surplus into capital shortage areas, and, generally, helps to stabilize market conditions.

2. *Conventional and Insured or Guaranteed Mortgages*

Congress designed the FHA-insured mortgage in 1934.[3] Despite popular belief to the contrary, the mortgagor does not borrow directly from the

---

2. 1984 Statistical Abstract of the U.S. 517.
3. 12 U.S.C. §§1701 et seq., 48 Stat. 1246. The FHA (Federal Housing Administration) is a constituent agency within the Department of Housing and Urban Development.

The Mortgage Market

Federal Housing Authority. Instead, he obtains his financing from an "approved" mortgagee, who agrees to make the loan subject to FHA's commitment to *insure* the lender against any losses caused by mortgage default. An insurance premium, averaging one-half of one percent of the principal balance, is paid by the borrower; aggregate premium collections provide the reserve from which FHA reimburses lenders for their losses.

The Veterans' Administration program, a homecoming present to GI's returning from World War II (and since extended to include nearly all latter-day veterans), was part of the Servicemen's Readjustment Act of 1944, popularly styled the GI Bill of Rights.[4] The VA loan resembled the FHA mortgage in requiring that the loan originate (except in areas where funds are unavailable)[5] with a private lender. It differs from the FHA mortgage by eliminating the premium for insurance. Instead, Congress has agreed to underwrite losses — up to a specified amount for each mortgage, but large enough to give the lender a comfortable margin for safety. With this assurance, the lender is said to have a *guaranteed* mortgage.

In the postwar years, FHA-insured and VA-guaranteed mortgages have been important sources of mortgage credit for single-family dwellings, and with FHA's growing diversity, for housing projects and other, more specialized, residential programs.

The *conventional* mortgage does not enjoy government backing. However, with the advent of several private mortgage insurers, even the conventional mortgage is often insured.

3. Mortgage Lenders

The resources, policies, and restraints of mortgage lenders largely determine what money will be available at any given moment for any given purpose. For descriptive ends, we can catalogue mortgage lenders into several major groupings, as shown in Table 2-1.

Of the institutions listed, those we have starred supply the bulk of mortgage funds for private investment. They are further described in the following pages.

a. Mutual Savings Banks

A mutual savings bank (savings bank) is owned by its depositors, whose earnings return to them as savings account interest or dividends. Deposi-

---

4. 58 Stat. 291. This section of the 1944 law was repealed in 1958, 72 Stat. 1273, and was replaced by provisions that now appear at 38 U.S.C.A. §§1801 et seq. (1984 Supp.).

5. The Administrator of Veterans Affairs is empowered to designate rural areas and small cities and towns as "housing credit shortage" areas when he finds that VA guaranteed loans are not generally available to veterans. If a veteran living in a designated area can show that he is unable to obtain a loan from a private lender at an interest rate not exceeding that for VA mortgages, he may obtain a direct loan from the Veterans Administration. 38 U.S.C.A. §1811 (1984 Supp.). It has not been an overworked provision.

TABLE 2-1

Financial Institutions	*Other Institutions*	*Individuals*	*Federal Agencies*
*Mutual savings banks	*Mortgage companies		*Government National Mortgage Assn. (Ginnie Mae)
*Savings and loan associations	*Federal National Mortgage Assn. (Fannie Mae)		*Federal Home Loan Mortgage Corp. (Freddie Mac)
*Commercial banks	Private non-insured pension funds		Farmers Home Administration
*Life insurance companies	State and local government retirement funds		
Real Estate Investment Trusts (REIT)	Fraternal benefit life societies		
	State-chartered credit unions		
	State and local housing finance agencies		

tors usually cannot vote, however; technically they are more like creditors of their institution. Management tends to vest in self-perpetuating boards of trustees, regulated by the state that issues the bank's charter.

Geographically concentrated in the capital surplus areas of the Northeast,[6] the 475 or so banks occur in fewer than 20 states; more than half are

---

6. Several historical factors explain the geographical concentration of mutual savings banks. These are enumerated in a 1952 report by the Commission on Money and Credit, Mutual Savings Banking, at 30-33:

"a. Most saving banks were formed before 1875. As the westward population movement intensified, the primary banking needs were for credit-creating facilities, which commercial banks were best able to meet. Such banks, especially those holding state charters, often provided savings facilities also.

"b. By the late nineteenth century, organizing a bank in stock form rather than as a mutual bank appealed to the promotional mentality of many bank organizers.

"c. In later years the demand for liberal mortgage credit terms speeded up the formation and growth of savings and loan associations, which attracted savers by their somewhat higher dividend rates (the result of more speculative portfolio practices and a heavier concentration of assets in higher-yield mortgages). The associations also appealed to organizers because of easier initial funding requirements and fewer restrictions on insider (trustee, director) profit-making."

in New York or Massachusetts. They have greatly expanded their lending activity to become heavy purchasers of FHA and VA loans originating in the burgeoning areas of the South and West. Two factors have supported this movement: the exemption of such loans from state laws barring mortgage investments on faraway real estate and the emergence of mortgage bankers to serve as out-of-town loan correspondents.

Net deposit gains provide the major source of new investment funds. Real estate loans continue as the savings banks' chief investment outlet, presently exceeding 60 percent of their overall portfolio. The approximate breakdown of loans by property groups is: one- to four-family dwellings, 70 percent; apartments, 15 percent; nonresidential, 15 percent.

b. Savings and Loan Associations (Building and Loan Associations)

The savings and loan association is by far the largest supplier of funds for residential mortgages. In a recent year, the nation's more than 5000 associations held 40 percent of the total mortgage debt on one- to four-family homes and 25 percent of the mortgages on multi-family units. The bulk of these mortgages are conventional; S & Ls have preferred to avoid the processing routine and the regulated interest ceilings of FHA and VA loans. And with the advent of FHLMC in 1970 (page 123 infra), the associations have their own secondary market operation that does not depend upon government mortgage guarantees.

Their concentration in residential financing has its roots in S & L history. The associations began as savings institutions that would lend only to their members and only to finance home purchases. Even today vestiges of that practice still survive; quite often, at the time he receives his loan, the borrower must accept nominal membership in the mortgagee association.

Membership associations are called *mutual*. Their depositors share in gross income and elect the governing board. *Stock* associations are privately owned and operate much like business corporations. These tend to be found among the larger state-chartered firms. All federally chartered S & Ls, as well as many of the state-chartered ones, are mutual associations.

A federal charter automatically involves membership in the Federal Home Loan Bank System. This carries with it regulation of loan policies, and a ceiling of the interest rate on deposits. But membership also confers the limited but valuable privilege of borrowing funds with which to make new mortgage investments or to meet short-term runs by depositors. A federal charter also requires that deposits be insured with the Federal Savings and Loan Insurance Corporation (FSLIC). State-chartered associations may also obtain FSLIC insurance; to do so, they submit to membership in and regulation by the FSLIC and the Federal Home Loan Bank System.

c. Commercial Banks

The 14,800 commercial banks, which may be either state or nationally chartered, obtain their funds from four sources: (a) demand deposits, (b) time deposits, (c) borrowing (from the capital market or the Federal Reserve banks), and (d) bank capital accounts.[7] In 1975, these resources totalled nearly one trillion dollars. One decade later, they had doubled.

Much of this growth has come in time deposits, which now comprise the principal source of commercial bank funds. To accommodate these deposits, commercial banks have materially stepped up their mortgage loan activity. Real estate loans still occupy a modest percentage (21.0) of the investment portfolio, but the dollar volume, $307.3 billion by 1983, is impressive.

Commercial banks heavily invest in nonresidential mortgages; these comprise one-third of the mortgage volume. But commercial banks are also the second largest acquirer of mortgages on one- to four-family homes; these loans are mostly conventional.

Because their major role has been to provide short-term credit, commercial banks have had to endure more rigorous controls on their long-term mortgage activity than do savings banks. On a conventional home mortgage loan, for example, commercial banks could not offer the loan-to-value ratio or the mortgage duration that would ordinarily be available from the savings bank next door. However, federal deregulation of the banking industry, inaugurated by the Depository Institutions Deregulation and Monetary Control Act of 1980[8] and furthered by the Garn-St. Germain Depository Institutions Act of 1982[9] has removed these constraints from federally chartered commercial banks. In turn, state legislatures seeking parity for state-chartered institutions have given them expanded powers.[10] This has narrowed the differences in mortgage terms between those available from commercial and savings banks.

Commercial banks are the major source of construction loan financing and, in the home mortgage field, besides placing mortgages for their own account, serve two important functions: they often originate and later service loans that are resold to secondary lenders; they supply interim credit to mortgage companies who, in their turn, originate and service loans. From this latter activity has grown a practice known as "warehousing," which works as follows: The mortgage company is given a revolving line of credit; as individual loans are closed and recorded, the mortgage

---

7. In addition, commercial banks — qua pension fund trustees — control huge investment portfolios.

8. Pub. L. 96-221, 94 Stat. 132, 142-145.

9. Pub. L. 97-320, 96 Stat. 1469.

10. For example, prior to 1983, New York State limited its state-chartered commercial banks to 80 percent conventional loans on newly built one-family houses, while letting savings banks make 95 percent mortgages. N.Y. Banking Law §§103, 235(6) (McKinney Supp. 1977). In February 1983, Governor Cuomo signed legislation that eliminated loan-to-value ratios and amortization requirements for mortgages issued by state-chartered lenders.

company pledges them as collateral with the commercial bank, which holds them for eventual reassignment to the permanent lender. The role of the commercial bank in "storing" the mortgages for a few weeks or months is like that of a warehouser.

d. Life Insurance Companies

Life insurance companies gain their funds from the premium and investment income that remains after operating expenses, policy reserves, and policy claims are provided for. At $588 billion by year-end 1982, these funds enjoy an annual growth rate of 10.5 percent.

Life insurance companies engage in a wide variety of lending activity. Mortgage loans, comprising 24 percent of the total portfolio, are second only to corporate securities as an investment outlet. But this percentage has slipped badly in the past decade after a period of aggressive competition for mortgage placements that followed the creation of an extensive network of loan correspondents (mortgage companies and local commercial banks). From 1950 to 1983 the mortgage inventory has grown from $16 billion to $142.0 billion.

More so than any of the other major lenders, life insurance companies have concentrated on multi-family residential (which they sometimes own and manage as well as finance) and nonresidential properties. Only 12 percent (and still dropping) of their mortgage portfolio consists of loans on one- to four-family houses. This emphasis is easily understood: the insurance giants, some with assets in the billions, are easily able to commit the multi-millions needed to finance a large apartment project or a 40-story office building. Moreover, one $20 million loan is far more efficient for such large companies than four hundred $50,000 loans, particularly in view of the heavy reliance on mortgage correspondents. Investment on this scale holds a special interest for law students. As we shall see, much of the innovation that gives real estate financing a complexity undreamed of one generation ago has appeared in transactions involving insurance company loans. Some of the finest real estate lawyers in the country guide these loan operations.

All life insurance companies are state-chartered, regulated by their home states and wherever they operate. Companies are generally able to purchase real estate as well as to invest in mortgages, which allows such financing techniques as joint ventures and sale-and-leasebacks.

e. Mortgage Companies (Mortgage Bankers)

Before World War II, mortgage companies were virtually unknown. They are now a key intermediary, especially in the financing of home sales and newly built residential properties. Acting as a middleman, the mortgage company originates loans to local builders or home buyers, and then sells the loans to out-of-town banks and insurance companies, or to secondary market agencies such as the Federal National Mortgage Association, following on page 122.

Typically, the mortgage company becomes the servicing agent after the loans are sold. This involves collecting the mortgage payments and remitting them to the mortgage holder and seeing that the property is adequately insured and that real estate taxes are paid. The company receives a servicing fee, as well as a fee for originating the mortgage. Many companies further profit through their wholly-owned insurance and brokerage affiliates, which deal with the property owners the parent has helped to finance.

Mortgage companies are subject to state corporate laws and regulations. Those dealing in FHA loans must receive FHA approval and submit to a periodic examination and audit as to their capitalization and servicing ability. In general, however, mortgage companies suffer little regulation, although some states have begun to adopt licensing laws.

f. Real Estate Investment Trusts (REITs)

Mid-nineteenth century Massachusetts law would not let corporations hold real property for investment purposes. Undaunted, Bay State lawyers invented the real estate trust (soon to be called the "Massachusetts" or "business" trust) in which investors could pool their funds and gain such corporate advantages as limited shareholder liability, enterprise continuity, and free transferability of interests. Business trusts later became popular in other states where they were generally used for other than real estate investment. Most state courts have upheld the validity of business trusts but in many instances, statutes now limit somewhat the formation and operation of such trusts.

A substantial inducement to the formation of business trusts arose with their exemption from federal corporate income taxation by decisions such as Crocker v. Malley, 249 U.S. 223 (1919). This favored tax status was later removed from realty trusts and investment companies by the decision in Morrissey v. Commissioner, 296 U.S. 344 (1935), which extended the corporation tax to any business entity with sufficient corporate attributes to fall within the definition of an "association" under the Revenue Acts of 1924 and 1926.

Investment companies dealing in securities immediately sought legislative relief from the *Morrissey* decision, and succeeded in regaining most of their former tax advantages under the Revenue Act of 1936 §48(e) (49 Stat. 1669). The regulation of such investment companies was supplemented by the Investment Company Act of 1940 (54 Stat. 789), and the

Internal Revenue Code of 1939 (now §§851-855 of the Internal Revenue Code of 1954). Real estate trusts were not accorded similar grace, however, until Congress in 1960 enacted Pub. L. No. 86-779, 86th Cong., 2d Sess.

In approving Subchapter M of the Internal Revenue Code of 1954 §§856 to 858, Congress hoped to stimulate real estate investment through the spreading of risk among many small investors who could secure the benefit of expert management and, thus, finance projects collectively that singly they could not undertake. By qualifying as a real estate investment trust (REIT), investor pools could enjoy the attraction of limited liability without suffering the penalty of a corporate layer of taxation. Congress distinguished sharply, however, between active and passive real estate investment. In order to qualify for the tax avoidance benefit, the REIT had to satisfy stringent limitations as to its organization (unincorporated trust), management (by trustees), ownership (100 or more shareholders), assets (principally real estate and mortgages), and income. The income requirement, which Congress designed to meet the test of "passive" investment, had three separate elements. Their present form is described below:

The 95 percent test: At least 95 percent of the gross income of the trust must be derived from what can be described generally as investment sources. This test is similar to one provided for regulated investment companies, and for REITs it includes chiefly (1) dividends; (2) interest; (3) rents from real property; (4) gain from the sale or other disposition of stock, securities, and real property; and (5) abatements and refunds of taxes on real property.

The 75 percent test: This test requires that at least 75 percent of the gross income of the trust be derived from what might be termed investments in real property. This includes chiefly (1) rents from real property; (2) interest on obligations secured by mortgages on real property or on interests in real property; (3) gain from the sale or other disposition of real property; (4) dividends or other distributions on, and gain from, the sale or other disposition of transferable shares in other real estate investment trusts that meet the requirements of subchapter M; and (5) abatements and refunds of taxes on real property.

The 30 percent test: Like the 95 percent test, the 30 percent income test is patterned after a provision from the requirements for regulated investment companies. The purpose of this limitation is to discourage speculation and active trading operations by a REIT. The test requires that less than 30 percent of the gross income of the trust be derived from the sale or other disposition of stock or securities held for less than six months and real property held for less than four years (unless it is compulsorily or involuntarily converted within the meaning of §1033). In all the income tests, "gross income" only includes net gains, but the regulations magnify the effect of the 30 percent test by providing that losses are not netted against gains to determine the total gain from the disposition of property that has been held for an insufficient period.

To further the expressed congressional intent that REIT income be derived primarily from passive investments rather than from active business operations, the code contains a detailed definition of the term "rents from real property." This definition excludes three different sources of income that would otherwise be regarded as rental income: payments under a percentage lease based upon income or profits (but not upon receipts or sales); income from a tenant in which the REIT has a substantial ownership interest; and rents from property where the REIT either furnishes services to tenants or manages the property other than through an "independent contractor" from whom the trust does not derive or receive any income.

Having met the qualifications above, the REIT must then distribute at least 90 percent of its taxable income for the taxable year to its beneficiaries (shareholders) to avoid corporate income tax on its entire earnings. Once a 90 percent distribution has been made, the dividends paid are deductible from taxable income, and the trust is subject to corporate taxes only upon that portion of its earnings that has been retained. All distributions except those properly designated as capital gains dividends are treated by the shareholders as ordinary dividend income, except that no dividend-received deduction is allowed.

Originally, REITs were mostly "equity trusts"; that is, they owned income-producing properties. But by the early 1970s, so-called mortgage trusts dominated the REIT industry. Some mortgage trusts specialized in permanent mortgages; but most mortgage trusts became heavily active in short-term development and construction loans with maturities ranging from one to three years. All mortgage trusts depended for their earnings on the spread between the interest rates they received and the cost of the money they raised through equity offerings and by borrowing.

Between 1968 and 1973, REIT investments soared from $1.2 billion to $21.1 billion. Much of this expanded portfolio consisted of mortgage holdings, and all but $5.0 billion of the funds for acquiring these mortgages came from REIT borrowings. Typically, the REIT would borrow at or near "prime" and lend to the developer at prime plus three or four.

1974 was a year of disaster for the construction industry. Huge cost overruns, the result of rapid cost inflation in construction materials and, for that era, an unparalleled rise in prime interest rates (at one time as high as 12 percent); the disappearance of permanent financing; and—in many areas—a glut of newly built housing units prevented many developers from finishing their projects, marketing the units, and repaying the construction lender. REITs, in turn, found themselves squeezed by their own creditors, since the construction loans not only remained outstanding but also became non-interest-earning.

In January, 1975, Fidelity Mortgage Investors, a middle-sized REIT filed under Chapter XI of the Bankruptcy Act, and soon afterwards, other REITs followed. Among the twenty biggest 1974 losers on the New York Stock Exchange 18 were REITs including the five largest trusts of all — and 1974 was a dismal year in stocks generally. Only the willingness of the REITs' creditor banks to enter into yearly revolving-loan agreements, under which each creditor bank (sometimes 50 to 100 per REIT) would promise to forbear while the REIT tried to get straightened out, prevented total collapse of the REIT construction lenders. For a lively account of the REIT demise, see Robertson, How the Bankers Got Trapped in the REIT Disaster, Fortune 113 (March 1975).

Considerably shrunken, REITs remain on the investment scene. Their investments have shifted toward ownership of income-producing property, with 60 percent of their assets in the form of equity interests. REITs qua construction lenders now comprise less than 10 percent of the industry, and one doubts that they will ever again achieve dominance.

4. *Federally Chartered Secondary Market Lenders*

How does the secondary market work? We have already seen one aspect of the secondary market, the use of mortgage companies to originate loans that are then sold to banks and insurance companies who, in this context, are acting as secondary or "take out" lenders. But in the last generation, an enormous "public" secondary market has evolved, first to supplement and, then, to expand greatly the secondary role of private institutions. The initial catalysts for public intervention were the recurring cycles of tight money when the usual housing finance sources could not satisfy the demand for new loans. To stabilize the flow of mortgage credit, Congress formed three government-chartered secondary market corporations: the Federal National Mortgage Association (FNMA), the Federal Home Loan Mortgage Corporation (FHLMC), and the Government National Mortgage Association (GNMA).

At the core of this "tight money" operation is the agencies' readiness to buy residential mortgages from originating lenders — at prices and upon terms that are set in advance. Armed with a "take out" commitment, a lender can then serve its customers who need mortgage financing even though the lender is "all loaned up." The lender places the mortgage and then gets its money back at once by selling the mortgage at the commitment price to the secondary market corporation.[11]

---

11. Since some months usually elapse between the receipt of the take out commitment and the making of the mortgage loan, the originating lender may decide — if its funds situation has improved — to keep the mortgage itself. Thus, the take out commitment is really an option to sell (in stock market terms, a put), for which the lender pays a fee. The lender will try to pass on this charge, as well as any losses it will incur should it exercise the put and resell the mortgage, by collecting an origination fee from the borrower.

As we shall see, these intermediaries have access to the nation's credit markets, including investors who typically do not place their funds in residential mortgages. By drawing "outside" money into home financing, the secondary market corporations have much changed the pattern of housing credit. In the process, they have become a vital and increasingly active link in the mortgage network.

The secondary market also works contracyclically during the rare periods of easy credit. Originating lenders then tend to be glutted with new deposits that outstrip the demand for new mortgage financing. Since lenders must find investment outlets if they are to pay deposit interest, the secondary market corporations stand ready to *sell* seasoned mortgages from their own portfolios. For example, in 1982, FHLMC's net sales neared $500 million. But we have seen few easy credit intervals in the past several decades and in most years, the secondary market corporations have bought far more heavily than they have sold. (Table 2-2 infra, at 125.)

a. Federal National Mortgage Association (Fannie Mae)

Title III of the National Housing Act of 1934 authorized the Federal Housing Administrator to help create national mortgage associations (federally chartered but privately owned) that would buy and sell the fledgling FHA-insured mortgage in direct dealings with originating lenders. Congress hoped that a secondary market would give liquidity to government-backed mortgages and heighten lender confidence in this new mortgage currency. The FHA mortgage proved quite unpopular at first, and when a private secondary market failed to emerge, Congress in 1935 — as a "temporary" step — formed the RFC Mortgage Company. Between 1935 and 1948, this federal agency bought nearly 90,000 FHA-insured and VA-guaranteed mortgages.

In 1938, another federal secondary market began when the RFC, at President Roosevelt's request, launched the National Mortgage Association of Washington, which quickly (but not formally until 1954) became known as the FNMA. In that latter year, FNMA gained a mixed-ownership format, owned partly by the federal government and partly by private shareholders. It became a consistently profitable venture, averaging a 6.5 percent yearly return on its capital.[12]

Congress finally achieved its original concept of a privately owned and managed FNMA with passage of Title VIII of the Housing and Urban

---

12. This was not left to chance. Congress wrote into the statute that the FNMA Secondary Market Operations be "fully self-supporting." 12 U.S.C.A. §1719 (1980). The major sources of profit are the differentials (1) between the interest received by FNMA on its mortgage portfolio and the interest paid on its debentures and other borrowings and (2) between the prices received for mortgages sold and paid for mortgages purchased.

Development Act of 1968. As a private concern, FNMA is owned and run by its stockholders (the New York Exchange lists its stock); a 15-member board of directors (of whom five are named by the President of the United States) fixes policy. However, the Secretary of HUD retains general regulatory powers over FNMA; for example, the Secretary can require that a reasonable portion of the company's mortgage purchases be related to the national goal of providing adequate housing for low- and moderate-income families.

FNMA acquires its funds from three sources: from the sale of common stock (including required purchases by mortgagees using FNMA services); from retained earnings on its mortgage portfolio; and from borrowing. FNMA raises borrowed capital (which at year-end 1983 totalled $74.6 billion) by issuing debentures, short-term discount notes, subordinated capital debentures, and mortgage-backed bonds. Congress has given FNMA debentures and short-term discount notes (30 to 270 day maturities) "federal agency" status, which greatly expands their marketability.[13]

In 1968, FNMA adopted an "auction" or "free-market" mortgage commitment system. Previously, FNMA would periodically announce the discount or price at which it would purchase mortgages and then would purchase all mortgages offered at that price — if funds were available. Under the present system, FNMA announces at regular intervals the total volume of forward commitments it will make, for delivery *at the seller's option,* within two distinct time periods in the future: within four months and within 12 months. In each auction, prices of the mortgages accepted by FNMA rest on the lowest bids. *Quaere:* What factors might influence the setting of a bid price?

Although FNMA continues to invest heavily in FHA and VA mortgages, it runs a secondary market for conventional mortgages as well. Conventional mortgage holdings have markedly increased in the last few years, from 32.7 percent of FNMA's portfolio in December 1980 to nearly 60 percent by mid-1984. As of June 1984 FNMA held $83.2 billion in combined FHA/VA-insured and conventional mortgages holdings.

b. Federal Home Loan Mortgage Corporation (Freddie Mac)

The Federal Home Loan Mortgage Corporation has been known as the Mortgage Corporation since 1976. It was created in January 1970, primarily to broaden secondary market activity for conventional mortgages.

---

13. Federal agency status, inter alia, makes FNMA obligations "riskless assets" for state or local trust investments, eligible investments for national banks without regard to legal limits generally imposed on investment securities, collateral for Treasury Tax and Loan Accounts, security for public monies of the U.S. Government, acceptable purchases by the Open Market Committee of the Federal Reserve Bank, and so on.

Formed as a subsidiary of the Federal Home Loan Bank System, FHLMC deals mainly with savings and loan associations, although any financial institution having federally insured deposits (e.g., mutual savings and commercial banks) can enter the FHLMC market. As Congress intended, three-quarters of FHLMC volume has been conventional, the rest government backed.

The Mortgage Corporation receives no direct federal financing. Except for an initial $100 million stock purchase by the 12 Federal Home Loan Banks, FHLMC has obtained its mortgaging funds by selling bonds in the capital market and by reselling mortgages. FHLMC has also innovated several marketing formats. These include Participation Sales Certificates, which are participation interests (minimum denomination — $100,000) in specific mortgage holdings acquired by FHLMC; Guaranteed Mortgage Certificates, which also give ownership in a pool of mortgages but are designed to resemble bonds — i.e., offering semi-annual interest payments, periodic retirement of capital, and FHLMC's promise to redeem at par after 15 years; and an automated mortgage market information network (AMMINET), which gives subscribers continuous computerized quotations on packages of whole mortgages and participations that various lenders and the secondary market principals are currently offering to sell.

In 1983, FHLMC issued $28.2 billion in purchase commitments and actually bought $23.7 billion in mortgages. FHLMC does not operate on auction, as does FNMA, but deals exclusively on an "over-the-counter" basis. Under this system, FHLMC quotes the price it will pay, and would-be sellers submit their offers by telephone or mail to the FHLMC regional offices.

c. Government National Mortgage Association (Ginnie Mae)

Before its recharter in 1969, FNMA also ran — as part of its secondary market duties — a so-called special assistance program. This dealt with various government-backed mortgages for which private investors would have little enthusiasm. Unlike the regular secondary market operation, which was self-sufficient *and* money-making, the special assistance program relied entirely upon the United States Treasury for its financing. Congress would decide yearly which mortgages it would support and the special assistance arm of FNMA, with Treasury funds, would make the requisite purchases. Although private lenders would actually originate the mortgages, they did so only to resell them *at par* to FNMA. Cutting through the organizational facade, we essentially had a direct government lending program. It helped inter alia to finance moderate-income housing, housing for the elderly, housing in Guam and Alaska and on Indian lands, and rehabilitation.

To carry out this special assistance function after FNMA's 1969 con-

The Mortgage Market

version to free enterprise, Congress formed the Government National Mortgage Association (GNMA), a corporation within the Department of Housing and Urban Development. GNMA still deals almost exclusively in government-backed mortgages, but the scope and volume of its activity have gone well beyond the fairly limited role it first assumed. Until they were discontinued after 1983, much of this activity had centered on a series of *tandem programs,* which we describe below.

(1) The Tandem Programs

Tandem in its pure form described a two-party relationship between GNMA and FNMA in which GNMA bought mortgages at par from an originating seller and resold mortgages at a discount to FNMA. In buying "high" and selling "low," GNMA provided a subsidy that reduced borrowing costs. For example, during the credit crunch of 1974, Congress authorized GNMA to buy 7.75 percent government-backed mortgages when interest rates on home loans had soared to 9.5 percent. Lenders who originated these "low interest" loans got their money back on the sale to GNMA. Completing the tandem, GNMA then resold the mortgage to FNMA; the resale discount raised the effective interest yield, which FNMA would collect, to the 9.5 percent market level. On a $30,000 mortgage, maturity 30 years, the discount would come to $4440.

In 1983, the Administration proposed that the tandem program be ended, a recommendation Congress approved. This closed GNMA's special assistance phase, already overtaken by the agency's role as a mortgage guarantor.

(2) GNMA Guaranteed Mortgage-backed Securities Programs

This is an ingenious arrangement that has brought previously untapped capital sources into the mortgage market. Authorized by the Hous-

TABLE 2-2
Federal National Mortgage Association and Federal Home Loan Mortgage Corporation Secondary Mortgage Market Activity
(In Millions of Dollars)

	FNMA		FHLMC	
	Purchases	*Sales*	*Purchases*	*Sales*
1969	4,121			
1972	3,699	211	1,298	408
1975	4,263	1	1,646	791
1978	12,303	5	6,524	6,211
1981	6,112	2	3,800	3,531
1982	15,116	2	23,673	24,170
1983	17,554	3,528	23,089	19,686

TABLE 2-3
Mortgage Debt Outstanding
(In Billions of Dollars)

	June 1984
Mutual Savings Banks	148.8
Savings and Loan Associations	526.8
Commercial Banks	351.2
Life Insurance Companies	153.7
Federal and Related Agencies	155.4
Mortgage Pools or Trusts	304.5
Individual and Others*	288.7

(Data derived from Federal Reserve Bulletin, August 1984, A 37)

* Other holders include mortgage companies, real estate investment trusts, state and local credit agencies, state and local retirement funds, noninsured pension funds, credit unions, and U.S. agencies for which amounts are small or for which separate data are not readily available.

ing and Urban Development Act of 1968, the program allows mortgage originators, e.g., mortgage companies, to pool HUD and VA mortgages and to issue securities against them. GNMA guarantees the debt service payment on these securities, which is equivalent to the full faith and credit of the United States, and markets them to investment house syndicates, who bid competitively for the issues.

TABLE 2-4
Mortgage Debt Outstanding by Class of Property
June 1984
(In Billions of Dollars)

	One- to-four Family Houses	Multi-Family	Commercial	Farm
Mutual Savings Banks	105.8	19.1	23.8	
Savings and Loan Associations	413.3	45.8	67.7	
Commercial Banks	190.7	20.5	130.0	10.0
Life Insurance Companies	15.0	19.3	106.8	12.6
Federal and Related Agencies	93.1	11.4	.3	48.5
Mortgage Pools or Trusts	276.6	10.7	7.6	9.6
Individuals and Others	186.6	32.8	39.2	30.1

(Data derived from Federal Reserve Bulletin, August 1984, A 37)

To illustrate: X Mortgage Company originates $2.0 million in FHA-insured loans, maturity 30 years. It then issues a $2.0 million debenture against this pool of mortgages; the debt service on the debenture corresponds to that of the underlying mortgages. GNMA then guarantees the debenture — reducing the already modest risk (tied to the FHA insurance) below the vanishing point. Finally GNMA markets the debenture, often gaining a premium price for the security.

The program's importance to the mortgage market is increasingly apparent. Mortgage-backed securities have grown from $3 billion in 1973 to $304 billion by mid-1984. By the late 1980s two out of every three newly issued mortgages may be packaged and traded as securities.

(5) Redlining

Duncan, Hood and Neet, Redlining Practices, Racial Resegregation and Urban Decay: Neighborhood Housing Services as a Viable Alternative

7 Urb. Law. 510, 513-514, 517-518 (1975)

One of the more common instances of discrimination in mortgage lending is the almost universal practice of redlining. In its narrowest sense, the term "redlining" simply denotes the practice of denying mortgage financing on property located within certain geographical areas of a city. These areas are generally the older, rundown sections of the city — the ghetto and adjacent areas, and sections undergoing racial transition. Typically a lending institution simply delineates an area as being too risky for investment. This initial "disinvestment decision" by local lenders, often acting individually, results in an inability on the part of residents or potential residents of the area to secure conventional mortgage loans for the purchase or repair of neighborhood homes. Although the outright denial of mortgage money to sections of a city is not as blatant a practice as it once was, the same effects are achieved by subtle though often well-intentioned means. Some common techniques include: the charging of higher prices and the imposition of more stringent terms for loans in rundown, minority, or racially transitional neighborhoods; a shortening of the length of time for loan repayment; refusing to lend on homes past a certain age, or the setting of a minimum dollar amount for mortgages; underappraising homes in transitional neighborhoods; and, especially if F.H.A. insured mortgages are involved, the charging of discount "points" in such areas. Through the use of such techniques, redlining becomes a subtle practice which is difficult to detect and even harder to prove. . . .

As the process of neighborhood deterioration gains impetus, local financial institutions begin to implement some of the more subtle redlining practices in order to discourage loan applications in the area. Again, the motives for such practices may be primarily economic. Since the underlying basis of long-term financing is stability over an equivalent period of years, areas in transition are suspect to potential lenders. Therefore, conventional lenders must be lured into such areas by more favorable terms — relatively short-term mortgages and higher rate of return. Over time, and further deterioration of the neighborhood, these subtle practices commonly evolve into a final decision by local lenders to disinvest the area as "too risky" for conventional loans.

NOTES AND QUESTIONS

1. Two statutes directed against redlining are the federal government's Home Mortgage Disclosure Act of 1975 and Connecticut's Home Mortgage Disclosure Act, enacted in 1977. These statutes in part provide:

12 U.S.C.A. (1980):

§2801. Congressional Findings and Declaration of Purpose
(a) The Congress finds that some depository institutions have sometimes contributed to the decline of certain geographic areas by their failure pursuant to their chartering responsibilities to provide adequate home financing to qualified applicants on reasonable terms and conditions.
(b) The purpose of this chapter is to provide the citizens and public officials of the United States with sufficient information to enable them to determine whether depository institutions are filling their obligations to serve the housing needs of the communities and neighborhoods in which they are located and to assist public officials in their determination of the distribution of public sector investments in a manner designed to improve the private investment environment.
(c) Nothing in this chapter is intended to, nor shall it be construed to, encourage unsound lending practices or the allocation of credit.

§2802. Definitions
For purposes of this chapter — . . .
(2) the term "depository institution" means any commercial bank, savings bank, savings and loan association, building and loan association, or homestead association (including cooperative banks) or credit union which makes federally related mortgage loans as determined by the Board: . . .

§2803. Maintenance of Records and Public Disclosure—Duty of Depository Institutions; Nature and Content of Information
(a)(1) Each depository institution which has a home office or branch office located within a standard metropolitan statistical area, as defined by the Department of Commerce, shall compile and make available, in accordance with regulations of the Board, to the public for inspection and copying at the home office, and at least one branch office within each standard

metropolitan statistical area in which the depository institution has an office the number and total dollar amount of mortgage loans which were (A) originated, or (B) purchased by that institution during each fiscal year (beginning with the last full fiscal year of that institution which immediately preceded the effective date of this chapter).

(2) The information required to be maintained and made available under paragraph (1) shall also be itemized in order to clearly and conspicuously disclose the following:

(A) The number and dollar amount for each item referred to in paragraph (1), by census tracts . . . for mortgage loans secured by property located within any county with a population of more than 30,000, within that standard metropolitan statistical area, otherwise, by county, for mortgage loans secured by property located within any other county within that standard metropolitan statistical area.

(B) The number and dollar amount for each item referred to in paragraph (1) for all such mortgage loans which are secured by property located outside that standard metropolitan statistical area.

For the purpose of this paragraph, a depository institution which maintains offices in more than one standard metropolitan statistical area shall be required to make the information required by this paragraph available at any such office only to the extent that such information relates to mortgage loans which were originated or purchased by an office of that depository institution located in the standard metropolitan statistical area in which the office making such information available is located.

Itemization of Loan Data . . .

(b) Any item of information relating to mortgage loans required to be maintained under subsection (a) of this section shall be further itemized in order to disclose for each such item—

(1) the number and dollar amount of mortgage loans which are insured under title II of the National Housing Act or under title V of the Housing Act of 1949 or which are guaranteed under chapter 37 of Title 38;

(2) the number and dollar amount of mortgage loans made to mortgagors who did not, at the time of execution of the mortgage, intend to reside in the property securing the mortgage loan; and

(3) the number and dollar amount of home improvement loans.

Period of Maintenance . . .

(c) Any information required to be compiled and made available under this section shall be maintained and made available for a period of five years after the close of the first year during which such information is required to be maintained and made available.

1977 Conn. Pub. Acts, No. 77-153:

Sec. 2.

As used in this act: (a) "Financial institution" means any commercial bank, savings bank, savings and loan association or credit union which makes mortgage loans or home improvement loans; . . .

Sec. 3.

No financial institution shall discriminate, on a basis that is arbitrary or unsupported by a reasonable analysis of the lending risks associated with the applicant for a given loan or the condition of the property to secure it, in the granting, withholding, extending, modifying, renewing or in the fixing of the rates, terms, conditions, or provisions of any mortgage loan or home improvement loan on one to four family owner-occupied residential real property located in the municipality in which such financial institution has a home or branch office, or in any municipality contiguous to such municipality, solely because such property is located in a specific neighborhood or geographical area, . . .

Sec. 7.

Any applicant who has been discriminated against as a result of a violation of section 3 of this act and the regulations pursuant to this act may bring an action in a court of competent jurisdiction. Upon finding that a financial institution is in violation of this act, the court may award damages, reasonable attorneys' fees and court costs. No class action shall be permitted pursuant to the provisions of this section. . . .

Sec. 9.

If the [Bank] commissioner finds that a financial institution is violating the provisions of this act, he shall order the institution to cease its unlawful practices. A financial institution which continues to violate the provisions of this act after having been ordered by the commissioner to cease such practices.

Would you expect that either of these statutes would significantly curtail redlining? Why? Why not?

2. Do you think redlining should be eliminated; and if it should, how can this effectively be accomplished? Should institutional lenders that obtain customer savings from ghetto communities be required to loan these moneys within the communities from which they are obtained? Should an institutional lender that operates over an entire metropolitan area be required to make riskier or less profitable real estate mortgage loans in older, rundown sections of the central city than it makes in other parts of the metropolitan area? If so, should there be any exceptions (the South Bronx in New York City, for instance)? And, if so, should government subsidize the losses or reduced profits from loans in these rundown sec-

tions or should they be absorbed by the lender's owners or other customers?

3. Other federal legislation has potential for prevention of redlining, including the Civil Rights Acts of 1866 and 1964, the Fair Housing Act of 1968, and the Community Reinvestment Act of 1977. See Renne, Eliminating Redlining by Judicial Action: Are Erasers Available?, 29 Vand. L. Rev. 987 (1976); and Note, Redlining: Remedies for Victims of Urban Disinvestment, 5 Fordham Urb. L. J. 83 (1976). In Laufman v. Oakley Building and Loan Co., 408 F. Supp. 489 (S.D. Ohio 1976), the court concluded that redlining violates the Fair Housing Act of 1968. See also Note, Attacking the Urban Redlining Problem, 56 B.U.L. Rev. 989 (1976); Note, Redlining — The Fight Against Discrimination in Mortgage Lending, 7 Loy. U. Chi. L.J. 71 (1975); and Rose, The Redlining Controversy: One Viewpoint, 7 Real Est. Rev. 94 (Winter 1978). On the Federal Home Mortgage Disclosure Act of 1975's preemption of state law, see National State Bank, Elizabeth, N.J. v. Long, 630 F.2d 981 (3rd Cir. 1980).

B. THE CREDIT QUARTET

Some years ago Professor Charles Haar coined the phrase "credit trio" to describe the terms of a mortgage. The trio consists of down payment, length of mortgage, and rate of interest. By manipulating these terms, Congress, through its FHA and VA programs; and state officials, through their control over mortgage lenders, can make housing finance cheaper or more expensive, and home buying easier or more difficult. Since the 1930s, the juggling of mortgage terms has been a key feature of the nation's housing programs. In other areas as well, especially in the realm of the high-voltage operators, the shaping of the credit terms in a deal negotiation may ultimately determine whether the deal can be made. One talent that marks the real estate "pro" is the knack for working out the debt arrangements to make an otherwise dubious transaction feasible and even inviting.

We will discuss each member of Professor Haar's trio, but we have augmented it to a quartet. The fourth player: method of amortization.

1. *Down Payment and the Loan-to-Value Ratio*

Suppose that a buyer can make a $12,000 down payment on a $80,000 house. To complete the purchase, he or she will need a $68,000 mortgage loan. In describing the mortgage, we use the term *loan-to-value ratio,* which states the percentage relationship between the size of the loan (mortgage debt) and the real estate's appraised value;[14] in our example, the loan-to-value ratio would be 85 percent. In making a mortgage loan, regulated lenders must comply with any maximum loan-to-value ratio that federal and state laws have fixed for each group of lenders. Often the loan-to-value ceiling will also depend upon the class or age of property given as security. It is self-evident that as the loan-to-value ceiling rises, the buyer's cash down payment requirements drop, provided, of course, that lenders are willing to make maximum loans. During tight-money eras, lenders — as a matter of internal policy — may refuse to make loans at, or even near, the ceiling percentage.

Until the mid-1930s, official loan-to-value ceilings were set far below present levels. Typically, the pre-Depression home mortgage was not supposed to exceed 50 to 60 percent of appraised value. Such limits, strictly obeyed, would have weakened the housing boom of the 1920s, since, despite good times, few families had the $5000 or $10,000 in liquid assets needed for a cash down payment. To get around the conservative limit, lenders often stretched their appraisals to the point of incredulity; and if, despite the inflated ratio, a homebuyer remained shy of cash, easy access to second, third, and even fourth mortgages from the seller or from private lenders made it quite simple to acquire real estate with little of one's own money in the transaction.

When incomes and real estate values tumbled during the 1930s, overextended borrowers and lenders suffered alike. Mortgage deliquency reached all-time highs as more than one million American families lost their homes through foreclosure between 1930 and 1935. The real estate market became so depressed that in all of 1933 only 120,000 residential starts occurred, fewer than one-tenth the number eight years before.

Only heart massage seemed likely to quicken the economy, and the National Housing Act of 1934 proved a useful and enduring stimulant. It introduced the federally insured mortgage, a guarantee to lenders that the government, not they, would bear any loss resulting from a defaulted loan. Yet a willing lender is only one party to a real estate transaction; a borrower able to raise the down payment and handle the long-term debt is a vital second. To escape the Depression, something more than old forms was needed, and Congress responded by lifting the loan-to-value ceiling

---

14. "The exact legislative definition can be quite important. The wording in different statutes — 'appraised value,' 'estimated value,' 'reasonable normal value,' 'estimated replacement cost,' 'actual cost,' 'necessary current cost,' 'reasonable value — affects the size of the resulting down payment considerably. Accounting terms often conceal significant social policy decisions. [The] substitution of the words 'replacement value' for 'market value' may substantially reduce the amount of equity capital which the builder has to provide." Haar, Federal Credit and Private Housing 60 (1960).

for the FHA-insured mortgage well above any level once believed safe. For example, the purchaser of a $15,000 house could obtain a $13,500 FHA-insured mortgage, reducing his down payment requirement to $1500. Had the house been conventionally financed, the buyer would have needed at least $6000.

Fairly high loan-to-value ceilings have remained a key feature of government-backed mortgages,[15] with the ratio at times even reaching 100 percent.[16] And as their confidence in the economy returned after World War II, lenders specializing in conventional loans wanted also to deal with low down-payment borrowers. Entreaties to state legislatures and to Congress brought an easing of loan-to-value limits on noninsured loans, in some cases almost to the level of FHA and VA mortgages. To illustrate: California now lets its state-chartered savings and loan associations make a 90 percent loan on an owner-occupied one-family house. Cal. Fin. Code §7505 (West 1981). With the advent of private mortgage insurers, conventional lenders can now shift the risk of default on high loan-to-value mortgages.

Other factors that cushion the lender's risk when making seemingly dangerous loans are exacting credit standards, a steady full employment economy, and a housing demand that exceeds the available supply. Time also works in the lender's favor, even though, as we shall see, the rate of mortgage reduction usually begins quite modestly. The pressures of inflation and scarcity tend to force up real estate values, adding to the owner's equity wholly apart from mortgage reduction. Moreover, inflation also allows the debtor to repay fixed dollars of debt service with dollars of shrinking value, thereby making default itself less likely.

An introduction to leverage. The professional investor knows emphatically the value of *leverage,* a congenial exercise in applied arithmetic that allows one to catapult his yield by reducing his down payment. To explain how leverage works, let us start with an investor who buys a $10 million apartment house that throws off $1,500,000 after expenses. On an all cash purchase, he will earn a 15 percent cash yield on his investment. Suppose instead that he borrows to make the purchase: first $5,000,000, then $9,000,000. If the mortgages bear 12 percent interest, and if the annual

---

15. On occasion the federal government has lowered the permitted ratio to stifle housing demand. During the Korean War, when munition makers were competing with subdividers for steel and other material, the FHA ceiling on §203 mortgages (the one- to four-family home program) dropped from 95 to 85 percent.

16. During the peak building years of 1950 and 1955, no-down-payment VA loans accounted for 44 and 40 percent, respectively, of all new one- to four-family home sales. Haar, Federal Credit and Private Housing 58 n.4 (1960).

Congress, in 1961, initiated the §221(d)(3) program, which was intended to stimulate non-profit groups (such as hospitals, churches, labor unions, colleges) to produce housing for "moderate" income tenants. An essential feature of this program was the 100 percent mortgage.

debt service (that is, the combined amount of interest and principal reduction) is designed to pay off the mortgages in 25 years, the cash flow and cash yield appear below:

(a) $5,000,000 mortgage, $5,000,000 cash down payment

Cash flow before debt service	$1,500,000
Less debt service	$633,000
Cash flow after debt service	$867,000
Cash yield on $5,000,000 down payment	17.34%

(b) $9,000,000 mortgage, $1,000,000 cash down payment

Cash flow before debt service	$1,500,000
Less debt service	$1,139,400
Cash flow after debt service	$360,600
Cash yield on $1,000,000 down payment	36.06%

If we were to continue to project cash yield based on ever-shrinking down payments, the investment return would approach infinity. And by placing elsewhere the cash that mortgaging replaces, the investor can expand and diversify his holdings.

It is useful to understand how leverage can bring a geometric increase in investment return. Note that it depends upon the investor turning a profit on the borrowed funds; this, in turn, depends upon a favorable spread between the "points" (points equal percentage) of debt service and the "free and clear" rate of return on the investment. To illustrate this principle with the $5,000,000 mortgage:

(1)	Free and clear return (at 15%) on $5,000,000 of borrowed funds	$750,000
(2)	Debt service (at 12.66 points) on $5,000,000 mortgage	$633,000
(3)	Profit on the borrowed funds (1 minus 2)	$117,000
(4)	Profit on the equity or down payment funds	$750,000
(5)	Overall cash flow (3 plus 4)	$867,000

Thus our investor has enhanced his rate of return by adding the $117,000 profit on the borrowed moneys to the regular 15 percent yield that his down payment generates. By increasing the spread between free and clear return and debt service costs, or by increasing the ratio of borrowed to equity capital, the investor will improve his leverage advantage. To test your understanding, repeat this calculation for a $9,000,000 mortgage.

The Credit Quartet

It follows, inevitably, that leverage will produce negative results if the assumptions above are reversed and the mortgage debt service costs exceed the free and clear rate of investment return. Suppose, in our example, that the free and clear return on an all-cash investment is only $1,300,000 (13 percent) and that the investor can only obtain a 15-year mortgage on any moneys that he borrows. If we assume the same 12 percent interest rate, the annual debt service for each $1,000,000 of mortgage comes to $144,600 (14.46 points). We now have an unfavorable spread between the "points" of debt service and the "free and clear" rate of investment return. The impact on cash yield, assuming a $5,000,000 mortgage, appears below:

$5,000,000 mortgage, $5,000,000 cash down payment	
Cash flow before debt service	$1,300,000
Less debt service	$723,000
Cash flow after debt service	$577,000
Cash yield on $5,000,000 down payment	11.54%

And, as the borrowed funds increase, the disadvantage grows geometrically. You might work out the figures for a $6,000,000 mortgage, a $7,000,000 mortgage, etc.

With medicine, one dose may be restorative, five doses fatal. So, too, with leverage. If it is too great, it may ruin. The investor (and the lender) gamble that operating income will be enough to carry the debt. In the first example, where $5,000,000 was borrowed, $867,000 was left after debt service; when $9,000,000 was borrowed, only $360,600 remained. These amounts, $867,000 and $360,600, are the margin of solvency. If the margin disappears (rentals down, expenses up), the investor faces the uninviting options of finding cash elsewhere or defaulting on his loan, unless he is able to refinance the debt so as to reduce or postpone the debt service requirements. Needless to say, the slimmer the margin of solvency, the shakier the investment. History records more than one real estate empire that was leveraged into oblivion.

2. *Length of Mortgage*

The due date of a loan, i.e., its length or maturity, is the second of the credit quartet. Prior to the New Deal, real estate loans were seldom written for longer than 10 or 15 years.[17] But with the advent of the FHA-insured

---

17. In 1925, the average contract length for home mortgages issued by life insurance companies and savings and loan associations, respectively, was 6.0 years and 10.9 years. Haar, Federal Credit and Private Housing 58 n.3 (1960).

TABLE 2-5
Monthly Debt Service Related to Length of Mortgage
and Loan-to-Value Ratio
(in Dollars)

	10 years	25 years	40 years
Loan-to-Value Ratio			
50 percent ($40,000)	573.88	421.29	403.40
80 percent ($64,000)	918.21	674.06	645.44
90 percent ($72,000)	1,032.99	758.32	726.12

mortgage, and its policy of easier down payment requirements, the practice of relatively short-term loans had to be reexamined. All else equal, an $80,000 loan bears twice the debt service of a $40,000 loan. Higher loan-to-value ratios may bring more buyers into the market, but higher debt service payments will drive them away again. To hold down the level of debt service, Congress enabled the FHA to insure 25-year mortgages, for that time (1934) a revolutionary idea. Table 2-5 shows that extending the mortgage's length can help offset the debt service increase of a higher loan-to-value ratio. The figures cover a 12 percent mortgage and real estate valued at $80,000.

As the table shows, the debt service on a $64,000, 25-year mortgage costs little more than that on a $40,000, 10-year mortgage. Even a $72,000 mortgage, extended for 40 years, results in debt service less than one-third higher than that of the much smaller, short-term loan.

The combination, then, of higher loan-to-value ratios and longer maturities became the key to FHA's effort to energize the housing market. Both credit changes were needed to reflect the savings and the incomes of potential buyers. Congress has since further liberalized the maturities on government-backed loans, with 40-year terms now authorized for some programs and 30- and 35-year terms available for most others. Conventional loans have also become much longer.

A stretched-out loan is not all to the buyer's advantage. The longer he repays the loan, the more slowly his equity builds and the larger will be his total interest charges. A 12 percent, $40,000, 10-year mortgage, costs $28,880 in interest; the interest on a 25-year mortgage would come to $86,400! Some might boggle at this sum. Given, however, the migratory habits of American households, 25-year mortgages rarely go to term. Most mortgages are paid off long before maturity, when the property is sold to a refinancing buyer. Moreover, the differences are less startling when present value discounting is applied to the absolute amounts. And, the deductibility of home mortgage interest payments for taxpayers itemizing their expenses further shrinks the "actual" outlays.

The Credit Quartet

a. Mortgage Prepayment

In arranging for his loan, the borrower should recognize that he may someday want to prepay the mortgage, wholly or in part. The right to prepay is not automatic. Unless he has agreed otherwise, the lender may stand on the original bargain and insist that payments continue, as provided for, until maturity. Why is it, do you think, that courts have tolerated this stubbornness? Consider, for example, the case that follows.

Peter Fuller Enterprises v. Manchester Savings Bank
102 N.H. 117, 152 A.2d 179 (1959)

Bill in equity, in which plaintiffs seek, among other relief, reformation of certain mortgage notes and a determination of their right to pay off these notes which are secured by real and personal property mortgages.

There are two notes executed by plaintiff Peter Fuller Enterprises, Inc., and endorsed by Peter Fuller, the other plaintiff, payable to Manchester Savings Bank in the principal amounts of $200,000 and $50,000 and another payable to Amoskeag Industries, Inc. in the principal amount of $220,000. All three notes provide for quarterly payments of interest and principal payments in specified amounts payable monthly beginning April 28, 1958 to April 28, 1963 "whereupon the entire unpaid balance shall become due and payable; sixty (60) days default in payment of any interest or principal payment to make the entire balance due and payable."

[On February 13, 1959, plaintiffs tendered to the respective payees the interest due to date and the unpaid principal of each note which was refused. They claimed the tender was improperly refused and made no more payments. They further claimed that by their failure to make the payments due February 28, March 28, and April 28, 1959, the maturity of the notes had been automatically accelerated.]

Before a hearing on the merits, plaintiffs filed a motion the amended prayer of which was "that the said mortgages on the real estate and chattels of Peter Fuller Enterprises, Inc. held by defendants be now discharged upon the mortgagors furnishing such securities in substitution for said mortgages as the Court shall find justice requires."

At a hearing on said motion counsel for plaintiffs stated and offered to provide that they "may lose a sale that will be at least one hundred and fifty thousand dollars more advantageous to them than any other sale they have been offered" and "that a failure to discharge these mortgages, particularly the chattel mortgages, would subject the debtor to irreparable harm and damage and a very serious financial loss."

The Court (Griffith, J.) found for the purposes of the motion "that it would appear you [plaintiffs] might suffer substantial loss by the failure to discharge the mortgage at this time and that equity would seem to indicate that you were entitled to a discharge of the mortgage upon some basis that would completely secure the defendants as far as a monetary performance of their contract was concerned."

Thereupon the following issues were reserved and transferred to this court without ruling:

"1) Whether or not the Trial Court has authority at this stage of the proceeding and after its findings as disclosed in the record which findings were excepted to by the petitioners, to order a discharge of the mortgages described in the petition upon the condition that the petitioners substitute therefor a sum of cash, to be deposited in New Hampshire banks, equal to the unpaid principal and interest to April 1963, plus a sum sufficient to offset any loss in credits against the state tax levied on savings banks' assets, or by the furnishing of any other security which the Court might order to secure the petitionees.

"2) Whether or not the Trial Court has authority after

"a) a hearing on the merits, and

"b) a ruling that notes and mortgages described in the petition are valid instruments as written and not mature until 1963, and

"c) a finding that the petitioners might suffer substantial financial loss by reason of their failure to obtain discharges of the mortgages described in the petition

to order a discharge of the mortgages upon the condition that the petitioners substitute therefore a sum of cash, to be deposited in New Hampshire banks, equal to the unpaid principal and interest to April 1963, plus a sum sufficient to offset any loss in credits against the state tax levied on savings banks' assets, or by the furnishing of any other security which the Court might order to secure the petitionees, or by requiring said cash or other security to be paid on said notes according to their terms."

LAMPRON, Justice. . . . Every negotiable instrument is payable at the time fixed therein. RSA 337:85. The mortgages the dominant feature of which is security for the performance of the primary obligations evidenced by the notes become void upon payment according to terms or by legal tender thereof. RSA 479:6; Blaisdell v. Coe, 83 N.H. 167, 168, 139 A. 758, 65 A.L.R. 626. A mortgagor, however, in the absence of a provision so providing has no right to pay in advance of maturity. Buffum v. Buffum, 11 N.H. 451, 456; Trahant v. Perry, 253 Mass. 486, 149 N.E. 149; 1 Glenn Mortgages, s. 50, p. 319; 59 C.J.S. Mortgages §447, p. 695. Plaintiffs argue that by their failure to make the payments due as indicated above, the maturity of the notes has been automatically accelerated by their provision that "sixty (60) days default in any interest or principal payment to make the entire unpaid balance due and payable."

It is stated in an annotation in 159 A.L.R. beginning at page 1077 that a majority of jurisdictions hold that such a clause is not self-operative but leaves an option to the creditor whether or not to take advantage of it and that without some action on his part the full amount will not become immediately due merely on the happening of a default. See cases cited pp. 1084, 1085. The rationale of these decisions is that the provision is primarily for the benefit of the creditor who should be free to decide whether such protection is necessary under the circumstances of the default and the obligor should not be entitled to take advantage of his own wrong and cause an automatic change of maturity. P. 1088.

Other jurisdictions hold that under such a clause the entire principal of the note and mortgage becomes automatically due without the necessity of a declaration of the right or an election on the part of anyone. See cases cited. Id., pp. 1079, 1080. The basis of these holdings is that the provision exists for the benefit of both parties and courts have no right to make a new contract different from the expressed words of the parties. Id., p. 1082.

We have no decision in New Hampshire on this point but we are of the opinion that the better view is that such a clause should be interpreted not as self-operating but as conferring an option on the holder to accelerate the maturity and so hold for the following reasons. In many instances mortgage loans are made by lenders as an investment and the period for which they run can affect the rate of interest and other terms thereof. If an acceleration clause such as the one in this case were held to be automatic, the borrower by his own default could convert a mortgage from a five-year mortgage to a sixty-day mortgage. Keene Five Cent Sav. Bank v. Reid, 10 Cir., 123 F. 221, 224; Kleiman v. Kolker, 189 Md. 647, 57 A.2d 297. Furthermore even though in the instant case such an interpretation is considered a hardship, in most cases if the clause were self-operating, the holder could not exercise leniency in overlooking failures to make payments when due, thus the whole loan would be brought down on the head of the debtor at once. Chafee, Acceleration Provisions in Time Paper, 32 Harv. L. Rev. 765-769. . . .

The Trial Court has found for the purposes of the motion to discharge the mortgages in advance of a hearing on the merits that plaintiffs might suffer substantial loss by their failure to obtain these discharges at this time. . . .

The plaintiffs argue in support of the Trial Court's authority that since the mortgage is merely security for the debt the Court should have authority to substitute other security for it, provided it is equivalent in value, for if the creditors' rights to payment of the debt are fully protected they may not complain.

Defendants take the position that the Trial Court has no authority to interfere with the private contractual rights voluntarily entered into by the parties. They argue that any alteration of the security arrangement by the Trial Court is a substitution of the court's judgment for that of the mortgagees as to the adequacy of the security.

"In the nature of things obligations arising from contractual relations cannot justly and reasonably be displaced by other obligations. . . . There is no law or judicial power by which considerations of equity may reform contracts which are free from legal attack on grounds of fraud and mistake." Lemire v. Haley, 91 N.H. 357, 361, 362, 19 A.2d 436, 440. The hardship which will result to the plaintiffs in this case is not one "the possibility of which was not evident at the time the agreement was executed." Bourn v. Duff, 96 N.H. 194, 198, 72 A.2d 501, 504. Hardship resulting from what may prove to be an improvident bargain fairly and voluntarily assumed by contract does not entitle a party to be relieved of its undertaking in equity. 96 N.H. 198, 199, 72 A.2d 501. Cf. Caron Inc. v. Manchester Federal Savings & Loan Association, 90 N.H. 560, 10 A.2d 668. The answer to transferred issue No. 1 is "no." . . .

It is not the duty of this court nor do we deem it good practice to advise the parties in advance of hearing as to their rights under all possible facts which might be proved. White Mountain Freezer Co. v. Murphy, 78 N.H. 398, 403, 101 A. 357. No decision holding that a court will order a discharge of a mortgage the condition of which has not been performed so as to enable the mortgagor to make a profit on an advantageous sale has been presented to us. Nor has any statutory law in our state granting such authority to the Trial Court been brought to our attention. Cf. RSA 511:48-50, 53. Williams v. Mathewson, 73 N.H. 242, 60 A. 687; Perry v. Champlain Oil Company, 99 N.H. 451, 114 A.2d 885; Lefebvre v. Waldstein, 101 N.H. 451, 146 A.2d 270. Our answer to issue No. 2 is "no."

The bill in equity for reformation not having been heard on the merits the order is remanded.

All concurred.

NOTES AND QUESTIONS

1. Facts appearing in a letter from Donald R. Bryant, Esq., attorney for petitioners, help to illuminate the lawsuit. The disputed loans had financed the purchase of a local textile business. Amoskeag Industries, Inc., which was one of the creditors, was an organization of Manchester citizens interested in bringing industry to that city. Unluckily, the textile business turned out to be precarious and, by October 1959, only six months after signing the secured notes, the petitioners had decided to sell out if they could find a buyer. When efforts to sell the entire business collapsed, the petitioners obtained an offer for just the machinery from J. P. Stevens Company, which intended to move it to a Southern mill. The Stevens offer was $150,000 higher than any other offer that the petitioners received, but it could not be accepted unless the notes were paid

and the mortgage on the machinery discharged. The payee's clear interest was in obstructing the sale of the machinery to an out-of-state organization.

The case was settled, after the New Hampshire Supreme Court decision and before trial, by the payment of a 3 percent penalty ($12,925). One of the petitioner's claims was the oral promise of a prepayment privilege when the loans were made. Is there a problem of parol evidence? Of the statute of frauds?

2. One textwriter explains the lender's view relative to prepayment: "[T]his freedom of the mortgagee from anticipation is of increasing value as the mortgage becomes more and more an investment instrument, designed to secure a regular flow of income. Current institutional mortgages customarily exact substantial amounts as conditions of accepting prepayment." 3 Powell, Real Property 696.12 n.4 (1985); cf. also Dugan v. Grzybowski, 165 Conn. 173, 332 A.2d 97, 99 n.2 (1973).

3. As the Powell excerpt indicates, lenders will usually grant at least a limited, conditional privilege of prepayment, if the borrower bargains for such a privilege when seeking the loan commitment. But to exercise the privilege, the borrower must often pay a substantial premium, the so-called penalty. A sample prepayment clause appears below:

> The further privilege is reserved commencing with the first regular quarterly installment due date in the fourth loan year . . . and on any regular quarterly installment due date thereafter of making payments in multiples of Five Thousand ($5,000) Dollars on the principal in excess of . . . [Five Hundred Thousand Dollars in any one loan year — the approximate regular annual principal payment] provided . . . that any such payment in excess of the said Five Hundred Thousand Dollars ($500,000) in any one loan year shall be subject to a prepayment charge of three percent (3%) on such excess during the fourth loan year and declining one-quarter (¼%) each loan year thereafter. . . . Cf. Westminister Investing Corp. v. Equitable Assurance Society of the United States, 443 F.2d 653 (D.C. Cir. 1970).

4. The standard attack on clauses imposing a prepayment penalty has been that the penalty is a usurious exaction. The standard judicial response has been that the sum exacted is not interest, but an agreed upon payment for exercising a privilege. Secured Real Estate Loan Prepayment and the Prepayment Penalty, 51 Calif. L. Rev. 923 (1963), collects the cases and argues that perhaps particular prepayment penalties can be struck down as forfeitures disproportionate to the harm caused to mortgagees from prepayment. What *is* the lender's loss if the borrower seeks prepayment at a time when interest rates are generally higher than when the mortgage was first placed? On the other hand, suppose that interest rates have fallen below where the prepayment penalty will fully compensate the lender for

its reinvestment losses? Would it be fairer — to lender and borrower alike — for the parties to hinge the prepayment charge, if any, to the differential in interest rates; that is, the greater the drop in interest rates, the greater the prepayment charge? Might this system result in the borrower collecting a premium from the lender for prepayments made when interest rates have risen?

5. In representing a lender, would you advise that the prepayment charge not be called a penalty?

6. Borrowers sometimes find themselves in a Catch-22 situation. Mortgages commonly contain a "due-on-sale" clause, infra page 143, which allows for acceleration of the unpaid principal if the mortgagor's equity is sold without the mortgagee's consent. The same mortgage may also provide for a substantial prepayment penalty. Upon the sale of the mortgagor's equity, may the mortgagee both refuse to consent, thereby accelerating the debt, and insist that the prepayment penalty be collected? Some states have acted to forbid this "double jeopardy." Cf., e.g., N.Y. Real Prop. L. §254-a (McKinney's 1984-1985); Rogers v. Williamsburgh Savings Bank, 79 Misc. 2d 852, 361 N.Y.2d 531 (D. Ct. 1974) (statute validly applies to already existing mortgages).

7. Suppose that the mortgage allows no prepayment for five years and prepayment with penalty after five years. During the first five years, the mortgaged property is condemned. Is the mortgage entitled, as an item of damages in the condemnation award, to the premium it would have received in the event of prepayment? Cf. DeKalb County v. United Family Life Ins. Co., 235 Ga. 417, 219 S.E.2d 707 (1975) (mortgagee could not claim prepayment premium). Same result if condemnation occurred after five years? Suppose that the mortgaged premises are destroyed by fire. Is the mortgagee entitled to recover any prepayment premium from the fire insurance proceeds? Cf. Chestnut Corp. v. Bankers Bond and Mortgage Co., 395 Pa. 153, 149 A.2d (1959) (premium earned only when mortgagor voluntarily prepays).

8. Might it also be argued that the legal system should not force borrowers to remain shackled to debt when they have the wherewithal to become debt-free or, at least, debt-lightened? Suppose that a would-be borrower applies for a mortgage loan, and the lender agrees to issue a commitment. The borrower then changes his or her mind and refuses to take the loan. May the lender sue for specific performance? Isn't the bank in the *Peter Fuller* case getting specific performance?

9. The mortgage provides for monthly debt service of $100 and also allows prepayment without penalty. In the first year, the mortgagor makes the twelve regular monthly installments and also makes two extra payments of $100 each. The mortgagor makes no payments in the next two months. Has a default occurred?

10. The mortgage does not allow for prepayment. Your client is eager

to refinance (interest rates have dropped sharply), but the lender refuses to accept your client's tender. Someone has suggested to your client that he let the mortgage go into default; acceleration would then occur and the lender would be "tricked" into accepting a prepayment. Do you see any problems with this scheme?

11. Would the widespread adoption of variable interest mortgages, infra page 146, end most of the controversy over prepayment?

b. "Due-on" Clauses

> If the mortgagor "sells, conveys, alienates . . . said property or any part thereof, or any interest therein . . . in any manner or way, whether voluntarily or involuntarily . . . mortgagee shall have the right at its option, to declare said note . . . secured hereby . . . immediately due and payable without notice."

This "due-on" clause, a standard provision in mortgages and deeds of trust, became the hurricane eye of a decade-long controversy, which Congress finally quelled in 1982. At issue was whether courts would (or could) enforce such clauses, where the mortgagee's security was unthreatened by a transfer of title, and where the mortgagee hoped simply to gain from a fortuitous event a higher interest yield. In short: the transferee would be credit-worthy, but the lender would not approve a mortgage takeover at the original, lower interest rate.

The California courts led the assault on such clauses in a series of four decisions. The cases and their holdings were:

La Sala v. American Sav. & Loan Assoc., 5 Cal. 3d 864, 489 P. 2d 1113 (1971) (lender may enforce clause upon the further encumbering of the property only when reasonably necessary to protect the lender's security);

Tucker v. Lassen Savings & Loan Assoc., 12 Cal. 3d 692, 526 P.2d 1169 (1974) (lender may enforce clause upon the mortgagor's entering into an installment land contract for the sale of the security only when one of the lender's "legitimate interests" is threatened);

Wellenkamp v. Bank of America, 21 Cal. 3d 943, 582 P.2d 970 (1978) (lender may enforce clause upon the outright sale of the security only when reasonably necessary to protect against impairment to the lender's security or the risk of default);

Dawn Investment Co. v. Superior Court of Los Angeles County, 30 Cal. 3d 695, 693 P.2d 974 (1982) (expanded the *Wellenkamp* doctrine to include commercial as well as residential real property and private as well as institutional lenders).

In its opinions, the California court made clear that the lender's understandable desire to improve its portfolio return would not, in itself, be sufficient justification for accelerating the debt.

> Even when the lender is willing to waive its option to accelerate in return for the assumption of the existing loan at an increased interest rate, an inhibitory effect on transfer may still result. The buyer, faced with the lender's demand for increased interest, may insist that the seller lower the purchase price. The seller would then be forced to choose between lowering the purchase price and absorbing the loss with the resulting reduction in his equity interest, or refusing to go through with the sale at all. In either event, the result in terms of a restraint on alienation is clear.

21 Cal. 3d at 950-951, 582 P.2d at 975.

The courts of at least three other states (Arizona, Arkansas, and Michigan) also restricted enforceability of the "due-on" clause, as did at least five state legislatures (Colorado, Iowa, New Mexico, Virginia, and Utah). On the other hand, several courts saw no reason not to enforce the clause regardless of the lender's purpose. See, e.g., Miller v. Pacific First Federal Sav. & Loan Assn., 86 Wash. 2d 401, 405, 545 P.2d 546, 549 (1976) ("Equity should not depart from the law which requires it to enforce valid contracts [in order to] strike down the acceleration option simply because its exercise will let the [mortgagees], not the [mortgagors], make the profit on the interest rate occasioned by the increased cost of money," citing Tennessee decision); Mutual Federal Sav. & Loan Assn. v. Wisconsin Wire Works, 71 Wis. 2d 531, 239 N.W.2d 20 (1976) ("due-on" clause enforceable both in outright and installment sale: lender has right to protect itself against the contingency of increased interest rates).

Believing that restrictions on the lender's ability to accelerate a loan upon transfer of the security would adversely affect lenders due to the loss of cash flow, net income, and access to secondary mortgage markets, the Federal Home Loan Bank Board (FHLBB), in 1976, issued a regulation that curbed state power over "due-on" provisions with respect to loans held by federally chartered thrift institutions. The United States Supreme Court, in Fidelity Sav. & Loan Assn. v. De La Cuesta, 458 U.S. 141, 102 S. Ct. 3014 (1982), upheld the regulation, ruling that Congress had delegated to the FHLBB the power to preempt state law as to such institutions under its regime.

Persuaded that even broader relief was necessary, Congress passed the Garn-St. Germain Depository Institutions Act of 1982, Pub. L. 97-320, 96 Stat. 1469. This measure, and the regulations thereunder, cover essentially all lenders, individual and institutional, and all properties, residential and commercial. There remain, however, some key exceptions to the Act's coverage, which bar state interference with the enforcement of "due-on" clauses. One of these, which will have expired on October 15, 1985, involves so-called window-period loans — those loans made or assumed after governing state law had already barred the "unrestricted exercise of due-on-sale clauses upon outright transfers of property." Prior to the October 1985 date, state law would continue to govern—except as to federal thrift organizations, and any restrictive state would be free to extend its restrictions beyond 1985. (To our knowledge, no state has done so.) In addition, the Act does not cover certain specified transfers, where the states may continue, or initiate, curbs on the enforceability of "due-on" provisions. These transfers include:

1. The creation of a lien or other encumbrance subordinate to the lender's security interest, which does not relate to a transfer of rights of occupancy in the property;
2. A transfer by devise, descent, or operation of law on the death of a joint tenant or a tenant by the entirety;
3. A transfer to a relative resulting from the death of the borrower;
4. A transfer where the spouse or children of the borrower becomes an owner of the property;
5. A transfer resulting from a decree of dissolution of marriage, a legal separation agreement, or from an incidental property settlement agreement, by which the spouse of the borrower becomes an owner of the property.

NOTES AND QUESTIONS

1. In explaining its support for the 1982 legislation, Congress stated that restrictions on the enforceability of "due-on" clauses had led to inflated home prices, higher mortgage origination fees, higher interest rates on newly issued mortgages, the advantaging of existing home owners to the disadvantage of home buyers, and the encouragement of riskier lending practices. A "Due-on-Sale Task Force" assembled by the FHLBB concluded that the imposition of due-on-sale restrictions nationwide would create, within two years, annual losses exceeding $1.0 billion for federal and state savings and loan associations. Barad and Layden, Due-on-Sale Law as Preempted by the Garn-St. Germain Act, 12 Real Est. L.J. 138, 140 (1983).

2. Consider why Congress would except from its tight embrace "due-on-encumbrance" clauses, which states remain free to regulate, as California did in Tucker v. Lassen Savings & Loan Assn., supra, page 143. Is it clear that "due-on-encumbrance" clauses present different policy considerations from "due-on-sale" clauses? If so, is it also clear that lenders should be denied (rather than given) the extensive leeway when lenders seek to accelerate the debt in the event of further encumbrance? When, after the junior encumbrancing of mortgaged premises, might the senior mortgagee be worse off than before?

3. What lies behind each of the other Garn-St. Germain exceptions referred to above?

4. Variable interest mortgages are a second scheme for improving the current yield of the loan portfolio. See subsection b., below. Some observers believe that "due-on" clauses would rarely be exercised if variable interest mortgages became the standard mortgage vehicle.

3. Rate of Interest

a. Introduction

The third member of the quartet, the rate of interest, gets the greatest attention — and deservedly — from lenders, consumer advocates, lawmakers, and the housing industry. Because interest payments are the largest item of housing expense for many homeowners and landlords, interest rate levels have much to do with the ability of consumers to afford decent shelter and with the willingness of both homebuyers and suppliers to engage in new shelter investment. A family earning $25,000 yearly would exhaust its entire housing budget on interest costs alone if its shelter (whether owned or rented) were financed by a $50,000, 14.0 percent mortgage — not a fanciful illustration at all, since in many areas even modest dwellings can no longer be had or built for less than $60,000. During the early 1970s, the primary federal housing subsidy programs for lower-income families, the FHA sections 235 and 236 programs, were pegged to an interest reduction payment that lowered effective interest rates to as little as 1 percent.

Since the early 1950s, interest rates on home mortgages have risen more than three-fold. The forces of inflation and excessive borrowing demand have brought about this steep rise, not only for mortgage rates but also for the rates on comparable long-term government and corporate securities. See Table 2-6.

b. Variable-rate Mortgages

The fixed-rate mortgage suffers badly during any period when interest yields climb explosively. At any one time, a lender's mortgage portfolio will have an average age of more than five years; this *is* inevitable because of the relatively long-term maturities of mortgage debt. In a sharply upward cycle, the average yield on the bank's older mortgages may be far lower than the current yield on new mortgage investments and, in a worst case situation, may not even be competitive with the yields on high-grade short-term paper, such as large negotiable certificates of deposit. (See Table 2-6.) Since a lender's ability to pay dividends on its deposits is

TABLE 2-6
Money Market Rates: 1950 to 1983

	FHA-Insured Home Mortgages	Large Negotiable Certificates of Deposit (3-month)	Moody's Corporate Industrial Bonds	U.S. Government Long-Term Taxable Bonds
1950	4.15	(NA)	2.67	2.32
1955	4.65	(NA)	3.19	2.84
1960	6.16	(NA)	4.59	4.01
1965	5.47	4.35	4.61	4.21
1970	9.03	7.56	8.26	6.59
1975	9.19	6.44	9.25	6.98
1976	8.82	5.27	8.84	6.78
1977	8.68	5.64	8.28	7.06
1978	9.70	8.22	8.90	7.89
1979	10.87	11.22	9.85	8.74
1980	13.44	13.07	12.35	10.81
1981	16.29	15.91	14.50	12.87
1982	15.31	12.27	14.54	12.23
1983	13.11	9.07	12.25	10.84

Table Derived from 1976 Statistical Abstract of the U.S., pp. 494-495, 1985 Statistical Abstract of the U.S., pp. 504-505.

derived from the lender's earnings on its total portfolio, thrift institutions cannot swiftly adjust their overall dividend rate upward without first absorbing large losses on low-yield investments. Depositors, on the other hand, may move their accounts quite easily, migrating toward higher interest rates wherever they are found. Having "borrowed" short and loaned long (at *fixed* rates), the lender is fairly helpless to staunch the heavy outflow of funds. During the worst years (1977-1981), disintermediation—the financial equivalent of hemorrhage—nearly ruined the thrift industry.[18]

The variable-rate mortgage (VRM) has gained wide acceptance in the past decade in helping to bring stability to the home mortgage market. It permits the lender to lift interest rates on an existing mortgage to reflect current higher interest levels. (Conversely, the borrower will (usually) enjoy lower interest charges should interest levels drop.) In this way, the

---

18. The Brookings Institute studied the *real* value (i.e., the excess of contract interest over inflation rate) of investment income achieved by lenders making fixed-rate long-term mortgages from 1950-1980. The results showed a dramatic fall-off, despite steadily rising contract rates. For example, loans made in the years 1951-1959 carried an average contract rate of 5.02 percent, but the average *real* interest rate was 3.51 percent. For loans made from 1970-1975, although the average contract rate was 9.34 percent, the average *real* interest earned was only 1.73 percent. Strum, Financing Real Estate During the Inflationary 80s at 23 (1981).

lender can adjust the yield on his total portfolio to track rises (and falls) in the yield on new mortgage investments.

How the variable-rate mortgage works: Suppose that R borrows $50,000 on a VRM, which calls for an initial interest rate of 12.0 percent, a 25-year maturity, and annual debt service (based on monthly payments) of $6320. Five years later, interest rates have risen to 13.0 percent and a VRM adjustment is required. What is the VRM adjustment? Under present theory, it might take one of three forms:

(1) *Maturity remains constant; debt service rises to reflect increased interest rate.* At the end of five years, R will have reduced his mortgage balance from $50,000 to $47,825. The interest rate having risen to 13.0 percent, the debt service must be adjusted upward so as to pay off the unpaid balance, at the higher rate, in the remaining 20 years. The revised annual debt service installment: $6724. The annual debt service increase: $404.

(2) *Debt service remains constant; maturity extended.* This formula would seek to avoid entirely the risk of default that might follow higher debt service payments. In order to maintain the level of debt service, while adjusting for higher interest rates, the mortgage term must be extended. After five years, when R's mortgage balance is $47,825, the annual debt service of $6320 — adjusted for a 13.0 percent interest rate — will require another 32 years in which to amortize that balance. Thus, the VRM maturity must be extended twelve years.

(3) *Combination of debt service increase and maturity extension.* This formula would seek to reduce the risk of default that might follow higher debt service payments while avoiding extreme extensions of the mortgage term. The parties might agree, for example, that any maturity extension would not exceed a fixed duration — viz., 25 years; and that the borrower would pay higher debt service to complete the adjustment. In the illustration above, R would be obliged after five years to pay an adjusted annual debt service of $6475, to reflect an extended maturity from 20 to 25 years. The annual debt service increase: $155.

One key variable is the index to which interest rates are geared. For the borrower's protection, the index used should not be one that the lender can manipulate. Thus, an index based on changes in the dividend rate on deposits would clearly be unsuitable. Short-term rates, e.g., the rate on prime commercial paper, change too frequently and swing too widely to be a useful index. The Consumer Price Index measures *current* inflation whereas interest rates reflect *anticipated* inflation; thus, the CPI does not seem entirely suitable, either.

Other, more likely possibilities for a VRM index would be the yields on corporate industrial bonds and intermediate or long-term government securities. Reexamine Table 2-6 supra and consider how these yields would have impacted on the rates of older mortgages had VRM been around in 1965. As its advocates argue, might VRM even have made it cheaper for a homebuyer to borrow?

c. **Limitations on the Lender's Return**

(1) State Usury Laws — Historical Antecedents

Salin, Usury
15 Encyclopedia of the Social Sciences 193-197 (Seligman ed. 1934)

In the course of its history the concept of usury has covered a variety of meanings. Originally it referred to all returns derived from the lending of capital and carried no moral opprobrium. With the growing condemnation of the financial abuses of the moneylenders the term came to be confined to credit transactions carrying excessive charges and thus acquired a distinct ethical connotation. In the Middle Ages all direct payments for loans were deemed usurious and condemned as sinful. In modern times the term was again narrowed down and now it refers only to excessive loan charges, while the payment of moderate rates is covered by the more neutral term interest. . . .

The ethical nature of the concept of usury renders it impossible to formulate permanent and definite criteria of what constitutes a usurious transaction. As long as freedom of contract remains the corner stone of economic organization, it is not the economist but the legislator who must decide at what point a voluntary economic transaction constitutes an abuse of economic freedom and thus an act of usury. [I]n certain periods the moral views of the legislative bodies were identical with those of the majority of the people, while at other times there was a wide divergence in this respect, so that usages which were officially outlawed were nevertheless sanctioned in economic life. Thus while concepts such as price, wage, interest, are economic categories transcending time, usury is a historical category understood only in the light of the moral and legal norms prevailing in a particular period.

. . . The earliest prohibition of usury is to be found in the Mosaic code (Leviticus xxv:36 and Deuteronomy xxiii:20). The restriction, however, applied only to Jews; the taking of interest from aliens was permitted. In Athens the legislation of Solon intended to ease the financial burden of the agricultural population, limited the rate of interest. In Rome the Twelve Tables established a minimum of 10 percent. Subsequently Justinian reduced the legal rate considerably, to 6 percent for general loans, 8 percent for manufacturers and merchants, 4 percent for persons in high positions and 12 percent for the foenus nauticum [a loan advanced to finance maritime trade]. The more drastic restrictions of the Justinian code were inspired by the growing influence of the teachings of the ancient philosophers and of the young Christian church.

The ancient Attic philosophers [Plato and Aristotle] realized the social dangers inherent in a system which encourages the pursuit of gain for gain's sake, and by condemning moneylending they hoped to strike at the very roots of profit economy. The ban on gains derived from moneylending was also influenced by the naturalistic conception of money and interest. . . . Money, Aristotle held, is an inorganic object used as a medium of exchange and therefore cannot breed new coins. He who demands payment for the lending of money causes money to beget money and thus acts contrary to the laws of nature.

The antichrematistic tone of the ancient philosophers was in perfect accord with the teachings of the rising church. While the attitude of the church was based primarily on the Scriptural command Mutuum date nihil inde sperantes (Lend, hoping for nothing again, St. Luke vi:35), the theologians drew freely upon the anti-usury arguments of the philosophers. In the Roman church Ambrose of Milan formulated the principle which dominated ecclesiastic teaching for almost a thousand years: everything which accrues to the capital constitutes usury. While couched primarily in moral terms, this rigorous prohibition derived its social justification from the fact that under conditions of a primitive economy most loans were contracted by the needy for purposes of consumption and the borrower usually found himself in a worse position at the end than at the beginning of the loan period. Moreover because of the absence of business opportunities in the early Middle Ages, when the usury doctrine of the church took shape, the holder of funds did not forego any loss of profit by parting temporarily with his capital. The absolute prohibition of usury was further justified in terms of contemporary economic theory; it was argued that a loan transaction involving the transfer of ownership of the sum of money to the borrower really constituted a sale in which in accordance with the medieval principle of equivalence of exchange the lender, that is, the seller of money, might expect in return only the exact equivalent of the amount originally advanced. The fact that a period of time intervened between the offering and the return of the sum was dismissed with the argument that time is divine and can therefore command no price. Unlike the situation in ancient Greece and Rome, it was no longer necessary to determine at which rate a charge for money loan became usurious and punishable; all charges above the principal were held usurious. Usury was no mere transgression of the law but a mortal sin punishable by excommunication. This rigid measure originally applied only to the clergy but was subsequently extended to all lay Christians.

While the church consistently prohibited the charging of a price for loans throughout the Middle Ages, a person in need of money who was willing to shoulder the cost was never deprived completely of the possibility of borrowing money. Aside from the various devices designed to evade the anti-usury laws, as, for instance, the practice of sale and resale whereby the prospective lender fictitiously sold to the borrower a commodity on credit at a high price and simultaneously repurchased it for cash at a lower price, the difference constituting an interest charge for an actual loan, the medieval borrower could turn to the Jewish moneylenders and pawn-brokers, who did not come under the jurisdiction of the church and were tolerated in their moneylending operations. Later Christian traders, notably the Lombards and the Caorsini, engaged to an increasing extent in the banking business; and although they were generally condemned as usurers, they came in time to enjoy the privileges of the princes and even of the church. Under the impact of economic necessity the church authorities themselves began to reinterpret the all comprehensive concept of usury in favor of a more liberal policy toward financial transactions. Thus while it denied to the creditor the right to charge a price for his loans, the church permitted the collection of a fine in case the debtor did not return the principal at the time specified in the loan agreement. There developed the practice of inserting a penal clause (poena conventionalis) into the loan agreements whereby a nominal, brief, gratuitous loan period was set; after its expiration the debtor automatically was liable for the payment of the fine in addition to the repayment of the principal. But even in the absence of a penal clause the creditor was allowed, by invoking the principle damnum emergens, to recover for any damages he might have suffered as a result of the loan. It was but one step further to the application of the principle of lucrum cessans, whereby the lender had a right to idemnity if he could prove that he had to forego a potential profit as a result of the loan; this proof was rendered easier with the growth of investment opportunities, and later it was waived for merchants and manufacturers. . . .

Under the impact of capitalistic development the original conceptions of the church fathers receded into the background. By the eighteenth century the status of moneylending came to resemble that prevailing in ancient Rome; the question was no longer whether it was permissible to charge a price for capital but at what rate the charge became excessive and therefor usurious. Most states attempted to fix maximum rates of interest. But soon even such restrictions drew the attack of the advocates of the newly emerging doctrine of freedom of enterprise. . . . Of greatest significance was the demand for complete freedom put forward by Jeremy Bentham in his famous Defence of Usury (London 1787). In the name of personal liberty Bentham demanded the same degree of freedom for money trade as that prevailing in commodity trade. Taking as his point of departure the familiar argument that every rational person knows best how to defend his interests and that there is therefore no reason for government interference, he maintained that the state which aims to aid the poor by restricting the interest rate excludes them at the same time from the sources of credit. Similarly impressive was the common contention that a restriction of the rate of interest necessarily results in a shortage of capital and consequently in an increase in the cost of credit. . . .

The advances of economic liberalism wiped the anti-usury laws from the statute books of most countries. England removed its ban on usury in 1854, Holland in 1857, Belgium in 1865 and Prussia and the North German Federation in 1867. In the United States the overwhelming majority of the states still retain their anti-usury laws, but these have little effect on the actual movement of interest rates. The sweeping repeal of the anti-usury laws did, however, produce in most countries a flood of credit abuses, sufficient to warrant the prompt reintroduction of protective measures. In the latter part of the nineteenth century Germany, Austria and other countries and England in 1900 found it necessary to enact measures covering all cases in which the moneylender took undue advantage of the inexperience or carelessness of the borrower, particularly when the latter was led to accept excessive financial changes through fraud or misrepresentation on the part of the former. In some countries and in various states of the United States the whole field of small loans, most of which are in the nature of consumption loans, was placed under the special protection of the law to prevent financial exploitation of the small and as a rule economically weak borrower. . . .

NOTE

For a brief summary of various other rationales supporting anti-usury laws, including arguments by Adam Smith and John Maynard Keynes, see Benfield, Money, Mortgages, and Migraine — The Usury Headache, 19 Case W. Res. L. Rev. 819, 831-833 (1968).

(2) *Selected Usury Issues*

(a) When Is a Transaction "Usurious"?

Moran v. Kenai Towing and Salvage, Inc.
523 P.2d 1237 (Alaska 1974)

CONNOR, Justice. This appeal presents a dispute over the disposition of the proceeds from an insurance policy following a fire loss.

In 1968 Kenai Towing and Salvage, Inc., was the owner of certain improved real property in the vicinity of Kenai, Alaska. On the property was a building which had been erected by Kenai Towing & Salvage, Inc., at its own expense. The company was in financial difficulty. It approached Jack Moran for a loan. The parties agreed that as security for the loan Kenai would convey title to the real property to Moran, and Moran would then lease the property to Kenai with an option to purchase. This arrangement would enable Kenai to reobtain the property when the lease obligations had been fulfilled. The initial loan occurred in September of 1968. Including closing costs, it was in the amount of $11,586.38. Kenai executed a warranty deed conveying title to Moran. Moran executed a lease with an option to purchase in favor of Kenai; the monthly payments were to be $300, with each payment fully credited to the purchase price. The lease was dated September 4, 1968; the warranty deed was dated September 20, 1968.

Thereafter more money was sought by Kenai, and Moran lent an additional $7,515.88. The parties terminated the earlier lease with option and entered into a new lease with a purchase option dated October 24, 1968. This "lease with option" bound Kenai unconditionally to pay $500 a month for five years, commencing November 1, 1968. It also bound Moran unconditionally to convey title to Kenai upon receipt of the last lease payment. By August 11, 1969, the total paid under both leases was $5,100.

On July 13, 1969, a fire totally destroyed the building located on the real property.

Under the October 24, 1968, lease Kenai was to maintain fire insurance on the building at its own expense, in an amount of at least $60,000. The precise language of this clause in the lease was: "During the term of this lease, lessees shall, at their own expense, maintain fire insurance covering the interest of the lessor in the demised premises in an amount not less than Sixty Thousand Dollars ($60,000.00)." Kenai was unable to pay for the insurance. It was agreed that Moran would do so, and that Kenai would reimburse Moran therefor. The total annual premiums for the first year were $2,029.

The parties had intended the sale with lease-back transaction to be a method of securing repayment of the $19,767.26 lent by Moran to Kenai. Moran himself believed the property to be worth between $75,000 and $100,000. He had evinced no interest in buying the property as a permanent owner, and no negotiations had taken place between the parties as to an absolute sale of the property.

After the fire a dispute arose between the parties over the disposition of the insurance proceeds. Moran claimed entitlement to the entire amount of the insurance proceeds. Kenai took the position that Moran was entitled to the proceeds in an amount not exceeding the amount loaned, plus fire insurance premiums paid, less a reduction because of usury.

Kenai brought a declaratory judgment action against Moran. The fire insurers paid $52,500 into the registry of the court as the agreed amount of insurance payable on the loss. The case was tried by the court, and ultimately a judgment was entered which provided that from the fire insurance proceeds Moran should be paid $19,767.26, with interest at 8 percent plus the insurance premiums paid by him, less payments received, and that Kenai should be paid the balance of the proceeds, $33,471.67. Kenai was also awarded costs and an attorney's fee.

Moran appeals from the judgment, claiming various errors committed by the superior court. Kenai cross-appeals, claiming that the court erred in failing to find that the loan from Moran was usurious. . . .

We must first observe that the "lease with purchase option" in this case is really a device to secure repayment of a debt. It is no different functionally than a mortgage or contract for the sale of land. Hervey v. Rhode Island Locomotive Works, 93 U.S. 664, 23 L. Ed. 1003 (1877); McKeeman v. Commercial Credit Equipment Corp., 320 F. Supp. 938 (D. Neb. 1970); American Can Co. v. White, 130 Ark. 381, 197 S.W. 695 (Ark. 1917). . . .

The loan in this case was in the amount of $19,767.26. It was to be repaid in monthly installments of $500, beginning November 1, 1968, and continuing for five years. The amount to be paid by Kenai to Moran was, therefore, $30,000, over a five year period. Even if one were to assume no reduction of principal until the end of five years, the rate of interest is more than 10 percent. A simple interest rate, with a constant reduction of principal, would be considerably greater.

The maximum interest rate which could be charged lawfully on this type of loan in 1968 was 8 percent. On its face this loan was usurious.

In Metcalf v. Bartrand, 491 P.2d 747, 750 (Alaska 1971), we adopted the rule of Wilcox v. Moore, 354 Mich. 499, 93 N.W.2d 288 (1958). The court in *Wilcox* stated that in determining whether a transaction is usurious, a court must look to the real nature of the transaction, in order to avoid "the betrayal of justice by the cloak of words, the contrivances of form, or the paper tigers of the crafty." Id. at n.1, 291. Intent to violate the usury law will be presumed when the loan agreement unequivocally calls for an impermissible rate of return on the indebtedness. Metcalf v. Bartrand, supra, 491 P.2d at 750-751.

That the transaction here was cast in terms of a "lease with option to purchase" does not save it from the application of the usury statute. Lease-purchase contracts or contracts for the sale of land are often used as devices to disguise usurious loans. When this is the case, courts unhesitatingly pierce through the transaction to determine whether, in substance, a usurious loan was negotiated. Metcalf v. Bartrand, supra at 750-751; McKeeman v. Commercial Credit Equipment Corp., 320 F. Supp. 938 (D. Neb. 1970); Burr v. Capital Reserve Corp., 71 Cal. 2d 983, 80 Cal. Rptr. 345, 458 P.2d 185 (1969).

We hold, therefore, that the superior court's finding was clearly erroneous. Under the applicable statutory provision, usury results in a forfeiture of the entire interest on the debt. It follows that the judgment in this case must be modified. The superior court allowed Moran $2,102.60 as interest on the loans, computed at 8 percent. This amount must instead be deducted from the sum that Moran will receive under the judgment, and Kenai's share of the recovery should be increased accordingly.

We affirm the judgment, as modified. We remand for the entry of a modified judgment.

Affirmed in part, reversed in part.

The Credit Quartet

NOTES AND QUESTIONS

1. The successful usury defense requires that three elements be shown: (1) the transaction was in fact a "loan or forbearance"; (2) the debtor was in fact *required* to pay excessive "interest"; and (3) the lender had "wrongful intent," which most courts view as anything more than innocent mistake.

"Loan" transactions are usually quite straightforward. The borrower simply issues his note or bond to evidence the obligation. Rarely does the note reveal an interest rate that blatantly violates the usury limit except where the lender may wrongly believe that one of the usury exceptions applies, page 166 infra. The *Moran* case typifies the *disguised* loan where the parties, at the "lender's" instance, dress up the transaction to conceal its real nature. Some other disguises are described in Benfield, Money, Mortgages, and Migraine — The Usury Headache, 19 Case W. Res. L. Rev. 819, 866-873 (1968). These include "selling" part of the borrower's business to the lender for a nominal price, or "selling" real estate or other property to the lender at one price (the moneys needed) and agreeing unconditionally to repurchase the asset at a second, higher price, where the difference exceeds the allowable interest rates for the interval between sale and purchase.

"Forbearance" occurs when, at the loan's maturity, the lender agrees not to press collection of the debt until some later date. If the lender exacts a charge for agreeing to forbear, it will be treated as loan interest.

2. The borrower may bear many expenses in connection with a loan, but only expenses that are "interest" or interest-like are subject to the usury defense. Loan expenses include charges for credit reports, appraisals, title examinations, title insurance, mortgage preparation, surveys, inspections, tax and insurance escrows, recording, bank attorneys, loan "origination," and mortgage brokers. In making the interest calculation, should a court add any of these expenses to the contract rate? Cf. B. F. Saul Co. v. West End Park North, Inc., 250 Md. 707, 246 A.2d 591 (1968); Silverstein v. Wakefield, 112 So. 2d 406 (Fla. Dist. Ct. App. 1959).

3. The facts in D & H Development Co. v. Sherwood & Roberts, 93 Idaho 200, 457 P.2d 439 (1969), were these: Plaintiff needed $250,000 to buy a parcel of land for a shopping center development. The defendant agreed to make a land purchase loan and also to provide construction and permanent financing at the plaintiff's option. The land purchase loan was written for $306,000 and bore 8 percent interest (within the usury limit). However, before the plaintiff received the loan proceeds, $56,250 was deducted as a "commitment fee" for the defendant's agreement to make the several loans. After purchasing the land, plaintiff obtained construction and permanent financing on better terms from another source and then sued to recover treble "interest," which was the remedy under Idaho

law for one who has paid a usurious rate. The trial court awarded judgment for $224,118.85. On appeal, judgment was reversed and summary judgment was granted to the defendant. The court reasoned that the "commitment fee" was not interest since it covered not the use of the moneys borrowed but the privilege later of borrowing other moneys. Note, however, that the plaintiff testified that the commitment for the construction and permanent financing was forced upon him if he wanted the land purchase loan.

4. The facts in Phalen Park State Bank v. Reeves, 312 Minn. 194, 251 N.W.2d 135 (1977), were these: Borrowers obtained a $34,000 mortgage secured loan. However, the lender retained more than $11,000 in an escrow account to cover outstanding taxes and an attorney's lien against the property. In remanding for further hearings, the sharply divided appellate court held that the trial judge must consider whether, on these facts, the loan was usurious. How should the trial judge rule? One commentator recommends that all escrows be placed in the hands of a third party named by the borrower. 7 Real Est. L. Rep. 7-8 (June 1977). A practicable suggestion? A necessary suggestion?

Addition of 2% discount and taking of $900,000 in stock adds to int. charged and makes 14% loan usurious

Continental Mortgage Investors v. Sailboat Key, Inc.

354 So. 2d 67 (Fla. Dist. Ct. App. 1977)

PER CURIAM. The mortgagee, Continental Mortgage Investors, appeals an adverse judgment of $1,321,924.06 plus costs in favor of the mortgagor, Sailboat Key, Inc., in this foreclosure action based upon a determination that a loan agreement was usurious.

Burton Goldberg, president of Sailboat Key, Inc., entered into negotiations on behalf of Sailboat Key with Continental Advisors for financing the acquisition and development of an island in Biscayne Bay known as Fair Isle. Continental Advisors, which is based in Coral Gables, is the advisor of appellant, Continental Mortgage Investors (hereinafter referred to as CMI), a Massachusetts business trust with offices in Boston. On December 30, 1969 CMI sent a loan commitment letter to Sailboat Key setting out the following terms: (1) a 24-month loan in the principal amount of $3,350,000 bearing interest at 14% per annum; (2) a 2% discount on the face amount of the loan to be taken by CMI (i.e., $67,000); (3) as additional consideration, receipt by CMI of 50% of the stock of the borrower, Sailboat Key, Inc.; (4) the right of first refusal on construction loans; (5) designation of the laws of Massachusetts as governing; (6) a 1% commitment fee to be paid by borrower upon acceptance of the commitment; however, upon closing the loan within 30 days of the date thereof, the 1% fee would be credited against the discount of the loan. Burton Goldberg paid CMI the commitment fee of $33,500 on behalf of Sailboat Key. All the necessary documents were prepared by CMI's advisor in Florida, and on January 22, 1970, in the Boston offices of CMI, the parties executed these documents which included a loan agreement, a note secured by a first mortgage, personal guarantees of Burton Goldberg and his wife and stock pledge agreements. The 1% commitment fee was credited against the discount of the loan, and CMI began disbursing the funds to Sailboat Key. In August 1971 the loan was in default for Sailboat Key's failure to make the interest payments on the due dates and the parties reached the following settlement agreement: (1) CMI to advance an additional $400,000 for which Sailboat Key would execute a note; (2) CMI to sell all of its Sailboat Key stock to Burton Goldberg for $10,000; and (3) CMI to release its right of first refusal on all construction financing for the sum of $740,000 ($190,000 payable on or before November 30, 1971 and the remainder due on November 1, 1976). In accordance with the above terms, on October 22, 1971 the parties executed a modification of loan agreement. Sailboat Key then executed a $400,000 note and $740,000 note (which bore no interest) secured by mortgages in favor of CMI which further agreed to subordinate $550,000 of the $740,000 indebtedness in favor of an institutional lender providing $6,000,000 in financing. Thereafter, Sailboat Key borrowed $6,000,000 from Fidelity Mortgage Investors to refinance its land development loan, and on November 5, 1971 paid CMI all the funds advanced by it totaling $2,691,412.17 and the $190,000 due under the terms of the $740,000 note.

Subsequently, Fidelity Mortgage Investors and others filed a mortgage foreclosure action naming as defendants, among others, CMI and Sailboat Key. CMI as holder of a subordinated mortgage in the amount of $740,000 filed a cross-claim against Sailboat Key which answered and raised the defense of usury. Sailboat Key also cross-claimed against CMI for return of the principal amount paid and double the amount of interest exacted on the ground that CMI had received interest at a rate in excess of 25%. CMI answered the cross-claim and pled as defenses: (1) that Massachusetts law is applicable and under the laws of Massachusetts, the loan is not usurious; (2) that the 50% stock of Sailboat Key it received cannot be considered interest because the value thereof depended upon the success of the venture within the meaning of Section 687.03, Florida Statutes (1975); . . . Upon motion therefor, the cross-claims of CMI and Sailboat Key were severed from the main action. Sydney Lefcourt, certified public accountant, was appointed special master to make findings of fact with regard to the interest computations. CMI then voluntarily dismissed its cross-claim to foreclose the mortgage securing the $740,000 note. The special master in his report determined that the interest on the actual principal amount loaned exceeded 15% without considering the issue of whether the receipt of the 50% equity interest in Sailboat Key by CMI represented additional interest. CMI filed exceptions to the report and a hearing was held thereon and on Sailboat Key's cross-claim. After hearing the testimony presented, the trial judge concluded that (1) Florida law and not Massachusetts law was applicable because the only purpose in selecting Massachusetts law was to evade Florida's usury laws; (2) a 2% or $67,000 discount was taken and CMI's bookkeeping records so indicated; . . . (4) the stock in Sailboat Key which CMI received as additional consideration was valued at $987,500 when CMI took it and is considered as interest; . . . (6) in fact, CMI forced Sailboat Key to repurchase the stock from CMI (the 50% equity interest in the project) for $750,000; and (7) the $10,000 received for the stock, and the $190,000 payment on the $740,000 note were additional interest on the loan. The trial judge concluded that the 2% discount, the $10,000 cash payment and the $740,000 note are additional interest which resulted in an interest rate in excess of 25%. He then determined that the proper penalty is twice the amount of interest actually exacted and entered judgment for $1,321,924.06 plus costs in favor of Sailboat Key and further held that CMI could not recover the $550,000 balance on the $740,000 note.

A threshold question raised in this appeal is whether the laws of Massachusetts as appellant contends, or the laws of Florida as appellee argues is applicable to the instant transaction. . . . [The choice of laws issue is considered at page 161 infra. — EDS.]

CMI contends that the charge by the lender and the payment by the borrower of a 1% commitment fee is not an interest payment and cannot be included as interest in the computation to determine the rate of interest charged by the lender.

CMI argues that the trial judge erred in finding that a 2% as opposed to a 1% discount was charged and collected because the 1% commitment fee was credited against the discount as provided in the commitment letter of December 30, 1969 which reads in pertinent part:

> 14. **Commitment Fee:**
> A commitment fee of 1% of the loan amount shall be paid by the Borrower upon accepting this commitment, along with an executed copy of this letter. If within 30 days from the date of this letter the loan is closed in accordance with the terms and conditions as set forth herein, the above fee shall be credited against the discount of the loan. If, through no fault of the Lender, the loan is not closed in accordance with this letter, the fee shall be deemed fully earned by Continental Mortgage Investors.

While we agree with appellant that a commitment fee is not a charge for the use of money and cannot be categorized as interest, the events of the instant case demonstrate that, in fact, no commitment fee ultimately was charged. Although what was initially termed a commitment fee was paid by the borrower, the loan was closed within 30 days. Accordingly, CMI credited the fee to the 2% loan discount and, in effect, waived the commitment fee. The bookkeeping records of CMI also reflect a discount of 2%.

Appellant next urges as error, including in the computation of the interest its receipt of an equity position in the project of the borrower.

Pursuant to the terms of the loan agreement, CMI received 50% of the outstanding capital stock of Sailboat Key, Inc. Based upon the uncontested testimony, the judge found that at the time the stock was issued to CMI the parties agreed that the total value of all the Sailboat Key stock was $1,975,000 and, therefore, the value of CMI's 50% equity was $987,500. CMI basically contends that the value of the equity in the project which it received (a so-called "equity kicker") substantially depended upon the success of the venture and should have been excluded from the calculation of interest as provided in Section 687.03(4), Florida Statutes (1974):

> (4) If a loan exceeds $500,000 then, for the purposes of this chapter, interest on that loan shall not include the value of property charged, reserved, or taken as an advance or forbearance, the value of which substantially depends on the success of the venture in which are used the proceeds of that loan. Stock options and interest in profits, receipts, or residual values are examples of the type of property the value of which would be excluded from calculation of interest under the preceding sentence.

We remain unconvinced that the trial judge erred. First, the statute gives as examples of "equity kickers" stock options and interest in profits, etc., not shares of stock. Second, the value of the property must substantially depend upon the success of the venture. Here, the uncontroverted evidence showed the stock received by CMI was worth $987,500 at that time and this value did not depend upon the success of the venture. . . .

Affirmed.

NOTES AND QUESTIONS

1. In their concern with inflation, lenders have sought an even sturdier hedge against the declining dollar than record-breaking interest rates. Lenders frequently insist upon a profit-sharing set-up, which may take one of several forms. An insurance company counsel describes these sharing arrangements in Hershman, Usury and "New Look" in Real Estate Financing, 4 Real Prop. Prob. & Tr. J. 315 (1969). Consider as to each arrangement its vulnerability to the claim of usury:

    a. Lender's participation in income as contingent interest: The borrower agrees to pay to the lender a specified percentage of his income from the mortgaged property as well as the fixed interest on the loan. The percentage base is variously defined (e.g., gross income, gross receipts, net income, etc.). Cf. Jameson v. Warren, 91 Cal. App. 590, 267 P.372 (1928); Brown v. Cardoza, 67 Cal. App. 2d 187, 153 P.2d 767 (1944) (usury can result where fixed rate at or near the ceiling and the contingent fee places return substantially above the ceiling); contra Lyons v. National Savings Bank, 113 N.Y.S.2d 695 (Sup. Ct. 1952).

b. Lender's participation in proceeds of refinancing or resale: The borrower agrees that if he sells the property or refinances the mortgage above the existing balance, the lender will receive a percentage of the sales price or excess mortgage proceeds. Cf. Thomassen v. Carr, 250 Cal. App. 2d 341, 58 Cal. Rptr. 297 (1967) (usury did not result where lender received 30 percent of the developers' sales profit "in lieu of" interest).

c. Lender's participation by receipt of ownership interest: The lender receives an *ownership* share in the venture for which he pays little or nothing. Compare Mission Hill Development Corp. v. Western Small Business Investment Co., 260 Cal. App. 2d 923, 67 Cal. Rptr. 505 (1968) (parties intended to evade usury laws) with Bokser v. Lewis, 383 Pa. 507, 119 A.2d 67 (1956) (no intent found).

d. The sale and leaseback: The developer sells the real estate (sometimes the land and building, sometimes the land alone) to the lender at fair market value; the lender then leases the property back to the developer for a lengthy term. Extensive treatment of the sale and leaseback appears at Chapter Seven, infra.

The author also describes two nonsharing devices that lenders employ to enhance their interest yield.

a. The sale-buyback: The borrower sells the real estate to the lender who immediately resells the property at the *same price* to the developer on a long-term installment contract. By juggling the installment amounts and the length of the contract, the lender can realize an "interest" return greater than the return that he charged on a straight mortgage deal. (Concealment is the secret!)

To illustrate the sale-buyback: The contract price, $100,000, is payable at $8500 yearly for 35 years and 7 months. If the lender were to make a $100,000 mortgage loan bearing 7.25 percent interest, an annual payment of $8500 would self-amortize the loan in 26 years and 7 months. The additional nine years of contract payments raises the lender's average yield well above 7.25 percent.

Discussion of the long term installment contract appears at page 197 infra.

How does the "sale-buyback" differ, if at all, from the device which the court pierced in the *Moran* case?

b. The "wrap-around" mortgage: This usually involves the refinancing of an existing mortgage that either cannot be readily prepaid or enjoys so favorable an interest rate as to make prepayment unwise. We defer description and analysis of the wrap-around mortgage until page 219 infra.

2. *How to compute the interest rate:* Ordinarily, the computation of the basic interest rate involves a routine calculation. Where the lender collects "extras," however, the calculation becomes more difficult and may in-

volve vital policy choices. To take a simple illustration: The lender charges at the outset a $500 "origination fee" on a $10,000, 2-year loan bearing 6 percent interest: Is the first year's yield 11 percent (and possibly usurious)? Looking at this and similar transactions, the court would probably prorate the fee, treating it as interest earned over the entire loan period; this would result in an average yield of 8.5 percent yearly. French v. Mortgage Guaranty Co., 16 Cal. 2d 26, 104 P.2d 655 (1940); Home Savings and Loan Assn. v. Bates, 76 N.M. 660, 417 P.2d 798 (1968). The result would be unchanged even if the borrower prepaid the loan after one year. Why is that? Cf. French v. Mortgage Guaranty Co., supra; B. F. Saul Co. v. West End Park North, Inc., 250 Md. 707, 246 A.2d 591 (1968).

Where the interest charge is partly tied to a profit-sharing arrangement, should courts vary their usual practice of viewing the entire loan period? To illustrate the problem: On a $100,000, 10-year loan, the borrower agrees to pay annually 5 percent interest and 10 percent of his net profits; under this sharing arrangement, the bank receives $6000 ($5000 + $1000) in year one, and $13,000 ($5000 + $8000) in year two. The borrower then claims usury. If the court treats the profit-sharing arrangement as an interest equivalent, how should the interest rate be measured: year two alone; the average for years one and two; no measurement until the 10-year loan period ends?

(b) Choice of Laws

[Handwritten notes: No strong public policy against usury. Parties can specify in K that other state's law which allows int. rate applies to transaction. Any state's law can apply as long as there exists sufficient nexus to that state]

Continental Mortgage Investors v. Sailboat Key, Inc.
395 So. 2d 507 (Fla. 1981)

SUNDBERG, Chief Justice. This petition for writ of certiorari arises from a money judgment awarded to Sailboat Key, Inc., a Florida borrower. The award was based on a claim that an interstate loan made by Continental Mortgage Investors, a Massachusetts business trust, violated Florida usury laws. Chapter 687, Fla. Stat. (1975). Though a myriad of issues was presented by both sides, we find the conflict of laws issue to be dispositive. The question presented is whether the courts of this state will recognize a choice of law provision designating foreign law in an interstate loan contract which calls for interest prohibited as usury under Florida law but supportable under the chosen foreign law. We conclude that in an interstate commercial loan transaction with which several states have contacts and in which usury is implicated, Florida courts will recognize a choice of law provision provided by the parties so long as the jurisdiction chosen in the contract has a normal relationship with the transaction. Under the circumstances of this case, we hold that Continental Mortgage Investors, a real estate investment trust organized under the laws of Massachusetts with its only office in Massachusetts where it carries on its business, has a sufficient nexus with Massachusetts to support a choice of law provision in favor of that state's law.

. . . Based upon the special master's findings and after hearing testimony, the trial court, applying Florida law, found the entire loan agreement to be usurious and assessed a penalty of twice the interest charged, plus costs. The District Court of Appeal, Third District, affirmed the award, upholding the application of Florida law on the basis of public policy and a finding by the trial court that the parties' choice of Massachusetts law was made in bad faith and was an effort to avoid Florida usury laws. Continental Mortgage Investors v. Sailboat Key, Inc., 354 So. 2d 67 (Fla. 3d DCA 1977).

II. Conflict of Laws: Usury

A. Public Policy

As with most shibboleths, the invocation of strong public policy to avoid application of another state's law is unwarranted in this case. Although a few jurisdictions do attach such a public policy to their usury laws, it is generally held that usury laws are not so distinctive a part of a forum's public policy that a court, for public policy reasons, will not look to another jurisdiction's law which is sufficiently connected with a contract and will uphold the contract. See Ury v. Jewelers Acceptance Corp., 227 Cal. App. 2d 11, 38 Cal. Rptr. 376 (1st Dist. 1964); Santoro v. Osman, 149 Conn. 9, 174 A.2d 800 (1961); Big Four Mills, Ltd. v. Commercial Credit Co., 307 Ky. 612, 211 S.W.2d 831 (1948); Exchange Bank & Trust Co. v. Tamerius, 200 Neb. 807, 265 N.W.2d 847 (1978); 45 Am. Jur. 2d, Interest and Usury §19 (1969). The few courts that do rely on a public policy exception in a usury-choice of law situation invariably are dealing with the individual, and often consumer, borrower. See, e.g., Lyles v. Union Planters National Bank, 239 Ark. 738, 393 S.W.2d 867 (1965).[4] We do not think the mere fact that there exists in Florida a usury statute which prohibits certain interest rates establishes a strong public policy against such conduct in this state where interstate loans are concerned.

The usury statute itself, fraught as it is with exceptions, belies the imputation of a strong public policy. See §687.031, Fla. Stat. (1975). In 1975 The Florida Consumer Finance Act allowed interest on small loans as high as 30% per annum, in contrast to the general usury ceiling of 10% per annum. §516.031, Fla. Stat. (1975). The Savings Association Act made usury limits simply inapplicable to building and loan associations. §§665.395, 687.031, Fla. Stat. (1975). Under the Banking Code, banks could charge up to 18% per annum on certain loans. §659.181, Fla. Stat.

---

4. See also Comment, Usury in the Conflict of Laws: The Doctrine of Lex Debitoris, 55 Cal. L. Rev. 123, 178 (1967).

(1975). Florida has long recognized the general exception to usury laws of the time-price doctrine. See Davidson v. Davis, 59 Fla. 476, 52 So. 139 (1910). The usury law does not apply to the sale of bonds, or mortgages on those bonds, section 687.03(1), Florida Statutes (1975), or to the transfers of negotiable paper in certain cases, section 687.04, Florida Statutes (1975).

The legislature recently raised the maximum interest rates allowable under the usury laws, demonstrating that this public policy is at very least relatively flexible in a confrontation with commercial reality. See Ch. 79-274 §13, Laws of Florida. Nor do we consider usury protections fundamental to a legal system. The defense of usury is a creature entirely of statutory regulation, and is not founded upon any common-law right, either legal or equitable. Matlack Properties, Inc. v. Citizen & Southern National Bank, 120 Fla. 77, 162 So. 148 (1935). Finally, we note the limited effect of the usury laws upon a contract. "[T]he usury statutes in this jurisdiction do not have the effect of *invalidating* contracts for [usurious] interest . . . but only accord to the obligor the personal privilege of setting up . . . affirmative defenses of usury in respect to such contracts." Yaffee v. International Co., 80 So. 2d 910, 912 (Fla. 1955).

The cases cited by the district court are not strong support for its invocation of public policy. Bond v. Koscot Interplanetary, Inc., 246 So. 2d 631 (Fla. 4th DCA 1971), cert. denied, 283 So. 2d 866 (Fla. 1973), merely stands for the truism that an agreement against public policy is unenforceable, but does not delineate public policy in terms of usury. Davis v. Ebsco Industries, Inc., 150 So. 2d 460 (Fla. 3d DCA 1963) and C & D Farms, Inc. v. Cerniglia, 189 So. 2d 384 (Fla. 3d DCA 1966), are inapposite since they deal with covenants-not-to-compete, and do not help us understand the strength of the very different policies underlying the usury laws.

Finding no real support in our case law for the use of the public policy exception under these circumstances, and in view of the pervasive exceptions to the usury laws and the actual operation of these laws, we are unable, particularly in the commercial setting of this case, to glean any overriding public policy against usury qua usury in a choice of law situation.

B. CONFLICT OF LAWS RULE

The courts of this state have never directly confronted conflict of laws in a usury setting when another state's law chosen by the parties will uphold the agreement. A general rule for choice of laws in a contracts situation might be derived from Thomson v. Kyle, 39 Fla. 582, 23 So. 12 (1897), which followed the traditional place of execution and place of performance. We have applied this rule in contractual choice of laws situations to which Florida could probably apply its usury penalties, and the parties did not indicate a controlling law. Goodman v. Olsen, 305 So. 2d 753 (Fla. 1974), cert. denied, 423 U.S. 839, 96 S. Ct. 68, 46 L. Ed. 2d 58 (1975) (applying New York law to find no usury). But such a test is today of little practical value since these contacts are so easily manipulated in our mobile society.

Courts in almost every jurisdiction recognize that a usury claim presents a distinct choice of laws question. The rule that the overwhelming majority follows may be stated as follows:

> [W]ith respect to the question of usury, it may be stated as a well-established rule that a provision in a contract for the payment of interest will be held valid in most states if it is permitted by the law of the place of contracting, the place of performance, or any other place with which the contract has any substantial connection.

Fahs v. Martin, 224 F.2d 387, 397 (5th Cir. 1955). This "traditional" or "federal" rule is derived directly from Seeman v. Philadelphia Warehouse Co., 274 U.S. 403, 47 S. Ct. 626, 71 L. Ed. 1123 (1927), in which a Pennsylvania corporation made a loan to a New York borrower who sought protection of New York usury laws. The Supreme Court concluded that the parties could contract for a higher rate of interest allowed by either place of performance, place of execution, or a place with a vital and natural connection. Id. at 408, 47 S. Ct. at 627. Citing Miller v. Tiffany, 68 U.S. (1 Wall.) 298, 17 L. Ed. 540 (1864), the court explained that the qualification of "good faith" required in that case must not be taken too literally:

> The effect of the qualification is merely to prevent the evasion or avoidance at will of the usury law otherwise applicable, by the parties' entering into the contract or stipulating for its performance at a place which has no *normal relation* to the transaction and to whose law they would not otherwise be subject.

Id. at 408, 47 S. Ct. at 627 (emphasis added). This language makes clear that if a "normal relation" does exist, then good faith is not otherwise necessary to validate the transaction.

There is no disagreement among commentators in the conflict of laws field that this view is generally followed. Professor Beale wrote: "[T]he rule has become well settled in almost all jurisdictions, too well settled to be changed except by statute, that if a contract is made and to be performed in different states, and is usurious by the law of one of these places but not by that of the other, it is governed, according to the presumed intention of the parties, by the law of the place which makes it valid." 2 J. Beale, Conflict of Laws, §347.4 (1935) (footnote to multitudinous citations omitted). See also H. Goodrich & E. Scoles, Conflict of Laws, §111 (4th ed. 1964); G. Stumberg, Conflict of Laws, 237-40 (2d ed. 1951).

As Professor Beale noted, the historical rationale underlying this rule of validation was the presumption that the parties had contracted with reference to the law of the place where the transaction would be valid. See Atlas Subsidiaries, Inc. v. O. & O., Inc., 166 So. 2d 458, 461 (Fla. 1st DCA 1964). This rationale has become modified in modern times because of the frequent inclusion of specific choice of law provisions in commercial, multistate contracts. The focus is no longer on presumed intent, but rather on party expectations since the intentions of the parties are usually expressed. The Restatement (Second) has adopted a modified traditional rule in usury cases and justifies its position through preservation of party expectation.[7]

> A prime objective of both choice of law ... and of contract law is to protect the justified expectations of the parties. Subject only to rare exceptions, the parties will expect on entering a contract that the provisions of the contract will be binding upon them. . . . Usury is a field where this policy of validation is particularly apparent. . . . [T]he courts deem it more important to sustain the validity of a contract, and thus to protect the expectations of the parties, than to apply the usury law of any particular state.

Restatement (Second) of Conflict of Laws, §203, Comment b (1971). Thus, the rule of validation is generally viewed as the best means of furthering the parties' expectations. A final justification for the traditional rule is founded in the idea of commercial comity. Since practically every jurisdiction that has confronted this issue has adopted some form of the traditional rule, this state would be commercially singular if it did not apply favorable law of the state with a normal relation to a contract. Commercial stability in interstate trade depends on predictability and some degree of uniformity among the states in their willingness to honor commercial agreements. . . .

III. APPLICATION OF THE RULE

Here the parties did not stipulate to a jurisdiction having no normal relation to the transaction. On the contrary, several vital and natural elements exist which establish a relationship with Massachusetts. The record shows that Continental's only domicile and office is in Boston. It is uncontested

---

7. Restatement (Second) of Conflict of Laws §203 (1971) reads:

The validity of a contract will be sustained against the charge of usury if it provides for a rate of interest that is permissible in a state to which the contract has a substantial relationship and is not greatly in excess of the rate permitted by the general usury law of the state of the otherwise applicable law under the rule of §188.

A state has a "substantial relationship" if it has a "normal and natural relationship to the contract and the parties." Id. §203, comment c.

that Continental's principal place of business is Boston, and that in Boston the trust approves loans, handles all commercial banking arrangements, carries on relations with underwriters, and there pursues other means of raising funds for interstate loans. The record establishes that Continental was formed in 1961 in Boston, nine years prior to the Sailboat Key loan, for the legitimate business reasons of seeking special federal tax treatment as a real estate investment trust, utilizing the established and predictable business trust laws of Massachusetts. Massachusetts was the residence of the founding majority of trustees, and was the residence with the greatest number of trustees when the loan was made. In addition to the domicile-place of business contacts, which we consider most significant, the loan agreement was executed in Massachusetts, the loan was made payable in that state, and the funds were originally disbursed from that state.

. . . The factually supported contacts Continental has with Massachusetts, particularly in its domicile and place of business, establish that it has a vital, natural, and normal relationship with that state, and therefore, in this usury case, the laws of Massachusetts should apply as contractually agreed by the parties. Although it is undisputed by the parties that applicable Massachusetts law does not provide usury penalties awarded to the borrower, we are not totally convinced that Massachusetts would not afford the borrower some relief. There is some possibility that Massachusetts Annotated Laws ch. 271, §49 (1980), a criminal usury statute enacted in 1970, may be applicable. Recent Massachusetts cases, although upholding the loan agreement, have provided borrowers protected by the statute a modicum of relief by limiting interest collection to twenty percent. See Begelfer v. Najarian, — Mass. —, 409 N.E.2d 167 (1980); Beach Associates, Inc. v. Fauser, — Mass. App. —, 401 N.E.2d 858 (1980). Since we were not briefed on Massachusetts law, and the parties did not present detailed arguments at either the trial or initial appellate level, we are unable to resolve this issue. The present usury award to Sailboat Key cannot stand, however, since it was erroneously based on Florida law.

Accordingly, the petition for writ of certiorari is granted. The decision of the District Court of Appeal, Third District, is quashed, and this case is remanded to the district court with instructions to remand to the trial court for determination and application of Massachusetts law, the proceedings not to be inconsistent with our decision.

It is so ordered.

(c) Exempt Transactions

"The usury statute itself, fraught as it is with exceptions, belies the imputation of a strong public policy."

Continental Mortgage Investors v. Sailboat Key, Inc., 395 So. 2d 507, 509 (Fla. 1981)

The Credit Quartet

The realm of usury is fraught not only with exception, but also with paradox. The very word "usurious" strongly connotes an unclean act and, indeed, where usury occurs, the penalties often are stringent and sometimes even criminal. Yet usury law exemptions cover many more loan situations than do the ceilings. Major exemptions include the consumer loan, which may carry rates as high as 3 percent monthly when made by licensed regulated lenders; the credit sale of goods; loans by credit unions and pawnbrokers; and installment or industrial loans derived from the Morris Bank Plan — transactions that control most consumer and business borrowing outside the area of real estate finance.

Three exemptions play a considerable role in the land finance field. The first two, the corporate borrower exemption and the seller-financed transaction, are of long-standing importance. The third, contained in the Financial Institutions Deregulation and Monetary Control Act of 1980, is another key event in the growing federalization of real estate transactions.

(i) The Corporate-borrower Exemption

Feller v. Architects Display Building, Inc.

54 N.J. Super. 205, 148 A.2d 634 (App. Div. 1959)

SCHETTINO, J.A.D. Appeal was taken by the defendants Architects Display Buildings, Inc., a corporation of New Jersey (hereafter referred to as "Architects") and Charles S. Cohan, individually, from a Superior Court, Chancery Division, summary judgment foreclosing two mortgages, one in the amount of $250,000 and the other $50,000. . . .

The trial court pointed out in its oral findings and opinion on April 25, 1958 that:

"The defendant corporation has filed a defense by amended pleadings which seeks to set up in the main three legal defenses: (1) usury; (2) that the transaction was a violation of the Banking Act, and, (3) that there is a violation to the Real Estate Broker's Act."

In support of its amended answer and counterclaim, defendant Architects submitted three affidavits, as follows: (a) affidavit of its president, Charles S. Cohan, dated February 28, 1958; (b) affidavit of Charles S. Cohan, dated March 28, 1958, and (c) affidavit of Samuel D. Lewin, attorney and title searcher, dated March 28, 1958. No other proof was submitted or offered by Architects.

The facts are as follows: Architects had been constructing a building on premises located on Route 22, Mountainside, New Jersey, and had completed about 70% of the work. In order to complete it, it sought mortgage loans from a man named Sturm. He offered to lend to Architects

$250,000 in consideration for advance interest of $11,460 and a "service charge" of $28,540 which would leave a net of $211,000. Architects accepted the offer by a letter dated January 30, 1957 confirming the terms of the agreement. Pursuant to the terms, Architects on February 4, 1957 mortgaged its premises to Sturm for the sum of $250,000, due December 30, 1957. The mortgage secured Architects' promissory note of $250,000 to the order of Sturm. The mortgage provided that "In the event that said note and this mortgage are not paid on the due date the Mortgagor shall pay a service charge at the rate of 1/23 of 1% per day from the date of default to the date of actual payment." The mortgage also provided that "The within mortgage is given to secure advances to be made for the construction of a building on the mortgaged premises and to secure other charges, all in accordance with the terms of a commitment signed by the mortgagee and approved and accepted by the mortgagor; said commitment is dated January 30, 1957." The note incorporated all the terms of the mortgage. Payment of this note was personally guaranteed by Architects' president, Charles S. Cohan. Mr. Cohan, although not a lawyer, had studied for the bar.

On the same day all of Architects' stockholders, consisting of Charles S. Cohan, Florence B. Cohan, his wife, and Ethel Cohan, his sister, executed their consent to the execution of the mortgage and note and also executed a subordination of indebtedness to the loan of $250,000. By letter dated February 4, 1957 Architects also agreed that Sturm could assign to plaintiffs the original loan letter agreement dated January 30, 1957, the note, the mortgage and the assignment of a certain lease affecting the premises. On February 4, 1957 Sturm transferred to plaintiffs the mortgage and note. Architects admitted the receipt of the $210,000 in accordance with the loan agreement and admitted that no part of the $250,000, the interest or charges has been paid.

On April 24, 1957 Architects borrowed an additional $50,000 from plaintiffs. This loan was secured by a mortgage containing provisions to the effect that it was given to secure a series of 11 promissory notes. The mortgage provided that "In the event that any of the notes secured by this mortgage are not paid on the due date said note in default shall bear interest at the rate of 1/23 of 1% per day from the due date to the date of actual payment. . . . Architects admitted receipt of $41,000 of this stated loan of $50,000 pursuant to the terms of the agreement. The series of 11 notes was endorsed by Charles S. Cohan, individually. The first ten of said notes were each in the sum of $2,000, due and payable on the first day of each month starting with July 1, 1957 and ending on April 1, 1958, inclusive, and the eleventh note was in the sum of $30,000 due April 24, 1958. The notes due July 1, 1957 through November 1, 1957, inclusive were paid by Architects. The note due December 1, 1957 was not paid and remained unpaid for more than 15 days. Each note provided that "in the event of the non-payment of any one of said series and such default continues for a period of 15 days, then at the option of the holder of any of the said notes, all or any part of the remaining unpaid notes shall forthwith become due and payable." By reason of the default in the payment of the December 1, 1957 note plaintiffs exercised the right to claim the principal unpaid balance of $40,000 represented by the notes due December 1, 1957 through April 1, 1958, inclusive, and April 24, 1958, were immediately due and payable. Architects admits that the sum of $40,000 has not been paid and that no interest or charges thereon have been paid.

As we view the record, we agree with the trial court that the case was a proper one for summary judgment. . . . N.J.S.A. 31:1-6 provides:

"Corporation not to make defense of usury.

"No corporation shall plead or set up the defense of usury to any action brought against it to recover damages or enforce a remedy on any obligation executed by said corporation."

Our Supreme Court has stated in In re Greenberg,[19] 21 N.J. 213, 220, 121 A.2d 520 (1956), and Gelber v. Kugel's Tavern, 10 N.J. 191, 196, 89 A.2d 654 (1952), that if the corporate form is used to cloak a loan which in fact is intended to be a loan to an individual, the alter ego of the corporation, then this statutory provision will not bar the plea of usury. In *Gelber* the Supreme Court stated that if the corporation to which the loan was ostensibly made was specifically incorporated at the request of the lenders' agent and subsequent to the application for the loan, the defense of usury would apply. The court stated (10 N.J. at page 196, 89 A.2d at page 656):

". . . It is generally recognized . . . that an individual may recover usurious payments on loans made in fact to the individual though in form disguised as loans to a corporation and evidenced by obligations executed by it to hide the fact that the lender has exacted an illegal rate of interest from the real borrower."

The Supreme Court pointed out that on the evidence the jury should have been permitted to determine the reason for the incorporation and if the jury found it was created as a cloak to evade the usury law, then the corporate shell would not benefit the lender.

But in the case before us the undisputed history of Architects does not help defendants at all. Architects was incorporated on May 24, 1956. On May 29, 1956 it acquired title to the premises involved herein. In July 1956 it began to build and by January 30, 1957, according to Mr. Cohan's depositions, "The building was enclosed, with the exception of window-walls. . . . Oh, I would say about seventy percent" of the construction

---

19. In the *Greenberg* case, attorney Greenberg was suspended from the practice of law for one year. In the words of a headnote to the case: "Attorney having knowledge that corporate device was being used because of usury laws and that borrower with little education or knowledge of business matters was wholly unrepresented owed to borrower obligation to explain transaction and to deal with borrower frankly and fairly, or at least to notify borrower that she should have independent legal advice." — EDS.

was completed. We hold that the loans were made to an existing corporation.

Architects through its president contends that the obligations were entered into by Mr. Cohan and Architects as co-makers and therefore the defense of usury should apply as one of the borrowers was an individual who could have the benefit of the defense of usury. Mr. Cohan's depositions dissipate this contention. Mr. Cohan was a guarantor of the corporate obligation and not a co-maker. Mr. Justice Brennan in *Gelber* stated (10 N.J. at page 196, 89 A.2d at page 656):

". . . If, however, the loans are actually made to the corporation direct, usury is not a defense even to the endorsers of the corporate obligations issued for the loans, [citations]."

We hold that the defense of usury is not applicable.

A corollary point is raised with reference to the charge of 1/23 of 1% interest per day after default as being a penalty. As to the first loan, i.e., $250,000, the due date was December 30, 1957. For the period of time from the date of the loan, February 4, 1957 to December 30, 1957, plaintiffs received $11,460 advance interest payments plus the service charge of $28,540 which plaintiffs concede amounts to interest as well by deducting the amount from the face amount of the loan. By the terms of the loan no default could take place until after December 30, 1957. It is the general rule in the case of a corporate borrower that it is not illegal to provide for a higher rate of interest than the legal rate after maturity, but if such rate is unconscionably high it will be unenforceable because it amounts to a penalty. 3 Williston on Contracts, §781, p. 2196; 5 ibid., §1416, p. 3945; 6 ibid., §1969, p. 4803; cf. Restatement, Contracts, §536; cf. Ramsey v. Morrison, 39 N.J.L. 591 (Sup. Ct. 1877); cf. In re Tastyeast, Inc., 126 F.2d 879 (3rd Cir., 1942), certiorari denied Modern Factors Co. v. Tastyeast, Inc., 316 U.S. 696, 62 S. Ct. 1291, 86 L. Ed. 1766 (1942). Here the rate before maturity amounted to about 19% and the rate after maturity is 15.87%. The latter being less it is not unconscionable and so is enforceable.

However, as to the interest payments after default on the $50,000 loan, a different factual situation exists. There, advance interest in the amount of $8,500 was retained by plaintiffs for the period from April 24, 1957 to April 24, 1958. Default took place on December 1, 1957. Plaintiffs urged and the trial court agreed that interest at the default rate of 1/23 of 1% per day ran from December 1, 1957 which was within the period for which interest had been paid. On the basis of $8500, the interest rate on the $50,000 loan is computed to be 17%. Were we to allow an additional 1/23 of 1% per day the defendant would be paying 17% plus 15.87%, totalling 32.87%, on the unpaid $40,000 balance from the accelerated maturity date. This is clearly unconscionable and unenforceable as a penalty. Error was therefore committed in allowing any additional interest on the unpaid balance of that loan for the period from December 1, 1957 through April 24, 1958. The trial court was correct in allowing the 1/23 of 1% rate after the maturity date of April 24, 1958 to the date of judgment, May 9, 1958 and legal rate thereafter. . . .

Modified and remanded for action not inconsistent with this opinion and with costs.

NOTES AND QUESTIONS

1. The corporate borrower exemption has spread to about thirty states. New York was first, in 1850, after a bank had outraged the financial community by successfully pleading the usury law to avoid repayment of a loan that had saved it from permanent insolvency. Dry Dock Bank v. American Life Insurance & Trust Co., 3 N.Y. 344 (1850). In several other states, rate limits for corporate borrowers are above those for noncorporate borrowers.

What is the present justification for treating corporations less protectively? Cf. Benfield, Money, Mortgages, and Migraine—The Usury Headache, 19 Case W. Res. L. Rev. 819, 849 (1968).

2. In New York, the exemption does not apply to a corporation whose principal asset is a one- or two-family dwelling, when the corporation is organized within six months prior to the obtaining of a loan secured by the asset. N.Y. Gen. Obl. Law §5-521 (McKinney 1978). See also Ky. Rev. Stat. Ann. §360.025(2) (1983). Why this exemption within an exemption?

3. In Washington, a corporate borrower may plead the usury defense only when an individual is also liable on the loan. Wash. Rev. Code Ann. §19.52.030 (1978). In short: the immunity of the individual inures to the corporation. This reverses the situation in the main case where the disability of the corporation attaches to the individual. What are the arguments for and against each rationale?

4. An individual borrows at a usurious rate and gives a mortgage to secure the debt. He then transfers the real estate to a corporation, which takes title subject to the mortgage. May the corporation interpose the usury defense in a mortgage foreclosure action? Cf. Kahn v. Sohmer, 12 A.D.2d 659, 212 N.Y.S.2d 85 (1961).

5. For a discussion of the problems that a taxpayer would face if he incorporated to obtain loans that, as an individual, he could not lawfully obtain, see Note, Incorporation to Avoid the Usury Laws, 68 Colum. L. Rev. 1390 (1968); cf. also David F. Bolger, 59 T.C. 760 (1973).

(ii) The Seller-financed Transaction

Mandelino v. Fribourg

23 N.Y.2d 145, 242 N.E.2d 823 (1968)

BERGAN, Judge. Plaintiff, a real estate broker, purchased from defendants a building on Flatbush Avenue, Brooklyn, for $15,500. He paid $1,000 in cash and executed a purchase-money mortgage for $14,500. The purchase-money mortgage in terms required the payment of 7% interest. This was in January, 1964. The statute on usury then in effect (General Business Law, former §§370, 371) prescribed the rate of interest "on the loan or forbearance of any money, goods or things in action" should be 6%. (Cf. General Obligations Law, Consol. Laws c. 24-A, §5-501, as amd. by L. 1968, chs. 349, 944, 1072.)

The action is to declare the mortgage and the accompanying mortgage note executed on the same terms "usurious and void." At Special Term the complaint was dismissed on the ground a purchase-money mortgage, reflecting the agreement of the parties on the price of the land, did not come within the scope of the statutory clause "loan or forbearance" and hence was not usurious. The Appellate Division reversed the Special Term, holding that while the sellers were free to "enlarge the purchase money mortgage obligation" by reason of "the extension of credit thereon" they could not "exact interest in excess of the lawful rate prescribed in the statute."

This ruling means that the parties could have fixed mortgage principal of any amount agreeable to themselves but, having fixed it, could not in terms agree to interest at more than 6%. The Special Term's ruling meant that interest and principal were integral parts of the purchase price on the sale of land and that the mortgage in these circumstances was not a "loan" within the terms of the statute. It was not, of course, a "forbearance" in any event.

The basic question, then, is whether a purchase-money mortgage is to be regarded in law as a loan. A fairly well definable line of decisional law suggests it is not a loan. There never seems to have been a case in this court, however, where, as part of the expression of a sale of property made and entirely performable by a noncorporate individual within the State, a rate of interest has been stated baldly and explicitly on the face of the paper in excess of the statutory rate.

The cases that have usually arisen are those in which the excess interest was absorbed, in one way or another, in the total obligation; and occasionally an interest rate authorized in another State has played some part. In rigidly logical terms, whether the interest reflects itself in the total obligation or in an expressed percentage seems indistinguishable in principle. The statute prohibits the proscribed rate "directly or indirectly" (General Business Law, former §371; General Obligations Law, §5-501, subd. 2).

If it be held that the weight of authority of the decided cases in New York has in the past been not to treat a true purchase-money mortgage as a loan, the further question for the court is whether, as a matter of policy, this apparent exception to the interdiction of the usury statute should be continued in contemporary law.

It cannot be doubted that the question is of importance to the community in the purchase and sale of real property and, indeed, of sales of all kinds of property, and there is much to be said for the stability and certainty in commercial transactions that would result if the laws regulating interest be made to apply universally to all transactions according to the terms of the recently revised statute.

But if stare decisis remains a guiding principle and the logic of past cases is to be honored, it is difficult, indeed, to escape holding that the purchase-money mortgage in this present case is not a "loan" within the terms of the usury statute.

It has been noted that there seems no case in this court in which interest was stated baldly in the instrument above the statutory rate; but Weaver Hardware Co. v. Solomovitz (235 N.Y. 321, 139 N.E. 353) comes very close to that. One of four notes there considered is pertinent to the present problem. It was found, and this court stated explicitly by Hiscock, Ch. J., that there was "an agreement . . . for the payment of interest . . . in excess of the legal rate" (p. 327, 139 N.E. p. 354). Such a finding is the equivalent of a statement on the face of the instruments.

Nevertheless, in the claim by the payee who sold building material for which that note was given reflecting in its amount interest higher than the lawful rate, it was held insofar as it expressed an agreement as to price of material it was not usurious. "The laws against usury pertain to the loan and forbearance of money, and not to the purchase price of building materials," said the Chief Judge (p. 331, 139 N.E. p. 355). Since there was a segregation between other loans which had been made and the sale of goods, it was concluded that "the note under discussion was given solely and simply for the former price. There is no way in which usury could be injected into the note thus given so as to make it void" (p. 331, 139 N.E. p. 356).

From an analysis of cases stemming from the Statute of Anne in 1713, on which most American usury statutes are modeled, Williston reaches the conclusion that where property is sold "the parties may agree that the price, if paid after a certain time, shall be a sum greater by more than legal interest than the price payable at an earlier day" (6 Williston, Contracts [rev. ed.], §1685, p. 4766). This is so, he notes, even though "stated in the form of interest" greater than the legal rate. A leading English case on the usury statute of that country, consistent with Williston's view, is Beete v. Bidgood (7 B. & C. 453, 108 Eng. Rep. 792).

The general American rule is drawn together in the statement: "An owner of property may sell it at such a price and on such terms as he may see fit, and such a sale, if bona fide, is not usurious, but a usurious loan in the form of a sale will not be permitted" (91 C.J.S. Usury §18, subd. a, p. 588). . . .

In Cutler v. Wright (22 N.Y. 472 [1860]), a note had been executed, probably in New York but payable in Florida, for a sale of lands in the latter State. It called for interest at 8% which would have been permissible in

Florida. Judge Davies assumed that even if executed in New York it would be governed by the law of Florida (p. 474); but Judge Selden, concurring, felt that even if made and performable in New York and thus governed by New York law "the defence of usury cannot prevail. . . . To constitute usury, there must be either a present loan or a forbearance in respect to some debt previously existing; in such a case as this, there is neither," since he had noted earlier that the note "was not given for a loan of money or of goods, or for a preexisting debt of any kind, but upon a sale of lands" (p. 482). . . .

This principle seems to have been regularly followed at the Appellate Division. "There is no usury in the normal purchase money mortgage transaction where a seller demands a higher price because the consideration is not all in cash" (Butts v. Samuel, 5 A.D.2d 1008, 174 N.Y.S.2d 325 [2d Dept.]). To the same effect and in almost the same language see Bennis v. Thomas (14 A.D.2d 895, 221 N.Y.S.2d 350 [2d Dept.]). An instrument which appears on its face to be a purchase-money mortgage may in truth be a cloak for an actual loan at excessive interest and in this situation it may be deemed usurious (cf. Del Rubio v. Duchesne, 284 App. Div. 89, 130 N.Y.S.2d 572). But that is not this case. There is no doubt at all here that the instrument is what it purports to be: a purchase-money mortgage. And there is no subterfuge about it. The 7% is spelled out on its face. Thus it is either good or bad according to its express terms. . . .

Upon settled authority, then, the purchase-money mortgage here in issue is not void for usury. The order should be reversed, with costs in this court and in the Appellate Division; the order of Special Term dismissing the complaint reinstated, and the question certified answered in the negative.

Fuld, C.J., and Burke, Scileppi, Keating, Breitel and Jasen, JJ., concur.

Order reversed, etc.

NOTES AND QUESTIONS

1. Although the Appellate Division had ruled (incorrectly) that sellers must not exact interest greater than the statutory rate, the court would have let sellers "enlarge the purchase money mortgage obligation." What was meant by this?

2. Weaver Hardware Co. v. Solomovitz, 235 N.Y. 321 (1923), is the New York precedent on which the *Mandelino* decision heavily relies. This involved the credit sale of building materials, where the buyer's note for the unpaid price bore an admittedly usurious rate. Having recited that usury applies "only to the loan and forbearance of money, and not to

The Credit Quartet   175

the purchase price of building materials," the *Weaver Hardware Co.* opinion states no policy in support of this distinction, nor does the opinion explain why a credit sale is not a "loan" of money as well as a transfer of goods.

3. Precedent aside, what policies underlie (or oppose) the seller-financed exemption from the usury rule? Is it sufficient explanation that a sale "does not normally involve a necessitous borrower in the hands of a rapacious lender"? Nelson and Whitman, Real Estate Finance and Development 1036 (1976). Why would the purchaser agree to pay his seller an interest rate higher than the lawful ceiling? *No one else would loan to him*

4. Suppose that the seller has a "for cash," but also a higher "for credit" price? Should not the interest charge on the unpaid sales price be subject to the usury laws? Nebraska has enacted an Installment Loan Act requiring a seller to state both an all-cash and time-sale price and giving a buyer the opportunity to choose between them. The Act further places a simple interest ceiling upon the time-price differential between the cash and credit price. Cf. General Motors Acceptance Corp. v. Mackrill, 175 Neb. 631, 122 N.W.2d 742 (1963).

5. If the seller does charge the going interest rate on the unpaid balance of the purchase price, why should his "for credit" price be greater than his "for cash" price? Might the answer depend upon whether the buyer's notes can be resold at par?

6. "There is no usury in the normal purchase money mortgage transaction where a seller demands a higher price because the consideration is not all in cash. However, a lender of money may not utilize the form of a purchase money mortgage to cloak a usurious loan." Butts v. Samuels, 5 A.D.2d 1008, 174 N.Y.S.2d 325, 326 (1958). What facts might support the debtor's assertion that a purchase-money mortgage conceals a usurious loan?

7. The converse situation to the "usurious" seller-financed transaction is one where the buyer's purchase-money notes carry less than the market rate of interest. Why might both parties to a real estate transaction prefer a "nominal" interest rate upon the unpaid purchase price? See pages 417-435 infra.

(d) The Penalties for Usury

The penalties for usury range from forfeiture of the entire interest and principal to loss only of the interest portion that exceeds the statutory maximum. It can make quite a difference, as the summary below shows, whether the lender is caught red-handed doing business in New York, which falls in group (g), or in Alabama, which falls in group (a). Problem: X lends Y $30,000 payable in one year with interest at 20 percent. The legal rate is 12 percent. Before Y begins to repay, a court declares the loan usurious. What does Y still owe?

	Y *Owes*	X *Forfeits*	No. States*
(a)	$33,600	Excess interest only	8
(b)	$31,200	Twice the excess interest	4
(c)	$30,000	All interest	20
(d)	$24,000	All interest and portion of principal equal to the contract interest	2
(e)	$22,500	All interest and 25 percent of the principal	2
(f)	$15,000	All interest and 50 percent of the principal	1
(g)	$0	All interest and principal	6

* Derived from a table in Benfield, Money, Mortgages, and Migraine — The Usury Headache, 19 Case W. Res. L. Rev. 819, 886-891 (1968). This does not account for every state. A few minor variants do not appear.

What are the arguments for and against the three most popular sanctions: the loss, respectively, of excess interest, of all interest, of all interest and principal?

If, in the problem above, Y has already repaid the loan with contract interest, what are his remedies? Suits for recovery enjoy much less statutory recognition than is given to a usury defense. Fewer than thirty states permit recovery, the limitations period is brief (six months to two years), and the maximum recovery typically is the excess interest, or in some states, double or treble the excess interest. Why treat the debtor less protectively after he has already performed?

Usury is a misdemeanor in nearly a dozen states, and in several states the felony of criminal usury occurs when the rate exceeds an extortionate ceiling. See, e.g., N.Y. Penal Law §2401 (McKinney 1977) (25 percent).

(3) The Financial Institutions Deregulation and Monetary Control Act of 1980

The Financial Institutions Deregulation and Monetary Control Act of 1980

Pub. L. No. 96-221, 94 Stat. 132 (1980)

TITLE V — STATE USURY LAWS

PART A — MORTGAGE USURY LAWS

Mortgages

Sec. 501(a)(1) The provisions of the constitution or the laws of any State expressly limiting the rate or amount of interest, discount points, finance charges, or other charges which may be charged, taken, received, or reserved shall not apply to any loan, mortgage, credit sale, or advance which is—

(A) secured by a first lien on residential real property, by a first lien on stock in a residential cooperative housing corporation where the loan, mortgage, or advance is used to finance the acquisition of such stock, or by a first lien on a residential manufactured home;

(B) made after March 31, 1980; and

(C) [This subsection describes in detail the sorts of loans and lenders affected by the preemption. In effect, it extends to all significant lenders.]

(b)(1) Except as provided in paragraph (2) . . . , the provisions of subsection (a)(1) shall apply to any loan, mortgage, credit sale, or advance made in any State on or after April 1, 1980.

(2) . . . the provisions of subsection (a)(1) shall not apply to any loan, mortgage, credit sale, or advance made in any State after the date (on or after April 1, 1980, and before April 1, 1983) on which such State adopts a law or certifies that the voters of such State have voted in favor of any provision, constitutional or otherwise, which states explicitly and by its terms that such State does not want the provisions of subsection (a)(1) to apply with respect to loans, mortgages, credit sales, and advances made in such State. . . .

(4) At any time after the date of enactment of this Act, any State may adopt a provision of law placing limitations on discount points or such other charges on any loan, mortgage, credit sale, or advance described in subsection (a)(1).

(c) The provisions of subsection (a)(1) shall not apply to a loan, mortgage, credit sale, or advance which is secured by a first lien on a residential manufactured home unless the terms and conditions relating to such loan, mortgage, credit sale, or advance comply with the consumer protection provisions specified in regulations prescribed by the Federal Home Loan Bank Board. Such regulations shall—

(1) include consumer protection provisions with respect to balloon payments, prepayment penalties, late charges, and deferral fees;

(2) require a 30-day notice prior to instituting any action leading to repossession or foreclosure (except in the case of abandonment or other extreme circumstances);

(3) require that upon prepayment in full, the debtor shall be entitled to a refund of the unearned portion of the precomputed finance charge in an amount not less than the amount which would be calculated by the actuarial method, except that the debtor shall not be entitled to a refund which is less than $1; and

(4) include such other provisions as the Federal Home Loan Bank Board may prescribe after a finding that additional protections are required. . . .

NOTES AND QUESTIONS

1. The Deregulation Act was a comprehensive overhaul of the banking system; among its other features was a nationwide authorization of NOW accounts (interest-bearing checking accounts), the expansion of powers for thrift associations, and the relaxation of truth-in-lending requirements.

In explaining usury preemption, the Senate Report on the Deregulation Act spoke of the need "to ease the severity of the mortgage credit crunches of recent years and to provide financial institutions, particularly those with large mortgage portfolios, with the ability to offer higher interest rates on savings deposits." S. Rep. No. 96-368, 96th Cong., 1st Sess. 18 (1979).

2. Thirteen states have elected to preserve usury restrictions after April 1, 1983 for the residential first mortgage loans covered by the federal statute above. These states are: Colorado, Georgia, Hawaii, Idaho, Iowa, Kansas, Massachusetts, Minnesota, Nebraska, North Carolina, South Carolina, South Dakota, and Wisconsin. The federal preemption continues in the remaining states. Is it anomalous, in such states, that homeowners are no longer protected in their first mortgage borrowings, whereas business borrowers, who tend to be more streetwise, may continue to derive usury protection?

4. Method of Amortization

The fourth member of the credit quartet, method of amortization, describes the rate at which the borrower repays the loan balance. Prior to the 1930s, when most loans had short-term maturities, lenders did not press for interim principal reduction; although the borrower made periodic interest payments, the original debt usually remained intact until maturity. At maturity, the borrower would either repay the entire loan or renew the loan in part or full.

Since the 1930s, however, due largely to the influence of the FHA, most residential first mortgages have been *self-amortizing*, which requires periodic principal payments leading to the *gradual* elimination of the loan balance over the term of the loan. The more typical form of self-amortizing mortgage involves *level payment* debt service, that is, equal (usually monthly) debt service installments. Given this objective, the calculation of the (monthly) installment derives from a formula with three variables: original principal balance, the length of the loan, and the rate of interest. Tables that aid in the computation are readily available, for example, from banks and mortgage brokers.

You should be aware of the changing relationship between interest and principal in the level payment mortgage; with each installment the interest component gets smaller while the amortization grows. Take, for example, a $50,000, 12 percent, 30-year mortgage, carrying monthly debt service

TABLE 2-7
Monthly Level Payments (Dollars) to Amortize $1000
Various Amortization Periods and Interest Rates

Interest Rate Percent	Term in Years				
	10	15	20	25	30
14.0	15.53	13.32	12.44	12.04	11.85
13.0	14.93	12.65	11.72	11.28	11.06
12.0	14.35	12.00	11.01	10.53	10.29
11.0	13.77	11.37	10.32	9.80	9.52
10.0	13.22	10.75	9.65	9.09	8.78
9.0	12.67	10.14	9.00	8.39	8.07
8.0	12.13	9.56	8.36	7.72	7.34

Problem: Compute the level payment required monthly to amortize a $40,000, 15-year mortgage at 13.0 percent interest; a $60,000, 30-year mortgage at 10.0 percent interest.

of $514.50. Each installment of debt service goes first toward the payment of interest on the unpaid loan; whatever sum remains goes then into principal reduction. Allocation of interest and principal for the first three months and the final months appears in Table 2-8.

TABLE 2-8

Month	Installment	Interest	Principal	Principal Balance After Monthly Payment
1	$514.50	$500.00	$14.50	$49,985.50
2	514.50	499.86	14.64	49,970.86
3	514.50	499.71	14.79	49,956.07
—	—	—	—	—
—	—	—	—	—
—	—	—	—	—
360	514.50	5.00	509.50	0

Notice, also, how slowly amortization proceeds via the level payment mortgage. Table 2-9 shows the percent of unpaid debt remaining at 5-year intervals on this hypothetical loan.

TABLE 2-9

Year	Principal Balance	Percentage of Original Balance
5	$48,830	97.66
10	46,710	93.42
15	42,855	85.71
20	35,845	71.69
25	23,120	46.24
30	0	0

The usual alternative to a *level payment* self-amortizing mortgage is the so-called *constant amortization* (declining payment) loan, which one sees more often in investment situations. This method of amortization requires equal amounts of principal reduction in each installment. Again using the example of a $50,000, 12 percent, 30-year mortgage, the schedule of debt service appears in Table 2-10.

TABLE 2-10

Month	Installment	Interest	Principal	Principal Balance After Monthly Payments
1	$638.88	500.00	138.88	49,861.12
2	637.49	498.61	138.88	49,722.24
3	636.10	497.22	138.88	49,583.36
—	—	—	—	—
—	—	—	—	—
360	140.27	1.39	138.88	0

Over the thirty years, if the hypothetical mortgages go to term, the level payment mortgage will be far more costly. Why is that?

Since the income of many homebuying households tends to rise during the mortgage term, both in real and inflated dollars, this might argue for a mortgage whose debt service starts quite low and later steps up. (One close analogy is the life insurance policy calling for premium increases after three to five years in anticipation of the policy holder's greater income.) Such mortgage instruments, the *graduated payment* mortgage (GPM), now exist, although their use remains fairly limited. Because the monthly payments at the outset of the loan are lower than the amount necessary to amortize the loan on a fixed rate basis, this may result in negative amortization during the early years of the loan. Not every state permits that.

The "balloon" mortgage. As we have seen, mortgages are not always self-amortizing. A mortgage is said to have a "balloon" when regular debt service installments do not reduce the unpaid principal balance to zero. While mortgages are still occasionally written to require only interest payments for the entire term, more often the balloon mortgage carries a schedule of mortgage reduction lower than necessary to achieve self-amortization. For example, one might find a $50,000 mortgage calling for $2000 amortization yearly, all due in fifteen years. This mortgage would have a $20,000 balloon. The balloon arrangement offers the property owner the great advantage of higher cash flow during the mortgage term. He must be ready, however, when the loan matures either to refinance it or pay off the balloon.

C. ALTERNATIVE MORTGAGE INSTRUMENTS

We have already met several alternatives to the fixed rate long-term mortgage, including the variable rate mortgage (VRM), the graduated payment mortgage (GPM), and the equity participation or equity "kicker." These are only a few, however, of a diverse group of creative mortgage arrangements designed to respond to the recent inflationary pattern and ensuing credit crunch. They are further elaborated in the following excerpts.

Levin and Roberts, Future Forms of Financing— Lending Devices Addressed to Inflation and Tight Money

American Bar Association, Real Prop. Prob. and Tr. Sec., Financing Real Estate During the Inflationary 80's at 31-51 (1981)

B. SOME NEW FINANCING DEVICES

Various alternative mortgage instruments (AMIs) have been implemented or are being considered and refined to complement the FRM and to stimulate the real estate market in the United States. Many of these were initially developed for the residential market. They include the variable rate mortgage (VRM); graduate payment mortgage (GPM); graduated payment adjustable mortgage (GPAM); renegotiable rate mortgage (RRM); rollover mortgage (ROM), shared appreciation mortgage (SAM); price level adjusted mortgage (PLAM); deferred interest mortgage (DIM); and flexible loan insurance program mortgage (FLIP). These, along with equity participations, convertible mortgages, joint ventures, and loans with short terms and/or kicker interest, have become the principal means by which the institutional and noninstitutional lender have avoided the recent inflationary pattern and credit crunch in the commercial lending market.

C. OBJECTIVES OF THE NEW DEVICES

The various AMIs serve lender and borrower interests in different ways. Some (such as the VRM, RRM, ROM, PLAM and SAM) offer the lender protection against inflation which may, in turn, allow a lender to charge initially a lower rate of interest, bringing new borrowers into the market. Other AMIs (such as GPMs, DIMs and FLIPs), offer payment schedules that are more affordable for borrowers, without really providing benefits to lenders except in the resulting stimulation of the market. A portfolio of SAMs, for instance, should bring increased yields proportional to inflation's impact on the cost of funds, thus easing disintermediation pressures on lenders, and making more funds available for mortgage lending even in inflationary periods. More plentiful mortgage funds may lead to a higher demand for the funds and hence for new construction, to the benefit, indirectly, of much of the economy. However, for the lender there is always the risk that yields on SAMS will be reduced if inflation in real property values slows or ceases.

GPMs, on the other hand, do not improve a lender's cash flow or necessarily provide a hedge against inflation. But they do permit a borrower who projects a continuously rising cash flow to enter the market in anticipation of future income levels. The borrower's credit is an important factor here, as equity may be reduced by negative amortization in the early years of the loan. A lender may have to accept an increased risk of default in order to accommodate a borrower whose expectations are brighter than his current financial picture. . . .

II. THE VARIABLE RATE MORTGAGE AND DUAL RATE-VARIABLE RATE MORTGAGE

A. CHARACTERISTICS

A variable interest rate loan or mortgage is a long-term loan which increases or decreases with a referenced index that reflects changes in the cost of funds to the lender and/or the current market rate of interest. Future payments are not known at the time the loan is originated, but the interest rate could fall, along with the index, to the borrower's advantage. Because the lender is protected against inflation, a VRM can be less restrictive as to assumption and prepayment and can be offered for a longer term. . . .

Probably the best index one could use is a weighted average cost of funds to the lending institutions. A weighted average cost of funds is very stable, but has the disadvantage (from the borrower's point of view) of tending to move upward far more readily than downward. In the residential market, the FHA National Average Mortgage Rate would be a stable index. Other indices might include the CPI, the LIBOR, the prime rate and comparable AA utility bond or commercial paper rates. Some of these indices seem less suitable than others, because they reflect volatile short-term market conditions not directly related to the cost of mortgage funds.

Regardless of which index is chosen, the frequency of periodic adjustments is another important issue. The longer the intervals, the greater the stability and the probability that long-term trends will be reflected. To promote greater stability, a lender may require a minimum change in the index before requiring a corresponding change in the interest rate. . . .

Alternative Mortgage Instruments

The dual rate-variable rate mortgage is a loan which involves two distinct interest rates: a deferred short-term interest rate on the mortgage balance, and a current long-term interest rate on the principal payment. The short-term rate would reflect the current market interest rate. This provides the borrower with a payment plan that follows the projected income stream of the property and long term interest trends. It provides the lender with an overall yield reflecting short term interest rates, although the lender's cash flow may not keep up in the same fashion. . . .

III. Graduated Payment Mortgage and Graduated Payment Adjustable Mortgage
[CONTENTS OMITTED]

IV. Renegotiable Rate Mortgage and Roll-over Mortgage

A. CHARACTERISTICS

A renegotiable rate mortgage is a loan in which the payments are calculated on a long-term (e.g., twenty- or thirty-year) amortization schedule, with a short-term (e.g., five years) maturity or with frequent (e.g., every five years) mandatory rate adjustments. The short-term note may be secured by a long-term mortgage. The loan is renegotiated at the new interest rate (usually the then market interest rate) at the end of each designated period. The loan may be renewable either at the option of the borrower or of the lender. . . .

Canada has had experience with ROMs since the 1930s, but only since 1969 have ROMs come into widespread use. Under the terms set by law for government guaranteed (insured) mortgages, the ROM is renegotiated after a minimum of five years, with a twenty-five-year minimum amortization period. Borrowers may prepay up to 10 percent in each of the initial two years and the full amount thereafter without penalty. In 1976, the average interest rate of nongovernment insured mortgages in Canada was nearly 12 percent, while five-year term certificates paid over 10 percent. On the other hand, interest rates on five-year term certificates in June 1978 averaged 8¾ percent, while conventional single-family (roll-over) mortgages were priced just over 10 percent. Although relatively expensive, mortgage funds appear to be readily available in Canada.

In Canada, lenders are under no legal obligation to refinance the loan at the end of each five-year term, but experience has shown that they tend to do so for creditworthy borrowers. There is now some movement to the use of even shorter term loans, in an attempt to adjust the lenders' yield more precisely. The supply of mortgage credit is relatively uninterrupted, disintermediation pressures are reduced, and housing cycles seem slightly less pronounced than in this country. Nonetheless, caution must be used in drawing on the Canadian experience because of the obvious differences between Canada's economic and financial structures and those in the United States. . . .

V. Deferred Interest Mortgage

The DIM is a variant of the GPM, in which the lender defers a portion of the interest payments during the initial years and adds the amount of the deferred interest to the outstanding balance of the loan for payment in subsequent years. The terms of a DIM usually provide for a lower initial interest rate which is increased within five or ten years. In addition to the deferred interest, the lender may receive a fee upon resale of the residence. DIMs are a suitable form of mortgage in areas experiencing a rapid appreciation in home values and a high rate of turnover in the housing stock.

VI. The Flexible Loan Insurance Program

The FLIP is the brainchild of FLIP Mortgage Corporation in Flemington, New Jersey. This corporation packages the FLIP concept together with a computer program and markets the package to lenders. A FLIP is a type of GPM with a highly individualized payment program. On the purchase of a home, a buyer makes a down payment which is placed in an interest bearing account and takes out a loan, in effect, for the full purchase price. Each FLIP establishes a schedule of monthly deductions for principal and interest from the account to supplement the buyer's out-of-pocket payments on the loan. Consequently, it enables an initial reduction of the debt service until the exhaustion of funds in the account.

FLIPs were first tried in 1977 and proved popular with consumers. Nonetheless, their use has been hindered by lenders' reluctance to engage in highly leveraged residential transactions, and by a severely constricted secondary market. Since the introduction of FLIPs, neither FNMA nor FHLMC has been willing to purchase them.

VII. Tenants In Common Keeping Equity (Ticket)

The TICKET plan is a convenient form of financing the purchase of residential properties for buyers with limited funds to meet a seller's down payment requirements. Under the plan, an investor provides the buyer with the cash for the down payment and takes an interest as co-tenant of the property. The investor receives no debt service but shares in the gains or losses upon the sale of the property. The parties agree to sell or to refinance within five years. The buyer obtains financing for the balance of the purchase price from a third party lender. The investor's unsecured position as a co-tenant removes any problems of the buyers's compliance with the third party lender's restrictions on subordinate debt.

TICKET plans are offered in New Jersey by the Sterling National Realty Group. Ticket Corporation, the developer of the plan, is based in San Jose, California.

VIII. CONTINGENT INTEREST MORTGAGES

A. CHARACTERISTICS

Contingent interest mortgages are established forms of financing which, singly and in combination with other AMI devices, will be widely used in the current inflationary economy. Normally the borrower must service debt at a stated interest rate, either fixed or variable, plus a contingent interest component comprised of a portion of the proceeds it derives from the property. Considerations such as the borrower's initial and projected income from the property, the terms of the borrower's leases with its tenants, and the type of the property (office, retail, banking, apartment units, etc.) affect the terms of the contingent interest element. The method of computing contingent interest, what items are included or excluded, and the definitions of various terms require careful consideration, negotiation and drafting.

B. COMPUTATION

Contingent interest may be based on a percentage of gross receipts or of net income. Under a gross receipts formula, all of the borrower's revenues can be swept into the computation prior to any adjustments for expenses or for receipts which merely reimburse the borrower as a landlord. From the lender's viewpoint this method is more reliable and administratively convenient than use of a net income or cash flow approach. The lender may encounter difficulties ascertaining and keeping account of excluded and included items under a net income formula. However, a borrower agreeing to pay his lender a percentage of gross receipts runs a very real risk in an inflationary economy that operating expenses may increase more quickly and in a greater amount than income, and that his net cash flow after debt service will actually diminish. It is submitted that devices intended to protect lenders from the ravages of inflation should not also result in exacerbating the effects of inflation on the expense side for the borrower. Net income determined on a cash basis enables the borrower to meet its debt service obligations when due, but also raises the possibility that the borrower may elect to defer receipt of payments to a subsequent accounting period. Net income determined on an accrual basis offers the lender the certainty that income will be included in net income for a current accounting period without manipulation by the borrower, but the borrower may be placed at a disadvantage because it may lack the funds to meet the amount of its obligation. . . .

IX. Shared Appreciation Mortgage

A. CHARACTERISTICS

A SAM loan is generally defined as a loan which has a fixed interest rate set below the prevailing market rate over the term of the loan and contingent interest based upon a percentage of the appreciation of the property securing the loan payable at the earlier of maturity or payment in full of the loan or sale or transfer of the property. A SAM is the newest and probably most controversial of the AMIs now offered or under consideration in the United States and, therefore, will receive more extensive coverage in these materials than the AMIs and other devices previously discussed.

A SAM loan would call for equal monthly installments of principal and fixed interest in a sufficient amount to fully amortize the loan over a certain amortization period, although the term of the SAM would be shorter than its amortization period.

The contingent interest which is intended to compensate the lender for the differential between the market rate and the lower loan interest rate, would be a portion of the net appreciated value of the property which is to be paid at the earlier of the maturity date, payment in full of the loan or the sale, transfer, disposition or further encumbrance of the property securing the loan.

The terms of a typical SAM might be:

(a) a below-market fixed interest rate; plus
(b) a rate of contingent interest (i.e., the percentage share of any appreciation) sufficient to produce an effective gross yield in excess of the yield on a conventional FRM;
(c) a short loan term, usually not more than ten years;
(d) a longer amortization period of twenty to thirty years;
(e) appreciation to be determined either by the actual sales price or by appraisal, allowing recovery by the borrower of the cost of capital improvements;
(f) a sizable prepayment penalty during the early years of the loan term;

(g) acceleration of the loan maturity upon sale, transfer or refinancing;
(h) a conservative loan to value ratio.

An alternative form of SAM might provide for a fixed interest rate over a longer term and for a periodic reappraisal of the property (e.g., every five years). The borrower would pay as interest to the lender an amount equal to a percent of the increase in value of the property over the last appraisal. This amount would be payable in cash or by the lender taking a note from the borrower in this amount at the original interest rate, with the same amortization rate and maturity date as the original loan or with increased amortization or an extended maturity date. If the property were sold, the mortgagee would receive its share of the excess of the sales price over the last appraisal. . . .

X. THE PRICE LEVEL ADJUSTED MORTGAGE

A. CHARACTERISTICS

A PLAM is a mortgage which provides for periodic increases or decreases in the principal amount due, based on appraisals or on a predetermined price level index. The goal is to periodically adjust the outstanding debt so that the debt keeps up with inflation while the nominal interest rate remains constant. The lender, therefore, does not charge an inflation premium in the stated interest rate in anticipation of the declining value of the dollar and the lender's actual yield on the loan would be approximately the same as stated, regardless of inflation. Actual payments would rise with the rate of inflation, but the initial payments, because there is no necessity to charge an inflation premium, would theoretically be much lower than those on an FRM.

In a PLAM, the borrower would negotiate a fixed interest rate, a schedule for adjustment of principal and an index or other method for revaluing the principal. Assuming that inflation amounted to 10 percent per year, on an annual adjustment plan the outstanding mortgage balance would be increased by a factor of 10 percent plus accrued interest called for under the terms of the mortgage, from which would be deducted the total payments paid by the borrower for that year. The mortgage balance would then be adjusted at the end of each year during the term of the loan.

PLAMs are used extensively in Brazil but not in the United States. They involve the same practical problems of selecting an index or an appraisal process as the VRM or SAM, and the practice of adjusting principal offers no advantages over the practice of adjusting interest, and may involve additional legal problems. . . .

D. BASIC SECURITY TRANSACTIONS

1. Forms of Security Devices

a. The Mortgage

We have already used the word "mortgage" repeatedly and have done so as a layman would — to describe a loan on real property. The lawyer knows better. A mortgage is not the loan itself, but a security interest in property given to an obligee (usually a lender) to secure the loan or, occasionally, some other obligation. Such other obligation might be the promise of the obligor to act as surety for the debts of a third person; in that instance the mortgage would be called a collateral security mortgage. The party who holds a mortgage is called the *mortgagee;* the party whose property is subject to a mortgage is called the *mortgagor.* Very often neither the mortgagee nor the mortgagor will be the original mortgaging parties, since the mortgage will have been sold or assigned or the mortgaged property will have been transferred. The mortgages dealt with in this text are mostly mortgages on real estate, not mortgages on personalty, which are called chattel mortgages. We shall learn, however, that real estate mortgages may be either fee mortgages or leasehold mortgages; the common law treatment of leaseholds as "chattels real" causes some blurring of the distinction between real and chattel mortgages.

Where a mortgage is given to secure a loan, the loan usually is evidenced by the obligor's note or bond, which accompanies the mortgage. Although the terms often are used interchangeably, technically a bond is a sealed instrument and a note is an unsealed instrument; until the 1966 repeal of the federal excise tax on corporate bonds mooted the difference, a corporate mortgagor could avoid the tax by issuing a note instead of a bond. For an instance in which the archaic difference may still matter, see N.J.S.A. 2A:50-3 (1977); 79-83 Thirteenth Ave., Ltd. v. De Marco, 44 N.J. 525, 210 A.2d 401 (1965).

What does the mortgagee get when it receives a mortgage? The answer to that question has varied greatly over the course of centuries, but today, for most practical purposes, the mortgagee receives a lien[20] on the mort-

---

20. Even in states where conveyancing practice still uses language in the mortgage instrument that signifies the transfer of legal title to the mortgagee, all that he gets is a lien interest. At an earlier time, American courts differentiated between the interest of a mortgagee holding title and the interest of a mortgagee having a lien only; today, most of the differences have disappeared. There remains, however, one. In a few states, known as title states, the mortgagee has the continuing right to possession, as he does in England. In one or two other states, known as "hybrid" or "intermediate" theory states, the mortgagee is entitled automatically to possession immediately upon default. Everywhere else, the mortgagee must petition the court for the right possession — via a court appointed receiver — to protect the security from waste or dissipation of the rents; usually the petition is received and granted as part of a foreclosure proceeding.

gagor's property as of the time that the mortgage is recorded. (Between the mortgaging parties, the lien is effective when the mortgage is executed and delivered, but since most disputes over priority involve third parties, the critical date is that of recordation.) In an earlier era, the mortgagee obtained title to the mortgagor's property subject to divestment if the debt were paid on the due or law day. Often this arrangement meant hardship for the mortgagor, for a late tender of payment, late even by so little as one day, would not bring a return of title unless the mortgagee volunteered to give it. In time, chancery intervened in behalf of defaulting mortgagors by letting them "redeem" the property from the mortgagee if they tendered payment within a reasonable period after the law day. This equitable right of redemption[21] grew into an implied term of every mortgage bargain.

Now the mortgagee faced hardship — the hardship of uncertainty — for he could not be sure, after default, when his title would indefeasibly vest. A late tendering mortgagor might yet persuade chancery that the tender was not unreasonably delayed. Taking the initiative, mortgagees began to petition the courts to cut off, or foreclose, the mortgagor's equity of redemption. In this way, the procedural remedy of foreclosure was born. The decree of foreclosure, which was issued some months after the law date and upon notice to the defaulting mortgagor, vested the mortgagee's title to the real estate security; prior to the decree redemption was possible, but after the decree, it was not.

If, when foreclosure occurred, the real estate was worth more than the mortgage debt, still another source of hardship remained for the mortgagor. Since foreclosure vested title in the mortgagee, he stood to benefit, while the mortgagor stood to lose, from any surplus in property value. No restitution was necessary. By the early 1800s, state legislatures began to respond to the evident harshness of this situation; mortgagees who applied for a foreclosure decree were ordered to sell the property at a public sale and to pay over to the mortgagor (and to any junior lienors) the surplus moneys from the sale, i.e., the moneys not needed to satisfy the claims of the foreclosing mortgagee. (Sometimes, of course, the sales price fails to satisfy the debt, and this may give rise to further claim for a deficiency judgment.) In a substantial majority of states, *foreclosure by judicial sale* has become the exclusive or generally used process, and it is available everywhere. The process is supplanted, which for obvious reasons became known as *strict foreclosure*, survives in only a few states as a permitted remedy.[22]

---

21. Be sure not to confuse the equitable right of redemption, which the mortgagor holds until the default hardens into foreclosure, with the statutory right to redeem. The latter operates only after the equity of redemption is extinguished and entitles the mortgagor, in states where the right exists, to buy back the real estate from the purchaser at the foreclosure sale.

22. Strict foreclosure, while not permitted in the original foreclosure proceeding, may sometimes be used to correct an error in the original proceeding. Take this example: X, who holds a first mortgage, obtains a foreclosure decree and bids in (i.e., purchases) the property

One other form of foreclosure deserves mention, for it does not depend upon judicial decree. Where the mortgage instrument gives the mortgagee the power, and state law does not prevent its exercise, a sale arranged for by the mortgagee may be held to transfer the interest of the defaulted mortgagor. A *mortgage with power of sale* grew out of the efforts of English lawyers to avoid Chancery; by the mid-1800s, statutes confirmed the practice, and today, in England, the practice prevails. A 1975 study[23] indicates the widespread use of the power of sale in 24 American states. In England the sale may be held privately, the mortgagor being deemed protected sufficiently by the requirement that the sale must be "bona fide to a stranger and at a reasonable price." In the United States the sale is invariably public and statutes carefully regulate the conduct of the sale and the method of giving notice.

The purchaser in theory obtains the same rights in the property he would enjoy had he purchased at a judicial sale, since the mortgagee is selling the title as it existed when the mortgage containing the power of sale was given. Nevertheless, the costlier, slower, and more cumbersome judicial sale is frequently preferred because it creates a permanent court record of the events leading to the transfer of the mortgagor's interest, while the purchaser at a nonjudicial sale may have only the recitals in his deed to establish the regularity of his title.

State law varies as to whether a mortgagee may bid at any sale that he conducts pursuant to the power of sale. Generally he will be permitted to do so if the mortgage gives him the privilege or if the sale is actually conducted by a public officer. What arguments do you see for and against letting the mortgagee participate in the bidding?

If the sale results in surplus moneys, the foreclosing mortgagee will usually bring a bill of interpleader joining the mortgagor and junior lienors so that their rights to the surplus may be decided judicially.

b. The Trust Deed Mortgage (Deed of Trust)[24]

Many states, both in lien and title, recognize a device called a *trust deed* mortgage, which creates a three-party mortgage transaction. When the

---

at the public sale. Then X discovers that service on Y, who held a second mortgage or a subordinate judgment lien against the property, was omitted in the foreclosure action, so that his lien survives the decree. Rather than reinstitute the sale, X may be able to apply for a decree of strict foreclosure — upon notice to Y, of course — that would cut off Y's interest in the real estate and relegate Y to a claim against the mortgage proceeds. Whether the decree is granted or not would probably depend on the showing of the relationship between the value of the property and the sales price and on the cirumstances of Y's non-service.

23. American Bar Association Comm. on Real Est. Financing, Cost and Time Factors in Foreclosure of Mortgages, 3 Real Prop. Prob. and Tr. J. 413, 414 (1968).

24. Deed of trust should not be confused with the *land trust,* a device for concealing real estate ownership, which is especially popular in the Chicago area. See Garrett, Land Trusts, 1955 Ill. L. F. 655. Under the usual "Illinois" land trust, record title is held by a corporate

Basic Security Transactions

loan is made, the borrower deeds the real estate security to a trustee, usually an institution specializing in that role.[25] While the mortgage remains current, the trustee has few duties; mortgage payments go directly to the lender who is the trust beneficiary. At maturity, or whenever the loan is repaid, the trustee reconveys the property to its rightful owner. But if a default occurs, the trustee must arrange a public sale of the mortgagor's interest — much as would a mortgagee with power of sale.[26] The trustee will usually conduct the sale and deed the property to the highest bidder. The trustee may not, however, acquire the property himself.[27]

Assignment of the mortgage leaves the trust intact. The original lender transfers the note or other evidence of obligation. The assignee then becomes the trust beneficiary.

While the differences between the straight mortgage and the trust deed mortgage may have once been significant,[28] that no longer is so. Courts and legislatures recognize the functional identity between the two mortgage forms, and, in a lien state, for example, the rights and powers of the trustor-mortgagor do not end because he parts with legal title. Thus, the mortgagor retains the right to possession until a default occurs and there has been a public sale or appointment of receiver. The mortgagor may also sell, lease, or further mortgage the real estate, subject, of course, to the trust. Which of the two forms the lender uses depends mainly upon the custom within the state.

---

trustee (a bank or title insurance company), but the trustee's powers are restricted by an unrecorded trust agreement whereby the beneficiary (and "real" owner) retains full powers of management and control. Advantages asserted for the land trust, in addition to privacy of ownership, are avoidance of probate, facilitation of multi-ownership, and insulation of the real estate from the claims of judgment creditors.

25. It would be fairly unusual for the lender also to act as the trustee. Where such identity exists, courts have required, in the event of the obligor's default, that the trustee-lender sue to foreclose the debtor's interest rather than proceed under the power of sale. Spruill v. Ballard, 61 App. D.C. 112, 58 F.2d 517 (1932).

26. The trust beneficiary notifies the trustee that the default has occurred and directs him to arrange the public sale. After receiving the foreclosure request, the trustee owes the mortgagor no affirmative duty to investigate whether, in fact, there has been a default. Spires v. Edgar, 513 S.W.2d 372 (Mo. 1974).

27. Casa Monte Co. v. Ward, 342 S.W.2d 812 (Tex. Civ. App. 1961); Lee v. Lee, 236 Miss. 260, 109 So. 2d 870 (1959) (trustee's wife may not purchase); Whitlow v. Mountain Trust Bank, 215 Va. 149, 207 S.E.2d 837 (1974) (corporation in which trustee interested may not purchase).

28. For a good discussion of these differences, see Bank of Italy National Trust & Savings Assn. v. Bentley, 217 Cal. 644, 20 P.2d 940 (1933).

c. The Deed Absolute

Cunningham and Tischler, Disguised Real Estate Security Transactions as Mortgages in Substance[29]
26 Rutgers L. Rev. 1 (1972)

I. INTRODUCTION

Ever since the English Chancellors regularly began to allow redemption of mortgages after default, creditors have sought ways to have real property serve as security free from any right in the debtor to redeem. As one writer put it, "[T]he big idea is to find a form of a transaction that will have the practical effect of security, yet will be held not to be a security but to belong to a wholly different jural species and so be held immune from security law."[1]

Creditors may use two devices to create real property security without appearing to enter into a security transaction. A creditor may require his debtor to grant him land by absolute deed, under oral agreement or tacit understanding that he will reconvey only if the debtor pays the debt when due. Alternatively, a creditor may obtain from his debtor an absolute deed to real property and execute to his debtor some sort of written agreement (almost invariably withheld from public record) to reconvey the property to the debtor upon receiving payment of the debt. The written agreement to reconvey may take the form of an option to repurchase, an unconditional contract obligating the grantee to reconvey and the grantor to repurchase, or a lease back to the grantor with an option to repurchase at or before the end of the lease term. Some such options or contracts provide for the deposit in escrow of a deed of reconveyance.

The use of an absolute deed to secure a debt, with or without a written collateral agreement for reconveyance upon satisfaction, is designed to eliminate the "grantor's" equity of redemption and the necessity of foreclosure if the debtor defaults. The written instrument, whether option to repurchase, contract to reconvey, or other arrangement, usually contains provisions making time "of the essence" and forfeiting the grantor's right in case he fails to exercise the option or tender payment under the contract within the time limited.

Besides avoiding the expense and delay involved in foreclosure, the creditor often expects to gain other advantages by securing his interest with an absolute deed rather than a regular mortgage. These other advantages include the right to possession of the land prior to default, the right to possession of chattels severed from the land by the debtor or third parties, preventing the debtor from encumbering the land with further mortgages or judgment liens, and the possibility of enlarging the credi-

---

29. Most footnotes omitted.
1. Durfee, Cases on Security 4 (1951).

tor's security interest to cover future advances to the debtor without the execution of a new security instrument.

Under the old system of separate law and equity courts, law courts would not entertain an action to establish that an absolute deed had been given as security for a debt though equity courts had long done so. It is now well settled, however, that any deed which is absolute on its face but intended at the time of its execution to be mere security for a debt will be regarded as a mortgage in substance. Since in the past only equity courts would entertain suits to establish that an absolute deed had been given as security for a debt, the term "equitable mortgage" is used frequently to describe disguised real property security transactions. The term "equitable mortgage" has not been confined, however, to "cases in which the interest in the property in the hands of the creditor is the full legal ownership and the aid of equity is necessary to cut it down to a security interest and to establish the rights of the debtor as a mortgagor."[17] The term has also been used to describe a creditor's interest where his "only interest . . . in the property for security purposes is an equitable one." Because the term "equitable mortgage" may refer to either of these two quite disparate types of security arrangement, that term will not be used in the text of this article.

It is important to keep in mind that the crucial question is *not* whether the parties to a deed absolute on its face intended to create the relation of mortgagor and mortgagee, but whether they intended the deed to stand as security for a debt. Where the parties cast their transaction in the form of an absolute conveyance instead of a mortgage, they do *not* intend to create the relation of mortgagor and mortgagee. Thus, the real issue is whether the circumstances are such as to justify treating the transaction as a mortgage in substance though the parties did not so intend. If the purpose of a conveyance was security, it will be treated as a mortgage even though the parties may have agreed or understood that the debtor should have no right to redeem. The right to redeem after default is an inseparable incident of the mortgage relationship and, as with ordinary mortgages, the parties cannot contract against its exercise where their relationship is in substance that of mortgagor and mortgagee. . . .

II. The Absolute Deed Without Collateral Writing: Extrinsic Evidence

When the only written instrument before the court is a deed of conveyance absolute on its face, extrinsic evidence must be adduced to prove the conveyance was a security. Vice-Chancellor Van Fleet stated the rule in Winters v. Earl:[26]

---

17. Osborne, Mortgages 42-43 (2d. ed. 1970).
26. 52 N.J. Eq. 52, 53 (Ch. 1893), *aff'd mem.*, 52 N.J. Eq. 588, 33 A. 50 (E. & A. 1894). The quoted language is paraphrased from Sweet v. Parker, 22 N.J. Eq. 453, 457 (Ch. 1871). The English Court of Chancery permitted the introduction of parol evidence to establish that

Any legal means of proof may be used to establish the fact that the deed was executed as a security. In the absence of a written defeasance, the evidence in such cases usually consists of the declarations of the grantee; the relations subsisting between the parties at the time the deed was executed; the retention by the grantor, subsequent to the execution of the deed, of the possession of the land and the exercise of dominion over it, in making improvements and repairs, paying taxes and the like; the value of the property compared with the consideration actually paid or allowed; an understanding that the consideration should be repaid and the payment of interest on it subsequent to the date of deed.

It seems generally to be assumed that the admission of extrinsic evidence to establish that an absolute deed was given for security does not violate the parol evidence rule. The parol evidence rule excludes extrinsic evidence only when the parties intend to embody their entire agreement in one or more written instruments. An allegation that the deed was given for security is necessarily an allegation that the deed was not intended to embody the entire agreement of the parties. Extrinsic evidence is admissible for the dual purpose of establishing the truth of this allegation and proving the entire agreement of the parties. A parol agreement that a deed was given only for security would merely supplement the deed with respect to a matter regarding which the deed says nothing; the parol agreement would not vary or contradict the deed.

It might be supposed, however, that the Statute of Frauds would bar the use of extrinsic evidence to convert an absolute deed into a mortgage where there is no written evidence that the grantor retains any interest in the land conveyed.[30] Yet most courts have not considered the Statute of Frauds a bar to the establishment of the grantor's equity of redemption by parol evidence. In Sweet v. Parker,[31] the court said:

> The efficacy of the parol evidence is not to establish an agreement to reconvey, the specific performance of which this court will enforce, but to establish the true nature and effect of the instrument, by showing the object for which it was made. . . . The distinction between parol evidence to vary a written instrument, and parol evidence showing facts which control its operation, is employed to reconcile the allowance of such proofs with the statute of frauds, and the general rules of common law.

---

an absolute deed was given to secure a debt from an early date. See, e.g., Maxwell v. Mountacute, Prec. Ch. 526, 24 Eng. Rep. 235 (Ch. 1719); Thornborough v. Baker, 1 Ch. Cas. 283, 36 Eng. Rep. 1000 (Ch. 1675); Copleston v. Boxwill, 1 Ch. Cas. 1, 22 Eng. Rep. 664 (Ch. 1660).

30. The original English Statute of Frauds provided that no estate or interest in land should be created or transferred except by an instrument in writing signed by the person creating or transferring the same or by his agent. N.J. Stat. Ann. §§21:1-1, 25:1-2 (1940) are identical in substance. See the discussion in Smedley and Blunk, Oral Understandings at Variance with Absolute Deeds, 34 Ill. L. Rev. 189, 191-93 (1939), [hereinafter cited as Smedley and Blunk], expressing the view that there is a violation of the statute. For the difference between the operation of the Statute of Frauds and the parol evidence rule, see . . . Osborne, supra note 17, §83.

31. 22 N.J. Eq. 453, 457 (Ch. 1871).

This suggests that when the grantor establishes by parol evidence that the absolute deed was given as security for a debt, he establishes "an independent equity superior to the written agreement" — that the grantor's equity of redemption arises by operation of law.[32] There is authority elsewhere which supports this view[33] and the closely related view that despite the Statute of Frauds parol evidence is admissible to prevent a "virtual fraud" on the grantor and unjust enrichment of the grantee.[34] Other courts take the position that the Statute precludes enforcement of the creation or transfer of real property by parol but not retention by parol.[35] Some other courts have suggested that the strong judicial policy in favor of the equity of redemption outweighs the policy embodied in the Statute of Frauds sufficiently to justify derogation of the latter policy.[36]

---

32. Osborne, supra note 17, §84, at n.7.

33. "The parol evidence is admitted . . . not for the purpose of contradicting or varying the written instrument, but to show facts *dehors* the instrument creating an equity superior to its terms." Pierce v. Robinson, 13 Cal. 116, 131 (1859).

34. E.g., Jenkins v. Eldredge, 13 F. Cas. 462 (No. 7,266) (C.C.D. Mass. 1844); Taylor v. Luther, 23 F. Cas. 778 (No. 13,796) (C.C.R.I. 1835); Smith v. Smith, 153 Ala. 504, 508, 45 So. 168, 169 (1907); Campbell v. Dearborn, 109 Mass. 130, 136-37 (1872); Strong v. Stewart, 4 Johns. Ch. 167 (N.Y. Ch. 1819).

35. "[P]arol proof of an equitable mortgage . . . does not transfer to the mortgagor an interest in land. The oral proof simply limits the effect of a conveyance absolute in form to the agreed effect — a transfer as security." Bennett v. Harrison, 115 Minn. 342, 355, 132 N.W. 309, 314, 37 L.R.A. (N.S.) 521 (1911). Accord, De Bartlett v. De Wilson, 52 Fla. 497, 504, 42 So. 189, 191, 11 Ann. Cas. 311 (1906); Osborne, supra note 17, §85.

This theory is unpersuasive to the present writers, however. Suppose a landowner conveys in fee by absolute deed, orally reserving a life estate. Surely the oral reservation would not be effective on the theory that it did not involve the "creation or transfer" of any estate or interest.

36. The strong judicial policy in favor of the equity of redemption would seem to be the real source of the "independent equity" referred to in the text accompanying note 33 supra.

"The entire doctrine of equity, in respect to mortgages, has its origin in considerations independent of the terms in which the instruments are drawn. In form, a mortgage in fee is a conveyance of a conditional estate, which, by the strict rules of the common law, became absolute upon breach of its conditions. But, from an early period in the history of English jurisprudence, Courts of Equity interposed to prevent a forfeiture of the estate and gave the mortgagor a right to redeem, upon payment, within a reasonable time, of the principal sum secured, interest and costs. . . . And when the right to redeem has been once established, to prevent its evasion, the rule was laid down and has ever since been inflexibly adhered to, that the right is inseparably connected with the mortgage, and cannot be abandoned or waived by any stipulations entered into between the parties at the time, whether inserted in the instrument or not. . . . It is against the policy of the law to allow irredeemable mortgages, just as it is against the policy of the law to allow the creation of inalienable estates. . . . Unless parol evidence can be admitted, the policy of the law will be constantly evaded. Debtors, under the force of pressing necessities, will submit to almost any exactions for loans of a trifling amount, compared with the value of the property, and the equity of redemption will elude the grasp of the Court, and rest in the simple good faith of the creditor." Pierce v. Robinson, 13 Cal. 116, 125-27 (1859).

The most thorough discussion of the admissibility of parol evidence to establish that an absolute deed is in substance a mortgage will be found in Annot., 1916B L.R.A. 18.

III. THE ABSOLUTE DEED WITH COLLATERAL WRITING: EXTRINSIC EVIDENCE

When the court has before it both an absolute deed and a collateral writing obligating the grantee to reconvey to the grantor upon receipt of a stated sum of money, the court will, of course, look first at the written instruments. If the collateral writing clearly embodies a proviso for defeasance or a promise to reconvey upon payment of a sum of money acknowledged to constitute a debt, the only problem is to establish that the two instruments were executed as part of a single transaction. If the two instruments were executed as parts of a single transaction, they will be treated as parts of a single instrument constituting a mortgage. Where the defeasance or promise to reconvey is in writing the Statute of Frauds will not bar its enforcement and the parol evidence rule will not bar admission of extrinsic evidence to show that the defeasance or reconveyance instrument and the deed represent a single arrangement entered into at one and the same time. If the collateral writing is ambiguous, extrinsic evidence is of course admissible to remove the ambiguity and indicate whether the parties intended a security transaction.

IV. CRITERIA FOR DETERMINING WHETHER THE TRANSACTION IS A MORTGAGE IN SUBSTANCE

In general, the extrinsic evidence offered to show that an absolute deed or a conditional sale should be treated as a mortgage may include the following: declarations of the grantee; the relation of the parties when the deed was executed; the grantor's continued possession of the land and exercise of dominion over it; the grantor's continued payment of taxes on, and improvement of, the land; the difference between the land's value and the consideration; the grantor's payment of interest to the grantee; and an understanding that consideration is to be repaid. In both absolute deed and conditional sale cases, the court's decision is likely to turn upon the "three leading criteria" set out in the following passage from Pace v. Bartles:[43]

> First, was there a debt created, either at the date of the deed or existing prior thereto, from the grantor, or some other person, to the grantee, which was not paid and satisfied by the conveyance, but which survived and continued in existence, notwithstanding the grant, so that the grantee might have sued upon it? [S]econd, was the price named and paid considerably less than the value of the thing granted? The first of these criteria—the continuance of the debt—has always been looked upon as a strong circumstance, and as being almost, if not absolutely, controlling. Conspicuously in this the case in instances of an attempt to turn absolute conveyance into mortgages wholly

---

43. 47 N.J. Eq. 170, 175, 20 A. 352, 359 (Ch. 1890).

by parol. . . . A third criterion is found in the conduct of the parties with regard to the possession and use of the subject of the grant after the date of the grant. Does the grantor retain possession with the right to use it as if he was the owner? Does he pay for the use of it an amount just equal to the interest on the consideration named, and the like?

d. The Installment Land Contract

Warren, California Instalment Land Sales Contracts: A Time for Reform
9 U.C.L.A. L. Rev. 608, 609-619, 625-630 (1962)

. . . Low-cost housing can be marketed on a mass basis only through the use of financing devices that will allow the purchaser to go into possession under terms requiring a small down payment and relatively low monthly payments. [When] secondary financing is needed, [s]ellers can choose between two devices to offer low equity financing: (1) the seller may take back a second trust deed from the buyer, or (2) he may sell the land under land sale contract. [Herein] the seller retains title until [the buyer has paid in the contract price or, at least, until] the buyer has paid in enough money to warrant transforming the transaction into an executed sale with the remaining indebtedness secured by a trust deed.[3]

. . . [T]he use of the [instalment land contract] has expanded in recent years, and the early Sixties find this device enjoying its greateat popularity. Why is this? The following sections will analyze the reasons commonly put forth for the popularity of the instalment contract.

A. INSTALMENT CONTRACT AS MERCHANDISING DEVICE

One of the attributes of the instalment land sale contract that commends it to a builder or developer is its supposed superiority as a merchandising device. In many instances contract buyers have found it possible to go into possession of subdivision homes under a down payment no larger than one

---

3. The mechanics of the use of the instalment sale contract as an interim financing device follow: A house is appraised at $10,000, thereby entitling its builder to obtain a $7,500 conventional loan secured by a first trust deed. This leaves a $2,500 balance—a sum far greater than the purchaser of a home in this price range is likely to be able to pay. The builder may sell for a $500 down payment and either obtain the other $2,000 by giving a second trust deed or he may carry the $2,000 balance himself. The builder then applies part of each monthly payment to the $7,500 first trust deed note that he owes and the remainder to the second trust deed note, if a second was obtained. When enough money has been paid in by the buyer to pay off the second or discharge the balance carried by the builder, he deeds the land to the buyer subject to the trust deed securing the remainder of the $7,500 loan. The amount of the buyer's monthly payments is proportionately reduced. For a discussion of such a transaction by an experienced builder, see Hearings Before the Assembly Subcommittee on Real Estate Contracts and Trust Deeds 132-33 (1960). . . .

of the monthly payments and with almost no incidental expenses. Of even greater importance is the fact that these astonishingly liberal credit terms are made available to people with virtually no credit rating.

In contrast, if subdivision houses are sold outright with the buyer giving back a first and second trust deed, the down payment is usually larger and the closing costs may include escrow and recording fees as well as investigation and title insurance costs. . . . When everything is considered, the price the buyer pays for low down payment financing under an instalment sales contract is exorbitant. One seller found it could market houses under trust deed financing for $295 down, while only $95 down was required for instalment contract financing. Thus for only $200 more the buyer could avoid the considerable hazards of purchasing under a land sale contract detailed elsewhere [see pages 200-203 infra]. In addition, most of the incidental expenses of sale are not avoided by buying under instalment sale; they are merely postponed until the time when the buyer takes title, whereupon he is often obliged to pay a refinancing fee as well. . . .

Another expense associated with land sale contract financing results from the practice of vendors of charging buyers higher interest rates than those paid in turn by vendors to their lenders on the underlying trust deeds. Under straight trust deed financing the buyer pays interest on the first trust deed at the going rate which is usually well known throughout the community. Though second trust deed rates are less well established and widely known, any attempt to load the buyer-borrower with excessive interest charges on a second trust deed shows up plainly. High interest rates can be more easily hidden from the buyer in an instalment land contract; even though the buyer realizes that he is paying a premium in interest, he may reconcile himself to it on the ground the contract may only be a temporary arrangement until he can build up enough equity to qualify for a trust deed. . . .

B. TAX CONSEQUENCES

The instalment land contract method of financing land sales has tax advantages that trust deed financing does not enjoy with respect to the time the seller realizes a gain from the sale of land. Several tax court decisions, not acquiesced in by the Commissioner, have held that a cash-basis seller realizes no gain on a sale by instalment land contract until the sum paid by the buyer in instalments exceeds the seller's tax basis on the property. This allows a land contract vendor to postpone his tax liability for [some] years after the sale of a house and lot. . . . The tax treatment of repossession under an instalment land contract is also favorable, in that the repossessing seller's gain is only the sum received from the buyer applied to recovery of the seller's basis of the property, plus the value of any improvements affixed to the property, less depreciation on the property while held by the buyer.

Basic Security Transactions

[More extended treatment of the tax consequences from the use of the installment land contract appears at pages 388-398 infra.]

C. RECOVERY OF POSSESSION

The high default rate in subdivision purchases makes it imperative for the seller to have a fast and inexpensive method of cutting off the claims of defaulting buyers in the houses — or, in the case of raw land developments, in the lots — they contracted to buy in order that the property can be immediately resold. In the case of the sale of houses, an additional problem may be involved: that of ousting the buyer from possession. One reason commonly advanced to explain the prevalence of the instalment land contract is the belief that somehow this financing device is superior to trust deed financing with regard to the seller's remedies on default by the buyer. The lender's remedies under a trust deed are easily stated: he may sell the property under the power of sale contained in the trust deed and thereby cut off all right of redemption of the borrower. The whole process [in California] takes nearly four months; substantial attorney's fees may be incurred.

Cataloging the vendor's remedies under an instalment sale contract compels reference to the whole law of enforcement of contracts. In any inventory of the vendor's arsenal of remedies, the following are usually included: rescission, ejectment, quite title, suit for price, and damages for the breach. But providing the modern subdivision builder with some of these remedies is like giving a farmer a liquid-fuel missile to shoot a lingering crow — too cumbersome, too expensive. What the vendor really wants is that the buyer in default will go away quietly, and the evidence indicates that in the usual case enough pressure — this is sometimes called the "in terrorem" approach — can be brought to bear to retake possession without judicial coercion.[94]

The first step the vendor takes in insuring himself against post-default difficulties is to omit to acknowledge the contract so that it does not qualify for recording. Were the contract recorded, the land covered thereby could not be resold after default, without a release from the buyer, until a quiet title suit was concluded. Sometimes the contract form will include the contractual horrendum which states that the agreement is avoided upon recording the contract. It is doubtful that this clause is effective to attain anything more than the hostility of the judge who has to interpret the contract. However, the informed buyer can becloud the title by assigning the contract and recording the assignment. Perhaps this is one explanation for the frequent presence in contract forms of nonassignment clauses.

---

94. The vice-president of a company that had sold thousands of homes on land instalment sale contracts recalled only one case in eight years where vendees in default refused to move voluntarily. [Hearings Before the Assembly Committee on Real Estate Contracts and Trust Deeds 91 (1961).]

To cut off the buyer's interest in the property upon default, the vendor will commonly include one or the other of two clauses in the contract form. One simply recites that the buyer's rights terminate upon default and authorizes the seller to retake possession by self-help. The other purports to transform the relationship of vendor and purchaser into one of landlord and tenant upon default, thereby presumably granting to the vendor the summary remedy of unlawful detainer whereby possession can be retaken quickly.

I. Hazards of Purchasing Under Instalment Land Contract

[Professor Warren lists and discusses half a dozen hazards for the unlucky installment vendor. The list includes:]

A. *Failure of Land Sale Vendor to [Apply Installment Payments Against the Primary Indebtedness]*
. . . The savings and loan association or other lender financing the development of a subdivision to be marketed by instalment sales contracts deals only with its borrower, the legal title holder. If the land owner fails to appropriate the payments of the contract buyers to the discharge of the loans encumbering the land, the lender may foreclose. The fact that the vendees are not in default in the payments to the land owner is immaterial to the lender. As soon as the owner-vendor goes into default, the lender may file notice of default; it must then send such notice to all persons who have filed a request for such notice. Since the contract vendee normally does not file a request, the lender need not even apprise him of the fact that he may be in imminent danger of losing his home. . . .

B. *Difficulty in Requiring Performance of Vendor*
[Unless the buyer obtains a title report when he signs the contract, he has no real assurance that the vendor owns the land he has contracted to sell or that it is not encumbered beyond the contract price at the time of the sale. The buyer may also be faced with the possibility that the seller may die, transfer his interest to a minor, be out of state, or be in bankruptcy on or before the time of performance. Bankruptcy Act §70(b) states the trustee shall assume or reject any executory contract within sixty days after the adjudication. A federal district court has applied this section to installment land contracts[24] which would leave the installment vendee with a claim for damages instead of an interest in real property.]

---

24. In re New York Investors Mutual Group, Inc., 143 F. Supp. 51 (S.D.N.Y. 1956) [footnote in original article].

Basic Security Transactions

C. *Claims of Judgment Creditors*
[Statement of the problem: After the contract is signed, X obtains and dockets a judgment against the vendor. What are the rights of the vendee with respect to X? Does the result depend upon whether the vendee is in possession or not? Discussion of the issues raised by these facts appears in Miller v. Green, infra p. 705, and at notes 2 and 3, the rights of judgment creditors to recording act protection, pages 698-699 infra.]

D. *Mechanics' Lien Claimants* . . .

E. *Federal Tax Liens* . . .

F. *Further Encumbrance Clause*
An instalment contract buyer cautious enough to read through the boiler-plate of his form contract is likely to come upon a clause which says: "Seller shall have the right to encumber the property at any time or to refinance any existing encumbrance. . . ." The purpose of this clause is to allow the vendor to borrow more money on the security of the land sold without the further consent of the vendee. It is said that the further encumbrance clause is legitimately used by the builders to take advantage of the appreciation in value of tracts they have sold on instalment contract, for it enables them to go back to their lender and increase the amount of the loan to a sum not exceeding the unpaid balance of the contract.

Taken at face value this clause grants to the vendor the power to subject the interest of the buyer to the rights of encumbrancers subsequent in point of time to the sale of the land. It is not surprising that this clause has been subject to abuse by unscrupulous vendors. The most flagrant example of this occurred during the brief but tumultuous period during which the so-called "ten-percenters" flourished in this state.[62] The "ten-percenters" advertised that they would select and sell second trust deeds to investors at a sum that would yield ten percent earnings per annum. If no trust deed was available for sale to an investor, his money was accepted and ten percent interest was paid on it until a trust deed could be obtained. The response to advertisements of "secured ten percent earnings" was astonishing; "ten-percenters" found themselves with huge deposits of money and few trust deeds to sell. Clearly second trust deeds would have to be mass-produced to provide the requisite supply.

They were. In its simplest form, the process by which junior trust deeds were created operated in this way. The subdivision builder bought the raw land by giving the owner a subordinated trust deed. A construction loan was obtained by giving a first trust deed to a financial institution; when

---

62. For a short description of the activities of the "ten percenters," see Subcommittee on Real Estate Contracts and Trust Deeds, Final Report, 23 Cal. Assembly Interim Committee Reps. 72-77 (1960).

construction was completed, permanent first deed financing was obtained. Either before or after the houses were sold on instalment land contract, the builder or an assignee who had taken over the tract wrote trust deeds on each of the lots and sold them to "ten-percenters" at heavy discounts. In some cases the total indebtedness secured by a tract lot exceeded the purchase price of the property.

NOTES AND QUESTIONS

1. Evidence mounts that in California and elsewhere parties now use the installment land contract as a mortgage substitute even more widely than during the early 1960s, when Dean Warren wrote the above excerpts. Remember that the installment land contract entails a seller-financed transaction and replaces the seller's deed and the buyer's purchase-money mortgage.

Remember, too, that you should not confuse (even though courts sometimes do) the installment land contract with the contract of sale. The former is a financing device, a mortgage substitute. The latter is a marketing device that "codifies" the agreement between seller and buyer during the relatively short but necessary interval from the reaching of agreement to the "closing of title." Typically, the contract of sale is performed within 90 days, while the installment land contract remains executory for many years. Chapter Four, infra, treats the problems associated with the contract of sale.

Because their functions differ, doctrine relative to one device does (should) not necessarily apply to the other.

2. Remember, too, that you should not confuse the installment land contract with the "installment sale," I.R.C. §453, a federal income tax concept we shall examine later at pages 388-398 infra. The installment sale may involve a land contract, but it may also be structured around a deed and mortgage. When Dean Warren wrote his article, no California decisions dealt with the priority rights of the subsequent encumbrance over a vendee in (or out of) possession under an unrecorded installment land contract. Quite possibly, the state supreme court's insistence upon fair dealing between the parties to a real estate transaction, which one finds in the 1967 decision of Handy v. Gordon, 65 Cal. 2d 578, 422 P.2d 329, 55 Cal. Rptr. 769 (1967), would lead to the court's refusal to enforce the further encumbrance clause. For its part, the California legislature in 1963 made it a crime for one who sells property on an unrecorded installment contract to further encumber the property in an amount which, together with the existing encumbrances thereon, exceeds the amount due under the contract, or under which the total amount of payments that

would be due each month would exceed the monthly payments due under the contract, without the consent of the vendee. Cal. Civ. Code §2985.2 (West Supp. 1985).

3. Quite a few states have now legislated to give the installment land contract buyer greater protection against some of the perils described above. Maryland's statute requires inter alia that:

a. The contract shall be in writing, signed by all parties, and contain all terms;
b. The buyer shall be given a copy of the contract and shall have an unconditional right to cancel the contract until the copy is received;
c. The vendor shall record the contract within 15 days from its signing; otherwise, the buyer may cancel;
d. Unless the contract specifies an earlier date, the buyer may demand upon payment of 40 percent of the purchase price that he receive a deed on condition that he execute a purchase money mortgage for the unpaid balance and absorb specified closing expenses;
e. The vendor shall furnish to the buyer periodic statements showing the unpaid contract balance and the disbursement — for taxes, insurance, debt service, etc. — of the installment payments. [Md. Real Prop. Code Ann. §§10-102–108 (Supp. 1984).]

Ohio enumerates what every installment land contract must contain as a statutory minimum. This includes a statement of any encumbrances against the property, a provision that the vendor furnish evidence of title, a requirement of recordation, and a statement of any pending order of any public agency against the property. Ohio Rev. Code Ann., ch. 5313 §5313.02 (Baldwin 1980).

4. Congress has brought interstate land sales, often based upon installment contracts, within its regulatory ambit. Interstate Land Sales Full Disclosure Act, 15 U.S.C.A. §§1701-1720 (1982).

5. Courts and legislatures have also acted to relieve some of the harshness of the installment contract if the buyer defaults. Problems of contract default are treated at page 345 infra.

6. Further bibliography includes: Hetland, The California Land Contract, 48 Calif. L. Rev. 729 (1960); Rozynes, Florida Installment Land Contracts: A Time for Reform, 28 U. Fla. L. Rev. 156 (1975); Shanker, The Treatment of Executory Contracts and Leases in Bankruptcy Chapter X and XI Proceedings, 18 Prac. Law. No. 4, 15 (April 1972); Nelson and Whitman, Installment Land Contract — A National Viewpoint, 1977 B.Y.U.L. Rev. 541; Note, Remedying the Inequities of Forfeiture in Land Installment Contracts, 64 Iowa L. Rev. 158 (1978); Randolph, Updating the Oregon Installment Land Contract, 15 Williamette L.J. 181 (1979); Note, Installment Land Contracts: Developing Law in Virginia, 37 Wash. & Lee L. Rev. 1161 (1980).

Harris and Hines, Installment Land Contracts in Iowa[30]
1, 2-3 (1965)

Ownership of a farm of his own has been an objective of the American farmer since earliest times. Until about the time of World War I the aspiring young couple could go west and preempt, homestead, or buy with little or no cash a family-sized farm of their own. As the west became settled and competition for land became keen, young farmers found it increasingly difficult to attain ownership — tenancy increased rapidly and many young farmers remained hired men until middle aged, some permanently. The chief ways to become a farm owner were to be born or marry into the right family or to progress up the agricultural ladder from laborer to tenant to owner. Regardless of which procedure was used, credit became an essential element in the acquiring of control over farm land. . . .

With few exceptions until recently, land credit was available only to those who could make a substantial down payment — usually 50 percent or more of the purchase price and seldom less than 35 percent. This high-equity financing generally was associated with mortgage lending. Low-equity credit involving down payments of less than 35 percent was used sparingly. The installment land contract was usually the security device for purchasing land with a small down payment.

Land contracts were used in the Midwest during settlement times, particularly in the cut-over areas of the lake states, by the railroads in disposing of their land grants and by large speculative land companies in selling their holdings. Later land contracts were used to dispose of properties acquired by lenders at distress sales during the early 1930's. Since World War II, land contracts have enjoyed widespread popularity as a low-equity financing device in the sale of both urban and rural property. In Iowa the use of land contracts increased sixfold during the decade of the 1950's, from 7 percent to 42 percent of all farm real estate transfers.

THE PROBLEM

Recent trends in the use of credit to finance farm purchases furnish some insight into the nature and magnitude of the problem. Data on the use of land contracts in financing farm sales have become available only recently on a national basis. For the Midwest, they may be summarized briefly as follows:

1. Buyers of farm land are using credit increasingly to finance the transactions. . . .

[2. The average purchase price of the 154 farms was $28,422, with an average down payment of $5,861 (21.4 percent), leaving an unpaid princi-

---

30. Footnotes omitted.

pal sum of $22,561. The debt was to be repaid, with an average interest of 4.0 percent, over a term of 16.5 years. (This interest rate was competitive with the rate for comparable real estate mortgage loans.) At the end of the term, in the absence of prepayment, the remaining average contract debt balloon) was $6,516. . . . (Editor's summary of pp. 23-24.)

3. The relationship between interest rate and the consanguinity of the contracting parties was as follows (pp. 26-27):

Group	Average Interest Rate
Father-son	3.63
Other relatives	3.47
Friends	3.86
Strangers	4.33

4. Most of the contracts used the constant amortization (Springfield Plan) method of debt service. The average first-year payment was $1,999 — $1,106 principal and $893 interest. . . . (Pp. 32-33.)

5. Not a single unrecorded contract was found. Yet, in nearby Kansas, only an estimated 10 percent of all land contracts are recorded. The universality of recording in Iowa is best explained by the right given by statute to record a notice of forfeiture, which is sufficient to eliminate the buyer's record interest. . . . (P. 22.)

6. In almost half of the contracts surveyed, one of the parties was without his own legal counsel. Many of the unrepresented buyers depended upon the seller's lawyer to have the papers in proper order. . . . (P. 16.)

7. Each of the 154 contract buyers was asked a battery of thirteen questions to test his knowledge of land contract law and the contract provisions. Questions ranged from whether the buyer could prepay to whether he could redeem in case of forfeiture. The average of the scores was 6.0. Two buyers failed to answer any questions correctly and no buyer answered correctly more than eleven questions. . . . (Pp. 105-107.)]

Mixon, Installment Land Contracts: A Study of Low Income Transactions, with Proposals for Reform and a New Program to Provide Home Ownership in the Inner City

7 Hous. L. Rev. 523-535 (1970)

I. INTRODUCTION

The rich, the middle class, and the poor place a high value on home ownership. The rich have never had any difficulty becoming homeowners, and therefore will not be discussed further. Today, the middle class can buy a home with a small down payment, and with monthly installments which are lower than rent. But the poor are to a great extent precluded from becoming homeowners. And when low income families try to buy a house, they are likely to pay a high price for low quality housing. Further, they find their ambitions frustrated by a system which they neither understand nor control.

The Federal Government has helped middle income families become homeowners; it has indirectly ruled out home ownership for low income families. Forty years ago home ownership was as illusive a goal for middle class families as it is today for low income families because the mortgage banker required 30 to 40 percent equity on home purchase loans. If today's purchaser of a $30,000 subdivision home had to have $10,000 cash for a down payment, there would be few subdivisions and few middle class homeowners. In order to open the "system" to accommodate middle income home buyers, Congress created the Federal Housing Administration (FHA). . . .

It is obvious that the middle class home purchaser is aided by the Federal Government. How about the poor? In order to cut down on losses from foreclosures, the FHA established both minimum credit standards for its purchasers and guidelines for determining whether a given buyer could afford to make the payments. In a nation where millions of families exist on incomes below the poverty level, it is apparent that not everybody can meet FHA's businesslike standards. To its credit, the FHA and the other government programs did not ignore the poor completely. Instead, they categorized them as "renters," and through public housing programs and FHA low rent projects subsidized construction of thousands of housing units to be rented to the poor. The public housing program even set strict income limitations for occupancy, with the result that the public housing occupants are *required* to be poor.

Governmental programs thus establish a class distinction which is not based on any presence or absence of subsidy. Both the middle class and the poor receive housing subsidies from the Federal Government. The distinction is that the middle class is subsidized by tax deductions and encouraged to become *owners*, while the poor are subsidized more directly, but are required to be *renters*. As it turns out, the middle class's home ownership subsidy proves to be popular with the middle class; public housing and rent subsidy are not so popular with the poor.

Home ownership can be as high an ideal for the poor as for the middle class. In some localities, private sellers have sensed this demand for ownership by low income families, and sought to fill it. In one type of transaction, delapidated housing (perhaps moved onto a vacant lot from a new highway site) is sold to a low income purchaser for two or three times its cost. Or a tract developer may buy several hundred acres outside of the center city and separate it into lots and blocks. He then mortgages the land for construction costs, and builds small houses with marginal amenities. These are offered for sale to the poor. Neither the house nor the purchasers can qualify for FHA or VA financing.

Low income buyers of this type housing have a theoretical choice between two methods of financing their purchase. The first method is by a standard deed and mortgage transaction. Following the conservative lender's rule, the purchaser would pay about one-third down and get a deed to his property. He would borrow two-thirds of the purchase price from a moneylender, and execute a standard mortgage and promissory note to secure repayment of the loan. Thus, on a $10,000 house purchase, the buyer would pay $3,333 down, along with closing costs which can range as high as $400. It is a rare low income purchaser who can come up with this substantial cash downpayment. And if he can, it should be noted that he is buying on about the same terms as the unassisted buyer of 50 years ago.

The second method of financing housing purchases for low income buyers is through the use of the *installment land contract,* a merchandising technique that has become widely used for selling low income housing. This article will focus on the use of the installment contract, with primary emphasis on practices in the Houston, Texas area.

[Professor Mixon then analyzes the comparative transactional costs of the deed-mortgage and installment land sale methods. Although his data now is 15 years old, the relative costs, adjusted for inflation, will not have changed. — EDS.]

A. THE DEED-MORTGAGE TRANSACTION

Whatever its qualitative disadvantages for the contract vendee, the installment land transaction carries a distinct cost advantage over the standard deed and mortgage transaction. On a purchase financed by a $10,000 FHA loan, the cost to the purchaser at the closing is estimated by a board of realtors to be as follows:

Mortgagee's Title Policy	$ 15.00
Survey	30.00
Attorney's Fees	30.00
Recording Fee	15.00
Escrow Fee	5.00
Copies of Restrictions	5.00
FHA Appraisal Fee	35.00
Credit Report	7.50
Photographs	7.50
1% Brokerage	100.00
Total	$250.00

To the above amounts must be added the following prepaid items for which a purchaser must provide cash at the time of the closing:

FHA Mutual Mortgage Insurance Premium (1 month)	$ 4.14
Hazard Insurance Premium (1 year)	72.00
Hazard Insurance Premium (2 mo.)	12.00
Tax Proration (3½ mo.)	63.00
Interim Interest (15 days)	25.00
Total Prepaid Items	$176.14

The total of the closing costs and prepaid items is $426.14. In addition to these expenses, the purchaser must make at least a 3 percent down payment on his house. The FHA buyer therefore has to come up with about $735.00 cash at the time he purchases a $10,300 house.

It is appropriate to note that the buyer does not really get $10,300 worth of house if value is measured by cost of construction plus profit to the builder. Transactional costs eat into the seller's as well as the buyer's pocketbooks. Upon sale of the same $10,300 house, the seller must bear the following costs according to the board of realtors:

Owner's Title Policy	$117.00
Attorney's Fee	15.00
Recording Fee	3.00
Tax Certificates	5.00
Escrow Fee	5.00
Loan Discount (8%)	800.00
Total Seller's Costs	$945.00

In addition to the costs itemized above, the seller must oftentimes pay a real estate broker a commission for finding the buyer. Assuming a 5 percent commission, the seller's expenses could be as high as $1,450.

Calculated on the figures supplied by the board of realtors, a buyer who purchases a $10,300 house really pays $10,550 not counting prepaid items, but he gets only $8,850 worth of house ($10,300 less $1,450), calculated on the net return to the seller. The transactional cost load can eat up as much as $1,600, or about 15 percent of the cost of the house.

Although the above figures were applicable at a time when mortgage money was "tight" and the FHA discount correspondingly high, it is fair to say that the mortgage transaction is a costly one, both to the seller and to the buyer. Part of this cost is the fault of an archaic system of land titles which necessitates that a buyer demand title insurance to avoid the risk of total loss of his investment. However, the major costs come from merchandising the land through real estate brokers, and from the premium and discount demands which mortgage companies make as a condition to lending money at their disposal.

B. THE INSTALLMENT LAND CONTRACT

By contrast, the purchaser who bought a $10,300 house by the means of an installment land contract might have to pay only a little more than $86.16 in cash, this representing the first month's installment on the purchase price calculated at 8 percent interest and on a 20-year payout. Using an installment contract, the vendor would get a full $10,300 investment at a good interest rate. Although installment buyers are occasionally required to make somewhat greater down payments, there is still very little wasted money in the transaction.

The installment land contract eliminates these cost items incident to a mortgage transaction:

1. *Mortgagee's Title Policy*—($15.00)—The mortgagee's policy is required in a mortgage transaction because the mortgagee does not want to run the risk that the buyer's title will fail. The cost of the mortgagee's policy is low because it is issued as a companion to the buyer's $117.00 policy which is shown as a seller's expense. In the installment land sale there is no need for mortgagee's title insurance because functionally, the contract vendor stands in the place of the mortgagee as financer, and it is the vendor's own title which would be at issue. He therefore needs no further protection.
2. *Survey*—($30.00)—Both the title insurance company and the mortgagee want to be certain there is no encroachment onto the purchased land by neighboring landowners. In addition, they want to be sure the land described in the deed is still owned and possessed by the seller. Therefore, they require a survey. However, to the contract vendor, encroachments are not a particular transactional concern because presumably he is aware of what has been happening to his boundaries. A land sale contract vendee is not likely to be aware of the problem or of the need for a survey. Therefore, without either title insurance or a mortgage, there will generally not be a survey.
3. *Attorney's Fees*—($30.00)—This fee represents the cost of preparing the mortgage instrument and note. Because there is no mortgage or note in the installment sale, there is no fee for these services.
4. *Recording Fee*—($15.00)—This fee is for recording the mortgage. Because there is no mortgage in the installment land contract, there is no recording fee.
5. *Escrow Fee*—($5.00)—This represents the buyer's half of the fee normally paid to the title company for handling the closing. The installment land contract is a one-step transaction, and there is no formal closing with a third party participant; hence, there is no escrow fee.

6. *Copies of Restrictions*—($5.00)—This expense relates to residential subdivisions under private deed restrictions. The primary purpose of providing a copy of these restrictions is to let the buyer know what land use restrictions there are which are not insured against by the title policy. This is not applicable to the installment land sale.
7. *FHA Appraisal Fee*—($35.00)—The FHA requires an appraisal of the house to determine whether it is worth the amount of the loan. For housing sold under an installment land contract, there is no FHA financing, no appraisal, and no appraisal fee.
8. *Credit Report*—($7.50)—Since the mortgage lender relies on the personal financial status of the buyer, he wants to be certain the buyer does not have a bad credit reputation. However, the installment contract seller probably assumes that the people he deals with would not pass a standard credit report. If they could, they probably would not deal with him. There is therefore no credit report, and no fee in the installment land contract transaction.
9. *Photographs*—($7.50)—In the deed and mortgage transaction, photographs of the house go into the mortgage file. There is no mortgage file, and therefore no need for photographs in the installment land contract transaction.
10. *1 Percent Brokerage Fee*—($100.00)—The brokerage fee is paid to the mortgage company as a bonus for lending money, or to a mortgage broker as a fee for locating a moneylender. The FHA will not allow over 1 percent of the loan to be paid as a brokerage fee by the buyer. The remainder of any brokerage fee is shown as a seller's expense, and is in reality a discount to make up for the difference between the market rate of interest and the interest rate allowable under FHA regulations. Because the contract vendor normally finances the installment sale, there is no brokerage fee. The contract vendor is likely to make up for this, however, by charging a higher overall interest rate than would a mortgage lender.
11. *Prepaid Items*—The contract vendee is just as favored on prepaid terms.
    a. *FHA mutual mortgage insurance premium*—($4.14)—There is no mortgage insurance for the installment land contract, and hence no premium need be paid.
    b. *Hazard insurance premium*—($84.00 for 14 months)—The mortgagor in an FHA transaction has to provide a year's prepaid insurance; he later pays an amount sufficient to meet subsequent premiums into an escrow fund. The installment contracts examined in the study area do not have an advance payment provision covering insurance or tax escrow. This is one cost in the deed and mortgage transaction which is not

Basic Security Transactions

purely wasted, and which some installment land contract vendors have justifiably begun to impose upon vendees.

c. *Tax proration*—($63.00)—Tax payments are treated in a like manner as insurance premium payments. A monthly escrow payment for taxes is provided in the mortgage transaction but is seldom used in installment sales.

d. *Interim interest*—($25.00)—Interim interest is charged between the time the mortgage loan is made, and the first of the month, when payments begin. Although a close accounting might disclose otherwise, there is no indication that installment sellers charge interim interest.

12. *Costs to the Seller*—The following costs to the seller are eliminated in the installment land contract sale:

    a. *Owner's title policy*—($117.00)—The archaic system of land title recordation in this country is such that no purchaser can be sure that his title is good without an expensive title search or a title insurance policy. Even if a buyer is unaware of the need for a title policy, the mortgagee will require that a title policy be purchased. On the other hand, installment land contract buyers are unaware of the need for title insurance. They trust the seller unduly and are not protected by a third party such as a mortgagee. They probably could not get a policy of title insurance protecting their interest anyway. For these reasons, there is no money spent for a title policy.

    b. *Attorney's fees*—($15.00)—This fee covers preparation of the deed in the standard mortgage transaction. There is no such fee involved in the usual installment land sale. The installment form is simple and needs only the names of the parties, the description of the contract, the purchase price, and the interest rate entered. However, when, and if, the price of the land is paid, the seller must provide a deed. Thus, this fee is deferred until the contract is completed.

    c. *Recording fee*—($3.00)—In the mortgage transaction, this fee pays for recording the deed which the buyer receives from the seller. In the installment land sale, the deed will not be handed over until the end of the contract term. No fee will be paid until then. The primary instrument governing the rights of the parties during the interim, the installment contract, will not be recorded. The seller will not want the contract recorded, because in the event of a default, he can regain possession and resell the house without having to remove the first buyer's formal contract claim from the public records.

    d. *Tax certificates*—($5.00)—In the deed-mortgage transaction, it is to the buyer's and mortgagee's benefit to insure that taxes have been paid through the date of purchase. Hence, the mortgagee will secure from the seller a tax certificate. In the installment contract sale, it is equally important that a buyer know whether back taxes have been paid. However, without the institutional protection afforded by the presence of a mortgagee, there is little likelihood that the buyer will receive a tax certificate. There is therefore no fee.

e. *Escrow fee*—($5.00)—This is the seller's half of the fee paid to the title company for handling the closing. Because the installment land transaction is a simple one-step proceeding, there is no closing, no third party escrow agent, and therefore no fee.

f. *Loan discount*—($800.00)—This discount represents the usual amount paid by the seller to entice the mortgagee to lend at the FHA interest rate. As noted, FHA regulations prevent the buyer from paying more than 1 percent as brokerage points. Therefore, the seller must absorb any additional "points" required to get mortgage financing. In the installment land sale, there is no loan discount in the transaction because the contract vendor is the financer. The cost of money is reflected in the transaction, however, because the installment seller's rate of interest will be higher than the rate charged by the mortgagee.

g. *Real estate broker's fee*—($500.00)—In the study area, there was no indication of broker activity in the sale of installment land contract houses. Instead, the sale appears to be handled directly between the seller, or the seller's employees, and the buyer. Real estate brokers are useful when there is a geographically widespread area within which houses suitable to a given class of buyers may be found. But because the poor and minority groups are often limited to certain parts of the community by lack of money and social pressure, it may be fairly easy for seller and buyer to come together without the assistance of a real estate agent.

The overall cost picture can be summarized as follows: From the purchaser's standpoint, the cost advantages of the installment land contract are about $650.00, or the difference between the cash payment of $86.16 required for the installment land contract and the cash payment of $735.00 required for an FHA mortgage on the same house. Including both seller's and buyer's costs, the advantage for the installment land contract is about $2,100.00 or the difference between total cost of $86.16 for the installment land contract and $2,200.00 for the FHA mortgage transaction.

[Query: In evaluating the comparative figures above, consider what part of the land contract's cost advantage consists of risk-assumption (usually unwittingly) by the contract-vendee.]

Basic Security Transactions

PROBLEM

In his article on California installment contracts, Dean Warren alludes to the seller's ability to hide interest rates higher than the stated contract rate and sometimes even higher than third-party lenders would charge on second mortgages. This practice may further explain the installment contract's growing popularity and deserves to be carefully understood. Consider the following illustration:

Seller wishes to sell property for $50,000. The property carries a $30,000 first mortgage bearing 8 percent interest and $2,780 annual debt service. Buyer can raise $4,000 in cash and must finance the balance of the purchase price. The parties enter into an installment contract:

Contract Price:	$50,000
Down Payment:	$4,000
Contract Balance:	$46,000
Terms:	$5,814 yearly, which includes 12 percent interest on the unpaid contract balance

Now consider the first year's events. Buyer pays $5,814. From this payment, seller remits $2,780 to the holder of the first mortgage. This sum includes $2,400 interest (0.8 × $30,000) and $380 principal. Notice, however, that seller is actually getting 12 percent interest on the first mortgage part of the contract price, which the bank has financed, as well as on the $16,000 of the contract price that seller has financed. In short, seller receives a 4 percent override on the bank's investment in the property.

For the first year, seller's *effective* return is not the contract's stated 12 percent, but a concealed 19.5 percent!

	Interest
$16,000 at 12 percent	$1,920
[$30,000 at 4 percent]	$1,200
Total	$3,120

Rate of Return $\frac{\$ 3,120}{\$16,000} = 19.5$ percent

See if you can compute seller's effective interest return for the second year. Is it higher or lower than 19.5 percent?

Note, finally, that hidden interest charges occur only when the property has already been mortgaged and the mortgage rate is lower than the contract rate.

Do you see any relevance to our earlier discussion of leverage, page 133 supra?

Do you see any relevance to our earlier discussion of "due-on" clauses, page 143 supra?

e. Miscellaneous Security Devices

Although we will examine them more fully later, both the lease (with and without an option to purchase) and the sale-and-leaseback are financing devices in which the lessor extends credit to the lessee and retains a security interest — his right to reenter in the event of default. To think of a lease as a financing device may seem odd, until one realizes that the lessor has given his tenant the use of an asset having a specific value for a finite term, on condition that the tenant return the asset unimpaired at the end of the term and pay "interest" on the asset value during the term of the lease.[31] What makes the lease both a financing and security device is the landlord's reserved or statutory power to terminate the lease if the "debt service" is not paid. If this power did not exist, the landlord could sue only for damages for contract breach.

The sale-and-leaseback is a complex mortgage substitute that is becoming commonplace, especially where the assets have commercial value: industrial plants, office buildings, shopping centers, aircraft, etc. We will see why later in Chapter Seven infra.

2. Junior (or Secondary) Financing

a. Conventional Second Mortgages

Spellman, A Banker's Tour Through the Second Mortgage Market
148 Bankers Magazine 19-20, 22, 23, 24-25 (No. 2, Spring 1965)

To many commercial bankers, second mortgages are a fringe-type accommodation — legal, but not eminently respectable. This impression is by no means strange, since commercial banks are rigidly restricted by law to first mortgage lending, on the basis of prescribed ratios of the appraised values of property.

Nevertheless, a number of compelling facts about second mortgages command the banker's attention. With roughly half of our material wealth represented by real estate, even the vast amount of institutional first mortgage lending activity in this country leaves a great deal of capital still to be raised to finance commercial, industrial and residential realty. Significant sums of junior capital are needed, which — in contrast to conventional corporate demands for funds — are not generally available through routine investment banking channels.

---

31. How is the interest rate (i.e., the rental) determined? What is the relationship between interest rates on money and "interest" rates on real property? As a percentage of asset value, would you expect that rents on land would be higher or lower than rents on buildings? Why?

Much junior capital for real estate purposes is furnished by means of the second mortgage device. Both institutional lenders and individuals make such loans. Recently active in the institutional sector are finance companies, which have displayed a disposition to extend such accommodations for two important reasons: in order to diversify their activities, and to enter a relatively untapped area of considerable magnitude.

Commercial banks enter the second mortgage picture indirectly, but in a number of ways. First, banks have real estate customers and therefore must develop an awareness and knowledge of the second mortgage market. A realization that second mortgages can be obtained on short notice from secondary lenders permits a more accurate appraisal of the liquidity of these real estate accounts. Mortgageability as well as marketability of real estate customer assets are important to the bank credit analyst. Additionally significant is the fact that the second mortgage lender will often be willing to lend without recourse to the borrower, looking exclusively to the real estate as security.

Other avenues of contract are equally clear. Because banks lend at wholesale to finance companies, they must be familiar with the fields into which their borrowers are expanding. In addition, bankers must be *au courant* on availability of second mortgage money, to be able to refer their own customers to secondary lenders when their requirements for such additional funds arise. Frequently, the bank can fulfill its customer's needs in cooperation with a secondary lender. Financial guidance of this nature is part of the routine public service which banks customarily render to their depositors. . . .

WILLING LENDERS

The secondary mortgage market is made up of a variety of lenders wishing to obtain a high yield on relatively short-term paper. These include:

- Commercial financing companies, such as AIC Financial Corporation, Allied Concord Financial Corporation, Walter E. Heller & Co., Inc., Rosenthal & Rosenthal, Inc., James Talcott, Inc. and others seeking to expand their portfolios and diversify their commercial receivables by adding real estate lending to their portfolios.
- Real estate finance companies, such as Equity Capital Corporation, Kirkeby-Natus Corp., and The Mastan Company, Incorporated, having a capital structure similar to commercial financing companies, but oriented to real estate lending.
- Industrial corporations, such as Curtiss Wright Corp., List Industries, and Merritt, Chapman & Scott, and real estate holding companies such as Transcontinental Investing Corporation, which seek to invest their excess cash.
- Small Business Investment Companies which seek medium-term loans convertible into real estate equities.

- Other specialized lenders, such as The Sixty Trust, a pool of sixty private pension funds, and many individual funds.
- Foreign investors seeking dollar obligations at near-equity without the inconvenience of ownership.
- Private individuals and syndicates of private individuals.

In addition, Government Agencies, notably the Small Business Administration and the Area Redevelopment Administration, have available second mortgage funds at low rates as part of their program to provide small business with working capital, particularly in areas of high unemployment. State and local agencies such as the Pennsylvania Industrial Development Authority, the Rhode Island Development Council, and the New York City Industrial Development Corporation, make long-term low-rate second mortgages to encourage local industrial development. . . .

SAFE SECONDS

A second mortgage may sometimes be safer than a first mortgage on the same property, for the very reason that the second mortgage is for a shorter term. The idea of a junior position being safer than a senior position appears to be self-contradictory, but the term is the key. Consider a new office building fully rented. The tenants are substantial companies who have executed five-year leases for rentals which are comparable to the rentals for similar properties. The rental is sufficient to pay all taxes, expenses and debt service on the first mortgage (which is the usual 20-year self-liquidating institutional mortgage) plus an additional cash flow of X dollars. A second mortgage is granted for 5 times X dollars, less interest over the period and a margin of safety. Assuming that all of the tenants pay their rent, the second mortgagee's position will be liquidated in five years, while 90% of the original first mortgage will still be unpaid at the end of this period. In a sense the first mortgagee has, in exchange for his preferred position, underwritten the potential of the building for the remaining 15 years; for no one can guarantee that the leases will be renewed at comparable rentals or that economic conditions will be such that the space can be re-rented at that time, not to mention the fact that the first mortgagee is committed to a fixed interest rate for the entire term of its loan.

On the other hand, many second mortgages carry with them a considerable amount of risk. Where the economic success of the property is based largely upon the character and success of a business being conducted at the premises, the lender is not dealing with space as a commodity, but rather with management skill as an investment. So-called "specialty" properties, such as bowling enterprises, restaurants, nightclubs and, to a lesser extent, hotels, motels and nursing homes, are considered to fall into this category. The pattern of financing for these properties shows that the first mortgage is typically for a very low ratio to appraised value—generally 30% to 50%—to compensate for the added risk.

Many second mortgage loans are also made for the purpose of adding to, improving or renovating an existing property. The term "mezzanine" financing has been coined by some secondary lenders for these situations, it being felt that the first mortgagee has the "ground floor" financing. The improved income after the addition or renovation is then applied to liquidate the second mortgage.

Some illustrative examples of second-mortgage financing are in order:

A purchaser of an older office building approached a commercial finance company for a second mortgage loan to provide a portion of the purchase price. Although a new first mortgage could probably be obtained, it would take three or four months to process the application. The existing first mortgage had been reduced from $900,000 to $450,000 over a period of 10 years and was made at a time when the interest rate was 4%. The purchaser found it cheaper to obtain a $150,000 second mortgage from a commercial finance company at 10% per annum rather than to obtain a new $600,000 first mortgage at 6% per annum. In addition, he would save on closing costs and brokerage fees on the lesser sum and would not give up valuable prepayment rights which had come into effect after the first mortgage loan had become seasoned.

A California builder completed a subdivision of 100 homes in the Los Angeles area. Local savings banks were willing to provide long-term first mortgage money on a formula basis. To encourage sales, the builder offered second mortgages to purchasers with good credit backgrounds but who lacked the full down payment. The second mortgages were then discounted on a wholesale basis with a finance company. The builder was thus able to accelerate the disposition of his inventory of homes and save the cost of carrying them until sold. By discounting his mortgage paper, the builder raised sufficient cash to begin another development. The finance company obtained in bulk a desirable portfolio with a diversity of credit risks. . . .

Terms

Second mortgage rates generally vary from 9% up. Among the major lenders the rate rarely exceeds 15%. If the loan cannot be made at a rate in this range, professional lenders consider it too risky. The term of the loan depends in part on the lender's financial structure. Finance companies whose permitted borrowing ratios presuppose a short-term portfolio prefer maturities of up to three years and rarely exceed five years, while SBIC's operating under governmental regulations make relatively long-term loans since they are not permitted to make loans for less than five years. Many loans are written on a discount basis, so that the mortgage itself will appear on record to bear a conventional rate of interest, such as 6%, the true yield to the lender being undisclosed. In addition, the borrower will pay, as is customary, recording taxes and fees, stamp taxes, title insurance fees and premiums, legal and appraisal fees, and brokerage charges. . . .

Legal Matters

The documentation of a second mortgage transaction necessarily contains the same features as a first mortgage and the closing requirements are usually similar with certain covenants customarily added:

1. A default on the first mortgage is an event of default under the second mortgage.
2. The borrower will not amend the terms of the first mortgage, or of any lease, or cancel any lease, or accept any advance rentals except as contemplated by the leases, or grant any rent concessions not set forth in the leases.
3. The borrower will pay the first mortgage payments and all taxes, insurance, water rents, sewer charges and similar items and upon failure to do so, the second mortgagee may pay them and add them to the second mortgage debt.
4. The borrower shall, at the second mortgagee's request, enter into an escrow arrangement to provide for the first mortgage payments, and (if not previously escrowed by the first mortgagee) taxes, insurance and similar items.
5. The second mortgagee may accelerate the loan if the property is sold or there is a change of management.
6. The borrower will insure the property for an amount sufficient to cover the first and second mortgages and will also provide rent insurance or business interruption insurance where required.
7. The borrower will deliver to the second mortgagee an assignment of rents where required.[32]

The first mortgage should be examined for special provisions which may affect the second mortgagee's security. Since the second mortgagee will invariably find the property more easily marketable with existing first mortgage financing intact, an effort should be made to correct unusual default or acceleration provisions in the first mortgage. An "open end" clause in the first mortgage which may subsequently increase the first mortgage lien to the disadvantage of the second mortgagee should be similarly dealt with. Wherever possible, a certificate of reduction of mortgage, lienor's estoppel certificate, or similar certification by the first mort-

---

32. Consider the purpose of each of the seven covenants. — Eds.

gagee should be obtained, fixing the mortgage amount and certifying that, to the knowledge of the first mortgagee, no default exists under its loan.

Servicing

A second mortgage is serviced in the same manner as a first mortgage, except that the second mortgagee must at all times be vigilant as to the first mortgage covenants. The above technique involves creating an escrow for this purpose; an alternate is to have properly spaced payment dates, requiring the borrower to exhibit timely proof that the first mortgage payment has been made. A third is to have the borrower forward the first mortgage payments to the second mortgagee for transmittal prior to the due date of the payment.

Many second mortgagees also notify the first mortgagee of their interest, requesting that copies of notice of default be forwarded to them. Although first mortgagees are reluctant to enter into agreements obligating themselves to provide such notice, the reputable institutions will usually note their records and co-operate with the second mortgagee, especially since it is invariably in their interest to do so, as the second mortgagee may intervene and cure a first mortgage default.

Existing insurance may be adequate to protect the first mortgagee but not the second, and should be reviewed. The possibility of an inadequate amount of insurance is not remote in situations where the property has appreciated in value since the time the first mortgage was placed, and the old insurance may very well be inadequate. Where the second mortgagee is relying upon income from lease rentals, the need for rent insurance in addition to the usual fire and extended coverage should be considered.

b. The Wrap-around Mortgage

Lifton, Practical Real Estate in the '80s: Legal, Tax and Business Strategies
390-398 (2d ed. 1983)

The wrap around mortgage, sometimes also called the "all inclusive" or "overriding" mortgage, is another form of junior mortgage which is subordinated to one or more existing mortgages which remain outstanding and unsatisfied. It differs from the usual junior mortgage in that the face amount of the wrap around mortgage includes the amount of the existing prior mortgages as well as the amount of junior lien. Thus, if there is a first mortgage on the property of $1,000,000 and secondary financing of $300,000 is desired, the traditional method of financing would be to place a $300,000 second mortgage on the property junior to the $1,000,000 first mortgage, with each mortgage paid separately. Using a wrap around mortgage, however, the mortgage note would be for $1,300,000 and would provide for the payment to the wrap around mortgagee of an amount sufficient to pay interest and amortization *both* on the underlying first mortgage of $1,000,000 and on the secondary loan of $300,000. The wrap around mortgagee in turn would have the responsibility of making the payments on the underlying mortgage.

Originally, the wrap around mortgage was seen as a form that would offer institutional lenders greater flexibility in making secondary loans. Most institutional lenders either are proscribed by law or have policies against making second mortgage loans. It was believed, however, that even though a wrap around mortgage would still be treated as a non-conforming loan and consigned to the "basket" for allowable exceptions to conforming loans, lenders would feel more comfortable making the loan because of the unusual characteristics of the wrap around form. For the wrap around lender, this form affords better control of the mortgage payments since, as between the wrap around lender and the owner, the lender is in the position of a first mortgagee. All payments are made to the wrap around lender which in turn makes the payments to the underlying mortgagee. In case of default, the wrap around lender can continue to make payments on the underlying mortgage and if necessary, pay off the underlying mortgage so that the wrap around lender becomes the sole mortgagee. The wrap around form also has cosmetic advantages, making for a cleaner looking transaction. Many conservative lenders and investors are disturbed when they see more than one mortgage on a property. The single wrap around mortgage, even though it encompasses two or more mortgages, helps assuage these concerns.

While use of the institutional wrap around mortgage has been suggested for a number of situations, it probably is most practical in a high interest rate market where the existing first mortgage bears a rate sufficiently below market so that the borrower would not want to pay it off. If the existing mortgagee will not advance new funds at a favorable rate and conventional secondary financing is too expensive, a wrap around mortgage can be sought from a new lender. The mortgage will bear a contract interest rate higher than the interest rate on the existing first mortgage and less than the market interest rate for first mortgages. Since the contract rate is higher than the interest rate on the underlying mortgage, the differential will result in an effective rate to the wrap around lender that is higher than the contract rate. Yet the owner will have the advantage of a lower than market rate. Of course, as the underlying mortgage is repaid, the differential between the two rates declines and the effective rate to the wrap around lender is reduced. The effective rate is higher at the outset of the term, but once the underlying mortgage is paid off, the effective rate equals the contract rate. Therefore, the effective rate must be calculated for the entire term of the loan.

Despite perceived advantages to institutional lenders, the wrap around mortgage has not caught fire with them. It has found great favor, however, among non-institutional lenders, particularly syndicate organizers, as a form of purchase money financing. . . .

The wrap around mortgage is distinctive in the commitment of the wrap around lender to remit the debt service on the underlying mortgage directly to the underlying mortgagee. The wrap around mortgage, however, usually contains covenants by the borrower similar to those found in a second mortgage. Many of those covenants will parallel the covenants in the underlying mortgage so that a default of the underlying mortgage will be a default of the wrap around mortgage. The wrap around mortgage generally will include an escrow of real estate taxes and water and sewer charges which upon receipt by the wrap around lender will be remitted to the first mortgagee, if so required, or held by the wrap around lender. The borrower is often required by the wrap around lender to notify the first mortgagee that payments of debt service, any repayment or any payment after acceleration are to be accepted from the wrap around lender on behalf of the borrower. The borrower requests the first mortgagee to deliver to the wrap around lender all notices of default required to be given by the underlying mortgage. In the case of a purchase money wrap around mortgage, the buyer would be well advised to inform the underlying mortgagee of the purchase and request that the underlying mortgagee send him all notices of default. In addition, the buyer periodically should send requests for confirmation to the underlying mortgagee to be sure that the PM wrap around mortgagee is making all payments to the underlying mortgagee as payments are made by the buyer. The buyer should also be aware that having taken the position for tax or other purposes that the wrap around mortgage is a unified mortgage, in case of default on the wrap around portion, he may be forced to pay off the entire wrap around mortgage, including the underlying mortgage, or lose his property in foreclosure, even if he has made the payments required to keep the underlying mortgage current.

NOTES AND QUESTIONS

1. "Since the contract rate is higher than the interest rate on the underlying mortgage, the differential will result in an effective rate to the wrap around lender that is higher than the contract rate." Lifton, page 220 supra.

This differential between the contract rate and the effective rate on the wrap-around loan occurs because the wrap-around lender will derive the contract rate not only on the additional funds he has advanced but also on the outstanding balance of the underlying mortgage. To give an example:

> O owes M a balance of $1,000,000, which is secured by a first mortgage (the underlying mortgage). This mortgage, which originally was $1,200,000, bears 10 percent interest; the debt service of $36,000 is payable quarterly. O borrows an additional $500,000 from W, which is secured by a wrap-around mortgage of $1,500,000. The wrap-around mortgage bears 13 percent interest; the debt service of $57,135 is also payable quarterly. What is the *effective* interest rate on W's loan?

	Year	Interest
$500,000 at 13 percent		$65,000
[1,000,000* at 3 percent]		30,000
	Total	$95,000
Rate of Return $\dfrac{\$95,000}{\$500,000}$	= 19 percent	

* The principal balance of the underlying mortgage will decline somewhat because of the quarterly amortization payments.

Notice that we have already had an instance of a concealed effective rate that may (greatly) exceed the contract rate. Recall our discussion of the installment land contract at page 213 supra.

2. *The problem of usury:* "There are still unanswered legal and tax questions in connection with the wrap around mortgage, mostly affecting its use by institutional lenders. One involves the issue of usury. It could be argued that as long as the contract interest rate stated in the wrap around mortgage conforms to the usury laws the transaction is not usurious. However, the issue may be more complex than that. Not all states judge usury by the interest paid by the borrower but may consider the appropriate criterion to be the interest earned by the lender. And in many cases the effective rate received by the lender will exceed the statutory usury rate because of the differential between the interest rate on the underlying mortgage and the interest rate on the wrap around mortgage. Prudent counsel for lenders should carefully investigate the applicable state usury law on this issue." Lifton, supra, at 397.

Cf., e.g., Mindlin v. Davis, 74 So. 2d 789 (Fla. 1954) (loan usurious where, in a refinancing transaction, lender did not pay off existing mortgage as agreed but earned override on the interest rate differential between the old and new mortgages). Consider the following argument, which the lender might make:

> It matters not what interest is received, the interest paid determines the existence of usury. . . . Is there any difference between a wraparound

mortgagee making a profit on the spread (1) between the underlying mortgage interest rate and the wraparound interest rate, and (2) between the interest rate on an ordinary mortgage loan and the interest rate representing the lender's cost of borrowing from its lender? Does it really matter that the borrower found the lender's lender? [Galowitz, How to Use Wraparound Financing, 5 Real Est. L.J. 107, 125 (1976).]

See also Note, Wraparound Financing: A Technique for Skirting the Usury Law? 1972 Duke L.J. 785.

3. "Of course, as the underlying mortgage is repaid, the differential between the two rates declines and the effective rate to the wrap around lender is reduced." Lifton, page 220 supra.

This statement sets forth the most elusive aspect of the wrap-around loan, the underlying calculations of which are essential to your clear understanding. To return to the earlier example:

> In the first year of the loan, W's *effective* return on his $500,000 advance is approximately 19 percent. Notice, however, that for the year O's debt service payments total $228,540 ($57,135 × 4), and from these payments, W remits $144,000 ($36,000 × 4) to the underlying mortgagee, M. This means that W will have $84,540 *in cash* available to apply against his interest earnings on the $1,500,000 wrap-around loan. Since these earnings, as we saw in Note 1, will be $95,000, W lacks more than $10,000 of the cash needed for him to derive the effective yield of 19 percent.
>
> W handles this shortfall through a bookkeeping entry that accrues the $10,460 as interest income, which O "pays" from the proceeds of an additional loan. Therefore at the beginning of the second year, W will have advanced the approximate sum of $510,460 ($500,000 + $10,460), and it will be this amount on which W calculates his effective yield for year 2.

Year 2	Interest
$500,000 at 13 percent	$65,000
[$1,000,000 at 3 percent]	30,000
Total	$95,000

$$\text{Rate of Return } \frac{\$95,000}{\$510,460} = 18.61 \text{ percent}$$

The process described above is repeated through each year of the underlying mortgage. Once the underlying mortgage is paid off (in our example, in approximately thirteen years), the effective rate and the contract rate will be the same.

In applying a state's usury law to the wrap-around transaction, should courts regard as the relevant rate the effective yield to maturity or the higher yield in the earlier years?

4. *Prepayment of the underlying mortgage:* "The right to prepay the first mortgage at any time will be denied to the borrower, and his right to

prepay the WA mortgage will be strictly limited. Such restrictions are obviously necessary since the desired effective rate contemplates the continuation to maturity of the first mortgage in order that the differential in interest rate (leveraging) can be enjoyed for the longest possible period. For a like reason, prepayment of the WA mortgage is postponed to the later years—probably ten to fifteen years. A more exact statement is impossible to make, however, since the prepayment provision is always subject to negotiation. The terms of the first mortgage may also materially affect the WA mortgage prepayment provision.

"The borrower may also desire a prepayment provision in order to revert to the lower service of the first mortgage. Consequently, the call privilege in the WA mortgage is strenuously negotiated. The penalty payable may very well recognize the loss to lender of the effective rate to maturity.

"The WA borrower is, therefore, presented with two alternative amounts necessary to prepay the mortgage:

"(1) He can prepay in an amount equal to the unamortized balance of the WA mortgage, according to the amortization schedule, plus penalty, but with an obligation on the part of the WA lender to remit the unamortized balance, if any, on the first mortgage. This presumes the first mortgage, if outstanding, is then prepayable and that a satisfactory arrangement has been made concerning payment of the prepayment penalty (if any) on the first mortgage.

"(2) He can also prepay in an amount equal to the net investment plus agreed penalty. This privilege not only has the virtue of simplicity but it also permits the continuation of the first mortgage, if still outstanding." Gunning, The Wrap Around Mortgage . . . Friend or U.F.O.?, 2 Real Est. Rev. 35, 43 (Summer 1971).

5. *The problem of interest on interest.* As a matter of public policy, a few states bar lenders from charging their borrowers compound interest (interest on interest). In wrap-around financing, the deferred interest also accrues interest at the contract rate that becomes payable during the interval between the discharge of the underlying mortgage and the maturity of the WA mortgage.

6. "Yet the owner will have the advantage of a lower than market rate [despite having to pay an effective rate on the wrap around mortgage that exceeds the contract rate]." Lifton, page 220 supra.

This assertion warrants a short explanation. The relevant comparison, according to Lifton, is between the contract rate of the wrap-around loan and the contract rate of a separate second mortgage if the latter alternative were used. Once again, an example should be helpful:

O owes M a balance of $1,000,000, which is secured by a first mortgage (the underlying mortgage). This mortgage, which originally was $1,200,000, bears 10 percent interest; the debt service is $144,000 per annum. If O borrows an additional $500,000, to be secured by a second mortgage, the lender will require a 16 percent return, and will (usually) want the loan to be paid off on a relatively short-term basis of, let us say, 15 years.

Under this arrangement, the debt service on the second mortgage will come to $88,450 annually. Together with the debt service on the underlying mortgage, the two loans will cost $232,450 yearly until the first mortgage is repaid.

A wrap-around lender, on the other hand, will (usually) accept a lower contract rate than is needed on a second mortgage because of the potentially higher concealed rate and the lender's greater control over the combined loan transactions. Often this will lead to an aggregate reduction in debt service (thus, a better cash flow) for the borrower during the term of the underlying mortgage. When that mortgage matures, however, the borrower will then have heavier debt service installments until the wrap-around loan also matures.

7. *The income tax treatment of wrap-around interest:*

The payment and accounting peculiarities of this financing device also raise nice questions of income tax consequences. There may well be some doubt as to how much of the payments made by borrower can be deducted as interest. Does he use the interest component of the debt service required by the amortization schedule for the WA mortgage alone or of the difference in interest payments in the debt service for the WA mortgage and the first mortgage? Is deferred interest to be deductible, currently or when payable upon maturity of the first mortgage? The WA lender, on the other hand, has to determine how much of the payments actually received by him, whether or not retained, constitute taxable income. [Gunning, supra, at 48.]

See Rev. Rul. 75-99, I.R.B. 1975-12; Lane, The "Wrap Around" Mortgage: Tax Problems Related to Its Use in Connection with the Refinancing or Sale of Real Estate, 33 Ann. N.Y.U. Inst. on Fed. Tax 1235 (1975).

See also Rev. Rul. 68-643, 1968-2 C.B. 76 ("If interest is prepaid for a period more than 12 months beyond the end of the current taxable year, the deduction of such prepaid interest in the taxable year of payment will be considered as materially distorting income. Where a material distortion of income has been found to result from the deduction of prepaid interest, the service will require the taxpayer to change his method of accounting with respect to such prepaid interest in order to allocate it over the taxable years involved."); Sherman, Maximum Tax Leverage with the All-Inclusive Note, 4 Real Est. Rev. 115 (Summer 1974); Barnett, Use of the Wrap-Around Mortgage in Realty Sales: The Tax Advantages and Problems, 40 J. Tax. 274 (1974).

Section 208(a) of the Tax Reform Act of 1976 added §461(g) to the Internal Revenue Code. This provision goes even further than the 1968

Revenue Ruling in restricting the deductibility of prepaid interest. Although directed chiefly at widespread tax shelter abuses, §461(g) may arguably apply also to wrap-around mortgages:

> (g) Prepaid Interest.—
> (1) In general.— If the taxable income of the taxpayer is computed under the cash receipts and disbursements method of accounting, interest paid by the taxpayer which, under regulation prescribed by the Secretary, is properly allocable to any period—
> (A) with respect to which the interest represents a charge for the use or forbearance of money, and
> (B) which is after the close of taxable year in which paid, shall be charged to capital account and shall be treated as paid in the period to which so allocable. . . .

8. We will return later to the WA mortgage in two other problem contexts:

a) The problem of the intervening lien, page 232 infra;
b) The problem of the foreclosure sale bid, page 271 infra;

9. Further readings on the WA mortgage appear at Messenger, Wrap Around Mortgages: Valuation and Interest Accruals, 42 N.Y.U. Inst. on Fed. Taxn. 22-1 (1984); Randolph, Home Finance in the Shadow World: Unsolved Usury Problems Affecting Adjustable Rate and Wrap-Around Mortgages in Missouri, 51 U.M.K.C. L. Rev. 41 (1982); Comment, The Wrap Around Mortgage: A Critical Inquiry, 21 U.C.L.A. L. Rev. 1529 (1974); and Cochrane, Wrap-Around Mortgage Financing, 37 Legal Bull. 185 (1971).

[Handwritten annotation: If mortgagor required to make advances on mtge recorded before mechanic's liens, mortgagor's debt takes priority]

c. Risks of a Junior Encumbrancer: The Open-ended Mortgage

Kemp v. Thurmond
521 S.W.2d 806 (Tenn. 1975)

COOPER, Justice. This is an action to enforce mechanics' and materialmen's liens upon a house and lot owned by E. C. Thurmond III and wife, Doris Thurmond. The issue now before the Court is which lien has priority— the lien of petitioners, Builders Supply Company, Inc., and K – T Distributors, Inc., who furnished materials used in the construction of the house, or the lien secured by a trust deed held by the respondent. The Martin Bank, Martin, Tennessee.

In January, 1971, E. C. Thurmond applied to The Martin Bank for a construction loan in the amount of $25,000.00 with the funds to be used in the construction of a dwelling on a one acre lot which Thurmond proposed to buy from his brother-in-law.

By May, 1971, Thurmond had acquired the lot and had secured a commitment from the First Federal Savings and Loan Association of Fulton, Kentucky, to The Martin Bank that First Federal would loan $25,000.00 on the Thurmond house, when it was completed. Thurmond then went to The Martin Bank where the arrangements for the construction loan were "finalized" and a note and trust deed were executed. The total amount to be loaned Thurmond by The Martin Bank was $25,000.00 and the money was to be made available as needed for construction and in relation to the work performed. The construction loan was to be paid from the proceeds of the permanent loan.

The trust deed, which was recorded on May 17, 1971, describes the Thurmond indebtedness to the bank as follows:

". . . To secure and make certain prompt payment of ($2,500.00) Two Thousand Five hundred and No/100 Dollars borrowed money: Evidenced by a promissory note of even date by the said E. C. Thurmond, III and wife, Doris B. Thurmond payable to the Martin Bank, Martin, Tennessee. Said note to be paid on demand with interest at the rate of 8% per annum.

"2. This deed of trust secures in addition to the original amount of said loan stated hereinbefore, all renewals and extension of said loan and the note evidencing it and such ADDITIONAL SUMS as thereafter may be loaned by The Martin Bank, Martin, Tennessee to the first party, or their successors in title, prior to the cancellation of this deed of trust said additional loans in no event to exceed $22,500.00 in addition to the original amount loaned. The additional advances are to be due and payable as provided in the notes evidencing same and bearing interest at the rate of ___ percent per annum from date until paid, provided such note recites that the sum is to be secured by this trust."

In addition to the initial $2,500.00 loan, The Martin Bank loaned the Thurmonds $7,500.00 on June 18, 1971, $5,000.00 on August 11, 1971, and $10,000.00 on September 2, 1971, for a total of $25,000.00. These monies were used by Thurmond in constructing the house.

Petitioners' liens against the Thurmond property were perfected and relate to and date from the first visible commencement of work on the Thurmond house. T.C.A. §64-1104. The exact date of commencement of work is not set out in the record. However, it is conceded by all parties that no materials had been delivered to the Thurmond property and no labor had been expended on the Thurmond house at the time the trust deed was executed and recorded and the initial $2,500.00 was loaned the Thurmonds. It is also conceded that work was commenced on the property before the additional loans were made.

In determining whether advances made after the giving of a mortgage shall receive priority over intervening mechanics' liens, courts generally look to whether the mortgagee is <u>under an obligation, pursuant to the terms of his agreement with the mortgagor, to advance the sum or sums called for by the instrument</u>. Many courts, including this Court, "have recognized that where the making of the advances is obligatory upon the mortgagee or beneficiary, the lien of a mortgage or trust deed receives priority over mechanics' liens when the mortgage or deed has been recorded before the mechanic's lien attaches, despite the fact that advances are actually given subsequently to this time." Annot.: Mortgage-Mechanic's Lien—Priority, 80 A.L.R.2d 179, 191; Theilen v. Chandler, 9 Tenn. App. 345 (1928); Kingsport Brick Corp. v. Bostwick, 145 Tenn. 19, 235 S.W. 70 (1921). "In determining the priority of the lien of a party lending money under a trust deed and that of materialmen, it was wholly immaterial whether the party lending the money had advanced the entire amount at the time material was furnished if the obligation to advance the money existed." Theilen v. Chandler, 9 Tenn. App. 345 (1928).

Petitioners do not take issue with the above statement of applicable law, but insist that the Court of Appeals erred in finding that "it was an obligation on the part of The Martin Bank to make additional loans." The Martin Bank, in turn, insists that this Court is faced with a concurrent finding of fact by the chancellor and the Court of Appeals on the issue, and that the only question is whether there is any material evidence in the record to support the finding that The Martin Bank was under legal obligation to make additional loans up to $25,000.00.

While a finding of an obligation on the part of The Martin Bank to make additional loans to the Thurmonds may be implicit in the chancellor's holding that The Martin Bank's lien under the deed of trust included the advancements up to $25,000.00, the chancellor made no such specific finding. Absent this, we do not feel bound by the "concurrent finding of fact" rule, but have reviewed the record with a view of determining where the preponderance of evidence lies on the issue. On doing so, we find ourselves in agreement with the finding of the Court of Appeals that "The Martin Bank was under a legal obligation to make its advances, pursuant to its agreement with Thurmond to make those advances, so long as the work progressed. . . . Therefore, the lien (of The Martin Bank) is for the full amount of the recited amount to be advanced. The lien thereof relates back to the filing of the Trust Deed and it is superior to the appellant's lien."

The judgment of the Court of Appeals is affirmed. Costs in this Court

Basic Security Transactions

are adjudged against the petitioners, Builders Supply, Inc., and K-T Distributors, Inc., and their surety.

Fones, C.J., and Henry, Brock and Harbison, JJ., concur.

NOTES AND QUESTIONS

1. "In California, the courts have enunciated what, it has been said, may with propriety be denominated as the 'California rule,' which, although opposed elsewhere by authority of respectability, is also sustained by strong reason and eminent authority. The rule is that the lien of a mortgage does not operate to secure *optional* advances made under the mortgage after the mortgagee has acquired actual notice of an encumbrance subsequent in point of time to his mortgage, so as to defeat or impair the rights of the subsequent encumbrancer. This rule is likewise applicable to trust deeds. To the extent of advances made without actual notice, the mortgage has priority over all liens subsequent to its execution. Recordation of the mortgage is notice to subsequent encumbrancers that it constitutes a lien to the sum therein named. If they desire so to do, they may ascertain the actual condition of the security and by notice to the holder of the prior mortgage prevent any additional encumbrance of the property for further advancements by giving notice of their liens, in which case they are entitled to have the senior mortgagee limited to the recovery of such advances as he has made under his mortgage prior to receipt of actual notice of the vesting of the junior liens, but if they do not give notice, their rights must be held subject to the mortgage to the full extent of advancements made. The rule does not apply where the provisions in the first mortgage makes it obligatory upon the mortgagee to make the advances, for it would be manifestly unsound to hold that actual notice of a subsequent mortgage would deprive the mortgagee of his lien for advances he is compelled to make. . . ." Oaks v. Weingartner, 105 Cal. App. 2d 598, 600-601, 234 P.2d 194, 196 (1951) (emphasis added).

(a) Mortgages usually provide that if the premises are not kept in good repair, or if the real estate taxes or hazard insurance premiums are unpaid, the mortgagee may make such repairs as it deems necessary "properly to preserve the property" or may pay such taxes or premiums, and any sums so paid "shall be a further lien" under the mortgage. Acting under this paragraph, will the mortgagee have made an optional or obligatory advance? Cf. Woodruff v. National City Bank of Evansville, 272 F.2d 696, 697 (7th Cir. 1959). Should the advance for repairs be treated differently from the advance for unpaid taxes?

(b) A junior mortgagee pays an overdue installment on a prior mortgage to prevent default and foreclosure. Is this optional or obligatory?

(c) Construction loan agreements usually provide for successive advances to coincide with stages of completion: for example, disbursement of 20 percent of the loan when foundation set; 20 percent when building roofed in; 20 percent when interior plaster set; 20 percent when certificate of occupancy issued; 20 percent thirty days later. Acting under this arrangement, as in Kemp v. Thurmond, supra, will the mortgagee always have made an optional or obligatory advance? If the subsequent lienor who is disputing the mortgagee's priority has furnished labor or materials to the site, will his ground be more solid than, let us say, a judgment creditor's?

2. What are the arguments for and against the rule (in California and in most other states) that protects even optional advances unless the senior lienor gets actual notice of the intervening claims? To subordinate the advance, why should it not suffice that the intervening claim be recorded before the advance is made? For expression of a distinctly minority view, see Ladue v. Detroit, Milwaukee R.R., 13 Mich. 380, 87 Am. Dec. 759 (1865).

3. A Florida statute (Fla. Stat. Ann. §697.04 (1984)), erases the common law distinction between obligatory and optional advances and protects all such advances against subsequent lienors from the time the mortgage is filed for record. It matters not that the advance is made with actual notice of the intervening claims. Cf. Silver Waters Corp. v. Murphy, 177 So. 2d 897, 900 (Fla. Dist. Ct. App. 1965). What are the arguments for and against this statutory scheme?

4. Compare the treatment of future advances that appears in The Uniform Land Transactions Act:

§3-205: _____ Future Advances . . .
    (c) Obligations secured by a security agreement may include future advances or other future obligations, whether or not the obligation was incurred pursuant to commitment. However, except as to advances made under subsection (e), the maximum amount of the obligation secured may not exceed the maximum amount stated in the agreement. . . .
    (e) Future advances made or future obligation incurred by the holder of the security agreement:
    (1) for the reasonable protection of the security interest in the real estate, such as advances made for real property taxes, hazard insurance premiums, or maintenance charges imposed under a condominium declaration or a restrictive covenant, or
    (2) under a construction security interest to enable completion of the contemplated improvement are secured by the security agreement even though the security agreement does not provide for future advances or obligations or the advances cause the total of future advances or obligations to exceed the maximum amount stated in the security agreement.
    (f) The priority of future advances or obligations under this section over other purchasers including secured creditor is determined by Part 3.

Basic Security Transactions

Part 3. Priorities

*Section 3-301: Priority Between Conflicting Security Interests in
                the Same Collateral . . .*

(b) A recorded security interest takes priority as of the date of its recording as to advances or obligations thereafter made or incurred under the security agreement:

   (1) if made pursuant to a commitment entered into before the secured party had knowledge of an intervening interest, to the extent of the advances or obligations made thereunder which do not exceed the maximum stated in the record;

   (2) if not made pursuant to a commitment to make an advance or to incur an obligation made before the secured party had knowledge of an intervening interest, to the extent of advances made or obligations incurred before the secured party had knowledge of the intervening interest and which do not exceed the maximum amount stated in the record;

   (3) if made or incurred for the reasonable protection of the security interest in the real estate, such as payment for real properties taxes, hazard insurance premiums, or maintenance charges imposed under a condominium declaration or restrictive covenant, whether or not the advances or obligations exceed the maximum amount stated in the instrument or the secured creditor had knowledge of the intervening interest; or

   (4) if made under a construction security interest to enable completion of the agreed improvement of the real estate, whether or not the advances or obligations exceed the secured maximum amount stated in the instrument or the secured creditor had knowledge of the intervening interest.

(c) In all other cases the priority of a security interest . . . is determined according to the law governing recording and priority.

5. No state has yet enacted any significant part of The Uniform Land Transactions Act (ULTA). The ULTA Commissioners, believing that ULTA may have been too ambitious an undertaking, have spun off ULTA's Article 3 on Secured Transactions, and have reincorporated the Article, as well as "updated" its provisions, into a proposed Uniform Land Security Interest Act (ULSIA). Below, in tentative form, are the ULSIA paragraphs on Future Advances and Priority Between Conflicting Security Interests in the Same Collateral. Do these restate or modify the ULTA provisions above?

*Section 301. Priority Between Conflicting Security Interests in
              Same Collateral*

(a) So long as conflicting security interests remain unrecorded, the first to attach has priority.

(b) Except as provided in Section 302, the priority of a recorded security interest is determined according to the law governing recording and priority.

Section 302. Future Advances

(a) Obligations secured by a security agreement may include future advances, whether or not the future advances were made pursuant to commitment. However, except for future advances made to protect collateral, the maximum amount of those future advances secured at any time may not exceed the maximum amount stated in the agreement, together with interest accrued but unpaid on those advances.

(b) All future advances made to protect collateral are secured by a security agreement even though the agreement does not provide for future advances, or the advances cause the total obligation to exceed the maximum amount stated in the security agreement.

(c) (Except as expressly set forth in (insert reference to state mechanics' lien laws, if any)) future advances made under a recorded security agreement take priority as of the date of the recording:

(1) if made pursuant to a commitment entered into before the secured creditor had knowledge of an intervening interest, to the extent of the outstanding future advances that do not exceed the maximum amount stated in the record;

(2) if not made pursuant to a commitment entered into before the secured creditor had knowledge of an intervening interest, to the extent of future advances outstanding when the secured creditor obtained knowledge of the intervening interest and that do not exceed the maximum amount stated in the record.

(d) Future advances made to protect collateral take priority as of the date a security agreement is recorded, even though the secured creditor has knowledge of an intervening interest at the time such a future advance is made.

6. The wrap-around mortgage necessarily involves future advances. Consider, for example, the additional-funds WA mortgage. Even if the mortgagor makes his scheduled payments (the non-default situation), the WA mortgagee's net investment will rise yearly, via deferred interest, until the underlying mortgage is paid off. Suppose that an intervening lien appears during this interval, of which the WA mortgagee has knowledge. What is the priority status of this lien vis-à-vis subsequent installments of deferred interest?

7. The intervening lien presents more difficult problems of priority if the WA mortgagor fails to make his scheduled payments. As with all junior mortgagees, the WA mortgagee must decide whether to advance moneys to prevent an early default of the underlying mortgage. But curative advances of debt service of the first mortgage are voluntary payments. Suppose they are made after the WA mortgagee has knowledge of an intervening lien. What are the respective priorities? Does §3-301(b)(3) of the Uniform Land Transaction Act cover this situation? Does the doctrine of subrogation? Cf. Gunning, The Wrap Around Mortgage . . . Friend or U.F.O.?, 2 Real Est. Rev. 35, 45-47 (Summer 1972), supra.

Basic Security Transactions

3. Transfers of Encumbered Property

Owner purchased a $50,000 tract two years ago. She financed her acquisition through First Bank by a $40,000 mortgage that has since been paid down to $35,000. Owner decides to sell; the best price she can get is still $50,000, this from an offeror who, happily for our hypothetical, happens to have $15,000 cash.

The usual choice in arranging the sale is between refinancing and mortgage takeover. In the former, buyer pays seller $15,000, and mortgages the property to Second Bank for $35,000, which is used to pay off the original mortgage. Can you see the closing in which among the papers shuffled are seller's deed, buyer's $15,000 check, buyer's note and mortgage to Second Bank, Second Bank's check for $35,000 (made payable to whom?), and First Bank's release of mortgage?

If, on the other hand, buyer takes over seller's mortgage, he gives seller the $15,000, takes seller's deed, and enters possession. But his possession and ownership are dependent upon his (or somebody's) keeping up the payments on First Bank's mortgage. If that mortgage incurs a default, buyer stands to lose the property. Also, there is another usual consequence to default; not only may the lender, by one or another procedure, take the security in satisfaction of his debt, he may also recover the deficiency from seller[33] (absent a release or a discharge, infra), should the security not bring as much as the debt. Hence, in a takeover transaction, seller is at risk of a concurrence of a decline in the value of the sold property and a default by her buyer, events which do tend to concur. One way of reducing that risk is to get the buyer not only to take the property *subject to* the bank's security interest, but also to have buyer promise seller that he, buyer, will maintain the payments. With such a promise, known as buyer's *assuming the mortgage*, seller can recover from buyer any deficiency liability imposed on seller by the lender.

Keeping in mind that the major variations are refinance or takeover, and that the two forms of takeover are "subject to" or "assumption," determine why the following statements are true:

a. The more the seller has paid off on principal, and the more the property has risen in value since the original First Bank loan, the more likely the parties will need to handle the deal by refinancing;

b. The seller will sometimes, but not always, try to insist — where the buyer can make the choice — that the deal be handled by refinancing instead of takeover;

c. The lower (higher) the market interest rate at the time of resale

---

33. This implies, of course, that the seller is or has been obligated on the mortgage debt. When will this not be the case?

relative to the original mortgage interest rate, the more (less) likely that First Bank would prefer takeover to refinancing;
d. Where there is no difference between the terms of the existing mortgage and the mortgage available through refinancing, mortgage takeover is cheaper for the buyer;
e. The shakier the income prospects of the property, the less likely buyer will be willing to *assume* the mortgage;
f. The greater the intrinsic value of the buyer's agreement to assume the mortgage, the less likely he will agree;
g. First Bank would prefer that buyer *assume* the mortgage, rather than take *subject to*.

a. Has the Mortgage Been Assumed?

Daugharthy v. Monritt Associates

293 Md. 399, 444 A.2d 1030 (1982)

DAVIDSON, Judge. In recent years, the wrap-around mortgage has achieved widespread use in the financing of real estate transactions. S. M. Guerin, Selected Problems in Wrap-Around Financing: Suggested Approaches to Due-On-Sale Clauses and Purchaser's Depreciable Basis, 14:3 U. Mich. J.L. Ref. 401, 401 (1981). This case concerns the application of principles of real property law to wrap-around mortgages. More particularly, this case presents a question concerning the circumstances under which an assumption of the obligation to pay a debt embodied in a pre-existing deed of trust will be implied when a buyer has executed a subsequent deed of trust providing that it is "subject to and wraps around" the pre-existing deed of trust.

In 1977, the appellants, Alan L. Daugharthy and Elizabeth Daugharthy, sold certain real property to the appellee, Monritt Associates, a Maryland Limited Partnership, for $200,000.00. At settlement, Monritt gave the appellants a promissory note and a deferred purchase money deed of trust dated 21 September 1977 (pre-existing 1977 deed of trust) securing the principal sum of $163,036.00 with interest at the rate of 8½% per annum. The pre-existing 1977 deed of trust provided in pertinent part:

> The parties agree that the said deferred purchase price Deed of Trust *shall be assumable by a later purchaser,* should grantor herein sell the property to a third party, provided, however, that the note holders, or assignee or assignees, shall have the right to change the rate of interest to a prevailing rate of interest as of the time of such assumption. (Emphasis added.)

In 1980, Monritt (seller) sold the property to Joseph Gerald Kurtinitis and Sandra Kurtinitis (buyers) for $275,000.00. At settlement, the buyers gave the seller a promissory note and a deferred purchase money wrap-around deed of trust (1980 wrap-around deed of trust) securing a principal sum of $235,000.00 with interest at the rate of 10% per annum. The 1980 wrap-around deed of trust provided in pertinent part:

> This Deed of Trust *is subject to and "WRAPS AROUND"* that certain Deed of Trust dated September 21, 1977 and recorded in Liber 5035 at Folio 135 of the Land Records of Montgomery County, Maryland. The unpaid principal balance of the indebtedness secured by said Deed of Trust, as of January 21, 1980, is approximately $158,347.00 and that amount is *included* in the indebtedness of $235,000.00 secured hereby. *The holder* of the promissory note secured hereby, *in accepting monthly payments* hereunder, *agrees to pay from such payments the monthly payments as required by the terms of the aforementioned Deed of Trust* as such payments become due and payable on the Note secured by said Deed of Trust dated September 21, 1977 and recorded in Liber 5035 at Folio 135. *In the event the holder* of the promissory note secured hereby *fails to make the payments* as required under the terms of the above referred "WRAPPED AROUND" Deed of Trust *the grantor herein shall be entitled to pay such installment due on said "WRAPPED AROUND" Deed of Trust* and to apply such payment as a credit against the next installment due under the promissory note secured hereby. . . .
>
> The grantor further agrees to comply with all of the terms, covenants and conditions of said "WRAPPED AROUND" Deed of Trust, *other than with respect to the liability for the payment of the principal sum and/or the payment of the monthly installments of principal and interest due under said Deed of Trust.* In the event the grantor shall fail to so comply with any of the terms, provisions and conditions of said "WRAPPED AROUND" Deed of Trust and such failure shall result in a default thereunder, *except with respect to the payment of the monthly payments of principal and interest and the liability for the payment of the principal sum,* such failure on the part of the grantor herein shall automatically constitute a default under this Deed of Trust. . . . (Emphasis added.)

The settlement sheet applicable to this transaction showed the $235,000.00 indebtedness under the 1980 wrap-around deed of trust as a debit to the seller against the $275,000.00 purchase price.

In 1980, the appellants notified the buyers and the seller that they viewed the 1980 wrap-around deed of trust as an assumption of the pre-existing 1977 deed of trust and were electing to increase the rate of interest on the obligation embodied in the preexisting 1977 deed of trust from 8½% per annum to 14% per annum. The buyers responded that they had taken the property "subject to" the pre-existing 1977 deed of trust and that the transaction did not involve an assumption of the debt embodied in that pre-existing encumbrance. Thereafter, the appellants notified the seller that they were demanding the unpaid balance and accrued interest outstanding on the pre-existing 1977 deed of trust and that failure to respond within 10 days would result in the immediate institution of foreclosure proceedings.

On 31 March 1980, in the Circuit Court for Montgomery County, the seller filed a Bill of Complaint for Declaratory Judgment and for Injunction to Stay Foreclosure. The complaint requested a declaration that the seller was not in default under the pre-existing 1977 deed of trust and that it was not liable for payment of an increased rate of interest. The complaint also sought an injunction against the appellants prohibiting them from instituting a foreclosure proceeding.

After a hearing on cross motions for summary judgment, the trial court found that the 1980 wrap-around deed of trust embodied an express agreement that the buyers had not assumed the obligation to pay the debt arising from the pre-existing 1977 deed of trust. The trial court granted the seller's motion for summary judgment and denied the appellants' motion for summary judgment. On 9 February 1981, the trial court entered a decree declaring that the seller was not in default of payments due under the pre-existing 1977 deed of trust. The trial court's order enjoined the appellants from accelerating the sum due under the pre-existing 1977 deed of trust, from increasing the rate of interest under that encumbrance, and from instituting foreclosure proceedings.

On 23 February 1981, the appellants filed an appeal to the Court of Special Appeals. On 9 April 1981, they filed a petition for a writ of certiorari to this Court. We issued a writ of certiorari before consideration by that Court.

Here, as in the trial court, the appellants' basic contention is that the buyers assumed the obligation to pay the pre-existing 1977 deed of trust. This position is premised upon three factors. Relying on Brice v. Griffin, 269 Md. 558, 307 A.2d 660 (1973), the appellants initially assert that an assumption must be implied because the settlement sheet reflects that the buyers elected to deduct the amount due on the pre-existing 1977 deed of trust from the purchase price. The appellants further assert that an assumption must be implied because the buyers are in fact making the payments due under the pre-existing 1977 deed of trust. In support of this position, they point out that the 1980 wrap-around deed of trust expressly provides that the seller must make the monthly payments due under the pre-existing 1977 deed of trust from monthly payments made by the buyers under the 1980 wrap-around deed of trust. Additionally, the appellants allege that an assumption must be implied because the pre-existing 1977 deed of trust requires a subsequent purchaser to assume the obligations of that encumbrance. In support of this position, they point out that the pre-existing 1977 deed of trust expressly provides that that encumbrance "shall be assumable by a later purchaser." The appellants conclude that because the buyers assumed the obligations of the pre-existing 1977 deed of trust, the appellants were justified in demanding a change in the rate of interest. We do not agree.

In Maryland, there is a distinction between the sale of property "subject

Basic Security Transactions

to" an existing mortgage or deed of trust and such a sale with an assumption of an existing mortgage or deed of trust. Ordinarily, when there is a sale of property subject to an existing mortgage or deed of trust, the purchaser does not become personally responsible for payment of the obligation. However, when there is an assumption of an existing mortgage or deed of trust, the buyer undertakes personal responsibility for the payment of the obligation arising under the existing encumbrance. The purchase of property subject to a specified encumbrance is not an agreement to assume and pay the encumbrance. In order to establish that an assumption has occurred, there must be an agreement, express or implied, written or parol, incorporated in or separate from the deed conveying the property. Such an agreement may be shown so long as it does not tend to vary or contradict the material terms of the deed. In the absence of an express contrary agreement, an assumption will be implied when the amount due under the trust obligation has been deducted from the purchase price. *Brice,* 269 Md. at 560-61, 307 A.2d at 661-62; Rosenthal v. Heft, 155 Md. 410, 419-21, 142 A. 598, 602-03 (1928); Chilton v. Brooks, 72 Md. 554, 558-59, 20 A. 125, 126-27 (1890).

These principles were most recently articulated in *Brice.* There, the sellers sold the buyers a building for $64,221.23. The buyers were to take title "subject to a first and second deed of trust." The settlement statement showed the amounts due under the first and second trust as debits against the purchase price indicating that the buyers had elected to deduct the amounts due under the first and second trust from the purchase price.

This Court held that in the absence of an express contrary agreement the buyers' election to deduct from the purchase price the amounts due under the pre-existing deeds of trust constituted an agreement to assume the obligation to pay the amounts due under the pre-existing deeds of trust. In reaching this result, this Court said:

> The law is clear in this State that the mere purchase of a property subject to an existing mortgage or deed of trust does not create a personal obligation on the part of the purchaser to pay it. But, the law here is equally clear, if the purchaser assumes the payment of an existing mortgage or deed of trust as a part of the purchase price of the property, then, in that event, it becomes his duty to satisfy the obligation, and to protect his vendor against any demands that may be made for payment of the debt it secures. *Whether the purchaser as between a vendor and vendee assumes the payment of such an existing obligation is a matter for agreement, which may be either express or implied, written or parol, and even separate from the deed conveying the property; but, in the absence of an express contrary agreement, an assumption will be implied when, as here, the amount then due under the trust obligation has been deducted from the purchase price.*

In this case, the appellants contracted to take title to the apartment property "subject to the first and second deed of trust." Standing alone, and without relating it to the agreed upon purchase price, that language would mean that Brice and Gaddis acquired only the equity of redemption and thereby assumed no personal responsibility to pay the obligations created by the existing deeds of trust. But here, as the settlement sheet demonstrates, instead of paying the purchase price in full, appellants elected to deduct from that price the sums due under the two existing trusts. In these circumstances, what we said in Rosenthal v. Heft, [155 Md.] at 420, [142 A. at 603,] a case with a factual pattern remarkably similar to the one here, is appropriate:

> When [the purchaser] elected to "deduct" the amount due on the mortgages from the "purchase price," he must have "deducted" it to pay the mortgagees, for otherwise, instead of deducting it from the purchase price, he would have bought the equity of redemption for the difference between the amount due on the mortgages, and the purchase price, but, in the absence of any evidence qualifying the language of the contract and the deed, we cannot assume that the [vendor] intended, and that [the vendee] understood, that he was to retain out of the purchase price the amount due on the mortgages, without any obligation on his part to pay the mortgages, so as to exonerate the [vendor] from any liability on account thereof. A more reasonable assumption is that by that arrangement he undertook, as a part of the purchase price, to pay the mortgages when and as they became due.

It is reasonable to make the same assumption here. *Brice,* 269 Md. at 560-62, 307 A.2d at 661-62 (citations omitted) (emphasis added).

Thus, this Court reaffirmed the principle that in the absence of an express contrary agreement, an assumption will be implied when the amount due under a trust obligation has been deducted from the purchase price.

Here, unlike *Brice,* there was an express agreement between the buyers and seller governing, as betweem them, the obligation to pay the amount due under the pre-existing 1977 deed of trust. The 1980 wrap-around deed of trust provides that it is "subject to" the pre-existing 1977 deed of trust. It states that the balance of the indebtedness secured by the pre-existing 1977 deed of trust is included in the amount of indebtedness secured by the 1980 wrap-around deed of trust. It further states that the seller, who receives the buyers' monthly payments under the 1980 wrap-around trust, agrees to pay monthly payments to the appellants under the pre-existing 1977 deed of trust. It additionally states that in the event of the seller's default, the buyers are entitled, but not obligated, to make monthly payments due under the pre-existing 1977 deed of trust to the appellants. Finally, the 1980 wrap-around deed of trust expressly provides that the buyers are not personally liable for the payment of the amounts due under the pre-existing 1977 deed of trust.

The language of the 1980 wrap-around deed of trust is plain and unambiguous. It establishes the seller's obligation to pay the amount due under the pre-existing 1977 deed of trust. More important, it negates an intention on the part of the buyers to assume personal responsibility to pay the obligations arising under the pre-existing 1977 deed of trust. In light of the express language embodied in the 1980 wrap-around deed of trust governing the obligations of the buyers and the seller to pay the amounts due under the pre-existing 1977 deed of trust, we can only conclude that the buyers did not agree to assume personal responsibility to pay the obligations arising under that pre-existing encumbrance.

Under the circumstances here, the seller was not in default of payments due under the pre-existing 1977 deed of trust. The trial court did not err in enjoining the appellants from accelerating the sum due under the pre-existing 1977 deed of trust, from increasing the rate of interest under that encumbrance, and from instituting foreclosure proceedings. Accordingly, we shall affirm the judgment of the trial court.

Judgment affirmed.

NOTES AND QUESTIONS

1. The statute of frauds also requires a writing for contracts that are not to be performed within a year. In the usual case, where the mortgage has some years to run, would not a mortgage assumption be within the statute? Yet the cases seem to give little attention to the point. Osborne, Nelson and Whitman, Real Estate Finance Law 255 (1979).

2. Some states, among them California and New York, have special statutes dealing with the manner of mortgage assumption. New York requires that (a) the assumption be set forth in a writing (usually the deed) stating the amount assumed and (b) that the writing be signed *and* acknowledged at the time of the conveyance. N.Y. Gen. Oblig. Law §5-705 (McKinney 1978). California requires that the assumption agreement appear in the conveyance itself. Cal. Civ. Code §1624(7) (West 1985).

3. Pennsylvania, seemingly alone in this country, treats a conveyance subject to a mortgage as the grantee's implied assumption of the debt, the indemnity running in favor of the grantor only. See Masgai v. Masgai, 460 Pa. 453, 333 A.2d 861 (1975). A similar rule prevails in England and Canada. Osborne, Mortgages 709 (1951).

4. A recorded mortgage states that all persons in whom title to the mortgaged premises is hereafter vested shall be personally obligated on the debt. The premises are transferred to X who refuses to assume the mortgage. Is X personally bound? See Seventeenth and Locust Streets Corp. v. Montcalm Corp., 54 F.2d 42 (3d Cir. 1931).

b. Mortgage Takeover: The Rights of the Grantor as Against the Grantee

The grantor has no claim against a non-assuming grantee that he personally pay the debt. But the land remains liable (as principal), not only to the claim of the mortgagee, but also — via subrogation — to the claim of the grantor who, facing personal liability, pays off the debt after a mortgage default. Procedurally, the grantor who has made good on the default is likely to ask the mortgagee to assign both the mortgage and mortgage debt to a nominee of the grantor. Assignment is believed necessary in the first instance in order to retain the priority which the mortgagee held in the property against the technical rule that *payment* of the mortgage debt discharges it and releases the mortgage. Osborne, Nelson and Whitman, Real Estate Finance Law 262 (1979). Use of a nominee, while not essential, becomes a helpful tactic where foreclosure is expected, since the grantor will sometimes be a party defendant as the original mortgagor.

At least one court has rejected the concept of subrogation where the grantor has paid off the mortgage debt. Best Fertilizers of Arizona, Inc. v. Burns, 116 Ariz. 492, 570 P.2d 179 (1977). That decision has been deemed incorrect "both technically and in terms of fairness." Osborne, Nelson and Whitman at 262-264.

When the mortgage is assumed, the grantor adds to his rights against the land, rights against the grantee personally. While the grantor certainly may sue for reimbursement after he has had to pay the debt, most courts also let the grantor recover from the delinquent grantee as soon as default occurs.[34] The grantor may also have the right to compel an assuming grantee to exonerate him by paying the debt to the mortgagee. Marsh v. Pike, 10 Paige Ch. 595 (N.Y. Ch. 1844).

c. Mortgage Takeover: The Rights of the Mortgagee as Against the Assuming Grantee

Osborne, Nelson and Whitman, Real Estate Finance Law
268-275 (1979)

As a generalized proposition the bases of recovery by the mortgagee against an assuming grantee are two: (1) by virtue of a direct and independent right of the mortgagee; (2) by virtue of enforcing the promise of the assuming grantee derivatively, i.e., through the right against him of the mortgagor or other transferor. Different reasons are assigned in different states for adopting one or the other of these solutions. Frequently identical results are reached regardless of purported theory. Not only do the theory and rules governing a given rationale vary from state to state, but they change in the process of development in the same state. Further, in single

---

34. Three arguments are enlisted against the majority holding: the assumption agreement is one of indemnity, i.e., reimbursement; the grantor's right is based not on contract but on his right as a surety to compensation against his principal; the grantee might be subjected to two judgments for the same debt. The danger of a double judgment is perhaps more theoretical than real, since the grantor can be compelled to hold the moneys collected as trustee for the mortgagee.

jurisdictions there has been a shift from one basis to another and sometimes more than one has been recognized simultaneously. The result of such changes is that many of the decisions are outdated. Hence, any precise classification of jurisdictions is difficult, would be transient and not particularly helpful. Nevertheless, an analysis of the theories themselves is important to understanding fundamental mortgage law concepts. . . .

THIRD PARTY BENEFICIARY

The first and most important view is that the mortgagee is allowed to sue the assuming grantee simply as a third party beneficiary of a contract. The great weight of authority accepts this view. . . . Where the third party beneficiary doctrine is accepted as the foundation of the mortgagee's right, it is clearly an independent one enforceable by an action at law.

"SURETYSHIP" SUBROGATION

A second group of cases, applying a "suretyship" theory, invoke what is called the doctrine of equitable subrogation. As used here, it means that the mortgagee-creditor is enabled to reach a right in the hands of his debtor, the mortgagor, against a third party, the assuming grantee, on the theory that the mortgagor-debtor has become a surety-debtor. In order for the principle to apply a "suretyship" situation must exist. A suretyship situation requires a triangle with the person at each foot of the triangle being bound to the creditor at the apex by their respective contracts. Where there is only one person owing a single obligation to another person no suretyship situation can exist. For a person's duty to be that of a surety, in addition to his obligation to the creditor, there must be a separate one, the principal, for whose performance it stands surety. In a mortgage, to begin with, there is a personal obligation running between the mortgagor and the mortgagee. There is also, existing between the mortgagee and the land in the hands of the mortgagor, a relationship normally referred to as a security interest in the property. When the land is transferred by the mortgagor to a grantee, as between the continuing personal duty of the mortgagor to the mortgagee and the continuing relationship between the mortgagee and the land now in the hands of another, the situation may be treated with some certainty as one of suretyship.

. . . But the suretyship situation to which the cases purport to apply the principle is a different and additional one in which the assuming grantee personally, not the land, is the principal. If the assumption creates a new direct right in the mortgagee against the assuming grantee, a suretyship situation results in which the new right is the principal obligation and the old right against the mortgagor becomes that of a surety. However, unless the mortgagee does acquire such a separate right against the assuming grantee in addition to his continuing personal right against the mortgagor no suretyship relation in the ordinary sense can exist. If the assuming grantee is not personally a principal, i.e., obligated directly to the mortgagee, his promise to the mortgagor to pay the debt cannot be regarded as the collateral security given by him, as principal, to the mortgagor, as his surety, for indemnity against liability to the mortgagee. It follows that, if the situation is really one of suretyship, the courts actually are recognizing that the contract of assumption creates a new right in the mortgagee against the assuming grantee — a result in substance no different from that which recognizes openly that it does so under the doctrine that the beneficiary of a contract may enforce it.

Equitable Assets

The equitable assets theory was initially advanced by Professor Williston. Under this approach, instead of looking at the assuming grantee's promise to the grantor-promisee as indemnity security in the latter's hands as surety, given to him by the principal obligor, it is regarded as an asset of the mortgagee's only debtor, the mortgagor, of a sort which can be reached only by the aid of equity.

The theory has certain distinct merits. On the one hand it avoids both the difficulty of giving reasons why a person who is not privy to a contract may nevertheless maintain an action on it against the promisor and the practical objection to permitting it that the promisor may be exposed to possible double liability on one promise. On the other hand, it escapes the fictitious, or apparently contradictory, aspects of the "suretyship" solution which seems to create, or at least recognize the existence of, a primary personal obligation of the assuming grantee running to the mortgagee and yet holds that the only way to realize on that obligation is by reaching, in equity, security in the form of a promise to indemnify given by the grantee-promisor as principal to his grantor-promisee as surety.

Nevertheless certain aspects of the theory have been criticized. For one thing, the asset is a peculiar sort of one in that, unlike other assets, it is available only to one particular creditor, the mortgagee. Another possible criticism of the doctrine is that, by offering a good, if not perfect solution of the problem, it tends to retard the complete triumph of the third party beneficiary direct right rule.

Miscellaneous

In some jurisdictions statutes give the mortgagee a right against the assuming grantee either expressly or by construction. In a few others the courts, predicating the relief upon the substantive rights of a mortgagee against the mortgagor and of the latter against his assuming grantee, permit the mortgagee to proceed directly against the grantee to avoid plurality of actions and harassment of the mortgagor.

Basic Security Transactions

NOTE

Where there are successive purchasers of the mortgaged property, each one assuming the mortgage, the mortgagee may enforce the debt against any one (or all) of them. But the chain of assumption sometimes stops and then resumes as in the following diagram:

E (*Mortgagee*)

↕

R (*Mortgagor*) ↔ A (*Non-Assuming Grantee*) ↔ B (*Assuming Grantee*)

If a mortgage default occurs, is B personally subject to E's claim on the debt?

Schneider v. Ferrigno

110 Conn. 86, 147 A. 303 (1929)

MALTBIE, J. This action is brought by the holders of a certain mortgage to recover upon a condition contained in a deed of the mortgaged premises to the defendant wherein he assumed and agreed to pay the mortgage. It was originally executed by Ethel M. Holmes Case to one Paradise, being a fourth mortgage for $15,475 upon certain premises owned by her. Paradise sold the note and mortgage to David Miller and Miller sold them to the plaintiff Baggish and to Samuel Schneider, who took title to his half interest in the name of his wife, the other plaintiff. Before he acquired his interest in the note and mortgage, Schneider purchased the equity of redemption, taking title subject to the mortgages upon the premises. Later he entered into negotiations with the defendant for the exchange of the premises for certain real estate owned by the defendant, but, when the terms came to be arranged, Schneider was unwilling to assume certain mortgages on the defendant's premises and to execute purchase-money mortgages to him, so he proposed to transfer his premises to a brother-in-law, Krawitzky, and then have him make the exchange. Accordingly he did transfer the premises to Krawitzky, who assumed and agreed to pay the mortgages upon it, including the one in suit, "as part consideration for this deed," and Krawitzky and the defendant then made the exchange, the defendant also assuming and agreeing to pay the mortgages on the premises Krawitzky conveyed to him. The defendant later lost title to the premises by reason of a strict foreclosure of an incumbrance prior to that held by the plaintiffs. The trial court decided for the defendant solely upon the ground that, in view of the fact that Schneider had not himself assumed payment of the mortgage upon the property, the break in the chain of assumptions prevented a recovery by the plaintiffs upon the assumption agreement in the deed to the defendant, and that he did not intend to make a contract for the benefit of the holders of the note and mortgage in suit.

The appellants seek many corrections in the finding, but, in the view we take of the case, none of them are material. The basic question presented is, "Can the holder of a mortgage make liable one who, upon acquiring title to the premises, has assumed and agreed to pay that mortgage, despite the fact that, in the chain of title from the original maker of the mortgage, some owner of the equity of redemption has not assumed and agreed to pay it?" Where such situations have come before the courts, in the absence of statutory provision, different conclusions have been reached. Those which deny a right of recovery advance various reasons. Wiltsie, Mortgage Foreclosure (4th Ed.) §246, states that such a conclusion is based upon the fact that there is no consideration for the assumption, but that can hardly be so; the agreement to assume is but one term in the contract by which the lands are acquired, and, if that contract as a whole is supported by a valuable consideration, it cannot be said that any one term lacks such support. Williston, Contracts, §386, suggests as the basis for the conclusion that, where the grantor of the equity of redemption was not himself liable by reason of an assumption of the mortgage and hence had no interest in the assumption of it by his grantee, the only intelligent object which can be attributed to him is to guard against a supposed or possible liability on his part, and he cannot be assumed to have intended to confer a benefit upon the holder of the mortgage; but it is difficult to see why, if his object is assumed to be to protect himself against a possible liability, his mental attitude is any different than it would be, had he sought to protect himself against a definite liability fixed by his own agreement to pay the mortgage. The cases which deny liability, such as the leading case of Vrooman v. Turner, 69 N.Y. 280, 285, 25 Am. Rep. 195, do not seem fully to recognize the extent and force of the rule which permits a third party beneficiary to sue upon a contract as it has now been developed.

The controlling test now is, Was there any intent to confer a right of action upon the third party? Amer. Law Inst. Restatement, Contracts, §§133, 135; Byram Lumber & Supply Co. v. Page, 109 Conn. [256], 146 A. 293. If the grantor of the equity of redemption who has not assumed the mortgage has no object to protect himself, an intent to confer a right to sue upon the holder of the mortgage would be the most natural motive to assign to him in requiring his grantee to agree to pay it. It is true that difficulties might be encountered in an attempt to work out the problem upon the equitable doctrine whereby, as between a mortgagor and his grantee who assumes and agrees to pay the mortgage, the latter becomes the principal debtor and the former occupies the position of surety, at least as it is applied in many jurisdictions, but with us that principle applies only as between the mortgagor and the grantee of the equity of redemption, and does not of itself affect the right of the mortgagee. Savings Bank of Ansonia v. Schancupp, 108 Conn. 588, 592, 144 A. 36. As regards the latter, the basis of a recovery upon an agreement by a grantee of the equity

of redemption to pay the mortgage is stated in Tuttle v. Jockmus, 106
Conn. 683, 689, 138 A. 804, 806, as follows: "The right of the mortgagee
to bring an action upon an assumption of the mortgage by the grantee of
the equity of redemption is ordinarily based upon the principle which
permits a third party to bring an action upon a contract made for his
benefit." . . .

The conclusion of the trial court that it was not the intention of the
defendant to make a contract for the benefit of the holders of the note in
suit we understand to refer to the intention which the law attributes to him
by reason of the assumption of the mortgage under the circumstances of
this case. Of course, the question is, What intent is disclosed by the terms of
his agreement read in the light of the surrounding circumstances, not such
actual intent as he may have entertained? Quinby Co. v. Sheffield, 84
Conn. 177, 193, 79 A. 179; Easterbrook v. Hebrew Ladies' Orphan Society, 85 Conn. 289, 295, 82 A. 561, 41 L.R.A. (N.S.) 615.

The trial court was in error in holding that the plaintiffs could not hold
the defendant liable upon his assumption of the mortgage because of the
break in the claim of assumptions due to Schneider's failure to assume it.
As the case was decided solely upon this ground, we remand it for further
proceedings according to law.

There is error, and a new trial is ordered.
All the Judges concur.

NOTES AND QUESTIONS

1. Restatement (Second) of Contracts §302 provides as follows:

(1) Unless otherwise agreed between promisor and promisee, a beneficiary
of a promise is an *intended* beneficiary if recognition of a right to performance in the beneficiary is appropriate to effectuate the intention of the
parties and either

(a) the performance of the promise will satisfy an obligation of the
promisee to pay money to the beneficiary; or

(b) the circumstances indicate that the promisee intends to give the
beneficiary the benefit of the promised performance.

(2) An *incidental* beneficiary is a beneficiary who is not an intended beneficiary. [Italics added.]

An intended beneficiary may enforce the promise. Id. at §304. An
incidental beneficiary acquires no such right. Id. at §315.

Restatement §§302(1)(a) and (b) preserve the distinction between
"creditor beneficiary" and "donee beneficiary," the two strands of third-party beneficiary doctrine under the common law. Read together, would
these two paragraphs cover every broken chain assumption case? Can we
infer, whenever the grantor inserts an assumption clause in the deed, that
he or she is either obliged to the mortgagee or intends to give the mortga-

gee the benefit of the assumption? Should such intent be disregarded if the grantor mistakenly believes that he or she is personally obliged? In this connection, Restatement §312 provides:

> The effect of an erroneous belief of the . . . promisee as to the existence or extent of a duty owed to an intended beneficiary is determined by the rules making contracts voidable for mistake.

The illustrations to §312 include the following case, supposedly based on Schneider v. Ferrigno:

> A, the owner of Blackacre, mortgages it to C for $5000. A transfers Blackacre subject to the mortgage to X, who does not assume or agree to pay the mortgage debt. X transfers Blackacre to B, who with knowledge of all the facts assumes and agrees to pay the mortgage debt. B is liable to C for the amount of the debt. (Illustration 3.)

Where B shows by clear and convincing evidence that his promise was inserted in the deed by mistake of the scrivener, contrary to the contract between X and B and without their knowledge, C would have no claim. (Illustration 4.)

2. Some jurisdictions still do not let the mortgagee recover against a grantee whose assumption follows a break in the chain. See, e.g., Dail v. Campbell, 191 Cal. App. 2d 416, 12 Cal. Rptr. 739 (1966).

3. "It is true that difficulties [in extending liability to the grantee] might be encountered in an attempt to work out the problem upon the equitable doctrine whereby, as between a mortgagor and his grantee who assumes and agrees to pay the mortgage, the latter becomes the principal debtor and the former occupies the position of surety. . . ." Schneider v. Ferrigno, at 244 supra. What are the difficulties?

d. Mortgage Takeover: Defenses to the Mortgagee's Suit on the Debt

(1) Discharge of Grantor as Surety—Grantor's Defense I

First Federal Savings & Loan Assn. of Gary v. Arena
406 N.E.2d 1279 (Ind. App. 1980)

CHIPMAN, Judge.

CASE SUMMARY

First Federal Savings and Loan Association of Gary, (First Federal), appeals from a grant of summary judgment in favor of Michael and Grace

Arena, (Arenas), in a foreclosure action brought by First Federal against the Arenas and their grantee, Sanford G. Richardson, as well as various lienholders.

First Federal asserts it was erroneous for the trial court to hold that altering the mortgages' interest rate was a material change which discharged the Arenas from personal liability on the mortgages. According to First Federal, a reservation of rights clause contained in the supplemental agreements to the mortgages executed by the Arenas and First Federal, permitted First Federal in its dealings with Mr. Richardson to increase the rate of interest on the mortgages without first affording the Arenas notice or obtaining their consent, while still retaining the Arenas' liability on the mortgages. The trial court, however, found the reservation of rights clause did not authorize First Federal to so act and entered judgment in favor of the Arenas.

We affirm the judgment of the trial court.

FACTS

On May 26, 1965, the Arenas executed a note, mortgage, and supplemental agreement with First Federal. The note provided for a loan of $32,000 at an interest rate of 5¾%, and the mortgage securing this note provided for advances of up to $6,400. March 11, 1966, the Arenas were granted an advance of $5,100, and in consideration, they executed a modification and extension agreement which provided they would owe a new balance of $36,664.81, and the interest rate would be increased to 6%. A separate note, mortgage, and supplemental agreement were also executed by the Arenas in relation to this advance.

March 10, 1969, the Arenas conveyed the real estate which was the subject of both the May 26, 1965, and March 11, 1966, mortgages to Sanford G. Richardson by warranty deed subject to the two mortgages to First Federal. The same day, without notice to or the consent of the Arenas, Mr. Richardson and First Federal entered into a modification and extension agreement, under the terms of which Richardson assumed both of the mortgages in question, and the time for payment was extended to twenty years; there was also a change in the interest rate from 6% to 7¼%. Thus, this agreement, signed only by Richardson and First Federal, was designed to be a modification of First Federal's earlier agreement with the Arenas by extending the time of payment and modifying the terms of payment to which the Arenas and First Federal had agreed.

After June 27, 1975, Richardson failed to make the payments due under the March 10, 1969, modification and extension agreement. As a result, a default on the mortgages and notes occurred and a suit in foreclosure was filed on behalf of First Federal against the Arenas, Richardson, and several lienholders. . . .

Decision

Conclusion — By reason of an expressed provision to that effect in the supplemental agreements between the Arenas and First Federal, the Arenas were not released from liability upon extension of the mortgage in the agreement between Mr. Richardson and First Federal; however, this agreement not only extended the time for payment, but it also modified the terms of payment by increasing the interest rate. It is our opinion the trial court properly found the Arenas had not consented to such a change in interest rates and, therefore, were released from liability.[3] Arenas' grantee and First Federal could not modify the original mortgagors' agreement without the mortgagors' consent.

The focal point in this controversy is the meaning to be accorded a reservation of rights clause which appeared in the supplemental agreement executed by the Arenas when they obtained the initial mortgage and later secured the advance. The agreement provided:

> THE UNDERSIGNED, Michael Arena and Grace Arena, Husband and Wife, . . . , hereinafter referred to as the Mortgagor, hereby executes and delivers to FIRST FEDERAL SAVINGS AND LOAN ASSOCIATION OF GARY, . . . , hereinafter referred to as the Mortgagee, this Supplemental Agreement, pursuant to a Mortgage executed and delivered concurrently herewith, and this Supplemental Agreement is expressly made a part of said Mortgage, ...
> THE MORTGAGOR COVENANTS: . . . . .
> 6. That in the event the ownership of said property or any part thereof becomes vested in a person other than the Mortgagor, the Mortgagee may, without notice to the Mortgagor, deal with such successor or successors in interest with reference to this mortgage and the debt hereby secured in the same manner as with the Mortgagor, and may forbear to sue or may extend time for payment of the debt, secured hereby, without discharging or in any

---

3. If the full amount due on foreclosure did not exceed the value of the property at the time of the execution of the Modification and Extension Agreement, it was proper for the trial court to completely discharge the Arenas. Mutual Ben. Life Ins. Co. v. Lindley, (1932) 97 Ind. App. 575, 183 N.E. 127; Stevens, Extension Agreements in the "Subject-To" Mortgage Situation, 15 U. Cin. L. Rev. 58 (1941). As a corollary, if the value of the land at the time of this agreement was less than the amount of the mortgage on the property, the Arenas should have remained liable to the extent of this difference.

Although it was improper for the trial court to hold there was a complete discharge without also holding the value of the land at the time of the March 10, 1969, agreement fully supported the mortgage loan, First Federal never raised any error regarding the extent to which the Arenas were discharged . . . ; consequently, we can only assume the amount due on foreclosure on March 10, 1969, would have been less than the value of the property at that time.

We note, since Mr. Richardson offered to purchase the real estate in question for $37,000, and the aggregate balance remaining unpaid when Mr. Richardson and First Federal executed the Modification and Extension Agreement was $33,393.83, it appears the value of the land, in fact, did exceed the amount due, and thus, a complete discharge would have been proper.

way affecting the liability of the Mortgagor hereunder or upon the debt hereby secured;

First Federal asserts the reservation of rights language set out above permitted it, in dealing with Richardson, to increase the interest rate and extend the time of payment without first obtaining the Arenas' consent while still retaining their liability. Appellant takes the position that the portion of paragraph six providing for no discharge modified forbearing to sue and extending time for payment as well as dealing in the same manner as with the mortgagor; therefore, since the interest rate was increased when the Arenas were given their additional advance, according to First Federal, raising the interest rate in its agreement with Richardson would merely be dealing with him in the same manner as it had dealt with the Arenas and, consequently, should not result in a discharge.

The Arenas, on the other hand, contend the reservation of rights clause in the Supplemental Agreement made no reference to the alteration or modification of the interest rate but rather, referred only to an extension of the time for payment or the decision to forbear to sue.

While it is true paragraph six indicates First Federal could deal with successors in interest to the mortgage in the same manner as with the mortgagor, we hold the resolution of whether this meant First Federal and the Arenas' grantee would be permitted to increase the interest rate without affecting the Arenas' liability was a question of law for the trial court since the rules applicable to construction of contracts generally apply to the construction of an agreement whereby a purchaser of mortgaged premises assumes the payment of the mortgage. 20 I.L.E. Mortgages §193. . . .

The essence of the appeal before us then is whether the trial court correctly concluded that as a matter of law, the scope of the reservation of rights clause found in paragraph six did not include altering or modifying the interest rate, and consequently, First Federal did not reserve the right to modify and increase the interest rate from 6% to 7¼% without the consent of the Arenas. We hold the trial court's entry of summary judgment in favor of Arenas was proper.

When the Arenas conveyed the real estate to Richardson subject to the existing mortgages to First Federal, the land became as to said parties, the primary source of funds for payment of the debt. Mutual Ben. Life Ins. Co. v. Lindley, (1932) 97 Ind. App. 575, 183 N.E. 127. No technical relation of principal and surety arose between the Arenas and their grantee from this conveyance, but an equity did arise which bears a close resemblance to the equitable rights of a surety. As a result, the Arenas assumed a position analogous to that of a surety, and the grantee became the principal debtor to the extent of the value of the land conveyed. Mutual Ben. Life Ins. Co. v. Lindley, supra; Warm, Some Aspects of the Rights and Liabilities of Mortgagee, Mortgagor and Grantee, 10 Temple L.Q. 116 (1936).

While a mortgagor in such a situation may consent in advance to future modifications or agree his liability will not be discharged by subsequent agreements between his grantee and the mortgagee, such clauses are to be strictly construed against the mortgagee, see Friedman, Discharge of Personal Liability on Mortgage Debts in New York, 52 Yale L.J. 771, 788 (1943), since it would be unjust to subject the mortgagor to a new risk or material change to which he has not consented. Consequently, a reservation of rights clause will not prevent a discharge of liability where the modification in question exceeds the scope of the consent in the clause. This should come as no surprise since the mortgagor occupies the position of a surety, and the law of suretyship provides that a surety is entitled to stand on the strict letter of the contract upon which he is liable, and where he does not consent to a variation and a variation is made, it is fatal, see American States Insurance Co. v. Floyd I. Staub, Inc., (1977) Ind. App., 370 N.E.2d 989; White v. Household Finance Corp., (1973) 158 Ind. App. 394, 302 N.E. 2d 828; therefore, an agreement between the principals for a higher interest than called for by the original contract will, if made without the surety's consent, release him from all liability. 74 Am. Jur. 2d Suretyship §47 (1974); see also 4 Am. Jur. 2d Alteration of Instruments §55 (1962).

The fact First Federal dealt with the grantee shows it knew of the Arenas' conveyance, and knowing of this conveyance, it was incumbent upon First Federal not to deal with the grantee in such a manner as would jeopardize or alter the surety-principal relationship. Warm, Some Aspects of the Rights and Liabilities of Mortgagee, Mortgagor and Grantee, 10 Temple L.Q. 116 (1936). The modification and extension agreement in question provided Mr. Richardson would personally assume the mortgage debt and thus, inured to the benefit of First Federal, but at the same time, the terms of the Arenas' earlier mortgage were changed to the detriment of the Arenas. If this increase in the interest rate was beyond the scope of the reservation of rights clause, the Arenas were thereby discharged, and the grantee became the sole debtor on the mortgages.

We hold the trial court properly rejected First Federal's argument that by increasing the interest rate it was merely dealing with Mr. Richardson in the same manner as it had dealt with the Arenas, and therefore, according to paragraph six, the Arenas should not have been discharged.

While it is true paragraph six indicated First Federal could deal with successors in interest to the mortgage in the same manner as with the mortgagor, this provision did not say First Federal could do so with impunity. We agree with the trial court that the portion of this paragraph providing for no discharge only modified forbearing to sue or extending the time for payment; consequently, the mortgagor would not be discharged from liability if the mortgagee simply extended the time for payment of the debt or opted not to bring suit, but these were the only situations where the mortgagee knew to a certainty his actions in dealing

Basic Security Transactions 251

with the grantee would not discharge the mortgagor. The reservation of rights clause in paragraph six did not apply to activities which allegedly came within the ambit of dealing in the same manner as with the mortgagor. At the risk of being redundant, we again note, paragraph six stated in part:

> 6. [T]he Mortgagee may, without notice to the Mortgagor, deal with . . . successors in interest with reference to this mortgage and the debt hereby secured in the same manner as with the Mortgagor, *and* . . . . (our emphasis)

The punctuation used clearly sets this portion of paragraph six apart from the remainder of the paragraph which then goes on to provide the mortgagee

> may forbear to sue or may extend time for payment of the debt, . . . , without discharging or in any way affecting the liability of the Mortgagor hereunder or upon the debt hereby secured.

In order to give the reservation of rights clause the expanded application urged by First Federal so that it also applied to dealing in the same manner as with the mortgagor, it would be necessary to ignore the punctuation used and the maxim that such clauses should be strictly construed against the mortgagee. Further, such a construction would change the reservation of rights provision from applying in two definite situations to an open-ended invitation to argue there was no discharge because the mortgagee either could have or in fact had dealt with the mortgagor in the same manner; the possible activities which arguably could then come within this clause's application would be indefinite.

We hold the construction of the supplemental agreement between the Arenas and First Federal was a question of law for the trial court, which correctly held paragraph six did not authorize First Federal and the Arenas' grantee to alter the terms of payment on the mortgage debt by increasing the interest rate without affecting the Arenas' liability.

Judgment affirmed.

Miller, P. J., and Young, J., concur.

NOTES AND QUESTIONS

1. Consider, in the following situations, whether the grantor, as surety, will be discharged from further obligation on the mortgage debt.

   (a) Mortgage covers tracts 1 and 2. For nominal consideration the mortgagee releases the lien of its mortgage from tract 2. At the time, the value of tract 1 exceeds the mortgage balance. Cf. Shine Laundry Inc. v. Washington Loan & Banking Co., 112 Ga. App. 827, 146 S.E.2d 371 (1965).

(b) Mortgagee waives his claim to a deficiency judgment against the grantee whose default on the mortgage resulted in foreclosure. Cf. Wagoner v. Brady, 221 App. Div. 405, 175 N.Y. 223 (1927).

2. Why should the grantor, who is principally obligated on the debt, not remain so even after a transfer of the mortgaged premises to an assuming grantee? And especially, after a transfer to a nonassuming grantee? What explains the application of suretyship law to the post-transfer relationship of mortgagee and grantor? For expression of a minority view, see Shockey v. Page, 354 S.W.2d 698 (Tex. Civ. App. 1962), and the dissenting opinion in Wagoner v. Brady, supra.

3. Where the mortgagee gives the grantee an extension, should full discharge of the grantor result, or discharge only to the value of the mortgaged property at the time of the extension? Suppose that the mortgagee can show that the real estate increased in value during the extension period or that the deficiency was less than it would have been had no extension occurred?

(2) Failure to Exhaust Other Remedies — Grantor's Defense II

Statement of the Problem. E holds a note signed by R; the note is secured by a mortgage. R sells the mortgaged property to X who assumes the mortgage. Default then occurs. Without bringing foreclosure, E sues R on the debt. R answers that the suit is premature. Result? See generally Osborne, Nelson & Whitman, Real Estate Finance Law at 264 (1979). Suppose, instead, that E proceeds to foreclosure and the foreclosure sale produces a deficiency. E sues R on the deficiency without first attempting to collect from X. R again answers that the suit is premature. Result?

(3) Subsequent Change of the Contract of Assumption — Grantee's Defense I

Statement of the Problem. E holds a note signed by R; the note is secured by a mortgage. R sells the mortgaged property to X who assumes the mortgage. Thereafter, before any default occurs, X and R mutually rescind the assumption agreement; E is not a party to the rescission. Default then occurs and the foreclosure sale produces a deficiency. E sues for a deficiency judgment. X pleads the rescission agreement. Result? Would it make a difference whether the rights of the mortgagee against an assuming grantee were direct or derivative? Would the result be different if the mortgage was already in default when the parties rescinded? If E had already begun his foreclosure suit? See generally Osborne, Nelson and Whitman, Real Estate Finance Law at 283-286 (1979).

Basic Security Transactions

(4) Usury in the Original Transaction — Grantee's Defense II

Statement of the Problem. In a suit by the mortgagee, may the grantee plead usury where the mortgage transaction was originally tainted? Compare Central Holding Co. v. Bushman, 238 Mich. 261, 213 N.W. 120 (1927) (defense of usury is personal to the original mortgagor), with National Mutual Building & Loan Assn. v. Retzman, 69 Neb. 667, 96 N.W. 204 (1903) (defense of usury may be asserted by the grantee, at least in the instance when the grantor and grantee adjust the sales price to reflect their belief that the mortgage loan was usurious). Should the privilege of the usury plea depend on whether the mortgagee is suing to foreclose or is seeking a deficiency judgment?

4. Remedies of Secured Creditors

a. Preforeclosure Rights

Lifton, Real Estate in Trouble: Lender's Remedies Need an Overhaul
31 Bus. Law. 1927, 1931-1934 (1976)

Three different conceptual approaches to the mortgage and the mortgagee's right to possession in case of default are embodied in state mortgage acts and judicial decisions. In the majority of states, even where the mortgage instrument uses language that signifies a transfer of title, the mortgagee only gets a lien or security interest in the property which can be activated by foreclosure sale. When a default occurs, unless the owner voluntarily turns over possession, the mortgagee has little hope of getting physical possession except through foreclosure proceedings.

A few title states, however, like the early common law, still treat the mortgage as a conveyance of the property to a lender to be returned to the borrower when the mortgage debt is discharged. In theory, the lender also gets the continuing right to possession which he agrees not to exercise unless there is a default. In another small group of so-called "intermediate" theory states, courts talk in terms of the right to possession being retained by the mortgagor until default, but after default automatically accruing to the mortgagee. Despite these theoretical differences, even in the title and intermediate states, modern courts are reluctant to grant a mortgagee physical possession of the property. And even where physical possession may be available, restraints on the mortgagee and the risks of possession may dissuade lenders from seeking it. In some jurisdictions, a mortgagee in possession may have minimum power over the property. It may not be compensated for its own management efforts or be able to recover money advanced for improving or maintaining the property during its possession.[21] The mortgagee in possession also may risk having to account to the owner under stringent rules of accounting for decisions on renting and operating the property if the owner later redeems the property.[22] As a result of these limitations, rather than seek physical possession to protect itself against the owner skimming off the income while the property deteriorates the lender will usually look to the traditional remedies granting constructive possession. These are contained in standard mortgage provisions for assignment of rents and for appointment of a receiver in case of default.

Generally, an assignment of rents can be activated in title, intermediate and some lien states by the mortgagee's serving notice on the tenants in the property to pay their rents to the mortgagee.[23] Although an assignment of rents is of no value in a property like a hotel, restaurant or theatre with daily operating income, it may be more effective in the case of a property with monthly tenants. Frequently, however, when the mortgagee attempts to activate an assignment of rents, the tenants will react to the conflicting demands for rent from the owner and the mortgagee by not paying rent to either until the issue is resolved in court. And many courts, particularly in lien states, are unwilling to deliver the rents to the mortgagee even if such action is warranted, preferring instead to appoint an independent receiver to collect and apply the rents.

Convincing the court to appoint a receiver, though, is not always easy. In some jurisdictions a provision in the mortgage for appointment of a receiver upon the mortgagee's demand is sufficient as a matter of course to get a receiver installed.[27] But in a few states it has been almost impossible to get a receiver appointed because of legislation enacted during the depression years to protect homeowners and farmers.[28] In between, are those

---

21. Although a mortgagee generally is entitled to credit for maintenance expenditures, credit for improvements is more difficult to recoup. See Osborne §§168, 169. This distinction may be very difficult to make in day-to-day management of a property.

22. Hall v. Goldsworthy, 136 Kan. 247, 14 P.2d 659 (1932); Osborne §§164, 167; 59 C.J.S. (2d) Mortgages §§305, 318, 336; See Pioneer Building & Loan Assn. v. Compton, 138 S.W.2d 884 (Tex. App. 1940) (mortgagor may recover from mortgagee for failure to perform its obligation to use reasonable diligence to rent the property). The mortgagee in possession may also face problems under the Interstate Land Act or the Securities & Exchange Act. Kaster, Hershman & Roegge, Realty Interests, Default and Resale, 52 Practising Law Institute (1975).

23. Freedman's Sav. & Trust Co. v. Shepherd, 127 U.S. 494 (1888); Osborne §150. Some lien states view an assignment of rents as security for the loan which may not be activated short of foreclosure or appointment of a receiver. See Dime Savings Bank v. Altman, 275 N.Y. 62, 9 N.E.2d 778 (Ct. App. 1937), *reargument denied*, 275 N.Y. 545 (1937). Other jurisdictions treat it as an absolute assignment of rents and give the beneficiary mortgagee the right to the rents upon default. See Kinnison v. Guaranty Liquidating Corp., 18 Cal. 2d 256, 115 P.2d 450 (1941). See also In re Ventura-Louise Properties, 490 F.2d 1141 (9th Cir. 1974).

27. In Westchester County, for example, it may take no more than a week to get a receiver appointed. See Kaster, Hershman & Roegge, supra note 22, at 155, citing similar rapid appointment of a receiver in New York, California, and Washington.

28. 59 C.J.S.2d Mortgages §656. In South Dakota a provision for consent to appointment of a receiver is against public policy and unenforceable. S.D. Compiled Laws Ann. §44-8-7

Basic Security Transactions

courts which require proof that the security is impaired and sometimes also that the borrower is insolvent.[29] Courts differ considerably on what constitutes impairment and what is required to prove it. Where the court's criterion is replacement value rather than economic value, it is difficult to prove that the property is impaired unless the building is being so poorly maintained that physical inspection shows a sharp deterioration in value. Impairment may also be demonstrated where the economic values have plummeted dramatically; for example, where utilities are cut off because of nonpayment and large numbers of tenants are leaving.

The mortgagee may present expert testimony from the appraiser who made the original loan appraisal that because of the economic decline of the property — the failure to reach certain rental levels, for example — the present value of the property is less than the appraised value on which the loan was based. In the case of certain institutional lenders, the mortgagor may counter by noting that under state law the lender was prohibited from making a loan of more than 75 percent of the property's value[30] so that the economic value of the property had to fall more than 25 percent for the loan to be impaired. It is difficult for a lender to admit what is often true — that the original loan exceeded 75 percent of value, and therefore any significant loss of value endangers its mortgage.

The struggle to have a receiver appointed can take too much time, in the face of what appears to be obvious need. In the case of one apartment hotel in Miami, for example, after defaulting on a mortgage of $7,500,000, the owner sold the property for $12,000 in cash to two out-of-state speculators. A purchase of defaulted property with a yearly gross income of $4,000,000 for a cash price that low inevitably suggests that the purchaser has in mind quickly recouping the cash portion of his purchase price from any available funds, as well as taking advantage of whatever else he can milk from the property. The buyers of this property quickly retrieved their investment and more at the expense of the creditors. They purchased three Cadillac cars for $65,000 in due bills and entered into favorable long-term leases with members of their families. Yet, it took

---

(1967). Although in a foreclosure by judicial action, the court may appoint a receiver if authorized by law, the criteria for appointment are stringent. Id. §21-21-2. See In re Federal Shopping Way, Inc., 457 F.2d 176 (9th Cir. 1972), discussing the Washington statute prior to its amendment in 1969. See also Investors Syndicate v. Smith, 105 F.2d 611 (9th Cir. 1939).

29. 3 Powell §465, at 696.14; 59 C.J.S.2d Mortgages §656. Some courts hesitate to appoint a receiver, even in the face of a mortgage provision for appointment which recites that "such appointment shall be made as a matter of absolute right to (lender) and without reference to the adequacy or inadequacy of the property mortgaged or to the solvency or insolvency of the mortgagor." 3 Powell, §465, at 696.15.

30. Regarding loan-to-value ratios permitted to life insurance companies, see generally, Gunning & Roegge, Contemporary Real Estate Financing Techniques, 3 Prop., Probate & Trust J. 325 (1968). New York State, for example, limits its state chartered commercial and savings banks to making 75% loans on improved real estate. N.Y. Banking Law §§103(4), 235(6)(a) (McKinney Supp. 1971). National banks are limited to 90% of appraised value if the property is improved by a building and 66⅔% if unimproved. 12 U.S.C. §371 (Supp. IV, 1974).

almost two months from the time the mortgagee requested the court to appoint a receiver to get a receiver appointed.

Finally, a receiver is too often chosen by the court because of his political connections or friendship rather than his managerial ability and real estate knowhow. And the award for a receiver's fees can eat up a good part of the property's income.

(1) Mortgagee in Possession

Myers–Macomber Engineers v. M.L.W. Construction Corp.

271 Pa. Super. 484, 414 A.2d 357 (1979)

WIEAND, Judge. Does a mortgagee who goes into possession of an incomplete condominium development upon default in the terms of a mortgage by the mortgagor owe a duty to use undistributed mortgage funds to satisfy the mortgagor's unpaid debts? The lower court held that a mortgagee in possession becomes a quasi trustee with a responsibility to satisfy outstanding, job related claims against the mortgagor. We disagree and reverse.

M.L.W. Construction Corporation was the owner and developer of a series of condominiums on a nineteen acre tract in East Pennsboro Township, Cumberland County. HNC Mortgage and Realty Investors agreed to lend construction money in the amount of $5,850,000.00, which sum was secured by a construction mortgage. After $2,900,000.00 had been advanced, the developer defaulted. HNC thereupon exercised the right given by the terms of the mortgage to assume control of the project as a mortgagee in possession. Subsequently, HNC foreclosed on its mortgage and purchased the incomplete development at sheriff's sale. The project was completed by a contractor employed by HNC.

The appellee, Myers–Macomber Engineers, had performed site-preparation work pursuant to a contract with M.L.W., for which it is owed an unpaid balance of $11,298.98. In this action of assumpsit appellee alleged that M.L.W. had breached its contract to pay for services rendered. M.L.W. did not contest the claim. In a separate count against HNC, appellee contended that the lender was liable for the value of engineering services on theories of unjust enrichment. The trial court submitted this issue to a jury, which returned a verdict in favor of appellee and against HNC for $11,000.00. Motions for new trial and judgment n. o. v. were denied, and judgment was entered on the verdict. HNC appealed.

"Mortgagee in possession" is a term applied to the special status of a mortgagee who has obtained possession of property from the mortgagor

Basic Security Transactions

with the consent of the latter. See generally: 55 Am. Jur. 2d Mortgages §§184, 185, 193-196; Osborne, Mortgages §§160-176 (2d ed., 1970). Such consent is usually contained, as here, in the mortgage agreement. This remedy avoids the drastic step of foreclosure, while enabling the mortgagee to protect and preserve its security interest. The mortgagee does not thereby limit its right to foreclose, and, upon foreclosure, the mortgagee may purchase the property at sheriff's sale. Girard Trust Company v. Dempsey, 129 Pa. Super. 471, 476, 196 A. 593, 595 (1938). Frequently, foreclosure becomes necessary despite the salvage efforts of a mortgagee in possession. If the mortgagor should avoid foreclosure by paying off the mortgage debt while the mortgagee is in control of the property, however, the mortgagee must surrender possession to the mortgagor, for the mortgagor has retained his title to the real estate throughout the mortgagee's occupancy. Elliot v. Moffett, 365 Pa. 247, 74 A.2d 164 (1950); Malamut v. Haines, 51 F. Supp. 837 (M.D. Pa. 1943).

When a mortgagee goes into possession, he does not become the owner of the real estate. Provident Trust Co. of Philadelphia v. Judicial Building and Loan Asso., 112 Pa. Super. 352, 171 A. 287 (1934); Malamut v. Haines, supra. Rather, he becomes a quasi trustee, managing the property for the benefit of the mortgagor, but at the same time protecting his own interest. Zisman v. City of Duquesne, 143 Pa. Super. 263, 18 A.2d 95 (1941); McNicholas' Appeal, 137 Pa. Super. 415, 9 A.2d 200 (1939). As a mortgagee in possession, his duty is to comport with the same standard of conduct as a prudent owner, i.e., he must manage the property in a reasonably prudent and careful manner so as to keep it in a good state of preservation and productivity. Landau v. Western Pennsylvania National Bank, 445 Pa. 217, 282 A.2d 335 (1971); Integrity Trust Co. v. St. Rita Building & Loan Asso., 317 Pa. 518, 177 A. 5 (1935). See also: Osborne, Mortgages §168 (2d ed., 1970). The mortgagee in possession has a duty to collect the rents and profits which accrue during his occupancy and apply them to the mortgage debt. Provident Trust Co. of Philadelphia v. Judicial Building & Loan Asso., supra. Moreover, the mortgagor is entitled to an accounting from his mortgagee who has taken possession. Landau v. Western Pennsylvania National Bank, supra; Winthrop v. Arthur W. Binns, Inc., 160 Pa. Super. 214, 50 A.2d 718 (1947).

The fiduciary duty of a mortgagee in possession, however, is owed only to the mortgagor. Thus, the mortgagee cannot be required to account to a second mortgagee for income received while the mortgagee was in possession, McNicholas' Appeal, supra; or to a creditor of the mortgagor, Supreme Council of the Royal Arcanum v. Susque Frozen Foods, 44 Northumberland L.J. 13 (1972). Similarly, a mortgagee in possession is not liable to a purchaser at sheriff's sale for taxes owed on the property. Fassitt v. North Tioga Building & Loan Asso., 133 Pa. Super. 146, 2 A.2d 499 (1938).

It follows that in the absence of a valid agreement by which the mortgagee has assumed or guaranteed payment of the mortgagor's debts, the mortgagee cannot be required to pay unsecured claims held by creditors of the mortgagor. Such creditors must look to the mortgagor upon whose credit they relied.

Appellee argues that the mortgagee will be unjustly enriched if it is permitted to retain the benefit of appellee's engineering work. Reliance is placed on the principle that when a person receives a benefit from another, and it would be unconscionable for the recipient to retain that benefit, the doctrine of unjust enrichment requires the recipient to make restitution. Binns v. First National Bank of California, Pennsylvania, 367 Pa. 359, 80 A.2d 768 (1951); DeGasperi v. Valicenti, 198 Pa. Super. 455, 181 A.2d 862 (1962); Restatement of Restitution, §1; 66 Am. Jur. 2d Restitution and Implied Contracts §3. See also: Roman Mosaic & Tile Co., Inc. v. Vollrath, 226 Pa. Super. 215, 313 A.2d 305 (1973). This equitable doctrine imposes on the recipient an obligation in the nature of quasi contract. L. Simpson, Contracts, §5 at 5, (2d ed., 1965); A. Corbin, Contracts, §19 at 44 (1963). The most significant requirement for recovery on quasi contract, however, is that the enrichment to the defendant *must be unjust.* Annot., 62 A.L.R.3d 288, 294 (1975).

In the instant case, appellant was not enriched unjustly. When appellant took possession of the condominium project it had already advanced to the developer the sum of $2,900,000.00. Included in the monies advanced was the entire amount budgeted for site preparation. Thus, it was not unjust that it received the benefit of such engineering work when it was compelled by the developer's default to take possession of the incomplete building project. Moreover, it does not appear that the mortgagee, after purchasing the real estate at sheriff's sale and employing its own contractor to complete the project, was able to dispose of the completed project at a profit.

The legislature in Pennsylvania has by statute provided the mechanics' lien as a means by which a contractor or subcontractor can obtain security for work done. Other security can be acquired by contract. If the right to file a mechanics' lien has been waived, if a contractor chooses to rely upon the personal credit of the party with whom he contracts, a court should not rewrite the contract of the parties or legislate a right to receive payment from a mortgagee who has been compelled to go into possession to preserve its security. Such a rule would do much to impair the availability of capital upon which the building industry so greatly depends. In any event, if additional remedy is needed, it should come from the legislature and should not be decreed by judicial fiat. East Penn Contracting Corp. v. Merchants National Bank of Allentown, 37 Leh. L.J. 268 (1977), *aff'd,* 254 Pa. Super. 613, 387 A.2d 114 (1978).

Reversed and remanded for the entry of judgment n.o.v. in favor of appellant.

NOTE ON MORTGAGEE IN POSSESSION

Apart from an agreement by the parties to the contrary, there is considerable authority giving the mortgagee right to possession of the mortgaged premises in those states that treat the mortgagee as having title rather than just a lien on the mortgaged land. In lien states, the mortgagor generally is considered to have the right to possession. However, in title states the parties usually agree that the mortgagor shall retain possession; but in both lien and title states, the mortgage may provide, as it did in the *Myers–Macomber* case, that if the mortgagor defaults, the mortgagee has the right to take over possession. The usual reasons for the mortgagee taking possession following default by the mortgagor are to protect and preserve the security or to acquire income from the property and apply it to the outstanding debt. The mortgagee, and perhaps the mortgagor as well, may prefer that the mortgagee assume possession than that a receiver do so. It is often hoped that if the mortgagee takes over possession, foreclosure will not be necessary, but by taking over possession the mortgagee ordinarily does not give up the right to foreclose later.

The mortgagee in possession has certain legal obligations to the mortgagor, who continues to hold a substantial interest in the property. The mortgagee must account to the mortgagor for rents and profits from the land and disposition of these rents and profits. The mortgagee may not commit acts of waste. There is uncertainty, however, as to how far the mortgagee may go in making repairs and improvements to the property, whether or not the mortgagee may recover for repairs and improvements made, and whether or not he or she may be compensated for the management of the premises.

What criteria do you believe should determine what repairs and improvements to the property mortgagees in possession may make, their right to reimbursement for repair and improvement costs and from whom, and whether or not they can be compensated for their management services?

(2) Appointment of a Receiver

Wingfoot California Homes Co. v. Valley National Bank of Phoenix

74 Ariz. 287, 248 P.2d 738 (1952)

DE CONCINI, Justice. The plaintiff, Valley National Bank, appellee herein, on June 26, 1951, filed a verified complaint against defendant, appellant, Wingfoot California Homes Co., praying for a money judgment and for foreclosure of certain mortgages. These mortgages were on 43 lots in

Chandler, Arizona, where the defendant had constructed a housing development known as Wingfoot Gardens. A copy of the complaint and summons, together with an order to show cause why a receiver should not be appointed, was served on the defendant. The defendant made no response to the order to show cause but was represented at the hearing on the order, held July 11, 1951. A receiver was appointed by the court on July 27, 1951. The appellant's assignment of error is to the effect that the lower court erred in appointing a receiver because:

1. It was without jurisdiction so to do, and
2. The appointment of a receiver was an abuse of discretion by the lower court.

• It is defendant's contention that the lower court had no jurisdiction to appoint a receiver in this case even though the parties contracted for the appointment of a receiver, under certain conditions, when the mortgages were executed. Defendant's contention here is correct as an abstract principle of law since it is well stated that parties may not by contract or stipulation confer jurisdiction on a court, Baker v. Varney, 129 Cal. 564, 62 P. 100; Lewis v. Shaw, 77 Cal. App. 99, 246 P. 86. The right of a court to appoint a receiver must exist under the law independent of a contract in question. However, where the court has acquired jurisdiction to appoint a receiver, and this appointment is sought for a legitimate purpose, it may proceed upon the consent of the parties interested. Logan v. Mauk, Tex. Civ. App., 126 S.W.2d 513.

Section 62-503, A.C.A. 1939, provides in part as follows:

"A mortgage is a lien upon everything that would pass by a grant of the property, but does not entitle the mortgagee to the possession of the property, unless authorized by the express terms of the mortgage. . . ."

• By this section, then, it can readily be seen that if in its opinion a receiver is necessary for the protection and preservation of the property, the court has jurisdiction to appoint a receiver in the instant case to take possession of the mortgaged property for the benefit of the mortgagee. The above statute confers upon the court the jurisdiction to appoint a receiver if conditions warrant it. The mortgages sought to be foreclosed included the "rents, issues, and profits", and also provided "that in any action to foreclose this mortgage a receiver shall, upon the application of the plaintiff in such action and without notice to the defendants, be appointed by the court to take charge of said property. . . ."

The sole remaining issue is whether the court abused its discretion. Appellant's brief and its extensive argument before the court relies on the proposition, that, because it did not have utility easements as it believed it had when it started to build, it was delayed and put to extraordinary expense. While that may be true there is nothing in this record to show that this condition was caused by the plaintiff. The hearing on the order to show cause did not litigate that question nor was it before the court in the form of testimony except that the appellant had been delayed and put to

Basic Security Transactions 261

extraordinary expense. The only testimony connecting the plaintiff with the utilities was as follows:

"*Q.* Mr. Dunlop, you started to relate who is responsible for this failure to get your utility easement, all that sort of thing, which cost you a large sum of money. Do you know at whose door we can lay that?
A. The escrow was handled by the Valley National Bank, and they did not get the signature from the party on the agreement. And after he had his money and hadn't signed then he said, 'No'. And we had to go around Hell's half acre, under the Southern Pacific Railroad into the City of Chandler another way. We had quite a to do about it during the time."

There was no evidence in the record which tended to show that the plaintiff had the duty to procure the utility easements for the defendant nor was that question presented to the lower court; therefore the defendant cannot now raise that question on appeal.

• There was conflicting testimony as to the value of the mortgaged property. One witness testified that the property was worth less than the balance due on the notes. The defendant admittedly was collecting about $2,000 per month in rent and was delinquent in five monthly payments on the note and mortgage and had actually collected over $6,000 since making his last payment. From the foregoing, we believe that the trial court did not abuse its discretion.
• Where there is a danger of a loss to the mortgagee the court acts within its discretion to appoint a receiver. Prudential Insurance Co. of America v. Puckett, 216 Iowa 406, 249 N.W. 142; Hastings v. Wise, 89 Mont. 325, 297 P. 482; Broad & Market Nat. Bank v. Larsen, 88 N.J. Eq. 245, 102 A. 265.

Judgment affirmed.
Udall, C.J., and Standford, Phelps and La Prade, JJ., concur.

NOTES ON THE APPOINTMENT OF A RECEIVER

1. In the instant case, the mortgage included both the real estate and the "rents, issues, and profits" (standard language). Was this a factor in the court's discretion?
2. Who gets to be appointed as receivers? May the mortgagee be named? May his attorney?
3. The order of appointment will usually direct the receiver "to take charge of, use, operate, manage and control the property . . . to conduct the business thereof, to collect the rents, issues, profits and income thereof, to apply the same to the payment of all usual and necessary expenses of said property, including taxes, mortgage payments, manage-

ment costs and all other regular and necessary costs of the operation of the business operated on said premises." Where the income fails to cover all usual and necesssary expenses, who decides what bills are paid? How is it decided? Suppose the buildings department issues a notice of code violation that requires a capital expense to cure. Does the order above empower the receiver to incur the expense?

(3) Transfer in Lieu of Foreclosure

Harbel Oil v. Steele
83 Ariz. 181, 318 P.2d 359 (1957)

JOHNSON, Justice. This is an appeal from a judgment in favor of Horace Steele and Ethel Steele, Texas Independent Oil Company, a corporation, Blakely Oil, Incorporated, a corporation, defendants-appellees, and against Harbel Oil Company, a corporation, plaintiff-appellant. The plaintiff-appellant will thereafter be referred to as plaintiff. The defendants-appellees, Horace Steele and Ethel Steele, will be referred to as defendants (Steele), and the defendant-appellee, Texas Independent Oil Company, a corporation, as defendant (Texas). It was agreed in the pretrial order that the defendant (Texas) is the successor in interest to the assets and liabilities of Texas Independent Oil Company, a copartnership, composed of the defendants (Steele). The parties further stipulated that defendant (Texas) and defendant Blakely Oil, Incorporated, a corporation, for the purpose of this proceeding, stand in the same position as the other defendants.

The material facts briefly stated are: Plaintiff had acquired a twenty-year lease of vacant land located in Phoenix, Arizona, from Dr. E. A. Cruthirds, for the purpose of erecting and operating a gasoline service station. In order to finance the construction thereof the defendants (Steele) agreed to loan plaintiff the sum of $10,000 which was to be repaid in monthly installments with interest. The cost of the station in excess of $10,000 was to be paid by plaintiff but the record is silent as to the actual cost. As security for the loan the parties executed four instruments: (1) an assignment of the Cruthirds lease for a term of four years and five months (or until the loan was repaid), (2) a sublease back to plaintiff, (3) a conditional sales and loan agreement (covered the equipment in the station), and (4) a products contract whereby plaintiff agreed to purchase the products of defendants (Steele).

The sublease provided that upon the failure of plaintiff to observe the terms and conditions of the Cruthirds lease and of the sublease, or to pay the monthly rent, then the defendants (Steele) may declare the sublease at an end and recover possession as if said premises were held by forcible detainer. The conditional sales and loan agreement provided that defendants (Steele), in case of default, shall be entitled, as its option, to take possession of the equipment and retain any monies paid as liquidated damages.

Thereafter, plaintiff was in default in the payment of rent under the sublease for the months of May, June and July, 1950, and in default of four monthly payments under the conditional sales and loan agreement (less than $500 having been paid). On July 7, 1950, defendant (Texas) served upon plaintiff a letter setting forth the above defaults, declaring the sublease at an end and requesting possession of the premises and equipment. On July 15, 1950, plaintiff voluntarily surrendered and defendant (Texas) took possession of the premises and equipment. Subsequently, defendant (Texas) made improvements to the premises and sub-leased to defendant, Blakely Oil, Incorporated.

On October 24, 1952, plaintiff by letter advised defendant (Texas) it desired to redeem the premises and its possession by full payment and satisfaction of the existing mortgage indebtedness upon defendant (Texas) rendering a complete accounting. No accounting was made and this suit was instituted.

The complaint seeks a finding that the instruments in question are a mortgage, for an accounting, and other related relief.

The trial court properly found from the admissions in the joint answer and the stipulations of the parties that said instruments were executed as security for the loan. However, plaintiff makes six assignments of error, all of which will be resolved upon a determination of the issue as to whether the trial court erred in holding the instruments to be a chattel mortgage, and that such mortgage had been foreclosed in compliance with section 62-527, A.C.A. 1939 (A.R.S. §33-757).

The instruments having been admitted to be a mortgage we are not confronted with the question of whether documents which on their face appear absolute are in fact a mortgage. We are, however, presented with the issue of whether the mortgage in question is a real property mortgage or a chattel mortgage. The assignment of the Cruthirds lease to defendants (Steele) is the basic instrument securing the loan. One of the estates in land less than a freehold is an estate for years. Section 71-101, A.C.A. (A.R.S. §33-201). Estates for years are chattels real. Section 71-103, A.C.A. 1939 (A.R.S. §33-202). The assignment of the Cruthirds lease for a term of four years and five months (or more if the loan remains unpaid) is a chattel real. At common law a lease for years, being a chattel real, is personal property; and unless it has been modified by statute, a leasehold interest, though a chattel real, is personal property and subject to the rules governing personal property.

We do not think, as urged by plaintiff, it is necessary to determine the question of whether our legislature, in enacting the various statutes involving real property, intended to abolish the common law rule as applied to chattels real. The real question in issue is whether a leasehold estate for a term of years is an interest in real property capable of being transferred under the provisions of the statute, section 62-501, A.C.A. 1939 (A.R.S. §33-701). This section provides as follows:

"Interest in real property mortgageable — Formalities in making — *Any interest in real property capable of being transferred may be mortgaged.* The mortgage can be created, renewed, or extended, only by writing, executed with the formalities required of a grant of real property, and may be acknowledged, certified and recorded, in like manner and with like effect." (Emphasis supplied.)

A leasehold estate for a term of years is an interest in land capable of being transferred. It possesses many characteristics of an ordinary chattel, and has some aspects of real property as it passes a present interest in land. . . .

We have held a statute must be interpreted in conformity with the language used by the legislature. Mayberry v. Duncan, 68 Ariz. 281, 205 P.2d 364. The language of section 62-501, supra, is not limited to real property but states any interest in real property capable of being transferred may be mortgaged. Although a chattel real is personal property it nevertheless transfers an interest in real property. Obviously the instruments in question constituted a real property mortgage within the purview of the statute. The related remedial statute, section 62-515, A.C.A. 1939 (A.R.S. §33-721), requires that mortgages of real property shall be foreclosed by action in court. In Davis v. First Nat. Bank, 26 Ariz. 621, 229 P. 391, we held mortgages of real property may not be summarily foreclosed, but only by action in a court of competent jurisdiction.

Defendants contend there was a mutual agreement to rescind the sublease and surrender the premises. This argument and the cases cited relate to a landlord and tenant relationship, and is without merit as to defense to the requirement that a mortgage of real property shall be foreclosed by action in a court. Equity favors the right to redeem and will not deny the right except upon strict compliance with the steps necessary to divest it. Romig v. Gillett, 187 U.S. 111, 23 S. Ct. 40, 47 L. Ed. 97. . . .

The judgment is reversed and the case remanded for proceedings not inconsistent herewith.

Udall, C.J., and Phelps and Struckmeyer, JJ., concur.

Windes, J., dissents.

NOTE ON "DEED" IN LIEU OF MORTGAGE FORECLOSURE

Consider whether the court in the *Harbel* case misconstrued the statute that requires foreclosure by court action. Arguably, the statute does not cover the facts at issue here, even if the mortgage was of real property. In any event, Arizona is one of the few states that does not recognize a voluntary conveyance by the mortgagor of his equity of redemption when made to the mortgagee in accord and satisfaction of the mortgage debt. Accepting a deed in lieu of foreclosure has definite advantages for the mortgagee, but the giving of the deed may also have some advantages for the mortgagor. What are these advantages? And what are the disadvantages? On balance, do you prefer Arizona's insistence upon court action?

b. Foreclosure

Mortgagor default may result in mortgagor loss of all interest in the mortgaged premises. A mortgage is a secured transaction and the secured lender has the right to satisfaction of the debt by resort to the security if the borrower is delinquent in paying the debt. The procedure whereby the mortgagor's interest in the mortgaged land is sold or taken over by the mortgagee in full or partial satisfaction of the outstanding obligation is known as foreclosure. There are detailed statutory procedures, with considerable variation from state to state, as to how foreclosures are to be carried out but the usual procedure followed includes an auction sale, the property going to the highest bidder.

In a judicial foreclosure action it is important that the plaintiff join as defendants all persons whose interests in the mortgaged premises are subordinate to the plaintiff's interest. These commonly include, among others, the original mortgagor, the present owner of the property if it has been conveyed by the mortgagor, junior mortgagees and lien holders, and any additional persons, such as lessees or easement holders, who claim a less than fee interest in the land created subsequent to the mortgage. Failure to join any of these persons means that the foreclosure will not terminate their interest in the land. If a deficiency decree can be had in a foreclosure proceeding, still other parties may be joined who presently have no interest in the land but may be personally obligated for the mortgage debt, such as mesne transferees who assumed the mortgage before conveying the property, or guarantors of the debt. Persons whose interests are senior to those of the foreclosing plaintiff are normally not joined, as the foreclosure cannot terminate their interests. Thus a foreclosing second mortgagee normally will not join the first mortgagee. The usual plaintiff in foreclosure proceedings is the original mortgagee, but others may have foreclosure rights, including the assignee of a mortgage and the executor or administrator of a deceased mortgagee.

Foreclosure laws reflect efforts by the legal system to balance fairly the interests of debtors and creditors, but the resulting laws often fail to satisfy fully either group. The history of foreclosure laws is marked by many statutory and case law modifications seeking to adjust this balance, usually resulting in more favorable treatment of debtors.

(1) Types of Foreclosure

Prather, Foreclosure of the Security Interest
1957 Ill. L. F. 420, 427-430

Methods of Foreclosure

After a default by the borrower, the lender or his successor in interest must seek to realize upon the real property security by selling or acquiring ownership of the land, at the same time extinguishing any equitable rights belonging to the borrower. The process is called foreclosure, which in its dictionary definition means "to shut out; exclude or bar."

In the early days of English mortgage law there was no necessity for foreclosure. The courts enforced the mortgage in accordance with its written terms, and a failure of the borrower to pay his debt when due simply extinguished all of his rights in the land. Because of the gradual development of a borrower's equitable right to redeem the land at a later date, however, foreclosure became necessary to extinguish the right.

Methods of foreclosure vary greatly from state to state. In some states foreclosure is quick and cheap; in others it is a long and expensive process.

Foreclosure procedures available for use must be sought under the laws of the state where the property is situated. While the diversity of state foreclosure laws is formidable, the most prevalent methods in use are foreclosure by sale in judicial proceedings, and foreclosure by exercise of a power of sale contained in the mortgage. . . . Although in some states one method is exclusive, in many states the mortgagee may elect which method he will pursue, including an election to proceed on the note alone, on the mortgage, or on both concurrently.

Strict Foreclosure. In jurisdictions which permit its use, strict foreclosure usually is one of several remedies, although ordinarily it is confined to cases where (1) the mortgagor is insolvent, (2) the mortgaged premises are not of sufficient value to pay the debt, and (3) there are no outside creditors or encumbrancers. The process begins with a complaint or a petition to foreclose. The complaint is brought against not only the owner but all persons who may have the right to redeem, including a spouse, tenants, and junior lien holders, if any. After summons either by personal delivery, or by publication and mailing of notice where personal summons is not possible, the defendants are given the opportunity to introduce defenses such as invalidity of the mortgage, prior payment, or failure of consideration.

After hearing any defenses, the court will determine if there has been a default and if the mortgagee has the right to foreclose. A decree or judgment is then entered, setting out the amount due to the lender, and specifying a period, ordinarily from two to six months, in which the borrower may redeem by payment of the amount due. The decree provides also that if the property shall not have been redeemed within the period specified, the borrower and all persons claiming under him shall be forever barred and foreclosed. As of the time the specified period expires, the mortgagee becomes the sole owner of the property. No sale of the premises is involved.

Some courts have called strict foreclosure a harsh remedy since it transfers the property to the mortgagee without a sale, the value appearing not to be taken into account.

Foreclosure by Sale in Judicial Proceedings. Under this method, the procedure is identical with that of strict foreclosure until the point that judgment or decree is about to be entered. At this time, the procedure becomes different, due to the widespread belief that if the land is sold at a public sale it might bring more than the mortgage debt, leaving something for the borrower. Although judicial sale predominates in most parts of the country, it later will be shown that in practical operation the theory seldom works out in accordance with the original purpose.

At the time of entering the decree, the court determines the amount due to the mortgagee. The decree provides that a specified period of notice shall be given to the public that the property is to be sold at public auction. The notice, usually by newspaper publication, must include a description of the property, the time, place, and terms of the sale, and the officer designated to conduct the sale. The officer usually is a master in chancery, a sheriff, or other officer appointed or authorized by the court.

The mortgagee customarily is permitted to bid at the auction, and in practice, the mortgagee almost invariably is the only or the highest bidder. If such bids are confined to the unpaid amount of the mortgage, the mortgagee may avoid parting with any cash. The bid price is merely applied to the mortgage debt.

Upon receiving a report of the auction, the court will determine the equity and propriety of the sale, and if it approves, the officer is ordered to execute either a deed to the purchaser or, as in Illinois, a certificate of sale. If the state law does not provide statutorily for a further period in which the borrower may redeem, the purchaser at this point becomes the sole and absolute owner of the land.

Foreclosure by Exercise of Power of Sale. In a great many states, a mortgage may be foreclosed without recourse to the courts, and the usual method is that of foreclosure by exercise of a power of sale contained in the security instrument. Power of sale mortgages are used primarily because they afford a less expensive as well as a more convenient and expeditious mode of foreclosure, and the mortgagor is not required to pay the greater expenses of a regular foreclosure action.

Foreclosure by power of sale specifically must be authorized in the mortgage instrument. Such clauses spell out what shall be considered a default, and, in the event of such default, confer power on the mortgagee (or trustee in the case of a trust deed) to sell the property after public notice at public auction.

Ordinarily personal notice of the proposed sale to the borrower is necessary, but certain states permit notice by advertisement. In order to be able to bid in at his own sale, the mortgagee or trustee must have expressly provided such authorization in the mortgage instrument, otherwise he is barred from the bidding. A deed is issued by the mortgagee as conductor of the sale to the highest bidder. Almost invariably this is the mortgagee himself. Again, while the equity of redemption is cut off by the process, statutory redemption may or may not be allowed, depending upon state statutory provisions. While the purchaser at the sale obtains immediate possession in states having no period of redemption, in states allowing a redemption period the majority allow the mortgagor to remain in possession, although the statute or the mortgage may contain different stipulations as to rents. To exercise the power of sale there is no need for the mortgagee to make entry. . . .

Lifton, Real Estate in Trouble: Lender's Remedies Need An Overhaul
31 Bus. Law. 1927, 1936-1941 (1976)

The usual way for the mortgagee to realize on its security is to foreclose on the property and see it sold to a third party or buy it in the foreclosure sale. The laws governing mortgage foreclosure are the outgrowth of efforts by the courts and legislatures to balance two competing claims: the secured lender's right to its security and the owner's right to whatever value the property has above the mortgage loan.

Under the common law rule, if the debtor failed to pay a mortgage on the due date, title would permanently vest in the mortgagee. Equity courts first developed the "equity of redemption" to give the debtor a period of time after the due date to pay the loan and redeem his property. When mortgagees complained that they were unable safely to convey title to a buyer without fear that the equity of redemption later would destroy the sale, the courts permitted them to "foreclose" the equity of redemption after notice and the expiration of a stated period of time. But this "strict foreclosure" did not protect the value in the property in excess of the mortgage from being wiped out. Thus, starting in the early 1800s, the concept evolved of selling the property in an open auction with appropriate safeguards to enable the owner to realize any value above the mortgage.

If real estate were traded in a ready auction market like listed securities, the foreclosure sale would have resolved the problem of the mortgagee's and owner's competing equities. The security would be sold on the market, the debt repaid to the lender and any excess returned to the owner. But real estate does not trade freely in an auction market. Most real estate buyers are not accustomed to all-cash purchases, and require the flexibility of face-to-face negotiation to tailor a transaction to meet the economic and tax needs of the parties. Under the best of circumstances it takes time and most often a knowledgeable broker to find a buyer for real property. Under the circumstances of a forced auction sale, it is almost impossible to find a buyer. As a result, in about 99 percent of public foreclosure sales the mortgagee ends up as the only bidder in the sale and buys the property in. An auction sale is particularly ineffective during periods of economic depression and collapsed real estate values. Yet, it is in periods of economic strain that large numbers of foreclosures occur and mortgagors get wiped out, eliciting the concern of voters, judges and legislators. And the courts and legislators have responded by formulating a variety of laws and procedures aimed at protecting the owner from losing his equity in the property.

A major consequence of this concern for the owner is that an action for foreclosure by judicial sale has to be tried as any other civil action. With inevitable discovery, trial calendar delays and other incidents of litigation it might take months or years to complete, particularly if the owner interposes counterclaims. Moreover, in a number of instances, judges have held off or threatened to hold off foreclosure by out-of-state mortgagees for long periods of time to force a settlement with local property owners or local mechanic lienors. In one case, the court found sufficient "sweat equity" deserving its protection in testimony that the owner had worked so diligently on the property that he suffered a heart attack! Finally, judicial foreclosure can be an expensive proceeding involving fees for attorneys, trustees and sheriffs.

A more effective foreclosure remedy, generally used in eighteen states, is a power of sale provision, giving the mortgagee or trustee the right to arrange for the sale of the property after appropriate notice, usually by advertisement. Because it does not require judicial action, this method sharply reduces foreclosure time and costs. In addition, although to foreclose under a power of sale the lender may have to give up any claim to a deficiency judgment, it has the advantage of avoiding statutory rights of redemption. . . .

A major obstacle encountered by mortgagees in twenty-six states is the statutory "rights of redemption" which gives the owner and certain others having an interest in the property the right for a specified time after foreclosure to redeem the property from the purchaser in the foreclosure sale at the sales price. These statutes are intended as a threat to force the mortgagee and other potential bidders to bid the full value of the property on the foreclosure sale in order to preclude the owner from later seeking to redeem the property at the below-market sales price.

Redemption periods range from six months to as much as 18 months, and there is a split of authority as to whether the right can be waived. The statutes also differ regarding the rights of the purchaser during the redemption period. In some states the purchaser is denied title and possession of the property during the redemption period; the mortgagor stays in possession, collects the rents and operates the property. If the property has been abandoned, it may have to remain vacant during the redemption period. Other statutes give possession to the purchaser but mandate appointment of a receiver to collect the earnings during the period. In these cases, the purchaser does not get any cash flow from the property until termination of the redemption period.

Most states with statutory rights of redemption permit the purchaser to take possession and operate the property during the redemption period. Some, however, limit the redemption price to the face amount of the mortgage plus foreclosure costs, so that the purchaser is not reimbursed for managing the property or for money spent on property improvements. Under these circumstances, a practical purchaser will not take a chance on rehabilitating the property during the redemption period. In some states, even rents collected by the purchaser while in possession, must be deducted from the redemption price.

The effect of these statutes is to diminish the interest of outside bidders in the property. If the mortgagee buys in the property, it ties up the mortgagee's funds for long periods of time, making the procedure more costly and delaying the day when the mortgagee can safely undertake rehabilitation of the property. Yet, experience with the statutes demonstrates that statutory rights of redemption are almost never exercised.

The mortgagee which operates foreclosed property may face added problems. In some states operation of foreclosed properties will subject the mortgage lender's entire portfolio in the state to state tax. In other states a mortgagee operating foreclosed property may be required to qualify to do business in the state. This presents a problem if the mortgagee is an out of state bank which cannot legally qualify to do business in the state. Such a mortgagee may have to engage a trust company, which can qualify, to operate its property and make independent decisions as to leasing, selling, and capital improvements; decisions which should properly be made by the mortgagee. Alternatively, the mortgagee may use a subsidiary which, to be completely separate from the parent, may require different officers and employees. In both cases the lender must be concerned that if its insulation from the trust company or the subsidiary is not sufficient, it will be deemed to be doing business illegally which may mean loss of its ability to enforce its other securities in the state.

NOTES

1. It is commonly asserted that a foreclosure sale is more favorable to the mortgagor than strict foreclosure. Why?

Basic Security Transactions

2. To whom and when is foreclosure by exercise of power of sale likely to be more favorable than foreclosure by sale through judicial proceedings?

3. Under what circumstances might foreclosing plaintiffs in judicial foreclosure proceedings join as defendants persons whose interests are senior to those of the plaintiffs?

4. If a mortgage is in default, generally the mortgagee may either bring an action on the secured debt or foreclose, and in most jurisdictions may pursue these remedies concurrently or successively so long as the debt has not been fully satisfied. However, if the mortgagor also has a claim against the mortgagee concerning the property covered by the mortgage, problems can arise under the *single action* doctrine that may prevent the mortgagee from obtaining full satisfaction of the debt. The single action doctrine, where applicable, requires that a defendant who is sued but has a claim arising out of the same transaction on which the suit is based must either file a counterclaim or lose that claim. The single action doctrine seeks to have related claims considered and resolved in one proceeding. A 1984 Missouri case illustrates how a mortgagee can lose his or her claim from failure to counterclaim as required. In Westoak Realty & Investment, Inc. v. Hernandez, 682 S.W.2d 120 (Mo. Ct. App. 1984), a builder-lender foreclosed under a power of sale but the sale left a deficiency; the builder-lender was then sued by the buyer-borrower for construction contract damages relative to the property in question, but defaulted; the builder-lender then brought an action on the note against the buyer-borrower for the deficiency. It was held that the builder-lender was barred from recovery on the note because the builder-lender failed, in the buyer-borrower's damage action, to counterclaim for the amount owed on the note.

(2) *Selected Foreclosure Problems*

(a) Foreclosure Sale Terms and Conditions: Price Adequacy and Chilled Bidding

Manoog v. Miele
350 Mass. 204, 213 N.E.2d 917 (1966)

REARDON, Justice. This case involves a deficiency judgment and is here on the defendant's exceptions to the judge's refusal to give certain instructions to the jury and to his exclusion of a question during trial. The facts are as follow.

On December 4, 1958, the defendants executed a $45,000 note secured by a mortgage on certain parcels of real estate. They defaulted on this note in May, 1962. Following notice on October 5, 1962, of his intention to foreclose, the plaintiff took possession of the premises on

October 23, 1962. On October 26, 1962, nineteen days before the foreclosure sale, the plaintiff Manoog entered into an agreement with one Barber for the purchase and sale of the property described in the mortgage. Under the agreement Barber gave Manoog a $2,000 deposit and contracted to purchase the premises from him for $45,000, subject however to the acquisition of title by Manoog at the foreclosure sale. Manoog described the contract purchase price of $45,000 as a "fair price for that property" on October 26, 1962. The agreement further provided that Manoog was to receive from Barber as part of the purchase price a ten year mortgage in the sum of $35,000 at six per cent interest and was to pay a broker's commission. Manoog "talked" to the defendant Snow about the agreement before it was executed but did not then or later disclose the purchase price. Before the foreclosure sale Manoog permitted Barber to occupy the premises and to bring trucks upon the property. At the foreclosure sale held on November 14, 1962, there were seven or eight people in attendance, including Barber, and the auctioneer made a general solicitation for bids. Manoog, however, was the sole bidder and, when his bid of $40,000 was accepted, he gave the auctioneer a $2,000 deposit in accordance with the terms of the sale as advertised. Sometime thereafter Manoog sold the land to Barber for $45,000. In this action the jury assessed a deficiency of $5,488.67 against both defendants. This figure reflected the total of the unpaid balance of the note, unpaid interest thereon to the date of sale, taxes paid by Manoog, and the costs of sale, with credits to the defendants for rents received by the plaintiff prior to sale, and such amounts as they had prepaid for the real estate taxes.

1. The question which was put to the plaintiff and excluded was, "You expected to keep the $45,000.00 when you passed papers on that property without disclosing it to Snow or Miele?" There was evidence that the plaintiff had never disclosed to the defendants the details of his agreement with Barber. Since the plaintiff never in fact disclosed the price, whether or not he had intended to disclose it was of no importance. The question asked was thus immaterial and the judge did not err in excluding it.

2. The judge, in charging the jury on the responsibilities of the mortgagee in the circumstances described above, cited and quoted from West Roxbury Co-op Bank v. Bowser, 324 Mass. 489, 492, 87 N.E.2d 113, 115, where it was said, "It is familiar law that a mortgagee in exercising a power of sale in a mortgage must act in good faith and must use reasonable diligence to protect the interests of the mortgagor. . . . The burden is on the mortgagor (the defendants here) to prove that the mortgagee has failed in that duty. . . . When, as was the fact here, 'a mortgagee . . . is both seller and buyer, his position is one of great delicacy. Yet, when he has done his full duty to the mortgagor in his conduct of the sale under the power, and the bidding begins, in his capacity as bidder a mortgagee may buy as cheaply as he can, and owes no duty to bid the full value of the property as that value may subsequently be determined by a judge or a

jury.'" The judge continued his charge, "Now, the defendants have introduced evidence and a fact that is not disputed is that prior to the foreclosure sale plaintiff made an arrangement with one Mr. Barber to sell the property to him at a price of $45,000. The defendant[s] . . . [claim] that under those circumstances there was a breach of the duty owed by the mortgagee in the mortgagee's conduct of the foreclosure sale. That is a question of fact that you will have to determine. It is not a question of law, but I can instruct you the defendant[s] . . . [argue] that you have a price differential there. . . . You are entitled to ask yourselves, also, these questions. Acting in good faith and with reasonable diligence, should Mr. Manoog have said to Mr. Barber when they were negotiating for a property, 'Look, the property is going to be sold at a foreclosure sale. Why don't you show up at the sale and bid for yourself?' Should he have refrained from entering into an agreement as a matter of good faith with Mr. Barber or were the terms of the agreement he entered into substantially different from the terms of the mortgage foreclosure itself so that it had no effect on the bidding? These are questions, Mr. Foreman, ladies and gentlemen, that you are going to have to decide and not questions of law upon which the Court can give you any instructions. So that with respect to the issues in the case, you must decide this issue. First, did the plaintiff act in good faith and did he exercise reasonable diligence in the conduct of the foreclosure sale? If your answer is the Plaintiff did act in good faith and in the exercise of reasonable diligence in the conduct of the foreclosure sale, then you would be warranted in finding for the plaintiff. . . ." In addition to giving the portions of the charge quoted above, the judge had granted one of the requests of the defendants for instructions to the jury to the effect that "[t]he mortgagee, in foreclosing his mortgage has the duty of good faith and reasonable care to secure the highest price that the property can bring." The judge, however, denied the defendants' request that he charge the jury that the "[p]laintiff, as foreclosing mortgagee is a trustee for the benefit of all persons interested, including the Defendant[s]."

There was no necessity for the judge to go further than he did in delineating the obligations of the mortgagee in this instance. The principles drawn from the *West Roxbury Co-op Bank* case cited by the judge provided appropriate guidelines for the jury on the facts which had been laid before them. The sense of the charge given to the jury was that the duty of acting with good faith and reasonable diligence imposed on the mortgagee was a strict one. What the judge had to say about the mortgagee's duties placed them in their proper perspective before the jury. The jury would have been confused rather than assisted by the employment of the word "trustee" in the judge's charge, for there is no built-in magic in that word which would have added any more in the way of guidance than the judge conveyed without using it.

3. The defendants requested an instruction to the effect that "[t]he

conduct of the Plaintiff in bidding $40,000.00 at the foreclosure sale, when prior to the sale he had entered into an agreement to sell the property for $45,000.00 constitutes bad faith." There was no error in refusing to give this instruction. The question which it raised was whether the defendants had "chilled" the sale. Lexington Trust Co. v. McCabe, 313 Mass. 733, 735, 49 N.E.2d 435. Whether a sale has been "chilled" is a complex question of fact which cannot be said to hinge solely upon the existence of a differential between the agreement price and the foreclosure sale price. See Cambridge Sav. Bank v. Cronin, 289 Mass. 379, 383, 194 N.E. 289.

A knowledgeable mortgagee should not be allowed to assume a position such that he preempts the field of bidders and discourages other potential bidders at a sale. He is not to be permitted to indicate in advance to other potential bidders that it is his intention to bid a price beyond a reasonable figure at the foreclosure sale unless they agree to buy the property from him at a reasonable price once he has bought the property at the foreclosure sale at a price which is unreasonably low. Such behavior by a mortgagee might result in a substantial deficiency to be later collected from the mortgagor. On the other hand, the law must not be such as to discourage a mortgagee from dealing prior to the foreclosure sale with persons who might otherwise not be interested in the property. A smaller deficiency to be met by the mortgagor may well be occasioned by a mortgagee's knowledge of the availability of a person who will purchase from the mortgagee subsequent to a mortgagee's acquisition of title at the foreclosure sale. See Dexter v. Shepard, 117 Mass. 480, 485-486.

In the instant case it appears that the mortgagee placed the property with a broker for sale. Having found a possible purchaser the mortgagee contracted to accept a purchase money mortgage at a reasonable rate of interest. In determining whether the mortgagee "chilled" the sale, as the defendants charged, it would have been relevant to inquire whether the purchaser could have procured similar financing elsewhere, whether the purchaser was a good or a bad credit risk, and whether the interest rate of six percent was more favorable than otherwise might have been expected from the nature of the premises. These are only some of the factors pertinent in an inquiry as to whether the mortgagee had in fact "chilled" the sale or whether, alternatively, he had so contracted with a purchaser as to be able himself to offer a price at the foreclosure sale which would most minimize the mortgagor's deficiency. The matter was adequately treated by the judge's charge which noted the existence of the price differential, the difference in the terms of the purchase sale agreement and the foreclosure sale, and their effect as a question of fact upon the plaintiff's duty of diligence and good faith.

4. The judge properly denied the defendants' request for a charge that the failure of the plaintiff to disclose to them that he had entered into a contract to sell the property for $45,000 constituted bad faith. The judge

Basic Security Transactions

charged instead that this conduct was only one of several factors to be considered in a determination of whether there had been bad faith on the part of the mortgagee.

Exceptions overruled.

NOTES ON FORECLOSURE OF THE EQUITY OF REDEMPTION

1. Why do you think that Barber agreed to purchase the land from Manoog, subject to Manoog acquiring title at the foreclosure sale, rather than purchasing the property himself at the foreclosure sale?

2. Considering that foreclosure sale transactions are forced auction sales, what is a proper price frequently has caused courts difficulty when fairness of the sales has been challenged. Mere inadequacy of price, assuming there has been no rigged bidding and all required statutory procedures have been followed, is generally not sufficient to upset a foreclosure sale. Yet, in extreme cases of price inadequacy, courts have invalidated such sales. For example, in Johnson v. Jefferson Standard Life Insurance Co., 5 Ariz. App. 587, 429 P.2d 474 (1967), a foreclosure sale price of $5,000 for property worth $73,000 was set aside; and in First Wis. Nat. Bank of Oshkosh v. KSW Investments, Inc., 71 Wis. 2d 359, 238 N.W.2d 123 (1976), a trial court order confirming a foreclosure sale was reversed when the trial court had accepted a $23,000 bid, based on the building being a vacant shell, when there was evidence that, improved as a bar-restaurant, the property was worth five or six times that much. Also, in Central Financial Services, Inc. v. Spears, 425 So. 2d 403 (Miss. 1983), a foreclosing mortgagee, who 12 days after the foreclosure sale resold the foreclosed land for 2½ times its foreclosure sale price, was required by the Mississippi Supreme Court to pay over his profit to the mortgagors on the grounds that the foreclosure price was unconscionably low.

As the principal case indicates, chilled bidding also may result in a mortgage foreclosure sale being upset. For instance, in Fitzpatrick v. Federer, 315 S.W.2d 826 (Mo. 1958), the Missouri Supreme Court held that a foreclosure sale should be set aside on a showing that the buyer had conspired with others not to compete in bidding and to share in the profits of buying at a low price. In some states, statutes have sought to prevent unduly low foreclosure sale prices by means of appraisal restrictions. Thus, in Louisiana, a sale price may not be lower than two-thirds of the value set by a required appraisal. However, if there is no bid at or above the appraised amount, the property must again be advertised and offered for sale, and may then normally be sold for whatever cash price it will bring. La. Code Civ. Proc. Ann. art. 2336 (West 1960). The Louisiana requirements are discussed in Comment, Deficiency Judgments in Louisiana, 49 Tul. L. Rev. 1094 (1975).

(b) Constitutionality of Power of Sale Procedures

Warren v. Government National Mortgage Assn.

611 F.2d 1229 (8th Cir. 1980), cert. denied, 449 U.S. 847 (1980)

McManus, District Judge. This is an appeal by Vivian Warren (plaintiff) from a final judgment in favor of Government National Mortgage Association (GNMA), holding no violation of her fifth amendment rights resulting from an extrajudicial foreclosure under a deed of trust. In her complaint, predicated principally under 28 U.S.C. §1331 (federal question), plaintiff sought declaratory and mandamus relief.

Plaintiff and her husband[2] were the owners of a residence in Kansas City, Missouri, which they purchased in August of 1966 from the United States Department of Housing and Urban Development (HUD). As part of the purchase price, they executed a note, secured by a deed of trust, to the Federal National Mortgage Association (FNMA). Thereafter, by Congressional Act, FNMA was converted into GNMA, a private corporation wholly-owned by the federal government. 12 U.S.C. §1716 et seq. Plaintiff's note and deed of trust were transferred and assigned to GNMA. The deed of trust included a "Power of Sale" clause,[3] which in the event of default permitted the trustee to initiate an extrajudicial foreclosure sale in accordance with Missouri statutory procedures.[4]

In September of 1970, the successor trustee under the deed of trust — a private attorney retained by GNMA and not otherwise employed by the federal government — mailed a letter, first class not registered nor certified receipt, to the plaintiff and her husband, notifying them that GNMA deemed the payments on the note to be in default and that, as holder of the

---

2. Plaintiff and her husband were separated at the time the action was filed and he was not an original party. Thereafter, by amendment, he was made a party defendant as a necessary party who would not join as plaintiff. FRCP 19(a). Summons was issued and served, and the husband defaulted.

3. The deed of trust was executed on "FHA Form No. 2139m (Revised August 1962)," which was then the standard printed form devised, approved and provided by the FHA for use in connection with federally insured loans on property situated in the State of Missouri. Compare 24 CFR §203.17. The deed of trust form included the following pertinent language, referred to here as the "Power of Sale" clause:

> NOW, THEREFORE, . . . if default be made in the payment of said note herein provided . . . then the whole of said note and interest thereon to date of foreclosure shall become due and payable and this deed shall remain in force; and said Trustee or his successor . . . , at the request of the legal holder of the aforesaid note, may proceed to sell the property . . . at public vendue . . . to the highest bidder for cash, first giving twenty days public notice of the time, terms and place of sale and of the property to be sold by advertisement in some newspaper published in said Jackson County, Missouri, and upon such sale shall execute a deed conveying the property so sold to the purchaser thereof.

4. Missouri statutory law permits the extrajudicial foreclosure of deeds of trust, which in Missouri are commonly used as security agreements in lieu of mortgages. Rev. St. Mo. §433.410 et seq. (1969).

note, GNMA had elected to declare the entire principal due. The letter, therefore, demanded payment of the entire balance but contained no mention or threat of foreclosure by a trustee's sale. For whatever reasons,[5] plaintiff made no response to the letter.

Thereafter, GNMA foreclosed against plaintiff by causing the trustee to advertise in a newspaper, used almost exclusively for such legal notices, and to conduct a public sale, all in compliance with the power of sale clause in the deed of trust. GNMA was the purchaser at this sale.

After the foreclosure sale, plaintiff was notified by letter of the sale and demand was made for possession on or before October 26, 1970. She did not vacate the premises and GNMA brought an action for unlawful detainer in the Missouri Magistrate's Court, securing a judgment in that case on January 11, 1971. GNMA secured possession of the property by a writ of restitution on or about April 7, 1971.

Plaintiff's challenge rests essentially on her contention that she was denied fifth amendment due process rights to notice and hearing *prior* to the foreclosure sale.[6] We affirm on the basis of no federal government action.

---

5. The record indicates that plaintiff had only a fifth grade education and neither she nor her husband could read. In a related case, she testified that she couldn't remember ever receiving the letter. Cf. Warren v. GNMA, 521 S.W.2d 441, 442 (Mo. en banc 1975).

6. Plaintiff originally filed this suit alleging additionally that the Missouri statute authorizing such extrajudicial foreclosures violated the fifth and fourteenth amendments, and sought both a declaratory judgment voiding the sale and injunctive relief.

The parties stipulated that the courts of Missouri had never passed on the constitutional issues presented in the case, and the trial court determined that it was a proper cause for abstention and dismissed the case on that basis.

On appeal, this court affirmed the application of the abstention doctrine, but reversed the dismissal, directing the plaintiff to file a suit in state court, and directing that the case remain on the federal court docket until determination of the constitutional issues by the Supreme Court of Missouri. Warren v. GNMA, 443 F.2d 624 (8th Cir. 1971).

The Supreme Court of Missouri decided the fourteenth amendment issue against the plaintiff. Warren v. GNMA, 521 S.W.2d 441 (Mo. en banc 1975). The rationale for the decision is found in Federal National Mortgage Association v. Howlett, 521 S.W.2d 428 (Mo. en banc 1975) (decided the same day as the *Warren* case). The Missouri Court only discussed the fourteenth amendment constitutional question and stated:

> We hold that the foreclosure of the deed of trust on appellant's property was pursuant to the *contractual* provisions in the deed of trust and *not by authority of state law*. It follows that appellant's contention that state action was present on the theory that the power of sale exercised by the trustee was conferred by state statute is overruled. (Emphasis added).

The Missouri Supreme Court relied upon the reasoning and result in Bryant v. Jefferson Fed. Sav. & Loan Assoc., 166 U.S. App. D.C. 178, 509 F.2d 511 (D.C. Cir. 1974). After the *Warren* decision, similar result was reached in cases involving extrajudicial foreclosures, Charmicor, Inc. v. Deaner, 572 F.2d 694 (9th Cir. 1978); Northrip v. FNMA, 527 F.2d 23 (6th Cir. 1975); and Barrera v. Security Bldg. & Inv. Corp., 519 F.2d 1166 (5th Cir. 1975). These cases hold that the fact that state statutes regulate and govern the procedures to be followed in an extrajudicial foreclosure of real estate under power of sale clause contained in a mortgage or deed of trust does not establish that the foreclosure constituted state action.

Subsequent to the Missouri Supreme Court decision in *Warren*, this case was reactivated in the federal district court below, limited to the fifth amendment issues.

The Due Process Clause of the Fifth Amendment to the United States Constitution provides that: "No person shall . . . be deprived of . . . property, without due process of law; . . . " It applies to federal government not private action, Public Utilities Comm'n v. Pollak, 343 U.S. 451, 461, 72 S. Ct. 813, 96 L. Ed. 1068 (1952); while the fourteenth amendment due process clause applies to the states, see, e.g., Moose Lodge No. 107 v. Irvis, 407 U.S. 163, 172-73, 92 S. Ct. 1965, 32 L. Ed. 2d 627 (1972); Shelley v. Kraemer, 334 U.S. 1, 13, 68 S. Ct. 836, 92 L. Ed. 1161 (1948). The standard for finding federal government action under the fifth amendment is the same as that for finding state action under the fourteenth amendment. See, e.g., Geneva Towers Tenants Org. v. Federated Mortgage Investors, 504 F.2d 483, 487 (9th Cir. 1974); Ponce v. Housing Authority of Tulare County, 389 F. Supp. 635, 648 (E.D. Cal. 1975). That standard is that there must exist "a sufficiently close nexus between the [government] and the challenged action of the regulated entity so that the action of the latter may be fairly treated as that of the [government] itself." Jackson v. Metropolitan Edison Co., 419 U.S. 345, 351, 95 S. Ct. 449, 453, 42 L. Ed. 2d 477 (1974).

It is undisputed in this case that GNMA is a corporate entity, wholly-owned by the federal government, 31 U.S.C. §846. It was created by the partition of the FNMA under the National Housing Act of 1968, 12 U.S.C. §1716 et seq., and is under the management and control of the Secretary of HUD, 12 U.S.C. §§1723(a) and 1723a(d). It has no capital stock, 12 U.S.C. §1717(a)(2)(A). The economic benefits and burdens of its administration inure to the Secretary of the Treasury, 12 U.S.C. §1722. Moreover, under 12 U.S.C. §1717(b)(1), it is authorized to purchase, service, sell or otherwise deal in mortgages insured under 12 U.S.C. §§1701-1750g by the Federal Housing Authority (FHA).[7] Thus, GNMA is not only wholly-owned by the federal government but it also operates under federal government authority.[8]

---

7. GNMA is authorized to deal only in mortgages or deeds of trust insured under federal programs and is not, unlike FNMA, authorized to deal in "conventional mortgages." Compare 12 U.S.C. §§1717(a)(2)(A) & 1717(b)(1) with 12 U.S.C. §1717(a)(2)(B) & 1717(b)(2). Thus, GNMA was authorized to deal in plaintiff's deed of trust in this case because that deed of trust was insured by FHA under §203 of the National Housing Act, 12 U.S.C. §1709.

8. Although the pertinent legislative history is somewhat unclear with respect to Congress' intent in bifurcating the old FNMA into two distinct corporate entities — FNMA and GNMA — in 1968, it is fairly certain that Congress was primarily motivated by "the emphasis of recent years of increased reliance on private sponsorship under our housing programs and participation by private enterprises in the financing and production of housing." H.R. Rep. No. 1585, 90th Cong., 2d Sess. reprinted in [1968] U.S. Code Cong. & Admin. News, pp. 2873, 2874. To that end, Congress decided to place the former FNMA's secondary market operation in a new privately owned corporation (with the continued designation FNMA) and its special assistance, management and liquidating functions in the new GNMA. Id., U.S. Code Cong., supra, at 2875; see also id., at 2943-48, 3004-09.

Thus, if considered purely as a matter of statutory and organizational form the new GNMA could perhaps be viewed as more "governmental" than its counterpart FNMA. We, however, read the legislative history to indicate Congress' intent as being essentially to

To recognize these relational facts, however, does not end the federal government action inquiry for, as was the case in Public Utilities Comm'n. v. Pollak, 343 U.S. 451, 72 S. Ct. 813, 96 L. Ed. 1068 (1952), the deciding issue in this regard is not simply whether GNMA is a government-owned or authorized corporation; rather, it is whether as such GNMA's foreclosure action pursuant to the contractual power of sale clause in the deed of trust was so closely linked to federal government regulation that it can in actuality be viewed more as the action of the federal government itself than that of GNMA. Compare also Jackson v. Metropolitan Edison Co., 419 U.S. 345, 356-57 & n.16, 95 S. Ct. 449, 42 L. Ed. 2d 477 (1974).

In approaching the latter issue, we emphasize that the power of sale clause as contained in the deed of trust is a contractual power having its genesis in the deed of trust itself and as such exists independent of any statute otherwise governing it. Compare, e.g., FNMA v. Howlett, 521 S.W.2d 428, 432 (Mo. en banc) *appeal dismissed* 423 U.S. 909, 96 S. Ct. 210, 46 L. Ed. 2d 137 (1975); Warren v. GNMA, 521 S.W.2d 441 (Mo. en banc 1975). As a party to the contract, and even though it was a governmentally-owned and authorized entity, GNMA had a right to resort to its contractual remedies just as a purely private entity had. See Atlantic Mutual Ins. Co. v. Cooney, 303 F.2d 253, 259 (9th Cir. 1962). Accord Rex Trailer Co., Inc. v. United States, 350 U.S. 148, 151, 76 S. Ct. 219, 100 L. Ed. 149 (1956).

We therefore are of the general opinion that mortgage foreclosures through power of sale agreements such as the one at issue here are not in and of themselves powers of a governmental nature. Compare Northrip v. FNMA, 527 F.2d 23, 31 (6th Cir. 1975); Bryant v. Jefferson Federal Savings and Loan Assoc., 166 U.S. App. D.C. 178, 180-81, 509 F.2d 511, 513-14 (D.C. Cir. 1974). The trial court implicitly recognized this when it concluded that "a wholly-owned government agency can enforce a valid *contractual* provision for foreclosure without running afoul of the constraints of the Fifth Amendment, under all circumstances in which the foreclosure of the same contract by a private lender would be held not to violate the requirements of due process." Warren v. GNMA, et al., Civil Action No. 19006-2, Memorandum Opinion and Judgment at p. 6 (W.D. Mo., February 12, 1979) [Designated Record on Appeal p. 117].

Plaintiff's major contention in this regard is that, all these considerations notwithstanding, federal government action is implicated in this case

---

dissociate as far as possible the newly created entities, however characterized as to form, from the federal government in regard to their respective secondary mortgage market functions.

In short, in terms of substance as opposed to form, we view the functions served by GNMA as being no more governmental than those served by the new FNMA, and accordingly we consider the cases holding the new FNMA's secondary mortgage market functions to be essentially "private action" as persuasive authority on the federal government action issue presented in this case. Compare Roberts v. Cameron–Brown Co., 556 F.2d 356, 358-60 (5th Cir. 1977); Northrip v. FNMA, 527 F.2d 23, 30-33 (6th Cir. 1975).

because the deed of trust form was specifically approved by HUD regulations, 24 CFR §203.17, and therefore GNMA's foreclosure action pursuant to that deed of trust was by implication also specifically approved by HUD. If this court were to accept plaintiff's argument, every FHA guaranteed mortgage held either by GNMA, FNMA or a private lending agency would be placed in the same position of constitutional uncertainty simply by virtue of the fact that the mortgage form must also be approved by a federal agency under HUD regulations. Moreover, plaintiff's argument ignores the point that the central inquiry is not whether the form of the deed of trust is approved by federal regulations, but rather it is whether there exists a sufficiently close nexus between the government regulations and the challenged activity specifically at issue so that the challenged activity itself may be fairly treated as truly that of the federal government directly. Cf. Jackson v. Metropolitan Edison Co., 419 U.S. 345, 351, 95 S. Ct. 449, 42 L. Ed. 2d 477 (1974). Accord, Roberts v. Cameron-Brown Co., 556 F.2d 356, 358 (5th Cir. 1977), ["The government must be involved *with the activity* that causes the actual injury." (emphasis added)].

The challenged activity specifically at issue in this case is GNMA's extrajudicial foreclosure pursuant to the power of sale terms of the deed of trust, performed in accordance with Missouri laws. Plaintiff cites 24 CFR Pts. 200 & 203 generally as support for her argument that the Secretary of HUD, vicariously through GNMA, directly regulates GNMA's foreclosure procedures here. We find nothing in those general provisions, however, constituting direct federal government regulation of GNMA's servicing policies, including what methods it may use to protect its financial interest in the mortgage on default.

Concededly, the Commissioner of the FHA is required to approve the form of the mortgage or deed of trust before it is eligible for FHA insurance under 24 CFR §203.17, but that regulation does not dictate what foreclosure provisions are to be included in the deed of trust. Indeed, 24 CFR §203.17(b), (c) and (d) explicitly set forth certain provisions which must be included in any mortgage or deed of trust approved under subpart 203. If the Secretary of HUD had intended to regulate the specific *method* of foreclosure to be adopted by an investor in an insured mortgage, the regulations would certainly have directly and expressly set forth that method in 24 CFR §203.17.

Moreover, it is admitted in this case that the foreclosure of plaintiff's deed of trust was according to its own terms and under the extrajudicial foreclosure statutes of Missouri. There is nothing in the record to indicate that the powers otherwise exercisable by officers or employees of the federal government were in any way applied or used in this foreclosure of plaintiff's deed of trust. In fact, the foreclosure was conducted by the successor trustee strictly in accordance with Missouri law pursuant to his position as the contractually appointed trustee and not as a government employee.

Further, the only direct government involvement in the relations with the mortgagor or grantor of the deed of trust after default can be found in 24 CFR §203.355. The regulation contemplates that if a claim is to be made under the mortgage insurance certificate then the mortgagee must take whatever steps, including foreclosure if and as permitted under state law, that are necessary to vest title to the property in either its name, or in the name of the commissioner. The rule, however, does not make explicit what specific foreclosure methods or procedures are to be adopted by the mortgagee. Thus, we view it as insufficient to conclude that the power of sale foreclosure methods at issue here were that of the federal government itself.

We conclude generally, therefore, that the federal government has neither mandated nor approved the method of foreclosure to be followed in the event of default; nor could it since the foreclosure procedures must accord with Missouri law. Since federal government regulation was not directly and substantially linked to the challenged foreclosure activity complained of by plaintiff and at issue here, no "federal government action" exists and plaintiff has no cognizable constitutional claim under the fifth amendment.

For the foregoing reasons, we affirm the judgment of the District Court. We need not reach waiver and other issues raised by plaintiff.

NOTES

1. In Ricker v. United States, 417 F. Supp. 133 (D. Me. 1976), sufficient federal government action was held to exist for the fifth amendment to apply when the Farmers Home Administration, a federal agency, foreclosed pursuant to Maine law under a power of sale mortgage provision. The *Ricker* opinion states at page 138: "It cannot be doubted that the Rickers [the mortgagors] were 'deprived of . . . property without due process of law' in violation of the Fifth Amendment. First, the foreclosure and sale were initiated and carried out by federal employees acting on behalf of the federal government: they plainly were bound to observe the requirements of the Fifth Amendment." Insufficient notice and the failure to provide a hearing were held to constitute the due process deprivations.

2. A number of power of sale foreclosure statutes have been challenged as violating the fourteenth amendment because they allegedly involve the use of state power to take property without due process of law. In these challenges, plaintiffs have relied on the authority of such cases as Snaidach v. Family Finance Corp., 395 U.S. 337 (1969), and Fuentes v. Shevin, 407 U.S. 67 (1972). Some of these challenged mortgage foreclosure statutes have been upheld, including the Missouri statute in Federal National Mortgage Assn. v. Howlett, 521 S.W.2d 428 (Mo. 1975). However, some have been held unconstitutional, such as a North Carolina

statute, as applied, in Turner v. Blackburn, 389 F. Supp. 1250 (W.D.N.C. 1975), and a Delaware statute in Brown v. Federal National Mortgage Assn., 359 A.2d 661 (Del. 1976). See generally 3 Powell, The Law of Real Property §466[1] (1985).

Some states have recently amended their power of sale foreclosure statutes to require efforts at notice which will increase the probability that those against whom foreclosure is sought will actually receive notice of the impending action. Illustrative of such statutes is Tex. Prop. Code Ann. §51.002 (Vernon 1984), now requiring notice by certified mail in addition to posting it on the courthouse door.

(c) Omitted Parties

Springer Corporation v. Kirkeby-Natus
80 N.M. 206, 453 P.2d 376 (1969)

NOBLE, Chief Justice. Kirkeby-Natus (hereafter termed Kirkeby) foreclosed its first mortgage covering 403 acres of lands securing an indebtedness of $521,458.11, bidding in the land for $323,625.00, and obtained a deficiency judgment for $197,833.11. Springer Corporation (hereafter termed Springer) held a second mortgage on 94.96 acres of the land mortgaged to Kirkeby, securing an indebtedness of $77,800.00. By reason of an abstractor's error, Springer was not made a party to the Kirkeby foreclosure. Springer then brought this action to foreclose its second mortgage. Kirkeby, in this suit, by counterclaim, was granted foreclosure of its first mortgage against Springer. Springer was held entitled to redeem from the Kirkeby foreclosure, within nine months after the date of the judgment in this case, but only upon payment of the full amount paid by Kirkeby for the entire 403 acres bought at the foreclosure sale — $323,625.00, plus $13,041.07, being the unpaid balance of the deficiency judgment. Springer has appealed. The cross-complainants have likewise appealed.

The trial court found that Kirkeby had received a credit of $184,792.04 on its deficiency judgment, leaving a balance of $13,041.07. Springer appears to contend that a greater credit should have been allowed but Findings 24 and 25, so determining, have not been attacked as being unsupported by the evidence and, accordingly, are binding on this court on appeal. Cooper v. Bank of New Mexico, 77 N.M. 398, 423 P.2d 431; Baca v. Gutierrez, 77 N.M. 428, 423 P.2d 617. Also, it is clear that the findings are amply supported by the proof.

It is settled in this jurisdiction that the rights of one who is not a party to a mortgage foreclosure action are not affected by any judgment rendered therein nor by a foreclosure sale pursuant thereto. Conway v. San Miguel County Board of Education, 59 N.M. 242, 282 P.2d 719; Mann v.

Whitely, 36 N.M. 1, 6 P.2d 468. See also Annot., 134 A.L.R. 1490, 1492. Thus, the failure to join Springer, a junior lien holder, left its rights, including its equity of redemption, unaffected and unimpaired.

The fact that Springer was not a party to the Kirkeby foreclosure, however, does not deprive Kirkeby of the benefit of its judgment against those parties who were before the court in its foreclosure action. Mann v. Whitely, supra. The counterclaim in the instant case constituted a separate and independent action to foreclose the Kirkeby mortgage against the Springer rights. Kirkeby, relying on §§24-2-19 and 24-2-19.1, N.M.S.A. 1953, argues that Springer was only entitled to redeem within nine months from the date of sale held pursuant to the Kirkeby foreclosure.

It is clear to us that since Springer's rights, including its right of redemption, were not impaired or affected by the original Kirkeby foreclosure to which Springer was not a party, its right of redemption only accrues upon the entry of a judgment foreclosing its rights in a separate and independent action, or the judgment on the counterclaim in the instant case. John Hancock Mut. Life Ins. Co. v. Mays, 152 Kan. 46, 102 P.2d 984.

Relying on Green v. Dixon, 9 Wis. 532 (1859); 2 Wiltsie on Mortgage Foreclosure (4th Ed.) §1071; and 2 Jones on Mortgages (8th Ed.) §1375, Springer argues that because it was not made a party to the Kirkeby senior mortgage foreclosure proceeding, and because Springer's junior mortgage only covers some 95 acres out of the 403 acres securing the senior mortgage, it should be permitted to redeem from the Kirkeby sale pro tanto by paying only the pro rata part of the amount for which the property sold at the Kirkeby sale. We cannot agree.

This question is one of first impression in New Mexico and appears to have been resolved by relatively few courts of other jurisdictions. It is a general rule that a mortgage is an entire thing, and must be redeemed in its entirety, and that a mortgagee cannot be required to divide either his debt or his security. 2 Jones on Mortgages (8th Ed.) §1372; Annot., 134 A.L.R. 1490, 1511. An exception pointed out by the author, supra, at §1375, indicating that where an owner of the land has not been made a party to the foreclosure of the senior mortgage, and the senior mortgagee is the purchaser at the sale, the owner not made a party may redeem pro tanto upon the theory that the senior mortgagee, by such purchase, voluntarily severed his right and obtained an indefeasible title to part of the land and a defeasible title to another part, affords some color for the Springer argument. See also 2 Wiltsie on Mortgage Foreclosure (4th Ed.) §1071; Monese v. Struve, 155 Or. 68, 62 P.2d 822. Our research discloses that the statement in Wiltsie has support only in Green v. Dixon, supra. 2 Jones on Mortgages, §1375, states a similar exception, relying only on Green v. Dixon, supra, and Wilson v. Tarter, 22 Or. 504, 30 P. 499. The basis of these decisions and the exceptions stated in Wiltsie and Jones is criticized by the author in 2 Glenn on Mortgages (1943) §299.1, who says the rule is objectionable because of a false premise, that is, it assumes that the senior mortgagee in his second independent action to require the junior lien holder to elect whether to redeem, is asking a favor of equity, and thus can be forced to accept a partial redemption as the price of equity. Glenn argues that, in fact, the senior mortgagee is not asking a favor, and that partial redemption should not be allowed merely because the junior encumbrancer happened to be omitted as a party in the first foreclosure. The exception to the general rule is likewise criticized in a note, 50 Harvard L. Rev. 990. See 25 Ill. L. Rev. 720. 2 Glenn on Mortgages, supra, at 1257, points out that the real relief of a partial encumbrancer lies in invoking the rule of marshalling by which the junior encumbrancer may require a senior mortgagee to exhaust his remedy against property other than that covered by the partial mortgage of the junior encumbrancer. That doctrine was applied in Hinners v. Birkevaag, 113 N.J. Eq. 413, 167 A. 209, at the instance of an omitted junior mortgagee, who established the relative values of the respective tracts in the subsequent independent action.

The Wisconsin Supreme Court, in Buchner v. Gether Trust, 241 Wis. 148, 5 N.W.2d 806, without reference to its earlier decision in Green v. Dixon, supra, appears to have rejected the reasoning of the earlier case. In *Buchner,* the court expressly said that the rights of a junior encumbrancer not made a party to the foreclosure of the senior mortgage are "unimpaired and unchanged by the defective foreclosure." The court further said: ". . . Except for the dictum in the *Winter* case, [Winter v. O'Neill, 241 Wis. 280, 5 N.W.2d 809] we discover no case holding that the rights of the junior claimant are improved or increased by the defect in the foreclosure proceedings. In accordance with quite elementary principles of justice, his position is preserved and equity will not permit that he suffer any disadvantage from the failure to include him as a party. It would be utterly unfair to do more than this."

The Supreme Court of Florida, in Quinn Plumbing Co. v. New Miami Shores Corp., 100 Fla. 413, 129 So. 690, 73 A.L.R. 600, discussed Green v. Dixon, supra, and specifically rejected the reasoning by which a junior encumbrancer, who was not a party to the foreclosure of the senior mortgage, is permitted to redeem pro tanto from the senior mortgage. In Key West Wharf & Coal Co. v. Porter, 63 Fla. 448, 58 So. 599, 610, Am. Ann. Cas. 1914A, 173, the Florida court said of the holder of a junior mortgage covering only a portion of the land held as security for a senior mortgage: ". . . Their portions of said land, as well as all the residue of said mortgaged tract, are bound for the payment of the whole of both mortgages; and the courts have no power to release any part of the land from the lien of the mortgages by affixing thereto a sum, less than the entire sum of the mortgages, which, when paid, shall release such part from the lien of the mortgages. . . ."

The only absolute right of a junior mortgagee, as against a senior mortgagee, is the right to redeem from the senior mortgagee. 3 Jones on Mortgages (8th Ed.) §1781. The rights of an omitted junior encumbrancer remain precisely as they were before the proceedings were instituted to foreclose the first mortgage. They are neither enlarged nor diminished by the defective foreclosure. McGough v. Sweetzer, 97 Ala. 361, 12 So. 162, 19 L.R.A. 470.

The judgment appealed from must be reversed, however, and the cause remanded because the judgment provided that Springer should have a period of nine months from the date of the entry of the judgment in the instant case within which to redeem the property from the mortgage foreclosure sale in Cause No. A-12537 on the docket of the district court of Bernalillo County. Section 24-2-18, N.M.S.A. 1953, provides that no property shall be sold under a mortgage foreclosure proceeding until sixty days after the date of the entry of the foreclosure judgment. Section 24-2-19, N.M.S.A. 1953, gives a person entitled to redemption nine months from the date of such foreclosure sale within which to redeem therefrom. Construing the two statutory provisions together, as we must, it is apparent that a person entitled to redeem is thus given at least eleven months from the date of the foreclosure judgment within which to redeem. We have said that because Springer was not a party to the first foreclosure action, it will not be permitted to suffer any disadvantage from the failure to include it as a party. It is apparent that the judgment in the instant case shortened Springer's period of redemption by sixty days. This was error.

What we have said makes it unnecessary to discuss other questions argued or briefed. It follows that the judgment appealed from should be affirmed in all respects except that the judgment must be vacated and a new judgment entered granting Springer eleven months from the date of such judgment within which to redeem from the Kirkeby foreclosure sale.

It is so ordered.

Moise and Tackett, JJ., concur.

NOTES

1. The mortgagor's interest commonly is called an equity of redemption, whether or not the mortgage is in default. The equity of redemption is to be distinguished from the statutory right to redeem, which arises after foreclosure by sale and permits the mortgagor to redeem for a specified period of time following the foreclosure sale or judgment. About half the states provide for statutory rights to redeem. Absent such statutory rights, defaulting mortgagors may redeem only until foreclosure sale or decree. Statutory rights of redemption can create sufficient uncertainty about future ownership so as to deter for many months alienation or development of the land.

2. Why should a senior mortgagee be permitted to foreclose the interest of a junior mortgagee? And why should a junior mortgagee of less land

than that covered by the senior mortgage not be permitted to redeem pro tanto by paying the pro rata portion of what the property was sold for at foreclosure sale? Are the reasons given in the principal case satisfactory?

(d) Effect of Foreclosure on Tenant's Rights

Conference Center Ltd. v. TRC
189 Conn. 212, 455 A.2d 857 (1983)

PETERS, Associate Justice. The issue in this case is whether a tenant has been constructively evicted when served with a demand for immediate possession by a mortgagee initiating foreclosure proceedings against the tenant's landlord. The plaintiff, Conference Center Limited, brought an action against its tenant, the defendant TRC—The Research Corporation of New England, seeking damages for the defendant's allegedly wrongful abandonment of the leasehold premises. The defendant, in its reply, raised a number of special defenses based upon the foreclosure action brought by Hartford Federal Savings and Loan Association against Conference Center Limited. The trial court, after a hearing, granted the defendant's motion for summary judgment and the plaintiff has appealed.

The underlying facts are established in the pleadings of the parties and in two memoranda of decision by the trial court, one by Wright, J., sustaining the defendant's objections to the plaintiff's motion to strike the defendant's first, second and third defenses, and one by O'Donnell, J., granting the defendant's motion for summary judgment on these three special defenses. No issue has been taken on this appeal with any of the facts thus established.

The plaintiff, Conference Center Limited (hereinafter CCL) and the defendant, TRC—The Research Corporation of New England (hereinafter TRC) entered into a two-year commercial lease on July 7, 1977. The tenant, TRC, took possession of the premises on September 12, 1977.

The leasehold premises were subject to a prior mortgage executed on May 5, 1972, by the plaintiff's predecessor in title to the Hartford Federal Savings and Loan Association (hereinafter the Bank), and duly recorded. On January 19, 1978, when the plaintiff had been in default on the mortgage for many months, the Bank initiated foreclosure proceedings. In that action, the Bank served the defendant with a demand for immediate possession of the leasehold premises. Thereafter, on February 27, 1978, the defendant vacated the premises and returned the keys thereto to the plaintiff. This litigation ensued.

In response to the plaintiff's complaint seeking damages arising out of the defendant's alleged breach of its leasehold contract, the defendant filed both an answer denying breach and several special defenses. The first three of these special defenses grew out of the foreclosure action and maintained that the foreclosure proceedings had resulted in: (1) a termination of the lease; (2) a breach of the covenant of quiet enjoyment in the lease; and (3) a constructive eviction. The plaintiff filed a motion to strike these defenses. The trial court, Wright, J., in sustaining the defendant's objections to the motion to strike, treated these three special defenses jointly and focused primarily upon the claim of constructive eviction. The court held that "[i]n yielding possession upon demand, defendant acted at its peril and assumes the burden of proving that the Bank's request was made under a paramount title. . . . Under these circumstances, the plaintiff's motion to strike the first, second and third special defenses is premature."

Some seven weeks after the pleadings had been closed, the defendant moved for summary judgment. In response, the plaintiff attempted belatedly to amend its reply to the defendant's special defenses. The proffered amendment sought to raise, by way of avoidance, the defendant's anticipatory determination to vacate the premises even before the foreclosure had begun, and the assurance given the defendant by the Bank that the defendant's possession would not actually be disturbed.

The trial court concluded that this amendment should be disallowed because it came too late. The court further concluded that, whether or not the amendment were allowed, there existed no genuine issue of material fact. Adopting the legal principles articulated in the memorandum of decision on the earlier motion to strike, the court granted the defendant's motion for summary judgment.

In its appeal from this judgment, the plaintiff CCL raises three issues: (1) the trial court erred in denying its motion to strike, since initiation of a foreclosure action by a mortgagee does not constitute a constructive eviction of the mortgagor's tenant; (2) the trial court erred in denying its motion to amend; and (3) the trial court erred in granting the motion of the defendant TRC for summary judgment, since there were unresolved issues of material fact. While we agree with the trial court that the motion to strike and the motion to amend were properly denied, we conclude that the court acted prematurely in granting the defendant's motion for summary judgment. . . .

This court has not previously ruled on the effect that a paramount mortgagee's institution of foreclosure proceedings has on rights and liabilities under a subsequent, and hence subordinate, lease. To resolve this issue, we must take account of three convergent areas of the law: under mortgage law, the right of a mortgagee in a "title" jurisdiction to possession of mortgaged premises; under landlord-tenant law, the right of a tenant to enforce a covenant of quiet enjoyment; and under commercial law, the right of a contracting party to adequate assurance of receiving due performance.

It is undisputed that a mortgagee in Connecticut, both by common-law rule and by statute, is deemed to have taken legal title upon the execution of a mortgage on real property. . . . If, after default, the mortgagee exercises his right to possession by an actual entry upon the mortgaged premises, such an entry, because it constitutes an eviction of the tenant, results in the termination of the tenant's lease. Pabst Brewing Co. v. Thorley, 145 F. 117, 122 (2d Cir. 1906), *cert. denied,* 203 U.S. 597, 27 S. Ct. 784, 51 L. Ed. 333 (1906); Net Realty Holding Trust v. Nelson, 33 Conn. Sup. 22, 25, 358 A.2d 365 (1976); Kratovil, supra, §20.05; Lesar, Landlord and Tenant §3.48 in 1 Am. Law of Property (1952); Osborne, supra, §144, pp. 237-38; 1 Tiffany, Real Property (3d Ed.1939) §139; Restatement (Second), Property §4.3.

Mere institution of a foreclosure action by a landlord's mortgagee does not, however, ineluctably lead to the tenant's dispossession. In Collins v. Sears, Roebuck & Co., 164 Conn. 369, 376-77, 321 A.2d 444 (1973), this court upheld, as not violative of public policy, a provision in a lease which required a tenant to pay additional rent "in the event of the institution of a foreclosure proceeding by the Landlord's present or future mortgagee against the premises of which the leased premises are a part." Id., 372n, 321 A.2d 444. Although the tenant in *Collins* voiced a concern that the rent escalation clause might be triggered by a collusive foreclosure, we dismissed that concern as speculative. Id., 377, 321 A.2d 444. *Collins* impliedly recognized both the possibility that foreclosure actions will prompt negotiations that lead to withdrawal of the foreclosure and the commercial desirability of arrangements between landlord and tenant that facilitate a working out of the mortgagor's financial difficulties.

From the vantage point of mortgage law, it is important therefore to note that the Bank in this case held title to the leasehold premises, and that this title was paramount to that of both the plaintiff CCL and the defendant TRC. The Bank manifested some intention to implement its paramount title, upon CCL's default, by commencing a foreclosure action in which it served the defendant with foreclosure papers demanding immediate possession. At the time when the defendant abandoned the premises, the Bank had not, however, exercised its power to enter into possession nor had it demanded a new lease from the defendant.

The Connecticut law of constructive eviction is equally not in dispute. The classic statement is that found in Amsterdam Realty Co. v. Johnson, 115 Conn. 243, 248, 161 A. 339 (1932), where this court held that "[a] constructive eviction arises where a landlord, while not actually depriving the tenant of possession of any part of the premises leased, has done or suffered some act by which the premises are rendered untenantable, and has thereby caused a failure of consideration for the tenant's promise to pay rent." A tenant is constructively evicted when compelled to yield possession to a third party with title paramount to that of its landlord. Such a constructive eviction may occur in advance of an actual eviction, "for, if he cannot hold lawfully, the law is not so unreasonable as to require him to hold unlawfully at the peril of a suit and certain judgment against him." Camp v. Scott, 47 Conn. 366, 369 (1879). To prove a constructive ouster, however, the facts must demonstrate that the person with paramount title "[made] a re-entry on the premises, or in some other positive manner [asserted] the forfeiture of the lease." Id., 374. Whether there has been such interference with the tenant's peaceful enjoyment of the premises as to render the leasehold untenantable cannot be determined by general principles but depends instead on an "inquiry in every instance [into] the facts of the particular case. By this is meant the situation of the parties to a lease, the character of the premises, the use to which the tenant intends to put them, and the nature and extent by which the tenant's use of the premises is interfered with by the injury claimed." . . .

Authorities from other jurisdictions have discussed the point in time when a tenant is constructively evicted by a mortgagee's action to foreclose a paramount mortgage on the leasehold premises. Focusing on the requirement that the tenant demonstrate actual and serious deprivation of the use contemplated by the parties to the lease, the cases have refused to conclude that a constructive eviction necessarily follows from the mere initiation of foreclosure proceedings. See John R. Thompson Co. v. Northwestern Mutual Life Ins. Co., 31 F. Supp. 399, 400 (N.D. Ohio 1937); Standard Livestock Co. v. Pentz, 204 Cal. 618, 625-26, 269 P. 645 (1928); Hyde v. Brandler, 118 A.2d 398, 399-400 (D.C. 1955); Metropolitan Life Ins. Co. v. Childs Co., 230 N.Y. 285, 289, 130 N.E. 295 (1921). The secondary authorities, building upon these cases and a few others, have universally agreed with the Restatement (Second), Property §4.3, comment d (1977), that "[t]he institution of foreclosure proceedings by a mortgagee who has a paramount title is not an eviction of the tenant." See, e.g., 3 Friedman on Leases §§29.201, 29.202 (1978); 3 Thompson on Real Property §1132, p. 499 (1959).

The defendant TRC urges us to reject these authorities because they emanate from jurisdictions that have rejected the "title" theory of mortgages. We find them distinguishable for a different reason. Read closely, the cases and the secondary authorities recognize that the overarching issue is not the particular step taken by the foreclosing mortgagee but rather its effect on the tenant's continued capacity to enjoy the use of the leasehold property. The Restatement itself, earlier in comment d to §4.3, acknowledges that the tenant has been constructively evicted "[w]here the tenant has not been ousted from possession by the assertion of the paramount title but the assertion prevents the use contemplated by the parties." Friedman opines that "[n]ormally, the institution of possessory proceedings . . . is no breach of a covenant of quiet enjoyment." 3 Friedman on Leases §29.202, p. 1089 (1978). Since the law of constructive eviction is fact-bound, no conclusive effect can be attached to the institution of mortgage foreclosure proceedings. In the proper circumstances; see Thomas v. Roper, supra, 162 Conn. 346-47, 294 A.2d 321; initiation of such proceedings may well constitute a constructive eviction; under other circumstances it will not.

From the vantage point of the law of constructive eviction, it is therefore significant that while there has been a formal demand for possession of the leasehold premises, the letter attached to the plaintiff's affidavit opposing summary judgment creates uncertainty about the extent of the mortgagee's intended interference with the defendant TRC's continued occupancy.[2] While offering the defendant some assurances, the letter, as the plaintiff CCL conceded at oral argument, falls short of committing the Bank to acceptance or ratification of the defendant's lease.

Put together, the law of mortgages and the law of landlord and tenant demonstrate that while the defendant TRC may have a valid defense to the plaintiff CCL's cause of action, the defendant has yet to prove it. At this juncture, it is clear that the trial court, Wright, J., was correct in refusing to strike TRC's first three defenses and to leave TRC to its proof. The trial court, O'Donnell, J., was, however, in error in concluding that TRC was entitled to summary judgment, since the actual impact of the foreclosure proceedings as a constructive eviction raises a genuine issue of material fact. Because a remand is therefore required in order for this question to be fully considered, it is useful to inquire what commercial law may add to fair resolution of the dispute between the parties.

The Connecticut law concerning commercial insecurity, although not in terms applicable to real property cases, provides by analogy a useful resource to enable contracting parties to deal with uncertainties about forthcoming performance. Under Uniform Commercial Code §2-609, General Statutes §42a-2-609, a contract

> imposes an obligation on each party that the other's expectation of receiving due performance will not be impaired. When reasonable grounds for insecu-

---

2. The letter, dated January 26, 1978, was addressed to the defendant and signed by the assistant vice president of Hartford Federal Savings and Loan Association. It reads:

"Gentlemen:

"Hartford Federal Savings and Loan Association is instituting proceedings to foreclose the mortgage which it holds on 936 Silas Deane Highway, Wethersfield, Connecticut. It is the understanding of Hartford Federal Savings and Loan Association that each of you is occupying some space in the building and may have a lease. For technical legal reasons, you are being joined as party defendants in the foreclosure. In the event that the foreclosure goes to a conclusion and Hartford Federal Savings and Loan Association takes over as sole owner of the premises, it intends to have you stay in possession of your area provided that a mutually agreeable leasing arrangement can be worked out between you and Hartford Federal Savings and Loan Association. Hartford Federal Savings and Loan Association does not know the rental and other terms under which you are occupying the premises. Therefore, it would be helpful if you could send a copy of your lease to me at Hartford Federal Savings and Loan Association and if you do not have a written lease, kindly set forth your monthly rental arrangement in a letter to me.

"I would appreciate it if you would send this material as soon as possible so that we can come to a mutual understanding in respect to your future occupancy of the premises.

"Very truly yours,
DONALD A. RYDER
Assistant Vice President"

rity arise with respect to the performance of either party the other may in writing demand adequate assurance of due performance and until he receives such assurance may if commercially reasonable suspend any performance for which he has not already received the agreed return.

Failure to provide adequate assurance within a reasonable period of time "is a repudiation of the contract." As we stated in a recent sale of goods case interpreting §2-609, when there is reasonable doubt about whether a contracting party's default is substantial, the injured party may be well advised to temporize by suspending further performance until it can ascertain whether the defaulting party is able to offer adequate assurance of future performance. Nonetheless, even under the code, the defaulting party's conduct may be sufficiently egregious so that, without more, such conduct in and of itself constitutes substantial impairment of the contract and a present breach. Cherwell–Ralli, Inc. v. Rytman Grain Co., 180 Conn. 714, 718, 433 A.2d 984 (1980). See generally White & Summers (2d Ed. 1980), Uniform Commercial Code §6-2.

This court has in the past looked to operative principles contained in the Uniform Commercial Code for a source of law that informs real property transactions as well as sale of goods transactions. Just as in Hamm v. Taylor, 180 Conn. 491, 494-95, 429 A.2d 946 (1980), we invoked the provisions of Uniform Commercial Code §2-302, General Statutes §42a-2-302, to provide a framework for resolving an issue of unconscionability with respect to a real property mortgage, so we may look to Uniform Commercial Code §2-609 for assistance in determining whether there has been that substantial interference with possession or enjoyment which is the essence of constructive eviction. Cf. Holt v. Seversky Electronatom Corporation, 452 F.2d 31, 36 (2d Cir. 1971).

We note that courts in other jurisdictions have required a tenant who contemplates abandonment of the premises because of constructive eviction first to give his landlord notice and a reasonable opportunity to provide adequate assurance. See Pague v. Petroleum Products, Inc., 77 Wash. 2d 219, 221, 461 P.2d 317 (1969); Northwestern Realty Co. v. Hardy, 160 Wis. 324, 326, 151 N.W. 791 (1915); accord 3 Friedman on Leases §29.301, pp. 1107-1108 (1978); Lesar, Landlord and Tenant in 1 Am. Law of Property §3.51, p. 283 (1952). That case law provides a further link to Uniform Commercial Code §2-609, for the cases and the statute both recognize the desirability of providing an opportunity for dialogue to establish whether the parties intend to repudiate or to fulfill their contractual obligations.

Finally, we find support for recourse to §2-609 as a source of general law in the provisions of §251 of the Restatement (Second) of Contracts. Those provisions, which are not limited to contracts for the sale of goods, permit any obligee with reasonable grounds for insecurity to demand adequate assurance of due performance and to treat as a repudiation an obligor's failure to respond with an adequate assurance within a reasonable time.[3] Courts in other jurisdictions have applied §251 to the resolution of disputes under construction contracts. See David Nassif Associates v. United States, 644 F.2d 4, 12 (Ct. Claims 1981); L. E. Spitzer Co. v. Barron, 581 P.2d 213, 216-17 (Alaska 1978); Carfield & Sons, Inc. v. Cowling, 616 P.2d 1008, 1010 (Colo. App. 1980).

Recourse to the commercial doctrine of insecurity is equally appropriate for the resolution of disputes concerning constructive eviction, for such disputes frequently require inferences to be drawn about future conduct and future expectations for beneficial enjoyment of the leasehold premises. Foreclosure proceedings may provide the incentive for finding alternate financing which discharges the paramount mortgage, so that the tenant's possessory use may remain utterly unimpaired. John R. Thompson Co. v. Northwestern Mutual Life Ins. Co., 31 F. Supp. 399, 400 (N.D. Ohio 1937). Access to a continued stream of rental payments, because it facilitates a workout of the mortgage, is therefore in the interest of both the landlord and the mortgagee. See the discussion of Collins v. Sears, Roebuck & Co., 164 Conn. 369, 321 A.2d 444 (1973), supra, and Kratovil, Modern Mortgage Law and Practice §§20.03, 20.05 (1981); Osborne, Mortgages (2d Ed. 1970) §144.

From the vantage point of commercial law, the Bank's institution of mortgage foreclosure proceedings which formally demanded surrender of possession by TRC certainly gave TRC reasonable grounds for insecurity, as that term is used in Uniform Commercial Code §2-609. At that time, TRC became entitled to request some form of adequate assurance of due performance.[4] On a full trial, the parties will be able to present evidence whether some kind of request for assurance triggered the Bank's letter of January 26, 1976, and whether, measured according to commercial standards; U.C.C. §2-609(2); that letter, or other communications, offered adequate assurance of due performance. It bears emphasis, however, that failure adequately to respond to TRC's insecurity, although it would strengthen TRC's case for constructive eviction, is not essential to

---

3. "[2 Restatement (Second) Contracts] §251. WHEN A FAILURE TO GIVE ASSURANCE MAY BE TREATED AS A REPUDIATION

"(1) Where reasonable grounds arise to believe that the obligor will commit a breach by non-performance that would of itself give the obligee a claim for damages for total breach under §243, the obligee may demand adequate assurance of due performance and may, if reasonable, suspend any performance for which he has not already received the agreed exchange until he receives such assurance.

"(2) The obligee may treat as a repudiation the obligor's failure to provide within a reasonable time such assurance of due performance as is adequate in the circumstances of the particular case."

4. Since Uniform Commercial Code §2-609 is applicable only by analogy, there is no need to incorporate its formal requirement that a request for assurance must be made in writing, if the circumstances demonstrate that the landlord knew or had reason to know of the tenant's insecurity.

TRC's defense if TRC can otherwise establish breach of the warranty of quiet enjoyment. See Cherwell-Ralli, Inc. v. Rytman Grain Co., supra. In any case, issues arising out of the law of commercial insecurity, like those of constructive eviction generally, because they are necessarily fact-bound, require a full trial and preclude summary judgment.

Applying these various legal principles to the decisions of the trial court, we conclude that Wright, J., was correct in denying the plaintiff's motion to strike the defense of constructive eviction, and that O'Donnell, J., was in error in granting the defendant's motion for summary judgment. Only a full trial can establish whether the defendant was in fact constructively evicted or was entitled, for lack of adequate assurance, to infer that its lease had been terminated.

There is error, the judgment is set aside, and the case is remanded for further proceedings consistent with this opinion.

In this opinion the other Judges concurred.

NOTES

1. Do you believe that it is appropriate or helpful to consider the Uniform Commercial Code as an authoritative source in deciding real property issues such as those raised above in the Connecticut *Conference Center* opinion?

2. A lease senior in time to a mortgage generally remains in effect following foreclosure, the person acquiring the property following the foreclosure becoming the lessor under the terms of the senior lease. A lease junior in time to a mortgage can be extinguished by foreclosure of the mortgage if the lessee is joined as a defendant in the foreclosure proceedings. Mortgagees sometimes intentionally do not join such junior lessees as foreclosure defendants. Why this conscious determination not to join junior lessees?

(e) Risks of a Junior Encumbrancer: Senior Lien Default

All mortgagees face some risk of loss when default occurs. The value of the security may not adequately cover the unpaid debt (which will include interest arrearages, curative advances, and foreclosure costs) and the mortgagor, even if personally liable, may be unable to pay the deficiency. The junior mortgagee, however, faces a special problem — that of "cover" — if default occurs in the senior mortgage. When the senior mortgagee sells the security under a power of sale or foreclosure decree, the junior mortgagee must look to the "surplus" proceeds of sale to realize anything on his security interest. As the following problems reveal, this is often, at best, a chancy prospect for the junior mortgagee — one, if at all possible, he would do well to avoid.

PROBLEMS

A owns a building that is appraised at $500,000 and is encumbered with two mortgages. X holds the first mortgage of $400,000. Y holds the second mortgage of $50,000.

1. The first mortgage (but not the second mortgage) is in default. X forecloses.

(a) At the foreclosure sale, X is prepared to make the opening bid. What amount might you suggest? How much new cash must X raise to bid $400,000?

(b) At the foreclosure sale, X has opened the bidding at $400,000. Except for Y, no other bidders appear. Y bids to protect his security interest. What amount might you suggest? How much new cash must Y raise to satisfy his bid?

(c) At the foreclosure sale, Z, a stranger, bids $430,000. In advising Y as to whether to continue the bidding, what factors would you weigh?

2. The second mortgage (but not the first mortgage) is in default. Y forecloses.

(a) Who should be joined in the foreclosure action?

(b) At the foreclosure sale, Y is prepared to make the opening bid. What amount might you suggest? How much new cash must Y raise to satisfy his bid?

3. The clauses below routinely appear in a junior mortgage.

§5567. *Second Mortgage Clause.*

This mortgage is subject and subordinate to _____ mortgage _____ given to secure the payment of _____ dollars and interest, recorded in the office of the _____ , of the County of _____ in liber _____ of section _____ of mortgages, _____ now _____ prior lien _____ on said premises.

AND IT IS HEREBY EXPRESSLY AGREED, that should any default be made in the payment of any installment of principal or of the interest on _____ said prior mortgage, and should such installment of principal, of such interest remain upaid and in arrears for the space of ten days, or should any suit be commenced to foreclose _____ said prior mortgage, then the amount secured by this mortgage and the accompanying bond, shall become and be due and payable at any time thereafter at the option of the owner or holder of this mortgage.

AND IT IS HEREBY FURTHER EXPRESSLY AGREED, that should any default be made in the payment of any installment of principal, or of the interest on _____ said prior mortgage, the holder of this mortgage may pay such installment of principal, or such interest and the amount so paid, with legal interest thereon from the time of such payment, may be added to the indebtedness secured by this mortgage and the accompanying bond and shall be deemed to be secured by this mortgage and said bond, and may be collected thereunder. Modern Legal Forms §5567 (Supp. 1967).

(a) Is the first mortgagee obligated to accept a tender made in behalf of the mortgagor pursuant to the third paragraph above?

Basic Security Transactions

(b) In the absence of the third paragraph above, would the junior mortgagee be privileged to make a tender if the mortgagor objected?

(c) If you represented the junior mortgagee, what provisions might you ask for, in addition to the standard clauses, to strengthen your client's status?

4. *Non-monetary Defaults:* Not every mortgage default results from the borrower's failure to pay his debt service installments currently. The typical loan agreement places other duties on the borrower (e.g., avoidance of waste, restoration of premises after casualty, payment of real estate taxes) that may lead to a default if the violation is not cured, and — more worrisome — certain other obligations (e.g., avoidance of insolvency, nontransfer of the mortgaged premises without the lender's consent) may lead to a default, with its attendant acceleration and foreclosure, that the junior lienor would be unable to cure.

Do you have any drafting or negotiating suggestions for placing the junior lienor somewhat less at peril under these circumstances?

(f) Foreclosure of a Wrap-around Mortgage

J. M. Realty Investment Corp. v. Stern
296 So. 2d 588 (Fla. Dist. Ct. App. 1974)

PER CURIAM. Defendant-appellant seeks review of an order denying defendant's motion for relief from final judgment of foreclosure.

Plaintiff-appellee, Richard I. Stern, for $220,000 sold five apartment buildings, which at the time were encumbered by a $150,000 first mortgage held by the Dade Federal Savings and Loan Association (DFS), to the defendant-appellant, J. M. Realty Investment Corporation. Defendant corporation paid the plaintiff $35,000 in cash and executed a purchase money mortgage in the sum of $181,953.77 which represented the aggregate of the first mortgage to DFS and the amount due plaintiff as a second mortgage.[1] By the terms thereof, the purchase money mortgage executed by the defendant was considered to be a "wrap-around" mortgage and plaintiff mortgagee was obligated thereby to make the payments on the senior DFS mortgage. Pursuant thereto, on November 15, 1971 defendant-appellant began to make the required $1,526.95 monthly payments to the plaintiff. However, defendant defaulted on the payment due June 15, 1973 and on subsequent payments, and plaintiff thereupon instituted the

---

1. $ 35,000   cash
     150,000   DFS mortgage
      35,000   *second mortgage to seller

    $220,000   total

* The $3,046.23 difference between $35,000 and $31,953.77 represents credits for prepaid rents, security deposits, taxes, etc.

instant action to foreclose the mortgage. While the action was pending, plaintiff continued to make the monthly payment on the DFS senior mortgage. DFS was not made a party to the foreclosure suit. The court entered a final judgment of foreclosure, determined that the amount owed plaintiff by the defendant was $185,850.62 for principal and accrued interest, plus court costs and attorneys' fees, and ordered that if payment was not forthcoming, the property was to be sold. The judgment further provided that the Clerk of the Court shall pay the DFS, the holder of the first mortgage, the principal, interest and prepayment penalties owing, unless plaintiff is the successful bidder at the sale, in which case the clerk shall not pay off the first mortgage. Subsequent thereto, defendant filed a motion for relief from final judgment of foreclosure wherein it alleged that less than $50,000 was actually owed to plaintiff, since the remainder of the judgment was owed to DFS which was not a party to the action and did not desire prepayment of its mortgage. After a hearing was held thereon, the trial judge denied the motion and defendant appeals the denial thereof.

On appeal, appellant mortgagor contends that the plaintiff, the holder of a junior mortgage, cannot by foreclosure of its mortgage and without joinder or request of the senior mortgagee, compel the acceleration and prepayment of the junior mortgage.

We have determined that in essence appellant mortgagor is seeking to have the court either modify or rewrite the provision of the subject "wrap-around" mortgage so that appellant may be allowed to pay off the difference between the balance due on the DFS mortgage and the balance due on what is argued as the plaintiff seller's second mortgage, rather than being required to pay the full amount of the "wrap-around" mortgage. This court cannot and will not modify the terms of the instant mortgage as we are powerless to rewrite contracts in order to relieve one of the parties thereto from the apparent hardships of an improvident bargain. Savage v. Horne, 159 Fla. 301, 31 So. 2d 477 (1947).

Further, we find that the plaintiff seller's corporation by the terms of the wrap-around mortgage was liable on the DFS mortgage and in absence of satisfaction thereof, the corporation's liability thereon would continue.

Finally, we note that the exercise of power pursuant to Fla. Stat. §702.07, F.S.A., which was relied upon by defendant-appellant to set aside the judgment of foreclosure, is within the discretion of the trial judge and appellant has failed to demonstrate an abuse thereof. Cf. Maule Industries, Inc. v. Seminole Rock & Sand Co., Fla. 1956, 91 So. 2d 307.

Accordingly, for the reasons cited hereinabove the order herein appealed is affirmed hereby.

c. Postforeclosure Redemption Rights

In about half the states, statutes provide for redemption after foreclosure for a period, varying among the states, from six months to two years.

These postforeclosure rights are often referred to as statutory redemption and are to be distinguished from preforeclosure equity of redemption rights. Those entitled to redeem after foreclosure include junior lienors as well as mortgagors and their successors. In most states the mortgagor has the right to possession during the period in which redemption is permitted. The amount that must be paid to redeem is usually the foreclosure sale price plus the expenses of foreclosure. Priorities exist for the right to redeem if more than one person has redemption rights, the mortgagor normally having the highest priority.

If a mortgagor or his successor redeems, junior liens are often considered to be revived. If a junior lienor redeems, he acquires the rights of the foreclosure sale purchaser and this interest can become a full title if no one with superior redemption rights redeems by the close of the redemption period. However, as illustrated by the next case, First Vermont Bank & Trust Co. v. Kalomiris, this is not true everywhere, and it may be necessary for the redeeming junior lienor to foreclose separately the mortgagor's interest in order to terminate all rights of the mortgagor.

(1) Effect of Redemption

First Vermont Bank & Trust Company v. Kalomiris
138 Vt. 481, 418 A.2d 43 (1980)

HILL, Justice. Defendant, Thunder Road Enterprises, Inc. (TRE), owned property in the Town of Barre on which plaintiff, First Vermont Bank and Trust Company, held a first mortgage. On January 30, 1978, TRE sold the property to defendant, Kalomiris, who assumed TRE's first mortgage to plaintiff, and who gave a second mortgage on the same property to TRE. Kalomiris subsequently defaulted on both mortgages.

On November 30, 1978, plaintiff commenced an action to foreclose Kalomiris' equity of redemption in the premises. In its petition, plaintiff named both Kalomiris and TRE as defendants. The lower court issued a judgment of foreclosure that provided that Kalomiris was to redeem on or before August 13, 1979, or else "said Anastasias Kalomiris and all persons claiming under him shall be foreclosed and forever barred from all equity of redemption on the premises." The judgment further provided that if Kalomiris failed to redeem, TRE could redeem on August 14, 1979.

Kalomiris failed to redeem by the date specified. On August 14, 1979, TRE redeemed, and the court issued a certificate of redemption which permitted TRE to apply for a writ of possession. Three days later, Kalomiris moved for relief from that part of the certificate of redemption that granted possession to TRE. The court granted the motion and struck the part of the certificate which stated that TRE "may have a writ of possession of the premises." It is from this order that TRE appeals.

TRE argues that the failure of Kalomiris to redeem the premises pursuant to the terms and conditions of the judgment of foreclosure coupled with TRE's subsequent redemption terminated all of Kalomiris' right, title and interest in the property. As a result, TRE claims that it was entitled to a writ of possession under 12 V.S.A. §4528, which states, in part: "If the premises are not redeemed agreeably to the decree, the clerk of the court may issue a writ of possession." We disagree.

Kalomiris' equity of redemption would have been forever foreclosed had TRE or one of the other named defendants not redeemed. Ward v. Seymour, 51 Vt. 320, 324 (1878). But when TRE, as second mortgagee, redeemed the premises it was a satisfaction of the judgment of foreclosure, and TRE became by operation of law subrogated to the rights of First Vermont Bank in the mortgaged property. Id. See also Phelps v. Root, 78 Vt. 493, 498-99, 63 A. 941, 942 (1906); Wheeler v. Willard, 44 Vt. 640, 644-45 (1871); Bullard v. Leach, 27 Vt. 491, 495 (1854). In effect, TRE became first mortgagee, as well as second mortgagee, because when the judgment of foreclosure was satisfied it had the consequence of "keep[ing] the mortgage on foot." Wheeler v. Willard, supra, 44 Vt. at 644. Therefore TRE was not entitled to a writ of possession, since it did not foreclose on Kalomiris' equity of redemption, either by cross claim in the original foreclosure action or by an independent action. Ward v. Seymour, supra.

It should be noted that while many of the older cases speak in terms of the second mortgagee becoming an assignee in equity on redemption, see Ward v. Seymour, supra; Wheeler v. Willard, supra; Bullard v. Leach, supra, further examination reveals that the Court actually was referring to the doctrine of subrogation, not assignment. Subrogation is an equitable doctrine that arises by operation of law, while assignment is a volitional transaction between parties. See 9 G. Thompson, Real Property §4800 (1958 repl.) (citing Ward v. Seymour, supra, at 610 n.36). In this case, had there been an assignment of the mortgage from First Vermont Bank to TRE while the foreclosure was pending, "the assignment would have carried with it the foreclosure, and it would have become available in the hands of the assignee." Frisbee v. Frisbee, 86 Me. 444, 447, 29 A. 1115, 1116 (1894). Because no such assignment was made, however, TRE could not take advantage of First Vermont's foreclosure. And, as noted above, since it did not foreclose on Kalomiris' equity of redemption on its own, it was not entitled to a writ of possession.

Affirmed.

NOTES

1. Could TRE have redeemed if it had not taken back a second mortgage from Kalomiris?
2. Why do you think TRE, prior to redeeming, did not obtain an assignment of the mortgage held by First Vermont Bank? Is it likely that

TRE sought such an assignment but the Bank refused to assign or insisted on a substantial payment for an assignment which TRE would not pay? Or is it probable that the advantages of an assignment never occurred to TRE or its attorney?

3. There is authority contra to the principal case on rights in the land acquired by the redeeming junior encumbrancer. See, for example, Franklin v. Jameson–Wohler, 15 N.D. 613, 109 N.W. 56 (1906), taking the position that the redeeming junior encumbrancer acquires all the rights of the purchaser at the sale, and after the redemption period has expired is entitled to a deed vesting title in him. A statute leading to the same result is Minn. Stat. Ann. §580.27 (1947). Which position is preferable? Should the redeeming junior encumbrancer receive title or only a security interest? If the redeeming junior encumbrancer can receive title upon redeeming, will this exert pressure on the senior mortgagee to bid the property up to fair value at the foreclosure sale; and, if so, should this be a decisive policy consideration in choosing between the two positions?

4. In states that permit postforeclosure redemption, more than one person with rights to redeem may wish to redeem. A problem then can arise as to which of these persons has a preferred right to redeem. The usual position is that if there are several junior lienors, seniority determines the preference. For example, a second mortgagee will be given redemption rights over a third mortgagee. The privilege of redemption may be given in successive periods to junior lienors in accord with their seniority. But if a junior lienor redeems, he may be subject to re-redemption by a more senior party during the post-foreclosure period. See generally Durfee and Doddridge, Redemption from Foreclosure Sale—the Uniform Mortgage Act, 23 Mich. L. Rev. 825, 845 (1925); and 4 American Law of Property §16.177 (Casner ed. 1952).

Why is it not inevitable that if a junior party chooses to redeem, the senior party with redemption rights will also choose to redeem? Why is it that some parties with redemption rights seek to redeem and others do not?

(2) Federal Preemption

United States v. Stadium Apartments, Inc.

425 F.2d 358 (9th Cir. 1970)

DUNIWAY, Circuit Judge: This case presents the question whether state redemption statutes should apply when the Federal Housing Authority (FHA) forecloses a mortgage which it has guaranteed. We hold that such statutes do not apply.

The federal statute here involved is Title VI of the National Housing Act, 12 U.S.C. §§1736-1746a. The stated objective of Title VI is "to assist in relieving the acute shortage of housing . . . available to veterans of World War II at prices within their reasonable ability to pay. . . ." 12 U.S.C. §1738(a). The statute confers authority upon the Secretary (formerly the Commissioner) "to make such rules and regulations as may be necessary to carry out the provisions of this subchapter." 12 U.S.C. §1742. Such regulations were promulgated, and those that were in force in November 1949, when the mortgage here in question was executed and insured appear in the 1947 Supplement to the Code of Federal Regulations. (24 C.F.R. §580 (1947 Supp.).) Citations to C.F.R. in this opinion are to the 1947 supplement.

The way in which the Act and regulations operated are well illustrated in this case. In 1949, appellee Stadium Apartments, Inc., desired to construct, under Title VI, an apartment house in Caldwell, Idaho. It applied to Prudential Insurance Company for a loan. Such a loan was eligible for insurance under 12 U.S.C. §1743(a). The conditions for eligibility are set out in 12 U.S.C. §1743(b). The mortgagor must be approved by the Secretary, who can impose certain regulations upon both the mortgagor and the property mortgaged. Certain terms of the mortgage are also prescribed. Application for approval was made, as required by 24 C.F.R. §§580.1-580.7. The FHA then issued a commitment of insurance, as required by 24 C.F.R. §580.8. The mortgage was executed upon a form prescribed by FHA, and accepted for insurance. 24 C.F.R. §§580.10-580.37. The amount of the insured loan was $130,000. The mortgage contained this provision: "The Mortgagor, to the extent permitted by law, hereby waives the benefit of any and all homestead and exemption laws and of any right to a stay or redemption and the benefit of any moratorium law or laws."

Stadium Apartments defaulted in 1966, and Prudential assigned the mortgage to the Secretary of Housing and Urban Development, pursuant to 12 U.S.C. §1743(c). The Secretary paid Prudential the amount then due, as required by 12 U.S.C. §1743(c). The United States then obtained a default judgment foreclosing the mortgage, 12 U.S.C. §§1713(k), 1743(f). The district judge, in spite of the foregoing provision, framed the foreclosure decree to allow for a one-year period of redemption, as provided by 2 Idaho Code §11-402. The question is whether this was error.

Stadium Apartments, Inc., having defaulted, is not represented here. Because the question is of some importance, we were disturbed that the government had chosen to appeal this uncontested case, when hitherto the FHA has at times consented to decrees providing for post-sale redemption rights as required by state laws. We therefore determined, following the initial oral argument in which only government counsel appeared, that the Attorneys General of the states within our circuit and of the Territory of Guam should be invited to submit amicus curiae briefs. The State of California has done so, taking a position opposed to that advocated by the government. Washington, Arizona and Guam adopt California's view. We were also unsure that the government's position in this case comported with the policies of various federal lending agencies; hence, we requested information from the government regarding such policies, as well as relevant statistics on past lending practices. Armed with this information, and additional briefs, and having now had the benefit of further oral argument, we are more fully prepared to render our decision.

It is settled that the applicable law is federal. In a decision that has become a leading case on the question, United States v. View Crest Garden Apts., Inc., 9 Cir., 1959, 268 F.2d 380, 381, arising under the National Housing Act, Title II, 12 U.S.C. §1707 ff. we held: "But we do find it to be clear that the *source* of the law governing the relations between the United States and the parties to the mortgage here involved is federal. (Citations omitted) . . . It is therefore equally clear that if the law of the State of Washington is to have any application in the foreclosure proceeding it is not because it applies of its own force, but because either the Congress, the FHA, or the Federal Court adopts the local rule to further federal policy." 268 F.2d at 382.

The first question is whether the Congress adopted state law in its definition of "mortgage" and "first mortgage." California argues that it did. The language relied upon appears in 12 U.S.C. §1736(a), and reads: "The term 'mortgage' means a first mortgage on real estate, in fee simple, or on a leasehold (1) under a lease for not less than ninety-nine years which is renewable; or (2) under a lease having a period of not less than fifty years to run from the date the mortgage was executed; and the term 'first mortgage' means such classes of first liens as are commonly given to secure advances on, or the unpaid purchase price of, real estate, under the laws of the State in which the real estate is located, together with the credit instruments, if any, secured thereby."

We rejected California's argument in *View Crest,* supra, where identical language in 12 U.S.C. §1707 was relied upon. We said: "The argument is that in adopting the state definition of 'first mortgage,' Congress intended to adopt *all* the incidents of the mortgage relation under state law including remedies on default and the appointment of receivers. That this is not the case is clear from reading section 1713 of the same Act which defines certain acts as being in default (part g) and sets out certain remedies that the FHA can pursue such as institution of foreclosure (part k) proceedings without reference to whether or not there is such a remedy for the default described in the State where the property is located. Moreover, there is no apparent reason for assuming that Congress in incorporating by reference certain duties under state law also meant to restrict the United States to the state remedies for breach of those duties. . . ." 268 F.2d at 382.

We proceeded to point out the convenience inherent in defining "first mortgage" in terms of local law, thus making available local recording acts, and continued: "A different set of factors come into play when the planning stage and the working stages of the agreement have been terminated.

After a default the sole situation presented is one of remedies. Commercial convenience in utilizing local forms and recording devices familiar to the community is no longer a significant factor. Now the federal policy to protect the treasury and to promote the security of federal investment which in turn promotes the prime purpose of the Act — to facilitate the building of homes by the use of federal credit — becomes predominant. Local rules limiting the effectiveness of the remedies available to the United States for breach of a federal duty can not be adopted." 268 F.2d at 383.

We think that the validity of this approach is emphasized by the fact that the definition relied upon does *not* refer to state law in defining "mortgage"; it does so only in defining "first mortgage." And the statute now before us, like the statute considered in *View Crest*, defines default without reference to state law (12 U.S.C. §1743(c)) and provides for remedies without reference to state law (12 U.S.C. §1743(c)) and incorporating the provisions of §1713(k). No other federal statute is relied upon.[3]

We conclude that the Congress did not adopt state redemption statutes as part of the federal law.

The second question is, did the FHA adopt those statutes? California says that it did, relying on two arguments. First, it points to the regulations. 24 C.F.R. §580.18 provides: "The mortgage must contain a provision or provisions, satisfactory to the Commissioner, giving to the mortgagee, in the event of default or foreclosure of the mortgage, such rights and remedies for the protection and preservation of the property covered by the mortgage and the income therefrom, as are available under the law or custom of the jurisdiction." No similar provision exists for the mortgagor. Instead, 24 C.F.R. §580.21 merely provides: "The mortgage may contain such other terms, conditions and provisions with respect to . . . foreclosure proceedings . . . and other matters as the Commissioner may in his discretion prescribe or approve." To be eligible for insurance the mortgage must be executed on a form approved by the Federal Housing Commissioner. (4 C.F.R. §580.10.)

We cannot find in this language an adoption of state redemption statutes. If anything can be said for it, it is that §580.21 permits a provision against such rights.

Second, California points to the waiver language contained in the mortgage, quoted above in our statement of facts, and particularly to the phrase "to the extent permitted by law." This phrase, California says, must refer to Idaho law, because (1) there is no other law to which it can refer and (2)

---

3. 28 U.S.C. §2410(c) provides for a one-year post-sale right of redemption as a condition of jurisdiction over the United States when the United States is a junior lienor. This provision is made inapplicable to the National Housing Act by 12 U.S.C. §1701(k).

the mortgage form was prepared for use in Idaho. The argument is buttressed by the contention that there are no federal homestead or exemption laws, or rights to a stay, or redemption or moratorium laws. . . . We agree that such laws are state laws, but the question is, what law is referred to as permitting that their benefits be waived? It must be the law applicable to this mortgage, which is, as we have seen, federal law. And there is no federal law which says that FHA cannot condition its participation upon waiver of the benefit of such state laws. The provision is in general terms, applicable in any state; it is obviously not specifically adapted to Idaho law. We find the waiver provision merely precautionary, and not an adoption of the local law.

Finally, we come to the third question: should the federal courts adopt the local law granting a post-foreclosure sale right of redemption in those states where it exists? Here, both authority and policy convince us that they should not.

Every federal appellate case dealing with the government's foreclosure remedy under insured mortgages applies federal law to assure the protection of the federal program against loss, state law to the contrary notwithstanding. Most of the cases cite and apply the principles of *View Crest.* Many cases rely upon express provisions in the mortgage that are in conflict with local law, but frequently couch the decision in broader terms. Several of these cases involve appointment of a receiver pending foreclosure. One such case holds that the government can collect and retain the rents during the period of redemption (consented to by the government), contrary to local Idaho law. . . .

Many cases simply rely on principles of federal law, in the absence of directly applicable federal statutes or regulations.

Through all of these cases there runs a dominant rationale, that stated by us in *View Crest,* supra — "Now [after default] the federal policy to protect the treasury and to promote the security of federal investment which in turn promotes the prime purpose of the Act — to facilitate the building of homes by the use of federal credit — becomes predominant. *Local rules limiting the effectiveness of the remedies available to the United States for breach of a federal duty can not be adopted.*" (268 F.2d at 383, emphasis added.)

California relies heavily upon two cases, United States v. Yazell, 1966, 382 U.S. 341, 86 S. Ct. 500, 15 L. Ed. 2d 404, and Bumb v. United States, 9 Cir., 1960, 276 F.2d 729. We are convinced that the facts of these two cases are distinguishable.

Here, too, we deal with the remedy, and as we have seen, in every such case involving federally insured mortgages, the courts have applied federal law "for the protection of the treasury and to promote the security of the federal investment."

Reasons of policy dictate the same result. In the first place, only 26 of the states provide for post-foreclosure redemption. The periods of redemption vary widely.[4] So do other conditions to redemption and the rules governing right to possession, right to rents, making repairs, and other matters arising during the redemption period. . . . There is a split of authority as to whether the right of redemption can be waived. Similarly, there is a split of authority as to the right of the mortgagee to recover the value of improvements made during the redemption period. It would be contrary to the teaching of every case that we have cited to hold that there is a different federal policy in each state, thus making FHA "subject to the vagaries of the laws of the several states." Clearfield Trust Co. v. United States, 1943, 318 U.S. 363, 367, 63 S. Ct. 573, 575, 87 L. Ed. 838. Which policy is to be the federal policy, that of the states which do not provide for a period of redemption, or that of those which do? And if the policy is to be the latter, is it to embrace, in each state, all of the special rules applicable in that state alone? Is it to be expanded to establish a federal right of redemption in each state where none exists under local law?

In response to our request, the government has informed us of the views of federal agencies involved in the lending or insuring of funds for private housing purposes. These include, in addition to the Federal Housing Administration, the Farmers Home Administration of the Department of Agriculture, acting under 42 U.S.C. §1471 ff., and the Veterans Administration, acting under 38 U.S.C. §1800 ff. We quote the government's response: "The Farmers Home Administration, the Federal Housing Administration, and the Veterans Administration have informed us that their experience has indicated that the imposition of post-foreclosure-sale redemption periods makes the foreclosure remedy more costly and administratively time-consuming in those states whose local law so provides. Generally, the reasons given in support of this conclusion are . . . that existence of a post-sale period for redemption chills bidding at the foreclosure sale, forcing the United States to buy the property at the sale and to

---

4. The following is a list, supplied by the government, of the state laws imposing post-foreclosure redemption periods, other than Idaho, and the periods prescribed: "7 Alabama Code (Recomp. 1958) 727 (2 years); Alaska Statutes 09.45.190, 09.35.250 (1 year); 4 Ariz. Rev. Stat. 12-1282 (6 months); 3A Ark. Stat. 1947 Ann. 30-440 (1 year); Cal. Code Civ. Proc. 725a (1 year); Colorado Rev. Stat. (1963) 118-9-2 (6 months); 77 Ill. Ann. Stat. 18c (1 year); 4 Kan. Stat. Ann. 60-2414 (6 to 18 months); Kentucky Rev. Stat. 426.220 (1 year); 14 Maine Rev. Stat. Ann. 6204 (1 year); Mich. Stat. Ann. 27A.3140, M.C.L.A. §600.3140 (6 months); Minn. Stat. Ann. 580.23 (6 months); 29 Vernon's Ann. Mo. Stat. 443.410 (1 year); 7 Rev. Code Mont. 93-5836(2) (1 year); 1 Rev. Stat. 21.210 (1 year); 5 N. Mex. Stat. Ann. 24-2-19, 24-2-19.1 (9 months); 6 N. Dak. Cent. Code 32-19-18 (1 year); 1 Or. Rev. Stat. 23.560 (1 year); S.D. Comp. Laws (1967) 21-52-1 et seq. (1 year); Tenn. Code Ann. 64-801 (2 years); Utah Rules Civ. Proc., Rule 69 (f) (3) (6 months); 4 Vermont Stat. Ann. Title 12, App. III, Rule 39 (1 year); Rev. Code Wash. Ann. 6.24.140 (8 months or a year); Wyoming Stat. 1-480 (6 months).

Wisconsin postpones the foreclosure sale until a one year period for redemption after judgment has expired. Wisconsin Stat. Ann. 278.10(2)."

Basic Security Transactions

hold it (paying meanwhile the costs of maintenance) until the expiration of the period, when it finally can give good title to a purchaser." Additional reasons stated by the government are quoted [below].[7]

We do not find the policy arguments presented by California convincing. First, it is argued that the purpose of the redemption statutes is to force the mortgagee and others to bid the full market price at the sale. We assume that this is the purpose; we are not convinced that the statutes accomplish it. What third party would bid and pay the full market value, knowing that he cannot have the property to do with as he wishes until a set period has gone by, and that at the end of the period he may not get it, but instead may be forced to accept a payment which may or may not fully reimburse him for his outlays? In some states he cannot get possession. In some states if he does get possession and collects rents, they will be deducted from his reimbursement. . . . In some states, if he makes repairs, he will not be repaid for his outlays. These are precisely the problems which the federal government should not have to face. It is not in the real estate business. It should not have to hold and manage properties for any period longer than is absolutely necessary for it to get back its money. It should not be subjected to the risk that the property will deteriorate, and it should not be left with no means to protect itself against such losses.

---

7. "The Farmers Home Administration has stated that where post-sale redemption periods have been imposed, the mortgaged property may, after sale and before expiration of the redemption period, 'stand unoccupied and unattended for considerable periods of time and consequently [may] deteriorate substantially in value, to the detriment of the financial interest of the United States and without concomitant benefit to any other party.' Similarly, the Veterans Administration reported to us that where a post-sale redemption period is imposed unless the former owner redeems timely, the mortgagee or his assignee are obligated to pay holding costs during the redemption period, i.e., taxes, public improvements, if any, the cost of repairs to preserve the security and the cost of hazard insurance premium when necessary. There is also for consideration the interest normally accruing on the outstanding investment. Moreover, many of these properties have been abandoned and must remain vacant during redemption periods. In many instances they are subject to extreme vandalism during these periods which is, of course, costly to the holder.

"Most pertinent to the present case, of course, were the comments of the Federal Housing Administration concerning foreclosures on multi-family projects like that involved here. The Federal Housing Administration reported to us: 'It is perhaps the normal situation to find any project in foreclosure to be in need of substantial repair. Many mortgagors, during a period of diminishing income, utilize the net income to keep the mortgage current as long as possible, keeping maintenance expenses to a bare minimum. When the evil day arrives that the income will no longer cover the mortgage payments, he falls into default, and the subject of the foreclosure action is a property which requires substantial expenditures to place it in properly habitable condition, and to make it attractive to the rental market. With the notable exception of Alabama, redemption statutes permit a foreclosure purchaser to receive from a redemptioner little more than the price bid at the foreclosure sale, so that a purchaser is well advised to keep rehabilitation expenses to an absolute minimum until the redemption period expires. As a practical matter, this delays the day when FHA, as such purchaser can safely embark on a program involving capital expenditures, thereby delaying the day when the property may be placed in condition for its best use and for advantageous sale which will reimburse the insurance fund for a portion of the loss incurred as a result of the mortgagor's default.'"

Our doubts as to whether the statutes accomplish the purpose is reinforced by the fact that in many states, partly because of those statutes, real estate financing is almost exclusively secured by trust deeds with power of sale. This is certainly true in California, and the statutory right of redemption does not apply to such sales. One is tempted to inquire why, if public policy so strongly favors a post-sale period of redemption, the legislature has not applied it to sales under trust deeds? Perhaps it is because the redemption statute has, in some states, made the use of mortgages almost a dead letter.

Moreover, the policy of FHA is to bid the fair market value at the foreclosure sale. For this purpose, it has the property carefully appraised before bidding. See Book 2, Volume VII, Sec. 72926 of the FHA Manual. It is authorized by 12 U.S.C. §1713(k) to "bid any sum up to but not in excess of the total unpaid indebtedness secured by the mortgage, plus taxes, insurance, foreclosure costs, fees, and other expenses. . . ." It bids fair market value for its own protection as well as that of the mortgagor and other lienors. It is limited to the amount specified because the objective is to recover its loss on the mortgage insurance, not to put the government in the business of buying and speculating in real property. Presumably, if the property is worth more, others will increase the bid, the government will be paid in full, and the excess will go to junior lien holders and, if there be sufficient funds, to the mortgagor.

It is also suggested that a purpose of the redemption statutes is to protect junior lienors. Perhaps. But if the objective of the statutes is to obtain bids equal to market value, and if as is argued, the bidding would be lower in the absence of the statutes, then junior lienors could more easily protect themselves in the latter situation. They could buy the property at the sale for less. It is always open to the junior lienors to protect themselves by bidding. They take with notice of the senior lien. Here, the government's judgment was for $93,804.97; its bid was $55,100. The court found the value of the property to be $58,000. The deficiency judgment is for $37,728.88. This is a singularly inappropriate case in which to be concerned about junior lien holders. They simply have no equity in the property. There is no evidence that second mortgagees or contractors are less willing to extend credit on the security of junior liens in the states that have no redemption statutes than they are in the states that do, or in California when the first lien is almost always secured by a trust deed rather than by a mortgage.

Nor is it accurate to say that the application of state redemption rights does not tie up government funds; as this case illustrates, it does do so. Under 12 U.S.C. §1743(c) the mortgagee has the option of assigning the mortgage to the Secretary and being paid the full amount of the guarantee, instead of itself foreclosing. As might be expected, that is what Prudential did in this case. Why would any mortgagee do otherwise, when by so assigning it can receive the full benefit of the insurance without having to incur the expense and risk attendant upon foreclosure? Under the statute, Prudential received the full benefit of the insurance — government obligations equal to the then total value of the mortgage, in this case more than $90,000. If the redemption period applies, the government must wait a year to get its money back — and it may not then get it all, or even as much as it bid.

We conclude that the Idaho statute providing for right of redemption is not here applicable.

Finally, we note that the district court's decision did not purport to balance state and federal policies in allowing the period of redemption. Instead, it reasoned that Prudential (the original mortgagee) would have been subject to the redemption rights provided by state law, and that the United States could have no more rights than Prudential. Even assuming arguendo that Prudential would have been subject to state law, it does not follow that the federal government is limited to the remedies of the private mortgagee.

That portion of the judgment providing for a right and period of redemption is reversed and the matter is remanded to the district court with directions to modify the judgment in a manner consistent with this opinion.

ELY, Circuit Judge (dissenting): I respectfully dissent. The majority, with broad strokes, erases highly significant redemptive rights created by statute in the Territory of Guam and eight of the states comprising our Circuit as well as equitable rights of redemption hitherto applied by the courts of Hawaii. These rights are deeply rooted in history, founded on an equitable principle applied through centuries to protect the temporarily disadvantaged without working significant prejudice against his creditor. The approach which I take is made, not only in the interests of local mortgagors involved in the federal housing program, but also in the interests of the federal program itself. I do not dispute the fact that federal abrogation of state-created rights is often necessary for the protection of federal programs, but I have been unable to accept the majority's proposition that its dramatic result is here warranted by an overpowering motive of federal self defense. Time after time, the Congress of the United States has created programs through which private loans are guaranteed by the federal government. In not one of those programs has Congress ever prescribed that, in connection with those programs, state redemptive rights, either statutory or equitable, are eliminated. To me it is inconceivable that the members of Congress, when they enacted the many federal lending programs now extant, were either ignorant of, or blind to, the existence of state redemptive rights in foreclosure proceedings. When the Country's legislators have apparently deemed it unnecessary, in protecting the interests of the federal government, to strike down the states' rights in question, I think it presumptuous that a federal court should substitute its policy judgment to the contrary. My Brother Duniway's opinion, while written with his characteristic scholarship and technical precision, does not, insofar as I can see, demonstrate the existence of any controlling precedent requiring the conclusion which is reached. In this light, as well as in that of other considerations which I shall discuss, I respectfully submit that the majority's opinion constitutes an unnecessary intrusion into the legitimate local affairs of nine western states, and of the Territory of Guam, and moreover, represents an unwarranted judicial usurpation of federal legislative power.

I can accept the assumption that federal law is controlling. United States v. View Crest Garden Apts., Inc., 268 F.2d 380 (9th Cir. 1959). But my proposition is that we should give effect to the pertinent and equitable state law by incorporating it into the federal program. The Supreme Court did exactly that with respect to a state coverture law in United States v. Yazell, 382 U.S. 341, 86 S. Ct. 500, 15 L. Ed. 2d 404 (1966), and our court did the same with respect to a state "bulk sale" statute in Bumb v. United States, 276 F.2d 729 (9th Cir. 1960). The controlling criterion on the question is whether the state law can be given effect without either conflicting with federal policy or destroying needed uniformity in the pertinent federal law in its operation within the various states. United States v. Yazell, supra at 352, 86 S. Ct. 500. Thus, we should first reach an understanding of the purpose and effects of state redemption statutes.

The statutes can best be understood through a brief review of their historical development. The original method of mortgage foreclosure was known as strict foreclosure, a method whereby, on default, the mortgagee obtained a court decree awarding the mortgagor's interest in the security to the mortgagee. This offensive procedure was subject to severe defects, the most obvious of which was that the mortgagor faced the possibility of forfeiting all his equity in the property in the event that the property was worth more than the unpaid balance on the debt.

The harshness of strict foreclosure led to the concept of foreclosure by sale. Theoretically, the property was to be sold to the highest bidder with the mortgagee having first claim to the proceeds and the mortgagor obtaining his equity in the form of whatever surplus remained. This approach was expected to yield more even results by allowing the competitive market to set the value of the land instead of the "value" being set at the amount of the unpaid debt as was the fact under strict foreclosure. Unfortunately, this expectation was frustrated by reason of the immense advantages favoring the mortgagee at the sale. First, it was unnecessary for the mortgagee to raise and expend any cash up to the amount of the unpaid debt. Secondly, there would not often be an interested outside buyer, or junior lienholder with cash, at the precise time of the sale. Thus, the senior mortgagee was assured of being almost always the only bidder at the sale. The junior lienors, in particular, suffered under this method since their interests were cut off by judicial sale. Since they had no weapons with which to force the sale price above the amount of the senior's claim, they often realized nothing on their claims.

The response of many jurisdictions to the unsatisfactory results of the foreclosure-by-sale procedure was the adoption of a statutory redemption period. The basic design of statutory redemption consists of giving the mortgagor and those claiming under him (including junior lienors) the right to redeem the property from the purchaser at the sale within a specified period by paying, *not* the balance of the debt secured, but the price paid at the sale. The objective of the redemption right is that the mortgagee or other bidders, if any, shall bid not less than the fair market value of the land, since otherwise the purchaser risks being divested of the land by redemption at less than its market value.

The key to understanding the statutory redemption right lies in the proposition that the statute's operation is in the nature of a threat. When redemption is exercised, it is thereby evidenced that the mortgagee has not bid adequately at the sale and the statute has not had its intended effect. On the other hand, if the threat functions successfully and the mortgagee does bid adequately, then the mortgagor and junior lienors, if any, will have been satisfied to the full value of the property and there will be no reason for exercising the redemption right. If he bids the full market value of the property, then the mortgagee may rest secure in the knowledge that it will not be redeemed. See generally Durfee & Doddridge, Redemption From Foreclosure Sale, 23 Mich. L. Rev. 825, 827-834 (1925); Note, Redemption From Judicial Sales, 5 U. Chi. L. Rev. 625, 626 (1938).

With the foregoing as background, the relation of redemption statutes to the federal housing policies can be more clearly analyzed. The particular program involved here, War Housing Insurance, is only one of many administered under various Acts of Congress. This program, as the majority notes, is designed to stimulate housing for veterans; other programs are designed for rural housing, poverty relief, urban renewal, etc. All of the programs have as their basic goal the stimulation of construction by guaranteeing that lenders, contractors, and suppliers will not suffer losses on extending credit to builders and owners. Of course, some programs are more concerned with the owners and their need for housing than they are with the market for mortgages. This would be true, for instance, of a program designed to supply single-family housing while it would not be as crucial a consideration in the construction of multiple dwelling units. Thus, protection of the mortgagor's interests takes on greater or less significance depending on the type of program involved. It seems crystal clear to me, however, that the type of balancing involved in deciding what rights the mortgagor should have requires legislative attention to the entire scope of housing programs. I will deal with the Congress' role in this question later.

It seems no less clear to me that, disregarding the question of protection of the individual mortgagor, the goals of *any* federal housing program could not be served by the majority's decision. From the viewpoint of a mortgagor in a state with redemption provisions, and in the light of the majority's decision, it would be more desirable to finance privately than to finance through an FHA guaranteed mortgage. Even more important, potential junior lienors, such as contractors and suppliers, will be less willing to extend credit under these circumstances. Nor can junior lienors protect themselves, as the majority suggests, by bidding at the foreclosure sale. I have already explained that one reason for the existence of the redemption statutes is that the enormous leverage of the foreclosing mortgagee is not matched by junior lienors, who typically have very small cash reserves and never have the first "paid up" interest.

Thus one effect of the majority's decision will be to lower the attractiveness of FHA financing in states that have enacted redemption statutes. Other states have other methods of protecting both mortgagors and junior lienors that will not be matched in the redemption states.[1] Therefore, the uniformity among the states for which the Government argues cannot possibly be furthered by the majority's decision. Instead, uniformity would be furthered by conforming federal programs with state law.

The Government, and also the majority, make several arguments designed to show that redemption statutes are neither important nor necessary. The first is that the statutes do not work because no third party will bid at the sale, knowing that he will be subject to redemption. The statutes, as I have tried to explain, are not the least bit concerned with the actions of third parties since they were necessitated by the observation that third parties do not ordinarily bid at foreclosure sales in any event. Instead of trying to stimulate bidding at the sale, they set up the more realistic possibility that the property will be redeemed if the mortgagee's bid is inadequate.

The majority also asserts that redemption rights are unimportant because most financing in modern times is accomplished through the use of trust deeds, which do not provide for redemption rights. There may be valid reasons for the distinction,[2] but we need not be concerned with them here. What is important is that the legislatures of the states have allocated certain rights to each method of financing with the result that a choice is available depending on the nature of the transaction and the needs of the parties. Once the parties have selected either method, they should accept all its consequences. Moreover, if redemption rights truly are of negligible importance, then it could be said that the Government has wasted much valuable time in pursuing a frivolous appeal!

---

1. Some states provide for a statutory appraisal and prohibit foreclosure for less than a certain percentage of that value, while other states depend on anti-deficiency legislation and upset prices. See Jones, Mortgages §1611(a).

2. Originally, the distinction lay in the conceptualistic notion that the grantor conveyed all his interest through the trust deed, so that, unlike a mortgagor, he had nothing on which to base a right of redemption. More recently, the distinction has been based on such facts as that creditors cannot obtain deficiency judgments when property is sold under a trust deed and that notice requirements are more extensive under trust deeds. See, e.g., Comment, Comparison of California Mortgages, Trust Deeds and Land Sale Contracts, 7 U.C.L.A. L. Rev. 83, 88 (1959); Comment, Trust Deeds: Suit Upon Note Before Security Has Been Exhausted, 20 Calif. L. Rev. 318, 321 (1932).

The Government argues at one point that the policies of the redemption right are satisfied by the alleged practice of the FHA carefully to appraise the fair market value of the property and to make its bid accordingly at the foreclosure sale. It is interesting to note that the Government argues elsewhere that the effect of redemption statutes is to *depress* bidding at the sale. But it is even more interesting, and remarkable, that a federal statute expressly prohibits the agency from bidding more than the unpaid balance on the debt! 12 U.S.C. §1713(k), as incorporated by 12 U.S.C. §1743(f).

Even if we assumed that the FHA contravened the prohibitory statute and was in some way bound to continue its asserted practice, such unilateral action of the FHA could not satisfy the premise of the redemption statutes. That premise is that the fair market value is realizable only through the interplay of competing economic forces. This premise is not satisfied by judicial sale because of the demonstrated falsity of the assumption, made by the majority, that a third party will come in to force the price up to market value at the sale. The fact that competing economic forces are necessary is amply shown in the case at bar, since the value of the land was set by the court according to the testimony of one Government witness. This value was less than one-half the original purchase price and far below the unpaid balance on the debt. The Government obtained a deficiency judgment for the difference between the set value and the unpaid debt. The Government then proceeded to buy in the property at the sale for an amount *less than the market value set by the court.*

Remaining unconvinced by the argument that the redemption statutes are unimportant and unnecessary, I can turn to other contentions made by the majority. The first is that the Government should not be required to maintain the premises during the redemption period. The majority asserts that the FHA does not have the manpower or the funds to place and keep the property in good repair, especially since the expense of improvements made by the purchaser-mortgagee is not recoverable as part of the redemption price. The first answer to this argument is that some redemption statutes specifically include the cost of upkeep and repair in the redemption price. E.g., Cal. Code Civ. Proc. §702. In addition, this is one element of redemption that could be molded to fit the Government's legitimate interests, as this court did in Clark Investment Co. v. United States, 364 F.2d 7 (9th Cir. 1966).

I note with some incredulity that the majority cites *Clark Investment* for the proposition that Idaho law requires deduction of collected rents from the redemption price. In *Clark Investment,* this court held that the Idaho law could not be applied to the United States when property is redeemed from it. That decision itself clearly shows that the right of redemption can be maintained without any harm to the FHA because the courts can tailor certain elements of redemption to the benefit of the United States.

Clark Investment also demonstrates that the FHA is not necessarily confined to the same risks and burdens that other financers face. For example, during the redemption period, it can actually make a profit on the property with no more burden on its manpower than any other purchaser would have. Moreover, there is no reason why the Government should not accept a large share of the risks mentioned by the majority. The very purpose of the entire federal housing program is to provide badly needed housing that could not otherwise exist. I cannot imagine why the United States would venture into such a program if it were not willing to accept risks, possibly even greater risks than would be accepted by the normal financing institution.

Nor am I persuaded that redemption periods inordinately tie up federal funds. Since the FHA is limited in its bid to the amount of the unpaid debt, it can expect to have property more valuable than that amount redeemed rather promptly. In the case of less valuable property, it will have to live with the fact that it is facing a loss, no matter what happens. One way in which this loss could be ameliorated would be to hold the property during the period of redemption, a period in which the agency can realize a valuable return on its money in the form of rents. If this is deemed to be too severe a burden upon the FHA, then the Congress is best equipped to recognize any such supposed burden and to relieve the agency from it.

Next, the Government argues, albeit weakly, that the issue is foreclosed by prior case law standing for the proposition that remedies under the federal housing programs must be uniform, without regard to the laws of the individual states. The cases cited by the Government do not support such a broad proposition. Principal reliance is on Clearfield Trust Co. v. United States, 318 U.S. 363, 63 S. Ct. 573, 87 L. Ed. 838 (1943), and United States v. View Crest Garden Apartments, 268 F.2d 380 (9th Cir. 1959). *Clearfield Trust* dealt with the question of what law should be applied to the case of a forged endorsement on a United States check. There, the Court noted that a single piece of commercial paper issued by the United States may easily be involved in several transactions in different states. Therefore, the possible confusions and uncertainty required a uniform rule that could be constructed by the courts. Here, we have a single transaction within a single state and there can be no uncertainty or divergence of results if the state law is applied.

View Crest Garden Apartments is much closer to the facts of this case, since it dealt with whether to apply state law in the appointment of a receiver after default on an FHA mortgage. The court relied principally on the distinction between the rights of the parties and the remedies available for the protection of those rights. After pointing out that Congress had adopted state laws for convenience in defining the rights of the parties, the court went on to note that after default the need for convenience had terminated and that the then paramount interest was furtherance of the policies of the act by attempting to insure certainty of return on the investment. In the opinion's bearing on our case, certain of its language is remarkably significant. That language is, "It is urged that to hold that federal law applie[d] would result in great hardship to mortgagors who would thereby be deprived of all rights under state law such as the right of redemption. We do not think that such a conclusion necessarily follows. A court confronted with that question could determine it by weighing the federal interest against the particular local policy involved. *If the considerations weighed by the court suggest an adoption of local law, such as the local rule on redemption, that could be done.*" Id. at 383 (emphasis added).

Although the court in *View Crest* evidently believed that redemption is more in the nature of a right than a remedy (or means of cutting off a remedy), I prefer not to rest on a conclusionary use of labels. Accepting the court's guidance that the involved interests should be weighed, I fail to see in what way the state interest conflicts with the true and most praiseworthy interests of the federal government. Certainly the minor inconveniences suffered by the FHA in managing the property is outweighed by the benefit to the national program in protecting the interests of contractors and suppliers. Therefore, we need not balance national interest against state interest but could simply give effect to all the policy considerations underlying both federal and state law.

Finally, I come to the Government's lame contention that the failure of Congress to provide for redemption rights is the equivalent of an express provision that state redemption laws should not be recognized. The logical absurdity of this argument is, of itself, sufficient to subvert the contention. But the abundant statutory and regulatory language apparently adopting state law in this context should not be overlooked. For example, the statutory definition of the rights of the United States itself provides that "the term 'first mortgage' means such classes of first liens as are commonly given to secure advances on, or the unpaid purchase price of, real estate, *under the laws of the State, in which the real estate is located*, . . ." 12 U.S.C. §1707(a) (emphasis added). The regulations provide, "The mortgage must contain a provision or provisions, satisfactory to the Commissioner, giving to the mortgagee, in the event of default or foreclosure of the mortgage, such rights and remedies for the protection and preservation of the property covered by the mortgage and the income therefrom, *as are available under the law or custom of the jurisdiction.*" 24 C.F.R. §580.18 (1968) (emphasis added). Even the waiver in the present mortgage, on which the Government relied so strongly in the court below, provides that it is effective "to the extent permitted by law." Surely, we must presume that this language refers to the law of Idaho, for the federal law contains no such corresponding provisions to be waived or to which the waiver could be applicable.

At the very least, it seems unusual for the Government to argue that congressional silence can be equated with express abrogation of state-created rights. It is especially significant that, as we were informed on oral argument, the FHA has introduced several bills to achieve the result reached here, but Congress has consistently refused to adopt this approach. The Supreme Court has stated on more than one occasion that rights should not be displaced or eliminated without the clearest legislative mandate. United States v. Shimer, 367 U.S. 374, 81 S. Ct. 1554, 6 L. Ed. 2d 908 (1961); Mitchell v. Robert De Mario Jewelry, Inc., 361 U.S. 288, 80 S. Ct. 332, 4 L. Ed. 2d 323 (1960). I could not hold that silence on the part of Congress can be taken to effect an abrogation of time-honored state rights, derived from the most exalted principles of equity and so carefully designed, not only for the protection of debtors and creditors alike, but also for the promotion of the general economic welfare of the public at large.

I would affirm.

NOTES

1. In United States v. Ellis, 714 F.2d 953 (9th Cir. 1983), the Ninth Circuit Court of Appeals adopted as federal common law a State of Washington postforeclosure redemption right. The Washington statute permits redemption within one year of foreclosure sale. In the *Ellis* case, the Farmers Home Administration (FmHA) had made direct loans to a Washington farmer and the loans were secured by a mortgage. When the mortgagor defaulted on loan payments, FmHA foreclosed and the judgment specifically provided that the mortgagor would have no redemption rights; the district court relied principally on United States v. Stadium Apartments in so providing. On appeal by the mortgagor, the Ninth Circuit, in holding for the mortgagor on the redemption issue, said:

> Statutory rights of redemption give the mortgagor power to force the sale price closer to true market value. When sale at foreclosure is at an inadequate price, the purchaser (normally the mortgagee) runs the risk that the mortgagor or a junior lienor, given the additional time to arrange financing, will exercise his right. In order to avoid this risk the mortgagor will bid adequately. The mortgagee and junior lienors, if any, will then be satisfied to the true value of the property and there will be no reason for exercising the redemption right. See generally, *Stadium Apartments*, 425 F.2d at 368-69 (Ely. C.J., dissenting); Durfee & Doddridge, Redemption From Foreclosure Sale, 23 Mich. L. Rev. 825, 827-834 (1925).

> Considering the dynamics of foreclosure and redemption, we fail to see how adoption of state law in this case is inconsistent with the federal policy of helping farmers through financial difficulty. Allowing the government the unchecked powers of a credit bidder at foreclosure sale would appear to defeat that purpose. It also is apparent that those who supply farmers with equipment, fertilizer, seed and the like would be reluctant to provide those necessities on credit, as is commonly done, knowing that the government holds the power to force them, as junior lienors, to a loss in the event of

foreclosure. Farmers unable to operate on a cash basis would be forced from the field. The alternative would be to seek primary financing from private lenders at less attractive rates than offered by the FmHA. Either result is inconsistent with the federal policy of strengthening the farming segment of the economy.

In the *Ellis* case do you believe that the Ninth Circuit should have gone further and overruled *Stadium Apartments* as to postforeclosure redemption rights whenever the United States government or a federal agency forecloses a mortgage in a state that permits postforeclosure redemption?

2. Since the *Stadium Apartments* case was decided, the Ninth Circuit Court of Appeals has considered other mortgage matters in which it has had to decide whether or not to adopt state debtor-protection requirements when the federal government has been the creditor. In some instances, state debtor protections have been imposed; in others, they have not been. Holding that state debtor protections should be applied are United States v. Crain, 589 F.2d 996 (9th Cir. 1979), Arizona guarantor protection law held applicable to an action by the Small Business Administration to recover from guarantor of a mortgage debt without first proceeding against the mortgage security; United States v. MacKenzie, 510 F.2d 39 (9th Cir. 1975), Nevada limited-deficiency statute and Arizona redemption rights held applicable to foreclosing of security for a Small Business Administration loan; and United States v. Stewart, 523 F.2d 1070 (9th Cir. 1975), California antideficiency statute held applicable to the Veterans Administration that on default had sold its security for less than the amount due. Holding state restrictions not applicable are United States v. Haddon Haciendas Co., 541 F.2d 777 (9th Cir. 1976), California antideficiency statute not applied against the federal government in a waste claim as to FHA insured property; and Branden v. Driver, 441 F.2d 1171 (9th Cir. 1971) California antideficiency statute not applied to a Veterans Administration loan situation. Is Judge Ely's statutory interpretation argument in his *Stadium Apartments* dissent weakened by Congressional failure to legislate following the above line of Ninth Circuit cases, including United States v. Ellis?

3. A consequence of the federal government's vast real estate credit support and loan activities is its major involvement with mortgage defaults, including foreclosing of mortgages and acquisition and sale of foreclosed properties. Each year federal agencies bring thousands of foreclosure proceedings and they continuously hold a large inventory of land parcels that they have purchased at foreclosure sales or have otherwise acquired when mortgagors have defaulted. On the government's problems with defaulted properties see Daniel, What's the Best Way to Handle Foreclosed Properties? HUD Seeks the Answer as the Default and Foreclosure Figures Climb, 32 J. Housing 323 (1975). And see HUD: The Reluctant Homeowner, 3 HUD Challenge 20 (Jan. 1972).

d. Deficiency Judgments

A real estate mortgage transaction involves the transfer of an interest in land by the mortgagor to the mortgagee as security for payment of a debt. The mortgagor has promised to pay the debt and has in addition provided the mortgagee with security to back up that promise. If the mortgagor defaults, the mortgagee generally can resort to the security through foreclosure, and if this fails to produce enough to pay the amount due, the mortgagee can obtain a deficiency judgment against the mortgagor for the balance still owed. Of course, if foreclosure produces more than what the mortgagor owes, the mortgagor is entitled to the excess. In case of default by the mortgagor, a mortgagee commonly may, but seldom will, sue on the debt without seeking resort to the security.

In some states deficiency judgments have been highly controversial and restrictions have been placed on mortgagees obtaining such judgments. These restrictions, many of them originating in the depression of the 1930s, reflect popular feeling that mortgage debtors who lose their homes or farms or other lands, especially in adverse economic times, have lost enough and should not be subject to further liability on the underlying debts. It is also felt that foreclosure sales frequently do not bring fair market prices, being forced sales often in depressed periods; hence their prices should not be the basis for determining deficiencies. Deficiency judgment restrictions are mostly statutory and take different forms, such as no deficiency judgment if a certain type of mortgage is foreclosed — a purchase money or nonjudicial power of sale mortgage, for example; or the deficiency may only be sought in a foreclosure proceeding; or the deficiency must be based on a separate determination of fair or reasonable value of the foreclosed property rather than on the foreclosure sale price. Antideficiency legislation varies considerably among the states, and many states have no serious deterrents to a mortgagee securing a deficiency judgment, plus accrued interest and foreclosure expenses, whenever a foreclosure sale price is insufficient to pay off the mortgage debt.

New York Real Property Actions Law
§1371 (McKinney 1979)

1. If a person who is liable to the plaintiff for the payment of the debt secured by the mortgage is made a defendant in the action, and has appeared or has been personally served with the summons, the final judgment may award payment by him of the whole residue, or so much thereof as the court may determine to be just and equitable, of the debt remaining

unsatisfied, after a sale of the mortgaged property and the application of the proceeds, pursuant to the directions contained in such judgment, the amount thereof to be determined by the court as herein provided.

2. Simultaneously with the making of a motion for an order confirming the sale, provided such motion is made within ninety days after the date of the consummation of the sale by the delivery of the proper deed of conveyance to the purchaser, the party to whom such residue shall be owing may make a motion in the action for leave to enter a deficiency judgment upon notice to the party against whom such judgment is sought or the attorney who shall have appeared for such party in such action. Such notice shall be served personally or in such other manner as the court may direct. Upon such motion the court, whether or not the respondent appears, shall determine, upon affidavit or otherwise as it shall direct, the fair and reasonable market value of the mortgaged premises as of the date such premises were bid in at auction or such nearest earlier date as there shall have been any market value thereof and shall make an order directing the entry of a deficiency judgment. Such deficiency judgment shall be for an amount equal to the sum of the amount owing by the party liable as determined by the judgment with interest, plus the amount owing on all prior liens and encumbrances with interest, plus costs and disbursements of the action including the referee's fee and disbursements, less the market value as determined by the court or the sale price of the property whichever shall be the higher.

3. If no motion for a deficiency judgment shall be made as herein prescribed the proceeds of the sale regardless of amount shall be deemed to be in full satisfaction of the mortgage debt and no right to recover any deficiency in any action or proceeding shall exist. . . .

NOTES

1. The New York statute both confirms the mortgagee's right to a deficiency and limits the deficiency to the difference between the amount of claim and the "fair and reasonable market value," not to the difference between the amount of claim and the foreclosure sale price. In practically every state the mortgagee may obtain a judgment for a deficiency — usually without benefit of statute. Through the years, however, courts and legislatures have devised methods to protect the debtor from being victimized by superficial bidding at the sale. There are, of course, provisions for the giving of notice, the time, place, manner and terms of conducting the sale. A court of equity may refuse to confirm a sale or may set it aside upon evidence of chilled bidding or upon a showing of inadequacy so gross as to "shock the conscience or raise a presumption of fraud or unfairness." See

Ballentyne v. Smith, 205 U.S. 285 (1907). Where foreclosure is by power of sale, the mortgagee is not permitted to buy unless the mortgagor has given his consent or, under some statutes, a public officer conducts the sale. Nearly half the states allow the mortgagor (and junior lienors) to redeem from the foreclosure sale upon payment of the sale price plus specified interest; these *statutory rights to redeem*, dating back to the panic of 1837, were intended to dissuade a perfunctory bid on the theory that too low a price would invite redemption. (Since the redemption period may run six months or longer, redemption may cause the very lackluster interest on the part of potential bidders it was expected to prevent.)

The depression of the 1930s gave new impetus to the effort to protect mortgage debtors, for even in normal times the result of a forced sale does not usually reflect the "reasonable" market value of the property. Some states, like New York, abandoned the sale price as the presumptive measure of fair value and forced the mortgagee who was seeking the deficiency judgment to prove "fair and reasonable market value." Fine in theory, except during the 1930s no market existed. Wrestling with this conundrum, some lower courts went back to pre-depression values, until the New York Court of Appeals held that the statute intended to set up a new "equitable standard" in lieu of market value, in which market transactions, if any, were only one item. See Heiman v. Bishop, 272 N.Y. 83, 4 N.E.2d 944 (1936). The values found on the new test were said to approximate tax assessments. See Friedman, Personal Liability on Mortgage Debts in New York, 51 Yale L.J. 382, 396 (1942).

The United States Supreme Court has approved the New York statute both as an emergency measure — Honeyman v. Jacobs, 306 U.S. 539 (1939) — and as a permanent provision applying to existing and future mortgages — Gelfert v. National City Bank, 313 U.S. 221 (1941). In both cases, however, the purchaser was also the mortgagee. Should the result be different if the purchaser is a third party?

2. Military personnel are entitled to the benefits of The Soldiers' and Sailors' Civil Relief Act of 1940, 50 U.S.C. app. §§501-591 (1981 & Supp. I 1983). This law tolls the statute of limitations during military service, permits the mortgagor to reopen foreclosure after his release from duty on proof of a meritorious defense, and authorizes a court to stay foreclosure or execution on a money judgment. The serviceman must be able to show, however, that military service has "materially affected" his ability to meet his debts or to defend an action. See Goldman, Collection of Debts Incurred by Military Personnel: The Creditor's View, 10 Tulsa L.J. 537 (1975); and Osborne, Nelson & Whitman, Real Estate Finance Law §§8.8-8.10 (1979).

3. Deficiency judgments are possible with strict foreclosure, as is illustrated by a Connecticut statute providing for a judicial valuation and deficiency judgment on motion after the time for redemption has expired. Conn. Gen. Stat. Ann. §49-14 (West Supp. 1984).

Ross Realty Co. v. First Citizens Bank & Trust Co.
296 N.C. 366, 250 S.E.2d 271 (1979)

Plaintiff instituted this action to recover from defendant $106,601.86 plus interest, the amount allegedly due on a promissory note executed by defendant in favor of plaintiff. In its answer defendant admitted execution of the note but alleged that it was given to secure the balance of the purchase price of real estate and that defendant had offered to reconvey the real estate to plaintiff.

Pursuant to stipulations entered into between the parties, the trial court found facts summarized in pertinent part as follows:

(1) Plaintiff is a corporation organized and existing under the laws of the State of North Carolina with its office and principal place of business in Mecklenburg County. Defendant is a North Carolina banking corporation having an office in Mecklenburg County. Defendant is trustee of the Profit Sharing Retirement Plan and Trust of Thermo Industries, Inc., and affiliated companies.

(2) By deed dated 25 March 1974 and duly recorded on 19 June 1974 in Mecklenburg County Registry, plaintiff conveyed to defendant certain real estate located in the City of Charlotte. As part of the purchase price for said real estate, defendant executed under seal a note for the balance of the purchase price for said real estate, payable to the order of plaintiff, in the amount of $126,000. Said note provided by its terms that it was for the balance of purchase money on real estate.

(3) To secure plaintiff seller the payment of the balance of said purchase price, a purchase money deed of trust conveying said real estate as security for payment of said note was executed by defendant; said deed of trust is dated 1 April 1974 and was duly recorded in Mecklenburg County Registry on 19 June 1974. F.T. Miller, Jr., is named trustee in said deed of trust which by its terms provides that it secures a note which is for the balance of the purchase money of the real estate.

(4) Defendant failed to make the payment which was due on 1 October 1976 and refuses to make any further payments on the note aforesaid. Plaintiff is still the owner and holder of the note and deed of trust aforesaid.

(5) Prior to the commencement of this action defendant tendered to plaintiff, in lieu of foreclosure, a deed to convey to plaintiff all the interests of defendant in the real estate embraced in the deed of trust.

(6) Plaintiff refused to accept the deed offered in lieu of foreclosure.

(7) Said note and deed of trust were given as payment for and security for the balance of the purchase price of the real estate referred to in the deed and deed of trust aforesaid.

The trial court concluded as a matter of law that the provisions of G.S. 45-21.38 are inapplicable to the subject matter of this action; that this action was brought solely to effect collection of the balance due on a purchase money note without recourse to or foreclosure of the deed of trust securing the same; that G.S. 45-21.38 "abolished deficiency judgments arising out of the sale of real property securing a balance purchase money note; however, in this case, such security was abandoned, resulting in there being no foreclosure and no sale of said real estate."

The court rendered judgment against defendant for the amount prayed and defendant appealed. . . .

BRITT, Justice. Defendant contends the Court of Appeals erred in affirming the trial court's conclusion of law that the provisions of G.S. 45-21.38 are inapplicable to the subject matter of this action and in entering judgment based on that conclusion. We think the contention has merit.

G.S. 45-21.38 provides in pertinent part as follows:

> Deficiency judgments abolished where mortgage represents part of purchase price. — In all sales of real property by mortgagees and/or trustees under powers of sale contained in any mortgage or deed of trust executed after February 6, 1933, or where judgment or decree is given for the foreclosure of any mortgage executed after February 6, 1933, to secure to the seller the payment of the balance of the purchase price of real property, the mortgagee or trustee or holder of the notes secured by such mortgage or deed of trust shall not be entitled to a deficiency judgment on account of such mortgage, deed of trust or obligation secured by the same: Provided, said evidence of indebtedness shows upon the face that it is for balance of purchase money for real estate. . . .

Decision in this case depends upon the interpretation or construction of the quoted statute. "In the interpretation of statutes, the legislative will is the all-important or controlling factor. Indeed, it is frequently stated in effect that the intention of the legislature constitutes the law. Accordingly, the primary rule of construction of statutes is to ascertain and declare the intention of the legislature, and to carry such intention into effect to the fullest degree. A construction adopted should not be such as to nullify, destroy, or defeat the intention of the legislature." 73 Am. Jur. 2d Statutes §145, p. 351.

Through the years this court has adhered to the principle that the legislative intent is a controlling factor in the construction of statutes. "The object of all interpretation of statutes is to ascertain the meaning and intention of the Legislature. . . ."

In State v. Bell, 184 N.C. 701, 705, 115 S.E. 190 (1922), this court in construing a statute relating to the abandonment of children said: "In our endeavor to ascertain the purpose of the statute, we should also have due regard to the rule that the spirit and reason of the law shall prevail over its letter, especially where a literal construction would work an obvious injustice. (Citations.)" . . .

While the statute now codified as G.S. 45-21.38 is not artfully drawn, we think the manifest intention of the Legislature was to limit the creditor to

Basic Security Transactions

the property conveyed when the note and mortgage or deed of trust are executed to the seller of the real estate and the securing instruments state that they are for the purpose of securing the balance of the purchase price.

We have found very helpful an article (cited in the Amicus briefs) by Professors Brainerd Currie and Mark S. Lieberman appearing in the 1960 Duke Law Journal, pages 1 et seq. We quote a portion of the article:

> Nothing in the way of conventional legislative history is available to shed light on the purpose of the legislation. There are no committee reports and no record of the legislative debates; even contemporary editorial comment is lacking. We are not, however, entirely without evidence on which to base a judgment. The year 1933 was one of deep depression, and North Carolina, along with other states, was concerned with the economic distress associated with wholesale mortgage foreclosures. The act which has been quoted—chapter thirty-six of the Laws of 1933—was the first in a series of legislative attempts at the same session to deal with the mortgage problem. It was enacted on February 6. On February 9, the legislature approved a joint resolution requesting a voluntary moratorium until November 1, 1934, on all principal payments secured by mortgages on farm lands and homes, so long as interest and taxes were paid. On April 18, chapter 275 was enacted, dealing rather comprehensively with the foreclosure problem. Section one empowered the courts, prior to confirmation of any foreclosure sale of real estate, to enjoin the sale or its confirmation on the ground that the amount bid or price offered was inadequate and inequitable and would result in irreparable damage. Section two authorized the courts, prior to confirmation, to order resale upon such terms as might be just and equitable. Section three provided that in suits for deficiency judgments after the exercise of a power of sale, the mortgagor, if the holder of the obligation was the purchaser at the sale, could defend by showing that the property was fairly worth the amount of the debt secured by it at the time and place of sale. All of these provisions applied to existing mortgages; they included, without being limited to, purchase-money mortgages. On May 15, the time within which actions for deficiencies might be brought was limited to one year from the date of sale. Currie and Lieberman, Purchase-Money Mortgages and State Lines: A Study in Conflict-of-Laws Method, 1960 Duke Law Journal 1, 11-12.

Most of the enactments mentioned now appear in Chapter 45, Article 2B of the General Statutes. The writers of the article concluded, among other things, that the 1933 General Assembly intended to protect vendees from oppression by vendors and mortgagors from oppression by mortgagees. Moreover, the authors examined the specific problem which this court confronts in the case sub judice.

> [T]he legislature was concerned about the situation in which the vendor finances the sale, and was particularly concerned for the protection of the purchaser in that situation. The question may well be asked: If that was the

purpose, why confine the remedial statute to deficiency judgments when the mortgagee could inflict substantially the same injury on the mortgagor simply by suing on the personal obligation. . . . The only answer is simply that legislatures do not always see the whole problem, and are not always astute to close all the loopholes. The evidence is strong that the legislature wanted to furnish protection to the purchaser where the vendor did the financing. The only alternative possibility is that there was something distasteful about the action to recover a deficiency under a purchase-money mortgage, as an action, which was not shared by actions on personal obligations, suits for specific performance, and actions to recover mortgage deficiencies brought by third-party mortgagees. This is manifestly absurd. . . . [T]he policy was one of protecting the purchaser where the vendor did the financing; the North Carolina legislature simply did not do an efficient job of insuring the effectiveness of the policy. Id. at 23-24.

Where the Legislature has enacted a statute to achieve a specific aim, it is incumbent upon the court to construe the statute in a manner which effectuates that legislative purpose. In Underwood v. Howland, supra 274 N.C. at 478, 164 S.E.2d 2, 6 in an opinion by Huskins, J., this court said:

Furthermore, " . . . where a strict literal interpretation of the language of a statute would contravene the manifest purpose of the Legislature, the reason and purpose of the law should control, and the strict letter thereof should be disregarded. [Citations omitted.]"

Plaintiff relies very heavily on the opinion in Page v. Ford, 65 Or. 450, 131 P. 1013 (1913). Plaintiff correctly states that the Oregon court, construing an anti-deficiency statute similar if not identical to ours, held that their statute — literally construed — did not prevent the holder of a note given for the purchase price of the land, and secured by a mortgage, from disregarding the mortgage and bringing an action for personal judgment on the note. Plaintiff has urged us to construe G.S. 45-21.38 similarly, but this we refuse to do.

We do not attempt to distinguish our statute from that of Oregon, nor the facts in this case from those before the court in *Page*. We note only that the Oregon court, using the same approach to statutory construction employed by the Court of Appeals in its consideration of this case, mechanically construed the language of the statute while failing to attempt to determine the purpose which the Legislature sought to accomplish. We feel compelled to follow the long tradition of this court which is to ascertain, if possible, the intent of our Legislature in interpreting statutes and to respect the rule "that the spirit and reason of the law shall prevail over its letter."

Our conclusion that the Legislature did not intend to allow suit upon the note in purchase-money mortgage situations is also buttressed by what appears to have been the only contemporary commentary on the statute. In an article written by members of the faculty of the U.N.C. Law School a brief summary of the statute is followed by this observation: "The effect of this (the statute) is to limit the creditor to the property conveyed, when for the purchase money, changing in that respect the present statute. This applies only to such contracts as are made after the ratification of the Act, Feb. 6, 1933." A Survey of Statutory Changes in North Carolina in 1933, 11 N.C. Law Rev. 191, 219 (1933).

Furthermore, the procedure attempted by plaintiff in the case at hand would circumvent the spirit and purpose of the statute in question. The Court of Appeals acknowledges in its opinion that its literal construction of the statute creates an "anomalous situation" which enables a creditor to easily evade the effect of the statute. After obtaining judgment on a note, a plaintiff could foreclose the deed of trust, apply the proceeds from the sale to the judgment, and then proceed with execution against the judgment debtor's general assets. Or, a plaintiff could ignore the deed of trust and proceed with execution against the judgment debtor's assets including the real estate covered by the deed of trust. Clearly, the General Assembly did not intend to allow such circumvention.

In the recent case of State v. Shook, 293 N.C. 315, 317, 237 S.E.2d 843, 845 (1977), this court, in an opinion by Exum, J., construing G.S. 15A-943(b), said:

> We must, of course, construe the meaning of the statute in accordance with the ascertainable intent of the legislature. In re Arther, 291 N.C. 640, 231 S.E.2d 614 (1977); Stevenson v. City of Durham, 281 N.C. 300, 188 S.E.2d 281 (1972). In construing a statute to determine its legal effect, we may infer the legislative intent by looking to the purpose of the statute, the evils which it is designed to remedy and the effects of alternative constructions. In re Arthur, supra.

Having in mind the purpose for which G.S. 45-21.38 was adopted, the perceived problem which the statute seeks to remedy, and the effect which a literal construction of the statute produces, we are compelled to construe the statute more broadly and to conclude that the Legislature intended to take away from creditors the option of suing upon the note in a purchase-money mortgage transaction. This construction of the statute not only prevents its evasion, but also gives effect to the Legislature's intent.

Finally, plaintiff argues that a ruling against it in this case would place sellers of real estate at a serious disadvantage in the present-day market place. This argument is not persuasive. The seller still has the prerogative of determining the amount of the down payment as well as the amounts and due dates of the future payments; in case of default the seller gets the land back while the purchaser loses his down payment and any other payments made on the purchase price.

For the reasons stated, the decision of the Court of Appeals is reversed and this cause is remanded to that court who will order the judgment appealed from reversed and vacated.

Reversed.

NOTES

1. Should the literal meaning of a statute be followed by a court even though this leads to a result apparently inconsistent with the objective or purpose of the statute? Should courts correct what legislatures clearly provide for in their enactments?

2. Why does the North Carolina antideficiency statute apply to a purchase money mortgage or deed of trust but not to a mortgage or deed of trust if the lender is someone other than the seller? Are borrowers faced with unique risks relative to deficiencies in purchase money secured transactions?

3. California bars deficiency judgments when the security is sold pursuant to a power of sale in either a mortgage or deed of trust. Cal. Civ. Proc. Code §580(d) (West 1976). Why are deficiency judgments barred if these kinds of foreclosure sales have taken place?

4. Referring to some of the more restrictive antideficiency legislation, the Powell treatise states: "[This legislation] is a recognition of the modern shift in mortgage theory from a personal relationship predicated upon acquaintance and the believed solvency of the borrower, to an investment device largely handled by corporations. It is hoped that more states will enact similar statutes." 3 Powell, The Law of Real Property §473 (1985). Do you believe that antideficiency statutes are so desirable that more states should enact them?

In his article on mortgagees' remedies, Robert Lifton makes this statement: "Most commercial real estate loans are made against the value of the property. Only in special circumstances is the borrower's credit a factor in the loan. Consequently, most mortgage lenders surveyed for this article replied that they would willingly trade off the right to a deficiency judgment for faster and more effective foreclosure remedies." Lifton, Real Estate in Trouble: Lender's Remedies Need An Overhaul, 31 The Business Lawyer 1927, 1942 (1976). How, if at all, does this statement affect your conclusion as to the desirability of more antideficiency legislation?

e. Bankruptcy Considerations

Many mortgagors against whom foreclosure is being sought or recently has been obtained are insolvent and faced with the possibility or even probability of bankruptcy. Despite the protection provided by mortgagees holding security interests, bankruptcy can affect mortgagees' rights. This casebook is not the appropriate place to deal comprehensively and in detail with the relation of bankruptcy to the law of mortgages, but attention should be directed to some important respects in which bankruptcy can affect mortgage foreclosures. One respect is that bankruptcy proceedings may result in a stay of the mortgagee's right to initiate or continue foreclosure proceedings. These stays may be brief or lengthy but in some instances can last until the bankruptcy case is closed. Another important respect in which bankruptcy can affect mortgage foreclosures is that some mortgage foreclosure sales can be set aside as actually or constructively fraudulent if made within a year prior to the debtor's bankruptcy at a price that is not a fair equivalent for the property. Two controversial cases concerned with these aspects of bankruptcy are considered in the materials that follow.

Johnson v. First National Bank of Montevideo, Minnesota
719 F.2d 270 (8th Cir. 1983), cert. denied, 465 U.S. 1012, 104 S. Ct. 1015 (1984)

Ross T. ROBERTS, District Judge. This case presents a troublesome question concerning whether a bankruptcy court possesses the authority to toll or suspend the running of a statutory redemption period created by state law in connection with real estate mortgage foreclosures.

The First National Bank of Montevideo ("First National") appeals from an order of the District Court for the District of Minnesota. That District Court order affirmed a bankruptcy court order which enjoined First National from taking further action to foreclose a lien on certain real estate, and stayed the expiration of the redemption period allowed by Minnesota law. For the reasons set forth below we reverse the judgment of the district court, and remand for further proceedings consistent with this opinion.

The relevant facts are undisputed. Curtis H. Johnson and Gloria Jean Johnson ("debtors") are the principal officers and shareholders of Oak Farms, Inc., and Oak Farms Service Co., both Minnesota corporations engaged in agricultural business pursuits. In 1978 Oak Farms, Inc. executed a mortgage on certain parcels of real estate located in Yellow Medicine and Lac qui Parle counties, Minnesota, to secure a $300,000 promissory note in favor of First National. In 1979, Oak Farms, Inc., Oak Farms Service Co., and the Johnsons executed a second mortgage to First National on the same property to secure nineteen additional promissory notes totaling approximately $650,000. Each mortgage contained a clause allowing First National to sell the mortgaged property at public auction in the event of default.

Following the debtor's default in September of 1980, First National commenced foreclosure proceedings. A sheriff's auction was held on October 31, 1980, in conformity with the requirements of Minnesota statutes. At that auction First National purchased the mortgaged property for the sum of $566,355.34.

Minn. Stat. §580.23(2) provides that a mortgagor shall have twelve months following the sale of real estate within which to redeem the property by paying the sale price plus interest from the date of the sale. In this instance that redemption period would have expired on or about October 31, 1981. Approximately three weeks prior to the expiration date, however, without having redeemed the property, the debtors filed a joint petition for reorganization under Chapter 11 of the Bankruptcy Code (the "Code"), and an adversary complaint alleging, in part, that they had substantial equity in the mortgaged property and were entitled to an order staying the expiration of the redemption period.

At a hearing convened before the bankruptcy court on October 16, 1981, Curtis Johnson testified that he estimated the value of the mortgaged property at $2,720,000 and that the encumbrances against the property totaled $2,043,000. Based upon Johnson's testimony, on October 20, 1981, the bankruptcy judge found that "an exigency exists, and that the debtors have substantial equity in [the] real property." Upon these findings, he enjoined First National from taking any further action to foreclose the property and ordered that the running of the statutory redemption period be stayed until further order or until the bankruptcy cases concerning the property were closed, all pursuant to 11 U.S.C. §105.[3] On March 17, 1982, the district court affirmed the bankruptcy court's order.

This Court subsequently granted First National leave to appeal pursuant to 28 U.S.C. §1292(a), subject to reconsideration should it be determined that the grant of permission to appeal was improvident. We now conclude that this matter is properly before us for review under §1292(a)(1), which grants the courts of appeal jurisdiction over "appeals from . . . [i]nterlocutory orders of the district courts . . . granting, continuing, modifying, refusing or dissolving injunctions, or refusing to dissolve or modify injunctions. . . ."

The appropriate starting point for our analysis is to recognize the general rule that a bankruptcy court possesses only the jurisdiction and powers expressly or by necessary implication conferred by Congress. . . . Although a bankruptcy court is essentially a court of equity, . . . its broad equitable powers may only be exercised in a manner which is consistent with the provisions of the Code. . . .

The issue as to whether the broad powers granted the bankruptcy court by §105(a) — to "issue any order . . . necessary or appropriate to carry out the provisions of [the Code]" — empowers the court to suspend the running of a statutory period of redemption is a matter of first impression among the circuit courts. An examination of the reported decisions of

---

3. Subsection (a) of §105 provides as follows:
"The bankruptcy court may issue any order, process, or judgment that is necessary or appropriate to carry out the provisions of this title."

those district courts and bankruptcy courts which have considered the matter reveals a wide divergence of opinion.

Section 2(a)(15) of the Bankruptcy Act, from which §105(a) is derived, allowed a bankruptcy court to issue such orders as might be necessary to prevent the defeat or impairment of its jurisdiction and to protect the integrity of the bankruptcy estate. 2 Collier on Bankruptcy ¶105.01 at 105-1 et seq. (15th ed. 1983); see also, In Re Merritt Lumber Co., 336 F. Supp. 325 (E.D. Penn. 1971); In Re Northern Boneless Meat Co., 9 B.R. 27 (D.C.S.D.N.Y. 1981). Although §105(a) is in certain respects broader in scope than its predecessor, the general equitable powers granted to the bankruptcy court by the statute are not unlimited, particularly in instances where property rights created and defined by state law are involved.

Article I, section 8 of the United States Constitution provides that Congress shall have the power to establish uniform bankruptcy laws throughout the United States. Where Congress has chosen to exercise its authority, contrary provisions of state law must accordingly give way. It is equally well-settled, however, that state laws are suspended only to the extent of actual conflict with the bankruptcy system provided by Congress, so that in the absence of any conflict between the state and bankruptcy laws, the law of the state where the property is situated governs questions of property rights. . . .

The importance of state law in determining property rights was emphasized in Butner v. United States, 440 U.S. 48, 99 S. Ct. 914, 59 L. Ed. 2d 136 (1979), a case concerning whether the right to rents collected during the period between the mortgagor's bankruptcy and the foreclosure sale of the mortgaged property was to be determined by state law or by a federal rule of equity. Writing for a unanimous Court, Justice Stevens declared that in those areas where Congress has not chosen to define by statute the property rights of parties to a bankruptcy proceeding, state law is determinative:

> Property rights are created and defined by state law. Unless some federal interest requires a different result, there is no reason why such interests should be analyzed differently simply because an interested party is involved in a bankruptcy proceeding. Uniform treatment of property interests by both State and federal courts within a state serves to reduce uncertainty, to discourage forum shopping, and to prevent a party from receiving "a windfall merely by reason of the happenstance of bankruptcy." [citation omitted] 440 U.S. at 55, 99 S. Ct. at 918.

The Supreme Court did of course recognize in *Butner* that "[t]he equity powers of the bankruptcy court play an important part in the administration of bankrupt estates in countless situations in which the judge is required to deal with particular, individualized problems." 440 U.S. at 55-6, 99 S. Ct. at 918. From the fundamental principles embraced by the *Butner* opinion, however, as well as from the language of §105(a) itself, it follows that, absent a specific grant of authority from Congress or exceptional circumstances, a bankruptcy court may not exercise its equitable powers to create substantive rights which do not exist under state law. See In Re Perry, 25 B.R. 817, 821 (Bkrtcy. D. Md. 1982); In Re Dunckle Associates, Inc., 19 B.R. 481, 485 (Bkrtcy. E.D. Penn. 1982); and cf. In Re Trigg, 630 F.2d 1370, 1375 (10th Cir. 1980). To conclude otherwise, and thus to hold that a bankruptcy court may, as a matter of course, suspend the running of a statutory period of redemption pursuant to §105(a), would be to enlarge the debtor's property rights beyond those specifically set forth by the Minnesota legislature and by Congress in §108(b). Despite the broad equitable powers bestowed by §105(a), we therefore find ourselves in agreement with those courts which have held that §105(a) may not be invoked to toll or suspend the running of a statutory period of redemption absent fraud, mistake, accident, or erroneous conduct on the part of the foreclosing officer. In Re Martinson, 26 B.R. 648, 654 (D.C.D.N.D. 1983); Matter of Markee, 31 B.R. 429, 432 (Bkrtcy. D. Idaho 1983); In Re James, 20 B.R. 145, 150-1 (Bkrtcy. E.D. Mich. 1982); In Re Headley, 13 B.R. 295, 297-98 (Bkrtcy. D. Colo. 1981); but cf., Bank of Commonwealth v. Bevan, 13 B.R. 989 (D.C.E.D. Mich. 1981); Bank of Ravenswood v. Patzold, 27 B.R. 542 (D.C.N.D. Ill. 1982).

Although the bankruptcy court here did not purport to create a uniform rule that the redemption period is tolled whenever a petition in bankruptcy is filed, we cannot agree with the district court that the bankruptcy court's order was a proper exercise of its equitable authority to deal with a "particular, individualized problem" under the standards outlined above. The bankruptcy court, after hearing certain evidence found only "that an exigency exists, and that the debtors have substantial equity" in the property. One might well anticipate that in many instances the debtor will indeed enjoy substantial equity in the property in question. It is precisely this concern, however, which the Minnesota legislature addressed by providing for a one-year period of redemption. As will be developed in detail below, whatever "exigency" may be said to have existed due to the timing of the expiration of that period was susceptible to alleviation by the specific provisions of §108(b).[5] There is no claim that First National or any other party was guilty of any wrongdoing which adversely affected the debtors' ability to redeem the property within the statutory period.

---

5. Section 108(b) provides as follows:

(b) Except as provided in subsection (a) of this section, if applicable law, an order entered in a proceeding, or an agreement fixes a period within which the debtor or an individual protected under section 1301 of this title may file any pleading, demand, notice, or proof of claim or loss, cure a default, or perform any other similar act, and such period has not expired before the date of the filing of the petition, the trustee may only file, cure, or perform, as the case may be, before the later of—

(1) the end of such period, including any suspension of such period occurring on or after the commencement of the case; and

(2) 60 days after the order for relief.

"[E]quity is available to protect property rights of the innocent debtor from the wrongful acts of other persons; however, equity does not extend to situations in which the debtor is simply unable to make the required payment within the prescribed time." In Re Headley, supra at 297. Nor have the debtors identified any federal interest which would, under the spirit of *Butner,* justify interference with clearly expressed state law and thwart First National's reasonable expectation that, upon expiration of the redemption period, it would obtain full title to the property. Given these circumstances, we hold that the bankruptcy court erred in ordering that the running of the statutory period of redemption be stayed pursuant to §105(a).

Although the district court rested its decision solely upon §105(a), the potential application of two other statutes — namely, 11 U.S.C. §362(a)[6] and §108(b) — has been briefed and argued on appeal by the parties. Since an appellate court is entitled to affirm a district court's judgment on grounds other than those relied upon by the district court, Brown v. St. Louis Police Dept., 691 F.2d 393, 396 (8th Cir. 1982); Chambers v. Omaha Public School Dist., 536 F.2d 222, 227 (8th Cir. 1976), a complete disposition of the present appeal therefore requires us to determine whether the decision below may be sustained by virtue of either of these two statutes.

Courts which have considered the present question under §362(a) and §108(b) have been virtually unanimous in concluding that, upon the filing of a petition in bankruptcy by a debtor, one of the two sections operates to stay the expiration of a statutory redemption period. The courts are in sharp disagreement, however, as to which section is the fount of such authority, and as to the extent of the relief granted. One line of cases, anchored by In Re Jenkins, 19 B.R. 105 (D.C.D. Colo. 1982), and In Re Johnson, 8 B.R. 371 (Bkrtcy. D. Minn. 1981),[7] stands for the proposition

---

6. Section 362(a) provides in pertinent part as follows:

(a) Except as provided in subsection (b) of this section, a petition filed under section 301, 302, or 303 of this title operates as a stay, applicable to all entities, of —
   (1) the commencement or continuation, including the issuance or employment of process, of a judicial, administrative or other proceeding against the debtor that was or could have been commenced before the commencement of the case under this title, or to recover a claim against the debtor that arose before the commencement of the case under this title;
   (2) the enforcement, against the debtor or against property of the estate, of a judgment obtained before the commencement of the case under this title;
   (3) any act to obtain possession of property of the estate or of property from the estate;
   (4) any act to create, perfect, or enforce any lien against property of the estate;
   (5) any act to create, perfect, or enforce against property of the debtor any lien to the extent that such lien secures a claim that arose before the commencement of the case under this title. . . .

7. See also, Eaton Land & Cattle Co. v. Rocky Mountain Investments, 28 B.R. 890 (Bkrtcy. D. Colo. 1983); In Re Shea Realty, Inc., 21 B.R. 790 (Bkrtcy. D. Vt. 1982); In Re H & W Enterprises, Inc., 19 B.R. 582 (Bkrtcy. N.D. Ia. 1982); In Re Sapphire Investments, 19 B.R. 492 (Bkrtcy. D. Az. 1982); Matter of Dohm, 14 B.R. 701 (Bkrtcy. N.D. Ill. 1981).

that the automatic stay provisions of §362(a) should be liberally construed to suspend the running of a statutory period of redemption. Other decisions, holding to the contrary with respect to §362(a), have instead found that §108(b) is the sole applicable statute, and that its automatic extension of a redemption period provides the only relief available. See, e.g., In Re Martinson, supra; In Re Ecklund & Swedlund Development Corp., 17 B.R. 451 (Bkrtcy. D. Minn. 1981); In Re Owens, 27 B.R. 946 (Bkrtcy. E.D. Mich. 1983). We conclude that the latter group of cases more accurately construe the language and legislative history of the two sections.

Preliminary to an examination of §362(a), it is important to identify the debtors' remaining interest in mortgaged property following a foreclosure sale, and to determine whether that interest constitutes property of the bankruptcy estate.[8] It is long-settled under Minnesota law that foreclosure extinguishes the mortgage and that the purchaser at the foreclosure sale acquires a vested right to become the absolute owner of the property upon expiration of the redemption period, or, in lieu thereof, to receive the payment of the purchase price plus interest. In Re Klein, 9 F. Supp. 57, 59 (D. Minn. 1934); In Re Stacy, 9 F. Supp. 61, 64 (D. Minn. 1934), and cases cited therein. The mortgagor, on the other hand, retains only the equity of redemption, plus the rights to possession, rents, and profits of the property during the period of redemption. Id. Accordingly, it is only the right of redemption, rather than the property itself, which passes into the bankruptcy estate if the redemption period has not expired at the time the bankruptcy petition is filed. (4 Collier on Bankruptcy ¶541.07[3]) at 541-30 (15th ed. 1983).

Section 362(a) prohibits the "commencement or continuation . . . of a judicial, administrative, or other proceeding," the "enforcement" of a judgment obtained prior to bankruptcy, or any other "act" to obtain possession of property of the estate or to create, perfect, or enforce any lien against property of the estate. The fundamental purposes of the automatic stay imposed by §362(a) against such actions are two-fold: to provide the debtor with a breathing spell from the collection efforts of creditors, and to protect creditors by insuring that the assets of the estate will not be dissipated in a number of different proceedings. S. Rep. No. 989, 95th Cong., 2nd Sess. 54-5, reprinted in (1978) U.S. Code Cong. & Ad. News 5787, 5840-41; H.R. Rep. No. 95-595, 95th Cong., 2nd Sess. 340, reprinted in (1978) U.S. Code Cong. & Ad. News 5963, 6296-97. Although a stay under the circumstances involved here would be consistent with these broad policies, we are of the view that §362(a) cannot be read to stay the mere running of a statutory time period.

---

8. Section 541(a)(1) defines property of the estate as "all legal or equitable interests of the debtor in property as of the commencement of the case." In characterizing the nature and extent of the debtor's interest in property, however, federal courts must look to state law. Georgia Pacific Corp. v. Sigma Service Corp., 22 B.R. 984 (Bkrtcy. M.D. La. 1982).

We respectfully disagree with those courts which have held that an automatic transfer of property, following the expiration of a period of redemption, constitutes either an "act" or "proceeding," or the "enforcement" of a right, within the meaning of §362(a). See In Re Johnson, supra at 374; Matter of Dohm, 14 B.R. 701, 702 (Bkrtcy. N.D. Ill. 1981). That Congress intended §362(a) to prohibit only certain types of *affirmative actions* is evidenced by its use of the terms referenced above and by a corresponding failure to use terms which appropriately describe the suspension or extension of a statutory time period. In Re Ecklund & Swedlund Development Corp., supra at 455; see also, In Re Pridham, 31 B.R. 497 (Bkrtcy. E.D. Cal. 1983); In Re New Town Mall, 17 B.R. 326, 328 (Bkrtcy. D.S.D. 1982). It is also instructive to note that although Congress did not, in §362(a), specifically empower the bankruptcy court to suspend the running of a statutory period of redemption, it had no difficulty expressing such authority when it amended §203 of the Bankruptcy Act in 1935 to provide for the tolling of statutory redemption periods in cases involving the reorganization of family farming operations. 49 Stat. 942 (1935).

Section 362(a) was designed to codify, in a single section, the scattered provisions of the Act and the former Bankruptcy Rules which governed the stay of various actions.[9] 2 Collier on Bankruptcy ¶362.01 at 362-5 (15th ed. 1983). The clear majority of cases decided under the prior provisions relating to automatic stays held that the filing of a petition in bankruptcy did not toll or extend the running of a statutory period of redemption. . . . If we assume, as it is proper to do, that Congress acts with knowledge of existing law, . . . it follows that, absent a clear manifestation of contrary intent, a newly-enacted or revised statute is presumed to be harmonious with existing law and its judicial construction. . . . This presumption is especially valid where, as in the present case, the language of the statute under consideration is substantially identical to that of the previous statutes. In Re Ecklund & Swedlund Development Corp., supra at 455. A careful review of that portion of the legislative history of the Code relating to §362(a) reveals no evidence that Congress intended to change the result reached in such cases as In Re Klein, supra. We conclude, therefore, that §362(a) does not operate to toll or suspend the running of the one-year statutory period of redemption created by Minn. Stat. §580.23(2).

The opposite result has been reached in jurisdictions which require that some affirmative action be taken by a creditor or by a third party in order to transfer full title to property upon the expiration of the period of redemption. See In Re Jenkins, supra; Eaton Land & Cattle Co. v. Rocky Mountain Investments, 28 B.R. 890 (Bkrtcy. D. Colo. 1983); In Re Sap-

---

9. See, §§116(4), 148, 314, 414, 428, and 614 of the Act and Bankruptcy Rules 401, 601 10-601, 11-44, 12-43, and 13-401.

phire Investments, 19 B.R. 492 (Bkrtcy. D. Az. 1982). Under the statutory scheme adopted by Minnesota, however, once the sheriff's certificate is issued to the successful bidder following the foreclosure sale, no further proceedings are required to vest absolute title to the property in the holder of the sheriff's certificate, assuming the debtor takes no steps to redeem the property. Minn. Stat. §580.12; In Re Klein, supra at 59; In Re Minnesota Urban Developers, Inc., supra at 446. First National, as purchaser at the foreclosure sale, thus had the right to expect either full title upon the expiration of the redemption period or, in lieu thereof, payment of the full purchase price plus accrued interest. Even accepting the debtors' argument that §362(a) is designed in part to preserve the status quo as of the date of the petition in bankruptcy, their right remains only to redeem the property within the period established by statute. To hold that §362(a) operates as an automatic stay of the running of the statutory period of redemption would be to enlarge property rights created by state law, a result we view as unjustified by the language of §362(a) and as unintended by Congress.

Our conclusion regarding §362(a) is also based in part upon the presence in the Code of §108(b). That latter section, derived from §11(e) of the Act, provides that where the debtor "may file any pleading, demand, notice, or proof of claim or loss, cure a default, or perform any other similar act," and the period for so doing has not expired as of the filing of the petition in bankruptcy, the trustee is given until the end of such period, "including any suspension of such period occurring on or after the commencement of the case," or 60 days, whichever is later, to perform that act.[11] The relationship between §362(a) and §108(b) was treated at length in Bank of Commonwealth v. Bevan, supra, the case which underlies the district court's opinion below and one of the few cases to consider all three statutes involved in this controversy (i.e., §§362(a), 108(b), and 105(a)). In *Bevan*, the mortgagor filed a petition for reorganization under Chapter 11 of the Code following foreclosure of the mortgaged property. The bankruptcy court subsequently entered an order pursuant to §362(a), indefinitely extending the statutory redemption period. In reviewing the bankruptcy court's order the district court noted that, unlike the language of §362(a), which does not appear to affect the running of specific time periods, §108(b) explicitly grants the trustee additional time in which to perform an act such as that of redemption. Reading the two sections together, the court held that the automatic stay provisions of §362(a) do not override the extension of time provision contained in §108(b). "While a stay tolling the running of the statutory period would give the debtor

---

11. Although the language of §108 refers only to the trustee, it is generally agreed that the debtor-in-possession is also entitled to the statute's privileges. In Re Interstate Restaurant Systems, Inc., 26 B.R. 298, 301 (Bkrtcy. S.D. Fla. 1982); In Re Santa Fe Development Etc., 16 B.R. 165, 167 n.1 (9th Bkrtcy. App. Pan. 1981); but cf., Matter of Dohm, supra at 702.

greater protection than that contemplated by §108," the court reasoned, "where one section of the Bankruptcy Code explicitly governs an issue, another section should not be interpreted to cause an irreconcilable conflict." Id., at 994. Thus, the court concluded:

> An interpretation of §362(a) as an indefinite stay of the statutory period of redemption would render §108(b) superfluous. If §362(a) automatically stays the running of the statutory right to redeem until the stay is lifted pursuant to §362(c) or (d), the pertinent time allotments of §108(b) are completely extraneous as statutory time periods designed to control the trustee's activity. Moreover, if §362(a) is interpreted to provide for the automatic stay of time periods for an indefinite amount of time, then subsections (a) and (b) of §108, which define minimum and maximum time periods for the trustee to act, directly conflict with §362(a). Id., at 994.[12] . . .

Given our conclusion that the bankruptcy court lacked authority under either §105(a) or §362(a), to stay indefinitely the expiration of the statutory period of redemption, it becomes apparent that the only extension of time available to the debtors was that provided by the express terms of §108(b). Since their petition in bankruptcy was filed on October 8, 1981, some three weeks prior to the expiration of the one-year statutory period of redemption, the debtors had sixty days from the former date, or until December 8, 1981, within which to redeem the mortgaged property. That sixty-day period having passed without the debtors redeeming the property, full title vested automatically in First National in accordance with Minnesota law.

The decision of the district court is reversed and the case is remanded to the district court for further proceedings consistent with this opinion.

NOTE

For more extended discussion of bankruptcy stays pertaining to mortgage lenders' rights, see Lifton, Practical Real Estate in the 80's: Legal, Tax and Business Strategies 297-306 (1983); Kennedy, Automatic Stays Under the New Bankruptcy Law, 12 U. Mich. J.L. Ref. 3 (1978); Nimmer, Real Estate Creditors and the Automatic Stay: A Study in Behavioral Economics, 1983 Ariz. St. L.J. 281; and Whalen, Lenders' Rights in Bankruptcy Stays, 45 Mortgage Banking No. 1, 57 (1984).

---

12. Despite its determination that the bankruptcy court incorrectly cited §362(a) as the basis for its order staying the running of the redemption period, however, *Bevan* affirmed the bankruptcy court's action, holding that the stay was a permissible exercise of the broad grant of discretionary authority embodied in §105. Id., at 996. Although, for the reasons stated previously, we disagree with the *Bevan* court's view of §105(a), we are persuaded that its conclusions with respect to §362(a) and §108(b) are sound.

Comment, Mortgage Foreclosure as Fraudulent Conveyance: Is Judicial Foreclosure an Answer to the *Durrett* Problem?

1984 Wis. L. Rev. 195-197, 214-218, 234-235

Mortgage foreclosure proceedings are intended to strike a delicate, equitable balance between two parties: the mortgagee and the mortgagor. Ideally, such proceedings permit a mortgagee to execute on its security within a reasonable time and recover its investment, while protecting the defaulting mortgagor's equity in the property. Over the years, foreclosure law has responded to the competing claims of mortgagees who seek prompt enforcement of their contracts and mortgagors who desire protection of their equity. Unfortunately, the law has not been able to fully respect the interests of each party. In at least one respect, foreclosure law tips the balance in favor of a mortgagee and its right to enforce expeditiously its contract because one of the basic rules is that inadequacy of a foreclosure sale price alone, will not be grounds to set the sale aside. As a result of this rule, a mortgagor, upon foreclosure, may lose its equity in the foreclosed property.

In the last few years, perhaps because of record high mortgage foreclosure rates and an unprecedented increase in bankruptcy cases, courts have begun to see attempts by bankruptcy trustees to upset the foreclosure process. A conflict between state foreclosure law and federal bankruptcy law arises when a defaulting mortgagor petitions for bankruptcy within a year after its property is foreclosed and the bankruptcy trustee moves to have the sale set aside. In such cases the trustee claims that the foreclosure sale was made without adequate consideration, thereby depriving the bankruptcy estate of the former mortgagor's equity in the foreclosed property.[10] Consequently, the bankruptcy trustee claims the sale is voidable as a fraudulent transfer pursuant to section 548(c)(2) of the Bankruptcy Code.[11]

Most of these bankruptcy challenges to the foreclosure process have involved foreclosure sales that lack judicial supervision. The courts ad-

---

10. The commencement of a bankruptcy proceeding creates a bankruptcy estate. 11 U.S.C. §541 (1982). The estate includes all legal or equitable interests of the debtor in property as of commencement of the case, as well as certain property interests that the trustee is able to recover from transferees of the debtor. Id. See also infra note 121 and accompanying text. A secured party's interest in collateral never becomes property of the estate. The secured party is given a right to the value of the collateral or the loan amount, whichever is less. 11 U.S.C. §506 (1982). However, when the value of the collateral exceeds the amount of the obligation, the estate has an equity interest in the property. J. R. Trost, G. Treister, L. Forman, K. Klee & R. Levin, The New Federal Bankruptcy Code 175 (1979). The estate, administered by the bankruptcy trustee, see infra note 120, is liquidated and distributed to creditors according to the priority and amount of their claims. 11 U.S.C. §726 (1982).

11. 11 U.S.C. §548(c)(2) (1982). These provisions are partially reprinted infra note 121.

dressing the issue have been willing to find the sales potentially voidable as fraudulent transfers and, assuming an inadequate sale price, to order them set aside. Although such decisions give effect to bankruptcy policy, they run squarely contrary to the basic foreclosure law rule that inadequacy of price alone will not be grounds to set aside a foreclosure sale. Thus, a conflict of policy has developed between state foreclosure law and federal bankruptcy law — the former attempting to protect the parties to the mortgage, the latter attempting to protect the general creditors of the mortgagor.

This conflict may become more pervasive in the future. Judicial foreclosure, which requires confirmation of the sale by the court, is the most commonly used method of foreclosure in the United States. Although the procedure is more expensive and time consuming than nonjudicial foreclosure, it has one primary advantage: it provides a more stable and thus more readily marketable title. . . .

The question arises whether bankruptcy courts will extend the cases voiding nonjudicial foreclosure sales to judicially confirmed foreclosure sales. If they do, the primary advantage of judicial foreclosure may be lost. Certain titles, once assumed stable, potentially would become subject to attack as fraudulent transfers. Courts might be tempted to extend the principles developed in nonjudicial foreclosures because even judicially approved sales rarely bring the fair market value of the foreclosed property. . . .

Judicial foreclosure is intended to sever *fairly*, but more important to the mortgagee and prospective purchasers, to sever *finally*, the interests of the mortgagor from the property. If a judicial sale of foreclosed property could be challenged successfully after confirmation, the primary benefit of the procedure, stable title, would be lost. It appears that a method already used to avoid nonjudicial foreclosure sales of mortgaged property could be employed to successfully challenge judicial sales of such property, even a year or more after the sale has been judicially confirmed. The method involves a bankruptcy trustee avoiding the sale, if made at a bargain price, as a fraudulent conveyance under section 548 of the Bankruptcy Code. . . .

Bankruptcy proceedings are designed to achieve two fundamental and complementary goals: (1) the deterrence of a creditors' race for the bankrupt's assets under normal state law collection procedures; and (2) the promotion of equality of distribution among similarly situated creditors.[117] Assuring that these goals are met requires some means of restrain-

---

117. See H.R. Rep. No. 595, 95th Cong., 2d Sess. 177-78, reprinted in 1978 U.S. Code Cong. & Ad. News 5963, 6138. A third goal of bankruptcy policy is to rehabilitate the bankrupt. Local Loan Co. v. Hunt, 292 U.S. 234, 244 (1934); Wilson v. City Bank, 84 U.S. (17 Wall.) 473, 486 (1873).

ing waste, fraud and unfair distributions of the debtor's assets. The Bankruptcy Code[118] provides these means.

Once the debtor files a bankruptcy petition, the Code's automatic stay provisions work to preserve the bankrupt's estate by restraining almost all proceedings intended to create, collect, or enforce claims against the debtor until the case is completed or the stay is vacated.[119] In addition, to prevent undermining of the equal distribution policy prior to bankruptcy, the bankruptcy trustee[120] is given powers to avoid certain transactions made within a limited time prior to bankruptcy that are not in the best interest of all the creditors. Among the "avoiding powers" given the trustee is the power to set aside, as constructively fraudulent, transfers made by the debtor within one year of the debtor's bankruptcy unless, among other things, the debtor received a "reasonably equivalent value" in exchange for the transfer.[121] Section 548(a)(2) of the Bankruptcy Code

---

118. The Bankruptcy Reform Act of 1978, 11 U.S.C. §§101-151104 (1982). This act replaced the Bankruptcy Act of 1898.

119. See 11 U.S.C. §541 (1982) (property of the estate). Because of the automatic stay, participation in the bankruptcy action becomes the only permissible method of proceeding against the debtor. Id. §362. Stays should be dissolved unless reasonably necessary. In re Empire Steel Co., 228 F. Supp. 316, 319 (D. Utah 1964). However, when a debtor has an equity interest in property being sought by a creditor, a court will find a stay reasonable. See, e.g., First Pa. Bank, N.A. v. Bailey (In re Bailey), 23 Bankr. 222, 223 (Bankr. D. Pa. 1982). Stays restrain uncompleted and pending foreclosure proceedings. Thus, stays can freeze the disposition of property for years.

120. The bankruptcy trustee is an officer appointed by the court to investigate the acts and conduct of the debtor and to manage the bankrupt's estate. See 11 U.S.C. §704 (1982) (duties of trustee).

121. The fraudulent transfers and obligations provisions are contained in id. §548, which states in part:

(a) The trustee may avoid any transfer of an interest of the debtor in property, or any obligation incurred by the debtor, that was made or incurred on or within one year before the date of the filing of the petition, if the debtor—. . .
(2)(A) received less than a *reasonably equivalent value* in exchange for such transfer or obligation; and
(B) (i) was insolvent on the date that such transfer was made or such obligation was incurred, or became insolvent as a result of such transfer or obligation;
(ii) was engaged in business, or was about to engage in business or a transaction, for which any property remaining with the debtor was an unreasonably small capital; or
(iii) intended to incur, or believed that the debtor would incur, debts that would be beyond the debtor's ability to pay as such debts matured. . . .
(c) [A] transferee or obligee of such transfer or obligation that takes for value and in good faith has a lien on any interest transferred, may retain any lien transferred, or may enforce any obligation incurred, as the case may be, to the extent that such transferee or obligee gave value to the debtor in exchange for such transfer or obligation.
(d)(1) For the purposes of this section, a transfer is made when such transfer becomes so far perfected that a bona fide purchaser from the debtor against whom such transfer could have been perfected cannot acquire an interest in the property transferred that is superior to the interest in such property of the transferee, but if

grants the trustee this power to allow maximization of the pool of assets available to the unsecured creditors.[122] The trustee may exercise this avoiding power irrespective of the actual intent of the parties to the transfer; no actual fraud need be found.[123]

The ability of a trustee to void fraudulent transfers stems from an English statute enacted in 1570[124] and is designed to protect against a debtor's incentives or tendencies toward waste, fraud and unfair distributions of assets that may injure the creditors. It forces the debtor "to give primacy to so-called legal obligations, which are usually the legitimate, conventional claims of standard contract and tort creditors, as opposed to the interests of self, family, friends, shareholders, and shrewder or more powerful bargaining parties." [125] The rule against fraudulent transfers increases the probability that a debtor's assets will be available to pay creditors and thereby reduces both the risks and costs associated with unsecured lending. . . .[126]

Following the Fifth Circuit's 1980 decision in Durrett v. Washington

---

such transfer is not so perfected before the commencement of the case, such transfer occurs immediately before the date of the filing of the petition.
  (2) In this section—
    (A) "value" means property, or satisfaction or securing of a present or antecedent debt of the debtor, but does not include an unperformed promise to furnish support to the debtor or to a relative of the debtor.

The Bankruptcy Code does not provide the trustee with a means of determining a "reasonably equivalent value." Instead, the "Code endeavors to establish an objective standard, as to the adequacy of consideration, by utilizing the phrase 'reasonably equivalent value'." Colletti, A Title Insurer Looks at the Avoidance Provisions of the Bankruptcy Reform Act of 1978, 15 Real Prop., Prob. & Tr. J. 588, 595 (1980).

The bankruptcy trustee is given additional powers to challenge specific transactions not in the best interest of creditors. See, e.g., 11 U.S.C. §544(a) (1982) (granting the rights and powers of an execution creditor and a bona fide purchaser of the debtor's real property as of the time of filing of the petition); id. §544(b) (power to set aside transfers void under state fraudulent conveyance law); id. §547(d) (power to set aside preferential transfers made within 90 days before filing of the petition, or one year if the transfer was made to insiders); id. §545 (power to avoid the fixing of certain statutory liens).

  122. G. Pettigrew, Federal Bankruptcy Code: Theory into Practice 124 (1982). The intent of the statute is to permit the trustee to recover, for the benefit of unsecured creditors, assets of the debtor that have been "fraudulently" transferred beyond their reach. See also V. Countryman, Cases and Materials on Debtor and Creditor 127 (2d ed. 1974).
  123. Gillman v. Preston Family Inv. Co. (In re Richardson), 23 Bankr. 434, 447 (Bankr. D. Utah 1982) ("Congress did not make bad faith, fraud, collusion, unfairness, or oppression elements of the trustee's course of action."). Cf. Bankruptcy Act of July 1, 1898, ch. 541, 30 Stat. 544 §67(d)(1)(3)(version at 11 U.S.C. §67(d)(1)(e)(1976))(repealed 1978)(required the element of "good faith").
  124. Statute of Elizabeth, 13 Eliz. I, ch. 5 (1570). See also 11 U.S.C. §548 note (1982). See generally 1 G. Glenn, Fraudulent Conveyances and Preferences §60 (rev. ed. 1940).
  125. Clark, The Duties of the Corporate Debtor to Its Creditors, 90 Harv. L. Rev. 505, 510-11 (1977).
  126. See Jackson & Kronman, Secured Financing and Priorities Among Creditors, 88 Yale L.J. 1143, 1148-49 (1978-79) (If fraudulent conveyances "were legally enforceable, creditors would either refuse to lend at much below the unsecured rate or would have to incur substantial costs in policing their loans. . . .").

National Insurance Co.,[127] section 548(a)(2) of the Bankruptcy Code has been used with increasing frequency as a means of attacking nonjudicial foreclosure sales that do not bring a "reasonably equivalent value" in exchange for the foreclosed property.[128] *Durrett* was the first decision to hold that a regularly conducted, nonjudicial foreclosure sale made pursuant to a deed of trust could be set aside as a fraudulent conveyance if, among other things, the sale was made without "fair consideration."[129]

The *Durrett* case involved a foreclosure sale in 1977 where the mortgagee, who was the sole participant, purchased the property by bidding the balance due on the note.[130] Nine days after the sale, the debtor filed a petition for arrangement under Chapter 11 of the Bankruptcy Act;[131] then, acting as a debtor-in-possession,[132] he sought to have the sale set aside as being a fraudulent transfer under section 67(d) of the Bankruptcy Act.[133] On appeal the Firth Circuit had little trouble deciding that the sale of the property under the terms of the deed of trust was a transfer by the debtor, despite the fact that the trustee of the deed of trust possessed the deed to the foreclosed property at the time of the sale. The court concluded that the sale was within the Act's definition of "transfer" because it was accompanied by a change of possession. It also held that the sale price equal to 57.7% of the property's fair market value was not a "fair equiva-

---

127. 621 F.2d 201 (5th Cir. 1980).

128. See Abramson v. Lakewood Bank & Trust Co., 647 F.2d 547 (5th Cir. 1981) (per curiam), *cert. denied*, 454 U.S. 1164 (1982); Lawyer's Title Ins. Corp. v. Madrid (In re Madrid), 21 Bankr. 424 (Bankr. 9th Cir. 1982); Rosner v. Worcester (In re Worcester), 28 Bankr. 910 (Bankr. C.D. Cal. 1983); Cooper v. Smith, (In re Smith), 24 Bankr. 19 (Bankr. W.D.N.C. 1982); Gillman v. Preston Family Inv. Co. (In re Richardson); 23 Bankr. 434 (Bankr. D. Utah 1982); Perdido Bay Country Club Estates, Inc. v. Equitable Trust Co. (In re Perdido Bay Country Club Estates, Inc.), 23 Bankr. 36 (Bankr. S.D. Fla. 1982); Wickman v. United Am. Bank in Knoxville (In re Thompson), 18 Bankr. 67 (Bankr. E.D. Tenn. 1982); Alsop v. Alaska (In re Alsop), 14 Bankr. 982 (Bankr. D. Alaska 1981), *aff'd*, 22 Bankr. 1017 (D. Alaska 1982).

129. 621 F.2d at 204.

130. Id. at 203.

131. 11 U.S.C. §§701-799 (1976) (repealed 1978). Chapter 11 arrangement is an option for some business debtors seeking reorganization or rehabilitation rather than a liquidation of assets. Creditors look to future earnings of the bankrupt, rather than property held by the bankrupt to satisfy their claims. See generally G. Pettigrew, supra note 122, at 257. The various chapter proceedings under the 1898 Act have been consolidated to form Chapter 11 of the 1978 Bankruptcy Reform Act, 11 U.S.C. §§1101-1174 (1982).

132. Normally, in Chapter 11 cases the debtor continues to manage its business. Such a debtor is referred to as a "debtor-in-possession" and is given most of the duties and powers of a bankruptcy trustee. See supra notes 120-21 and accompanying text. See also G. Pettigrew, supra note 122, at 258-60.

133. Section 67(d) of the Bankruptcy Act is the predecessor of §548 of the 1978 Bankruptcy Reform Act and has been substantially recodified by §548. Section 67(d) provided:

> Every transfer made and every obligation incurred by a debtor within one year prior to the filing of a petition initiating a proceeding . . . is fraudulent . . . if made or incurred without fair consideration by a debtor who is or will be thereby rendered insolvent, without regard to his actual intent. . . .

Bankruptcy Act of July 1, 1898, ch. 541, 30 Stat. 544 §67(d) (version at 11 U.S.C. §107(d) (1976)) (repealed 1978). Cf. 11 U.S.C. §548 (1982), reprinted supra note 121.

lent" for the transfer, and suggested that no less than 70% of fair market value would constitute fair equivalent value. Finally, because the sale occurred within one year of the debtor's bankruptcy and left him insolvent, the court ruled it void as a fraudulent conveyance. . . .

. . . *Durrett* and its progeny, which advance the bankruptcy goal of promoting an equitable distribution of a debtor's assets, unfortunately introduce uncertainties into the foreclosure process which make it difficult for mortgagees to realize on their security. At present, a mortgagee who completes a foreclosure sale cannot be certain whether it has accomplished its objective by recovering its investment or whether, at some future time, a bankruptcy court will avoid the sale or penalize the mortgagee who purchased the foreclosed property for later reselling it. These uncertainties introduced into the foreclosure process by *Durrett*, directly conflict with the policy of foreclosure law that a lender is entitled to have its contract with the mortgagor promptly enforced according to state law; these uncertainties weaken the value of a mortgagee's security and contribute to increased credit costs.

To reconcile the conflicting policies of bankruptcy and foreclosure law, the bankruptcy courts should consider awarding an irrebuttable presumption of price adequacy to judicially supervised and confirmed foreclosure proceedings. Federal bankruptcy courts should consider the state court supervision of a foreclosure as adequate to protect a mortgagor's creditors from an improvident sale of the foreclosed property. In turn, state courts should confirm foreclosure sales with an eye toward bankruptcy policy. Finally, the judicial foreclosure process should provide a bankruptcy court with further evidence that the confirmed price is reasonable because judicial foreclosure is designed to encourage third-party participation at foreclosure sales. An irrebuttable presumption of price adequacy awarded to judicially confirmed foreclosure sales would maintain the integrity of mortgage financing without sacrificing the interests of a defaulting mortgagor's unsecured creditors. Failure to award the presumption would, among other things, leave mortgagees without assurances that they could effectively realize on their security.

NOTE

For other discussions of the *Durrett* case reflecting the concern over vulnerability of prebankruptcy foreclosures, see Coppel and Kann, Defanging *Durrett:* The Established Law of "Transfer," 100 Banking L.J. 676 (1983); Alden, Gross and Borowitz, Real Property Foreclosure as a Fraudulent Conveyance: Proposals for Solving the *Durrett* Problem, 38 Bus. Law. 1605 (1983); and Zinman, Houle and Weiss, Fraudulent Transfers According to Alden, Gross and Borowitz: A Tale of Two Circuits, 39 Bus. Law. 977 (1984).

f. Some Suggested Changes in Mortgage Lenders' Remedies

Lifton, Real Estate in Trouble: Lender's Remedies Need an Overhaul
31 Bus. Law. 1927, 1942-1945 (1976)

The starting point for a more rational approach to the real estate lender's remedies is recognition that the rules that are appropriate for mortgages on homes and small farms should not control the treatment of mortgages on investment real estate like office buildings, shopping centers, multi-family housing, or user-owned real estate like factories or warehouses.

The laws presently governing mortgages on homes or small farms properly take into account the borrower's need for greater protection because of his relatively unsophisticated position and his weaker bargaining power. They also satisfy the emotional and political command that the law should lean over backwards to give a debtor maximum opportunity to protect his home or farm from foreclosure. In the case of commercial real estate, however, the borrower is equally, if not more, sophisticated than the lender; their bargaining powers are comparable and their equity claims are essentially the same — they each represent competing business interests. Some states already distinguish between the two categories of real estate; for example, assigning shorter statutory redemption periods to commercial property than to homes.[69] But further differentiation is required. The legislatures and courts should create new treatment for commercial mortgages which recognizes the national and local economic interests in effective and less expensive enforcement of lender's remedies with due, but not exaggerated, consideration for the debtor's equity. Since lending institutions and real estate investors have to operate throughout the country under the burden of as many different laws as there are states, a *Uniform Act for Remedies of Commercial and Industrial Real Property Lenders* would be most desirable. Realistically, however, the chances are slight that the states will relinquish their prerogatives to individual mortgage laws. One can only hope that they will adopt as many of these recommendations as possible.

The appropriate legislation should provide that in case of default, within 45 days after the mortgagee's request the court will appoint the

---

69. See, e.g., Mich. Stat. Ann. §27A-3240 (Supp. 1975) (established shorter redemption periods for commercial or industrial real estate and multifamily homes in excess of four units); N.D. Cent. Code §32-19.1-.01 (Supp. 1975) (foreclosure and deficiency rules for less than ten acre real estate). See also Holtz & Griem, Mortgage Foreclosures New Procedures under P.A. 104 of 1971, 51 Mich. State Bar J. 164 (March 1972). Great Britain also makes a distinction between actions by a mortgagee for possession of a dwelling property or of other property. Samuels, Actions by Mortgagees for Possession, 34 Conveyancer and Prop. Law. 324 (1970).

mortgagee or its designee as a receiver for the property. The debtor will have the opportunity within the 45 day period to challenge the appointment by showing that the debtor will be irreparably damaged by such an appointment. This would put the burden on the debtor to prove that he has an equity in the property above the mortgage debt and that appointment of a receiver will diminish that equity, or that appointment of the lender or his designee as receiver will damage the property. Should the arguments on the issues be delayed the receiver will be appointed pending the hearing. The Act should require the receiver to account to the court periodically with respect to the earnings, expenditures and status of the property. At each accounting, the owner should have an opportunity to challenge the receiver's actions and have the receiver discharged if the receiver has failed to operate the property prudently. Assuming that the receiver engaged recognized management, it is doubtful that the owner will ever argue this position strenuously. The court should be empowered to approve advances by the lender of additional funds either to complete unfinished property or to maintain finished property in good repair where there is a showing that such advance is called for to maintain the physical or economic value of the property. Any expenditures under these circumstances should be treated like advances under a certificate of indebtedness in bankruptcy proceedings and should be reimbursed to the lender out of the first monies earned by the property or generated on its sale, ahead of other creditors and the owner. Actually, it is doubtful that the other creditors or the owner would object to the mortgagee's expenditures on the property. Such objections, for the most part, have represented an attempt to seek bargaining leverage rather than to protect the best interests of the property.

A new law enabling the mortgagee or its designee quickly to be appointed receiver will relieve most of the pressure to satisfy the mortgagee's need for immediate foreclosure to protect its security. But speedy and less expensive foreclosure is still required if the lender is to realize on its debt. A valuable first step would encourage the use of the deed-in-lieu of foreclosure since that carries out the desires of borrower and lender without tying up already overcrowded courts in unnecessary litigation. State transfer taxes should be drafted so that they do not obstruct the use of a voluntary deed. In addition, as part of the review of the bankruptcy laws suggested below, it would be worthwhile to consider eliminating from the preference category a voluntary conveyance of defaulted property to a first mortgage lender for no cash consideration to the owner (other than reasonable legal fees to his attorney) when the lender on its part waived all rights to a deficiency judgment. To protect against improper transfers such a provision might apply only where the first mortgage represented a cash advance of no less than $500,000 made at least four months before the conveyance and when the lender was an unrelated institution subject to regulatory control, such as a bank or insurance company.

The proposed Act should also provide the lender with the alternative of choosing between foreclosure by judicial sale or foreclosure under power of sale so long as notice of the sale is also given to the owner. Deficiency judgment should be available only in the case of foreclosure by judicial sale which provides the owner more time to sell the property and generate interest in the sale. In that case, where the lender has relied on credit collateral, and a sophisticated borrower aware of the difficulty of realizing full value on a foreclosure sale undertook to pledge its credit, the lender should be entitled to the benefits of its bargain without the frustration of appraisal or "market value" tests. Furthermore, in connection with commercial, multifamily residential and industrial real estate, the statutory right of redemption should be eliminated since it restricts the lender's ability to sell the property without adding significant protection for the property owner. In those states that still insist on retaining the equity of redemption concept, its use should be limited to properties where an independent appraiser engaged by the court — not by either of the parties — finds that the property has value over and above the mortgage. Even in that event the equity of redemption period should not exceed three months.

Finally, those states, where a foreclosing lender may be treated as doing business in the state, should amend their laws to give the lender a reasonable time, perhaps with a minimum of six months, after foreclosure, during which it can operate the foreclosed property in the state without being treated as doing business there. A "reasonable time" should be calculated to give the lender sufficient time to sell the property, and failing that, to engage independent management.

Madway and Pearlman, A Mortgage Foreclosure Primer: Part III, Proposals for Change

8 Clearinghouse Rev. 473, 478-479 (November 1974)

As indicated earlier, most efforts to reform mortgage foreclosure procedures have attempted to balance the competing interests of lenders, who seek quick and inexpensive procedures, against the interests of homeowners in adequate notice, a right to a hearing prior to any action that cuts off their rights and maximum opportunities to cure any alleged default and obtaining reinstatement of the mortgage. We submit that a foreclosure procedure should be directed toward a third goal of equal or perhaps greater importance than the first two: reducing the incidence of mortgage foreclosures.

The need for adoption of such a goal is well illustrated by recent reports of a nationwide practice on the part of mortgagees under the FHA single

Basic Security Transactions

homeownership programs of "quickie" foreclosures on the homes of low and moderate income families who are supposed to be the beneficiaries of those programs. While this practice may well violate federal law and regulations, no present state law imposes any real impediment to this practice.

Accordingly, we propose the establishment of a foreclosure scheme which would attempt to reduce the incidence of foreclosure, while at the same time ensuring that mortgage lenders may protect their security and that homeowners have an adequate opportunity to raise defenses to foreclosure and cure any defaults. The heart of this scheme is the establishment, under the supervision of the judiciary, of a foreclosure commissioner or other appropriately denominated officer who would have primary responsibility for overseeing the whole foreclosure process. The officer would have both a judicial and a mediatory function. Mortgagees would notify the commissioner of any default. He, in turn, would then have the responsibility of preparing notices to the mortgagor and other parties holding recorded liens against the property. Such notices would be designed clearly to warn the mortgagor of the threat to his home, the need for immediate action to protect it and advise him of matters such as the basis for the asserted default, the rights to cure and reinstatement or redemption, the right to sell the mortgaged premises subject to the mortgage, and the right to any surplus in the event of a foreclosure sale. Finally, the notice would inform the homeowner that upon request, the commissioner will direct a representative of the mortgagee with full power to act to attend a meeting with the mortgagor conducted by the commissioner for the purpose of exploring in good faith the question of whether there is a basis upon which foreclosure may be avoided, such as an agreement on the part of the mortgagee to forbear and to recast the obligation. The notice would also advise the mortgagor that, if he has any defenses to the foreclosure, he has a right to a full evidentiary hearing before the commissioner at which he may be represented by counsel. The notice would also suggest to the mortgagor that he immediately contact an attorney and that, if he could not afford to pay a private attorney, he should contact the local Legal Aid Society or Legal Services program or any local bar association. The telephone numbers of such organizations should be included in the notice.

If, within twenty working days of the notice, the mortgagor fails to request either a meeting or an evidentiary hearing on any defenses he may wish to offer, the commissioner may then order that a sale of the mortgaged premises occur within some reasonable period of time thereafter. During that period, the mortgagor's rights would be limited to curing the default, provided that the right has not been exercised more than once in the preceding six months or to redeeming by paying off the outstanding balance of the obligation. Any sale would be conducted by the commissioner with appropriate standards for advertisement and either a bidding procedure designed to maximize the sale price or a provision for private sale, at the commissioner's discretion. The bid purchaser at the sale would take title free from any claims by the mortgagor and other lien holders of record who had been properly notified. There would be no post-foreclosure sale statutory right of redemption. Protecting the title of the bid purchaser and eliminating post-sale redemption rights, in jurisdictions where such rights exist, would meet one of the major objections of mortgagees, because these practices tend to depress foreclosure sale prices significantly.

In the event that the mortgagor requests a meeting under the auspices of the commissioner with the mortgagee, and the mortgagee either fails to attend such a meeting or refuses to discuss in good faith a basis for avoiding foreclosure, the commissioner could then decline to proceed with the foreclosure. This decision would be reviewable by an appropriate appellate court.

To minimize the possibility of abuse, the commissioner would have the power to award attorney's fees to either party. Furthermore, upon finding that a mortgagor's defenses were frivolous or not offered in good faith, the commissioner could grant summary relief to the mortgagee. It is anticipated that, in most cases, foreclosure under this proposal could be completed within the ten-week period that ULTA envisages.

In instances where the mortgagee can demonstrate either that the mortgaged premises have been abandoned or are being subjected to waste to an extent that the security is undermined or impaired, the commissioner would be authorized to grant the mortgagee immediate possession. At this point, there would be an expedited procedure for a rapid sale of the property. The traditional remedy in cases of waste, where the mortgagee seeks to protect the security interest, is to provide for the appointment of a receiver. This procedure is traditionally time-consuming and expensive. Under the scheme proposed here, there would be no necessity for the appointment of a third party who would have to be compensated by the mortgagee or out of the proceeds of the sale. Moreover, in appropriate cases, possession could be accomplished within a matter of days, instead of weeks or months.

We submit that the scheme sketched out above provides the basis for reducing the incidence of foreclosure, while at the same time addressing the problem of the mortgagee's need to move quickly to protect his security interest in instances where it is threatened, and of assuring the maximum price at the foreclosure sale by eliminating post-sale redemption and protecting the bid purchaser's title. At the same time, it accords the mortgagor an ample opportunity to cure any default and obtain reinstatement and to have a full evidentiary hearing, with appropriate prehearing discovery opportunities, on the merits of any defenses without the necessity for posting a bond and seeking an order restraining a sale, as would be necessary under traditional power-of-sale foreclosure statutes.

g. Remedies of the Installment Land Contract Vendor

The installment land contract seller may have a number of remedies available to him if the buyer defaults, including self-help recovery of possession, forfeiture, rescission, specific performance, damages for breach of contract, or suit to recover possession. Some of these remedies, in the context of a contract buyer's failure to close, are considered in Chapter Four. However, the remedies of self-help and forfeiture merit consideration at this point because of their importance to the installment land contract as a security device.

Note, Reforming the Vendor's Remedies for Breach of Installment Land Sale Contracts
47 S. Cal. L. Rev. 191, 205-206 (1973)

The remedies available to the vendor range from private self-help actions to formal judicial proceedings. Frequently, however, the vendor need not take any action upon default by the vendee since the latter may have vacated the premises before notification that he is in default. However, some form of coercion is ordinarily necessary. . . .

Of all the remedies available to the vendor, private enforcement or self-help is by far the most effective. There are three reasons for its effectiveness, and each is directly related to the fact that low income groups are the primary source of installment land sale contract vendees. First, low income groups are generally confused by the complexities of real estate transactions and thus are more likely to accept and acquiesce in the demands of the vendor; second, these groups tend to be unaware of their legal rights; and third, even if they were cognizant of their legal rights, low income families are financially incapable of pursuing legal actions.

Because these private-enforcement remedies are so effective, a large and diversified arsenal of self-help techniques has been developed. For example, there is what may be called "friendly persuasion," which involves notifying the vendee that he is in default and requesting him either to pay his arrearages or vacate. Another of the vendor's noncoercive means of reacquiring possession is to promise the vendee that if he will vacate and sign a quitclaim deed, the vendor will not pursue legal actions against him. This ploy, if successful, yields exactly what is desired by the vendor — the repossession of the property without troublesome and costly legal proceedings.

Also included in the vendor's arsenal of self-help remedies are the "in terrorem" approaches. These may include ominous-sounding letters from an attorney threatening the vendee with legal action if he refuses to vacate, a threat from the vendor to physically evict the vendee, or a visit from a sheriff who has been induced to warn the vendee that if he does not vacate the sheriff will forcibly remove the vendee, his family and their belongings.

Which of these self-help remedies a vendor will use depends upon his individual integrity and business policy. However, it is certain that he will employ at least some of them before going to the time and expense of formal legal proceedings.

NOTES ON THE RECOVERY OF POSSESSION BY SELF-HELP

1. Warren, California Instalment Land Sales Contracts: A Time for Reform, 9 U.C.L.A. L. Rev. 608, 630-631 (1962):

In Jordan v. Talbot,[98] the California Supreme Court, though faced with a landlord-tenant problem, made pronouncements which appear to limit severely the vigor of the self-help clause as an effective remedy of a land sale vendor. Here the plaintiff was in possession under a written lease which provided that upon default by the lessee the lessor "shall have the right to take possession forthwith." The defendant lessor entered the premises by a passkey in the absence of the defaulting lessee, had her furniture and other possessions removed by a storage company and stored for her account, and refused to allow her to reoccupy the premises. The court held the lessor guilty of forcible entry and detainer when he unlocked the door of the lessee's apartment without her consent and entered, even though no actual force or violence was involved. In the course of this decision the court expressly disapproved a case which held that an instalment land contract vendor who entered the premises of a defaulting vendee without force and under a self-help clause was not guilty of forcible entry or detainer. The result of *Jordan* is that a vendor entering the premises without the consent of the vendee under a self-help clause may be subject to suit under the forcible entry and detainer statutes however peaceable his entry. If the vendee will not leave voluntarily the vendor must now go to law.

In accord with Jordan v. Talbot on the invalidity of landlord lockouts are Mendes v. Johnson, 389 A.2d 781 (D.C. 1978); Freeway Park Build-

---

[98]. 55 Cal. 2d 597, 361 P.2d 20 (1961). See 9 U.C.L.A. L. Rev. 453 (1962), for an extended discussion of the possible consequences of this important decision in land sale contracts and conditional sales. The doctrine of repossession by self-help, though frowned upon in the civil law, survives in Anglo-American law as a relic of a more crude age of legal order. However unsavory its past or anomalous its present, the remedy of repossession by self-help is enthusiastically supported by vendors as an economic necessity in this age of mass distribution of chattels and real estate by low down payment merchandising. One suspects that with increasing judicial and legislative attention being drawn to the protection of instalment sale consumers, the self-help doctrine will come increasingly under the kind of hostile scrutiny it was given by Justice Traynor in the *Jordan* case.

ing, Inc. v. Western States Wholesale Supply, 22 Utah 2d 266, 451 P.2d 778 (1969) and Brooks v. LaSalle National Bank, 11 Ill. App. 3d 791, 298 N.E.2d 262 (1973). Also see Annot., Right of Landlord Legally Entitled to Possession to Dispossess Tenant Without Legal Process, 6 A.L.R.3d 177 (1966).

2. Are mortgagees of real property as likely to attempt self-help remedies in default situations as are installment land contract vendors and landlords?

Carlson v. Hamilton
8 Utah 2d 272, 332 P.2d 989 (1958)

HENRIOD, Justice. Appeal from a judgment for money paid by plaintiff buyers to defendant sellers under a real estate contract which the former breached. Reversed. Costs to defendants.

The subject of the contract was a farm with a home situate thereon. The sale price was $22,000, with $1,000 annual instalments, the purchasers to pay the taxes also. Such payments were met the first year, but plaintiffs failed to make payments the second year, notifying defendants that they would be unable to carry out the terms of the contract. Defendants advised plaintiffs that if they would pay the taxes and the interest the payment of the $1,000 principal would be forgotten for the time being. Even so, plaintiffs again indicated to defendants that they would not meet the commitments made under the contract. Under the circumstances defendants resumed possession of the property which at the time was not occupied by plaintiffs or anyone else.

Defendants did not sue for specific performance or for the arrearages resulting by plantiffs' default, as defendants well may have done. Instead, they chose to take back the property and retain the amounts paid as liquidated damages, which the contract clearly provided they could do.

Plaintiffs brought suit to recover everything they had paid under the contract before default, being the sum of $6,680. The evidence indicated that considerable damage had been done to the house and property during the two years plaintiffs occupied them. The trial court made findings as to the amount of damage done and added it to a reasonable two-year rental value, concluding the plaintiffs had paid $2,119.94 more on the contract than defendants actually had been damaged. Plaintiffs were awarded judgment for that amount, apparently under the theory that in Perkins v. Spencer, 121 Utah 468, 243 P.2d 446, we determined that a defaulting buyer could require the return of all sums paid in over and above actual damage caused the seller.

Perkins v. Spencer is no authority for such doctrine. The spirit of that case calls for adhesion to a principle that equity historically has indulged, —that it abhors unconscionability shocking to such degree that the function of equity would be misconceived and misapplied by the enforcement of such unconscionability, even though it may have been the subject of contract.

Such unconscionability is obvious in the *Perkins* case, where, after a breach committed only four months after execution of the contract, an exaction of over 27% of the entire purchase price was attempted, — $2,725 where the price was $10,000, and where the seller demanded the entire balance of the price before conveying the property. In the instant case, the amount of damage that the contract said could be considered as liquidated damages was $2,119.94. Occupancy had been enjoyed a full two years. The bona fides of the sellers generously was demonstrated by a volunteered waiver of the principal for the time being if the buyers would but pay the taxes and interest. The amount of damages here was but 9½% of the purchase price, an amount that would exceed but little the real estate commission that would have to be paid on resale of the property that defendants took back without fault on their part, from those who caused all the difficulty by breaking the contract.

The two cases are poles apart, the one obviously being punctuated by unconscionability, the other appearing to call only for the exaction of a reasonably small percentage of the price for a breach that would cause delay for repairs, time lapse for re-sale, and possibly other items of damage susceptible of little but conjectural measurement.

People should be entitled to contract on their own terms without the indulgence of paternalism by courts in the alleviation of one side or another from the effects of a bad bargain. Also, they should be permitted to enter into contracts that actually may be unreasonable or which may lead to hardship on one side. It is only where it turns out that one side or the other is to be penalized by the enforcement of the terms of a contract so unconscionable that no decent, fair-minded person would view the ensuing result without being possessed of a profound sense of injustice, that equity will deny the use of its good offices in the enforcement of such unconscionability. We think no such case is presented here.

In Peck v. Judd [7 Utah 2d 420, 326 P.2d 712, 717,] Mr. Justice Worthen poignantly expressed the thought when he said "It is not our prerogative to step in and renegotiate the contract of the parties. . . . There is no reason why we should consider the vendee privileged . . . unless the conditions . . . are unconscionable . . . and . . . we should recognize and honor the right of persons to contract freely and to make real and genuine mistakes when the dealings are at arms' length." He pointed out also that buyers ofttimes reap a handsome harvest by the appreciation of real estate values, but that equity will not interfere to require the buyer to share such increment with the seller. "Courts of equity," he said, "should not interfere except when sharp practice or most unconscionable result is to be prevented."

McDonough, C.J., and Crockett, Wade and Worthen, J.J., concur.

NOTES ON FORFEITURE OF EQUITY

1. Suppose that in Carlson v. Hamilton, seller had sued to cancel the installment contract because of buyer's default. Could buyer then claim successfully that the contract was an "equitable" mortgage for which foreclosure would be the only appropriate method for cutting off his interest? If yes, would buyer then be entitled to redemption prior to the decree? For what sum? If buyer did not have the moneys to redeem, would seller then be able to keep all moneys received?

2. Courts have become increasingly reluctant to enforce forfeiture provisions in installment land contracts. Their declared reasons for refusing to apply these clauses may be unconscionability, as in the Utah case of Perkins v. Spencer, discussed in the Carlson v. Hamilton opinion; a desire for granting buyers who are behind in their payments a right of repayment similar to a mortgagor's equity of redemption right; or waiver of the forfeiture right by the seller having accepted one or more late payments. For judicial limitations on forfeiture, see Osborne, Nelson and Whitman, Real Estate Finance Law §3.28 (1979). Also, some states have sought to ease the forfeiture hardship on installment contract buyers by statutes giving buyers a grace period following default in which to comply with the terms of the contract. Arizona is one such state, and its statute provides in part:

> D. Forfeiture of the interest of a purchaser in the property for failure to pay monies due under the contract may be enforced only after expiration of the following periods after the date such monies were due:
> 1. If there has been paid less than twenty percent of the purchase price, thirty days.
> 2. If there has been paid twenty percent, or more, but less than thirty percent of the purchase price, sixty days.
> 3. If there has been paid thirty percent, or more, but less than fifty percent of the purchase price, one hundred and twenty days.
> 4. If there has been paid fifty percent, or more, of the purchase price, nine months.
> E. For the purpose of computing the percentage of the purchase price paid under subsection D of this section, the total of only the following constitutes payments on the purchase price:
> 1. Down payments paid to the seller.
> 2. Principal payments paid to the seller on the contract.
> 3. Principal payments paid to other persons who hold liens or encumbrances on the property, the principal portion of which constitutes a portion of the purchase price, as stated under the contract.

Ariz. Rev. Stat. Ann. §33-742 (West Supp. 1985).

One claimed advantage of installment land contracts is that they enable persons of modest means to buy their own homes, as little or no down payment usually is required. Forfeiture, a quick and simple method of termination in case purchasers default, is one of the attractions that installment land contracts have for sellers and makes them more willing to enter into such transactions. Do you think that grace periods seriously deter use of the installment land contract as a security device in the sale of real estate? Are such contracts subject to so much abuse and capable of creating so much hardship on buyers that with or without grace periods on default they should be prohibited? Is the best solution that provided by the Uniform Land Transactions Act §§3-102 and 3-501, in which transactions intended to create security interests in land, including mortgages and installment land contracts, are treated similarly, with the same rights and remedies in case of default?

3. Other ways in which states by statute have sought to protect the installment land contract purchaser are to permit the purchaser of residential property to secure a deed and mortgage after 40 percent or more of the purchase price has been paid. Md. Real Prop. Code Ann. §10-105 (Michie 1981); to require judicial foreclosure and sale for the seller to recover possession on default if the purchaser has made payments for at least five years or has paid 20 percent or more of the purchase price. Ohio Rev. Code Ann. §5313.07 (Anderson 1981).

CHAPTER THREE

Basic Tax Considerations of the Real Estate Transaction*

The Internal Revenue Code has done even more than Quia Emptores to revolutionize real estate transactions. So common an event as the sale or purchase of a family home is fraught with tax considerations, even though more compelling matters of personal preference and need usually control the choice. For transactions in which the primary purpose is not to provide housing for the taxpayer, tax factors are essential to the investment decision: to sell or not to sell, to invest or not to invest, to buy or to lease, to buy outright or to finance, to sell outright or to give credit to the buyer, etc. Moreover, the financial shaping of the transaction, the legal arrangements that the parties agree to, and the forms of organization that are employed may determine whether the investor realizes his or her tax objectives. The real estate lawyer can no more remain ignorant of taxes than can the physician of antibiotics (or, for that matter, of taxes).

A. CLASSIFICATION OF REAL PROPERTY

The taxability of real estate investment and transfer depends initially upon the purpose for which the property is held. With respect to real property, the Code offers four general categories: (1) property held solely as a personal residence; (2) property held for the production of income; (3) property held for use in a trade or business; and (4) property held primarily for sale to customers.

---

* Editors' caveat: major tax reform proposals now before Congress (Spring 1986) may result in significant changes for real estate investment. Under consideration are: longer depreciation write-off periods; curtailed deductibility of property taxes and second-home mortgage interest; repeal of the investment tax credit; and a smaller rehabilitation tax credit.
   All Code references in this chapter are to the Internal Revenue Code of 1954.

1. Property Held Solely as a Personal Residence

During the period such property is held, the home owner is entitled to deduct the following expenses: interest paid under any mortgage that is a lien against the home,[1] real property taxes,[2] and losses caused by casualty or disaster.[3] All other expenses incurred by the home owner are nondeductible. These include depreciation,[4] maintenance and repair,[5] insurance,[6] and any loss suffered upon disposition.[7] A condominium unit held as a personal residence is taxed as if it were a one-family detached dwelling.[8] Special Code provisions,[9] which will be examined later, allow the owner of a cooperative apartment to obtain tax treatment roughly equivalent to that accorded other home owners.

Although losses on disposition are nonrecognized, any gain realized on the sale or exchange of a personal residence would normally be taxable[10] as capital gain, since the Code regards one's residence as a capital asset.[11] However, taxpayers over 55 who have owned and used the home as a principal residence for at least three out of the five years preceding the sale

---

1. I.R.C. §163(a); Treas. Reg. §1.163-1(b). The interest is deductible even though the taxpayer is not directly liable upon the bond or note secured by such a mortgage. Ibid. In at least two states, Maryland and Pennsylvania, land is sometimes held subject to ground or quit rents—a feudal relic that permits the grantor of a "fee simple" to reserve a token rental. If the ground rent is redeemable, that is, if by statute the owner may discharge any further duty to make ground rental payments by paying to the grantor a specified sum, then the ground rents paid (but not the lump sum payment in redemption) are deductible as interest. Payments of irredeemable ground rentals are treated as rent and are nondeductible for the taxpayer who uses his or her home solely as a personal residence. I.R.C. §§163(c), 1055; Treas. Reg. §§1.163-1(b), 1.1055-1.

2. I.R.C. §164(a)(1); Treas. Reg. §§164-1(a), 3(b). Real property taxes do not include special assessments paid for local benefits such as streets or sidewalks when the property subject to the tax is limited to the property benefited. I.R.C. §164(c)(1); Treas. Reg. §1.164-4(a). If, however, the special assessment is made for the purpose of maintenance and repair or for the purpose of meeting interest charges with respect to such benefits, they are deductible. Treas. Reg. §1.164-4(b)(1). A further exception from the nondeductibility of special assessments is available for some exactions levied by special taxing districts in existence on December 31, 1963. Treas. Reg. §1.164-4(b)(2).

3. I.R.C. §§165(c)(3), (h); Treas. Reg. §§1.165-7, -11. The first $100 of loss per casualty is nondeductible. Moreover, beginning in 1983, no such loss is deductible unless the total amount of all casualty and theft losses sustained by the taxpayer during the taxable year (as determined after subtracting the first $100 of each loss) exceeds 10 percent of the taxpayer's adjusted gross income. I.R.C. §165(h)(1).

4. See I.R.C. §167(a); Charles F. Neave, 17 T.C. 1237 (1952).

5. I.R.C. §262; Treas. Reg. §1.262-1(b)(3). Expenditures for improvements or additions to the residence that prolong the life of the property or increase its value are added to the basis. I.R.C. §§1012, 1016(a)(1), 263(a)(1); Treas. Regs. §§1.1012-1(a), -1(b),1.1016-2, 1.263(a)-1, -2.

6. I.R.C. §262; Treas. Reg. §1.262-1(b)(2).

7. I.R.C. §§165(c), 262; Treas. Reg. §§1.165-9, 1.262-1(b)(4).

8. See generally Anderson, Tax Aspects of Cooperative and Condominium Housing, 25 N.Y.U. Inst. on Fed. Taxn. 79 (1967); Rev. Rul. 64-31, 1964-1 C.B. 300.

9. I.R.C. §216.

10. I.R.C. §61(a)(3).

11. I.R.C. §1221.

Classification of Real Property

may elect to exclude up to the first $125,000 of gain.[12] For all other cases, recognition of the gain *must* be postponed if the provisions of I.R.C. §1034 are satisfied.[13] Under §1034 if the taxpayer buys another "principal residence"[14] within the period beginning two years before and ending two years after the sale of the preceding "principal residence," gain is recognized only to the extent that the adjusted sales price of the old residence exceeds the cost of the new residence.[15]

"Adjusted sales price"[16] means the amount realized (the sales price less expenses such as commissions, legal services, title abstract charges, etc.),[17] reduced by any "fix-up costs" (i.e., noncapital outlays incurred to make the house more readily salable), where the work is performed within ninety days of the making of contract of sale. "Sales price" is the value of property and cash that the seller receives plus the unpaid principal of any mortgages against the property that are not discharged at transfer, whether the buyer assumes the mortgages or takes subject to them and whether or not the seller is personally liable on the debt.[18]

To illustrate the workings of §1034, consider the following example: Taxpayer purchases a house and lot for $40,000 in 1978. During 1979, taxpayer adds two rooms to the house at a cost of $5000. In 1985, taxpayer sells the house, receiving $70,000, paying the broker $4200 and the law-

---

12. I.R.C. §121; Treas. Reg. §1.121-1, -2, -3, -4. If the property was held by a husband and wife jointly as community property, and if a joint return is filed, §121 is available only once in a taxpayer's lifetime, and the taxpayer may elect the exemption when he or she wishes. If the taxpayer acts within a specified time period, taxpayer may rescind an election previously made. I.R.C. §§121(b)(2), (c); Treas. Reg. §§1.121-2(b), -4.

13. Section 1034 is mandatory if the requirements for deferral are met. Section 121, however, offers the taxpayer over 55 the election to defer.

14. I.R.C. §1034(a); Treas. Reg. §1.1034-1(c)(3). A taxpayer may have several homes, but the Code recognizes only one as principal residence. Cf. William C. Stolk, 40 T.C. 345, 356 (1963), aff'd per curiam, 326 F.2d 760 (2d Cir. 1964). Thus, if a taxpayer has a summer home that is used three months yearly and another home that is used the rest of the year, only the latter would qualify under §1034. Further, if the taxpayer owned the summer home and rented the principal residence, any gain on the sale of the summer home would be immediately taxed. Levine, Real Estate Transactions, Tax Planning 361-362 (1976). Estate lawyers will see the parallel in the distinction between residence and domicile.

15. I.R.C. §1034(a); Treas. Reg. §1.1034-1(c)(1). "A residence any part of which was constructed or reconstructed by the taxpayer shall be treated as purchased by the taxpayer." I.R.C. §1034(c)(2). However, only those costs of construction, reconstruction, and improvements that are attributable to the four year period centering on the sale of the old residence may be included in determining the cost of the new residence for purposes of §1034. Id. In addition, the Regulations indicate that "the mere improvement of a residence, not amounting to reconstruction, does not constitute the 'purchase' of a residence." Treas. Reg. §1.1034-1(b)(9). The §1034 time limits are strictly observed. For example, even if the taxpayer begins construction of the new home expecting in good faith to satisfy §1034, and through no fault of taxpayer, occupancy is delayed beyond the statutory limit, taxpayer loses the benefit of deferral. Richard W. Henzel, T.C.M. 1965-250; Rev. Rul. 75-438, 1975-2 C.B. 334; John F. Balyley, 35 T.C. 288 (1960); Rev. Rul. 69-434, 1969-2 C.B. 163.

16. I.R.C. §1034(b); Treas. Reg. §§1.1034-1(b)(3), (4).

17. Treas. Reg. §1.1034-1(b)(4); Mrs. F. A. Griffin, 19 T.A. 1243 (1930); I.T. 2340, VI-1 C.B. 43; Rev. Rul. 54-380, 1954-2 C.B. 155.

18. Treas. Reg. §1.1034-1(b)(4)(ii). Discussion of mortgage assumption and taking subject to a mortgage begins at page 233 supra.

yer $700. Buyer takes title subject to a $20,000 mortgage. Two months before the sales contract is signed, taxpayer repaints several rooms — at the broker's suggestion — at a cost of $2000. Before the end of 1985, taxpayer pays $80,000 for a new residence and moves into it. Assuming that taxpayer occupied both houses as taxpayer's principal residence, what are the consequences of the above transactions?

1. Does the cost of the new residence exceed the "adjusted sales price" of the old residence?

Sales Price	$70,000	(including the $20,000 mortgage balance)
Less: Commissions	−4,200	
Lawyer's fees	− 700	
Amount realized	$65,100	
Less: Fix-up costs	−2,000	
Adjusted sales price	$63,100	

Since the $80,000 cost of the new residence exceeds the "adjusted sales price," §1034 requires present nonrecognition of the entire gain.

2. What is the taxpayer's gain? The taxpayer's gain or loss on the sale of the residence is the difference between the amount realized on the sale and the basis in the property.[19] For our purposes, a home owner's basis is the amount that owner paid for the property increased by any capital expenditures made during the holding period.[20]

Sales price	$ 70,000
Less: Commissions	− 4,200
Lawyer's fees	− 700
Amount realized	$ 65,100
Less: Adjusted basis cost	−40,000
Capital improvements	− 5,000
Gain on sale	$ 20,100

The nonrecognized portion of taxpayer's gain, in this case the entire $20,100, will be reflected in the basis of the new residence, which will be reduced by the amount of nonrecognized gain.[21] Thus taxpayer's $80,000 new residence will carry a $59,900 basis.

If, in the above example, the taxpayer had spent only $60,000 for the

---

19. I.R.C. §1001.
20. I.R.C. §§1012, 1016(a), 263; Treas. Reg. §§1.1012-1(a), -1(b), 1.1016-2, 1.263(a)-1, -2.
21. I.R.C. §1034(e); Treas. Reg. §1.1034-1(e)(2). One should carefully note that the $2,000 "fixing up expense" qualifies neither as a capital outlay, which the taxpayer may add to the adjusted basis pursuant to §1016(a) of the Code, nor as a selling expense, which the taxpayer may subtract from the consideration received pursuant to §1001.

Classification of Real Property

new residence, taxpayer would not have qualified for the full benefit of §1034.

Adjusted sales price	$ 63,100
Cost of new residence	−60,000
Adjusted sales price not invested in new residence (taxable gain)	$ 3,100
Gain	$ 20,100
Taxable gain	− 3,100
Nonrecognized gain	$ 17,000
Basis of new residence	$ 43,000

Section 1034 is also available where the taxpayer's principal residence is a condominium or a unit in a qualifying stockholder-cooperative. For example, a taxpayer might sell a condominium and buy a one-family detached house and, if each were a principal residence, bring the transaction within §1034.[22]

Before leaving the topic of taxpayer residence, we should mention that a personal residence may sometimes be used partially for business purposes, thus entitling the taxpayer to deductions for depreciation and maintenance expenses for the part of the residence so used. Discussion of the tax treatment of a combined residence-business use appears in numerous recent articles. See, e.g., Davis and Heller, An Update on Section 280A: Home Office and Vacation Home Deductions, 14 Tax Adviser 525 (1983); Eichenbaum, The Office at Home, 10 J. Real Est. Taxn. 63 (1982); Kulsrad, Recent Statutory and Judicial Developments Have Liberalized Home Office Deductions, 56 J. Taxn. 344 (1982); Lang, When a House Is Not Entirely a Home: Deductions Under Internal Revenue Code §280A for Home Offices, Vacation Homes, Etc., 1981 Utah L. Rev. 275; Rice, The Controversy with the I.R.S. Over the Rental of Personal Residences, 9 J. Real Est. Taxn. 143 (1982); Ward, Home Office Deductions: The Development and Current Status of Section 280A(c)(1), 13 Cum. L. Rev. 195 (1982-83).

2. *Property Held for the Production of Income (Investment Property)*

Two categories of real property qualify as "property held for the production of income": property held solely for investment (i.e., property held "for future use or future realization of the increment in

---

22. Rev. Rul. 64-31, 1964-1 C.B. 300 (condominiums); I.R.C. §1034(f); Treas. Reg. §1.1034-1(c)(3) (stock-cooperatives).

value. . . .")[23] and property currently producing income, but not used in a trade or business. As with property held solely as a personal residence, interest[24] and taxes[25] are deductible. The owner may also deduct all the ordinary and necessary expenses incurred in managing, conserving, or maintaining the property.[26] Moreover, owner is given a limited election between deducting the "carrying charges" or capitalizing them. If the parcel is unimproved, interest, taxes, and all other carrying charges may be capitalized;[27] if the parcel is improved, however, only specified carrying charges, which do not include real estate taxes, may be capitalized as a matter of right.[28] A taxpayer, having no current income against which to offset tax, interest, and other deductions, may, thus, apply these outlays toward lowering his or her eventual gains on resale.[29]

In addition, ownership of improved real estate held for the production of income entitles the taxpayer to an allowance for depreciation.[30] This allowance, as will be seen, offers one of the chief inducements to real estate

23. Treas. Reg. §1.1031(a)-1(b).
24. Since 1969 the Code has limited the interest deduction on money borrowed to acquire investment assets. Tightened further in 1976, the deduction may not exceed the taxpayer's net investment income for the year (not including long-term capital gains), plus $10,000. I.R.C. §163(d).
25. I.R.C. §164(a). Construction period interest and taxes are an exception to this rule. Under I.R.C. §189 taxpayers are required to capitalize interest and taxes attributable to the construction period of all realty that does *not* fall within one of the following categories: low income housing; property that is not and cannot reasonably be expected to be held for the production of income or for use in a trade or business; and residential realty acquired, constructed, or carried by regular corporations. Beginning in 1984, 10 percent of the amount capitalized is deductible in the year in which it is paid or accrued. The remainder is amortized over the nine-year period commencing with the year the property is ready to be placed in service or to be held for sale. Phase-in provisions apply to amounts paid or accrued after 1975 and before 1984. As an alternative to §189, taxpayers may elect to capitalize construction period interest and taxes under §266. See note 27 infra.
26. I.R.C. §212; Treas. Reg. §1.212-1(b) (individual taxpayer); I.R.C. §162 (corporate taxpayer).
27. I.R.C. §266; Treas. Reg. §1.266-1(a), (b)(1).
28. Id. The enumerated carrying charges, for which capitalization is always possible are interest, employee taxes, sales taxes, and other necessary expenditures for the "development of the real property or for the construction of an improvement or additional improvement to such real property, up to the time the development or construction work has been completed." Treas. Reg. §1.266-1(b)(1)(ii). With respect to other taxes and carrying charges, the Commissioner must agree to capitalization. Treas. Reg. §1.266-1(b)(iv). Cf. Smyth v. Sullivan, 227 F.2d 12 (9th Cir. 1955), *aff'g* Sullivan v. Smyth, 44 Am. Fed. Tax Rep. (P-H) 920 (N.D. Cal. 1953).
29. Losses are deductible and may be used to offset income from other sources, since the transaction presumably is engaged in for profit. I.R.C. §165(c)(2). If such other income is insufficient to absorb the loss, however, the taxpayer may not carry the excess loss backward or forward under the carryover provisions of I.R.C. §172. (For an individual, §172 applies only to property used in a trade or business.) Taxpayer might find it beneficial, therefore, to elect to capitalize some or all of his or her carrying charges, so as to reduce the current deductions that do taxpayer no immediate good taxwise and to provide an increased basis that can be of tax benefit in future years.
Corporate taxpayers are free of the "trade or business" limitations of §172. They are entitled to carry over operating losses from any rental property.
30. I.R.C. §167(a)(2).

investment, for it is an important source of so-called tax-sheltered income. Current production of income is not essential for the asset to be depreciable.[31] To qualify, the owner need only show that the purpose in holding the property was acquisition of current or future income.

The only case in which real property that is neither held solely as a personal residence nor held primarily for sale to customers might fail to qualify for depreciation is the case in which the owner's use of the property is "not engaged in for profit" as defined by §183. This section sharply limits the deductibility of all expenses beyond interest, taxes, and casualty losses, arising from such activities.[32]

Typically, §183 concerns owners of resort condominiums who hire out their units to transient renters. The statute provides that unless a rental activity earns a profit in any two of five consecutive years, the taxpayer must overcome a presumption of a §183 not-for-profit[33] activity; the regulations still make this fairly simple, however, for an owner who derives no personal pleasure or recreation from the unit.[34] But Congress in 1976 sought to stiffen the requirements for taxpayers making excessive personal use of a vacation facility. If the owner or related persons occupy the unit for more than 14 days annually (or 10 percent of the "fair rental" days, whichever is greater), the taxpayer shall be deemed to be using the unit for personal purposes.[35] Should that occur, the owner's deductions may not exceed gross rental income;[36] in other words, there can be no net operating losses. Where the taxpayer's personal use is not excessive under the statutory standard, the two-years-in-five test of §183 will continue to control.[37] Finally, the 1976 law would treat as de minimis any rental activity during the year of two weeks or less. The taxpayer would be able to

---

31. William C. Horrmann, 17 T.C. 903, 907 (1951), *acq.* 1952-1 C.B. 2. "The term 'production of income' under Section 212 [deduction of all ordinary and necessary expenses] is broadly construed to include 'not merely income of the taxable year but also income which the taxpayer has realized in a prior taxable year or may realize in subsequent taxable years; and is not confined to recurring income but applies as well to gains from the disposition of property.' This broad definition has been held to be applicable under Section 167, and therefore there is no difference between property held for investment and property for the production of income. George W. Mitchell, 47 T.C. 120 at 128, *acq.* 1967-1 C.B. 2." Anderson, Tax Factors in Real Estate Operations 25, n.10 (4th ed. 1976).

32. I.R.C. §183; Treas. Reg. 1.183-1(b). Regardless of the venture's unprofitability, items otherwise deductible — viz. real estate taxes, interest, casualty losses — remain so. Beyond these items, however, aggregate deductions (except for the "as-of-right" deductions) cannot exceed the property's gross income. Moreover, the taxpayer cannot begin depreciating the property until first itemizing all other deductible expenses.

33. I.R.C. §183(d).

34. Treas. Reg. §183-2(b). This regulation specifies nine factors that bear on the taxpayer's motive or intent to carry on the activity for profit despite its nonprofitable record. These factors include: the time and effort expended; the expertise of the taxpayer's advisors; the businesslike manner of the taxpayer's bookkeeping; the likelihood of future appreciation; and the element of personal pleasure or recreation.

35. I.R.C. §280A(a), (b), (d).

36. I.R.C. §280A(c)(5).

37. I.R.C. §280A(f)(3).

exclude gross rentals but would not receive the deductions that come with an income-producing activity.[38]

The sale or exchange of property held for the production of income is a capital transaction.[39] Capital losses deductions are limited, however, either to the extent of capital gains (in the case of corporations), or to capital gains plus a maximum of $3000 against other taxable income (in the case of noncorporate taxpayers).[40] Gains that stem from the taxpayer's use of accelerated depreciation, page 373 infra, are subject to the depreciation "recapture" provisions of §1250,[41] which may result in some of these gains being taxed as ordinary income. More on recapture later.

3. Property Held for Use in a Trade or Business

It can be vexatious to distinguish this category from the one preceding. In defining capital asset, §1221(2) excludes property used in the taxpayer's trade or business.[42] Instead, trade or business assets held for more than six months are treated as §1231 property[43] — a classification that will usually result in a tax advantage if the taxpayer suffers a loss on a sale or exchange. Consider the following example. Taxpayer owns two parcels, A and B, having held them for several years. Each parcel has a $50,000 basis. The parcels are sold for $60,000 and $30,000 respectively. In the year of the sale taxpayer has $10,000 of other ordinary income.

If both parcels are §1221 (capital) assets, taxpayer will be deemed to have suffered a net long-term capital loss,[44] which would be computed as follows:

Long-term capital gain[45]	(Parcel A)	$10,000
Less: Long-term capital loss[46]	(Parcel B)	($20,000)
Net long-term capital loss		($10,000)

---

38. I.R.C. §280A(g).
39. I.R.C. §1221.
40. I.R.C. §§165(f), 1211; Treas. Reg. §1.1211-1. Only 50 percent of an individual's long-term capital loss may be offset against ordinary income. The taxpayer may utilize the capital loss carryover provisions of I.R.C. §1212 and Treas. Reg. §1.1212-1.
41. I.R.C. §1250; Treas. Reg. §1.1250-1–5.
42. I.R.C. §1221(2).
43. I.R.C. §1231(b)(1). Prior to 1977, the minimum holding period for §1231 property was more than six months. For the transition year 1977, the minimum holding period was more than nine months. Beginning in 1978, the minimum period was extended to more than one year, but once again, for property acquired after June 22, 1984 and before January 1, 1988, Congress has reduced the minimum period to more than six months.
44. I.R.C. §1222(8).
45. I.R.C. §1222(3).
46. I.R.C. §1222(4).

Classification of Real Property

Only $3000 of a capital loss in any one year may be used to offset other income.[47] Therefore, taxpayer's income for the transaction year is $7000.

If the parcels are treated as §1231 (trade or business) assets, any excess of §1231 losses over §1231 gains becomes an ordinary loss;[48] as such, the $10,000 may be applied fully to offset taxpayer's other income.[49] Thus in the above example, taxable income would be zero. Moreover, if there is any unabsorbed loss, taxpayer can utilize the carryover provisions of §172,[50] which are far more generous than the capital loss carryover provisions of §1212.[51]

In the case of a gain on a sale or exchange, where the taxpayer has made only one transaction in the tax year, it will not matter whether the asset is governed by §1221 or §1231, since net gains from §1231 transactions are treated as capital gains.[52] If taxpayer has made multiple transactions, however, that include offsetting (but not outweighing) §1231 losses, taxpayer might prefer to have the profitable transactions taxable under §1221.[53]

During the holding period, property used in a trade or business receives the same tax treatment as property held for the production of income, with the technical exception that (trade or business) expenses are deductible under §162[54] rather than under §212 (expenses for the production of income).[55] Since the taxpayer usually does not have to declare prior to any

---

47. I.R.C. §1221(b). If taxpayer is a corporation, no part of the capital loss may be applied against other income. I.R.C. §1211(a). For all taxpayers, the unused capital loss may be carried over to succeeding years. I.R.C. §1212. However, each dollar of offset absorbs two dollars of net long-term, capital loss. §§1211(b), 1212(b). In the textual example, the taxpayer would have only $4,000 of carryover loss.

48. I.R.C. §1231(a).
49. I.R.C. §165(c)(1).
50. I.R.C. §172.
51. I.R.C. §1212.
52. I.R.C. §1231(a). The Deficit Reduction Act of 1984 has added an important qualification. If the taxpayer has incurred net §1231 losses for the preceding five year period beginning in 1982, his §1231 gains will be treated as ordinary income to the extent of any "unrecaptured" net §1231 losses. I.R.C. §1231(c).

53. Anderson, Tax Factors in Real Estate Transactions 14 (2d ed. 1965), gives the following example: "Owner purchases a small apartment of four rental units. The property costs him $40,000, but after 10 years of rental, its basis is reduced to $20,000. Owner then sells the apartment for $30,000, realizing a $10,000 gain. In the same year, he has reported the sale of two meat coolers used in his businesses for more than six months at a loss of $5000." What result?

	Apartment Held as Income Producing	Apartment Held for Use in Business
Capital Gain	$10,000	
§1231 Gain		$10,000
§1231 Loss	($5,000)	($5,000)
Net §1231 Gain or Loss	($5,000)	$5,000

54. I.R.C. §162.
55. I.R.C. §212.

sale or exchange whether he or she regards the property as a §1221 or a §1231 asset, the circumstances of the transaction itself may well cause an after-the-fact decision by taxpayer (and commissioner) as to which section should apply. The courts have not had an easy time of it, and one can only say — especially as regards taxpayers who are relatively inactive in their real estate ventures — that the decisional law is muddled.[56]

4. Property Held Primarily for Sale to Customers

Property held "*primarily for sale to customers* in the ordinary course of [the taxpayer's] trade or business" is discussed separately because it, too, is excepted from the §1221 definition of capital asset.[57] Unlike "trade or business" assets, however, which are also excepted by §1221 but advantageously treated under §1231, all property held primarily for sale to customers is an "ordinary" asset, and any sale or exchange transaction will result in ordinary income or loss.

During the holding period prior to sale, the taxpayers may deduct "trade or business" expenses,[58] interest,[59] state and local taxes,[60] and losses.[61] The allowance for depreciation, however, does not apply to property held primarily for sale to customers,[62] unless the property also is used to produce current income.[63]

Taxpayers whose activity makes their income subject to ordinary gains treatment are called "dealers," as distinguished from "investors" — taxpayers able to utilize §§1221 or 1231. Owners who subdivide their

---

56. Compare Grier v. United States, 120 F. Supp. 395 (D. Conn. 1954), *aff'd per curiam*, 218 F.2d 603 (2d Cir. 1955), with Leland Hazard, 7 T.C. 372 (1946), *acq.* 1946-2 C.B. 3. In *Grier*, taxpayer had inherited a one-family house that was being rented. When he sold the house at a loss, taxpayer sought to qualify the event as a (§1221) capital loss, because the Code then made it advantageous for him to to so. Over the commissioner's vigorous opposition, the court agreed with the taxpayer's designation. In *Hazard*, decided a few years earlier, the tax court had held that the rental by a lawyer of his former residence constituted a trade or business to him, which permitted him to obtain §1231 treatment of his loss. The irony of *Grier* is that the commissioner's argument was consistent with his acquiescence in *Hazard*. Lest you conclude that the overriding principal is "taxpayer always wins," examine McNeill v. Commr., 251 F.2d 863, 866 (4th Cir. 1958).

A recent analysis of the §§1221(2) and 1231 cases concludes that the law "focuses on the extent of the taxpayer's *activities* in relation to the property, with extensive activities indicating the presence of a trade or business." 2 Guerin, Taxation of Real Estate Dispositions §16.17 (1982).

57. I.R.C. §1221(1).
58. I.R.C. §162(a).
59. I.R.C. §163(a).
60. I.R.C. §164.
61. I.R.C. §165.
62. I.R.C. §167(a).
63. Compare Camp Wolters Enterprises, 22 T.C. 737, 754 (1954), *aff'd*, 230 F.2d 555 (5th Cir. 1956), *cert. denied*, 352 U.S. 826 (1956), with I.T. 1342, I-1 C.B. 169 (1922).

Classification of Real Property 361

property before sale are almost certainly dealers,[64] unless they can qualify the transaction under the more liberal, but tricky, provisions of §1237.[65]

Since only this form of property results in ordinary income upon its sale (after six months), the taxpayer who is not a confirmed dealer (and even the confirmed dealer, as to any unusual activity) will usually fight the Internal Revenue Service commissioner's effort to designate him as a "dealer." The courts have been deluged with such disputes; consider how you would decide the following illustrative cases:

  1. Homebuilder acquires 28-acre tract for intended subdivision, but resells 16-acre portion to commercial buyer after deciding not to develop residentially. Ordinary or capital gains?[66]
  2. Dwelling units, originally constructed as rental units, are later sold. Ordinary or capital gains?[67]
  3. Building supply company acquires customer's unsold houses in settlement of account and makes a further profit on their sale. Ordinary or capital gains?[68]
  4. An investor in rental real estate, forced to raise funds to pay off a debt, sells fourteen homes in one year, thirty-one the next, and twelve in the following year. Ordinary or capital gains?[69]
  5. A dealer sells his personal residence. Ordinary or capital gains?[70]
  6. A dealer sets up a separate investment account, in which he places a small multi-family dwelling. A few years later the building is sold. Ordinary or capital gains?[71]

---

  64. Palos Verdes Corp. v. United States, 201 F.2d 256 (9th Cir. 1952).
  65. I.R.C. §1237. This section permits the owner, who is not a dealer, to subdivide a parcel and report part, and perhaps all, of the gains from the sale of the lots, as long-term capital gain. But the making of any substantial improvements in order to ready the lots for sale will bar the use of §1237, unless the tract has been held for more than 10 years. (Streets, sewers, and drainage works all are substantial improvements.) It makes no difference whether the owner alone makes the improvements, or whether they are made through an agent or contractor, a member of the owner's family, a controlled corporation, a special improvement district, or a contract vendee as a condition of the contract. Furthermore, the taxpayer must have held the tract (unless taxpayer inherits and then sells immediately) for more than five years to reap the benefits of §1237. Finally, the section is not available to corporations. For a more detailed discussion, including sample tax computations and an opinion that §1237 may booby trap the taxpayer, see Anderson, Tax Planning of Real Estate 203-211 (7th ed. 1977). See also 2 Guerin, Taxation of Real Estate Dispositions §§16.27-16.35 (1982).
  66. See Maddux Construction Co. v. Commr., 54 T.C. 1278 (1970); cf. also Frank H. Taylor and Son, Inc., 32 T.C.M. 362 (1973).
  67. See, e.g., Galena Oaks Corp. v. Scofield, 218 F.2d 217 (5th Cir. 1954); Curtis Co. v. Commr., 232 F.2d 167 (3d Cir. 1956).
  68. See, e.g., Thompson Lumber Co., 43 B.T.A. 726 (1941). But cf. Houston Endowment, Inc. v. United States, 606 F.2d 77, 81 (1979).
  69. See, e.g., McGah v. Commr., 210 F.2d 769, 771 (9th Cir. 1954).
  70. See, e.g., Walter R. Crabtree, 20 T.C. 841 (1953), acq. 1954-1 C.B. 4.
  71. Compare Jones v. Commr., 209 F.2d 415 (9th Cir. 1954), with Rollingwood Corp. v. Commr., 190 F.2d 263 (9th Cir. 1951).

One point of confusion centered on the word "primarily," which forms part of the §1221(1) phrase. In the following decision, the United States Supreme Court tried to settle its meaning.

Malat v. Riddell[72]
383 U.S. 569 (1966)

PER CURIAM. Petitioner was a participant in a joint venture which acquired a 45-acre parcel of land, the intended use for which is somewhat in dispute. Petitioner contends that the venturers' intention was to develop and operate an apartment project on the land; the respondent's position is that there was a "dual purpose" of developing the property for rental purposes or selling, whichever proved to be the more profitable. In any event, difficulties in obtaining the necessary financing were encountered, and the interior lots of the tract were subdivided and sold. The profit from those sales was reported and taxed as ordinary income.

The joint venturers continued to explore the possibility of commercially developing the remaining exterior parcels. Additional frustrations in the form of zoning restrictions were encountered. These difficulties persuaded petitioner and another of the joint venturers of the desirability of terminating the venture; accordingly, they sold out their interests in the remaining property. Petitioner contends that he is entitled to treat the profits from this last as capital gains; the respondent takes the position that this was "property held by the taxpayer primarily for sale to customers in the ordinary course of his trade or business," and thus subject to taxation as ordinary income.

The District Court made the following finding: "The members of [the joint venture], as of the date the 44.901 acres were acquired, intended either to sell the property or develop it for rental, depending upon which course appeared to be most profitable. The venturers realized that they had made a good purchase price-wise and, if they were unable to obtain acceptable construction financing or rezoning . . . which would be prerequisite to commercial development, they would sell the property in bulk so they wouldn't get hurt. The purpose of either selling or developing the property continued during the period in which [the joint venture] held the property.

The District Court ruled that petitioner had failed to establish that the property was not held *primarily* for sale to customers in the ordinary course

---

72. Footnotes omitted.

Classification of Real Property

of business, and thus rejected petitioner's claim to capital gain treatment for the profits derived from the property's resale. The Court of Appeals affirmed, 347 F.2d 23. We granted certiorari (382 U.S. 900) to resolve a conflict among the courts of appeals with regard to the meaning of the term "primarily" as it is used in §1221(1) of the Internal Revenue Code of 1954.

The statute denies capital gain treatment to profits reaped from the sale of "property held by the taxpayer *primarily* for sale to customers in the ordinary course of his trade or business." (Emphasis added.) The respondent urges upon us a construction of "primarily" as meaning that a purpose may be "primary" if it is a "substantial" one.

As we have often said, "the words of statutes—including revenue acts—should be interpreted where possible in their ordinary, everyday senses." Crane v. Commissioner, 331 U.S. 1, 6. And see Hanover Bank v. Commissioner, 369 U.S. 672, 687-688; Commissioner v. Korell, 339 U.S. 619, 627-628. Departure from a literal reading of statutory language may, on occasion, be indicated by relevant internal evidence of the statute itself and necessary in order to effect the legislative purpose. See, e.g., Board of Governors v. Agnew, 329 U.S. 441, 446-448. But this is not such an occasion. The purpose of the statutory provision with which we deal is to differentiate between the "profits and losses arising from the everyday operation of a business" on the one hand (Corn Products Co. v. Commissioner, 350 U.S. 46, 52) and "the realization of appreciation in value accrued over a substantial period of time" on the other. (Commissioner v. Gillette Motor Co., 364 U.S. 130, 134.) A literal reading of the statute is consistent with this legislative purpose. We hold that, as used in §1221(1), "primarily" means "of first importance" or "principally."

Since the courts below applied an incorrect legal standard, we do not consider whether the result would be supportable on the facts of this case had the correct one been applied. We believe, moreover, that the appropriate disposition is to remand the case to the District Court for fresh fact-findings, addressed to the statute as we have now construed it.

Vacated and remanded.

Mr. Justice Black would affirm the judgments of the District Court and the Court of Appeals.

Mr. Justice White took no part in the decision of this case.

Except for its effort at definition, the Supreme court in *Malat* offers lower courts little help in disposing of the frequent disputes between taxpayer and commissioner over "dealer" classification. As a result, the case law remains in disarray, as evidenced below.

Byram v. Commissioner
555 F.2d 1234 (5th Cir. 1983)

Gee, Circuit Judge.

"If a client asks you in any but an extreme case whether, in your opinion, his sale will result in capital gain, your answer should probably be, 'I don't know, and no one else in town can tell you.'"[1]

Sadly, the above wry comment on federal taxation of real estate transfers has, in the twenty-five years or so since it was penned, passed from the status of half-serious aside to that of hackneyed truism. Hackneyed or not, it is the primary attribute of truisms to be true, and this one is: in that field of the law — real property tenure — where the stability of rule and precedent has been exalted above all others, it seems ironic that one of its attributes, the tax incident upon disposition of such property, should be one of the most uncertain in the entire field of litigation. But so it is, and we are called on again today to decide a close case in which almost a million dollars in claimed refunds are at stake. Doing so requires us to survey the development of this law in our circuit and to consider what application here, if any, the recent decision in Pullman-Standard v. Swint, 456 U.S. 273, 102 S. Ct. 1781, 72 L. Ed. 2d 66 (1982), is to find.

Facts

The trial court, sitting without a jury in this taxpayer's suit for refund, found the following facts:

During 1973, John D. Byram, the taxpayer, sold seven pieces of real property. Mr. Byram was not a licensed real estate broker, was not associated with a real estate company which advertised itself, and did not maintain a separate real estate office. He advertised none of the seven properties for sale, nor did he list any of them with real estate brokers. To the contrary, all of the transactions were initiated either by the purchaser or by someone acting in the purchaser's behalf.

None of the properties sold was platted or subdivided. Byram devoted minimal time and effort to the sales in question, occupying himself chiefly with his rental properties. Byram's income for 1972 and 1973 included substantial amounts of rental income and interest income.

The district court's findings do not reflect the following additional facts, which apparently are not disputed by the parties. From 1971

---

1. Comment, Capital Gains: Dealer and Investor Problems, 35 Taxes 804, 806 (1957) quoted in 3B Mertens, Law of Federal Income Taxation §22.138 n.69 (Zimet & Weiss rev. 1958); Biedenharn Realty Co. v. United States, 509 F.2d 171, 175 (5th Cir. 1975), *rev'd en banc*, 526 F.2d 409 (5th Cir.), *cert. denied*, 429 U.S. 819, 97 S. Ct. 64, 50 L. Ed. 2d 79 (1976); Thompson v. Commissioner, 322 F.2d 122, 123 n.2 (5th Cir. 1963); Cole v. Usry, 294 F.2d 426, 427 n.3 (5th Cir. 1961).

through 1973, Byram sold 22 parcels of real property for a total gross return of over $9 million and a net profit of approximately $3.4 million. The seven properties at issue in this case sold for approximately $6.6 million gross, resulting in a profit of approximately $2.5 million. Six of the seven properties were held by Byram for periods ranging from six to nine months, intervals just exceeding the then-applicable holding periods for long-term capital gains. The seventh property had been held for two years and six months.

Although, as noted above, Mr. Byram received substantial rent and interest income in 1973, nevertheless his rental activities for that year resulted in a net tax loss of approximately $186,000. He received rental income from only one of the seven properties sold in 1973. The record does not reflect the exact relative amounts of income attributable to the sales in question and Byram's other activities.

Certain facts are disputed by the parties. The government asserts in its brief that Byram had entered into contracts to sell at least three of the seven properties in issue before he actually acquired them. Byram first responds that the record reflects only two such instances, not three; and at oral argument the government appeared to concede the point. As to those two transactions, Byram asserts that he acquired the right to purchase the properties by executing a contract before he entered into a contract to sell them; it was only closing on the purchases that postdated his contracts to sell. Finally, the government asserts, and Byram denies, that by virtue of Byram's civic activities in Austin, Texas, Byram's business of selling real estate was well-known in the community.

Based on its subsidiary findings indicated, the district court made ultimate findings that Byram held each of the seven properties for investment purposes and not primarily for sale to customers in the ordinary course of his trade or business. Judgment was therefore entered granting Byram the capital gains treatment that he sought. The government brought this appeal.

. . . Profits derived from the sale of "capital assets," known as "capital gains," are entitled to favorable tax treatment under the Internal Revenue Code (the "Code"). See 26 U.S.C. §§1201, 1202. The term "capital asset" is defined in relevant part as "property held by the taxpayer," not including property held "primarily for sale to customers in the ordinary course of [the taxpayer's] trade or business." Id., §1221. The district court found that Byram "was not engaged in the real estate business" during the relevant years and that each of the seven properties in issue was held "for investment purposes and not primarily for sale to customers in the ordinary course of [Byram's] trade or business." Accordingly, the district court held that Byram was entitled to treat the profits from his 1973 sales as capital gains and ordered an appropriate refund. Our first task is to decide the correct standard by which to review the district court's principal finding[3] that Byram's holding purpose was for investment rather than for sale. The choice of a standard will determine the outcome of many cases; if the issue is treated as factual, the district court's decision is final unless clearly erroneous, F.R.C.P. 52(a), but if a question of law is presented, we may decide it de novo.

The question whether the characterization of property as "primarily held for sale to customers in the ordinary course of [a taxpayer's] trade or business" is an issue of fact or one of law has engendered tremendous controversy and conflict both in this[4] and in other[5] circuits. Recognizing the conflict in our own cases, a panel recently attempted to resolve it by breaking the statutory test down into its component parts, see note 3, supra, some of which we held "are predominantly legal conclusions or are 'mixed questions of fact and law,' whereas others are essentially questions of fact." *Suburban Realty,* 615 F.2d at 180 (footnote omitted). As we shall see, it must now be admitted that, because we were forced to struggle with

---

3. In Suburban Realty Co. v. United States, 615 F.2d 171 (5th Cir.), *cert. denied,* 449 U.S. 920, 101 S. Ct. 318, 66 L. Ed. 2d 147 (1980), we recognized that the Code definition of "capital asset" gives rise to at least three inquiries:

(1) was taxpayer engaged in a trade or business, and, if so, what business?
(2) was taxpayer holding the property primarily for sale in that business?
(3) were the sales contemplated by taxpayer "ordinary" in the course of that business?

Id. at 178 (footnote omitted).

In many situations, these questions are analytically independent. For example, it will oftentimes be beyond dispute that a taxpayer is engaged in the real estate business with respect to certain properties, yet *other properties* may not be held primarily for sale in that business, or *particular sales* may be outside its ordinary scope. See, e.g., Wood v. Commissioner, 276 F.2d 586 (5th Cir. 1960); Maddux Construction Co. v. Commissioner, 54 T.C. 1278 (1970). However, in the present case the three statutory questions tend to merge into one, because the existence of a business, Byram's holding purpose, and the "ordinariness" of sales must all be determined by characterization of the same transactions. Moreover, because we decide below that Byram's holding purpose must be treated as an issue of fact, and that the district court's finding is not clearly erroneous, the holding below must be left undisturbed and we need not address related questions arguably posed by the statute.

4. See *Suburban Realty,* 615 F.2d at 180, collecting cases treating the issue as one of law, e.g., Houston Endowment, Inc. v. United States, 606 F.2d 77, 83 (5th Cir. 1979); United States v. Winthrop, 417 F.2d 905, 910 (5th Cir. 1969); Galena Oaks Corp. v. Scofield, 218 F.2d 217 (5th Cir. 1954); and another line of cases treating the question as essentially factual, e.g., United States v. Burket, 402 F.2d 426, 429 (5th Cir. 1968); Thompson v. Commissioner, 322 F.2d 122, 127 (5th Cir. 1963).

5. Three other circuit courts of appeals treat the issue as one of fact. Philhall Corp. v. United States, 546 F.2d 210 (6th Cir. 1976); Brown v. Commissioner, 448 F.2d 514 (10th Cir. 1971); Municipal Bond Corp. v. Commissioner, 382 F.2d 184 (8th Cir. 1967). Two circuits treat it as a question of law, following our cases that so hold. Turner v. Commissioner, 540 F.2d 1249 (4th Cir. 1976); Jersey Land & Development Corp. v. United States, 539 F.2d 311 (3d Cir. 1976). In other circuits, the issue is apparently unsettled. Compare Sovereign v. Commissioner, 281 F.2d 830 (7th Cir. 1960) (fact question) with Hansche v. Commissioner, 457 F.2d 429 (7th Cir. 1972) (treats question as open); compare Estate of Segel v. Commissioner, 370 F.2d 107 (2d Cir. 1966) (applies clearly erroneous standard) with In re Joseph Kanner Hat Co., 482 F.2d 937 (2d Cir. 1973) (bankruptcy case; dicta that de novo review applies). See also Cruttenden v. Commissioner, 644 F.2d 1368 (9th Cir. 1981) (open question); Parkside, Inc. v. Commissioner, 571 F.2d 1092, 1095 n.5 (9th Cir. 1977) (only one panel member accepts position that issue is one of fact).

this circuit's longstanding distinction between "subsidiary facts" and "ultimate facts," this attempt to clarify the law was not entirely successful. . . .

Fortunately, it is unnecessary once again to traverse the conceptual thicket of ultimate and subsidiary facts so carefully husbanded by this court through the years. The Supreme Court has levelled it. Pullman-Standard v. Swint, 456 U.S. 273, 102 S. Ct. 1781, 72 L. Ed. 2d 66 (1982).

In *Swint*, the Court reviewed a decision of this court holding that by setting up and perpetuating a particular seniority system, an employer and two unions had discriminated against black employees in violation of Title VII of the Civil Rights Act. 42 U.S.C. §2000e-2(h). In order to establish discrimination in the operation of a seniority system, it is necessary to prove discriminatory intent. Id.; *Swint*, 456 U.S. at 275-277, 102 S. Ct. at 1783-1784, 72 L. Ed. 2d at 72-73. Analyzing the issue in the manner suggested by this court, the district court found that the seniority system did not result from an intention to discriminate. Treating the issue of discriminatory purpose as one of ultimate fact, this court independently reviewed the record and made its own finding of discrimination.

Reversing that decision and rejecting our authorities on which it rested, the Supreme Court held that our accepted rule allowing de novo review of ultimate facts is incompatible with the dictates of Rule 52, Federal Rules of Civil Procedure. 456 U.S. at 285-287, 102 S. Ct. at 1788-1789, 72 L. Ed. 2d at 78-79. The Court emphasized that Rule 52 "broadly requires" that findings of fact be accepted unless clearly erroneous, and that it does not divide findings of fact into categories. Id.

The Court recognized the "vexing nature of the distinction between questions of fact and questions of law," and noted that Rule 52 provides little guidance in drawing the line. Id. 456 U.S. at 287, 102 S. Ct. at 1789, 72 L. Ed. 2d at 79. Indeed, the ultimate fact doctrine itself probably can be understood best as an abortive attempt to resolve the law/fact dilemma by making that elusive distinction less determinative. Elusive or not, *Swint* tells us that it is a distinction Rule 52 requires us to draw.

Though the characterization of issues as ones of law or fact may be difficult in some cases, the present case is not one of them. . . .

The purpose for holding property, like the purpose for maintaining a seniority system at issue in *Swint*, is a question of intent and motive.[9] As such, it is a question of pure fact, and is neither a question of law nor a mixed question of law and fact. See 456 U.S. at 287, 102 S. Ct. at 1789, 72

---

9. We have uniformly held that the statutory exception for property "held" for sale to customers, 26 U.S.C. §1221, requires an inquiry into a taxpayer's intent. See, e.g., *Surburban Realty*, 615 F.2d at 182-85; Biedenharn Realty Co. v. United States, 526 F.2d 409, 422-23 (5th Cir.) (en banc), *cert. denied*, 429 U.S. 819, 97 S. Ct. 64, 50 L. Ed. 2d 79 (1976). Moreover, the fact that the taxpayer's subjective state of mind is not controlling and an objective inquiry must be made by the court does not render the issue any less one of intent or any less factual. See Commissioner v. Duberstein, 363 U.S. 278, 286, 290-91, 80 S. Ct. 1190, 1199, 4 L. Ed. 2d 1218, 1225, 1228 (1960).

L. Ed. 2d at 79. The factors usually cited to justify plenary review of holding purpose are the same factors that the Court found unpersuasive in determining the proper standard of review in *Swint*. For example, both issues involve a consideration of all facts and circumstances, with emphasis on particular significant factors. Compare James v. Stockham Valves & Fittings Co., supra note 6 (relevant considerations under Title VII) with *Suburban Realty*, 615 F.2d at 176, 182-85 (factors relevant to holding purpose under the Code). Similarly, both issues require the district court to use a reasoning process in analyzing the facts and to apply certain legal standards in making its finding. See note 9, supra. Resolution of either issue can determine the outcome of a case. None of those considerations affected the *Swint* Court's conclusion that the issue of discriminatory intent is neither a question of law nor a mixed question of law and fact, but is a pure question of fact. We see no reason to subject a district court's determination of holding purpose to a different standard of review than that applied to a district court's finding of discriminatory intent. The district court's finding in the present case that Bryam held his property for investment rather than for sale to customers in the ordinary course of his business must be accepted unless it is clearly erroneous.

The record and the district court's findings of fact indicate that in determining Byram's holding purpose, the court considered all the factors this court has called "the seven pillars of capital gains treatment":[10]

> (1) the nature and purpose of the acquisition of the property and the duration of the ownership; (2) the extent and nature of the taxpayer's efforts to sell the property; (3) the number, extent, continuity and substantiality of the sales; (4) the extent of subdividing, developing, and advertising to increase sales; (5) the use of a business office for the sale of the property; (6) the character and degree of supervision or control exercised by the taxpayer over any representative selling the property; and (7) the time and effort the taxpayer habitually devoted to the sales.

United States v. Winthrop, 417 F.2d 905, 910 (5th Cir. 1969). Recent cases have placed particular emphasis on four of these factors, noting that frequency and substantiality of sales is the most important factor, and that improvements to the property, solicitation and advertising efforts, and brokerage activities are also especially relevant considerations. *Biedenharn Realty*, 526 F.2d at 415-16; *Surburban Realty*, 615 F.2d at 176. At the same time, it has been repeatedly emphasized that these factors should not be treated as talismans. *Winthrop*, 417 F.2d at 911. Rather, "each case must be decided on its own peculiar facts. . . . Specific factors, or combinations of them, are not necessarily controlling." *Biedenharn Realty*, 526 F.2d

---

10. In application, these "pillars" have come more nearly to resemble the walls of a maze. See, e.g., *Suburban Realty*, 615 F.2d 171; *Biedenharn Realty*, 526 F.2d 409.

at 415 (quoting Thompson v. Commissioner, 322 F.2d 122, 127 (5th Cir. 1963)).

The district court found most of the *Winthrop* factors absent in Byram's case. Byram made no personal effort to initiate the sales; buyers came to him. He did not advertise, he did not have a sales office, nor did he enlist the aid of brokers. The properties at issue were not improved or developed by him. The district court found that Byram devoted minimal time and effort to the transactions.[11] The government does not contend that any of these findings are clearly erroneous. Rather, the government argues that the frequency and substantiality of Byram's sales, together with the relatively short duration of his ownership of most of the properties, establishes that Byram intended to hold the properties for sale in the ordinary course of his business. In light of our decision regarding the standard of review, the government's argument must be that the district court clearly erred in finding these factors outweighed by the other relevant evidence. We cannot reasonably say that the district court's finding that Byram held his properties for investment was clearly erroneous.

The record reveals that during a three-year period, Byram sold 22 parcels of real estate for over $9 million, netting approximately $3.4 million profit.[12] Though these amounts are substantial by anyone's yardstick, the district court did not clearly err in determining that 22 such sales in three years were not sufficiently frequent or continuous to compel an inference of intent to hold the property for sale rather than investment. Compare *Suburban Realty,* 615 F.2d at 174 (244 sales over 32-year period); *Biedenharn Realty,* 526 F.2d at 411-12 (during 31-year period, taxpayer sold 208 lots and twelve individual parcels from subdivision in question; 477 lots were sold from other properties). This is particularly true in a case where the other relevant factors weigh so heavily in favor of the taxpayer.

---

11. This factor has been slighted in recent cases, not because it is unimportant, but because it was irrelevant to our consideration of the activities of large corporate organizations. See e.g. *Suburban Realty,* 615 F.2d 171; *Houston Endowment,* 606 F.2d 77; *Biedenharn Realty,* 526 F.2d 409. However, in a case like the present one, where the government seeks to show that an individual taxpayer is holding property for sale in a certain business, the quantum of that individual's activity becomes very relevant. Long before the proliferation of tests and factors engulfed the capital gains field, this court made the common sense observation that the word "business" means "busyness; it implies one is kept more or less busy, that the activity is an occupation." Snell v. Commissioner, 97 F.2d 891, 892 (5th Cir. 1938); see also Stern v. United States, 164 F. Supp. 847, 851 (E.D. La. 1958) ("[A] court should not be quick to put a man in business . . . simply because he has been successful in earning extra income through a hobby or some other endeavor which takes relatively small part of his time.") *aff'd* 262 F.2d 957 (5th Cir.), *cert. denied,* 359 U.S. 969, 79 S. Ct. 880, 3 L. Ed. 2d 836 (1959). The district court was entitled to give great weight to Byram's time and effort devoted to sales in determining whether he held his property for sale in the ordinary course of his business.

12. Although only the seven sales completed in 1973 are at issue in this case, prior years' activities are relevant to the characterization of the 1973 transactions. See Thompson v. Commissioner, 322 F.2d 122, 127 (5th Cir. 1963).

"[S]ubstantial and frequent sales activity, standing alone, has never been held to be automatically sufficient to trigger ordinary income treatment." *Surburban Realty,* 615 F.2d at 176. Moreover, Byram's relatively short holding periods for some of the properties do not tip the balance in favor of the government. Ranging from six to nine months, these periods exceeded the then-applicable threshold for long-term capital gain treatment. In establishing those thresholds, Congress clearly expressed its intent that sales of otherwise qualified capital assets held for six to nine months be accorded capital gains treatment. To avoid frustration of that intent, a court should avoid placing too much weight on duration of ownership where other indicia of intent to hold the property for sale are minimal.[13]

Mr. Byram has presented us with a close case. Had we been called upon to try or retry the facts, perhaps we would have drawn different inferences than did the district court. However, *Swint* has relieved us of that duty. Our review of the evidence convinces us that the district court was not clearly erroneous in finding that Byram held his properties for investment and not for sale in the ordinary course of his trade or business. . . .

NOTES AND QUESTIONS

1. Compare Goodman v. United States, 390 F.2d 915 (Ct. Cl. 1968), decided against the taxpayers. The Goodmans were New York City lawyers who specialized in real estate law. Their practice gave them opportunities to buy and sell realty for their own interests, as well as for clients and associates. They were not licensed real estate brokers. During the three tax years in question, the Goodmans sold 32 different realty interests. Of these, 15 had been held less than six months and only five had been held as long as five years. In each instance, the taxpayers' investment was that of a minority membership within the ownership syndicate. The taxpayers' net income from the sale or disposal of their real estate interests during this period exceeded by roughly one-third their net income from the practice of law. To the trier of fact, this evidence demonstrated that the taxpayers bought and held the various property interests primarily for sale to customers.

2. *Goodman* illustrates the professional taxpayer who also "invests" heavily in real estate. Why should it matter that the Goodmans earned

---

13. A variation of the argument based on short holding periods is that Byram's execution of contracts to sell two properties before acquiring title to them indicates lack of investment intent. The record shows that Byram contracted to purchase one of the properties and a portion of the other before engaging to see them. See Record, Volume IV, p. 307-07, 310; Plaintiffs' Exhibits 15, 19, & 20. For these, the timing of passage of title is irrelevant for our purposes. Even if we assume that Byram contracted to sell the remaining portion of property before acquiring it, our view of the district court's finding remains unaltered. Though this fact undoubtedly favors the government's position, the district court reasonably could have found it outweighed by the other evidence.

Classification of Real Property

more from real estate than from the practice of law? Suppose that the taxpayers' major source of income had been legal fees: would this change the result? Should it? Compare *Goodman* with Robert L. Adam, 60 T.C. 996 (1973), where taxpayer, a full-time CPA, obtained capital gains treatment on nine resales of property over a four-year period.

3. Does the Code discriminate against taxpayers whose livelihood comes partly from real estate investments? Suppose that the Goodmans had invested in corporate securities, including real estate corporations, and had churned their portfolio with the same frequency and profitability; would their gains be taxed at ordinary or capital rates? Does the §1221 phrase "primarily for sale *to customers*" explain satisfactorily the differing treatment of real estate and corporate securities? Cf. Chirelstein, Federal Income Taxation 317 (4th ed. 1985).

4. Even taxpayers who are real estate dealers may still seek investor status as to occasional properties. See, e.g., Richard Pritchett, 63 T.C. 149 (1975), where taxpayer real estate broker held investment properties in his own name and used partnerships or corporations for his regular dealings. In according capital gains treatment to the taxpayer's "investments," the court stressed the absence of advertising or subdivision, and the relatively long holding periods.

5. Section 1236 offers the securities dealer (e.g., underwriter, floor specialist) a method to insulate his securities' "investments" from §1221(1) status. The dealer must elect before the close of the day on which the securities were acquired whether to hold the property as an investment. He is bound by the election. What are the merits of a similar election in the real estate field?

6. The factual converse to *Malat* is the fairly typical case of the taxpayer who acquires investment property but later sells the property much as a dealer might — by subdivision, improvements, heavy advertising, or the use of brokers. The taxpayer may then claim that he has done so merely to *liquidate* the investment most feasibly and at the best price, and that he did not intend to enter into the subdivision business. For contrasting results, compare Estate of Josephine Clay Simpson, 21 T.C.M. 371 (1962), with Winthrop v. Tomlinson, 417 F.2d 905 (5th Cir. 1969). Suppose that taxpayer has paid $100,000 for property, that he can resell it for $200,000 without subdivision and sales promotion, and that his "liquidation" activity will net $350,000. Does the Code allow an allocation of gain between investment and dealership activity?

7. A closely related situation arises when a long-term investor in an apartment building decides to convert his project to a cooperative or condominium and sell off the units individually. Is there any way for the taxpayer to avoid §1221(1)? See page 1009 infra.

8. Where several taxpayers share interests in the same real property, as in *Goodman,* must they all be treated alike, i.e., as dealers, or nondealers? Cf. Riddell v. Scales, 406 F.2d 210, 212 (9th Cir. 1969); Tibbals v. United

States, 362 F.2d 266, 278 (Ct. Cl. 1966). Suppose that X, a dealer, owns a controlling interest in the X corporation; will X's status taint the corporation's? Cf. Royce W. Brown, 54 T.C. 1475 (1970), aff'd, 488 F.2d 514 (10th Cir. 1971); contra C. Frederick Frick, 31 T.C.M. 286 (1972).

9. The taxpayers in *Goodman* must have depreciated the properties that they sold during the years 1953-1955. What is the consequence for a taxpayer who takes depreciation before learning that he is a "dealer"?

10. Further readings include Friedlander, To "Customers": The Forgotten Element in Characterization of Gains on Sales of Real Property, 39 Tax L. Rev. 31 (1983); Weiss and Dallman, Tax Planning for Real Estate Transactions 269-274 (1983); 2 Guerin, Taxation of Real Estate Dispositions §§16.01-16.26 (1982); Levine, Real Estate Transactions: Tax Planning and Consequences §§331-338 (1981); Goggans and Englebrecht, Investors vs. Dealers: Tax Implications of Investor vs. Dealer Status in Real Estate, 9 J. Real Est. Taxn. 169 (1981); Note, Real Estate and Section 1221: Business as a Pattern of Activity in the Definition of a Capital Asset, 35 Tax Law. 225 (1981).

B. COST RECOVERY (DEPRECIATION) AND OTHER INVESTMENT INCENTIVES

Depreciation systems are a means of allocating the cost of an asset over the years of its projected useful life. If an asset is subject to wear and tear, wasting, or obsolescence, its owner's net worth is gradually reduced by the declining value of the property. For both accounting and taxation purposes, the basic aim of depreciation deductions is to determine more accurately the net gains or losses incurred by the owner during each year of the asset's ownership, by recognizing the yearly losses attributable to the decline of the asset as they are incurred, rather than delaying recognition until the property is disposed of.

Incidental to its theoretical purpose, the allowance for depreciation may also be a powerful incentive to develop and acquire property to the degree that it permits the investor to defer taxes, to convert ordinary income into capital gains, and, where depreciation results in or adds to a loss, to reduce taxes on income from other sources. Since 1981, with the passage of the Economic Recovery Tax Act (ERTA), this hitherto incidental aspect of the depreciation system has been elevated by Congress to one of its primary concerns. Under the new label "cost recovery," §168 permits accelerated depreciation deductions for both real and personal property over statutory "recovery periods" far shorter than the projected

Cost Recovery (Depreciation) and Other Investment Incentives

useful lives of the assets. As a result, the tax shelter afforded by depreciation has vastly expanded, and incentives to acquire and develop property have increased accordingly.

1. ACRS: Cost Recovery for Property Acquired After 1980

a. Eligible Property

The Accelerated Cost Recovery System (ACRS) applies only to "recovery property."[73] Such property is defined with few exceptions as "tangible property of a character subject to the allowance for depreciation — (A) used in a trade or business, or (B) held for the production of income,"[74] which was placed in service by the taxpayer after 1980.[75] Although ACRS is mandatory for all eligible property, several elections allow the taxpayer to remove specified types of property from its ambit — e.g., election of the straight-line method[76] or the §179 special expensing allowance.

Depreciable property generally includes property that is subject to wear and tear, to decay or decline from natural causes, to exhaustion and to obsolescence. Thus, that part of the cost of real property attributable to raw land is nondepreciable.[77] Allocation of the cost of real estate between improvements and the land on which they rest must be based on documentation of the relative fair market values of the buildings and land at the time of acquisition.[78] Disputes sometimes arise over the depreciability of land preparation costs — e.g., for clearing, filling, and grading. Generally such improvements are treated as nondepreciable land expenses, unless they are "so closely associated with assets such as . . . storm sewers . . . that they will be retired, abandoned, or replaced contemporaneously with these assets."[79]

Unlike previous systems, ACRS makes no distinctions between new and used or residential and commercial properties. Moreover, it prohibits the use of component depreciation, thus requiring the application of a single cost recovery method to an entire building and all its structural components — e.g., air conditioning, wiring, and plumbing.[80]

---

73. See I.R.C. §168(e)(2), (3), (4).
74. I.R.C. §168(c)(1).
75. I.R.C. §168(e)(1).
76. I.R.C. §168(b)(3).
77. Proposed Reg. §1.168-3(a)(1), 49 Fed. Reg. 33, 5957 (1984).
78. Treas. Reg. §1.167(a)(5).
79. Rev. Rul. 80-93, 1980-1 C.B. 50.
80. I.R.C. §168(f)(1).

b. Cost Recovery Periods

ACRS establishes four basic recovery periods—3, 5, 10, and 18 years—and assigns all recovery property to one of these periods.[81] Most realty falls within the eighteen-year class.[82] However, the taxpayer may elect, on a property-by-property basis, to extend the cost recovery of any real estate over either a thirty-five or forty-five-year period.[83]

c. Cost Recovery Methods

Only three cost recovery methods are utilized in ACRS: accelerated cost recovery (based on 175% declining balance) and straight-line method, which are permissible for all recovery property; and the 200% (double) declining balance method, which is permissible only for low income housing.[84] These methods are incorporated into tables prescribed by the Secretary for determining the percentage of the unadjusted basis of depreciable real property that may be recovered in a given year of ownership.[85] Although the tables in the regulations already include the necessary calculations under these methods, it is useful to understand how the applicable percentages for each year are computed.

Problem. X acquires an apartment house for $560,000, his purchase price allocated between land, $60,000, and improvements, $500,000. X elects to recover his cost over an eighteen-year period, although he estimates the property's useful life at forty years. At the end of forty years, X believes the apartment house will have a salvage value of approximately $40,000. Compute the cost recovery allowance for the first and second year by the straight-line method, and the 175% and 200% declining balance methods.

Straight-line. The computation is made by applying a constant multiple to a constant balance. Under ACRS, X disregards the estimated useful life and salvage value of the improvements, but must subtract the cost allocable to land.[86] This leaves a constant balance of $500,000. X then multiplies this sum by the reciprocal of the recovery period—in the case of an eighteen-year period, approximately 5.55 percent ($500,000 × .0555 = $27,750). The depreciation for the second and each succeeding year remains unchanged.

---

81. I.R.C. §168(c)(2).
82. I.R.C. §168(c)(2)(D). Between 1981 and 1984, real estate enjoyed a 15-year recovery period.
83. I.R.C. §168(b)(3).
84. I.R.C. §§168(b)(2)(A), (3)(A).
85. I.R.C. §168(b)(2)(A); Proposed Reg. §§1.168-2 (b), (c).
86. Proposed Reg. §1.168-2(a), 49 Fed. Reg. 33, 5943 (1984). Normally, when using the straight-line method, the taxpayer must first subtract the salvage value from the property's depreciable basis.

175% Declining Balance. The computation is made by applying a constant multiple to a changing balance. The constant multiple is equal to 175 percent of the straight-line rate for the given period, or approximately 9.62 percent. This percentage is multiplied by the undepreciated balance[87] — in our example, $500,000 in the first year — to result in an allowance of $48,125. In the second year this process is repeated; since the undepreciated balance has declined to $451,875, the product also declines ($451,875 × .0962 = $43,470). In succeeding years the drop continues; if charted the depreciation would resemble a hyperbolic curve.

200% Declining Balance. The computation is the same as for 175% declining balance, except that the constant multiple is equal to twice the straight-line rate for the given period (eighteen years) or approximately 11.1 percent. Thus, the first year's allowance is $55,555, and the second year's allowance is $48,888.

d. Prorating First and Last Year Allowances

The cost recovery allowance for eighteen-year real property that is placed in service or disposed of during a given taxable year must be prorated by multiplying the otherwise applicable allowance by a fraction, the numerator of which is the number of months that the property was in service during that year, and the denominator of which is twelve.[88]

In the case of all other recovery property, no cost recovery deduction is allowed in the year of disposition,[89] and the half-year convention incorporated in the ACRS tables allows one-half of the full first-year cost recovery deduction, regardless of when the property was first placed in service during the taxable year.[90]

e. Anti-churning Rules

Since ACRS generally affords far greater cost recovery deductions than the depreciation system applicable to property acquired prior to 1981, "anti-churning" rules are necessary to prevent taxpayers from transmuting their property into "recovery property" by "disposing" of it in ways that result in their continued use of the property transferred.

Section 168(e)(4) states that ACRS is not applicable to real estate acquired by a taxpayer after 1980 whenever any of the following conditions pertains: (1) The property was owned or used at any time during 1980 by

---

87. Taxpayers using declining balance methods never need account for salvage value in computing depreciation. This apparent leniency results from the impossibility, under this method, of reducing the basis to zero.
88. I.R.C. §168(b)(2); Proposed Reg. §1.168-2(a)(3).
89. Proposed Reg. §1.168-2(a)(2), 49 Fed. Reg. 33, 5943 (1984).
90. I.R.C. §168(b)(1).

the taxpayer or a "related person." [91] (2) The taxpayer is leasing the property to a person who owned or used it at any time during 1980 (or to someone related to such a person).[92] (3) The taxpayer acquired the property in a like-kind exchange, or by involuntary conversion, repossession, or rollover of low-income housing, and the basis of the property acquired includes an amount representing the adjusted basis of other property owned by the taxpayer (or a related person) prior to 1981.[93] However, to the extent of any "boot" received in the transaction, ACRS applies. (4) The property was acquired by the taxpayer in a nonrecognition transaction such as the liquidation of a subsidiary, a transfer to a controlled corporation, a reorganization, or a transfer to or from a partnership. As in the case of like-kind exchanges, ACRS treatment is denied only to the extent that the property's basis is a carryover basis.[94] (5) The property was acquired in any other transaction described in the Regulations as having as one of its principal purposes the avoidance of the anti-churning rules.[95]

2. Depreciation of Property Acquired Prior to 1981

The rules in force prior to the enactment of ERTA continue to govern real property acquired and placed in service prior to 1981. In addition, property acquired in transactions that run afoul of §168(e)(4)'s anti-churning rules must be depreciated according to the pre-1981 rules. Unlike ACRS, the earlier system requires that depreciation allowances reflect the property's useful life and, where the convention requires it, the property's salvage value.

a. Useful Life

An asset's useful life is "the period over which the asset may reasonably be expected to be useful to the taxpayer in his trade or business or in the production of his income."[96] Under the pre-1981 rules, two methods can

---

91. I.R.C. §168(e)(4)(B)(i). "Related persons," for purposes of the anti-churning rules, include the following: spouses; siblings; ancestors and lineal descendants; corporations and individuals owning more than 10 percent of the value of their outstanding stock; two corporations, at least one of which was a personal holding company for the preceding tax year, where an individual owns more than 10% of the value of each corporation's outstanding stock; a settlor and trustee of a trust; trustees of separate trusts having the same settlor; a trustee and a beneficiary of the same trust or separate trusts having the same settlor; a partnership and a partner owning more than 10 percent of its capital or profits; organizations engaged in trades or businesses under common control. I.R.C. §168(e)(4)(D).
92. I.R.C. §168(e)(4)(B)(ii).
93. I.R.C. §168(e)(4)(B)(iii).
94. I.R.C. §168(e)(4)(C).
95. I.R.C. §168(e)(4)(F).
96. Treas. Reg. §1.167(a)-1(b).

be used to establish the useful life of an asset: the taxpayer himself can estimate the period (thus subjecting himself to a potential dispute with the IRS), or he can refer to certain guideline lives suggested by the Service.[97] Taxpayer estimates must reflect a variety of considerations listed in the Regulations.[98] The guideline lives for various types of buildings range from forty to sixty years.[99]

b. Salvage Value

Once the asset's useful life is established, the taxpayer must estimate the amount that can be obtained upon its disposition when it is no longer useful to him. Unless a declining balance method of depreciation is used, this amount must be subtracted from the asset's depreciable basis in calculating the depreciation allowance.[100]

c. Depreciation Methods

Under the pre-1981 rules, the function of real property, and whether it is new or used, determine permissible methods of depreciation. The greatest flexibility is accorded to new residential rental property. This is defined as new property, from which at least 80 percent of the gross yearly rental income is derived from dwelling units.[101] Such property may be depreciated according to the straight-line method, the sum-of-the-years'-digit method,[102] the double declining balance method, or any other

---

97. See Rev. Proc. 62-21, 1962-1 C.B. 418.
98. Treas. Reg. §1.167(a)-1(b) prescribes the following factors: "wear and tear and decay or decline from natural causes, (2) the normal progress of the art, economic changes, inventions, and current development within the industry and the taxpayer's trade or business, (3) the climatic and other local conditions peculiar to the taxpayer's trade or business, and (4) the taxpayer's policy as to repairs, renewals and replacements."
99. Rev. Proc. 62-21, 1962-1 C.B. 418, includes, e.g., the following guideline lives: apartments — 40 years; dwellings — 45 years; hotels — 40 years; office buildings — 45 years; stores — 50 years; warehouses — 60 years.
100. Treas. Reg. §1.167(a)-1(c).
101. I.R.C. §167(j)(2)(B).
102. According to this method, the computation is made by applying a changing multiple to a constant balance. It can best be illustrated by application to the problem facts discussed on page 374 supra. Under the pre-1981 rules, the depreciable basis is the cost of the improvements less their salvage value, in our example $460,000. The rate by which the $460,000 is multiplied changes yearly, and is determined by a fraction where "[t]he numerator . . . changes each year to a number which corresponds to the remaining useful life of the asset (including the year for which the allowance is being computed), and whose denominator . . . remains constant [and] is the sum of all the years' digits corresponding to the estimated useful life of the asset." Treas. Reg. §1.167(b)3. Thus, the first year's fraction is set at

$$\frac{40}{40 + 39 + 38 \ldots + 1} \quad \text{or} \quad \frac{40}{820}$$

method that does not result in a greater allowance during the first two-thirds of the useful life of the property than would double declining balance.[103]

New nonresidential realty receives the next most favorable treatment. Its owners may choose between the straight-line method, the 150% declining balance method, and any other method that does not result in greater deductions during the first two-thirds of the property's life than would result from the 150% declining balance method.[104]

Used residential realty is treated still less generously. If the property has a useful life of at least twenty years, it may be depreciated under the declining balance method at a rate of up to 125%, or, alternatively, under the straight-line method.[105]

All other used realty acquired prior to 1981 must be depreciated by the straight-line method.[106]

d. Component Depreciation

For property placed in service prior to 1981, unlike post-1980 property, component depreciation is permissible.[107] Instead of estimating the useful life of the building as a whole, the taxpayer may divide the building into its components — bare shell, roof, wiring, plumbing, etc. — assign useful lives and salvage values to each separately, and compute independent depreciation allowances for each part. This may help to shorten the property's effective useful life.[108]

3. *Depreciation Recapture*

"Recapture" is a means of preventing taxpayers from transforming ordinary income into capital gains. The problem arises when taxpayers

---

and the depreciation rate is 4.88 percent. The first year's depreciation is $22,448. In the second year the rate declines, since the numerator of the fraction drops to 39 while the denominator remains unchanged. The second year's depreciation is

$$\frac{39}{820} \times \$460,000 = \$21,878$$

103. I.R.C. §167(j)(2)(A).
104. I.R.C. §167(j)(1).
105. I.R.C. §167(j)(5). A special exception is made for "substantially rehabilitated property." Such property, as defined in I.R.C. §167(o) (repealed 1981) may be treated for depreciation purposes as if the taxpayer were the original owner.
106. I.R.C. §167(j)(4).
107. Milbrew, Inc., 1981 T.C.M. (P-H) 610, *aff'd*, 710 F.2d 1302 (7th Cir. 1983).
108. While the IRS has ruled that the depreciation allowance for an asset should be the same regardless of whether unitary or component depreciation methods are used, Rev. Proc. 62-21, 1962-1 C.B. 418, the Tax Court has indicated that the resultant allowances need not necessarily be the same. The Merchants National Bank of Topeka, 1975 T.C.M. (P-H) 238, *aff'd*, 554 F.2d 412 (10th Cir. 1977).

Cost Recovery (Depreciation) and Other Investment Incentives

who have offset cost recovery deductions against their ordinary income (and reduced their basis in an asset accordingly) pay tax at the time of property disposition only at capital gains rates on the amount by which their basis has been reduced. The Code's solution is to provide, under certain circumstances, that gains attributable to basis reductions caused by cost recovery allowances will be taxed as ordinary income.

a. Recapture for Realty Placed in Service After 1980

Which ACRS recapture rules are applicable to a parcel of realty generally depends on how long the property is held, whether it qualifies as residential property or low-income housing, and how it is transferred. However, in no case may the amount recapturable as ordinary income exceed the taxpayer's "gain" on the disposition.[109] "Gain" in this sense is defined as "the excess of the amount realized (in the case of a sale, exchange, or involuntary conversion), or the fair market value of such property (in the case of any other disposition), over the adjusted basis of the property.[110]

If real property, residential or nonresidential, is held less than one year, the entire amount of cost recovery deductions taken by the taxpayer is recapturable as ordinary income to the extent of gain on a taxable disposition.[111]

Where realty is held more than one year, but does not qualify either as subsidized low-income housing[112] or as residential realty,[113] and accelerated cost recovery deductions have been taken, then all gain is likewise treated as ordinary income to the extent of all depreciation deductions taken.[114] However, if the straight-line method was used for most nonresidential realty held at least one year, then *none* of the taxpayer's gain is recapturable.[115] For this reason, it often makes sense for the owner of such

---

109. I.R.C. §1250(a)(1)(A)(ii).
110. Id.
111. I.R.C. §1250(b)(1).
112. This category is defined for recapture purposes in I.R.C. §1250(a)(1)(B).
113. "Residential rental property" is identically defined for both depreciation and recapture purposes. See I.R.C. §§1245(a)(5)(A), 167(j)(2)(B).
114. I.R.C. §§1245(a)(1), (5).
115. Real property is subject to §1245's more stringent recapture provisions only if it qualifies as either "§1245 property" or "§1245 recovery property." I.R.C. §§1250(c), 1250(d)(11), 1245(a)(1). "§1245 recovery property" includes "all recovery property" (as defined in §168(c)(1)) *except* eighteen-year real property which is (1) residential rental property, (2) used predominantly outside the United States, (3) depreciated under the straight-line method, or (4) subsidized low-income housing. I.R.C. §1245(a)(5). "§1245 property" includes elevators and escalators and real property amortizable under certain rapid write-off provisions, as well as amusement park structures, manufactured homes, and certain special industrial structures. I.R.C. §1245(a)(3). All other real property is subject to §1250 recapture.

Accordingly, when nonresidential realty is depreciated under the straight-line method, it

realty to recover his cost by the straight-line method (rather than through an accelerated method) over an eighteen-year period — despite the resultant decreased present value of his stream of deductions.

Where residential realty is concerned, only "additional depreciation" deductions — i.e., those in excess of what is permissible under the straight-line method — are subject to recapture as ordinary income.[116]

If property qualifies as low-income housing, recapture is phased out at the rate of one percentage point per month for every month the taxpayer owns the property after the first 100 months.[117] Thus, if such property is held for 150 months, the amount of depreciation recaptured as ordinary income is decreased by 50 percent; and if the low-income housing is held for 200 months, no recapture at all ensues.

As noted earlier, the recapture rules are also subject to limitations based on the type of transaction by which a disposition is effected. For instance, transfers by gift, at death, through nontaxable like-kind exchanges, involuntary conversions, partnership contributions, corporate reorganizations and liquidations, and dispositions of a principal residence do not trigger the recapture provisions.[118] The basic reason for these exceptions is to avoid chilling certain nonrecognition transactions with the threat of recapture, since the additional depreciation will eventually be taxed on a subsequent transfer.

b. Recapture for Realty Placed in Service Before 1981

The rules governing depreciation recapture for real property underwent two major changes between 1964 and 1981, through provisions of the Tax Reform Acts of 1969 and 1976. As a result, the recapture rules for pre-1981 property depend on when the particular deductions were taken.[119]

The post-1975, pre-1981 recapture rules are identical to the ACRS rules, except where nonresidential realty held at least one year is concerned. Under ACRS all depreciation of such property is recaptured when an accelerated method of cost recovery has been used. However, under the previous system, nonresidential realty is treated as favorably as dwell-

---

avoids classification as §1245 recovery property, and under §1250(b)(1), no recapture occurs upon disposition. Whereas, if accelerated depreciation is taken for nonresidential realty, it qualifies as §1245(a)(1) property and all gain attributable to depreciation deductions is taxed as ordinary income.

116. I.R.C. §§1245(a)(5)(A), 1250(b)(1).
117. I.R.C. §1250(a)(1).
118. See I.R.C. §1250(d).
119. See I.R.C. §1250(a).

ings, in that only depreciation in excess of straight-line allowances is recaptured.[120]

4. Minimum Tax

The rationale for the minimum tax, as first instituted by the Tax Reform Act of 1969, was to make certain that taxpayers with sizable incomes pay at least a certain level of tax. Its importance for real estate transactions stems largely from the classification of the capital gains deduction and the excess of accelerated cost recovery deductions over straight-line allowances (figured on an eighteen-year period) as items of tax preference subject to minimum tax.[121] Since 1982, the tax has been divided into two provisions: the "add-on tax," for corporate taxpayers,[122] and the "alternative tax," which pertains solely to noncorporate taxpayers.[123]

a. The Add-on Minimum Tax

The corporate minimum tax operates essentially as follows. The taxpayer first determines the total amount of all tax preference items claimed on its return.[124] From this sum, it subtracts the greater of $10,000 or its "regular taxes." [125] A flat 15 percent tax is then imposed on the resulting amount, in *addition* to the regular income tax.[126] Hence, the name "add-on tax."

b. The Alternative Minimum Tax

Unlike the corporate tax, the alternative minimum tax is payable only to the extent that it exceeds the "regular tax" payable.[127] The tax base generally consists of the taxpayer's adjusted gross income, plus the total amount of all tax preference items, decreased by certain allowable deduc-

---

120. This is because §1245(a) applies to §1245 recovery property only when it is disposed of after 1980.
121. I.R.C. §§57(a)(2), (9), (12).
122. I.R.C. §56.
123. I.R.C. §55.
124. In addition to accelerated depreciation and the capital gains deduction, the list of tax preferences includes, e.g., the dividend exclusion and the excess of depletion over the adjusted basis of the property. I.R.C. §57(a).
125. The "regular taxes," for purposes of the add-on minimum tax, are calculated under §56(c) by deducting from the taxes otherwise payable the minimum tax, penalty taxes on accumulated earnings and personal holding companies, and most tax credits.
126. I.R.C. §56(a).
127. I.R.C. §55(a). "Regular tax" for purposes of the alternative minimum tax is defined in §55(f)(2).

tions.[128] This base is further reduced by a $30,000 exemption ($20,000 in the case of a married person filing a separate return, and $40,000 in the case of a joint return) and then multiplied by a flat 20 percent rate to yield the alternative minimum tax.[129] No refundable tax credit may be used to reduce the alternative minimum tax payable in a given year.[130] However, if a taxpayer has certain unused credits, these credits will not be reduced to the extent of his alternative minimum tax liability for that year, and may be carried over or carried back to other years.[131]

5. Tax Credits

a. The Investment Tax Credit

Most real property does not qualify for the investment tax credit.[132] For this reason, a comprehensive discussion of requirements for the credit is not attempted here. However, since the credit is a powerful investment incentive (generally worth far more than a deduction of equal amount), and since substantial components of real estate developments may be eligible for it, a general understanding of investment tax credit operation is useful.

Property eligible for the investment credit generally includes tangible personal property placed in service after 1980, which is of a character subject to the allowance for depreciation, and used in a trade or business or held for the production of income.[133] It also includes, for example, certain depreciable, post-1980 real property (other than buildings or their structural components) that "is used as an integral part of manufacturing . . . or of furnishing transportation, communications, electrical energy, gas, water . . . or . . . constitutes a research facility used in connection with any of the [above] activities. . . ."[134] All such property must have a useful life of at least three years.[135] Personal property used in connection with residential realty usually does not qualify for the credit.[136]

---

128. I.R.C. §55(b). The allowable deductions include, e.g., charitable contributions, casualty losses in excess of 10 percent of adjusted gross income, medical expenses in excess of 10 percent of adjusted gross income, certain estate tax deductions, gambling losses, interest paid on debts incurred prior to July 1, 1982 to buy, build, or substantially renovate one's home, and other interest to the extent of net investment income included in minimum taxable income. Special provisions are made for the deduction of net operating losses. I.R.C. §55(d).
129. I.R.C. §55(a)(1), (f)(1).
130. I.R.C. §55(c)(1).
131. I.R.C. §55(c)(3).
132. I.R.C. §48(a)(1)(B).
133. I.R.C. §48(a)(1)(A).
134. I.R.C. §48(a)(1)(B).
135. I.R.C. §48(a)(1).
136. I.R.C. §48(a)(3).

Cost Recovery (Depreciation) and Other Investment Incentives

The amount of the credit is generally 10 percent of the "qualified investment" in the property[137] — except in the case of three year property, which receives an effective credit of only 6 percent.[138] The taxpayer's depreciable basis in the eligible property must be reduced by one-half of the amount of the credit claimed,[139] unless the taxpayer elects to claim a reduced credit (8 percent in the case of five year or more recovery property, and 4 percent in the case of three year property).[140]

Three limitations are imposed on the amount of investment tax credit that may be claimed by a taxpayer. First, no credit is allowed to individuals and certain corporations for amounts that are not "at risk," if the taxpayer is engaged in business activities subject to I.R.C. §465.[141] Second, a taxpayer may claim the credit for a maximum of $150,000 of used property per year.[142] Finally, the amount of credit claimed in a single year may not exceed $25,000 of tax liability plus 85 percent of the taxpayer's tax liability in excess of $25,000.[143] Unused credits may be carried back three years and forward fifteen.[144]

The investment tax credit may also be subject to recapture, if eligible property is disposed of or becomes ineligible for the credit before the end of the useful life or recovery period on which the credit was based.[145] The amount captured is a percentage of the credit and depends on the number of years the property was held before disposition.[146]

b. The Rehabilitation Tax Credit

While the general investment tax credit applies principally to personal property, the rehabilitation tax credit is available only for buildings. To qualify, a building must have been (1) "substantially rehabilitated," (2) placed in service before the beginning of the rehabilitation, and (3) left with at least 75 percent of its preexisting external walls intact.[147] In addition, unless the building is a certified historic structure, it must have been placed in service for the first time at least thirty years before the rehabilitation began.[148] A building has been "substantially rehabilitated" only if "qualified rehabilitation expenditures" during a two-year period selected

---

137. I.R.C. §46(a)(2)(B). "Qualified investment" is defined in §46(c).
138. I.R.C. §46(c)(7)(B).
139. I.R.C. §48(q)(1).
140. I.R.C. §48(q)(4).
141. I.R.C. §48(c)(8). Note that real estate activities are not subject to the §465 limitation.
142. I.R.C. §48(c)(8).
143. I.R.C. §46(a)(3).
144. I.R.C. §46(b).
145. I.R.C. §47(a).
146. I.R.C. §§47(a)(1),(5).
147. I.R.C. §48(g)(1)(A).
148. I.R.C. §48(g)(1)(B).

by the taxpayer in accordance with the Regulations are both greater than the adjusted basis of the property and greater than $5,000.[149]

If a building qualifies, only that portion of its basis that is attributable to "qualified rehabilitation expenditures" is eligible for the credit.[150] This amount is then multiplied by the "rehabilitation percentage" to obtain the amount of the credit.[151] The "rehabilitation percentage" is 25 percent in the case of certified historic structures,[152] 20 percent if at least forty years have elapsed between the date the building was first placed in service and the date on which rehabilitation commenced, and 15 percent for all other qualified buildings.[153] The taxpayer's basis in a qualified building must be reduced by the full amount of the rehabilitation credit claimed, unless the building is a certified historic structure, in which case only 50 percent of the amount of the credit need be subtracted.[154]

6. *Election to Expense Assets in Lieu of Depreciation*

Like the regular investment tax credit, the §179 election is unavailable for most real property. In general, it applies to all property eligible for the credit, except property held for the production of income (rather than for use in a trade or business) and property that is not acquired by "purchase."[155] "Purchase" in this context is specially defined to exclude transfers among certain related persons, or members of affiliated groups of corporations, and transfers in which the basis of the transferred property is at least partly a carryover basis.[156]

Section 179 allows a taxpayer to deduct a limited portion of the cost of qualified property in the year in which it is placed in service.[157] Through 1987, the prescribed ceiling is $5,000; for the years 1988 and 1989, the limit rises to $7,500; thereafter the limit becomes $10,000.[158]

---

149. I.R.C. §48(g)(1)(C). "Qualified rehabilitation expenditures" are generally defined as expenses properly chargeable to capital amounts that are incurred after 1981 for property that has an ACRS recovery period of eighteen years, in connection with the rehabilitation of a qualified building. I.R.C. §48(g)(2)(A). Enlargement expenditures do not qualify for the credit. I.R.C. §48(g)(2)(B)(iii). The regular two-year period may be extended to five years, if the rehabilitation "may reasonably be expected to be completed in phases set forth in architectural plans and specifications completed before the rehabilitation begins." I.R.C. §48(g)(1)(C)(ii).
150. I.R.C. §48(a)(1)(E).
151. I.R.C. §§46(a)(2)(F), (c)(2).
152. I.R.C. §46(a)(2)(F)(i). The requirements for "certified historic structures" are set out in §48(g)(3).
153. I.R.C. §46(a)(2)(F).
154. I.R.C. §48(q)(3).
155. I.R.C. §179(d)(1).
156. I.R.C. §179(d)(2).
157. I.R.C. §179(a).
158. I.R.C. §179(b).

A First Look at Tax Shelter

Election under §179 has a number of financial consequences. First, the investment tax credit may not be claimed for any amount expensed.[159] Second, gain on a disposition of expensed assets may be subject to recapture as ordinary income.[160] Third, expensed amounts are ineligible for §453 installment sales treatment upon disposition.[161] Thus, if expensed property is sold on the installment method, any amount previously expensed is treated as a payment received in the year of sale, and taxed as ordinary income to the extent of gain realized. As a result, the advisability of expensing qualified assets in lieu of claiming ACRS depreciation and the investment tax credit depends, inter alia, on the length of the recovery period allowed for the given asset, the rates of taxation during the years the asset is owned, and the time value of money to the taxpayer.

C. A FIRST LOOK AT TAX SHELTER

Cost recovery produces a cash stream (or cash flow) that is not immediately subject to taxation at its source. Why not? It is because the owner obtains a deduction for which he or she has no current expenditure. "Tax sheltered" income via cost recovery is what real estate investment is very much about. Consider first the following example:

X purchases a building for $5,000,000 (exclusive of land). The first year's gross revenue is $1,000,000. Operating expenses, exclusive of debt service, total $400,000. Ignoring debt service (for the moment), compute X's taxable income. Compare with X's cash stream.

Taxable Income (before debt service)		Cash Stream (before debt service)	
Gross Revenue	$1,000,000	Gross Revenue	$1,000,000
Less: Operating Expenses	(400,000)	Less: Operating Expenses	(400,000)
Cost recovery (assume 18 year recovery period)	(600,000)		
Taxable Income	0	Cash Stream	$600,000

In short, in this first year, X takes $600,000 out of the property free of taxes on ordinary income.

---

159. I.R.C. §179(d)(9).
160. I.R.C. §1245(a)(2)(D).
161. I.R.C. §453(i).

We should remember, however, that real estate seldom is owned free and clear. And for good reason! Think "leverage"! Let us, therefore, add to our calculations debt service on a hypothetical $3,000,000 mortgage, at the assumed rate of 10 percent interest and $100,000 yearly amortization.

Taxable Income		Cash Stream	
Gross Revenue	$1,000,000	Gross Revenue	$1,000,000
Less: Operating		Less: Operating	
Expenses	(400,000)	Expenses	(400,000)
Cost Recovery	(600,000)	Debt Service	
		Amortization	(100,000)
Interest	(300,000)	Interest	(300,000)
Taxable Income (loss)	($300,000)		$200,000

Not a bad outcome! X will still be able to withdraw $200,000 of nontaxable cash from the property and, in addition, report a $300,000 taxable loss, which can be used to shelter income derived from other sources.

From this example, you are about to grasp two key realities of real estate investment. First: Whenever cost recovery exceeds mortgage amortization, tax-sheltered income results; in fact, the amount of tax-sheltered income is measured exactly by the excess of cost recovery over amortization (in our example: $600,000 − $100,000 = $500,000). Second: A tax loss — available to offset taxable income from other sources — can coexist with a cash flow.

Do not conclude, however, that tax-sheltered income forever escapes taxation. The reckoning occurs if, and when, the asset is sold. (By retaining ownership until death, the taxpayer may avoid the *taxable* day of reckoning, altogether.) In our example, if X were to resell the property after six years for the exact cost, $5,000,000, X would still realize a gain measured, in effect, by the accumulated cost recovery enjoyed during the holding period. And, as we have seen, that gain may be subject to recapture, in part or full, as ordinary income. But even if, because of recapture, the taxpayer's aggregate tax has not changed, the interest value of the tax deferral may be considerable.

The collapse of tax shelter. When property is held free and clear, the owner receives tax-sheltered income until his depreciable basis is reduced to zero. But if the property is mortgaged, an untaxed stream of cash depends on the continuing surplus of cost recovery over amortization. Should amortization ever exceed cost recovery, the owner will have earned taxable income that is not reflected in cash. Most taxpayers would regard this prospect bleakly.

To illustrate the collapse of tax shelter, suppose that X has borrowed $4,000,000 and is required to pay 10 percent interest and $400,000 yearly amortization. Suppose also that X has decided to use straight-line recovery

A First Look at Tax Shelter

on a thirty-five-year basis. Now look at the comparison between taxable income and cash stream.

Taxable Income		*Cash Stream*	
Gross Revenue	$1,000,000	Gross Revenue	$1,000,000
Less: Operating Expenses	(400,000)	*Less:* Operating Expenses	(400,000)
Cost recovery	(140,000)*	Debt service Amortization	(400,000)
Interest	(400,000)	Interest	(400,000)
Taxable Income	$60,000	Cash Stream	($200,000)

* rounded off.

In this example, X must pay a tax on $60,000, even though the property does not throw off enough cash to meet the debt service. The size of the "negative" tax shelter is measured by the same formula we employed a moment ago, that is, cost recovery − amortization; here this comes to $140,000 − $400,000 = ($260,000). In short, the taxable income exceeds cash flow by $260,000.

Tax shelter seldom collapses during the first years of ownership. In our example, by starting with accelerated cost recovery, X would increase the first year's deduction to $600,000 — greater than the amortization — and couple a paper tax loss to a negative cash stream. Moreover, no sane investor would gladly accept mortgage terms, the first year's amortization of which would wipe out that investor's tax shelter from the start. (However, a revenue shortfall or unexpectedly high operating expenses may have the same effect.) As the holding period continues, however, the danger of collapse often increases. Two factors, singly or in combination, are responsible: the cost recovery gets smaller, and/or the amortization gets larger. Decreasing allowances for cost recovery result from the declining balance method of depreciation upon which accelerated cost recovery is based. Rising amortization exists, as you have learned, page 178 supra, in any mortgage that provides for constant debt service. The simplest way to retain indefinite tax shelter is to use straight-line recovery and obtain a mortgage with constant amortization at a level below that of cost recovery. But this invites other problems. Constant amortization may mean that the early installments of debt service will greatly exceed those for a level payment mortgage; otherwise the mortgage either cannot amortize itself or must be written over a much longer term (often not possible). Furthermore, the owner who does not maximize his depreciation must either lose or, at least defer, the first year's tax advantages.

The owner who is faced with the loss of tax shelter should consider two actions: (1) sell or exchange the property; (2) refinance the mortgage. The first option is self-evident, although the owner's desire to sell is no guarantee of a favorable market response. The taxpayer who elects the second option and refinances the mortgage will be seeking initially lower amortization. (*Query:* without reducing the principal balance, how can this be achieved?) But, as in the case of a sale, refinancing may not be possible or propitious when tax factors make it urgent: prepayment may be barred or expensive; interest rates may have risen; mortgage money may be unavailable; or the property might not support the terms sought. In short, the investor who decides to maximize tax-sheltered income must recognize both the inherent risks and the uncertainty of successful countermeasures.

D. TAX STRATEGY: HOW TO POSTPONE TAXES ON THE SALE OF REAL PROPERTY

1. *The Installment Sale*

The buyer rarely pays all cash when acquiring real property. If buyer borrows entirely from third parties (such as a commercial lender), the seller will receive full cash for his equity. Often, however, the seller will extend purchase money financing for some (perhaps the entire) part of the unpaid price. Absent the installment sale provisions of the Code, first enacted in 1954, full gain realization might result in serious hardship for the seller who agrees to accept the buyer's liabilities in lieu of cash.

Section 453, the installment sale provision, was significantly amended in 1980. To provide greater structural convenience, three Code sections replaced omnibus §453: new §453 — sales of real property and casual sales of personalty; §453A — sales by dealers in personalty; and §453B — treatment of gain or loss on the disposition of installment obligations. The 1980 revision has also:

1. eliminated the requirement that no more than 30 percent of the selling price be received in the taxable year of the sale;
2. eliminated all uncertainty as to whether two or more payments are essential for §453 treatment. A sale is now eligible for installment reporting even if there is only a single installment — that is, one lump sum made in a taxable year subsequent to that in which the sale occurs;
3. reversed the formerly elective feature of §453. Instead, as to gains from the sale of realty (and nondealer personal property), installment reporting will automatically apply to a qualified sale unless the taxpayer chooses against tax deferral. (*Query:* under what circumstances might the taxpayer make that election?)

Tax Strategy: How to Postpone Taxes on the Sale of Real Property

The mechanics of installment sale reporting were not changed by the 1980 amendments. These mechanics are illustrated below.

a. Definitions

If a transaction qualifies as an installment sale under §453, gain is realized *and* taxable only as the seller actually receives the sales proceeds. The installment method does not apply to losses.

Selling price is the total consideration agreed upon for the property. It includes cash, the buyer's notes, other property received by the seller, and the amount of any mortgage being transferred with the real estate, whether the buyer assumes the mortgage or takes subject to it. The selling price is *not* reduced by sales commissions or other expenses of sale. Temp. Reg. §15a.453-1(b)(2)(ii).

Gross profit is the selling price less the adjusted basis; the latter is increased (other than in the case of a dealer) to include commissions, attorney's fees, and other sales expenses. Temp. Reg. §15a.453-1(b)(2)(v).

Contract price, in most cases, equals the seller's cash equity in the property and is the amount seller will eventually receive in cash, including payment on the buyer's notes, or in other property. In addition, any excess of mortgage over basis will be included in the contract price. Temp. Reg. §15a.453-1(b)(2)(iii).

Gross profit ratio is the ratio of the gross profit to the contract price. Temp. Reg. §15a.453-1(b)(2)(i).

Payments received in the taxable year are best considered in terms of the initial year and each subsequent year. In the first taxable year, the payments would include cash or other property (e.g., the notes of someone other than the buyer) received at or before the closing, together with any installments of principal (but not of interest) received by the seller in reduction of the buyer's notes. In addition, in the instance where buyer takes over an outstanding mortgage whose balance exceeds the seller's basis in the property, the excess of mortgage over basis will be deemed a first year's payment. In each subsequent year, principal reduction payments would be subject to tax.

Although the buyer's notes, ordinarily, are not regarded as payments until reduction or disposition occurs, if the seller receives a demand note, or a readily tradeable corporate or governmental obligation, the face amount of the note received will be includable in income at the very outset. Also, as a result of the 1984 amendments, any gain that would be treated as ordinary income under the recapture provisions of §§1245 or 1250 will be fully recognized in the initial year even though this exceeds the payments actually received. Any recapture income so recognized is added back to the basis of the property for the purpose of determining the gross profits and the gross profit ratio.

b. Illustrations

(1) *Mortgage less than the seller's basis.* On September 1, 1986, X (calendar year taxpayer) sells property having a $300,000 basis and subject to a $250,000 mortgage, for $400,000. The terms are: $50,000 cash; $250,000 by the buyer's assumption of the first mortgage; and $100,000 by the buyer's giving back his note and second mortgage. The buyer makes a note reduction payment of $40,000 on December 1, 1986. He also makes a $50,000 principal payment on the first mortgage before the end of 1986. Assume no recapture income.

What is seller's 1986 taxable gain? This is a qualifying transaction, without regard to the percentage of the selling price that X receives in the year of sale (1986), so long as some part of the unpaid price will not be received until after 1986. X must elect out of §453 if he does not wish to enjoy deferral of gain recognition, §453(d).

The taxpayer must report as income that proportion of the payments received in 1986 which the gross profit bears to the total contract price. Here, the gross profit ratio is $\frac{\$100,000}{\$150,000} = \frac{2}{3}$. The 1986 payments are $50,000 (cash down payment) + $40,000 (principal reduction of the buyer's note) = $90,000. (The buyer's $50,000 payment on the existing mortgage is *not* included.) Therefore, in 1986, X's taxable gain is $60,000. The 2/3 ratio will also be applied to future years' installments.

(2) *Mortgage exceeds the seller's basis.* In the problem above, assume that the seller's basis is $220,000.

What is seller's 1986 taxable gain? We must add to X's 1986 payments the $30,000 excess of mortgage balance ($250,000) over adjusted basis ($220,000). This would increase his 1986 payments to $120,000.

Moreover, the transfer of property subject to a mortgage in excess of basis will also change both the contract price and, necessarily, the gross profit ratio. In this instance, the contract price rises from $150,000 to $180,000, since the $30,000 mortgage excess must be added to the $150,000 cash that X will eventually get for his equity. Gross profit also rises to $180,000 ($400,000 − $220,000). Thus the gross profit ratio is 100 percent, and X in 1986 must report as a taxable gain the entire $120,000 in payments received. The 100 percent ratio will also be applied to future years' installments.

The 1980 revision also eliminated a broad potential for further tax avoidance through the "closely related parties" gimmick. That ploy, and its counter, are discussed in the Senate Report:

> Under present law, the installment sale statutory provision does not pre-

clude installment sale reporting for sales between related parties. Further, the statutory provision does not preclude installment sale reporting for sales of marketable securities although the seller might readily obtain full cash proceeds by market sales.

Under the existing statutory framework, taxpayers have used the installment sale provision as a tax planning device for intra-family transfers of appreciated property, including marketable securities. There are several tax advantages in making intra-family installment sales of appreciated property. The seller would achieve deferral of recognition of gain until the related buyer actually pays the installments to the seller, even if cash proceeds from the property are received within the related party group from a subsequent resale by the installment buyer shortly after making the initial purchase. In addition to spreading out the gain recognized by the seller over the term of the installment sale, the seller may achieve some estate planning benefits since the value of the installment obligation generally will be frozen for estate tax purposes. Any subsequent appreciation in value of the property sold, or in property acquired by reinvestment of the proceeds from the property sold on the installment basis, would not affect the seller's gross estate since the value of the property is no longer included in his gross estate.

With respect to the related buyer, there is usually no tax to be paid if the appreciated property is resold shortly after the installment purchase. Since the buyer's adjusted basis is a cost basis which includes the portion of the purchase price payable in the future, the gain or loss from the buyer's resale would represent only the fluctuation in value occurring after the installment purchase. Thus, after the related party's resale, all appreciation has been realized within the related group but the recognition of the gain for tax purposes may be deferred for a long period of time. . . .

. . . Under the bill, the amount realized upon certain resales by the related party installment purchaser will trigger recognition of gain by the initial seller, based on his gross profit ratio, only to the extent the amount realized from the second disposition exceeds actual payments made under the installment sale. Thus, acceleration of recognition of the installment gain from the first sale will generally result only to the extent additional cash and other property flows into the related group as a result of a second disposition of the property. In the case of a second disposition which is not a sale or exchange, the fair market value of the property disposed of is treated as the amount realized for this purpose. For these purposes, the portion of the amount realized from a second disposition will not be taken into account to the extent attributable to any improvements which had been made by the related installment purchaser.

The excess of any amount realized from resales over payments received on the first sale as of the end of a taxable year will be taken into account. Thus, the tax treatment would not turn on the strict chronological order in which resales or payments are made. If, under these rules, a resale results in the recognition of gain to the initial seller, subsequent payments actually received by that seller would be recovered tax-free until they have equaled the amount realized from the resale which resulted in the acceleration of recognition of gain.

In the case of property other than marketable securities, the resale rule will apply only with respect to second dispositions occurring within 2 years of the initial installment sale. (96th Cong., 2d Sess., U.S. Sen., Comm. on Fin., Rpt., Installment Sales Revision Act of 1980, pp. 12-15.)

While the arithmetic of §453 may trouble you briefly, especially the treatment of mortgage excess, far more troublesome have been the efforts of taxpayers to qualify a transaction that deviates from the straightforward examples given above. Consider the following case.

Commissioner v. Stuart
300 F.2d 872 (3d Cir. 1962)

GANEY, Circuit Judge. This is a review of a decision of the Tax Court at the request of the Commissioner of Internal Revenue. The question presented is whether or not that Court correctly held that the sale or other disposition of taxpayers' real property was made in 1954 within the meaning of §453(b) of the Internal Revenue Code of 1954, 26 U.S.C.A. §453(b), as the taxpayers maintained, rather than in 1955, as the Commissioner contended.

The basic facts are not in dispute and, as obtained from the opinion of the Tax Court, may be stated as follows: In 1954, the taxpayers, husband and wife, owned and resided upon a 187.74 acre farm near Beverly, New Jersey. On April 21, 1954, they entered into a written agreement to sell the land to the purchasing agent ("Buyer") of Levitt & Sons, Inc., which was then engaged in the development of Levittown, New Jersey. In pertinent part the agreement provides:

> WITNESSETH, That the Seller and Buyer respectively agree to sell and buy ALL THAT CERTAIN tract and parcel of land . . . consisting of approximately 187.74 acres . . . for the price of . . . $150,000.00 . . . under the following conditions:
>
> 1. (a) A payment of . . . $1,500.00 . . . made herewith is to be applied on account of the purchase price.
>
> (b) A further payment of . . . $1,500.00 . . . shall be made on or before July 20, 1954, to be applied on account of the purchase price.
>
> (c) A further payment of . . . $12,000.00 . . . shall be made on or before October 20, 1954, to be applied on account of the purchase price.
>
> 2. Settlement is to take place at Burlington County Abstract Company, 451 High Street, Burlington, New Jersey, on the 20th day of April, 1955, at 2 o'clock P.M., which time is of the essence of this agreement, when the Seller shall deliver a general warranty deed for the said premises, at which time the balance of the purchase price is to be paid. Buyer shall have the right to advance the settlement date by no more than six months, by giving thirty days notice in writing to the Seller of his intention to do so.

Tax Strategy: How to Postpone Taxes on the Sale of Real Property

The above consideration is to be delivered to Burlington County Abstract Company to be disbursed after the insurance company selected by Buyer has completed the necessary continuation search to cover the record date of said deed.

3. In the event that the Buyer shall fail to make any of the payments called for hereunder, or shall fail to make settlement in accordance with the terms hereof, then and in that case all sums paid on account by the Buyer shall be forfeited to the Seller as liquidated damages, and Buyer shall be released from all obligation and liability, including any right of the Seller to bring an action for specific performance, and all rights and liabilities of both parties to this agreement shall cease and determine.

4. The title to be delivered shall be marketable title and insurable by the title insurance company selected by the Buyer. . . .

6. Actual possession is to be given to the Buyer on October 20, 1955. . . .

9. This agreement includes all fixtures permanently attached to the building or buildings . . . and appurtenances; also specifically includes the following items:

9A. Seller shall have the right to completely harvest all crops planted for the year 1954, & 1955, up to October 20, 1955.

9B. Seller shall have the right to remove all buildings and trees from the premises in question.

9C. Seller shall have the right to occupy and use the dwelling and all buildings up to October 20, 1955.

10. Buyer shall have the right at any time or times prior to settlement to enter upon the premises for the purpose of making test borings or test excavations, or any other work of a similar nature, provided, however, that in such event Buyer shall reimburse Seller for any damages that may be thereby inflicted upon the crops or other installations of the Seller. . . .

The agreement was modified in order to change the provision for payment in full of the $135,000 balance of the purchase price at settlement to payment of $85,000 in cash, plus a purchase money mortgage in the amount of $50,000, payable in installments of $20,000 on April 1, 1956, and $30,000 on April 1, 1957. Although the taxpayers began searching for another abode during May of 1954, they continued to live in the dwelling located upon the land until May of 1956. Levitt & Sons, Inc., made use of the land in accordance with paragraph 10 of the agreement. It does not appear when settlement took place. On this point, the Tax Court said: "Settlement was made and title to the land transferred more than a year prior to May of 1956." On account of the purchase price the taxpayers received $15,000 in 1954, $85,000 in 1955, $20,000 in 1956, and $30,000 in 1957. For the taxable years ending in 1954 and 1955, taxpayers reported the gain from the sale or other disposition of their real property pursuant to §453(b) of the Code. The Commissioner determined that they were not entitled to use the installment method of reporting the gain from the disposition of their property, recomputed their returns in accordance with the long term provisions of the Code, and assessed a deficiency for the year 1955. Taxpayers petitioned the Tax Court for a redetermination of the deficiency.

Before one who sells real property on an installment plan extending over a taxable year may take advantage of §453(b) of the Code, not more than thirty percent of the selling price may be received in the year of the sale or other disposition of the property. There is no question that the taxpayers received less than thirty percent of the selling price in 1954 and more than thirty percent in 1955. There is a dispute as to whether the sale or other disposition of the property took place in 1954 or 1955.

The Tax Court stated: "In the case before us there was already a binding agreement on April 21, 1954, between the respective parties to buy and sell real property. So binding was the agreement that it was necessary that the buyer be relieved by paragraph 3 of the agreement of the obligation to specifically perform thereunder in consideration of the payment of $15,000 liquidated damages. By the agreement taxpayers immediately disposed of all the incidents of ownership in their land and the right of the purchaser to exercise the incidents of ownership thereafter was absolute with the exception that petitioners were permitted to occupy the dwelling therein for a fixed period and that legal title was not to pass until the settlement date. See Wiseman v. Scruggs, 281 F.2d 900 (C.A. 10, 1960)." (19 T.C.M. 1311, 1314). The real property is situated and the agreement was made in New Jersey. We look to the law of that State to determine what disposition was made of the property in 1954 and 1955. [Citations omitted.]

We agree with the Tax Court that an enforceable agreement came into existence upon the signing of the document on April 21, 1954. However, it did not bind the Buyer to perform his promises. Except for the forfeiture of installments already paid, paragraph 3 of the agreement permitted him to terminate the agreement with impunity at any time prior to settlement. Under New Jersey law, that paragraph transformed the agreement into one of option. Such an agreement, as distinguished from an agreement of sale, imposes no binding obligation on the holder of the option. Sooy v. Henkelman, 104 N.J.L. 540, 142 A. 17 (1928); Wellmore Builders, Inc. v. Wannier, 49 N.J. Super. 456, 140 A.2d 422 (1958).

In the case before us the Buyer kept the option alive by paying the installments amounting to $15,000 as they became due. He could have refused to make any more down payments after making the first $1,500 and would have been relieved of any obligation to pay more. The option to buy was not exercised until the Buyer tendered a purchase money mortgage in the face amount of $50,000, payable as agreed, plus $85,000 in cash on April 26, 1955, at which time he received a deed to the land. Until that time he had only an inchoate right; he was not entitled to the deed before then. Bright v. Forrest Hill Park Development Co., 133 N.J. Eq.

170, 31 A.2d 190, 198 (Ch. 1943). Thus the agreement did not create an unconditional obligation to sell and an unconditional obligation to buy, which were absolute and enforceable at the time of the signing. There never was an unconditional liability on the part of the Buyer for the balance of the purchase price until settlement was completed. At that time a sale of the real property took place, over a year after the signing of the agreement.

The inchoate right to acquire the land by the Buyer prior to the sale of the real property was not a "disposition" of property within the meaning of §453(b) of the Code. Hence the ultimate finding by the Tax Court that the taxpayers made a sale or other disposition of their land on April 21, 1954, within the meaning of that section, was clearly erroneous.

The decision of the Tax Court will be reversed.

STALEY, Circuit Judge (dissenting). One of the reasons for adopting the installment plan of reporting income was to relieve taxpayers from having to pay an income tax in the year of sale based on the full amount of anticipated profits when in the tax year they received in cash only a small part of the sales price. Commissioner of Internal Revenue v. South Texas Lumber Co., 333 U.S. 496, 68 S. Ct. 695, 92 L. Ed. 831 (1948). Section 453 being remedial, "manifestly it is to be construed liberally in favor of the taxpayers to give the relief it was intended to provide." Bonwit Teller & Co. v. United States, 283 U.S. 258, 263, 51 S. Ct. 395, 75 L. Ed. 1018 (1931); Kelly-Springfield Tire Co. v. United States, 81 F.2d 533 (C.A. 3, 1935). The majority here is doing just the contrary.

Whether the instrument here in question should be construed as an option or contract of sale depends not on any particular words but on the manifested intent of the parties. "In determining whether a conveyance is, or is not, effective, and if effective, just what its effect is, the intent of the conveyor is always an important, and often the decisive factor." Restatement, Property, §11, comment *d*, (1936). Intent is, of course, a question of fact, and the Tax Court's finding in this regard must be affirmed unless clearly erroneous. In the agreement here, the buyer expressly agreed to buy and the taxpayers to sell. The taxpayers disposed of all incidents of ownership in the land, and the right of the purchaser to exercise the incidents of ownership was absolute with certain exceptions which in themselves clearly show that the parties intended to enter into a binding agreement. During the year 1954, the buyer paid taxpayers $15,000 as he was required to do by the agreement. The remainder was to be paid at the time of settlement. The taxpayers specifically reserved the right to harvest the crops during all of 1954 and part of 1955, and to remove all buildings and trees and to retain occupancy and use of the structures until 1955. Shortly after the agreement was signed, the taxpayers began looking for a new farm in New York and Maryland, and as early as February 1955 bought one in New Jersey. As one of the taxpayers testified, "The farm was sold and we hunted for a farm right away." In 1954, the buyer sent numerous employees and heavy equipment on the land in order to prepare for construction. In accordance with the agreement the deed to the property was delivered in 1955. These facts clearly show that the parties intended a sale.

It is accepted that where an agreement is made in which there are mutual promises to buy and sell, such an agreement is not turned into an option by the fact that there is also a provision for forfeiture of down payment as liquidated damages in case of a failure by the purchaser to perform. 1 Corbin on Contracts §274, pp. 921-922 (1950). The fact that the extent of purchaser's liability in case of breach was to be determined by the liquidated damages clause is of itself unimportant, for the Commissioner's own regulation under the section here involved, Treas. Reg. 1.453-5 (1958), establishes a procedure for reporting income in the event the purchaser fails to perform. . . .

It was the Commissioner who, by regulation, first expressly authorized the use of installment reporting. In holding those regulations ultra vires, the Board of Tax Appeals in B. B. Todd, Inc., 1 B.T.A. 762 (1925), indicated that the regulations had been promulgated in order to reduce the over-all tax paid. Immediately thereafter, Congress, in the Revenue Act of 1926, §212, authorized installment reporting. That provision was reenacted as §44 of the Revenue Act of 1928 and the Internal Revenue Code of 1939, and §453 of the Internal Code of 1954. See Commissioner of Internal Revenue v. South Texas Lumber Co., supra.

Here, one of the taxpayers testified that they intended to take advantage of the relief contained in §453 and in fact adjusted the selling price in accordance with the tax savings that would result from payments on the installment plan. It appears that the taxpayers originally asked for a larger selling price, which was reduced because of a suggestion by the buyer's counsel that since payments would be made on an installment basis, there would be a tax savings. The sale was consummated as agreed to. Under these circumstances, to hold as the majority does would negate the intent of Congress.

NOTES AND QUESTIONS

1. As the Stuarts' attorney, how would you have handled the transaction to gain §453 qualification?
2. *Disposition of the buyer's installment obligations.* The 1980 Revision Act treats more clearly the seller's sale or other disposition of the buyer's installment obligation, which earlier was a matter of greater uncertainty. The seller has derived a gain (or loss) measured by the difference between the amount realized, in the case of a sale or exchange, and seller's basis in the obligation. The basis here is the excess of the obligation's face value

over the income (i.e., profit represented by the note) that the seller would have received if the obligation were paid in full. §453B.

> Example: Taxpayer sold property with a basis of $25,000, for $50,000. Taxpayer received $10,000 in cash and $40,000 in notes. Prior to receiving any installment payment toward the $40,000 notes, Taxpayer sells the notes for $32,000. Taxpayer's profit ratio is 50 percent ($25,000/$50,000), resulting in a $20,000 basis in the notes. Thus, the income upon sale of the notes is $12,000 ($32,000 proceeds − $20,000 basis).

The seller also derives income if he or she disposes of the buyer's obligations other than by sale or exchange, for example, through a gift or dividend distribution. (Transfers at death are expressly excluded, §453B(c).) In this instance, the seller's income is measured by the excess of the obligations' face value over their basis — in our example above, $20,000.

What continues to cause some uncertainty, even after the 1980 Revision Act, is the question of *when* a disposition has occurred. Borrowing against the installment obligation pledged as security does not necessarily cause a disposition, a pleasing outcome, for it suggests that the seller may have her cake and eat it too. United Surgical Steel Co. v. Commr., 54 T.C. 1214 (1970), *acq.* 1971-2 C.B. 3; Schaeffer v. Commr., T.C.M. 1981-27. A court may read through the pledge, however, and treat it as a sale or discount, especially if the seller borrows the face amount of the obligation and the lender makes the collections. Alsworth-Washburn Co. v. Helvering, 67 F.2d 694 (D.C. Cir. 1933).

Other situations where the issue of disposition has arisen include:

(a) substitution of a mortgage for the land contract (no disposition: Rev. Rul. 55-5, 1955-1 C.B. 331);
(b) transfer of obligation to grantor trust (disposition, unless grantor deemed to have retained ownership under trust rules: Rev. Rul. 81-98, 1981-1 C.B. 40).

Section 453B and the Treasury Regulations also list several other dispository and nondispository events. The former includes cancellation of the obligation; the latter includes transfers between spouses or incident to a divorce, contribution to or distribution from a partnership, and various corporate organization and reorganization situations.

2. The Deferred Payment Method

In some instances of an installment sale, the taxpayer cannot readily determine gross profit and, derivatively, the gross profit ratio, because of the indeterminacy of the selling price. This situation arises when the contractual right to full payment is contingent upon future events, or the fair market value of the buyer's obligations is not readily ascertainable.

Prior to 1980, sellers in such situations could use the "deferred payment" method to report their gain. Under this approach, the authority of which derived from a reading of §1002, the taxpayer asserted that until the contingency was altogether removed or the value of the buyer's obligations ascertainable, the amount of *realized* gain — a prelude to recognition of any gain — could not be measured. Thus the first receipts of cash (or other property) from the buyer would be treated as a return of capital — a nontaxable event — to be applied in reduction of basis. Not until recovery was complete, that is, not until the basis was reduced to zero, would taxability begin. Thereafter, *all* receipts would be taxable. Regulations accepting this approach in principle appeared at Treasury Regulation §1.453-4,6, although the taxpayer still had to persuade the Commissioner and the courts of the indeterminacy of the selling price. See, e.g., Jones v. Commissioner, 60 T.C. 663 (1973), *nonacq.* 1980-1 C.B. 2, *rev'd and remanded,* 524 F.2d 788 (9th Cir. 1975), *on remand,* 68 T.C. 837 (1977), *aff'd in unpublished order,* (9th Cir. 1980).

Congress, in 1980, sought to curtail use of the deferred payment method. Section 453(j) directs the Secretary of the Treasury to issue regulations providing for "ratable basis recovery" in transactions where the gross profit or the total contract price (or both) cannot be readily ascertained. The ensuing (temporary) regulations distinguish between two situations. Where the buyer's obligations bear a fixed amount, a cash method seller must treat as an amount realized in the year of sale the obligations' fair market value, which shall be considered as worth no less than the fair market value of the property sold (less other consideration received); an accrual method taxpayer may make some adjustment to reflect any contingency as to when payments are to be made. But under no circumstances will an installment sale for a fixed amount obligation be considered an "open transaction." Temp. Reg. §15a.453-1(d)(2).

In the second situation, where the seller's *right* to payment is contingent upon future events, the Regulations provide for "ratable basis recovery." This technique is described in extensive detail, which does not warrant restatement here. Temp. Reg. §15a.453-1(c). Deferred payment thus remains an option of sorts, but its use has become far more limited, and where available, its advantage also more limited.

3. *Tax-free Exchanges Under Section 1031*

Section 1031 has become an increasingly popular vehicle for real estate tax deferral. Although the section was first intended chiefly to permit tax-free replacements of tangible personal property (for example), industrial machines, §1031's broad compass, and the courts' readiness to construe the section generously have given real estate operators an option for gain deferral that is often worth exploring.

Section 1031(a) provides for nonrecognition of gain or loss when the taxpayer exchanges property held for productive use in a trade or business or for investment solely for "like-kind" property held either for productive use in a trade or business or for investment. When the conditions are met, nonrecognition is required. Various forms of property are excluded, however, from §1031(a) treatment even if the purpose for which the property is held satisfies the Code. Chief among the excluded categories are stocks, bonds, security interests, and, since 1984, partnership interests. Because it does not meet the qualifying purpose requirement, a private residence or dealer property would not be eligible for §1031(a) treatment either.

Whether the exchanged properties, if otherwise qualifying, are also "like-kind" is sometimes uncertain. The Regulations state that like-kind refers to the nature and character of property and not to its grade or quality, and give some surprising illustrations: improved real estate for unimproved real estate; a leasehold of a fee with thirty years or more to run, for a fee interest in real estate. Treas. Reg. §1.1031(a)-1(b). Shortly, we will see a like-kind dispute, page 410 infra.

a. The Mechanics of Section 1031

Problem A: X owns an apartment building that he has held for investment. The adjusted basis is $1,000,000. The building's fair market value is $5,000,000. Y owns a ranch with a fair market value also of $5,000,000. X wishes to acquire the ranch, which Y is willing to *sell* at its market value.

If X were to sell the apartment building to a third person, let us say, Z, for $5,000,000, he would suffer a net capital gain of $4,000,000 (assuming no recapture), on which his federal capital gains tax would come to $800,000. (X must also consider state income taxes, and possibly the minimum tax for tax preferences.) However, if X exchanged the building directly for Y's ranch, and held the ranch for a qualifying purpose, §1031(a) would require nonrecognition. The acquired property would receive the carryover basis of $1,000,000. §1031(d).

Since Y, presumably, wants to cash out on the transaction, he will not wish to retain the apartment building and will resell it (shortly) to a third person, Z, for $5,000,000. Do you see why, on these facts, the exchange between X and Y is *not* nonrecognizable as to Y?

If you are wondering whether §1031(a) covers this three-corner deal, in which Z — not a direct party to the exchange — is the ultimate acquirer of X's apartment house, the *Biggs* case, following, should supply the answer.

> Problem B: X owns an apartment building that he has held for investment. The adjusted basis is $1,000,000. The building's fair market value is $5,000,000. Y owns a ranch with a fair market value of $4,000,000. In order to effect an exchange between X and Y, Y agrees to pay $1,000,000 in cash.

Section 1031(a) does not qualify this exchange because X has not received *solely* like-kind property. The nonqualifying property, cash, is called "boot," and §1031(b) handles exchanges, otherwise qualifying, that involve the receipt of boot. This section provides that gain, if any, shall be recognized in the amount of any money, and in the fair market value of any nonqualifying property, received by the taxpayer; in our example, X must recognize a $1,000,000 net capital gain.

Despite the $1,000,000 gain recognition, X's new basis in the apartment house remains $1,000,000. Section 1031(d) commands a carryover basis in the newly acquired property decreased by the amount of any money received and increased by the amount of any gain recognized. To test whether this treatment is sensible, consider what X's ultimate gain would be if he were to resell the ranch at its $4,000,000 market value.

Purchase money notes would be regarded as a cash equivalent on this exchange, and X would be taxed on their fair market value. Note, however, that if the exchange is one that would otherwise result in a nonrecognized *loss* to the taxpayer, the receipt of money or "other property" does not result in partial recognition. §1031(c).

> Problem C: X owns an apartment building that he has held for investment. The adjusted basis is $1,000,000. The building's fair market value is $5,000,000, but the building is subject to a $2,000,000 mortgage. Y owns a ranch with a fair market value of $3,000,000. X and Y exchange their properties.

The amount of any mortgage liability attached to the transferred property, which the transferee either assumes or takes subject to, is treated as boot and, thus, as potentially taxable under §1031(b). Treas. Reg. §1.1031(b)-1(c). Accordingly, in our example, X must recognize a $2,000,000 gain on the exchange.

The basis provision, §1031(d), would again result in a carryover basis of $1,000,000 for the ranch. Y's $2,000,000 mortgage takeover is viewed as the exact equivalent of "money received" under §1031(d), so that X must first adjust his basis downward to reflect that event before adjusting it upward to reflect gain recognition. To test whether this treatment is sensible, consider what X's ultimate gain would be if he were to resell the ranch at the $3,000,000 market value.

Tax Strategy: How to Postpone Taxes on the Sale of Real Property

Consider, also, the effect of a mortgage takeover on Y's basis for the apartment house, if Y were to bring the exchange within the ambit of §1031. To assist in that consideration, assume that Y's basis in the ranch prior to the exchange was $1,500,000.

Often mortgages will be present on both sides of the transaction. See if you can work through the following problem.

> Problem D: X owns an apartment building that he has held for investment. The adjusted basis is $1,000,000. The building's fair market value is $5,000,000, but the building is subject to a $2,000,000 mortgage. Y owns a ranch that he has held for investment. The adjusted basis is $1,500,000. The ranch's fair market value is $4,000,000, but the ranch is subject to a $1,500,000 mortgage. X and Y effect an exchange of the two properties. X receives $500,000 in cash.
> What is X's gain recognition, if any?
> What is Y's gain recognition, if any?
> What is X's basis in the ranch after the exchange?
> What is Y's basis in the apartment building after the exchange?

Biggs v. Commissioner
632 F.2d 1171 (5th Cir. 1980)

HENDERSON, Circuit Judge. The Commissioner of Internal Revenue appeals from the decision of the United States Tax Court holding that a transfer of real property effected by the taxpayer, Franklin B. Biggs, constituted an exchange within the meaning of §1031 of the Internal Revenue Code of 1954. We affirm.

The numerous transactions which form the subject of this suit are somewhat confusing and each detail is of potential significance. Thus, it will be necessary to recount with particularity the facts as found by the Tax Court.

Biggs owned two parcels of land located in St. Martin's Neck, Worcester County, Maryland (hereinafter referred to as the "Maryland property"). Sometime before October 23, 1968, Biggs listed this property for sale with a realtor. The realtor advised Biggs that he had a client, Shepard G. Powell, who was interested in purchasing the property.

Biggs and Powell met on October 23, 1968 to discuss Powell's possible acquisition of the Maryland property. Biggs insisted from the outset that he receive real property of like kind as part of the consideration for the transfer. Both men understood that Biggs would locate the property he wished to receive in exchange, and Powell agreed to cooperate in the exchange arrangements to the extent that his own interests were not impaired.

On October 25, 1968, Biggs and Powell signed a memorandum of intent which provided, in pertinent part, the following:

I. PURCHASE PRICE: $900,000 NET to SELLERS. . . .
   c. $25,000.00 down payment at signing of contract, . . .
   d. $75,000.00 additional payment at time of settlement, which shall be within ninety (90) days after contract signing, making total cash payments of $100,000.00.
II. MORTGAGE:
   a. Balance of $800,000.00 secured by a first mortgage on Real Estate to SELLERS at a 4% interest rate; 10 year term. . . .

The memorandum contained no mention of the contemplated exchange of properties. Upon learning of this omission, Biggs' attorney, W. Edgar Porter, told Powell that the memorandum of intent did not comport with his understanding of the proposed transaction. Powell agreed to have his attorney meet with Porter to work out the terms of a written exchange agreement.

Biggs began his search for suitable exchange property by advising John Thatcher, a Maryland real estate broker, of the desired specifications. Subsequently, Biggs was contacted by another realtor, John A. Davis, who had in his inventory four parcels of land located in Accomack County, Virginia, collectively known as Myrtle Grove Farm (hereinafter referred to as "the Virginia property"). Biggs inspected the property, found it suitable, and instructed Davis to draft contracts of sale.

As initially drawn, the contracts named Biggs as the buyer of the Virginia property. However, at Porter's suggestion, they were modified to describe the purchaser as "Franklin B. Biggs (acting as agent for syndicate)." The contracts were executed on October 29th and 30th, 1968, and contained the following terms:

Paid on execution of contract	$ 13,900.00
Balance due at settlement	115,655.14
Indebtedness created or assumed	142,544.86
Total—Gross Sales Price	$272,100.00

Upon signing the contracts, Biggs paid $13,900.00 to the sellers of the Virginia property.

Because Powell was either unable or unwilling to take title to the Virginia property, Biggs arranged for the title to be transferred to Shore Title Company, Inc. (hereinafter referred to as "Shore"), a Maryland corporation owned and controlled by Porter and certain members of his family. However, it was not until December 26, 1968 that the purchase was authorized by Shore's board of directors. On January 9, 1969, prior to the transfer to Shore, Biggs and Shore entered into the following agreement with respect to the Virginia property:

   1. At any time hereafter that either party hereto requests the other party to do so, Shore Title Co., Inc. will and hereby agrees to convey unto the said Franklin B. Biggs, or his nominee, all of the above mentioned

Tax Strategy: How to Postpone Taxes on the Sale of Real Property 403

property, for exactly the same price said Shore Title Co., Inc. has paid for it, plus any and all costs, expenses, advances or payments which Shore Title Co., Inc. has paid or will be bound in the future to pay, over and above said purchase price to Shore Title Co., Inc., in order for Shore Title Co., Inc., to acquire or hold title to said property; and it [is] further agreed that at that time, i.e.—when Shore Title Co., Inc. conveys said property under this paragraph and its provisions, the said Franklin B. Biggs, or his nominee will simultaneously release or cause Shore Title Co., Inc. to be released from any and all obligations which the latter has created, assumed or become bound upon in its acquisition and holding of title to said property.

2. All costs for acquiring or holding title to said property by both the said Shore Title Co., Inc. and Franklin B. Biggs, or his nominee shall be paid by the said Franklin B. Biggs, or his nominee at the time of transfer of title under paragraph numbered 1 hereof.

On or about the same date, the contracts for the sale of the Virginia property were closed. Warranty deeds evidencing legal title were delivered to Shore by the sellers. Biggs advanced to Shore the $115,655.14 due at settlement and, by a bond secured by a deed of trust on the property, Shore agreed to repay Biggs. Shore also assumed liabilities totalling $142,544.86 which were secured by deeds of trust in favor of the sellers and another mortgagee. Biggs paid Thatcher's finder's fee and all of the closing costs.

On February 26, 1969, Shore and Powell signed an agreement for the sale by Shore of the Virginia property to Powell or his assigns. Payment of the purchase price was arranged as follows:

Upon execution of the agreement	$100.00
Vendee assumed and covenanted to pay the following promissory notes, all secured by deeds of trust on Virginia property:	
To Shore Savings & Loan Association	58,469.86
To those from whom Shore acquired the Virginia property	84,075.00
To Franklin B. Biggs	115,655.14
Balance due at settlement	13,900.00
Total purchase price	272,200.00

The next day, February 27, 1969, Biggs and Powell executed a contract which provided that Biggs would sell the Maryland property to Powell or his assigns upon the following terms:

Cash, upon execution	$ 25,000.00
Cash, at settlement	75,000.00
First mortgage note receivable from Mr. Powell	800,000.00
Total	$900,000.00

The contract further stated:

Sellers and Purchaser acknowledge the existence of a Contract of Sale dated February 26th, 1969, between Shore Title Co., Inc., Vendor-Seller; and Shepard G. Powell or Assigns, Vendee-Purchaser, copy of which is attached hereto and made a part hereof, whereby that Vendor has contracted to sell and that Vendee has agreed to buy from that Vendor at and for the purchase price of Two Hundred Seventy Two Thousand Two Hundred Dollars ($272,200.00) . . . [the Virginia property]. As a further consideration for the making of this Contract of Sale . . . for the sale and purchase . . . of . . . [the Maryland property] the said Shepard G. Powell or Assigns, for the sum of One Hundred Dollars ($100.00) in cash, in hand paid, receipt whereof is hereby acknowledged, does hereby bargain, sell, set over and transfer unto said Franklin B. Biggs all of the right, title and interest of the said Shepard G. Powell or Assigns in and to said Virginia property and said Contract of Sale relating thereto, upon condition that the said Franklin B. Biggs assumes and covvenants to pay (which he hereby does) all of the obligations assumed by the said Shepard G. Powell under the aforesaid Contract of Sale between him and Shore Title Co., Inc.; and said Franklin B. Biggs hereby agrees to hold Shepard G. Powell or Assigns harmless from any liability under any and all of said obligations on said Virginia property, and the said Shepard G. Powell and said Franklin B. Biggs do hereby jointly and separately agree to execute and deliver any and all necessary papers to effect delivery of title to said Virginia property to said Franklin B. Biggs and to relieve said Shepard G. Powell from any and all obligations assumed by him thereon.

On the same date, Powell and his wife assigned their contractual right to acquire the Maryland property to Samuel Lessans and Maurice Lessans. The Lessanses, in turn, sold and assigned their rights to acquire the Maryland property to Ocean View Corporation (hereinafter referred to as "Ocean View"), a Maryland corporation, for $1,300,000.00 by an agreement dated May 22, 1969. The purchase price was comprised of $150,000.00 to be paid into escrow at the time the contract was signed, an $800,000.00 note executed by Ocean View in favor of Biggs at the time of settlement, a $250,000.00 note from Ocean View to the Lessanses, and a $100,000.00 note from Ocean View to the real estate agents at closing.

Ocean View was incorporated on May 21, 1969. At the first meeting of its board of directors, the corporation was authorized to acquire the Maryland property and, also, to quit-claim any interest it might have in the Virginia property. It is undisputed, though, that neither the Lessanses nor Ocean View had any interest whatsoever in that property.

On May 24, 1969, Shore executed a deed conveying all of its right, title and interest in the Virginia property to Biggs. Powell and his wife, the Lessanses and Ocean View all joined in executing the deed as grantors, despite their apparent lack of any cognizable interest in the property. This instrument provided that:

[T]he said Shore Title Co., Inc., a Maryland corporation, executes this deed to the Grantee herein for the purpose of conveying the . . . Virginia property hereinafter described by good and marketable title, subject to the assumption by the Grantee herein of the obligations hereinafter referred to, and all of the other Grantors herein join in the execution of this deed for the purpose of releasing and quit-claiming any interest in and to the property described herein and for the purpose of thereby requesting Shore Title Co., Inc. to convey said property to the Grantee herein in the manner herein set out. . . .

By the same deed, Biggs agreed to assume and pay the notes in favor of the mortgagee and the owners from whom Shore had acquired the Virginia property, in the total sum of $142,544.86. On May 29, 1969, Biggs executed a deed of release in favor of Shore indicating payment in full of the $115,655.14 bond.

On May 26, 1969, Biggs and his wife, Powell and his wife and the Lessanses sold the Maryland property to Ocean View. Contemporaneously, Ocean View executed a mortgage in the face amount of $800,000.00 in favor of Biggs. Also on this date, all of the contracts were closed. Ocean View received the deed to the Maryland property and Biggs accepted title to the Virginia property.

Biggs reported his gain from the sale of the Maryland property on his 1969 federal income tax return as follows:[1]

Selling price of Maryland property	$900,000.00	100.00%
Exchange-Virginia property	298,380.75[a]	33.15%
Boot	$601,619.25	66.85%
Selling price Maryland property	$900,000.00	
Basis-date of exchange	186,312.80	
Gain	$713,687.20	
Not recognized-exchange (Sec. 1031 I.R.C.) 33.15%	236,587.31	
Taxable gain	$477,099.89	53.011%

[a] Such figure included finders' fees and legal costs incident to the acquisition of the Virginia property.

Biggs elected to report the transaction under the installment sales provision of §453 of the Code. The Commissioner issued a notice of deficiency based upon his determination that there was no exchange of like-kind properties within the meaning of §1031. The Tax Court disagreed, and ruled in favor of Biggs.[2]

Section 1031 provides, in pertinent part, that the gain realized on the exchange of like-kind property held for productive use or investment shall

---

1. Biggs admits that, even if the transaction qualifies as a §1031 exchange, he used an incorrect method to calculate the gain to be recognized.
2. The Tax Court opinion is reported at 69 T.C. 905 (1978).

be recognized only to the extent that "boot" or cash is received as additional consideration. The Commissioner does not deny that Biggs fully intended to carry out an exchange that would pass muster under §1031. It was undoubtedly for this purpose that Biggs insisted from the beginning of his negotiations with Powell that he receive property of like kind as part of the consideration for the transfer of the Maryland property. Cf. *Alderson v. C.I.R.*, 317 F.2d 790 (9th Cir. 1963). However, as this court made clear in *Carlton v. United States*, 385 F.2d 238 (5th Cir. 1967), the mere intent to effect a §1031 exchange is not dispositive. Indeed, the Commissioner's primary contention is that, under the authority of our holding in *Carlton*, Biggs failed to accomplish an exchange because the purchaser, Powell, never held title to the Virginia property.

The facts on which *Carlton* was decided parallel those which we now consider in several respects. Carlton, the taxpayer, wished to trade a tract of ranch land for other property of a similar character in order to obtain the tax benefits afforded by §1031. This intent was made explicit in the negotiations and resulting option contract entered into by Carlton and General, a corporation which desired to purchase the ranch property. Carlton proceeded to locate two parcels of suitable exchange property, negotiate for the acquisition of this property, and pay a deposit on each parcel. General executed the actual agreements of sale and then assigned its contract rights to purchase the exchange property to the taxpayer. However, the crucial factor which distinguishes *Carlton* from the instant case is that General actually paid cash for the ranch property which Carlton then used two days later to purchase the exchange property. A panel of this court held that the receipt of cash transformed the intended exchange into a sale:

> [W]hile elaborate plans were laid to exchange property, the substance of the transaction was that the appellants received cash for the deed to their ranch property and not another parcel of land. The very essence of an exchange is the transfer of property between owners, while the mark of a sale is the receipt of cash for the property.

385 F.2d at 242 (footnote and citations omitted).

Although the payment and receipt of cash was the determinative factor, the court went on to cite additional reasons to support its holding of a sale, rather than an exchange:

> Further, General was never in a position to exchange properties with the appellants because it never acquired the legal title to either the Lyons or the Fernandez property. Indeed, General was not personally obligated on either the notes or mortgages involved in these transactions. Thus it never had any property of like kind to exchange. Finally, it cannot be said that General paid for the Lyons and Fernandez properties and merely had the properties deeded directly to the appellants. The money received from General by the

appellants for the ranch property was not earmarked by General to be used in purchasing the Lyons or Fernandez properties. It was unrestricted and could be used by the appellants as they pleased.

385 F.2d at 242-243. The Commissioner maintains that this language in *Carlton* establishes as an absolute prerequisite to a §1031 exchange that the purchaser have title to the exchange property. We do not agree with this interpretation. The *Carlton* decision was based on the aggregate circumstances discussed therein and, as we have noted, the most significant of these was the receipt of cash by the taxpayer. In the present case, the transfer of the Maryland property and the receipt of the Virginia property occurred simultaneously, and the cash paid to Biggs at the closing constituted "boot." Also in contrast to the facts found in *Carlton,* Powell, as contract purchaser, did "assume [ ] and covenant [ ] to pay . . . promissory notes, all secured by deeds of trust on the Virginia property," plus the balance due at settlement. We cannot ignore the legal obligations and risks inherent in this contractual language, even though Powell was subject to such risks only for a short period of time. Also, the unrestricted use of funds which was a problem in *Carlton* is of no concern here because Biggs received cash only upon the closing of all transactions.

Thus, we are left with the sole consideration that Powell never acquired legal title to the Virginia property. Yet, if we were to decide, as the Commissioner urges, that this factor alone precludes a §1031 exchange, we would contravene the earlier precedent established by this court in W. D. Haden Co. v. C.I.R., 165 F.2d 588 (5th Cir. 1948). *Haden* also involved a multi-party exchange in which the purchaser, Goodwin, never held title to the exchange property. However, since Goodwin had contracted to purchase the property, the court held that the taxpayer had effected a like-kind exchange, stating that the purchaser "could bind himself to exchange property he did not own but could acquire." 165 F.2d at 590.

Our resolution of the title issue is also tangentially supported by language contained in the Ninth Circuit's recent opinion in Starker v. United States, 602 F.2d 1341 (9th Cir. 1979). Briefly stated, the *Starker* facts involved a transfer of the taxpayer's real property to the purchaser, Crown Zellerbach Corp., in exchange for the corporation's promise to acquire other real property in the future and convey it to the taxpayer. The government argued that this arrangement did not qualify for §1031 treatment because the transfers were not simultaneous and, alternatively, the contract right received by the taxpayer was personal property and, hence, not like-kind to the real property he had conveyed. The Ninth Circuit disagreed and, in response to the latter argument, stated:

> This is true, but the short answer to this statement is that title to real property, like a contract right to purchase real property, is nothing more than a bundle of potential causes of action: for trespass, to quiet title, for interfer-

ence with quiet enjoyment, and so on. The bundle of rights associated with ownership is obviously not excluded from section 1031; a contractual right to assume the rights of ownership should not, we believe, be treated as any different than the ownership rights themselves. Even if the contract right includes the possibility of the taxpayer receiving something other than ownership of like-kind property, we hold that it is still of a like-kind with ownership for tax purposes when the taxpayer prefers property to cash before and throughout the executory period, and only like-kind property is ultimately received.

602 F.2d at 1355. Of course, we need not, and do not, express either acceptance or disapproval of the ultimate holding in *Starker*. However, the Ninth Circuit's discussion of the title versus right-to-purchase problem is, we believe, consistent with our own analysis.

We must also reject the Commissioner's assertions that the Tax Court applied the so-called "step-transaction doctrine" incorrectly, and that the transactions which occurred here were in substance a sale for cash of the Maryland property and an unrelated purchase of the Virginia property. The step-transaction doctrine was articulated in Redwing Carriers, Inc. v. Tomlinson, 399 F.2d 652 (5th Cir. 1968):

> [A]n integrated transaction may not be separated into its components for the purposes of taxation by either the Internal Revenue Service or the taxpayer. (Citation omitted.) In Kanawha Gas and Utilities Co. v. Commissioner, 5 Cir. 1954, 214 F.2d 685, 691, our Court through Judge Rives said:
>
>> In determining the incidence of taxation, we must look through form and search out the substance of a transaction. . . . [cases cited] This basic concept of tax law is particularly pertinent to cases involving a series of transactions designed and executed as parts of a unitary plan to achieve an intended result. Such plans will be viewed as a whole regardless of whether the effect of so doing is imposition of or relief from taxation. The series of closely related steps in such a plan are merely the means by which to carry out the plan and will not be separated.

399 F.2d at 658. The Tax Court found that the many transactions leading to the ultimate transfers of the Maryland and Virginia properties were part of a single, integrated plan, the substantive result of which was a like-kind exchange. This finding is amply supported by the evidence. Biggs insisted at all times that he receive like-kind property as part of the consideration for the transfer of the Maryland property. Powell agreed to this arrangement and assured Biggs of his cooperation. Biggs was careful not to contract for the sale of the Maryland property until Powell had obtained an interest in the Virginia land. When he and Powell did enter into an agreement of sale on February 26, 1969, the exchange was made an express condition of the contract. Biggs also avoided the step which was fatal to the taxpayer's intended exchange in *Carlton;* i.e., he did not receive any cash prior to the simultaneous closings of the properties on May 26, 1969.

Under these circumstances, the Tax Court correctly determined that all transactions were interdependent and that they culminated in an exchange rather than a sale and separate purchase.

Finally, we examine the Commissioner's claim that Shore was serving as an agent for Biggs throughout the transactions, and that the accomplishment of the intended exchange was thereby precluded. Admittedly, the exchange would have been meaningless if Shore, acting as Biggs' agent, acquired title to the Virginia property and then executed the deed conveying title to Biggs. For, in essence, Biggs would have merely effected an exchange with himself. Cf. Coupe v. C.I.R., 52 T.C. 394 (1969). However, while the Tax Court refused to find, in contrast to its decision in *Coupe*, that Shore acted as an agent for the purchaser, Powell, it also specifically determined that Shore was not an agent of Biggs. Rather, Shore accepted title to the Virginia property, albeit at Biggs' request, merely in order to facilitate the exchange. We believe that this is an accurate characterization of Shore's role in the transactions. Consequently, we reject the Commissioner's agency notion also.

Undoubtedly, the exchange of the Maryland and Virginia properties could have been more artfully accomplished and with a greater economy of steps. However, we must conclude on the facts before us that the taxpayer ultimately achieved the intended result. Accordingly, the decision of the Tax Court is affirmed.

NOTES AND QUESTIONS

1. In commenting upon *Biggs* and similar §1031-styled disputes, one writer has stated:

These cases have generally set forth a very liberal trend as to when an exchange will be recognized. Both the courts and the Service have indicated that it is permissible for the party seeking to effectuate an exchange to locate and designate the property for the [second party] to acquire. The courts have also held that it is not necessary for the [second party] to acquire legal title to the property for purposes of the exchange, although the IRS has not conceded this point. . . . Despite this liberal trend, taxpayers are advised not to ignore completely the formalities of the exchange transaction or to assume that any transaction will qualify as an exchange simply because that is their intent. . . . The documents to the transaction should clearly set forth the parties' intent that an exchange take place. If the [second party] will not be acquiring legal title to the property which is being acquired for the purpose of the exchange, it is certainly preferable that the documents reflect that the [second party] hold a beneficial interest in such property for a period of time. Care should be taken in the documentation so as not to suggest that the [second party] is acquiring the property as the agent of the party seeking to effectuate the exchange.

Madden, Taxation of Real Estate Transactions — An Overview, B.N.A. Tax Mgmt. Portfolio 480, at A-101 (1984).

2. *Bigg's* counterpoint appears at Allen v. Commr., 43 T.C.M. 1045 (1982). There the court denied §1031 treatment when it found that the escrowed closings were not "mutually interdependent."

The facts were these: The taxpayer (T), owner of a rental property, located an apartment complex that she desired to obtain through a trade. When approached by T, the owner of the apartment complex (X) said that he was interested only in receiving cash. Thereupon, T found a third party (Y) willing to buy T's rental property. To consummate the transactions, two escrows, each with separate companies, were used: 1) T and X opened an escrow account for the purchase of the X property; 2) T and Y opened an escrow account for the sale of the T property. Each transaction was subject to several conditions. Nothing in the record indicated, however, that the successful completion of either transaction was a condition of the other.

> The two transactions in this case were related only in the sense that the proceeds of the sale of the (T) property were, in fact, used for the purchase of the (X) property and may have been necessary for it. We do not think that this is sufficient for the transactions to be viewed as independent steps pursuant to an exchange of one property for the other. Instead, we think that the transactions are better characterized as a sale and reinvestment of the proceeds.

Id. at 1046.

3. *Delayed exchanges.* In Starker v. United States, 602 F.2d 1341 (9th Cir. 1979), the court allowed §1031 treatment despite the fact that the second partner was given up to five years to find suitable exchange property. Because the second party was contractually bound to perform within that five-year period, the court viewed taxpayer's contractual entitlement to a property to be "named later" as equivalent to ownership therein for purposes of effectuating a like-kind exchange. *Starker* exchanges became widespread, but the Tax Reform Act of 1984 has greatly curtailed the opportunity to delay selection of the second property. Section 1031(a)(3) requires that the exchange property be identified within 45 days of the day on which the taxpayer gives up the property to be relinquished, or that the exchange property be received on the earlier of either 180 days after the transfer of the taxpayer's property or the due date (including extensions) of the taxpayer's return for that year.

Magneson v. Commissioner
753 F.2d 1490 (9th Cir. 1985)

BOOCHEVER, Circuit Judge. We are faced in this case with an issue of first impression in the Courts of Appeals: whether property acquired in a like-kind exchange with the intention of contributing it to a partnership under Internal Revenue Code §721 is "held" for investment within the meaning of Internal Revenue Code §1031(a).

Petitioners Norman and Beverly Magneson exchanged a fee interest in one piece of real estate for a fee interest in another. The same day they contributed the acquired real estate to a limited partnership in return for a general partnership interest. The Magnesons claim nonrecognition of gain on both the exchange and the contribution under sections 1031(a) and 721 of the Internal Revenue Code. The Tax Court held that the taxpayers qualified for nonrecognition, 81 T.C. 767 (1983), and the Commissioner appeals. We affirm.

The Magnesons were the sole owners of an apartment building in San Diego, California (Iowa Street Property). They held the property for productive use in trade or business or for investment within the meaning of section 1031(a). N.E.R. Plaza, Ltd. (NER) was the sole owner of commercial property in San Diego, California, known as the Plaza Property (Plaza Property).

Pursuant to a prearranged transaction consummated on August 11, 1977, the Magnesons transferred their fee interest in the Iowa Street Property to NER in exchange for a ten-percent undivided fee interest in the Plaza Property. Thereafter, on the same day, both the Magnesons and NER transferred their interests in the Plaza Property to U.S. Trust, Ltd. (U.S. Trust), a limited partnership under California law. In exchange for cash and their ten-percent interest in the Plaza Property, the Magnesons received a general partnership interest in U.S. Trust consisting of a ten-percent equity interest and a nine-percent interest in net profits and losses. U.S. Trust was formed for the purpose of acquiring, holding, and operating the Plaza Property. The Magnesons paid no tax on the gain realized from their exchange of the Iowa Street Property for the Plaza Property, claiming nonrecognition treatment under section 1031(a). They also paid no tax on the gain realized from their contribution of the Plaza Property to U.S. Trust, claiming nonrecognition treatment under section 721.

The parties agree that the contribution of the Plaza Property to U.S. Trust qualifies for nonrecognition of gain under section 721, which provides that "[n]o gain or loss shall be recognized to a partnership or to any of its partners in the case of a contribution of property to the partnership in exchange for an interest in the partnership." The parties also agree that the Iowa Street Property and the Plaza Property are like-kind properties within the meaning of section 1031(a), which in 1977 provided:

> No gain or loss shall be recognized if property held for productive use in trade or business or for investment (not including stock in trade or other property held primarily for sale, nor stocks, bonds, notes, choses in action, certificates of trust or beneficial interest, or other securities or evidences of indebtedness or interest) is exchanged solely for property of a like kind to be held either for productive use in trade or business or for investment.

For purposes of this opinion we will use the phrase "held for investment" when discussing the holding requirement of section 1031(a), because the distinction between productive use and investment is not at issue.

I. THE HOLDING REQUIREMENT OF SECTION 1031(a)

The Commissioner argues that the exchange of the Iowa Street Property for the Plaza Property cannot qualify for nonrecognition under section 1031(a) because the Magnesons did not "hold" the Plaza Property for investment. The Magnesons contend that holding the property to contribute to a partnership is "holding" the property for investment. The court found for the Magnesons. The majority concluded that the contribution of the Plaza Property to U.S. Trust was a continuation of the Magnesons' investment unliquidated but in a modified form, and that therefore the Magnesons did hold the Plaza Property for investment. 81 T.C. at 771-72. We review the Tax Court's conclusions of law de novo, noting however that its opinions are entitled to respect because of its special expertise in the field. California Federal Life Insurance Co. v. Commissioner, 680 F.2d 85, 87 (9th Cir. 1982).

To qualify for nonrecognition treatment under section 1031(a), the taxpayer must, at the time the exchange is consummated, intend to hold the property acquired for investment. Regals Realty Co. v. Commissioner, 127 F.2d 931, 934 (2d Cir. 1942); see Margolis v. Commissioner, 337 F.2d 1001, 1003-05 (9th Cir. 1964). Numerous cases have held that the taxpayers' intent at the time of the exchange to liquidate their interest in the property acquired disqualifies the exchange from nonrecognition under section 1031(a). See, e.g., Regals Realty, 127 F.2d at 933-34 (intent to sell); Click v. Commissioner, 78 T.C. 225, 233-34 (1982) (intent to give as gift); Lindsley v. Commissioner, T.C.M. (P-H) 1983-729, at 3047-48 (intent to give to charity); Land Dynamics v. Commissioner, T.C.M. (P-H) 1978-259, at 1107-08 (intent to sell). But see Wagensen v. Commissioner, 74 T.C. 653, 658-59 (1980) (intent at time of exchange to hold for productive use not negated by desire to give eventually to children). It is stipulated that the Magnesons intended at the time of the exchange to hold the property for contribution to U.S. Trust. Therefore, the Magnesons' exchange can only qualify under section 1031(a) if contributing property to a partnership in return for an interest in the partnership is "holding" the property for investment within the meaning of section 1031(a).

We have found no precedent on point at either the Tax Court or the circuit court level. Revenue Ruling 75-292, 1975-2 C.B. 333, relied on by the Commissioner, addresses a related question: whether a like-kind exchange followed by a transfer for stock under section 351[2] to a controlled

---

2. Section 351 provides, in pertinent part:
   (a) General rule—No gain or loss shall be recognized if property is transferred to a corporation by one or more persons solely in exchange for stock or securities in such corporation and immediately after the exchange such person or persons are in control (as defined in section 368(c)) of the corporation.

corporation qualifies for nonrecognition under section 1031(a). The Service ruled that the property transferred to the corporation was no longer held by the taxpayer, and gain was recognized on the exchange. Id. at 334. Revenue rulings, however, are not binding on this court. Ricards v. United States, 683 F.2d 1219, 1224 & n.12 (9th Cir. 1981) (rulings not dispositive although entitled to consideration as "body of experience and informed judgment"). More significantly, transfer to a corporation in exchange for shares is distinguishable from transfer to a partnership for a general partnership interest in several important ways.

First, a corporation is a distinct entity, apart from its shareholders, whereas a partnership is an association of its partner-investors. Shareholders have no ownership interest in the assets of a corporation; partners own the assets pf a partnership. Shareholders have no participation in daily management of corporate assets and very little participation in long-term management; general partners are the managers of the partnership. Thus when the owner of property transfers it to a corporation in exchange for shares, he relinquishes ownership and control of the property. In contrast, he retains both in a transfer to a partnership for a general partnership interest.

Second, a like-kind exchange followed by a section 351 transfer, viewed as a whole, results in the exchange of property for stock. The parenthetical clause of section 1031(a) expressly excludes stock as property eligible for exchange, but there is no such prohibition on exchange of partnership interests. Long v. Commissioner, 77 T.C. 1045, 1066-68 (1981) (rejecting Commissioner's argument that partnership interests fit within exclusionary clause as choses in action or evidences of interests). Revenue Ruling 75-292 is therefore inapplicable to this case.

The central purpose of both sections 721 and 1031(a), as stated by the Treasury Regulations, is to provide for nonrecognition of gain on a transfer of property in which the differences between the property parted with and the property acquired "are more formal than substantial," and "the new property is substantially a continuation of the old investment still unliquidated." Treas. Reg. 1.1002-1(c), T.D. 6500, 24 Fed. Reg. 11910 (1960). The regulations reflect the legislative history of the predecessor of section 1031(a). See H.R. Rep. No. 704, 73d Cong., 2d Sess. 12, reprinted in 1939-1 C.B. (pt. 2) 554, 564; Starker v. United States, 602 F.2d 1341, 1352 (9th Cir. 1979) (section 1031 "designed to avoid the imposition of a tax on those who do not 'cash in' their investments in trade or business property"). Furthermore, as the Tax Court noted, the regulations unequivocally describe section 721 as representing a continuation, not a liquidation, of the old investment. The case law, the regulations, and the legislative history are thus all in agreement that the basic reason for nonrecognition of gain or loss on transfers of property under sections 1031 and 721 is that the taxpayer's economic situation after the transfer is fundamentally the same as it was before the transfer: his money is still tied up in investment in the same kind of property. Koch v. Commissioner, 71

T.C. 54, 63-64 (1978); see *Starker,* 602 F.2d at 1352; Biggs v. Commissioner, 69 T.C. 905, 913-14 (1978), *aff'd,* 632 F.2d 1171 (5th Cir. 1980). This principle exactly describes the Magnesons' situation. Before the two transactions, their investment was a fee interest in income-producing real estate. They exchanged this property for other income-producing real estate, which they held as tenants in common with NER. The Magnesons and NER then changed the form of their ownership of that real estate from tenancy in common to partnership. They still own the income-producing real estate, and they have taken no cash or non-like-kind property out of the transaction. The Magnesons' transactions therefore fit squarely within the central purpose of section 1031. They exchanged their investment property for like-kind investment property which they continue to hold for investment, albeit in a different form of ownership.

The Commissioner, and the dissenting Tax Court judges, argue that the differences between ownership as tenants in common and ownership as a partnership are so substantial that the Magnesons cannot be regarded as having continued to hold the property for investment under section 1031(a) after the partnership contribution. . . .

. . . In application of federal tax statutes, state law controls in determining the nature of the legal interest the taxpayer holds in the property sought to be taxed. Federal law does not create or define property rights; it merely attaches tax consequences to the interests created by state law. Aquilino v. United States, 363 U.S. 509, 512-13, 80 S. Ct. 1277, 1279-80, 4 L. Ed. 2d 1365 (1960). The dissent and the majority therefore correctly looked to California law to determine and compare the nature of tenancy in common and partnership ownership.

In California, a tenant in common owns an undivided interest in and is entitled to possession and enjoyment of the entire property. Dimmick v. Dimmick, 58 Cal. 2d 417, 422, 374 P.2d 824, 826, 24 Cal. Rptr. 856, 858 (1962). Title to his interest is vested in him, he may encumber it or sell it independently of his co-tenants, Meyer v. Wall, 270 Cal. App. 2d 24, 30, 75 Cal. Rptr. 236, 240 (1969), and the interest is devisable and descendible, see Wilkerson v. Thomas, 121 Cal. App. 2d 479, 482, 263 P.2d 678, 680 (1953). Similarly, a partner is co-owner with his partners, as a tenant in partnership, of specific partnership property. Cal. Corp. Code §15025(1) (West Supp. 1984). A general partner has the right to possess partnership property for the purposes of the partnership, although title is not vested in him. Cal. Corp. Code §15025(2)(a) (West Supp. 1984). However, a partner's interest in specific partnership property is not assignable without concurrent assignment by all other partners, Cal. Corp. Code §15025(2)(b) (West Supp. 1984), nor subject to attachment except for partnership debt, Cal. Corp. Code §15025(2)(c) (West Supp. 1984), nor subject to marital property rights, Cal. Corp. Code §15025(2)(e) (West Supp. 1984). On the death of a partner, his interest in specific partnership property vests in the surviving partners, not in the deceased partner's devisees or heirs. Cal. Corp. Code §15025(2)(d) (West Supp. 1984).

The Tax Court minority concluded from these differences that the transformation of the Magnesons' tenancy in common into a partnership interest "so changed their legal relationship to that property as to disqualify the exchange from section 1031(a) treatment." We disagree. While there are significant distinctions, we do not believe that they are controlling in determining the holding for investment issue. First, we note that the crucial question in a section 1031(a) analysis is continuity of investment in like-kind property. Therefore, the critical attributes in the taxpayer's relationship to the property are those relevant to holding the property for investment. As both tenants in common and as general partners, the Magnesons owned an interest in the Plaza Property. As both tenants in common and as general partners, the Magnesons had the right to possess and control the property. While it is true that section 15025(2)(a) limits their possession and control to partnership purposes, the partnership purpose was to hold for investment. Under these circumstances their control as general partners is of the same nature as their control as tenants in common, in each case holding the property for investment.

The significant differences between the tenancy in common and the partnership interests lie in the voluntary and involuntary alienability of the property. Basically, the tenancy in common interest is freely alienable, but specific partnership property is not. Because the whole premise of section 1031(a) is that the taxpayer's intent is *not to alienate* the property, we believe that alienability distinctions are not dispositive. If at the time of the exchange, as here, the taxpayer intends to contribute the property to a partnership for a general partnership interest, and the partnership's purpose is to hold the property for investment, the holding requirement of section 1031(a) is satisfied despite the limited alienability of specific partnership property.

The Commissioner contends that the Tax Court majority, in focusing exclusively on the continuity of investment principle underlying section 1031(a), ignored the equally important technical requirements of the section itself. Treasury Regulation 1.1002-1(b) provides:

> The exceptions from the general rule requiring the recognition of all gains and losses . . . are strictly construed and do not extend either beyond the words or the underlying assumptions and purposes of the exception. Nonrecognition is accorded by the Code only if the exchange is one which satisfies both (1) the specific description in the Code of an excepted exchange, and (2) the underlying purpose for which such exchange is excepted from the general rule.

The Commissioner contends that this double test applies, and that even if this transaction satisfies the "underlying purpose" prong of the test, it still fails to qualify under the "specific description" prong because technically the partnership and not the taxpayers holds the acquired property. This circuit, however, rejected an analogous argument in *Starker,* 602 F.2d at 1352-53, refusing to give such a narrow construction. The Commissioner argued in *Starker* that the language of the regulation quoted above, as applied to section 1031(a), required simultaneous transfer for section 1031(a) nonrecognition. After analyzing the legislative history of section 1031(a) and concluding that it did not support the Commissioner's position, the court stated:

> [T]here is a second sound reason to question the applicability of Treas. Reg. §1.1002-1: the long line of cases liberally construing section 1031. If the regulation purports to read into section 1031 a complex web of formal and substantive requirements, precedent indicates decisively that the regulation has been rejected.

Starker, 602 F.2d at 1352; see, e.g., Coastal Terminals, Inc. v. United States, 320 F.2d 333, 336-39 (4th Cir. 1963) (cash option did not preclude section 1031(a) nonrecognition because taxpayer intended to take cash only if no property available); Alderson v. Commissioner, 317 F.2d 790, 793 (9th Cir. 1963) (three-corner exchange); *Biggs,* 69 T.C. at 913-14 (four-corner exchange); 124 Front Street, Inc. v. Commissioner, 65 T.C. 6, 17-18 (1975) (taxpayer can advance money toward purchase price of property to be acquired); Coupe v. Commissioner, 52 T.C. 394, 405-09 (1969) (taxpayer can locate and negotiate for the property to be acquired); J. H. Baird Publishing Co. v. Commissioner, 39 T.C. 608, 611 (1962) (taxpayer can oversee improvements on the land to be acquired). Applying the *Starker* manner of construing the section, we decline to read into section 1031(a) the requirement that the taxpayer continue to hold the acquired property by the exact form of ownership in which it was acquired. So long as, as in this case, the taxpayers continue to own the property and to hold it for investment, a change in the mechanism of ownership which does not significantly affect the amount of control or the nature of the underlying investment does not preclude nonrecognition under section 1031(a).

II. THE STEP TRANSACTION DOCTRINE

As an alternate position, the Commissioner contends that the step transaction doctrine should be applied in this case and would preclude section 1031(a) nonrecognition. Under this doctrine, the court must view the transaction as a whole even if the taxpayer uses a number of steps to consummate the transaction. See Commissioner v. Court Holding Co., 324 U.S. 331, 334, 65 S. Ct. 707, 708, 89 L. Ed. 981 (1945). A taxpayer may not secure, by a series of contrived steps, different tax treatment than if he had carried out the transaction directly. Crenshaw v. United States, 450 F.2d 472, 475-78 (5th Cir. 1971), *cert. denied,* 408 U.S. 923, 92 S. Ct. 2490, 33 L. Ed. 2d 333 (1972). Viewed as a whole, the Commissioner argues that the Magnesons have exchanged their fee interest in the Iowa Street Property for a partnership interest in U.S. Trust, which the Commissioner contends is not like-kind property under this court's decision in

Meyer, 503 F.2d at 557-58 (general and limited partnership interests not like-kind).

Initially, we note that it may not be appropriate to collapse the steps of this transaction, because it is not readily apparent that the transaction could have been achieved directly. The Magnesons started out with the Iowa Street Property, which was worth one tenth of the Plaza Property. NER owned 100% of the Plaza Property. NER and the Magnesons wanted to end up owning the Plaza Property together in a partnership, and the Magnesons wanted to pay for their share with the Iowa Street Property. The Magnesons could have sold the Iowa Street Property, used the proceeds to buy ten percent of the Plaza Property, and then formed the partnership with NER, but that would have added a step to the transaction, rather than being a more direct route than that taken. Alternatively, NER and the Magnesons could have formed the partnership with the Iowa Street Property and ninety percent of the Plaza Property, and then the partnership could have exchanged the Iowa Street Property for the remaining ten percent of the Plaza Property. Again, this is no more direct than the method by which the Magnesons chose to carry out the transaction. Between two equally direct ways of achieving the same result, the Magnesons were free to choose the method which entailed the most tax advantages to them. *Biggs,* 69 T.C. at 913 (quoted in *Starker,* 602 F.2d at 1353 n.10). . . .

Our holding in this case is limited to those situations in which the taxpayer exchanges property for like-kind property with the intent of contributing the acquired property to a partnership for a general partnership interest. Further, the taxpayer must show, as the Magnesons have here, that the purpose of the partnership is to hold the property for investment, and that the total assets of the partnership are predominantly of like kind to the taxpayer's original investment.

Affirmed.

E. ORIGINAL ISSUE DISCOUNT (OID)

Smith, Tax Shelter Topics
14 Real Est. Rev. 14 (Winter 1985)

THE TAX REFORM ACT OF 1984 REDUCES PROPERTY VALUES UP TO 26 PERCENT

As predicted in this column in the Summer 1984 issue,[1] Congress passed the Tax Reform Act of 1984[2] (TRA), which completely rewrote the rules

---

1. David A. Smith, Tax Shelter Topics: Accrued But Unpaid Interest—A Hot Tax Shelter Technique Under Fire, 14 Real Estate Review—(Summer 1984).

2. By the time Congress was through improving the health of the nation's economy, the

for treating accrued but unpaid interest for tax purposes. Congress also extended the depreciable life for most real estate from fifteen to eighteen years, increased penalties for tax shelter sponsors, promoters, and investors, and required that all tax shelters be registered with the IRS *before* they are sold.

TRA cuts the value of nearly all real estate. As the author will show below, some particular types of real estate are as much as 26 percent less valuable after TRA than they were before. Most forms of accrued but unpaid interest investments have been severely wounded and may not recover. Many deserved extinction; some did not. None escaped unscathed.

THE NEW ORIGINAL ISSUE DISCOUNT (OID) RULES

The IRS chose to attack accrued but unpaid interest by extending the original issue discount (OID) rules to cover purchase money financing: that is, financing issued in connection with the purchase of property.

The Concept

OID is a provision of the Internal Revenue Code designed to provide proper recognition, over the expected holding period, of income on an instrument that carries a below-market interest rate.

Suppose, for instance, that an investor purchases, for $24.72, a zero-coupon bond (a Zero) with a ten-year maturity and a face amount of $100. Between now and ten years from now the bond pays nothing. On the tenth anniversary it pays $100. Somewhere between the purchase of the Zero and its redemption the investor has made $75.28 (the difference between the $100.00 received in year 10 and the $24.72 outlay made in year 1).

- When did the investor earn that money?
- Was it ordinary income or capital gain?

The OID rules solve these problems by calculating the implied compound interest rate that sets $24.72 in year zero equal to $100 in year 10. In our example, this rate is 15 percent. That is, if instead of buying the Zero our hypothetical investor had put $24.72 into an account earning a constant 15 percent, and reinvested the proceeds every year for ten years, at the end of that period he would have $100 — the same amount as if he had bought the Zero.

Since the investor's purchase of the Zero is economically equivalent to investing and reinvesting for ten years at 15 percent, the OID rules require

---

Tax Reform Act of 1984 had been included in a larger bill, the Deficit Reduction Act of 1984, which also included the Spending Reduction Act of 1984. Note that when spending goes down, it is a reduction, but when taxes go up, it's always a reform.

[TABLE 3-1]
Annual Interest Earned by a Zero Coupon Bond

Terms of the Zero

Face Amount:	$100
Required Yield Rate:	15%
Term:	10 Yrs.
Purchase Price:	$24.72

Year	Principal Amount at Beginning of Year	Interest Earned	Ending Principal Amount
1	$24.72	$3.71	$28.43
2	28.43	4.26	32.69
3	32.69	4.90	37.60
4	37.60	5.64	43.24
5	43.24	6.49	49.72
6	49.72	7.46	57.18
7	57.18	8.58	65.76
8	65.76	9.86	75.62
9	75.62	11.34	86.96
10	86.96	13.04	100.00

him to report income just as if that is what he had done.[3] His annual earnings are shown in [Table 3-1]. Each year the investor must report the amount in the "Interest Earned" column of [Table 3-1] as ordinary income, *even though he receives no cash.*[4] The investor has accrued but unpaid *ordinary income.* When at the end of ten years the Zero is paid off, the investor has no capital gain because the entire $75.28 of income has already been reported as interest income.

Applied to examples such as this, the OID rules have a pleasing logic, and this is probably why they were originally implemented for transactions in which original issues (of a new security) were sold at a discount from par. The OID rules provide a rational method for accounting for a disparity between issue amount and issue price. They also create a reverse tax shelter because taxes are paid before cash is received.

Rule Changes

The new legislation applies the OID rules to purchase money financing. But purchase money financing is not sold at a discount — it is tendered at par. This, says the IRS, is a distortion. However, the IRS insists it be

---

3. The rules also require the issuer to amortize the discount according to the same method, so they enforce a matching of income and expense between the two parties to the OID purchase.

4. It's worth noting that the price of a zero-coupon bond increases as it ages, and (assuming market interest rates remain stable) as a bond ages and nears maturity, its market value rises according to the OID schedule.

considered as having been discounted to cash, according to rules that it will set forth. (As will be seen below, the solution the IRS proposes creates problems of its own.)

TRA extends the OID provisions to all forms of purchase money financing, not just the limited forms to which it was previously applicable. Specifically, TRA:

- Mandates deduction of interest for tax purposes on the so-called economic accrual of interest, which basically means compound interest.
- Requires deferred-payment noteholders to report accrued but unpaid *income* concurrently with the deduction by the borrower/buyer of accrued but unpaid interest.
- Increases the safe harbor rate required on purchase money transactions from 9 percent to 110 percent of the yield to maturity of comparable Federal obligations.

Since long-term Treasury bills today yield about 13 percent, this means purchase money notes issued in 1985 must carry rates of roughly 14.25 percent.

IMMEDIATE CONSEQUENCES OF THE TAX REFORM ACT

These changes have two types of consequences: immediate and marketplace. Immediate consequences are those changes that can be calculated directly, as listed below in a "before and after" example. Marketplace consequences are the reactions by the investment community to the changed relative merits of different investments.

As the example below will demonstrate, the immediate consequences are the following:

- Deductions from noncash costs are "back-ended."
- Tax costs are higher when a borrower fails to pay a nonrecourse note when due and the property is foreclosed.
- The relative merit of prepaying a purchase money note (versus holding it to maturity) is increased.
- The benefits to a taxpaying seller of holding a deferred-payment note are practically eliminated.

The Example

Consider a simplified example. On January 1, 1984, a buyer purchases a building for $1 million from a cash-basis seller. Both buyer and seller are in

Original Issue Discount

the maximum brackets (50 percent ordinary income, 20 percent capital gain) and have after-tax discount rates of 10 percent. The buyer pays for the purchase by giving the seller a $1 million purchase money note bearing interest at 9 percent simple.

The building is well located but is encumbered by a net lease that has fifteen years remaining and that provides for annual payments equal to the building's operating expenses plus $1. Accordingly, the buyer expects to hold it for fifteen years, during which time it will produce no income at all, and then to sell it as soon as its temporary encumbrances expire. Since there will be no cash available for debt service during the holding period, interest on the note is accrued for payment upon maturity.

Before TRA Consequences

The rate on the note is the lowest permitted under Section 483 as it applied during 1984, and so no restatement is required. The buyer's tax consequences of this transaction are shown in [Table 3-2].

By the end of the fifteen-year holding period, the buyer has depreciated $1 million. He has also deducted accrued but unpaid interest of $1.35 million and in the process he has raised his terminal indebtedness to $2.35 million.

The net present value of the buyer's holding period benefits (before residuals and before termination taxes) is $688,849. To pay his nonrecourse indebtedness, he must sell the property for $2.35 million. For it to be worth this much, it must appreciate 5.86 percent per year.

After TRA Consequences

Once the rules of TRA are in effect, the buyer who does not wish the terminal indebtedness resulting from the purchase to rise above the $2.35 million of the old structure, encounters a problem. He cannot tender a $1 million, 9 percent note because the IRS will restate it. The lowest rate the IRS will accept will be 14.3 percent, compounded annually. At this percentage rate, the revised principal amount of the note required to produce a terminal payment of $2.35 million is a mere $316,501, *less than one-third* of the old principal amount. The resulting new benefit schedule is shown in [Table 3-3].

The interest accruals in the early years are far below those that were possible under the pre-TRA structure. In fact, not until year 9 do the benefits under the new structure exceed those under the old structure. When the investment ends in year 15, the net present value of the holding period benefits is only $548,939, a full 20 percent lower than under the old structure. A comparison of old versus new tax benefit schedules is made in graphic form in [Table 3-4].

[TABLE 3-2]
Buyer's Tax Consequences as the Result of Hypothetical Transaction
(Before the Tax Reform Act of 1984)

(1)	(2)	(3)	(4)	(5)	(6)	(7)	(8)	(9)	(10)
Year	Date	ACRS Depreciation Percentage	ACRS Depreciation	Accrued but Unpaid Interest on Note	Total Deductions	After-Tax Benefits	Discount Factor	Discounted After-Tax Benefits	Ending Balance of Purchase Money Note
1	1984	12%	$ 120,000	$ 90,000	$ 210,000	$ 105,000	1.0000	$105,000	$1,090,000
2	1985	10	100,000	90,000	190,000	95,000	1.1000	86,364	1,180,000
3	1986	9	90,000	90,000	180,000	90,000	1.2100	74,380	1,270,000
4	1987	8	80,000	90,000	170,000	85,000	1.3310	63,862	1,360,000
5	1988	7	70,000	90,000	160,000	80,000	1.4641	54,641	1,450,000
6	1989	6	60,000	90,000	150,000	75,000	1.6105	46,569	1,540,000
7	1990	6	60,000	90,000	150,000	75,000	1.7716	42,336	1,630,000
8	1991	6	60,000	90,000	150,000	75,000	1.9487	38,487	1,720,000
9	1992	6	60,000	90,000	150,000	75,000	2.1436	34,988	1,810,000
10	1993	5	50,000	90,000	140,000	70,000	2.3579	29,687	1,900,000
11	1994	5	50,000	90,000	140,000	70,000	2.5937	26,988	1,990,000
12	1995	5	50,000	90,000	140,000	70,000	2.8531	24,535	2,080,000
13	1996	5	50,000	90,000	140,000	70,000	3.1384	22,304	2,170,000
14	1997	5	50,000	90,000	140,000	70,000	3.4523	20,277	2,260,000
15	1998	5	50,000	90,000	140,000	70,000	3.7975	18,433	$2,350,000
		100%	$1,000,000	$1,350,000	$2,350,000	$1,175,000		$688,849	

Average annual appreciation in building price required to pay debt in Year 15 is 5.86%

[TABLE 3-3]
Buyer's Tax Consequences as the Result of Hypothetical Transaction with Revised Purchase Money Note After The Tax Reform Act of 1984
(Ignoring Extension of ACRS Lives)

(1) Year	(2) Date	(3) ACRS Depreciation Percentage	(4) ACRS Depreciation	(5) Accrued but Unpaid Interest on Note	(6) Total Deductions	(7) After-Tax Benefits	(8) Discount Factor	(9) Discounted After-Tax Benefits	(10) Ending Balance of Purchase Money Note
1	1985	12%	$ 37,980	$ 45,260	$ 83,240	$ 41,620	1.0000	$ 41,620	$ 361,760
2	1986	10	31,650	51,732	83,382	41,691	1.1000	37,901	413,492
3	1987	9	28,485	59,129	87,614	43,807	1.2100	36,204	472,621
4	1988	8	25,320	67,585	92,905	46,452	1.3310	34,900	540,206
5	1989	7	22,155	77,249	99,404	49,702	1.4641	33,947	617,455
6	1990	6	18,990	88,296	107,286	53,643	1.6105	33,308	705,751
7	1991	6	18,990	100,922	119,912	59,956	1.7716	33,844	806,674
8	1992	6	18,990	115,354	134,344	67,172	1.9487	34,470	922,028
9	1993	6	18,990	131,850	150,840	75,420	2.1436	35,184	1,053,878
10	1994	5	15,825	150,705	166,530	83,265	2.3579	35,312	1,204,583
11	1995	5	15,825	172,255	188,080	94,040	2.5937	36,257	1,376,838
12	1996	5	15,825	196,888	212,713	106,356	2.8531	37,277	1,573,726
13	1997	5	15,825	225,043	240,868	120,434	3.1384	38,374	1,798,769
14	1998	5	15,825	257,224	273,049	136,524	3.4523	39,546	2,055,993
15	1999	5	15,825	294,007	309,832	154,916	3.7975	40,794	2,350,000
		100%	$316,501	$2,033,499	$2,350,000	$1,175,000		$548,939	

[TABLE 3-4]
Comparison of Deferred Payment Deductions From Hypothetical Purchase Money Note, Pre-TRA 84 and Post-TRA 84

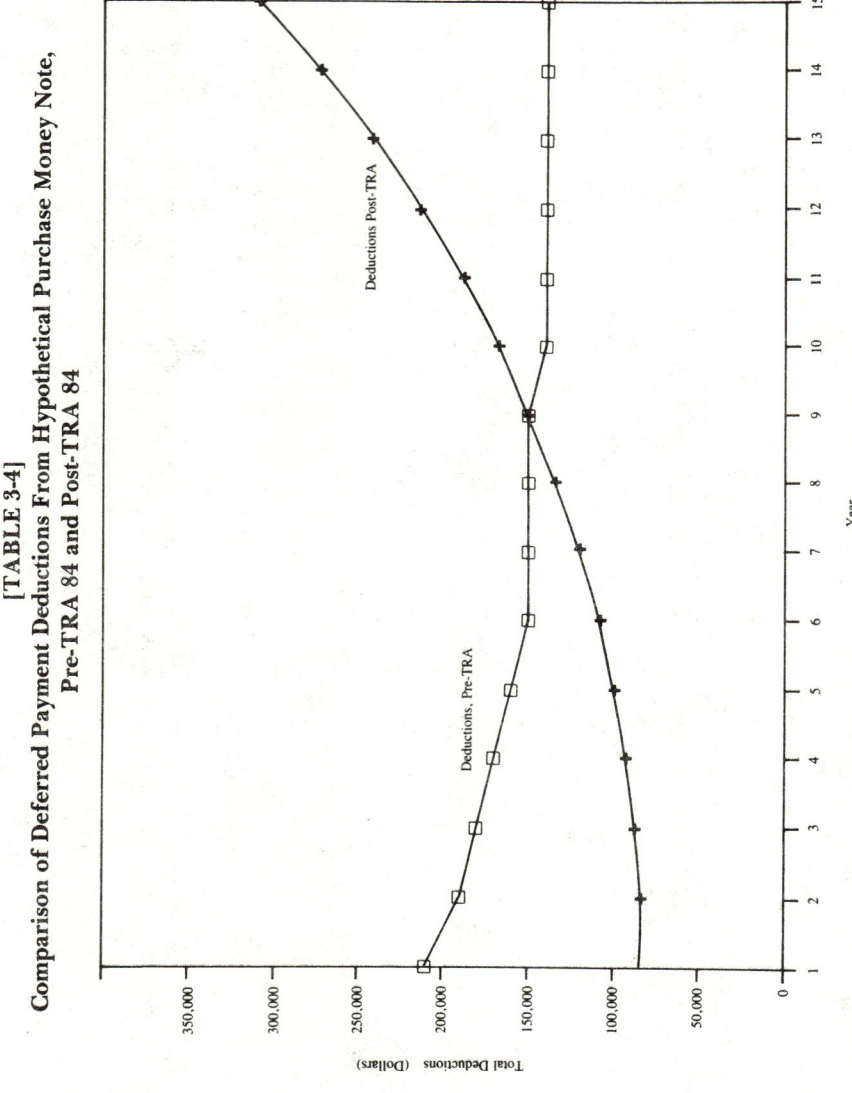

Original Issue Discount

What is the difference between the old and new structures?

- *Conversion of depreciation to interest.* Approximately $683,499 of depreciable basis that was available pre-TRA has been converted into accrued but unpaid interest, and, in consequence, it is deducted later.
- *Deferral of interest deductions.* The $1.35 million of accrued but unpaid interest that was due under the pre-TRA note was deducted in equal fifteenths ($90,000 per year). Under the new structure, seven years of pre-TRA deductions are deducted in the last four years. In fact, the last year's accrued but unpaid interest (post-TRA) equals that deducted in the first five pre-TRA years *combined.*
- *Resulting decline in benefits.* The net present value of these tax benefits has been cut 20 percent.

Seller Consequences of TRA

From the point of view of the buyer, tendering a deferred-payment note is about 20 percent less attractive than it was before the rules changed. But it is upon the seller/noteholder that the real havoc has been wreaked. This is shown in [Table 3-5].

Two immediate consequences are the following: (1) much of the seller's capital gain is converted to ordinary income; and (2) the seller pays taxes before the receipt of cash.

☐ *Seller's capital gain converted to ordinary income.* Under the old structure, the seller/noteholder paid $975,000 in taxes ([Table 3-5], column (5)) on his $2.35 million in total receipts—and he paid it all at the end. Under the new rules, the noteholder pays $1,111,700 ([Table 3-5], column (9)), an increase in taxes of approximately 11 percent.

☐ *Seller pays taxes before receipt of cash.* The change in the time value implications of the note is even worse; it has become a reverse tax shelter in which income is taxed before any cash is received. It is assumed that the noteholder is in the same tax situation as the buyer (50 percent ordinary income bracket, 10 percent after-tax discount rate). Consequently, the note that was worth 36 percent of par under the old rules is now worth a mere 14 percent of par under the new ones—a whopping 60 percent decline.

Other Consequences If Note Is Not Paid at Maturity

All of these consequences occur so long as the note is paid in full upon its maturity. There are at least three other possibilities to consider: (1) default at maturity; (2) prepayment before maturity; and (3) extension after maturity.

☐ *Default at maturity.* If at the termination date the property has not appreciated enough to pay off its debt and the noteholder forecloses and

[TABLE 3-5]

Buyer's Tax Consequences from Hypothetical Transaction with Purchase Money Note Before and After the Tax Reform Act of 1984

(Ignoring Extension of ACRS Lives)

| (1) | (2) | Pre-TRA Consequences ||| | Post-TRA Consequences |||| (11) |
| | | (3) | (4) | (5) | (6) | (7) | (8) | (9) | (10) | |
Year	Discount Factor	Ordinary Income	Capital Gain	Taxes Payable	Discounted After-Tax Value of Taxes Payable	Ordinary Income	Capital Gain	Taxes Payable	Discounted After-Tax Value of Taxes Payable	NPV of Cash Received
1	1.0000	0		0	0	$ 45,260		$ 22,630	$22,630	
2	1.1000	0		0	0	51,732		25,866	23,514	
3	1.2100	0		0	0	59,129		29,565	24,434	
4	1.3310	0		0	0	67,585		33,792	25,389	
5	1.4641	0		0	0	77,249		38,625	26,381	
6	1.6105	0		0	0	88,296		44,148	27,412	
7	1.7716	0		0	0	100,922		50,461	28,484	
8	1.9487	0		0	0	115,354		57,677	29,598	
9	2.1436	0		0	0	131,850		65,925	30,755	
10	2.3579	0		0	0	150,705		75,352	31,957	
11	2.5937	0		0	0	172,255		86,128	33,206	
12	2.8531	0		0	0	196,888		98,444	34,504	
13	3.1384	0		0	0	225,043		112,521	35,853	
14	3.4523	0		0	0	257,224		128,612	37,254	
15	3.7975	$1,350,000	$1,000,000	$975,000	$256,748	$294,007	$316,501	$ 241,954	63,714	$618,828
Total		$1,350,000	$1,000,000	$975,000	$256,748	$2,033,499	$316,501	$1,111,700	$475,084	$618,828

reclaims the property, the buyer has a forgiveness of interest that is taxable at ordinary income rates rather than a simple capital gain. The economic consequences to the buyer of failing to pay the note when it is due have become more severe. A buyer will, therefore, think twice before overpaying for a property, even with a nonrecourse note, and he will work harder to avoid foreclosure.

☐ *Prepayment before maturity.* As a year-by-year comparison of the total indebtedness shows (compare column (10) of [Table 3-2] with column (10) of [Table 3-3]), if the note is prepaid at any time before its maturity, the lower-face, higher interest rate note mandated under the new laws[5] has a lower balance in each year prior to year 15. Thus at sale the buyer would report additional deductions to "catch up" on the interest and principal "understated" by OID.

By taking two useful tools (simple interest and single-digit interest rates) out of businessmen's hands, the government has intruded upon the economic marketplace. This is nothing unusual — the government does it all the time. The legislative process seldom excises tumors neatly, but usually hacks away healthy flesh in the bargain.

☐ *Extension after original maturity.* Suppose that each note contained a provision that allowed the buyer to extend the term of the note until the restrictions are lifted. The terms of the simple interest note would continue to increase its principal value at the rate of a fixed $90,000 per year. If the property continued to appreciate at the same rate at which it had been appreciating, its future value would continue to be higher than the total indebtedness. In year 16, for instance, the outstanding balance of the debt increases only 3.83 percent.

That appreciation rate will not suffice for the higher-rate, compound interest note. In year 16, the post-TRA note will accrue $336,050 of interest — more than three and one-half times as much as the pre-TRA note. Assuming that the property was worth just enough to pay off its indebtedness in year 15, it would have to appreciate 14.3 percent in year 16 just to stay even. And it will continue to have to do this every year until the note is finally paid off.

Prepaying a deferred-interest note is now more attractive than it was under the old law. Similarly, failing to pay on the original target date is more expensive, whether the buyer defaults or is able to obtain an extension of the term of the note.

---

5. The law does not insist that the taxpayer use a rate of 110 percent of the federal rate, but if the taxpayer uses something else, the government can recalculate the note at *120 percent* of the federal rate. The net present value of these payments is actually about 2.5 percent worse for the borrower than that of the 110 percent rate. Thus the 110 percent rate is economically mandated.

MARKETPLACE CONSEQUENCES OF THE NEW OID RULES

The new rules are effective for transactions entered into on or after January 1, 1985.[6] This led, in the fourth quarter of 1984, to frenetic activity as the last deals of various investment types were offered and sold. Many sellers who had deferred selling to take advantage of anticipated high prices found instead that the last quarter of 1984 was a market constrained mainly by the throughput capacity of the investment bankers able to structure and market deferred-payment transactions. Many missed the boat entirely.

The marketplace consequences of the new OID rules are likely to be the following:

☐ The number of transactions using deferred-payment financing will drop substantially. Those transactions that continue to use deferred-payment financing will use much less of it.

☐ Most forms of real estate are now between zero and 25 percent less valuable than they were. (As shown below, the longer ACRS life is partly responsible for this value drop.) The more leverage applied to the purchase, the more new rules hurt. The average value drop is about 10 percent.[7]

☐ Resyndications, which were an excellent way for owners of existing subsidized housing to liquidate their positions, will now become a rarely used technique suitable only in exceptional circumstances. This is because in subsidized housing resyndications (and some net lease transactions) accrued but unpaid interest is an integral part of the buyer's investment decision. Therefore, in the future, either the seller will be a tax-exempt entity or there will have to develop a secondary market for the *purchase* of secondary notes by tax-exempt entities at prices close to par. Otherwise, the properties will simply not be sold.

☐ In 1984, prudent buyers were willing to pay appraised value for a property, provided that the secondary financing portion of the purchase price was funded with a 9 percent note. In 1985, such buyers will now insist on buying for substantial discounts from appraised value, to offset the above-par secondary financing they must now tender.

☐ It will be much harder to develop satisfactory workouts for troubled real estate properties that need cash infusions. Recognizing this, HUD lobbied for a subsidized housing exemption to the new rules, but it was unsuccessful in stopping Treasury's juggernaut.

---

6. The law provides exemptions for any transaction in which the total consideration is $250,000 or less. Although this lower limit protects such established financing as automobile loans or seller house financing, it is so low that it is causing sellers of large houses or modest farms considerable discomfort. There is now some political agitation to protect these areas by carving out additional exemptions to the new provisions.

7. Properties that were sold during 1982-1984 have not lost holding period value. They have already locked in the benefits of favorable financing. But an owner who sold Phase I of a property for price P will probably find, in 1985, that Phase II will sell for something less than P.

Original Issue Discount

□ Investors who purchased property in 1982-1984 using deferred-payment financing probably bought bargains and will find it much harder, in 1985 and beyond, to purchase an equivalent stream of tax shelter benefits. The following consequences emerge:

- Prices for high-grade tax shelters will rise. Deductibility ratios to investors will decline. The high-volume buyer's market that existed in 1984 will probably evolve into a smaller-volume seller's market by late 1985. The volume of very high write-off real estate tax shelters sold in 1985 will probably be lower than in 1984.
- There will be a dropoff in real estate activity in early 1985 as the stunned marketplace gropes to react to its new environment. Sellers who spurned yesterday's offer and failed to consummate a deal in 1984 will wish they could have it back. They will find they cannot.
- Isolated resales of interests in partnerships that purchased property in 1982 through 1984 using deferred-payment financing will probably command a premium in the marketplace, since their stream of deductions will now cost more in the marketplace.

OTHER PROVISIONS OF THE NEW TAX ACT

This column has concentrated on the OID provisions of the Tax Reform Act. Three other provisions will have a major effect on the real estate market:

- Extending ACRS life;
- Registration provisions; and
- Compliance provisions.

ACRS

Congress extended the ACRS life for non-low-income housing from fifteen to eighteen years. As shown in [Table 3-6], this reduces the holding period value of one dollar of depreciable basis from 31.2 cents to 28.9 cents—a 7.5 percent drop.

Combined with the drop in benefits from deferred-payment financing, the effect is reduction in value of up to 26 percent. [Tables 3-2 and 3-3] show that the decline in value attributable to the change in treatment of purchase money financing is 20.31 percent. The discounted tax benefits of the hypothetical transaction declined from $688,849 ([Table 3-2], col. (9)) to $548,939.

$$1 - (548,939/688,849) = 20.31\%$$

As shown in [Table 3-6], the decline in value attributable to the change in ACRS is up to 7.42 percent:

$$1 - (0.578361/0.624697) = 7.42\%$$

[TABLE 3-6]
Comparison of Net Present Value Of ACRS Depreciation Before and After
Tax Reform Act of 1984
(Residential Non-Low-Income Property)

10% Buyer Annual Discount Rate

Years	Old Law ACRS Factor[a]	New Law ACRS Factor[b]	Discount Factor	Net Present Value, Old Law Depreciation	Net Present Value New Law Depreciation
1	12%	10%	1.0000	0.120000	0.100000
2	10	9	1.1000	0.090909	0.081818
3	9	8	1.2100	0.074380	0.066116
4	8	7	1.3310	0.060105	0.052592
5	7	7	1.4641	0.047811	0.047811
6	6	6	1.6105	0.037255	0.037255
7	6	5	1.7716	0.033868	0.028224
8	6	5	1.9487	0.030789	0.025658
9	6	5	2.1436	0.027990	0.023325
10	5	5	2.3579	0.021205	0.021205
11	5	5	2.5937	0.019277	0.019277
12	5	4	2.8531	0.017525	0.014020
13	5	4	3.1384	0.015932	0.012745
14	5	4	3.4523	0.014483	0.011587
15	5	4	3.7975	0.013167	0.010533
16		4	4.1772	0.000000	0.009576
17		4	4.5950	0.000000	0.008705
18		4	5.0545	0.000000	0.007914
Total	100%	100%		0.624697	0.578361

[a] From tables promulgated by the Treasury Department.
[b] At the time we went to press, the Treasury had not issued new tables, but we're willing to bet they'll be pretty close to the above.

So the combined maximum decline is:

$$1 - ((1 - 0.2031) \times (1 - 0.0742)) = 26.22\%$$

Registration Provisions

Any person who organizes certain types of "tax shelter" offerings in which investments are initially sold on or after September 1, 1984 will have to register those offerings with the Secretary of the Treasury. Each registered shelter will be supplied with its own number (after all, this *is* 1984), which the promoter must furnish to investors and which each investor must include on his tax return.

The registration provisions are probably intended to do several things. They will make sure that, if a partnership is audited and adjustments made, *all* investors affected by the adjustments will have their taxes adjusted as well. Under the current system, it is easy for the IRS to lose track of the implementation of tax adjustments on individual investors who are scattered throughout the country.

Since the registration number will include information on the promoter, if the IRS audits a given partnership and finds a pattern of abusive behavior, it will be more likely to target the other partnerships sponsored by that promoter for audit as well. For this reason, investors would be wise to ask tax shelter sponsors about their IRS audit track record.[8]

Under the regulations now proposed for defining a "tax shelter," the IRS may find that it has cast its net too wide and caught too many fish. One would expect a technical clarification that focuses on investments in which net tax benefits to a 50 percent bracket taxpayer exceed capital contributions. Once the rules are clarified, some investment types will doubtless adjust their deductibility ratios to be just below the registration level.

Compliance Provisions

The penalty for underpayment of interest on "tax motivated transactions" is now 120 percent of the otherwise applicable rate. Fortunately, "tax motivated transactions" are defined as transactions in which there are valuation overstatements of 150 percent or more or transactions that use accounting methods specified in the regulations as capable of producing substantial distortion of income.

The regulations also focus on appraisers who aid or assist in the preparation of an appraisal, knowing that the appraisal will result in an understatement of tax liability of another person. Such appraisers may be disciplined

---

8. A properly constructed audit track record should divide audits into three elements: no change, adjusted, and pending. For the latter two classifications, the proposed reduction should be quantified, indicating the percentage of total losses challenged and, if settled, the percentage finally lost.

by the Treasury (presumably fined) and their appraisals may be disregarded in IRS audits or administrative proceedings.

CONCLUSION

For real estate investments, the new OID rules are by far the most significant change in the tax act, more significant even than the extension of ACRS from fifteen to eighteen years. Accrued but unpaid interest is, if not extinct, certainly an endangered species.[9] Economics in real estate are more important than ever.

NOTE

As Smith's note 9 indicates, the real estate industry fought back from the 1984 setbacks like a wounded animal, gaining later in 1984 some temporary relief, and, finally in 1985, some modest improvements. Below is the Conference Committee summary of the Imputed Interest Rules as of mid-1985, followed by our summary of the amendments that the conferees agreed to.

Conference Report of the Simplification of Imputed Interest Rules

(H.R. Rep. No. 99-250, 99th Cong., 1st Sess. (1985)

I. SIMPLIFICATION OF GENERAL IMPUTED INTEREST RULES

A. THE IMPUTED INTEREST RULES

Present Law

The Imputed Interest Rate

Overview

Under the imputed interest rules, whether there is adequate stated interest in a debt instrument issued for nonpublicly-traded property is determined by reference to an appropriate "test rate." Where adequate interest is not stated, the imputed interest rules recharacterize a portion of the principal amount of the debt instrument for income tax purposes using a somewhat higher "imputation rate." The amounts of principal and inter-

---

9. After the new OID rules were enacted into law, but even before they took effect, Congress was inundated with mail lambasting the new rules as haphazard and unworkable. Accordingly, before it adjourned for the fall campaign, Congress passed a set of exemptions or clarifications that defer OID's implementation until June 30, 1985. When Congress reconvenes, the whole issue will be reexamined . . . and probably backpedaled still further.

est as recharacterized will generally determine the seller's "amount realized," the buyer's basis in the property, and the amount of interest deductions and interest income for the buyer and the seller, respectively. The test rate for a debt instrument subject to the imputed interest rules is the rate in effect on the first day there is a binding contract for the sale or exchange of the property. All test and imputation rates are applied using semiannual compounding.

"Test Rates" and "Imputation Rates"

General Rule. — For sales or exchanges after December 31, 1984, of new property eligible for the investment credit, and for all sales or exchanges after June 30, 1985, the test rate is 110 percent of the "applicable Federal rate," and the imputation rate is 120 percent of the "applicable Federal rate."

Special rule for certain transactions before July 1, 1985. — For sales or exchanges after December 31, 1984, and before July 1, 1985, of property other than new property eligible for the investment credit, the test rate for "borrowed amounts" not exceeding $2 million is 9 percent. The test rate for borrowed amounts exceeding $2 million is a "blend" of 9 percent on the first $2 million and 110 percent of the applicable Federal rate (the "AFR") on the excess. In applying the $2 million limitation, all sales or exchanges that are part of the same transaction (or a series of related transactions) are treated as one transaction, and all debt instruments arising from the same transaction (or a series of related transactions) are treated as one debt instrument. The imputation rate for transactions during this same period is 10 percent for borrowed amounts up to $2 million and a blend of 10 percent and 120 percent of the AFR for borrowed amounts exceeding $2 million.

Other lower test and imputation rates. — The test rate for certain sales of homes and farm property after June 30, 1985, may not exceed 9 percent. This exception generally is limited to $250,000 for sales of homes and $1 million for sales of farms.

Applicable Federal rate. — The applicable Federal rate ("AFR") for a debt instrument is the lower of two published rates, one specified by the Tax Reform Act of 1984 (the "1984 Act") and one specified in temporary Treasury regulations. The statutory rate is based on the weighted average of yields over a period of six months for marketable obligations of the United States Government with a comparable maturity. Such rates are redetermined at six-month intervals for three categories of debt instruments: short-term maturity (three years or less), mid-term maturity (more than three years but not in excess of nine years), and long-term maturity (more than nine years).[1]

---

1. Appropriate adjustments to the rates are to be made for application to debt instruments, the interest on which is wholly or partly exempt from tax (sec. 1288).

The rates determined under the temporary Treasury regulations are intended to reflect more accurately the current marketplace.[2] These rates are computed monthly using the same methodology described above, except that the rates reflect the average yields for one-month periods. In any month, the lower of the six-month rate or the monthly rate is the AFR. However, in cases where the monthly rate for either of the two preceding months is lower than the AFR for a particular month, the test rate for that month is the lower of the two such rates.

Exceptions. — The imputed interest rules do not apply to the obligor on a debt instrument incurred in the acquisition of personal use property, to the sale of certain patents, to certain annuities, and to transactions involving a sale of property with a sales price of not more than $3,000.

Method of Accounting

Interest income and expense on debt instruments that are issued for property and that do not require the current payment of interest generally must be accounted for on the accrual method of accounting unless one of the following exceptions apply.

The accrual accounting requirement does not apply to (1) debt instruments issued for nonpublicly-traded property in transactions that are excepted from the imputed interest rules, (2) debt created in the sale of certain small businesses and farms, (3) debt created in the sale of a principal residence, and (4) debt created where the total payments are less than $250,000.

Assumptions

The assumption of the following debt obligations in connection with the sale or exchange of property, or the taking of property subject to such debt obligations, does not result in the application of the imputed interest rules, provided that the terms and conditions of the obligation are not modified in connection with the sale: (1) loans that were made before October 15, 1984, and assumed after December 31, 1984, in connection with the sale of property the purchase price of which does not exceed $100 million and (2) all loans assumed in connection with the sale of a residence, certain farms, and certain trades or businesses.

---

2. The mechanism provided by the temporary regulations is intended to respond to a problem that may exist where interest rates decline after the period in which the Federal rates were determined.

EDITORS' SUMMARY OF CONFERENCE AGREEMENT

1. The imputed interest shall be the same as the test rate (i.e., there is no higher "penalty rate" where inadequate interest is stated).
2. Where the amount of seller financing does not exceed $2.8 million, the imputed interest rate generally may not exceed 9 percent.
3. Where the amount of seller financing is greater than $2.8 million, the imputed rate generally shall be 100 percent of the AFR.
4. An imputed interest rate of 110 percent of the AFR, however, applies to sale-leaseback transactions.
5. Indexing of the $2.8 million threshold for the 9 percent rate begins after 1989.
6. The accrual accounting requirement will not be applied in the following situations:

   a. the *stated* principal amount of the debt instrument does not exceed $2.0 million;
   b. the debt instrument must arise from the sale of property by a cash-basis taxpayer who is not a dealer in the type of property sold;
   c. the lender and the borrower must jointly elect to account for the interest item on the cash receipts and disbursements method of accounting;
   d. indexing of the $2.0 million threshold for these "cash method debt instruments" begins after 1989.

7. If an existing debt instrument is assumed in connection with the sale or exchange of property (or if the property is acquired subject to an existing debt instrument), the imputed interest rules will not apply to such existing debt instrument unless either the terms of the existing debt instrument are modified in connection with the transaction or the nature of the transaction is changed.

In order to "help pay" for the estimated revenue loss occasioned by these liberalizing changes, the conferees also agreed to extend the minimum recovery period for domestic real property qualifying as recovery property from 18 to 19 years.

CHAPTER FOUR

The Contract of Sale: Duties and Remedies

A. THE BUYER FAILS TO CLOSE: PLANNING FOR DEFAULT OR CLEANING UP THE MESS

1. Is There an Enforceable Contract?

a. Financing and Other Conditions

Kovarik v. Vesely

3 Wis. 2d 573, 89 N.W.2d 279 (1958)

Action by the plaintiffs Emil H. Kovarik, Jr., and Lorraine Mary Kovarik, his wife, to recover from the defendants George Vesely, Sr., Viola Vesely, his wife, and Henry Gardner a $4,000 down payment made by the plaintiffs to the defendants pursuant to contract on the purchase of land. The defendants Vesely counter-claimed for specific performance of the contract.

The contract was in writing dated July 6, 1956, and was drafted in the form of an offer to purchase by the Kovariks with an acceptance of such offer, such offer and acceptance being incorporated in one document. The purchase price was stated to be $11,000, of which $4,000 was paid by the Kovariks to Gardner, real estate broker for the Veselys. The contract provided that the $7,000 mortgage was payable in the form of a "$7,000 purchase money mortgage from the Fort Atkinson Savings & Loan Ass'n." The following special condition appeared in the body of the offer to purchase: "This offer is contingent upon buyer's ability to arrange above described financing."

The Kovariks shortly after entering into the contract made a written application to the Fort Atkinson Savings & Loan Association for the $7,000 mortgage loan on the premises being purchased. Kovarik testified that the terms and conditions of the loan were not inserted in this application at the time it was signed by him. Therefore, it may be assumed that they were inserted by the association after such signing of the application and before the same was acted upon. There is no claim made on this appeal that the insertion of such terms was not authorized by the Kovariks.

On August 10, 1956, the Kovariks learned that the association had rejected their loan application, a fact then already known to the defendants. On the same day Kovarik demanded return of the $4,000 down payment from Gardner. Gardner informed Kovarik that the latter would have to see Vesely about the matter because Gardner had no authority to pay back the $4,000. Kovarik then also on that day asked Vesely for the return of the money. Vesely refused such demand and suggested that Kovarik employ a lawyer.

The Kovariks then employed Attorney Williamson as their counsel who on August 17, 1956, conferred with a member of the law firm retained by the Veselys. The latter tendered the abstract of title to Mr. Williamson and advised him that the Veselys were willing to take back a first mortgage on the same terms and conditions as the Fort Atkinson Savings & Loan Association. Attorney Williamson refused such tender of the abstract, and in behalf of his clients also rejected the proposal with respect to the Veselys accepting the $7,000 first mortgage as payment of the balance of the purchase price.

Under date of September 9, 1956, the Kovariks instituted action to recover the down payment and the Veselys counter-claimed for specific performance. The action was tried to the court without a jury and the trial judge under date of June 14, 1957, filed a memorandum opinion reciting the facts and determining the legal issues in favor of the defendants. . . .

. . . [F]ormal findings of fact and conclusions of law were entered in conformity with the trial judge's memorandum opinion. Finding of Fact No. 5 reads as follows:

"That the buyers applied for a loan from the Fort Atkinson Savings & Loan Association in the amount of Seven Thousand Dollars, which loan would run for fifteen years and bear interest at the rate of five percent per annum, payable monthly, and it further provided for monthly payments of Eight Dollars per thousand or Fifty-six Dollars per month to apply first upon the interest and the balance upon the principal plus one-twelfth of the taxes based upon the preceding year for the term of fifteen years, and these terms of financing were satisfactory to the buyers."

Judgment was entered August 21, 1957, dismissing the plaintiff's complaint, and decreeing specific performance of the contract as prayed for in the counterclaim. The judgment requires the Kovariks to execute a $7,000 note and mortgage to the Veselys upon the purchased premises, the terms of such note and mortgage being those set forth in Finding of Fact No. 5. From such judgment the plaintiffs have appealed.

CURRIE, Justice. . . . The three issues confronting the court on this appeal are:

(1) Is the contract of purchase and sale, which was entered into be-

The Buyer Fails to Close

tween the plaintiff buyers and the defendant sellers, void because of failure to comply with the statute of frauds (sec. 240.08, Stats.)?

(2) How are the words of the contract, "This offer is contingent upon buyer's ability to arrange above described financing," to be construed?

(3) Was the offer of the defendant sellers to accept a $7,000 mortgage upon the same terms as those set forth in the prior loan application to the Fort Atkinson Savings & Loan Association timely made?

It is the contention of counsel for the buyers that the contract fails to comply with the statute of frauds because the terms of the $7,000 mortgage are not set forth therein. On the other hand, it is the position of the attorneys for the sellers that such mortgage terms were set forth in the written loan application which the buyers signed and filed with the Fort Atkinson Savings & Loan Association, and that such application, although a separate writing, constitutes part of the "memorandum" of purchase and sale.

The general rule is that the memorandum required by the statute of frauds may consist of several writings. [Citations omitted.] It is also not essential to the validity of such memorandum that a particular writing shall have been made with the intention that it constitute a memorandum of the contract. Restatement, 1 Contracts, p. 286, sec. 209.

The fact that the buyers mortgage loan application came into existence subsequent to the date on which the contract was signed by the parties is also immaterial. . . . Annotation 85 A.L.R. 1184, 1193.

In Kelly v. Sullivan, [252 Wis. 52, 30 N.W.2d 209], this court held that, when separate writings are necessary to spell out a memorandum of sale and they do not refer on their face to the same transaction, they cannot be construed together to constitute the memorandum required by the statute unless physically annexed to each other. In the *Kelly* case the separate writing particularly relied upon was unsigned by the defendant seller, who was the party sought to be charged. The New York court of appeals in the recent case of Crabtree v. Elizabeth Arden Sales Corp., [305 N.Y. 48, 110 N.E.2d 551], has held that the separate writings, even though one or more are unsigned, are sufficient to constitute the required memorandum, provided that when read together they appear to refer to the same transaction, or the connection between them and the transaction can be established by parol testimony. In so holding, the New York court in effect overruled a number of earlier New York decisions to the contrary. It is unnecessary for us to go that far in the instant case in order to hold that the loan application constitutes part of the memorandum of sale. We do not consider that Kelly v. Sullivan, supra, rules the instant case, because here the loan application is a separate writing subscribed by the Kovariks who are the parties against whom it is sought to enforce the contract.

We experience no difficulty in determining that the loan application to the Fort Atkinson Savings & Loan Association is a separate writing which is to be construed together with the original contract of the parties, and that together they constitute a sufficient memorandum to comply with sec. 240.08, Stats.[1] Kenner v. Edwards Realty & F. Co., 1931, 204 Wis. 575, 581, 236 N.W. 597.

Counsel for the buyers also contend that the contract falls within the statute of frauds because the offer made in behalf of the sellers, to accept a $7,000 first mortgage having the same terms as stated in the loan application to the Fort Atkinson Savings & Loan Association, was made verbally and not in writing. The evidence of such offer is material on the issue of whether the event had occurred which removed the stated contingency from the plaintiff's offer to purchase. Proof of the occurrence of such event is not required to be part of the statutory memorandum. For example, let us suppose that, instead of the Fort Atkinson Savings & Loan Association having rejected the buyers' loan application, its chief executive officer had verbally informed both the buyers and the sellers that such application had been approved by the association and the loan granted, and the buyers had then refused to conclude the purchase of the premises. It is clear that in such a situation the buyers would not be permitted to assert that the contract was void under the statute of frauds because the association had verbally granted their loan application instead of doing so in writing.

We now turn to the issue of the proper construction of the contingency clause of the contract. It is not seriously argued but that as drafted the terms of the $7,000 mortgage financing were to be left to the discretion of the buyers. However, when they signed the application to the Fort Atkinson Savings & Loan Association, and such application set forth the terms of the loan applied for, they had exercised such discretion and were bound thereby. Therefore, the question boils down to whether the stated contingency of the contract was removed by the sellers offering to accept a $7,000 mortgage on the same terms. The exact contract wording is, "This offer is contingent upon buyer's ability to arrange *above described financing.*" Such issue is to be resolved by determining whether the words *"above described financing"* refer to the terms of the mortgage loan sought from the Fort Atkinson Savings & Loan Assocation, or do they also necessarily import that the loan itself must be procured from the named association.

This problem of interpretation is not unlike that facing a court when it endeavors to solve the problem of whether time is of the essence of a contract for the sale of real estate. In such a situation evidence of surrounding circumstances as to the acts of the parties may be material. . . . In the instant case, Kovarik testified that in negotiating the contract it was the seller Vesely who suggested the Fort Atkinson Savings & Loan Association as the source of financing the $7,000 purchase money mortgage. Kovarik was asked the following question and gave the following answer thereto:

---

1. Wis. Stat. §240.08 (1967), cited by the court, voids only contracts of sale of which there is no memorandum signed *by the seller.* — EDS.

"Q. It didn't make any difference to you from whom the loan was secured did it? A. As long as it was from a reliable loan company or a bank. I had tried to borrow money from the local bank and they turned me down."

Kovarik's testimony stated no reason of any kind with respect to why the Kovariks preferred having the mortgage loan come from the association rather than from the Veselys. Neither was there any claim advanced in such testimony that at the time of making the contract it was of material consequence to the Kovariks that the loan be obtained from the association rather than some other source. The trial court could reasonably infer from the absence of any such testimony, and from the above related evidence, that the words of the contingency clause of the contract, *"above described financing"* were intended by the parties to have reference to the ability of the buyers to finance the balance of the purchase price by means of a mortgage loan of $7,000 on terms of their own choice, and that the source of such financing was not a material part of the condition.

The pertinent findings of fact by the trial court are Nos. 6 and 7, reading as follows:

"6. That the buyers did not intend by the words, 'above described financing,' to mean that such loan must be secured from the Fort Atkinson Savings & Loan Association.

"7. That the buyers were interested in financing a Seven Thousand Dollar mortgage and not in any particular loaning agency."

Such findings are not against the great weight and clear preponderance of the evidence. Therefore, we approve the interpretation of the contract made by the trial court, that the buyers' offer to purchase was not contingent upon the $7,000 mortgage being obtained from the Fort Atkinson Savings & Loan Association.

The last point to be considered is whether the sellers' offer of August 17, 1956, to take back the $7,000 purchase money mortgage upon the same terms as contained in the prior loan application to the association was timely made. Counsel for the buyers contend that it was not because the buyers a week before had attempted to rescind the contract, and had then demanded back their down payment, as a result of learning of the rejection by the association of the buyers' loan application. This argument ignores the fact that the closing date specified in the contract was "on or before September 1, 1956." The sellers' offer to accept the mortgage was well in advance of September 1, 1956, and the buyers had no right to rescind the contract prior to the closing date because of inability to secure the $7,000 mortgage loan. Furthermore, the contingency clause was self-executing and not in the nature of one granting an option to cancel.

There are other issues raised in the briefs which have received careful consideration, but we deem it unnecessary to discuss them in this opinion.

Judgment affirmed.

FAIRCHILD, Justice (dissenting). I interpret the contract as one which is conditional upon the willingness of a specified third party to make a loan to the buyers upon the security of the property being purchased. The third party having been unwilling to make the loan and there being no suggestion of lack of good faith on the part of the buyers in making the application and seeking the loan, the buyers have no further obligation under the contract and their down payment should be returned.

I do not view the contract as ambiguous and do consider the testimony of one of the buyers as to what he intended as immaterial. Many offers to purchase are made which contain similar contingencies. Whatever may be the subjective intention of a buyer in any particular case, one can readily think of reasons why a buyer may make an offer contingent upon financing by a specific lending institution or through a particular type of loan. Examples of such reasons are: That the buyer will feel more confident of his own judgment of the price he is to pay if a lending institution is willing to make a loan; That the buyer would rather have the matter, in the event of default, in the hands of an established lending institution than in the hands of an individual who might be less able, if not less willing, to adjust matters reasonably. . . .

Gerruth Realty Co. v. Pire
17 Wis. 2d 89, 115 N.W.2d 557 (1962)

This is a suit to recover on a $5000 [down payment note] promissory note given to the plaintiff by the defendants as a down payment on the purchase of real estate under an offer of purchase.

The defendants were interested in purchasing two commercial properties in Beloit, Wisconsin, one owned by Mayer Putterman and the other owned by the plaintiff Gerruth Realty Co. On May 15, 1960, the defendants Walter E. Pire and Emily Pire, his wife, signed an instrument designated "Deposit Receipt and Purchase Agreement" on a printed form of the Beloit Real Estate Board which was accepted by the plaintiff. This form which is substantially an offer to purchase, was filled out by the real estate broker for the plaintiff, and provided for the usual details. The purchase price for the plaintiff's property was $30,000; $5,000 of which was the down payment, evidenced by a note payable at the time of closing. The balance of the purchase price was to be paid in cash. The offer to purchase contained a typewritten paragraph to the effect the offer was conditioned upon the defendants' buying the Putterman property for $40,000 and the offer was void unless the closing of the purchase of the two properties took place simultaneously. During the negotiations, there was some talk of financing. The defendants were under the impression they would have no difficulty financing the purchase but insisted upon a clause for their protection. The real estate broker inserted the following clause in the offer: "This offer to purchase is further contingent upon the purchaser obtaining the proper amount of financing."

The Buyer Fails to Close

On the trial, it was proven the defendant Walter E. Pire attempted to borrow $75,000 from the Second National Bank in Beloit with whom he did business and which had mortgages on his house and business. No formal application was made, but in discussing the matter the defendant was told that a borrowing limit to one person was $100,000 which would be exceeded because of his other loans. In order to come within this limit, it was suggested the defendant might incorporate his business. There was testimony the usual and customary commercial loans by banks in Beloit on commercial property for holders of good credit could not exceed 66⅔ percent of the value of the property. The defendant notified the plaintiff he could not go through with the contract because of his inability to obtain the proper amount of financing. The plaintiff and the Puttermans offered to finance the purchase of the properties to the extent of $45,000, which was refused by the defendants.

The case was tried to the court without a jury. The court found the "subject to financing" clause was a condition precedent to the performance of the contract on the part of the defendants, who in good faith had attempted to obtain the financing which they would require to consummate the purchase but were unable to do so. The court concluded the defendants were entitled to a dismissal of the complaint. From the judgment dismissing the complaint, the plaintiff appeals.

HALLOWS, Justice. Contracts of purchase or offers to purchase containing "subject to financing" clauses are fairly common and the clauses have been construed frequently as constituting a condition precedent to the buyer's performance. The initial question in reference to such a contract is whether it is definite enough to be sustained or if indefinite, whether it may be given a meaning which renders the contract certain. Courts are not inclined to strike down such a contract for uncertainty if the deficiency can be supplied consistent with reasonableness in the interest of preserving the contract which parties thought they made. A contract is certain which may be made certain from the surrounding circumstances. . . .

. . . On this theory, the plaintiff argues the clause "contingent upon the purchaser obtaining the proper amount of financing" must be construed in the light of current practices in the community with respect to financing of similar transactions. The defendants contend the clause in the light of the circumstances gave the option to the defendants to determine what the proper amount of financing was in relation to his particular needs. It was this latter view which the trial court adopted. However, any interpretation, which allows one party to a contract to determine without limitation and in a subjective manner the meaning of an ambiguous term, comes dangerously close to an illusory or aleatory contract [see 3A Corbin on Contracts, ch. 38, at 399 (1963)], if it does not in fact reach it.

The evidence does not disclose what was said concerning the amount and details of the financing of the purchase excepting the defendants thought they would have no difficulty in arranging financing. An inference might be drawn from the fact the down payment was not cash but in the form of a promissory note for $5,000 payable on the closing and the offer was also conditioned upon the purchase and simultaneous closing of the Putterman property, that the defendant would need to borrow a large part, if not the total amount, of the purchase price of both properties. The transcript of the evidence is barren of any communicated details of the amount or terms of the financing which the defendants had in mind, if they had any, or tentative ones, or what was understood by the real estate broker representing the plaintiff. Apparently both parties had something in mind when this clause was inserted in the offer to purchase for the benefit of the defendants. The real estate broker presumably familiar with the difficulties, details and terms of financing, might have asked the defendants for more details, but was apparently content with putting something in writing and having it signed by the purchasers.

The problem presented is whether there is sufficient evidence upon which this court can ascertain the intention of the parties, i.e., whether there was a meeting of the minds, even objectively, concerning the meaning of this clause. If it is impossible to fairly ascertain such intention, the contract must fail for indefiniteness. The facts of this case are distinguishable from Kovarik v. Vesely (1958), 3 Wis. 2d 573, 89 N.W.2d 279, 280 in that an essential term (the amount of financing) is not designated. In *Kovarik*, the clause "contingent upon buyer's ability to arrange 'above described financing,'" referring to his $7,000 purchase money mortgage from the Fort Atkinson Savings and Loan Association was held to give the purchaser the option to select the terms of financing, which he exhausted upon making an application to the Fort Atkinson Savings and Loan Association. The court construed, in view of the evidence, that the particular lending institution was not an essential term of the clause and it made no difference from whom the buyer obtained his loan.

In the two cases which we were able to find in which the amount of the financing was not stated in the contract, the court did not hold the contract void. In Reese v. Walker (Ohio Mun., 1958), 151 N.E.2d 605, the facts are somewhat analogous. There, the contract for the purchase of real estate contained the clause "contingent upon securing necessary financing." The court held the buyers had the right to determine the terms of financing they needed and the seller was in no position to complain if the buyers honestly determined what kind of a loan they needed. A similar view was taken in Zigman v. McMackin (1958), 6 A.D.2d 907, 177 N.Y.S.2d 723, wherein the contract obligated the purchaser to apply for a purchase money mortgage loan of not more than $10,000 at 5% due in 15 years or longer. In both these cases, the court found a meaning from the circumstances surrounding the execution of the contract and from the purposes the parties sought to accomplish, namely, a loan in such amount or on such terms as the buyer in good faith considered necessary for his purposes.

We do not reach the question of good faith on the part of the defendants in the instant case in determining the amount of the financing because we believe the contract can not be made certain by the surrounding circumstances. In our view, the good faith issue arises only after the determination of the meaning of the ambiguous phrase. True, if we could interpret the contract from the surrounding circumstances that it was intended to give the defendant buyers the sole right to determine the amount of financing, then they would be required to determine in good faith the amount of the loan which they honestly needed. Since financing is such an important element in the purchase of real estate, it is to be wondered why so little attention is paid to this important element in the contract or offer of purchase by those dealing in the sale of real estate.

We cannot find in the evidence any indication upon which even a reasonable inference can be drawn that the parties contracted knowingly and in light of any current practices in the community of Beloit with respect to financing of similar transactions. The evidence sets forth what the current practices were but there is no evidence both parties had them in mind at the time the offer to purchase was executed. Likewise, we cannot agree this clause gave the defendants the exclusive or absolute option or privilege to determine the proper amount of financing, without holding the contract illusory. The contract, and the evidence also, are silent as to all the other terms and conditions of the loan, many of which terms and conditions are interrelated and vary with the security and the borrower. The evidence shows the defendant Walter E. Pire attempted to or at least desired to borrow from his bank $5,000 more than the combined purchase price of the two properties, which the court inferred the defendant intended to use for remodeling. Such a loan was beyond the limit of current practices in the community. The defendant met other difficulties in attempting to finance the purchase which he had not anticipated, namely, the bank's policy of not loaning in excess of $100,000, to a customer. If this evidence is taken as indicating what the defendants had in mind at the time they signed the offer of purchase, it was not communicated to the agent of the plaintiff.

It seems to us, if we were to adopt either the interpretation contended for by the plaintiff or that urged by the defendants, we would be making, in fact, a contract for the parties by supplying an essential term thereof rather than interpreting what they mutually meant by an ambiguous term. We find the task of interpreting this contract, on the evidence presented, impossible and must hold the contract void for indefiniteness.

Judgment affirmed.

NOTES

1. *Foreplay.* There is considerable variation, by geography and transaction type, among the sorts of writings which appear sequentially as a real

estate transaction moves toward consummation. Normal papering of a simple deal might involve: (1) the seller's listing agreement, (2) a brief "offer to purchase" or "binder" signed only by the buyer and accompanied by his deposit (or perhaps an even briefer "deposit receipt" signed only by the broker), and (3) a formal contract signed by both buyer and seller. Or perhaps after the listing agreement, the broker will obtain buyer's signature to a detailed contract, which will then be submitted to seller for signing, and then the parties will meet to prepare escrow instructions.

Is buyer bound by a "binder"? More generally, at which point in such sequences are seller and buyer contractually obligated one to another? The many cases on this topic (Friedman, Contracts and Conveyances of Real Property §1.3 (4th ed. 1984)), are handled by the courts in terms familiar from first year contracts courses: preliminary negotiations, indefiniteness, significance of "Formal contract to follow," etc. It has not seemed worthwhile to us to repeat material from a contracts course in lengthy and systematic application to all the papers and processes in a real estate transaction. But since you now know something about financing, the principal cases and the notes which follow will enable you to focus on the contracting process with that knowledge via the following question: How much must buyer and seller understand and say about their deal's financing in order to reach an enforceable bargain? Later on in the book (pages 553-588) we'll recur to deal with formation and formulation questions in the context of boundary descriptions.

2. *Blank clauses.* In Grayson v. LaBlanche, 107 N.H. 504, 225 A.2d 922 (1967), the parties signed a contract to purchase real estate for $28,000. The contract contained a clause, with the blank not filled, reading: "This agreement is contingent on the buyer obtaining a conventional mortgage of _____ at his terms or obtaining an FHA mortgage." Defendant buyer tried two banks, the second at the urging of seller, but could not get a mortgage. The court excused the buyer and ordered a refund of his deposit stating: "[W]hile pristine precision in financing provisions may be recommended to attorneys and real estate brokers, this quality is frequently missing in the litigated cases. Absolute and exact certainty in contracts for the sale of realty is not required, but reasonable certainty is a requisite. . . . While the court cannot make a contract for the parties, this does not prevent it from ascertaining from the evidence whether the parties made a binding contract and what it was in spite of some ambiguity arising from a term that is missing or left blank. . . . [D]efendant's obligation to purchase was dependent on his ability to obtain a conventional mortgage in a reasonable amount."

3. *Vagueness in payment provisions.* S has a property subject to a $10,000 mortgage. He and B enter a contract which, inter alia, describes B's payment obligation as "$15,000 subject to the existing mortgage." This clearly means that B must pay S $5000 and acquire the property

subject to the mortgage. Or else it clearly means that B must pay S $15,000 and acquire the property subject to the mortgage. Or maybe the language is too uncertain for a contract to have been formed. Or perhaps the language is ambiguous and its meaning can be determined by resort to parol. But in the latter case, the contract may fall because of the Statute of Frauds. See Friedman, Contracts and Conveyances of Real Property §1.3, at 104-105 (4th ed. 1984).

See also Moog v. Palmour, 15 Ga. App. 602, 155 S.E. 2d 692 (1967), in which Judge Frankum gave the following opinion: "Where a contract for the sale of a described tract of realty provides that the fixed and definite purchase price of $704,500 as set forth therein, is to be paid as follows: Purchaser to buy subject to an existing first mortgage (which is fully described); that 'This loan balance after January 1966 payment estimated at $555,000; seller to accept purchaser's equity in property known as 2998 Grandview Ave., N.E. in the amount of $23,500; purchaser to pay cash in the amount of $22,000; seller to accept purchase money note and security deed on above property in the amount of $104,000,' with interest rate, term and monthly payments on such note fully described, such contract was too vague, indefinite and uncertain to be enforced. No closing date of the sale contemplated by the contract was definitely provided for therein, and it will, therefore, be presumed that the parties contemplated that the contract would be consummated within a reasonable time after the offer to buy made by the purchaser was accepted by the seller. However, under the clear and unmistakable terms of the contract, should the closing date in fact turn out to be some date other than January, 1966, the estimated balance of the loan to be assumed by the buyer would necessarily vary from the figure of $555,000, set forth in the contract. But the contract does not state whether the fixed and definite figure of $22,000 cash to be paid by the buyer or the fixed and definite figure of the $104,000 purchase money note to be given by the buyer shall be varied to arrive at the fixed and definite figure of $704,500 as the total purchase price. For example, if, upon closing the sale, it should be found by the parties that the loan balance, instead of being $555,000, is in fact only $545,000, the question arises: Is the buyer to pay $32,000 in cash and give a note for $104,000, or would the seller be required by the terms of the contract to accept only $22,000 in cash and accept a note for $114,000, so as to make the fixed and definite purchase price of $704,500? The contract furnishes no key by which a court, in construing its terms, can say that either one or the other of these alternatives is required. It is, therefore, too vague and indefinite to be enforceable. . . ."

4. *Financing conditions: practices and attitudes.* Raushenbush, Problems and Practices with Financing Conditions in Real Estate Contracts, 1963 Wis. L. Rev. 566, contains an excellent treatment of the Wisconsin cases. It follows an earlier excellent article by Aiken, "Subject to Financing" Clauses in Interim Contracts for Sale of Realty, reprinted in part at

page 513 infra. In addition, the Raushenbush article describes practices prevalent in Wisconsin transactions, and it notes that "subject to" clauses present some difficulties in brokerage commission cases (at 596-603). The article also contains the results of a 1960 survey involving a dozen Wisconsin attorneys, 17 out of 100 Madison realtors, and 61 out of 500 Milwaukee realtors (the author believes that his sample reached a more sophisticated group of brokers than the usual).

In the Raushenbush survey most (but not all) respondents described themselves as rarely using loose language like "subject to financing," and as generally specifying size of loan, interest rate, duration, payments, and the results of a failure to obtain the specified financing. One question was, "Do you think general language like 'subject to financing' requires the buyer to use 'reasonable effort' to get a reasonable loan?" Eight of nine responding lawyers and two thirds of the brokers said yes. On the question, "Can you say what is a reasonable loan?" about half of the respondents said yes, half said no.

Indoe v. Dwyer
176 N.J. Super. 594, 424 A.2d 456 (Law Div. 1980)

GAYNOR, J.S.C. These cross-motions for summary judgment involve primarily the scope and effect of an attorney approval clause in a contract for the purchase of real estate. A secondary question relates to the binding effect upon a husband of such a contract executed solely by the wife where the only evidence of the husband's interest was a provision in the contract providing that the deed was to be taken in both names. The primary issue presented is one of first impression and, in our opinion, must be resolved by an interpretation which permits an unlimited application of the attorney approval provision in the contract.

The facts of the case are not in dispute. In August 1976 plaintiffs listed their home in Bernardsville for sale at a price of $235,000. The property was not sold and it was listed again in 1977 at the same price. In August 1977 defendant Christine Dwyer was shown the house by a realtor in the absence of plaintiffs. She returned the following weekend with her husband, defendant John Dwyer, for a further inspection. No offer was made because defendants determined they were not interested in purchasing the property.

The following February Mrs. Dwyer inquired of the realtor as to whether plaintiffs' home was still available for purchase. Being informed that it was, but that an offer was then being considered, Mrs. Dwyer contacted her husband, who was on a business trip, and obtained his approval to submit a bid for the property. Accordingly, an offer of $225,000 was submitted orally by Mrs. Dwyer to the realtor. Later that day a realtor's printed form of contract for the sale and purchase of real

The Buyer Fails to Close

estate was prepared by the realtor and presented to Mrs. Dwyer for signature. Believing the document to be merely a "bid" and that if acceptable to plaintiffs a purchase contract would thereafter be prepared, with the assistance of counsel and which would include terms acceptable to her husband and their attorney, Mrs. Dwyer signed the agreement. That evening the contract was presented to plaintiffs and executed by them.

When a copy of the fully executed document was returned later the same evening to Mrs. Dwyer she was informed that, contrary to her expectations, plaintiffs did not intend to include the wall-to-wall carpeting in the sale. She thereupon called her attorney who instructed her to deliver a copy of the agreement to him the following morning. Two or three days later Mr. Dwyer returned from his trip and conferred with their attorney concerning the contract. Following this conference defendants' attorney notified plaintiffs and the realtor that, as attorney for defendants and in accordance with the provisions of the agreement, he was withholding his approval of the contract, and accordingly defendants would not proceed with the transaction. It was indicated that such disapproval was not based upon the price or financing terms. Pretrial discovery disclosed that such notification was given because the carpeting was not included in the sale and there was no specification in the agreement as to what personal property was indicated; the concern of defendants as to the close proximity of the swimming pool to the kitchen doors; the lack of provisions for potability and septic system tests; the shortness of the time period for satisfaction of the mortgage contingency; the inadequacy of the agreement in that Mr. Dwyer was not a signatory thereto, and other intangible considerations.

As indicated, the form utilized by the realtor was the "Standard Form of Real Estate Contract Adopted by the New Jersey Association of Realtor Boards for Use by New Jersey Realtors." The property was described by reference to the municipal tax map, and the purchase price, deposit and mortgage amount were handwritten insertions. The type of deed to be delivered was specified as "C. vs. Grantor," and the rate of interest on the mortgage to be obtained by the purchaser was stated as "prevailing rate." The agreement contained typed contingency clauses for the obtaining of a $75,000 conventional mortgage within 20 days and a termite inspection within 7 days. No provision was made for the inclusion in the sale of any personal property, except for gas and electric fixtures, etc., if any, as provided by the printed language of the form. The agreement also contained the following typewritten provision, which is being relied upon by defendants in opposing plaintiffs' motion for summary judgment for breach of the contract and in support of their motion for a dismissal of the complaint:

> This contract, except as to price and financing terms (if any), is contingent upon approval by the respective attorneys for purchasers and sellers within three (3) business days of the date hereof. The parties agree that such ap-

proval shall be deemed to have been given, and this contingency satisfied or waived, unless an objection or amendment or addition or other express statement witholding (sic) approval is made in writing within said three day period and delivered to the realtor or exchanged between the respective attorneys if they are known to each other.

Inasmuch as there does not exist any dispute concerning the material facts relating to the issues presented, it is appropriate that the motions of the parties be determined in a summary proceeding. R. 4:46-2; Judson v. Peoples Bank & Trust Co. of Westfield, 17 N.J. 67, 110 A.2d 24 (1954).

It is plaintiffs' contention that defendants breached the contract by their failure to consummate the purchase in accordance with the agreement and that their attorney's notification of disapproval was not sufficient to excuse them from such performance. They assert that the "attorney approval clause" in the contract does not permit disapproval for unspecified reasons nor for any of the reasons as disclosed by defendants' answers to interrogatories. Plaintiffs argue that it would be unreasonable to conclude otherwise because of the specific language precluding an objection based upon price or financing terms. Additionally, they contend that a reasonable interpretation of the clause would not support a claim that the parties intended *carte blanche* disapproval rights after entering into what purports on its face to be a legally binding contract. Rather, a more logical conclusion is that the intention of the parties was to provide for a disapproval based upon legal deficiencies of the contract, which would be matters within the special expertise of an attorney.

On the other hand, defendants argue that there was no breach of contract as the inclusion of the subject clause in the agreement rendered its efficacy contingent upon the approval of either party's attorney and, so long as there is no showing of bad faith, the contract is not enforceable in the event of a disapproval by the stipulated counselor. Also, defendants suggest that the reasonable expectation of a purchaser and seller of residential property is that such a provision, in a contract presented to them for execution by a real estate broker or salesperson, grants the right to obtain the unfettered approval or disapproval of their attorney.

While a clause providing for approval of the contract, within a specified time, by the attorney for either party, has not been judicially construed or applied, there appears to be varying interpretations ascribed to such a provision by professionals and others who are involved in real estate transactions. Thus, some may interpret it as meaning that the right of approval is restricted to negotiating the inclusion or exclusion of certain standard clauses, or the modification of included provisions, while others consider that the right is unlimited, thereby permitting the attorney to disapprove the contract for any reason. Under the latter interpretation there is no requirement that the disapproval be reasonable or even that the other contracting party be informed of the reasons for such disapproval. The effect of an unlimited right of disapproval is to place the parties in the same position they would have been if they had been able to consult with an attorney before signing the contract. See Horn, Residential Real Estate Law and Practice in New Jersey §1.1.

Although the effect of a general attorney approval clause in a contract for the purchase of real estate has not been judicially passed upon, a somewhat analogous issue has been presented in cases involving contractual provisions requiring that title to the subject property be satisfactory to the purchaser's attorney. Varying conclusions have been reached as to the manner in which the attorney may exercise such contractual right of approval or disapproval. One line of cases holds that any dissatisfaction with the title is to be tested by objective standards, the test being whether the title meets the standard of marketability, or whether the objections are reasonable. [Citations omitted.] A different view is represented by the group of cases which consider that such provisions constitute the attorney as the sole judge of his dissatisfaction, subject only to the limitation that the decision be arrived at in good faith and not be arbitrary or capricious. [Citations omitted.]

The objective approach, i.e. where the dissatisfaction is tested by the standard of marketability, proceeds on the basis that a clause making the title subject to an attorney's approval is nothing more than an expression of that which is implied in every real estate purchase contract, namely, that the title shall be good and marketable. Accordingly, the purchaser is required to be satisfied with a title which is in fact marketable. Any claim of dissatisfaction must therefore be judged by what the law holds to be a merchantable title, and title cannot be rejected by a simple expression of dissatisfaction based on insufficient legal reason.

Those cases which apply what might be termed the subjective criterion consider that, by providing for an attorney's approval of title, the contracting parties have bargained for something more than a good or marketable title, namely, the attorney's acceptance of the title as satisfactory. It being competent for parties to so stipulate, the attorney's disapproval is conclusive if made in good faith, although in the opinion of others, including the court, the title may be good as a matter of law. Such an interpretation follows the apparent intention of the parties that the attorney be the sole and final arbiter as to the acceptability of the title. To conclude otherwise would deny to the purchaser his right under the contract to the benefit of his attorney's judgment as to the sufficiency of the title. . . .

While these rules are not controlling of the present case, it seems that where the contract permits disapproval thereof by either party's attorney as to its sufficiency or acceptability in general, and not only as to the state of the title, there is even more justification for considering that the right granted by such a provision should not be diluted or denied by requiring that the attorney's judgment be measured by some standard, other than good faith, or another's opinion. The purpose of such an attorney approval clause is to provide the purchaser or seller with the opportunity of obtaining legal advice with respect to the transaction, and its value lies in the fact that the contract may be canceled upon receiving such advice. Parties to a real estate transaction are entitled to the benefit of the judgment of a trusted counselor, and an approval contingency is designed to accord this right to those who, for some reason, enter into a purchase and sale agreement before reviewing the matter with their attorney.

Applying these observations to the present case compels the conclusion that the disapproval of the contract by defendants' attorney effectively terminated the contract. The clause in question expressly made the agreement contingent upon the attorney's approval, except as to price and financing terms, and thereby bound the parties to abide the opinion of either party's attorney with respect to the efficacy of the contract, limited only by the requirement that the attorney act in good faith. The disapproval voiced by the defendants' attorney was an exercise of his judgment, and his reasons therefor were not subject to review or contradiction. The contract cannot be rewritten to qualify the clear and express language of the agreement by limiting the applicability of the attorney approval contingency to those circumstances where the reason for disapproval meets some standard or the concurrence of the plaintiffs, or their attorney. Defendants are entitled to the fruits of their bargain. There is no basis for a claim of bad faith or capriciousness on the part of defendants, or their attorney, in the use of this contingency provision, which would render the notice of disapproval ineffective.

We would also note that a contract for the purchase and sale of a residence determines the rights and responsibilities of the parties as to the entire transaction and is of such importance in this respect as to require preparation or, in the least, preliminary review by an attorney. A text writer has described the significance of the contract in the following manner:

> The contract of sale is the key to the real estate transaction. It is the critical document which fixes the fundamental rights and obligations of the parties from the time it is signed through the closing of title and, in many cases, even beyond. [Horn, Residential Real Estate Law and Practice in New Jersey, §1.1.]

The complexity of the law of contracts and of real property demand that one qualified by education and experience determine the legal sufficiency of a real estate sale agreement and advise the prospective seller or purchaser as to the rights and obligations arising thereunder. Objective counseling by one's own attorney as to the practicability or desirability of undertaking the sale or purchase is also often necessary to avoid precipitous actions which may prove to be legally, financially or socially disadvantageous.

The conclusion reached herein is in accord with the public policy as expressed by the Legislature by including the right of rescission in recent statutes pertaining to retail installment sales, financing of home repairs and the disposition of land in subdivisions. See N.J.S.A. 17:16C-61.5; N.J.S.A. 17:16C-99; N.J.S.A. 45:15-16.12(d).

Our determination that the contract was terminated by operation of the attorney approval contingency provision renders it unnecessary to consider the secondary question concerning the liability of defendant John Dwyer.

Accordingly, plaintiffs' motion for summary judgment for damages is denied and defendants' motion for summary judgment dismissing the complaint is granted.

NOTE

New Jersey now requires that every sales "contract" prepared by a broker open as follows:

> THIS IS A LEGALLY BINDING CONTRACT THAT WILL BECOME FINAL WITHIN THREE BUSINESS DAYS. DURING THIS PERIOD YOU MAY CHOOSE TO CONSULT AN ATTORNEY WHO CAN REVIEW AND CANCEL THE CONTRACT. . . .

In rejecting a buyer's suit for specific performance, where sellers consulted an attorney who disapproved of the contract but gave no reasons for his disapproval, the New Jersey Superior Court wrote:

> For represented parties to a contract, like those involved here, there is really nothing wrong with such a clause. Attorneys offer advice on a limitless range of matters. Clients rely upon them not only for legal advice but also for emotional support, financial guidance, and common sense. They do not often come to their attorneys with their deals all made, save only the limited contributions of the scrivener. For those reasons, there is nothing surprising about a contract provision that effectively creates a timeout period for discussion and advice from a trusted counsellor. That advice can be on details or on price and, to be effective, has to be uncontrolled. Plaintiffs fear price was the problem here and believe they were simply outbid by a latecoming buyer. That may be so. If it is, it is a possibility contemplated and legitimized by the attorney review clause.

Trenta v. Gay, 191 N.J. Super. 617, 621-622, 468 A.2d 737, 739 (Ch. Div. 1983).

b. The Subordination Agreement

Uncertainties as to the availability of *acquisition* financing lead to "subject to" clauses of the sort discussed above; uncertainties as to the availability of *development* financing lead to clauses which present their own special problems. (Although these problems do not arise in the setting of buyer nonclosure, and the topic thus digresses from our main theme, development financing clauses do present planning and doctrinal problems allied to those of acquisition financing.)

Suppose that the buyer has acquired a large tract for shopping center development and has given the seller a mortgage to cover part of the acquisition price. Buyer approaches a bank for construction money. Though the bank, if permitted to do so by lending laws, might be willing to lend with only buyer's equity in the land as its security (i.e., as a second mortgagee), it may instead insist on subjecting the entire fee to its security interest. If it so insists, buyer can secure the development loan only with seller's contemporaneous consent to subordinate his mortgage to the bank's loan.

Previsioning a bank's insistence on a first mortgage, the original contract might:

(1) say nothing about the matter of subordination, leaving the matter to be worked out between buyer, seller, and bank when the development loan is sought; or
(2) contain a provision that buyer and seller are to agree to subordination when the development loan is sought; or
(3) contain one of two types of automatic subordination clause:
   (a) open — whereby seller agrees to subordinate his mortgage to any loan buyer might procure; or
   (b) restricted — whereby, for example, seller agrees to subordinate his mortgage to a *development* loan of, say, not more than $100,000 repayable in *ten years* at not to exceed *8 percent* interest.

Stenehjem v. Kyn Jin Cho

631 P.2d 482 (Alaska 1981)

OPINION

BURKE, Justice. Kurt Stenehjem, the prospective purchaser of a parcel of unimproved land with frontage on the new Homer by-pass road, appeals from the superior court's refusal to specifically enforce his contract with Kyn Jin Cho and Sun Shik Cho, and from the court's failure to award him damages for the Chos' refusal to complete the transaction. Judge James A. Hanson ruled that the contract should not be enforced in light of a provision requiring the Chos to subordinate the deed of trust to be given to them by Stenehjem to any deed of trust that Stenehjem might give to an "F.D.I.C. insured lending institution." We affirm the court's decision not to enforce the contract with the subordination agreement, but we remand

The Buyer Fails to Close

the case for consideration of whether specific enforcement is proper without the subordination clause, or for an award of compensatory damages.

The essential facts are not disputed by the parties. The Chos purchased the property at issue in March, 1977 for approximately $40,000. They subsequently listed the property for sale with a real estate broker for $200,000. After Stenehjem made two offers on the property that were not acceptable to the Chos, the parties signed an agreement dated August 29, 1977. Subsequently, disputes arose between the parties and though attempts were made to find a satisfactory solution, the Chos ultimately refused to perform under the August 29 agreement, and Stenehjem brought this action. . . .

I

. . . In the present case, the Chos resisted specific performance on the ground that the subordination provision contained in the agreement made the agreement uncertain. Stenehjem responds that the provision was sufficiently certain to allow the court to invoke its equitable power "to frame a decree which assures performance on both sides. . . ." The Chos do not contend that there is uncertainty as to any other provision of the agreement, and plainly the agreement contains ample details concerning the property in question, the down payment, assumption of the prior lien, and the mortgage to be given by Stenehjem to the Chos. Therefore, resolution of the question concerning the subordination clause could allow us to find that the agreement was sufficiently definite and certain. . . .

. . . We believe that it is consonant with our past decisions to find that the clause expresses the parties' intentions with reasonable certainty. While we discuss below whether this provision can be enforced in accordance with equitable considerations governing an award of specific performance, that problem results not from uncertainty as to what was intended, but from a concern that the provision leaves a seller without adequate security. Here the parties have plainly stated the subordination procedure to be allowed, and we therefore hold that the agreement has binding legal effect between the parties. . . .

II

A

. . . We therefore must consider whether the trial court erred in refusing to grant specific performance of the contract. As we have previously stated:

> An action for specific performance is equitable in nature. The decision to specifically enforce a contract is within the discretion of the trial court and

will be reversed on appeal only where it is against the clear weight of the evidence. Moran v. Holman, 501 P.2d 769 (Alaska 1972); Jameson v. Wurtz, 396 P.2d 68 (Alaska 1964).

Hausam v. Wodrich, 574 P.2d 805, 809 (Alaska 1978).
The inclusion of a subordination clause in a land sale contract raises the issue of whether the buyer's performance is sufficiently secured to allow specific performance consonant with equitable principles of fairness. We recognized in *Rego* that specific performance should be refused "if a substantial part of the agreed exchange for the performance to be compelled is as yet unperformed and its concurrent or future performance is not well secured to the satisfaction of the court." Rego v. Decker, 482 P.2d at 839, quoting Restatement of Contracts §373 (1932).[4]

Understanding the security problems created by the inclusion of a subordination clause requires familiarity with the reasons for its use and the disadvantages incurred by a seller who agrees to subordinate. The purpose of a subordination agreement is explained by one commentator as follows:

> Typically, when an individual purchases a large amount of raw acreage for the purpose of subdivision and resale, he has neither the entire purchase price nor the capital for the construction. Therefore the buyer will usually operate on long term credit. This credit often takes the form of purchase-money security in favor of the seller, and a construction loan secured by a deed of trust on the property in favor of a third party lender, normally an institutional lender.
>
> A problem arises because the commercial lender is required by statute to hold the first deed of trust on the property. However, the purchase money security is usually the senior lien. Therefore it is necessary, in order to obtain the construction loan from the institutional lender, that the buyer obtain the promise of the seller to waive his statutory priority and accept the junior lien on the property. This waiver is "subordination."

[Comment, 52 Calif. L. Rev. 157 (1964) (hereinafter cited as Subordination Comment).]

Here, Stenehjem was to pay the Chos $40,000 in cash, and assume their debt of $30,500 to the prior owners of the property. The remaining $129,500 of the purchase price was to be paid in semi-annual installments of $6,000 including interest at nine percent. At that payment schedule, repayment would take slightly over forty years. The Chos were to subordi-

---

4. To the same effect is Restatement (Second) of Contracts §377 (Tent. Draft No. 14, 1979).
While the dissent argues that the conditions of the adjacent §378 are not met here, and thus that specific performance is available, it is apparent from an examination of the Restatement that both sections offer grounds for denial of specific performance.

nate Stenehjem's obligation to them to another loan he planned to obtain from an "F.D.I.C. insured lending institution."

It is widely recognized that a subordination agreement is unfavorable to the seller and can greatly increase the risk the seller incurs in the transaction. As one commentator notes:

> When he agrees to subordinate, the seller undertakes substantial risks and becomes a de facto partner in the land development venture. . . . If land values decline or the project turns out to be a poor business investment, the seller may lose his investment because the amount of the construction loan may exceed the ultimate market value of the improvements. Likewise, if construction loan money is misspent by the developer, the property may not appreciate in value sufficiently to provide funds from which the seller can be paid when the property is sold. Should the developer default on the construction loan, foreclosure of the senior lien by the construction lender extinguishes all junior security interests in the property. When such a default by the developer occurs, the seller must either reinstate the construction loan and finish the project himself or redeem the senior lien by paying the entire indebtedness owed by the developer to the lender. Either course of action is usually a practical impossibility without refinancing from another lending agency because the construction loan is typically several times larger than the purchase money loan. In return for the risks he assumes the seller receives an inflated purchase price for his land.

Comment, Purchase Money Subordination Agreements in California: An Analysis of Conditional Subordination, 45 So. Cal. L. Rev. 1109, 1111-12 (1972) (hereafter cited as Purchase Money Subordination) (footnotes omitted). Of course, the amount of the purchase price is meaningless if the seller never receives it, and the courts have expressed reluctance to enforce subordination agreements unless the agreement gives the seller substantial protection from the risks described above by specifying details of the loan to be obtained.

As Stenehjem points out, the subordination agreement here was entered into at a time when the parties did not know the exact nature of the financing that he would eventually receive. This is not uncommon, and Stenehjem therefore urges us not to impose commercially unreasonable standards of certainty. We concur that a land sale contract containing a subordination agreement need not contain every term of the subsequent financing to be sufficiently certain to allow enforcement. However, as we explain below, sufficient terms must be present in the agreement, or be subject to implication in fact or in law, to allow the court to conclude that the agreement is sufficiently fair to both parties to warrant exercise of the court's equitable power.

The courts have thus required that the subordination clause "contain terms that will define and minimize the risk that the subordinating liens will impair or destroy the seller's security." [7] Handy v. Gordon, 65 Cal. 2d 578, 55 Cal. Rptr. 769, 770-771, 422 P.2d 329, 330-31 (1967) (citations omitted). In *Handy,* the court refused to enforce a contract that it found left the "defendants with nothing but plaintiff's good faith and business judgment to insure them that they will ever receive anything for conveying their land." Id., 55 Cal. Rptr. at 771, 422 P.2d at 331. Here, Stenehjem contends that the subordination provision in question adequately secures the Chos' investment and we therefore turn to this question. We first examine each point asserted by Stenehjem to offer security and then consider the agreement as a whole.

B

Stenehjem argues first that the Chos were adequately secured by the payment terms of the contract. He points to the provisions for cash payments of $40,000, and for his assumption of the $30,500 obligation owed by the Chos. Stenehjem maintains that this obligation would have had to have been paid off by him before a development loan could have been obtained. He says these payments, totalling slightly over a third of the purchase price, "constitute a sufficient undertaking to assure that he would complete his performance."

As authority for this proposition, Stenehjem cites Restatement of Contracts §373, Comment b (1932). Section 373 states that the performance of the party seeking specific enforcement must be adequately secured. In Comment b, the Restatement recognizes that

> the plaintiff may already have so far partly performed and so deeply invested his funds and labor, that his own economic interest constitutes an adequate security to the defendant. . . .

Id.[8] Thus, in Adams v. Waddell, 543 P.2d 215 (Alaska 1975), we affirmed a decree of specific performance where the lessees who held an option to purchase had spent over twice the purchase price on improvements prior to exercising the option. Here, however, while Stenehjem's self-interest indeed dictates that he attempt to fulfill all his obligations, the fact that the Chos may receive one-third of the purchase price gives them no security as to the remainder when the remaining portion is subordinated to a loan that would be a senior lien on the property. Instead, if Stenehjem's attempt

---

7. Stenehjem has cited cases upholding agreements which did not contain such terms. See note 12 infra. However, he does not disagree that the contract must afford sufficient security for his performance in order for the court to require specific performance. To the extent that the decisions of other courts do not require such security as a predicate for enforcement, they are not in accord with our decisions or with equitable considerations and we decline to follow them.

8. Restatement (Second) of Contracts §377, Comment a (Tent. Draft No. 14. 1979), restates this proposition without significant alteration.

The Buyer Fails to Close

to develop the property fails in one of the ways discussed above, the Chos will have received only one-third of the purchase price.

Stenehjem next argues that the Chos are secured by his personal liability and "creditworthiness." He points out that the Chos have recourse against him in the event he defaults on either loan. . . .

. . . The commentators are in agreement that the availability of personal liability of the buyer gives little security to the seller. While Stenehjem is indeed solvent now, if the Chos were to seek recovery against him it would be at a time when Stenehjem had defaulted on his obligation to an institutional lender and presumably would be insolvent. See Subordination Comment, supra, at 158 n.7; Comment, The Supreme Court of California 1971-1972: Application of Antideficiency Statute to Construction-Subordination Arrangement, 61 Calif. L. Rev. 273, 545 (1973); 13 Santa Clara Law., 170, 173 (1972).

We recognize that a seller who accepts a mortgage from the buyer in an ordinary land sale transaction takes the risk that the buyer will become insolvent at a later date. There the seller is secured by the value of the land, to which the seller has recourse in the event of a default. Where the seller agrees to subordinate, however, it is the senior lienholder who has recourse to the land, and the seller can look only to the buyer's personal liability.

Here, Stenehjem presented no evidence indicating that he has large financial resources sufficient to provide some security in the event his planned development is unsuccessful. On the contrary, he is 27 years old, had been a general contractor for approximately four years at the time of trial, and has lived in Homer only since 1977. While Stenehjem contends that the Chos had an opportunity to investigate his financial responsibility, we do not believe this opportunity justifies a decision to require specific performance in light of the equitable considerations that govern such a decision.

Stenehjem argues next that the parties' agreement impliedly limited the use of any loan Stenehjem obtained to development of the property, and that this limitation adequately secures the Chos' position. The basis for this contention is that loan money used in development adds to the value of the property, and that in the event of a default the property would be worth enough to cover both the outstanding development loan and the money owed to the seller. Purchase Money Subordination, supra, at 1112-13. Here, we agree that the factual context of the agreement between the Chos and Stenehjem shows that a loan for development purposes was contemplated. And even if it were not possible to make this factual implication, we believe that such a limitation could be implied in law as well. . . .

Stenehjem can point to no case, however, in which it was held that the limitation of a senior lien to development purposes was determinative of the enforceability of the agreement. The mere fact that a loan is spent on construction does not mean that the property increases in value in an amount equal to the loan. Subordination Comment, supra, at 157 & n.5.

> [T]here is not always a direct relation between the construction expenses and a rising land value. Excavations and foundations are of negligible value when the project fails. The large increase in value is realized only when the improvements obtain a significant market value.
>
> The assumption that the cumulative value of the construction and purchase money liens do not exceed the value of the property is therefore inaccurate.

Id. at 157 n.5. Thus, we think this limitation is important only if the agreement as a whole provides adequate security.

Stenehjem also contends that the fact that the agreement requires a development loan be obtained from an F.D.I.C. lending institution provides additional security to the Chos. While Stenehjem failed to offer evidence to the trial court as to the effect of this provision, he argues that the court was required by former Rule 43(a)(1), Alaska R. Civ. P., to take judicial notice of federal and state statutes limiting the amount that banks may lend upon the security of unimproved real estate. We believe the statutes cited by Stenehjem fail to add certainty or security to his agreement with the Chos.

The statutes purport to set limits on the amount of a loan based on a set percentage of the property's appraised value.[10] It would seem that the appraised value would have to include the value of the improvements to be constructed with the loan proceeds. The cost of improvements commonly exceeds the cost of the underlying land, and thus a construction loan would not be limited to a percentage of the land value. This conclusion is in accord with the testimony at trial, as both Stenehjem and the real estate broker handling the transaction acceded to the suggestion that a loan of $1,000,000 could theoretically have been obtained by Stenehjem in a senior position to the obligation owed the Chos.

No evidence was submitted to the trial court concerning these statutes, and thus we have no way of knowing whether they are enforced or whether enforcement provides any security to a subordinating seller. No authority suggests that the statutes make a subordination agreement enforceable, and we decline to so hold here.

Stenehjem also argues that the limitation to F.D.I.C. institutions "guarantee[s] the general soundness of the institution's banking practices," and both Stenehjem and the real estate broker testified that the limitation protected the Chos by preventing subordination to other than a reputable

---

10. AS 06.05.206(c) allows banks to make construction loans on real estate of up to 80 percent of the appraised value where specified improvements are made. Under 12 U.S.C. §371(a)(1), national banking associations are limited to loans of 75 percent on the appraised value of real estate that is to be improved. However, 12 U.S.C. §371(f) allows banks to make loans in excess of that amount as long as the total amount of such loans does not exceed 10 percent of the total amount that a bank may invest in real estate loans.

lender. The institutional lender commonly controls disbursements of loan proceeds, making them progressively as work is performed, after on-site inspections. Subordination Comment, supra, at 157 n.5. These practices are intended to assure the lender and the seller that the value of the property increases as the loan proceeds are spent, so that in the event of a default the property can be sold for an amount equal to both outstanding loans. [Miller, Starr and Regalia, Subordination Agreements in California, 13 U.C.L.A. L. Rev. 1298, 1299 n.5 (1966) (hereinafter cited as California Subordination)]; Purchase Money Subordination, supra, at 1112-13. However, it has been recognized that while correlating disbursement of the loan with the progress of construction work offers significant protection to the lender, who has recourse to the land as well as the improvements in the event of a default, the subordinating seller is not afforded much protection because the default may occur at a time when the amount of construction does not correlate to an increase in property value. Purchase Money Subordination, supra, at 1112 n.12; Subordination Comment, supra, at 157 n.5.

Requiring that the loan be obtained from an institutional lender does afford protection to the seller insofar as it provides some assurance that the less significant details of the financing will be handled properly, and it has been suggested that this limitation obviates the need to specify these details in the original agreement. California Subordination, supra note 5, at 1305. However, the limitation to an institutional lender is only pertinent to incidental parts of the transaction, where specification would make the agreement unwieldy, and does not substitute for provision in the agreement of the major terms of the loan. Id.[11]

C

We have considered each of Stenehjem's contentions concerning the subordination clause individually, but we agree that the ultimate decision as to the agreement's enforceability requires us to consider it as a whole, and

---

11. The authors of California Subordination . . . at 1305, state:

There are innumerable other provisions of the new loan which might be specified. For example, should the amount of possible prepayment charges and late "penalties" be determined? Should the detailed provisions of the note and deed of trust to be delivered to the third party lender be specified? Should the agreement describe the type or nature of the improvements to be constructed on the property? These limitations could probably be inserted in the agreement; such specificity may be unwieldy. The seller can obtain sufficient protection by simply limiting the source of the new loan funds to a federal or state-chartered bank or savings and loan association, or an insurance company, and by providing that the provisions of the new loan, except for the limitations as to amount, term, interest rate, and amortization period and terms, shall be as required by the lender. Such lenders have established loan and security instruments with standardized provisions and, to some degree, they are subject to government regulation.

(Footnotes omitted.)

decide whether it is sufficiently certain and just to warrant enforcement. We reiterate that this decision is vested in the trial court's discretion in the first instance and that a court may fill gaps in a contract where it is necessary to make the agreement amenable to enforcement, but such gap-filling must be in accord with the parties' intentions.

Here, we have construed the agreement to require the Chos to subordinate two-thirds of the purchase price to a loan to be obtained from an F.D.I.C. lending institution to be used for the construction of improvements on the land. As so construed, the subordination provision fails to (1) limit the amount of the loan to which the Chos would subordinate, (2) limit the interest rate of that loan, (3) set maximum and minimum payment periods for the loan, or (4) describe the method of repayment of the loan. The courts and commentators have stated that inclusion of provisions concerning these items serves to give a seller sufficient security that the buyer will perform so as to enable a court to enforce the agreement. [Citations omitted.][12]

In particular, a limit on the amount of the senior lien allows the seller a measure of control over the scope of the construction project to be undertaken. If the construction loan is reasonably proportional to the value of the underlying land, or if it does not exceed the value that the improvements add to the land, then in the event of a default the seller may have the opportunity to cure the default and avoid the loss of his security. A limit on the interest rate of the construction loan also limits the risk which the seller undertakes in subordination since it may prevent commencement of a construction project with an unsuitably high risk of failure. The interest rate also affects the size of the payments on the loan, which may affect the seller's ability to take over the project.

A restriction on the maximum duration of the senior lien allows the seller to avoid being placed in a subordinated position for an overly long time. A specified minimum term for the construction loan insures that the loan does not fall due prior to the return on the buyer's investment, and thus makes it more likely that the buyer will be able to meet each payment as it comes due, and that the seller will not have to make overly burdensome payments should he or she have to take over the construction loan. Subordination Comment, supra, at 163-64; California Subordination, supra note 5, at 1303.

---

12. As we noted in note 7 supra, there are cases enforcing agreements absent terms that give protection to the seller. See, e.g., White & Bollard, Inc. v. Goodenow, 58 Wash. 2d 180, 361 P.2d 571, 574 (1961) (enforcement allowed where seller "was content to trust the purchaser to see that the terms were reasonable." Rivers v. Rice, 233 Ga. 819, 213 S.E.2d 678, 680 (1975) (refusing injunction against foreclosure sale by senior lienholder, citing Ideal Realty Co. v. Reese, 122 Ga. App. 707, 178 S.E.2d 564, 565-66 (1970), an action for damages where the seller had the option of agreeing to subordinate). There are also California cases upholding subordination clauses containing only a few terms of the senior loan, but all involve situations different from that presented here. See Annot., . . . 26 A.L.R.3d at 868-71; California Subordination, at 1305 n.27.

A description of the method of repayment also serves to give the seller some control over the project and allow the protection of his or her interests in the event of a default, particularly if payments are limited to a stated amount, or if they equally amortize the loan. Id.

The agreement here has been construed to limit the use of loan proceeds to development of the land, and we have noted this protects the seller by providing some assurance that the loan serves to increase the value of the property.[13]

The agreement before us limits the use and the source of Stenehjem's financing, but we believe this is insufficient to give the Chos any significant assurance that a development plan undertaken by Stenehjem will not create unwarranted risks for them. Such risks include the possibility that the project will be of such magnitude that they will be unable to rescue it in the event of a default, or that the financing will give inadequate consideration to their interests. As we have noted, while limitation of the use of loan proceeds to development purposes offers some security to the seller, the likelihood that the amount of construction will not correlate with an increase in the value of the property prevents this provision from sufficiently securing the seller's investment.

Where the seller agrees to subordinate to the buyer's obligation, he or she remains vitally interested in the progress and ultimate success of the development project. A court's determination of whether an agreement is sufficiently certain and fair to allow specific enforcement must therefore take into account the amount of recognition the agreement accords to this interest. Here, we do not believe that the agreement affords adequate security for the Chos' investment and it does not include terms widely recognized as providing such protection.[14]

Stenehjem asks us to judicially fill the gaps in the subordination clause so as to enable enforcement, but he does not suggest any way that this could be accomplished and have any basis in the agreement of the parties. We

---

13. While not reflected in the cases, it has been suggested that the subordination provision also specify whether loan proceeds may be used to pay the cost of obtaining the loan, and that a limit on the loan fee to be paid also be stated. Subordination Comment, supra at 164; California Subordination, . . . at 1304; Purchase Money Subordination, supra, at 1118 n.35.

14. Stenehjem argues that the amount of profit the Chos may realize on their sale to him should be considered in deciding whether the agreement should be enforced. However, as we have pointed out, such profits mean little if the Chos never receive them because of the agreement's failure to give them adequate security. Stenehjem cites no case which has used this as a basis to decide the question, and we decline to give the purported profit any significant weight. We note instead, that even with the inclusion of terms to minimize a seller's risk in agreeing to subordination, this procedure still has significant risks for a seller. 13 Santa Clara Law., supra, at 173. Thus where steps have been taken to give the seller protection, the fact that the seller receives a premium makes the agreement fair to both sides and allows enforcement even though some risk remains.

For these reasons, we also reject the intimation of the dissent that the possibility of a large profit obviates the need for a court to determine if the performance of both parties to an agreement is adequately secured.

likewise see no way to accomplish this task. . . . [D]etailed specification of terms would be necessary that would put the court in the inappropriate position of drafting a subordination clause for the parties. We have never undertaken to do this, and therefore we uphold the trial court's decision not to decree specific enforcement with the subordination clause. In so doing, we do not hold that the provisions discussed above must be included to make a subordination clause enforceable, but we note that such provisions are a valuable guide to an agreement's fairness, and that in light of this agreement's failure to otherwise provide the sellers with security, enforcement must be declined.

III

Stenehjem contends that even if enforcement is denied because the agreement fails to provide the Chos with adequate security, the court can use its equitable powers to enforce the contract without the subordination provision. In essence, his argument is that the trial court abused its discretion in not conditioning an award of specific performance on his willingness to forego the benefits of the subordination clause. . . .

We . . . believe that Stenehjem has suggested a sensible way to give the parties the benefit of their bargain and at the same time give adequate security for his performance. However, we do not find it appropriate for this court to mandate that such a decree issue, as the trial court should have an opportunity to consider the issue and, if it thinks appropriate, to take testimony concerning the effect of this remedy.[15]

IV

Stenehjem's final attack on the trial court's judgment is on the court's failure to award damages for the Chos' refusal to perform the contract.

---

15. We have previously noted that the buyer desiring inclusion of a subordination provision in a land sale contract must usually pay a premium purchase price for the land. Therefore, there may be instances in which the court, in making a decision to enforce a contract without the subordination provision, should consider whether the purchase price is still fair if the buyer does not receive the benefit of utilizing the subordination procedure. As Corbin has recognized:

> In some cases specific performance may be an available remedy as to part of a promised performance and not be available as to the remainder. . . . In these cases the court may decree specific performance of the first part, with compensatory damages as to the remainder that is unperformed.

5A A. Corbin . . . §1160, at 185 (footnote omitted). Accord, D. Dobbs, Law of Remedies §12.10, at 849-50 (1973).

Of course, the court is free to determine that the price is fair even without the subordination provision, particularly where, as here, the buyer argues that he be allowed to purchase the land without the clause, or where it is not apparent that subordination influenced the price term of the contract. It is also possible that lack of evidence concerning a fair price absent the subordination provision would lead the court to decline to adjust the price, since remedies for breach of contract should have a basis in the agreement of the parties.

The Buyer Fails to Close

Obviously there is no need to consider this issue if specific performance is granted, but in view of our disposition of that question, we think it appropriate to consider the question of damages to aid the trial court in the event it determines specific performance is improper.

We have already determined that the agreement between the parties here constitutes a binding contract, but that it does not warrant specific enforcement because of the equitable considerations inherent in that remedy. However, as we recognized in *Rego,* damages may be awarded in situations where specific performance is inappropriate. Rego v. Decker, 482 P.2d at 838. Gulbenkian v. Gulbenkian, 147 F.2d 173, 175-76 (2d Cir. 1945); 5A A. Corbin, supra, §1161, at 200-01; 11 Williston, Law of Contracts §1444, at 985 (Jaeger ed. 1968); Restatement of Contracts §370, Comment b (1932). Also, a Florida court has held that damages are available where specific performance was denied because a subordination clause and other provisions lacked sufficiently certain terms. Lasseter v. Dauer, 211 So. 2d 584, 585 (Fla. App. 1968). Accord, Benson v. Chalfonte Development Corp., 348 So. 2d 557, 560 (Fla. App. 1976); therefore, if the court does deny specific performance it should make an award of damages for the breach of the agreement by the Chos, relying on the testimony previously taken on this subject, unless the court finds it necessary to augment the record.

Reversed and remanded for further proceedings consistent with this opinion.

Compton, J., not participating.

Matthews, Justice, joined by Rabinowitz, Chief Justice, dissenting.

I agree with the majority's interpretation of the parties' contract. As so interpreted, I believe the contract should be specifically enforced.

In my view the question which should be asked in each case where specific enforcement is sought is whether the transaction is a fair one. Of course, adequate security is relevant to the question of fairness, but it is not determinative in every case, because a transaction can be fair, and unsecured, or unfair, and well secured.

Restatement (Second) of Contracts §378 (Tent. Draft No. 14, 1979), describes the types of unfairness which will preclude the application of equitable remedies. It takes the position that

(1) Specific performance or an injunction will be refused if such relief would be unfair because

   (a) the contract was induced by mistake or by unfair practices,
   (b) the relief would cause unreasonable hardship or loss to the party in breach or to third persons, or
   (c) the exchange is so grossly inadequate or the terms of the contract are otherwise unfair.

The record discloses no evidence of mistake or unfair practices in the inducement to contract. Nor would specific enforcement of the agreement cause unreasonable hardship or loss to the Chos. Consequently, here the fairness question depends solely on whether the agreed upon consideration is grossly inadequate or the terms of the contract are otherwise unfair. On this record, I think that neither conclusion can be justified.[1]

A subordination agreement is a contract term over which parties frequently bargain. A buyer is often willing to pay a higher price for a contract which includes a subordination clause than for one which does not because the clause will reduce, or eliminate, the need for the buyer to come up with additional capital in order to obtain bank financing for the proposed project.

The record indicates here that the sale was quite favorable to the Chos. They paid approximately $40,000.00 for the property in March of 1977. Less than two months later they listed it for $200,000.00 and sold it for that price to Stenehjem in August of the same year. The terms of the contract provide for $40,000.00 in cash payments to the Chos, assumption of the Chos' debt of $30,500.00 to the prior owners, payment of the remaining balance, $129,500.00 in semi-annual installments of $6,000.00 including interest at nine percent. On this record it appears that the amount which the Chos stand to gain under the contract is not disproportionate to the risks which they must bear.

NOTES AND QUESTIONS

1. "We believe that it is consonant with our past decisions to find that the [subordination] clause expresses the parties' intentions with reasonable certainty." Stenehjem v. Kyn Jin Cho, at 455 supra.

Why, in the first instance, is a subordination clause, which is silent as to (nearly) all of the significant details, nevertheless "certain"? Compare the Alaska court's treatment of the subordination clause, in this respect, with the Wisconsin court's treatment of the financing clause in Gerruth Realty Co. v. Pire, at page 442 supra.

2. "We recognize that a seller who accepts a mortgage from the buyer in an ordinary land sale transaction takes the risk that the buyer will become insolvent at a later date. . . . Where the seller agrees to subordinate, however, it is the senior lienholder who has recourse to the land, and the seller can look only to the buyer's personal liability." *Stenehjem*, at 459 supra.

As we have seen, a seller may often accept a purchase money *second* mortgage to finance the sale of seller's property. Is it true that only the

---

1. It is unusual to find unfairness in the exchange itself without evidence of artifice, sharp practice or the like in its inducement. See Restatement (Second) of Contracts §378, Comment b. See also 5A A. Corbin, Corbin on Contracts §1165 at 224-26 (Rev. ed. 1964).

senior lienholder has recourse to the land in such a case? Is the same true in the subordination case? By analogy to the subordination case, might a seller who has agreed to take back a purchase money second mortgage resist specific performance of the sales contract on equitable grounds?

3. "[T]herefore, if the court does deny specific performance it should make an award of damages for the breach of the agreement by the Chos. . . ." *Stenehjem,* at 465 supra.

What *are* Stenehjem's damages? In computing damages, should the court consider that the Chos may have agreed to pay a premium to obtain so favorable a subordination clause?

4. Lascher, Subordination Clauses in Court: Is California Unfair to Unfairness?, 1 San Fern. V.L. Rev. 1, 24-25 (1967), offers an interesting insight into the motives of some buyers for seeking an *automatic* subordination clause. Lascher writes that by the early 1960s, state courts had cast so strong a doubt over the validity of such clauses that in fact California institutional lenders would not rely on these clauses as conferring the required first-mortgage status, but would demand a contemporaneous subordination. The author continues:

> Why . . . does a person who acquires a parcel of land for the purpose of development nevertheless want an automatic subordination agreement and want it so badly that he is willing to fight through the courts for it?
>
> The answer is obvious to anyone who has had the remotest relationship with the field, and indisputable: The purchaser who buys the land primarily for motives of contemplated economic development to be made upon the land, does *not* want the automatic subordination agreement.
>
> **A. Performance of the Automatic Subordination Agreement Is Not the Motive, in the Typical Case**
>
> But somebody does. The prospective purchaser to whom a substantial and short range profit is available, *from the very agreement itself* (without any of the bother or risk of development) is the one who wants to enforce automatic subordination agreements.
>
> Why? Because the law places in his hands an advantage which almost inevitably will make it imperative for the land owner to buy his peace, thereby turning a neat profit for the purchaser by dint of no activity more strenuous than drafting an automatic subordination agreement and talking a land owner into signing it.
>
> Whatever one may think of the abstract business ethics of such an enterprise, it is nevertheless completely sanctioned by law (and even, during the second phase described above, as much encouraged by it). And it is a fundamental of our legal institutions that there is nothing unlawful about doing that which the law permits. The law not only permits this, but it also supplies the last ingredient necessary to its effectuation: the power to tie up the seller's land by the recordation, simultaneously with the filing of the complaint, of a lis pendens (as it is inevitably known in California, although technically described as "a notice of pendency of an action").

B. The Seller, Under a Lis Pendens, Faces a Choice of Three Unpalatable Options

As a practical matter, the seller who has blundered into one of these transactions but has seen the light, and against whose land—typically his sole substantial asset and possibly even sole source of livelihood—a lis pendens has been imposed, faces three unpalatable alternatives: (1) going through with the transaction on terms which are financially maniacal, from his standpoint; (2) spending two, three or four years in litigation, during which time he cannot sell even a portion of his land, lease it for a period of a year or more, or even borrow upon it; (3) mitigating his loss by paying whatever it takes to buy a dismissal and mutual recission, just so long as the asking price is less than the contemplated cost of either of the other alternatives (which it seldom fails to be).

5. *Negotiation and drafting exercise.* Assume that the Chos are legitimate developers who wish to build a 20-unit residential subdivision on the Stenehjem acreage, and that each home, including the lot, will have an approximate appraised value of $60,000 when completed. Together with a classmate, negotiate and draft a subordination agreement that is mutually acceptable and likely to be specifically enforceable in the Alaska courts. One of you should act as the buyer's lawyer, the other as seller's lawyer. In carrying on the negotiations, consider the seller's interest in security and specificity, and the buyer's interest in profit and flexibility. You should not feel entirely constrained by the original contract price of $200,000, or the $40,000 cash down payment.

6. Seller agrees to subordinate her purchase money mortgage to a construction loan. Upon subordination, the development begins but is abandoned in midstream. The construction lender starts foreclosure, joining the seller as a defendant. Seller discovers that the construction lender has failed to limit the use of the loan proceeds to construction purposes. Does seller have any remedy? Cf. Middlebrook-Anderson Co. v. Southwest Savings & Loan Assn., 18 Cal. App. 3d 1023, 96 Cal. Rptr. 338 (1971); Note, Purchase Money Subordination Agreements in California: An Analysis of Conditional Subordination, 45 S. Cal. L. Rev. 1109 (1972).

2. *Seller's Damages*

Absent an agreement for liquidated damages, a seller's damage recovery is measured by the difference between the contract price and the market value of the property as of the date for performance. A seller may also recover some incidental damages as well as consequential damages to the extent permitted under the rule of Hadley v. Baxendale.

The Buyer Fails to Close 469

Although problems of land valuation in the contexts of eminent domain and taxation have generated a complex body of law, and real estate appraisal is an increasingly sophisticated operation (cf. 2 Am. Jur. Proof of Facts, Appraisals §1 (1959)), in land breach of contract actions the appellate opinions rarely explore valuation questions. Occasionally, attention is paid to the problem of whether values influenced by feverish land speculation are relevant to damage measurement. 1 Bonbright, Valuation 357 (1937). There is some dispute as to the admissibility on the issue of valuation of sales prices of "comparable" property, and of the original cost of the land to the seller. 2 Wigmore, Evidence §463 (3d ed. 1940).

a. Fixing Damages by Resale

If seller sells the property some few days after buyer's breach for more than the contract price, it does not necessarily follow that he sustained no compensable damage: "Why should a later rise in the value of the land or superior acumen of the vendor in securing a sale above the market value work to the benefit of the defaulting buyer?" asks McCormick, Damages 711 (1935), citing nothing. Contrariwise, consider Shurtleff v. Marcus Land & Investment Co., 59 Cal. App. 250, 211 P. 244 (1922). In this case, the buyer agreed to pay $58,000; he then defaulted, and twenty-one days after his breach, seller resold to X for only $52,000. A month later X sold to the original buyer for $54,500. In seller's action for damages against buyer, the trial court found that the land was worth $60,000 as of the breach; the court had received in evidence, in addition to the above, expert testimony of the potential uses of the property, and of the $60,000 valuation. The ensuing $1 judgment for seller was affirmed.

More generally, it seems to be the law that seller's realization on resale, if not too remote in time from the date of breach, is *evidence* of value on the date of breach but does not of itself operate to fix damages. Interesting is the rule that the contract price itself is also evidence of the value on the date of the breach, at least where the contract and breach dates are not too far apart. Fleischer v. Cosgrove, 145 Cal. App. 2d 14, 301 P.2d 911 (1956).

While on the topic of resale, it is essential to note that there is likely to be conversation between buyer and seller after the breach and prior to the resale, and that such conversations may be given the legal effect of an agreement to liquidate damages via resale. Barr v. McGlothin, 176 Va. 474, 11 S.E.2d 617 (1940), permits the seller, by postbreach letter to buyer, to bind the buyer to the damages fixed by resale.

It may also be argued that the conversations concerning resale bar *any* damage action by seller. See pages 500-502 infra.

b. Expenses of Resale, of Initial Sale

Royer v. Carter
37 Cal. 2d 544, 233 P.2d 539 (1951)

TRAYNOR, J. [Plaintiff seller was awarded damages by the trial court, measured in part by the difference between the unpaid contract price ($23,000, defendant having paid $1000 down) and the $18,500 realized by resale three months after the breach. This was held error in the face of undisputed proof that the property was declining in value between the dates of breach and resale.]

Defendant contends that the trial court also erred in allowing as additional damages $45 in escrow charges, $40 in title charges, and $420 in broker's fees paid in connection with the first sale. When, as under section 3307,[2] the measure of damages is designed to assure to the vendor the benefit of his bargain, additional damages should not be allowed for expenses that would have been incurred had the contract been performed. To do so would place the vendor in a better position than he would have been in had there been no breach. Civil Code, §3358. Thus, plaintiff would have paid the expenses from the proceeds of the sale had the contract been performed. If she is given the equivalent of the proceeds of the sale under section 3307 she is not also entitled to expenses that she would have incurred in any event.

In many cases, however, the vendee's breach may make it necessary for the vendor to incur additional expenses to realize the benefit of his bargain. Given the rule that the value of the property to the seller under section 3307 is ordinarily the market value at the time of the breach, Employees' Participating Assn. v. Pine, 91 Cal. App. 2d 299, 301, and cases cited, injustice could result if the vendor were not allowed to recover damages for additional expenses caused him by the vendee's breach. Thus in a case where the property is sold at the market value and that value remains constant until after the breach, and the property is then resold at the same price, the vendor could recover no damages under section 3307. He would be forced to pay, however, in addition to the expenses of the first sale, the expenses of the resale. When such additional expenses are the natural consequence of the breach, they may be recovered in addition to those provided for in section 3307. [Citations omitted.] The statements in Morgan v. Dibble, 43 Cal. App. 116, 184 P. 704, and Maloney v. Houston, 51 Cal. App. 585, 197 P. 611, indicating that section 3307 provides the exclusive measure of damages were not necessary to the decisions in those cases and are disapproved.

---

2. "The detriment caused by the breach of an agreement to purchase an estate in real property, is deemed to be the excess, if any, of the amount which would have been due to the seller, under the contract, over the value of the property to him."—EDS.

It does not follow that the actual expenses of the first sale will necessarily be equal to the additional expenses caused by the vendee's breach. If all of the contemplated expenses of the first sale are actually paid and the property does not change in value, ordinarily the additional expense of reselling made necessary by the breach will be equal to those incurred in the first sale. In the present case, however, it appears that all the contemplated expenses of the first sale were not paid and that the cost of reselling at the market value at the time of the breach would have been less than the cost of selling at the contract price. Under the terms of her agreement with the broker plaintiff was not obligated to pay the full commission on the first sale in case of defendant's default. She paid only $420, thus saving $780 of the anticipated expense of the first sale.

Since the cost of a sale under the usual brokerage contract is five percent of the purchase price, what the cost would have been at the time of defendant's breach cannot be determined in the absence of a finding of the market value of the property at that time. On retrial, the trial court, in computing the additional damages caused by defendant's breach, should allow an amount equal to the difference between the cost of selling the property at its value at the time of the breach and $780, the amount the anticipated expenses of the first sale were reduced by defendant's default. . . .

c. The Middleman Seller

McDaniel v. Daves, 139 Va. 178, 123 S.E. 663 (1924): In January, X agreed to sell a tract to S for $13,000, closing for the following January. S made an initial payment of $1500. In May S agreed to sell the land to B for $15,000, closing for the following January; B made an initial payment of $1000. B was aware of the S-X contract. B defaulted, and thereafter, under unexplained circumstances, S paid X an additional $500 for a release from the S-X contract. Nothing appears in the opinion as to the market value of the property, although inferences can perhaps be drawn from the prices in the two contracts and from the fact that S paid X $500 for a release.

S sued B for damages of $3000, as the difference between the unpaid balance on the S-B contract and that on the S-X contract, viz. $2500, plus the $500 paid for a release.

The court restricted S's recovery against B to $1000, and quoted a New York decision in support:

> The [trial] court adopted and applied the wrong measure of damages in permitting plaintiff to prove the market value of the land, and in basing the damages on the difference between the market value and the contract price. This is the proper and usual rule where the vendor actually owns the land,

but it is wholly inapplicable where he has to purchase it himself in order to fulfill his contract. In such case, his loss cannot exceed the difference between what it would cost him to acquire the land and what the defendant promised to pay. It may be that, if his contract with the owner was at a price far below the market price, he could not recover the whole difference; but he certainly cannot recover more. If his contract with the owner was at a price below the market price, he would not be damaged to the extent of the difference between those prices by the defendant's refusal to complete the purchase, because that difference would be represented by the land, which he presumably could sell at the market price. The true measure of damage in a case like the present, assuming an obligation on the part of the defendant to purchase and ability on the part of plaintiff to put himself in a position to convey would be the difference between what it would cost plaintiff to acquire the property and the contract price, not exceeding, however, the difference between the fair market value and the contract price.

The quote, whether or not apposite, is from an Appellate Division decision, Booth v. Milliken, 127 A.D. 522, 525, 111 N.Y.S. 791, 795 (1908), *aff'd*, 194 N.Y. 553, 87 N.E. 1115 (1909). In Tague Holding Corp. v. Harris, 250 N.Y. 422, 165 N.E. 834 (1929), the New York Court of Appeals held, on facts similar to *McDaniel*, that seller was entitled to recover the difference between the face amount of the contract with the buyer and the net amount owed to X less buyer's down payment to seller (there was no payment for a release involved in *Tague*).

3. *Retention of Deposit*

Farrand, Conveyancing Contracts[3]
300-305 (1964)

Estate agents expect every purchaser to do his duty by paying a deposit. We have all got the message. This is rarely, if ever, queried on behalf of purchasers. Whether it should be would largely turn, of course, on the advantage to vendors of requiring a deposit. So what is this advantage?

As Lord Macnaghten has said: "Everybody knows what a deposit is. The purchaser did not want legal advice to tell him that. The deposit serves two purposes—if the purchase is carried out it goes against the purchase money—but its primary purpose is this, it is a guarantee that the purchaser means business" (in Soper v. Arnold (1889), 14 App. Cas. 429, at p. 435). The question, therefore, is how the deposit acts as a guarantee. The short answer, again as everybody knows, is that "if the contract is not performed by the payer [the deposit] shall remain the property of the

---

3. This is an excellent one-volume treatment of English law on land transfer contracts. Much of the text and most citations have been edited out of the excerpt which follows.

payee" (per Fry, L.J., in Howe v. Smith (1884), 27 Ch. D. 89, at p. 101). . . . This however, calls for closer consideration. . . .

The rule is that if a purchaser be so much in default as to discharge the vendor from the contract, the purchaser as a punishment will lose and the vendor as a consolation will gain the deposit (ibid. . . .). In colloquial conveyancing, the vendor may rescind the contract and forfeit the deposit. . . . The vendor may do this even without any express enabling provision in the contract—it is implied from the primary purpose of paying a deposit (see Hall v. Burnell [1911] 2 Ch. 551). He may also forfeit the deposit where the purchaser resists the enforcement by action of the contract as not observing the evidential requirement of [the Statute of Frauds], but not where he himself resists enforcement on this ground (Gosbell v. Archer (1835), 2 Ad. & El. 500), nor, of course, where there has never been any concluded contract at all to enforce in any way (e.g., agreement "subject to contract," see Chillingsworth v. Esche [1924] 1 Ch. 97).

What is more, the vendor has been held entitled to keep the deposit although it may exceed any loss he has suffered (see Hinton v. Sparkes (1868), L.R. 3 C.P. 161), and even to sue for such an excessive deposit where it has not for some reason been paid before the purchaser's default (see Wallis v. Smith (1882), 21 Ch. D. 243). . . . All this springs directly from the primary purpose of requiring a deposit and is hardly to be doubted. Yet the present writer in all conscience must confess his difficulty in seeing how equity came to tolerate this. Why, in other words, was it not relieved against as a "penalty"?

The two may perhaps be compared for a moment. What again is a deposit? "It comes shortly to this—that a deposit, if nothing more be said about it, is, according to the ordinary interpretation of business men, *a security* for the completion of the purchase" (per Bowen, L.J., in Howe v. Smith (1884), 27 Ch. D. 89, at p. 98). What is a penalty? "If the intention is to *secure* performance of the contract by the imposition of a fine or penalty, then the sum specified is a penalty" (per Lopes, L.J., in Law v. Redditch Local Board [1892] 1 Q.B. 127, at p. 132). Once more, what is a deposit? "[I]t is not merely a part payment, but is then also in earnest to bind the bargain so entered into, and creates by the fear of its forfeiture a motive in the payer to perform the rest of the contract" (per Fry, L.J., in Howe v. Smith, supra, at p. 101, the leading case). And a penalty? "The essence of a penalty is a payment of money stipulated as in terrorem of the offending party . . ." (per Lord Dunedin in Dunlop Pneumatic Tyre Co., Ltd. v. New Garage & Motor Co., Ltd. [1915] A.C. 79, at pp. 86-88, the leading case). . . .

Lastly one may reflect on the true test of a penalty, namely, any sum which is not a genuine pre-estimate of damage. The traditional 10 percent on a sale of land represents pure practice and is never even a perfunctory pre-estimate. . . .

In the result the present writer feels that the deposit on a sale of land with its potential forfeiture is open to equitable attack. He would, however, be somewhat surprised to find such an attack succeed against the traditional 10 percent. . . .

Kraft v. Michael
166 Pa. Super. 57, 70 A.2d 424 (1950)

DITHRICH, Judge. This appeal is from the discharge of a rule to show cause why a judgment by a confession should not be opened. The judgment was entered on a note given by appellants in part payment for premises which they had agreed to purchase from appellee and his wife. The agreement, entered into by Kindler & Furman, real estate agents for appellee, and the appellants, husband and wife, provided that the latter would purchase appellee's residence at 320 North Oak Avenue, Clifton Heights, Delaware County, Pennsylvania, for the total consideration of $16,000.

The terms of the settlement were as follows: $50 in cash upon the signing of the agreement, $1,550 within five days to be secured by judgment note payable one day after date, and the balance in cash on or before August 27, 1948. The agreement was dated May 28, 1948. Prior to the time stipulated for settlement appellants requested and secured an extension of time to October 1, 1948, but they subsequently defaulted in their agreement.

Paragraph 10 of the agreement provided: "Should the Buyer violate or fail to fulfil and perform any of the terms or conditions of this agreement then and in that case all sums paid by the Buyer on account of the purchase price or consideration herein may be retained by the Seller, either on account of the purchase price, or as liquidated damages for such breach, as the Seller shall elect, and in the latter event the Seller shall be released from all liability or obligation and this agreement shall become null and void." The agreement further provided that the agents' commission of $500 should be earned and payable only on completion of settlement and payment of the full purchase price.

After appellants had breached their agreement they obtained a rule to show cause why the judgment should not be opened. The petition to open stated, in part, that (1) appellee is a member of the Delaware County Bar and that the husband appellant is a chief petty officer in the United States Navy, and at no time were he and his wife represented by counsel; (2) the admitted breach was a result of their inability to sell and convey their residence; and (3) that appellee had later sold his property for a sum in excess of the sum for which appellants had agreed to purchase it.

A complete answer to the first phase of appellants' petition is found in the opinion of Judge Sweney discharging the rule to open judgment. He said: "Plaintiff is a member of the Bar of this County and is also the District

Attorney. Defendants would have us infer that this is of oppressive significance, especially in view of the fact that defendants had no attorney. There is no testimony before us that the defendants dealt with the plaintiff. The realtors procured the defendants to purchase this property and the inference is that negotiations were conducted between the parties through the agency of the realtors. We find no evidence which indicates that defendants were persuaded or prevented from securing their own attorney. The plaintiff stands before us as any other litigant no higher and no lower."

The fact that appellants were unable to go through with the agreement because they were unable to dispose of their own property, assuming that to be a fact, is of no consequence, as there was no stipulation to that effect in the agreement.

Whether the sum of $1,600, comprising the cash payment and the judgment note, shall be construed as liquidated damages or as a penalty is, as stated by the learned court below, "the real question here involved." The guiding principle and general rule applicable in cases of this kind is summarized in Streeper v. Williams, 48 Pa. 450, 454, as follows: "Upon the whole, the only general observation we can make is, that in each case we must look at the language of the contract, the intention of the parties as gathered from all its provisions, the subject of the contract and its surroundings, the ease or difficulty of measuring the breach in damages, and the sum stipulated, and from the whole gather the view which good conscience and equity ought to take of the case."

Considering the language of the agreement in the instant case in that light, we can come to no other conclusion than that the sum stipulated bore such a reasonable relation to the purchase price that the court below did not err in treating it as liquidated damages and not as a penalty.

The averment that the property was later sold for more than the amount that appellants had agreed to pay for it would not be proper ground for opening the judgment, assuming it to be a fact. The same point was squarely raised and met in Sanders v. Brock, 230 Pa. 609, 79 A. 772, 35 L.R.A., N.S., 532. The Court in passing upon it said, in an opinion by Mr. Justice Mestrezat, 230 Pa. at pages 613, 614, 79 A. at page 773: "The plaintiff bases his right to recover back the $2,000 on the fact that, the defendant having resold the property for a sum in excess of the price agreed to be paid by the plaintiff, the defendant was not injured by the plaintiff's breach of the contract and must therefore return the sum paid on the purchase money." In respect thereof the Court said, 230 Pa. at pages 614, 615, 79 A. at page 773: " 'No rule in respect to the contract (for the sale of real estate) is better settled,' says Nelson, J., in Hansbrough v. Peck [5 Wall. 497], 72 U.S. 497, 506 [18 L. Ed. 520], 'than this: That the party who has advanced money, or done an act in part performance of the agreement, and then stopped short and refuses to proceed to its ultimate conclusion, the other party being ready and willing to proceed and fulfill all his stipulations according to the contract, will not be permitted to recover back what has thus been advanced or done.' " . . .

True it is that this Court in Ellis v. Roberts, 98 Pa. Super. 49, 60, upon which appellants chiefly rely, said that an advance payment of $2,500 on the purchase of a $16,800 property, or 15 percent of the purchase price, considered "In the light of the amount of the purchase price, the knowledge which plaintiff had of defendants' financial condition, the relation which the sum agreed upon as liquidated damages bears to the purchase price and *all the other circumstances,* we are led to the conclusion that plaintiff intended the provision in the contract for liquidated damages to compel specific performance by defendants. This made it a provision for a penalty and precludes plaintiff from recovering more than just compensation for the breach of the contract by defendants, and requires us to open the judgment." (Italics supplied.)

However, in that case the sum claimed as liquidated damages included not only a down payment of $100 and a judgment note for $2,000, but $400 additional, made in payments of $25 per week by the purchaser for a period of sixteen weeks. It should further be borne in mind that the relation which the sum agreed upon as liquidated damages in the instant case bears to the purchase price, to wit, 10 percent, is considerably less than the 15 percent relationship in Ellis v. Roberts, supra.

Restatement, Contracts, provides: "§339. Liquidated Damages and Penalties. (1) An agreement, made in advance of breach, fixing the damages therefor, is not enforceable as a contract and does not affect the damages recoverable for the breach, unless (a) the amount so fixed is a reasonable forecast of just compensation for the harm that is caused by the breach, and (b) the harm that is caused by the breach is one that is incapable or very difficult of accurate estimation." . . .

We are in entire accord with the conclusion of the learned court below that $1,600.00 on a total price of $16,000.00 or a ratio of 10% is not unconscionable or in the nature of a penalty."

Judgment affirmed.

NOTES

1. *Broker's rights.* Does seller's retention of deposit in lieu of seeking other remedies subject seller to commission liability to broker? Does buyer's breach, in addition to causing loss of deposit, subject buyer to commission liability to broker? See, e.g., Ellsworth Dobbs, Inc. v. Johnson, 50 N.J. 528, 236 A.2d 843 (1967); and Rothman Realty Co. v. Bereck, 73 N.J. 590, 376 A.2d 902 (1977).

If buyer fails to consult an attorney before entering a sales contract (and few residential buyers have attorneys at the contract stage), is anyone under a duty to advise buyer of the utility of a financing condition?

2. *Penalties and specific performance.* The *Kraft* court's quotation from Ellis v. Roberts states the standard objection to a penalty clause: "We are

led to the conclusion that plaintiff intended the provision in the contract for liquidated damages to compel specific performance by Defendants. This made it a provision for a penalty. . . ." But the law generally as to sales of real estate permits seller to get a court to require buyer to specifically perform. Why can't the parties use a contract device to compel a performance that the law will compel absent the device?

Freedman v. Rector, Wardens & Vestrymen of St. Mathias Parish
37 Cal. 2d 16, 230 P.2d 629 (1951)

TRAYNOR, Justice. On October 8, 1947 plaintiff signed a deposit agreement with Clarence Urban, a real estate broker, for the purchase of two lots owned by defendant. He paid $2,000 down and agreed to pay the balance of $16,000 into escrow within thirty days. [Thereafter a dispute as to seller's title obligation arose, in the course of which buyer wrote letters in November and December which had the legal effect of repudiating the contract. In January 1948 seller sold the lots to a third party for $20,000. Buyer then commenced this action for specific performance, or in the alternative, return of his deposit. Buyer's specific performance action failed because he was held to have repudiated.]

. . . The question remains whether plaintiff is entitled to the return of any part of his down payment. Since defendant resold the property for $2,000 more than plaintiff had agreed to pay for it, it is clear that defendant suffered no damage as a result of plaintiff's breach. If defendant is allowed to retain the amount of the down payment in excess of its expenses in connection with the contract it will be enriched and plaintiff will suffer a penalty in excess of any damages he caused. Under our recent holdings in Barkis v. Scott, 34 Cal. 2d 116, 208 P.2d 367, and Baffa v. Johnson, 35 Cal. 2d 36, 216 P.2d 13, plaintiff could recover that excess under section 3275 of the Civil Code, if his breach was neither wilful, fraudulent, nor grossly negligent.[4] The trial court found, however, on substantial evidence, that plaintiff's breach was wilful. It is necessary to consider, therefore, the question left open in the *Baffa* case, namely, whether a vendee under such circumstances may recover the excess of his part payment over the damage he caused the vendor.

As was pointed out in the *Baffa* case, if the right to restitution rests solely on the provisions of section 3275, a vendee who has been guilty of a wilful default must be denied relief. We have concluded, however, that the

---

4. Section 3275 provides: "Whenever, by the terms of an obligation, a party thereto incurs a forfeiture, or a loss in the nature of a forfeiture, by reason of his failure to comply with its provisions, he may be relieved therefrom, upon making full compensation to the other party, except in case of a grossly negligent, willful, or fraudulent breach of a duty."
—EDS.

damage provisions of the Civil Code together with the policy of the law against penalties and forfeitures provide an alternative basis for relief independent of section 3275.

"Few questions in the law have given rise to more discussion and difference of opinion than that concerning the right of one who has materially broken his contract without legal excuse to recover for such benefits as he may have conferred on the other party by part performance. . . . A satisfactory solution is not easy, for two fundamental legal policies seem here to come in conflict. On the one hand, it seems a violation of the terms of a contract to allow a plaintiff in default to recover — to allow a party to stop when he pleases and sell his part performance at a value fixed by the jury to the defendant who has agreed only to pay for full performance. On the other hand, to deny recovery often gives the defendant more than fair compensation for the injury he has sustained and imposes a forfeiture on the plaintiff. The mores of the time and place will often determine which policy will be followed. But the second of these opposing policies has steadily increased in favor in recent years." (5 Williston on Contracts [Rev. ed.] §1473, p. 4118.)

In adopting a rule allowing restitution to the defaulting vendee the Supreme Court of Utah stated:

. . . "The rule contended for by respondent, carried to its logical sequence, would forfeit every dollar paid by appellant and still leave the respondent in possession of the land even if appellants had paid the last installment but one, and then defaulted. In answer to this, it may be said that such is not the case at bar. But where are we going to draw the line?" Malmberg v. Baugh, 62 Utah 331, 340, 345, 218 P. 975, 978; see also, McCormick on Damages, §153, p. 616; Corbin, The Right of a Defaulting Vendee to the Restitution of Installments Paid, 40 Yale L.J. 1013.

The failure of courts adopting a contrary viewpoint to recognize that they are permitting unjustifiable penalties for breach of contract has led to the comment that "The law, while looking with righteous abhorrence on forfeitures, and washing its hands of their enforcement, after the manner of Pontius Pilate, yet has been reluctant to intervene with affirmative relief or to formulate any consistent principle condemning the validity of cutthroat provisions which in their essence involve forfeitures. Although the law will not assist in the vivisection of the victim, it will often permit the creditor to keep his pound of flesh if he can carve it for himself." (Balantine, Forfeiture for Breach of Contract, 5 Minn. L. Rev. 329, 341.)

To permit what are in effect punitive damages merely because a party has partially performed his contract before his breach is inconsistent both with section 3294[1] of the Civil Code limiting the right to exemplary dam-

---

1. "In an action for the breach of an obligation not arising from contract, where the defendant has been guilty of oppression, fraud, or malice, express or implied, the plaintiff, in addition to the actual damages, may recover damages for the sake of example and by way of punishing the defendant."

ages and sections 1670[2] and 1671[3] dealing with liquidated damages. "A penalty need not take the form of a stipulated fixed sum; any provision by which money or property would be forfeited without regard to the actual damage suffered would be an unenforceable penalty." Ebbert v. Mercantile Trust Co., 213 Cal. 496, 499, 2 P.2d 776, 777. Such penalties cannot reasonably be justified as punishment for one who wilfully breaches his contract. Not only does section 3294 of the Civil Code express the policy of the law against the allowance of exemplary damages for breach of contract regardless of the nature of the breach, . . . but if a penalty were to be imposed it should bear some rational relationship to its purpose. A penalty equal to the net benefits conferred by part performance bears no such relationship. It not only fails to take into consideration the degree of culpability, but its severity increases as the seriousness of the breach decreases. Thus a vendee who breaches his contract before he has benefited the vendor by part performance suffers no penalty, whereas one who has almost completely performed his contract suffers the maximum penalty.

Moreover, to deny the remedy of restitution because a breach is wilful would create an anomalous situation when considered with section 3369 of the Civil Code. That section provides that "Neither specific nor preventive relief can be granted to enforce a penalty of forfeiture in any case . . ." and precludes the court from quieting the vendor's title unless he refunds the excess of the part payments over the damage caused by the vendee's breach. Baffa v. Johnson, 35 Cal. 2d 36, 39, 216 P.2d 13; Barkis v. Scott, 34 Cal. 2d 116, 121, 208 P.2d 367, and cases cited. Unless the same rule is adopted when the vendee seeks restitution, the rights of the parties under identical fact situations will turn on the chance of which one first seeks the aid of the court. . . .

The provision of the contract providing that on plaintiff's default defendant could retain the down payment cannot be enforced as a valid clause providing for liquidated damages. Although such a provision in a contract for the sale of real property is presumptively valid, if the down payment is reasonable in amount, . . . when as in this case the evidence establishes that it would not "be impracticable or extremely difficult to fix the actual damage," Civil Code, §1671, such a provision may not be enforced as one for liquidated damages. [Citations omitted.]

Since a commission of $900 was retained by the broker from the down payment it is clear that defendant received from plaintiff at most $1,100. Defendant contends, however, that there were other expenses incurred in connection with the escrow that reduced the amount of the down payment

---

2. "Every contract by which the amount of damage to be paid, or other compensation to be made, for a breach of an obligation, is determined in anticipation thereof, is to that extent void, except as expressly provided in the next section."

3. "The parties to a contract may agree therein upon an amount which shall be presumed to be the amount of damage sustained by a breach thereof, when, from the nature of the case, it would be impracticable or extremely difficult to fix the actual damage."

received. Since the trial court erroneously concluded that plaintiff could recover no part of his down payment, no finding was made as to the fraction that accrued to the net benefit of defendant. Accordingly, a new trial limited to that issue is appropriate. . . .

The judgment is reversed insofar as it denies plaintiff restitution of any part of his down payment and the trial court is directed to retry the issue of the amount thereof to which he is entitled. In all other respects the judgment is affirmed. Each party is to bear his own costs on this appeal.

Gibson, C.J., and Shenk, Edmonds, Carter and Spence JJ., concur.
SCHAUER, Justice. I would affirm the judgment in its entirety.
Rehearing denied; Schauer, J., dissenting.

Hetland, The California Land Contract[5]
48 Calif. L. Rev. 729, 736-745 (1960)

III. THE MARKETING CONTRACT

A. THE LIQUIDATED DAMAGES CLAUSE

1. *The Problem.* According to Civil Code section 1671, "the parties to a contract may agree therein upon an amount which shall be presumed to be the amount of damage sustained by a breach thereof, when, from the nature of the case, it would be impracticable or extremely difficult to fix the actual damage."

In Freedman v. The Rector, the buyer agreed to pay $18,000 for the property involved, gave a $2,000 deposit, then unjustifiably repudiated the contract and demanded the return of his $2,000 deposit. Because the seller shortly thereafter resold the property for $20,000 and thus suffered no *actual* damage, the court ordered the return of that part of the buyer's $2,000 that exceeded the seller's expenses of the first sale, saying, "Although such a provision [retention of down payment by vendor] . . . is presumptively valid, if the down payment is reasonable in amount . . . when as in this case, the evidence establishes that it would not 'be impracticable or extremely difficult to fix the actual damages' . . . such a provision may not be enforced as one for liquidated damages."

The court could not have meant what it seemed to say. "Presumptively valid" and "evidence in this case establishes" do not belong in the same sentence. If the validity of a liquidated damages clause under section 1671 depends upon the evidence in the case showing actual damages with little difficulty, then each case must be litigated to determine, through hindsight, whether or not the actual damages can be fixed and how much they

---

5. Many footnotes have been omitted.

are.⁶ And regardless of the final result the parties have had to litigate actual damages, the avoidance of which, presumably, was a major reason for using a liquidated damages clause in the first place. Under a pessimistic reading of *Freedman*, either the court means damages "in this case" are not extremely difficult to fix *because* the vendor *subsequently* sold at a profit or it means that the damages are never "extremely difficult" in a deposit receipt land contract case because Civil Code section 3307 provides a ready measure of damages. Either alternative leads to the same result. Even without a subsequent resale the parties could, with or without expert testimony, prove the value on the date of the breach and thus no case would be within section 1671. So never, except in the case where actual damage roughly equates the liquidated damages as shown by subsequent events, could there be a good liquidated damages clause — but then it is really a judgment for actual damages anyway, the parties having had to show damages rather than their anticipated difficulty in proving them.

But to look back at the time of trial and consider whether or not it turned out to be too difficult to ascertain damages in light of what happened at and after the breach is not what section 1671 contemplates. The usual approach is to consider whether, at the time the contract was made, it appeared that damages would later be difficult to ascertain,³⁸ and this [*ex ante*] limits the evidence to whether or not it would so appear to the parties at the time of the contract, regardless of how it appears in view of subsequent developments. Surprisingly, though, the California Supreme Court has gone even further than the traditional approach in finding prospective impracticality. In two cases,³⁹ both of which were filed February 6, 1953, and neither of which mentioned *Freedman*, the supreme court enforced the liquidated damages clause because it appeared that at the time of the contract it would not have been practicable or reasonably possible to fix the *probable* damage resulting from breach. Thus, section 1671 was interpreted not only to require the court to look at the situation in light of the facts known at the time of the contract, but also to look only to the difficulty or impracticality of predicting an actual amount of damages at that time rather than to the then apparent difficulty the parties could expect in ascertaining actual damages after the event. In both cases moreover the

---

6. Compare 1 Restatement of Contracts §339, quoted in Kraft v. Michael, page 476 supra, and Comment e of the Restaters, which declares: "If the parties honestly but mistakenly suppose that a breach will cause harm that will be incapable or very difficult of accurate estimation, when, in fact the breach causes no harm at all or none that is incapable of accurate estimation without difficulty, their advance agreement . . . is not enforceable." —Eds.

38. See, e.g., 5 Corbin, Contracts §1060 at 294 (1951); Dunbar, Drafting the Liquidated Damage Clause — When and How, 20 Ohio St. L.J. 221 (1960); 3 Williston, Contracts §683 at 2201 (2d ed. 1936); Comment, 5 Stan. L. Rev. 822 (1953); Note, 27 So. Cal. L. Rev. 209 (1954).

39. Atkinson v. Pacific Fire Extinguisher Co., 40 Cal. 2d 192, 253 P.2d 18 (1953); Better Food Markets, Inc. v. American Dist. Tel. Co., 40 Cal. 2d 179, 253 P.2d 10 (1953).

actual damages were probably a definite amount and easily ascertainable.[40]

This approach would sustain a liquidated damages clause in practically every case, at least with respect to section 1671 requirements, because rarely will the parties know with any certainty just what damages a breach will entail, market condition, time of breach, other commitments of the parties, and so forth, being infinitely variable. Possibly the court was concerned with the requirement that the amount of liquidated damage be a reasonable estimate by the parties of actual damages and read this requirement into section 1671's test. But even if the court backs off somewhat and holds that section 1671 really relates to apparent impracticality in later fixing actual damages rather than in impracticality in prospectively predicting the amount of actual damages, the clear holding that "the court should place itself in the position of the parties at the time the contract was made . . ." indicates that the court had something else in mind with its earlier *Freedman* approach. " 'It is the look forward, and not backward, that we are called upon to take.' This rule is too well settled to admit of further discussion."

Still, the vendor in *Freedman* had to return part of the deposit.

2. *Need for a Workable Clause.* But if the defendant in *Freedman* resold at a profit anyway, why worry about his extra "pound of flesh"?[42] Putting "people" back into the picture helps to answer the question and perhaps helps to demonstrate that the court chose an earnest money case to correct an abuse under a security instrument.

Let us use *Freedman's* figures and supply what could often be the background facts, not *Freedman's* facts, but not uncommon facts either. By August 1, the seller, let's call him Shylock — the court does[43] — has had his house shown by various members of a multiple listing service at $24,500. He had previously turned down an offer of $22,000, but upon the August 1 expiration of the broker's listing he was offering the house at $23,000, there no longer being a commission involved. He was selling because he

---

40. Caveat: These cases, factually, involved a disclaimer or limitation of liability, but they were treated as though they involved a liquidated damages clause and the opinions are solely liquidated damage opinions.

42. "Although the law will not assist in the vivisection of the victim, it will often permit the creditor to keep his pound of flesh if he can carve it for himself." Freedman v. The Rector, 37 Cal. 2d 16, 21, 230 P.2d 629, 632 (1951), quoting from Ballantine, Forfeiture for Breach of Contract, 5 Minn. L. Rev. 329, 341 (1921). Notice, incidentally, that even this statement, as shown by its reference to debtor and creditor rather than to buyer and seller related to the parties to the security contract, not the earnest money contract.

43. The court in *Freedman* called the creditor a vivisectionist, supra note 42, and referred to the law as Pontius Pilate (washing its hands of the whole affair) in an earlier part of its quote from Ballantine. It is Ballantine, supra note 42, who calls him Shylock, 5 Minn. L. Rev. 329, 347 (1921). Calling the law Pontius Pilate suggests names for the debtor and creditor but they seem quite inappropriate, so I chose to take the rest of Ballantine, call the creditor "Shylock," and pin this on the court, too — it is in the same vein. Clearly, however, this is an unfair inference from the court's use of the quote. The use of "Shylock" is, admittedly, exaggerating the court's position.

The Buyer Fails to Close

had taken a job in Florida; he had to be there by September 1 and it was important to him to move his family and get his children started in school. He already had earnest money on a house in Florida. It was an excellent buy, but his purchase contract was contingent upon selling his California house by September 1, so monetary loss in the out-of-pocket sense was not involved.

Against this background, a buyer — call him DeFault to distinguish him from a later buyer — offered him $18,000 on a deposit receipt contract dated August 1. Shylock countered; DeFault sat tight at $18,000 but finally agreed to raise his deposit from his initial $500 to $2,000 and to remove a financing contingency upon Shylock's insistence that if DeFault should back out, Shylock should have something to cover his loss on the realistic leisurely sale value. Closing was set for August 29 and time was made of the essence.

On August 15 DeFault's wife saw the house for the first time and did not care if it was a steal, she simply would not live there. So DeFault defaulted and demanded his money back. Shylock could have sued for specific performance, but this contract was attractive to him only if he could have closed in time to complete his Florida purchase by September 1. The same time factor coupled with the fact that he would not have had any damages under Civil Code section 3307 anyway, the property being worth more than the contract price at the time of breach, was the answer to an action for damages.

Shylock was "stuck." He had lost his Florida bargain, he and his family could not move together, his children had to change schools in the middle of the year, and all he had to show for it was DeFault's $2,000 — so far. Without the time factor pressing him, Shylock went back on the market at a realistic $23,500, listing again with a broker. On August 25 the broker brought him an offer for $21,200, leaving $20,000 net to Shylock after commission. He accepted, the deal was closed on September 30, and DeFault sued for restitution.

DeFault, according to *Freedman*, has the burden of proving that Shylock's damages are less than the amount retained. That's easy. He can show the contract price and the higher resale within a short time. His realtor would testify that the property was worth more than $18,000 at the time of breach and Shylock would admit the same fact on cross-examination. He can also bring out that Shylock had no commission to pay and that there were no expenses connected with the sale. He would have shown thereby the facts of *Freedman*.

Then it would be Shylock's turn. He could try to explain about the children in school, the difficulties involved in finding a new house in Florida, that the house he finally bought in Florida was not as good but cost a lot more, and that his low price to DeFault was a "hurry" price. But will the courts listen, or are they inclined to say — "Talk about money, Shylock — what did you lose?"

Suppose the court would be sufficiently impressed with the possibility that loss of the Florida bargain was a forseeable consequential loss to let Shylock really show how good it was — where is the real burden of proof? Shylock could bring in a Florida expert or two to talk about value, but there is only $2,000 at stake and experts are just more than he can afford.

Finally, Shylock might try to say something to the effect that these were the very things DeFault and he had in mind when they considered the amount of the "forfeiture." But he cannot dispute that the evidence in his case shows that damages "would not be 'impracticable or extremely difficult to fix. . . .'" And, undoubtedly, if "damages" mean actual damages, and if "evidence in this case" means the clause should be considered in retrospect, they are not.

Admittedly, one will not find Shylock's facts often in the cases. But the reason is not that some variation is not typical, but instead that these facts are generally irrelevant. Time makes it worth minus X dollars to sell for reasons legally irrelevant but extremely relevant to the parties at the time the contract is made. Penalties and forfeitures are prohibited because they are unconscionable. But if the law is going to interfere with the freedom to contract for liquidated damages (or even a forfeiture in the dollar sense) based upon the justice of the thing, it must at least decide where justice is by considering all of the factors of the equation. One can argue that damages of any kind based upon Shylock's evidence would be compensating for "pain and suffering" resulting from breach of a contract. And perhaps it is. The parties made a contract using a "forfeiture" clause with that in mind. If the courts say they cannot use it, then do they have to say they will look at the factors that impelled its use in deciding whether or not it is unconscionable? Perhaps money must be the only common denominator and certainly it must be the only manner of expressing damages. But this brings us right back to *Freedman* — is it really true that it is not difficult or impractical to measure damages in a typical deposit receipt case regardless of resale appearances?

Considering only the dollar amounts, it is easy to detect a penalty. But there are reasons for overlooking dollars and supporting the parties' use of the liquidated damages clause. Shylock's unprovable loss is only part of it. Avoiding the expense of trial, avoiding the expense of expert witnesses to prove value, taking away the club of a litigious vendee who knows that his threatened lawsuit is potentially dangerous enough to "nuisance out" a settlement,[45] saving the developer from depressing the value of the rest of his tract by proving resale at a loss to be resale at true value[46] — these, too, have some bearing on the problem.

---

45. Litigation of the occasional abuse where the amount chosen is, prospectively, far in excess of any reasonable expectation of damages is a far different matter than potential litigation over every deposit simply because the value of the property has not dropped.

46. This reason seems to have motivated a New York legislative commission in recommending a percentage liquidated damage clause. See Note, 52 Harv. L. Rev. 129 (1938).

Granting that the defaulting vendee should be allowed to test whether or not the amount involved is so disproportionate to the amount that could reasonably have been expected by the parties to be potential damage that it qualifies as a penalty, the desirability of a workable clause demonstrates that the issue should be put back in the "prospective" context so that the liquidated damages clause is in fact, as the *Freedman* court said, "presumptively valid."

3. *Around Freedman.* Assuming the desirability of a liquidated damages clause in the marketing contract, the problem of avoiding *Freedman* apparently remains. But the problem is only apparent, not real. *Freedman's* liquidated damages language was dicta[48]—but of greater importance, it was dicta aimed at the installment contract and the court simply did not intend to comment upon liquidated damages under a deposit receipt or earnest money contract.

All of *Freedman's* arguments are installment arguments; the abuses it seeks to avoid are security device abuses; its authorities are security device authorities; it was, in short, an installment land contract case with deposit receipt facts. This, perhaps, explains *Freedman's* definition of "unjust enrichment" to the vendor and "penalty" to the vendee, i.e., any amount in excess of the vendor's actual damage. This, too, is the installment device argument.

To have an enforceable liquidated damages clause, the proponent must show that at the time of making the contract it appeared to be impractical or extremely difficult to fix actual damages and he must show that the amount selected bears some reasonable relation to probable actual loss. The second ingredient, however, is not a matter of looking back to see what the damages actually were, but is instead a matter of determining whether or not the parties adopted a reasonable formula for selecting, or otherwise made a reasonable attempt to select, an amount. If the formula or approach is proper, the court should not compare the amount selected with actual damage; but if the method used by the parties does not represent a legitimate attempt to anticipate probable actual loss, the court should look to the amounts involved to determine the penalty question.

There seems little question that the usual installment contract formula, forfeiture of all payments made, simply is not an adequate attempt by the parties to forecast something akin to possible damages. So in the installment cases, the first step, determination of whether or not the parties have used a reasonable method of determining amount, need not even be considered in the usual (forfeiture of payments) case and the court is justified

---

48. The deposit receipt in *Freedman* did not make liquidated damages the sole *money* remedy of the seller. Thus the clause was not a true liquidated damages clause and the discussion of liquidated damages was totally unnecessary. See, e.g., McCarthy v. Tally, 46 Cal. 2d 577, 297 P.2d 981 (1956); Atkinson v. Pacific Fire Extinguisher Co., 40 Cal. 2d 192, 253 P.2d 18 (1953); Better Food Markets, Inc. v. American Dist. Tel. Co., 40 Cal. 2d 179, 253 P.2d 10 (1953).

in looking immediately to the penalty question in deciding the case based upon actual damages. This was the *Freedman* approach, and this is why the *Freedman* approach is the installment contract approach; it omits the first step, as it should in most installment contract cases, viz., it omits the initial determination of reasonableness.

Since a California court may enforce a liquidated damages clause in a marketing contract, the court's approach presumably will be to treat each part of the question in its proper order. Thus the court should first decide whether at the time the contract was made the parties were justified in thinking damages might be impracticable or difficult to ascertain. If it should appear that they were, the issue no longer is whether the vendor is getting more than actual damages but only whether or not at the time of the contract the parties chose an amount, or a formula likely to lead to an amount, that represented a reasonable endeavor to estimate fair compensation for any loss that might be sustained. . . .

4. *The Clause.* At the contract drafting stage there are several things that could be done to improve the vendor's position under the clause. There are, perhaps, more devices which can substantially impair it. The suggestion was once made, for example, that an express waiver of Civil Code section 3275 might be enforceable. Overlooking issues such as whether or not section 3275 is a matter of public policy, the short answer is that the court has consistently refused to enforce an agreement suggesting a forfeiture and an express waiver adds nothing to an express agreement. And, of course, the liquidated damages-forfeiture problem now has gone far beyond the nonwillful plaintiff of section 3275.

Another common approach which seems more detrimental than beneficial is to phrase the contract in terms of an option and thus avoid the liquidated damages clause. If the suggestion contemplates a bona fide change in the customary real estate marketing structure so that a prospective residential purchaser would actually purchase an option pending determination of marketability of title, termite inspection, financing possibilities, and so forth, it would probably avoid the forfeiture problem. But how much would the average purchaser pay for a bond fide option? Assuming he actually purchases an option and has received full value even though his decision not to exercise it was based upon failure of one of the normal contingencies, it is difficult to imagine he will be willing to pay much for it. Even if the option is made contingent upon these things, and the buyer's problem solved, it would be surprising to find the normal residential seller willing to take his property off the market for long on the strength of an option rather than a binding agreement to purchase. And it seems unlikely that realtors would encourage a marketing device that generally would produce a lower fund out of which the realtor could claim his commission if the sale were not closed.

If, on the other hand, the buyer is liable for damages upon his refusal to perform except for items expressly made contingent, the agreement is no

The Buyer Fails to Close

longer an option, but is again the same old deposit receipt or earnest money contract dressed up in different language. If the option suggestion contemplates that the deposit receipt be made to look like an option when in fact it is not, the result of litigating it seems obvious. Thus, it is surprising to find a watered down form of this suggestion in the California Real Estate Association standard form "deposit receipt." The "forfeiture" clause of the form reads: "If Buyer fails to pay the balance of said purchase price, or to complete said purchase as herein provided, the amounts paid hereon may be retained by Seller at his option as consideration for the execution of this agreement by Seller." But usually the buyer does not pay the seller an amount as consideration for the execution of the agreement; he makes a down payment on the property in question, and to the extent the seller keeps it, he keeps it as a forfeiture[61] and not as consideration for the execution of the agreement.

Taken literally, the Real Estate Association form with its pseudo option requires the buyer to forfeit his deposit "as consideration" for the agreement even if the sale is not closed because of the failure of an express contingency.[62] It was inevitable, perhaps, that someone would try to take it literally and keep the deposit when the failure of an express contingency prevented the closing. The supreme court, of course, recognized that the consideration for the bilateral agreement was the mutual promises of the parties and that the deposit was part performance of the buyer's obligation, not consideration for the right to disapprove the contingencies.[63]

The option clause in the standard form is unlikely to excite judicial sympathy for other reasons, the major one being its total ambiguity in the hands of those dealing with it. It provides that the seller can, at his option, keep the deposit. Does this mean his option is to keep it or to return it, as many buyers apparently believe,[64] or are led to believe,[65] or does it mean that the seller's option is to keep it or to elect to sue for actual damages, keeping the deposit only as a setoff against actual damages? The court has given it the latter interpretation, as it should,[66] but seemingly this intended result was sufficiently hidden by the draftsman so that only the astute buyer could recognize it.

If the seller were willing to limit himself to liquidated damages the court

---

61. This would not be liquidated damages because the provision under which payments were retained does not include the requirements for a liquidated damage clause. While there are cases under which the court has allowed retention as "consideration for the execution of the agreement" they are lease cases and the consideration seems to be for holding the property off the rental market. Since it is time that is for sale under a proposed rental, the lease result probably would not affect the result of a case involving sale (rather than sale of its use) of the property.

62. Other than marketability of title which is treated differently within the form itself.

63. Rodriguez v. Barnett, 52 Cal. 2d 154, 338 P.2d 907 (1959).

64. Cf., e.g., Royer v. Carter, 37 Cal. 2d 544, 233 P.2d 539 (1951).

65. Cf., e.g., Fleischer v. Cosgrove, 145 Cal. App. 2d 14, 301 P.2d 911 (1956).

66. Royer v. Carter, supra note 64.

probably would enforce the provision in most cases. An enforceable liquidated damages clause should be binding upon the parties and should be the limit of money damages; it should be a true liquidation of damages. Assuming that in most residential sale cases the seller would be willing to retain the deposit and to forego other remedies, and assuming that in most cases the buyer expects to lose his deposit if he willfully breaches, making liquidated damages the exclusively *money* remedy would usually be in accord with the expectation of the parties and certainly is a sine qua non of an enforceable clause. This does not mean, however, that the agreement must be an option. The contract would remain specifically enforceable, but if the seller prefers money damages he would be limited to or, for that matter, enriched by, the deposit or earnest money upon which the parties have agreed.

Even a printed standard form could satisfy these requirements, assuming, of course, as would necessarily be the case, that the amount is a matter left open to be individually considered in each contract. Agreeing on the amount creates no new problems for the realtor or seller since present practice often includes some give and take on the amount of the deposit, and retention is generally within the contemplation of the parties. It seems then that if the form unambiguously so provided and gave the typical reasons for the use of the clause, the court would have little difficulty sustaining it. This probably was what the court meant in *Freedman* when it said the clause is "presumptively valid." Evasive devices simply will not get past the court; perhaps the draftsmen should, instead, be candid.

[Handwritten margin note: Seller's consequential damages reduced if he subsequently sells for higher price, Buyer gets credit]

Smith v. Mady
146 Cal. App. 3d 129, 194 Cal. Rptr. 42 (1983)

[Handwritten margin note: JB for Π revised]

SCHAUER, Presiding Justice. Defendants, who were defaulting purchasers under an agreement to buy real property from plaintiff sellers, appeal from a judgment after a non-jury trial. On appeal the question presented is whether a defaulting buyer of realty is entitled to credit, against consequential damages charged to buyer, an increased price obtained by the seller upon a quick resale.

The essential facts are not in dispute. In September of 1980, plaintiffs and defendants entered into a written agreement by which defendants were to purchase respondent plaintiffs' residence for a purchase price of $205,000. The sales escrow was to close in early December of 1980. However, defendants defaulted and the sale did not take place. On December 7, 1980, within a few days after the expected close of escrow and breach by defendants, plaintiffs entered into another contract to sell the property to third parties. Under this second sales agreement, the purchase price was $215,000. The second sale proceeded to close in February of 1981.

The instant lawsuit was commenced on December 5, 1980, for breach of the first sales contract. Upon trial the court recognized that there were no "benefit-of-the bargain" damages under Civil Code section 3307[1] since the purchase price in the rapid resale established that the value of the property at the time of the breach was in excess of the contract price of the earlier sale. However, the trial court found consequential damages under Civil Code section 3300,[2] suffered by sellers for costs of insurance, gardening, property taxes, utilities and encumbrance interest payments incurred between the default and the subsequent sale. The trial judge declined to offset the consequential damages with the increased resale proceeds, remarking upon the separate character of the resale transaction in comparison with the sale to defendants which gave rise to the breach. A judgment for plaintiffs in the sum of $2,648.34[3] was entered and this appeal followed.

The sole issue is whether a defaulting purchaser of real property is entitled to credit, against damages from his default, the increase in proceeds of a subsequent, but rapid, resale at a higher price. We resolve the issue in the affirmative and reverse.

Under the provisions of Civil Code, section 3307, "The detriment caused by the breach of an agreement to purchase an estate in real property, is deemed to be the excess, if any, of the amount which would have been due to the seller, under the contract, over the value of the property to him." But the view that this section is exclusive, and precludes other consequential damages occasioned by the breach, was rejected in Royer v. Carter (1951) 37 Cal. 2d 544, 550 [233 P.2d 539]. Under Civil Code, section 3300, other damages are recoverable, usually embracing the out-of-pocket expenses lost by failure of the transaction. (Wade v. Lake County Title Co. (1970) 6 Cal. App. 3d 824 at p. 830, 86 Cal. Rptr. 182.)

The Supreme Court in *Royer* (at p. 550 [233 P.2d 539]) stated that: ". . . the vendee's breach may make it necessary for the vendor to incur *additional expenses* to realize the benefit of his bargain . . . [and] [w]hen such *additional expenses* are the natural consequence of the breach, they may be recovered in addition to those provided for in section 3307." (Italics added.) The *Royer* opinion deals specifically with the expenses which the

---

1. Civ. Code, §3307 provides: "The detriment caused by the breach of an agreement to purchase an estate in real property, is deemed to be the excess, if any, of the amount which would have been due to the seller, under the contract, over the value of the property to him."

2. Civ. Code, §3300 provides: "For the breach of an obligation arising from contract, the measure of damages, except where otherwise expressly provided by this Code, is the amount which will compensate the party aggrieved for all the detriment proximately caused thereby, or which, in the ordinary course of things, would be likely to result therefrom."

3. The sales contract between plaintiffs and defendants provided for reasonable attorneys' fees for the prevailing party in litigation arising out of the agreement, and the trial court awarded plaintiffs such fees in the sum of $750, in addition to the $2,648.34. Since plaintiffs are not prevailing parties in view of the reversal on this appeal, the award of attorneys' fees for trial and appeal services is left to the trial court on the remand. (Schoolcraft v. Ross (1978) 81 Cal. App. 3d 75, 82, 146 Cal. Rptr. 57.)

innocent vendor would incur in a second sale. More recent cases have shed further light on the scope of "additional expenses" which *Royer* sanctioned.

In Allen v. Enomoto, 228 Cal. App. 2d 798, 803-805 [39 Cal. Rptr. 815], the court allowed the vendor's out-of-pocket expenses for fire insurance, mortgage interest and real property taxes on the subject property. The award was premised on a finding that the vendor had continued diligently to attempt to resell the subject property and that the resale was made within the shortest period of time possible. The unspoken premise of such a holding is that the vendor (who still wishes to sell the property) actually has had to pay out-of-pocket expenses proximately caused by the vendee's breach. (Abrams v. Motter (1970) 3 Cal. App. 3d 828 at pp. 849-850, 83 Cal. Rptr. 855, footnote omitted.)

In both *Abrams* and Sutter v. Madrin (1969) 269 Cal. App. 2d 161, 74 Cal. Rptr. 627, it was recognized that ". . . resale . . . should be made with reasonable diligence to qualify the vendor to an allowance . . ." (id. at p. 169, 74 Cal. Rptr. 627) for consequential damages incurred after the breach. Additionally, both cases acknowledged that a vendor's continued ownership after a purchaser's default may have a "use" value which should be offset against expenses of the continuing ownership. (Id. at p. 168, 74 Cal. Rptr. 627; Abrams v. Motter, supra, 3 Cal. App. 3d at p. 850, 83 Cal. Rptr. 855.)

The facts in *Sutter* differ somewhat from the instant case in that the *Sutter* defaulting purchaser was seeking restitution of a portion of his deposit under the real estate sales contract. However, we find the fundamentals reviewed in *Sutter* to be equally applicable here. Also pertinent is ". . . the line of cases beginning with Freedman v. Rector etc. of St. Matthias Parish, 37 Cal. 2d 16 [230 P.2d 629, 31 A.L.R.2d 1], which have allowed recovery to a defaulting vendee in order to prevent the vendor from being unjustly enriched as a result of the vendee's default, even where the default has been wilful. [Citations omitted.] As indicated by these cases the underlying purpose of the *Freedman* doctrine is to prevent the unjust enrichment of the seller at the expense of the buyer by requiring the former to refund to the latter payments made under the contract in excess of damages suffered by the seller." (Branche v. Hetzel (1966) 241 Cal. App. 2d 801 at p. 807, 51 Cal. Rptr. 188.)

The principle we draw from the precedents is that a vendor of real property is not to be ". . . placed in a better position by the buyer's default. This result is directly prohibited by section 3358 of the Civil Code."[4] [Citations omitted.]

Although it is well settled in the foregoing authorities that damages under Civil Code section 3307 for the difference between the contract

---

4. Civ. Code, §3358 provides: "Except as expressly provided by statute, no person can recover a greater amount in damages for the breach of an obligation, than he could have gained by the full performance thereof on both sides."

price and property value may be insufficient to give the vendor the benefit of his bargain and he is entitled also to resale expenses and some costs of continued ownership, he <u>should not be permitted to receive a windfall at the purchaser's expense.</u> We discern no reason to deprive the defaulting purchaser of benefitting from a higher price on resale after continued ownership by seller while crediting the purchaser, as required under *Abrams* and *Sutter,* with the value of use to the seller during continued ownership.

In cases where the resale at a higher price occurs at a time much more distant from the breach than here, the vendor may show a lower property value at the moment of breach as well as increased costs of continuing ownership. However, in the case at bench the resale took place within a few days after the breach and established the value of the property at the time of breach. Realistically, the vendors here had sold their property to defendants at a price lower than the then value of the real estate. Sellers argue that the damages awarded only place them in the same position they would have been in had the defendants performed the contract, but a sufficient response is that had defendants performed plaintiffs would be in a worse position. By the resale sellers have obtained a $10,000 increment which is more than sufficient to absorb the $2,648.34 in increased costs of continuing ownership.

Inasmuch as under *Abrams* and *Sutter* the vendor has an obligation to resell promptly in order to obtain consequential damages and the resale price may fix the property value as a basis for Civil Code section 3307 damages, we are impelled to conclude that there is no inherent separateness in the original sale and subsequent resale transactions. The increased resale price should not be disregarded in considering an offset to consequential damages awarded to a vendor against a defaulting purchaser of real property.

The judgment is reversed and the cause remanded.

Johnson and Paez, JJ., concur.

NOTES AND QUESTIONS

1. In the light of California's reluctance to allow the vendor to "profit" from the vendee's breach, can you think of circumstances where, after the fact, a court might validate a liquidated damages clause, even though the resale price exceeded the contract price? Should the validity of a liquidated damages clause ever depend upon conditions at the time of breach, rather than upon the foreseeability of such conditions from the parties' vantage at the time of contract formation? In that vein, why should the parties ever believe beforehand that it would be "impracticable" to fix damages should the buyer breach?

2. If there is weight of authority, the Pennsylvania decision of Kraft v.

4. Rescission

a. Time and the Essence

Kasten Construction Co. v. Maple Ridge Construction Co.

245 Md. 373, 226 A.2d 341 (1967)

HORNEY, Judge. The question presented by this appeal is whether the Maple Ridge Construction Company (Maple Ridge), as buyer, is entitled to require the Kasten Construction Company (Kasten), as seller, to specifically perform a contract in which settlement for the sale for certain building lots was to have been made in sixty days but the time was not stipulated as being of the essence.

The contract of sale, dated December 4, 1964, provided for the sale and purchase of a tract of land in Section 4 of the Maple Ridge Subdivision in Anne Arundel County consisting of thirty-four "finished" lots designated as 20-A and 20-B through 36-A and 36-B. The contract further provided that Maple Ridge was to have an option to purchase ninety-four other lots in the subdivision within twelve months from the date of the contract of sale and was given the first refusal to purchase approximately five hundred of the remaining lots in Sections 3 and 4. Subsequently, when financing difficulties were encountered, the settlement date was extended in writing to on or before March 19, 1965, but again time was not stated to be of the essence. Maple Ridge had requested a longer extension, but it was refused by Kasten and later requests for extensions were also refused.

Although Kasten in the interim between the making of the contract of sale and the extended settlement date had bulldozed several of the streets or roads and stabilized them with gravel, it had made little progress toward providing Maple Ridge with the finished or completed lots it needed to begin constructing homes. No agreement had been made between Kasten and the County with respect to street and drainage easements and there had been delays in connection with the construction of the curbs and gutters and the installation of public utilities. And while a proposed agreement and bond was completed by the County department of public works on March 3, 1965 and delivered to Kasten promptly, it was never executed and returned. Moreover, although Kasten recorded a deed of "covenants, restrictions and conditions" purporting to cover Sections 3 and 4 of Maple

Ridge, which it was agreed was required before the houses to be thereafter constructed would be eligible for FHA financing, Maple Ridge was never consulted or afforded an opportunity to participate in formulating the specifications contained in the restrictions. Maple Ridge, however, in addition to engaging an architect to prepare plans for houses to be constructed in the development and the renting of a trailer to be used on location as an office at a total outlay of $12,000, had continued trying to obtain the type of financing it hoped to get before the extended settlement date expired without having to use such of the personal funds of its president as were available to the corporation. In the meantime the settlement date came and went and neither party made a demand on the other. But when Maple Ridge notified Kasten five days after the expiration of the extension that it had applied for a title examination and it would take about three weeks to complete it, Kasten in turn notified Maple Ridge that the contract of sale had expired, as had the extension, and that it considered the contract null and void and no longer in force. Subsequent negotiations were unsuccessful and this suit for specific performance was brought.

On the evidence and the exhibits produced at the hearing, the chancellor, having found that although the buyer was dilatory in making the necessary financial arrangements and in applying for a title examination, it had tendered full performance of the terms of the contract within a reasonable time after the expiration of the extended settlement date; that the seller, besides acting as if time was not of the essence, had been somewhat lackadaisical in the performance of its part of the contract; and that the seller had suffered no loss that could not be compensated by the payment of interest, decreed specific performance of the contract of sale.

On appeal, Kasten, claiming that the chancellor erred in decreeing specific performance, contends that its refusal to grant further extensions was clear indication that time was of the essence and should therefore have been inferred from the circumstances. Maple Ridge, however, claiming that a specified date for settlement did not mean that the parties intended time to be of the essence, contends that it was not and that the delay in making settlement was reasonable under the circumstances.

In a case involving specific performance, where the intention of the parties is always the controlling factor, the general rule is that time is not of the essence of the contract of sale and purchase of land unless a contrary purpose is disclosed by its terms or is indicated by the circumstances and object of its execution and the conduct of the parties. Of course, one may lose his right to specific performance by gross laches and unreasonable delay in paying the purchase money. Ordinarily, however, time is held to be of the essence only when it is clear that the parties have expressly so stipulated or their intention is inferable from the circumstances of the transaction, the conduct of the parties or the purpose for which the sale was made. . . . Applying these tests to the facts of this case, we think the chancellor was correct in decreeing that Maple Ridge was entitled to specific performance. Under the circumstances, it was not necessary to regard the stipulation fixing the original and extended times for payment of the purchase price as imposing a condition requiring strict and punctual compliance in order to entitle the buyer to specific performance. . . . Nor, even though the buyer was somewhat neglectful in not paying the balance of the purchase money on the day it was due, can it be said that the delay, particularly in view of the fact that the seller was in no hurry to perform its part of the contract, was unreasonable. . . . In any event, the buyer was required to compensate the seller for whatever loss it sustained by the payment of interest. Moreover, the mere fixing of a particular date for the completion of a contract for the sale and purchase of land is not regarded as being of the essence with respect to payment but treats the provision as formal rather than essential.

Although the seller relies principally on Stern v. Shapiro, 38 Md. 615, 114 A. 587 (1921), Doering v. Fields, 187 Md. 484, 50 A.2d 553 (1947), and Levy v. Baetjer, 198 Md. 240, 81 A.2d 644 (1951), to support the claim that the chancellor erred in granting specific performance, all of these cases are distinguishable on the facts from the case at bar. In *Stern*, the provision that the down payment was to be forfeited in the event settlement was not made within the time specified, warranted the inference that time was of the essence. Here, a forfeiture was neither provided nor contemplated. In *Doering*, the buyers not only made no effort to settle within the agreed time, but despite an extension were still unable to pay the balance of the purchase money at the expiration of the extended period. Here, although the extended time had expired, the president of the corporate buyer had tendered full performance within a reasonable time thereafter. In *Levy*, the express provision that time was of the essence was held not to have been waived by the extension of the settlement date. Here, the very absence of the essentialness of time without more distinguishes that case from this.

The further claim that the presence of a stipulated settlement date in the contract of sale impels an inference that time was to be of the essence is likewise without merit. In Soehnlein v. Pumphrey, it was said (at p. 338 of 183 Md., at p. 845 of 37 A.2d): "The accepted doctrine is that in the ordinary case of contract for the sale of land, even though a certain period of time is stipulated for its consummation, equity treats the provision as formal rather than essential, and permits the purchaser who has suffered the period to elapse to make payments after the prescribed date, and to compel performance by the vendor notwithstanding the delay, unless it appears that time is of the essence of the contract by express stipulation, or by inference from the conduct of the parties, the special purpose for which the sale was made, or other circumstances surrounding the sale.". . . When there has been a delay, as there was in this case, the important question is whether it was reasonable. The chancellor found that it was and we cannot say that he erred in so doing.

Decree affirmed; appellants to pay the costs.

Doering v. Fields
187 Md. 484, 50 A.2d 553 (1947)

MARBURY, Chief Judge. Appellees brought this complaint in the Circuit Court of Baltimore City to obtain specific performance of a contract for the sale to them of leasehold property, 4313 Glenmore Avenue in Baltimore City. The chancellor granted them a decree, and it is from that decree that this appeal is taken.

On August 31, 1945, the appellants and the appellees entered into an agreement by which the appellants sold and the appellees purchased the property, subject to a $90 ground rent, at the price of $7500, "of which $500 have been paid prior to the signing hereof and the balance to be paid as follows; cash within 45 days from date of contract." The contract was on a printed form which contained the words "time is of the essence of this contract." These words were erased. At the end of the 45-day period, not having received any word at all from the appellees, the appellants consulted their attorney. He sent a letter to the appellees advising them that he represented the appellants and notifying them that unless settlement was made within ten days from date, the contract would be declared off and the deposit forfeited as liquidated damages for its breach. This letter was dated October 17, 1945, was mailed in Baltimore, October 18th, and was received on October 20th by the appellees. Upon receipt of this letter the appellees went to see the real estate agent through whom they had been brought in touch with the appellants, and on October 22, 1945, made an application to a building association, to which they were directed by the real estate office, for a loan of $6000 on the Glenmore Avenue property. This loan which would net $5700 was approved by the building association on October 29th. This fact was communicated to the appellants' attorney, but as the ten days had expired, appellants declined to convey the property. As a result this suit was brought.

The appellees had a home on Brookwood Avenue which they anticipated selling and applying the proceeds to the purchase of the Glenmore Avenue property. They had listed this property with a real estate agent on August 13th, but it was not sold until November 26th, and when it was sold it was for $1000 less than the amount at which it had been listed. The appellees admitted they were not in any position to carry out their agreement until they had sold the Brookwood house. They had not engaged any lawyer to examine the title to the Glenmore property during the 45-day period, nor did they make any effort to arrange for a loan on the property or in any way to prepare themselves to carry out the agreement. Neither of the appellees had told the appellants that their purchase was dependent on selling their own house. The representative of the real estate company who made the sale said she was told that the Brookwood house had to be sold before the appellees could make payment for the Glenmore house, but there is no evidence that this was communicated to the appellants.

At the time when this contract was made, and during the entire period up to the time the suit was filed, the Court will take judicial notice that there was a severe housing shortage throughout this country and in Baltimore City. Federal agencies and State agencies were trying to arrange some method by which houses could be built, primarily for returning soldiers, but even this was very difficult in view of the shortage of building materials. The City was overcrowded with people who had come there for work or other purposes during the War, rents were frozen by the O.P.A., and as a result a great many people, in order to find a place to live, were buying houses at almost any price. As a result, there was a fluctuating and rising real estate market. Those are facts which must be taken into consideration in the decision of this case. . . .

. . . The rule is well established that while courts will ordinarily decree specific performance of contracts for the sale of real estate, unless there is some reason to the contrary, this is not a matter of right but is a question addressed to the sound discretion of the Court under the circumstances of the particular case.

The complainant must seek relief promptly. . . . In Pomeroy's Equity Jurisprudence, 5th Ed., Vol. 2, paragraph 400, it is stated in a discussion of the maxim that he who seeks equity must do equity, "By virtue of this principle, a specific performance will always be refused . . . when the specific performance would be oppressive upon the defendant, or would prevent the enjoyment of his own rights, or would in any other manner work injustice." The same author in Vol. 4, paragraph 1409, states: "Although time is not ordinarily essential, yet it is, as a general rule, material. In order that a default may not defeat a party's remedy, the delay which occasioned it must be explained and accounted for. The doctrine is fundamental that a party seeking the remedy of specific performance, and also the party who desires to maintain an objection founded upon the other's laches, must show himself to have been 'ready, desirous, prompt, and eager.'" . . .

. . . In each case the Court decides whether it is right and just that a specific performance should be decreed. If the vendee has not unduly delayed, if the vendor is not hurt, then the decree will be granted. But if these elements do not appear, the equity court will decline to interfere and will leave the parties to their legal remedies.

In the case before us the vendors signed a contract to sell their home. That contract was on a form which contained the statement that time was to be of the essence of the contract. The fact that this statement was in fine print would not have destroyed its effect had it been left in the signed agreement. Nor do we think the fact that it was stricken out before execution emphasizes or increases the elastic nature of the period of 45 days inserted. That stands in this contract just as it would have stood had the other statement never been in the printed form. Had the vendor's attention been specially directed to the erasure, and a reason given and accepted for it, the situation might be different. But there is no evidence that this was done, so we consider the contract as if no such clause had ever been in the original form upon which the agreement was superimposed.

The vendors assumed, as they had a right to assume, that the vendees intended to carry out the purchase within the 45 days provided for that purpose. It is true that they are presumed to know that such a period in a contract affecting real estate is relative and is not to be interpreted absolutely literally. It is just as true that it means something. It is not to be totally disregarded. It is an approximation of what the parties regard as a reasonable time under the circumstances of the sale. The vendors, therefore, had a right to expect that the vendees would be ready *about* that time. The vendees, on the other hand, were under an obligation to make the necessary efforts to consummate their purchase within the period they had agreed upon. They could not sit by and do nothing, and then claim a further indefinite period. That would tie the hands of the vendors, perhaps prevent them from finding another home within their means, in a rising real estate market, or, at any rate, keep them from the use of the purchase price they expected to get. In the speculative condition which then obtained in real estate in the City of Baltimore, the payment of interest would not compensate them for the lapse of time.

There is no evidence that the vendors were told that the vendees had to sell their own home before they could carry out their agreement. Certainly, it was no part of the contract itself, and no sensible persons would tie up their property upon such a condition, even in an active real estate market. And it was not true, in fact, because the vendees, when they finally said they were ready to consummate the purchase, were going to finance it through a building association without waiting to sell their own property.

When the 45 days had expired the vendors consulted their attorney, and were told they could not consider the sale terminated unless they gave the vendees notice to that effect. The latter were given such a notice, requiring them to settle in 10 more days. Then for the first time the vendees did something. They applied for a loan, and had one approved after 12 days. Then they advised the attorney for the vendors of this fact, but even then they were not ready. The title had not been searched, the deed and the mortgage still had to be prepared, and more delay would ensue. How much more is purely problematical.

Had the vendees made the slightest effort within the 45 days to carry out the contract, they would be in a different position. Since they sat by, doing nothing at all, the vendors were compelled to wait, at least until the expiration of what might be a reasonable time. But since a time, presumed to be reasonable by all parties was fixed in the contract, they were not obliged to wait indefinitely after that time had expired. Under the circumstances, ten days more was enough. It cannot be reasonable or just for a court to require appellants to be put at such a disadvantage. That is not what is meant by saying that time is not of the essence of a contract for the sale of real estate. It does not mean that one party can rely upon that principle to do nothing and embarrass the other. It means that neither party will be held strictly to the time limited, not that either party will be at liberty to disregard it entirely. The statement of the time limit is not nugatory, because it is not literally construed. "Courts of Equity have regard to time so far as it respects the good faith and diligence of the parties." Story, Eq. Jur., 14th Ed., paragraph 1064.

There is another indication that the appellees were not eager to get the property. They did not take action at once. Their property was sold on November 26th, although it is not clear from the evidence whether that was the date they signed the contract or whether the sale was consummated then. In either event, they waited until January 18, 1946, before bringing their suit, although they knew by November 1st that the appellants intended to consider their contract at an end. This is not the diligent prosecution of their rights expected of parties eager and willing to buy. This delay is entirely unexplained in the testimony.

We do not think the vendees have so conducted themselves as to justify them in asking the Court now to enforce the contract they completely neglected and we do not think the Chancellor was justified in taking such action under the circumstances. For these reasons the decree will be reversed.

Decree reversed and bill dismissed with costs.

NOTES ON TIME AND THE ESSENCE

1. Uniform Land Transactions Act:

§2-302 Time of performance; time of essence
  (a) The time for performance is a reasonable time after the making of the contract and tender must be at a reasonable hour and after reasonable notice to the other party of intention to tender. If the contract does not fix the time for performance, either party may fix a time for performance if the time is not unreasonable and is fixed in good faith.
  (b) Except as provided in subsection (d), even though the contract specifies a particular time for performance, the failure of one of the parties to tender his performance at the specified time does not discharge the other party from his duties under the contract unless:

The Buyer Fails to Close

(1) the failure to perform, under the circumstances, is a material breach, or
(2) the contract explicitly provides that failure to perform at the time specified discharges the duties of the other party.

(c) The phrase "time is of the essence" or other similar general language does not of itself provide explicitly that failure to perform at the time specified discharges the duties of the other party.

(d) If the contract specifies a particular time for performance, either party, by reasonable and good faith notice to the other before that date, may specify effectively that failure to perform on the specified date will discharge him from his own duties under the contract.

(e) If the contract specifies a particular time for performance, and a failure to tender performance at the specified time does not discharge the other party (subsections (b) and (d)):

(1) the time for performance is a reasonable time thereafter; and
(2) the rules of subsection (a) as to time for tender and fixing of time for performance apply. . . .

2. *Forfeiture.* Suppose S sells to B under a contract of sale for $20,000, closing for January 20. B, pursuant to the contract, gives S a $2000 down payment. The contract provides that the $2000 is to be applied toward the price, but in the event of default by the buyer, the seller may retain the $2000 sum as liquidated damages. B is unable to close on January 20, but he tenders $18,000 plus two days interest on $18,000 as full payment on January 22. S refuses to consummate the transaction. B commences a suit for specific performance and tenders the amount as above. If the court decides that in the particular case time is not of the essence and therefore specific performance will be granted to B, could it also decide that B's default lost him the $2000 liquidated damages sum and that he must pay $20,000 — the selling price — if he wants the property?

3. *Buyer tender.* If a buyer sues for specific performance, must he pay the full price into the registry of the court at the time he commences that action?

Consider the practical remarks of Judge Crockett on the validity of an insufficient funds check as a tender. The following is from his concurring opinion in Sieverts v. White, 2 Utah 2d 351, 356, 272 P.2d 974, 997 (1954):

> Though the practice may not be one to be commended, it is not uncommon, in various types of financing of business transactions, to write a check with the expectation of transferring funds or credit from one account to another, or arranging credit with the bank, or depositing money to cover commitments, if and after, a check is accepted. If such a check were refused there would be no practical use of arranging for the money or credit to cover it. This might entail considerable inconvenience, difficulty or even hardship, to

no useful purpose. Serious injustices might result if the offeree in such a transaction could defeat proof of tender simply by showing that the offeror had not sufficient funds in the bank to cover the check at the time it was offered.

The offeree, of course, has a right to reject the tender by check when it is made. This is perfectly proper if he states the ground of his objection, but it is only reasonable that the person making a tender has a right to know the ground of the objection, so that if it be well taken he may protect himself by conforming thereto within the required time. If the offeree has failed to state an objection, or objects on other grounds, it would be manifestly unfair to permit him to defeat proof of tender by check on the sole ground that there were not sufficient funds to cover the check at the time the tender was made, because the offeror may have arranged for payment of the check if it had been accepted. This reasoning is reflected in our statute which requires the person to whom a tender is made to "specify any objection" he has thereto or be "deemed to have waived it."

[margin note: if rejecting tender, must state objection]

4. *Waiver.* The basic A.L.R. annotation on the vendor's waiver of vendee's delay is at 107 A.L.R. 345 (1937). (The annotation is some sixty pages long, but most of the cases covered involve defaults in payments under installment land contracts.) In the waiver cases, a large legal significance is attributed to apparently trivial variations in postdefault behavior. Cf. our discussion of postdefault behavior and measuring damages on resale, page 469 supra.

In Evelyn v. Raven Realty, 215 Md. 467, 138 A.2d 898 (1958), the court held that in order to take advantage of seller's waiver of a time condition, the buyer must be able to show that he could have performed at the essential date.

Waiver gets even more complicated when there is a broker in the transaction whose enthusiasm for a consummated commission-producing deal may exceed the enthusiasm of the party whose rights he is waiving. See, for example, Horan v. Blowitz, 13 Ill. 2d 126, 148 N.E.2d 445 (1958).

5. *Problems of election for the seller in responding to buyer's default.* Certain kinds of buyer default and seller response may bring into play all the uncertainties of the law of anticipatory repudiation, but we will omit this topic. Such default and responses may also involve the law of election of remedies—in respect to substantive rules, not pleading rules. A brief discussion on election follows, authoritative support for which will be found in 5 Corbin, Contracts, c. 66, Election of Remedies, and §§1236-1237, Rescission (1963). This note treats the subject in an elementary fashion; Corbin, of course, does not.

S and B entered a contract for the sale of a house for $60,000, closing for January 4. On January 4, B failed to close. Three months later S sold the premises to X for $55,000. S sues B for damages.

Can B claim that S has elected himself out of the damages remedy? After all, upon the buyer's default, the seller had two distinct remedial choices: he could have enforced the contract—specifically via specific performance or substitutionally via a damage action — or he could have treated it as ended by buyer's breach. It follows that resale of the premises evidences the seller's choice of the second line, which precludes a later change of mind and recovery of damages. Buyers have made this argument, usually without success.

Alternatively, can the buyer, on the facts given, defend by arguing that the contract of sale was terminated by mutual assent? Parties to an executory contract can, of course, agree to cancel the contract. Therefore B might claim that he has indicated his intention to cancel by not closing, and that S, through the resale, has indicated his acquiescence and acceptance of the cancellation. This argument has met with as little success as the first, although there is in fact authority for both. Even if the defense is plausible on its face, seller can respond on two points: (a) If a land transfer contract is required to be in writing under the statute of frauds, the cancellation contract must also be in writing. (b) If buyer's breach terminated his rights under the contract, then seller received no consideration for his promise to cancel. The authorities on these points are split.

Both of buyer's arguments from resale are based on the idea of rescission of the contract. In the first, buyer seeks to charge seller with an *election to rescind* for breach. In the second, buyer charges seller with an *agreement to rescind*. (Corbin, in 5 Contracts §1236 (1963), frowns upon the use of "rescission" in other than the mutual sense.)

How much help is buyer given toward either of his two theories by any or all of the following facts?

(a) There is a question as to whether time was of the essence of the contract.
(b) Upon buyer's failure to close, buyer heard seller remark, "Good. That was a bad deal anyway."
(c) Seller listed the property for resale at a $65,000 price.
(d) Buyer was not informed of the listing for resale.
(e) The only witness to the negotiations which led up to the contract of sale was the real estate broker, who died one month after the closing date.
(f) Buyer had properly recorded the contract of sale, but, after the closing failed, buyer, at the seller's request, executed a release of record.

This discussion may be useful in dealing with the case that follows.

Cohen v. A.F.A. Realty Corp.

250 N.Y. 262, 165 N.E. 285 (1929)

PER CURIAM. In an action by the vendor for the specific performance of a contract for the sale of real estate, the Trial Term dismissed plaintiff's complaint and granted judgment on the counterclaim of defendant A.F.A. Realty Corporation for the return of the down payments on the purchase price. The Appellate Division reversed, ordered judgment for specific performance, and dismissed the defendant's counterclaim.

An appeal was then taken to this court. After the entry of judgment on the order of the Appellate Division, the plaintiff-respondent conveyed the premises in question to a third party. He so states in his brief, and the appellant consents that the statement be received as a part of the record. He also seeks on this appeal to abandon his claim for specific performance of the contract, asks that the action therefor be discontinued without costs, and the judgment, so far as it affects appellant's counterclaim, be affirmed.

The question is whether the plaintiff, having put it out of his power to carry out the judgment, may retain the money paid on account of the purchase. If these facts had appeared on the trial, the complaint would have been dismissed, and defendant A.F.A. Realty Corporation would have had judgment on its counterclaim. Plaintiff, instead of curing his title of technical legal defaults, would have made it worse. Inability to perform on his part would have defeated recovery. The same rule should apply when he conveys after obtaining judgment. The plaintiff should not be permitted to convey the land and still retain the payment of the purchase money. When the action is to enforce a contract which the vendor has put it out of his power to perform, the vendee cannot be subjected to damages for not receiving that which the vendor could not convey. Bigler v. Morgan, 77 N.Y. 312, 319. Cf. Bloomgarden v. Hoffmann, 116 App. Div. 719, 102 N.Y.S. 20. . . .

The judgment of the Appellate Division should be reversed, and judgment ordered against plaintiff in favor of defendant A.F.A. Realty Corporation for the sum of $8,000, with interest theron from August 5, 1925, with costs in this court.

Cardozo, C.J., and Pound, Crane, Lehman, Kellogg, O'Brien and Hubbs, JJ., concur.[7]

b. The Buyer Ties Up the Property

Where the transaction has not closed because of a buyer time default, buyer, if time was of the essence, will have lost his bargain and perhaps his deposit; but if timely tender was not a condition, buyer may yet have rights in the deal. Suppose, as in the preceding principal cases, litigation is required to resolve the crucial issue of the significance of a time default. Is it

---

7. It has also been held (presumably because of inadequate pro-seller draftsmanship) that if buyer has not only defaulted at closing but has also stopped payment on the "deposit" check, an action by seller against buyer on the check is a contract affirmance and cannot be maintained if seller has resold the land. 5 Corbin, Contracts §1075, at 422 (1963).— Eds.

The Buyer Fails to Close

inevitably true that buyer will, as in those cases, have to assume a plaintiff's position via an action for specific performance? Will seller, with down payment in hand (or shared with the broker), simply be able to sit tight?

Seller, if he wishes to resell, might not be able to lie back waiting for buyer to commence suit. Could seller resell to a buyer whose purchase would be subject to loss in the original buyer's subsequent specific performance action? There might, of course, be many willing subsequent buyers, depending on price, or on seller's willingness to enter an indemnification agreement, but property subject to a litigation possibility is often hard to sell or borrow against.

To be sure, a third person, if unaware of the original buyer's contract, might acquire bona fide purchaser status to cut off buyer's specific claim to the land. But seller would probably have to be a liar for his purchaser on resale to become a bona fide purchaser — or at least a seller as nice as you and us would surely tell a new purchaser of the original buyer's armed presence in the wings.

Accordingly, buyer, after default, might have to become a plaintiff to establish his rights, if any; seller might have to become a plaintiff to free the land from buyer's rights, if none.

Seller is subject to the difficulty just mentioned simply from having entered into a contract with buyer which has been defaulted with ambiguous effect. But there are several devices by which buyer can make it even worse, can darken the cloud which hangs over the land. These, next treated, are available to a buyer who has possible rights in a time ambiguity situation. They are perhaps available also to a buyer who has pretty clearly forfeited his rights by delay, but who would like to create a little or a lot of nuisance value to be bought off by seller.

Lis pendens. At page 467 supra, in connection with automatic subordination clauses, excerpts from an article by Lascher are reprinted in which the author points out how, in filing a specific performance action, the buyer can also file a lis pendens against the subject property. Lis pendens is a notice which, when properly recorded, communicates to the world that an action is pending which might take the land from seller (the owner of record) and transfer it to the plaintiff-buyer. No one buying from seller after the filing of the lis pendens can become a bona fide purchaser so as to prevail over the original buyer, should the latter be successful in his specific performance action. However frivolous that action, the lis pendens is likely to cut down seller's freedom to deal with the property.

Recording the contract of sale. Somewhat the same result can be achieved by buyer's recording his contract of sale. With this contract of record, if seller, after buyer's default, tries to sell the property to a new buyer, that buyer will find the contract when the public records are explored. Of course he will see that the contract called for buyer performance as of a given date, and that the date has passed. Will he then feel free to buy the property from seller without worrying about a claim from buyer? Only if he has a firm grasp of the law of "time of the essence," which is relatively ungraspable, and only if he knows exactly how the buyer and seller conducted themselves through the course of the defaulted transaction. In other words, the recorded contract will inhibit a new purchaser.

However, there are circumstances under which the buyer may not be able to record the contract of sale: (a) The contract of sale may contain a provision in which buyer promises not to record, or a provision by which the contract is voided upon recordation; (b) The seller may simply sign the contract of sale without acknowledging his signature, the latter formality being a usual prerequisite to recording. Installment sellers often use these devices to discourage or prevent contract buyers from putting the contract on record. See page 199 supra.

Certainly, seller does not want a recorded interest interfering with his power to deal with the property. Just as certainly, buyer would like something recorded: not only is recordation a weapon in his time-of-the-essence struggle with the seller; but it also serves to protect the buyer's executory interest from being cut off by seller's financing arrangements. Suppose, for example, that seller is a subdivider. Following the contract of sale to the buyer, the seller may borrow money for property development, giving the lender a security interest in the property. If buyer's interest is not recorded and seller later defaults on the loan, the security interest may prevail over buyer.

In spite of any contract arrangements which might prohibit recording by the buyer, it might nonetheless be possible for buyer to record. First, Hetland, in The California Land Contract, 48 Calif. L. Rev. 729, 746 (1960), suggests that an antirecording provision may be against public policy. Second, if the contract is unrecordable because seller's signature is not acknowledged, this obstacle might be bypassed — buyer might be able to get the instrument recorded by the recording officer. Third, Hetland also suggests a method by which the contract may be recorded indirectly: buyer might assign the contract to a straw man, and take an assignment back in a document which is acknowledged by the straw man and which incorporates the original contract. Under either of the latter devices, the contract will be of record, but perhaps not as usefully as where the recorded document is something signed in acknowledged form by the record owner (seller). There is a question as to whether anyone needs to pay attention to such aberrantly recorded contracts of sale and as to whether they give constructive notice of a buyer's interest — a question which will be covered further in Chapter Five. But even though the effects of such recordings are doubtful, they may yet be intimidating. For example, a title insurance company may be scared off from writing a policy on which seller's future capacity to deal with the property might depend.

There is one further device available to the buyer who wishes to record in spite of the need of an acknowledged signature. Buyer can simply forge the acknowledgement and record the contract. Whatever temporal or spiritual punishment may come to the buyer as a consequence of this forgery, it does not subject him to civil liability to the seller, even where the seller loses a deal because of the "forgery-enabled" recording. Can you see why? Kirsch v. Barnes, 153 F. Supp. 260, 157 F. Supp. 671 (N.D. Cal. 1957). *Actual malice necessary for defamation of title*

Rogers Carl Corp. v. Moran
103 N.J. Super. 163, 246 A.2d 750 (App. Div. 1968)

LEONARD, J.A.D. Defendants appeal from an adverse judgment entered against them in plaintiff's action for slander of title and upon defendants' counterclaim for specific performance.

The trial court, at the conclusion of all of the testimony, denied defendants' motion for a dismissal of plaintiff's action but granted plaintiff's motion for a direction of verdict in its favor on the liability phase of the case. The court thereupon submitted to the jury solely the issue of damages and the jury returned a verdict in favor of plaintiff and against defendants for $655.33 compensatory damages and $5 punitive damages.

This action springs from a contract executed between the parties on January 7, 1966, wherein plaintiff agreed to sell and defendants agreed to buy certain vacant land and a house to be constructed thereon by plaintiff. The total contract price was $23,500, to be paid as follows: $100 down; $400 cash and a $1500 promissory note, when defendants obtained a $16,000 mortgage commitment; and the balance of $5500 in cash and the mortgage money at the closing.

By an addendum to the contract the parties agreed that the mortgage loan "shall be obtained from City Federal Savings and Loan Association only" (City Federal), the company from which plaintiff had obtained a construction mortgage.

By letter dated January 27, 1966 City Federal advised defendants that their application for a mortgage loan had been approved and that attorneys Adams and Rockoff would "prepare our required documents and furnish us with title insurance." Defendant Lawrence Moran remonstrated with Englemann, president of plaintiff, over the mortgagee's designation of its closing attorney, taking the position that Foley, defendants' attorney in the transaction, who was also on a list of approved closing attorneys of City Federal, should so act. Englemann said the designation could not be changed and, according to Moran, said there was "no deal." Englemann testified he had his discussion on this subject with Foley and that the latter was adamant about being the closing attorney for the mortgagee, even after Englemann inquired of City Federal whether that arrangement satisfied it and received and transmitted a negative response. The Morans also refused to make the cash payment or deliver the $1500 note.

On February 16, 1966 Adams and Rockoff, attorneys for the mortgagee, wrote to defendants that in view of their failure to make payment of the cash deposit and execute the promissory note, the agreement was rescinded by the seller. Coincidentally, the Morans recorded their contract with plaintiff in the county clerk's office on the very same date—February 16, 1966. Defendant Lawrence Moran on February 22, 1966 wrote to City Federal that defendants accepted the commitment "except that the attorney who is to prepare the necessary documents and title insurance is your approved attorney, Francis C. Foley," purportedly in accord with an original understanding between defendants and Englemann to that effect. This controversy as to the attorney was never resolved, both parties holding steadfast to their respective positions.

On February 22 plaintiff wrote to defendants, returning their $100 deposit check and stating that "[W]e regret that you were unable to complete the purchase of the property. . . ." On March 4 defendants' attorney, Foley, by letter sent defendants' deposit check to Adams and Rockoff, advising them that defendants had no intention of cancelling their contract and that he was holding the balance of the deposit for the seller and "will deliver the same when the controversy with respect to your representation of Mr. Moran is disposed of." In the same letter Foley stated that the contract between plaintiff and defendant was recorded on February 16.

Thereupon, plaintiff instituted the present action for slander of title, seeking compensatory and punitive damages and the removal of the contract from record. The basis of plaintiff's claim, as disclosed by the pretrial order, was that defendants "willfully, wantonly, maliciously and with the intention to damage plaintiff, recorded the contract" and in so doing acted "in bad faith."

Nevertheless, at the commencement of the trial and before the jury was drawn, the judge, albeit without objection by counsel, stated that the question involved was whether plaintiff or defendants "breached the contract." From then on the record discloses that the only issue considered and resolved by the court was "breach of contract."

However, defendants in arguing their motions for dismissal made at the end of plaintiff's case at the conclusion of all the testimony, argued that plaintiff did not carry its burden of proving that defendants acted "maliciously" and that the evidence disclosed that defendants acted in "good faith" upon "probable cause" prompted by "a reasonable belief." The court, in denying these motions and in granting plaintiff's motion for a directed verdict, did not determine the issue of malice or good faith but merely concluded that there was "no factual question with respect to the breach of contract by the defendants and that they therefore had no right to record the contract."

Upon the record, we agree with the court's conclusion that defendants breached their contract and that therefore they were not entitled to specific performance thereof, and that plaintiff was entitled to have the contract removed from record. Defendants had no legal right to name the mortgagee's closing attorney. The fact that the mortgage commitment designated closing attorneys other than Foley did not constitute a failure to provide defendants with a suitable mortgage commitment consistent with the contract. Consequently, upon defendants remaining adamant in naming the mortgagee's closing attorney and refusing to pay the cash and deliver the note called for by the contract, plaintiff had the right to rescind. Nevertheless, the foregoing conclusions do not support the trial court's entry of a directed verdict in favor of plaintiff on its action for slander of title.

Malice, express or implied, is an essential element of the cause of action for slander of title. . . . Plaintiffs do not deny that proof of malice or bad faith in the recording of the contract by defendants was a requisite for their establishment of a cause of action for slander of title, but contend that factor is conclusively shown by the proofs.

A rival claimant is privileged to disparage another's property in land by an honest assertion of an inconsistent legally protected interest in himself. Restatement of Torts, §647, pp. 364-365 (1938).

As the court said in Andrew v. Deshler, "If the words are spoken by a stranger, the law presumes malice. But if the party is himself interested in the matter and announces the defect of title, bona fide, either for the purpose of protecting his own interest or preventing the commission of a fraud, the legal presumption of malice is rebutted. Malice is of the gist of the action, and the real point on the question of malice is whether the defendant made the statement bona fide and under an honest impression of its truth, or whether he made it maliciously, for the purpose of slandering the plaintiff's title" (45 N.J.L. at pp. 169-170).

Where a defendant acts in pursuance of a bona fide claim which he is asserting honestly, although without right, as eventually appears from an adjudication by a court of competent jurisdiction, such defendant will not be penalized in damages for asserting such a bona fide claim in good faith. . . .

As previously noted, the contract here involved made no provision as to whose attorney was to prepare the closing documents and the title search. Moreover, defendants attempted to establish that City Federal had a "policy" or custom whereby it allowed a purchaser-mortgagor to use his own attorney to handle the closing for the mortgagee, particularly when that attorney was on City Federal's "approved" list. The court sustained plaintiff's objection to this evidence on the ground that the contract could not be altered by oral evidence. This ruling was erroneous insofar as it affected plaintiff's claim for slander of title. Since the contract was silent as to the closing attorney, custom and usage of the trade would be admissible on the issue of defendants' good or bad faith. The jury could well have considered that such proof indicated that defendants acted in good faith in insisting that Foley act as the closing attorney.

Under all the circumstances, we are of the opinion that the issue of whether defendants exceeded the just bounds of their privilege i.e., whether they were actuated by an honest, bona fide purpose to protect their own interest or by a malicious design to defame plaintiff, was one for the jury resolution. Andrew v. Deshler, supra, 45 N.J.L. at pp. 170-171.

The fact that defendants breached their contract with plaintiff is not per se proof of malice. It is merely one fact that the jury should consider together with all the other circumstances, in evaluating defendants' conduct. . . .

5. Specific Performance

Centex Homes Corp. v. Boag

128 N.J. Super. 385, 320 A.2d 194 (Ch. Div. 1974)

GELMAN, J.S.C., Temporarily Assigned. Plaintiff Centex Homes Corporation (Centex) is engaged in the development and construction of a luxury highrise condominium project in the Boroughs of Cliffside Park and Fort Lee. The project when completed will consist of six 31-story buildings containing in excess of 3600 condominium apartment units, together with recreational buildings and facilities, parking garages and other common elements associated with this form of residential development. As sponsor of the project Centex offers the condominium apartment units for sale to the public and has filed an offering plan covering such sales with the appropriate regulatory agencies of the States of New Jersey and New York.

On September 13, 1972 defendants Mr. & Mrs. Eugene Boag executed a contract for the purchase of apartment unit No. 2019 in the building under construction and known as "Winston Towers 200." The contract price was $73,700, and prior to signing the contract defendants had given Centex a deposit in the amount of $525. At or shortly after signing the contract defendants delivered to Centex a check in the amount of $6,870 which, together with the deposit, represented approximately 10% of the total purchase of the apartment unit. Shortly thereafter Boag was notified by his employer that he was to be transferred to the Chicago, Illinois, area. Under date of September 27, 1972 he advised Centex that he "would be unable to complete the purchase" agreement and stopped payment on the $6,870 check. Centex deposited the check for collection approximately two weeks after receiving notice from defendant, but the check was not honored by defendants' bank. On August 8, 1973 Centex instituted this action in Chancery Division for specific performance of the purchase agreement or, in the alternative, for liquidated damages in the amount of $6,870. The matter is presently before this court on the motion of Centex for summary judgment.

The Buyer Fails to Close

Both parties acknowledge, and our research has confirmed, that no court in this State or in the United States has determined in any reported decision whether the equitable remedy of specific performance will lie for the enforcement of a contract for the sale of a condominium apartment. . . .

Under a condominium housing scheme each condominium apartment unit constitutes a separate parcel of real property which may be dealt with in the same manner as any real estate. Upon closing of title the apartment unit owner receives a recordable deed which confers upon him the same rights and subjects him to the same obligations as in the case of traditional forms of real estate ownership, the only difference being that the condominium owner receives in addition an undivided interest in the common elements associated with the building and assigned to each unit. . . .

Centex urges that since the subject matter of the contract is the transfer of a fee interest in real estate, the remedy of specific performance is available to enforce the agreement under principles of equity which are well-settled in this state.

The principle underlying the specific performance remedy is equity's jurisdiction to grant relief where the damage remedy at law is inadequate. The text writers generally agree that at the time this branch of equity jurisdiction was evolving in England, the presumed uniqueness of land as well as its importance to the social order of that era led to the conclusion that damages at law could never be adequate to compensate for the breach of a contract to transfer an interest in land. Hence specific performance became a fixed remedy in this class of transactions. See 11 Williston on Contracts (3d ed. 1968) §1418A; 5A Corbin on Contracts §1143 (1964). . . .

While the inadequacy of the damage remedy suffices to explain the origin of the vendee's right to obtain specific performance in equity, it does not provide a *rationale* for the availability of the remedy at the instance of the vendor of real estate. Except upon a showing of unusual circumstances or a change in the vendor's position, such as where the vendee has entered into possession, the vendor's damages are usually measurable, his remedy at law is adequate and there is no jurisdictional basis for equitable relief. But see Restatement, Contracts §360, comment c. The early English precedents suggest that the availability of the remedy in a suit by a vendor was an outgrowth of the equitable concept of mutuality, i.e., that equity would not specifically enforce an agreement unless the remedy was available to both parties. . . .

Our present Supreme Court has squarely held, however, that mutuality of remedy is not an appropriate basis for granting or denying specific performance. Fleischer v. James Drug Store, 1 N.J. 138, 62 A.2d 383 (1948). . . .

The disappearance of the mutuality of remedy doctrine from our law dictates the conclusion that specific performance relief should no longer be automatically available to a vendor of real estate, but should be confined to those special instances where a vendor will otherwise suffer an economic injury for which his damage remedy at law will not be adequate, or where other equitable considerations require that the relief be granted. . . .

Here the subject matter of the real estate transaction — a condominium apartment unit — has no unique quality but is one of hundreds of virtually identical units being offered by a developer for sale to the public. The units are sold by means of sample, in this case model apartments, in much the same manner as items of personal property are sold in the market place. The sales prices for the units are fixed in accordance with schedule filed by Centex as part of its offering plan, and the only variance as between apartments having the same floor plan (of which six plans are available) is the floor level or the building location within the project. In actuality, the condominium apartment units, regardless of their realty label, share the same characteristics as personal property.

From the foregoing one must conclude that the damages sustained by a condominium sponsor resulting from the breach of the sales agreement are readily measurable and the damage remedy at law is wholly adequate. No compelling reasons have been shown by Centex for the granting of specific performance relief and its complaint is therefore dismissed as to the first count. . . .

NOTES

1. *The general content of a decree of specific performance entered against buyer.* "[An] appropriate decree may enter requiring specific performance on the part of the vendee, by a fixed time, after the vendor has deposited in court, for the vendee, a conveyance to him of a good title to the land; failing acceptance of the deed and payment of the purchase price and interest by the vendee, it may thereupon be contingently decreed that the land be sold to satisfy the vendor's demand, and that execution against the vendee issue to enforce the payment of the unpaid balance of the purchase price and interest that the net proceeds of the sale fail to satisfy. . . ." Morgan v. Lewis, 203 Ala. 47, 82 So. 7 (1919).

Seller can also recover in his specific performance action, a judgment for any consequential damages caused by buyer's delay to the extent permitted by Hadley v. Baxendale. Some old cases hold that invocation of the specific performance remedy precludes recovery of such damages, 5A Corbin, Contracts §1222 (1963), but they are judged to be unimportant today.

2. *Justifications for seller specific performance.* Conventional justifications for giving seller the specific performance decree are mentioned in the *Centex* case. A fuller statement, from the comments to the Restatement

The Buyer Fails to Close

(Second) of Contracts §360 comment e (1981), follows. Considering all the reasons given, are you persuaded that the condominium should be exempted from the general rule? Or rather that the general rule is inappropriate for sales in subdivisions as well as condominiums?

> *e. Contracts for the sale of land.* Contracts for the sale of land have traditionally been accorded a special place in the law of specific performance. A specific tract of land has long been regarded as unique and impossible of duplication by the use of any amount of money. Furthermore, the value of land is to some extent speculative. Damages have therefore been regarded as inadequate to enforce a duty to transfer an interest in land, even if it is less than a fee simple. Under this traditional view, the fact that the buyer has made a contract for the resale of the land to a third person does not deprive him of the right to specific performance. If he cannot convey the land to his purchaser, he will be held for damages for breach of the resale contract, and it is argued that these damages cannot be accurately determined without litigation. Granting him specific performance enables him to perform his own duty and to avoid litigation and damages.
>
> Similarly, the seller who has not yet conveyed is generally granted specific performance on breach by the buyer. Here it is argued that, because the value of land is to some extent speculative, it may be difficult for him to prove with reasonable certainty the difference between the contract price and the market price of the land. Even if he can make this proof, the land may not be immediately convertible into money and he may be deprived of funds with which he could have made other investments. Furthermore, before the seller gets a judgment, the existence of the contract, even if broken by the buyer, operates as a clog on saleability, so that it may be difficult to find a purchaser at a fair price. The fact that specific performance is available to the buyer has sometimes been regarded as of some weight under the now discarded doctrine of "mutuality of remedy" (see Comment c to §363), but this is today of importance only because it enables a court to assure the vendee that he will receive the agreed performance if he is required to pay the price. The fact that legislation may have prohibited imprisonment as a means of enforcing a decree for the payment of money does not affect the seller's right to such a decree. After the seller has transferred the interest in the land to the buyer, however, and all that remains is for the buyer to pay the price, a money judgment for the amount of the price is an adequate remedy for the seller.

3. Welling v. Crosland, 129 S.C. 127, 158-159, 123 S.E. 776, 787 (1924), Justice Fraser, dissenting:

> . . . Courts of equity have never decreed specific performance in hard cases. The plaintiffs have their land and have always had it. They have also a $10,000 bonus. If they had alleged that they could have sold it to others and the sales (to real purchasers and not other unfortunates) have failed by reason of the violation of this contract to purchase, the position would have appealed to the court of equity, but they have not so alleged.

Mr. Justice Hydrick, in one of his many excellent opinions, said that courts should not be ignorant of or refuse to recognize matters of current history that were known to every one.

It has also been said by another "that communities, as well as individuals, go crazy at times." Such a time occurred in 1920. Forty-cent cotton upset us. The boll weevil was rapidly approaching, and the nearer it came the higher went the price of cotton lands. Many of our most progressive and thrifty citizens were obsessed with the idea that cotton would go higher still. Speculation in lands was wild and all too nigh universal. The price of cotton went down and with it the price of land. Lands were not worth the boom prices after the boom had past. Vendors who had contracts of sale demanded the contract price. They came into the court of equity and demanded that the vendee be required to comply with their contracts. If the court of equity had granted their demand, then, as the price of lands had fallen and the vendee could not pay the boom prices, there would have been a sale of the land at much less than the contract price and a judgment for the deficiency taken. This judgment for a deficiency would, in many instances, have paralyzed the activities of the judgment debtor. This state was in danger of a financial slaughter of its most thrifty citizens. In that emergency the court of equity said, "No; we will not be a party to this slaughter. We have a discretion in specific performance and we will, in our discretion, refuse specific performance. You may go into a court of law and allow a jury to say what your loss has been." For once the courts of law could do justice, when a jury could say how much the vendor had lost; but the court of equity under specific performance would do a great wrong, bound as it was by the letter of the bond. It was demanded of the court of equity that it give the pound of flesh, for no other reason than that it was so nominated in the bond. When the courts of equity shall decree specific performance for no other reason than that it is so nominated in the bond, it should change its name, because it has departed from its traditions and done despite to the memory of its chancellors. The broken contract was not ignored, but the parties were sent to a jury who could say what the vendor had lost.

4. *Burdensome land.* Olszewski v. Sardynski, 316 Mass. 715, 717-718, 56 N.E.2d 607, 608 (1944), delivered by Judge Lummus:

The facts that the plaintiff is the vendor and that performance by the vendee would consist entirely or primarily of the payment of money have never prevented specific performance. Commonly the remedy at law of a vendor is not adequate. Every piece of real estate has some unique disadvantage as well as advantage. The eagerness of buyers to acquire some properties is matched by the joy with which sellers part with others. Ownership of real estate is burdensome even when profitable. It hampers mobility. Years may be required to find a buyer. When at last a buyer is found, and a contract made which is broken by the buyer, the owner, with the real estate still on his hands, finds that at law he can recover only the excess, if any, of the price over the value as judicially appraised. [Citations.] For these reasons to say nothing of more technical ones (Fry, Spec. Perf., 6th Ed. 1921, §72), . . . a vendor is regularly granted specific performance unless some ground for denying it exists in the particular case.

There are frequent references in the literature to seller's specific performance being necessary to permit seller to gain the benefit of his bargain by dumping some peculiar disadvantages which might inhere in a specific tract of land. However, in our reading of some hundred cases in which a buyer was, on one or another ground, resisting a specific performance action by seller, we discovered no case in which there was even a hint that seller was trying to get rid of something burdensome.

Nevertheless, the references to such a basis for specific performance by seller are so frequent that the relation of land disadvantages and seller specific performance should be explored. Suppose that S owns a hillside tract in Los Angeles on which is located a house so constructed that it threatens to rain destruction on a lowland neighbor's house. S's house was constructed in its threatening condition for a previous owner by an incompetent and now insolvent builder. If the house drops on the neighbor, S, qua owner, is liable. Somehow S has managed to get B to agree to buy the premises for $30,000, although with the impending liability no reasonable man would pay anything for the house. B fails to close, being unable to obtain financing from any reasonable lender. These facts being disclosed to a court of equity, will the court order B to take title? If it does so, will this relieve S of future liability to the neighbor? See generally 2 Harper and James, The Law of Torts §27.21 (1956); Prosser, Torts §62 (3d ed. 1964).

Aiken, "Subject to Financing Clauses" in Interim Contracts for Sale of Realty[8]

43 Marq. L. Rev. 265, 295 (1960)

[At pages 295 ff., the author deals with the seller's remedies in cases in which (a) buyer's obligation is "subject to" financing, (b) buyer does not obtain financing and fails to close, but (c) the court finds that acceptable financing was available and that buyer is therefore in breach (Kovarik v. Vesely, page 437 supra, is such a case). After dealing with deposit problems, the author notes that seller might sue buyer for damages under the conventional formula: contract price minus fair market value of property at the time of the breach minus deposit.]

In circumstances in which the value of the property is fairly stable, and in which the value of the property was not too badly overpriced, this

---

8. Some footnotes omitted.

formula will yield no net recovery to the seller. The significant circumstance which bears heavily on the advisability of this remedy in "subject to financing" cases is that, to establish availability of the financing, the seller must establish an adequate security value in the property itself. This process will tend to defeat the seller's attempt to establish a low market value under the formula.

But the acute lawyer, representing the seller in such situations, will elect a different remedy: that of specific performance. The sole drawback of this course, assuming a financially responsible buyer, is that the resale of the property is necessarily postponed pendente lite. That problem, however, may be present regardless of the form of action selected, assuming inability to negotiate settlement of the dispute, so that it constitutes no insuperable objection.

The most important practical advantage gained by proceeding in specific performance is that it enables seller to separate his proofs on the question of security-value from those on the question of fair market value, and effectively shifts the burden on the latter question. In addition, seller places himself in a position to recover the "demurrage" on the property (taxes, interest, insurance, upkeep, heating, repairs etc.) over and above the basic contract debt.

The procedure is this: Seller commences suit praying that buyer be required specifically to perform by paying the balance of purchase price, plus demurrage, and alleging that, upon such payment, seller will himself perform by conveyance. Buyer's most usual answering plea sets up the contingency. This plea failing, judgment is entered for the full balance due on the contract, ordering payment within a reasonable period, and directing that, unless such amount is paid as ordered, the subject property (treated as equitably belonging to the buyer) be advertised and sold at equitable foreclosure sale to meet the judgment.[72] To this point, the only question which has arisen respecting the value of the property is that respecting its security value, in connection with the availability of financing, and the seller's position is that such value was — at time of breach — adequate.

Subsequently, the foreclosure auction is held. Prominent among the bidders, and going as high as he must, is the seller-plaintiff. Following the auction, the matter comes back into court for confirmation — and determination of deficiency. If defendant-buyer intends now to defeat or lessen the impending deficiency, he has the burden of showing that the auction *did not* realize fair market value, against the presumption that it did. The inquiry now is not concerned with fair market at time of breach, but with

---

72. . . . The procedure should be carefully distinguished from that followed in mortgage foreclosures, under Ch. 278, Wis. Stats. The provisions of Ch. 281, Wis. Stats., governing the procedure, are sketchy at best; and the matter is largely governed by judicial custom.

fair market at time of sale; and opinion evidence offered on behalf of buyer is ranked against the fact of the open public auction sale.

The court's alternatives, even assuming its dissatisfaction with the bid, are limited: it may present plaintiff-seller with an option to reduce or waive his deficiency or submit to a resale; it may order resale, including an upset price; or it may simply order a resale. Meanwhile, the costs and demurrages continue to run against the buyer's account. Ultimately, he must either purchase or go bankrupt. If the necessary financing is in fact unavailable (regardless of the legal finding on the point), the buyer's only course is bankruptcy. The credit purchase which buyer originally contracted to make has been converted into a present cash liability.

The spectre of this outcome will disincline many purchasers to hazard either the action or the appeal undertaken by the buyer in Kovarik v. Vesely. The risk of loss is entirely disproportionate to the possibility of gain by recovery of the deposit money. The innocent-appearing and obscure words, "subject to financing," have evolved into a monster.

Whatever may be said for or against the construction which the courts have placed upon the clause itself, it would seem that the practice of granting specific performance on seller's plea in such cases is inequitable and unwarranted. No rule is better supported by authority than is the rule that equity will not enforce a contract which is doubtful and unclear in its terms. In the sense of this rule, a degree of clarity substantially in excess of that required for legal enforceability has been consistently required.

It can scarcely be gainsaid that "subject to financing" contracts are tentative and unsettled in their inception. By definition, they are contingent; and in the vast majority of cases, the precise meaning of the contingency is lost in a cloud of doubts. Only in clear cases can the finding that the contingency was satisfied so far as "material" be made without substantial doubt, regardless of whether or not it is "against the great weight and clear preponderance of the evidence." [78] To permit the invocation by seller of the equitable powers of the court against this background seems improper.

More especially is this true when we consider that the contract which is specifically enforced under the decree is essentially unlike the one which the parties originally entered into. Buyer and seller both envisioned the necessity of third-party financing as the sine qua non of the transaction. It is inconceivable that buyer would have entered into the transaction at all had it been put to him as a cash proposition, with the money to come from his own assets. Even assuming that the buyer's failure to procure the financing and to complete the purchase was entirely deliberate, the hard fact of the matter is that equity cannot after the event, restore the availabil-

---

78. The latter standard was employed in Kovarik v. Vesely [supra] in affirming the trial court's finding respecting "immateriality" of the loan-source provisions, in support of specific performance at seller's behest.

ity of such financing so that the purchase may proceed essentially as per contract. Its decree of specific performance, under such circumstances, amounts realistically to a hollow gesture, stripping the contract of its most vital provision.

The only apparent reason advanced for allowing the remedy to the seller is because, had seller defaulted, the same remedy would have been available to the buyer. This reasoning constitutes an affirmative application of the doctrine of mutuality of remedy—a doctrine which has never possessed any but the haziest logical support, and one which at least in its affirmative applications, has been thoroughly discredited.[81] In plain fact, the seller's action for specific performance is nothing but a debt-collection device; and no reason has ever been suggested why the legal remedy is inadequate for those purposes.[82] Indeed, once the specific performance decree has worked its tactical magic by dispensing the seller from proving his legal damage, all aspects of its equitable nature disappear, and the debt collection proceeds by ordinary legal processes.

Pursuing the mutuality concept a bit further, however, we find a common practice of attempting to block, by contract, even the buyer's well-established right of specific performance upon seller's attempted default. By insertion of the customary avoidance clause, the standard interim contract provides that should seller fail to make title as he undertakes to do, and buyer is unwilling to waive the default, the agreement shall be null and void. Not even a damage action is allowed to buyer, to say nothing of specific performance. Under this common form of contract, therefore, not even the mutuality doctrine seems to permit seller's action.

NOTE: VENDOR'S LIEN

The contract of sale is entered, B promising to pay, at a future closing, $30,000 for Blackacre. Subsequently B becomes insolvent. Is S thereafter obliged to close, passing title to Blackacre to B, and becoming a general creditor of B for the $30,000? If so, of course, he will not be paid in full: B's assets, augmented now by Blackacre, are not sufficient to pay his debts, augmented by the $30,000.

S is not so harshly treated. Contract theory provides a sufficient basis for

---

81. . . . The logical separation of affirmative and negative applications of the doctrine requires a feat of mental gymnastics, but is most easily understood as a technique for avoiding the usual requirements for invocation of equity. If a petitioner for specific performance can show no grounds for equitable relief on his own account, he pleads the rule. Likewise, if one resisting the petition cannot disprove petitioner's grounds for equitable relief, he invokes the negative rule. Since a seller, unable by reasonable measures to remove clouds, incumbrances, or other title defects, may resist specific performance (see Specific Performance of Land Contract Where Vendor Will be Compelled to Acquire, or Incur Expense in Clearing Title, 171 A.L.R. 1299), should not the negative application of the rule deny the relief on seller's petition? The rule itself prompts the dog to chase its tail.

82. Quite the contrary. The most telling argument in favor of granting specific performance to the seller is that it is the practical equivalent of the legal remedy.

The Buyer Fails to Close

his victory: seller's performance obligation does not mature prior to B's tender of his payment obligation. But under a "property" theory, seller can also win; it can be said that, until paid, S has a "lien" on Blackacre for the price. This seems an odd form of words for cases in which S still holds title; how can one have a lien on that in which he has the fee? But once the contract of sale is entered, S and B, both between themselves and as to third parties, are complexly interlocked, an interlocking sometimes described by saying that B is owner or equitable owner for some purposes. With B so characterized as a sort of owner, S's lien is on B's sort of ownership.

The law of a particular jurisdiction then may characterize seller as having a vendor's lien in the fact situation with which this entire chapter has so far dealt, namely, a buyer's failure to close. If such a characterization obtains, seller is given an additional remedy upon buyer's default, i.e., foreclosure of his lien under relevant local practice. In most important respects involving an insolvent buyer, vendor's lien foreclosure and a seller's specific performance action achieve the same results, but there may be differences in timing, expense, procedure, and the like. For an extensive annotation on vendor's lien, which among other things contrasts vendor's lien foreclosure with a seller's specific performance action, see Annot., 77 A.L.R. 270 (1932).

It has been mentioned that it seems inelegant to say that seller has a vendor's lien in property of which he has not yet divested himself of title. You will then be pleased to know that the term is most generally used not to describe the seller's rights where buyer has not closed, but rather to describe seller's rights in two quite different types of transactions involving the buyer who has already received a deed. Were you to consult the vendor's lien A.L.R. annotation listed above, you would find that only a little of it deals with the problem of the nonclosing buyer.

The concept of "vendor's lien" is most usually applied to a specific form of purchase-money security transaction used in several states. In this form seller gives buyer a deed in exchange not for cash but rather for buyer's promise to pay. The deal is then instrumented by a recordable document in which seller is described as having a "lien" on the transferred title.

There is still another usage for the vendor's lien term. In nonstandard transactions where somehow seller has transferred title to the buyer without having received either payment or a formal recordable security interest, there is some common law learning that seller is to be treated as having a lien on the premises for the purchase price. The result of this characterization is to give seller an extra remedy against buyer, and also to give the seller rights to the property against some (mostly donative) transferees.

It should be noted that inasmuch as this part of the book concentrates on buyer-seller relationships, no attention has been paid to the relations which buyer and seller have with the world of tax authorities, creditors, and relatives when seller is said to have a vendor's lien.

B. STRAWS, SPECULATORS, AND SHARPIES

1. Liability Limitation

Houtz v. Hellman
228 Mo. 655, 128 S.W. 1001 (1910)

LAMM, P.J. . . . [The trial court awarded plaintiff Houtz a decree for specific performance of a contract whereby defendant Hellman, a widow acting through a power of attorney exercised by her son, Charles, contracted to sell described property to Houtz for cash.]

. . . A domestic corporation, the Burdeau Real Estate Company, a habitant of St. Louis, was the real purchaser of the property. We will hereinafter call it the "company." Its plan was to keep itself in the shadow until the exigencies of the case forced it into the sunlight. There is a resort in that great city known as the "Golden Lion." It seems beer is sold there. Houtz, the plaintiff, serves at the Golden Lion, presumably assembling such proportions of beer and foam in each customer's glass as leaves the Golden Lion an increment of profit on the sale. At a certain time the corporate eye of the company was fixed on Houtz as a present holding receptacle for its land titles, and a future conduit through which such titles might pass to subsequent purchasers, without liability to the company as warrantor. Whether Houtz acted as such receptacle and conduit from love of gain or received a recompense in mere sentimental ways is dark, but he assumed the role of such mysterious convenience whereby the company killed two birds with one stone, viz., pocketed the gains of the traffic in land titles and avoided the liability for loss. There is no evidence that defendant or her agent, Charles Hellman, knew Houtz was used by the company as such convenience. At a certain time one Charles J. Moser heard . . . that defendant's property was on the market. Moser is also in the real estate line, having some casual but undisclosed connection with the company, at least in this transaction. Armed with such information, Moser went to a place called Real Estate Row on Chestnut street. He there met a man named Hamburg, who seems also to have such undisclosed connection (whatever it was) with the company, as induced him to refer to it as "his client." At any rate, these two laid their heads together and agreed that an attempt should be made to buy the lot for Hamburg's "client." Hamburg did not disclose his "client's name" to Moser, and the mystery was cleared up only by the appearance of the company on the stage at the final scene. Moser presently met Charles Hellman. A price was agreed upon, and the contract of sale was prepared in duplicate in the name of Houtz. A check evidencing the earnest money ($250) was given by the company payable to Houtz and indorsed to Hellman, Hamburg paying Moser $50 for his services and getting $50 from his then undisclosed principal for his. Charles Hellman refused to close the transaction with

Straws, Speculators, and Sharpies

Moser without Houtz's signature to the contract. Thereupon Moser took it away to procure such signature. He returned ostensibly with Houtz's signature thereto, and turned Hellman over a duplicate of the contract so signed, thereby completing the contract. At the trial neither Houtz or Hamburg testified, and when it was discovered, as it was, that the signature of Houtz on defendant's duplicate was not the same as his indorsement on the check for the earnest money, the investigation in that regard was stopped at that point by an admission in open court to the effect that Houtz did not sign defendant's duplicate, that (to quote) "the contract signature is not the identical signature of Mr. Houtz," but was written on the paper by Mr. Burdeau, the representative of the company. Mr. Burdeau testified that: "Houtz was a straw man for me. He represents me in this matter." Plaintiff's testimony also shows that the plan of the company was to borrow from one Love the entire purchase price in the name of Houtz, and secure the loan on the lot in question. We gather that the money so borrowed was to be used in the purchase of the lot, that Houtz was to make the loan simultaneously with getting his deed from defendant — one hand washing the other. There is evidence, however, that the company had money in the bank sufficient to make a tender of the purchase price in the first instance, and, if a tender was necessary, intended to use its own money in making one. To show that Houtz was able and willing to perform at the time of the trial, a certified check from the company of that date payable to his order, for the amount of the purchase price, was introduced in evidence. This is sufficient of the record to pass upon the following question, viz.: Should a chancellor, armed with a discretion, specifically enforce the contract under the circumstances just disclosed? In other words, does plaintiff come into a court of equity with clean hands? On that question we rule: (a) That, for the purpose of disposing of the precise question now up, the matter of Houtz's ability to perform, through a loan or through a temporary advancement of the purchase price by the company for the purposes of a tender, or payment, is not decisive. Therefore, by way of elimination, we put it to one side for the present. (b) The contract was not in the form of an option, but in a form involving mutuality — that is, an obligation to sell on one side and impliedly to purchase on the other. Under the statute of frauds, Houtz's signature was necessary to the contract in order to bind him and support a suit by defendant for specific performance on Houtz's failure to perform. Defendant, through her agent, as was her clear right, demanded such signature as a condition precedent to consummating the contract. That demand was answered with a false and sham signature, and defendant, relying on its genuineness, closed the deal by delivery of the contract.

In this condition of the record the case does not call for judicial comment on the business morality of the secret and deceptive use of a "man of straw" in real estate contracts — a questionable practice, the product of insincerity and mere commercialism. By the term "man of straw" we understand one of no substance, one in name only, an irresponsible person having no property to respond in damages, who loans himself out to others to sign contracts as a purchaser knowing he is acting a lie — an office no honorable man should fill, and no honorable man should ask another to fill. When a case comes here in which a litigant, innocent of the deception practiced on him, is fraudulently misled and injured by the man of straw method, and raises such issue by his pleading, we can deal with it. But, under the power and discretion lodged in a chancellor in cases of specific performance, we think the case does call for comment on the business morality of using not only a man of straw as a contracting party but the shade of a shade, viz., the straw name of a "man of straw," to induce the owner of real estate to become bound in a contract of sale. Look at it. If the widow Hellman had sued Houtz on the contract and he had pleaded non est factum, and the fact had appeared that he had not signed it, it is no answer to say that she could have shown that the company was authorized to sign his name and bind him. This, for more reasons than one. In the first place, it is not shown that the company had any such authority. In the next place, holding the hidden key to the concealed fact, the company was itself in ambush, and its connection with the transaction was in the shade. So Hamburg was in the shade and concealed even from Moser his client's name. What right have people, moving with such studied and serpentine sinuosity, to throw the burden upon a real estate owner of ferreting out the facts essential to making a binding mutuality in a contract of sale, when such owner was entitled to straightforward dealing and a genuine signature to his contract, free from any such burden or danger? None this court knows of. Nor is it any answer to say, as was said at our bar, that by suing on the contract Houtz ratified it and became bound. The widow Hellman was entitled to have him bound at the start. She gave no option to have him bound or not bound as he might elect at some future time. If the price of real estate had gone down instead of up, as it did, and she had sued him for specific performance, she had the right to rest on a certainty that the party to be charged had signed the contract, not upon a mere possibility of being able to prove that the fictitious signature was authorized, or the contract ratified. On this view of the case, the contract sued on was a trick, an intended deception and snare. The story of its birth, told in the language of this record, brings a blush and makes justice avert her face for very shame. Whether, then, we look at the nominal plaintiff or (through such parody on a man) to the corporate company, claiming to be the beneficiary in the contract and is here seeking to gather in its fruits under cover of its straw man's name, neither of them came into a court of equity with clean hands. Therefore a chancellor should not lift a finger by way of performance, and we shall not. . . .

. . . Nothing herein is to be construed as affecting plaintiff's right to a return of the $250 of earnest money. . . .

The premises considered, the decree was for the wrong party. Let the

Judgment be reversed and the cause remanded, with directions to enter a decree in favor of defendant, dismissing plaintiff's bill. It is so ordered. All concur.

NOTES TO HOUTZ v. HELLMAN

1. *The uses of straws.* Keeping in mind that a dummy or no-asset subsidiary corporation is in many aspects equal in sinuousity to a "Houtz," straws are used for a large variety of legitimate and illegitimate purposes.

Thus, straws are used to counter some of the sillier rules of the law of estates and future interests, as where a husband, wishing to convert his fee ownership of Blackacre into a joint tenancy with his wife, is in some states required and allowed to use a straw intermediary as grantee of the fee and grantor in joint tenancy.

Straws are used for evading or avoiding the beneficial owner's duties to tax or regulatory authorities, and to creditors. Straws are used to conceal the beneficial buyer's identity from a seller who might, with knowledge, refuse to sell to that buyer, or demand more money; the legitimacy of this use will be treated below in this chapter.

Finally, straws are used, as the *Houtz* case mentions, to limit the beneficial buyer's liability to (a) seller, (b) lender, or (c) subvendee.

2. *Straws: liability on the mortgage debt.* Friedman, Contracts and Conveyances of Real Property[9] 169-171 (4th ed. 1984):

> When the nominee is used to spare the real party in interest from liability on a mortgage debt, temporary title is taken in the name of an individual or corporate nominee, who executes the mortgage instruments and then conveys the premises, subject to the mortgage, to the principal. The insulation of the principal from liability on the mortgage debt is based, in part, on the rule of law that a conveyance subject to a mortgage (as distinguished from an assumption thereof) imposes no personal liability under the mortgage or the debt thereby secured, on the grantee. It is also based on two rules relating to instruments executed by an agent (the nominee in this situation) and to which the principal is not a party. The principal is not liable, as indicated above, if the instrument is under seal,[10] nor if the instrument is negotiable. The use of nominees for this purpose is recognized as legitimate unless the mortgagee has been led to believe the real party in interest is personally liable. And an owner, who conveys to or shunts title through a nominee, in order to have the latter execute the mortgage instrument, is not liable on the mortgage debt or for a deficiency judgment. Nor may the mortgagee, in most cases, succeed in reaching the principal, on the theory of being subro-

9. Extensive citations omitted.
10. Here the author refers back to text stating the common law rule: A principal who is not mentioned in an instrument made by his agent under seal is not liable on the instrument. Citing 32 A.L.R. 162 (1924). —Eds.

gated to the claim of an agent (the nominee) against his principal for exoneration from liability or reimbursement for his loss, it being understood that

> A "straw" is a conduit, usually an impecunious person who cannot respond in damages to anyone and who ordinarily, for this reason, does not expect to be indemnified in the event he suffers a loss. Nor usually does a person who uses a straw in this type of transaction expect in any way to be liable. . . . This is usually understood by all the parties concerned.

The nominee is almost invariably irresponsible financially. One of the few cases allowing subrogation against the principal is based largely on the fact that the nominee was a person with substantial income. The court refused to believe the parties intended this nominee to assume a liability of over $100,000 in return for a $25 fee.[22] And in a Pennsylvania case a nominee, who defied precedent by subsequently acquiring means and paid a deficiency judgment recovered against him, recovered judgment against the principal for reimbursement.[23]

Note: Friedman, dealing with jurisdictions in which the seal does not have the insulating effect described above, recommends that in all the nominee's instruments a clause be included whereby the other party recognizes the nominee as principal and agrees not to look to anyone other than the nominee.

When the deal is written up with such explicitness in freeing the beneficial borrower from personal liability on the mortgage, you begin to wonder why there's any point to using a straw here at all. If the parties bargain for a loan under which there is to be no liability beyond the mortgaged premises, why not have the beneficial borrower borrow in his own name under an instrument negativing undesired liability? In living the lie of a straw transaction, neither of the parties is fooling the other, so why bother?

3. *Straws: purchase options.* Consider again buyer's use of a straw as a device for concealment from seller. Suppose that the real buyer furnishes down payment money to an impecunious straw, who then enters a contract in his own name with a seller who had insisted on a bilateral contract, granting no option. Then straw assigns the contract to the real buyer, who figures he has a de facto option for the down payment. If he wants the property, he closes; if he doesn't want it, he retreats back into the shadows.

If the facts can be flushed out, seller may have two shots at imposing liability for breach on the real buyer. Buyer might be liable on the contract (putting aside the seal rules mentioned above) as undisclosed principal,

---

22. Halsey v. Brown, 177 Misc. 415, 30 N.Y.S.2d 646 (County Ct. 1941).

23. Aronson v. Heymann, 56 Pa. Super. 501 (1914). The opinion cites the Pennsylvania rule, followed in a minority of the states, that whereas a conveyance subject to a mortgage does not make the grantee personally liable to the mortgagee on the mortgage debt, it makes the grantee an indemnitor of the mortgagor against liability. But it will be noted that the *Halsey* case, note 22 supra, reaches substantially the same result in New York, which follows the majority rule, to the effect that a conveyance subject to a mortgage imposes no liability, either direct or indirect, on the grantee.

and he might also be liable if the instrument of assignment does not clearly state that the assignee is to succeed only to the straw's rights, and that the assignee by acceptance does not thereby assume the straw's duties. This is the general law of contracts, Restatement (Second) of Contracts §328; but the Restatement expresses no opinion as to whether the rule applies to an assignment by a purchaser of his rights under a contract for the sale of land, in view of the leading New York case of Langel v. Betz, 250 N.Y. 159, 164 N.E. 890 (1928), which refuses to find an assumption absent a specific assignee agreement to assume.

[margin note: real purchaser can assume straw's rights but not obligations?]

4. *Agency theories for principal's liability.* In Houtz v. Hellman, the pecunious Burdeau, upon signing the contract in the impecunious Houtz's name, became liable on one of two theories. Either Burdeau was Houtz's agent, in which case Burdeau's signature bound Houtz, and Houtz being then bound as agent for an undisclosed principal (Burdeau), the undisclosed principal became liable. Or, Burdeau was not Houtz's agent, in which case Burdeau became liable for breach of warranty of authority (but not as undisclosed principal, because if he wasn't Houtz's agent, he obviously couldn't be his principal). Anyway, what did the wily Burdeau hope to achieve by signing Houtz's name? Or by using a company check for the down payment?

2. Overreaching by Buyer

Seller has finally gotten Blackacre off his hands at $10 an acre, and he drives by the property one day to discover the property being mined for gold. Where seller thereafter acts to rescind, the case will be argued in terms of the law of fraud and mistake, and that of the undisclosed principal. But no systematic development of these generally familiar bodies of law will be attempted here; we will simply give a quick look at land transfer problems of information and disclosure about "gold." The principal hidden value cases which follow involve types of "land" as diverse as rural mineral property in Arkansas in 1904, property at the edge of a small Kentucky town in the 1950s, and a redemption right in a New Jersey suburb in the 1960s. We believe these "lands" have enough in common to justify juxtaposition in the "hidden value" context, and that something useful can be learned even without detailed information as to how buyers and sellers obtain and exchange information with respect to present and latent value in the several types of transactions involved.

[margin note: K enforced even though buyer did not tell seller of possible mineral deposits where min. deposits in area were generally known and price was basically fair]

Storthz v. Arnold
74 Ark. 68, 84 S.W. 1036 (1905)

HILL, C.J. Mary and Bettie Arnold, ignorant negro girls, aged respectively 18 and 16 years, owned, with their infant brother, a tract of 160 acres of land in Saline county. It had come to them through their deceased father, who had lived upon it at one time. A small part of it had once been in cultivation, the improvements were of little value and the taxes unpaid, and the time for redeeming from a tax sale nearing expiration. Such was the condition when one Jones, a man of their race and an attorney, called to see them at the home of their half-sister, with whom they lived, in the city of Little Rock. He told them of the imminent danger of the land being lost on account of nonpayment of taxes, and, after attempting to frighten them about the land, offered $25 for the interest of the elder sister. This was declined, and negotiations continued, Jones renewing his offers. Finally he brought about an interview between them and Storthz, whom he claimed to represent. He told them Storthz would not give over $300 for the two interests, if that, and that he would get mad and leave. Storthz came, offered $50 each, which was declined, and got mad and left as predicted. He came back in a few minutes and said that he would give $300 for the two interests because the girls were orphans, but that the land was not worth it — that it would not sprout peas. The offer was accepted, $150 paid the adult sister; and in a few days an application was made to Pulaski circuit court for the removal of the disabilities of Bettie, at which hearing her relatives appeared and some others. The order was made removing her disabilities for the purpose of making the sale, which was then consummated, and the money paid. Storthz paid the witnesses and relatives who appeared at said hearing small sums for their services in attending same. These suits were brought to set aside the conveyance as fraudulent, in that the lands contained valuable bauxite deposits, and that Storthz knew this and the girls were ignorant of it, and he knowingly imposed on their ignorance. The suits are similar, except in Bettie's case there was a tender of the purchase price. There is a conflict in the evidence as to the statements and conduct of Storthz when the tender was made, but it is not considered material.

The evidence is conflicting as to whether there are bauxite deposits on the land, and consequently as to its value. It is clear that the price is a good one if the land is not valuable for mineral deposits, and their presence is a matter of speculation and conjecture. There is no development upon this land, and witnesses differ as to the surface indications and the effect and certainty of surface indications. Mineral rights in this vicinity have sold in many instances at $1 per acre. The principal witness for the girls has offered $1,100 for the tract, or $766.66 for these two interests, or twice the amount paid by Storthz. This was some time after the sale to Storthz, and this witness places the value at the time Storthz bought at $800 for the entire interest, which is $350 more than the basis upon which Storthz bought. From the standpoint of the witnesses for the girls, the price is not so shockingly disproportionate of the value, even this speculative value, as to call for the interposition of equity. On the other hand, the evidence for Storthz shows his price to be a fair one, and just such price as other parties in that vicinity owning similar lands were running on an average. "Fraud without damage, or damage without fraud, will not do." Carvill v. Jacks, 43 Ark. 455. . . .

It is evident that Storthz wanted this land for the bauxite deposits which he believed existed in it, and that he was buying it for the mineral value of it. He says that he bought in order to put this in with some other tracts in that vicinity which he was bargaining to sell to a bauxite development company. His purchase was not secret, all the nearest relatives and the girls participated in the deal, and there was no concealment other than his evident belief that it had value as bauxite lands, or that he could induce this company to so believe. Was such conduct sufficient to avoid his purchase, even if the value was grossly inadequate (which, as seen, is doubtful)? In Dugan v. Cureton, 1 Ark. 31, 31 Am. Dec. 727, Chief Justice Ringo said: "It has been repeatedly held that it is not every willful misrepresentation, even of a fact, which will avoid a contract upon the ground of fraud, if it be of such a nature that the other party had no right to place reliance on it, and it was his own folly to give credence to it; for courts of equity, like courts of law, do not aid parties who will not use their own sense and discretion upon matters of this sort." Mr. Justice Walker, in Yeates v. Pryor, 11 Ark. 58, thus stated the rule:

> The misrepresentation, in order to affect the validity of the contract, must relate to some matter of inducement to the making of the contract, in which, from the relative position of the parties and their means of information, the one must necessarily be presumed to contract upon the faith and trust which he reposes in the representations of the other on account of his superior information and knowledge in regard to the subject of the contract; for if the means of information are alike accessible to both, so that, with ordinary prudence or vigilance, the parties might respectively rely upon their own judgment, they must have been presumed to have done so, or, if they have not informed themselves, must abide the consequences of their own inattention and carelessness.

These principles have often been announced, and these cases followed, in subsequent decisions of this court. While these girls were ignorant and young, yet they were surrounded by their grown relatives, who participated in and evidently approved of the sales. The bauxite development in the vicinity of this land was evidently known to all of them; if not, it was solely on account of their own inattention and carelessness. If they gave credence to Storthz's assertion that he was buying of them land that "would not sprout peas" because they were orphans, their folly must pay the penalty. The evidence shows, however, that they refused the early offer, and evidently stood out for the price they wanted, and finally got it. They do not seem to have been carried away with Storthz's representations, and stiffly refused his various offers, even to the point of making him mad and causing him to leave them, which seems to have been characteristic of his trading. On the whole case, the court is of opinion that the sales must stand.

NOTES TO STORTHZ v. ARNOLD

1. *Procedural settings for issues of overreaching.* Cases on land buyer's overreaching are collected in 3 American Law of Property 56-61 (Casner ed. 1952). They fall into the following procedural classes:

   (a) Seller, after contract but before closing, brings an equitable action to cancel the contract.
   (b) Seller refuses to close, and defends against buyer's action for damages or specific performance.
   (c) Seller, after closing, brings an action to cancel the deed.
   (d) After closing, buyer has conveyed to a bona fide purchaser; seller sues buyer for damages or to impress a trust on buyer's receipts under his resale transaction.

Of course, the cases also feature variations on whether the "buyer" and the person who will ultimately "mine" the hidden value are legally related as agent and principal, or as buyer and subvendee.

2. *The chancellor's conscience.* On page 511 supra, you read a dissenting opinion in which Justice Fraser of the South Carolina Supreme Court found it inequitable to permit seller to obtain specific performance against a buyer who bought at the top of a then-ending speculative boom. The Supreme Court of South Carolina in Schmid v. Whitten, 114 S.C. 245, 103 S.E. 553 (1920), denied specific performance to a buyer who, during a boom, contracted to buy (with no down payment) and resold. The court found that, as to buyer, "the only inference from the record is that he was on the make," and as to the country, "one of the curses of the country at present is the gambling speculative craze, whereby a lot are out for easy money and a desire for quick riches." A buyer who is turned down by a squeamish chancellor can always go to the law for his damages remedy; but see Frank and Endicott, Defenses in Equity and "Legal Rights," 14 La. L. Rev. 380 (1954): in a startling number of cases, a plaintiff sent to the law side for being a bad guy winds up with nothing at all.

Although Schmid v. Whitten has not been followed outside of South Carolina, it is well-settled that equity will not grant specific performance to a buyer if the consideration is unconscionable or grossly inadequate. In another case, the trial court, which applied this rule to refuse buyer specific performance, was reversed in Banner v. Elm, 251 Md. 694, 248 A.2d 452 (1960). The buyer, who was assembling acreage, bought defendants' tract in October at 30 cents per square foot, but in November paid a neighbor 75 cents per square foot, and in December paid another neighbor one dollar per square foot.

3. *Options.* Presupposing that he has given consideration as appropriate, an optionee on a land purchase can obtain specific performance. However, for a reason perhaps connected with the theme of this chapter, the rule is that the optionee must strictly comply with the option's terms. See Annot., Time Specified in Real Estate Contract for Giving Notice of Exercise of Option to Purchase as of Essence, 72 A.L.R.2d 1127 (1959).

4. *Purchase for public use.* The Port of New York Authority has been judicially commended for using a dummy brokerage firm to buy up land for a bridge approach (Boyle Holding Corp v. Medgreen Holding Corp., 154 Misc. 189, 276 N.Y.S. 670 (1933)). However, the law of Nebraska provides that eminent domain cannot be used in land acquisition unless the condemnor has made a prior bona fide attempt to agree on value with the landowner (Higgins v. Loup River Public Power District, 157 Neb. 652, 61 N.W.2d 213 (1958)). There is a general eminent domain rule stating that the owner is not entitled to compensation for any value added to his land by the project for which the condemnation is sought.

MAJOR v. CHRISTIAN COUNTY LIVESTOCK MARKET, INC., 300 S.W.2d 246 (Ky. 1957): One year after seller acquired some acreage at $300 an acre as an addition to his 150-acre farm home, buyer bought five and one-half acres from seller at $600 an acre. Buyer represented that he was buying the acreage for the purpose of building a home. The deed to buyer contained restrictions against the following: (1) use in liquor business; (2) use in the amusement business; (3) use for tourist cabins; (4) any use interfering with natural drainage; or (5) sale or lease to any person of African descent.

One month after acquiring the tract in suit, buyer conveyed it to a newly incorporated livestock company, of which the buyer was president and 25 percent owner. When the company commenced construction of a stockyard, plaintiff seller first sought an injunction on nuisance grounds, which was denied. Plaintiff seller then sued to rescind. In deciding for defendant, the trial court found that buyer had purchased the property in good faith for a home site and had later changed his mind. The court of appeals, in affirming, decided that the finding of fact was adequately supported by evidence and stated:

"[Seller] had the five restrictions inserted in the deed. Had he been as insistent when he executed the deed to [buyer] as he is now that the property should not be used for a livestock market, he could have obviated all controversy by putting such a restriction in the deed. The weakest part of [seller's] case is he inserted the restrictions he thought important, but did not put in the deed a restriction against using this property for a livestock market."

BRETT v. COONEY, 75 Conn. 388, 53 A. 729 (1902): Plaintiffs sold their unrestricted summer beach home to a buyer who said he was buying the premises for a summer home, but who was in fact buying for, and who immediately conveyed to, the defendant. Defendant had previously been trying to buy into the neighborhood to run a boarding house; she had failed because plaintiff and his neighbors regarded boarding houses and the defendant as undesirable neighbors. Defendant argued that plaintiff, having received a fair price, could not rescind; fraud without damage, said defendant, is no wrong. The court found that although plaintiff had sustained no pecuniary damage from the fraud, he was entitled to rescind because he had been fraudulently deprived of his jus disponendi. But query that plaintiff had sustained no damage: if aware that a boarding house keeper wanted the property, would not plaintiff, qua economic man, have gotten a little something extra for selling out his neighbors? Or would this sell-out opportunity be reflected in seller's "fair" price to an unobjectionable buyer?

Somehow related to the problem of the *Brett* case is the law's disfavor of use restraints imposed by a seller who is planning to leave the neighborhood.

HERSCH v. SILBERSTEIN, 424 Pa. 486, 227 A.2d 638 (1967): Plaintiff-appellants sought to rescind as to their conveyance of a one-acre lot adjoining their home. Defendant-appellees Silberstein had represented that they were buying for their own use, but in fact were buying for and immediately conveyed to Negro defendant-appellees, Cross.

The opinion by Judge Cohen notes the trial court's finding that the price was adequate. It cites §304 of the Restatement of Agency: "A person with whom an agent contracts on account of an undisclosed principal can rescind the contract if he was induced to enter into it by a representation that the agent was not acting for a principal and if, as the agent or principal had notice, he would not have dealt with such principal." The court also notes that appellants described themselves as bringing the action not "because they had any prejudice against negroes, but solely because of the fraud practised upon them." The opinion concludes that there was no cognizable damage and no fraud.

Bron v. Weintraub
42 N.J. 87, 199 A.2d 625 (1964)

WEINTRAUB, C.J. In 1935 the Township of Woodbridge sold certain vacant lands for unpaid taxes and itself was the buyer at the sale. In 1940 it foreclosed the tax sale certificates in the former Court of Chancery. That proceeding ran against Danwil Developers, Inc., as owner. However, in 1929 that company had conveyed to El-Ka Holding Co., Inc., which in turn conveyed to Harry Weintraub in 1931. Weintraub apparently was the secretary of both corporations. He died intestate in 1933, survived by two sisters who lived in California. The searcher did not pick up the conveyances just mentioned and hence the 1940 foreclosure suit ran only against Danwil Developers, Inc., as we have said.

In 1952 Woodbridge conveyed the lands to a developer who erected homes and sold them for $10,000 to $11,000 each. Ten such parcels are here involved. In 1959 one of the homes was resold and a search in that connection revealed the failure to bar the Weintraub interests. The township was asked to foreclose those interests, and it started a suit to that end. N.J.S.A. 54:5-86.1 et seq. Judgment was entered fixing November 13, 1959 as the date by which the unknown heirs of Weintraub had to redeem or be barred. At the eleventh hour Hudson Trading Corporation and Frank Altomare redeemed on the basis of deeds obtained from the Weintraub heirs (the deeds ran to Hudson which in turn conveyed a quarter interest to Altomare).

The present actions ensued, the householders seeking to quiet title and Hudson and Altomare demanding possession and mesne profits. Hudson and Altomare conceded the householders were equitably entitled to remove the improvements or to buy the land at its value unaffected by the improvements. The trial court entered a judgment under which the householders would have to pay for the land the sum of $19,555.11, found to be its value as of the time of the deeds to Hudson and Altomare, plus mesne profits of $2,856.91. Hudson had paid the Weintraub heirs but $400. The Appellate Division affirmed and we granted certification. 40 N.J. 507 (1963).

The householders urge that Hudson and Altomare be declared constructive trustees and be required to convey title upon payment of the $400 they gave the Weintraub heirs. Alternatively they say the lands should be valued as of a date prior to the date of the deeds to Hudson, and that, whatever date is approved, the lands should be valued without enhancement due to streets, sidewalks, sewers, and curbing. As to the last proposition, it is unclear whether the appraisers had excluded those items in valuing the "unimproved" land.

We need consider only the first proposition, that Hudson and Altomare should receive no more than what they paid the Weintraub heirs, since we are satisfied the householders are entitled to prevail upon it.

Here ten homes were purchased in the bona fide belief that title was good. The defect in the 1940 foreclosure was discovered in 1959, some 28 years after the original owners of the vacant land had last paid a penny of taxes. The municipality started a second suit to perfect the title, and in that action it was necessary to advertise as against the Weintraub heirs. In that way Hudson learned of an opportunity to make some money out of the predicament of these householders.

Hudson located Weintraub's sisters in California. Exactly when we do not know, but on November 7, only six days before the date fixed for redemption, one Herbert Harvey wrote to them. His letter opened with a statement that it related to "lots in Middlesex County, New Jersey, in which, according to the record, the late Harry Weintraub had an interest." That the interest was ownership in fee was not disclosed. The letter correctly said the property was sold for taxes in 1935 and a foreclosure action was brought in 1940, but added only that the foreclosure action was deemed "possibly defective." It continued that "you might claim an interest" and we are writing to inquire whether you "will furnish a voluntary release of your possible claim" for a "courtesy consideration" of $50 "for the release." It adds that "The required instrument, in the form of a quitclaim deed, is enclosed." We interpolate that trial counsel for Hudson and Altomare placed on the record:

"It is Mr. Harvey's practice to take quit-claim deeds. I say that of all the deeds he gets, 90 percent are quit-claim deeds. He knows by law a quit-claim deed is just as good as any other kind of a deed."

Mr. Harvey was well informed in that regard, R.S. 46:5-1 et seq., but we assume, as no doubt he did, that the recipient of his letter would likely think only of some claim to be released to the existing holder of title in fee. Indeed the letter said the deed "will have the effect of releasing any claim which you have or may have in the land therein described." Finally the letter noted that "this instrument will serve its purpose only if it reaches us without delay—actually no later than November 13, which seems practically return mail." Appreciation was promised for "your cooperation" and the letter closed "With thanks for your courtesy in the matter."

This letter was palpably deceptive. It was deceptive as to the nature of the outstanding interest. It was deceptive as to identity of the parties on whose behalf it was written. In the latter respect, if no more appeared, it would permit an inference that Harvey led the Weintraub heirs to believe he was acting for the householders, and upon such a finding a constructive trust could be imposed in their favor. Bell v. Smith, 159 Fla. 817, 32 So. 2d 829, 175 A.L.R. 695 (Sup. Ct. 1947), annotated 175 A.L.R. 700 (1948). The cause, however, was not tried on the theory of fraud, and since we are told there were further communications with the Weintraub heirs not spread on the record, we should not decide the case on that basis. Nonetheless we refer to the fraudulent nature of this communication as a sample of the kind of thing to be expected if we hold that strangers may exploit these situations.

Let us look at the interests involved and the impact of Hudson's activities upon them.

We are dealing with tax titles. Contrary to early hostility to such titles, the policy today is to support them, thereby to aid municipalities in raising revenue. To that end N.J.S.A. 54:5-85 provides:

"The provisions of this article shall be liberally construed as remedial legislation to encourage the barring of the right of redemption by actions in the Superior Court to the end that marketable titles may thereby be secured."

Everybody knows that taxes must be paid. True, there may be instances in which the individual concerned is unaware of his property interest, but such cases are rare. Usually the owner omits to pay knowing the end result will be a tax sale. It is therefore understandable that the Legislature found it fair to bar the right to redeem by a strict foreclosure, i.e., by a judgment that payment be made by a fixed date, in default of which the right to redeem shall end, rather than by a sale as in the case of the foreclosure of a mortgage. The point we stress is that, whereas with respect to the initial sale for taxes, the statute intends to attract third parties to the opportunity to acquire the property and provides for public notice to that end, N.J.S.A. 54:5-25 and 26, there is no like policy to invite the public to participate with respect to the foreclosure of the right to redeem. . . .

Hence the foreclosure process concerns only the holder of the tax sale certificate and the holders of existing interests in the property. Hudson learned of this situation, not because it was the policy of the law to advertise to solicit its interest, but because of the fortuitous circumstance that the foreclosing municipality had not located the Weintraub heirs. If they had been found, they could have been served without the need for publication. R.R. 4:4-5. In short, our rules of court called for this public notice solely to reach the holders of existing interests, but Hudson read a communication intended for another and sought to turn that information to its own gain, thereby depriving the householders of a chance to work out their misfortunes with the holders of the outstanding interests upon a basis presumably no more onerous than the basis upon which Hudson acquired those interests.

In attacking the legality of Hudson's activity, the householders appeal to public policy, the ultimate source of justice. Public policy has been described but never quite defined. . . . [The court quotes from several cases which do not quite define public policy.]

With respect to the factual pattern before us, no one disputes the right of the holders of existing interests to convey them to third persons if they wish. What is challenged is the legality of the intrusion into the scene by third persons who seek only to further their own interests rather than the interests already on hand. As we have pointed out, the policy of the statute is to support tax titles, a policy which overall is burdened by the conduct before us. The burden upon individuals situated as are the householders in this case is evident enough. These manifest hurts should not be tolerated unless it can be said that some other legitimate interest or advantage is served. We find none. We see no social value or contribution in the activities of Hudson. On the contrary, decent men must sense only revulsion in this traffic in the misfortunes of others.

We are not aware of any precedent precisely in point, although reference could appropriately be made to the established hostility toward so-called "heir-hunting." See Carey v. Thieme, 2 N.J. Super. 458, 466 (Ch. Div. 1949); Annotation, 171 A.L.R. 351 (1947); note, 7 Vand. L. Rev. 104 (1953). In any event, public policy is more than a mere summation of its past applications. . . . As Judge Desmond said in Latham v. Father Divine, 299 N.Y. 22, 27, 85 N.E.2d 168, 170, 111 A.L.R.2d 802 (Ct. App.

1949), the applicability of the concept of a constructive trust "is limited only by the inventiveness of men who find new ways to enrich themselves unjustly by grasping what should not belong to them." We have no doubt the common conscience condemns the conduct of Hudson and Altomare as an undue interference with the rights of the householders. Hudson and Altomare having acquired the outstanding title under "circumstances which render it unconscientious for the holder of the legal title to retain and enjoy the beneficial interest, equity impresses a constructive trust on the property thus acquired in favor of the one who is truly and equitably entitled to the same." 4 Pomeroy, Equity Jurisprudence (5th ed. 1941) §1053, p. 119. <u>The householders are equitably entitled to the property upon the payment of the sum of $400 plus simple interest</u> from the date of the payment to the Weintraub heirs.

The judgments are therefore reversed and the matters remanded to the trial court with direction to enter judgments in harmony with this opinion.

From Appellant's Brief

The plaintiffs are ordinary, unsophisticated homeowners, presumably living on their properties with their families. They are in the lower income bracket or perhaps the lower middle income bracket, depending upon one's definition of these categories. Their homes were purchased in 1953 for between $10,000.00 to $11,000.00. They may be veterans of the United States armed forces for their purchases were made possible only through provisions in our Federal laws which in effect permitted practically the entire purchase price to be financed by long-term, low-interest mortgages. When they purchased their homes, they relied on the mortgage company as to their title, for their only contact was with the attorney for the mortgage company. They did not obtain title insurance, indeed they may not even have known what title insurance was. All they knew was that like many other people throughout the country and many more thereafter, they were buying a home in a development and ready to start a new life. They did their best every month to meet the mortgage and tax payments and presumably tried within their limited means to maintain the home. Their families grew and attended school. Presumably they participated in the civic, social and recreational affairs of the municipality and the neighborhood in which they lived. They went to work during the week and relaxed on weekends. They attempted in our installment-purchase age to make ends meet periodically. Their ownership of their homes constituted the foundation upon which their entire life was based: job, family, political, social, cultural, recreational and civic activities, all were premised on the home. A destruction or interruption of their peaceful possession would destroy or interrupt all that flowed therefrom.

Herbert Harvey reads newspapers. He reads the legal notices in the newspapers and attempts to learn therefrom the names of those who are

Straws, Speculators, and Sharpies

having some problem with the title to their property. He tries to determine who may have an outstanding interest in someone else's land; he is most interested in those people who have an outstanding interest but don't know that they have one. The ingredients of his livelihood are innocent mistakes made by those who acquire what appears to be good title and lack of knowledge on the part of those who have an interest which makes the title not good. His talents include the discovery of the concurrent existence of these ingredients, the location of the people with an interest, and a somewhat less than candid approach to them for the purpose of buying that interest. In effect, they are led to believe that they really don't own anything but they should "release" it just to clear title. His activities result in advising persons of the ownership of possible interests, of whose existence they never knew nor ever relied in the ordering of their lives; his activities result in the purchase of same and in the assertion of these interests in the form of claims of one sort or another by Mr. Harvey or his designees; they result in a small payment to the unsuspecting owner, a large profit to Mr. Harvey, and misery and tragedy to the couple formerly living in the home, to their children, their families and the community in which they live. His activities in no way preserve or protect private property in the ordinary sense. They merely preserve and protect a legal interest which, but for his activities, would have expired in due time silently and without damage to anyone's life or to society; his activities protect and preserve a legal interest called "property" but upon which no social or economic structure was ever based; they awaken a legal interest solely for the purpose of destroying.

In short, Mr. Harvey, Hudson Trading and Altomare are "title raiders." They are like vultures, feeding on the mistakes and ignorance of innocent victims. When they find their prey, they feed without remorse or conscience. Using the complexities of a highly-developed society as their working tools, they seize on the accepted, insignificant and common-place decisions and activities of ordinary men whom they observe from afar. They ascertain a speck, a pinpoint of vulnerability—perhaps a decision not to hire a lawyer since the mortgage company would be there, or since someone told him he didn't need one; a bleary-eyed searcher who misses a number and another who relies on the search—and they pick and pick at this point of vulnerability until it becomes a fatal wound. . . .

From Respondent's Brief

While appellants' salvo may have poetic charm and melodramatic effect, these literary qualities have been purchased at the expense of accuracy and fair dealing. Respondents consider it entirely unfitting and unseemly that a petition should be addressed to the highest court of this state which is based on bogus emotional appeal, wanton exaggeration, and the temperament and tone of gossip and rumor. The untenability of appellants' legal position is neither strengthened nor veiled by their barrage of irresponsible personal invective and sham sentimentality. Their lyrical tragedy of the impending forces of evil invading the federally-financed hearthrug of innocence and virtue is an irrelevant, inaccurate and grossly unwarranted portrayal.

In casting Hudson and Mr. Harvey as the villains of the piece, appellants completely overlook the fact that neither in any way caused their present plight — neither in any way had anything to do with the patent invalidity of their titles, with the construction of the improvements, or with their purchases. Appellants Bron have obviously no one but themselves to blame. They can hardly claim innocence, having purchased with full notice of the title defect and obviously having chosen to take their chances notwithstanding the manifest nullity of title. As to the others, their situation results primarily from their imprudence in having chosen not to hire their own lawyers when they bought their homes.

When appellants chose the reforeclosure technique as the device for eliminating the outstanding Weintraub interest, they actually invited redemption. Now they claim to have been victimized because redemption was made. Their imputation of some element of criminality in the act of reading legal notices in newspapers is absurd — one presumes that such notices are printed for the express purpose of being read by the general public. While appellants complain so bitterly of respondents' investigation which revealed the existence of the Weintraub heirs, nowhere do they suggest that they undertook an investigation similarly designed to locate these people in order that they might also negotiate with them for the purchase of their interest. Appellants obviously gambled with the probability of cutting off the Weintraub interest without payment to anyone of consideration. It was they who hoped to get something for nothing and they lost their gamble.

Appellants make the shocking statement that but for respondents, the legal interest of the Weintraub heirs "would have expired in due time, silently and without damage to anyone's life or to society," (Ab11-19 to 20), meaning, it is supposed, that their gamble would have succeeded through ignorance and the silence of the grave. Do appellants seriously suggest that one's unawareness of an inheritance is good cause for depriving him of it altogether? Certainly the law of descent represents a significant and protectible social interest. Appellants themselves point out that the taxes on the property were unpaid only after Harry Weintraub's death, at which time and for long thereafter his heirs had no knowledge of his ownership of the lands. Thus they could never have abandoned their interest therein, as appellants have suggested. They simply did not know of it. . . .

Furthermore the dirge of appellants' utter financial doom is greatly exaggerated, particularly in view of the fact that they are not remediless as against their grantors and those whose negligence caused and contributed to their present situation. For the past ten years, they have had the undisturbed and uninterrupted use of the property. They made these purchases by means of little or no down payment, long term, V.A. mortgages. Their actual cash investment in the property was therefore little or nothing. As a matter of simple mathematics, this Court may take judicial notice of their small monthly payments. According to the amortization tables published by the Financial Publishing Company of Boston, the monthly payment required to amortize an $11,000 direct reduction mortgage loan at five percent interest over a twenty year period is $72.60, which even with taxes added is a modest rental figure. While the exact mortgage principal, interest rates and term are not precisely specified, it is at least clearly inferrable that the interest rate is less and the term longer than above hypothesized. Furthermore the judgment does not deprive the appellants of the houses themselves, the appreciation of the value of the buildings attributable to the high increase during the past ten years in building reproduction costs, and the benefit of any home improvements they may have made.

This much alone is clear. If the appellants are anyone's victims, they are the victims of the title and mortgage company (one and the same here), and the insidious practice pervading new home purchasing whereby a residential developer's searching and title costs are passed onto the buyer through a conflict of interest situation involving dual and sometimes triple representation, a situation recently condemned by this Court in In re Kamp, 40 N.J. [588] (1963). These purchasers were not independently represented. But whether or not an attorney acted solely in their interests, some attorney probably did purport to act for them in the closing of the title and the mortgage. It is represented that they paid for the search and other closing fees (Ab4-1 to 3). They apparently were led to believe that their title interests were fully protected. Presumably someone actually did or should have certified title to them. . . .

C. SELLER'S OBLIGATIONS

1. *Destruction of Premises During the Executory Interval*

Bixby, The Vendor-Vendee Problem: How Do We Slice the Insurance Pie?
19 The Forum 112-114 (1983)

An executory contract for real property involves an agreement to sell property with a subsequent transfer of title. Between the time of the agreement and transfer of title, damage to the property may occur. The parties can contractually agree [on] who is to bear the risk of loss. In the absence of contractual agreement, the courts have developed three primary rules to allocate risk of loss between vendor and vendee.

The first rule leaves the risk of loss on the vendor until title passes. After a loss a vendee may elect to complete the contract or rescind it. There may be an additional election to abate the price. Placing the risk on the vendor has been called the "Massachusetts" rule. It has been followed in only a few states.

The second rule places the risk of loss on the vendee after the contract has been signed. This rule is based on the 1801 English case, Paine v. Meller. The vendee is considered to have all the indicia of ownership except title, that is, he is the equitable owner. This rule is referred to as the doctrine of "equitable conversion." Although in many instances the vendee may have possession of the property, the doctrine of equitable conversion does not require possession. Risk of loss shifts to the vendee immediately. Limited exceptions occur if the vendor for some reason was not in a position to convey title.

The equitable conversion rule is followed by a majority of American jurisdictions despite being severely criticized for placing a substantial burden on a vendee (risk of loss) without corresponding benefits. The continuing vitality of the equitable conversion rule is probably due to the presence of insurance. There is a reasonable probability the vendor had a preexisting property insurance policy. American courts almost uniformly impose a trust on the proceeds of the vendor's insurance policy for the benefit of the vendee in states following the equitable conversion rule. This is consistent with the asserted layman's concept that insurance runs with the property. The English accomplished the same result by statute when their courts refused to give the vendee the benefit of a vendor's insurance.

The third common law rule focuses on possession of the property. The person in possession bears the risk of loss until title is transferred. It is asserted the possession test is preferable because it places the risk of loss on the party likely to have the most interest in protecting the property. The possession test was adopted in the Uniform Vendor and Purchaser Risk Act promulgated by the National Commissioners on Uniform State Laws. This act has been adopted in eleven states. The possession rule is also used in the more recent Uniform Land Transaction Code. . . .

The foregoing risk of loss rules for executory real estate transfers are relatively straightforward. It is the judicial effort to provide insurance coverage to a person who is not a party to the insurance contract which creates most problems in vendor-vendee situations. In trying to give an uninsured the benefit of insurance on a case by case basis, courts have rejected certain principles of insurance. While these insurance principles are often tested in other situations, the vendor-vendee cases seem to trigger more conflicts more often.

The insurance principles often ignored by courts in deciding vendor-vendee cases include: the insurance policy is a personal contract; insurance is intended to provide indemnity; insurance covers the insurable interest of the insured; an insurer is subrogated to the rights of its insured; and loss is determined as of the date of the occurrence.

[handwritten: Follows Mass. rule. Seller bears risk]

Skelly Oil Co. v. Ashmore
365 S.W.2d 582 (Mo. 1963) (en banc)

HYDE, Judge. [In March 1958, defendant-sellers were the owners of improved business premises. The premises were subject to a $7200 mortgage and were leased to a tenant through 1961 at a rental of $150 per month.

Defendants, that same March, agreed to sell the premises, subject to the lease but free of the mortgage, to Skelly Oil Company for $20,000. Skelly, owning premises adjacent to those in the suit, planned at some later date to combine the tracts for a gas station. The closing was set for April 16, 1958. On April 7, 1958, the building on the lot was destroyed by fire without fault of either party. Seller had a $10,000 insurance policy, and, according to its terms, the insurance company paid off the $7200 mortgage and gave the $2800 balance to defendants. Plaintiffs sued for a decree compelling defendants specifically to perform but seeking an abatement in the purchase price of $10,000 as the amount of the insurance policy proceeds. The trial court decreed plaintiffs' requested relief; defendants appealed. The opinion states the facts, dismisses defendants' contention that there was no enforceable contract, and continues:]

The contract of sale here involved contained no provision as to who assumed the risk of loss occasioned by a destruction of the building, or for protecting the building by insurance or for allocating any insurance proceeds received therefor. When the parties met to close the sale on April 16, the purchaser's counsel informed vendors and their attorneys he was relying on Standard Oil Co. v. Dye, 223 Mo. App. 926, 20 S.W.2d 946, for purchaser's claim to the $10,000 insurance proceeds on the building. . . . It is stated in 3 American Law of Property, §11.30, p. 90, that in the circumstances here presented at least five different views have been advanced for allocating the burden of fortuitous loss between vendor and purchaser of real estate. We summarize those mentioned: (1) The view first enunciated in Paine v. Meller (Ch. 1801, 6 Ves. Jr. 349, 31 Eng. Reprint 1088, 1089) is said to be the most widely accepted; holding that from the time of the contract of sale of real estate the burden of fortuitous loss was on the purchaser even though the vendor retained possession. (2) The loss is on the vendor until legal title is conveyed, although the purchaser is in possession, stated to be a strong minority. (3) The burden of loss should be on the vendor until the time agreed upon for conveying the legal title, and thereafter on the purchaser unless the vendor be in such default as to preclude specific performance, not recognized in the decisions. (4) The burden of the loss should be on the party in possession, whether vendor or purchaser, so considered by some courts. (5) The burden of loss should be on vendor unless there is something in the contract or in the relation of the parties from which the court can infer a different intention, stating "this rather vague test" has not received any avowed judicial acceptance, although it is not inconsistent with jurisdictions holding the loss is on the vendor until conveyance or jurisdictions adopting the possession test. . . .

We do not agree that we should adopt the arbitrary rule of Paine v. Meller, supra, and Standard Oil Co. v. Dye, supra, that there is equitable conversion from the time of making a contract for sale and purchase of land and that the risk of loss from destruction of buildings or other substantial part of the property is from that moment on the purchaser. Criticisms of this rule by eminent authorities have been set out in the dissenting opinion of Storckman, J., herein and will not be repeated here.

We take the view stated in an article on Equitable Conversion by Contract, 13 Columbia Law Review 369, 386, Dean Harlan F. Stone, later Chief Justice Stone, in which he points out that the only reason why a contract for the sale of land by the owner to another operates to effect conversion is that a court of equity will compel him specifically to perform his contract. He further states: "A preliminary to the determination of the question whether there is equitable ownership of land must therefore necessarily be the determination of the question whether there is a contract which can be and ought to be specifically performed *at the very time when the court is called upon to perform it.* This process of reasoning is, however, reversed in those jurisdictions where the 'burden of loss' is cast upon the vendee. The question is whether there shall be a specific performance of the contract, thus casting the burden on the vendee, by compelling him to pay the full purchase price for the subject matter of the contract, a substantial part of which has been destroyed. The question is answered somewhat in this wise: equitable ownership of the vendee in the subject matter of the contract can exist only where the contract is one which equity will specifically perform. The vendee of land is equitably entitled to land, therefore the vendee may be compelled to perform, although the vendor is unable to give in return the performance stipulated for by this contract. The non sequitur involved in the proposition that performance may be had because of the equitable ownership of the land by the vendee, which in turn depends upon the right of performance, is evident. The doctrine of equitable conversion, so far as it is exemplified by the authorities hitherto considered, cannot lead to the result of casting the burden of loss on the vendee, since the *conversion depends upon the question whether the contract should in equity be performed.* In all other cases where the vendee is treated as the equitable owner of the land, it is only because the contract is one which equity first determines should be specifically performed.

Seller's Obligations

"Whether a plaintiff, in breach of his contract by a default which goes to the essence, as in the case of the destruction of a substantial part of the subject matter of the contract, should be entitled to specific performance, is a question which is answered in the negative in every case except that of destruction of the subject matter of the contract. To give a plaintiff specific performance of the contract when he is unable to perform the contract on his own part, violates the fundamental rule of equity that . . . *equity will not compel a defendant to perform when it is unable to so frame its decree as to compel the plaintiff to give in return substantially what he had undertaken to give* or to do for the defendant.

"The rule of casting the 'burden of loss' on the vendee by specific performance if justifiable at all can only be explained and justified upon one of two theories: first, that since equity has for most purposes treated the vendee as the equitable owner, it should do so for all purposes, although *this ignores the fact that in all other cases the vendee is so treated only because the contract is either being performed or in equity ought to be performed;* or, second, which is substantially the same proposition in a different form, the specific performance which casts the burden on the vendee is an incident to and a consequence of an equitable conversion, whereas in all other equity relations growing out of the contract, the equitable conversion, if it exists, is an incident to and consequence of, a specific performance. Certainly nothing could be more illogical than this process of reasoning." (Emphasis ours.)

For these reasons, we do not agree with the rule that arbitrarily places the risk of loss on the vendee from the time the contract is made. Instead we believe the Massachusetts rule is the proper rule. It is thus stated in Libman v. Levenson, 236 Mass. 221, 128 N.E. 13, 22 A.L.R. 560: When "the conveyance is to be made of the whole estate, including both land and buildings, for an entire price, and the value of the buildings constitutes a large part of the total value of the estate, and the terms of the agreement show that they constituted an important part of the subject matter of the contract . . . the contract is to be construed as subject to the implied condition that it no longer shall be binding if, before the time for the conveyance to be made, the buildings are destroyed by fire. The loss by the fire falls upon the vendor, the owner; and if he has not protected himself by insurance, he can have no reimbursement of this loss; but the contract is no longer binding upon either party. If the purchaser has advanced any part of the price, he can recover it back. Thompson v. Gould, [supra] 20 Pick. [37 Mass.] 134, 138. If the change in the value of the estate is not so great, or if it appears that the buildings did not constitute so material a part of the estate to be conveyed as to result in an annulling of the contract, specific performance may be decreed, *with compensation for any breach of agreement,* or relief may be given in damages." (Emphasis ours.) . . . An extreme case, showing the unfairness of the arbitrary rule placing all loss on the vendee, is Amundson v. Severson, 41 S.D. 377, 170 N.W. 633, where three-fourths of the land sold was washed away by the Missouri River (the part left being of little value) and the vendor brought suit for specific performance. Fortunately for the vendee, he was relieved by the fact that the vendor did not have good title at the time of the loss, although the vendor had procured it as a basis for his suit. However, if the vendor had then held good title even though he did not have the land; the vendee would have been required to pay the full contract price under the loss on the purchaser rule. (Would the vendee have been any better off if the vendor had good title from the start but did not have the land left to convey?) The reason for the Massachusetts rule is that specific performance is based on what is equitable; and it is not equitable to make a vendee pay the vendor for something the vendor cannot give him.

However, the issue in this case is not whether the vendee can be compelled to take the property without the building but whether the vendee is entitled to enforce the contract of sale, with the insurance proceeds substituted for the destroyed building. We see no inequity to defendants in such enforcement since they will receive the full amount ($20,000.00) for which they contracted to sell the property. Their contract not only described the land but also specifically stated they sold it "together with the buildings, driveways and all construction thereon." While the words "Service Station Site" appeared in the caption of the option contract and that no doubt was the ultimate use plaintiff intended to make of the land, the final agreement made by the parties was that plaintiff would take it subject to a lease of the building which would have brought plaintiff about $6,150.00 in rent during the term of the lease. Moreover, defendants' own evidence showed the building was valued in the insurance adjustment at $16,716.00 from which $4,179.00 was deducted for depreciation, making the loss $12,537.00. Therefore, defendants are not in a very good position to say the building was of no value to plaintiff. Furthermore, plaintiff having contracted for the land with the building on it, the decision concerning use or removal of the building, or even for resale of the entire property, was for the plaintiff to make. Statements were in evidence about the use of the building and its value to plaintiff made by its employee who negotiated the purchase but he was not one of plaintiff's chief executive officers nor possessed of authority to bind its board of directors. The short of the matter is that defendants will get all they bargained for; but without the building or its value plaintiff will not.

We therefore affirm the judgment and decree of the trial court.

Eager, Leedy and Hollingsworth, JJ., concur.

Storckman, J., dissents in separate opinion filed.

Westhues, C.J., and Dalton, J., dissent and concur in separate dissenting opinion of Storckman, J.

STORCKMAN Judge (dissenting). . . . I cannot assent to the holding that the plaintiff is entitled to specific performance on any terms other than those of the purchase contract without reduction in the contract price. . . .

Seller's Obligations

The evidence is convincing that Skelly Oil Company was buying the lot as a site for a service station and that in so using it they not only wanted the Jones's lease terminated but intended to tear down and remove the building in question. The contract documents support this conclusion. Both the option and the letter of acceptance refer to the property as a "service station site" and contain escape clauses permitting Skelly to avoid the purchase agreement if proper permits could not be obtained or if zoning laws prohibited such use. From the time the option was first granted on July 31, 1957, through its various extensions, until the letter of March 4, 1958, Mr. Busby, Skelly's real estate representative, was cooperating with and urging Mr. Ashmore and his attorney to secure a termination of the Jones's lease (which was on the entire property) even to the extent of filing an ejectment suit against the lessee. Then after the fire Skelly's legal department prepared as one of the closing documents an agreement to be executed by the Ashmores and the Jones for mutual cancellation of the lease. The purchase contract calls for an assignment of the Jones's lease by the Ashmores to Skelly and its honoring the lease; but, at the request of Mr. Busby, the Ashmores on April 17, 1958, with the approval of their attorney, executed and delivered to Mr. Busby the mutual cancellation agreement. This conduct is consistent with its prior activities, but is inconsistent with plaintiff's present contention that the building and its rental under the lease represented a substantial part of the consideration for the purchase of the real estate.

Count 1 of the petition is for specific performance in accordance with the terms of the purchase contract; Count 2 seeks a declaration that the defendants hold the $10,000 insurance proceeds in trust for the benefit of the plaintiff and that the defendants be required to pay the proceeds to the plaintiff or that the amount thereof be applied in reduction of the purchase price of the property. Count 2 alleges that the concrete block, single-story building which was used as a grocery store was totally destroyed by fire, that the defendants collected the insurance thereon, and that "said building was a valuable appurtenance on said real estate worth more than $10,000.00 and that its destruction reduced the value of said real estate more than the sum of $10,000.00."

In spite of the issue made by Count 2 as to effect of the destruction of the building upon the value of the real estate, the trial court refused to permit cross-examination of plaintiff's witness to establish that the purpose and intent of Skelly was to remove the building from the premises when the lease was terminated, and the court rejected defendants' offer of proof to the same effect. In this equity action the testimony should have been received. It did not tend to vary or contradict the written contract but dealt with an issue made by plaintiff's petition based on a partial destruction of the subject matter subsequent to the acceptance of the option. Nevertheless, there was other evidence from which it could be reasonably inferred that the use of the real estate as a filling station site necessitated the removal of the building. Mr. Ashmore testified that he originally asked $27,000 for the property but reduced his price on Mr. Busby's representation that the improvements had no value to Skelly and that Skelly would be glad to have Mr. Ashmore remove them.

The plaintiff introduced no evidence of the market value of the property before or after the fire in support of the allegations in Count 2. The amount paid by the insurance company is of little or no benefit as evidence of the actual value of the building because of the valued policy law of Missouri which provides that in case of the total destruction of a building by fire, insurance companies shall not be permitted to deny that the property insured was worth at the time of issuing the policy or policies the full amount for which the property was insured. Sections 379.140 and 379.145, R.S. Mo. 1959, V.A.M.S. Defendants' evidence tended to prove that the real estate was worth more as a site for a service station after the fire than before and that the value of the real estate after the fire was in excess of $20,000.

The claim of neither party is particularly compelling insofar as specific performance in this case is concerned. The destruction of the building by fire, its insurance, and the disposition of the insurance proceeds were matters not contemplated by the parties and not provided for in the purchase contract documents. Skelly's representative did not know that Mr. Ashmore carried insurance on the building until after the fire, and he then told Mr. Ashmore that despite the fire the deal would be closed on the agreed date. Skelly's present claims are an afterthought inconsistent with its conduct throughout the negotiations and prior to the closing date.

In short, as to both Skelly and the Ashmores, the destruction of the insured building was a fortuitous circumstance supplying the opportunity to rid the property of a vexatious lease, to dispose of the building, and at the same time resulting in a windfall of $10,000. And the problem, in fact the only seriously contested issue between the parties, is which of them is to have the advantage of this piece of good fortune. Skelly contracted to pay $20,000 for the property. If it is awarded the $10,000 windfall, it will receive a $20,000 lot for $10,000. If the Ashmores retain the $10,000, they will in fact have realized $30,000 for a piece of property they have agreed to sell for $20,000.

In claiming the proceeds of the Ashmores' fire insurance policy, Skelly did not contend that the value of the real estate as a service station site had decreased. After learning of the fire and the existence of the insurance policy, Skelly's counsel did some research and, as he announced when the parties met in Joplin to close the deal, Skelly was relying on a case he had found, Standard Oil Company v. Dye, 223 Mo. App. 926, 20 S.W.2d 946. And in its basic facts the case admittedly is quite similar to this one although there were no attendant circumstances such as we have in the present case. The doctrine of [this case] laboriously evolved from Paine v. Meller, (1801) 6 Ves. Jr. 349, 31 Eng. Reprint 1088, is "that a contract to sell real property vests the equitable ownership of the property in the purchaser, with the corollary that any loss by destruction of the property through casualty during the pendency of the contract must be borne by the purchaser." The twofold rationale of this doctrine is a maxim that "equity regards as done that which should have been done," from which it is said the "vendor becomes a mere trustee, holding the legal title for the benefit of the purchaser or as security for the price." 27 A.L.R.2d 444, 448, 449. All of the experts and scholars seem to agree that this doctrine and its rationale is misplaced if not unsound. . . . As to the maxim, Williston said, "Only the hoary age and frequent repetition of the maxim prevents a general recognition of its absurdity." 4 Williston, Contracts, §929, p. 2607. As to the corollary, Williston points out that while the purchaser may have an interest in the property, it is equally clear that the vendor likewise has an interest, and as for the vendor's being a trustee for the purchaser observes, "However often the words may be repeated, it cannot be true that the vendor is trustee for the purchaser." 4 Williston, Contracts, §936, p. 2622. See also Pound, The Progress of The Law— Equity, 33 Har. L.R. 814, 830.

Nevertheless, adapting this doctrine and following a majority opinion in another English case, Rayner v. Preston, (1881) L.R. 18 Ch. Div. 1 (CA), the rule as stated in the Dye case has evolved: "Where the purchaser as equitable owner will bear the loss occasioned by a destruction of the property pending completion of the sale, and the contract is silent as to insurance, the rule quite generally followed is that the proceeds of the vendor's insurance policies, even though the purchaser did not contribute to their maintenance, constitute a trust fund for the benefit of the purchaser to be credited on the purchase price of the destroyed property, the theory being that the vendor is a trustee of the property for the purchaser." Annotation 64 A.L.R.2d 1402, 1406. Many jurisdictions have modified or do not follow this doctrine, some take the view that the vendor's insurance policy is personal to him, and Parliament has enacted a statute which entirely changes the English rule. 4 Mo. L.R. 290, 296. The rule is not as general as the annotator indicated, and as with the rule upon which it is founded, all the experts agree that it is unsound, their only point of disagreement is as to what the rule should be. . . .

Professor Williston was of the view that the risk of loss [pending transfer of legal title] should follow possession (4 Williston, Contracts, §§940, 942), and that view has been written into the Uniform Vendor and Purchaser Risk Act 9C U.L.A., p. 314 and 1960 Supp., p. 82. Eight states have adopted that act and four of those, California, New York, South Dakota, and Oregon, are listed among the fifteen jurisdictions said by the A.L.R. annotator (64 A.L.R. 1406) to follow the Dye case. . . .

Vance is of the opinion that a rule of "business usage" should be adopted, but he ruefully adds, "Here we have another instance in which business usage substitutes the insurance money for the insured property, despite the general rule that the two are not legally connected; and, as usual, the courts are sluggishly following business." Vance, Insurance §131 p. 781. Dean Pound assails Vance's contention that the insurance money is any part of the thing bargained for and he also vigorously attacks the theory that the vendor is a trustee for the vendee. 33 Har. L.R., 1. c. 829, 830. . . .

Automatic application of the doctrine that "equity regards that as done which ought to be done," in the circumstances of this case, begs the question of *what ought to be done*. Because the insurance proceeds may be a windfall to those legally entitled does not necessarily mean that justice will be accomplished by transferring them elsewhere. The substance of the purchase contract and the use to which the property is to be put must be considered. A resort to equity should involve a consideration of other equitable principles or maxims such as the equally important maxims that "equity follows the law" and "between equal equities the law will prevail."

A valid legal excuse is a sufficient reason for refusal of specific performance. . . . Destruction of a particular thing upon which the contract depends is generally regarded as a legal excuse for nonperformance. . . .

If plaintiff's contention is that there has been a substantial failure or impairment of the consideration of the contract by reason of the destruction of the building, then I do not think that the Ashmores should be entitled to specific performance, and because of the theory of mutuality it would seem that Skelly would not be entitled to specific performance unless it was willing to perform its legal obligations under the purchase contract as drawn. We would not be justified in making a new contract for the parties to cover the building insurance, and a court of equity will not decree specific performance of a contract that is incomplete, indefinite or uncertain. . . . Nor can the courts supply an important element that has been omitted from the contract. . . .

If the subject matter of the purchase contract was not as well or better suited to Skelly's purpose after the fire than it was before, then it appears from the authorities above discussed that Skelly could avoid the contract entirely or that it could clearly establish the amount and manner in which it was damaged. What would the situation be if the building had not been insured or for only a small amount? The fact that the building was insured and the amount thereof are hardly determinative of Skelly's alleged injury.

But Skelly did not after the fire or in this action elect to abandon the contract although the Ashmores gave it the opportunity to do so rather than to sell at the reduced price. It is quite evident that Skelly has received one windfall as the result of the fire in that the lease is terminated and the site can be cleared at less cost. It has not shown itself to be entitled to another, the one now legally vested in the Ashmores. Ideally the purchase contract should be set aside so that the parties could negotiate a new one based on the property in its present condition. But the plaintiff by its election to take title has foreclosed this possibility. . . . As the opinion stands, the adoption of the Massachusetts rule is more imaginary than real. The equitable conversion theory is *applied,* not the Massachusetts rule.

The opinion simply awards the *proceeds* of the fire insurance policy. It does not, and could not on the evidence in the present record, ascertain the compensation or damages, if any, to which Skelly is entitled by reason of the destruction of the building. Evidence of this sort was excluded by the trial court. Count 2 of the plaintiff's petition claims the insurance proceeds on the theory of a trust fund as a matter of law and that seems to be the basis of the majority opinion's award of the insurance fund to the purchaser. This is the antithesis of the Massachusetts rule which contemplates the ascertainment of the amount of compensation or damages that will assure the vendee receiving the value for which it contracted, and no more. . . .

Although the entire court now seems to be in agreement that the theory of equitable conversion should not be adopted and that the equitable rules which should govern are those that require an allowance of compensation or damages to fit the particular case, nevertheless a majority of the court have concurred in an opinion which makes the amount of insurance proceeds the yardstick. This is the rejected doctrine of equitable conversion regardless of the name given to it. . . .

NOTES

1. *Specific performance with abatement.* Suppose seller's performance is defective; he cannot supply the promised structures, or structural quality, or acreage, or quality of title. As with cases where he fails to perform on time, if his nonperformance is not too bad ("too bad" being the concept to be explored), he can yet get specific performance, leaving buyer to cross-claim for damages, in law or equity as locally appropriate, or perhaps entitling buyer to get an "abatement" in seller's specific performance action of so much of the price as the court decides to apportion to the flaw.

Can seller use his flawed performance to escape buyer's action for specific performance? Not where buyer is willing to pay the full price for whatever performance seller can render. But is buyer entitled to specific performance with an abatement? Suppose the Blackacre contract is for $40,000; the house, insured for $20,000, burns down; the jurisdiction is one which puts "risk of loss" on the seller; the jurisdiction is one which holds that the seller's insurance proceeds are "his"; the land is worth $24,000 after the fire. Specific performance with abatement?

Abatement problems will be more fully developed in connection with title flaws, pages 629-630 infra.

2. *Risk following possession.* In *Skelly Oil,* seller's tenant was in possession at the time of the fire; buyer bought subject to that tenant's rights, the tenant had not yet given a red rose or otherwise attorned to the buyer. How would a rule that the risk follows the possession be applied?

3. *Equitable conversion.* Whether the concept of equitable conversion is

question-begging or question-solving as applied to executory interval fires, it is, in either case, unnecessary. There is plenty of contract doctrine to do any legal job that needs doing in these cases. The relevant contract doctrines (frustration, impossibility, independent conditions, implied conditions and promises, failure of consideration, etc.) are supposedly bottomed on intent, and so the premises of our free society require them to be honored in determining disputes between free actors in a free land-money exchange. Those same premises require that results not be derived from a depersonalization of the parties into "owner" and "not owner" via property doctrine. It has never been suggested that concepts of equitable conversion would control an explicit agreement between the parties as to their relations in the event of an interim fire.

Anyway, Skelly Oil started the transaction involved in the principal case by acquiring an option on the site, although Skelly had picked up the option (converted it into a bilateral contract) before the fire. Who in the world, other than a considerable number of courts (see A.L.R. 1225 (1926)), would say that a fire during the period of an otherwise enforceable but as yet unexercised option would leave the optionee remediless — remediless in spite of the fact that the jurisdiction would award to a bilateral contract buyer a post-fire specific performance decree with abatement for insurance proceeds? The concept of equitable conversion is involved here, but it does not fully serve the optionee, partly because of the equally derided concept of mutuality. See page 516 supra.

However, determining whether buyer or seller is owner or equitable owner of Blackacre during the executory interval is important for many legal purposes whether or not fire loss allocation ought to be one of them. The characterization is central in determining — or at least describing — the relations of the buyer and seller not with each other, but with third persons.

For example, after Blackacre is under contract to buyer, does a creditor of the seller reach seller's interest in Blackacre by levy on Blackacre or by garnisheeing buyer? The law of a state provides that the real property of an intestate deceased descends to his heirs but that his personalty shall devolve on his personal administrator for distribution according to a statutory formula; S dies intestate, who gets what? Does the date of contract or of deed measure the holding period of "property" for Internal Revenue Code purposes? In the next case, a seller's relation to his insurance company turns on whether or not he continued, after contract, to be the "owner." This is, of course, just an elementary refresher of the point that questions of "ownership" for buyer and seller are numerous.

Yet it is surprising that the questions just posed are answered in terms of ownership. At any given moment in the United States there are thousands of properties in executory interval, the buyers and sellers of which are netted into the complex of legal relationships between Blackacre and the world of third persons. The surprise is that the intestacy statutes, or the

Seller's Obligations

Internal Revenue Code, or the Bankruptcy Act or whatever body of law controls the particular relationship rarely deals specifically with the executory interval phenomenon and leaves it to be disposed of by the larger generalizations of ownership.

Finally, practical aspects of executory interval planning for a land transaction may involve these third party relationship questions as importantly as buyer-seller problems inter se. But the problems are as much those of creditors' rights and taxation as they are of land transfer, and it is to the former categories of instructional organization that we consign them.

Vogel v. Northern Assurance Co.
219 F.2d 409 (3d Cir. 1955)

GOODRICH, Circuit Judge. This is an appeal from a decision in an insurance case. With a stipulated loss of $12,000 the plaintiff finds himself in the happy possession of a judgment against two insurance companies which aggregates $15,000. The insurance companies, quite naturally, appeal.

The whole question is one of Pennsylvania law. The property insured against fire was located in Pennsylvania; the insurance policies were written and delivered in Pennsylvania. Our sole problem is to determine as best we can the Pennsylvania law which governs this situation.

The undisputed facts present a question with all the tantalizing niceties of the type which examiners pose to law students. Indeed, the problem of the case can be posed in the form of a hypothetical examination question. Here it is:

S, a seller of real property, (in the actual case a man named Shank) agrees to sell the land to V, the vendee, for $15,000. (The vendee's real name in this case is Vogel so the initials fit happily.) S then takes out fire insurance on the property in the amount of $6,000; V does likewise but in the amount of $9,000. Before S conveys the property to V a fire occurs, damaging the house on the land to the extent of $12,000. V goes ahead and completes his part of the purchase agreement and receives a deed from S. Following this, S assigns to V all of his rights against the insurance company under the policy. V then sues both S's insurer (Northern Assurance Company, Ltd.) and his own insurer (Mount Joy Mutual Insurance Company). Was the district court correct in giving judgment against each company even though the total recovery exceeds the stipulated loss by $3,000?[2]

---

2. The hypothetical statement oversimplifies the fact situation just a little. The actual chronological order of events in this case was as follows: Prior to August 29, 1950, the property was owned by one Riddle who had entered into an agreement of sale with Shank. On August 29, 1950, Shank entered into an agreement of sale with Vogel. On October 3, 1950, Shank received a deed to the property from Riddle. It was not until October 16, 1950, that Shank made his insurance contract with Northern Assurance Co. The next day, October 17,

We start the analysis with the well-settled rule in Pennsylvania, derived from English law, that when a contract to sell land is made the equitable ownership passes forthwith to the buyer. The seller's "title" which he retains until final conveyance is but a "security title" and the risk of loss or advantage of gain is borne by the buyer. [Citations omitted.]

The seller with this security title may take out fire insurance to protect his interest. The Pennsylvania decisions say unequivocally that as between the seller and the insurance company the seller is the owner of the property. [Citations omitted.]

. . . Of course, upon the performance of the contract of sale, the seller no longer has an insurable interest. [Citations omitted.] The Pennsylvania cases demonstrate very clearly, however, that a seller of real estate, having taken out fire insurance, can collect from the insurance company under the policy for a loss occurring prior to the date of settlement. The reason assigned is that the rights and liabilities of the parties to the insurance contract become fixed when the loss occurs. It is not a valid argument, according to these authorities, that the seller has suffered no loss because the vendee has later completed the contract of sale and paid the seller. [Citations omitted.]

So far, so good. Is the insurance money thus collected by the seller his own to do with as he pleases? May he use it to buy himself a new car, give it to a favorite grandchild or otherwise dispose of it as people do who have some extra money? In this particular case, S, instead of collecting the money, assigned his rights against the insurance company to V. The district judge indicates that he thinks that S was under no obligation to do this. See Vogel v. Northern Assur. Co., D.C.E.D. Pa. 1953, 114 F. Supp. 591. If that were so and this insurance money, or the claim to it, belonged to S free and clear, then his gift of the insurance proceeds to V, or to anybody else, would certainly be none of the insurance company's business. It would simply be a case where a man is allowed to do what he pleases with his own.

We think the district court was mistaken on this point because under Pennsylvania law the seller becomes the trustee of the property and rights incident thereto and holds them in trust for the vendee. [Citations omitted.] The most recent case in Pennsylvania which involved this point directly is Dubin Paper Co. v. Insurance Co. of North America [361 Pa. 8, 63 A.2d 85, 8 A.L.R.2d 1393 (1949)]. In the *Dubin* case the loss occurred prior to the date of settlement of the contract of sale. The vendee having performed his contract, the seller upon receiving checks from his insurance companies to cover the fire loss returned them to the insurance companies. Then the vendee brought an action in equity against the insur-

---

1950, Vogel entered into the insurance contract with Mount Joy Mutual Insurance Co. The fire occurred seven days later on October 28, 1950, which was prior to the date of settlement. On November 24, 1950, Vogel received the deed to the property after paying Shank the full purchase price. On December 1, 1950, Shank assigned all his "right, title, interest, right of action and claim" that he had against Northern to Vogel.

Seller's Obligations

ance companies and the seller to compel the insurance companies to pay the proceeds to the seller and to have the court declare that the seller hold the proceeds as trustee for the plaintiff. The problem was discussed at length by Chief Justice Maxey. The conclusion was that the action was well brought and that the plaintiff was entitled to the relief for which he prayed.

This decision clearly shows that the insurance money which S collects from the insurance company after he has been paid by the vendee is not his to keep or spend but in equity belongs to the vendee. As we read the *Dubin* and earlier Pennsylvania cases no other conclusion is possible. So, in this particular instance, when V has complied with the terms of the contract of sale, the proceeds due on the insurance which S had taken out was something to which V was equitably entitled. That means that in this case V (Vogel) may clearly maintain his action against the insurance company which was the insurer on S's contract.

Northern makes two arguments with considerable plausibility. One is that the insurance which S takes out covers only the security title which he has. If he gets his money from the vendee he suffers no loss and should not be allowed to recover anything against the insurance company. Northern also argues that it is entitled to subrogation to the insured's right to the extent that the insured has a claim over and above the amount of his loss. Both of these arguments are pretty good. But in this case the federal court is bound to apply state law as best it can. The state law has been settled, and firmly settled, against Northern's arguments by the series of decisions which we have already cited above.

Then we pass to the claim of V against his insurer. This insurance policy was taken out by V himself in the amount of $12,000, but contains a three-fourths value clause. There is no doubt that a vendee who has made a contract of sale to buy land can himself take our insurance. . . . This is only common sense; if the vendee bears the risk of loss he certainly has a risk which he can insure against. What is there, then, to prevent V from recovering against the insurance company for the loss which it agreed took place?

Mount Joy argues that it is excused from paying because there was in the policy a place for the noting of other insurance and the insured gave Mount Joy no information on this. Therefore, it says, this provision being one to guard against fraud in over insurance, it does not have to pay anything. As pointed out by the district judge, however, these policies were taken out on different interests. S took out a policy to protect his interest as seller; V took out a policy to protect his interest as an equitable owner. The settled interpretation of the "other insurance" clause is that the other insurance must be "on the same interest and subject, and against the same risk." 3 Richards on Insurance 1667 (5th ed., Freedman, 1952). The district court was correct in holding the other insurance clause inapplicable.

Furthermore, it is to be pointed out that what S assigned to V was not an insurance policy. He assigned to V his claim against the insurance company for a loss which had already taken place and which left him with a claim against the insurance company. [Citations omitted.] And under the Pennsylvania cases which we have set out above that claim was for the face of the policy, not for the protection of S's security title.

This brings us to an affirmance of a judgment for $15,000, $3,000 more than the loss. This, it is true, seems incongruous in view of the often stated generalization that fire insurance is indemnity insurance. Vance on Insurance §14 (3d ed., 1951); 1 Richards on Insurance 3. The incongruity, if there is one, reaches clear back to 1853 in the settled rule in Pennsylvania that the seller can recover fully against the insurance company for a loss occurring between the time of the agreement and final settlement even though the buyer has taken title according to the terms of the contract. We have no doubt that the ingenuity of insurance counsel will draft a provision whereby total recovery can be limited to actual loss if that is an object to be desired. And if this Court has failed in its examination of Pennsylvania law on the subject, it will be compelled to take the course over.

The judgment of the district court will be affirmed.

NOTES TO SKELLY AND VOGEL

1. Shortly after the *Vogel* case was decided, the Pennsylvania Supreme Court refused recovery in excess of the loss to a vendee in a situation similar to that in *Vogel*. In Insurance Company of North America v. Alberstadt, 383 Pa. 556, 561, 119 A.2d 83, 86 (1956), Alberstadt owned a land parcel that Patterson bought at a sheriff's sale held for delinquent taxes. Alberstadt and Patterson separately took out fire insurance policies on the property. The property then suffered fire loss of $3,175, and thereafter Patterson paid the sheriff for the property and received a sheriff's deed. In its opinion, the court said:

> Since Patterson is entitled to the $3,175 [as equitable and later legal owner] for which Alberstadt must account to him, may he also recover the amount of his own policy, $2,500 from North America Company? The answer to this question must be in the negative. Since fire insurance is only a contract of indemnity and its object is not to permit a gain by the insured but only to compensate him for a loss, it is obvious that he cannot recover insurance in an amount greater than the loss which he sustained. If he himself had had policies in these two insurance companies he could not, of course, have collected from either or both of them more than the amount of the damage occasioned by the fire, and the companies, under the pro rata clauses of their policies would have been entitled to prorate the loss. . . . Here, however, virtually the same situation exists, because if Patterson were allowed recovery of the proceeds of both policies he would likewise be enjoying the fruit of

Seller's Obligations

two insurances on the same subject, the same risk, and the same interest, namely his own, and in an amount greater than his actual loss, which, as already stated, the law will not permit. His recovery is limited, therefore, to the sum of $3,175 which will be paid by the insurance companies in the proportion of their respective policies of $3,500 and $2,500.

Cf. Smith v. Prudential Property and Casualty Ins. Co., 508 F. Supp. 452 (W.D. Pa. 1980), policy terms construed to require pro rata allocation of actual loss between vendor's insurer and vendee's insurer, hence the *Vogel* doctrine is inapplicable. Cf. also Reliance Ins. Co. v. Allstate Indemnity Co., 514 F. Supp. 486 (E.D. Pa. 1981), contract of sale placed risk of fire loss on vendor, and as vendor and vendee have separate insurable interests, vendee's insurer need not pay anything to vendor, even though the loss exceeded the vendor's coverage.

2. *Transfers during insurance period.* If equitable conversion turns buyer into equitable owner of Blackacre, why is he not also equitable owner of the insurance policy? Because the insurance policy does not run with the land (Vance on Insurance 96 (3d ed. 1951)), so that the promised conveyance of legal title to Blackacre at the closing will not carry legal title to the insurance policy.

Saying that the fire policy does not run with the land obscures the point that fire policies, in terms, only give coverage during the insured's continued ownership of the premises. However, it should be clear from the *Vogel* case that mere entry into an executory contract does not work such a change of ownership as to eliminate coverage, although, as the case indicates, there is an issue as to whether coverage continues on the whole value of the premises or only on seller's security title. (Vance, supra, at 834-835.)

Termination of coverage upon transfer of the *insured premises* reflects the insurer's concern over adverse risk alterations. A further concern on the part of the company, that it not get entangled in adverse claims situations, has led to clauses requiring company consent for either transfers of the policy itself or of matured claims under the policy.

An unconsented transfer of the policy probably, or of a claim certainly, does not relieve the insurer from liability, simply suspending its obligation to pay until the rights of the parties to the assignment are adjusted inter se (Vance at 99; Corbin on Contracts §§873, 888).

3. *Transaction planning.* As the fully insured seller plans with his buyer for the executory interval, the parties will keep the following considerations and questions in mind:

(a) Seller may be willing to escrow his insurance policy but will be unenthusiastic about assigning it.

(b) There are possibilities of decisions on an insurer's post-contract liability that make insurance policy assignment risky as a device for buyer-seller protection.

(c) Many questions will be unresolved by a clause in the sale contract reading "risk of loss from fire or other destruction of the premises is on the seller."

(d) Suppose buyer takes out his own coverage for the executory interval so that both parties are insured, but they do not expressly contract concerning risk of loss and allow the Uniform Vendor and Purchaser Risk Act or a seller's risk common law rule to govern. The house burns, buyer waives his rescission or other rights and pays the full price. At this point seller has no loss, and hence can get no recovery from his insurer. Buyer then attempts to recover his loss from his insurer. Has buyer had a loss? If so, is his insurance company, after settlement with buyer, subrogated to buyer's pre-waiver rights against seller? If that subrogation subjects seller to a money liability to buyer's insurer, is seller then entitled to a recovery against his insurer?

(e) The phone number of the insurance company is listed in the Yellow Pages.

4. *Other executory interval changes: Rezoning and eminent domain.* Steinway and Sons contracted to buy from two separate tract owners, intending, as was known to both sellers, to use the tracts as a unit for construction of a business building and adjacent warehouse. After contract and before closing, a rezoning of one of the tracts precluded the intended use. Steinway was held excused as to the rezoned tract but not as to the other. Anderson v. Steinway & Sons, 178 A.D. 502, 165 N.Y.S. 608, *aff'd*, 221 N.Y. 639, 117 N.E. 575 (1917); Biggs v. Steinway & Sons, 229 N.Y. 320, 128 N.E. 211 (1920).

An eminent domain taking of all or part of the land during the executory interval presents problems closely analogous to those of destruction by fire or otherwise. Both eminent domain and rezoning cases can be argued against the buyer in common law terms of equitable conversion and by conventional contract principles; but they have a special pro-buyer doctrinal feature. In the usual contract for the sale of land, the buyer is excused if seller cannot, at closing, supply him with a deed carrying *marketable title* to the land. A fire loss will not be regarded as clouding seller's title, but a post-contract zoning change or eminent domain might be so regarded. Mixing this extra doctrinal feature with the equitable conversion and contract principles has of course produced a pattern of results for rezoning and condemnation cases fully as incoherent as that of the fire cases described in *Skelly Oil*. See Friedman, Contracts and Conveyances of Real Property §4.12 (3d ed. 1975).

Bixby, The Vendor-Vendee Problem: How Do We Slice the Insurance Pie?
19 The Forum 112, 127-128 (1983)

As a preliminary matter the courts should abandon the doctrine of equitable conversion as it applies to the allocation of risk of loss between vendor

Seller's Obligations

and vendee for destruction of real property in the executory period. The Massachusetts rule or the possession rule of the Vendor and Purchaser Risk Act is more logical. Even with the adoption of a more logical risk of loss rule, the desire of courts to provide insurance to someone not insured will continue to create conflicts with insurance principles. Consideration might be given to legislation which would give either vendor or vendee the benefit of the other's insurance. Attorneys and others involved in the transfer of real property should consider the conflict between risk of loss rules and insurance principles in drafting sales documents.

Recognizing that problems will still arise, the following guidelines for handling vendor-vendee cases are suggested.

1. The cases involving a single policy are the most difficult. (a) In states following the equitable conversion rule, the trust doctrine will undoubtedly continue to be used to give the vendee the benefit of a vendor's insurance. The trust doctrine should be recognized as a counterbalance to the harshness of the equitable conversion risk of loss rule. (b) In states following the Massachusetts rule or the possession rule for allocating risk of loss, there is less justification for imposing the trust doctrine. Cases such as Long v. Keller, [104 Cal. App. 3d 312, 163 Cal. Rptr. 532 (1980), court refused to give vendee the benefit of vendor's insurance] should be followed. (c) Efforts to impose a trust for the benefit of a vendor when insurance is purchased by the vendee should be scrutinized carefully and generally should be rejected absent strong equitable considerations. (d) In the absence of a trust doctrine, courts may still negate subrogation by a vendor's insurer by interpreting the intent of the executory sales contract.

2. The double coverage cases are less troublesome. (a) In double coverage cases when there is no overlap between policies the courts should follow the underlying risk of loss rule and permit subrogation. An exception would be where subrogation is waived by the sales agreement. (b) In double coverage situations where there is an "overlap" among policies, the courts should be flexible. Nonetheless, the courts should not prorate between policies unless there is at least a partial identity between or among the named insureds or designations historically considered equivalent to an "insured," such as a mortgagee.

NOTE

Do Bixby's recommendations merit adoption, and if so, why?

2. *Boundary Description and the Binding Effect of Writings*

Suppose S sells part of his ranch to B, a developer; B takes possession of his new property. He then sets concrete markers at each of its four corners, marks off the interior into streets that he dedicates to the public and into lots that he sells and that are promptly built up by his buyers. As time passes, the lots become the subject of the usual sorts of devolutionary and intervivos transfer, and each of them accumulates a reasonable amount of ownership complexity: a mortgage or an easement, or a power of termination for condition broken, a tax lien, and so on.

Then somebody takes a closer look at the deed from S to B. It appears that some sort of mistake was made, for B has located each of the four concrete markers nine feet west of the spot where it apparently should have been to mark the boundaries of the property apparently conveyed by S to B in the original deed. Furthermore, the street dedications and all the conveyances of the lots were prepared in relation to the description in the original deed rather than by reference to the concrete markers, but all the lots were physically laid out with reference to the markers. What a mess; everybody's driveway is where his neighbor's rumpus room should be. Every owner's actual occupancy encroaches on a neighbor; every owner is in turn encroached upon.

There are several ways out. One is to have all the owners, the friendly folks in the neighborhood (*and* the banks, municipalities, absentee owner's, unborn heirs, etc.) execute the necessary quitclaims and releases to conform ownership to occupancy. This, of course, they will do, if they can be found; if they are all that nice (if a municipality, for example, can quit claim in the face of a taxpayer's suit objection that all sales of municipal property must be by competitive bidding); and if too large a strain is not put on the generosity of one of the owners who recognizes that he only encroaches to the extent of an overwide driveway while his encroaching neighbor is, inter alia, a very expensive subsurface utility distribution pipe.

Failing a neighborhood concordat, the law of adverse possession may do the job, if time has run, if necessary tackings are permitted, and if each adverse claimant had the required state of mind during the possessory period. And even if the requirements for the acquisition of adverse title are not met, the possession-confirming body of law dealing with the establishment of boundaries by acquiescence or practical location can in some cases be invoked to cure discrepancies between instrumented lines and occupied ones.

The following sections center on two other approaches. First of all, if it is a particular reading of the deed from S to B that gives rise to the mess, perhaps a different reading will dispel it. Second, even if the reading that gives rise to the difficulty is the true one, perhaps it is legally permissible to show that S and B really meant that B was to have the markered area, even though the conveyance described something nine feet off. Accordingly, these sections present material on conventional methods of boundary description, and on legal techniques for resolving error and ambiguity, whether by interpretation or by conforming a document's erroneous or ambiguous description to true intention otherwise ascertained.

Seller's Obligations

As to the latter problem, the material will be more of the same — rules of interpretation based on presumed intent, statute of frauds, parol evidence rule, and the like. These doctrines, however, will be extra sharply focussed; where-do-you-draw-the-line is, in boundary cases, not entirely metaphorical.

a. Boundary Description Methods

A new property description originates in subdivision. If an owner of a tract wishes to transfer the *entire* tract, he is most likely to convey by using the description under which he acquired the property. However, if a *portion* of the tract needs to be designated, as for intervivos or testamentary gift, listing with a broker, or for describing a bargain between owner and a buyer, a new description has to be created.

Boundary descriptions are operational statements; they tell the reader, "Go to such and such a place, look for some markers or make some measurements at various orientations, and when you are finished, you will have traced out on the ground that which I am trying to describe." More technically, a description, to have legal effect, is supposed to be one with which a competent surveyor can identify a particular tract of land to the exclusion of all other tracts.

(1) Metes and Bounds Descriptions

O owns Blackacre, which he believes to be a 160-acre tract, squarely oriented north and south, bounded on the west by the neighboring Smith property, on the north by a road. On Blackacre is a single spectacular oak tree — known to all the world as the Eastern Oak — located exactly 660 feet from O's west boundary and 1320 feet south of the road.

O bargains to transfer the northwest 40 acres of the tract to B. It is easy to work out a description of the 40 acres, in part because of the happy location of the oak, and in part because two sides of the tract to be conveyed run along the exterior boundaries of O's tract.

"Beginning at the Eastern Oak, thence 660 feet West to the J. B. Smith property, thence North to the Ross Road, thence along the road East 1320 feet, thence South 1320 feet, thence West to the place of beginning, containing 40 acres, all located approximately 5 miles Northwest of Tuba City, Wayne County, Illinois."[11]

This description is made up of a sequence of *calls*, operational instructions to the reader as to how to trace out on the ground the lines that bound the intended tract. Walking through the calls we have:

---

11. The description could have started elsewhere, ignoring the oak: "Beginning at the intersection of the East line of the Smith property and the Ross Road, thence East 1320 feet, thence South 1320 feet, thence West 1320 feet, thence North 1320 feet to the place of beginning."

First Call: **From the Eastern Oak 660 feet West to the J. B. Smith property.** This call begins with a *monument*—the Eastern Oak. If an owner does not have a *natural monument* so happily located, he may set up a stake, an *artificial monument,* at the desired location, It would be even simpler to set an artificial monument at the southeast corner of the carved out area, phrasing the description from that.

The monument call is followed by a *distance*— 660 feet; a *course*— west; and an *adjoiner*— the J. B. Smith property. Since course and distance have been called from the oak, the adjoiner call is really not needed in this case to locate the terminus of the first line (but the possible uses of an apparently surplus adjoiner call should become clear later). If the distance call were omitted, so that the description read, "From the Eastern Oak to the J. B. Smith property," then somehow the property line of the Smith tract would have to be located. Assuming for now that "the J. B. Smith property" means what J. B. Smith owns, rather than what he in fact occupies, the likely way to find out Smith's boundaries is by examining the property description in the deed by which neighbor Smith acquired ownership. But query: If the distance call were omitted, how would the Smith line be located for the purposes of O's deed if the deed by which Smith acquired his land described his western boundary as "the West line of the tract adjoining on the East"?[12]

Second Call: **Thence [from the point located as per first call] North to the Ross Road.** This call has a course and an indication to the road; the latter can be conceived of as a monument in its physical existence, or as an adjoiner if conceived of as something owned by someone other than the grantor (more on roads later).

Third Call: **Thence [from the point located as per second call] along the road East 1320 feet.** This contains a double course indication: *East* and *along the road,* and a distance indication.

Fourth Call: **Thence [from point indicated by third call] South 1320 feet.** This indicates a course and a distance. Would it be better if the grantor set a concrete marker at the southeast corner of the tract, and called, "Thence to the concrete marker"?

Fifth Call: **Thence [from point indicated by fourth call] West to the place of beginning.**

Sixth Call: **Containing 40 acres.** This is a call for quantity.

Seventh Call: **All located approximately 5 miles Northwest of Tuba City, Wayne County, Illinois.** This, of course, is the anchorage of the description and probably ought to have been mentioned first; it tells where the starting point, Eastern Oak, is to be found.

(2) Description by Fractional Part

It would be simple for O to convey the square tract to B by stating: "The N.W. ¼ of my farm." For application, this requires (a) anchorage of

---

12. Cf. the business usage: "Don't call us, we'll call you."

"my farm," (b) a decision as to whether "N.W. ¼" means a square in the corner or a tract marked off by a diagonal between the north and west boundaries (usually the former). It is also important that somebody representing owner remember the above conveyance. Otherwise when the S.W. corner is later sold it might be described as "the S.W. 40 acres of my farm." This would create difficulties if upon measurement it was discovered that the western half of the farm contained 70 or 90 acres.

(3) Description by Government Survey

The tract for B which we are considering might be described as follows: "the N.W. ¼ of the N.W. ¼ of section 6, Township 3 North, Range 2 West of the Third Principal Meridian, containing 40 acres," which, to the initiate, will indicate that a United States government survey is being used to anchor the description of the new tract, that the property is somewhere in Illinois, and that maybe a mistake has been made.

Much of the land in the United States has been public land of the United States government at one time or another (major exceptions are land in the original colonies, Texas, and some southwestern states where Spanish grants were honored). In preparing public lands for management and for fractionated transfer to myriad private owners, it was necessary to describe them. By a succession of statutes starting before 1800, the Congress directed the division of public land into *sections,* one mile on a side, containing 640 acres. Congress did not instruct the Bureau of Land Management to send out surveyors to look for elm trees in Kansas with which to anchor the description of the public land sections; rather the survey took reference points from longitude and latitude. The surveyors were instructed to locate on the ground and mark by monuments a series of some 35 points, e.g., for central Illinois: lat. 38°28′27″N, long. 89°08′54″W; for Colorado, Kansas, Nebraska, South Dakota, and Wyoming, a single point; for Oklahoma, yet another (with lat. 36°30′50″N, which should recall the Missouri Compromise) and so on. From each such monumented point the line of longitude was conceptually extended on the ground as "Principal Meridian." Each Principal Meridian was named or numbered for convenient subsequent reference: e.g., the Third for central Illinois, the Sixth for Colorado, the Choctaw (or Indian) for Oklahoma. Each line of latitude was similarly projected from the point as a *base line.* From these lines, a grid was built of *townships,*[13] each six miles square, and within each township 36 *sections,* each one mile square. All of this was to be accomplished by measurements on the ground, and the placement of monuments (stakes, cement markers, plates set into rock) to mark the township, and section, and sometimes quarter-section corners.

Once the survey was made, in any subsequent transaction with respect to land covered by the survey, one could speak of such and such a section,

---

13. More formally "Congressional Township," to be distinguished from the New England township, a governmental unit.

know that the ground was monumented to enable its location, and know that it consisted of 640 acres squarely oriented north and south; or at least that would be true if the survey were ideal.

Lapses from the ideal were inevitable, and one lapse was inherent. The townships were supposed to be a gridded succession, north and south, east and west, of six-mile-square areas covering the major part of the United States. However, the curvature of the earth and the convergence of longitudes toward the North Pole is such that a township could be six miles square, or it could be oriented north-south, but it couldn't be both. Thus suppose you start at the anchor point for the Third Principal Meridian; go six miles west, then six miles north, then return east to the meridian, and then go south back to the starting point. You will not have described a six-mile-square area; because of longitudinal convergence, the southern boundary of the tract just described will be 50-some feet longer than the northern boundary — 50 feet being the approximate amount of longitudinal convergence at Illinois latitudes for each six miles of progress toward the Pole.

Accommodation for this tension between the desire for squareness and the desire to use longitudes as township boundaries was incorporated into the system; for our purposes it is only necessary to note that neither desire won out completely and therefore that there are many townships that do not consist of the ideal six-mile square with its ideal 36 sections, each one mile square and containing 640 acres.

There were additional deviations. The surveys, often made years apart, had to be fit into each other's monuments, and this fitting had to take into account not only the curvature-correction patterns just noted but also the inevitable inaccuracies caused by measuring instrument variation, terrain difficulties, haste induced by the presence of nearby hostiles, and natural or larcenous disappearance[14] or shifting of monuments. It would then happen that a surveyor working to create a proper six-mile-square township could not fit this to the monuments of neighboring surveys; he was then instructed to normalize as many sections as possible, working from south to north, and east to west — hence the remark above that Section 6 presents special problems. There is a uniform convention for numbering the sections within a township; since 6 is always the section in the northwest corner of a township, it is likely to be monumented other than for a square 640 acres; hence a description reading "N.W. ¼ of N.W. ¼ of *Sec. 6 containing 40 acres*" makes you wonder.[15]

14. "[In Lebanon] we saw rude piles of stones standing near the roadside, at intervals, and recognized the custom of marking boundaries which obtained in Jacob's time. There were no walls, no fences, no hedges — nothing to secure a man's possessions but these random heaps of stones. The Israelites held them sacred in the old patriarchal times and these other Arabs, their lineal descendants, do so likewise. An American, of ordinary intelligence, would soon widely extend his property, at an outlay of mere manual labor, performed at night, under so loose a system of fencing as this." From Innocents Abroad, by Samuel Clemens.

15. When the northwest quarter of the northwest quarter of a section is described as containing 40 acres, one further inquiry is suggested. It is common to have roads and

The description by government survey that heads this subsection is a fractional part description and also contains an acreage call.

(4) Description by Plat Reference

"Tracts 7 and 8 of J. B. Miller's Subdivision of the N.W. ¼ of Section 6, Township 3 North, Range 2 West of the Third Prime Meridian, recorded in Registry of Deeds Book 17, etc."

A private owner may, as did the government, decide to break up his lands into tracts of various sizes and shapes for one or another management or disposition purpose. He then causes a map or plat to be made in which, after anchoring the exterior limits of the area being mapped, the several portions of the area are mapped in *their* exterior dimensions, and receive designations ("Lot 2," "Tract 1," etc.) that are thereafter convenient for use. In usual course, the map descriptions will be anchored by monumentation (a stake, a marking in a sidewalk, etc.), but the map itself will be a form of metes and bounds description, showing footages, areas, orientations, and adjoiners. With luck the monumentation and the map will be consistent.

Platting, of course, is most usual with respect to subdivision of once-rural land for sale to residents of the growing city. The plat will show streets, parks, etc. Its registration and approval are key points in public regulation of land planning.

(5) Multiple Description—"Being" Clauses

It is common to find a description that uses:

(a) *a lot number,* which requires reference to a plat with a metes and bounds description;
(b) *a separate metes and bounds description with complex calls,* e.g., "hence (from the oak tree) south 45° 13′ east 4500 feet along the Smith property line to the elm tree";
(c) *an adjoiner description;*
(d) *an area designation;* and, to top it all off,
(e) *"being" clauses,* which might involve such notations as "Being the same premises"—or "Being the north 50 acres of those same premises"—"conveyed to Jones by Green by deed recorded Deed Book 47, Page 118. . . ."

This latter clause, of course, calls for the descriptions in the recorded deed, which in turn might contain a being clause.

---

highways laid out on section lines. Since the tract under description has section lines for both its northern and western boundaries, if chunks have been taken off the section for roads along each line, there won't be 40 acres left for the northwest corner. In our initial illustration, of course, there was a road on the north line, but none on the west.

(6) Plane Coordinates

There is increasing use of a plane coordinate system of boundary description, stimulated by the United States Coast and Geodetic Survey and validated by enabling legislation in a number of states. The Coast and Geodetic Survey has a series of stations scattered around the country, and any spot in the United States can be *described* by reference to a conceptual grid of lines running north and south, east and west, from the several stations. Any spot thus described can also be *located* at any time in the future by an elementary surveying technique using any three of the stations as monuments. Obviously, this is more permanent and precise monumentation than "neighbor Wilson's fence." Descriptions using this system call for points thus: "Coordinates North 1, 470, 588; East 416, 239." and give a reference to the particular survey on which the coordinates are based.

b. Professionals and Boundary Description

(1) The Lawyer

Once involved in boundary litigation, an attorney errs if he does not supplement his law school education on the topic with a short non-credit course from his experts. At any level of practice, attorneys who must use descriptions for their paper work can probably function perfectly well in transaction planning by having a reasonable proofreading system to verify a secretary's copy of someone else's description. After all, if Blackacre has been bought and sold and mortgaged and devised for a hundred years on the basis of a particular legal description used in instrument after instrument, chances are pretty good that the next transaction in Blackacre can be handled with the same description. And if Blackacre, by the march of progress, gets turned into Blackacre Terrace, descriptions of the now-subdivided lots will be prepared by surveyors rather than the subdivider's attorney; a lot buyer's attorney will rely on the survey rather than make up his own verbalization of the exterior lot lines of his client's purchase.

If the attorney does choose to concern himself with the old or new description that is at the base of his transaction, he can, even in the office, perform some checks.

Anyone who knows that north is at the top of the page and who can use a protractor can draw a map from a metes and bounds description. Some common errors in descriptions, however, will produce unmappability — as where four boundary lines are described running in order east, south, west and south, the last south being a transcriber's mistake for an intended north. Some errors map out into suspiciously odd shapes, as where, through number transposition, there is a misstatement of the angle at which two lines are to be projected. These can be caught in the office.

Some errors can be caught only by going to the site. Any layman can follow some of the description's directions by pacing off: if the description calls for projection of a line 50 feet from a road, and after 40 feet of pacing you run into a neighbor's back fence, a problem is raised.

Finally, there are errors that cannot be discovered without a surveyor's talents and instruments.

How many of these verifying operations ought a prudent attorney perform or have performed? There is no substantial body of case law in point or other authority from which a standard of conduct can be drawn, but the attorney's duties are presumably in large part a function of the bar's usual behavior in his area.

Owen v. Neely, 471 S.W.2d 705 (Ky. 1971), 59 A.L.R.3d 1171, holds that a title examining attorney is not entitled to summary judgment where sued by a client who paid a seller for more land than the seller owned in reliance on the attorney's certification of title, even though the certification was expressly made subject to such facts as would be revealed by an accurate survey and by personal inspection of the premises. The attorney, who had obtained a survey, noticed while preparing the deed some discrepancies between the record description and the survey description but relied on the survey. Whether the attorney upon discovering the discrepancies should have made further inquiries was not a question that could be resolved on summary judgment.

(2) The Surveyor

In preventing mistakes in conveyancing it is not uncommon to have surveys precede the closing for purposes of running the lines from the description to the ground and also for noting visible third party intrusions, wires, pipes, and the like. A firm that originally prepares a plat, one of whose lots is being transferred, is able to do transfer surveys more expeditiously than a newcomer.

In the event of a mistake in which a surveyor is involved, there are of course possibilities of his being liable in some circumstances to some plaintiffs. One interesting case is Taft v. Rutherford, 66 Wash. 256, 119 P. 740 (1911), in which a surveyor was held liable for $1267 damages to his client who mislocated a building in reliance on the negligently erroneous survey. It was held to be no defense that the surveyor offered, in line with area custom, a $12 survey, and a more expensive guaranteed survey, and that the client had selected the former.

BIBLIOGRAPHY

The following works on surveying receive frequent legal references: C. Brown, W. Robillard, and D. Wilson, Evidence and Procedures for Boundary Location (2d ed. 1981); C. Brown, Boundary Control and Legal Principles (2d ed. 1969); F. Clark, Surveying and Boundaries (3d ed.

1959); and R. Skelton, The Legal Elements of Boundaries and Adjacent Properties (1930). Procedures for surveying of public lands are considered in Bureau of Land Management, U.S. Dept. of the Interior, Manual of Instructions for the Survey of the Public Lands of the United States, Technical Bull. 6 (1973). On surveys, see also Cook, Land Data Systems: The Next Steps, 43 U. Cin. L. Rev. 527 (1974); Boyd and Uelman, Re-Surveys and Metes and Bounds Descriptions, 1953 Wis. L. Rev. 657; and Fegtly, Historical Development of Land Surveys, 38 Ill. L. Rev. 270 (1944).

The one unavoidable legal work that treats boundary problems is Patton on Titles. Volume 3 of the American Law of Property series is by one of the co-authors of Patton and follows its organization.

Indispensable on problems of establishing intention in conjunction with property description are, of course, Corbin on Contracts and 9 Wigmore, Evidence §§2460-2477 passim (3d ed. 1940). Further references will be given within.

c. Informal Descriptions

[handwritten: Memorandum w/ mistake in legal description not sufficient to satisfy Sof Fr]

Martin v. Seigel
35 Wash. 223, 212 P.2d 107 (en banc 1949)

SCHWELLENBACH, Justice. This is an appeal from a decree dismissing an action for specific performance of a contract to sell real property.

On March 2, 1948, respondents listed their property for sale with Frank L. McGuire, Inc. The listing agreement described the property as:

		Addition	City of Seattle
1 N 10′ Lot	32 Blk.	Pontius 2nd	King County Washington

The address was given as 309 E. Mercer.

On June 24, 1948, the following Earnest Money Agreement was entered into. It was upon a printed form, and we italicize those portions which were written.

Seattle, Washington
June 24, 1948

Received From *Lois M. Martin (widow)* the sum of *$1,000.00* dollars as part payment on this his (her) agreement to purchase from Frank L. McGuire, Inc., Agent for owner, the following real property: *at 309 E. Mercer and furniture as per inventory* in the City of Seattle, County of *King*, State of Washington, at the agreed price of *$18,500* Dollars, the balance of the down payment to be paid as follows: *$1500.00 including earnest money* Dollars within ten (10) days of the time when seller shall furnish an abstract brought to date or title insurance policy showing marketable title, and the remainder of said purchase price to be paid as follows: *$150.00 per month or more including 5% interest for one year. $200.00 or more per month including 5% interest thereafter until paid.* [Parts of the instrument are omitted.]

This property is sold on the basis of the contract between Frank L. McGuire, Inc., and the owner and not on any verbal statements made by the agent, and all such statements and representations not covered by this receipt are hereby waived.

Purchaser to have possession on or before ten (10) days after deal is closed.

This deposit taken subject owner's approval, and broker shall have five (5) days in which to obtain said approval.

> Frank L. McGuire, Inc.
> Agent
>
> *Lois M. Martin* [signed]
> Purchaser
>
> By *G.W. Dunn* [signed]
> Salesman

I hereby approve this sale, accept the price and agree to the terms herein and agree to pay Frank L. McGuire, Inc., my agent, 5% commission for making above sale. I hereby authorize my said agent to give tenants legal notice to vacate premises.

> Dated this _____ day of _____ 19__
>
> *Karl Seigel* [signed] Owner
> *Jeanne Seigel* [signed] Owner

On August 5, 1948 a policy of title insurance was furnished, which described the property:

"In the County of King, State of Washington

"Lot one (1) and north 10 feet of lot two (2) block thirty-two (32), Supplementary Plat of Pontius Second Addition to Seattle, according to plat thereof recorded in volume 5 of plats, page 76, records of said county."

This is the correct legal description.

The trial court made Finding No. 8: "That the earnest money receipt, Exhibit 3, is not a sufficient memorandum to satisfy the Statute of Frauds, nor does it incorporate by reference any other instrument, either Exhibit 1 or otherwise, that does contain an adequate legal description sufficient to satisfy the Statute of Frauds; that parol evidence would have to be resorted to, to connect the real estate described in the plaintiff's complaint with that described in Exhibit 1 and Exhibit 3, and that therefore the Exhibit 3 is void and not enforceable. . . ."

The general rule with regard to the sufficiency of legal descriptions to satisfy the statute of frauds in contracts for the sale of real property is stated in 49 Am. Jur. 658, Statute of Frauds, §349:

". . . In general, a description of the property in a contract for the sale of real estate may be sufficient to satisfy the statute of frauds even though it is not in such particulars as to render unnecessary a resort to extrinsic evidence to apply the description to the subject matter; the description is considered sufficient if with the assistance of external evidence it can be applied to the property intended to the exclusion of all other property. It follows that evidence of extrinsic circumstances is admissible within limitations in aid of a description the words of which standing alone would not identify the subject matter of the contract positively. A writing relied upon to constitute the memorandum must in and of itself furnish the evidence that the minds of the parties met as to the particular property which the one proposed to sell and the other agreed to buy; when such evidence is not found in the writing, it cannot be supplied by parol, but if it is found there, parol evidence of extrinsic circumstances may be resorted to for the purpose of specifically designating the property to which both parties are shown to have referred by the terms of the writing."

In 37 C.J.S., Frauds, Statute of, §188, p. 674, we find the following: "In transactions affecting urban property a description of the property by street and number is a sufficient description where the city or town in which it is located is stated either in the caption or the body of the instrument or may be ascertained from the writing. Ordinarily, however, an omission of the city or town in which the property is located renders the description insufficient where it contains nothing from which the omitted statement may be inferred."

In Broadway Hospital & Sanitarium v. Decker, 47 Wash. 586, 92 P. 445, 446, we affirmed a judgment dismissing an action for specific performance, where the memorandum described the property to be sold as: "House No. 322 Broadway" because the writing did not show the state, county, or city where the property might be found. See also, West v. Cave, 98 Wash. 237, 167 P. 747, where the property was described as the "J. T. Arrasmith place." Rogers v. Lippy, 99 Wash. 312, 169 P. 858, L.R.A. 1918C, 583, where the writing stated: "my stock ranch located in sections 9, 17 and 21, township 3 south, range 13 east, Sweetgrass county, Mont." Nelson v. Davis, 102 Wash. 313, 172 P. 1178, 1179, "One lot and store building in Wenda(e)ll, Idaho, in the county of Goodling, state of Idaho."

In Martinson v. Cruikshank, 3 Wash. 2d 565, 101 P.2d 604, the memorandum covered "the following described property situated in the County of Lewis, State of Washington, to-wit: '160 Acres, more or less, in Section

2, Township 13 N, Range 2 East.'" In affirming a judgment dismissing an action for reformation and specific performance, we said: "In a long line of decisions we have held that, in order to comply with the statute of frauds, a contract or deed for the conveyance of land must contain a description of the land sufficiently definite to locate it without recourse to oral testimony." [Citing cases.]

We also quoted from 22 C.J. 1290, §1719: "'The rule that where a contract upon its face is incomplete resort may be had to parol evidence to supply the omitted stipulation applies only in cases unaffected by the statute of frauds. If the subject matter of the contract is within the statute of frauds and the contract or memorandum is deficient in some one or more of those essentials required by the statute, parol evidence cannot be received to supply the defects, for this would be to do the very thing prohibited by the statute.'"

In Fosburgh v. Sando, 24 Wash. 2d 586, 166 P.2d 850, we reiterated the rule that a contract for the conveyance of land is void under the statute of frauds, when such a contract does not contain a description of the land sufficient to locate it without recourse to oral testimony. The contract attempted to convey land in King county described as: "Blue Bird Auto Court, No. 14241 Pacific Hi-Way Commencing at the North West corner of the intersection of Highway 99 and South 144th Street thence Northerly 60 feet to point of beginning thence approximately 207 feet thence Westerly approximately 300 feet, Thence Southerly approximately 265 feet, Thence Easterly approximately 93 feet, Thence Northerly 60 feet, Thence Easterly 120 feet point of beginning. All in Section 15, Township 23 North, Range 4 E.W.M." . . .

It will thus be seen that this court is at variance with the more liberal rule which permits parol testimony to explain what particular property the parties had in mind when they contracted to transfer real property described merely by a street number. We do not care to recede from the rule adopted by us, which has been stated in a long line of decisions over a number of years, and known and followed by the members of the bar and title men. We do not apologize for the rule. We feel that it is fair and just to require people dealing with real estate to properly and adequately describe it, so that courts may not be compelled to resort to extrinsic evidence in order to find out what was in the minds of the contracting parties.

In the present case, appellant contends that the description in the earnest money receipt is sufficient because the property is described not merely by street number, but also by city, county and state; and that this court should therefore adopt the liberal rule relative to descriptions of urban property as set forth in 37 C.J.S., Frauds, Statute of, §188, p. 674, supra. While neither party has cited us any decision of this court in which the question of the sufficiency of such a description has been squarely presented, we find that it was before the court in one instance. In Thompson, Swan & Lee v. Schneider, 127 Wash. 533, 221 P. 334, 335, the action was brought for the specific performance of a contract to trade two pieces of real estate. In granting specific performance, this court held that the description, "An eight-room house and two lots at 5822, 46th Street, S.E. Portland, Ore.," was a sufficient legal description because "the property was bounded on two sides by streets and on the other two sides by fences and pointed out to appellants." We note that that point in the Thompson case has been cited but once since it was decided in 1923; see Kauffman v. Marlborough Investment Co., 154 Wash. 396, 282 P. 377. However, the decision in that case is not based on the Thompson case, for in the Kauffman case the description included not only the street address, but also a correct description by lots, block number and addition. We feel that the sufficiency of the description in the Thompson case is not in keeping with the trend of our later decisions noted earlier in this opinion. That trend has been away from indefinite and vague legal descriptions, and in the direction of preciseness and accuracy.

In the interests of continuity and clarity of the law of this state with respect to legal descriptions, we hereby hold that every contract or agreement involving a sale or conveyance of platted real property must contain, in addition to the other requirements of the statute of frauds, the description of such property by the correct lot number(s), block number, addition, city, county and state. In so far as the Thompson case, supra, conflicts with this rule, it is hereby overruled.

Applying the above rule to the facts in the present case, it is apparent that the legal description of the property in question is insufficient and, therefore, the agreement set forth in the earnest money receipt is within the statute of frauds and, hence, unenforcible.

The judgment is affirmed.

Simpson, C.J., and Beals, Robinson, Mallery, Hill, Grady, Hamley and Donworth, JJ., concur.

NOTES

1. In Tenco, Inc. v. Manning, 59 Wash. 2d 49, 368 P.2d 372 (1962), it was held that a defective land description may be corrected by reformation if the defect resulted from mutual mistake. Mutual mistake exists only if the intentions of the parties were identical at the time of the transaction but the written agreement did not express these intentions; however, reformation does not lie if the agreement expresses the intent of the parties but the description is merely incomplete. Williams v. Fulton, 30 Wash. App. 173, 632 P.2d 920 (1981).

Most courts are more liberal than the Washington courts in upholding incomplete descriptions of land parcels. This contract of sale description was upheld in Ray v. Robben, 225 Ark. 824, 826, 285 S.W.2d 907, 908 (1956): "A tourist court consisting of ten cabins, furnished, including all

Seller's Obligations

extra bedding, located on one full lot and a fractional part of adjoining lot. Said location being 3408 Midland Blvd., Fort Smith, Ark." A street number in a sales contract was also upheld as adequate in Johnson v. Watson, 70 Nev. 443, 272 P.2d 580 (1954). Statute of frauds requirements were considered met for a lease contract description of "all those improvements and that parcel of land located at 2270 Guadalupe Street, in the City of Austin, County of Travis, and being the same property now occupied by lessee herein as a tenant of lessors." Hoover v. Wukasch, 152 Tex. 111, 113, 254 S.W.2d 507, 507 (1953). An easement deed description was held sufficient in providing that "two tower lines . . . over upon and across that certain tract or parcel of land situated in _____ Township, Wake County, North Carolina, formerly known as West lands" parallel with present tower line beginning on lands of Bettie Reavis across property of grantors to lands of E. B. Crow." Carolina Light & Power Co. v. Waters, 260 N.C. 667, 669, 133 S.E.2d 450, 452 (1963). In the *Carolina Light & Power* case, the opinion includes this language: "Where property either real or personal has a known and commonly used and recognized name, the use of this name to describe and identify the property sold is an adequate description, that is, it is sufficient to permit the introduction of evidence to show that the property claimed is in fact the property named. Individuals are usually identified by their names, but other means may be used to identify them, such as, for instance, fingerprints or scars. For the purpose of identifying the property made subject to the easement, plaintiff was entitled to put in evidence the deed to it and then by parol proof show that the property was 'formerly known as West lands.' "

2. *The statute of frauds: its character as a legal norm.* The statute of frauds is treated by the courts as a principle rather than as a statute whose force is a function of language and legislative intent. See 2 Corbin, Contracts §275. Perhaps this explains why the Washington Supreme Court in each of the preceding cases neither bothers to cite nor quote the statutory text. However, we are unable to find *any* Washington statute that requires a writing for a contract for the sale of land. The only relevant provision of the Washington statutes appears to be Wash. Rev. Code Ann. §64.04.010 (1966), which states, "Every conveyance of real estate, or any interest therein, and every contract creating or evidencing any encumbrance upon real estate, shall be by deed. . . ."

In deciding whether the results of the Washington cases above would have been changed had the court read the quoted statute, one question would involve the original English statute of frauds. Was the original statute received into Washington as a part of the common law? And if so, was it displaced by subsequent legislation occupying the field of required writings? See Neff, The English Statute of Frauds in Washington, 34 Wash. L. Rev. 124 (1959). Under Section Four of the English statute, "any contract or sale of lands . . . or any interest in or concerning them [may be sued on only if] the agreement upon which such action shall be brought, or some memorandum or note thereof, shall be in writing. . . ." Washington does have a real estate brokers' statute of frauds. Wash. Rev. Code Ann. §19:36.010 (1978).

3. *Street numbers.* A description such as "309 E. Mercer Street," without mention of city, county, and state, is potentially ambiguous in that as many cities might have such an address as there are ships named "Peerless." The extrinsic fact that the seller happens to own only one of these myriad lots is suggestive but not conclusive. Although land is not sold "short" as regularly as is stock, people often intend to assume legal obligations to transfer real estate that they do not own (expecting to acquire it in time to perform), and sometimes they are held to such obligations irrespective of intent. Hence, if there is a 309 E. Mercer Street in Seattle, and another in Eastport, Maine, and seller only owns the one in Seattle, and has never heard of Eastport, still "the devil himself knoweth not the mind of man."

Even the full address—"309 E. Mercer Street, Seattle, King County, Washington"— is potentially ambiguous. Does the street number refer to the lot that received that number in the subdivision plat or tax map or planning map from which the street number originated? Suppose that since being numbered the lot has been expanded or contracted by the successive owners, who perhaps bought or sold additional footages at the back or sides of the property?

4. *Other informal descriptions.* (a) O contracts to convey to B property described as "out of the 40 acres which I own by deed from X, the farmhouse and buildings and the three acres surrounding same." Is this description sufficient under the statute of frauds? In the 1858 Tennessee case of Hodge v. Blanton, 38 Tenn. (1 Head) 560, plaintiff transferred 400 acres to defendant. The description excepted "A small lot reserved for a burying ground, two poles square, around the grave where [plaintiff's daddy and two other relatives] are now buried." There were three graves side by side. Defendant then interred a deceased slave-child three feet from one of the three graves. Plaintiff went to law, in trespass. However, he apparently did not argue that the deed containing the vague exception was void, nor did defendant argue that the vague exception was itself void. Rather, plaintiff urged that the two poles square should be measured excluding the graves, and defendant that the graves should be included. Held, in affirming a jury verdict and judgment for the defendant: The language of the exception meant that the boundaries of the reserved lot were to be laid out two poles square by making the graves a common center.

(b) O contracts to convey to B a property described as "out of the 40 acres which I own by deed from X, the farmhouse and building and three acres." Should the contract be construed as nonambiguously giving B rights to the buildings and also to an undivided 3/40 interest in the entire 40 acres? Considering what B and O would be likely to do after such a decision, Solomon himself would approve. 1 Kings 3:16-28. See also Harris v. Woodard, 130 N.C. 580, 41 S.E. 790 (1902).

5. *Reformation and the statute of frauds.* (a) Suppose you are a seller, owning acreage, some of which you contract to convey to buyer. The boundary description is improperly prepared and purports to bind you to transfer more property than you had intended. Other things being equal, are you worse off if the misdescribed excess is property that belongs to you or if it is property actually belonging to your neighbor?

(b) S and B orally agree to the transfer of the east half of Blackacre. S does not own the west half, having sold that half of the property to X 10 years before. By error, the only document signed by the parties is a contract of sale that describes Blackacre in its entirety as its subject matter. Normally, one would think that S would attempt to reform down his written obligation, defensively; but S wishes to rescind the contract and instead it is B who seeks reformation. There are cases indicating that the writing can be reformed to describe the east half of Blackacre; as thus reformed it can be enforced against S. In so doing these cases reject S's contention that there is no writing describing the real bargain and that the transaction thus fails for noncompliance with the statute of frauds.

S's contention, though it may be rejected, is consistent with Restatement (second) of Contracts §509, which denies reformation and consequent enforcement to any executory contract within the statute (although it might be argued that buyer's earnest money is a partial performance). See Palmer, Reformation and the Statute of Frauds, 65 Mich. L. Rev. 421 (1967), which argues that the Restatement position, taken in 1932, is contra to the then and subsequent weight of authority, as well as to the high principles of the statute of frauds.

(c) Reformation down of an excess description may be argued to be not inconsistent with the statute of frauds. There *is* a writing that describes the actually intended transfer; the erroneous description obviously is a writing that describes a whole, and therefore each part of the whole. 1 Euclid 1? But where the deal is for Blackacre and the writing describes the east half of Blackacre, clearly enforcement after reformation would violate the statute. See Palmer, note 5(b) supra.

6. *Executed transactions within the statute of frauds.* To say that a contract is unenforceable through a failure to comply with the statute of frauds hardly disposes of cases where the parties have acted in reliance upon the defective instrument. If it is the buyer who uses the statute to justify withdrawal, seller, under some decisions, may charge buyer with expenses incurred in preparing the premises to meet buyer's specifications, even though the rejecting buyer has received no benefit. Similarly, where seller asserts the statute, buyer may recover his down payment and perhaps other reliance outlays. 3 Williston, Contracts §536.

There is an enormous number of cases, generally involving family rather than commercial transfers, in which there has been an intended but improperly papered transfer of ownership accompanied by change of possession. The change of possession, if continued for some uncertain length of time and accompanied by the possessor's paying taxes and perhaps making improvements, will, in most jurisdictions, entitle the possessor to prove the transfer in spite of the statute of frauds. See Annot., 101 A.L.R. 923 (1934). Furthermore, many states have Occupants and Claimants acts, under which one in possession by mistake may, after his ouster, recover the value of improvements made to the land during his possession. 41 Am. Jur. 2d, Improvements §5. This, of course, supposes that the possession has not continued for the length of time and under the state of mind necessary to transfer title by adverse possession.

d. Error and Ambiguity in Metes and Bounds Descriptions

Each illustration below consists of a sample description and discussion that should indicate to the reader problems that might arise when a description is incorrect. Each description below has been incorporated into a contract of sale by which seller and buyer have bargained for the transfer of a 110-foot square piece of land comprising the southeast corner of seller's tract. In each description we have introduced an error — either an error concerning the *subject* contracted for, or an error in the *description* of that subject.

1. *"Starting at the iron stake marked S-B, thence East 101 feet, thence South 110 feet, thence West 110 feet, thence North to the place of beginning."*

In this description, there is a scrivener's error: The first call should have been written, "East 110 feet," but a number transposition produced "East 101 feet." Make a map of this description. The first three lines will be easy to draw, but the fourth will be impossible. If it goes "North" it will not reach the "place of beginning," and vice versa.

2. *"Starting at an iron stake marked S-B, thence East to the J.B. Smith line, thence South 110 feet, thence West 110 feet, thence North to the place of beginning."*

Draw a map of this description, starting with the second and third lines to do so. The map can be completed by projecting the fourth line north from the terminus of the third line, and back projecting the first line from the origin of the second line. The first and fourth lines will intersect at the stake. There is nothing wrong with the face of the description. However, the iron stake was to have been set 110 feet west of the Smith property line to serve as an artificial monument with reference to which the parties would contract and describe. By an error, again of transposition in numeration, instruction for setting the stake called for a stake set "101 feet" west of the Smith line; and that's where the stake was set. Hence, applying the description to the ground would start without difficulty: The iron stake is

Seller's Obligations

found; east is paced to the Smith line, then south 110 feet, then west 110 feet; but the last call cannot be honored. Again, going north will not bring you to the place of beginning, and vice versa.

3. *"Starting at an iron stake marked S-B, thence East 101 feet, thence South 110 feet, thence West 110 feet, thence to the place of beginning."*

Here, as in the first illustration, the stake is properly set, but a scrivener's error transposed a proper "110" into a "101" in the first call. In contrast with the first illustration, however, there is no difficulty in completing the map, since the embarrassment of the word "North" has been eliminated from the fourth call; nor will there be any difficulty in applying the description to the ground. The problem with this description, in fact, is that it describes something other than the subject of the parties' bargaining. It serves to mark out an area that is not square and whose north line is only 101 — instead of 110 — feet long. Furthermore, it describes an area whose east line is 9 feet west of the east boundary of the tract out of which the bargained property was carved.

In the above cases, error has produced (1) an unmappable description, (2) a mappable but inapplicable description, and (3) a perfect description that does not correspond with intent. As to what sorts of errors and descriptions will produce these several results, consider these generalizations:

(a) Although an increase in the complexity of a description multiplies the chances that an error will be made, it also increases the chances that any error will appear to have been made. Thus the errors are identical in Illustrations 1 and 3. The startling difference in effect is produced simply by the presence of a detail, "North," indicated in the last call of Illustration 1.

(b) When an error is made that results in an inability to map or to apply a description to the ground because of a call conflict, it may or may not be true that the call in which the error is made is the one that is impossible to honor. In Illustration 1, the error is in the first call; the impossibility of mapping is in the last call.

(c) When there is an error arising from a misconception of subject matter, whether that error will find expression in an inapplicable description depends on whether the description calls to a fact about which the misconception exists. In illustration 2, the draftsman, believing that there was a stake 110 feet from the neighbor's line, drew up a description that called for that stake *in relation to* the line as an adjoiner. The description then proved inapplicable when sought to be applied to the actual stake, which was only 101 feet from the line. But suppose that the draftsman, even though under the same delusion, had written his description differently: "starting at the stake, thence east 110 feet, thence south 110 feet, thence west, 110 feet, thence north to the place of beginning." In spite of his delusion he has produced a description that will map, and also one that will apply to the ground. In this case, however, although the description works, it works wrong. It describes and applies to a unique piece of land, but it's the wrong land; since the real stake is nine feet away from the assumed stake, the description has marked out a nine-foot slice of neighbor Smith's property, and has failed to refer to an intended portion of S's land.

Cribbet, Principles of the Law of Property
169-171 (2d ed. 1975)

The cases on legal description are legion but a "feel" for the judicial construction problem may be obtained by a look at ten canons of construction. They are as follows.

1. The construction prevails which is most favorable to the grantee, i.e., the language of the deed is construed against the grantor. If the deed contains two descriptions, the grantee can select that which is most favorable to him. This canon is based on the presumption that the grantor drafted the deed and, if an ambiguity has resulted, he has only himself to blame. As in insurance law, where the policy is typically construed against the insurer, this canon is frequently the unstated premise in a case otherwise inexplicable.[18]

2. If the deed contains two descriptions, one ambiguous and the other unambiguous, the latter prevails in order to sustain the deed. This is not so likely to happen with modern, short form deeds but with the old, prolix instruments it was not uncommon.

3. Extrinsic evidence will be allowed to explain a latent ambiguity but a patent ambiguity must be resolved within the four corners of the deed.[19] This old chestnut has lost much of its validity but it still must be reckoned with. It was based on the idea that if the defect was latent (not apparent to the parties when the deed was drafted) evidence of surrounding circumstances should be admitted to clarify intent, but if it was patent (apparent on the face of the document) the parties must have been aware of it when the deed was executed and no extrinsic evidence is necessary. It has long been clear that this canon is easily controlled by the determination of what is latent or patent and many writers have called for abolition of the distinction.[20]

4. Monuments control distances and courses; courses control distances; and quantity is the least reliable guide of all.[21] In a metes and

18. See Hall v. Eaton, 139 Mass. 217, 29 N.E. 660 (1885) which makes little sense on any other basis.
19. Walters v. Tucker, 281 S.W.2d 843 (Mo. 1955).
20. McBaine, The Rule Against Disturbing Plain Meaning of Writings, 31 Cal. L. Rev. 145 (1943). In a footnote it is pointed out that the distinction "is gradually disappearing" and the hope is expressed that the time will soon come "when it will be of interest only to students engaged in tracing the history of law through periods of formalism to a period of realism."
21. Pritchard v. Rebori, 135 Tenn. 328, 186 S.W. 121 (1916).

bounds description, it is relatively easy to start with a known monument (the side of a road, a stream, a rock, etc.), move in a stated direction or course for a set distance, and end up with an impossible description because one of these elements is in error. This canon tries to set up a priority of reliability, based on presumed intent of the parties. Most monuments would be difficult to mistake so they are probably identified correctly. A course, "northerly at a 90° angle," is more certain than a distance, "thence eighty feet," since most people cannot measure distances with any degree of accuracy with the naked eye. Quantity, which is always hard to estimate, logically brings up the end of the list.

5. Useless or contradictory words may be disregarded as mere surplusage. The difficulty with this canon is patent. Which are the useless or contradictory words? Nonetheless, it states a useful truth since many prolix, confusing descriptions can be pared down to meaningful size to sustain a deed.

6. Particular descriptions control over general descriptions, although a false particular may be disregarded to give effect to a true general description. Any more questions?

7. A description, insufficient in itself, may be made certain through incorporation by reference. This is a particularly useful canon since it enables shorthand reference to be made to involved descriptions in other documents. It can create major merchantability problems, however, if the instrument referred to is not recorded and hence not available for title search.

8. If an exception in a deed is erroneously described, the conveyance is good for the whole tract and title to all of the land passes. Frequently, the grantor will convey Blackacre "except for" a described area. If the description of the exception is faulty, it could be argued that the entire deed should fail but this canon would sustain the larger grant at the expense of the grantor who made the error.

9. When a tract of land is bound by a monument which has width, such as a highway or a stream, the boundary line extends to the center, provided the grantor owns that far, unless the deed manifests an intention to the contrary.[22] The converse of this canon would lead to undesirable policy results. Suppose A, who owns to the center of a highway, conveys to B, but the description uses the edge of the road as one boundary. Years pass and the highway is vacated so that the easement of public use is removed. At this point, the narrow strip of land becomes valuable due to the discovery of oil or a change in the direction of urban growth. Who owns the strip? If the parties thought of it at all, they probably intended to transfer whatever land the grantor owned since the retention of a strip under an existing highway would be unreasonable. To prevent endless litigation over nar-

---

22. Bowers v. Atchison, T. and S.F. Ry. Co., 119 Kan. 292, 237 P. 913, 42 A.L.R. 228 (1925).

row strips and gores of land, the courts, in general, have followed the rule stated above.

10. A description in a deed includes the appurtenances to the tract even though they are not specifically mentioned in the deed.[23] Normally, only that portion of the land passes to the grantee which is specifically described in the deed. However, there are interests in the land which are appurtenant to the described tract in such a way that they have no existence apart from their parasitical attachment to the host premises. Thus, if A owns Blackacre and has an access road across Whiteacre to the highway, a conveyance of Blackacre to B will include the appurtenant easement even though not described in the conveyance. . . .

A study of the canons will reveal that they overlap in their statements of law and that some of them are contradictory. Moreover, it should be clear that any one of them will yield to a clear manifestation of intent, which is always the courts' major guideline. Even so, they serve a useful purpose, if only as a point of departure, and do give some degree of predictability in an uncertain area of the law.

Cities Service Oil Co. v. Dunlap
100 F.2d 294 (5th Cir. 1938)

SIBLEY, Circuit Judge. The appellant, Cities Service Company, is by assignment and succession the holder of a producing oil and gas lease on a tract of land in Gregg County, Texas, made in 1930 by the heirs of J. F. Rogers. In 1934 appellee B. P. Dunlap obtained a lease upon a narrow strip of land about 68 feet wide by 880 yards long along the west side of the J. F. Rogers tract (less two acres sold off at the northwest corner) from the heirs of J. F. Rogers and his three brothers, W. H. Rogers, F. E. Rogers and J. W. Rogers. The four Rogers brothers were the heirs of Louisa Rogers, who owned a rectangular tract of about 320 acres. They in February, 1899, divided it by assigning to J. F. Rogers a tract in the northwest corner, to W. H. Rogers a tract in the northeast corner, while F. E. Rogers and J. W. Rogers together took the south portion. The lease made in 1934 to Dunlap rests on the theory that a strip of land 66 or 68 feet wide along the west side was left undivided in 1899.

The lease of 1934 was recorded, and appellant as the holder of the lease of 1930, claiming the strip to be within its lease, filed in the District Court a bill to remove the cloud on its title, making Dunlap and all the Rogers parties. The defendants denied the material allegations of the bill touching the west boundary of the J. F. Rogers land, and by cross-bill set up that a call in the deed to J. F. Rogers for the "Wiley Davis northeast corner" as the northwest corner of the J. F. Rogers tract was inserted by the drafts-

---

23. Stockdale v. Yerden, 220 Mich. 444, 190 N.W. 225 (1922).

Seller's Obligations

man through inadvertance and mistake, and that the course and distance in the deed were correct and located that corner about 66 feet east of the Wiley Davis corner, and that the strip thus left between the east side of the Davis land and the west side of the J. F. Rogers land was purposely left undivided to be controlled in common; and there was a prayer to quiet title in them and their lessee. In answer to the cross-bill the complainant denied these allegations and asserted that it and its predecessors in the lease were purchasers for value in good faith and without notice of the mistake in the J. F. Rogers deed. On full findings of fact the District Court held that the extrinsic evidence of what happened in the partition, and of the intention in locating the west line of the J. F. Rogers land, was admissible; that the strip in question was not a part of the tract set off to J. F. Rogers, but that his west line began at a point 880 yards west of the northeast corner of the original tract and went thence south to a "gear shaft" corner, and that the reference to Wiley Davis' corner was inserted in the deed by mistake. The title was accordingly quieted in the defendants. There was no express finding as to whether the complainant or its predecessors, or any of them, was a bona fide purchaser for value without notice. This appeal followed.

The principal questions made are: That the parol extrinsic evidence was not admissible; that the call for the Davis corner overrules the course and distance which fell short of it; that if that call be ignored the tract was nevertheless one adjoining a road, and by legal construction would include the land under the road; that the mistake, if any, was not correctible against bona fide purchasers; and that if all these contentions fail, still the one-fourth interest of the J.F. Rogers heirs in the strip should be held

The first lease copied exactly the calls of the partition deed to J. F. Rogers, as follows: "Being a part of the G. A. Thomas HR; starting at the N.E. corner of Lot No. 2, which is the N.W. corner of W. H. Rogers' tract, Lot No. 1, running west 440 yards to Wiley Davis' N.E. corner; thence south 880 yards; thence east 224 yards; thence north 310 yards at 12° east of north; thence east 754 yards; to W. H. Rogers' line; thence north 574 yards to the starting point; containing 68⅕ acres more or less." On its face this survey is out of balance. The total west measurement is 440 yards. The east measurements are 224 and 574 yards, a total of 798 yards beside the easterly gain in the line which runs 310 yards 12° east of north. All agree that the partition deeds, which are of the same date and between the same parties, recite the same consideration, and each in form a warranty deed to the grantee from the other tenants in common and duly recorded, are to be construed together as one transaction. Comparing them, it appears that the east and west line set down in the deed to J. F. Rogers as 754 yards long continues as a part of the south boundary of Lot No. 1 for 66 yards further. This entire line appears in the deed to the F. E. and J. W. Rogers part as 220 yards long, showing that 754 is a clerical error for 154, because 154 plus 66 makes 220 yards. Thus corrected, the J. F. Rogers east and west measurements approximately balance. They also work out correctly on the land. The northeast corner of the original tract is known, and is the northeast corner of Lot No. 1. The northwest corner of Lot No. 1 is by the deed to W. H. Rogers fixed 440 yards to the west, and was in 1930 a marked corner. That is the northeast corner of Lot No. 2, the J. F. Rogers tract, and the beginning and ending point for the calls in the deed to him. The northwest corner (ignoring the Wiley Davis corner) is called for as 440 yards to the west. Thence the course is south 880 chains, the deed mentioning no marker there but there being at this point a heavy iron shaft with a beveled gear on it planted, as is testified, soon after the survey to mark the corner and it has been reputed to be the corner ever since. The courses and distances following thence, after the correction of 754 to 154 yards, reach the west line of Lot No. 2 and proceed along it to the beginning with fair accuracy. On the other hand, if the north line of Lot No. 2 is not stopped at 440 yards but is continued about 66 feet to Wiley Davis' N.E. corner, which was a known point in 1899 and ever since, and if the survey is continued thence, the beveled gear shaft will be missed at the southwest corner by 66 feet, the west lines of Lot No. 1 will not be reached by that distance, nor will the beginning point be.

In the effort to include just the land the parties intended, which is the true object in all questions of boundary, shall the measurement of 440 yards for the north line prevail, or shall the call for Wiley Davis' northeast corner control? The appellant correctly contends that there is a presumption that the parties intended to divide all their land and especially not to leave a narrow strip off to one side; and that it is a general rule that courses and distances, because of the greater possibility of error in them, will yield to a call for a fixed monument, including the line or corner of an adjoiner. [Citations omitted.] But the presumption stated is rebuttable; and the rule not without exceptions. It sometimes appears that the measurements are more likely correct than the call for some monument or adjoiner, or that such call was inserted by error; and when that is clearly true the mistaken call will be rejected and the measurements followed even in cases at law. [Citations omitted.] In the present case the scope of the admissible evidence is enlarged by the pleaded issue that the reference to the Wiley Davis corner got into the deed through mistake. On that issue, the case being in equity, parol and other extrinsic evidence of what was done and said was plainly admissible. The court properly heard the testimony of persons who were present at the survey, and it clearly showed that the northwest corner of Lot No. 2 was deliberately and purposely put about a chain's length east of the Wiley Davis corner so as to leave a strip undivided and under the control of all four tenants in common for the purpose of a road. The planting of the heavy gear shaft at the same distance from the Davis line at the south end powerfully sustains this testimony. Most evidently it marked a permanent corner. The evidence was admissible, and it well warranted the finding of the judge that the reference to the Wiley Davis corner as the corner of Lot No. 2 was inserted by mistake in drafting the deed. Appellant argues that the field notes of the survey contradict the witnesses as to where the surveyor went and how he located the corners of Lot No. 2. It so happens that the field notes of Lot No. 2 have not been found. Those for the other lots do not show the surveyor at or near the Wiley Davis corner, or measuring the north line 440 yards or any other length, for this line was not common to the other lots. Only the field notes for Lot No. 2 would show what was done at or near the northwest corner of that lot. There is no contradiction of the witnesses by the field notes introduced.

But appellant argues that equity will not correct a mistake as against a bona fide purchaser for value without notice, and that there is no proof that it and its predecessors in the lease were not such. The answer is that there is no sufficient proof that they were. In the law of negotiable instruments presumptions are indulged as to bona fides and want of notice, but in equity a claim to the favored position of a bona fide purchaser for value without notice is a matter of affirmative defense, and he who asserts it has the burden of proving it. . . . It fairly appears that these lessees paid value in developing the lease, but there is no evidence at all that at the time they paid they did not know that the west line was not the east line of Davis, or that the call for 440 yards on the north line would not reach Davis' corner, rendering the corner questionable. No well was drilled or expenditures made on this disputed strip. There being no proof of bona fides or want of notice, this plea was not sustained. The district judge held the evidence touching the intention of the parties to be admissible on the ground that the deed was ambiguous irrespective of the equitable power to correct a mistake in the deed. The cases cited above go far to sustain him, but we find it unnecessary to determine that question in view of the equitable issues pleaded.

Appellant strongly argues that although it be established that the call for the Wiley Davis corner does not belong in the deed, under settled rules of law the conveying of the land adjoining a road will carry the grantor's title to the servient fee up to the center of the road, and if the grantor has no land beyond the road the grantor's title to its further edge will pass. Such is the general rule applied both to highways and streets and alleys, non-navigable streams and railroad right-of-way. 8 Am. Jur., Boundaries, §36, 39, 22, 25; 11 C.J.S., Boundaries, §31, 35, 45. It is based on the presumed intention of the parties that the grantor would not reserve a long, narrow strip under such way or stream for which he had no use, and partly on public policy in that such strips are likely to give rise to litigation in the distant future. But it is not unlawful to retain such a strip. If the intention to do so is clear, the contrary presumption must yield. And if the conveyance as made does not reach the highway or stream, it cannot be extended to it to avoid creating a separately owned strip. There was in

1899 no highway or street or alley covering the strip in question. A highway ran east and west through the land to be partitioned near its center. The Rogers brothers had run a sawmill on their land, and had hauled logs along the line of Davis to this highway. It was not a publicly worked way, or an established road. About this time, the date not being clearly fixed, Davis wished to confine the travel across his place, and he testifies he gave fifteen feet along the east edge of his land for a north and south road. Several witnesses say they helped cut the road out fifteen or twenty feet wide, cutting the line trees on the Davis line because they were in the road. The big pine at the Wiley Davis northeast corner was cut close to the ground and its stump was in the middle of the road. It was thereafter a country road open to all, although little used. The fences, where there were any, on either side were sixty or seventy feet apart, but not straight, and probably were not regarded as correct line fences. The land, as we understand, was mostly in woods. The actual road was thus only twenty feet wide, and supposed to be half on the land of Davis. Assuming it to have been in existence in 1899, the northwest and southwest corners which the surveyor fixed for Lot No. 2 were about sixty-six feet from the center of this road and fifty-six feet from its margin. Neither the deed nor the field notes say anything about a road. This is not a case in which a road is mentioned as a boundary, nor one in which the boundary fixed is in fact the edge of a road either public or private. The only thing that tends to make the strip in contest a road, or the equivalent of a road, is the parol evidence that the Rogers brothers during the survey informed the surveyor, as found by the court, that "They would leave the 66 feet out of the partition and use the same jointly, and keep it like it was; the same 66 foot tract was then being used in part as a logging road." There was no covenant to dedicate the strip to the public as a road. It was subjected to no easement over the whole of it so as to convert the whole strip into a roadway. There is a plainly expressed intention not to add the strip to Lot No. 2 but to retain joint control and ownership of it. Since the deed as prepared said nothing about a road as a boundary, there was no occasion to make a reservation of the land, though to some extent on its far edge it was used for a road. The case presented is not one requiring an extension of the deed beyond its true calls. In recent years a broad public road occupying most of the strip has been laid out, but this development years after the making of the deed cannot have the effect of extending its scope. 11 C.J.S., Boundaries, §35(4).

Appellant lastly contends that its lessors at the date of its lease owned in any event a fourth interest in the strip, and it is covered by the lease because of the words in it which follow the description first above quoted: "and being the same land described in a deed from J. W. Rogers, W. H. Rogers and F. E. Rogers, February 28, 1899, Recorded Vol. R, pages 59-60, Deed Records Gregg County, Texas, save and except two acres out of the northwest corner sold to R. M. Wood, it being the intention to include all land owned or claimed by lessor in said surveys." . . . The only survey definitely mentioned consists of the courses and distances just before recited. The reference to the recorded deed to J. F. Rogers imports its contents into the lease, and there is a similar "survey" in it. The "intention clause" if applied to these adds nothing to the lease. It is, however, attempted to make it refer to the original grant to G. A. Thompson (Thomas is the name used in the lease) which contained 640 acres, but the lease does not mention any survey in that connection. The uncertainty is too great to warrant any application of this clause to land outside the limits of the surveys which are definitely set forth. Furthermore, if other land can be included under this clause the original lessee's interest in it was not transferred to the appellant, for his deed of assignment recites the description of the J. F. Rogers deed as above quoted, omitting the "intention clause," and then transfers "all rights, title and interest of the original lessee and present owner in and to said lease and rights thereunder in so far as it covers the above described tract." If the lease covered any additional land, the original lessee did not transfer his interest therein.

Judgment affirmed.

[After the decision of the court of appeals, the Supreme Court granted certiorari, and remanded. Next printed is the court of appeals opinion on remand, 115 F.2d 720 (5th Cir. 1940).]

SIBLEY, Circuit Judge. Our former opinions in this case are reported, Cities Service Co. v. Dunlap, 100 F.2d 294, 101 F.2d 314. The contentions are there fully stated. We did not therein undertake to construe and apply the description in the deed to J. F. Rogers under which appellant claims, to determine whether it included the strip of land in dispute by reason of the call for the Wiley Davis northeast corner as the northwest corner of the tract conveyed, because we thought the evidence clearly showed that this call was inserted by mistake and that the deed might be reformed so as to omit it, since it was not shown that appellant was an innocent purchaser for value. On certiorari to the Supreme Court it was held that under a rule peculiar to Texas the burden was on appellees to prove that appellant was not a bona fide purchaser for value, and the cause was remanded to us for further consistent proceedings. Cities Service Co. v. Dunlap, 308 U.S. 208, 60 S. Ct. 201, 84 L. Ed. 196. Since the record does not show what appellant paid for its lease or with what knowledge or in what faith it paid whatever it did pay, we must and do hold that the deed cannot be reformed.

Our present task, therefore, is to take the deed as it is written and determine whether at law it conveys the disputed strip. This is not a case of parol partition of land, as appellees argue, but one in which the results of the partition were expressed in mutual deeds. The deed to J. F. Rogers fixes what he got in severalty. The descriptive words are: "Being a part of the G. A. Thomas H.R.; starting at the N.E. Corner of Lot No. 2, which is the N.W. corner of the W. H. Rogers tract, Lot 1; Running West 440 yards to Wiley Davis N.E. corner; thence South 880 yards; thence East 224 yards; thence North 310 yards at 12 deg. East of North; Thence East 154[1] yards to W. H. Rogers line; Thence North 572 yards to starting point, containing 68⅕ acres, more or less." The language imports an actual accurate survey. It mentions a located beginning point, and a line 440 yards west therefrom to the Davis corner, another located point. No other natural or artificial object is mentioned, but the courses and distances around to the beginning point are exactly stated, and the included acreage. On its face there is neither indefiniteness nor contradiction, so that no patent ambiguity appears. But in the effort to trace the lines on the ground it is at once found that the distance from the known beginning corner to the Davis corner is not 440 yards, but one chain or 66 feet more. This discrepancy alone would make no great difficulty and would not amount to an ambiguity, because it is well settled that a distance is generally overruled by a call for a fixed object, the law esteeming that a mistake in the measurement, or in recording it, is more likely than one about the fixed object. But if we so decide and continue according to the deed, no other fixed objects being mentioned, it develops that we do not get back to the beginning point at all, but 66 feet west of it. If we force the course of the last line so as to reach the beginning point it will not have the direction nor the length called for, and the acreage included will be excessive. On the other hand, if we stop on the first line at 440 yards instead of going on to the Davis corner, we find that the remaining lines, run according to the deed, do take us back to the beginning corner and include the acreage called for. There is in this situation a real doubt as to whether the call in the first line for the Davis corner or for a corner at 440 yards is correct. That is a latent ambiguity which requires construction; and may justify a resort to extrinsic evidence, not to contradict the deed, but to explain its true meaning. Without such evidence we should conclude that the call for 440 yards was correct and the Davis corner in error. The oral evidence leaves no doubt about it. The disputed strip was not included. . . .

. . . An innocent purchaser is protected from reformation in equity, but not from construction at law of the deed as written. If the muniments of title he holds are beset with ambiguity, a court of law will resolve that ambiguity according to its own methods. See Miller v. Lemm, Tex. Com. App., 276 S.W. 211, and cases cited. . . .

We repeat our ruling in our first opinion that the coverage of the deed cannot be enlarged as bounded by a public or private road. The deed did not itself mention any road, and there was in fact no road, either established by the public authorities or created by dedication and acceptance or

---

1. It is conceded that 154 yards, and not 754 as stated in the first opinion, is the true call.

prescriptive use. The wagon trail fifteen feet wide, partly on the land of Davis and partly on the disputed strip, did not touch the land conveyed.

The judgment of the District Court is affirmed.

On Rehearing: 117 F.2d 31 (5th Cir. 1941)

PER CURIAM. It is urged on motion for rehearing that the description we have construed and applied refers to another fixed object, to wit "W. H. Rogers' line." We did not and do not so regard it for his line was originated in and is a part of this very partition survey. It did not exist before, and cannot be considered a controlling monument.

Touching the presumed inclusion is a conveyance of a strip of land devoted to a road, we are referred to the case of Cantley v. Gulf Production Co., Tex. Sup., 143 S.W.2d 912. The deed there construed expressly referred to the road, and to the partition decree and map which clearly showed it, though it was never opened. The court held that the servient fee in the strip was annexed to the abutting lots, and a conveyance of them carried the strip. We rest the present decision on the point that there is in this case no mention of a road in any of the title papers, and there was no abutting road in fact.

Motion denied.

NOTES

1. *Risk of errors in descriptions.* Land description errors can arise from a variety of causes, including inaccurate surveys, copying errors by typists, and incorrect designations by sellers in showing land to buyers. A good example of error possibilities and their persistence is Schultz v. Rudie, 275 Wis. 99, 80 N.W.2d 804 (1957). In *Schultz,* parties to a land sale visited the ground and pointed out the intended portion for transfer. A contract of sale was entered that contained a description that differed from what was pointed out. Then a deed was delivered with a description that differed from the two previous descriptions. The trial court was upheld in its decree reforming the deed to conform to the parties' original orally expressed intention, but on the appeal it was discovered that the description in the decree (different from all previous ones) failed to effect this.

Justice Gillespie of the Mississippi Supreme Cou. in an article entitled Some Animadversions on Land Line Cases, 33 Miss. L.J. 159 (1962), gives some suggestions for avoiding errors in preparing litigation and decrees for boundary line cases.

2. *Reformation and the bona fide purchaser.* A seller who mistakenly overconveys, or a buyer who mistakenly receives an underconveyance,

cannot obtain reformation against a bona fide purchaser. This is the rule announced (and finessed) in *Cities Service*. As a practical matter, how likely is it that one will be able to acquire the status of bona fide purchaser where a mistakenly described conveyance is involved? Keep in mind that a buyer of real property is charged with notice of the rights of persons in *possession* of the premises.

3. *Non-called monuments.* Suppose that a description applies to mark out a unique tract. Suppose further that 15 feet east of the tract thus defined one of the following appears: (a) The east line of grantor's property; (b) A fence marking the east line of the grantor's property; (c) The center line of a 30-foot highway easement running along the east edge of grantor's property, grantor owning in fee to the center of the highway.

In each of the above hypotheticals, adjoiner, fence, and road have not been called in the description.

After conveying the tract to B_1, who enters possession, grantor sells the balance of his property to B_2 by describing it as "my farm [properly described] except [tract conveyed to B_1]." Litigation ensues over the 15 feet between B_1 and B_2. What results are suggested by *Cities Service?*

A similar problem arises where grantor conveys a chunk out of the center of his property to buyer under a description that unambiguously applies. However, ten feet north of each northern corner thus described are discovered monuments set by the surveyor who surveyed and monumented the property for the transaction with buyer. The monuments have not been called in the description. For an excellent discussion of the large number of cases that deal with discrepancies between description and survey monuments, see Browder, Boundaries: Description v. Survey, 53 Mich. L. Rev. 647 (1955). This topic is further developed in Browder, Practical Location of Boundaries, 56 Mich. L. Rev. 487 (1958), in relation to the law of change of boundary line by adverse possession, practical location, and acquiescence. See also Comment, Boundary Law: The Rule of Monument Control in Washington, 7 U. Puget Sound L. Rev. 355 (1984).

4. *Deed calls for quantity.* People often talk about land values in terms of property in a downtown area selling for $250,000 a front foot, or of undeveloped property off to the southeast of a growing city selling at $15,000 an acre; and land sale prices are sometimes figured, say, at so much an acre. Someone buying Blackacre for its historic value qua Blackacre is not the same legal-economic fellow as the buyer who sees its lovely elms as bulldozeable impediments to his carving it up into the largest number of resaleable lots permitted by zoning laws.

Suppose Blackacre is sold as such, but is conceived by the parties and priced as so many acres permitting so many lots or as carrying such an agricultural production quota as is permitted by federal statutes. Then Blackacre turns out to have more or less acres than had been assumed as the basis of the bargain.

Seller's Obligations

Parol evidence can be used to prove the basis of the bargain, and the regular remedy pattern comes into play—rescission or reformation, breach of warranty, price abatement or enhancement for overage and underage, etc. See 3 Corbin, Contracts §604.

The fact that a quantity call is used as a part of a property description does not mean that the transaction was premised on a quantity.

e. Errors Affecting Many Parcels

Van Deven v. Harvey
9 Wis. 2d 124, 100 N.W.2d 587 (1960)

Action to establish a boundary line, to quiet title, for an injunction, and for other equitable relief.

The plaintiffs and the defendants are owners of adjoining lots in block 8 of Lake Forest Park subdivision in the village of Whitefish Bay in Milwaukee county. The tract of land, of which block 8 is a part, was subdivided in the year 1892, and all of the lots in said block are improved and occupied. The plat of the subdivision was recorded in the office of the register of deeds of Milwaukee county on February 20, 1892.

Block 8 in said subdivision is bounded on the north by East Birch avenue, an east-west street, and on the east by North Lake Drive, a street running in a northwesterly and southeasterly direction. Block 8 consists of 24 lots numbered consecutively 1 to 24, both inclusive, with lot No. 1 being on the extreme west and lot No. 24 being on the extreme east of the block and adjoining North Lake Drive. According to the recorded plat lot No. 1 is 72.34 feet in width, lot 2 is 40 feet in width, lot 23 is 60 feet in width, and lot 24 is 45.96 feet in width. Lots 3 through 22 are each 50 feet in width. These measurements are the frontages on East Birch avenue. The south line of the block is longer, due to the direction in which North Lake Drive runs. Plaintiffs are the owners of lot 23 and the defendants are the owners of lot 24.

On the 3d day of January, 1938, plaintiffs' predecessors in title to lot 23 were Joseph M. Bell and Katharina Q. Bell, his wife. At that time the defendants' predecessor in title to lot 24 was the Old Line Insurance Company. On that date the respective owners of the two lots in question entered into a written agreement which recited that garages and driveways had been built on each lot and that in case any of them encroached upon the lot of the other party such encroachment should be deemed and considered those of licensor and licensee only and not an easement. The agreement provided that it would bind the parties and their successors in title and that it might be cancelled upon giving 60 days' notice of revocation of the license. The agreement was duly recorded.

On the 29th day of February, 1952, David W. Goodman and Ethel Goodman, his wife, the then owners of lot 23, caused to be served upon the defendants herein, who were then the owners of lot 24, a written notice cancelling said agreement and license. Thereafter the Goodmans erected a curb consisting of plank and concrete and a picket fence on what they claimed to be the boundary between lots 23 and 24. On March 16, 1955, the Goodmans, having set the stage for this suit, conveyed lot 23 by warranty deed to the present plaintiffs. These plaintiffs removed the fence but refused to move the curb which shuts off the defendants from the use of their garage and have enjoined the defendants from removing said curb.

In their complaint the plaintiffs alleged that the east boundary of their lot is as designated on the recorded plat at a point 45.96 feet west of the northeast corner of defendants' property. By way of counter-claim the defendants alleged that the true east boundary of the plaintiffs' premises and the west boundary of the defendants' premises is to be measured south from a point 47.38 feet west of the northeast corner of block 8.

The case was tried to the court without a jury. Two surveyors testified upon the trial, one for each side. Both surveyors agreed, and it is undisputed that the actual measurement of the north line of block 8 is 1,219.72 feet, whereas an addition of the frontages allotted to the respective lots on the recorded plat amount to 1,218.30 feet, so that there is an excess in the block over the plat measurement of 1.42 feet.

The trial court filed findings of fact and conclusions of law wherein it was determined that the 1.42 feet overage in block 8 was intended by the original surveyor and subdivider to belong to lot 24. Judgment was entered on February 19, 1959, dismissing plaintiffs' complaint, fixing the boundary as prayed for in the counterclaim of the defendants, dismissing the injunction that restrained the defendants from removing the curb, and for costs and disbursements to the defendants. The plaintiffs appealed.

BROADFOOT, Justice. Upon the trial the original drawing of the plat by the surveyor, R. C. Reinertsen, was introduced in evidence. He had continued his work as a surveyor until 1915, when he sold his business and all of his records to a successor. The surveyor for the defendants, as a successor in interest, had all of the original records in his possession. The figures upon the original drawing in black ink corresponded with the recorded plat. However, the original drawing showed some additional figures in red ink. The length of the north boundary of lot 24 on the original drawing was marked in black ink as 45.96 feet. Underneath that figure in red ink appeared the figures 47.38.

In order to establish the authenticity of the drawing there was introduced in evidence the affidavit of Donald J. Reinertsen, son of the original surveyor. He had worked with his father until 1915. The son was not called as a witness but the affidavit was received under a stipulation that if he were called as a witness he would testify to the statements made in the affidavit. The son stated that the figures in red ink upon the original drawing were in the handwriting of the original surveyor, R. C. Reinertsen.

The trial court based his decision in this case on an inference he drew from the figures in red ink that appeared thereon. In his memorandum decision the trial court said:

"The evidence disclosed that the recorded plat here in question was made in 1892 by a surveyor named R. C. Reinertsen. The latter is now deceased.

"The survey notes attached to the affidavit of Donald J. Reinertsen, and marked document 'B,' clearly indicate that the surveyor who originally prepared the recorded plat not only knew of the existence of the overage but actually allocated, and placed it in Lot 24.

"While it is true that the said Donald J. Reinertsen, if he were called as a witness, would testify that he does not know when said R. C. Reinertsen made the red and black numerals contained in document 'B', nevertheless it does appear that said numerals were made in the handwriting of said R. C. Reinertsen.

"The appearance of document 'B' clearly indicates that it is a very old document. It contains survey notes prepared by said R. C. Reinertsen of the block in question. It is safe to infer, in the absence of direct evidence, from the circumstances present that document 'B' was made by said R. C. Reinertsen prior to the preparation of the recorded plat which was prepared in 1892. There would be no reason for making these notes after the completion and recording of the plat.

"In any event, whether we assume that document 'B' was prepared prior to 1892 or prior to 1915, it was made by R. C. Reinertsen, and it is obvious from said document, and the court finds, that the original surveyor included the overage in question in Lot 24. The difference between the numerals 45.96 appearing in black ink in the square containing 'Lot 24' and the numeral 47.38 appearing in red ink in the same square is 1.42, the exact amount of the overage here in question."

The trial court also stated that the overage of 1.42 feet in the block was located in lot 24 according to the intention of the original surveyor and subdivider. We cannot agree with the trial court that the exhibit supports an inference that the surveyor effectively placed the overage in lot 24. There is no testimony that the subdivider ever knew of the mistake in the measurement. Any inference as to the intention of the original subdivider is based upon the inference as to the intention of the surveyor. When we speak of the subdivider we refer to the owner of the tract that was subdivided. If the mistake had been discovered in 1892 or soon thereafter and had been called to the attention of the subdivider, the matter of the overage could have been settled very easily at that time.

Our determination requires a reversal of the judgment.

In the trial court the plaintiffs urged the application of the apportionment rule, a well-known rule that is often applied when there is a variance between the actual measurements of a subdivision and the measurements of the lots therein as shown by the recorded plat. The leading case in Wisconsin is Pereles v. Magoon, 78 Wis. 27, 46 N.W. 1047. Also see 97 A.L.R. 1227, where the *Pereles* case is cited in a footnote along with other Wisconsin cases. In the *Pereles* case this court said (78 Wis. at page 31, 46 N.W. at page 1049):

"This court has repeatedly held, in effect, that where a piece of land is subdivided into lots, and a plat of the subdivision recorded, and the actual aggregate frontage of such lots is *less* than is called for in the plat, the deficiency must be divided among the several lots in proportion to their respective frontage, as indicated by the plat. [Citations omitted.] This is certainly not inconsistent with section 770, Rev. St. These cases have been cited approvingly in a recent case in Kansas, where it is held that, 'on a line of the same survey, and between remote corners, the whole length called for, it is not to be presumed that the variance was caused from the defective survey in any part, but it must be presumed, in the absence of circumstances showing the contrary, that it arose from imperfect measurement of the whole line; and such variance must be distributed between the several subdivisions of the line in proportion to their respective lengths (citations). The same principle maintains where the actual measurements are in excess of the dimensions specifically designated upon the plat, as in case of a deficiency. . . ."

The trial court discussed the apportionment rule at length in a carefully written memorandum decision. He cited authority to the effect that there are exceptions to the rule. He determined that it could not be applied in this case for three reasons, which he stated to be as follows:

"That the 'apportionment rule' cannot be applied in this case because none of the owners of lots 1 to 22, inclusive, in block 8 are parties to this action.

"That, in any event, to apportion the overage of 1.42 feet among all the owners of the lots in block 8 would involve a change of the occupational boundary lines of all of said lots and result in encroachments of buildings, fences, driveways and hedges upon adjacent lots.

"That to apply the 'apportionment rule' in this case would result in allocating a small fraction of an inch of said overage to the defendants' lot and allowing the remainder of said overage to go to the plaintiffs by default since none of the owners of the remaining lots in said block 8 are before the court."

As authority for his first reason he cited a statement in 11 C.J.S. Boundaries §124, p. 737. In footnotes sustaining the contention C.J.S. cited a California, Indiana, and Illinois case. The trial court quoted from the California case Hoffman v. Van Duzee, 19 Cal. App. 2d 517, 65 P.2d 1330.

We cannot agree with the first reason given by the trial court. In the case of O'Brien v. McGrane, 27 Wis. 446, and the *Pereles* case, and in Wisconsin cases in which the *Pereles* case has been cited as shown by Shepard's Wisconsin Citations, that rule has not been followed. In the case of Wiegman v. Alexander, 4 Wis. 2d 118, 90 N.W.2d 273, 91 N.W.2d 335, it appeared that an adjoining landowner would be directly affected. We did not say that adjoining landowners must be made parties but did state that they would not be bound by any decision made in the action. Apparently that is as far as this court has gone in holding that all other owners in a tract would have to be made parties to an action if the apportionment rule is to be applied. The other lot owners in the block were not necessary parties to the action, but the decision herein is not binding on them.

The second and third reasons given by the trial court are valid reasons for not applying the apportionment rule in detail as requested by the plaintiffs. The surveyor for the defendants testified that he had checked all of the occupational lines between the various lots in the block. Some were marked by fences, some by hedges, and other physical evidence. In line with the occupational boundaries, which corresponded with the frontages shown on the recorded plat when measured from lot 1 eastward, he found crosses chipped in the sidewalk in front of the properties. Upon the west side of lot 23, owned by the plaintiffs, was a fence that corresponded almost exactly with the location of that line as shown on the recorded plat when measured from the west. There was evidence that these occupational boundary lines and the corresponding crosses had been there for some time.

There was further evidence of a cross in the walk at a point 47.38 feet west of the northeast corner of block 8 that apparently at one time marked the boundary between lots 23 and 24. Except for the agreement entered into in 1938 that would have constituted evidence that the boundary line between the two lots had been established at that point. However, the agreement negated the effect of this evidence.

Upon this record, and with the understanding that none of the other lot owners are bound by this decision, it is apparent that the boundary lines between all of the lots except those of the plaintiffs and the defendants, have been established. Whether this was done by adverse possession or by agreement we cannot tell from this record. Lines can be established by oral agreement or by implied agreement if followed by acquiescence and possession. 1 Patton, Titles, (2d ed.) p. 425, sec. 159; 11 C.J.S. Boundaries §64, p. 635 ff. Because of the time element involved, because the lots are improved and occupied, and because of evidence of the establishment of the boundaries up to the division between lots 23 and 24, a strict application of the apportionment rule would be inequitable in the manner pointed out by the trial court. Allotting a fraction of an inch to each lot owner could only cause confusion.

The evidence of the fence on the west line of the plaintiffs' property is justification for the third reason given by the trial court. If a fraction of an inch of the overage is allotted to the defendants the plaintiffs, so far as this record is concerned, could retain the balance of the overage. Plaintiffs have sought the equitable powers of the court. The inequitable result that would follow the strict application of the apportionment rule is evident and is justification for not applying the rule as requested by the plaintiffs.

Upon this record and with our desire to make it clear that the other lot owners in block 8 are not bound by this judgment, we can only apply the apportionment rule as between the parties to this action, allotting one-half of the overage to the plaintiffs and the remaining half to the defendants. The northernmost part of the boundary between the two lots then is fixed at a point 46.67 feet west of the northeast corner of block 8.

It is apparent from our determination that the curb constructed by the predecessors in title of the plaintiffs will encroach upon lot 24. Provision for its removal should be made in the judgment to be entered herein.

3. Quality

a. Introduction: Caveat Emptor

As recently as the 1950s there was a reasonably coherent body of law dealing with seller's responsibilities to buyer as to structures on the sold premises. The law was "caveat emptor": the warning to the buyer was generally, "Guard yourself at all times," and particularly, "Look before you sign," "Don't assume, ask," and "Get it in writing."

One could find in the authorities a whole series of propositions that made up the "caveat emptor" system. They were all derived from the general bodies of contract and tort law, and as you read below a selection from the more important of the rules you will find nothing startling. To be sure, you ought to doubt whether there ever was a time and place where every proposition listed was rigidly applied to defeat every disappointed buyer, and you ought to recognize that some of the propositions have been weakened in recent years in their general applicability, whatever may be true about land sales. Nevertheless, here are propositions that defeated many a buyer in many a case.

NOTE: CAVEAT EMPTOR AS A SYSTEM OF PROPOSITIONS

1. *Promissory obligations of the seller: seller has contractual quality responsibilities only to the extent that he makes express warranties in contract of sale or deed.*

   (a) There are no implied warranties of quality in the sale of real estate.

   (b) Seller's oral promises preceding the contract of sale are unavailing to buyer because of the parol evidence rule.

Seller's Obligations

(c) Seller's oral promises preceding the contract of sale are made unenforceable by the statute of frauds.

(d) Seller's oral promises between contract of sale and deed are unavailing to buyer because not supported by consideration.

(e) Express warranties in the contract of sale but not contained in the deed are unavailing to buyer because of the doctrine of merger. (This is a variant of the parol evidence rule.)

(f) An express quality warranty in the deed inures only to the grantee and does not run with the land.

(g) The remedy for breach of an express quality warranty is damages, not rescission.

(h) Breach of an express quality warranty does not subject the warrantor to liability for consequential damages, particularly personal injury damages.

2. *Duties of the seller not to misrepresent.* Here is a sampling of propositions from the tort law of misrepresentation: innocent, negligent, and intentional:

(a) *Nondisclosure:* (1) Seller has no duty to disclose any quality defect detectable by inspection. (2) Seller has no duty to disclose a concealed defect unless buyer proves that the defect is actually known to seller. (3) Seller has no duty to disclose a concealed defect known to him unless he knows that buyer is unaware of the defect and that the buyer would regard the defect as material.

(b) *Intentional misrepresentation:* (1) Seller's words are an unenforceable oral promise, rather than a duty-laden representation of fact. (2) Seller's quality affirmation is a mere opinion. (3) Buyer's inspection shows he does not rely on the representation. (4) Buyer's opportunity to inspect shows that he has no right to rely on the representation.

(c) *Agency problems:* (1) A real estate broker is not authorized to make quality representations to prospective purchasers. (2) Seller who authorizes a broker to make quality representations is not liable for intentional misrepresentations made by the agent.

(d) *Regulatory statutes:* Statutory duties imposed on seller by building codes or like regulatory statutes do not run to buyer.

(e) *Remedies:* (1) Buyer's remedy for misrepresentation is restricted to rescission. (2) A buyer who, after discovering a defect, keeps up mortgage payments while deciding on a course of action, has waived the tort. (3) The statute of limitations runs from the date of the tort, not the date of its discovery.

When it came to purchase of new homes from builder-vendors, all the rules that denied buyer protection unless he had it in writing got their bite from the fact that the instrumentation of the transaction was in the hands of the seller. In the last significant case that reaffirmed the one-time nationwide rule that there were no implied warranties in the sale of a new home, Steiber v. Palumbo, 219 Ore. 479, 347 P.2d 978 (1959), the court noted that the transaction's documents did not contain any mention at all of the structure being sold.

The material that follows shows how caveat emptor has been nationally undercut in the last 15 years in a common law process that is still under development. This legal change also should come as no surprise to persons who have studied recent products law and recent landlord-tenant decisions.

You must note that we are dealing systematically only with private remedies for disappointing housing, and not with building codes, criminal statutes, conditional public subsidy programs, antitrust laws, and myriad other institutional and governmental constraints on the housing seller. The prophylaxis of a tightly administered building code might be enormously more protective to buyers than the opportunity to engage in expensive, time-consuming, nerve-frazzling, common law litigation — even if successful. And it may be that a vigorous, innovative, competitive housing supply industry would be the best protection of all.

b. Implied Warranty

In the sale of new homes in most American states, the doctrine of caveat emptor has been largely replaced and buyers are protected by implied warranties of fitness and habitability. This is a relatively new doctrine in the United States for the sale of homes, first appearing in the late 1950s and steadily spreading ever since; its rate of adoption has been particularly rapid for a new real property concept that is largely the creation of judicial case law.[16] Implied warranty doctrine as it relates to housing sales is still evolving and there is a question as to how far it will be extended — whether it will become widely applicable to used home purchases, for example — and what defenses to implied warranty claims will be available to builder-vendors.

Implied warranty of habit. extends to subsequent purchasers

Richards v. Powercraft Homes, Inc.
139 Ariz. 242, 678 P.2d 427 (1984)

GORDON, Vice Chief Justice. Each of the several individually named plaintiffs purchased houses in the Indian Hills subdivision near Casa Grande, Arizona at varying times during 1975, 1976, and 1977. The houses had

---

16. For a state-by-state listing of case authority as to recognition of implied warranties of fitness in new home sales, see Note, 15 St. Mary's L.J. 673 n.27 (1983). On implied warranty protection of used home buyers, see Note, Builders' Liability for Latent Defects in Used Homes, 32 Stan. L. Rev. 607 (1980); and Note, 35 Baylor L. Rev. 670 (1983).

Seller's Obligations

been built by defendant Powercraft Homes beginning in 1974. Plaintiffs Woodward, Fillion, Schaar, and Grant purchased their homes directly from Powercraft while plaintiffs Richards, Farina, and White bought repossessed homes from Farmers Home Administration. After occupying the houses, each plaintiff discovered numerous defects. The defects included, inter alia, faulty water pipes, improperly leveled yards that resulted in pooling and flooding with any rain, cracking of the interior and exterior walls, separation of the floors from the walls, separation of sidewalks, driveways, and carports from the houses, and doors and windows which were stuck closed or which could not be locked because of misalignment. Powercraft was notified of many of these defects and attempted some repairs. The repairs in most cases provided only temporary or partial relief from the problems.

In the spring of 1978, each of the plaintiffs filed a complaint with the Arizona Registrar of Contractors. The Registrar found that Powercraft had failed to follow certain plans and specifications in the building of each home and that it had failed to properly compact the soil beneath each house before building commenced. Powercraft's contractor's license was revoked on December 6, 1978.

Plaintiffs filed suit against Powercraft on August 17, 1979 alleging violation of the Consumer Fraud Act, A.R.S. §44-1521 et seq., and breach of the implied warranty that houses be habitable and constructed in a workmanlike manner. A jury awarded the plaintiffs $210,000 in compensatory and punitive damages. Powercraft appealed; the Court of Appeals affirmed in part and reversed in part. Richards v. Powercraft Homes, Inc., 139 Ariz. 264, 678 P.2d 449 (App. 1983). The Court of Appeals ordered the consumer fraud count dismissed, the punitive damage award vacated, and the verdicts in favor of plaintiffs Richards, Farina, and White set aside. The plaintiffs petitioned this Court to review the Court of Appeal's opinion. We have jurisdiction pursuant to Ariz. Const. art. 6, §5(3) and Ariz. R. Civ. App. P.23. While we approve the Court of Appeal's decision regarding the consumer fraud claim and the punitive damages, we vacate that portion of the Court of Appeal's decision regarding the verdicts of plaintiffs Richards, Farina, and White. The jury verdict in favor of those three plaintiffs against defendant Powercraft for the breach of the implied warranty of habitability is reinstated for the reasons set forth below.

In setting aside the verdicts in favor of Richards, Farina, and White, the Court of Appeals held that "there must be privity to maintain an action for breach of the implied warranty of workmanship and habitability," *Richards*, supra, 139 Ariz. at 266-267, 678 P.2d at 451-452. One basis cited for that holding was this Court's decision in Flory v. Silvercrest Industries, Inc., 129 Ariz. 574, 633 P.2d 383 (1981). In *Flory*, we held that warranties implied pursuant to A.R.S. §44-2331 (the Arizona version of U.C.C. §2-314(2)) require privity. We specifically stated:

> It is important to note that what we have said herein regarding the requirement of privity to recover for breach of warranty under the Uniform Commercial Code is limited to those actions.

Id. at 579, 633 P.2d at 388. In the instant case, the warranty at issue is not implied pursuant to A.R.S. §44-2331.[1] Rather, it is imposed by law. In Columbia Western Corp. v. Vela, 122 Ariz. 28, 592 P.2d 1294 (App. 1979), builder-vendors of new homes were held to impliedly warrant that construction has been done in a workmanlike manner and that the structure is habitable. The issue before us now is whether this implied warranty extends to subsequent buyers of the homes.[2]

The courts of several states have confronted this issue. Many of those courts have refused to extend the implied warranty of habitability to remote purchasers or to those not in privity with the builder-vendor. See, e.g., H.B. Bolas Enterprises, Inc. v. Zarlengo, 156 Colo. 530, 400 P.2d 447 (1965); Coburn v. Lenox Homes, Inc., 173 Conn. 567, 378 A.2d 599 (1977); Strathmore Riverside Villas Condominium Assn., Inc. v. Paver Development Corp., 369 So. 2d 971 (Fla. App. 1979); Oliver v. City Builders, Inc., 303 So. 2d 466 (Miss. 1974); John H. Armbruster & Co. v. Hayden Company-Builder Developer, Inc., 622 S.W.2d 704 (Mo. App. 1981); Herz v. Thornwood Acres "D," Inc., 86 Misc. 2d 53, 381 N.Y.S.2d 761 (Justice Ct. 1976), *aff'd*, 91 Misc. 2d 130, 397 N.Y.S.2d 358 (App. Term. 1977); Brown v. Fowler, 279 N.W.2d 907 (S.D. 1979). Others, however, have rejected the imposition of a privity requirement and have allowed remote purchasers to maintain a cause of action against a builder-vendor for breach of the implied warranty of habitability. See, e.g., Blagg v. Fred Hunt Co. Inc., 272 Ark. 185, 612 S.W.2d 321 (1981); Redarowicz v. Ohlendorf, 92 Ill. 2d 171, 65 Ill. Dec. 411, 441 N.E.2d 324 (1982); Barnes v. Mac Brown & Co., Inc., 264 Ind. 227, 342 N.E.2d 619 (1976); Hermes v. Staiano, 181 N.J. Super. 424, 437 A.2d 925 (Law Div. 1981); McMillan v. Brune-Harpenau-Torbeck Builders, Inc., 8 Ohio St. 3d 3, 455 N.E.2d 1276 (1983); Elden v. Simmons, 631 P.2d 739 (Okl. 1981); Terlinde v. Neely, 275 S.C. 395, 271 S.E.2d 768 (1980); Gupta v. Ritter Homes, Inc., 646 S.W.2d 168 (Tex. 1983); Moxley v. Laramie Builders, Inc., 600 P.2d 733 (Wyo. 1979). We find the latter group of cases to be more in line with the public policy of this state and hold that privity is not required to maintain an action for breach of the implied warranty of workmanship and habitability.

---

1. Article 2 of the Uniform Commercial Code, A.R.S. §44-2301 et seq., applies only to the sale of "goods" as that word is defined in §§44-2305 and -2307. Sales of realty, and structures affixed thereto, are not within the purview of that definition. Anderson, 1 Uniform Commercial Code §2-105:32 at 572 (3d ed. 1981).

2. This issue is considered in a recent article, Comment, Implied Warranties in New Homes and Their Extension to Subsequent Purchasers in Arizona, 1983 Ariz. St. L.J. 113 (1983).

We agree with the persuasive comments of the Wyoming Supreme Court in *Moxley,* supra, that:

> [t]he purpose of a warranty is to protect innocent purchasers and hold builders accountable for their work. With that object in mind, any reasoning which would arbitrarily interpose a first buyer as an obstruction to someone equally deserving of recovery is incomprehensible.

600 P.2d at 736. In addition, such reasoning might encourage sham first sales to insulate builders from liability.

Since *Columbia Western,* an original homebuyer in this state has been able to rely on the builder-vendor's implied warranty. The same policy considerations that led to that decision — that house-building is frequently undertaken on a large scale, that builders hold themselves out as skilled in the profession, that modern construction is complex and regulated by many governmental codes, and that homebuyers are generally not skilled or knowledgeable in construction, plumbing, or electrical requirements and practices — are equally applicable to subsequent homebuyers. Also, we note that the character of our society is such that people and families are increasingly mobile. Home builders should anticipate that the houses they construct will eventually, and perhaps frequently, change ownership. The effect of latent defects will be just as catastrophic on a subsequent owner as on an original buyer and the builder will be just as unable to justify improper or substandard work. Because the builder-vendor is in a better position than a subsequent owner to prevent occurrence of major problems, the costs of poor workmanship should be his to bear.

The implied warranty of habitability and proper workmanship is not unlimited. It does not force the builder-vendor to "act as an insurer for subsequent vendees" as the Court of Appeals feared, *Richards,* supra, 139 Ariz. at 267, 678 P.2d at 452. It is limited to latent defects which become manifest after the subsequent owner's purchase and which were not discoverable had a reasonable inspection of the structure been made prior to purchase. We adopt the standard set forth by the Indiana Supreme Court in *Barnes,* supra.

> The standard to be applied in determining whether or not there has been a breach of warranty is one of reasonableness in light of surrounding circumstances. The age of a home, its maintenance, the use to which it has been put, are but a few factors entering into this factual determination at trial.

264 Ind. at 229, 342 N.E.2d at 621. The burden is on the subsequent owner to show that the defect had its origin and cause in the builder-vendor and that the suit was brought within the appropriate statute of limitations. Defenses are, of course, available. The builder-vendor can demonstrate that the defects are not attributable to him, that they are the

result of age or ordinary wear and tear, or that previous owners have made substantial changes.

In the present case, the plaintiffs met their burden and proved that the defect had its origin and cause in Powercraft. There was no indication that the original owners substantially changed the structure of the homes. The cracking of the exterior and interior walls, the separation of the floors from the walls, and the separation of the sidewalks, driveways, and carports from the homes were due to improper compacting done by Powercraft prior to building the houses coupled with an apparent systematic lack of reinforcement in the floors, walls, ceilings, and roofs of the houses. Such improper compaction and lack of structural reinforcement could not have been determined from a reasonable inspection prior to purchase. Each of the plaintiffs moved into their homes before the end of 1977. The defects became manifest only after extraordinarily heavy rains in early 1978. Therefore, all of the plaintiffs, whether or not in privity with Powercraft, are entitled to the jury verdicts rendered in their favor.

The decision of the Court of Appeals that the consumer fraud count be dismissed and that the punitive damage award be vacated is approved; the decision of the Court of Appeals that the verdicts in favor of plaintiffs Richards, Farina, and White be set aside is vacated; the verdicts in favor of plaintiffs are affirmed in all other respects. The case is remanded for further proceedings not inconsistent with this opinion.

NOTES

1. In most of the cases granting recovery for implied warranty breaches involving sales of new homes, the defendant is the builder-vendor. But liability has also been imposed when the defendant is not the builder-vendor of a new home. E.g., Starfish Condominium Assn. v. Yorkridge Service Corp., 295 Md. 693, 458 A.2d 805 (1983); and Lane v. Trenholm Bldg. Co., 267 S.C. 497, 229 S.E.2d 728 (1976).

2. *Personal injuries: implied warranty and negligence.* In Schipper v. Levitt and Sons, Inc., 44 N.J. 70, 207 A.2d 314 (1965), the unattended 16-month old child of tenants of the original new-home buyer was badly scalded after turning on the hot water taps in the bathroom sink.

There is a device called a mixing valve, then costing builders about $10 installed, which reasonably assures moderation of hot water temperatures enroute to the faucet. The builder, in producing the thousands of homes known as Levittown of which the home rented by adult plaintiffs was one, had decided not to install a mixing valve but rather to include a statement in its Home-Buyer's Guide as to how to turn on the faucets so as to reduce the hot-water risk.

The court held that the mass builder vendor had a duty of reasonable care, which was not satisfied by its Home-Buyer's Guide notice, which was not cut off by the acceptance of the house by the first buyer, and that extended not only to first buyer but also to persons who might reasonably be expected to use the premises: the opinion was sweeping and fit the builder vendor's liability in tort squarely into the law previously developed as to product manufacturers. In addition the court held that defendant on the facts had breached an implied warranty of fitness for residential use that ran to the infant and adult plaintiffs.

3. *Implied warranty: law and economics.* Builders after *Schipper* will either install $10 mixing valves or insure at some cost (if they can find insurance carriers who will not insist on mixing valves). Will this raise the price per house $10? What is the general relation between a seller's price and his costs? What is that relation in mass housing? Is a mass seller's pricing mechanism sensitive enough to respond to a $10 cost charge? If the builder doesn't raise its price will it skimp on something else? If it doesn't increase prices or skimp, will the profit drop impede entry into the supply of housing? If it does raise $10, will this shut some buyers out of the market? If it does raise prices, does this represent an outrageous imposition of a mixing valve cost on people who read the Home-Owner's Guide with care, in favor of the irresponsibles (aged 16 months and over) who don't?

4. What arguments can be advanced in support of implied warranties of fitness and habitability in new home sales but not as to such warranties in used home sales?

5. In at least two states, used home purchasers are protected by statutorily created implied warranties that the builder warrants. Minn. Stat. Ann. §§327A.01 and .02 (West 1981); and N.J. Stat. Ann. §§46:3B-2 and 4 (West Supp. 1985).

6. Implied warranties of fitness for the intended purpose have been held to exist in construction contracts, even those involving commercial or industrial structures. E.g., Markman v. Hoefer, 252 Iowa 118, 106 N.W.2d 59 (1960); and Robertson Lumber Co. v. Stephen Farmer Cooperative Elevator Co., 274 Minn. 17, 143 N.W.2d 622 (1966).

7. On the measure of damages for breach of implied warranties, Hoagland v. Celebrity Homes, Inc., 40 Colo. App. 215, 216, 572 P.2d 493, 494 (Colo. App. 1977), in accord with substantial authority, states:

> When the warranties of workmanlike construction or suitability for habitation are breached, damages may be measured in two ways. The ordinary measure is the difference between the actual value at the time of sale and what the value would have been if it had been as warranted. When, however, the buyer retains the property, the measure of damages may appropriately be the cost of bringing the property into conformity with the warranty. Glisan v. Smolenske, 153 Colo. 274, 387 P.2d 260. This latter measure of damages was properly applied in this case.

8. Construction lenders run a risk of being held liable under implied warranties of quality if the lenders are co-joint venturers with builders or

owners and share ownership or profits and losses. There is some authority holding construction lenders who are not co-joint venturers liable in negligence for defectively built homes. The lead case for such lender liability, with little subsequent support, is Connor v. Great Western Savings and Loan Association, 69 Cal.2d 850, 73 Cal. Rptr. 369, 447 P.2d 609 (1968). In the *Great Western* case, the majority took the position that since the developers' lender had sufficient power over the construction process through control over loan funds, it had a duty to exercise reasonable care to prevent the construction and sale of seriously defective homes to home buyers. The *Great Western* case is a 4-3 decision and there are strong dissents. Among cases holding lenders not liable for defective construction are 1000 Grandview Assn. v. Mt. Washington Associates, 290 Pa. Super. 365, 434 A.2d 796 (1981); and Smith v. Continental Bank, 130 Ariz. 320, 636 P.2d 98 (1981). In the *Smith* case it was held that the lender was not liable for defective construction because it did not do the construction work, even though it foreclosed during the course of construction on property it was financing, had another construction company complete the structure, and then sold to the plaintiffs who later claimed breach of implied covenants of quality against the lender. The bank was not, according to the Arizona Court, a builder-vendor.

G-W-L, Inc. v. Robichaux

643 S.W.2d 392 (Tex. 1982)

SONDOCK, Justice. This is a suit brought under the Texas Deceptive Trade Practices Act by John and Merila Robichaux because of alleged defects in a new house purchased from builder-vendor G-W-L, Inc. d/b/a Goldstar Builders ("Goldstar"). The trial court rendered judgment for the Robichaux after a jury trial. The court of appeals affirmed. 622 S.W.2d 461. We reverse the judgments of the courts below and render judgment that plaintiff take nothing.

The Robichaux contracted with Goldstar for the construction of a house. The contract provided that Goldstar would design, build, and provide the materials for the house. The construction was completed by Goldstar but the roof of the house had a substantial sag in it. The Robichaux sued for breach of express and implied warranties. The jury found that no express warranties were breached, but found that Goldstar had failed to construct the roof in a good workmanlike manner and that the house was not merchantable at the time of completion. Judgment was rendered awarding the Robichaux damages under the Deceptive Trade Practices Act, plus attorney fees.

Goldstar's first point of error is that the court of appeals erred in holding that the implied warranty of fitness created by Humber v. Morton, 426

Seller's Obligations

S.W.2d 554 (Tex. 1968) was not waived because the parties agreed that there were no express or implied warranties. The promissory note signed by the Robichaux contained this provision:

> This note, the aforesaid Mechanic's and Materialmen's Lien Contract and the plans and specification signed for identification by the parties hereto constitute the entire agreement between the parties hereto with reference to the erection of said improvements, there being no oral agreements, representations, conditions, warranties, express or implied, in addition to said written instruments.

In Humber v. Morton, supra, this Court held that a builder-vendor who built and conveyed a house impliedly warranted that the house was constructed in a good workmanlike manner and was suitable for human habitation. Both parties acknowledge that the *Humber* warranty applies to real estate transactions of this nature. Additionally, both parties agree that this implied warranty can be waived by proper language. The question presented, therefore, is what is sufficient to exclude the implied warranty of fitness created in Humber v. Morton, supra. This question was reserved in Watel v. Richman, 576 S.W.2d 779 (Tex. 1978), and has not been addressed by this Court.

The court of appeals stated that the language waiving the implied warranty must be "clear and free from doubt." 622 S.W.2d 464. We agree. This standard is consistent with the better-reasoned decisions in other states addressing the exclusion of the implied warranty of habitability. See Sloat v. Matheny, 625 P.2d 1031 (Colo. 1981); Belt v. Spencer, 585 P.2d 922 (Colo. Ct. App. 1978); Rapallo So. Inc. v. Jack Taylor Dev. Corp., 375 So. 2d 587 (Fla. Dist. Ct. App. 1979); Arnold v. New City Condominiums Corp., 78 A.D.2d 882, 433 N.Y.S.2d 196, *appeal dism'd* 53 N.Y.2d 823, 422 N.E.2d 583, 439 N.Y.S.2d 922 (1980); Griffin v. Wheeler Leonard & Co., 290 N.C. 185, 225 S.E.2d 557 (1976).

The court of appeals held, however, that the language of disclaimer in this case did not meet that test. With this we do not agree. The language in the contract that states "no . . . warranties, express or implied, in addition to said written instruments" could not be clearer. The parties to a contract have an obligation to protect themselves by reading what they sign. Thigpen v. Locke, 363 S.W.2d 247 (Tex. 1962). Unless there is some basis for finding fraud, either actual or constructive, the parties may not excuse themselves from the consequences of failing to meet that obligation. Courseview, Inc. v. Phillips Petroleum Co., 158 Tex. 397, 312 S.W.2d 197 (1957); Indemnity Insurance Co. v. N. America v. W. L. Macatee & Sons, 129 Tex. 166, 101 S.W.2d 553 (1936).

Although this is a question of first impression, we do not write on an entirely clean slate. In Pyle v. Eastern Seed Co., 198 S.W.2d 562, 563 (Tex. 1946), this Court faced a similar question. In the *Pyle* case, a seed buyer sued the seed company for breach of warranty when the seed delivered was not the variety provided for in the contract. The seed company argued that the contract contained a waiver of all warranties because the contract provided that "Eastern Seed Co. gives no warranty, express or implied, as to description, purity, productivity, or any other matter of any seed we may send out. . . ." Id. at 563. In holding that the buyer could not recover for breach of warranty, this Court stated:

> Neither of the parties here are under guardianship or incompetent to contract. There is no claim that the contract signed was not the one agreed upon, or that both parties did not fully understand what they were agreeing to. Plaintiff [seed seller] plainly undertook to relieve itself from liability in case of intermixture, and defendant agreed that it should be relieved. It is not claimed that the contract is void, because contrary to public law or to public policy, and, if not, effect should be given to it. . . . If it be conceded that the contract is one-sided, it must also be conceded that the parties had a right to make a one-sided contract if they saw fit.

See also Allright, Inc. v. Elledge, 515 S.W.2d 266 (Tex. 1974) (limitation of liability in bailee's written parking contract need not be called to consumer/bailor's attention); W. R. Weaver Co. v. Burroughs Corp., 580 S.W.2d 76 (Tex. Civ. App.— El Paso 1979, writ ref'd n.r.e.) (disclaimer in an equipment lease agreement need not meet the conspicuousness requirement of Tex. Bus. & Com. Code Ann. §2.316).

The Robichaux cite MacDonald v. Mobley, 555 S.W.2d 916 (Tex. Civ. App.— Austin 1977, writ ref'd n.r.e.), for the proposition that the provisions in the Texas Business and Commerce Code for exclusions or modifications of warranties should be applicable to the implied warranty of fitness created in Humber v. Morton, supra. See Tex. Bus. & Com. Code Ann. §2.316 (1968). In MacDonald v. Mobley, supra, the builder-vendor defended on the grounds that the sales contract excluded the *Humber* warranty pursuant to §2.316 of the Business and Commerce Code. The court of appeals agreed that the provisions of §2.316 were applicable, but held that the language used was not effective to exclude the warranty of fitness because it was not "conspicuous," as required by §2.316(b). Id. at 919.

The provisions of Chapter 2 (Sales) of the Business and Commerce Code are not applicable to the construction and sale of a house. The Legislature thus far has not included real estate transactions within the scope of Chapter 2. Chapter 2 is limited to transactions involving the sale of "goods." Tex. Bus. & Com. Code Ann. §2.102 (1968). Goods are defined as "all things . . . that are *movable* . . . at the time of identification to the contract. . . ." Tex. Bus. & Com. Code Ann. §2.105 (1968). The Code additionally makes it clear that the sale of a home is not normally "movable." Section 2.107 provides that "a contract for the sale of . . . a

Seller's Obligations

structure or its materials to be removed from realty is a contract for the sale of goods within this chapter if they are to be severed by the seller."

Additionally, building contracts involve the sale of both services and materials. In such hybrid transactions, the question becomes whether the dominant factor or "essence" of the transaction is the sale of the materials or the services. See Freeman v. Shannon, 560 S.W.2d 732 (Tex. Civ. App.—Amarillo 1977, writ ref'd n.r.e.). The contract in this case provided that Goldstar would "build, construct, and complete . . . and furnish and provide all labor and material to be used in the construction and erection thereof." Clearly, the "essence" or "dominant" factor of the transaction was the furnishing of labor and the performance of work required for constructing the house. See Robertson Lumber Co. v. Stephens Farmers Co-op Elevator, 274 Minn. 17, 143 N.W.2d 622 (1966); Markman v. Hefner, 252 Iowa 118, 106 N.W.2d 59 (1960).

Goldstar's second point of error complains that the court of appeals erred in holding that the implied warranty of merchantability could be applied to this transaction. Since we conclude that Chapter 2 of the Business and Commerce Code is not applicable to this real estate transaction, we hold that the trial court and court of appeals erred in applying the implied warranty of merchantability contained therein.

The judgments of the courts below are reversed and judgment is rendered that plaintiff take nothing.

Spears, J., dissents with an opinion in which Ray and Robertson, JJ., join.

SPEARS, Justice, dissenting.

I respectfully dissent.

I do not agree with the majority that the language "no warranties, express or implied" is sufficient to exclude the builder's implied warranty of fitness. The better rule is the waiver must be in *clear and unequivocal* language specifically naming the warranty that is being disclaimed. See Sloat v. Matheny, 625 P.2d 1031 (Colo. 1981); Herlihy v. Dunbar Builders Corp., 92 Ill. App. 3d 310, 47 Ill. Dec. 911, 415 N.E.2d 1224 (1980).

In analogous areas of contract law this court has held clauses ineffective if not clear and specific, and I see no reason not to apply that same rule here. For example, in order for an indemnity agreement to protect an indemnitee from its own negligence the obligation must be expressed in clear and unequivocal terms. Eastman Kodak v. Exxon Corp., 603 S.W.2d 208 (Tex. 1980); Fireman's Fund Insurance Co. v. Commercial Standard Insurance Co., 490 S.W.2d 818 (Tex. 1972). Similarly, in McMillan v. Klingensmith, 467 S.W.2d 193 (Tex. 1972), we held unless a party is expressly named in a release, he is not released.

The warranty of habitability is implied in law to protect innocent consumers, and to hold builders accountable for their work. To effectuate the public policies underlying the implied warranty, a court should not consider the warranty waived except by very express and specific language which clearly reflects that the buyer knew the implied warranty did not attach to the sale of his home.

In the sale of a new home, the builder warrants that the house is constructed in a good and workmanlike manner, and is suitable for human habitation. Humber v. Morton, 426 S.W.2d 554 (Tex. 1968). An effective waiver must give the buyer notice that he is waiving his warranty of habitability. The ordinary consumer when signing a contract for sale would not even conceive of the possibility that his house would not be built in a good and workmanlike manner. For that reason the waiver must at least be specific and express enough to inform the buyer specifically what he is waiving. An effective waiver of the implied warranty of fitness in the sale of a new home should refer to a warranty of "habitability" or disclaim "good and workmanlike manner." In this case the language "no warranties express or implied" is not sufficient to notify the purchaser that he is waiving his implied warrant of habitability.

Other states have various requirements for effectively waiving the implied warranty of habitability. I believe the better reasoned authorities are those that at least require specific and express language. E.g., Sloat v. Matheny, 625 P.2d 1031, 1034 (Colo. 1981); Peterson v. Hubschman Construction Co., 76 Ill. 2d 31, 27 Ill. Dec. 746, 748, 389 N.E.2d 1154, 1156 (1979); Crowder v. Vandendale, 564 S.W.2d 879, 881 (Mo. 1978); Casavant v. Campopiano, 114 R.I. 24, 327 A.2d 831, 834 (1974).

I would, therefore, affirm the judgments of the court's below.

Ray and Robertson, JJ., join in this dissenting opinion.

NOTES

1. Should disclaimer clauses in home sale contracts be held invalid as against public policy if they provide, even in clear and unequivocal language, for waiver of the buyer's rights under implied warranties of fitness and habitability?

2. In addition to disclaimer clauses, other defenses that may be successfully raised against a home buyer's assertion of implied warranty breaches include statutes of limitations, limited express warranties, reasonable care shown in construction, and proof that defects are so minor as not to be covered by the warranty. These defenses are discussed in Note, Implied Warranties in New Home Sales — Is the Seller Defenseless?, 35 S.C.L. Rev. 469 (1984).

c. Express Warranty

Many contracts for the sale of real property contain express warranties as to the quality of the premises being sold. However, ambiguity in warranty terms often leads to conflict and litigation, even when the contract is in writing. Recovery on asserted oral warranties may be especially difficult, as the oral statements relied upon may be considered merely expressions of opinion, not promises; and if promises, they may be unenforceable under the Statute of Frauds.

Garriffa v. Taylor

675 P.2d 1284 (Wyo. 1984)

CARDINE, Justice. This is an appeal from an action to recover damages for breach of an express warranty. Judgment was entered in favor of plaintiffs-appellees in the amount of $1,650, the cost of installing a septic tank, plus court costs, for a total judgment of $1,692.75.

We will reverse.

FACTS

The appellants sold a house to the appellees. Approximately nineteen months after appellees had moved into the house, they replaced the septic tank and sent the bill for the cost of replacement to appellants with a request for payment. Appellants refused payment and this suit was initiated.

Appellants had lived in the house for five years prior to the time of sale. Prior to that time, appellant, Marla Garriffa, had lived in the house for ten years with her parents, the previous owners. The house was at least forty years old. The preprinted real estate listing form had a category entitled sewerage. Above this the real estate agent had typed "Septic." These forms are prepared from information provided by the sellers. While the appellees were looking at the property, Mrs. Taylor asked Mrs. Garriffa where the septic tank was located. Mrs. Garriffa indicated that the tank was located north of the house. Mrs. Taylor also asked Mrs. Garriffa if the tank had been pumped; Mrs. Garriffa replied that they had not pumped the tank but that they had used chemicals to keep the system working properly. Appellees testified that there were some problems with the sewerage system several months after they moved into the house, but nothing was done.

Nineteen months after taking possession and occupying the house, the appellees contacted a septic tank sales and service company to pump the tank. When they dug into the area north of the house, they did not find a septic tank. However, they found two pipes running out of the house. At the end of the pipes appellees testified that there was an accumulation of rocks, dirt, and debris. The appellees then employed a contractor who installed a new septic tank. Appellees did not notify appellants concerning any of this until after the installation of the septic tank. They then forwarded them the bill, which appellants refused to pay. Appellees contend that there was an express warranty by the appellants that the property had a septic sewer system and that this warranty was breached because no septic system existed. Therefore, they contend that appellants are liable for the cost of installing the septic tank.

Appellants raised several issues for review, however, we need only address one to dispose of this case — whether or not there was an express promise or warranty enforceable against the appellants regarding the existence and durability of a septic system.

Contracts for the sale and purchase of land may include an express warranty on the sellers' part as to the physical quality or condition of the property.

> . . . It has been held that such an express warranty of quality is governed by the common law principles applicable to warranties of quality in the sale of goods. . . . 77 Am. Jur. 2d Vendor and Purchaser §336.

An express warranty is created by any affirmation of fact made by the seller to the buyer which relates to the goods and becomes a part of the basis of the bargain. 67 Am. Jur. 2d Sales §442. The primary question is whether there were any affirmations of fact or promises which amounted to an express warranty or whether the representations were merely opinions. General Supply and Equipment Co., Inc. v. Phillips, Tex. Civ. App., 490 S.W.2d 913 (1972). The standard generally used is that:

> . . . [W]hen a seller asserts a fact of which the buyer is ignorant, and the buyer relies on the assertion, the seller makes an express warranty; but, when the seller merely states his opinion or his judgment upon a matter of which the seller has no special knowledge, . . . then the seller's statement does not constitute an express warranty. . . . Lovington Cattle Feeders, Inc. v. Abbott Lab., 97 N.M. 564, 642 P.2d 167, 170 (1982). See also, Scovil v. Chilcoat, Okl., 424 P.2d 87 (1967).

In order for an express warranty to exist, there must be some positive and unequivocal statement concerning the thing sold which is relied upon by the buyer and which is understood to be an assertion concerning the items sold and not an opinion. Maupin v. Nutrena Mills, Inc., Okl., 385 P.2d 504 (1963). A representation which expresses the seller's opinion, belief, judgment, or estimate does not constitute an express warranty. Scheirman v. Coulter, Okl., 624 P.2d 70 (1980). It is important to consider whether the seller asserts a fact about which the buyer is ignorant or whether he merely states an opinion or judgment upon a matter of which the seller has no special knowledge and upon which the buyer might be expected to have an opinion or to exercise his own judgment. Carpenter v.

Alberto Culver Co., 28 Mich. App. 399, 184 N.W.2d 547 (1970). All the circumstances surrounding a sale are to be considered in determining whether there was an express warranty or merely an expression of opinion. Lovington Cattle Feeders, Inc. v. Abbott Lab, supra; Price Brothers Co. v. Philadelphia Gear Corp. 649 F.2d 416 (6th Cir. 1981), *cert. denied* 454 U.S. 1099, 102 S. Ct. 674, 70 L. Ed. 2d 641.

The question of whether an express warranty exists is for the trier of fact. Scheirman v. Coulter, supra. In the absence of special findings of facts, the reviewing court must consider that the judgment carries with it every finding of fact which is supported by the evidence. Hendrickson v. Heinze, Wyo., 541 P.2d 1133, 1135 (1975). However, where nonconflicting evidence admits of only one conclusion, a contrary conclusion cannot stand. Wyoming Farm Bureau Mutual Ins. Co. v. May, Wyo., 434 P.2d 507 (1967).

In this case there is not a conflict in evidence; therefore, we must look at the undisputed facts in relation to the requirements necessary for an express warranty. There was uncontradicted testimony by the real estate agent that the phrase, "Septic" on the real estate listing agreement is interpreted as meaning that it does not have city sewer, "[i]t has some sort of a septic system." There was also testimony by appellee that appellant had stated that there was a septic system located north of the house and that they had not had any difficulty with the system. There was no testimony presented that they had had problems with the system, knew of any present difficulties, or that they had information which they did not disclose. Appellee testified concerning the septic system:

"*Q. (By Mr. Tate)* You said on your direct examination you didn't look at the system when you bought it; is that correct?
"*A.* We looked at what we could see.
"*Q.* You can't look at a sewage system when you buy an old house.
"*A.* That's true.
"*Q.* It would be pretty impractical.
"*A.* That's right.
"*Q.* And if the Garriffas never dug that system up, they really wouldn't know what was under there themselves either.
"*A.* They wouldn't know what was under the ground, no."

We do not find that these statements were sufficient to form an express warranty concerning the septic sewerage system. The house was at least forty years old. Appellants stated that they had never had any problem with the septic system and that the tank had not been pumped. There was no testimony contradicting these statements. The statements were very general. They related to appellants' experience in the house. Appellants were not dealers of septic systems, nor were they people who had a special knowledge about these matters. Guess v. Lorenz, Mo. App., 612 S.W.2d

831 (1981). Representations of fact which are capable of determination are warranties, but the mere expression of an opinion is not. Young & Cooper, Inc. v. Vestring, 214 Kan. 311, 521 P.2d 281 (1974).

We find that these statements merely expressed the sellers' opinions and beliefs concerning the septic system and did not constitute an express warranty. If both parties are free from fault, there is no compelling reason to require the seller, instead of the purchaser, to bear the loss. Cook v. Salishan Properties, Inc., 279 Or. 333, 569 P.2d 1033 (1977). Appellees purchased a forty-year-old house not connected to the city sewer. Sewage was moved from the house by a septic system installed forty years earlier. What kind of system was installed forty years earlier we do not know. We do know that these systems do not last forever. When, more than a year after purchase of the house, this system did not function as expected, appellees, without demand or notice to appellants, employed a contractor of their choice and installed a new septic tank. They now ask that appellants be required to pay for that new septic tank. That was not their bargain. Because appellants' statements did not constitute an express warranty, we will reverse with instructions to the trial court to enter a judgment in accordance with this opinion.

P.B.R. Enterprises v. Perren
243 Ga. 280, 253 S.E.2d 765 (1979)

PER CURIAM. In this case the appellees, as purchasers of a house and grantors of a subordinate deed to secure debt, sued the appellants, sellers-grantees. The complaint alleged substantially that the house had been still under construction and that the defendants had orally agreed, at the time of closing and both prior and subsequent thereto, to make the necessary repairs and changes and to complete the construction; that, unknown to the plaintiffs at that time, there were certain latent, structural defects in the construction of the house, of which the defendants failed to advise the plaintiffs; that the defendants orally agreed that no payment would be due them under their deed to secure debt until the orally promised repairs and work were performed; that the defendants have failed to comply with the plaintiffs' demands for completion of the work; that the defendants have commenced advertising for a foreclosure of their second mortgage, which would result in the plaintiffs' loss of their home, their equity therein, their good credit rating, and their adequate remedy at law; that the plaintiffs had had to make numerous emergency repairs to the house because of the defendants' failure to do the promised work; that the defendants had made wilful misrepresentations of material facts as to the structural soundness of the house and had failed to abide by a one-year warranty allegedly granted to the plaintiffs. The prayers for relief were for a tempo-

Seller's Obligations

rary injunction against the impending foreclosure; money damages for the cost of repairing the alleged structural defects; a set-off of the sum due under the mortgage (in the original amount of the principal) against the amount for the repairs; and punitive damages, interest and costs. *[relief asked]*

The trial judge, after a hearing, overruled the defendants' motions for directed verdict and to dismiss, and granted the temporary injunction, contingent upon the plaintiffs' payment into the registry of the court of the sum due under the defendants' mortgage and the monthly installments thereon until further order of the court. The defendants appeal. *Held*:

1. Subject to certain exceptions, the doctrine of caveat emptor applies to the sale of realty, there are no implied warranties as to the physical condition of the property sold, the purchaser buys at his own risk, and the purchaser cannot have an abatement of the purchase price on account of the seller's misrepresentations unless he exercised ordinary diligence to discover the falsity of the representations. Collier v. Sinkoe, 135 Ga. App. 732(2, 3), 218 S.E.2d 910 (1975) and cits.

2. The plaintiffs relied on three alleged oral contracts with the defendant sellers, i. e., that there was a one-year warranty on the house, that the sellers would repair all defects in the house, and that the sellers would forbear to foreclose their second mortgage until such promised repairs and completion of construction were made. As far as the record discloses, none of these promises was reduced to writing in the sales contract, the warranty deed, the deed to secure debt, or elsewhere. "Both this court and the Court of Appeals have followed the general rule that antecedent sales contracts covering the purchase and sale of real property merge in a subsequent deed involving the same property. Thus, where in a contract for sale of land the parties execute a preliminary sales contract and subsequently reduce that contract to a finality evidenced by a deed to secure debt, the terms of the preliminary contract, where not otherwise reserved, are merged into the deed, and those terms, conditions or recitals contained in the preliminary sales contract which are not included in the deed are considered as eliminated, abandoned or discarded. [Cits.]" Jordan v. Flynt, 240 Ga. 359, 362, 240 S.E.2d 858, 861 (1977). Thus, the oral promises of a one-year warranty and a forbearance to foreclose, which were included in neither the sales contract nor in either of the deeds, were unenforceable. *[oral promises merged into written deed or K so no longer exist]*

3. As to the promise for effecting completions and repairs on the house after the delivery of possession of the property and the warranty deed, such promises generally may be found to have survived the closing and not merged in the deed. Cullens v. Woodruff, 137 Ga. App. 262(1), 223 S.E.2d 293 (1976) and cits. Again, however, in order for such promise to survive the closing and not merge in the deed, it must have been included in the sales contract, which it was not in the case sub judice. The plaintiffs did not seek rescission based on the vendor's misrepresentations, and "no remedy is generally available for any breach by the vendor of any

promise contained in the contract but *omitted in the deed.*" Walton v. Petty, 107 Ga. App. 753, 756, 131 S.E.2d 655 (1963).

4. The complaint did allege, however, that, unknown to the plaintiffs at the time of closing and prior and subsequent thereto, there were certain latent structural defects in the construction of the house, of which the defendants failed to advise the plaintiffs. In Wilhite v. Mays, 140 Ga. App. 816, 818(3), 232 S.E.2d 141, 143 (1976),[1] the Court of Appeals held that "in cases of passive concealment by the seller of defective realty, we find there to be an exception to the rule of caveat emptor, which exception is applicable to the instant case. That exception places upon the seller a duty to disclose in situations where he or she has special knowledge not apparent to the buyer and is aware that the buyer is acting under a misapprehension as to facts which would be important to the buyer and would probably affect its decision. Prosser, Law of Torts 697-698 (4th Ed. 1971); Keeton, Fraud—Concealment and Non-Disclosure, 15 Tex. L. Rev. 1, 37-39 (1936). See Rothstein v. Janss Inv. Corp., 45 Cal. App. 2d 64, 113 P.2d 465 (1941) (improperly filled ground); Kaze v. Compton, 283 S.W.2d 204 (Ky. 1955) (drain under house causing yard to flood); Williams v. Benson, 3 Mich. App. 9, 141 N.W.2d 650 (1966) (termites); Brooks v. Ervin Construction Co., 253 N.C. 214, 116 S.E.2d 454 (1960) (house located on improperly filled ground)." Although some of the alleged defects were made known to the purchasers by the vendors' oral promises to repair, and other defects may have been discoverable by the purchasers' exercise of reasonable diligence to investigate and inspect, there remains the possibility that others of the defects come within the exception created or recognized by the Court of Appeals and approved by this court in Wilhite v. Mays, supra.

5. However, we hold that the trial court erred in granting the temporary injunction. "This state has long recognized the equitable maxim that '[h]e who would have equity must do equity, and give effect to all equitable rights in the other party respecting the subject-matter of the suit.' Code Ann. §37-104. Pursuant to this basic principle of equity, this court has held that 'a borrower who has executed a deed to secure debt is not entitled to an injunction against a sale of the property under a power in the deed, unless he first pays or tenders to the creditor the amount admittedly due." Wright v. Intercounty Properties, 238 Ga. 492, 233 S.E.2d 160 (1977). Accord, Mickel v. Pickett, 241 Ga. 528(9), 247 S.E.2d 82 (1978). In this case, the plaintiffs made no tender of the amount due. The fact that the trial judge, as a condition for the grant of the temporary injunction, required payment into the registry of the court of the installments due under the defendants' mortgage and the monthly installments due thereon until further order of the court does not constitute tender to the defendants.

Judgment reversed.

1. *Affirmed,* Wilhite v. Mays, 239 Ga. 31, 235 S.E.2d 532 (1977).

Seller's Obligations   607

NOTES

1. In a case involving representations by sellers that filled-in land being sold was fit for buyer's proposed restaurant building, the court in Stanford v. Owens, 46 N.C. App. 388, 265 S.E.2d 617 (1980), held the statements to be opinions not rising to the level of affirmations of fact or promise so required for an express warranty. In so holding, the court, at 265 S.E.2d 621, quotes as follows from an earlier North Carolina case:

> Assertions concerning the value of property which is the subject of a contract of sale, or in regard to its qualities and characteristics, are the usual and ordinary means adopted by sellers to obtain a high price, and are always understood as affording to buyers no ground for omitting to make inquiries for the purpose of ascertaining the real condition of the property. Affirmations concerning the value of land or its adaptation to a particular mode of culture or the capacity of the soil to produce crops or support cattle are, after all, only expressions of opinion or estimates founded on judgment, about which honest men might well differ materially.

2. In a suit involving warranties, in which the party charged had not signed the contract, it was held that conveyance of the parcel by defendant followed by plaintiff taking possession constituted sufficient performance under the doctrines of full or part performance to bar the defendant from raising the statute of frauds as a defense. Scribner v. O'Brien, Inc., 169 Conn. 389, 403, 363 A.2d 160, 168 (1975).

3. Since 1973, a substantial percentage of new home construction in the United States has been by builders participating in the Home Owners Warranty Program (HOW) sponsored and administered by the National Association of Home Builders. Under the HOW program participating builders must provide certain express warranties to buyers as to quality of work and materials. The warranties are backed by insurance paid for by the builders but the cost presumably is passed on to the buyers. A conciliation and arbitration scheme for buyers' complaints against builders is also part of the program. On the HOW Program, see Note, The Home Owners Warranty Program: An Initial Analysis, 28 Stan. L. Rev. 357 (1976).

4. Federal agencies that insure or guarantee mortgage loans are directed by Congress to require warranties of quality by builders or sellers of new homes financed by these insured or guaranteed mortgage loans. 12 U.S.C. §1701j-1 (1983), applicable to HUD; and 38 U.S.C. §1805 (1983), applicable to the Veterans Administration. The warranty requirements in the two statutes are very similar. The HUD statute provides in part:

> *§1701j-1* (a) The Secretary of Housing and Urban Development is authorized and directed to require that, in connection with any property upon which there is located a dwelling designed principally for not more than a

four-family residence and which is approved for mortgage insurance prior to the beginning of construction, the seller or builder, and such other person as may be required by the said Secretary to become warrantor, shall deliver to the purchaser or owner of such property a warranty that the dwelling is constructed in substantial conformity with the plans and specifications . . . on which the Secretary of Housing and Urban Development based his valuation of the dwelling: . . . Provided further, that such warranty shall be in addition to, and not in derogation of, all other rights and privileges which such purchaser or owner may have under any other law or instrument. . . .

5. Should there be a requirement that all sales contracts for new housing being sold to persons who intend to live in the housing include government specified warranties of quality? If not, why not?

4. Seller's Title Obligation

a. Introduction

Systems of title assurance. A buyer who has contracted to purchase Blackacre wants some protection against the possibility that there are flaws in seller's title. In a rare case, seller may turn out to have no legal or equitable interest at all in Blackacre. In a more common one, seller's ownership of Blackacre may fall short of the full unencumbered fee that buyer expects, so that buyer, in order to acquire "Blackacre," would have to pay not only the contract price to seller, but also some money to a third person. Whichever of these title shortages may exist, buyer doesn't want to have to close if seller's title turns out to be defective. Buyer also would like some kind of protection in the event that it's not discovered that seller doesn't own the property until after buyer has paid for it and taken a deed.

As you are already abundantly aware, there are different systems in effect for providing the requisite assurances to buyer, including title insurance and an attorney's title opinion without title insurance. In the former, buyer's payment obligation generally does not mature unless a title company will insure the title, and that insurance provides protection (however adequate) against after-discovered flaws. In the latter system, buyer's payment obligation generally does not mature unless an attorney certifies that seller's title is *marketable* (which means reasonably flawless, as will be developed later). Protection (however adequate) against after-discovered errors is furnished by seller's liability on covenants of title contained in the deed and by causes of action against abstracter or certifying attorney for negligence, fraud, etc.

The general topic of title assurance is not treated as a unit in this book. It has seemed useful to us to pull together buyer-seller remedy problems for

Seller's Obligations

title flaws before you are presented with the extensive material in Chapter Five, dealing with title insurance, devices for de-flawing titles, and the recording system upon which most title assurance depends.

The contract obligation and the deed. Under the caveat emptor system as to quality, you will recall that buyer was expected to guard himself as to premises quality *before* signing the contract. A different system obtains as to the quantity and quality of title; here buyer's contractual obligations in the usual case are contingent upon seller's being able to transfer a "marketable title" to the buyer. But suppose that B accepts S's deed to Blackacre at the closing, and it thereafter turns out that S did not have marketable title. Once B has accepted S's deed, he has no *contract-of-sale* remedies against S for title flaws. The doctrine of merger gives B *postclosing* rights against S only to the extent that S has given a *deed* containing express warranties against the particular loss-causing event or circumstance.

Of the sorts of deeds, soon to be more fully described, there are quitclaims in which S makes no title warranty, and there are warranty deeds in which he does. If B has taken a quitclaim, he generally has no recourse against S, and if he's taken a deed with warranties too narrow to cover the actual loss, he also has no recourse — always, of course, excepting that provided by the law of fraud and mistake. To reinforce these points, consider the following hypotheticals:

1. S contracts to sell the Brooklyn Bridge to B. Later S gives and B accepts and pays for a deed of conveyance of all of S's right, title, and interest in and to the Brooklyn Bridge. S makes no warranties in the deed. B then discovers that S at no time had any right, title, or interest in or to the Brooklyn Bridge. B sues for his money back. Result? Restatement (Second) of Contracts §413 provides: "The acceptance of a deed of conveyance of land from one who has previously contracted to sell it discharges the contractual duties of the seller to the party so accepting, except such as are embodied in the deed."

2. S contracts to sell the Brooklyn Bridge to B. The contract further provides that conveyance is to be by quitclaim deed but it is silent on S's title obligation. Comes time for closing, and B's attorney discovers that S does not have marketable title. S contends that he can nevertheless enforce the contract against B by delivering the quitclaim. Result? S is wrong; the leading case is Wallach v. Riverside Bank, 206 N.Y. 434, 100 N.E. 50 (1912).

3. S agrees to sell Blackacre to B. By the closing date, B's attorney, through checking the public records and a survey (to negate unrecorded possessory claims), decides that S does have a marketable title. He so advises his client, at the closing. The contract is silent as to S's deed obligation. S tenders a quitclaim deed. B's attorney doesn't want B to accept the deed; if it should later turn out that S doesn't have marketable title, B will have no rights against S. The contract is silent as to type of deed. Does the seller, in addition to his obligation to furnish "marketable title,"

also have an obligation to give a warranty deed? *Or,* is a contract for the sale of land that is silent as to type of deed too indefinite to be enforced? The answer to the second question is "no." The answer to the first varies by jurisdiction; great weight is given to local conveyance customs. 3 American Law of Property §11.56 (Casner ed. 1952).

Types of deed: quitclaim and warranty. It oversimplifies to classify instruments into two categories, *warranty deeds* in which seller-grantor has responsibility for after-discovered title flaws and *quitclaims* in which he does not. Each term is used to describe a number of different sorts of instruments, and the classification into quitclaim or warranty deed has significance for legal issues other than title liability. Thus a warranty deed serves to pass title from grantor to grantee where grantor acquires that title *after* the delivery of the deed, while a mere quitclaim supposedly does not. Yet courts, in the after-acquired property situation, have strained to thrust particular instruments into the former category, so that an instrument entitled *quitclaim deed* (as against mere *quitclaim*) has been held to carry after-acquired property. Comment, Quitclaim Deed in Texas, 18 Baylor L. Rev. 618 (1966).

Type of instrument has also been sometimes critical on the issue of whether buyer is a bona fide purchaser, it being supposed that anyone who would be content with a quitclaim must at least have been suspicious of seller's title, and paid a lower price accordingly. The desire to produce a hybrid under which buyer could acquire the status of bona fide purchaser without seller being liable for postconveyance difficulties, has been met in several ways. There are statutes that declare that a quitclaim grantee can be a bona fide purchaser. Or sellers can give an instrument that is entitled and reads like a conventional *warranty deed,* but which contains a clause stating that seller is not liable on the warranties. As a third solution, the bargain and sale deed has been pressed into service as a warranty-free instrument in some jurisdictions. But buyers have jibbed a little at the bargain and sale deed's lack of any title assurance, so that at some times and places, grantors under these deeds have inserted a modest "covenant against grantor's acts," a warranty that grantor has not done or suffered to be done anything that has weakened the title. Friedman, Contracts and Conveyances of Real Property §7.1 (3d ed. 1975).

A warranty deed is one which contains one or more of six "covenants for title."[17] These covenants split into two triads, the first of which consists of the covenants of *seisin, right to convey,* and *against encumbrances.* The first two generally guarantee that grantor owns what he purports to grant, and the last that the estate is free of liens, mortgages, easements, etc. except as

---

17. On covenants for title, see 3 American Law of Property §§12.124-131 (Casner ed. 1952); 6A Powell, The Law of Real Property §§895-902 (1984); and Levin, Warranties of Title: A Modest Proposal, 29 Vill. L. Rev. 649 (1983-84).

otherwise noted in the deed. The first two are generally regarded as indistinguishable, and in the cases they blur into the last.

This first group represents guarantees against title flaws extant at the date of the conveyance and thus differ in form from the second triad in which grantor promises in the future to defend and hold grantee harmless against hostile claimants or encumbrancers. Of this latter triad, the covenants of *quiet enjoyment* and *warranty* are again indistinguishable, and the last, that of *further assurances,* is little used in the United States.

You will notice that the first triad is phrased in present tense and the second is phrased in future tense. This has resulted in controversy over whether the first group can run with the land so as to benefit subsequent grantees. Since these covenants are broken, if at all, upon delivery of the deed, they become mere choses in action, which do not run. However, some courts have found that the chose in action passed to a subgrantee by implicit assignment when the subgrantee received his deed. The future-phrased covenants do run with the land. (*Query:* How can a covenant for title run with the land to a subgrantee when the original grantor didn't own the land for the covenant to run with?)

One further consequence of the difference between present and future covenants is that legal persons under statutory or other disability from incurring contingent liabilities (e.g., banks, trustees) are generally supposed to be unable to covenant within the second triad. If these disabled legal persons covenant at all, it is likely to be simply by the single covenant against encumbrances, and a warranty deed thus confined is often known as a special warranty deed. As a last caveat against overaccepting this wildly overgeneralized note on deeds, you should note that the expression "warranty deed" in *some* places is held to mean what we have just finished describing as a special warranty deed. Note also that many states have statutes that impute one or more warranties into any instrument headed "Deed," or using the word "grant" or "convey." See, e.g., Cal. Civ. Code §1113 (West 1982).

The protection afforded by the warranties is not generous; the warrantor's liability generally is limited to the consideration he received for the land. McCormick, Damages §185 (1932). You can see how negligible a recovery this would produce for an evicted buyer of California land who sues against a remote grantor-warrantor. Covenantee may also recover his expenses in reasonable though unsuccessful defense of the title. There will be no case treatment of covenants for title below; there is only a thimbleful of appellate cases in recent years.

The cases that follow deal with preclosing problems. The first is designed to concretize the text above about marketable title. The second and third cases introduce some special remedy problems, and the last case opens up the special title difficulties of the buyer on installment land contract.

b. Marketable Title[18]

Melcer v. Zuck
95 N.J. Super. 252, 230 A.2d 538 (Ch. Div. 1967)

LANE, J.S.C. This action was instituted for specific performance of an agreement to sell real estate, to set aside a subsequent conveyance of the real property and, in the alternative, for damages for breach of the contract.

[Defendants Zuck agreed to sell to plaintiff a 295-acre tract for $29,750. The tract was unimproved back land, 70 percent under water, and did not front on any public road. The agreement (dated March 13, 1965) set closing for April 20, 1965, and contained a provision, "Sellers guarantee ingress and egress from the main road to the premises in question."]

Plaintiff's attorney obtained a title report from Lawyers Title Insurance Corporation which showed, in addition to an outstanding mortgage, the following exceptions:

No. 7 — Interest outstanding in the heirs of Aaron Burke.
No. 8 — Possible outstanding dower interest of Annie Burke, widow of Aaron Burke.
No. 9 — Possible outstanding dower interest of Charlotte Smith.
No. 10 — Rights of ingress and egress to a public road will not be insured.

Because of these exceptions, there was no closing in April. Subsequently, plaintiff's attorney obtained an affidavit for the title company as a result of which the title company deleted exceptions Nos. 7, 8 and 9.

Subsequently, the closing was fixed for May 25, 1965. There was no closing at that time because plaintiff insisted upon an abatement of the purchase price due to the fact that his attorney did not believe that defendants could guarantee ingress and egress from a main road. In addition, on May 25, 1965, when Mr. Zuck went to the office of plaintiff's attorney to close, defendants were in no position to close because Mr. Zuck did not have a deed and affidavit of title, nor was Mrs. Zuck present at the meeting to sign any papers.

Although the Zucks took the position that as of May 25, 1965 their agreement with plaintiff was at an end, they nonetheless continued to try to contact their real estate broker throughout the summer in connection with this transaction.

---

18. On marketable title, see 4 American Law of Property §18.7 (Casner ed. 1952); 6A Powell, The Law of Real Property §925[2][b] (1984); Friedman, Contracts and Conveyances of Real Property ch. 4 (4th ed. 1984); Bayse, Clearing Land Titles (2d ed. 1970); and 8A Thompson, Commentaries on the Modern Law of Property §§4482-4486 (1963).

Seller's Obligations

As a result of certain conversations between Mr. Zuck and persons apparently representing plaintiff, the closing was fixed for October 22, 1965 with an abatement of the contract price. On that date, the Zucks appeared at the office of plaintiff's attorney and agreed to give a $1,000 abatement in the purchase price as an alternative to their guaranteeing an ingress and egress. While the closing statement was being prepared the Zucks refused to complete the closing because plaintiff's attorney insisted upon withholding funds sufficient to pay the mortgage on the premises and to pay a judgment against the Zucks that then appeared of record. The position of the Zucks was that they had sufficient monies and would make the payments themselves. Of course, this position on their part was untenable because the contract obligated them to convey by deed "free from all encumbrances." . . .

Subsequently, the property was sold to R.G.B. Construction Co., Inc., for $40,230 by an agreement dated November 5, 1965. In that agreement there was a specific reference to ingress and egress as follows:

"It is understood and agreed by and between the parties hereto that the Seller has made no representation with regard to any right of ingress or egress to the property hereinabove described and that the Seller agrees to convey and the Purchaser agrees to accept whatever rights the Seller may have with regard to ingress and egress."

At the time of the contract between plaintiff and the Zucks, the value of the property was between $40,000 and $45,000. The agreement to sell to R.G.B. Construction Co., Inc., establishes the value as of October 22, 1965 at $40,230.

There was nothing in the contract or the offer to purchase that required the Zucks to provide a right of ingress and egress that would be insurable by a title insurance company. It is admitted that the title was not unmarketable because of the question as to ingress and egress. In Love v. Fetters, 98 N.J.L. 784, 121 A. 607 (E. & A. 1923), the court pointed out that there is a difference between a title that is marketable in the usual sense and a title that a title company would insure. See also Korb v. Spray Beach Hotel Co., 24 N.J. Super. 151, 93 A.2d 578 (App. Div. 1952). The question is whether the Zucks were justified in not closing on October 22. . . .

[Defendants argued that they had no duty to accept a price abated for lack of access; in their view the property carried more than sufficient legal rights of access. The court examined each "right" of access adverted to by defendants and found that none of them could be exercised as of right by the owner of the tract in suit; each access depended on the continuing consent of neighbors.]

It follows, therefore, that the Zucks should have conveyed the property on October 22, in accordance with the contract and their subsequent agreement as to an abatement in the contract price. . . .

The Zucks contend that the plaintiff should be barred by the doctrine of laches.

That doctrine might apply to the cause of action for a specific performance but it would not bar a cause of action for breach of contract until the expiration of the time limit set forth in the statute of limitations for such actions. The complaint has already been dismissed under N.J.S.A. 46:21-3 on a motion for summary judgment as to the subsequent grantee, R.G.B. Construction Co., Inc. Specific performance, therefore, cannot be ordered. The complaint was timely filed to recover damages for breach of the contract. Although the statute of limitations does not apply in its terms to courts of equity, proceedings in equity to enforce a legal right are within the spirit and meaning of the statute.

Defendants also contend plaintiff should be barred by the doctrine of unclean hands; at some time subsequent to the contract, the subject matter of this suit, plaintiff obtained an interest in a piece of property which would have given access to a main highway from the Zuck property. The testimony shows that plaintiff's interest in such land was not obtained until August 1966. There is no showing here of any fraudulent conduct on plaintiff's part that vitiates in important particulars the situation in respect to which judicial redress is sought.

In regard to the damages to which plaintiff is entitled, defendants contend that he is limited by a provision in the agreement between the parties which stated:

"In the event title to the above described premises is found to be unmarketable upon an examination thereof, the only obligation of the seller shall be the return of the deposit and all monies of the purchaser paid unto the seller; providing, however, that the seller will reimburse the purchaser for legal expenses incurred in the examination of the title to the hereinabove described premises which, however, shall not exceed the sum of $150.00; and upon receipt of the same by the purchaser, the rights and liabilities of the parties hereto, their respective heirs, executors, administrators or assigns, shall cease and terminate and this contract then to become null and void."

It is inconceivable that under the circumstances of this case plaintiff should be limited by that provision. Defendants had it within their power to make the title marketable by allowing plaintiff's attorney to withhold sums sufficient to pay the mortgage and the judgment. Such is the normal practice in real estate transactions.

By failing so to act, defendants should not be allowed to limit the amount of damages to which plaintiff is entitled.

[Plaintiff, having received back his deposit and having failed to prove the cost of title examination, was awarded loss of bargain damages of $11,480 with interest from October 22, 1965.]

On Appeal: 101 N.J. Super. 577, 245 A.2d 61 (App. Div. 1968)

KOLOVSKY, J. We reverse. We are satisfied from our review of the record that plaintiff did not establish a claim for relief either under the terms of

Seller's Obligations

the written contract of March 13, 1965, or by reason of what occurred thereafter. . . .

At the outset it is essential to determine exactly what the contract obligated the seller to convey — what was the estate the purchaser had bargained for. The tract does not front on any state, county or municipal road. The only reference to rights of ingress and egress thereto appears in the statement that the "sellers guarantee ingress and egress from the main road to the premises in question." However, it is clear that the contract did not contemplate that the purchaser was merely to have the benefit of the seller's warranty that ingress and egress would continue to be available. Cf. Jersey Estates Corp. v. Weintraub, 140 N.J. Eq. 216, 217, 53 A.2d 817 (Ch. 1947).

We agree with the trial court and with plaintiff's contention that the contract obligated defendants to convey not only the 298-acre tract but also "legally recognizable" right-of-way easements furnishing ingress and egress from the main road to the tract.

At the trial Zuck offered proofs as to seven roads and rights of way allegedly available, some of which were being used for ingress to and egress from the 298-acre tract. After analyzing those proofs the trial court concluded that "the Zucks could not honor their guarantee of ingress and egress from a main road to their premises" (95 N.J. Super., at p. 258, 230 A.2d, at p. 542), this based on the court's ruling that "there was no proof that any easement had been established over any of the properties through which these ways went," either by prescription or dedication (95 N.J. Super., at pp. 257-258, 230 A.2d at p. 541).

Although Zuck vigorously challenges the correctness of the trial court's analysis and findings with respect to the legal existence of the rights of way, we find it unnecessary to deal with that challenge for our disposition of the case. Assuming the correctness of the court's ruling, it constitutes a determination that the Zucks were unable to convey good or marketable title to the estate, which included the rights of way they had agreed to convey.

Unless plaintiff acquired additional rights by reason of what occurred after the execution of the contract of March 13, 1965, that determination of lack of marketable title brings into operation the contract provision limiting the sellers' obligation in the event title is found to be unmarketable to the return of the deposit and search fees not exceeding $150. It is settled that such a provision for limitation of liability is valid and enforceable. . . .

We have not overlooked the statement in the trial court's opinion that "it is admitted that the title was not unmarketable because of the question as to ingress and egress." (95 N.J. Super., at p. 257, 230 A.2d at p. 541). Altogether, apart from the fact that such an admission or stipulation as to what the law is is not binding upon the court, . . . the record does not support the statement. That was not the position taken by plaintiff in his pleadings, in the pretrial orders, or indeed on this appeal. We find nothing persuasive in the opinion to the contrary expressed at the trial by the attorney who represented plaintiff in the transaction. As far as defendants are concerned, there was no stipulation by them that marketability of title would not be involved if in fact defendant was obligated to convey good or marketable title to an easement of ingress and egress.

On that background, we next consider the sequence of events following the execution of the agreement of March 13. Plaintiff's attorney ordered and obtained a title report from Lawyers Title Insurance Company which, as was to be anticipated, repeated the statement in its prior report[19] that "rights of ingress and egress to a public road will not be insured." Zuck had, of course, not agreed that his title would be such as a title company would insure. . . . Plaintiff's attorney made no effort otherwise to ascertain whether there were "legally recognizable" rights of ingress and egress. Instead, he, on plaintiff's behalf, insisted that plaintiff was entitled to an abatement in the purchase price, the abatement originally demanded being $6000.

Defendant refused to grant any abatement. The impasse led to a final blow-up on May 25, 1965, with plaintiff's attorney on that day demanding of and receiving from the broker Bowne the $2975 which had been deposited under the contract, telling the broker that the matter "would be going probably into court and he wanted to hold the deposit during litigation." . . .

In view of the contract provision governing the rights of the parties in the event title was unmarketable, providing that in such event "the only obligation of the seller shall be the return of the deposit and all moneys of the purchaser paid unto the seller" plus search fees not exceeding $150, there was no justification for plaintiff's insistence on an abatement. If there were no legally recognizable rights of ingress and egress, so that title was in fact unmarketable, all that plaintiff was entitled to was a return of the deposit moneys — which he had already obtained through the cooperation of the broker — and search fees not exceeding $150.

So, too, the contract provision was a bar to specific performance with an abatement which was the relief sought in the complaints filed herein and in the first pretrial order entered on October 6, 1966. Epstein v. Mundweiler, 97 N.J. Eq. 375, 377, 127A. 547 (E. & A. 1925); Guaclides v. Kruse, 67 N.J. Super. 348, 361, 170 A.2d 488, certification denied 36 N.J. 32, 174 A.2d 658 (1961), although of course it would not bar a vendee from seeking specific performance without an abatement. Epstein v. Mundweiler, supra. . . .

The relief granted by the trial court was in fact not damages in lieu of specific performance with an abatement; it was damages in lieu of specific performance of a new agreement, a modification agreement allegedly entered into in October 1965 under which Zuck's guarantee of ingress and

---

19. The title report here referred to is the one that was prepared for the transaction in which defendants Zuck acquired the property.— EDS.

egress was eliminated in consideration of his agreement to reduce the purchase price by $1000. . . .

It is clear that the alleged oral modification under which defendant ceased to be obligated to deliver marketable title insofar as it related to ingress and egress, in exchange for an abatement of $1000 in the purchase price, was unenforceable because it was not in writing as required by the statute of frauds. . . .

Further, altogether apart from the question of the application of the statute of frauds and even ignoring the testimony of defendant and his witnesses, we are satisfied that in the absence of any testimony from Flaum, the person who allegedly entered into the modification agreement on plaintiff's behalf, the only inference fairly to be drawn from the testimony of plaintiff's witnesses is that the arrangement for the closing was not a binding contractual modification but rather an attempt to get the transaction and title closed. Since such tentative understanding for the purpose of closing failed, plaintiff's rights and defendants' obligations must be measured by the written contract of March 13.

The judgment is reversed and the cause remanded to the Chancery Division with direction that judgment be entered in favor of defendants Benjamin Zuck and Rose Zuck.

NOTES

1. *The meanings of marketable title.* A seller who contracts to sell Blackacre thereby assumes an obligation to convey a "marketable title"; this note will treat the main aspects of that concept. The treatment will be brief in contrast with, say, the 300-page basic annotation on marketable title in American Law Reports (57 A.L.R. 1253 (1927)), or the 125 pages of assorted cases devoted to the topic in the earliest commercial land transactions casebook: Handler, Cases on Vendor and Purchaser (1933). In this note, to some extent, we will deal with matters more fully developed in Chapter Five in conjunction with recording, quiet title actions, and the like.

Marketable title disputes readily group into two categories: what kind of ownership in Blackacre seller is committed to transfer to buyer; what kind of proof of that ownership buyer must be given.

(a) What kind of ownership in Blackacre is seller committed to transfer to buyer? What seller is selling will seldom be described simply as "Blackacre with appurtenances," but it is useful to start with the obligation entailed by so simple a subject-matter description. Blackacre having been described as subject, seller is obligated to pass a fee simple absolute in those premises, and the fee must be free of *encumbrances*. In its largest meaning, encumbrances includes, inter alia, leases, liens (mortgage, tax, etc.), marital rights, easements, private use restrictions, or encroachments

(Blackacre must not be encroached upon by a neighbor's structure even if the structure unlawfully encroaches; buyer is not to be regarded as having to buy the law suit for its removal. Blackacre's structures must not unlawfully encroach on a neighbor.)

Seller's title obligation having been defined as "Blackacre in fee simple absolute free of encumbrances," three sorts of disputes arise. The first picks up all the substantive law of property, mortgages, creditor's rights, etc. Did the will by which the seller acquired Blackacre pass fee simple absolute or some lesser estate? Was a mortgage satisfied by payment to the mortgagee after the mortgagee had assigned? And so on.

Another sort of dispute involves the question of what kind of language serves to cut down how much of seller's normal obligation. Thus, a seller, having leased the premises before entering the contract of sale, will of course only promise to sell Blackacre "subject to lease." Suppose the closing is delayed, that the lease expires during the delay period, and that seller renews the lease during that period. Or seller may sell "subject to easements": does this excuse seller if it is discovered that there is an encroachment by a neighbor that hasn't lasted quite long enough to have become a prescriptive easement? Of course, allied to these cases are those involving the use of extrinsic evidence to cut down seller's obligation, and evidence of mistake to avoid it.

Finally, it turns out that there are some kinds of use interferences that define out as easements or encroachments, and thus as encumbrances, but that nevertheless ought not be regarded as violations of seller's marketable title obligation. This third category of marketable title disputes centers on classifying use encumbrances as violative or not. Thus, suppose that seller promises expressly or impliedly to convey Blackacre free of encumbrances and that Blackacre is described in the contract by a metes and bounds description that extends to the center of the public street that abuts Blackacre and that provides its access to the outside world. The street is an easement, it's an easement on Blackacre as described, but its presence nevertheless does not cause seller to lack marketable title. The rule just announced proceeds from the premise that the street is beneficial, so that any reasonable buyer ought to be pleased with its presence. You can readily imagine disputes as to whether the burden of a particular street exceeds its benefits. Just as buyer is deemed to have assented to a beneficially encumbering easement, so also he is usually deemed to have assented to *easements* and *encroachments*, whether or not beneficial, that were visible upon an inspection of the premises. Seller will argue that if the buyer went out to the premises and saw overhead wires or the like, he obviously was willing to assent to take subject to those wires if he didn't insist on an express clause obligating seller to get rid of them before closing. Buyer will, of course, argue that he obviously expected seller to make the usual encumbrance-free transfer, inasmuch as seller didn't ex-

Seller's Obligations

pressly except the wires from his contract obligation. The cases fall on both sides of this dispute. For the seller, there are cases that require the buyer to take subject to encumbrances that were seen even though not excepted. There are also cases that excuse seller for visible encumbrances whether or not seen by buyer in the particular case.

(b) What kind of proof of ownership must seller furnish to buyer? Seller ownership of Blackacre free of flaws is one thing; proof of that ownership another. Taking the easiest case, suppose that seller is in possession of Blackacre and that visual and seismographic inspection of the premises discloses no hint of adverse interests. Suppose further that seller is the grantee of Blackacre in fee simple absolute by a recorded deed, the grantor of which in turn was the grantee of a recorded deed and so on all the way back to the first transaction in which Queen Isabella deeded the property to Miles Standish. Nevertheless, *if* the deed to seller was a forgery and *if* seller had taken possession the day before the inspection as a disseizor vi et armis, seller would not be the owner of Blackacre. Therefore as part of the marketable title requirement must seller as a regular matter furnish proofs to buyer that the deed to him was not a forgery? Or that none of the other deeds were? Or that a recorded deed dated 1876, which recites no consideration, was in fact delivered so as to pass title by gift? Or that all the grantors were sane? And so on.

These cases, generally, are those in which both record and possession facts suggest that seller is the true unencumbered owner of Blackacre, and the law is that seller on that state of appearances has satisfied his obligation to prove his title unless buyer has some colorable information to suggest that the record and possession appearances are invalid.

The reverse case is one in which seller really does own Blackacre, but the necessary record regularity is lacking. Thus, record title to a strip on the edge of Blackacre is in X, but seller and his predecessors have been in full adverse possession of the strip for 126 years. *Or,* the last recorded deed to Blackacre has as its grantee, George W. Johnson, and the seller's name is George W. Johnson. Would a buyer's lawyer advise his client to pay George W. Johnson for Blackacre, when George W. Johnson is clearly the owner? Suppose an affidavit can be obtained from the grantor in the recorded deed that he intended to convey to George W. Johnson, and that he delivered possession to George W. Johnson? This would make buyer's lawyer feel somewhat better in allowing the deal to close, but then he'd worry about the fact that although he trusts the grantor (a nice old man) and has his affidavit, how will the situation appear when his buyer-client, say five years hence, becomes a seller of Blackacre?

In most cases of this sort, where record appearances *to some degree* belie, but the seller *to some degree* can prove ownership; the seller really does own Blackacre. He can establish this with varying delays and amounts of expense by getting affidavits, releases from the apparent record interest holder, and finally by an action to quiet title. Which steps he will have to take, if any, for which kinds of flaws will be developed at Chapter Five infra.

Yet, in a case in which buyer contends that record flaws deprived seller of marketable title, why can't seller simply prove that he owns Blackacre in that very proceeding, and thus defeat buyer's damage action or sustain his own? *Query:* In a proceeding for specific performance of a contract to buy Blackacre, brought by George W. Johnson as seller against the buyer, with an adjudication for plaintiff on a finding that he, George W. Johnson, was the true owner, would this adjudication bind true owner George W. Johnson, who appears after buyer has reluctantly complied with the decree and who sues to eject buyer? The fact that no res judicata effect can be given to the seller-buyer proceedings against the record claimant is the commonly asserted ground for denying record supplementation by proof in such proceedings (at least, where there is more color to the potential record claim than arises from a probable typographical transposition).

The last paragraph suggests that there is a kind of dispute generated by the face of the record that the court can resolve in buyer-seller litigation. It may be that seller is the true owner of Blackacre in light of all the deeds of record only if such and such a statute really docked all the tails in North Carolina. No fact being in dispute, there is no need for res judicata to bar against future claims by the tenant in tail, and the stare decisis effect of the holding will adequately protect a buyer forced to comply with his contract of purchase. Where the dispute arises from construction of a particular instrument, categorization of the issue as one of fact or law largely determines its resolvability in buyer-seller proceedings.

On the point of the last paragraph, however, it may be that the buyer-seller deal will be interpreted as not requiring buyer to stay tied up in the transaction until legal uncertainties are resolved, even if that resolution would provide adequate protection against potential future adverse claimants.

2. *Some administrative problems.* Contract or custom will provide that seller furnish or buyer procure the proofs of seller's title during the executory interval. Buyer's attorney, busy man that he is, is expected to get to his title examination with reasonable diligence and to notify seller's attorney promptly of any flaws that he discovered. There are many cases in which buyer's interim behavior is held to have waived a flaw in seller's title or to have waived any time-of-the-essence requirements on seller to have his title in proper shape by the closing date.

One final point about closing procedures as related to marketable title: If Blackacre is covered by a $12,000 mortgage, and is to be conveyed free and clear to buyer for $20,000, seller cannot convey requisite title without paying off the mortgage and getting it released of record. Seller will probably pay off the mortgage out of the buyer's $20,000. Hence seller cannot clear the title without the buyer's money, and buyer need not give the money before seller has cleared the title. In the absence of an escrow mechanism, a three-party closing is a device used to solve this insoluble.

c. Title Standards

In supplementing statutes and judicial case law on titles, many states also have title standards approved by the conveyancing bar, usually a bar association committee or section, that are used as guides in determining whether or not titles are marketable. Title standards are not government enacted or declared laws and are not binding on courts. However, they are a form of privately created law generally followed by lawyers and on occasion cited by courts in their opinions, and hence have much the same effect as laws created by governments. In these respects they resemble such other forms of privately created law as bar association codes of ethics, where not adopted as formal rules of court, and opinions of bar association professional ethics committees.

Professor Lewis Simes, a great figure in American land law of a generation or so ago and a leading advocate of title standards when they initially were being adopted, was the principal author of the statement that follows on the value of title standards.

Simes and Taylor, Model Title Standards
1-3 (1960)[20]

THE FUNCTION AND SCOPE OF UNIFORM TITLE STANDARDS

A uniform title standard may be described as a statement officially approved by an organization of lawyers, which declares the answer to a question or the solution for a problem involved in the process of title examination. A brief reference to the task of the title examiner will show why such standards are needed.

Perhaps there is no greater delusion current among inexperienced conveyancers than that land titles are either wholly good or wholly bad, and that the determination of the person who has the title is merely a mathematical process of applying unambiguous rules of law to the abstract of the record. Yet the experienced conveyancer knows that the process of determining the marketability of a title is much more like determining whether, under all the facts, a man has a cause of action for negligence,

---

20. On title standards, see also Basye, Clearing Land Titles §7 (2d ed. 1970); and Payne, Increasing Land Marketability Through Uniform Title Standards, 39 Va. L. Rev. 1 (1953).

than it is like the calculation of the amount of income tax a person owes on a given date.

No record, or abstract of the record, gives all the facts from which marketability must be determined. Thus, if the grantee in one recorded deed is Joseph Fremont and the grantor in the next is also Joseph Fremont, it is highly probable that these are one and the same person. But the record does not enable us to know whether it was delivered, whether it was a forgery, or whether the grantor was of sound mind when he executed it. Yet it is patently impossible for the title examiner to make a factual investigation to determine these things. He must decide, not whether it is absolutely certain that a given person has title, but whether it is reasonable to conclude from the facts which he can be expected to investigate, that this person has title.

As to many fact situations which are constantly recurring, a completely uniform practice of conveyancers is recognized. Thus, all conveyancers presume that the use of an identical name in one deed as grantee and in the next deed as grantor indicates that these names refer to the same person. All conveyancers presume, in the absence of evidence to the contrary, that a recorded deed has been delivered, that it was not a forgery, and that the grantor had the capacity to execute it. These presumptions may be described as a part of that body of recognized procedures known as the practice of conveyancers.

Now while, as to such matters as those already named, the practice of conveyancers is uniform, as to other matters there are notable variations. Thus, such questions as the following may be involved: whether a recorded conveyance should be questioned which does not have a notary's seal, or does not have a statement of the date on which the notary's commission expires; or, if a conveyance is made by a corporation, whether it should be questioned because there is no resolution on record showing the action of the corporation to make the conveyance, or showing whether the people who executed it as officers were in fact such officers at the time. As to these matters some title examiners may reach one conclusion and others the opposite conclusion. Uncertainties may also arise as to pure matters of law. Thus, a new probate procedure act may have been passed, and there may be a difference of opinion among members of the bar as to its constitutionality.

If the practice of conveyancers is not uniform, the tendency always is for the standards of the overmeticulous conveyancer to determine the standards of all conveyancers. Lawyer A feels that a title should be passed even though there are certain defects in the recorded acknowledgment, and he realizes that the majority of experienced, competent conveyancers would agree with him. But he also knows that Lawyer B would refuse to pass the title and would require a quiet title suit. Since Lawyer A is aware that his client may some day wish to sell the land to someone who employs Lawyer

B to pass on the title, he will be inclined to impose the same overmeticulous standard as Lawyer B. Like Gresham's law, the result will be that bad title standards drive out good standards.

The remedy for this situation is either uniform title standards or legislation or both. Although Lawyer A may not dare to approve a title solely on his individual judgment, the situation is different if his judgment is backed by the official action of a bar association.

NOTE

Examples of typical title standards appear below.

Kansas Title Standards Handbook (1975):

12.6 When Is Title Marketable?
Problem: When shall the title of the surviving joint tenant be considered marketable?
Standard 12.6: When it appears that (1) Proof of death of the deceased joint tenant has been made as provided in preceding Standard 12.4; (2) A showing of non-tax liability for Kansas inheritance taxes has been made (see Standard 12.7); (3) Nine months has elapsed after the death of the deceased joint tenant.

15.6 Foreclosure of Mortgage—What Release Is Necessary When Judgment Released?
Problem: If a mortgage is foreclosed, and the judgment of foreclosure is properly released and satisfied on the judgment docket, should the old mortgage be released by the mortgagee?
Standard 15.6: The note and mortgage were merged into the judgment and a satisfaction of the judgment is a satisfaction and release of the mortgage. No separate release of the mortgage is necessary.

Report of the Title Standards Committee, Oklahoma Bar Association, 54 Okla. B.J. 2379 (1983):

7.1 Bar or Presumption of Nonexistence of Marital Interests
Marketability of Title is not impaired by the possibility of an outstanding marital interest in the spouse of any former owner whose title has passed by instrument or instruments which have been of record in the office of the county clerk of the county in which the property is located for not less than ten (10) years after the date of recording, where no legal action shall have been instituted during said ten (10) year period in any court of record, having jurisdiction, seeking to cancel, avoid or invalidate such instrument or instruments on the ground or grounds that the property constituted the homestead of the party or parties involved.

d. Remedies

Mokar Properties Corp. v. Hall
6 A.D.2d 536, 179 N.Y.S.2d 814 (1958)

BOTEIN, Presiding Justice. This appeal is from an order of Special Term denying a motion by defendants which sought primarily to dismiss the complaint for failure to state a cause of action and on the ground that the claim was released. The complaint, grounded on the alleged failure to convey real property, sets forth three causes of action.

The first cause, against the individual defendants Lawrence and Melville Hall, alleges that they contracted in writing to sell to plaintiff two parcels of real estate in Manhattan improved with apartment houses. In the contract, a copy of which was annexed to the complaint, the Halls represented that they were record owners of the properties and that they would give title such as a responsible title company would approve and insure. Plaintiff paid $25,000 down on the signing of the contract and agreed to pay an additional $145,000 on the closing of title, the balance being subject to outstanding mortgages.

The contract provided that the purchaser agreed to deliver to the sellers' attorneys, at least seven days before the date fixed for closing title, a written statement of objections to title which the purchaser believed made title unmarketable. Pursuant to this provision, the Halls were timely notified prior to the date fixed for closing that the Title Guaranty & Trust Company required documents indicating the regularity of the transfer of the property in question from Melhar Realty Company, Inc., the previous record owner, to the Halls, who owned two-thirds of its corporate stock. Alleged consideration for the transfer was cancellation of an outstanding debt owed to the Halls by the corporation. The Halls were required by the title company either to show the unanimous consent of the stockholders to the transfer or to bring an action to bar any claim by Mathesius, the remaining stockholder; to provide proof of the solvency of the corporation at the time of conveyance so that the transfer would not be subject to attack by creditors; and to obtain a clearance on taxes chargeable against the corporation on dissolution.

It is further alleged that on the date set for closing, plaintiff tendered $145,000 as provided in the contract. However, the Halls failed to produce any of the documents required by the contract, or to provide any of the necessary instruments and assurances in connection with objections to title, and failed to tender the deed to the premises. The contract provided:

"In the event that the seller is unable to convey title in accordance with the terms of this contract, the sole liability of the seller will be to refund to the purchaser the amount paid on account of the purchase price and to pay the net cost of examining the title, which cost is not to exceed the charges fixed by the New York Board of Title Underwriters, and upon such refund and payment being made this contract shall be considered cancelled."

Two weeks after the closing date, defendants repaid to plaintiff the sum of $25,862.50, representing the down payment on the contract plus costs of title examination; but plaintiff claims to have lost the benefit of its bargain and seeks additional damages of $50,000.

... It is defendants' position that the complaint itself alleges that they were unable to convey marketable title, so that with the return of the deposit and the payment of the costs of examining title, their liability under specific contract provisions came to an end. ...

Plaintiff, on the other hand, has alleged that the defaults of the Halls were willful and deliberate, and that the objections to title were such as were created by the defendants and could have been avoided or cured by them. ...

Upon failure of a vendor to convey real property as required by contract, the damages recoverable by a purchaser are dependent to some extent on the cause of the failure. Where the vendor has acted in good faith but is unable to give good title, the purchaser may recover only the amount he has already paid on the purchase price, together with necessary expenses incurred pursuant to the contract, such as costs for investigating title and reasonable attorney's fees. [Citations omitted.] Where the vendor acts in bad faith or willfully disregards the contract, the purchaser may also be entitled to recover for the loss of his bargain. [Citations omitted.] Of course, the parties to a contract may agree to extend or restrict the liability consequent upon a breach; or they may agree that no damages will be payable at all once the status quo ante has been restored.

The contract in this case purported to limit the liability of the vendor to refund of the amount payable on account of the purchase price and payment of the net costs of examining title. But such restriction was to be applicable only "[i]n the event that the seller is *unable* to convey title in accordance with the terms of this contract" (emphasis supplied). A limitation conditioned on such inability contemplates the existence of a situation beyond the control of the parties. Implicit in such a limitation is the obligation to act in good faith. A party under circumstances such as have been alleged cannot exculpate himself from liability by reliance on a condition precedent when his own conduct is the cause of the nonperformance of that condition. ... The vendor is under a duty to take affirmative action to convey a marketable title according to his contract of sale (Smith v. Browning, 225 N.Y. 358, 122 N.E. 217). If the vendor has contracted to convey, knowing that there are circumstances that will render it impossible to do so, or if he is able with the reasonable expenditure of money and effort to remedy defects in title and neglects or refuses to do so, he has not acted in good faith; and he cannot then limit his damages by shielding himself behind such self-created or easily scaled barriers.

The complaint having alleged that the default of the defendants was willful and deliberate, a triable issue is raised as to whether in fact defendants acted in good faith or whether their alleged inability to convey marketable title was due entirely to circumstances beyond their control. If defendants were unable or made no effort to obtain the consent of the remaining stockholder because they had transferred the corporate property to themselves without full disclosure of its value; if they were unable to show proof of the solvency of the corporation because they had stripped it of all its assets; and if they were unable to obtain tax clearances because they had willfully failed to meet their tax obligations, it could be found that they were undertaking to convey a title which, when they entered into the contract, they themselves knew they had rendered unmarketable. They should then be required to remedy the defects rather than to terminate the contract, or failing that, respond in damages, as sought in this complaint. In the event of an ordinary breach of an agreement to convey, the contractual provision defining and limiting the vendor's liability would govern. The allegations of willful and deliberate default in this case make inapplicable here the general rule that a reasonable contractual provision for a compensation in lieu of damages difficult of ascertainment will be upheld.

[The order was affirmed insofar as it denied the motion to dismiss the first cause of action.]

NOTE

The doctrine of Flureau v. Thornhill. The limitation of liability clause in the principal case restates the doctrine of Flureau v. Thornhill, sometimes called the English rule.

Flureau, 96 Eng. Rep. 635, 2 W. Bl. 1078 (1776), holds that the buyer's recovery for seller's breach through inability to make title is confined to money back plus transaction expenses, but both *Flureau* and Bain v. Fothergill, L.R. 7 H.L. 158 (1874), in which the House of Lords put its approval on the Common Pleas decision in *Flureau,* contain dicta subjecting seller to the usual loss-of-bargain damages where his breach is a result of willfulness or bad faith, and the dicta have been converted into holdings in later cases.

Does the *Flureau* decision, in its special favoring treatment of real estate sellers over other types of contracting parties, comport with a theory that common law decisions, in whatever doctrinal form expressed, represent skillful efforts by wise judges to adapt rules of law to emergent social needs, or with a theory that such decisions are conscious or unconscious effectuations of the interests of dominant social or economic classes? The briefly reported facts of this case, decided Easter term, 1776, simply disclose a seller and buyer, not otherwise described, of a leasehold worth about £250 sold at an auction, and the principal dispute seems to be not about the issue for which the case is famous, but rather whether buyer could recover for losses sustained when some government securities that he sold to raise cash for his purchase went up in value after he sold them, so that he wound up without the leasehold and with depreciated cash on his hands.

Flureau seems to lay down an aberrational rule of damages, but maybe it simply effectuates well-established contract principles concerning mutual mistake of fact, or impossibility of performance, or even the rule of Hadley v. Baxendale —"One reason for the rule lay in the fact that in England a contract for sale of real estate was closed almost directly. But in the United States, long-term options are given, as well as long-term executory contracts, so that while in England there was practically no fluctuation in the value of realty during the short time necessary for the closing of the contract, there may be considerable change in the value of the property under American practices." Carnahan, The Kentucky Rule of Damages for Breach of Executory Contracts to Convey Realty, 20 Ky. L.J. 304, 314 (1932).

Many states have *Flureau* as part of their common law (Kentucky) or by statute (California), while others have rejected it at common law (Maine) and by statute (North Dakota).

Valley Associates Corp. v. Rogers
4 Misc. 2d 382, 158 N.Y.S.2d 231 (1956)

EAGER, Justice. This action by a vendee for specific performance was tried before the undersigned without a jury. It was established that the defendant, Jerome Rogers, and the plaintiff, a corporation, did, on December 4, 1953, enter into a contract in writing by which the defendant agreed to sell and the plaintiff agreed to purchase certain improved real property situate in the Village of Elmsford for the sum of $40,000. The contract was received in evidence and the making and terms thereof are not disputed. It appears, however, that, at the time of making of the contract the defendant owned but an undivided one-half interest in the property which he had contracted to sell. The other undivided one-half interest was owned by his sister Juliette Rogers. She did not sign nor authorize the contract and refused to join in a conveyance of the property pursuant to the terms of the contract. Therefore, on February 2, 1954, the defendant returned uncashed the plaintiff's check given for the down payment. The defendant refused to deliver a conveyance of the premises and took the position that he should be released from the contract because he was unable to convey title to the premises. The plaintiff, however, alleges and has proved due performance of all of the conditions precedent on its part to be performed, and readiness, ability and willingness to take title and pay the price as agreed.

Now, it is clear that the defendant well knew at the time he entered into the contract that he owned but an undivided one-half interest. I further find that the plaintiff corporation also had notice of this fact before the making of the contract. The president of the plaintiff corporation was well aware of the fact that defendant's sister had an interest in the premises. He had discussed the matter with the sister; and the defendant, at the time of preliminary negotiations, expressly made known to the said president that his sister had an interest in the premises. . . .

The parties expected that the defendant's sister would go along with the contract as agreed upon between plaintiff and defendant. She, however, refused, and is not a party to the action. Therefore, the court is not in a position to decree specific performance directing defendant to convey the entire title. The court will not attempt to decree the impossible. . . .

The plaintiff, however, requests a decree of specific performance directing conveyance by defendant of his undivided one-half interest with abatement of one-half of the purchase price. It is determined, however, that such a decree should not be rendered.

Now, it is to be borne in mind that the parties, at the time of the making of the contract, knew that the defendant owned but a half interest in the property. Having that knowledge, they nevertheless contracted for the conveyance by the defendant and acquiring by the plaintiff of the entire title to the premises. And, then, as per provision in the written agreement, they expressly agreed as follows:

"If the seller *for any reason* is unable to convey a marketable title to the premises *as herein provided,* then, and in such event, the seller will return to the purchaser the amount paid on account of the purchase price and also the net cost actually incurred by the purchaser for the examination of the title to the premises, which said cost is not to exceed the usual net fees of a reputable title company in effecting the examination of title in cases where insurance is not obtained, less the usual attorneys' discount, and *thereupon this contract shall terminate* without other or further damage to either party as against the other." (Emphases added by the Court.)

Under special circumstances, such a provision may not bar specific performance where the purchaser is willing to overlook defects in title and pay the price in full. But, under the circumstances here, where the parties knew that the seller possessed but an undivided one-half interest, and where, without his fault, he is unable at the time of closing to give any title whatever to the other undivided half interest, this special provision is to be taken as clear indication of the intent of the parties that the contract was to be terminated except for the seller's obligation to return the down payment, if any, and pay title costs as agreed. The provision should be given that effect because, after all, the problem is to be solved by giving effect to the intention of the parties. In fact, to grant a decree of partial specific performance as now sought would have the effect of making and decreeing the enforcement of a contract not intended by the parties.

In any event, and independent of the existence of the above quoted provision, it is clear that this court would not, under the circumstances here, be justified in rendering a decree compelling defendant to convey his undivided one-half interest. The contract being one for the conveyance of the entire title and the complaint being framed to secure such a conveyance, a decree for partial performance is not to be rendered unless it affirmatively appears on the trial that such a decree is proper and necessary in the interests of justice. [Citations omitted.] Whether or not a decree of specific performance is to be rendered in a specific case rests within the sound discretion of the court, and the circumstances here are not such as to warrant the exercise of discretion in plaintiff's favor to grant it the decree sought. . . .

NOTES ON SPECIFIC PERFORMANCE WITH ABATEMENT

1. *Abatable flaws.* Refresh yourself on the availability of abatement when the house burns down during the executory interval (see discussion in Skelly Oil Co. v. Ashmore, page 537 supra, and Note 1, page 545 supra).

(a) Seller's right to specific performance with abatement: Where the deficiency is an outstanding liquidated encumbrance, easily paid off, seller is entitled to specific performance with abatement. He is similarly entitled where the deficiency is acreage or footage deemed to be unsubstantially related to the buyer's purposes in purchasing.

(b) Buyer's right to specific performance with abatement: Do you think that the specific performance abatement remedy will be more or less freely granted to buyer than seller? In a leading English case, Rudd v. Lascelles 1 Ch. 815 (1900), the court, in denying buyer specific performance with a £1000 abatement (for a restrictive covenant) on a £3500 price, says, among other things, that the remedy should be available to buyer only where the actual subject matter is substantially the same as that contracted to be sold. The court further states that it should be refused in cases of great hardship or where the deficiency is difficult to value, and also where the court cannot assume that vendor would have contracted to sell the title actually owned at the abated price. But the court in Fidelity Chemical Products v. Rubino, 1 N.J. Super. 184, 63 A.2d 539 (App. Div. 1949) saw no reason to infer hardship or unconscionability simply from allowing buyer an abatement of $4400 on a $7500 price (the property turned out to lack the promised access and was bisected by a railroad right of way) where seller had purchased the property from the town for $2000 seventeen days before the contract with plaintiff buyer.

2. Flureau *and the measure of abatement.* Assuming that a *Flureau* clause in the contract does not defeat buyer's right to specific performance with an abatement, is the clause relevant in valuing the title deficiency for the purpose of determining the amount of the abatement?

3. *The nonsigning wife.* Transmute the *Valley Associates* case from one of nonsigning sister with an undivided half interest to one of a nonsigning wife with a dower or similar interest. Clearly, if the husband agrees to sell Blackacre, he cannot convey marketable title unless he can convey to buyer free of the wife's interest, which, of course, requires her consent. Keeping this in mind, is it true that *Valley Associates* provides a perfect out for a married couple dissatisfied with the price they have agreed to take?

5A Corbin, Contracts §1160, states as a general rule: "If one has contracted to transfer complete title, and his wife, who has a dower interest, refuses to join in the deed, the vendor can compel a transfer of such interest as the promisor has, with an abatement for the value of the wife's interest," and adds, "It has been so held even though the vendee knew when the contract was made that the wife had an interest and was not bound to join in the conveyance."

But the section continues with citations and analysis that suggest reasons why some courts have been less willing to enforce and abate for dower than in the usual case. Forcing the sale of husband's interest alone has not led to arguments about whether conjugal rights run with the land or whether buyer or wife gets the twin bed next to the window; but postdecree buyer-wife relations are more difficult than postdecree buyer-sister relations, since the latter can be, of course, handled by partition, while the inchoate dower continues to float indestructibly over the property. Dower rights also seem difficult to value for purposes of setting an abatement figure. Finally some courts have refused buyer a decree with abatement against the husband on the curious ground that a court of equity ought not lend itself to a device that would indirectly be coercive of the wife.

If husband lists with broker, and broker finds willing buyer, but the transaction does not close because of the wife's failure to join, broker has nevertheless earned his commission even under a contract conditioning broker's rights upon "closing" or the like. But query: If broker was aware of the wife's opposition to the listing, can broker still collect? Annot., 10 A.L.R.3d 665 (1964).

e. **The Installment Buyer**

Warren, California Instalment Land Sales Contracts: A Time for Reform

9 U.C.L.A. L. Rev. 608 (1962)

Under California law, the young man who carries his bride over the threshold of a new tract house purchased on instalment contract has not

Seller's Obligations

been a good bet to "live happily ever after"—at least not in that house. In fact, the instalment land contract and the marital agreement he has just entered into have something in common: a good bit can happen to the contracting party that he had not anticipated at the time he made the deal. The man who leaves an apartment to buy a home under contract loses a landlord but gains a vendor, and, though he can but dimly perceive it at the time, the health, wealth, and honesty of that vendor are matters of vital concern to him. The danger in the buyer's position lies in the fact that record title to the property he is buying is in the vendor who may before time for conveyance die, become mentally incompetent, go into bankruptcy, move back to Iowa, neglect to pay his income tax, fail to keep up the payments on the trust deed covering the subdivision, suffer a judgment, refuse to pay off the people who built the houses in the tract, give a further trust deed on the land, or do as one land sale vendor in California did recently: transfer his interest to a six-year old Indian boy in El Reno, Oklahoma.

[This excellent article draws on Hearings before the California Assembly Subcommittee on Real Estate Contracts and Trust Deeds in 1961 for cases in which installment buyers lost their homes under circumstances unforeseen by them and which a sloppy-thinking layman would call unfair. The article in part discusses the forfeiture of past installments problem; more relevantly, it also considers the extent to which installment buyer's rights in Blackacre will be subordinated to persons who, after the contract of sale, acquire interests in the property via seller's continued record ownership. The article analyses the extent to which buyer's rights, although unevidenced of record, prevail over subsequent interests because evidenced by buyer's possession. It also considers whether buyer's recording of the unacknowledged installment contract could preclude priority for after-contract interests.]

Luette v. Bank of Italy National Trust & Savings Assn.

42 F.2d 9 (9th Cir. 1930)

KERRIGAN, District Judge. This is an appeal from an order dismissing a third amended and supplemental bill of complaint and from the decree of dismissal entered thereon.

The complaint alleges that the plaintiffs entered into a contract in June, 1926, with the predecessor in interest of the defendant for the purchase of a certain parcel of real property. The purchase price was $6,500, $1,625 of which was paid at the time of the execution of the contract. The balance was to be paid in monthly installments, which plaintiffs paid to July, 1928; the complaint showing that such payments would continue to May, 1933, under the contract. Plaintiffs allege in effect, construing all of the allegations as to defendant's title together, that defendant has record title to the property in question, and that an adverse claim has been asserted through the filing of homestead claims upon the theory that title to the land is in the United States, the outcome of which claims is uncertain; the matter being now before the Department of the Interior on appeal. It may be fairly concluded from the description of the present state of these homestead proceedings that the decision in the first instance in the Land Office was unfavorable to the homestead right, and that the appeal is that of the claimants; in other words, that the Land Office has held that the land in question is not part of the public domain.

Plaintiffs allege that, on discovery of the existence of the homestead claims, they demanded of defendant that it exhibit its title, and offered, if and when defendant should do so, to pay the amount due under the contract, but that defendant has refused to exhibit its title and, on demand, has refused to repay to plaintiffs the sums already paid upon the contract. The prayer of the complaint is that defendant be enjoined from canceling the contract of plaintiffs and forfeiting plaintiffs' rights thereunder, and that plaintiffs be relieved from paying further installments pending the outcome of the proceedings before the Department of the Interior. Plaintiffs further pray that, in the event the court is unable to grant the relief prayed for, the contract between plaintiffs and defendant be rescinded, and that plaintiffs have judgment for the moneys already paid under the contract. In seeking to rescind, plaintiffs allege that the only thing of value received by them is the contract of sale itself, which they tender.

In considering whether this complaint states a cause of action, its aspect as a bill for an injunction must be disregarded, as plaintiffs state no ground for the intervention of equity to preserve all of their rights under the contract pending the determination of defendant's title, while at the same time relieving them from the duty of performing their part of the bargain. There is no allegation that defendant is, or is likely to become, insolvent, nor any pleading of other equities to justify such relief. The question therefore is whether the complaint states grounds for rescission of the contract.

The vendees under an executory contract here seek to rescind on account of an uncertainty as to the state of the vendor's title, at a time long prior to the date when the vendor will be required to convey title under the installment contract. The complaint shows that the plaintiffs attempted to put the vendor in default by demanding that the title be exhibited and tendering the balance due. The rule has long been settled in California that there can be no rescission by a vendee of an executory contract of sale merely because of lack of title in the vendor prior to the date when performance is due. Joyce v. Shafer, 97 Cal. 335, 32 P. 320; Shively v. Semi-Tropic Land & Water Co., 99 Cal. 259, 33 P. 848; Brimmer v. Salisbury, 167 Cal. 522, 140 P. 30. And the vendee cannot place the vendor in default by tendering payment and demanding a deed in advance of the time and under circumstances not contemplated by the contract. Garberino v. Roberts, 109 Cal. 126, 41 P. 857; Hanson v. Fox, 155 Cal. 106, 99 P.

489, 20 L.R.A. (N.S.) 338, 132 Am. St. Rep. 72. In the present case the pleading does not show the vendor to be in default, as under the contract, assuming a defect to exist, the time within which title must be perfected does not expire until May, 1933.

In this connection an attempt is made to strengthen plaintiffs' position by averring that, in the event that the homestead claims are allowed and the whole tract in which plaintiffs' lot is situated is declared to be part of the public domain, defendant will be financially unable to procure title to the whole tract, and hence can never perform its obligation to convey title to plaintiffs. The whole tract contains over 16,000 acres. Plaintiffs' lot comprises about one-fourth of an acre. The complaint does not show that defendant would be unable, for financial or other reasons, to procure title to the one-fourth acre which it has contracted to convey to plaintiffs and with which alone plaintiffs are concerned.

There remains to be considered the question as to whether certain allegations of fraud bring this case within the rule that, even though the vendor is not in default, the vendee may rescind an executory contract for material fraudulent misrepresentations of the vendor as to a matter of title upon which the vendee was justified in relying. Crane v. Ferrier-Brock Development Co., 164 Cal. 676, 130 P. 429; Brimmer v. Salisbury, 167 Cal. 522, 530, 140 P. 30. Plaintiffs allege that they are inexperienced in business and relied upon the defendant for fair treatment, being accustomed to put complete trust in and rely upon banks and bankers. The latter allegation is insufficient to establish a fiduciary relationship between plaintiffs and defendant, as there is no suggestion that defendant voluntarily assumed a relation of personal confidence with plaintiffs. Ruhl v. Mott, 120 Cal. 668, 53 P. 304. The parties to the contract must therefore be regarded as having dealt at arm's length. Viewing the pleading in this light and looking to the averments as to the state of the title referred to above, it appears that plaintiffs have not charged defendant with material misrepresentations, unequivocally averred to be false, upon which plaintiffs relied to their injury.

The orders appealed from are affirmed.

NOTES

1. *Cases relied on in* Luette. (a) *Joyce:* After buyer defaulted, seller sold the land to a third person before the contract dates for final payment and deed delivery. Buyer contended that this sale worked a rescission of the contract and on that theory sued to recover installments previously paid.

(b) *Shively:* Again defaulting buyer tried to avoid forfeiture of installments by characterizing seller's postbreach resale as a rescission. Seller graciously admitted that the resale was a rescission. Buyer won.

(c) *Brimmer:* Buyer was sued on a note, the purported consideration for which was seller's foregoing suit after buyer failed to pay an installment. Buyer defended on a ground of no consideration, contending that the installment was excused because after the contract was entered but prior to the installment date seller had sold the land to a third person. *Held,* the sale did not excuse the installment, buyer not having proved that seller did *not* make the resale contract subject to buyer's rights.

(d) *Hanson:* When installment buyer discovered that seller's only title was a void tax deed, he tendered all undue installments and demanded a deed and proof of marketable title. Seller's failure to comply with his demand was held not to be a default that entitled buyer to rescind and recover back past installments.

2. *Installment financing alternatives and interim title deficiencies.* Luette does contain glimmers of hope for installment buyers, and it perhaps understates them. It is true that there is a well-settled rule that in an installment land contract buyer's promises to pay are independent of and not conditioned on seller's duty to deliver a deed carrying marketable title. This is extensively annotated in Tender of Deed as Condition Precedent to Action for Purchase Price or on Note Therefor, 35 A.L.R. 108 (1925). Yet, cases are numerous in which buyer's payment obligation is held to be suspended by an unassumed and unexpected initial or supervening significant deficiency in seller's title. 1 Restatement of Contracts §§283, 284. Further, even where buyer is inferentially held to have agreed to risk an interim title deficiency, he is not regarded as assuming the risk of a seller in solvency which will prevent seller's clearing the title by the time for deed performance.

Suppose that instead of embodying his installment obligation in a contract that may be assigned or sold by seller to a bank (as in *Luette*?) buyer rather borrows the purchase price on an installment note and mortgage from a bank, and then discovers a title shortage during the installment period. Or suppose that the shortage is discovered after the buyer gives the seller a purchase money installment negotiable note and mortgage that seller has sold to a bank.

The title shortage might be of so grievous and threatening a character as would permit buyer to suspend payment on a note running to seller if seller still held the note, although the court might hold that unless buyer were evicted, he ought to continue paying seller and seek relief by independent action against seller on seller's deed covenants. See 18 Baylor L. Rev. 104 (1966). If buyer would have had no defense against seller, he has none against the bank. But even if buyer has a defense where he has been seller-financed by mortgage and the seller still holds the paper, if either of the two bank financing methods is used, the defense disappears. In the second method mentioned above, the bank is a holder in due course, and in the first it is a direct lender whose repayment rights against buyer are not clearly defeated by buyer-borrower's having bought a bum title with its money.

Seller's Obligations

Considering that buyer under an installment land contract with a title failure is more likely to get judicial relief as to unpaid installments than is one who takes a deed and gives a note and mortgage, and considering the sorts of title risks to which the installment buyer might be subject as compared to mortgage buyer (see excerpt from Warren, page 630 supra), which device is better for buyer?

In the note and mortgage case, the bank is likely to search the title to make sure of its security. Having lent to buyer after such a search, would the bank lose its usual rights to recover against buyer in spite of after-discovered title flaws?

3. *Seller's title shortage and the defaulting installment buyer.* If buyer discovers seller's title shortage during the installment period, and if he withholds payments, he may turn out to have guessed wrong in assuming his power to do so. If a court so rules, he will be in default, subject to whatever harsh or gentle rules the jurisdiction provides for relief from default and from forfeiture of past installments. Whatever the forfeiture rules may be, and whether or not buyer's default precedes or follows and is or is not motivated by seller's title flaw, is it not true that buyer should be relieved of forfeiture to the extent that the flaw depreciates the value of the subject premises? Weidner v. Hyland, 216 Wis. 12, 255 N.W. 134 (1934), suggests not, although the point was not directly raised.

Compare the analogous Duke v. Garret, 276 S.W.2d 587 (Tex. Civ. App. 1955). In this case, seller sold on a deed with a vendor's lien retained for buyer's installments. Both parties knew that seller's title was deficient because of an outstanding mineral interest, but seller was obligated to cure that deficiency. Buyer defaulted, and seller sued for the unpaid price and for foreclosure of his vendor's lien. Buyer sought to offset the value of the mineral interest that seller had not yet acquired. *Held:* buyer's failure to continue his payments, coupled with his failure to relinquish possession and deed, constituted a failure to do equity, which deprived buyer of his right to the offset.

CHAPTER FIVE
Title Protection

This chapter is concerned with the scope and methods of land title protection in the United States. Alternative means of title protection are critically analyzed and attention is centered on some of the more important problem areas. Considerable statutory material is dealt with, as basic legal policies in this field are frequently set by statute and an understanding of what these statutes do and are expected to do is essential. Included within the concept of title protection are devices not only for safeguarding title interests once acquired, but also for compensating in cases of loss of actual or apparent title rights. Title protection can also entail steps to clear defective titles once defects are apparent. This chapter stresses the two principal means of land title protection currently relied on in the United States: the recording acts and title insurance. These devices are cornerstones of the prevailing system by which American land titles are made comparatively safe and secure.

Title protection in the United States works well enough to enable intensive land development by a great variety of public and private interests. But American title protection is complex and costly, with some degree of uncertainty in almost every title. The margin of uncertainty can be substantially eliminated in most instances, but at present this can be an expensive and long drawn out process. Through reform of the law and of institutional procedures, greater efforts should be made to reduce the system's deficiencies. This chapter considers some of the prospects for achieving such a goal.

One reason for the complexity and cost of American title protection is the complexity of our land title law. The great diversity of legal interests in land permitted by our legal order makes the unraveling and appraising of outstanding legal interests in any particular land parcel difficult and expensive. In part this is inherent in the nature of land, particularly in an advanced modern society where much of the wealth is in private hands. Land parcels are valuable and permanent, and most of them can be used simultaneously by different persons. They also are ideal forms of security for extension of credit and, at the local government level, a major source of tax income. Increasingly, too, they are the subject of government regulation and subsidy. These factors have led to wide dispersal of legal rights in individual land parcels. Most parcels have had a complex title history, with termination of some old interests in doubt and present rights frequently divided among owners, lenders, users, and government instrumentalities.

Continued reliance on the recording acts as the basis of title protection also contributes to cost and complexity. Reasonably well suited to a newly settled, sparsely populated rural nation, the recording acts have become less and less satisfactory as American title histories have lengthened, the number of parcels has increased and the volume of public land records, notably in urbanized areas, has multiplied at an enormous rate. Recording act weaknesses have been compounded by the fact that maintaining public records essential to the system has been almost entirely a function of local government, the least effective and innovative level of American government. Further complications result from the public records not being the sole source of title data under the recording acts. A miscellany of private records, including unrecorded original instruments, may be relevant considerations, and so may the physical condition of the land itself and the character of its occupation, insofar as these factors indicate the existence of unrecorded interests. Other off-record information may also be significant. Even the state of mind of purchasers becomes important: when they took did they have actual notice of unrecorded interests? Patchwork legal changes and development of new title service groups, especially the title insurance companies, have helped in adapting the recording acts to changed circumstances; but these have been more palliatives than cures. Torrens registration, a system of title protection potentially more satisfactory than recording, has failed to catch hold in the United States, and its future prospects here are doubtful, for recording is so well established that a major shift to Torrens would hurt too many interests.

The American law of title protection has an important impact on a number of different groups, each having somewhat different interests in title protection, and consequently different and even conflicting views as to what ends title protection laws should serve. These include persons who own or think they own land interests; those desirous of buying land interests or lending on the security of such interests; unpaid creditors of persons owning land interests; professional title searchers and examiners, including those who also insure titles; and government instrumentalities that maintain public records pertaining to land titles. There are others, but these groups are the most obvious and most directly concerned. They further comprise subgroups, whose interests in title protection and title protection laws may be in conflict. For example, title insurers and lawyers in private practice compete for work, and more than one person may make claim to the same or overlapping ownership rights in the same land parcel.

Most ends that title protection laws serve tend to benefit some groups and harm others, benefit and harm usually being expressed in monetary terms as title protection normally is conceived of in those terms. Some possible ends are these:

1. A fast, accurate, and inexpensive means of ascertaining the legal status of the title to any particular land parcel;
2. Land titles in every community generally certain enough so as not to impede the marketability of land interests or deter land development;
3. Encouragement of land marketability by protecting bona fide purchasers without notice;
4. Protection of interests in land of those persons whose interests are known or readily ascertainable;
5. Protection of interests in land of those persons unable adequately to protect themselves, such as persons under disability and those unaware that they own land interests;
6. Assurance of compensation to those who have suffered losses in land transactions without fault on their part but through the bad faith or negligence of others;
7. No government out-of-pocket expenditures on land title records for privately held land interests beyond what is necessary for effective performance of government tax and regulatory functions; and
8. Fair compensation to those performing title protection services.

NOTE

It is comparatively simple to determine what ends title protection laws should further in the best interests of any one group. But how should a legislature or court resolve the questions and priorities of ends when dealing with title protection problems? Whose ends should they seek to serve? If your answer is the public interest, or the community at large, what does this mean in the title protection context, and how should a legislature or court approach the diversity of worthy interests and the ends that would best serve each, as listed above? If these questions cannot be satisfactorily answered in the abstract, consider them as they relate to the legal problems raised in succeeding chapters.

A. THE RECORDING ACTS

Fundamental to title protection in the United States are the recording acts, statutes in effect in every state.[1] The term "recording acts" has a variety of

---

1. On recording acts generally, in addition to the standard real property texts, see the following: Burke, American Conveyancing Patterns (1978); Lane & Edson, Land Title Recordation Systems: Legal Constraints and Reforms (1978), prepared for the U.S. Department of Housing and Urban Development, pursuant to a contract with Booz, Allen & Hamilton; U.S. Depts. of Agriculture and Commerce, Land Title Recording in the United States: A Statistical Summary (1974); Symposium on Title Recordation, 22 Am. U.L. Rev.

meanings, but here it is used in a narrow sense common to discussions of real property law. It means only those statutes that provide for land conveyancing records to be maintained by recorders of deeds (or equivalent public officials) and that establish priorities among successive purchasers of land interests. Under some circumstances these acts reverse the common law rule that priority among successive purchasers of land interests from the same grantor is dependent on priority in time of execution. Although they differ in detail, all the recording acts provide for (1) centralized filing of documents creating or transferring land interests, (2) maintenance of systems of public records, consisting primarily of copies of the filed documents, and (3) priorities for those interests appearing in the public records as against those that do not.

Public land records provided for by the recording acts are generally maintained in the office of a designated public official of the county where the lands are located. In many states this official bears the title of county recorder of deeds. Most of the records he keeps are open for public inspection and are the principal source of land title data sought by professional searchers. But records kept pursuant to the recording acts are not the only sources of information about land titles; and, on theories of notice or priority irrespective of notice, interests not apparent from an examination of these records may be outstanding and superior to any others. Such interests may be ascertainable from other public records, including court and tax records, and from an examination of the premises. Title examinations frequently involve inspection of these other sources, but some outstanding land interests still may not be uncovered, nor may any reasonable kind of search prove successful. The existence of such interests is an off-record risk that usually cannot be eliminated, although through title insurance or other means the risk may be passed on to someone else. However, known title defects, including interests with priority under the recording acts, frequently can be eliminated by such means as purchase of outstanding claims, passage of time and operation of limitations or curative acts, and suits to quiet title. Professional title searchers and examiners who negligently fail to locate title defects or report on them, may be liable in tort or contract.

American recording acts were highly developed by the close of the colonial period.[2] In their early evolution they were probably influenced by English legislation, by the statute of enrollments and registry acts for the counties of Middlesex and York, and by English judicial decisions that purchasers with notice of unregistered conveyances were not protected by

---

239 (1973); Cross, Weaknesses of the Present Recording System, 47 Iowa L. Rev. 245 (1962); Philbrick, Limits of Record Search and Therefore of Notice, 93 U. Pa. L. Rev. 125, 259, 391 (1944-1945); and Note, Recording Statutes: Their Operation and Effect, 17 Washburn L.J. 615 (1978).

2. On the history of the recording acts, see 4 American Law of Property §§17.4 and 17.5 (Casner ed. 1952); and 6A Powell, The Law of Real Property §904[1] (1984).

the registration statutes. But a general system of recording never developed in England as it did in the United States, and original title instruments kept in private hands have been the main sources relied on in title examinations of English lands. Registration somewhat similar to that provided for by the American Torrens system has, however, largely replaced this so-called title deeds system in England.

It is conventional to classify American recording acts into three main groups, emphasizing the varied significance of notice and the act of recording. The three types are often referred to as race, notice, and race-notice statutes. Under the race type statute, a purchaser who records has priority over any interest then unrecorded, whether or not the purchaser had notice of the unrecorded interest when he took title. In other words, the race to the recorder's office determines who prevails. Under a notice type statute, a purchaser takes priority over all prior unrecorded interests of which he had no notice when he took. Once such a purchaser takes title, it is advisable for him to record in order to protect himself from subsequent purchasers, but he need not record to be protected against prior but unrecorded interests of which he had no notice. Race-notice type statutes are similar to notice statutes, except that for a purchaser under a race-notice statute to prevail over a prior unrecorded interest of which he had no notice when he took, he must record before the prior unrecorded interest holder does. Thus, under a race-notice statute, the subsequent uninformed purchaser is not accorded automatic protection against a prior unrecorded but recordable interest, as is the case under the notice statute. The term race-notice is applied to statutes so designated because under them both the race and the notice are material to determination of priority.

Only two states, Louisiana and North Carolina, have race statutes applicable to conveyances generally; several other states have them for mortgages. Of the remaining states, about half have notice statutes and half have race-notice statutes.[3] Arizona, Illinois, and Massachusetts are among the notice states; and California, Michigan, and New York among the race-notice ones.

Filing for record under the recording acts is not essential to validity of an unrecorded but recordable instrument. Such an instrument is valid between the parties and is effective as against subsequent takers not protected by the recording acts. When recording act priorities do not apply, then priority among successive conflicting interests in the same land parcel normally is determined by the common law preference for the interest senior in time of execution.

Public records kept pursuant to the recording acts also have evidentiary value in judicial proceedings. In many states the recorded copies of instru-

---

3. For a listing of states by types of recording statutes, see 4 American Law of Property §17.5, n.63 (Casner ed. 1952 and Supp. 1977).

ments are primary evidence, with no requirement that the original be produced or accounted for. In other states contents of an instrument may be proven from the recorded copy, but only after accounting for the original.

The recording acts, with their stress on readily accessible public land records and priorities for interests appearing in these records, have been largely responsible for creating enough certainty in American land titles to meet the needs of a highly developed industrial society extensively based on private property rights. But there are serious weaknesses in the recording acts that have resulted in more title uncertainty than is necessary and high costs of title protection to minimize the risks inherent in the system. Weaknesses in the recording acts include: the extensive and complex searches that must be made, both on and off record, to determine the apparent state of a title; inefficiently maintained and indexed public records; the risk of outstanding title interests that cannot be ascertained from any reasonable search; and limited effectiveness of recording due to possible errors by recorders and chain of title restrictions on search obligations. What was no doubt a very good system in earlier days when title histories were short and searches comparatively easy is now a cumbersome and expensive procedure, particularly in highly urbanized communities. Following are representative recording acts, including examples of race, notice, and race-notice statutes.

Washington Revised Code Annotated
(1966)

§65.08.070. *Real property conveyances to be recorded.* A conveyance of real property, when acknowledged by the person executing the same (the acknowledgment being certified as required by law), may be recorded in the office of the recording officer of the county where the property is situated. Every such conveyance not so recorded is void as against any subsequent purchaser or mortgagee in good faith and for a valuable consideration from the same vendor, his heirs or devisees, of the same real property or any portion thereof whose conveyance is first duly recorded. An instrument is deemed recorded the minute it is filed for record.

Florida Statutes Annotated
(West 1984)

§695.01. *Conveyances to be recorded.* (1) No conveyance, transfer or mortgage of real property, or of any interest therein, nor any lease for a term of 1 year or longer, shall be good and effectual in law or equity against

The Recording Acts 643

creditors or subsequent purchasers for a valuable consideration and without notice, unless the same be recorded according to law; nor shall any such instrument made or executed by virtue of any power of attorney be good or effectual in law or in equity against creditors or subsequent purchasers for a valuable consideration and without notice unless the power of attorney be recorded before the accruing of the right of such creditor or subsequent purchaser.

Arkansas Statutes Annotated
(1971)

§51.1002. *Lien attaches when recorded.* Every mortgage of real estate shall be a lien on the mortgaged property from the time the same is filed in the recorder's office for record, and not before; which filing shall be notice to all persons of existence of such mortgage.

Indiana Code Annotated
(Burns 1980, Supp. 1985)

§32-1-2-11. *Conveyances and leases — recorded deed required.* No conveyance of any real estate in fee simple, or for life, or of any future estate, and no lease for more than three [3] years from the making thereof, shall be valid and effectual against any person other than the grantor, his heirs and devisees, and persons having notice thereof, unless it is made by a deed recorded within the time and in the manner provided in this chapter.

§32-1-2-16. *Recording required — effect.* Every conveyance or mortgage of lands or of any interest therin, and every lease for more than three [3] years shall be recorded in the recorder's office of the county where such lands shall be situated; and every conveyance, mortgage or lease shall take priority according to the time of the filing thereof, and such conveyance, mortgage or lease shall be fraudulent and void as against any subsequent purchaser, lessee or mortgagee in good faith and for a valuable consideration, having his deed, mortgage or lease first recorded.

NOTES

1. Without reference to interpretive judicial opinions, it is not always possible to determine with accuracy whether a particular recording act falls in the race, notice, or race-notice group. But from the statutory language appearing above, how do you think each of the enactments is classified?

2. What are the advantages and disadvantages of each of the three types of recording acts? On balance, which type is preferable? Should the answer vary depending on whether a locality is within a metropolitan area or is outside such an area and is largely rural or small town? Under a race type statute, are titles more certain?

3. A period following delivery during which a purchaser could record and still have priority over a subsequent purchaser was at one time provided for in the recording acts of a number of states, and earlier, in some of the American colonies. The period of grace varied from five days to two years. Webb, The Law of Record of Title §7 (2d ed. 1891). Due to the retroactive effect of recordation, persons buying interests in land were always in danger of being subject to unrecorded interests of which they had no notice. The reason for grace periods apparently was poor communication and slow mail service, which meant that instruments executed in England and other distant places would be long delayed in reaching the office of the locality where the land was located. Most grace period recording act provisions have been repealed, although a few survive. See, e.g., Pa. Stat. Ann. tit. 42, §8141 (Purdon 1982), 10 days for purchase money mortgages. On early recording act provisions of this kind see Hackman, Time for Recording Title Instruments, 19 Lawyer & Banker 12, 16 (1926). Similar grace periods with retroactive effect upon filing in the public records are still fairly prevalent for mechanics' and materialmen's liens.

1. Administration

Assembly and maintenance of public records upon which effective operation of the recording acts depends is the administrative responsibility of local government, principally of the counties in most parts of the United States. When documents are submitted for recordation, employees of the recorder's office accept them, note the time of initial filing, copy the documents, bind the copies in large books, and index each copy in some manner that will facilitate location of it. Originals are normally returned to the persons who submitted them for recordation, usually transferees or their representatives. Index and document books are permanently stored, usually on open shelves, available for inspection during regular office hours by members of the public. Except for a few localities where past collections have been destroyed by fire or other holocaust, and apart from occasional pilfering or negligent failure to properly copy or store, recorders' offices normally contain copies of all documents recorded since the early days of settlement in the community. In much of the United States the earliest recorded document pertaining to any particular land parcel is likely to be a patent from the federal government, an instrument

The Recording Acts

similar to a deed, issued when the parcel passed from the federal domain into private hands.

There are approximately three thousand counties or their functional equivalents in the United States. This means that not only is administration of public land records heavily decentralized, but there are inevitable variations in the details and caliber of administration. Some counties do a good job, some a very poor job; and the quality and methods of operation tend to vary with population size, number of land parcels in the county, local real estate activity, competence of local government personnel, and nature of state statutory provisions pertaining to public land records. As is to be expected, public recorders' offices differ greatly in the volume of documents handled and in the size of their document accumulations. In the great metropolitan counties these offices are vast and busy places housing large staffs of employees, the hundreds of thousands of new recordings which come in annually, and tremendous collections of past recordings maintained for public inspection. At the other extreme are offices in sparsely settled rural communities with relatively few land transactions. These offices may have only a few dozen document books, and a total of only two or three new recordings a day may be unusually heavy. Quite clearly, many of the operational problems of such offices are very different from those in metropolitan or even middle-sized communities.

Although sets of public records and the officials who process and maintain them are essential to the administration of a recording act system, private skill groups have developed that are also essential to a workable recording act system. These include groups that use the public records, or information gleaned from such records, to sell services to their customers or clients, for example, abstracters, lawyers, and title insurers, who, as part of their own work, commonly prepare and maintain private land records, in large part summaries or evaluations of relevant public records. Such records include abstracts prepared and sold by abstract companies and the title plant compilations maintained by many title insurers and abstracters. The manufacturers of data processing machinery constitute another essential skill group. These companies are increasingly being called on to help devise methods of data storage and retrieval for both public and private land record offices. And manufacturers' research staffs, in their work on more efficient means of handling masses of data, are influencing the probable future of land title search and examination.

Title insurance is sufficiently important so that it is considered separately in this chapter. However, it should be underscored at this point that private title insurance as it has developed in the United States is built upon the recording acts and systems of public land records. In determining exceptions to insurance coverage of any particular land title, title insurers' ultimate sources of data are primarily the public land records. This is true even of those companies maintaining their own title plants.

In the United States there are three major forms of title search and examination, each dominated by a different skill group or combination of skill groups. In the first, lawyers in private practice make both searches and examinations and provide their clients with title opinions, usually in writing. These opinions ordinarily state who has title, indicate whether or not title is marketable, and describe any defects.

Under the second form of search and examination, lawyers in private practice do the examining and provide their clients with opinions but do not search the public records. Searching is done by professional abstracters who prepare written summaries of the titles to individual land parcels as disclosed by the public records. These summaries, or abstracts as they are called, are histories of the titles to particular parcels. An abstract has a series of entries, normally arranged chronologically, each entry a synopsis of or excerpt from a recorded document or other public record relevant to the land title in question. To the extent that the abstract is an accurate and complete reflection of the public records, it will have an entry for every step in the public record history of the title: every deed, mortgage, will, judicial decree, or other instrument or event bearing on the title and appearing in the public records will be referred to in a separate abstract entry. By carefully examining these entries a competent lawyer can determine the nature of the record title, including its current marketability. The companies that prepare abstracts are staffed by specialists in title searching, although few abstracters are lawyers. Many title insurance companies originally started as abstract companies, and some of the insurers still prepare and sell abstracts.

The third major form of title search and examination is one in which both search and examination functions are performed by a title insurance company as preliminary steps to issuance of title insurance policies. When a policy is ordered, company employees assemble and evaluate data requisite to insurability. Those employees who search rarely are lawyers; those who examine often are.

In counties where there is not enough title work to justify search and examination staffs, some companies, on request, will issue policies based on opinions of expert title lawyers in private practice. Thus title insurance is fairly frequent even under lawyer or lawyer-abstracter forms of title search and examination. In New England and most rural and small-town communities in the United States, title searches and examinations generally are still monopolized by lawyers or lawyers and abstracters. The Far West is an exception to this, for there and in most of the larger urban areas demand for title insurance is so great that insurers do a high percentage of all searches and examinations. Where title insurance companies have moved into title searching and examination, private practitioners of law have often been displaced in performing one or both of these functions. In some communities, especially most major metropolitan centers, this displacement is almost complete, and the title work of lawyers in private practice is restricted to clearing defective titles and negotiating with title insurers to limit the scope of coverage exceptions. The shift away from title work has had important implications for the private practice of law, as at one time such work was a major source of income to lawyers in all parts of the United States. This loss of title searching and examination illustrates the vulnerability of lawyers in private practice to competition from specialized, high volume businesses and professions. Other occupations that have been particularly effective in cutting in on the work of private law firms include collection agencies, banks in their probate and trust work, and accountants dealing with tax matters.

NOTES

1. As one would expect, there are different ways of going about title work and differences of opinion over which procedures are best. The following two excerpts illustrate points of view on scope and emphasis in abstracting and examining.

Bermond, Standardization of Abstracting, 38 Title News 10, 11-12 (Oct. 1959): "Some of the abstracts submitted to me for examination . . . are merely outlines or chains of title, little more than an index or list of the matters appearing of record. Others are virtual copies of everything on the public records. The former is, of course, too little. The latter, too much. What the examiner needs, and all he needs or desires is an abstract of the essential and intrinsic facts and information on record sufficient to base an intelligent opinion on the title.

"No matter how useful such undertaking may be at the local level, the full advantages of such organized efforts toward standardization cannot be realized without the establishment of a state-wide system. It is true that some abstracting problems may be inherent to particular locations, but the bulk of all of the problems are present, and the answers are the same all over any one state. . . .

"Most important of the causes of overmeticulous abstracting and title examination is fear. The fear may be of two sorts — First, we may be afraid of ourselves, lacking confidence in our own ability or judgment as to what is a proper conclusion on some point — Second, we may be afraid of what the next abstracter or examiner will require. It is from this latter type of fear that a vicious circle arises. No abstracter or examiner wants his reputation injured by having the next abstracter or title examiner call attention to something, however non-meritorious, that he has overlooked or disregarded. Unless some means of escape are provided, the type or pattern for abstracting and title examination will tend to be established in any community by those who raise the most objections irrespective of their triviality or lack of merit. Standardization is the most obvious cure for this. Fear that our own judgment may be wrong is quickly dispelled if we can find our particular question already answered in a standard upon which our fellow abstracters and examiners, including recognized specialists, have agreed as a rule of practice."

McQuiston, Scope of the Abstract: Investigations Aside From the Abstract, 14 Okla. L. Rev. 437, 454-455 (1961): "Purpose of title examination is to assist the client in making a real estate deal. Title opinions should not be composed to display the examiner's profound knowledge of the law nor to point out ignorance of those who have dealt with the title before. Of course, the examiner should make reasonable and necessary requirements. Sometimes an intelligent client experienced in real estate affairs will complete the deal without requiring expenditure of unusual title clearance costs, provided the title is safe, although not strictly marketable. This practice is pointed out in a recent article concerning the title opinion. [Mosburg, Title by Adverse Possession, 13 Okla. L. Rev. 125 (1960).] Experienced clients, it is pointed out, are careful to have and demand a thorough examination and, although at times they act independently of their lawyer, their judgment is always based on a clearly analyzed title as shown in the examiner's written opinion. The writer of the article believes it is the examiner's duty to set forth possible defects that raise a reasonable question of safety or marketability, and particularly, it is essential to call the client's attention to the possibility of unabstracted prior claims such as unrecorded rights of persons in possession, encroachments, unfiled mechanics' and materialmens' liens, unmatured installments of special assessments not certified by the abstract and to warn of the necessity of investigating governmental zoning regulations applicable to the particular property.

"Conversely, the author states, if an examiner were so inclined he could point out numerous pitfalls against which even a bona fide purchaser has no adequate safeguard, such as the possibility of forgery, non-delivery of deeds, undisclosed minority or incompetency of grantors, false recitals of identity or marital status. These are risks a client always takes unless he chooses to purchase a policy of title insurance. In such cases the law of averages is overwhelmingly in favor of safety of the title. Calling these things to the client's attention would merely create a sense of insecurity, so it is recommended that the opinion be silent as to such matters."

2. In many states, abstracters are licensed. See Eckhardt, Abstracters' Licensing Laws, 28 Mo. L. Rev. 1, 54-55 (1963). In discussing the desirability of licensing, Eckhardt has this to say: "From the point of view of the general public it would be desirable if all abstracters were financially responsible, had adequate plants, were professionally competent, had regulated fees, and were liable to anyone relying on the abstract to his damage, with limitation running from the date of injury. As a practical matter, this ideal is unattainable, and it becomes a matter of balancing the potential for good against the potential for evil in the particular proposal. As a rule this

will turn upon an analysis of the plant requirement and its related grandfather clause: Will the proposed act tend to bring all plants up to an adequate level, or will it tend to create a monopoly and perpetuate an inadequate plant?

"Further, from the public point of view, will the act be so stringent that in some counties no one will provide abstracting services? Inferior abstract service is better than no abstract service at all. The problem is not the same as with legal and medical services, because one can drive to a lawyer or doctor in the next county, but abstracting necessarily must be done locally.

"The question from the point of view of the abstracter is really two or more questions, because abstracters fall into several groups, each with different interests at stake. A majority of abstracters can and do meet the minimum requirements any licensing act might impose, viz., they are financially responsible (frequently by insuring the risk), have adequate plants, and are managed by competent personnel. They would like a license act in order to improve their weaker fellows, and to give the industry the prestige and status they think will come with licensing. They are sincere in believing there will be improvement both as to personnel and as to plant, and minimize or ignore the monopolistic tendency of some acts.

"On the other hand, many in the upper group of abstracters fear that any regulatory legislation will open the door to other regulation they do not desire, such as a schedule of maximum fees. They are not opposed to an abstracters' board of examiners composed of high-grade abstracters, but do fear what a board of political hacks might do (the political climate of course will vary from state to state and from time to time).

"Those abstracters who could not meet some or all of the basic requirements have a vital interest in defeating any license act, unless by grandfather clauses or otherwise their continuance in business is assured. This group is not represented in published discussions of the question because many of them are not active in or even members of their state and national associations."

3. In much of the United States, titles are customarily examined back to their inception in the federal government. However, in the older eastern sections of the nation, such lengthy checking frequently is not done. In the East it is customary to examine transactions back for only a set period of years, commonly sixty years, and perhaps thereafter to a warranty deed. Why this more limited examination? What added risks, if any, are incurred in not checking back further?

4. Why do you think that preparation of abstracts of title has not generally become a local government service performed on a fee basis by government employees? Does it not make sense for those who maintain the public records to prepare abstracts of them? Some states authorize by statute recorders of deeds or other local officials to make and sell abstracts. See, for example, Ill. Rev. Stat. c. 115, §24 (1981) and Wis. Stat. Ann.

§59.58 (1957). However, little of the abstract preparation market has been taken over by public authorities.

5. On the current and anticipated future character of abstracting in various parts of the United States, see Abstracting: State of the Art, 53 Title News No. 8, at 6 (1974). A good summary of problems encountered in abstract examination appears in Kubicek and Kubicek, Selected Topics in Examination of Abstracts of Title, 26 Drake L. Rev. 1 (1977).

2. Protection Provided

a. Recordable Instruments

The trend has been to broaden the recording acts by increasing the kinds of conveyancing instruments that are recordable and as such can give constructive notice and priorities. Most title instruments are recordable: deeds, mortgages, leases, contracts of sale, options, grants of easements, etc.[4] Wills and short term leases are common but not universal exceptions. At one time, instruments pertaining only to equitable interests in land were not recordable in many states, but this has been changed almost everywhere. However, considerable variation exists among the states concerning the recordability of certain kinds of instruments peripheral to modern recording classifications, including affidavits and assignments of interests relating to land.[5]

Before an instrument is entitled to be recorded, certain statutory prerequisites usually must be met. A widespread requirement is that a deed, mortgage, or other instrument creating, transferring, or terminating interests in land must be acknowledged before a notary public or other designated official, and the states differ on what essential statements the acknowledgment must contain. An alternative to acknowledgment commonly provided is the right to have a subscribing witness to execution of the instrument prove the validity of the instrument and its execution by declarations before an authorized official.[6] In most states instruments not properly acknowledged or proven are not entitled to constructive notice

---

4. Examples of relatively recent cases holding certain kinds of interests not recordable are Thomas v. Roth, 386 P.2d 926 (Wyo. 1963), affidavit; Coggins v. Mimms, 373 So. 2d 964 (Fla. App. 1979), affidavit; Hellweg v. Bush, 74 S.W.2d 89 (Mo. App. 1934), mortgage assignment; Auslander v. Strain, 278 App. Div. 615, 101 N.Y.S.2d 831 (1951), written instrument of dedication.

5. Some recording acts give broad meaning to the term "conveyance." For example, Cal. Civ. Code §1215 (West 1982), provides: "The term 'conveyance' . . . embraces every instrument in writing by which any estate or interest in real property is created, aliened, mortgaged, or incumbered, or by which the title to any real property may be affected, except wills."

6. See, for example, Ore. Rev. Stat. §§93.440 and 93.480 (1981).

The Recording Acts

even if accepted by a recorder and placed of record. But some states have curative acts that fully validate such instruments as recordable after they have been in the proper records for a certain number of years.[7] And, generally, unacknowledged and unproven instruments are valid between the parties, their privies, and those with actual notice.[8] A few states have requirements that each deed presented for recording shall contain prescribed information about the grantee; and there are statutory provisions that before a deed may be recorded, taxes on the property involved must be paid and the ownership change noted in the tax assessment books.[9] Failure to meet these latter requirements generally does not prevent the instrument from giving constructive notice if placed of record.

NOTES

1. Why do you think many states do not provide for the recording of probated wills or short term leases?

2. If unacknowledged and unproven deeds are valid between the parties and their privies, why should they not be recordable? The following statutory provision has been enacted in this or comparable form in a minority of states. Is such a provision desirable?

"Deeds, mortgages and other instruments of writing relating to real estate shall be deemed, from the time of being filed for record, notice to subsequent purchasers and creditors, though not acknowledged or proven according to law; but the same shall not be read as evidence, unless their execution be proved in manner required by the rules of evidence applicable to such writings, so as to supply the defects of such acknowledgment or proof." Ill. Rev. Stat. c. 30, §30 (1981).

3. In Prudential Insurance Co. of America v. Holliday, 191 Neb. 144, 214 N.W.2d 273 (1974), two of three co-owners of a ranch mortgaged their undivided two-thirds interest but one of the mortgagors did not acknowledge the instrument. The mortgage was recorded and the court held the recording to be constructive notice only as to the interest of the co-owners who had acknowledged the instrument.

4. Mass. Ann. Laws c. 183, §6 (West 1977) provides: "Every deed presented for record shall contain or have endorsed upon it the full name, residence and post office address of the grantee and a recital of the amount

---

7. See, for example, Cal. Civ. Code §1207 (West 1982), providing that the defective instrument will impart notice if of record one year. Many such curative statutes require that the defective instrument be in the records for five or ten years before it has recording effect. Also see the discussion of curative acts, infra.

8. But see Nordman v. Rau, 86 Kan. 19, 119 P. 351 (1911).

9. Md. Real Prop. Code Ann. art. 21, §3-104 (Michie 1981). And see Wash. Rev. Code Ann. §82.45.090 (Supp. 1985), requiring that before a conveyance or sale instrument is accepted for recording, any tax due on sale of such real estate shall be paid.

of the full consideration thereof in dollars or the nature of the other consideration therefor, if not delivered for a specific monetary sum. The full consideration shall mean the total price for the conveyance without deduction for any liens or encumbrances assumed by the grantee or remaining thereon. All such endorsements and recitals shall be recorded as part of the deed. Failure to comply with this section shall not affect the validity of any deed. No register of deeds shall accept a deed for recording unless it is in compliance with the requirements of this section."

What is the purpose of this section?

b. Purchasers and Creditors

For a subsequent taker to be entitled to priority under the recording acts as against prior unrecorded interest holders, he must have paid for his land interest; and payment must have been substantial in relation to the value of the interest acquired. Donees as subsequent takers are not protected by the recording acts;[10] and in some states certain classes of creditors are not protected even though they have acquired interests in particular land parcels.[11] However, a number of statutes expressly include creditors, or at least designated kinds of creditors,[12] and universally mortgagees are included as protected subsequent takers.

Horton v. Kyburz
53 Cal. 2d 59, 346 P.2d 399 (1959)

SCHAUER, Justice. In this action to have defendant declared the constructive trustee for plaintiff of an undivided one half interest in real property, plaintiff appeals from a judgment which decrees that he has no interest in such property. Plaintiff alleged and the trial court found facts sufficient to

---

10. Colorado is an exception to this. In Colorado donees are protected by the recording acts. Colo. Rev. Stat. §38-35-109 (Supp. 1984), as interpreted in Eastwood v. Sheed, 166 Colo. 136, 442 P.2d 423 (1968).

11. Judgment creditors, for example, are not protected as subsequent takers under some recording acts. They have been held to lose out to prior grantees from judgment debtors, even though the prior grantees' deeds were unrecorded when the judgment liens became effective. Johnson v. Casper, 75 Idaho 256, 270 P.2d 1012 (1954); and Kartchner v. State Tax Commn., 4 Utah 2d 382, 294 P.2d 790 (1956).

12. Illustrative of a broad creditor protection statute is Ky. Rev. Stat., §382.270 (1970): "No deed or deed of trust or mortgage conveying a legal or equitable title to real or personal property shall be valid against a purchaser for a valuable consideration, without notice thereof, or against creditors, until such deed or mortgage is acknowledged or proved according to law and lodged for record. As used in this section 'creditors' includes all creditors irrespective of whether or not they have acquired a lien by legal or equitable proceedings or by voluntary conveyance."

raise a constructive trust under the view of Notten v. Mensing (1935), 3 Cal. 2d 469, 473-477 [1-6], 45 P.2d 198, and Ryan v. Welte (1948), 87 Cal. App. 2d 897, 901-903 [4-6], 198 P.2d 357; i.e., plaintiff's father and step-mother orally agreed that all their property would go to the survivor for life and that the survivor would will such property one half to plaintiff and one half to those relatives of the step-mother whom she chose; in reliance on the oral agreement the spouses put their property in joint tenancy and plaintiff's father forebore to make any testamentary or other disposition of his property to members of his own family which would have been effective in the event the step-mother survived him, which she did; the step-mother took the subject realty as surviving joint tenant, conveyed it to herself and defendant, her relative, as joint tenants, and on her death defendant took as surviving joint tenant. But defendant alleged and the trial court found that he gave "good and valuable consideration" for the conveyance and took as a bona fide purchaser.

Plaintiff urges that as a matter of law defendant is not a bona fide purchaser because (1) there is no evidence that he gave consideration adequate to cut off plaintiff's equity, because (2) the evidence establishes that defendant took with constructive notice of plaintiff's equity, and because (3) there was no agreement between defendant and plaintiff's step-mother that defendant would receive *all* the subject property on her death but rather defendant alleged and the trial court found that defendant gave "good and valuable consideration" for the agreement of plaintiff's step-mother to convey "a joint tenancy interest" which plaintiff asserts, is only a one half interest. Plaintiff also contends that the trial court erred (4) in admitting, over objection, evidence of assertedly "self-serving" oral declarations of plaintiff's deceased step-mother, (5) in admitting, over objection, the will of plaintiff's step-mother, which states that she devises her entire estate to defendant, and (6) in rejecting evidence of the value of the subject realty shortly before the institution of this action, offered on the issue of adequacy of the consideration given by defendant.

We have concluded that plaintiff's contentions, considered (as they must be) on the basis of facts found by the trial court from conflicting evidence, do not impel reversal.

Plaintiff is the son of Robert and Annie Horton, who were divorced prior to 1916. In 1916 Robert married Elizabeth. They remained married until Robert's death in 1931. There was no issue of their marriage. Robert throughout his life had a close and affectionate relationship with plaintiff, and plaintiff often visited Robert and Elizabeth in their home.

In 1930 Robert and Elizabeth purchased and took up residence on the subject property, a ranch of 223 acres. During their marriage they had orally agreed that all property owned by either of them would go to the survivor for life and the survivor on his or her death would will such property one half to plaintiff and one half to those relatives of Elizabeth whom she might select.² In reliance on their oral agreement they put all their property, including the subject ranch, in joint tenancy and Robert made no will or other disposition of his property to any members of his own family in the event Elizabeth should survive him. On February 18, 1930, he made a will which would have devised the entire ranch to plaintiff if Elizabeth had predeceased Robert.

Defendant is Elizabeth's grandnephew. She took defendant into her home in 1932, when he was four years old, and their relationship was similar to that of mother and son.

From the time of Robert's death until 1949 Elizabeth leased the ranch for grazing purposes for $125 a year. In 1948 Elizabeth sold 63 acres of the ranch to the United States government for $50 an acre.

On February 15, 1954, without plaintiff's knowledge Elizabeth conveyed the ranch to defendant and herself as joint tenants. She caused this deed to be recorded on February 19, 1954. The trial court found "That said conveyance . . . was made for good and valuable consideration in that prior to 1954 ['About the end of '49' and 'Quite a few times' thereafter, according to defendant's testimony] said Elizabeth A. Horton informed defendant, Norvin R. Kyburz, that if said Norvin R. Kyburz would maintain and improve said real property during the lifetime of said Elizabeth A. Horton that she would convey to him a joint tenancy interest in said real property; that for more than seven (7) years prior to the death of said Elizabeth A. Horton on October 11, 1956, said Norvin R. Kyburz did improve and maintain said property.⁴ . . . That at no time prior to the

---

2. The evidence of this oral agreement is as follows: Plaintiff testified that on January 18, 1931, the day following his father's death, plaintiff and his wife, at Elizabeth's request, called at the home of plaintiff's aunt and uncle (Robert's brother) where Elizabeth was visiting. There Elizabeth told plaintiff, in the presence of his wife, aunt, and uncle, that "The reason I wanted to see you was, your father and I had an agreement that if he died first, I was to have the use of all the property until I died; and then it was to be divided to — his half was to go to you, and I could leave my half to anyone I wished, on my side of the family. . . . Now, it won't do you any good to start any trouble, because all the property is in joint tenancy, and that is the way it is going to be." Plaintiff's wife, uncle, and aunt gave substantially similar testimony. Also plaintiff, his wife, and his aunt each testified that Robert, prior to his death, had made statements to the effect that "I am going to give this ranch to Vincent [plaintiff] when I die."

4. Defendant testified that before 1949 he had done some work in maintaining and repairing the ranch property and other property of Elizabeth; that "About the end of '49 [when defendant was 21 years of age] she said if I would continue helping her with her maintaining her places and the ranch, she would leave them to me"; that thereafter Elizabeth repeated the substance of this statement "Quite a few times" and defendant from time to time worked on Elizabeth's property and contributed some of his money to its improvement and maintenance; that in 1954 "She told me as long as I was putting part of my money in on the ranch that she would protect me too, that she would give me a joint tenancy deed and that is when she went to Judge Mundt."

Judge Albert H. Mundt testified that in 1954, while he was engaged in the private practice of law, Elizabeth asked him to draw a joint tenancy deed of the ranch to herself and defendant; that "I suggested to her that it would not be in her best interest to do so in that it was taking control of the property from her and putting it at least partially in control of her nephew. She informed me at that time that she not only wanted to do so but was obligated to do so because she had agreed with him previously that if he would assist her and maintain

filing of the plaintiff's complaint herein did . . . defendant, have any knowledge that said plaintiff claimed any right, title or interest in and to said real property. . . . That defendant . . . is a bona fide purchaser of said real property . . . and to enforce against said defendant the oral agreement made and entered into between [Robert and Elizabeth] . . . would be harsh, oppressive and unjust."

Sufficiency of Consideration paid by Defendant to Elizabeth. Plaintiff urges that because "This entire proceeding is one in equity and involving equitable considerations" defendant, to establish his position as bona fide purchaser, must show not merely that he gave value for the conveyance but that he gave "adequate consideration" in the sense that such adequacy is necessary to obtain specific performance of a contract. To uphold this contention would appear to contravene rules of contract and real property law long established in this state. When the Legislature in 1872 enacted as code law the familiar rule (Civ. Code, §3391) that "Specific performance cannot be enforced against a party to a contract . . . 1. If he has not received an *adequate* consideration for the contract . . ." (italics added) it also dealt with subjects pertinent to the present action by enacting the following rules:

"No implied or resulting trust can prejudice the rights of a purchaser . . . of real property for value and without notice of the trust." (Civ. Code, §856.)

"Any benefit conferred, or agreed to be conferred, upon the promisor, by any other person, to which the promisor is not lawfully entitled, or any prejudice suffered, or agreed to be suffered, by such person, other than such as he is at the time of consent lawfully bound to suffer, as an inducement to the promisor, is a good consideration for a promise." (Civ. Code, §1605.) The term "good consideration" in section 1605 is equivalent to the term "valuable consideration." (Aden v. City of Vallejo (1903), 139 Cal. 165, 168, 72 P. 905, rejecting the earlier view, expressed in Clark v. Troy (1862), 20 Cal. 219, 224, that "A good consideration is such as that of blood, or of natural affection. A valuable consideration is such as money or the like.") The Clark case refused to accept the contention, similar to that advanced by the present plaintiff, that the expression "valuable consideration" in the former Conveyancing Act did not mean "only that amount of money, or its equivalent, which would support a contract at common law — that is, one dime or one cent" but rather meant "such a consideration as would support an executory contract in a Court of Equity" (at page 222 of 20 Cal.), and held that "The inadequacy of price is a circumstance proper to be considered in determining the question of good faith, but it will not the less fall within the legal definition of a valuable

---

that property and other properties that she would convey the property to him in joint tenancy and upon her death he would get all of it. And she told me that he had complied with his agreement and that he had done certain work the nature and extent of which I do not recall."

consideration, however disproportionate it may be to the value of the land" (at page 224 of 20 Cal.).

This remained the rule under the 1872 enactment of section 1107 of the Civil Code, which provides that "Every grant of an estate in real property is conclusive against the grantor, also against everyone subsequently claiming under him, except a purchaser . . . who in good faith and for a valuable consideration acquires a title . . . by an instrument that is first duly recorded." (See Civ. Code, §5; Cain v. Richmond (1932), 126 Cal. App. 254, 260, 14 P.2d 546; cf. United States v. Certain Parcels of Land (U.S. Dist. Ct., S.D. Cal., C.D. 1949), 85 F. Supp. 986, 1006, footnote 17.)

It has been pointed out that "The recording laws were not enacted to protect those whose ignorance of the title is deliberate and intentional, nor does a mere nominal consideration satisfy the requirement that a valuable consideration must be paid. Their purpose is to protect those who honestly believe they are acquiring a good title, and who invest some substantial sum in reliance on that belief." (Beach v. Faust (1935), 2 Cal. 2d 290, 292, 40 P.2d 822.) But here there is evidence that defendant gave more than "mere nominal consideration." He testified that he and Elizabeth did the following work on the ranch: "Well, we fixed the fences. We put in the northeast fence which was about a little over a quarter of a mile, and I built the northwest fence. It is about a quarter of a mile, about ready to fall down, and a couple of cross fences. We had three wells drilled. We paid fifty percent apiece . . . on the wells. Put an aluminum roof on the barn and jacked it up and poured a foundation on the north end of it and pillars through the middle and through the south end. We run water to the corral and across the road; put in pressure pumps and separator house. We knocked the front of it off and rebuilt that, reroofed it; put a foundation in the front of it and put a cement floor in it. We built a three-car garage out of aluminum; and the clearing of the land and the reservoir around the hill; and the seeding of the south side; and there is about an acre of permanent pasture besides the brush clearing and burning and stuff that we had done before that." Defendant paid for half the roofing and half the cost of bulldozers to clear part of the land. He bought the seed, pump, and sprinkler pipe for the permanent pasture. The clearing of brush and repair of fences were done prior to 1949. The wells were drilled in 1954 and 1955. The record is silent as to just when the rest of the work was done, but it can be inferred that it was after 1949 because from the time of Robert's death until 1949 Elizabeth "leased [the ranch] out for cattle grazing," and after 1949 defendant "started running stock on it."

Plaintiff argues that defendant could have done little work on the ranch after the making of the 1949 agreement because from September, 1949, until September, 1953, he was in the armed services and thereafter he worked full time at various jobs. These circumstances were for the appraisal of the trier of fact; they do not show as a matter of law that defendant's contribution to the maintenance and improvement of the realty was barely nominal. Plaintiff further argues that work of defendant done after the 1954 conveyance by Elizabeth to herself and defendant as joint tenants could not have been consideration for such conveyance since defendant was co-owner of the property. But the consideration for which Elizabeth bargained and which defendant gave was *continued* help in maintaining the property, not help merely until Elizabeth should convey a legal interest in the property to defendant.

Also pertinent to the subject of consideration is plaintiff's attack on the trial court's refusal to admit evidence that in 1956, shortly after Elizabeth's death and shortly before the institution of this action, defendant agreed to sell the ranch (then reduced to 160 acres) for $950 an acre. The trial court took the position that evidence of value in 1956 was not relevant. It appears that evidence of the value of the property in 1956, when defendant received full legal title as surviving joint tenant, would be relevant to the question of "inadequacy of price [which] is a circumstance proper to be considered in determining the question of good faith" necessary to constitute defendant a bona fide purchaser (Clark v. Troy (1862), supra, 20 Cal. 219, 224), but that exclusion of the evidence was not prejudicial because had it been received it would have required interpretation by other evidence to connect it controllingly with value in 1954 (when Elizabeth executed the joint tenancy deed to herself and defendant). Furthermore, insofar as relates to the reasonableness of the original oral offer made by Elizabeth to defendant in 1949, the value in 1956 would be entitled to little, if any, weight. It will be recalled that there was evidence that in 1949 Elizabeth ceased to rent the ranch (then comprising 223 acres) for $125 a year and sold 63 acres of it to the United States government for $50 an acre. This 63 acres apparently had some connection, not adequately explained, with construction of Folsom Dam. The finding of the trial court, as hereinabove mentioned, is that "prior to 1954 said Elizabeth . . . informed defendant . . . that if [defendant] . . . would maintain and improve said real property during the lifetime of said Elizabeth A. Horton that she would convey to him a joint tenancy interest in said real property; that for more than seven (7) years prior to the death of said Elizabeth A. Horton on October 11, 1956, said Norvin R. Kyburz did improve and maintain said property."

Concerning the value of the ranch the following may also be mentioned: In the course of a colloquy as to admissibility of evidence of its value in 1956, defendant's counsel remarked, "the court may well take judicial notice of the fact that in this particular area that we are concerned here with that there has been a vast increase in property values owing to Folsom dam being erected or construction there and in the past six or seven years." The court replied, "Yes, what I had in mind when I was inquiring of Mr. Paras [plaintiff's counsel], value—" and Mr. Paras interjected a comment on the consideration allegedly given by defendant. From the foregoing colloquy it is not apparent whether the court felt that it could take judicial notice of the rising value of the ranch for its bearing on defendant's good faith, but it does at least appear that the matter was brought to its attention.

Plaintiff cites Bank of Ukiah v. Gibson (1895), 109 Cal. 197, 200, 41 P. 1008, for the proposition that a mere promise of the purchaser is not value within the rule which protects a bona fide purchaser. The proposition is generally sound (Davis v. Ward (1895), 109 Cal. 186, 189-190, 41 P. 1010; Rest. Trusts 2d (1959), §302) but it does not necessarily control the factual situation here. At the time of plaintiff's attack on the conveyance, the contract was fully executed; any implied promise of the purchaser-defendant to render services and assist in maintaining the ranch had been performed; at least some services had been rendered which were accepted by Elizabeth as full performance.

Evidence Assertedly Establishing that Defendant was Put on Notice of Plaintiff's Claim. Plaintiff urges that the following testimony of defendant shows that defendant had constructive notice of plaintiff's interest, i.e., that defendant had "actual notice of circumstances sufficient to put a prudent man upon inquiry as to a particular fact" and "by prosecuting such inquiry, he might have learned such fact" (Civ. Code, §19):

Q. Norvin, during the time that you lived with your aunt [great aunt Elizabeth], did your aunt ever say anything to you about . . . plaintiff Vincent Horton getting any of her property?
A. No sir.
Q. Did you ever have any conversation with her concerning the possibility of his coming in on any of the property?
A. Between '55 and '56 she brought it up one day that if anything happened to her that she didn't want my mother or her sister to come in on the will or anything. And I brought it up about did she think that Vincent would ever try to come in.
Q. I see. You asked her if she thought that Vincent would ever come in?
A. Yes, sir.
Q. What was her answer?
A. She didn't think he would. . . .
Q. May I ask why you asked that question?
A. Because Vincent was the only one on the other side that I thought would have anything to say about it or — well, that is the only one we ever saw.
Q. Can you tell me what made you think that he might have anything to say about it?
A. No, I don't — he was the only one I could think of.
Q. Just occurred to you to ask that question about Vincent, is that correct?
A. Well, it came up that spur of the moment. It was over —
Q. You brought it up?

A. I brought it up about Vincent but she started about the other party.
Q. Was this after 1953 when you had this conversation?
A. '53? It was '49.
Q. This conversation concerning Vincent was in '49?
A. Oh, '55 and '56.
Q. '55 and '56?
A. Yes, sir.
Q. I see. It was after your father had died?
A. He died in '53.
Q. You indicated that he died in '53 and this conversation took place afterwards?
A. '55, yes sir.
Q. And is that the only conversation you ever had with your aunt concerning Vincent Horton?
A. Yes.

The foregoing conversation held after Elizabeth had executed and caused recordation of the joint tenancy deed to herself and defendant in 1954, and after defendant had furnished some consideration for the conveyance, does not as a matter of law show that defendant was put on notice of plaintiff's equitable claim. It shows that defendant was concerned with the possibility that plaintiff might assert some claim but neither the conversation alone nor the conversation coupled with the rather small and indefinite, but valuable, consideration which defendant gave for the ranch shows that defendant deliberately remained ignorant of a state of facts as to which he should have been put on notice.

Plaintiff's Claim that Defendant was at Most a Bona Fide Purchaser of a One Half Interest in the Ranch. Defendant alleged and the trial court found that prior to 1954 Elizabeth agreed that if defendant would maintain and improve the ranch "she would convey to him a joint tenancy interest in said real property." Since "A joint interest is one owned by two or more persons in equal shares . . ." (Civ. Code, §683) plaintiff argues that under the agreement between Elizabeth and defendant Elizabeth undertook to convey and defendant gave consideration for only a one half interest in the ranch; plaintiff says that Elizabeth did not agree not to sever the joint tenancy and urges that the joint tenancy deed did not convey to defendant the one half interest which Elizabeth had orally agreed with Robert was to go to plaintiff.

Judge Mundt, however, testified that when (in 1954) Elizabeth asked him to prepare the joint tenancy deed she said that she had agreed with defendant "that she would convey the property to him in joint tenancy and upon her death he would get all of it" and defendant testified that Elizabeth said "if I would continue helping her with her maintaining her places and the ranch, she would leave them to me." The foregoing testimony supports the view that defendant gave consideration for Elizabeth's promise not merely to put the ranch in joint tenancy with defendant but also to leave it in joint tenancy so that the right of survivorship would operate. The trial court stated that "I think everyone has been telling the truth in the case. . . . I believe all the folks in the case." It is apparent that the case was tried on the theory that defendant claimed as bona fide purchaser of the entire interest in the ranch, and that if the trial court had specifically found concerning the present contention of plaintiff its finding would have been adverse to plaintiff and in accord with the above quoted testimony of Judge Mundt and defendant. Therefore, under familiar rules of appellate review, we must reject plaintiff's argument that the judgment decreeing that defendant is the owner of the ranch and plaintiff has no interest in it is not supported by the allegation and finding that Elizabeth agreed to convey to defendant a joint tenancy interest. . . .

While on the record it may seem to some of us that, were we triers of fact, we might have reached findings differing in some respects from those declared by the trial judge, we recognize that we did not see and hear the witnesses and, hence, on conflicting evidence have neither right nor power to disagree with the trier of fact.

For the reasons above stated the judgment is affirmed.

NOTES

1. Why should not donees or those paying nominal consideration be protected as subsequent takers? Is there sufficient merit to the valuable consideration requirement to justify its retention? Can it be justified as bolstering the notice requirement on the theory that in many situations the meager consideration paid indicates that the transferees involved must have had notice?

2. There is considerable authority to the effect that a mortgagee is not a taker for value under the recording acts if he accepts a mortgage to secure a preexisting debt. Brown v. Mifflin, 220 Ark. 166, 246 S.W.2d 567 (1952); and Salem v. Salem, 245 Iowa 62, 60 N.W.2d 772 (1953). But there are cases holding that he does qualify as a taker for value if at the time he accepts the mortgage he gives up some significant legal right. Thus extending time for payment or forbearance from suit may be such a relinquishment of a right. Tripler v. MacDonald Lumber Co., 173 Cal. 144, 159 P. 591 (1916); and Manufacturers and Traders Trust Co. v. First National Bank in Fort Lauderdale, 113 So. 2d 869 (Fla. Dist. Ct. App. 1959). But cf. Gabel v. Drewrys Ltd., 68 So. 2d 372 (Fla. 1953), where the forbearance was not for any definite time so the mortgagee was held not a taker for value.

3. Suppose that a subsequent taker without notice makes a partial payment and then becomes aware of a prior unrecorded interest. What should be the respective rights of the prior and subsequent interest holders?

The Recording Acts

In Seguin v. Maloney-Chambers Lumber Co., 198 Ore. 272, 253 P.2d 252, 256 P.2d 514 (1953), X conveyed standing timber to A. This instrument of conveyance was not recorded. Later X contracted to convey to B the land on which the trees were located, including the timber previously sold to A. B paid $5000 toward the purchase price, the balance to be paid in installments, and B to receive a deed upon all payments being made. When B contracted to buy and when he paid the $5000, he was unaware of the conveyance from X to A. But before B made any further payments, he was informed of the timber conveyance from X to A. In a quiet title proceeding brought by B against A, the court held that A's interest in the timber was superior to B's, except that B was declared to have a lien on the standing timber minus the value of timber cut and removed by B.

Why should A receive the timber and B, in essence, receive back his payment? Why should not B receive the timber but be required to pay A for the value of the timber as of the contract date or date of partial payment, minus payments by B before B obtained notice? What criteria should resolve this question? Is this one of those legal problems in which one solution is no more appealing than another, hence the court must act arbitrarily? Should the proportion of the contract price paid by B before notice be an important consideration? Should it make any difference whether the subsequent taker's interest is legal or equitable?

4. Under these facts, should A have a cause of action of any kind against X or B? Assume the transactions occurred in the following chronological order:

X-A, mortgage delivered
X-B, deed delivered
B-C, deed delivered
X-B, deed recorded
B-C, deed recorded
X-A, mortgage recorded

Assume that B is a donee from X who knew of the X-A mortgage when he took delivery of his deed, but that C is a bona fide purchaser who paid the full value of the property and was unaware of the X-A mortgage when he took delivery. Does your answer vary depending on whether the applicable recording act is a race, race-notice, or notice one?

Osin v. Johnson
243 F.2d 653 (D.C. Cir. 1957)

BURGER, Circuit Judge. Appellant, a woman of more than average business experience, agreed to sell a parcel of improved real estate to appellee

Johnson and subsequently executed and delivered a deed, taking back a note for the full purchase price of $30,000. There was no down payment. Johnson represented to appellant that he would prepare, execute and record a trust on the property to secure his purchase money note.

After delivery of the deed to him, Johnson recorded the deed but did not prepare and record the trust instrument as he had promised appellant he would do. For this breach of faith and fraud Johnson was thereafter indicted, tried and convicted and testimony in the criminal case forms part of the record in this case.

Without disclosing appellant's prior unrecorded lien against his title, Johnson borrowed $11,000 from appellee Perpetual Building Association, executing deeds of trust against the property. Later Johnson borrowed an additional $3300 on second deeds of trust from appellee Glorius. Thereafter, creditors of Johnson obtained judgments which became liens on the real estate under D.C. Code, §15-103 (1951 ed.).[1] When foreclosure proceedings were commenced under the trust deeds executed by Johnson, appellant brought this suit for equitable relief, joining the trust holders, with the judgment creditors of Johnson subsequently intervening.

The trial court properly heard the case without a jury since this suit was plainly addressed to the equity jurisdiction of the court. The trial judge found that appellant conveyed title to Johnson knowingly and in reliance on Johnson's assurances that he would record all the documents including the deed of trust which secured the purchase money note. Upon this finding the court concluded that appellee trust holders and judgment creditors had acquired interests in the property superior to that of appellant's unrecorded claim.

Appellant contends she did not knowingly execute and deliver the deed, and that Johnson fraudulently procured her signature on an instrument represented to be a sales contract. Cf. Baker v. Morton, 1870, 12 Wall. 150, 79 U.S. 150, 20 L. Ed. 262; Brown v. Pierce, 1868, 7 Wall. 205, 74 U.S. 205, 19 L. Ed. 134. Compare Restatement, Contracts §494 with §495 (1932). However, appellant's pre-litigation actions and letters expressly refute this contention and provide ample basis for the trial court's

---

[1] "Every final judgment at common law . . . for the payment of money from the date when the same shall be rendered, every judgment of the municipal court when docketed in the clerk's office of the District Court . . . shall be a lien on all the freehold . . . estates, legal and equitable, of the defendants bound by such judgment . . . in any lands, tenements, or hereditaments in the District. . . ."

Appellant's Brief urges us to take judicial notice of certain facts of record in the cases of Umbricht v. Johnson, No. M-7187-55, Municipal Court of District of Columbia, and Hakim v. Johnson, No. 771-55, United States District Court for the District of Columbia, to wit: Umbricht sold Johnson an Oldsmobile car taking Johnson's note for $1875, against which Johnson later paid $400. Hakim sold a Cadillac car to Johnson taking the latter's note for $4,500 upon which he later defaulted.

It would appear from the nature of these transactions that neither judgment creditor dealt with Johnson in reliance on the state of the record title as to the realty.

finding contrary to her testimony.[2] Nor do we find merit in appellant's other allegations of error on the part of the trial court.

I

The trial court apparently did not consider whether Johnson's fraudulent conduct might give rise to the imposition of a constructive trust on the real estate in appellant's favor, although appellant's prayer for equitable relief, while not specifically requesting this remedy, was sufficiently broad to enable a court of equity to impress a trust upon the property.

A constructive trust is a purely equitable device which can be applied with great flexibility. It arises by operation of law from the occurrence of an unconscionable act for which no traditional relief is available. A constructive trust can be imposed whenever one unfairly holds title or a property interest and where the holder would be unjustly enriched if permitted to retain such interest. Specifically, the acquisition of property through the fraudulent misrepresentation of a material fact has been held sufficient grounds to fasten a constructive trust on the property. Howard v. Howe, 7 Cir., 1932, 61 F.2d 577, certiorari denied, 1933, 289 U.S. 731, 53 S. Ct. 527, 77 L. Ed. 1480. Since the District Court in the instant case found that appellant was induced to convey her title to the real estate by a fraudulent promise of Johnson that he would execute and record a deed of trust, the court could have properly considered whether, under all the circumstances, a constructive trust should have been imposed. It thus becomes necessary to consider whether the existence of a constructive trust would give appellant a superior claim to the interests of the trust holders and Johnson's judgment creditors, should it be found that a constructive trust exists.

II

We turn first to the holders of the first and second deeds of trust. Whatever the nature of appellant's interest, the District Court was correct in holding the fraud in the relationship between appellant and Johnson did not give appellant a claim superior to that of the trust holders who occupy the position of bona fide purchasers. Colorado Coal and Iron Co. v. United States, 1887, 123 U.S. 307, 314, 8 S. Ct. 131, 31 L. Ed. 182; Davison v. Morgan, 1931, 60 App. D.C. 161, 50 F.2d 311.

---

2. The trial judge, in finding number 7, recited: "Plaintiff [Mrs. Osin], shortly after [the date she executed and delivered the deed], sought, and received, return of her deposits with the several utility companies for service to the aforesaid houses. She agreed that defendant Johnson should receive the rents for said properties thereafter and she no longer received them herself. She made no further efforts to sell the property and later went to Florida from which place she wrote letters on March 30, 1955, stating that she had sold the properties and had received back a purchase money deed of trust."

The record demonstrates, and the lower court so found, that the holders of the trust deeds were innocent purchasers for value without notice of appellant's prior equity, and thus they clearly fall within the purview of the recording act, D.C. Code, §45-501 (1951 ed.), protecting bona fide purchasers against unrecorded conveyances.[5] The logical and rational basis for preferring the bona fide purchaser over the grantor of the record title holder is that as between two innocent parties, i.e., appellant and the bona fide lenders such as Perpetual and other trust holders, appellant must yield to those who in good faith relied on the state of the record which her negligence allowed to exist. It would manifestly defeat the whole point of recording statutes to permit Mrs. Osin to assert her admitted equities at the expense of those who relied in good faith on a state of the record title which her acts created.

Even in the absence of recording acts or, as discussed under point III infra, if the recording statute is inapplicable, a bona fide purchaser's rights have always been held superior to prior equitable interests. A purchaser for value, without notice of the facts which lead to the creation of a constructive trust, will cut off the trust beneficiary's rights. Restatement, Restitution, §172 (1937); 4 Scott, Trusts §468 (2d ed. 1956). Therefore, the holders of the deeds of trust would prevail over appellant even if a constructive trust were to be imposed on the property.

III

The same rationale does not have equal validity when applied to judgment creditors of the fraudulent grantee. A judgment creditor possessing a statutory lien on property does not occupy a position equivalent to that of a purchaser for value and thus "if the land of the debtor is subject to equities, the judgment creditor's lien is subject to such equities." 3 Scott, Trusts §308.1, p. 2276 (2d ed. 1956). See also Restatement, Restitution §173, comment j (1937). As a matter of simple ordinary fairness, which is the essence of equity, there is every reason why a defrauded grantor of title should command a higher priority than creditors of the fraudulent grantee since such creditors usually do not rely on the record title in their extension of credit. The equitable considerations dictating the priority of an equitable right over subsequently acquired judgment liens was aptly summarized by this court many years ago:

---

5. "Any deed conveying real property in the District, or interest therein . . . executed and acknowledged and certified as provided in sections 30-216, 45-106, 45-302, 45-401 to 45-404 and delivered to the person in whose favor the same is executed, shall be held to take effect from the date of the delivery thereof, except that as to creditors and subsequent bona fide purchasers and mortgagees without notice of said deed, and others interested in said property, it shall only take effect from the time of its delivery to the recorder of deeds for record."

D.C. Code, §45-601 (1951 ed.) provides that deeds of trust are to be recorded and to take effect as against "bona fide purchasers and mortgagees and creditors" in the same manner as absolute deeds under §45-501.

The Recording Acts

"Unless precluded by the terms of some statute expressly intended to change it, the rule has always prevailed that the equity under a trust or a contract in rem is superior to that under a judgment lien. The claimant under the contract in rem has an equity to the specific thing which binds the conscience of his grantor; whilst the judgment creditor, who has advanced nothing on the faith of the specific thing, is entitled only to that which his debtor really has, at the time, or could honestly convey or encumber; his beneficial interest and nothing more." Hume v. Riggs, 1898, 12 App. D.C. 355, 367.

The appellee judgment creditors, however, point to the recording acts as altering the equitable rule and giving them a preference over appellant's unrecorded interest. This jurisdiction, like approximately half of the states, has adopted a recording statute which specifically lists "creditors" among those classes given precedence to prior interests not recorded. Despite early intimations to the contrary, it is now well settled that the statutory reference to "creditors" includes a good faith judgment creditor holding a statutory lien obtained under D.C. Code, §15-103, without the necessity of such creditor executing his lien by attachment or by "filing a bill in equity." Hitz v. National Metropolitan Bank, 1884, 111 U.S. 722, 4 S. Ct. 613, 28 L. Ed. 577; Atlas Portland Cement Co. v. Fox, 1920, 49 App. D.C. 292, 265 F. 444, 266 F. 1021. See also 4 American Law of Property §17.29 (Casner ed. 1952); 1919, 4 A.L.R. 434. thus, as to instruments required to be recorded *and capable of being recorded,* the recording act elevates a judgment creditor to the same legal plane as a bona fide purchaser for value.

But since the preference accorded a judgment lien depends upon the statute, it extends only to such interests as the statute requires to be recorded. It has long been acknowledged that recording acts similar to that enacted in the District of Columbia do not apply to interests incapable of record. Where an equitable interest is not created by a written instrument or conveyance but rather arises by operation of law, such an interest "is not within the statute and is not subject to the lien of a judgment [creditor]. . . ." 2 Freeman, Judgments 2043 (5th ed. 1925). Other jurisdictions have recognized that a constructive trust, by its nature not susceptible of record, is not within the reach of recording acts and thus retains priority over judgment liens. In re Rosenberg, D.C.S.D. Tex. 1925, 4 F.2d 581; East St. Louis Lumber Co. v. Schnipper, 1923, 310 Ill. 150, 141 N.E. 542; School District No. 10 v. Peterson, 1898, 74 Minn. 122, 76 N.W. 1126.

This jurisdiction has never passed directly on the question whether a creditor holding a statutory lien takes preference over an earlier equity incapable of being recorded. In American Savings Bank v. Eisminger, 1910, 35 App. D.C. 51, this court held the lien of a judgment creditor equal to the lien of a bona fide purchaser and thus superior to any secret trust *capable of being recorded,* but not so recorded. This qualification of recordability was carefully and precisely delineated by the court by repetition in these words: "We say, trust capable of being placed upon record, for that is the case here. *Whether* a resulting or constructive trust, *incapable of record,* and in the assertion of which there has been no laches, would yield to the lien also, *we intimate no opinion.*" American Savings Bank v. Eisminger, supra at 55. (Emphasis added.) The case now before us gives rise to precisely the possible situation envisaged by this court in the *American Savings Bank* case and as to which the court would then "intimate no opinion." We say "possible situation" for it is not the function of this court to resolve whether the facts warrant the imposition of a constructive trust since appellant failed to point out the possibility of such a course to the District Court. We decide only the question pointedly left open in American Savings Bank v. Eisminger, supra. For the reasons indicated above, and in line with the authority cited, we now supply that gap and hold if a new trial discloses (1) a constructive trust inherently incapable of recording and (2) no laches on the part of appellant in the assertion of her rights, that in such case Mrs. Osin's constructive trust will have priority over the judgment creditors of Johnson. But we qualify the above holding to this extent: a judgment creditor who is able to show affirmative reliance on the state of the record without notice of any infirmity should be entitled to the same standing as a bona fide purchaser. See 2 Freeman, Judgments 2043-44 (5th ed. 1925). Thus if a judgment creditor can satisfy the District Court that he, like the trust holders, extended credit on faith of Johnson's record title, he should be entitled to the same priority enjoyed by other bona fide purchasers, unless when the debt arose he had actual or constructive notice of Johnson's fraud on Mrs. Osin. D.C. Code, §45-501 (1951 ed.).

The judgment of the District Court also provided that appellant could elect to take a reconveyance of the property upon her returning to Johnson (for the benefit of Johnson's judgment creditors) the $680 Johnson had paid appellant on his purchase money note. We think that part of the judgments should be vacated and the ultimate disposition of the $680 abide the determination of the equities on a new trial.

The judgment below is affirmed as to the trust holders, Perpetual Building Association, Scrivener, Crowell, Laughlin, Sinclitico, Glorius and Sherman; reversed as to the intervenor judgment creditors Hakim and Umbricht, and the case is remanded for further proceedings.

Affirmed in part; reversed in part.

NOTES

1. Would the result in the principal case have been different as to the holders of deeds of trust if it had been shown that they did not search the recorded documents or have those documents searched in their behalf before they made the secured loans to Johnson? Under the recording acts, protection is normally extended to subsequent purchasers whether or not

they have searched the records or have relied on such a search, if a search would not, as in the *Osin* case, have disclosed the senior-in-time interest.

2. Whether or not the judgment creditors in extending credit relied on the title as recorded, should Mrs. Osin prevail over them when her negligence or poor judgment encouraged Johnson's wrongful conduct? She failed to set up the transaction with Johnson so that her interest assuredly would be promptly recorded, and had her interest been promptly recorded she clearly would have been protected against all of the defendants.

3. Should the judgment creditors prevail over Mrs. Osin if they did not rely on the recorded title before extending credit but did so rely before deciding to bring the actions against Johnson that resulted in the judgments?

c. Notice From Recording

The recording of an instrument does not necessarily mean that constructive notice of its contents will be held to exist. Even though an instrument is recordable and filed for record by someone entitled to protection of the recording act, it is possible under some circumstances that the instrument will not be given recording effect. It may, for instance, be outside the chain of title of some persons who may acquire an interest in the parcel involved, and recording is generally not constructive notice to such persons. Although an instrument may have been filed for record, a public official may have been negligent and as a result the instrument was never placed of record or indexed, or it may have been inaccurately transcribed onto the records or inaccurately indexed. In some states these circumstances prevent an instrument from having recording effect. Courts and legislatures often take the position that although an instrument is filed or placed of record, it should not be constructive notice if it is impossible to find it in the public records or if it can be found only by an unduly burdensome search. A common counter judicial or legislative policy is to protect those who have made a reasonable effort to record. Under the recording system, interests of those who record are frequently inconsistent with those of persons obligated to search, and in various situations a choice between the two must be made. In close cases, some courts and legislatures tend to favor those who record and others those who must search.

Kiser v. Clinchfield Coal Corp.
200 Va. 517, 106 S.E.2d 601 (1959)

WHITTLE, Justice. On October 26, 1951, Clinchfield Coal Corporation, hereinafter called Clinchfield, filed a bill in chancery against Mont B.

Kiser, et al., alleging title to the coal and minerals underlying a tract of 117 acres of land in Dickenson county. . . . The bill further alleged Mont B. Kiser and his lessees (appellants here) were mining coal and trespassing upon said land.

Upon the filing of the bill the court entered an order restraining the trespass until the case could be heard on its merits.

Appellants demurred to the bill, and without waiving their demurrer, answered the same. Depositions were taken, and upon a hearing, the circuit court on October 4, 1957, entered a decree overruling the demurrer, adjudging Clinchfield to be the owner of the mineral estate in the 117 acres. . . . A commissioner was appointed to ascertain the damages resulting from the alleged trespass. From this decree appellants appeal.

The record and briefs are voluminous, and there are some contentions made which we do not deem of sufficient merit to be considered. The material questions for decision are. . . .

III. Was Clinchfield entitled to a decree adjudging it the owner of the mineral estate underlying the 117-acre tract of land? . . .

Question No. III challenges Clinchfield's right to the mineral estate in the 117-acre tract. The record discloses that in 1884 the land here involved was a part of a large tract consisting of some 1400 acres owned in fee simply by James M. Kiser, father of Schofield, which is the common source of title of all parties to this controversy.

On January 31, 1884, James M. Kiser and wife conveyed the 117 acres by deed in fee simple to their son Schofield. There was no exception of the mineral estate. This deed was not recorded until November 30, 1888 and, as hereinafter pointed out, was never acknowledged by James M. Kiser. In the meantime, on December 7, 1887, James Kiser and wife, together with certain of their children not here involved, conveyed the mineral estate and certain timber to Tazewell Coal and Iron Company.

The evidence discloses that after the deed of 1884 to Schofield Kiser was executed, he held possession of the surface until December 12, 1891, when he executed a deed for the 117 acres to James M. Kiser and wife, which contained the following exception, "with the exception of the coal and minerals" and certain timber.

Thus, at the time of the conveyance of 1887 of the mineral estate by James M. Kiser and wife to the Tazewell company, Schofield was in possession of the surface of the land, and under the common law rule stated in Chapman v. Chapman, 91 Va. 397, 21 S.E. 813, his possession was sufficient to charge Tazwell with notice of Schofield Kiser's deed. However, by statute enacted by the General Assembly of January 15, 1900, the common law rule was abrogated by adding a proviso to the recording statute (Acts of Assembly 1899-1900, p. 89) to the effect that mere possession shall not be notice to subsequent purchasers for valuable consideration. Norfolks & P. Traction Co. v. C. B. White & Bros., 113 Va. 102, 73 S.E. 467; Code of 1950, §55-96. This was the law in effect on August 7, 1902, when Tazewell Coal and Iron Company executed two deeds to the land in question, one conveying to William Patrick an undivided three-fourths interest in the mineral estate, and the other conveying to L. C. Ware an undivided one-fourth interest in the mineral estate.

Thereafter, by mesne conveyances, the mineral estate passed to Clinchfield, at which time the proviso that mere possession shall not be notice to subsequent purchasers for valuable consideration was in effect. Thus, this proviso applied to all purchasers of the mineral estate since the enactment of the statute abrogating the rule in the *Chapman* case, and mere possession by Schofield or Mont Kiser since the effect date of the statute constituted no notice of Schofield's deed.

The record clearly discloses that Clinchfield in good faith, for valuable consideration, purchased in 1907 the mineral estate embraced in the deed from James M. Kiser to Tazewell, relying upon said deed and the recorded chain of title by subsequent conveyances from Tazewell and its successors in title. Therefore, if Clinchfield so purchased without notice of Schofield Kiser's deed, then Schofield's deed was and is void as to Clinchfield's deed of purchase.

Further, the record discloses that the only certificate of acknowledgment, or any other proof of execution of the deed by James M. Kiser to Schofield Kiser on January 31, 1884, appears to be a certificate of Jessie Wampler, a notary public, certifying the privy examination and acknowledgment of Elizabeth Kiser, wife of the grantor. Nowhere is it shown that James M. Kiser acknowledged the deed; therefore the deed was not duly admitted to record as to him. §§2500, 2501, Code 1887; now §§55-106 and 55-113, Code 1950.

It is argued by counsel for appellants that the attorney for Clinchfield who examined the title to the mineral estate prior to purchase must have had actual notice of Schofield's deed. It will be remembered that the deed from James M. Kiser to Schofield was not filed for recordation until after the conveyance of the coal and minerals by the deed from James M. Kiser to Tazewell, and an attorney examining the record as to the title to the mineral estate would not be called upon to look for the recordation of adverse conveyances in the name of James M. Kiser subsequent to the date of the recordation of the duly acknowledged deed from James M. Kiser to the Tazewell Coal and Iron Company. The deed to Schofield Kiser was not recorded until four years and ten months after its execution, and ten months after the recordation of the deed to the Tazewell company. See Bowman v. Holland, 116 Va. 805, 83 S.E. 393.

In order for a deed and its recitals to operate as constructive notice to a bona fide purchaser of land it must be a link in the purchaser's chain of title. No purchaser is chargeable with constructive notice of all matters of record but only with such as the title deeds of the estate refer to or put him on inquiry about. Lewis v. Barnhart, 145 U.S. 56, 12 S. Ct. 772, 36 L. Ed. 621; Flanary v. Kane, 102 Va. 547, 46 S.E. 312.

It was not uncumbent upon Clinchfield's attorney to search the record for adverse conveyances by James M. Kiser recorded after the recordation of the Tazewell Coal and Iron Company's deed.

Appellants further contend that even if Mont Kiser's paper title to the mineral estate is not good as against Clinchfield, he has title to the same by adverse possession by reason of Schofield's possession. This is not true under the circumstances here involved. After the severance of the surface estate from the mineral estate, color of title to the mineral estate alone and possession of the surface estate not held adversely, is not sufficient. Mont Kiser has shown no occupancy or use of any part of the mineral estate such as would constitute actual possession, and there is no merit in this contention. Clevinger v. Bull Creek Coal Co., Inc., 199 Va. 216, 219, 220, 98 S.E.2d 670, 672, 673; 58 C.J.S. Mines and Minerals §157, page 329.

The record title exhibited by Clinchfield shows that it has a good recorded paper title to the mineral estate which was conveyed by the deed of December 7, 1887 from James M. Kiser to Tazewell Coal and Iron Company, and the evidence shows that it has exercised acts of exclusive ownership over the same and is therefore the owner of the mineral estate in the 117 acres in controversy.

For the reasons stated the decree appealed from is affirmed.

NOTES

1. One of the links in Clinchfield's chain of title was weak: Tazewell was junior in time and not protected by the recording acts because it was on notice of Schofield Kiser's interest. Should this not have prevented Clinchfield from prevailing in the principal case?

2. What could Clinchfield have done to have discovered the Schofield Kiser interest and interests derived from him? Should Clinchfield have been obligated to search for and discover these interests?

3. Do you favor the Massachusetts or Vermont position or the one preferred by the court, as these positions are described in this excerpt from the opinion in Woods v. Garnett, 72 Miss. 78, 84-87, 16 So. 390, 391-392 (1894):

> When a conveyance is made to one who fails to record his deed until after another has received and recorded a conveyance from the grantor, but with notice of the first deed, what are the rights of the first grantee against a purchaser from the second, where such purchaser, having no actual knowledge of the facts, buys after the record of the prior deed? This question is determined by a construction of our registry act; for at the common law a second purchaser of the fee could take nothing, since by the first conveyance the grantor would have divested himself of all his estate and would have nothing to convey. Basset v. Nosworthy, 2 White & T. Lead. Cas. Eq. 1, and

note; Co. Litt. 290f, note 13. By our registry act, it is declared that the instruments thereby required to be recorded "shall be void as to all creditors and subsequent purchasers for valuable consideration without notice, unless they shall be acknowledged or proved, and lodged with the clerk of the chancery court of the county, to be recorded, in the same manner that other conveyances are required by this act to be acknowledged or proved and recorded; but the same as between the parties and their heirs, and as to all subsequent purchasers with notice, or without valuable consideration, shall nevertheless be valid and binding." Code 1880, §1212; code 1892, §2457. "Every conveyance, convenant, agreement, bond, mortgage and deed of trust shall take effect as to all subsequent purchasers for a valuable consideration, without notice, and as to all creditors, only from the time when delivered to the clerk to be recorded." Code 1880, §1213; Code 1892, §2458. In Massachusetts and Vermont it is held that a purchaser is not bound to examine the record after the date of a recorded conveyance, to discover whether the grantor therein has made another conveyance prior in time, but junior in record, but may safely purchase from the grantee in the first recorded conveyance, if he, the purchaser, has not actual notice of the prior deed, and no notice of the facts which make it his duty to prosecute inquiry. Connecticut v. Bradish, 14 Mass. 296; Trull v. Bigelow, 16 Mass. 406; Morse v. Curtis, 140 Mass. 112, 2 N.E. 929; Day v. Clark, 25 Vt. 397. And this is said to be the more reasonable rule by the annotators of the Leading Cases in Equity (Le Neve v. Le Neve, 2 White & T. Lead. Cas. Eq. 180), and by Mr. Jones (1 Jones, Mortg. §574). The decided weight of authority is, however, to the contrary, though Mr. Jones cites none of them as supporting the contrary rule except the New York decisions. . . . The question has never been decided in this state, though in Harrington v. Allen, 48 Miss. 492, there is a doctrine in which Judge Simrall, mistaking the facts of his case, seems to favor the Massachusetts rule. The decisions in Massachusetts and Vermont, while resulting in practically the same end, proceed on irreconcilable and opposite principles. In Massachusetts it is ruled that the purchaser from the grantee in the deed junior in date, but senior in record, need not examine the records after the date of registration of the conveyance to his grantor. Morse v. Curtis, 140 Mass. 112, 2 N.E. 929. In Vermont it is held that he is bound by the constructive notice afforded by the registration of the first deed, that it is notice to him of the fact that a deed prior to that of his grantor had been made, but it is not notice that his grantor had notice of the first deed; and so the conveyance to the first purchaser from the second grantee is preferred in Vermont, not because the purchaser is himself a purchaser without notice, for the registration of the prior deed is notice of its existence, nor because his grantor was a purchaser without notice, for that may or may not be true, but because the purchaser did not know that his grantor was not a bona fide purchaser; and thus, under the Vermont decisions, one may secure protection, as though he were a bona fide purchaser, when neither he, nor any one under and through whom he derives title, was in fact such purchaser. This rule has no recognition except in Vermont, so far as we have discovered. We think the Massachusetts decisions are erroneous, because they hold that one not bound by the registry law is protected by it. But for the registry law, where one has conveyed his title, he has nothing left to convey to another, and that other, with or without notice of the prior conveyance, would get nothing, for his grantor had nothing to convey. Now, the statute comes, and provides that, though a conveyance of the class named in the statute may be made, it shall, as to certain persons, viz. creditors and purchasers without notice, be valid only from a certain time, viz. the time when it is filed for record. In other words, the operation of the unrecorded conveyance is suspended until it shall be recorded as against creditors and purchasers without notice, and where recorded it does not operate by relation as against such persons from the day of its execution, but is effectual only from and of the date of its delivery for record. But where filed for record it has full scope and effect against the world. One who buys after that event can find no protection in the statute, for its terms have been complied with by the holder of the adverse title. It is no answer to say that it is inconvenient to the purchaser to examine a long and voluminous record, made after the record of the title of his grantor. To this the sufficient reply is that, but for the registry acts, he would not have even the protection which such records afford, but would deal at his peril with his grantor, and secure only such title as he might assert. If that grantor had good title because a purchaser for value, without notice, that is a defense to his vendee; but if such grantor was not such purchaser, then the validity of the title he conveys must depend upon the character of his vendee; and, if such vendee is not a bona fide purchaser under the common law or the statute, we cannot perceive from what source a principle can be deduced which will afford him protection. It seems clear to us that one who buys an estate cannot invoke the protection of the registry act as against a deed recorded under such act at the time of his purchase.

4. In McCahill v. Travis Co., 45 So. 2d 191 (Fla. 1950), it was held that there is a presumption that subsequent purchasers have no notice of prior unrecorded instruments, and the burden of overcoming this presumption is on those claiming under such instruments.

5. If a subsequent taker is on actual or constructive notice of an instrument, he generally is considered on constructive notice of matters referred to in the instrument pertaining to the title in question. If the recitals are indefinite and incomplete but suggest that prior claims against the title may exist, the subsequent taker generally is considered on notice of what a reasonable inquiry would disclose. Statutes in some states have sought to narrow the notice scope of recitals in instruments. For example, N.Y. Real Prop. Law §291-e (McKinney 1968), provides in part:

1. This section applies to any language, contained in a conveyance of real property in this state, which (a) excepts or reserves a part of any or all parts of the described premises which have been or may have been previously conveyed, or previously contracted to be sold or exchanged, by the grantor or by a previous owner, or (b) otherwise indicates that the premises or some part or parts thereof have been or may have been previously conveyed or that a contract has been or may have been previously made for the sale or exchange of all or some part or parts thereof, or (c) indicates that only such part of the premises described is intended to be conveyed as the

grantor, or a previous owner, has not previously conveyed or has not previously contracted to sell or exchange, and, in any of the cases described in this subdivision, fails to identify the premises previously conveyed or contracted to be sold or exchanged in any other manner than by indicating that a conveyance or contract has previously been made or indicating the fact or possibility that one or more conveyances or contracts have been or may have been previously made.

2. An exception, reservation or recital described in subdivision one of this section is (a) void as against a subsequent purchaser in good faith and for a valuable consideration, who has no other notice of the identity of the premises to which it refers, and (b) ineffective to give notice to such subsequent purchaser of the previous conveyance or contract so referred to or create any duty of inquiry with respect thereto, unless, in either case, such previous conveyance or contract is sufficient to identify the premises to which the exception, reservation or recital refers and is recorded as provided in this article before the recording of the instrument by which the subsequent purchaser acquires his estate or interest.

Why do you think this statute was enacted? What ends does it further?

Cross, The Record "Chain of Title Hypocrisy"
57 Colum. L. Rev. 787, 787-796 (1957)

Anyone reading part of the mass of recording act cases in almost any American jurisdiction will be confronted with the "chain of title" rationale often invoked to resolve priority between competing claimants to interests in land. The assertion is that a subsequent purchaser[1] will have priority over an earlier claimant to the same title unless the antecedent claim is revealed within the "chain" of the title which the subsequent purchaser believes he is getting. The concept has been evolved apparently to effect some practical protection by the recording acts. These acts commonly provide that an instrument shall be ineffective against certain competing claimants unless the direction of the statute is followed. The statute may make the instrument "void" as to the competitor or may state that if the statutory direction is followed the record of an instrument shall be notice to all the world. The chain of title concept is commonly used without regard to the possible importance of the particular form of statute.

I. THE RECORD CHAIN OF TITLE CONCEPT

From the rule that all conveyances are "innocent" it must follow that a current claimant can prevail only if he can establish that ownership has in

---

1. "Subsequent purchaser" is here used generically to include any person who by the force of the applicable recording act may be able to assert its protection, and it is assumed that he has the necessary qualities, e.g., actual good faith and payment of valuable consideration.

fact passed from the sovereign (theorectically) through his predecessors to himself, and hence that there is a chain or sequence of transactions ending in him. The record chain of title concept has an additional connotation, that of defining the length of each link in the sense of fixing the period of time for search in the records against a particular owner. Rather than strictly a chain of transfers it connotes a chain of owners or persons interested in the title. The typical statute says nothing of chain of title — it appears by a judicial gloss which has done much to conceal the inadequacy of the protection afforded by the acts. Consequently the needed corrections are not pressed.

Chain of title has been used in a geographical sense to disqualify, as not part of the chain to tract one, an instrument having the primary function of conveying tract two, even though as between the parties it creates rights in tract one and specifically so states.[5] The term had also been used to narrow the operative effect of record "notice to the whole world" (in some of the statutes), thus permitting disregard of the "wild deed" from a person who, so far as the records reveal, had no interest in the land.[6] This discussion has no principal concern with these two uses of the term.

From the practical necessities of search in the public records has evolved the meaning definitive of the length of each link. This is the method to determine whether a prospective vendor has the interest he purports to have, the records are examined to discover the sequence of transfers which support his assertion of title. Unless the origin of his title is known the search must extend backwards in time looking for the record of a conveyance to the vendor; then continuing backwards, search is made for the record of the instrument in which the vendor's grantor was the grantee, and continuing similarly as to each predecessor until the transfer from the sovereign is discovered, or in older states, far enough back until an apparently firm "root" is located. In an earlier time this must have involved thumbing through the actual volumes of the record, but since indexing has been directed by the legislatures, the initial search for the persons has been in the indexes. The history of transfer now discovered, the process is reversed and search is made to determine what each of the various owners did with or to the title during the period of his apparent ownership. As to

---

5. This meaning is involved in Glorieux v. Lighthipe, 88 N.J.L. 199, 96 Atl. 94 (1915) (restrictive covenant affecting lot 1 in deed to lot 2 — not in chain of title). Contra, Finley v. Glenn, 303 Pa. 131, 154 Atl. 299 (1931) (easement on lot 1 in favor of lot 2 created in deed to lot 2 — in chain of title).

Professors Merrill and Philbrick believe the "chain" is narrow. 2 Merrill, Notice §981 (1952); Philbrick, Limits of Record Search and Therefore of Notice, 93 U. Pa. L. Rev. 125, 169 (1944) (this article is in three parts, id. at 125, 259, 391). Mr. R. G. Patton does not agree. 4 American Law of Property §17.24 (Casner ed. 1952). Compare the analysis of Bowman v. Holland, 116 Va. 805, 83 S.E. 393 (1914) in Note, Title Search in Virginia, 26 Va. L. Rev. 385 (1940), with MacKenzie, Examining for Conveyances by a Grantor after He Has Conveyed Title of Record, 26 Va. L. Rev. 831 (1940).

6. 4 American Law of Property §17.17 (Casner ed. 1952).

each owner there should be a small overlap in time, i.e., the search is made from the day before execution of the deed to him (not the day of recording) until the day after recording of the deed from him (not the day of execution). Thus the length of the respective links is identified. A transaction by the then owner fairly discoverable of record within the duration of his link is in the chain of title, but all other transactions, though reflected in the records in fact, are not in the chain of title.[8] Under this approach the prospective purchaser has no concern with instruments thus determined to be out of the chain of title. Professor Philbrick asserts this is the proper meaning of the term.[9] Mr. R. G. Patton has concurred.[10] And where search or examination is made directly from the public records this meaning is apparently adopted to control the extent of search.

Since it is not now practicable to search in the actual record or transcription books, if it ever was for long, this then is the resulting proposition: A prospective purchaser can be confident he will get good title from his vendor if an examination of the indexes in the indicated manner, and a study of the transactions thereby discovered, reveal a chain of title without infirmity. But is this so? I suggest that to assert that such a "chain of title" assures ownership in the vendor is sheer hypocrisy.

II. The Infirmities of Chain of Title Reasoning

A. *The Immateriality of the Index.* The most glaring weakness stems from the rule that a grantee has established his position and barred a subsequent

---

8. "Chain of title" notice seems to be a one-way street—forward in time only, not backward even though the persons in the chain may initially be discoverable only by the "backward" search. Thus an instrument *in favor of* or *to* the record owner can be ignored. Philbrick, supra note 5, at 170 n.146. This is reasonable when the instrument is in his favor as creditor or mortagee, as in Pyles v. Brown, 189 Pa. 164, 42 A. 11 (1899) or Veazie v. Parker, 23 Me. 170 (1843). The searcher is not interested in any such position, but is it equally reasonable when the instrument is a deed which *might* be his necessary title deed? To illustrate: search against M to learn his source of title before 1920 when he conveyed to N. In 1918 M's name appears in the index as mortgagee—irrelevant; in 1917 he appears as grantee—relevant? In 1915 he appears as grantee from the real source of his title, and if search could run forward from 1915, in 1917 the searcher would be looking for deeds from M, not to him. Going backward in time, the reverse is true. Nonetheless the rule applied in the Veazie case, supra, was believed by the Texas court to answer the question of notice from the 1917 deed (in effect), and it could be ignored. Frank v. Heidenheimer, 84 Tex. 642, 19 S.W. 855 (1892).

The chain has a certain ephemeral quality in another "wild deed" problem. Suppose V contracts to sell to P, and P mortgages to M. The mortgage is recorded but the contract is not. Then A buys P out, pays V the balance due on the contract, receives and records the deed from V. A though he knows nothing in fact of the mortgage to M takes subject to it; his chain of title includes P and hence he must search for P's transactions. Simonson v. Wenzel, 27 N.D. 638, 147 N.W. 804 (1914). However, if A conveys to B who knows nothing of P, B as a bona fide purchaser for value will apparently take free of M's mortgage. Although it is in A's chain of title it is not in B's. Cf. Fullerton Lumber Co. v. Tinker, 22 S.D. 427, 118 N.W. 700 (1908) (rejection of this argument *because* of tract indexing).

9. Philbrick, supra note 5 (passim), particularly at 167, 179.

10. 4 American Law of Property §17.19 (Casner ed. 1952).

purchaser from the protection afforded by the recording act when the prior grantee has merely "filed" or "lodged" his instrument with the recording officer for record, without regard to what that officer does about transcribing it or making an index to the transcription. Nearly as fatal is the proposition that the grantee is secure against subsequent parties if the instrument is transcribed though not indexed at all or indexed in a misleading manner.

It is asserted that application of the chain of title approach is essential to accomplish the purpose of protection for the subsequent purchaser. Without denying the accuracy of this assertion, it may be observed that twenty-six states have decisions not overruled which hold that filing or lodging with the recording officer fulfills the grantee's duty, or that the subsequent purchaser gets no protection from the lack or inaccuracy of an index, and four more states have cases in which one or the other of these propositions is stated.

Under typical statutes the normal steps in recording are these: (1) filing the instrument with the recording officer and payment of the required fees; (2) notation by the officer in an entry or reception book if there is one, or preliminary entry in an index book; (3) actual transcription in the appropriate record book; (4) completion of the index(es) to the record; and (5) return of the instrument by the officer. Completion of these steps can be called full recording.[17] The cases cited above recognize that a prior grantee must start the recording process before a subsequent purchaser buys if he is to prevail against the subsequent purchaser, but in concluding that full recording is not required, the courts reason that, as recording is for the protection of the subsequent purchaser, he should bear the burden of the officer's inadequate performance. The applicable statute may provide that an instrument is void unless "lodged" or "filed" with the officer, or it may provide that an instrument is deemed recorded from the moment it is filed for record. The literal interpretation of the statute preserves as near as may be the grantee's position at common law. The factual patterns have varied, as the footnotes indicate. In some situations the instrument was still held by the officer, but there was no clue in the books to its existence; in others the instrument had been returned but the recording process was not completed; in others the instrument had been lost; in others the transcription was inaccurate. The rule of immateriality of the index has an understandable origin, even though it may not have current rationality. The need for an index apparently was not fully appreciated at first, and after the enactment of the recording acts, additional, independent statutes were passed directing the recording officer to prepare indexes to the records then in existence and henceforth to make indexes

---

17. There is inevitably an interval of time between the beginning and end of the process; careful search should reveal the existence of instruments in the officer's hands not yet transcribed or indexed. See Perkins v. Strong, 22 Neb. 725, 36 N.W. 292 (1888). This of course can be burdensome if hundreds or thousands of instruments are filed in a single day.

The Recording Acts

contemporaneously with the recording. The gap in time between the enactments fostered analysis of them separately.

From the standpoint of the recording process stated above the instruments are not really recorded. Of course some courts wisely so hold, and require more than mere "filing" with the officer; a few also conclude that indexing is a necessary part of recording. But wherever these positions, stated in the preceding paragraphs, are maintained, the record chain of title cannot reveal with certainty what the subsequent purchaser will get.

B. *The Time Element.* Even if there is full recording there are two situations in which the time element — the length of the link in the record chain — is particularly important: first, where the prior grantee's deed is recorded after the subsequent purchaser's deed is recorded; and second, where the prior grantee's deed is recorded before the grantor acquired the title which he purports to convey to the subsequent purchaser (the estoppel by deed or after-acquired title problem). Discussion of these problems can be simplified by use of symbols identifying X as the common grantor; A as the prior grantee with B and C as successors under A; and R as the subsequent purchaser with S and T as successors under R. A diagram may be helpful:

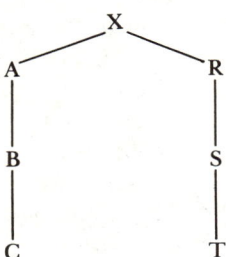

Thus the X-A transaction is prior in time of occurrence to the X-R transaction, and the A-B-C chain is prior in time of origin to the R-S-T chain.

1. The subsequent purchaser who records first. No problem in chain of title analysis arises when X is owner and conveys to A who records his deed before X conveys to R. The chain of title problem is presented when R records before A, but A records before the R-S transaction occurs. Even here there is no unresolved problem if R is within the protection of the recording act, because the title he secures with the aid of the act as a bona fide purchaser for value can be passed to S even though S knows of A's deed. However, when R knows of A's claim he is not protected by the act, and the question arises, can S who subsequently takes in actual good faith assert that he is protected by the act against A? Here the adoption or rejection of chain of title reasoning is crucial.

The practical mechanics of search are such that as to the period during which A records his deed, S will be searching for conveyances from R, having abandoned X as grantor on discovery of the X-R deed of record.

Since, according to the rationale, the X-A deed is not reasonably discoverable by S, he should take free of it. This may be called the Massachusetts view, whose object is protection of the subsequent purchaser. The contrary result may be called the New York view. In the latter, chain of title reasoning is believed not to be persuasive and emphasis is on protection of the prior grantee, A, when he has done all the statute specifically requires him to do. This is to record his deed; if he does not, the statute says certain persons are protected; if he does, no claimant getting into the picture thereafter (as S does) can get any protection from the statute. Difficulty of discovery is irrelevant. It is just unfortunate that the statute does not afford a greater practical protection to the subsequent purchaser. The New York view apparently finds acceptance in ten states and is the majority view.

2. *The estoppel by deed situation.* In the estoppel by deed area a preliminary distinction must be drawn. The operative effect of the estoppel by deed doctrine may be merely to prevent X from claiming title against his estoppel grantee, A (to whom X has "conveyed" before receiving title himself); or it may be that the title when secured by X automatically inures or passes to A. The latter approach, the inurement doctrine, is primarily important here. The competing claimants are A, the estoppel grantee, and R, to whom X conveyed after receiving title. Limiting his examination by the chain of title search, R will not discover A's deed in the record because as to the period of time in which A's deed is recorded R will be looking for conveyances by X's grantor not by X. Again, the recording statutes typically are silent. If as a matter of law the title is in A and he has recorded, he can assert that there is nothing in the usual statute by which he can be deprived of his title. The basic counter argument is that A was negligent in failing to discover from the record that X apparently had no title, while R has not been negligent and the spirit of the recording act requires that he should be protected. This may usually be true but it can hardly be said to be always true. An additional argument that the X-A deed is a nullity and recording is therefore meaningless seems to be an exaggeration. If the inurement doctrine is the rule in a jurisdiction by decision only (or if the estoppel by deed operates only to give A equitable protection against X), there may be fair reason to nullify it when it conflicts with the asserted protection given R by the statute. But if the inurement doctrine is the law by statute and the recording act does not specifically nullify it, there does not appear to be persuasive reason to prefer R through a claimed but unexpressed policy. It is asserted that the inurement doctrine in a majority of states gives way to the protection of the recording act for the subsequent purchaser, nonetheless there are several states where it has not given way, although the point was argued. These include, surprisingly enough, Massachusetts, which is strong on chain of title reasoning in the A against S controversy discussed above, as well as several other states in

[TABLE 5-1]

	Type of Statute[8]	Filing Sufficient or Index Immaterial[9]	A's delayed record binds S	Estoppel deed binds R[10]
Alabama	N	x		
Arizona	N			
Arkansas	N	x		
California	NR		x	
Colorado	N			
Connecticut	N	?		
Delaware	N			?
Florida	N	x		
Georgia	NR	x		?
Idaho	NR	?		x
Illinois	N(NR?)	x	x	x
Indiana	N			
Iowa	N		x	x
Kansas	N	x		
Kentucky	N	x		
Louisiana	R	x		
Maine	N			?

8. N, notice; R, race; NR, notice race. . . . In order to prevail, the subsequent purchaser must, in a notice jurisdiction, take without notice, while in a race jurisdiction, he must record first. In a notice-race jurisdiction, he must meet both requirements. In some states there was formerly a different type statute.

9. . . . A question mark denotes an equivocal statement in a case.

10. . . . A question mark indicates that the cases of the jurisdiction noted may not resolve the inurement-recording act conflict. . . .

which it is held that the title inures to A, no point being made of recordation, although in most cases A's deed was promptly recorded.

If in either of these last two situations A's priority is found, certainly it cannot be said that the chain of title passing from vendor back through A will establish the validity of the vendor's (X's) title!

C. *Recapitulation.* Combining the infirmities into a table presents this picture. [Reproduced in Table 5-1.]

NOTE

Assume a series of real estate transactions occurring in the following chronological order and each transaction nominally creating a first-mortgage interest in land: X, the fee owner, to A; X to B, B having no notice of the X-A mortgage; mortgage from X-A recorded; and then X to C, C having no actual notice of the X-A or X-B mortgages. At this point, who has what interests in a notice state, a race-notice state and a race state?

Note, The Tract and Grantor-Grantee Indices[13]
47 Iowa L. Rev. 481, 481-485 (1962)

A practical and convenient means of locating records which an owner of property must rely upon to prove his title and which a prospective purchaser must depend upon when making a title search is an indispensable part of a workable system of recordation. Therefore, it is not surprising to discover that statutory provisions providing for some system of indexing which affords a history of the ownership of land and which discloses instruments or encumbrances affecting title to real property have been enacted in every state. There are currently two types of indices in use: (1) the grantor-grantee index, and (2) the tract index. This should not be interpreted as meaning that a dual system of indexing has always been present in the United States, for under the land owned by the English, French, Mexican, and Spanish governments on the North American Continent, there were no numbered tract systems in existence which could serve as a basis for land description. This was, of course, directly related to the fact that a competent survey had never been made of the land owned by these countries. Under these circumstances, even tax levies had to be against the owners of the land rather than against the land itself. Therefore, it was only logical that when some system of indexing was finally adopted the alphabetical or grantor-grantee system of indexing was selected. Nevertheless, even after the United States Government acquired the land formerly held by foreign countries in what is now the United States and adequate Government surveys had been undertaken and completed, the grantor-grantee system of indexing was still retained as the basis of land description. However, it was gradually discovered that the grantor-grantee system of indexing was inadequate in many respects. This led several states to enact statutes establishing a tract or numerical system of indexing. Nevertheless, even those states which adopted the tract system of indexing retained the alphabetical system of indexing which they had established at an earlier date.

Under the grantor-grantee or alphabetical index, pages are assigned in the index to each letter of the alphabet. As an instrument is received at the recorder's office, it is first recorded and then indexed under the name of

---

13. On tract indexes by individual parcels or multiparcel areas, see also Booz, Allen and Hamilton, State-of-the-Art Report 132-135 (1978), prepared for the U.S. Department of Housing and Urban Development. Automated parcel indexes are also possible; they have been established and are being used by some title insurance companies. On such automated indexes, see id. at 135-139.

the granting party on the appropriate page of the index. In addition, the county recorder is usually required to make notations on the grantor's page which disclose the name of the other party to the transaction, the book and page of the record where this particular transaction can be found, a description of the property, the date when the instrument was executed, the date when the instrument was filed for recordation, and the nature of the instrument. These same notations are then made as the transaction is indexed under the name of the grantee or the receiving party. After both steps have been completed, the instrument is considered to have been properly indexed.

Under the tract indexing system each parcel of land in a certain area is assigned a separate page in the index and every subsequent transaction affecting this property will be noted thereon. Under the tract system of indexing, a "parcel of land" means any geographical unit of land which has been surveyed and platted, such as sections, blocks, and lots. In addition to describing the property, the tract index also discloses the character of the instrument which affects the title to the property, the date of the execution of the instrument, the date of the filing of the instrument for recordation, and the names of the parties to the transaction. Under this system, therefore, *all* the instruments which affect the title to a particular parcel of realty will be noted on one page of the index. For this reason and innumerable others, the uniform adoption of the tract index has been urged by many legal scholars. However, the reaction of the respective state legislatures to this proposal apparently has not been enthusiastic. This fact has led one respected scholar to exclaim: "Nevertheless, it is a rebuke to legislators, and to the legal profession, that . . . the courts must determine priorities on the basis of an outmoded and generally unused system of indices." However, in view of the persistence of this course of action and the likelihood that a jurisdiction will retain its grantor-grantee system of indexing even if it adopts the tract index, a comparison of the advantages offered by the two different systems when applied to established doctrines in the law of property would appear to be appropriate.

I. Relation of Indexing to Recordation

In property law, an index is generally defined as a means provided for pointing out or indicating where the record to a certain parcel of realty may be found. The implication created by such a definition is that an index constitutes no part of the record. Nevertheless, a split of authority exists on the issue whether indexing is in fact necessary to complete recordation. The prevailing view is that an index forms no part of the record. Therefore, the instrument filed constitutes constructive notice of its existence from the time it is delivered to the county recorder even though the recorder fails to index it. A great number of the decisions which support this view rely on the construction of the applicable state statutes in that recordation and indexing are usually provided for in separate sections of the state code. Therefore, the courts rationalize that had the legislators intended the index to be an indispensable part of the record without which the record would not impart constructive notice of its contents, they would have either provided for indexing in the same section of the code which provided for recordation or they would have specifically stated in the statutes that indexing was necessary to complete recordation.

The minority view considers indexing to be an essential part of recordation without which the record does not impart constructive notice of its contents. In some instances, state statutes are directly responsible for this view in that they expressly state that without indexing, the act of recordation is incomplete. However, the consideration of one of the fundamental purposes of the recording acts — affording protection to the subsequent purchaser — in conjunction with the state statute which requires indexing is the most common source of justification for this view. Accordingly, if this view were to be accepted, in many instances the record would be considered of no effect when there had been either an absence of indexing or improper indexing even though the complaining party had not relied on the index. This view is consistent with the result which is reached in all instances involving the filing of instruments and their transcription to the permanent record. This rule persists because a system of recording is not based on whether there is an actual search of the records but, rather, on whether proper documents have been provided so that *if* a party decides to make a title search, a complete record will be at his disposal. Regardless of the fact that the minority rule is based upon one of the underlying purposes of recordation, it is clear that the rule cannot solve all the problems which arise in the area of indexing. In the case of Barney v. McCarty some of these problems were faced by the Iowa Supreme Court. The plaintiff had acquired a mortgage which the county recorder had not indexed until twelve years after the time the plaintiff had presented his mortgage for recording. During this twelve-year period, the property in question was sold to the defendants who claimed to be purchasers for value without notice. On an appeal to the Iowa Supreme Court, the court affirmed the trial court's refusal to render a foreclosure decree ordering a sale of the property involved to repay the mortgage held by the plaintiff and pointed out that the Iowa code expressly required the filing of the instrument, the copying of the instrument into the record book, and the indexing of the instrument. Relying on the purposes for the establishment of a system of recordation, the court interpreted the legislative intent as requiring the indexing of an instrument before there could be valid recordation. Such a result undoubtedly places upon a grantee the burden of maintaining some surveillance over the actions of the county recorder until he records and properly indexes an instrument. It is obvious that the decision reached by the court in the Barney case affords a subsequent purchaser more protection than he receives under the rule that indexing is not essential to complete recordation in that in this instance, the *grantee* of the property rather than the subsequent purchaser suffers for the mistakes of the county recorder. Although a burden is undoubtedly imposed upon a grantee under this rule, nevertheless, the grantee is in a much better position to ensure the sufficient indexing of his instrument than is the subsequent purchaser. Requiring him to ensure that the instrument is indexed would not be harsh in view of the fact that a subsequent purchaser ordinarily would have no notice whatsoever of the prior transaction and could acquire none by investigating the index.

Another related problem is present in those jurisdictions which follow the rule that indexing is essential to recordation in that the courts usually conclude that recordation is complete only when there has been "sufficient" or "proper" indexing. Generally, the courts have considered an entry in an index "sufficient" or "proper" if it is complete enough to direct a searcher to the record, even though some detail required by statute to be indexed has been omitted or incorrectly reported. In view of the fact that an index is the only practical source for examining the state of the title to realty and, therefore, relied upon by all title examiners, the index should logically be made an essential part of the record without which the record does not impart constructive notice of the existence of an instrument. The adoption of a statute requiring this procedure would not only afford more security to land titles, but would also ensure greater protection of subsequent purchasers.

NOTES

1. As a matter of policy, should the chain of title limitation on constructive notice of recorded instruments be legally inapplicable in any county that has a public tract index whether or not that index is made an essential part of the record by statute or case law? Should it be inapplicable if a private tract index for recorded land transactions in the county is maintained by a private abstract company or title insurer and used in preparing abstracts or passing on applications for insurance?

2. Who should be preferred in defective indexing cases — parties who record or subsequent takers who are obligated to search the records? Should it make any difference that, although they rarely make later checks to determine if indexing has taken place, parties who record have it within their power to do so?

3. The prevailing position is that those who file instruments for recording assume the risk that the recorder's office will fail to transcribe or will accurately transcribe so that subsequent purchasers are on constructive notice only of instruments as copied into the public records. Patton

and Patton, Land Titles §64 (2d ed. 1957). Risk is often allocated differently in defective transcription cases from defective indexing cases: commonly to the person filing for record if there is an error in transcription, to the subsequent purchaser if there is an indexing error. How can such differences be justified? In both kinds of situations should not risk be on the same person?

4. Until an instrument filed for record has been transcribed by the recorder's office, the original is kept in the recorder's possession, available for examination by those searching titles. Transcription usually takes place within a few days. After transcription the original normally is returned to the party who filed it for record.

How long should the original be constructive notice if kept in the recorder's possession and not transcribed? In Whalley v. Small, 25 Iowa 184 (1868), a deed of trust was filed for record in 1842 and apparently through inadvertence never transcribed but kept in the recorder's office. In 1860, the grantor of the deed of trust conveyed the property and the grantee and subsequent takers through him were unaware of the deed of trust when they acquired their interests. In litigation over the title the Iowa Supreme Court held that the subsequent purchasers did not take subject to the deed of trust. In its opinion the court said at 189-190:

> In the nature of things, there must, of necessity, exist a period of time between the filing and recording. The law designs that during such reasonable time that may so intervene, the filing shall be notice of the instrument. But certainly, it would be extending great indulgence to officers and parties whose duty it is to record and procure the recording of the instrument, to give them more than a quarter of a century, the time which expired in this case, to record and index the instrument after it is filed, and yet, to hold that during all of this long period the deed, slumbering forgotten in some out-of-the-way receptacle of the recorder's office, operates as notice to the world of its contents, while at the same time the very parties who claim under it are ignorant of its existence. Such an interpretation of the law would defeat its very object.
>
> The filing fixes the time from which the notice of the instrument commences, under the presumption that reasonable diligence will be exercised to comply with the other directions of the law made for its lawful registration. Within what time this must be done, it is not for us now to determine, further than to hold, that a quarter of a century cannot be considered a reasonable or proper time to permit the instrument to lie unrecorded, and that the filing cannot be considered as imparting notice during this long period.

5. In most jurisdictions, if the copy of an instrument properly of record is destroyed or disappears, it continues to give constructive notice. Patton and Patton, Land Titles §23 (2d ed. 1957). A major risk, of course,

The Recording Acts

is destruction of public records by fire or other natural calamity; and there have been instances in which substantially all recorded instruments in a county have been lost when the structure in which they were stored was destroyed. Some states have legislation, often referred to as burnt record acts, specifically directed to this problem. Often these acts were passed following major holocausts and provide procedures for accommodating to the massive record losses that occurred. For example, see Ill. Laws 1871-1872, at 652-662, a burnt records act passed after the Chicago Fire of 1871; and Cal. Stat. 1906, Extra Sess., cc. 52-59, at 70-82, enacted following the San Francisco Earthquake of 1906.

Section 1 of the Illinois Burnt Records Act, Ill. Rev. Stat. c. 116, §5 (1981), provides:

> Whenever it shall appear that the records, or any material part thereof, of any county in this state have been destroyed by fire or otherwise, any map, plat, deed, conveyance, contract, mortgage, deed of trust, or other instrument in writing affecting real estate in such county, which has been heretofore recorded, or certified copies of such, may be re-recorded; and in recording the same the recorder shall record the certificate of the previous record, and the date of filing for record appearing in said original certificate so recorded shall be deemed and taken as the date of the record thereof. And copies of any such record, so authorized to be made under this section, duly certified by the recorder of any such county, under his seal of office, shall be received in evidence, and have the same force and effect as certified copies of the original record.

Under this section of the Illinois act, there is no obligation to re-record, and a subsequent purchaser takes subject to the recorded interest even if the record has been destroyed and not re-recorded. Gammon v. Hodges, 73 Ill. 140 (1874). But in Kentucky Coal & Timber Development Co. v. Conley, 184 Ky. 274, 211 S.W. 734 (1919), a duty was placed on a grantee to record his deed when the recorded copy was destroyed in a fire. Failure to record within a reasonable time resulted in the instrument being treated as though never recorded, and a subsequent purchaser without notice was held to have superior title. The court considered this "a case calling for the application of the rule that where the loss must fall on one of two innocent parties, it will be put on him whose negligence has made the loss possible."

6. Unless he has made a search of the public records, should a subsequent taker be preferred by the recording acts to a prior unrecorded interest holder? Unless he has actually relied on the public records, is the subsequent taker deserving of the acts' protection? What if the motive of the subsequent taker in not examining the public records is to avoid the risk of actual notice from discovery of instruments put of record that do not give constructive notice, such as defectively acknowledged deeds?

7. An Arizona statute provides as follows:

Any document evidencing the sale, or other transfer of real estate or any legal or equitable interest therein, excluding leases, shall be recorded by the transferor in the county in which the property is located and within sixty days of the transfer. In lieu thereof, the transferor shall indemnify the transferee in any action in which the transferee's interest in such property is at issue, including costs, attorney's fees and punitive damages. [Ariz. Rev. Stat. Ann. §33-411.01 (Supp. 1984-85).]

Why does the Arizona statute obligate recording by the transferor rather than the transferee? Under what kinds of situations may the statute result in liability of the transferor to the transferee?

d. Notice From Other Public Records

There are many kinds of public records pertaining to land titles other than those records required by the recording acts.[14] In no state are all these records centralized in one place, but some states have gone much farther than others in the degree of centralization provided for. In some states, the offices of recorders of deeds contain not only conveyancing records but a number of other kinds of land title records as well. Important land title records can also be found in public offices of various court clerks (for judicial records pertaining to land) and county treasurers (for property tax records evidencing tax liens on land).

In the course of their title searching, professional title searchers customarily check through public records other than those that the recording acts say must be kept. It is also customary in the course of their work for professional searchers to go to public offices other than those of recorders of deeds. Local variations exist in the broadness and intensity of these searches. As will be shown in the materials on title insurance, large abstract and title insurance companies often facilitate their title searches by duplicating many of the public land records for a particular county and keeping them on their own premises in more easily searchable form. These private collections of public records are known in the trade as title plants.

In considering different kinds of public records, special attention should be given to why the records are required and whom they are intended to benefit. In particular, what effect do the records have on land titles; and what inducement is there for prospective transferees of land interests to have the records searched?

---

14. You are reminded again of the narrow meaning here given to the term "recording acts." See the introductory comments at the beginning of this chapter. Note that the term is occasionally given a different usage by legal authorities, and some or all of the statutes authorizing other kinds of public records also sometimes are referred to as recording acts.

Lane and Edson, Land Title Recordation Systems: Legal Constraints and Reforms[15]
II-25 (1978)

A recurring complaint of title searchers is that they cannot limit their searching efforts to the records lodged in the recording office, but must also examine the records maintained in numerous other public offices. How many other public offices need to be visited varies with each state, and often with each county within a state. A thorough search of title might necessitate visits to the county offices of the tax assessor and sheriff, to the offices of the clerks of the county court of general jurisdiction and of the county probate court, to the offices of the city tax assessor and health department, to the office of the clerk of the city court of general jurisdiction, to the office of the clerk of the federal district court, and to state offices at the state capital with responsibility for the collection of state taxes and for corporate status. The principal events reflected in the documents that these offices maintain of concern to the title searchers are those directly affecting the property (such as lis pendens filings and unpaid real estate taxes), and those directly affecting the property owner with possible consequences on his title. Except for real estate taxes and special assessments, most of these documents are indexed only under an individual's or business name, as, for example, a defaulting taxpayer, a deceased owner, or a defendant to a judicial action.

Two common problems face title searchers seeking information about these kinds of events. One is the physical distance between the county recorder's office where the land conveyancing documents are maintained and the offices housing these other records. The distances and relative inconveniences vary, of course. In one suburban Philadelphia county, the recorder's office and the office of the county registrar of wills are on the same floor in the same building; in the next county, they are in different buildings separated by two miles of clogged urban streets. The relevant state offices are usually in the state capital which may be across the state. The separateness of these records and their different physical locations cause the process of title searching to take longer and cost more than if the records were integrated. The maintenance costs of private title plants must also be increased because of the more difficult logistics in continually collecting documents from so many different locations.

Another serious problem is that, except for real estate taxes and special property assessments, these records are indexed by the names of the individual or business property owners. Finding the correct names in volumi-

---

15. A report prepared for the U.S. Department of Housing and Urban Development, pursuant to a contract with Booz, Allen & Hamilton, Inc. Footnotes omitted.

nous name indexes can be difficult because of inadequate alphabetization and multiple and variant names. We need to take a closer look at this latter problem.

Whitehurst v. Abbot
225 N.C. 1, 33 S.E.2d 129 (1945)

Special proceeding for the sale of land for partition by Ada V. Whitehurst and others against Henry D. Abbott. From an adverse judgment, plaintiff appeals.

New trial.

Special proceedings for the sale of land for partition in which defendant filed answer denying the alleged title of plaintiffs and pleading sole seizin and adverse possession under color for more than twenty years. The answer having raised issues of fact, the cause was transferred to the civil issue docket of Camden County Superior Court for trial.

John L. Hinton, a resident of Pasquotank County, died testate in January 1910, and on January 29, 1910 his will was probated in common form in Pasquotank County. A copy of the will was certified to and recorded in the office of the clerk of the Superior Court of Camden County.

The will devised the lands of testator to his wife and his children other than J. C. Hinton who predeceased the testator. No provision was made in the will for the widow and children of the deceased son.

At the time of his death the testator owned a tract of land in Camden County known as the Abbott Ridge Farm containing 324 acres. On August 12, 1910, R. L. Hinton, son of the testator, purchased the interest of the other devisees and took deed therefor which was duly registered in the Camden County registry.

On September 30, 1918, the widow and children of J. C. Hinton, deceased, filed a caveat to the will of John L. Hinton. No notice of lis pendens was filed in Camden County or indexed or cross-indexed in the lis pendens docket in the office of the clerk of the Superior Court in Pasquotank County.

On July 24, 1919, R. L. Hinton, while the hearing on the caveat was pending, conveyed the Abbott Ridge Farm in Camden County to one T. G. McPherson.

On January 10, 1920, judgment was entered in the caveat proceedings sustaining the caveat on the grounds of mental incapacity and undue influence and declaring the will null and void. On appeal to this Court the judgment was affirmed. In re Hinton's Will, 180 N.C. 206, 104 S.E. 341. The judgment declaring the will null and void was not certified to Camden County and no marginal entry was made on the certified copy of the will as recorded in Camden.

On December 4, 1923, McPherson conveyed to defendant Henry D.

Abbott that part of the Camden County farm which is described in the complaint and is the subject matter of this action.

When the cause came on for hearing in the court below, the jury, by their answers to the issues submitted, found that T. G. McPherson and H. D. Abbott were each purchasers for value and without notice of the claim of plaintiffs. There was judgment on the verdict decreeing that plaintiffs have no right, title, or interest in the land in controversy and plaintiffs appealed. . . .

BARNHILL, Justice. R. L. Hinton was a devisee, executor, and propounder of the will of John L. Hinton. He purchased the interest of the other devisees in the Camden County property. He and the other devisees were dealing inter partes in the property of the estate. He conveyed the land after the caveat was filed. Any claim that he was an innocent third party and that his deed, executed pendente lite, conveyed a good title is without substance. To hold otherwise would open the door for parties to litigation to convey the subject matter of the litigation pending a hearing and thus render the court powerless to enforce its own decrees. Newbern v. Hinton, 190 N.C. 108, 129 S.E. 181.

As to T. G. McPherson, grantee of R. L. Hinton, a different question arises. Had he purchased before the filing of the caveat unquestionably under our decisions his title would have been unassailable. G.S. §31-39: Newbern v. Leigh, 184 N.C. 166, 113 S.E. 674, 26 A.L.R. 266; Whitehurst v. Hinton, 209 N.C. 392, 184 S.E. 66; Anno. 26 A.L.R. 270. But such is not the case. He acquired title to the property in Camden after the filing of the caveat from one of the devisees who was directly affected by the proceedings then pending in Pasquotank, the county in which the original will was probated. Is he charged with constructive notice of the claim of plaintiffs?

At common law a pending suit was regarded as notice to all the world. The complaint or cross-complaint, as the case might be, was the lis pendens and any person dealing with the property pendente lite was bound by the judgment rendered. Massachusetts Bonding & Insurance Co. v. Knox, 220 N.C. 725, 18 S.E.2d 436, 138 A.L.R. 1438; 34 Am. Jur. 363.

The ever-increasing volume of litigation rendered this common-law rule so harsh and burdensome upon abstracters that the Legislature intervened and adopted the modifying Acts now incorporated in Article 11, Chapter 1, General Statutes of North Carolina. Now the pending action does not constitute notice as to land in another county until and unless notice thereof is filed in the county in which the land is located. G.S. §1-116 et seq.; Collingwood v. Brown, 106 N.C. 362, 10 S.E. 868; Spencer v. Credle, 102 N.C. 68, 8 S.E. 901.

When a will is probated in common form, any interested party may appear and enter a caveat. G.S. §31-32. But a caveat is an in rem proceedings. In effect it is nothing more than a demand that the will be produced and probated in open court, affording the caveators an opportunity to attack it for the causes and upon the grounds set forth and alleged in the caveat. It is an attack upon the validity of the instrument purporting to be a will and not an "action affecting the title to real property." The will and not the land devised is the res involved in the litigation. Prospective purchasers were held to notice that probate jurisdiction was in Pasquotank County and if they acquired title without ascertaining the status of the proceedings in that county they did so at their peril. Hence the lis pendens statute has no application. So contend the appellants.

Thus we are called upon to decide the force and effect of the lis pendens statute as it related to a caveat proceedings.

The registration statute, G.S. §43-18, modifies the common-law rule of lis pendens. Its purpose is to stabilize titles by requiring recordation of all deeds, mortgages, or other paper writings which transfer or encumber the title to land. Our lis pendens statute, above cited, is designed to supplement the registration law and to provide a simple and readily available means of ascertaining the existence of adverse claims to land not otherwise disclosed by the registry. Notice under the Act is required to give constructive notice to prospective purchasers when the claim is in derogation of the record. Insurance Co. v. Knox, supra.

The effect of lis pendens and the effect of registration are in their nature the same thing. They are only different examples of the operation of the rule of constructive notice. One is simply a record in one place and the other is a record in another place. Each serves its purpose in proper instances. They are each record notices upon the absence of which a prospective innocent purchaser may rely.

Bearing this broad general purpose in mind it would seem to be apparent that the Legislature intended the term "action," as used in G.S. §1-116, to embrace all judicial proceedings affecting the title to real property or in which title to land is at issue.

Naturally proceedings in court are divided into various classifications. Each class has its own particular label. But the word "action," when unqualified, is an inclusive term and connotes all judicial proceedings of a civil nature maintained and prosecuted for the purpose of asserting a right or redressing a wrong. When qualified, as in the statute, by the term "affecting the title to real property," it includes and embraces all such proceedings wherein the title to real property is at issue.

Such is a caveat. Though not an adverse proceedings in the ordinary sense, interested parties are notified and given an opportunity to be heard. Legal rights are at stake and the issues raised are tried as in other civil actions.

While in one sense the will is the res involved in the caveat proceedings, it is quite clear that any final decree entered therein will directly affect the title to the land devised. The probated will constitutes a muniment of title unassailable except in a direct proceedings. G.S. §31-19. It operates as a conveyance of title to the land devised. Any action or proceedings contesting its validity directly assails the validity of such conveyance and necessarily involves the title. Hence the filing of notice under the lis pendens statute is essential to give constructive notice to those who are not directly interested in the proceedings. McIlwrath v. Hollander, 73 Mo. 105, 39 Am. Rep. 484.

But lis pendens notice under the statute is not exclusive. Nor is it designed to protect intermeddlers. When a person acquires an interest in property pending an action in which the title thereto is at issue, from one of the parties to the action, with notice of the action, actual or constructive, he is bound by the judgment in the action just as the party from whom he bought would have been. This rule seems to be universal and is considered by all the courts to be absolutely necessary to give effect to the judgments of the courts because, if it was not so held, a party could always defeat the judgment by conveying in anticipation of it to some stranger and the claimant would be compelled to commence a new action against him. Rollins v. Henry, 78 N.C. 342; Jarrett v. Holland, 213 N.C. 428, 196 S.E. 314.

"Our statute on the subject . . . only purports to deal with constructive notice and its effect on subsequent purchasers, but, where one buys from a litigant with full notice or knowledge of the suit and of its nature and purpose and the specific property to be affected, he is concluded or his purchase will be held ineffective and fraudulent as to decree rendered in the cause and the rights thereby established. Griswold v. Miller, 15 Barb. [N.Y.] 520; Corwin v. Bensley, 43 Cal. 253-262; Wick v. Dawson, 48 W. Va. 469-475, 37 S.E. 639; 25 Cyc. p. 1425; Bennett on Lis Pendens, p. 319." Morris v. Basnight, 179 N.C. 298, 102 S.E. 389, 391.

Plaintiffs offered evidence tending to show that when the court proceedings was being heard at the January Term, 1919, McPherson was present in court and that he talked about the case in the presence of his son and his brother, all prior to the time he purchased. Upon this evidence, which is uncontradicted, plaintiffs duly requested the court to give a peremptory charge on the second issue which is as follows: "Did T. G. McPherson purchase the lands in controversy for value and without notice of plaintiff's claim?"

The court declined to give the requested instruction. Instead it charged the jury that the burden rested upon the plaintiffs to show that McPherson "did not purchase it for value and that at the time he, T. G. McPherson, had notice of plaintiff's claim to the land in question" and that if they failed to so find they should answer the second issue "Yes." In this there was error prejudicial to the plaintiffs.

As heretofore stated a party directly interested in judicial proceeding affecting the title to real property cannot convey a good title to the res pendente lite. Even so, the grantee acquires a good title provided he purchases (1) for value, and (2) without notice, actual or constructive. Both conditions must appear. Hence the absence of either is fatal.

The uncontroverted evidence tends to show and it seems to be admitted that Hinton conveyed to McPherson pendente lite. This being true, his deed was ineffective and fraudulent as against the final decree in the pending action. Upon such showing plaintiffs were entitled to judgment, certainly as against McPherson, unless it should be made to appear that he purchased for value and without notice. This is an affirmative defense and he who claims to be a bona fide purchaser for value without notice so as to avoid the defective character of his deed has the burden of proving that fact. Hughes v. Fields, 168 N.C. 520, 84 S.E. 804; King v. McRackan, 168 N.C. 621, 84 S.E. 1027, affirmed on rehearing, King v. McRackan, 171 N.C. 752, 88 S.E. 226; 27 R.C.L. 737.

The conditions under which defendant acquired title are on this record immaterial. At that time there was no presumptively valid will of record operating as a muniment of title. It had been annulled by decree of court. It protects a purchaser only until vacated. G.S. §31-19. It follows that his title rests squarely upon the title possessed by his grantor.

If McPherson was an innocent purchaser for value, his deed to defendant conveyed title in fee to the land therein described. Conversely if McPherson purchased with notice, then immediately upon the entry of the final decree in the caveat proceedings invalidating the will, the plaintiffs, as heirs-at-law of J. C. Hinton, by operation of law, became seized and possessed of an undivided interest in the Camden County land. From that instant they were tenants in common with McPherson. His deed to defendant thereafter executed conveyed only such interest as he possessed and the vested interest of plaintiffs can be defeated only by twenty years' adverse possession pleaded by defendant.

But defendant insists that even though, at the time he purchased, the will was void, the certified copy thereof filed in Camden County was still of record without any notation or entry that would operate as notice to him of the judgment entered in Pasquotank County and that he had the right to rely on this record as a valid link in his chain of title. We cannot so hold.

Whatever may be the effect of Chap. 108, P.L. 1921, the rights of the parties to this action accrued prior to its enactment and are to be controlled by the law as it existed before the effective date of that statute.

At that time it was the original will as probated in the county in which the testator resided at the time of his death that constituted the muniment of title as to all land devised. C.S. §4145. Ownership under the will in nowise is made dependent upon the certified copy directed to be recorded in the county where the land lies. C.S. §4163. The only purpose of the certified copy disclosed by the pertinent statute was to give information to abstracters and to direct their attention to the source of title — the will as originally probated. Hence when the original will was annulled by judicial decree the certified copy ceased to have any force and effect for any purpose.

Nor is defendant protected by the provisions of Sec. 2 of the 1921 statute. At the time of its enactment the final decree had been entered. There was no valid will of record. If McPherson purchased with notice title had vested in plaintiffs. The Legislature was without authority to divest them of their title and revest it in McPherson. It is not to be presumed that the General Assembly so intended. In any event the Act cannot be so construed. Section 17, 19, Art. I, N.C. Const.

It follows that there must be a new trial in accord with this opinion. It is so ordered.

New trial.

NOTES

1. The North Carolina lis pendens statutes, N.C. Gen. Stat. §§1-116 to 1-120.1 (Michie 1983), are fairly typical of such enactments in many of the states. They provide as follows:

§1-116. *Filing of notice of suit.* (a) Any person desiring the benefit of constructive notice of pending litigation must file a separate, independent notice thereof, which notice shall be cross-indexed in accordance with G.S. 1-117, in the following cases:

(1) Action affecting title to real property;
(2) Actions to foreclose any mortgage or deed of trust or to enforce any lien on real property; and
(3) Actions in which any order of attachment is issued and real property is attached.

(b) Notice of pending litigation shall contain:

(1) The name of the court in which the section has been commenced or is pending;
(2) The names of the parties to the action;
(3) The nature and purpose of the action; and
(4) A description of the property to be affected thereby.

(c) Notice of pending litigation may be filed:

(1) At or any time after the commencement of an action pursuant to Rule 3 of the Rules of Civil Procedure; or
(2) At or any time after real property has been attached; or
(3) At or any time after the filing of an answer or other pleading in which the pleading party states an affirmative claim for relief falling within the provisions of subsection (a) of this section.

(d) Notice of pending litigation must be filed with the clerk of the superior court of each county in which any part of the real estate is located, not excepting the county in which the action is pending, in order to be effective against bona fide purchasers or lien creditors with respect to the real property located in such county.

§1-116.1. *Service of notice.* In all actions as defined in §1-116 in which notice of the pendency of the action is filed, a copy of such notice shall be served on the other party or parties. . . .

§1-117. *Cross-index of lis pendens.* Every notice of pending litigation filed under this article shall be cross-indexed by the clerk of the superior court in a record, called the "Record of Lis Pendens" to be kept by him pursuant to G.S. 2-42(6).

§1-118. *Effect on subsequent purchasers.* From the cross-indexing of the notice of lis pendens only is the pendency of the action constructive notice to a purchaser or incumbrancer of the property affected thereby; and every person whose conveyance or incumbrance is subsequently executed or subsequently registered is a subsequent purchaser or incumbrancer, and is bound by all proceedings taken after the cross-indexing of the notice to the same extent as if he were made a party to the action. For the purposes of this section an action is pending from the time of cross-indexing the notice.

§1-119. *Notice void unless action prosecuted.* The notice of lis pendens is of no avail unless it is followed by the first publication of notice of the summons or by an affidavit therefor pursuant to Rule 4(j)(1)c of the Rules of Civil Procedure or by personal service on the defendant within sixty days after the cross-indexing. . . .

§1-120. Cancellation of notice.— The court in which the said action was commenced may, at any time after it is settled, discontinued or abated, on application of any person aggrieved, on good cause shown, and on such notice as is directed or approved by the court, order the notice authorized by this article to be cancelled of record, by the clerk of any county in whose office the same has been filed or recorded; and this cancellation must be made by an endorsement to that effect on the margin of the record, which shall refer to the order.

§1-120.1 *Article applicable to suits in federal courts.* The provisions of this Article shall apply to suits affecting the title to real property in the federal courts.

2. In their detailed requirements, lis pendens statutes vary somewhat from state to state. For example, a common requirement is that for lis pendens to apply, descriptive information concerning the suit must be filed with a designated public official who maintains sets of records readily accessible to persons examining land titles. But statutes differ as to which public official shall be responsible for accepting and maintaining lis pendens records. Some states follow the North Carolina requirement that it be the clerk of the general court of first instance in the county where the land is located; for example, Fla. Stat. Ann. §48.23(1) (West 1976). Other states provide that it be the recorder of deeds; for example, Cal. Civ. Proc. Code §409 (West Supp. 1985). And in some, no special filing of notice is necessary, service of summons charges third persons with notice of pendency of suit. One such statute is Ohio Rev. Code Ann. §§2703.26 to 2703.27

The Recording Acts

(Page 1981), but only as to suits brought in the county where the land is located. Some states place a time limit on the effectiveness of lis pendens notices. In New York, for example, the effective notice period is three years. N.Y. Civ. Prac. Law §6513 (McKinney 1980).

3. One rationale for lis pendens is that it prevents parties to litigation from avoiding the effects of a possible adverse judgment by conveying out during pendency of the proceedings. So in most states the filing of a lis pendens can have consequences only for subsequent takers of interests in the land involved. Those who acquire their interests prior to filing of the lis pendens are generally unaffected by the litigation unless made parties. However, in some states, those who acquire interests in the land prior to the litigation, but fail to record prior to filing of the lis pendens, are also bound by any judgment as though they had taken subsequent to the lis pendens filing. See Bristol Lumber Co. v. Dery, 114 Conn. 88, 157 A. 640 (1932); and Jones v. Jones, 249 Miss. 322, 161 So. 2d 640 (1964). What justification can there be for making such prior unrecorded transferees subject to lis pendens doctrine?

4. There have been serious challenges recently to lis pendens statutes as providing inadequate notice and hearing opportunities and thereby violating procedural due process. On this problem see Lis Pendens: A Legislative Response to a Judicial Invitation, 7 Seton Hall Legis. J. 59 (1983), considering a New Jersey statute; Note, Connecticut's Lis Pendens Shapes Up: Williams v. Bartlett, 16 Conn. L. Rev. 413 (1984); and Note, A Proposal for Reformation of the Iowa Lis Pendens Statute, 67 Iowa L. Rev. 289 (1982).

First Federal Savings & Loan Assn. of Miami v. Fisher
60 So. 2d 496 (Fla. 1952)

CHAPMAN, Justice. On September 16, 1939, a final decree of divorce and property settlement was entered in the Circuit Court of Dade County, Florida, in the case of Freda Y. Fisher v. Porter G. Fisher. The following pertinent provisions are set out in the final decree: . . .

"Ordered, adjudged and decreed that the bonds of matrimony heretofore and now existing between complainant, Freda Y. Fisher, and the defendant, Porter G. Fisher, be and the same are hereby forever dissolved, and that the complainant and defendant are hereby divorced one from the other, a vinculo matrimonii; and it is hereby further

"Ordered, adjudged and decreed that the agreement heretofore entered into by and between the complainant and defendant herein, dated September 11, 1939, providing for the matters of custody of the child, P. Graham Fisher, his maintenance, the matters of alimony and property settlements, be and the same *is hereby in all respects approved.* . . ."

The following stipulations signed by Freda Y. Fisher and husband, Porter G. Fisher, were before the Court at the time of the entry of the divorce decree and property settlement on September 16, 1939, to wit:

"It is stipulated by and between the undersigned complainant and defendant and their respective solicitors in the above styled cause that, if a final decree of divorce is entered, said decree shall contain the following provisions. . . .

"6. Defendant is also to maintain the house at 531 49th Street, Miami Beach, Florida for a home for the complainant and her son. . . .

"7. *In the event defendant dies or remarries, then, in that event the defendant's interest in the house shall be conveyed to the son P. Graham Fisher.* . . ."

Some two or three months after the date of the decree, on November 13, 1939, Porter G. Fisher remarried and the second wife was Alma F. Fisher. On July 19, 1946, Porter G. Fisher and wife, Alma F. Fisher, made, executed and delivered their promissory note in the sum of $10,400 payable to the First Federal Savings and Loan Association of Miami. Simultaneously with the execution and delivery of the aforesaid promissory note they secured the payment thereof by execution of a mortgage to the Federal Savings Bank, which described the home owned by Porter G. Fisher located at 531 49th Street, Miami Beach, Florida. The mortgage was duly recorded in the office of the Clerk of the Circuit Court of Dade County, Florida. The home described in the mortgage supra was in the possession of Freda Y. Fisher and son, Porter G. Fisher, Jr., when the note and mortgage were executed by the husband, Porter G. Fisher, Sr., and the second Mrs. Fisher (Alma F. Fisher). It appears that the first Mrs. Fisher and son occupied the home pursuant to the divorce stipulations made a part of the final decree.

The Federal Savings and Loan Association, on February 9, 1949, filed foreclosure proceedings on the mortgage given it by Porter G. Fisher and wife, Alma F. Fisher. The proceeding progressed to a final decree, when the property was sold by a Special Master, and a Special Master's deed was executed conveying the residential property supra to the First Federal Savings and Loan Association. On June 25, 1950, Freda Y. Fisher filed in her divorce suit her motion for a final decree for arrears in support and also to enforce the provisions of paragraph 7 of the stipulations, to wit: "7. In the event defendant dies or remarries, then, in that event, the defendant's (Porter G. Fisher's) interest in the house shall be conveyed to the son P. Graham Fisher." The Chancellor below heard the parties on the motion and other appropriate pleadings and entered its order requiring Porter G. Fisher to convey his right, title and interest in the home occupied by Freda Y. Fisher and son situated at 531 49th Street, Miami, Florida, in accordance with the provisions of Section 7 supra of the stipulations signed by the parties when the divorce decree was entered. On May 25, 1951, Porter G. Fisher and wife, Alma F. Fisher, executed and delivered to Porter G. Fisher, Jr., a deed to the described property, pursuant to an order or decree of the Court below. It was recorded among the public records of Dade County, Florida, on June 4, 1951.

On August 15, 1951, Porter G. Fisher, Jr., filed in the Circuit Court of Dade County, Florida, his suit to quiet title as against the First Federal Savings and Loan Association and alleged that the Special Master's deed acquired by it through the foreclosure of its mortgage was subject to, inferior and subservient to the title conveyed to Porter G. Fisher, Jr., by his father, Porter G. Fisher, Sr., and wife, Alma F. Fisher, and said conveyance was a cloud which created doubt and suspicion as to the true fee simple title held and owned by Porter G. Fisher, Jr. That the title conveyed by the Special Master to the Federal Savings and Loan Association was made with full knowledge and notice of the provisions described in Section 7 of the divorce stipulation, which was approved and confirmed by the final decree of divorce. Section 7 thereof could have been ascertained by an examination of the final decree of divorce duly recorded among the public records of Dade County, Florida. Also, Freda Y. Fisher and son, Porter G. Fisher, Jr., were in the open, adverse and continuous possession of the home and were residing therein prior and subsequent to the date of giving the note and mortgage to the Savings Association. The Chancellor, by an appropriate decree, cancelled the Special Master's deed to the First Federal Savings and Loan Association as a cloud upon title as held by Porter G. Fisher, Jr. The Federal Savings and Loan Association appealed.

On this appeal counsel for the appellant Association contend that provision 7, supra, of the marriage agreement, which as approved and confirmed by the terms of the final decree of divorce entered between Freda Y. Fisher and husband Porter G. Fisher, Sr., was legally insufficient to constitute notice, implied or constructive, of the claims and interest of Porter G. Fisher, Jr., in and to the described property, although Fisher, Sr., had not lived or resided in the home from 1939 until giving the mortgage on July 16, 1946. He remarried within ninety days after the divorce decree was entered. It was the Chancellor's conclusion that the divorce decree and divorce stipulation were legally sufficient to constitute lawful notice of the interest of Porter G. Fisher, Jr., in and to the described property.

In the case of Sapp v. Warner, 105 Fla. 245, 141 So. 124, 143 So. 648, 144 So. 481, we held that notice is of two kinds: actual and constructive. Constructive notice has been defined as notice imputed to a person not having actual notice, for example: such as would be imputed under the recording statutes to persons dealing with property subject to those statutes. Actual notice is also said to be of two kinds: first, express, which includes what might be called direct information and, second, implied, which is said to include notice inferred from the fact that the person had means of knowledge, which it was his duty to use and which he did not use, or as it is sometimes called implied actual notice. Constructive notice is a legal inference, while implied notice is an inference of fact, but the same facts may sometimes be used to prove both constructive and implied actual notice. The foregoing rule has been reaffirmed by this Court. See Rinehart v. Phelps, 150 Fla. 382, 7 So. 2d 783.

The record reflects that Porter G. Fisher, Sr., under the terms of the divorce agreement, was to provide his first wife and son with a home and furnishings. It is not disputed that they lived in the original home of the parties located at 531 49th Street, Miami. It is not contended that P. Graham Fisher, Sr., ever lived in the home after the divorce decree, but married again within approximately three months thereafter. If the appellant had made inquiry as to the possession of the property upon which it later made a loan of $10,400 and accepted a mortgage, the fact would have developed that P. Graham Fisher, Sr., was not in possession of the property but the possession thereof was in his divorced wife. Under these circumstances we are forced to hold that the appellant failed to exercise, in the acceptance of the note and mortgage that decree of care as the law imposed upon it.

Another theory of the case is that the appellant, by searching the records in the office of the Clerk of the Circuit Court of Dade County, Florida, would have found the divorce decree and property settlement appearing upon the record, and a provision thereof which is viz.: "Ordered, adjudged and decreed that the agreement heretofore entered into by and between the complainant and defendant herein, dated September 11, 1939, providing the matters of custody of the child, P. Graham Fisher, his maintenance, the matters of alimony and property settlements, be and the same is hereby in all respects approved. . . ."

It is our view and conclusion that the decree appealed from should be and it is hereby affirmed on the authority of Sapp v. Warner, supra.

Affirmed.

Terrell, Roberts and Mathews, JJ., concur.

Sebring, C.J., and Thomas and Hobson, JJ., dissent.

NOTES

1. Is there any difference between constructive notice and implied notice, as those terms are used by the court in the principal case? And if there is a difference, does it serve any useful function to make such a distinction?

2. Judgments that create or declare interests in land are generally considered binding on subsequent takers of the land parcels involved. A broad range of judicial proceedings may result in judgments of this kind: suits to quiet title, eminent domain takings, mortgage foreclosures, divorce proceedings and will contests being but a few. By statute, judgments for money can in most states create liens on land owned by the judgment debtor; and such liens are also binding on subsequent takers, provided that

The Recording Acts 699

the necessary statutory formalities are followed. One common requirement for a judgment to be binding on subsequent takers of land interests is that it be made a matter of public record in the county where the land is located. Docketing in that county's court records or filing with its recorder of deeds is the usual means of giving a judgment this broader effect.

3. In many states, the requirements for federal court judgment liens are the same as those for liens of state court judgments. The federal statute authorizing this conformity provides:

> Every judgment rendered by a district court within a State shall be a lien on the property located in such State in the same manner, to the same extent and under the same conditions as a judgment of a court of general jurisdiction in such State, and shall cease to be a lien in the same manner and time. Whenever the law of any State requires a judgment of a State court to be registered, recorded, docketed or indexed, or any other act to be done, in a particular manner, or in a certain office or county or parish before such lien attaches, such requirements shall apply only if the law of such State authorizes the judgment of a court of the United States to be registered, recorded, docketed, indexed or otherwise conformed to rules and requirements relating to judgments of the courts of the State. [62 Stat. 958 (1948), 28 U.S.C. §1962 (1983).]

In most states, liens of federal judgments can arise only if docketed or put of record in some public office in the county where the land is situated. However, 28 U.S.C. §1962 does not apply to judgments not resulting in judgment liens but otherwise affecting land titles. Thus in Norman Lumber Co. v. United States, 223 F.2d 868 (4th Cir. 1955), the court held that an eminent domain judgment entered by a United States District Court in North Carolina did not have to be docketed and indexed in the office of a state court clerk in the county where the land was situated, even though a North Carolina statute so required. Not only was the judgment valid without compliance with the state statute, but it created rights in the condemnor superior to those of a purchaser without actual notice who bought from the condemnee some years later. In its opinion at 872, the court of appeals said:

"Whether docketing and cross indexing of federal judgments of condemnation with state court records should be required as a condition of validity as against subsequent purchasers from the condemnee is a matter for Congress, and, so far, Congress has not seen fit to take action with regard to the matter."

How could the purchaser from the condemnee in the *Norman Lumber Company* case have determined if title had been taken by proceedings brought in a federal court? Should Congress require docketing and cross indexing of federal judgments of condemnation with state court records? Why do you think Congress has not done so?

4. As land titles frequently pass by devise or descent, title searches

often must be made in the records of probate or other courts that have jurisdiction over administration of decedents' estates. Laws concerning wills, intestate succession, and the formalities of estate administration are, of course, important to land title search and examination. A host of troublesome legal problems can arise in connection with succession to real property interests by death.

    5. Under most recording acts, purchasers are charged with what a reasonable inquiry would disclose. Massachusetts has an unusual statute that provides: "A conveyance of an estate in fee simple, fee tail or for life, or a lease for a term of seven years, or an assignment of rents or profits from an estate or lease, shall not be valid as against any person, except the grantor or lessor, his heirs and devisees *and persons having actual notice of it*, unless it . . . is recorded in the registry of deeds for the county or district in which the land to which it relates lies. . . ." (Emphasis added.) Mass. Gen. Laws Ann. c. 183, §4 (West 1977). In Tramontozzi v. D'Amicis, 344 Mass. 514, 183 N.E.2d 295 (1962), it was held that a subsequent buyer did not have notice of an unrecorded mortgage noted in the probate estate inventory of a former deceased owner. Without an actual notice statute such as the one quoted above, it is quite possible that a court would hold the buyer to have had constructive notice of the mortgage, as he or his agent should have examined the inventory in the course of the title search.

United States v. Union Central Life Insurance Co.
368 U.S. 291, 82 S. Ct. 349, 7 L. Ed. 2d 294 (1961)

Opinion of the Court by Mr. Justice BLACK. . . . Robert G. Peters, Jr., and his wife, of Oakland County, Michigan, failed to pay their 1952 federal income taxes. In January 1954 an assessment for this delinquency was filed in the Internal Revenue Collector's Office at Detroit, Michigan, at which time a lien arose "in favor of the United States upon all property" of the two delinquent taxpayers.[1] Some 10 months after the Government's tax lien arose, Mr. and Mrs. Peters executed a mortgage on real property they owned in Oakland County to secure an indebtedness to the respondent Union Central Life Insurance Company. They defaulted in payment of the mortgage, and Union Central filed this action to foreclose in the Circuit Court of Oakland County, joining the United States as a party defendant because of its asserted lien.

    The company claimed priority for its mortgage over the earlier created federal lien because no notice of the federal lien had been filed with the register of deeds in Oakland County as then required by Michigan law.[2] For this alleged priority the company relied on §3672(a)(1) of the 1939

---

    1. Sections 3670 and 3671 of the Internal Revenue Code of 1939, in effect at that time.
    2. Act 104, Public Acts of Michigan of 1923, repealed April 13, 1956, by Act 107, Public Acts of Michigan of 1956.

The Recording Acts 701

Internal Revenue Code, as amended, providing that a federal tax lien shall not be valid as against any mortgagee until notice has been filed "In the office in which the filing of such notice is authorized by the law of the State or Territory in which the property subject to the lien is situated, whenever the State or Territory has by law authorized the filing of such notice in an office within the State or Territory." The Government, however, claimed that Michigan had not "authorized" filing within the meaning of the statute and that the case should be governed by §3672(a) (2) which provides that "whenever the State . . . has not by law authorized the filing of such notice in an office within the State," the notice may be filed in "the office of the clerk of the United States district court for the judicial district in which the property subject to the lien is situated." Since the federal lien had been filed in the District Court months before the mortgage was executed and filed in the county register of deeds' office, the Government claimed that its lien had priority. The Government's contention that Michigan had not "authorized" a state office for filing the federal tax notice was based on the fact that the Michigan law purporting to authorize such filing expressly required that a federal tax lien notice contain "a description of the land upon which a lien is claimed," even though the form long used for filing federal tax lien notices in the District Courts throughout the United States does not contain a description of any particular property upon which the lien is asserted. In support of its contention the Government pointed to the fact that in 1953 the Michigan Attorney General ruled that federal tax lien notices not containing such a description are not entitled to recordation, and it is stipulated that from the time of that ruling, up to 1956,[3] "it was the policy of the office of the Register of Deeds for said County of Oakland not to accept for recording notices of Federal tax liens which did not contain a legal description of any land."

Because the United States had not filed a notice complying with the Michigan law, the Michigan Circuit and Supreme Courts held the federal lien to be subordinate to the mortgage, 361 Mich. 283, 105 N.W.2d 196. While this holding is in accord with Youngblood v. United States, 141 F. 2d 912 (C.A. 6th Cir.), it conflicts with United States v. Rasmuson, 253 F. 2d 944 (C.A. 8th Cir.). In order to settle this conflict and because of the importance of the question in the administration of the revenue laws, we granted certiorari. 365 U.S. 858.

The Michigan requirement that notice of the federal tax lien be filed in Michigan is, of course, not controlling unless Congress has made it so, for the subject of federal taxes, including "remedies for their collection has always been conceded to be independent of the legislative action of the States." United States v. Snyder, 149 U.S. 210, 214. While §3672(a)(1) unquestionably requires notice of a federal lien to be filed in a state office when the State authoritatively designates an office for that purpose, the section does not purport to permit the State to prescribe the form or the

---

3. Act 104 was repealed April 13, 1956.

contents of that notice. Since such an authorization might well result in radically differing forms of federal tax notices for the various States, it would run counter to the principle of uniformity which has long been the accepted practice in the field of federal taxation. Moreover, a required compliance with Michigan law would mean that the federal tax lien would be superior to all those entitled to notice only as to the property described in the notice even though §3670 broadly creates a lien "upon all property and rights to property, whether real or personal, belonging to" a taxpayer. This language has been held to include in the lien all property owned by the delinquent taxpayer both at the time the lien arises and thereafter until it is paid.[4] It seems obvious that this expansive protection for the Government would be greatly reduced if to enforce it government agents were compelled to keep aware at all times of all property coming into the hands of its tax delinquents. Imposition of such a task by the Michigan law could seriously cripple the Government in the collection of its taxes, and to attribute to Congress a purpose so to weaken the tax liens it has created would require very clear language. The history of §3672 belies any such congressional purpose.

In 1893 this Court decided in United States v. Snyder, 149 U.S. 210, that the federal tax lien could be enforced against bona fide purchasers who had no notice of the lien, despite a state law attempting to defeat the lien unless it has been recorded. In order to grant relief from the *Snyder* rule, Congress in 1914 passed an Act requiring, much as the provision here in question did, that the tax liens should not be "valid as against any mortgagee, purchaser, or judgment creditor" until notice was filed with the clerk of an appropriate District Court, or, whenever a State authorized such filing, in the office of a county recorder of deeds.[5] This statute was amended in 1928 by adding that the lien would not be valid until notice was filed *"in accordance with the law of the State or Territory* in which the property subject to the lien is situated, whenever the State or Territory has by law provided for the filing of such notice. . . ."[6] (Emphasis supplied.) Following this in United States v. Maniaci, 36 F. Supp. 293, *aff'd,* 116 F.2d 935, both a United States District Court and a Court of Appeals refused to enforce a federal tax lien on Michigan property because the notice of lien, although filed both in a District Court and in the office of the proper Michigan register of deeds, did not contain the description of the property required by Michigan law. In this holding emphasis was placed on the clause added in 1928, requiring notice to be filed "in accordance with the law of the State or Territory in which the property subject to the lien is situated. . . ."

Less than two years after the *Maniaci* holding Congress again amended the lien notice provisions, struck out "in accordance with the law of the

---

4. Glass City Bank v. United States, 326 U.S. 265.
5. 37 Stat. 1016.
6. 45 Stat. 876.

State or Territory" and substituted the language in the section here controlling that notice was not valid until filed "In the office in which the filing of such notice is authorized by the law of the State or Territory." [7] The reports of the House and Senate Committees reporting this amendment point strongly to a purpose to get away from the ruling in the *Maniaci* case and make it clear that, while notice of a federal lien must be filed in a state office where authorized by a State, the notice is sufficient if given in the form long used by the Department "without regard to other general requirements with respect to recording prescribed by the law of such State or Territory." [8] The Department never accepted the *Maniaci* case and its practice has been to use forms which do not contain a particular description of any property owned by a delinquent taxpayer. The notice provisions were once more amended in the 1954 Code, this time providing that the notice shall be valid if in the Department form "notwithstanding any law of the State or Territory regarding the form or content of a notice of lien." [9] The House Report stated that this amendment was merely "declaratory of the existing procedure and in accordance with the long-continued practice of the Treasury Department." [10]

The Michigan law authorizing filing only if a description of the property was given placed obstacles to the enforcement of federal tax liens that Congress had not permitted, and consequently no state office was "authorized" for filing within the meaning of the federal statute. It was therefore error for the Michigan courts to fail to give priority to the Government's lien here, notice of which had been filed in the District Court in accordance with federal law.

The judgment of the Michigan Supreme Court is reversed and the cause is remanded to that court for proceedings not inconsistent with this opinion.

Reversed and remanded.

Mr. Justice Douglas dissents.

NOTES

1. The Uniform Federal Tax Lien Registration Act is now in effect in Michigan, Mich. Comp. Laws Ann. §§211.661 to 211.687 (Supp. 1985), and provides in part:

> Sec. 2. This act shall apply only to federal tax liens and to other notices of federal liens which under any act of Congress or any regulation adopted pursuant to an act of congress are required or permitted to be filed in the same manner as notices of federal tax liens.

---

7. 56 Stat. 957, §3672(a)(1) of the Internal Revenue Code of 1939, as amended.
8. H.R. Rep. No. 2333, 77th Cong., 2d Sess. 173. See also S. Rep. No. 1631, 77th Cong., 2d Sess. 248.
9. Section 6323(b) of the Internal Revenue Code of 1954.
10. H.R. Rep. No. 1337, 83d Cong., 2d Sess. A406-A407.

Sec. 3. (1) Notices of liens, certificates, and other notices affecting federal tax liens or other federal liens shall be filed pursuant to this act.

(2) Notices of liens upon real property for obligations payable to the United States and certificates and notices affecting the liens shall be filed in the office of the register of deeds of the county in which the real property subject to the liens is situated.

Sec. 5. . . .

(4) Upon request of any person, the filing officer shall issue his or her certificate showing whether there is on file, on the date and hour stated, any notice of lien, certificate, or notice affecting any lien filed under this act or former Act No. 162 of the Public Acts of 1967, naming a particular person, and if a notice or certificate is on file, giving the date and hour of filing of each notice or certificate.

Almost every state now provides by statute for local filing of federal tax liens. See generally 3 Powell on Real Property §495 (1984).

2. For many years considerable dissatisfaction with federal tax lien laws has existed. By passage of the Federal Tax Lien Act of 1966, 80 Stat. 1125, Congress sought to alleviate some of this dissatisfaction. Among other lien law changes made by the 1966 act, the Internal Revenue Code of 1954 was amended to give priority over federal tax liens to certain categories of claims or property interests, even though the claims or interests were created after filing of federal tax lien notices. Included in this list of "superpriority" claims are liens of general real estate taxes, liens for special assessments on real estate and some mechanics' liens. 26 U.S.C. §6323(b) (6) and (7) (1983).

3. Liens on real property for unpaid local and state general property taxes and special assessments can generally be determined from public records, and these records are regularly checked in the course of title examinations. In some places such tax liens are entered in separate tax lien records; in some an examination of tax assessment and payment records must be made. When unpaid, other local and state taxes can result in liens on real estate, and the existence of these liens ascertained from examining public records. Examples of such liens are N.Y. Tax Law §380 (McKinney 1975), income tax lien; and Va. Code §58.1-908 (1984), estate tax lien.

4. In addition to public records of tax liens, lis pendens, judgment liens, and priorities created by other judicial determinations, additional interests in or claims against particular land parcels may be discovered by searching the public records other than conveyancing records kept pursuant to the recording acts. Of major importance are mechanics' liens, a public record of which is required sooner or later to make liens of this kind valid. See, for example, N.Y. Lien Law §10 (McKinney Supp. 1984-85). Note, however, that as is indicated in Hadrup v. Sale, infra, mechanics' liens in many states can be off-record risks for a limited period of time. On possible invalidity of mechanics' lien statutes under the Fourteenth Amendment, see note 5 following Hadrup v. Sale, infra. Other public records that may disclose claims against land include records of attach-

ments of real property that may be made at the commencement of certain judicial proceedings, e.g., Me. Rev. Stat. tit. 14, §§4451 and 4454 (1980); and records of state liens on real property of certain welfare recipients, e.g., Ill. Ann. Stat. c.23, §3-10.2 (Smith-Hurd Supp. 1985).

5. Why do you think that all public records pertaining to land titles in each county, or at least a cross-reference to such records, are not centralized in one public office so as to facilitate title searching? What public records do you think should be so centralized that frequently are not?

e. Off-record Risks

All legally protected land interests are not apparent from a search of public records. Under many circumstances, title interests are recognized as valid even though their existence or validity is not disclosed by these records. Even a bona fide purchaser without actual notice can be subordinated to off-record interests, often but not always on the grounds that he has constructive notice.

Persons acquiring interests in land are generally obligated to physically examine the premises for indications of interests inconsistent with the record title. Inquiry of parties in possession may be required, especially if their right to possession does not appear of record. Further inquiry should be made if there is evidence of land use incompatible with the title as shown by the public records. If transferees fail to examine adequately the premises before they take, they are put on notice of what a reasonable examination would have disclosed. In some states, mechanics' and materialmen's liens may be created without first being put of public record, and for a period of time may bind even subsequent transferees. Merely because a land transaction appears of record and seems to be valid does not necessarily mean that it is valid or has created any legally recognized land interests. The underlying instrument may have been forged, never delivered when necessary, executed by a person without legal capacity, or for some other reason be void. Putting a void instrument of record generally has no effect as a validating act.

The above are just a few of the many off-record risks to land titles. Although they rarely cause losses to persons acquiring interests in land, these risks are a sufficient threat so that purchasers and lenders commonly take some precautions to avoid them, and they are major inducements to the acquisition of title insurance.

Miller v. Green
264 Wis. 159, 58 N.W.2d 704 (1953)

Prior to November 4, 1950, the defendant, Mary Green, owned a farm of 63 acres located in Pierce county. During November, 1949, she rented the farm to the plaintiff, Eugene M. Miller, for the year of 1950. He raised a crop thereon during the season of 1950. On November 4, 1950, Mrs. Green and the plaintiffs, Eugene M. Miller and his wife, made a land contract by the terms of which the latter agreed to buy the farm for $3,500, $400 having been paid as earnest money.

On November 29, 1950, the defendant, W. E. Hines, paid Mrs. Green $500 toward the purchase price of the same farm. On the next day Mrs. Green executed a deed conveying the farm to Hines. The deed was delivered on December 1, 1950, and recorded in the office of the register of deeds on the same day. Later Hines paid the balance of the purchase price, $3,300.

The Miller land contract was not recorded until March 7, 1951.

The action was commenced on March 8, 1951, to set aside the deed to W. E. Hines and Avis Hines, and for specific performance on the part of Mrs. Green of her agreement to convey to plaintiffs.

Judgment dismissing the complaint was entered on June 16, 1952. Plaintiffs appeal. . . .

CURRIE, Justice. Defendants Hines claim that their title under their deed is superior to the land contract interest of the plaintiffs inasmuch as their deed was recorded first. Section 235.49, Stats., provides as follows:

"Every conveyance of real estate within this state hereafter made (except patents issued by the United States or this state, or by the proper officers of either) which shall not be recorded as provided by law shall be void as against any subsequent purchaser in good faith and for a valuable consideration of the same real estate or any portion thereof whose conveyance shall first be duly recorded."

The question at issue on this appeal is whether the defendants Hines qualify under the foregoing statute as subsequent purchasers *"in good faith."* Plaintiffs contend that the defendants Hines do not so qualify because the plaintiffs were in possession of the premises on November 29, 1950, when the defendant W. E. Hines paid Mrs. Green $500 toward the purchase price of the farm, and that such possession constituted constructive notice of the plaintiff's rights under their land contract. This makes it necessary to review the evidence bearing on such possession by the plaintiffs, or either of them.

Approximately 40 acres of the 63-acre tract was cultivated land and the remainder was pasture and woods. The buildings on the farm consisted of a small log house, a barn, and some sheds, which were in a dilapidated condition; the house was unlivable; and such buildings had not been used for many years. The plaintiff Eugene M. Miller had leased the entire 63-acre tract for the crop season of 1950 and had grown crops on the cultivated 40 acres and had grazed livestock on the remaining portion. The crop had been harvested prior to November, 1950, and the livestock had been removed when cold weather came about November 22, 1950. However, starting November 4, 1950 (the date that the Millers contracted to purchase this farm tract), Miller's father, in behalf of the Millers, hauled between 59 and 60 loads of manure to the farm. First the manure was spread over the land, but then after a snowstorm came it was piled on a pile about 100 feet from the road, such pile being about 60 feet long and several feet high. Such hauling of manure was taking place on November 29, 1950 (the date that the defendants Hines made the $500 down payment on the purchase price), and continued until about December 8 or 9, 1950. Also in November, prior to the snowstorm, approximately 2 acres of land had been plowed by Miller, which plowed land was plainly visible from the abutting highway before the snowstorm.

The Hines farm was located about one half mile from this 61-acre tract, although the distance by highway was about one and one half miles. Part of the tract was visible from the Hines home. The defendant W. E. Hines testified that he knew that the plaintiff Eugene M. Miller had leased the tract for the crop season of 1950, but denied that he drove past the tract on the abutting highway during November, 1950, and denied having seen the plowing of the land, the hauling of the manure, or the manure pile on the land, although he admitted finding the manure pile there the following spring.

The general rule is that possession of land is notice to the world of whatever rights the possessor may have in the premises. The reason underlying this rule is well stated in Pippin v. Richards, 1911, 146 Wis. 69, 74, 130 N.W. 872, 874:

"The theory of the law is that the person in possession may be asked to disclose the right or title which he has in the premises, and the purchaser will be chargeable with the actual notice he would have received, had he made inquiry. Mateskey v. Feldman, 75 Wis. 103, 43 N.W. 733; Brinkman v. Jones, supra [44 Wis. 519]. In Frame v. Frame, 32 W. Va. [463], at page 478, 9 S.E. [901] at page 907 (5 L.R.A. 323), the court said: 'The earth has been described as that universal manuscript, open to the eyes of all. When, therefore, a man proposes to buy or deal with realty, his first duty is to read this public manuscript; that is, to look and see who is there upon it, and what are his rights there. And, if the person in possession has an equitable title to it, he is as much bound to respect it, as if it was a perfect legal title evidenced by a deed duly recorded.'"

An apt statement of this general principle of possession being constructive notice is stated in State v. Jewell, 1947, 250 Wis. 165, at page 171, 26 N.W.2d 825, at page 828, 28 N.W.2d 314:

"The possession of real estate is generally considered constructive notice of rights of the possessor, whether the possession is sought to be used for the purpose of charging a purchaser with notice of an outstanding equity, or whether it is sought to charge a subsequent purchaser with notice of an unrecorded instrument and thereby defeat his right to protection under the recording acts. It is so held in the United States courts and in 28 states of the Union. 55 Am. Jur. [Vendor and Purchaser] 1087, sec. 712, and cases cited."

The rule with respect to possession of a tenant constituting notice of any rights claimed by such tenant is stated in 5 Tiffany, Real Property, Third Ed., p. 73, sec. 1291:

"It has been decided in a number of states that, by the possession of a tenant under a lease, a purchaser is chargeable with notice, not only of the tenant's rights under the lease, but also of any right which he may have not under the lease, as, for instance, under an agreement by the lessor to sell the property to him."

The authorities generally hold that in order that possession may constitute constructive notice such possession must be "open, visible, exclusive and unambiguous." Ely v. Wilcox, 20 wis. 523, Wickes v. Lake, 25 Wis. 71; and 55 Am. Jur., Vendor and Purchaser, p. 1090, sec. 716. It will thus be seen that the requirements as to the type of possession that will constitute constructive notice are practically identical with the requirements of the type of possession necessary to constitute adverse possession. In view of the fact that the farm buildings were unusable, the plowing of the 2 acres of land after November 4, 1950, and the hauling of the manure practically every day throughout November were acts which not only were "open and visible," but also "exclusive and unambiguous." They were the customary acts of possession which could be exercised as to unoccupied farm lands at such time of year. Surely they would have been sufficient to have constituted acts of adverse possession, and it would appear that the rule as to acts of possession necessary to constitute constructive notice to a purchaser is no more strict. Wickes v. Lake, supra, is authority for the principle that actual residence on the land is not required in order to have sufficient possession to constitute constructive notice.

In George v. Stansbury, 1922, 90 W. Va. 593, 111 S.E. 58, both the plaintiff and defendants claimed title to a city lot. The plaintiff, during 1919, had maintained a garden on the lot, and the following year, although he did not have a garden there, he permitted the owner of a nearby lot who was excavating for a building to haul a large quantity of dirt from the excavation and dump it on the lot so as to fill a low place. It was during this second year that the defendants purchased the premises and obtained a deed which they recorded, while the plaintiff's title was not recorded. The West Virginia court held that the gardening during the one season, followed by the permitting of the dirt to be hauled in and dumped the second year, constituted sufficient possession to be constructive notice to the defendants of plaintiff's rights, and plaintiff was held to have the superior title. If hauling dirt onto a vacant lot constitutes sufficient possession to be constructive notice to a subsequent purchaser, surely hauling manure onto farm land, as in the instant case, should be held to be equally effective to constitute constructive notice.

In Lyman v. Russell, 1867, 45 Ill. 281, plaintiff purchased some farm land but did not record his deed. The defendants claimed under a subsequent mortgage executed by plaintiff's vendor. The question was whether there was such "actual, open, notorious and visible possession" of the lands by plaintiff as to constitute constructive notice to the subsequent mortgagees. Plaintiff's act of possession consisted of plowing some of the land in view of all who passed along the adjoining highway. The Illinois court held that the plaintiff's possession was sufficient notice to put a subsequent purchaser on inquiry, and should operate as notice of plaintiff's rights.

The learned trial court in the instant case apparently was of the opinion that, in order for the plaintiff Eugene M. Miller's possession of the premises to have been constructive notice to the defendants Hines that Miller claimed rights of ownership therein, there must have been some change in the type of his possession after November 4, 1950 (the date the Millers entered into the contract to purchase), and his possession prior thereto. This is very apparent from finding No. 5 of the findings of fact made by the trial court, such finding reading as follows:

"That the plaintiff, Eugene M. Miller, continued in possession of said premises, and continued to pasture livestock thereon until about November 22, 1950, when it was necessary to remove them because of the weather, and continued to make such use of the tillable land on said premises as the weather permitted during the month of November, 1950. That the defendant, W. E. Hines knew at that time of the oral lease between the plaintiff, Eugene M. Miller, and the defendant, Mary Green, for the 1950 season. That there was nothing in the use to which the land was put by the plaintiff, Eugene M. Miller, to indicate to the defendant, W. E. Hines, that [there] had been a change in the status of said plaintiff with relation to said land."

In other words the trial court found that there was possession of the premises by Millers from November 4, 1950, through to the end of that month, but there was no change in the type of possession. Apparently it was the theory of the trial court that the defendants Hines could assume, because of such lack of change in the character of possession, that the possession after November 4, 1950, was that of a tenant and not of a purchaser. The authorities, however, clearly establish that no such change in the character of possession is necessary.

8 Thompson on Real Property (Permanent Edition), p. 413, sec. 4516, states:

"If the tenant changes his character by taking an agreement to purchase, or he has this right under his lease and exercises his option to purchase, his possession amounts to notice of his equitable title as purchaser."

To the same effect see Anderson v. Brinser, 1889, 129 Pa. 376, 404, 11 A. 809, 18 A. 520, 521, 6 L.R.A. 205, wherein the Pennsylvania court stated:

"Knowledge of the existence of a lease will, of course, give constructive notice of all its provisions; but the possession, apart from the lease, we think, should be treated as notice of the possessor's claim of title, whatever that claim may be, for the lease may be but the first of two or more successive rights acquired by the tenant. While in the occupancy under a lease for years, the tenant may have purchased under articles, and entitled himself to an equity; or, indeed, he may have purchased the legal estate in fee, and failed to record his deed. Would it be supposed that a knowledge of the precedent lease would dispense with the duty of inquiry, and entitle a subsequent grantee to the protection of an innocent purchaser? . . . In Sugden on Vendors, (volume 1, 6th Amer., from 10th London, Ed., p. 265, §22,) it is expressly stated, and numerous authorities are cited in support of the statement, that if a tenant, during his tenancy, changes his character by having agreed to purchase the estate, his possession amounts to notice of his equitable title as purchaser."

It is our considered judgment that the acts of possession on the part of the plaintiff Eugene M. Miller throughout the remainder of the month of November, 1950, following the purchase of the tract by the Millers on November 4, 1950, constituted constructive notice to all the world which required a subsequent purchaser to make inquiry as to what rights, if any, the plaintiff Eugene M. Miller claimed to have in the premises. Subsequent purchasers could not safely assume, without inquiry, as did the defendants Hines, that, because Miller had theretofore been a tenant for the season, there had been no subsequent change in his rights from that of a tenant to that of a purchaser.

Judgment reversed and cause remanded with directions to enter judgment as prayed for in plaintiffs' complaint.

NOTES

1. Many courts have been reluctant to impute notice of an unrecorded title when acts of occupation are not exclusive, continuous, or readily apparent. There is a similar reluctance when the acts of occupancy occurred some considerable time in the past. Compare Miller v. Green with these cases holding that the indicated acts of occupancy did not constitute notice of the occupiers' titles: Sanford v. Alabama Power Co., 256 Ala. 280, 54 So. 2d 562 (1951), continuous occupation of the surface plus mining operations many years earlier (contest over mineral rights); Anderson v. Barron, 208 Ga. 784, 69 S.E.2d 874 (1952), infrequent visits to vacant land, posting no trespassing signs, occasional cutting and removal of timber, and payment of taxes; Hosier v. Great Notch Corp., 23 N.J. Misc. 1, 40 A.2d 196 (1944), planting and harvesting a corn crop; Paganelli v. Swendsen, 50 Wash. 2d 304, 311 P.2d 676 (1957), earlier construction of improvements and posting for sale signs; and Fohn v. Title Ins. Corp. of St. Louis, 529 S.W.2d 1 (Mo. 1975), advertising signs, not indicative of ownership, posted on the premises.

2. Why should a purchaser ever be on notice of what an examination

of the premises would disclose? In all of these cases, is not the difficulty caused by the willful or negligent conduct of the prior owner in failing to record, and should not the prior owner therefore be responsible for failing to perform this simple act?

Martinique Realty Corp. v. Hull

64 N.J. Super. 599, 166 A.2d 803 (App. Div. 1960)

FREUND, J.A.D. Plaintiff, the purchaser of a leasehold interest in a 55-apartment building in Passaic, commenced this suit against the tenants of one of the apartments for damages for the non-payment of rent allegedly due and owing under the terms of a five-year written lease. Defendants asserted the defense of payment, claiming that the entire rent for the term of the lease had been paid in advance to the former lessor, plaintiff's vendor, and that plaintiff purchased subject to all of defendants' rights as lessees. No basic facts being in issue, the Law Division granted defendants' motion for summary judgment on the ground that plaintiff was chargeable with notice of defendants' rights in and to the apartment, as created between defendants and plaintiff's assignor. Plaintiff files the instant appeal from that determination.

The apartment building in question was formerly owned by The Martinique, a New Jersey corporation. On August 5, 1957 the corporation entered into a five-year lease with defendants for a 1½ room apartment. The gross rental, including security deposit, was $8,450, the rent payable at the rate of $130 per month. Defendants immediately delivered to the landlord a check in the amount of $130, and on August 15, 1957, apparently in accordance with an oral arrangement, the entire rental balance was paid in advance by defendants in the form of a check for $8,320.

On or about October 22, 1957, at the lessor's suggestion, defendants agreed to exchange their apartment for a larger one in the same building. Since the rent on the larger apartment was $150 a month, it was agreed that defendants would make up the difference in annual installments of $240, besides providing additional security of $100. Accordingly, a new lease was executed; its terms ignore the prior advance payment and simply provide that rent will be paid to the landlord over a five-year term, commencing December 1, 1957 and terminating October 31, 1962, in the gross sum of $9,000, payable "in equal monthly installments of $150 in advance on the first day of each and every calendar month during said term." Both the additional security deposit of $100 and the sum of $240, covering the additional rental for the calendar year beginning December 1, 1957, were paid by check to the landlord. A letter dated October 23, 1957 was received by defendants from the lessor's agent, acknowledging the rent prepayment and the $240 annual payment arrangement. Defendants took possession of their new apartment in November 1957.

Subsequently, on December 16, 1957, The Martinique sold and conveyed title to the premises to Cambrian Estates, Inc., a New York corporation, taking back, at the same time, a long-term lease covering the apartment building. On April 29, 1958, the lease-hold interest of The Martinique was sold to the present plaintiff, a separate and distinct corporation. At the time of purchase, plaintiff caused an uneventful search to be made at the office of the Passaic County Clerk. (The Hulls did not record their lease until July 16, 1958.) It apparently relied upon its vendor's silence and its reading of paragraph 45(a) of the Martinique-Cambrian leaseback agreement of December 16, 1957, providing that "the lessee shall not without the prior written consent of the Lessor with respect to any lease now in existence or any renewal or extension thereof any space demised to any tenant, accept prepayment of rent in excess of one month prior to its due date."

In May of 1958 plaintiff mailed rent statements to all of its tenants. Defendants, having learned for the first time that ownership of the leasehold had changed hands, refused to tender any rent by reason of their prepayment.

Plaintiff's contention on this appeal is two-fold. It argues, first, that as the transferee of the leasehold interest, it was entitled to the benefit of all of the covenants between its predecessor and the Hulls. Secondly, it urges that it had a right to rely upon the terms of defendants' lease as written, and that the prepayment of rent is therefore no bar as such prepayment was inconsistent with the terms of the lease; further, that it had no notice, at the time of purchase, of defendants' advance payments, and that it was not, under the principle of Feld v. Kantrowitz, 98 N.J. Eq. 167, 130 A. 6 (Ch. 1925), aff'd, 99 N.J. Eq. 847, 132 A. 657 (E.&A. 1926), and 99 N.J. Eq. 706, 134 A. 920 (Ch. 1926), required to make inquiry of each tenant as to the latter's interest in the property outside of the written lease. Defendants respond by questioning the applicability of the *Feld* case, arguing that plaintiff was under a duty to make inquiry respecting the rights of lessees under their tenancies and that failure to make such inquiry charges plaintiff with notice of such rights. They further contend that the payment of rent by a tenant to his landlord in advance of the time stipulated in the lease for its payment is a discharge pro tanto from the claim of the lessor, and therefore a valid defense against the assignee of the lessor's interest.

Plaintiff is confronted at the outset by the specific statutory provision that the rights of a lessee of real estate for a term of years vis-à-vis his lessor survive the passing of the lessor's interest to another by assignment or otherwise. R.S. 46:8-3, N.J.S.A.; 51 C.J.S. Landlord and Tenant §44(2), p. 567. This is but an illustration of the general rule that the assignee of a contract right takes subject to all defenses valid against his assignor. N.J.S. 2A:25-1, N.J.S.A. While it may be contended that the applicability of these sections is limited by the penalties inherent in our recording act, R.S. 46:22-1 et seq., N.J.S.A., embracing leases for a term exceeding two years,

N.J.S.A. 46:16-1(a), the statute requires, however, that the prevailing purchaser be bona fide in nature.

An essential characteristic of the bona fide purchaser is his lack of notice of the interest of the unrecorded or late-recorded party. It is long settled that the purchaser of a lessor's interest in property has a duty to make inquiry as to the extent of the rights of any person in open, notorious and exclusive possession of the premises; if this duty is not discharged, then notice is imputed to the purchaser of all facts which a reasonably prudent inquiry would have revealed. [Citations omitted.] Such inquiry must be made of the tenant in possession, and if inquiry is made only of the former lessor, the tenant will not be precluded from asserting against the purchaser such rights as he possessed against the lessor. Arcade Realty Holding Corp v. Hildinger, 6 N.J. Misc. 1055, 1058, 144 A. 25 (Ch. 1928).

Moreover, it has been held, in a situation strikingly parallel to the one at hand, that the duty of inquiry is not discharged when an intending purchaser of a leasehold merely examines the written lease which the occupant has signed with the owner of record. The purchaser assumes at his peril that the instrument accurately defines the rights of the occupant. Caplan v. Palace Realty Co., N.J. 110 A. 584 (Ch. 1920). Vice-Chancellor Leaming stated unequivocally in the latter case that:

"If the purchaser is content to rely upon the representations of the landlord, either express or implied, to the effect that the writing contains . . . an accurate statement of the terms actually agreed upon, and fails to inquire of the tenant touching those facts . . . the purchaser's rights as against the tenant can rise no higher than those which were in fact enjoyed by the landlord under that instrument, and any right of reformation of the instrument for fraud or mistake which the tenant may have enjoyed against the landlord may in like manner be enjoyed against the purchaser." (110 A., at p. 585).

Plaintiff contends, however, that the duty of inquiry has been severely restricted, if not eliminated entirely, in cases involving a multi-tenanted office or apartment building. Reliance is placed exclusively on the opinions in Feld v. Kantrowitz, supra. There, an attorney, a tenant in a small office building, claimed that he had acquired, under an unrecorded assignment, an option to purchase a one-sixth interest in the building. The defendant, who had entered into a contract to purchase the entire property without notice of plaintiff's option and without making inquiry of the tenant, claimed status as a bona fide purchaser and asserted that defendant's unrecorded option was extinguished. The vice-chancellor took cognizance of the doctrine of inquiry notice but held that it did not apply to the situation before him. He reasoned that since an office building or apartment house is constructed for the very purpose of creating numerous tenancies, a purchaser should be able to assume that the occupants of the offices or apartments possess the designated status of tenants. Therefore, he concluded, "under these circumstances, to charge a prospective purchaser with notice of any right, title, or interest of one of the tenants, beyond the right of tenancy, would be absurd." 98 N.J. Eq., supra, at p. 169, 130 A., at p. 7. He further discussed the rule that to put the purchaser on inquiry notice, the tenant must be in exclusive possession, and concluded that the interest of one of numerous tenants of a large building does not satisfy the exclusivity requirement. The vice-chancellor's decision was affirmed on the sole ground that he had applied the proper procedural principles in denying plaintiff a preliminary injunction; the Court of Errors and Appeals expressly disclaimed any examination of the merits of the litigation. 99 N.J. Eq. 847, 849, 132 A. 657, (E. & A. 1926). Subsequently, the cause came on for final hearing, at which time the vice-chancellor reiterated his position, further stating that Caplan v. Palace Realty Co., supra, "does not, so far as my reading of the opinion reveals, refer in any way to the constructive notice arising from tenancy in a building such as the one involved in the case at bar." 99 N.J. Eq., supra, at p. 707, 134 A., at p. 920.

The precise holding in *Feld* would seem to be clearly distinguishable from the instant fact situation in that defendants are not herein asserting any interest "beyond the right of tenancy," that is, beyond a demand for recognition of the precise terms of their tenancy. To apply *Feld* to the instant situation would be to contravene the general rule that possession and occupancy of the premises by the tenant amount to notice of his advance payment of rent, and that such prepayment—honestly made, and in the absence of special circumstances putting the tenant on notice that he is prejudicing the rights of third parties—will protect the tenant against further liability for such rent to the landlord and all successors to his interest. 52 C.J.S. Landlord and Tenant §535, p. 348; 32 Am. Jur., Landlord and Tenant, §461, p. 378. Boteler v. Leber, 112 N.J. Eq. 441, 164 A. 572 (Ch. 1933), cited by plaintiff, is not opposed to this view. The court in *Boteler* left open the question of whether notice would affect the rights of the parties. Furthermore, the lease was expressly subordinated to the mortgage, thereby insulating the mortgagee's rights to the rents upon default.

On the other hand, we cannot in all candor overlook indications in the language of *Feld* broad enough to encompass the instant case, namely: (1) the vice-chancellor's statement (98 N.J. Eq., supra, at p. 172, 130 A., at p. 8), that he might decide differently if "dealing with the right of a tenant as such, even in this kind of a building, *that appears in his lease."* (Emphasis added.) Evidence of the prepayment of the Hulls did not, as we have noted, appear in their lease; and (2) the attempt to distinguish the *Caplan* case on the ground that a multi-tenanted building was not there involved, leaving the implication that the purchaser of such a building can justifiably rely exclusively on the tenants' leases as written.

We must therefore consider, to the extent it bears on the present appeal, the question which we left open in Schnakenberg v. Gibraltar Savings and Loan Assn., 37 N.J. Super. 150, 158, 117 A.2d 191, 196 (App. Div.

1955): "Whether the rights of a tenant in possession and the duties of a purchaser of realty vary with the size and character of the building. . . ."

At least with respect to the details of a tenant's *leasehold* arrangement with his landlord, we are convinced that the purchaser's duty of inquiry does not vary with the number of tenants occupying the property. The arguments advanced in favor of such a correspondence are of dubious validity. Inquiry notice is an equitable doctrine designed to effect a distribution of precautionary burdens in a situation involving two "innocent" parties. American Law of Property, §17.11, pp. 565-66. We see little merit in plaintiff's insistence that it would be exceedingly onerous to require inquiry of every tenant in a multi-tenanted building. The statement in *Feld*, 98 N.J. Eq., supra, at p. 169, 130 A., at p. 7, that it "would be absurd" to hold that "one contemplating the purchase of one of the great office buildings in the metropolitan district would be under a duty to personally interview every one of the hundreds of tenants occupying the offices thereof" ignores the very practical and effective device of the written communication. The duty to inquire is discharged by the exercise of due diligence or reasonable prudence, see Clawans v. Ordway B. & L. Assn., 112 N.J. Eq. 280, 284, 164 A. 267 (E. & A. 1933), and what such an inquiry fails to reveal is not further protected by the mere continued possession of the tenant. 4 American Law of Property, §17.12, p. 576. Under certain circumstances, written inquiry may be sufficient to discharge that duty.

We need not dwell upon the statement in *Feld* that no single occupant of a multi-tenanted building is in such exclusive possession as to warrant the invoking of the purchaser's duty of inquiry. For the period of his lease, the lessee is considered the exclusive owner and occupier of the demised premises. Longi v. Raymond-Commerce Corp., 34 N.J. Super. 593, 600, 113 A.2d 69 (App. Div. 1955). That the demised premises consist of one apartment rather than an entire building should not be of consequence. This is not a situation involving the interests of the various family occupants of a single house. See Rankin v. Coar, 46 N.J. Eq. 566, 22 A. 177, 11 L.R.A. 661 (E. & A. 1890); Annotation, 2 A.L.R.2d 857 (1948). Each apartment in the building under consideration is an entirely separate habitational unit, evidenced by a separate landlord-tenant arrangement.

We expressly refrain from a determination as to whether a purchaser's duty of inquiry extends to collateral interests of the lessee which are independent of his tenancy. We note, however, that the majority rule appears to extend the inquiry notice doctrine to cover certain collateral interests of the lessee, such as an option to purchase, see Annotations, 17 A.L.R.2d 331 (1951), 27 A.L.R.2d 1112 (1954), though perhaps not a claim of ownership of the fee. See Annotation, 74 A.L.R. 355, 357 (1931).

In any event, plaintiff, having failed to fulfill its duty of inquiry with respect to defendants' rights under their tenancy, is subject to the prior effective discharge by the latter of their rental obligations. Caplan v. Palace Realty Co., supra.

Judgment affirmed.

NOTES

1. What kind of written inquiries directed by a purchaser or mortgagee to the many tenants of a large building do you think might satisfy the court in the principal case that the purchaser or mortgagee was entitled to protection as a bona fide taker against tenants with unrecorded leases? Do you think it would make a difference if the structure involved were a large office building with many individual tenants rather than a large residential apartment house?

2. What do you think of the result in the following case? A went into possession of a farm as a tenant and later purchased from B, the owner, but failed to record the deed. Subsequently, B offered to sell the land to C. C inquired of A, the party in possession, as to what interest he had in the premises, and A said that he had a deed from B. C then checked the public records and, of course, found no record of such a deed. He asked B about the conveyance to A, and B denied that there ever had been a conveyance to A. C then purchased the farm from B, accepting delivery of a deed. In a contest between A and C, the court held for C, taking the position that C was a bona fide purchaser without notice of the deed from A to B. In its opinion, the court said: "Under all the circumstances shown here, we think, as did the Chancellor, that Alexander [C] made such inquiry as was reasonable and that the rule as to notice from possession did not apply so as to give priority to Gregory's [A's] deed." Gregory v. Alexander, 51 Tenn. App. 307, 316, 367 S.W.2d 292, 297 (1962).

Hadrup v. Sale
201 Va. 421, 111 S.E.2d 405 (1959)

MILLER, Justice. In this suit appellants, A. Hadrup, and W. C. Spratt and W. C. Spratt, Jr., partners, trading as Fredericksburg Pipe and Supply Company, assignees of A. Hadrup, seek to enforce a mechanic's lien taken out by them upon a house and lot owned by Thomas Battaile Sale, Jr., and Margaret B. Sale, appellees. From a decree of October 24, 1958, that declared the mechanic's lien to be invalid, we granted an appeal.

Some months prior to July 9, 1956, Hadrup entered into a contract with Normandy Village, Incorporated, owner of numerous lots in a residential subdivision known as Normandy Village, to do the plumbing and heating work in the building erected on lot 67, section 4. On July 9, 1956, Hadrup assigned in writing to W. C. Spratt and W. C. Spratt, Jr., partners, all sums of money due him under his contract.

Appellants, on July 29, 1957, filed in the appropriate clerk's office a memorandum of mechanic's lien in the sum of $1,265 for plumbing and heating work done by Hadrup on the house and lot. However, lot 67 had been purchased on March 19, 1957, by appellees from Normandy Village,

Incorporated. Appellees' deed was duly recorded but appellants had no actual knowledge of the sale until the day their lien was filed in the clerk's office.

About the time appellants filed their mechanic's lien, many other similar liens were filed against lots in the subdivision owned by Normandy Village, Incorporated, and its numerous grantees. Seven separate suits for various amounts were instituted by mechanic's lien claimants against Normandy Village, Incorporated, and other lot owners in the subdivision, and holders of liens on the lots.

By decree of January 10, 1958, these seven suits, in which numerous liens and claims of varying dignities and priorities were asserted against the same defendants and subject matter, were consolidated into a single cause and referred to a special commissioner to take evidence and report upon the inquires set out in the decree.

The inquiry pertinent to this appeal follows: "The validity of the mechanic's liens which have been asserted in these causes against the properties standing in the names of the parties hereto."

After hearing voluminous testimony from numerous witnesses and considering many exhibits, the commissioner reported that the work on the building on lot 67 was completed during the second week of August, 1957, and the mechanic's lien filed by appellants on the 29th day of July, 1957, was a valid lien against the house and lot in the sum of $1,265, with interest from July 27, 1957.

Exceptions were filed to the commissioner's report, and in an opinion that ruled upon the exceptions, the court found that no work was done by Hadrup on the house and lot bought by appellees on March 19, 1957, subsequent to their purchase, and that by the change of ownership on March 19, 1957, the work on the building was then "otherwise terminated" within the meaning of §43-4, Code 1950. As appellants did not file their lien within sixty days after March 19, 1957, the lien was held invalid. In its opinion the court said:

". . . Any work that Hadrup did on the house must have been done for the prior owner before 19 March, 1957, and Hadrup's lien against Sale's house should have been filed within sixty days after 19 March, 1957 whether the house was finished or not. When there is a change of ownership, that is notice to contractors and workmen who do no further work on the house, that the statute has begun to run and the lien even on an unfinished house must be filed within the limitation period from the date of sale."

In the decree which conformed to the opinion, the court held that appellants' mechanic's lien was invalid.

Appellants' assignment of error is that the court erred when it held that the sale and conveyance of the house and lot by Normandy Village, Incorporated, to appellees "otherwise terminated" the work on the building within the meaning of §43-4, Code 1950.

The material part of that section follows:

"A general contractor, in order to prefect the lien given by the preceding section, shall file at any time after the work is done and the material furnished by him and before the expiration of sixty days from the time such building, structure, or railroad is completed, or the work thereon otherwise terminated. . . ."

The question presented is solely one of law. It is: Did the conveyance of the house and lot "otherwise terminate" the work upon the building and make it necessary for Hadrup and his assignees to file their lien within sixty days of the date of sale?

No Virgina case has been cited to us nor have we found one that decides the specific question. The trial court relied upon and cited Bolton v. Johns, 1847, 5 Pa. 145, 47 Am. Dec. 404, and note. However, in that case the statute construed was materially different from our statute.

The effect of a conveyance of the property upon the right to assert a mechanic's lien is dependent upon the character of the mechanic's lien statute in force in the particular jurisdiction.

"The determination of what effect a conveyance of the real estate has upon the right to assert a mechanic's lien depends upon the kind of statute in existence in the particular jurisdiction. Under statutes which provide that the claimant shall, upon giving or filing notice, have a lien upon the property, a sale of it in good faith before the notice of lien is given or filed prevents the acquisition of any lien. On the other hand, under statutes which recognize the right to a lien from the date of the contract or the time of the commencement of the building or other improvement, or from the beginning of the performance of the labor or the furnishing of material for which the lien is claimed, a lien which has thus attached is not affected by a change of ownership during the progress of the work. This rule applies to property which is sold to a municipal corporation. Where there has been a change of ownership, a purchaser is chargeable with notice that a lien might attach to the property for the improvements. A purchaser before the time for filing a lien on the property has expired may be required to pay such lien although in purchasing he relies upon the representations of the vendor that the contractor's claims against the property have all been paid in full." 36 Am. Jur., Mechanic's Liens, §217, p. 140.

In Thorn v. Barringer, 73 W. Va. 618, 621, 81 S.E. 846, 847, in construing and applying mechanic's lien statutes somewhat similar to ours, the court said:

"Under our law Thorn's lien attached to the property, for all materials furnished by him under the contract and used in the building, as of the time that his furnishing the materials and the use of them began. Cushwa v. Improvement [Loan & Building] Association, 45 W. Va. 490, 32 S.E. 259. . . .

"One purchasing premises on which buildings are in process of erection must take notice of any mechanic's lien right that has attached prior to his purchase. He must inquire what contracts are in course of execution on a

The Recording Acts   719

property he is about to buy. He must further inquire what has been done and may be done under any such contracts that he finds. 'A party purchasing premises on which buildings are in the process of erection, having knowledge of the same, is bound to make inquiry as to the rights of parties furnishing materials or performing work thereon, and is charged with constructive, if not actual notice of their lien.' Phillips on Mechanics' Liens, sec. 227. 'The fact that the work is in progress, is a notice to all of the rights of the mechanic, and all conveyances made during that time are made subject to the mechanic's rights.' Rockel on Mechanics' Liens, sec. 150. . . ."

Of like import is Boisot, Mechanics' Liens (1897), §§312-316.

It should be observed that §43-4 provides that the general contractor, to perfect his lien, shall file his memorandum "at any time after the work is done and materials furnished by him and before the expiration of sixty days from the time such building . . . is completed, or the work thereon otherwise terminated." Burks, Pleading and Practice, 4th ed. §459, p. 891. This language, when fairly construed, means that an inchoate lien attaches when the work is done and materials furnished which may be perfected within the specified time. Wallace v. Brumback, 177 Va. 36, 41, 12 S.E.2d 801. There is nothing in the statute to indicate that the work on the building is "otherwise terminated" by a mere sale. Such a construction would impose an undue hardship upon the contractor and is not in keeping with the language or spirit of the statute.

The mechanic's lien asserted by appellants is declared to be invalid is reversed and the cause remanded for the entry of a decree not in conflict with the views herein expressed.

Reversed and remanded.

NOTES

1. For a period of time during and after construction, in some states, priority by statute is given to mechanics' and materialmen's liens over the interests of subsequent bona fide purchasers or encumbrancers of the land, whether or not, apparently, the bona fide purchasers or encumbrancers knew or could have known of the liens when they acquired their interests. See, e.g., Franks v. Wood, 217 Ark. 10, 228 S.W.2d 480 (1950); Starek v. TKW, Inc., 410 So. 2d 35 (Ala. 1982), but a fee purchaser of an existing, as distinct from a new, structure has priority; and Lenexa State Bank v. Dixon, 221 Kan. 238, 559 P.2d 776 (1977), dictum citing in support Warden v. Sabins, 36 Kan. 165, 12 P. 520 (1887). And see Ohio Rev. Code Ann. §§1311.13 and 1311.14 (Page 1979), with certain exceptions for property improvement mortgages.

Is it good public policy to give such benefits to the construction and building supply industries? Where mechanics' and materialmen's liens are off-record risks, how can a prospective purchaser or mortgagee protect himself against the possible existence of such liens? Prior to the time they are put of record, how can he even determine whether or not liens of this kind exist?

2. In Texas a mechanics' lien even has limited priority over a mortgage or other lien senior in time at inception or recording. This particular priority, however, extends only to improvements to the land severable without injury to the land or the improvements. Tex. Prop. Code Ann. §53.123 (Vernon 1984). There is uncertainty as to whether or not the preference is restricted to those removables provided by the claimant. How can such a superlien be justified? Texas mechanics' lien preferences are discussed in Youngblood, Coping With Texas Mechanics' Liens: A Lender's Guide to Priorities, 12 St. Mary's L.J. 889 (1981).

3. In some states, if a mechanics' lien has not been put of public record and a bona fide purchaser has no actual notice of it, he takes free of the lien. Illustrative cases so holding are Bryant v. Ellenburgh, 106 Ga. App. 510, 127 S.E.2d 468 (1962); and Walker v. Valley Plumbing, Inc., 370 S.W.2d 136 (Ky. 1963).

4. In addition to the bona fide purchaser's off-record risks considered above there are a scattering of other off-record risks he may run. Examples of some of these appear below. In no instance was the risk apparent from the face of the record, and yet the off-record interest was held paramount to that of the subsequent bona fide purchaser without notice. Chances of loss from such risks, however, are very slight, for incidents that could lead to these kinds of loss occur so infrequently. Furthermore, as to some of the risks, most prevailing case law is favorable to bona fide purchasers without notice, following the strong judicial preference for these innocent takers. This preference commonly is exerted quite independently of the recording acts, and the trend in the cases seems to be toward further extending the immunity of bona fide purchasers. When the bona fide purchaser is claiming through an instrument asserted to be invalid, he is more likely to prevail if the court labels the instrument voidable instead of void. His chances are also increased if the court finds negligent or dilatory conduct on the part of the other side or those through whom it is claiming. Off-record risk examples are these:

(a) Incapacity of a grantor. A grantor in the bona fide purchaser's chain of title did not have the legal capacity to convey because mentally ill or feeble-minded, so the transfer was held invalid. Erickson v. Bohne, 130 Cal. App. 2d 553, 279 P.2d 619 (1955); and Dewey v. Allgire, 37 Neb. 6, 55 N.W. 276 (1893). Contra Brown v. Khoury, 346 Mich. 97, 77 N.W.2d 336 (1956).

(b) Defrauding of a grantor. A grantor in the bona fide purchaser's chain of title was tricked into signing a mineral deed when he thought he was signing a mineral lease. As a result of this "fraud in the execution," the court held the instrument void, passing nothing to the grantee or to bona fide purchasers from the grantee. Hauck v. Crawford, 75 S.D. 202, 62 N.W.2d 92 (1953). Contra Marlenee v. Brown, 21 Cal. 2d 668, 134 P.2d 770 (1943); and Dixon v. Kaufman, 79 N.D. 633, 58 N.W.2d 797 (1953).

(c) Forgery of an instrument. A forged or altered instrument in the bona fide purchaser's chain of title prevents the bona fide purchaser from acquiring a valid interest. Martin v. Carter, 400 A.2d 326 (D.C. 1979); Prater v. Prater, 208 Miss. 59, 44 So. 2d 582 (1949); and Mosley v. Magnolia Petroleum Co., 45 N.M. 230, 114 P.2d 740 (1941).

(d) No delivery of an instrument. An instrument in the bona fide purchaser's chain of title was never delivered because the grantee surreptitiously removed the deed from the glove compartment of the grantor's automobile, so no interest passed to the grantee or to a bona fide purchaser from the grantee. Watts v. Archer, 252 Iowa 592, 107 N.W.2d 549 (1961). Similar result when an escrow agent improperly gave up possession of a deed contrary to the terms of the escrow agreement. Blakeney v. Home Owners' Loan Corp., 192 Okla. 158, 135 P.2d 339 (1943).

(e) No acknowledgment of an instrument. An instrument in the bona fide purchaser's chain of title was not acknowledged and hence was void by the law of the controlling state. A notary public apparently filled out the acknowledgment blanks, so that on its face the instrument appeared to have been properly executed. But the notary was not present at the execution of the instrument and the grantor never made any acknowledgment statements to the notary. Dixon v. Kaufman, 79 N.D. 633, 58 N.W.2d 797 (1953).

(f) Subsequent probated will. Heirs of a decedent conveyed land to a bona fide purchaser and later a will was probated leaving the land to someone other than the conveying heirs. The devisee under the will was held to take as against the bona fide purchaser. Reid's Administrator v. Benge, 112 Ky. 810, 66 S.W. 997 (1902); and Barnhardt v. Morrison, 178 N.C. 563, 101 S.E. 218 (1919). Contra Eckland v. Jankowski, 407 Ill. 263, 95 N.E.2d 342 (1950).

(g) Pretermitted after-born child. Devisee under a will, subsequent to probate, borrowed money secured by a deed of trust on the devised land. Years later, an after-born and pretermitted child of the testator brought suit to determine title to the land and was held to have an interest superior to the holder of the trust deed, even though the trust deed holder had been unaware of the child's interest when the loan was made and security accepted. Conroy v. Conroy, 130 Tex. 508, 110 S.W.2d 570 (1938). Accord Chicago B. & Q.R. Co. v. Wasserman, 22 F. 872. (1885).

(h) Prior adverse possession. A record owner of land lost title to it as the result of adverse possession by a neighbor. Thereafter the record owner sold the land to a bona fide purchaser. The bona fide purchaser acquired no title to the land even though at the time of purchase the adverse possessor was not occupying the land and an examination of the premises would have disclosed no indication of the adverse possessor's claim to the land. Mugaas v. Smith, 33 Wash. 2d 429, 206 P.2d 332 (1949).

As to each type of off-record risk illustrated above, what could a title searcher do to determine if a prior off-record interest exists? Would any of these search efforts be so costly that it would be unreasonable to expect them to be made?

On the subject of this note see Straw, Off-Record Risks for Bona-Fide Purchasers of Interests in Real Property, 72 Dick. L. Rev. 35 (1967).

5. Following the concept of due process enunciated in such cases as Snaidach v. Family Finance Corp., 395 U.S. 337 (1969) and Fuentes v. Shevin, 407 U.S. 67 (1972), the Connecticut mechanics' lien statute was held unconstitutional in Roundhouse Construction Corp. v. Telesco Masons Supplies Co., Inc., 168 Conn. 371, 362 A.2d 778 (1975), *vacated and remanded,* 423 U.S. 809 (1975), *reaff'd,* 170 Conn. 155, 365 A.2d 393, *cert. denied,* 97 S. Ct. 246 (1976). The Connecticut Supreme Court, in concluding that the mechanics' lien procedures provided for in its state's enactments did not meet constitutional due process requirements, stated: "Under Connecticut procedure, the party claiming the lien is not required to post any bond or provide any surety to protect the owner of the property subjected to the lien against damages from an unsupportable lien. . . . The filing and perfection of the lien may be done by a claimant entirely ex parte, without authorization, supervision or control by a judicial officer. . . . Most conspicuously absent from the Connecticut procedure is any provision whatsoever for any sort of a timely hearing, either before or after the recording of the lien, which would give the property owner an opportunity to be heard or require the lienor to justify his lien. The statutes allow the lien to continue for two years without any further action on the part of the lienor, during which time the owner of the property is without recourse in the courts to contest the merits of the claim underlying the lien. . . . The plaintiff argues that the 'taking' of the property under a mechanic's lien statute is de minimis. It is true that the deprivation which results from the filing of a mechanic's lien is not as obvious or as great as the dispossession of property under the statutes struck down in Fuentes v. Shevin, 407 U.S. 67, 92 S. Ct. 1983, 32 L. Ed. 2d 556, and Snaidach v. Family Finance Corporation, 395 U.S. 337, 39 S. Ct. 1820, 23 L. Ed. 2d 349, but the recording of a mechanic's lien, while it does not prevent alienation of the property, does, as a practical matter, severely restrict the opportunity for and possibility of its alienation." Following the decision in the *Roundhouse Construction Corp.* case, the Connecticut legislature extensively revised its mechanics' lien statutes in an effort to meet the Court's constitutional objection. Conn. Gen. Stat. Ann., §§49-33 to 49-40a (Supp. 1985).

Considerable law review commentary on constitutionality of various mechanics' lien statutes came along after *Snaidach, Fuentes,* and *Round-*

house Construction Corp. Examples are Frank and McManus, Balancing Almost Two Hundred Years of Economic Policy Against Contemporary Due Process Standards—Mechanics' Liens in Maryland After *Barry Properties,* 36 Md. L. Rev. 733 (1977); Note, Constitutionality of Mechanics' Liens Statutes, 34 Wash. & Lee L. Rev. 1067 (1977); Note, The Colorado Mechanics' Lien Statute: Is Due Process Provided?, 49 U. Colo. L. Rev. 127 (1977); and Comment, The Constitutional Validity of Mechanics' Liens Under the Due Process Clause—A Reexamination After *Mitchell* and *North Georgia,* 55 B.U.L. Rev. 263 (1975). Some states have recently revised their mechanics' lien statutes to provide greater due process protection. Two such statutory revisions are discussed in Comment, Nebraska Remakes the Mechanic's Lien: An Analysis of the Nebraska Construction Lien Act, 16 Creighton L. Rev. 128 (1982); and Note, Liens: Mechanics' and Materialmen's Liens: Conforming to New Statutes and the Bankruptcy Code, 36 Okla. L. Rev. 722 (1983).

Such cases as *Snaidach, Fuentes,* and *Roundhouse Construction Corp.* raise doubts about the validity of a number of state statutes pertaining to land interests, including some other mechanics' and materialmen's lien statutes and some lis pendens enactments. What should a title examiner do if he believes a mechanics' lien pertaining to a title he is giving an opinion on may be invalid under the *Roundhouse Construction Corp.* reasoning but the constitutionality of the mechanics' lien statute in the relevant state has never been adjudicated?

3. *Eliminating Title Defects*

Title defects, whether based on actual or potential claims and whether of record or not, may be eliminated in a variety of ways, one of the more common of which is through the passage of a prescribed period of time and operation of a statute of limitations or similar type statute that cuts off previously existing rights. Another common means is litigation, particularly the suit to quiet title, that can result in a decree clearing the title of some or all of its defects. Besides litigation, the defective title holder often has additional options for clearing his title, including, among others, such possibilities as buying up outstanding title interests; paying off lien or encumbrance claims; securing affidavits resolving troublesome questions of heirship, marital status, or identity of parties in the chain of title; surveying the premises so as to correct land description uncertainties; and recording a new instrument that rectifies errors in one that was previously recorded. On occasion, too, statutory changes in the substantive law may eliminate present or prospective title defects; for example, statutes abolishing dower.[16] In rare instances, substantive statutory modifications in

---

16. E.g., in one year, 1969, dower was abolished in Georgia, Ga. Laws 123; Maryland, Md. Laws, c. 3; and Oregon, Or. Laws c. 591, §78.

real property rights are even made for the express purpose of clearing title to a particular land parcel.

a. Statutes of Limitations, Adverse Possession, and Curative Acts

Legislatures have long attempted to make land titles more certain and to simplify the process of title search by enactments that cut off stale nonpossessory title claims.[17] Such enactments are usually classified as statutes of limitations. There has also been a long history of legislation that seeks to make titles more certain by validating defective instruments or transactions. The defects concerned are usually defects of form and until validated make the instruments or transactions partially or completely ineffectual. These latter kinds of statutes are commonly classified as curative acts, although not always clearly distinguishable from those labelled as statutes of limitations.[18] Adverse possession statutes also frequently operate to clear titles when the adverse holder has a questionable or clouded title, as he often does in adverse possession situations.

Weeks v. Rumbaugh
144 Neb. 103, 12 N.W.2d 636 (1944)

Nuss, District Judge. This action was commenced by appellee on April 11, 1942, to foreclose a mortgage executed and delivered on November 12, 1926, and filed on November 23, 1926. By its terms the mortgage was due on November 3, 1929, but interest had been paid thereon November 24, 1933, to November 3, 1933. The original mortgage was never refiled nor was a copy thereof ever filed. On May 15, 1940, the defendant, appellant here, bought the land in question for value. Since more than ten years elapsed after the maturity of the mortgage debt before the action was brought the defendant claimed the action was barred by the statute of limitations, specifically Section 20-202, Comp. St. 1929. The trial court ruled against defendant and he appealed.

The mortgage was by its terms due on November 3, 1929. It was

---

17. On statutes of limitations and curative and marketable title acts, see Basye, Clearing Land Titles (2d ed. 1970); Conine and Morgan, The Wyoming Marketable Title Act — A Revision of Real Property Law, 16 Land and Water L. Rev. 181 (1981); Burke, American Conveyancing Patterns ch. 3 (1978); Simes and Taylor, The Improvement of Conveyancing by Legislation (1960); Note, The Marketable Record Title Act and the Recording Act: Is Harmonic Coexistence Possible?, 29 U. Fla. L. Rev. 916 (1977).

18. For efforts to distinguish statutes of limitations and curative acts, see Basye, Clearing Land Titles 36-37 (2d ed. 1970); and Simes and Taylor, The Improvement of Conveyancing by Legislation 17, 37 (1960).

therefore barred on November 3, 1939, and the defendant below acquired good title, relieved of the lien of the mortgage, by his purchase for value on May 15, 1940, unless the period of limitation was postponed, extended or tolled by the payment of interest on November 24, 1933. The defendant claims that the amendment of 1925 (Laws 1925, Ch. 64) to Section 6 of the code of civil procedure, Section 20-202, Comp. St. 1929, did so bar the mortgage and the lien and that he acquired a title therefor free and relieved of the said lien.

The plaintiff on the other hand contends that under the decision of this court in Steeves v. Nispel, 132 Neb. 597, 273 N.W. 50, the amendment of 1925 was invalidated or circumscribed so that the payment of interest tolled the ten year period. There is no allegation that the amendment of 1925 was or is unconstitutional, nor is it claimed that the *Nispel* case so held. The amendment is therefore presumed to be constitutional. "The basic principle which underlies the entire field of legal concepts pertaining to the validity of legislation is that by enactment of legislation, a constitutional measure is presumed to be created. In every case where a question is raised as to the constitutionality of an act, the court employs this doctrine in scrutinizing the terms of the law. In a great volume of cases the courts have enunciated the fundamental rule that there is a presumption in favor of the constitutionality of a legislative enactment." 11 Am. Jur. 776, sec. 128.

In State v. Adams Express Co., 85 Neb. 25, 122 N.W. 691, 693, 42 L.R.A., N.S., 396, it is said: "In making the investigation we start with the presumption that the statute in question is a valid and constitutional exercise of legislative power. [Citations omitted.] In [Davis v. State, 51 Neb. 301, 70 N.W. 984] the rule is well stated as follows: 'Every legislative act comes before this court surrounded with the presumption of constitutionality, and this presumption continues until the act under review clearly appears to contravene some provision of the Constitution.' "

The burden of proof of the invalidity of any statute is therefore upon the one so claiming. "In consequence of the general presumption in favor of the validity of acts of the legislature and desires of the courts in resolving all doubts in favor of their validity, the rule has become established that courts will not search the constitution for express sanction or for reasonable implication to sustain a legislative enactment; the successful assailant must be able to point out the particular provision that has been violated and the ground on which it has been infringed." 11 Am. Jur. 795, sec. 132, and many cases cited.

The question relative to the constitutionality of the act must be presented to the trial court else it cannot be considered by this court. Howarth v. Becker, 128 Neb. 580, 259 N.W. 505; State v. Knudtsen, 121 Neb. 270, 236 N.W. 696; Mergenthaler Linotype Co. v. McNamee, 125 Neb. 71, 249 N.W. 92. In the first two cases above cited this court applied the rule notwithstanding that the person claiming the invalidity of the statute was successful in the district court. Thus in the case of Howarth v. Becker, supra [128 Neb. 580, 259 N.W. 506], it was said:

"The appellee contends that the trial court rightfully denied the application for two reasons, first, that the Moratory Act, section 20-21, 159, Comp. St. Supp. 1933, is unconstitutional. . . .

"We have carefully examined the record in this case and we fail to find that the unconstitutionality of section 20-21, 159, Comp. St. Supp. 1933, was pleaded or presented to the trial court for determination. This court has consistently held that in order for this court to consider the question of the constitutionality of a statute, it must first be raised and placed in issue in the trial court. First Trust Co. v. Glendale Realty Co., 125 Neb. 283, 250 N.W. 68; Bell v. Niemann, 127 Neb. 762, 257 N.W. 69. We therefore hold that the question whether the Nebraska Moratory Act violates the Nebraska Constitution is not determinable in this court on this appeal for the reason that it was not presented to the district court in this case."

For the foregoing reasons any question relative to the constitutionality of the amendment of 1925 cannot be considered, and this court must presume for the purpose of this proceeding, that the amendment is valid and constitutional.

The question then arises as to the proper consideration to be given to the amendment in question. It is entirely clear, as established by an overwhelming array of authorities, that the cardinal principle of construction or interpretation of a statute is to arrive at and give effect to the intention of the legislature. 25 R.C.L. 960. City of Lincoln v. Nebraska Workmen's Compensation Court, 133 Neb. 225, 274 N.W. 576; Kearney County v. Hapeman, 102 Neb. 550, 167 N.W. 792.

Since the act in question is clearly remedial it is well to call attention to several other pertinent rules, to-wit: "In construing a remedial statute three things must be considered, viz., 'the old law, the mischief and the remedy.'" Clother v. Maher, 15 Neb. 1, 16 N.W. 902. See also City of Lincoln v. Nebraska Workmen's Compensation Court, supra. Further, a remedial statute is to receive a liberal construction to carry into effect the purposes for which it was enacted. City of Lincoln v. Nebraska Workmen's Compensation Court, supra; State v. Fremont, E. & M.V.R. Co., 22 Neb. 313, 35 N.W. 118; Becker & Degen v. Brown, 65 Neb. 264, 91 N.W. 178. And that a statute of doubtful meaning should be construed, if reasonably possible, so as to carry out the purpose and intention of the legislature, and when this purpose is manifest it will prevail over a seeming conflict in the language. City of Lincoln v. Nebraska Workmen's Compensation Court, supra. State v. Ure, 91 Neb. 31, 135 N.W. 224.

With these rules in mind we proceed to a discussion of the law in question. Prior to the amendment of 1925 (Laws 1925, Ch. 64) to Section 6 of the code of civil procedure, that section provided that an action for the recovery of the title or possession of lands, tenements or hereditaments, "or for the foreclosure of mortgages thereon," could only be brought within ten years after the cause of action shall have accrued. Sec. 8507, Comp. St. 1922. By construing the above section with certain other sections, as this court held in Teegarden v. Burton, 62 Neb. 639, 87 N.W. 337, and McLaughlin v. Senne, 78 Neb. 631, 111 N.W. 377, should be done, the ten year period was extended under Section 22 of the code (Sec. 8522, Comp. St. 1922) by part payment, written acknowledgment of debt or promise to pay. It was likewise postponed by Section 7 of the code, (Sec. 8518, Comp. St. 1922) in favor of any person "under any legal disability"; under Section 17 (Sec. 8519, Comp. St. 1922) in favor of any person "within the age of twenty-one years, insane or imprisoned." Again, it was tolled by Section 20 of the code (Sec. 8520, Comp. St. 1922) against any person "out of the state, or shall have absconded or concealed himself." It is thus seen that the basic ten year period provided in Section 6 of the code could be postponed almost indefinitely for a variety of reasons, not one of which necessarily appeared on the face of the record. In the course of time a great many old unreleased mortgages accumulated on the records and clouded the titles. Since it was possible to extend the basic ten year period in the various ways above mentioned an examiner of titles in such case was compelled to assume that an old unreleased mortgage had been tolled in one of the ways mentioned and was still in effect.

On the contrary, in the case of mechanics liens, every one dealing with any land knew that when the period of two years had elapsed the lien could be disregarded with impunity and would cast no cloud upon the title. Goodwin v. Cunningham, 54 Neb. 11, 74 N.W. 315; Green v. Sanford, 34 Neb. 363, 51 N.W. 967. Although the two year period for the foreclosure of mechanic's liens was only one-fifth of the basic ten year period for the foreclosure of mortgages, that period had proved entirely satisfactory for many years and there has apparently never been any attempt to change it. If a definite period of limitation, not subject to extension for any reason, was satisfactory and desirable in the case of mechanics liens, there can be no reason why the same or a similar unqualified provision would not be equally desirable as to mortgages.

Evidently with some such thought the legislature in 1925 amended Section 6 of the code above mentioned by clarifying when the cause of action should be deemed to accrue. It provided that such cause should be assumed to accrue, "at the last date of the maturity of the debt or other obligation secured thereby, as stated in, or as ascertainable from the record of such mortgage. . . ." Later in the amendment it was provided: "At the expiration of ten years from the date the cause of action accrues on any mortgage as is herein provided, such mortgage shall be presumed to have been paid, and the mortgage and the record thereof shall cease to be notice of the mortgage as unpaid and the lien thereof shall then cease absolutely as to subsequent purchasers and encumbrancers for value; said period of ten years shall not be extended by non-residence, legal disability, partial payment, or acknowledgment of debt."

Bearing in mind the old law, the mischief and the remedy, there can be no doubt that the legislature intended by the above to fix a definite unconditional period of limitation which could be extended only as therein provided by a refiling of the mortgage or a sworn copy thereof. Clearly the legislature intended to bar all mortgages where, on the face of the record, the cause of action accrued more than ten years previously, and that, regardless of anything which might formerly have tolled or extended the period. Only by making the period completely immune from being extended for any reason except as provided in the act would the law serve any useful purpose. See 17 Nebraska Law Bulletin, 137, 144. This being true the law should be so construed as to subserve the legislative purpose. The words of the act: "shall not be extended by non-residence, legal disability, partial payment, or acknowledgment of debt," should not receive a narrow or strict interpretation, but should be broadly and liberally construed to exclude every method or manner of tolling the statute, unless the mortgage is refiled or a sworn copy thereof filed.

The beneficial features of this legislation so overwhelmingly outweigh the trifling inconvenience to holders of mortgages that no reason can be conceived of why the amendment should be strictly construed.

As applied to this case the words "partial payment" in the act clearly include payments of principal and interest. The notes in question provided for the payment of a certain amount of money as principal and a certain amount or rate of money as interest. The principal and interest together at any given time constituted the indebtedness. The payment of principal or of interest which does not pay and satisfy the entire indebtedness is clearly a partial payment and, therefore, within the very terms of the law. Consequently the period of limitations in this case was not extended or tolled by the partial payment of interest and the lien of the mortgage was barred.

The case of Steeves v. Nispel, supra, relied on by plaintiff does not sustain her. It merely held that unrecorded written extension agreements are not included under any of the terms, "Non-residence, legal disability, partial payment, or acknowledgment of debt," in the amendment of 1925, and therefore, such written extension agreement will toll the ten year period. It seems to the writer of this opinion that the court in that case gave to the amendment of 1925 and the terms just quoted altogether too strict and narrow an interpretation and application. The writer believes that the legislative intent is entirely clear that as against purchasers and lienors for value, nothing should toll the ten year period unless the mortgage is refiled or a copy thereof filed. However, whether the writer's criticism is or is not valid, the *Nispel* case goes as far in restricting the operation of the amendment as the court is disposed to go. It does not justify the additional restriction upon the act sought to be imposed herein. While the 1925 amendment may not, in specific terms, exclude written promises or extension agreements from tolling the period, it does, expressly and specifically, prohibit "partial payments" from so extending it.

The Recording Acts 729

It is unnecessary to consider the effect of the 1941 amendment, Laws 1941, c. 35, since the mortgage in question was fully barred many months before that amendment was adopted.

The judgment of the district court is reversed and the action dismissed. Reversed and dismissed.

NOTES

1. Certain kinds of claimants commonly are exempted from adverse application of statutes of limitation. Those often favored in this way are persons under legal disability, holders of future interests prior to rights becoming possessory, spouses with inchoate dower or curtesy rights, and federal and state governments. In addition, in many states, certain events can stop the running of the statutory period to the disadvantage of those who would otherwise benefit. Part payment of an overdue mortgage debt is an example of such a tolling of the limitations period. One result of these exempting and tolling preferences so far as land titles are concerned is to make statutes of limitations much less effective as title clearance and protection devices for those claiming interests in land against which old, stale claims are outstanding. Owners wishing to sell or mortgage may find that they do not have marketable title because of such claims. Decades of adverse possession may even be ineffectual to create good title.

A trend has long been apparent to cut down on exceptions to the running of limitations periods. One approach has been to eliminate the exceptions, at least in some situations. The Nebraska statute construed in Weekes v. Rumbaugh illustrates this. Another way of dealing with limitations exceptions is to place an absolute time limit on how long the exception may extend running of the period. An Oregon statute, for instance, does this: "If, at the time the cause of action accrues, any person entitled to bring [certain actions, including those for the recovery of real property] is:

"(1)   Within the age of 18 years,

"(2)   Insane, or

"(3)   Imprisoned on a criminal charge, or in execution under the sentence of a court for a term less than his natural life, the time of such disability shall not be a part of the time limited for the commencement of the action; but the period within which the action shall be brought shall not be extended more than five years by any such disability, nor shall it be extended in any case longer than one year after such disability ceases." Or. Rev. Stat. §12.160 (1981).

Still another way of weakening exceptions is to require an additional recording or a judicial proceeding to keep excepted interests alive. This approach has also been used more broadly to limit interests not treated as exceptions. The marketable title acts have incorporated this re-recording approach. Another is the following Iowa statute:

In all cases where the holder of the legal or equitable title or estate to real estate situated within this state, prior to January 1, 1970, conveyed the real estate or any interest in the real estate by deed, mortgage, or other instrument, and the spouse failed to join in the conveyance, the spouse or the heirs at law, personal representatives, devisees, grantees, or assignees of the spouse are barred from recovery unless suit is brought for recovery within one year after July 1, 1980. But in case the right to the distributive share has not accrued by the death of the spouse making the instrument, then the one not joining is authorized to file in the recorder's office of the county where the land is situated, a notice with affidavit setting forth affiant's claim, together with the facts upon which the claim rests, and the residence of the claimants. If the notice is not filed within two years from July 1, 1980, the claim is barred forever. Any action contemplated in this section may include land situated in different counties, by giving notice as provided by section 617.13. Iowa Code Ann. §614.15 (West Supp. 1985).

2. The following Oklahoma statute, Okla. Stat. Ann. tit. 16, §4 (West 1953, Supp. 1976-1977), was held constitutional in Saak v. Hicks, 321 P.2d 425 (Okla. 1958): ". . . a deed relating to the homestead shall be valid without the signature of the grantor's spouse, and the spouse shall be conclusively deemed to have consented thereto, where the same shall have been duly recorded in the office of the county clerk of the county where the real estate is situated for a period of ten (10) years prior to a date six (6) months after the effective date thereof, and thereafter when the same shall have been so recorded for a period of ten (10) years, and no action shall have been instituted within said time in any court of record having jurisdiction seeking to cancel, avoid or invalidate such deed relating to the homestead by reason of the alleged homestead character of the real estate at the time of such conveyance."

3. All American states have adverse possession statutes, a form of statute of limitations that can result in the adverse holder acquiring unencumbered title to the land. In many instances the adverse holder has a defective title and his adverse possession for the statutory period results in the claims against his title being terminated. Although state adverse possession statutes differ considerably in the details of their coverage, this North Carolina enactment is typical: "No action for the recovery or possession of real property, or the issues and profits thereof, shall be maintained when the person in possession thereof, or defendant in the action, or those under whom he claims, has possessed the property under known and visible lines and boundaries adversely to all other persons for twenty years; and such possession so held gives a title in fee to the possessor, in such property, against all persons not under disability." N.C. Gen. Stat. §1-40 (1969).

In some states the period of time required to make out title by adverse possession is shortened if the adverse holder also has a claim of title that although defective is sufficient to constitute color of title. The following are illustrative of such statutes:

Ill. Ann. Stat. c. 110 (Smith-Hurd 1984)

§13-109. Payment of taxes with color of title. Every person in the actual possession of lands or tenements, under claim and color of title, made in good faith, and who for 7 successive years, continue in such possession, and also, during such time, pays all taxes legally assessed on such lands or tenements, shall be held and adjudged to be the legal owner of such lands or tenements, to the extent and according to the purport of his or her paper title. All persons holding under such possession, by purchase, legacy or descent, before such 7 years have expired, and who shall continue such possession, and continue to pay the taxes as above set forth so as to complete the possession and payment of taxes for the term above set forth is entitled to the benefit of this Section.

Tex. Civ. Code Ann. (Vernon 1958)

Art. 5507. Suits to recover real estate, as against a person in peaceable and adverse possession thereof under title or color of title, shall be instituted within three years next after the cause of action accrued, and not afterward.

Art. 5508. By the term "title" is meant a regular chain of transfers from or under the sovereignty of the soil, and by "color of title" is meant a consecutive chain of such transfers down to such person in possession, without being regular, as if one or more of the memorials or muniments be not registered, or not duly registered, or be only in writing, or such like defect as may not extend to or include the want of intrinsic fairness and honesty; or when the party in possession shall hold the same by a certificate of headright, land warrant, or land scrip, with a chain of transfer down to him in possession.

In a few states, only persons with color of title may successfully acquire title by adverse possession. E.g., N.M. Stat. Ann. §37-1-22 (1978).

Dennen v. Searle
149 Conn. 126, 176 A.2d 561 (1961)

KING, Associate Justice. On September 18, 1941, Mary A. Searle conveyed a tract of land in Windsor to her four children as tenants in common. These children comprised the three plaintiffs in this action, Rena L. (Searle) Dennen, Ralph B. Searle and Inez C. Searle, and also Elbert A. Searle, the deceased husband of Mildred Beebe Searle, the defendant in this action. Although Mary A. Searle reserved a life estate in herself, this need not be considered, since she apparently died prior to the execution of the instrument here in controversy.

On June 21, 1948, all four children joined in the execution of an unartfully drawn instrument which is styled "Agreement" and which purports to change the rights and interests of the cotenants inter se and to convey to others certain remainder interests in the land. This instrument remained unrecorded until May 19, 1953. The defendant's husband died intestate on May 10, 1953, leaving, as those entitled to his estate, the defendant and her two children, Milton C. and Enid L. Searle. See General Statutes, §§46-12, 45-274. The defendant knew nothing of the agreement until after her husband's death. The plaintiffs are in possession of the property and claim that their rights in it are those purportedly given them under the agreement. The defendant and her two children, at some undisclosed time after her husband's death but prior to February 19, 1955, executed a mutual distribution of the estate of her husband wherein all of his interest in the tract question was set to her. No claim is made that this mutual distribution was executed prior to the effective date of the validating act hereinafter discussed.

The plaintiffs brought this action to quiet title under General Statutes, §47-31. They alleged possession in themselves and such other rights and interests in the property as were purportedly given them by the agreement, and also that the defendant claimed rights in the property adverse to them. They asked for a judgment determining her rights in the property and settling the title thereto. Since none of the remaindermen other than the defendant were made parties, their rights cannot be authoritatively determined, and we confine our consideration to the rights of the plaintiffs and the defendant in the property. The remaindermen should have been made parties, and we decide this case only because, as hereinafter appears, our construction of the agreement and our determination of the claims of law made in respect to it deprive the remaindermen of nothing. See cases such as Auchincloss v. City Bank Farmers Trust Co., 136 Conn. 266, 273, 70 A.2d 105.

The plaintiffs claim their interests in the property solely under and by virtue of the agreement, which they claim is a valid deed. The defendant asserts that the agreement is inoperative as a deed for a number of reasons. . . .

The defendant also claims that even if the instrument is a deed, it is inoperative for lack of any seal. Since there is no seal, the instrument fails to conform to the requirements as to the due execution of a conveyance of realty as set forth in General Statutes, §47-5, and on its face is inoperative as a deed. See Savings Bank of New Haven v. Davis, 8 Conn. 191, 212; Howe v. Keeler, 27 Conn. 538, 555; Bickart v. Sanditz, 105 Conn. 766, 772, 136 A. 580. The plaintiffs claim that this defect was cured by subsequent validating acts. At the legislative sessions of 1949, 1951 and 1953, acts were enacted, in substantially identical language, validating properly recorded conveyances which were defective because of the absence of a seal. None purported to validate a conveyance unless the conveyance had been recorded nor in fact did it. Mangusi v. Vigiliotti, 104 Conn. 291, 295,

132 A. 464. The agreement was recorded May 19, 1953, so that it was validated, if validation was possible, by the 1953 validating act, which, as a special act, took effect upon its approval by the governor on June 30, 1953. General Statutes, §2-32. The defendant claims that the validating act could not affect her, since its operative date was subsequent to that of her husband's death and at the moment of his death his interest vested in those entitled to his intestate estate, that is, the defendant and his heirs at law, the two children. See General Statutes, §§46-12, 45-274; Parlato v. McCarthy, 136 Conn. 126, 133, 69 A.2d 648; O'Connor v. Chiascione, 130 Conn. 304, 306, 33 A.2d 336, 148 A.L.R. 169; Ziulkowski v. Kolodziej, 119 Conn. 230, 233, 175 A. 780, 96 A.L.R. 1065; 2 Locke & Kohn, Conn. Probate Practice §266.

"What the Legislature may prescribe it may dispense with, and it may cure by subsequent act an irregularity of nonobservance of requirements which it originally might have dispensed with, provided that vested rights have not intervened." Sanger v. City of Bridgeport, 124 Conn. 183, 186, 198 A. 746, 748, 116 A.L.R. 1031. Since the requirement of a seal was prescribed by statute, there can be no question of the right of the General Assembly to cure the defect arising from the omission of a seal, as between the parties to the instrument. Ibid. Thus, if the agreement had been recorded, and its validation had occurred, before the death of Elbert A. Searle, the deed would have been effectually validated. He could have had no equitable justification for objecting to the validation. The question arises as to what equities this defendant has which her husband lacked. At the moment of his death, a one-third interest in his interest in the property vested in her. She paid nothing for it. She did nothing in reliance on the state of the record title. She was not a creditor of her husband's estate. Her position is not that of a bona fide purchaser for value, or even of a purchaser for value with notice. She has no equities other than those he had. See cases such as Finnegan v. LaFontaine, 122 Conn. 561, 568, 191 A. 337; Sanford v. DeForest, 85 Conn. 694, 698, 84 A. 111; Green v. Abraham, 43 Ark. 420, 425. In short, she could not by the mere act of inheritance gain interests, legal or equitable, in the property greater than those of the person from whom she inherited. Shadden v. Zimmerlee, 401 Ill. 118, 125, 81 N.E.2d 477. Her interest, to be sure vested at the time of her husband's death, but her interest was a one-third interest in his interest, with whatever infirmities his interest had, including the possibility of validation of the deed. First School District v. Ufford, 52 Conn. 44, 49; Watson v. Mercer, 8 Pet. 88, 33 U.S. 88, 110, 8 L. Ed. 876. The 1953 validating act was effective to cure the lack of a seal in the deed. . . .

The court correctly held that the defendant's interest in the property in question is limited to the remainder interest granted her under the final dispositive clause of the deed; that this interest is defeasible by the exercise of the power of sale given the surviving cotenants; and that neither she nor the other distributees of the estate of Elbert A. Searle acquired, either by descent or distribution, any interests in the property which survived the validation of the deed.

There is no error.

NOTES

1. The curative act held applicable in the principal case provides:

> Any deed, lease or other instrument made for the purpose of conveying, leasing or affecting real property, or pertaining to or affecting any interest therein, and recorded in the land records of the town in which such land is located, which deed, lease or other instrument was not sealed by the parties, or any of them; any deed, lease or other instrument made for the purpose of conveying, leasing or affecting real property, or pertaining to or affecting any interest therein, recorded in the land records of the town in which such land is located, the acknowledgment of which was not completed, or was erroneously taken or recited, or was taken by a person not having authority to take such acknowledgment or where the authority of the person taking such acknowledgment was not stated or authenticated, or where no acknowledgment by the parties, or any of them, to such deed, lease or instrument was taken, is validated. [1953 Conn. Spec. Laws c. 26, §7, at 1035.]

Why do you think the Connecticut legislature passed this kind of curative act rather than repealing the seal and acknowledgment requirements?

Note that subsequent to the above 1953 act, the Connecticut legislature has updated validations by a series of similar statutes enacted every two or more years. This practice of updating validations by a series of comparable curative acts has occurred in a number of states.

2. Some curative acts apply to defective instruments as they become of record for a set number of years. The following is illustrative of a broad statute of this kind:

> When any owner of land the title to which is not registered, or of any interest in such land, signs an instrument in writing conveying or purporting to convey his land or interest, or in any manner affecting or purporting to affect his title thereto, and the instrument, whether or not entitled to record, is recorded, and indexed, in the registry of deeds for the district wherein such land is situated, and a period of ten years elapses after the instrument is accepted for record, and the instrument or the record thereof because of defect, irregularity or omission fails to comply in any respect with any requirement of law relating to seals, corporate or individual, to the validity of acknowledgment, to certificate of acknowledgment, witnesses, attestation, proof of execution, or time of execution, to recitals of consideration, residence, address, or date, to the authority of a person signing for a corporation

who purports to be the president or treasurer or a principal officer of the corporation, such instrument and the record thereof shall notwithstanding any or all of such defects, irregularities and omissions, be effective for all purposes to the same extent as though the instrument and the record thereof had originally not been subject to the defect, irregularity or omission, unless within said period of ten years a proceeding is commenced on account of the defect, irregularity or omission, and notice thereof is duly recorded in said registry of deeds and indexed and noted on the margin thereof under the name of the signer of the instrument and, in the event of such proceeding, unless relief is thereby in due course granted. [Mass. Ann. Laws c. 184, §24 (West 1977).]

b. Suits to Quiet Title

Title to land can be adjudicated in a number of different kinds of proceedings, but the most important in many American states is the suit to quiet title. Suits of this sort are frequently brought to clear and thereby protect titles when owners wish to sell or mortgage, when defects have been discovered that make the titles unmarketable and less valuable, and when easier title clearance means are inadequate for the job. Only a small percentage of these proceedings are contested, either because the defendants' claims are of such dubious value as not to be worth the bother or, if service is by publication, so old and remote that the defendants, who may not even know they have claims, never receive actual notice of suit. The title clearance possibilities of suits to quiet title differ considerably from state to state. In a few states, broad in rem proceedings are provided for that can generally purge titles of all defects, if the suits are not successfully defended. More typically, however, requirements of personal service, relative ease of direct or collateral attack, and severe restrictions on who can bring such proceedings have greatly limited the potential of suits to quiet title. Both legislatures and courts have generally been reluctant to increase the title clearing effectiveness of the suit to quiet title device. Concern over summary deprivation of defendants' rights has apparently been the principal reason for this reticence. Constitutional considerations have occasionally been crucial, although it is clear that rather strongly pro-plaintiff quiet title legislation can be devised that will withstand constitutional attack.

Berry v. Howard
33 S.D. 447, 146 N.W. 577 (1914)

POLLEY, J. The record in this case shows that one Eberhart Thomson died intestate, on the 3d day of March, 1904, and that, at the time of his death, he was seized in fee of a 120-acre tract of land in Brown county; that, in

1905, this land was sold by the treasurer of the county for the taxes thereon; that, no redemption having been made from said sale, a treasurer's deed, purporting to convey the said land to the purchaser at the said tax sale, was issued on the 25th day of March, 1908; and thereafter, on the 11th day of May, 1908, the grantee in said treasurer's deed conveyed the said premises to the appellant in this action. The respondent is the administrator of the estate of the said Thomson, and this action, commenced within less than three years after the issuance of said deed, is brought for the purpose of having the said tax deed canceled and title to the premises in controversy quieted in the estate of the plaintiff's intestate. The case has been once before this court, upon an appeal from an order overruling a demurrer to plaintiff's complaint (Berry v. Howard, 26 S.D. 29, 127 N.W. 526, Ann. Cas. 1913A, 994) where plaintiff's right to maintain the action in his representative capacity is sustained; and it is conceded that said premises belong to the said estate, unless the title thereto was divested by the tax deed to defendant's grantor, and certain court proceedings that will be hereinafter noticed.

It is claimed by the respondent that there were numerous defects and informalities in the various proceedings leading up to the issuance of the tax deed, which render the deed voidable; but, in the view we take of the case, it will be unnecessary to consider more than one of these defects. Respondent's intestate was never married, but left surviving him, as his sole heirs at law, a sister and three brothers, to wit, Mary A. Hall, Halver Roass, Ole Silerud, and Martin Bjekness. At the time of, prior to, and ever since the death of the said Thomson, his said sister, Mary A. Hall, lived on land adjoining the land of Thomson; and it was at her house that he lived, and where he died. The trial court found as a fact that, upon the death of said Thomson, on the 3d day of March, 1904, the said Mary A. Hall took possession of, and remained in possession of, the said premises until after respondent was appointed administrator of Thomson's estate, on the 29th day of December, 1908, when he took possession thereof. Prior to the issuance of the tax deed upon which appellant bases his claim of title, his grantor undertook to serve the notice required by section 2212 of the Pol. Code. The notice attempted to be served in this instance was addressed as follows: "To Eberhart Tomson, otherwise known as Eberhart Thomson, the owner, person in possession and in whose name the S. 1/2 of the S.E. 1/4 and N.W. 1/4 of the S.E. 1/4, Sec. six (6), in township one hundred twenty-seven (127) north, range sixty-five (65) west 5th P. M., in Brown county, South Dakota, is taxed, and to all other persons in interest." Then follows the regular statutory notice of expiration of period of redemption and issuance of tax deed. This notice was served by the sheriff of Brown county, as the agent of the holder of the said tax sale certificate, upon one Martin C. Hall, who is a son of the said Mary A. Hall, and resided with her on land adjoining the disputed premises. It was also published in a legal newspaper in that county for the statutory length of time.

It is contended by the respondent, and the trial court so held, that this did not constitute service of the notice of issuance of tax deed as is required by said section 2212. In our opinion the court was correct in so holding. The contents and manner of service of the notice of the issuance of a tax deed has been the subject of consideration by this and other courts in the past. [Citations omitted.]

Section 2212 designates the persons upon whom notice of the issuance of tax deed must be served. It names two classes of persons upon whom service may be made and is in the alternative. It must be served "upon the owner . . . of the land so sold, and upon the person in possession of such land or town lot unredeemed, and also upon the person in whose name the land is taxed." It is optional with the holder of the certificate whether he serve the owner of the land or the person in possession thereof; but it is imperative, in all cases, that he serve one or the other of them and that he also serve the person in whose name the land is taxed. This gives the holder of the certificate the option: First, of serving the owner of the land, and also the person in whose name it is taxed; or, second, he may serve the person in possession and also the person in whose name the land is taxed. Of course, if the land is taxed to an "unknown" owner, then the notice cannot be served upon the person in whose name it is taxed, there being no such person to serve. In this case, Eberhart Thomson, the person in whose name the land was taxed, being dead, service on him could not be made; and, having been dead at the time the land was assessed for taxation, it should be treated as though it were a case where the land were taxed to an unknown owner. This is the rule adopted in Iowa under a similar statute: "As there was no person in existence to whom the land was assessed and taxed, the situation may be said to be analogous to that where lands are assessed and taxed under the heading as to ownership of 'unknown.'" Grimes v. Ellyson, 130 Iowa 286, 105 N.W. 418. The affidavit of service of the notice upon Martin C. Hall contains the averment that he was then in possession of the land; but, as the notice was not addressed to him, and as he was in no wise mentioned therein as the party who was to be affected by such notice, the service upon him was a nullity. Woods v. Hardy, supra. And, moreover, the court found that at this identical time the land was in the possession of Mary A. Hall. No attempt ever having been made to serve her as the party in possession, the notice, in order to have had any validity whatever, must have been served in one of the ways pointed out by the statute upon the owners of the land; but, as we have already seen, Mary A. Hall, Halver Roass, Ole Silerud, and Martin Bjekness were the owners of the land at the time of the attempted service of the notice; and, although Mary A. Hall lived upon land adjoining the premises to be affected by the notice, no attempt was ever made to serve her or to give notice to either of the other owners. Therefore the treasurer was wholly without jurisdiction to issue the deed.

But this deed, though irregularly issued and subject to cancellation, was yet color of title; and appellant, for the purpose of putting outstanding claims, if any existed against the disputed premises, at rest, immediately after he acquired his interest therein, commenced an action in the circuit court for Brown county, under the provisions of chapter 81, Laws of 1905. Said action was not only brought for the purpose of quieting the title to the real property involved in this action, but included a large number of segregated tracts situated in Brown county and was against a large number of persons who were named as defendants, and against the heirs, devisees, legatees, executors, administrators, and creditors of any deceased person, or persons, who might have, or claim to have, any interest in any of the described premises adverse to the claims of the plaintiff in that action. Said action was prosecuted to final determination, and decree therein was entered on the 11th day of September, A.D. 1908. This decree purports to quiet the title to the disputed premises in the appellant as against all the world, with the exception of the said Mary A. Hall and Martin C. Hall; and it is now urged by the appellant that, although the said tax deed may have been insufficient to bar a recovery in this action, such recovery is barred by the said decree.

In that action, the said Mary A. and Martin C. Hall were made defendants by name and were served personally with the summons and complaint. They both appeared and answered in the case: but upon the filing of their answers, the appellant, upon his own motion, and at his own costs, caused the dismissal of the said action as to those two defendants, and the decree entered in said action does not purport to quiet the appellant's title as against either of them. This left the one-fourth interest in the disputed premises, inherited from the said Eberhart Thomson by Mary A. Hall, undetermined, and, as to her, the said decree is not a bar or any hindrance to the assertion of her claim to a one-fourth interest in the said premises in this action. As to the interests of the other three heirs of Eberhart Thomson, a more difficult question is presented, and one that will require careful analysis of chapter 81, Laws of 1905. If they were in fact parties defendant to the said action, then the plaintiff is barred from the assertion of any claims on their behalf in this action, and such an attempt would be a collateral attack on said judgment and cannot be maintained.

From the language used in said act, its scope is as broad as it can well be made. The action which a claimant to an interest in real property is authorized by this law to maintain is virtually against all the world, and may determine every conceivable interest adverse to plaintiff, and against all claimants — whether known or unknown.

But there are some limitations that must be observed. In order to make one a party defendant to such action he must be named as such and served with a summons by some method pointed out by the Code, unless his name cannot, by the exercise of due diligence, be ascertained.

Neither of the said owners (Halver Roass, Ole Silerud, or Martin Bjekness) was made defendant by name; and therefore whether they were parties defendant to the suit depends upon whether proper diligence was exercised in the attempt to ascertain their names. Service of the summons in said action was made by publication, and the affidavit of the plaintiff therein, upon which the order of publication was issued, was received in evidence and is made a part of the record on the appeal in this action. This affidavit sets out, in great detail, the effort made by appellant to learn the whereabouts of certain of the named defendants as well as the names of others unknown. This effort consisted of inquiry of various parties in Brown county, an examination of the county records of that county, and some correspondence; but it is a significant fact that no inquiry was made of the said Martin C. Hall, whom appellant claims was in possession of the disputed premises, nor of Mary A. Hall, whom the court found as a fact to be in possession of said premises. Both these parties were named as defendants, both were served, and both answered. While neither of these answers appear in the record, it may be assumed that the answer of Mary A. Hall, who is the owner of a one-fourth interest in said land, set out her source of title. This must have suggested inquiry which, if made by appellant, would certainly have led to the identification and probable location of the other owners — thus enabling appellant to have made them parties by name and give them notice of the pendency of the action. Instead of doing this, appellant dismissed his action as to those two defendants and made no effort whatever to have their interests, if any, determined. This leads to the inference that the appellant did not desire to have the title to the disputed premises determined in said action, and that the said heirs of Eberhart Thomson were not parties to the said action, and the court was wholly without jurisdiction to adjudicate their rights.

"Due diligence," as used in section 2 of chapter 81, Laws of 1905, has the same meaning as it does where used in section 112, Code Civ. Proc., and requires the same good faith effort on the part of the plaintiff in an action prosecuted under said chapter 81 to ascertain the name of a party who is to be divested of his interest in real property as said section 112 does to ascertain his whereabouts. This court has indicated the character of effort that is required by section 112, and, as it is a matter of vital import in proceedings under chapter 81, we reiterate and quote at length from what we said in Grigsby v. Wopschall, 25 S.D. 564, 127 N.W. 605, 37 L.R.A. (N.S.) 206: "While, in this class of cases, it is not necessary that all possible or conceivable means should be used to ascertain the whereabouts of a defendant, still it is necessary that the affidavit for publication should show that all reasonable means have been used to discover the whereabouts of defendant, to the end that he may receive actual notice of the pendency of the suit against him. This is what is meant by the term 'due diligence.' In Coughran v. Markley, 15 S.D. 37, 87 N.W. 2, it is very aptly stated: 'Judgments which exclude persons from any interest or lien upon land should not be rendered without actual notice, when by the exercise of reasonable diligence actual notice can be given. There should be either actual notice or an honest and reasonable effort to give it. The statute contemplates, and trial judges should invariably require, that the party who institutes the suit shall in good faith make every reasonable effort to not only ascertain that the defendant cannot be served within the state, but to ascertain his whereabouts, in order that copies of the summons and complaint may reach him through the mails or otherwise.' Where a defendant, on whom service by publication is sought, has recently left the state, plaintiff should ascertain the place where he last resided, and it is also incumbent upon plaintiff to ascertain whether such defendant left any relatives or agents or other business associates in such vicinity, and, if so, inquiry should be made of them, as persons presumed to be most likely to know the present whereabouts of such defendant. Failing to find such relatives, agents, or business associates, inquiry should be made of the nearest and most immediate neighbors of such defendant as persons also presumed to be likely to know the whereabouts of such defendant. Inquiry of the postmaster at the last-known post office address of such defendant might readily lead to the discovery of his whereabouts. The affidavit for publication should show that all reasonable inquiry has been made of persons likely or presumed to know the whereabouts of the person sought to be notified by publication. Near neighbors might know of near relatives of defendant who resided in some other locality who could furnish the desired information. It is the use of all such reasonable means of this character that constitutes 'due diligence.' The affidavit should show that such sources of inquiry have been reasonably pursued and exhausted. Inquiries made of persons in a distant part of the county, or state, 20, 50, 100, or more miles from the locality where defendant last resided, who are not personally acquainted with and did not know defendant, are wholly worthless and wholly immaterial to establish 'due diligence.' Such persons are not likely or presumed to know the whereabouts of defendant.'' The record does not show that the defendant made any such good-faith effort to ascertain the names and location of the owners of the disputed premises as would authorize the court to adjudicate their rights as unknown owners. He not only failed to exercise reasonable diligence in ascertaining and bringing before the court all parties in interest, but he dismissed his action as to such parties as disclosed an interest in this particular piece of land. By doing this, he withdrew said premises from consideration of the court and left the court without jurisdiction to determine any of the interests therein; and, the court not having such jurisdiction in said action, the decree entered therein did not affect the title to the premises in question and is no bar to the maintenance of this action.

Nothing said herein is to be taken as an expression of opinion as to the constitutionality or unconstitutionality of chapter 81 of the Session Laws of 1095. The law as it stands not having been complied with, it is not necessary to pass upon the validity of the law itself. Neither is anything said herein to be taken as an expression of opinion as to whether or not chapter

The Recording Acts

81, Laws of 1905, authorizes a party to have litigated, in one action, claims to separate tracts of land, plaintiff's title to which is derived from different sources, and where no community of interest exists between the several defendants.

At the beginning of the trial, the appellant objected to any further proceedings in the action until the respondent had paid or tendered to appellant all taxes, interest, and penalties, legal costs and expenses, as provided by section 2214, Pol. Code. The objection was overruled, and this ruling is urged as error by appellant. The court followed the provisions of section 2225, Pol. Code, by ascertaining the amount to which appellant was entitled by reason of taxes paid and expense incurred on account of the land in controversy. Appellant was awarded judgment and given a lien on the premises for this amount. There was no error in this. Pettigrew et al. v. Moody, 17 S.D. 275, 96 N.W. 94.

This necessarily leads to the conclusion that the trial court was right, and the order and the judgment appealed from are affirmed.

American Land Co. v. Zeiss
219 U.S. 47, 31 S. Ct. 200, 55 L. Ed. 82 (1911)

As a result of the conditions caused in San Francisco by the great calamity of earthquake and fire, which befell that city in April, 1906, an extraordinary session of the legislature of California was convoked. One reason stated for the call was the necessity of providing for restoring the record title to land in San Francisco. An act to accomplish that purpose became a law upon its approval on June 16, 1906.

The Circuit Court of Appeals has certified the issues involved in a pending cause, the determination of which rests upon the validity of the statute just referred to. The pertinent facts arising on the record of the cause are stated in the certificate, and are hereafter set forth. The purpose contemplated is to obtain instructions as to whether the act in question "is violative of the Fourteenth Amendment of the Constitution of the United States," and whether by virtue of a decree rendered by the Superior Court of the city and county of San Francisco, referred to in the recital of facts, the American Land Company "has been deprived of its property without due process of law."

The following are the facts recited in the certificate:

"The appellant as complainant in the court below brought its bill in equity against the appellee to remove a cloud from its title to real property and to quiet its title thereto. The bill alleges on April 10, 1908, and at all the times prior thereto referred to in the bill, George H. Lent and Mary G. Coggeshall were severally the owners in fee simple of two adjacent lots of land in San Francisco, which lots are described in the bill. The lots and others similarly situated are known as City Slip and Water Lots. Under the provisions of an act of the legislature of the State of California, approved March 5, 1851 (Stats. of 1851, page 764), the State leased this property to the city of San Francisco for the term of ninety-nine years. The appellee is alleged to be the owner of the unexpired portion of this lease as successor in interest of the city's right, and to be entitled to the possession thereof until March 26, 1950. The bill alleges that the appellee has no right whatever other than this right of possession and occupation; that notwithstanding the premises, the appellee claims to be the owner in fee simple of said lands under a judgment and decree of the Superior Court of the State of California in and for the city and county of San Francisco, made and entered December 19, 1906, in a proceeding entitled 'Louis Zeiss, plaintiff, vs. All persons claiming any interest in, or lien upon the real property herein described, or any part thereof, defendants;' that said proceeding was brought under an act of the legislature of the State of California, entitled 'An Act to provide for the establishment and quieting of title to real property in case of the loss or destruction of public records,' approved June 16, 1906; that said claim of the appellee under said decree is without right, and said decree is void; that in the complaint in that proceeding the appellee, after properly setting forth the destruction of the records, alleged that he was the owner in fee simple, free of incumbrance, of the lands which are described in the bill in this case, and that he prayed for a decree of the Superior Court adjudging his title to be as set forth by him; that at the time of filing his complaint he filed his affidavit setting forth the character of the estate, the source of his title, his possession, and stating that he had made no conveyance of the land, that there were no liens on it, and that he did not know and that he had never been informed of any other person who claimed or may claim any interest or lien upon the property, or any part thereof, adversely to him. The affidavit contained no averment that inquiry of any kind had been made to ascertain whether such adverse claim did exist. It is shown in the bill that in said proceeding under said act of the legislature, summons was published in the Law Recorder for the space of two months, and was also posted on the land, and that after the period of publication of the summons the appellee herein obtained a decree of the court as prayed for by him. The bill further alleges that although the appellant's grantors were at all times citizens and residents of California, not seeking to evade but ready to accept service of summons, and easily reached for that purpose, no service was made upon them, nor did they in any way receive notice of the pendency of the action, nor did they gain any knowledge of the existence of the decree until more than a year after its entry. A demurrer was interposed to the bill in the court below for want of equity, which demurrer was sustained by the court and the bill was dismissed."

Mr. Chief Justice WHITE, after making the foregoing statement, delivered the opinion of the court. Although not objecting to an answer to the questions, nevertheless the American Land Company, which was the appellant below, suggests at bar a want of power to reply to the questions for a twofold reason: First, because the certificate on its face indicates that the court below was not in a state of mind which required the instruction of this court, but was merely desirous of provoking a direct decision by this court, to avoid the delay and the public inconvenience which otherwise might result. Second, because the certificate is so broad as simply to refer the whole case to this court for decision instead of presenting definite propositions of law for solution. While it may be that these suggestions find possible support, considering the record in a detached way, we think when the certificate is considered as a whole and the subject with which it deals is properly weighed the suggestions are without merit. We therefore pass to a consideration of the questions propounded.

It is apparent that the substantial considerations involved in the questions certified are embraced in the following, *a*, the authority of the State to deal with the subject with which the statute is concerned; *b*, upon the hypothesis of the existence of power, the sufficiency of the safeguards provided in the statute; *c*, upon the like hypothesis the adequacy of the proceedings had in the particular cause with which the certificate deals. We shall consider these subjects separately.

As to the power of the State. The conditions which led to the legislation in question were stated by the Supreme Court of California in Title Document Restoration Co. v. Kerrigan, Judge, 150 California, 289, 305. The court said:

"It is also a matter of common knowledge that in the city and county of San Francisco, at least, if not in other counties, the disaster of April last worked so great a destruction of the public records as to make it impossible to trace any title with completeness of certainty. That some provision was necessary to enable the holders and owners of real estate in this city to secure to themselves such evidence of title as would enable them, not only to defend their possession, but to enjoy and exercise the equally important right of disposition, is clear."

As it is indisputable that the general welfare of society is involved in the security of the titles to real estate and in the public registry of such titles, it is obvious that the power to legislate as to such subjects inheres in the very nature of government. This being true, it follows that government possesses the power to remedy the confusion and uncertainty as to registered titles arising from a disaster like that described by the court below. We might well pursue no further the subject of the power of the State to enact the law in question, and thus leave its authority to depend upon the demonstration necessarily resulting from the obvious considerations just stated. As, however, the question of power is intimately interwoven with the sufficiency of the procedure adopted, and as a clear comprehension of the scope of the power will serve to elucidate the question of procedure, we shall briefly refer to some of the leading cases by which the elementary doctrine of power over the subject of titles to real estate and the application of that doctrine to a case like the one in hand is settled beyond question. That a State has the power, generally speaking, to provide for and protect individual rights to the soil within its confines and declare what shall form a cloud on the title to such soil was recognized in Clark v. Smith, 13 Pet. 195. So, also, it is conclusively established that when the public interests demand the law may require even a party in actual possession of land and claiming a perfect title to appear before a properly constituted tribunal and establish that title by a judicial proceeding. Such was the method employed by the United States in settling as between itself and claimants under Mexican grants the title to property in California. Barker v. Harvey, 181 U.S. 481; Mitchell v. Furman, 180 U.S. 402; Botiller v. Dominguez, 130 U.S. 238; More v. Steinbach, 127 U.S. 70.

The question of what authority a State possesses over titles to real estate, and what jurisdiction over the subject it may confer upon its courts, received much consideration in Arndt v. Griggs, 134 U.S. 316. It was there held that, even as to ordinary controversies respecting title to land arising between rival claimants, the State possessed the power to provide for the adjudication of titles to real estate not only as against residents, but as against non-residents, who might be brought into court by publication. In the course of the opinion the court said (p. 320):

"It [the State] has control over property within its limits; and the condition of ownership of real estate therein, whether the owner be stranger or citizen, is subject to its rules concerning the holding, the transfer, liability to obligations, private or public, and the modes of establishing titles thereto. It cannot bring the person of a non-resident within its limits — its process goes not out beyond its borders — but it may determine the extent of his title to real estate within its limits; and for the purpose of such determination may provide any reasonable methods of imparting notice. The well-being of every community requires that the title to real estate therein shall be secure, and that there be convenient and certain methods of determining any unsettled questions respecting it. The duty of accomplishing this is local in its nature; it is not a matter of national concern or vested in the general government; it remains with the State; and as this duty is one of the State, the manner of discharging it must be determined by the State, and no proceeding which it provides can be declared invalid, unless it conflict with some special inhibitions of the Constitution, or against natural justice."

Manifestly, under circumstances like those here presented, the principle applies with equal force in the case of unknown claimants. Undisclosed and unknown claimants are, to say the least, as dangerous to the stability of titles as other classes. This principle received recognition and was applied in Hamilton v. Brown, 161 U.S. 256, where it was held to be competent for a State to make provision for promptly ascertaining, by appropriate judicial proceedings, who has succeeded to property upon the death of a person leaving such property within the State. It was said (p. 275):

The Recording Acts

"If such proceedings are had, after actual notice by service of summons to all known claimants, and constructive notice by publication to all possible claimants who are unknown, the final determination of the right of succession, either among private persons, as in the ordinary administration of estates, or between all persons and the State, as by inquest of office or similar process to determine whether the estate has escheated to the public, is due process of law; and a statute providing for such proceedings and determination does not impair the obligation of any contract contained in the grant under which the former owner held, whether that grant was from the State or from a private person."

The application of the doctrine of governmental power as just stated, to a condition like the one here in question was aptly pointed out by the Supreme Court of Illinois in Bertrand v. Taylor, 87 Illinois, 235, where, in considering the Illinois Burnt Record Act, the court said:

"It was demanded as a matter of safety in a great emergency. It was not calculated to take any reasonable being by surprise. It was known throughout the civilized world that a large part of the city of Chicago had been destroyed by fire and that the records of courts and the records of deeds were all destroyed. This naturally commanded the attention of all reasonable persons everywhere, and called upon them to attend and see what means would be adopted to mitigate the evils and dangers incident to the destruction. This legislation was not done in a corner, but before the observation of a civilized world. We cannot doubt the power of the general assembly to pass the act."

The Supreme Court of California, in the *Kerrigan* case, supra, addressing itself to the same subject, pertinently observed (pp. 313, 314):

"Applying the principles which have led the courts in cases like Arndt v. Griggs, 134 U.S. 316, and Perkins v. Wakeham, 86 California, 580, to sustain judgments quieting titles against non-residents upon substituted service, why should not the legislature have power to give similar effect to such judgments against unknown claimants where the notice is reasonably full and complete? The validity of such judgments against known residents is based upon the ground that the State has power to provide for the determination of titles to real estate within its border, and that, as against non-resident defendants or others, who cannot be served in the State, a substituted service is permissible, as being the only service possible. These grounds apply with equal force to unknown claimants. The power of the State as to titles should not be limited to settling them as against persons named. In order to exercise this power to its fullest extent, it is necessary that it should be made to operate on all interests, known and unknown. As was said by Holmes, C.J., in Tyler v. Judges of the Court of Registration, 175 Massachusetts, 71, in speaking of a statute which, in the particular under discussion, was similar to ours: 'If it does not satisfy the Constitution, a judicial proceeding to clear titles against all the world hardly is possible; for the very meaning of such a proceeding is to get rid of unknown as well as known claimants — indeed, certainty against the unknown may be said to be its chief end — and unknown claimants cannot be dealt with by personal service upon the claimant.'"

The power exerted by the act being then clearly within the legislative authority, we are brought to consider whether the lawful power was manifested in such a manner as to cause the act to be repugnant to the Fourteenth Amendment. And this brings us to the second proposition heretofore stated, viz:

The adequacy of the safeguards which the statute provides. As no complaint is made concerning the provisions of the statute relating to the designation of and notice to known claimants, we put that subject out of view and address ourselves to the provisions relating to unknown claimants or claims. The action which the statute authorizes may be brought by "Any person who claims an estate of inheritance, or for life in, and who is by himself or his tenant, or other person, holding under him, in the actual and peaceable possession of any real property" situated in a county where "the public records in the office of a county recorder have been lost or destroyed, in whole or in any material part, by flood, fire or earthquake." In the caption of the complaint the statute requires that the defendants shall be described as "all persons claiming any interest in or lien upon the real property herein described, or any part thereof." The summons is required to contain a description of the property affected by the suit and to be directed to "all persons claiming any interest in or lien upon the real property herein described, or any part thereof." The summons is to be published at least once a week for two months, and the defendants are commanded to appear and answer within three months after the first publication of the summons. A copy of the summons is required to be posted in a conspicuous place on each separate parcel of the property described in the complaint within fifteen days after the first publication of the summons. At the time of filing the complaint a notice of the pendency of the action, giving among other things a particular description of the property affected thereby, must be recorded in the office of the recorder of the county in which the property is situated, and it is made the duty of the recorder to enter, "upon a map or plat of the parcels of land, to be kept by him for that purpose, on the part of the map or plat representing the parcel or parcels so described a reference to the date of the filing of such notice and, when recorded, to the book and page of the record thereof." In considering the statute we are bound by the construction affixed to it by the Supreme Court of the State, and therefore treat as embraced within its terms that which the highest court of the State has declared the statute exacts, either expressly or by necessary implication. In the *Kerrigan* case, supra, it was held that the result of the provisions of the statute was "to require the complainant to designate and to serve as known claimants all whom, with reasonable diligence, he could ascertain to be claimants," a construction which, in effect declared that the statute prohibited the omis-

The Recording Acts

sion of a known claim or claimant, upon the conception that the rights of such claim or claimant would be foreclosed by the general designation and notice prescribed for unknown claimants. And in Hoffman v. Superior Court, 151 California, 386, where the doctrine of the *Kerrigan* case was reiterated and applied, the court, after holding that the statute requires the plaintiff in his affidavit to allege in terms "that he does not know and has never been informed" of any adverse claimants whom he has not specifically named, pointed out that failure of the plaintiff to make inquiry or to avail himself of knowledge which would be imputed to him because of facts sufficient to put him on inquiry as to the existence of adverse claims would be available "in any subsequent attack upon the decree, upon the ground that there was extraneous fraud of the plaintiff in making a false affidavit to obtain jurisdiction."

It is to be born in mind that it has been settled (Griffith v. Connecticut, 218 U.S. 563, and cases cited) that the Fourteenth Amendment does not operate to deprive the States of their lawful power, and of the right in the exercise of such power to resort to reasonable methods inherently belonging to the power exerted. On the contrary, the provisions of the due process clause only restrain those arbitrary and unreasonable exertions of power which are not really within lawful state power, since they are so unreasonable and unjust as to impair or destroy fundamental rights.

It is to be observed that the statute not only requires a disclosure by the plaintiff of all known claimants, but moreover at the very outset contains words of limitation that no one not in the actual and peaceable possession of property can maintain the action which it authorizes. No person can therefore be deprived of his property under the statute unless he had not only gone out of possession of such property and allowed another to acquire possession, or if he had a claim to such property or an interest therein, had so entirely failed to disclose that fact as to enable a possessor to truthfully make the affidavit which the statute exacts of a want of all knowledge of the existence of other claimants than as disclosed in his affidavit. Besides, it is to be considered that the statute, as construed by the California court, imposed upon the one in possession seeking the establishment of an alleged title the duty to make diligent inquiry to ascertain the names of all claimants. Instead, therefore, of the statute amounting to the exertion of a purely unreasonable and arbitrary power, its provisions leave no room for that contention. On the contrary, we think the statute manifests the careful purpose of the legislature to provide every reasonable safeguard for the protection of the rights of unknown claimants and to give such notice as under the circumstances would be reasonably likely to bring the fact of the pendency and the purpose of the proceeding to the attention of those interested. To argue that the provisions of the statute are repugnant to the due process clause because a case may be conceived where rights in and to property would be adversely affected without notice being actually conveyed by the proceedings is in effect to deny the power of the State to deal with the subject. The criterion is not the possibility of conceivable injury but the just and reasonable character of the requirements, having reference to the subject with which the statute deals. The doctrine on this subject was clearly expressed by the Court of Appeals of New York in In re Empire City Banks, 18 N.Y. 199, 215, where, speaking of the right of a State to prescribe in a suitable case for constructive service, it was said:

"Various prudential regulations are made with respect to these remedies, but it may possibly happen, notwithstanding all these precautions, that a citizen who owes nothing, and has done none of the acts mentioned in the statutes, may be deprived of his estate without any actual knowledge of the process by which it has been taken from him. If we hold, as we must, in order to sustain this legislation, that the constitution does not positively require personal notice in order to constitute a legal proceeding due process of law, it then belongs to the legislature to determine in the particular instance whether the case calls for this kind of exceptional legislation and what manner of constructive notice shall be sufficient to reasonably apprise the party proceeded against of the legal steps which are taken against him."

And in accordance with this view, the Supreme Court of California, in the *Kerrigan* case, pointed out that the statute furnished all the safeguards for which, in reason, it could have been expected to provide consistently with the condition dealt with. The court said (p. 312):

"Where, as here, the summons describing the nature of the action, the property involved, the name of the plaintiff, and the relief sought, is posted upon the property, and is published in a newspaper for two months, and a *'lis pendens'* containing the same particulars is recorded in the recorder's office and entered upon the recorder's map of the property, we cannot doubt that, so far as concerns the possible claimants who are not known to the plaintiff, the notice prescribed by the act is as complete and full as, from the nature of the case, could reasonably be expected."

The case of Ballard v. Hunter, 204 U.S. 241, is instructive on this feature of the case. In that case a judgment of the Circuit Court of Arkansas was affirmed which sustained the validity of a sale of lands for levee taxes. The Arkansas statute authorized the proceedings which had resulted in the sale, upon constructive publication against non-residents and unknown owners. Lands of Josephine Ballard were sold under the statutory proceeding, she not having knowledge of the existence of the suit or of the fact that the taxes had been assessed against her property. In the course of the opinion the court, speaking through Mr. Justice McKenna, said (p. 261):

"It is said, however, that Josephine Ballard was not made a defendant in the suit, though the records of the county showed that she was an owner thereof. But the statute provided against such an omission. It provided that the proceedings and judgment should be in the nature of proceedings in rem, and that it should be immaterial that the ownership of the lands might be incorrectly alleged in the proceedings. We see no want of due process in that requirement, or what was done under it. It is manifest that any criticism of either is answered by the cases we have cited. The proceedings were appropriate to the nature of the case.

"It should be kept in mind that the laws of a State come under the prohibition of the Fourteenth Amendment only when they infringe fundamental rights. A law must be framed and judged of in consideration of the practical affairs of man. The law cannot give personal notice of its provisions or proceedings to every one. It charges every one with knowledge of its provisions; of its proceedings it must, at times, adopt some form of indirect notice, and indirect notice is usually efficient notice when the proceedings affect real estate. Of what concerns or may concern their real estate, men usually keep informed, and on that probability the law may frame its proceedings; indeed, must frame them, and assume the care of property to be universal, if it would give efficiency to many of its exercises. This was pointed out in Huling v. Kaw Valley Railway & Improvement Company, 130 U.S. 559, where it was declared to be the 'duty of the owner of real estate, who is a non-resident, to take measure that in some way he shall be represented when his property is called into requisition; and if he fails to give notice by the ordinary publications which have been usually required in such cases, it is his misfortune, and he must abide the consequences.' It makes no difference, therefore, that plaintiffs in error did not have personal notice of the suit to collect the taxes on their lands or that taxes had been levied, or knowledge of the law under which the taxes had been levied."

While we are of opinion that the views just stated demonstrate the want of merit in the contention that the statute, because of the insufficiency of its requirements, was repugnant to the Fourteenth Amendment, a consideration of a provision of the general law of California, which by the construction of the Supreme Court of California is incorporated into the statute under consideration, would lead to the same result. Thus, in the *Hoffman* case, 151 California, 386, 393, the court said:

"In this connection it is proper to say that in determining whether or not due process of law is afforded, other statutes applicable to the proceeding may be considered. The provisions of §473 of the Code of Civil Procedure apply in such cases. Any person interested in the property and having no actual notice of the decree, may come in at any time within a year after its rendition and by showing that he has not been personally served with process and stating facts constituting a good defense to the proceeding—that is, facts sufficient to show that he has a valid adverse interest in the property—he may have the decree vacated, as to him and be allowed to answer to the merits."

The right conferred by §473 of the code, it is to be observed, is an absolute right, although the section declares that the court may impose "such terms as may be just." Holiness Church v. Metropolitan Church Association (Cal. App.), 107 Pac. Rep. 633; Gray v. Lawlor, 151 California, 352.

Under this construction it might well be held, if it were necessary to do so, as establishing a rule of limitation which it was in the power of the State to prescribe, in view of the circumstances to which the limitation was made applicable. See Tyler v. Judges, 175 Massachusetts, 71, and State v. Westfall, 85 Minnesota, 437. See also Illinois cases concerning the power to fix a short period of limitations to meet a disaster like the one to which the statute in question relates, collected in Gormley v. Clark, 134 U.S. 346, 347.

These views dispose of all the contentions concerning the repugnancy of the statute to the Fourteenth Amendment which we think it necessary to separately consider. In saying this we are not unmindful of a multitude of subordinate propositions pressed in the voluminous brief of counsel and which were all in effect urged upon the Supreme Court of California in the *Kerrigan* and *Hoffman* cases and were in those cases adversely disposed of, and which we also find to be without merit. Some of them we briefly refer to. We do not think it is important to determine the precise nature of the action authorized by the statute, since the method of procedure which was prescribed was within the legislative competency. So, also, we do not deem it important to discuss what constitutes a judicial proceeding, since the statutory proceeding provided by the act was within the authority of the State to enact, and that it was judicial in character has been expressly determined by the court of last resort of the State. Indeed, not only these, but all contentions proceed upon a misconception as to the legislative authority of the State and the effect thereon of the due process clause of the Constitution of the United States. The error which all the propositions involved was pointed out in Twining v. New Jersey, 211 U.S. 78, where, speaking by Mr. Justice Moody, the court said:

"Due process requires that the court which assumes to determine the rights of parties shall have jurisdiction (citing cases) and that there shall be notice and opportunity for hearing given the parties, (citing cases). Subject to these two fundamental conditions, which seem to be universally prescribed in all systems of law established by civilized countries, this court has, up to this time, sustained all state laws, statutory or judicially declared, regulating procedure, evidence and methods of trial, and held them to be consistent with due process of law."

3. *The adequacy of the proceedings pursued in the case referred to in the certificate.* As there is no claim that fraud, actual or constructive, was employed by Zeiss in obtaining the judgment complained of, and the proceedings confirmed to the California statute, the considerations previously stated entirely dispose of this question.

It follows that both of the questions certified must be answered in the negative.

And it is so ordered.

Comment, Enhancing the Marketability of Land: The Suit to Quiet Title
68 Yale L.J. 1245, 1265 (1959)

THE SUIT TO QUIET TITLE

The modern suit to quiet title is a statutorily authorized proceeding designed to establish a title's status by adjudicating the validity of adverse interests in real property. The suit may be in rem or quasi-in-rem; in either case, the court obtains jurisdiction to adjudicate all interests in the land at issue through its control of that land. When the suit is in rem, unknown parties served by publication may be bound by the decree. When the suit is quasi-in-rem, on the other hand, a decree can bind only those parties named by the petitioner's complaint and served process either actually or constructively.[102] . . .

The principal objective of the quiet-title suit should be to restore the saleability of titles impaired by known or record defects. In addition, the suit should impart commercial respectability to interests acquired through adverse possession—interests which are not recognized under today's recording systems, and which rarely command more than a fraction of their actual value. The suit should further protect ostensibly clear titles against the multitudinous unrecordable and misrecorded claims which repeatedly emerge to destroy the peaceful use and possession of land. Succinctly, then, the goal sought for the modernized suit to quiet title is a proceeding available to almost any interest-holder in which all adverse claims can be marshaled, examined and settled by a court whose decree, once rendered and docketed, is both the exclusive and conclusive determinant of title. To attain this objective, a new type of authorizing statute is needed. . . .

The basic problem, then, is convincing lawmakers not of their authority to adopt in rem legislation but of the need therefor. Almost half the present quiet-title statutes are essentially adversary—requiring personal jurisdiction or the joinder of known nonresident claimants—and are not founded solely on judicial control over the res. Underlying these statutes is

---

102. Whether an action is in personam, in rem, or quasi-in-rem involves an unsettled area of the law which has generated incessant controversy. See Mullane v. Central Hanover Bank & Trust Co., 339 U.S. 306, 313 (1950); Cook, The Powers of Courts of Equity (pts. 1-3), 15 Colum. L. Rev. 37, 106, 228 (1915); Fraser, Actions in Rem, 34 Cornell L.Q. 29 (1948); Walsh, Development in Equity of the Power To Act In Rem, 6 N.Y.U.L.Q. Rev. 1 (1928). . . .

a marked legislative disinclination to authorize a decree which would conclusively settle the rights of unjoined, unnotified and unrepresented parties. But obtaining personal jurisdiction over or joining unknown interest-holders is patently impossible. Their claims must accordingly be expunged ex parte or allowed to emerge at any time to subvert a previously rendered judgment. The choice is between an in personam or quasi-in-rem decree, which is worth little as a title determinant, and an in rem proceeding, which binds all adverse claimants despite possible inequities. . . .

NOTES

1. What are the inequities of broad suit to quiet title statutes, such as the one involved in American Land Co. v. Zeiss, that can clear all title defects? Should such statutes apply only to situations in which some holocaust has destroyed the public land records or should they be more generally applicable?

2. The significance of quiet title proceedings has been expanded somewhat by their inclusion in the Torrens registration system. The judicial proceeding required for Torrens registration in the United States is in effect a suit to quiet title. New Torrens registrations in this country, to the extent they occur, not uncommonly involve land parcels with known defective titles. The title clearing benefit of initial registration proceedings is a strong inducement to putting these properties into Torrens. Other benefits from registration may be merely incidental or bonus inducements. Ejectment, trespass, eminent domain, and specific performance of land sales contracts are among the many other judicial proceedings in which land title conflicts can be adjudicated and thereby cleared.

3. Many errors in land titles are not sufficiently serious to justify the time and expense of clearing them by suits to quiet title or other judicial proceedings; so less involved and less costly corrective devices may be used instead, including affidavits. Lawyers and title insurers, in determining marketability issues, often will accept affidavits by knowledgeable persons to explain apparent gaps in chains of title or clear other seeming title deficiencies. Issues that examiners frequently are willing to resolve by affidavit include questions of family history relating to titles—such as relevant births, deaths, survivors, and marital status—and questions of identity, for example, whether or not the same person conveyed out as earlier took title when there is a slight disparity in the public records between the name of a grantee and that of the next succeeding grantor. Title examiners also may accept affidavits alleging facts bearing on other significant title matters, including the acquisition of homestead rights and obtaining of title by adverse possession.

Affidavits pertaining to land titles have, however, posed problems as to

The Recording Acts

their recordability and admissibility in evidence. In a number of states they may not be recorded so as to give actual or constructive notice of the allegations they contain; and they are considered hearsay, thus may not be admitted in evidence before courts. On hearsay grounds, recitals of fact in deeds and other conveyancing instruments also have been held inadmissible evidence. But there is something of a trend to expand the recordability and evidentiary value of affidavits bearing on land titles, of which these Connecticut and Wisconsin statutory provisions are indications:

Conn. Gen. Stat. Ann. §47-12a (West Supp. 1984)

(a) An affidavit, stating facts relating to the matters hereinfter named, which may affect the title to or any interest in real estate in this state, made by any person having knowledge of the facts or competent to testify concerning them in open court, may be recorded in the land records of the town in which the real estate is situated; and, when so recorded, such affidavit, or a certified copy thereof, shall be admissible as prima facie evidence of the facts therein stated, so far as such facts affect title to real estate in any action involving the title to such land or any interest therein, if the affiant is dead or otherwise not available to testify in court.

(b) The affidavits herein provided for may relate to the following matters: Age, sex, birth, death, capacity, relationship, family history, heirship, names, identity of parties, marital status, possession or adverse possession, adverse use, residence, service in the armed forces, conflicts and ambiguities in description of land in recorded instruments, and the happening of any condition or event which may terminate an estate or interest.

(c) Every affidavit herein provided for shall include a description of the land, title to which may be affected by facts stated in such affidavit, and shall state the name of the person appearing by the record to be the owner of such land at the time of the recording of the affidavit. The town clerk shall index the affidavit in the name of such record owner.

Wis. Stat. Ann. §706.09 (West 1981 and Supp. 1984-85)

(1) *When conveyance is free of prior adverse claim.* A purchaser for a valuable consideration, . . . and his successors in interest, shall take and hold the estate or interest purported to be conveyed to such purchaser free of any claim adverse to or inconsistent with such estate or interest, if such adverse claim is dependent for its validity or priority upon: . . .

(i) *Facts not asserted of record.* Any fact not appearing of record, but the opposite or contradiction of which appears affirmatively and expressly in a conveyance, affidavit or other instrument of record in the chain of title of the real estate affected for 5 years. Such facts may, without limitation by noninclusion, relate to age, sex, birth, death, capacity, relationship, family history, descent, heirship, names, identity of persons, marriage, marital status, homestead, possession or adverse possession, residence, service in the armed forces, conflicts and ambiguities in descriptions of land in recorded instruments, identification of any recorded plats or subdivisions, corporate authorization to convey, and the happening of any condition or event which terminates an estate or interest.

Which of the above two statutes do you consider preferable, and what weaknesses are implicit in each statute as set forth?

4. Liability of Title Searchers and Examiners

For failure to do their work satisfactorily, professional title searchers and examiners may be liable in tort or contract. To their customers, and in some places even to others who rely on such work or for whose benefit it is carried on, this can be an additional form of protection. Abstracters, lawyers, and title insurance companies are the professionals most commonly involved, and carelessness is the usual reason for their unsatisfactory work. Risks of misconduct by search and examination professionals are spread by bonding or malpractice insurance, the latter also known as errors and omissions insurance.

Williams v. Polgar
391 Mich. 6, 215 N.W.2d 149 (1974)

WILLIAMS, Justice (To Affirm). While important, the issue in this case is a relatively narrow one.

Michigan already permits a buyer of property who has relied on a faulty abstract to his detriment to recover from the abstracter, even though there is no clear contractual privity between them, if the abstracter in fact knew the buyer would rely on the abstract.

This case presents the issue whether a faulty abstracter should likewise be liable to a buyer *he should have foreseen would rely* on the abstract as well as to the buyer *he knew would rely* on it. The question boils down to whether there should be liability for *foreseeable* as well as *known* reliance.

This Court has answered that question affirmatively in a related fact situation, and in categorical terms relieved Michigan jurisprudence of the restrictions of "privity." [2] In this opinion, we reaffirm our general decision eliminating privity and specifically apply it to abstracters.

There is a second issue in this case. When does liability accrue and what statute of limitations applies.

I. FACTS

Plaintiffs Williams purchased certain property situated in the City of Warren, Macomb County, from defendants Polgar on a land contract dated

---

2. Spence v. Three Rivers Builders & Masonry Supply, Inc., 353 Mich. 120, 90 N.W.2d 873 (1958).

August 1, 1959. At the time of purchase, as provided in the land contract, defendants furnished to plaintiffs an abstract of title certified to July 15, 1959 by Abstract and Title Guaranty Company. This abstract was originally issued on February 4, 1926 by the Macomb County Abstract Company and was extended by said company in 1936, 1937, 1943, 1944, 1945, 1946, 1948, 1951, and 1952. Defendant American Title Insurance Company is the successor in interest to Macomb County Abstract Company.

The abstract of title failed to include a deed dated May 1, 1926 which was recorded on May 24, 1926 in Liber 242 of Deeds at page 174 of Macomb County records. This deed conveyed the southerly 60 feet of the property in question to the Macomb County Board of Road Commissioners.

After execution of the land contract on August 1, 1959, plaintiffs learned, allegedly for the first time, of the existence of this omitted deed. As the result thereof, plaintiffs claim they were required to completely remove a building and that certain other damages were incurred.

Plaintiffs filed this action on April 21, 1971. All defendants filed motions for accelerated judgment based on the statute of limitations. The trial court held that plaintiffs' cause of action accrued no later than the execution of the land contract on August 1, 1959. Thus accelerated judgment was granted defendants. Plaintiffs were non-suited. The Court of Appeals reversed and remanded. 43 Mich. App. 95, 204 N.W.2d 57 (1972). Defendant American Title Insurance Company requested leave to appeal to this Court which was granted on December 12, 1972. 388 Mich. 812 (1972).

II. Effect of Accelerated Judgment

Under a motion for accelerated judgment by defendants the facts well pleaded by plaintiffs and the reasonable inferences therefrom must be considered most favorably towards plaintiffs. As the complaint adequately alleges the title company's negligent misrepresentation in the abstract, plaintiffs' reliance thereon and the damage caused thereby as well as the other matters appearing in the above statement of facts, this case presents at this point no dispute as to facts.

Where there is a person negligently injured by another, normally there is recovery therefor. Ubi injuria, ibi remedium.

Defendant title company here, however, seeks immunity from liability for the injury it caused plaintiff buyers, pleading two defenses. First, defendant pleads it is immune from suit because it is not in contractual privity with plaintiffs. Second, defendant pleads it is immune from suit because of the statute of limitations. We disagree.

III. Defense of Privity

A. Cessante Ratione Legis, Cessat et Ipsa Lex[3]

The early common law rule restricting liability to those in contractual privity with an abstracter was based on a system where abstracts would only be used by real estate owners. 1 Fitch, Abstracts and Titles to Real Property, §9, p. 9; and see §3. As time went on the actual usage of abstracts and the class of people relying on them expanded. This historical change in circumstance and the corresponding change in law is noted in numerous cases of which the following two quotations will serve as examples. The first, Brown v. Sims, 22 Ind. App. 317, 325, 53 N.E. 779, 781, 72 Am. St. Rep. 308 (1899) illustrates a judicial expansion of liability to a known third party beneficiary:

"It is very well known that the owner of real estate seldom incurs the expense of procuring an abstract of the title from an abstracter, except for the purpose of thereby furnishing information to some third person or persons who are to be influenced by the information thus provided. If the abstracter in all cases be responsible only to the person under whose employment he performs the service, it is manifest that the loss occasioned thereby must in many cases, if not in most cases, be remediless."

The second, Gate City Abstract Co. v. Post, 55 Neb. 742, 746, 76 N.W. 471, 472 (1898), represents judicial support of legislation that purports to create liability "for the payment by such abstracters of any or all damages that may accrue to any party or parties, by reason of any error, deficiency or mistake in any abstract":[4]

"By the common law, as we interpret it, the owner of real estate could

---

3. Justice Cardozo in extending a weigher's liability to a known third party beneficiary against the defense of privity, among other reasons stated: "Constantly the bounds of duty are enlarged by knowledge of a prospective use." In making this statement he relied upon, as we shall, a products liability case, his famous case of MacPherson v. Buick Motor Co., 217 N.Y. 382, 111 N.E. 1050, LRA 1916F, 696. Glanzer v. Shepard, 233 N.Y. 236, 240, 135 N.E. 275, 23 ALR 1425 (1922). In dicta, Judge Cardozo found this same lack of immunity specifically applicable to abstracters: "No such immunity, it has been held, protects the searcher of a title, who, preparing an abstract at the order of a client, delivers it to another to induce action on the faith of it." (Citations omitted.) 233 N.Y. 240, 135 N.E. 276.

4. Fifteen states have abstracter bond and liability statutes of this nature. Ark. Stats. Ann. 71-106; Colo. Rev. Stats. 1963 Chpt. 1-1-5; Idaho Code §54-101; Kans. Stat. Ann. 58-2802; Minn. Stat. Ann. §386.66; Mont. Rev. Code §66-2113; Rev. Stat. Neb. §76-501; Nev. Rev. Stats. Title 19, §240.330; New Mex. Stat. Ann. §70-2-6; N.D. Cent. Code §43-01-11; Okla. Stat. Ann. Title 1 §1; Oreg. Rev. Stats. §30.750; SDCL §36-13-15; Utah Code Ann. §1-1-12; Wyo. Stat. §33-12. A typical example of such a statute is Idaho Code §54-101:

"*54-101. Abstracters to give bond.*—It shall be a misdemeanor for any person or persons to engage in the business of compiling abstracts of title to real estate in the state of Idaho, and demand and receive pay for the same, without first filing in the office of the county recorder of the county in which such business is conducted, a surety bond to the state of Idaho, in the penal sum of $10,000, with a surety company authorized to do such business in Idaho as security condition for the payment by such abstracters of any or all damages that may accrue to any party or parties, by reason of any error, deficiency or mistake in any abstract or certificate of title, made and issued by such person or persons."

The Recording Acts

only utilize an abstract as an argument to reinforce his own assertions concerning the state of his title. It might be persuasive, but was without legal efficacy. He may now use it as evidence in an action to enforce the specific performance of a contract of sale, and in every other form of action in which the validity of his title or the existence or non-existence of liens or incumbrances are questions directly or collaterally involved. The right to use an abstract as evidence is not even limited to the person to whom it is issued. Any one may use it, and any one against whom it is employed may be injured in consequence of the certificate being false. Having thus widened the abstract's sphere of action, it was quite natural that the legislature should also widen the abstracter's liability." [5]

Responding to the actual change in use of abstracts and the additional classes of persons relying on them, at least six general court-created exceptions have been grafted onto the supposed common law requirement of strict contractual privity. These exceptions include: (1) abstracter's fraud or collusion, (2) theory of third-party beneficiary contracts, (3) theory of foreseeability of use by a third-party, (4) actual knowledge or notice of third-party, (5) agent for disclosed or undisclosed principal contracting with an abstracter, and (6) re-issuance or recertification of an abstract. See "Liability of Abstracter-Privity," 34 A.L.R.3d 1122, 1131, for cases supportive of each of these exceptions. See also 12 Vand. L. Rev. 783 (1959).

Whereas the common law rule limiting abstracter liability provided immunity from all who were injured by a faulty abstract except those in actual contractual privity, of the 35 jurisdictions (outside of Michigan) addressing themselves to this matter only seven retain a rule of strict contractual privity: Arizona, California, Florida, Illinois, Ohio, Texas and Wisconsin. On the other hand, 11 extend liability to known third-parties relying thereon: Alabama, District of Columbia, Hawaii, Idaho, Indiana, Maryland, Missouri, New Jersey, New York, Pennsylvania and Tennessee. Two jurisdictions have allowed recovery by undiscovered principals: Iowa and Washington. Fourteen purport to extend liability by statute to "any person" relying on the abstract: Arkansas, Colorado, Kansas, Minnesota, Montana, Nebraska, Nevada, New Mexico, North Dakota, Oklahoma, Oregon, South Dakota, Utah and Wyoming. And one jurisdiction extends liability to foreseeable relying third-parties by court decision: Louisiana.

---

5. Note also the discussion of the rationale for the Wyoming abstracter liability statute in "Abstracter's Liability in Examination of Title," 6 Wyo. L.J. 184, 185 (1952):

"The use of abstracts of title has expanded greatly in conveyancing transactions in recent years. The legislature took the increased use of abstracts into consideration and expanded their value in that an abstract could be used as evidence in any case in which validity of title was questioned either directly or collaterally, by anyone directly interested, whether the person to whom the abstract was issued or not. Having thus widened the abstract's sphere of use it was natural that the legislature should include within the protection of this statute any person who might suffer from fraud or mistake of the abstractor."

B. MICHIGAN HAS ABOLISHED PRIVITY REQUIREMENT

Michigan ended the last century and began this one firmly wed to the rule of contractual privity immunizing abstracters. Smith v. Holmes, 54 Mich. 104, 19 N.W. 767 (1884); Kenyon v. Charlevoix Improvement Co., 135 Mich. 103, 97 N.W. 407 (1903). By the end of the second decade it reluctantly broke away from strict privity in favor of a known third-party beneficiary. Beckovsky v. Burton Abstract & Title Co., 208 Mich. 224, 175 N.W. 235 (1919). Michigan thereby joined a category of 11 other jurisdictions just noted who had opened recovery to parties the abstracter knew would rely on the abstract. In *Beckovsky*, the plaintiff buyer actually accompanied the seller to the office of defendant title company and said he wanted an abstract but the contract in all truth was between the seller and the title company with the seller paying the title company for its work, although in order to avoid the title company's defense of privity, the trial court graciously put that question to the jury.

So *Beckovsky* extends liability to the faulty abstracter who knows a third-party beneficiary will rely on its abstract. The question remains, will liability likewise apply to the faulty abstracter who can reasonably foresee reliance by a third-party.

Michigan answered this question affirmatively in 1958 and categorically eliminated the requirement of privity. Spence v. Three Rivers Builders & Masonry Supply Inc., 353 Mich. 120, 90 N.W.2d 873 (1958). This was done in a products liability case where a plaintiff not in privity with a defendant building supply company purchased cinder-block building materials through a third-party building contractor. The supplies subsequently proved faulty to plaintiff's damage, just as the abstract did in the instant case. Defendant in that case, like the defendant in the instant case, relied on privity to bar plaintiff's action.

Justice Voelker, speaking for this Court, recognized that privity was more honored by exceptions than by the rule. However, this Court decried continued evasion of the rule and faced the issue squarely holding that privity was an unnecessary bar to recovery. . . .

C. PRIVITY CONCLUSION

Michigan's own jurisprudence records the categorical elimination of privity. This Court had previously extended abstracter liability consonant with the historical growth in reliance and use of abstracts and the corresponding changes in the law to known relying third-parties. Confronted now as of first impression with the question of abstracter liability to foreseeable relying third-parties, we have but to apply our own persuasive precedent of categorical elimination of privity to an analogous situation, and we do so.

IV. Abstracter Liability in Tort for Negligent Misrepresentation

On the basis of *Three Rivers* and a plethora of jurisdictions in the United States a good case is made for abolishing contractual privity and permitting suit in "negligence or implied warranty" by any foreseeable third-party who would and does rely on the abstract. We consider now the matter of suit in "negligence."

In Clark v. Dalman, 379 Mich. 251, 150 N.W.2d 755 (1967), for example, it was held that breach of a contract to repair, clean, and paint a water storage tank, also gave rise to an action in tort in favor of a non-contracting third-party. Chief Justice (then Justice) T. M. Kavanagh explained this relationship of a tort action to the underlying contract:

"Actionable negligence presupposes the existence of a legal relationship between parties by which the injured party is owed a duty by the other, and such duty must be imposed by law. . . . Such duty of care may be a specific duty owing to the plaintiff by the defendant, or it may be a general one owed by the defendant to the public, of which the plaintiff is a part. *Moreover, while this duty of care, as an essential element of actionable negligence, arises by operation of law, it may and frequently does arise out of a contractual relationship, the theory being that accompanying every contract is a common-law duty to perform with ordinary care the thing agreed to be done, and that a negligent performance constitutes a tort as well as a breach of contract.* But it must be kept in mind that the contract creates only the relation out of which arises the common-law duty to exercise ordinary care. Thus in legal contemplation the contract merely creates the state of things which furnishes the occasion of the tort. This being so, the existence of a contract is ordinarily a relevant factor, competent to be alleged and proved in a negligence action to the extent of showing the relationship of the parties and the nature and extent of the common-law duty on which the tort is based." (Emphasis added.) 379 Mich. 251, 260-261, 150 N.W.2d 755, 759, 760.

This Court recently reaffirmed these principles, citing *Clark*, in Nash v. Sears Roebuck & Co., 383 Mich. 136, 143, 174 N.W.2d 818 (1970). . . .

With respect to the particular type of tort action arising from breach of an abstracter's contractual duty, we hold it to be an action in negligent misrepresentation. Numerous cases and law review articles have debated the precise tort cause of action most appropriate in this context. The theories of fraud, deceit, warranty, and strict liability have all been the subject of extensive discussion with respect to professional misrepresentations of this sort. None of these theories has been found to adequately deal with this particular problem; negligent misrepresentation, on the other hand, precisely fits this situation.

The obvious difficulty with a fraud or deceit action is the requisite element of scienter. The issue we are dealing with in the instant case does not, on the pleadings, involve *intentional* misrepresentation. To supply the element of intent constructively is to do great violence to existing law on the subject of fraud. Note the discussion of this point by Prof. Francis Bohlen in Should Negligent Misrepresentations Be Treated As Negligence or Fraud, 18 Va. L.R. 703, 706-707 (1932):

"In all other fields of tort law the line is sharply drawn between intentional and unintentional injury. The persistence of this distinction can only be explained by recognizing the fact that it is in accord with the normal reactions of the mass of mankind. If negligent misrepresentation is called fraud, and, therefore, comes to be regarded by courts as tantamount thereto, there is danger that the unintentional character of the one and the intentional character of the other will be overlooked. There is danger that that liability, which is regarded both by lawyers and laymen as just where there is conscious dishonesty, will be imposed although there is no purpose to deceive. Call any two essentially different things by the same name and the two are likely to be treated as identical for all purposes."

Further, to treat this cause of action as sounding in warranty or strict liability might serve to extend an abstracter's duty beyond the duty anticipated by the original contract. It is important to repeat that the tort cause of action created by an abstracter's nonfeasance or misfeasance stems from the contractual duty originally imposed and does not render an abstracter liable for action beyond such contractually-imposed duty, i.e., to perform in a diligent and reasonably skillful workmanlike manner.

Thus, we adopt the tort action of negligent misrepresentation in this context. See 1 Harper & James, The Law of Torts, §7.6; 17 C.J.S. Contracts §154c. It should be noted that this action is premised on negligence in title search; an abstracter is not converted into a title insurer by virtue of our decision today.[13] We repeat that the only liability an abstracter has to an injured third-party is with respect to negligent performance of his or her contractual duty.

As to the measure of the duty required to be exercised by the abstracter, Chief Justice Kavanagh noted in Nash v. Sears Roebuck & Co., supra, 383 Mich. at page 142, 174 N.W.2d at page 821: "Every contract of employment includes an obligation, whether express or implied to perform in a diligent and reasonably skillful workmanlike manner."

This is clearly a form of the traditional negligence standard. Since the legal duty which, when breached, gives rise to a tort cause of action, springs from the contractual duty imposed, this *Nash* standard governs an

---

13. An abstracter, obviously, is not responsible for a legal conclusion as to whether good title exists on the basis of his or her abstract. Furthermore it should be noted, for example, that an abstracter would not be liable for failure to record items not contained in the public record nor part of the contract of employment.

The Recording Acts

abstracter's legal obligation to non-contracting parties. Because an abstracter is hired to determine what is in the public record, misstatements of, or failure to include, relevant items contained in that record are obviously examples of acts constituting failure to perform abstracting services in a diligent and reasonably skillful workmanlike manner.

This cause of action arising from breach of the abstracter's contractual duty runs to those persons an abstracter could reasonably foresee as relying on the accuracy of the abstract put into motion. The particular expert-client relationship accruing to a professional contract to certify the condition of the record of title reposes a peculiar trust in an abstracter which runs not only to the original contracting party. There is a clearly foreseeable class of potential injured persons which would obviously include grantees where his or her grantor or any predecessor in title of the grantor has initiated the contract for abstracting services with the abstracter.

V. Defense of Statute of Limitations

Defendants below were granted accelerated judgments on the basis of a plea of statute of limitations bar to this action. There is some textbook authority to the effect that the statute of limitations in an abstracter liability action begins to run from the date the abstract was furnished rather than from the time of the discovery of the error.

But the textbook authority referred to is predicated upon an action *in contract* not an action *in tort*. Consider for example, part of the applicable section in American Jurisprudence: ". . . the statute of limitations begins to run from the time of the occurrence of the breach of duty. . . ." 1 Am. Jur. 2d 245.

While such a breach of duty creating a cause of action *in a contract action* would date from the actual act of omission or misrepresentation, the cause of action *in a tort action* runs from the date the tort was committed, not the date the actor put his or her force wrongfully into motion. 20 Michigan Law & Practice (Statute of Limitations) §43; 51 Am. Jur. 2d (Limitations of Actions) §§107, 109. . . .

VI. Conclusion

For the reasons outlined above, we hold that there is a valid tort cause of action in the nature of negligent misrepresentation arising from a contract for an abstracter's services in favor of a non-contracting damaged third-party whose reliance on the abstract could be foreseen. In a tort action of this nature, the statute of limitations begins running from the date the injured party knew or should have known of the existence of the negligent misrepresentation, a date not clearly in evidence in this case. The accelerated judgment granted by the trial court was thus improper.

The judgment of the Court of Appeals is affirmed. This case is remanded to Macomb County Circuit Court for further proceedings not inconsistent with this opinion. Costs to the appellees.

T. M. Kavanagh, C.J., and Levin, Coleman, Brennan, T. G. Kavanagh, and Swainson, JJ., concur.

NOTES

1. In Florida, abstracters owe a duty of care in abstract preparation not only to the person with whom they contracted to provide the abstract, often the seller of the land, but also to the intended beneficiary of the contract for abstracting services, who is often the purchaser of the property. First American Title Insurance Co. v. First Title Service Co., 457 So. 2d 467 (Fla. 1984). But this liability to the beneficiary exists only if the abstracter knows or should know of the intended use by the beneficiary, and the Florida Supreme Court has specifically declined to extend an abstracter's liability more broadly to include all persons who foreseeably rely to their detriment on a negligently prepared abstract. Abstract Corp. v. Fernandez Co., 458 So. 2d 766 (Fla. 1985). Other courts have refused to extend the abstracter's liability to those who have not contracted for the abstracter's services. For example, Calamari v. Grace, 98 A.D.2d 74, 469 N.Y.S.2d 942 (1983). For arguments against the narrow privity position as applied to lawyers' negligence, see Note: Attorney Negligence in Real Estate Title Examination and Will Drafting: Elimination of the Privity Requirement as a Bar to Recovery by Foreseeable Third Parties, 17 New Eng. L. Rev. 955 (1981-82).

2. Lawyers engaged in title searching and examination may be held liable for negligent conduct in carrying out such work. See Annot., Liability of Attorney for Negligence in Connection With Investigation or Certification of Title to Real Estate, 59 A.L.R.3d 1176 (1974). For more general consideration of lawyer malpractice, see R. Mallen and V. Levit, Legal Malpractice (2d ed. 1981); and D. Stern and J. Felix-Retzke, A Practical Guide to Preventing Legal Malpractice (1983).

Should a lawyer be liable if in a title examination he makes errors of judgment concerning the law? Suppose he passes a title as marketable that a court later holds is unmarketable? Assume the lawyer had all the relevant facts before him but misinterpreted what turns out to be the controlling rule of law pertaining to the title point that resulted in the title being held unmarketable. Should he be liable for negligence then? What if his mistake was due to his ignorance of a lead case that had been decided on the point or of a clearly applicable title standard? Should a lawyer-specialist in title examinations be held to a different standard of care than a lawyer whose clients are aware that he only occasionally examines titles?

3. In Owen v. Neely, 471 S.W.2d 705 (Ky. 1971), a damage action was brought against a lawyer by his client for a description error not noted in the lawyer's title opinion. However, the lawyer's certificate to the effect that the title was merchantable was expressly made "subject to any information that would be revealed by an accurate survey of the real estate." In its opinion, the court said: "We are of the opinion that a lawyer certainly may protect himself by reservations and disclaimers expressly set forth in a certificate of title, but only if he has no reasonable grounds to suspect the actual existence of defects not mentioned. The average layman is not familiar with and ordinarily does not understand legal descriptions, and if his lawyer, accidentally or otherwise, receives information that should reasonably put him on notice of a defect we think it is his duty to investigate or report it to his client."

4. There are circumstances in which an attorney may be liable to nonclients for negligence. See Note, Attorney Negligence in Real Estate Title Examination and Will Drafting: Elimination of the Privity Requirement as a Bar to Recovery by Foreseeable Third Parties, 17 New Eng. L. Rev. 955 (1982). But in a recent case, the Supreme Judicial Court of Massachusetts held the mortgagee's attorney, who was negligent in a title examination, not liable to the mortgagors who had presumably relied on the attorney's title opinion in buying and mortgaging the land. Page v. Frazier, 383 Mass. 55, 445 N.E.2d 148 (1983). Influential in the court's decision was language in the mortgage application that the bank's attorney would represent the bank's interests and the mortgagors might retain their own attorney to represent their interests. The mortgagors did not retain an attorney.

5. With the abstracter's liability in the principal case compare the title insurer's liability in Jarchow v. Transamerica Title Insurance Company, at page 829 infra.

6. Another liability source that may be available to a grantee is the grantor. If the title turns out to have been defective at the time of transfer, the grantee took by warranty deed, and the defect was not expressly exempted from covenant coverage by the deed's terms, the grantee may be able to recover against the grantor for breach of the deed's covenants for title. Warranty deeds are discussed in Chapter Four at page 610 supra. Many states, by statute, provide for short form warranty deeds that result in some or all of the covenants for title being implied by inclusion in the granting clause of language to the effect that the grantor warrants the conveyed premises. See, for example, Ill. Ann. Stat. c. 30, §8 (Smith-Hurd Supp. 1985). Many owners' title insurance policies will continue even after conveyance to protect the grantor for liability under title covenants.

B. TITLE INSURANCE

In many parts of the United States, including nearly all metropolitan areas, title insurance is a major form of title protection.[19] It is an American innovation and little such insurance is written outside the United States.[20] The first American title insurance company was formed in 1876, and by World War II some title insurance was being written on lands in most all parts of the United States, with well-established companies in nearly all big cities. But the great expansion of this kind of coverage has come mostly since the mid-1940s, a period marked by extensive real estate activity, a tremendous volume of new subdivisions and a vast number of new conveyances and mortgages. Title insurance has grown in both absolute and relative terms, for it has gradually cut in on other forms of title protection, particularly title search and examination by lawyers in private practice. In a number of big cities private practitioners of law have been eliminated from both title search and examination; and in some areas, notably in the Far West, this has happened in many middle and small-sized cities as well. In these communities the title work of the private bar is reduced largely to occasional efforts at curing title defects that title companies will not insure or negotiating with title insurers to waive minor defects. But in all of New England and in much of the Midwest and South outside large metropolitan centers, private law firms still do a great deal of title examination work, and in some communities they do title searching as well.

There are two major types of title insurance operations. In one the title company merely insures in reliance on the title opinion of a lawyer in private practice, the lawyer making a title examination and he or an abstracter making the search. In the other the title company performs all functions itself, commonly maintaining a title plant to facilitate searching. A title plant consists principally of duplicate copies of public records pertaining to all land parcels in a particular county, arranged and indexed to enable accurate and speedy searching of titles for individual parcels. Most highly developed plants are in counties with large populations.

The phenomenal growth of title insurance is attributable to a series of factors. For one thing, the big national lenders, especially the life insur-

---

19. On title insurance generally, see American Bar Association, Title Insurance and You: What Every Lawyer Should Know!, 1979 A.B.A. Sec. Real Prop. Prob. and Tr. L.; American Land Title Association, The Title Industry: White Papers, Vol. 1 (1976); Burke, Law of Title Insurance (1986); Gage, Land Title Assuring Agencies in the United States (1937); Johnstone and Hopson, Lawyers and Their Work, c. 8 (1967); 7 Powell, The Law of Real Property, c. 92 (1984); Practicing Law Institute, Real Estate Law and Practice Course Handbook Series, Nos. 144 (1978), 204 (1981), 236 (1983), and 251 (1984); and Johnstone, Title Insurance, 66 Yale L.J. 492 (1957).

20. A modest amount of title insurance is now being written on lands in Canada, England, several Caribbean countries, and Mexico. Insurers of much of this coverage are U.S. title companies or their subsidiaries. Roller, Title Insurance — An International Perspective, 62 Title News No. 3, 7 (1983). See also Payne, Second Thoughts on the Future of Title Insurance in England, 124 Solic. J. 699 (1980).

ance companies, like the relatively standardized coverage given by mortgagees' policies wherever written. This makes it easier for these large volume operators to determine the acceptability of mortgages originated for them or that they purchase in the secondary market. They also like the risk insurance feature. Demand for title insurance by national lenders is probably the single most significant reason for expansion in this type of title protection since World War II. Another reason for title insurance growth is that in large metropolitan areas public records pertaining to land have become so voluminous and difficult to search that only specialists with a large volume of title work can operate efficiently. And only the mass volume operator can afford a title plant, an essential to maximum efficiency in many big counties. Still another reason why title insurance has expanded so is that, being businesses, title companies can and do vigorously solicit work, whereas their lawyer and Torrens competitors are inhibited from doing so, lawyers by their canons of ethics and Torrens registrars by the usual reluctance of government agencies to spend money promoting their services.

Title insurance differs from most other kinds of insurance in that it does not insure against future risks but only against those existing at the time coverage is obtained. Further, it is issued only after a careful title search and examination and excludes any risks of substance disclosed by this process. As a result, loss ratios are low, with principal risks being negligence in search and examination and relatively rare defects not apparent from customary public record searches. Only one premium is paid for title insurance, and this includes a charge for search and examination if made by the title company. It is common, at the time land is sold, for a title company to issue two separate policies of insurance for which separate premiums are paid: one policy to the mortgagee and the other to the purchasing owner. Owners' policies do not cover grantees from the insured; if a buyer wishes coverage he must order and pay for a new policy, even though his grantor was covered. Mortgagees' policies usually cover assignees. In addition to fee owners and mortgagees, long-term lessees and holders of valuable oil and gas rights frequently obtain title insurance coverage.

1. *Administration*

Many title insurance companies are licensed to do business in a number of states, and a few, directly or through subsidiaries, operate in almost every state. In recent years the big companies have been strengthening their national positions by buying up local and regional companies. Many title companies have branch offices and agencies located at various points throughout the area in which they do business. Orders are accepted at all these outlets, while searches and examinations are made only at some.

Companies that will insure in reliance on title opinions of lawyers in private practice usually will accept only opinions of lawyers experienced in title work whose work they trust, and the companies maintain lists of such lawyers.

There are considerable differences geographically within the United States in title insurance rates. When title insurance companies issue coverage in reliance on the opinion of a lawyer, the basic premium rate in some places may be as low as $2.50 per thousand dollars of coverage for a mortgagee's policy and $3.50 per thousand dollars of coverage for an owner's policy, with somewhat lower rates common for coverage in excess of $50,000 per parcel. In many places basic rates are higher, as much as double or more in some localities. Charges are, of course, considerably greater if the title company also does the searching and examining, a common practice if the company maintains its own title plant in the area. Lower rates may prevail if an owner's policy is issued simultaneously with a mortgagee's policy or if the insurer has recently issued a policy on the same property. It is the usual practice of title companies, when insuring a particular piece of property for a very large amount of money, to reinsure with other companies, thereby spreading the risk. This is not only sound business practice but in some states is required by law.

An alternative to the typical commercial title insurer is the bar-related form of insurance organization, a title company owned and operated by the lawyers in a state, generally those lawyers active in title work.[21] Essentially these organizations are efforts by the practicing bar to counter the competition of the traditional kind of commercial title company and to divert to lawyers engaged in title work some of the insurance profits from title coverage. The first of the bar-related title insurers was the Florida Lawyer's Title Guaranty Fund, established in 1947. Such bar-related insurers now write policies in about half the states but their percentage of the total title insurance market in the United States is small. However, the commercial insurers see them as serious competitive threats and claim that the bar-related insurers are in violation of the antitrust laws.

---

21. On bar-related title insurers, see Jackson, The Saga of the Bar Funds, 60 Title News No. 1, 18 (1981); and Rooney, Bar-Related Title Insurance: The Positive Perspective, 1980 S. Ill. U.L.J. 263 (1980). See also American Bar Association, Standing Committee on Lawyers Title Guaranty Funds, How-To-Do-It: Bar-Related Title Assuring Organizations (1976); American Bar Association, Standing Committee on Lawyers Title Guaranty Funds, Bar-Related Title Assuring Organizations (1976); Miles, Bar-Related Title Insurers: Their Benefits to the Bar and the Public, reprinted in American Bar Association, Title Insurance and You: What Every Lawyer Should Know!, 1979 A.B.A. Sec. Real Prop. Prob. and Tr. L. 45; Payne, Title Guaranty Funds: Symptom, Cure or Nostrum, 46 Ind. L.J. 208 (1971); and Roussel, Pera, and Rosenberg, Bar-Related Title Insurance Companies: An Antitrust Analysis, 24 Vill. L. Rev. 639 (1979).

Zerwick, Creation and Maintenance of a Title Plant
34 National Capital Area Realtor 11 (No. 1, 1966)

. . . Actually, there are many kinds of title plants. They vary in the way different title men get hold of the title evidence that go into the plant; they vary in the kind of books or indexes that are used; and they vary in the classification or organization of this title evidence. And, so far as I know, no one has satisfactorily proved that one type of plant is superior to all others. Indeed, title men find an abiding joy in parrying all evidence that might indicate that any system other than their own has anything to offer them.

One group of title men really uses the public recording offices as their title plant. Each title search is a laborious sifting through of the offices of the recorder, the tax collector, the city assessor, and the clerks of the various courts — perhaps municipal, state, county and even federal. He, the title searcher, brings back to his own shop a digest of all the information in the public title plant which evidence and [sic] augments or diminishes the title he is to reflect. With this information at hand, he analyzes and organizes it into an abstract, or a report of title, or a policy of title insurance, thus placing the information in the hands of the persons who are buying a lot, or borrowing money on the security of a parcel of real estate, or initiating a condemnation for public use, or simply furnishing information to an investor.

Other title people don't wait until a specific search is called for to go to the public records. They build and maintain a plant of their own. And that plant is a good plant to the extent that it exactly reflects or duplicates the original records at the courthouses and the city hall. The only difference at all is in the way those records are organized and indexed. The private title plant is economic to the extent that it improves the speed and accuracy with which a single title may be examined.

There are two extremes: the completely public records and a private plant embracing a reflection of *every* public record. Between the two lie all the title plants in the country.

Many title people omit some of the courthouse information — some of the information which is ultimately necessary in their final searches. They do a part of each final title search among the records at the source, work with the original documents, though they may create and maintain an index even to these records in their own private plant. . . .

The volume of public records is almost beyond the imagination of people not engaged in their use. In the last year before the County of Los Angeles started to microfilm its records, they bound and placed on reference shelves *each day* an average of 135 volumes of 450 pages each. That is about 35,000 heavy tomes a year. They were recording 4,500 instruments a day at that time (1958). Today the daily average is over 6,000.

. . . Private plants are not mere copies of the public records, but a re-organization of them. The basic information obtained must be exactly the same. But in the private plant there are two general classifications only — a classification by description of real estate which supplants the Grantor-Grantee Indexes and in which every instrument describing real estate is filed in such a manner that the searcher finds it through or by means of that description; and a classification by name, for those instruments which contain no description of property, like a judgment for money, a change of name, or an incorporation.

Thus the title searcher in the private plant quite often looks in but two places — a single tract or location index, and a single name index. Contrast this with the public records where there may be as many as twenty places or more where a search must be made. . . .

The creation of a title plant is a sort of crash maintenance project. A title plant is actually created as it is maintained. The tremendous job of bringing together the records from the beginning of the history of a county is merely a telescoping of the daily maintenance job — of doing what might ordinarily have accumulated over a hundred years, in as little as a year's time. . . .

. . . A title plant is never complete. It is never finished. It grows and changes with every market transaction involving real estate. The figures of speech which might be applied to it are many. As it refines the system of public records, it becomes the safety deposit vault of the land system of the community. Its facilities are a transportation system, a pipe line system accommodating the flow of title evidence. . . . It is largely manned by small, independent individuals and businesses making their living in a free economy by industry and service not duplicated, to my knowledge, elsewhere in the world.

Robinson, The Organization and Operation of Title Plants[22]

Due to the recording acts and related laws presently in force, a search of every lender and every purchaser is extremely prudent. But such searches can be highly complicated and difficult. The question then becomes: what can be done to make land title searches efficient and economical?

First, consider the principal public officials who maintain records that may affect titles to real estate:

1. Recorder of deeds, by whatever name or title he may have in a particular jurisdiction.

2. Clerks of the various municipal, county, state and federal courts in the area in which the real estate is located.

---

22. This article was written especially for this casebook by James W. Robinson, formerly Secretary of the American Land Title Association, Washington, D.C.

Title Insurance

3. Officers of the various municipalities and the county clerk, county treasurer, county assessor or other public official charged with the responsibility of maintaining records pertaining to general taxes, street assessments, sewer assessments, special charges for city services and other special taxes and levies.

A title searcher must draw on records maintained by all these officials, and on occasion others as well, if those who order title examinations are to be adequately protected. In a sparsely-populated county in a state where tract indices are maintained by the recorder, searches can readily be made directly from the public records; but in most metropolitan areas a complete title plant is needed for quick and thorough searching. Surprisingly sophisticated record-keeping systems are also found in offices of abstracting firms and title companies in many small and medium-sized communities throughout the nation.

In organizing and operating a title plant, several basic problems are encountered: how to obtain recorded data from the various public offices, a procedure commonly referred to as the "take-off"; how to index and arrange this data once obtained; and how to use plant data most advantageously after a plant has been set up.

Take-Offs

There are only a few ways in which take-offs are made. Either some kind of photocopy is made of relevant documents, or a typewritten or longhand copy or abstract is prepared of each such document. Photographing all recorded instruments and reproducing copies 80 percent of original size is now a common practice, as is microfilming.

The Tract Book System

The method of indexing data in title plants may be one of several. The oldest and the one most generally used is to maintain and keep up to date a set of bound or loose-leaf tract index books, with a separate page or "account" for each parcel showing its title history. Accounts are arranged in alphabetical order by platted subdivision name, followed by unplatted accounts in section, township and range number order, or in some other logical sequence for communities not covered by the rectangular survey system. Each transaction involving a parcel of land is then posted to the appropriate account, the index entry commonly showing the names of grantor and grantee, type of instrument, date of the instrument and its date of recording, and the book and page number or other filing designation of where a copy of the original document can be found. To facilitate title searches, subdivision accounts are usually broken down into lots, sectional accounts into quarter-sections. If microfilm copies of recorded instruments are part of a title plant, a punch card system can now be used to make both index and tab card entries. Each microfilm copy is inserted in a tab card with aperture. As microfilm becomes available, an operator using a typewriter card punch does two simultaneous jobs: typing and punching. As the tract index entry is being typed, identical information is also punched onto the aperture card. This is an example of the increased efficiency that mechanization is making possible in relation to land titles.

Card Index System

The card index system substitutes a card or cards for a page in the tract index. These cards are filed and posted in the same manner as the tract books are arranged. The advantage to a card system is its ease of handling and reproduction when titles are consolidated or split. However, cards readily become defaced, misfiled, or lost.

Folder System

Under this system a separate document folder is maintained for each parcel of land. Every folder contains an up-to-date index to all transactions of record for which there is a legal description tying it to the parcel in question. Many plants also include in the folder photocopies of indexed documents, so that most of what is needed for a title examination is included in one package. Folders are filed and numbered in an order that simplifies locating them, frequently in accord with their geographic locality, such as subdivision, block and lot.

Name Indices

Every complete title plant must have a "name" or "general" index file. All recorded instruments that cannot be indexed by legal description, such as money judgments against individuals that may create liens on land, are noted in one central index. In some areas a Soundex System of indexing names is used for maximum efficiency in locating names that are spelled differently but sound alike. In other areas the practice of posting and searching only the verbatim spelling of names in recorded instruments is followed.

Electronic Storage and Retrieval

Title companies have been experimenting with electronic storage and retrieval equipment as a means of indexing information relating to land titles. Portions of entire title plants (judgment indices, delinquent tax records, standard policy exceptions, etc.) have already been stored in computers and are in daily use in a few of the larger companies. Present high cost of equipment, lack of trained personnel, intricacies of the process, and rapid mechanical changes characteristic of advancing computer technology have combined to slow the conversion of title plants to a fully computerized process. The industry is a long way from push button title insurance, but investigation of the possibilities of electronic storage and retrieval is under continuing study.

Supplemental Data

In addition to the indices described above, and variations and combinations of these indexing systems, every abstract or title insurance company has accumulated a vast amount of internal material, developed as a by-product of the public records, which may expedite investigation of titles to real estate. This material consists of such items as tract opinions (title findings covering subdivisions and other large tracts of land), previously issued policies, corporate documents (charters and bylaws), starter files, subdivision atlases and other detailed maps, official surveys, legal opinions, affidavits and other memoranda, court decisions, government regulations and a cross-reference system for converting street addresses to legal descriptions. All these are part of the title plant and are regularly used.

Joint Title Plants

Whether or not a title or abstract company finds it profitable to maintain a title plant depends not only on the volume of recorded instruments and the quality of the records kept by public officials in a particular county, but also on the extent of competition. In a county with more than one title or abstract company, each company, if it is to maintain a complete plant, must duplicate the work and expense of its competitors for only a fraction of the available business. To avoid this costly repetition, a recent development in several large communities (Denver, Dallas, and Los Angeles) is a joint venture in which several title companies form a separate corporation to organize and maintain a single title plant, owned and used by all participating firms. Preliminary indications are that joint plants are working well, and more of them can be expected.

The Operation of Title Plants

Regardless of what system or combination of systems are employed to develop and index information, it is in the use of the title plant that all the installation and maintenance work finds fulfillment. The search operations described below will be performed by persons with different titles, depending upon local terminology. In a small operation, one person might perform several or all of the functions. But generally here is what happens when an order is placed for a title insurance policy or an abstract of title:

A "caption writer" determines that the legal description on the application is valid and can be identified and reconciled with descriptions incorporated in the title plant records. He also determines the period of time to be searched, usually back to a previous policy or abstract.

A "chain man" compiles a list of all recorded documents that during the period to be searched were posted against the described property in the basic index.

A "name searcher" compiles a list of all current items (judgments, probate matters, mechanic's liens, etc.) posted against the names of the individuals appearing in the chain of title for the search period.

A "tax searcher" records the year, purpose, and amount of any unpaid general property taxes and special assessments shown against the property.

These different work sheets are then assembled in a file and assigned for examination to a highly-trained, experienced employee or officer of the firm. Upon going over the file, he may order additional documentation to fill in apparent gaps or deficiencies. He may, for instance, ask for a full copy of certain original instruments, a survey or physical inspection of the premises, or an affidavit on some dubious factual point. But once satisfied that the file is sufficiently complete, he will prepare the abstract or, if a title insurance policy has been ordered, a preliminary report of title, to be followed at a subsequent time by the policy of insurance. A further step, after closing of a real estate transaction, may be a later date search to reflect recording of the deed or mortgage and any mortgage releases.

SUMMARY

A title plant is a gigantic consolidated bookkeeping system, compiled from many sources, reflecting pertinent matters pertaining to land titles as disclosed principally by public recording act, judicial and tax records. Given the present scattered, often poorly indexed and sometimes incomplete nature of public land records, privately owned and operated title plants are helpful and frequently essential to accurately and quickly determine the record ownership of real property in the United States. In many counties, especially those in and around large cities, it is doubtful if the surge of homebuying, road building, office and commercial construction and subdivision of lands, which has characterized the present century, could have been accomplished under prevailing laws had it not been for the development and use of private plants. And title plants everywhere have tended to cut the cost of title searches and examinations.

NOTE

Title insurers and abstracters everywhere have been converting segments of their title plants to computer access and it is possible that in the future there will be fully automated plants enabling all relevant documents to be retrieved readily on a display screen. Time consuming manual searches will be eliminated, titles can be examined merely by checking document copies called up on a screen, and title examination will become largely a paperless operation. But conversion of entire title plants to make easy computer retrieval possible is a very costly process, especially for large plants with records going back one hundred years or more, and this cost is a deterrent to conversion. How much automation to adopt and what equipment and systems to use are major issues in the title field, as is reflected by the frequency of articles on computerization appearing in Title News, the journal of the American Land Title Association. Typical of such articles are Thiss, Taming the Technological Tiger, 63 Title News No. 10, at 9 (1984); Stovall, Efficiency "From the Ground Up," 63 Title News No. 6, at 15 (1984); and Morgan et al., Automation in the Local Title Office, 63 Title News No. 1, at 7 (1984).

2. *Protection Provided*

Title insurance protects the insured from loss as the result of title deficiencies not excepted by the policy. Most policies contain a number of exceptions: any material defects uncovered by the insurer in its search of the particular title, and certain risks that, in standard printed clauses, the insurer excludes in all coverage of the kind in question. For an added premium, there are companies that will provide extended coverage by eliminating some of their standard exceptions. State insurance regulations in some states control the kinds of extended coverage permitted.

Most title policies insure the title against both record and off-record claims, subject, of course, to stated exceptions. Coverage of off-record risks is desired by many knowledgeable insureds because of the difficulty, often the impossibility, of ascertaining that such risks exist. However, one type of policy, sometimes referred to as a title guarantee, insures only the record title. The policy states, in essence, that the insured has good record title, subject to any listed exceptions, and then obligates the company to pay any losses incurred by the insured should the record title be otherwise. It provides not only protection against negligence in search and examination of the public records, but guarantees that the record title is as represented, thus protecting against non-negligent search and examination errors. This limited form of policy was extensively written at an earlier stage in the evolution of title insurance.

Many insurers insist that at the time of policy issuance, an owner insure for the full value of the fee and a mortgagee for the full amount of the mortgage. Additional coverage is not required by the policy if subsequently the value of the property goes up, although if this happens, the owner may deem it wise to increase the face amount of the policy, which

Text continues on page 794, following Sample American Land Title Association insurance policies.

AMERICAN LAND TITLE ASSOCIATION
LOAN POLICY-1970
(Rev. 10-17-70 and 10-17-84)

CHICAGO TITLE INSURANCE COMPANY

SUBJECT TO THE EXCLUSIONS FROM COVERAGE, THE EXCEPTIONS CONTAINED IN SCHEDULE B AND THE PROVISIONS OF THE CONDITIONS AND STIPULATIONS HEREOF, CHICAGO TITLE INSURANCE COMPANY, a Missouri corporation, herein called the Company, insures, as of Date of Policy shown in Schedule A, against loss or damage, not exceeding the amount of insurance stated in Schedule A, and costs, attorneys' fees and expenses which the Company may become obligated to pay hereunder, sustained or incurred by the insured by reason of:

1. Title to the estate or interest described in Schedule A being vested otherwise than as stated therein;
2. Any defect in or lien or encumbrance on such title;
3. Lack of a right of access to and from the land;
4. Unmarketability of such title;
5. The invalidity or unenforceability of the lien of the insured mortgage upon said estate or interest except to the extent that such invalidity or unenforceability, or claim thereof, arises out of the transaction evidenced by the insured mortgage and is based upon
   (a) usury, or
   (b) any consumer credit protection or truth in lending law;
6. The priority of any lien or encumbrance over the lien of the insured mortgage;
7. Any statutory lien for labor or material which now has gained or hereafter may gain priority over the lien of the insured mortgage, except any such lien arising from an improvement on the land contracted for and commenced subsequent to Date of Policy not financed in whole or in part by proceeds of the indebtedness secured by the insured mortgage which at Date of Policy the insured has advanced or is obligated to advance; or
8. The invalidity or unenforceability of any assignment, shown in Schedule A, of the insured mortgage or the failure of said assignment to vest title to the insured mortgage in the named insured assignee free and clear of all liens.

In Witness Whereof, CHICAGO TITLE INSURANCE COMPANY has caused this policy to be signed and sealed as of the date of policy shown in Schedule A, the policy to become valid when countersigned by an authorized signatory.

CHICAGO TITLE INSURANCE COMPANY

By: *[signature]*
President.

ATTEST: *[signature]*
Secretary.

AMERICAN LAND TITLE ASSOCIATION
OWNER'S POLICY FORM B-1970
(Rev. 10-17-70 and 10-17-84)

CHICAGO TITLE INSURANCE COMPANY

SUBJECT TO THE EXCLUSIONS FROM COVERAGE, THE EXCEPTIONS CONTAINED IN SCHEDULE B AND THE PROVISIONS OF THE CONDITIONS AND STIPULATIONS HEREOF, CHICAGO TITLE INSURANCE COMPANY, a Missouri corporation, herein called the Company, insures, as of Date of Policy shown in Schedule A, against loss or damage, not exceeding the amount of insurance stated in Schedule A, and costs, attorneys' fees and expenses which the Company may become obligated to pay hereunder, sustained or incurred by the insured by reason of:

1. Title to the estate or interest described in Schedule A being vested otherwise than as stated therein;
2. Any defect in or lien or encumbrance on such title;
3. Lack of a right of access to and from the land; or
4. Unmarketability of such title.

In Witness Whereof, CHICAGO TITLE INSURANCE COMPANY has caused this policy to be signed and sealed as of the date of policy shown in Schedule A, the policy to become valid when countersigned by an authorized signatory.

CHICAGO TITLE INSURANCE COMPANY

By: *[signature]*
President.

ATTEST: *[signature]*
Secretary.

IMPORTANT

This policy necessarily relates solely to the title as of the date of the policy. In order that a purchaser of the real estate described herein may be insured against defects, liens or encumbrances, this policy should be reissued in the name of such purchaser.

EXCLUSIONS FROM COVERAGE

The following matters are expressly excluded from the coverage of this policy:
1. (a) Governmental police power.
   (b) Any law, ordinance or governmental regulation relating to environmental protection.
   (c) Any law, ordinance or governmental regulation (including but not limited to building and zoning ordinances) restricting or regulating or prohibiting the occupancy, use or enjoyment of the land, or regulating the character, dimensions or location of any improvement now or hereafter erected on the land, or prohibiting a separation in ownership or a change in the dimensions or area of the land or any parcel of which the land is or was a part.
   (d) The effect of any violation of the matters excluded under (a), (b) or (c) above, unless notice of a defect, lien or encumbrance resulting from a violation has been recorded at Date of Policy in those records in which under state statutes deeds, mortgages, lis pendens, liens or other title encumbrances must be recorded in order to impart constructive notice to purchasers of the land for value and without knowledge; provided, however, that without limitation, such records shall not be construed to include records in any of the offices of federal, state or local environmental protection, zoning, building, health or public safety authorities.
2. Rights of eminent domain unless notice of the exercise of such rights appears in the public records at Date of Policy.
3. Defects, liens, encumbrances, adverse claims, or other matters (a) created, suffered, assumed or agreed to by the insured claimant; (b) not known to the Company and not shown by the public records but known to the insured claimant either at Date of Policy or at the date such claimant acquired an estate or interest insured by this policy or acquired the insured mortgage and not disclosed in writing by the insured claimant to the Company prior to the date such insured claimant became an insured hereunder; (c) resulting in no loss or damage to the insured claimant; (d) attaching or created subsequent to Date of Policy (except to the extent insurance is afforded herein as to any statutory lien for labor or material).
4. Unenforceability of the lien of the insured mortgage because of failure of the insured at Date of Policy or of any subsequent owner of the indebtedness to comply with applicable "doing business" laws of the state in which the land is situated.

Exclusions From Coverage

The following matters are expressly excluded from the coverage of this policy:
1. (a) Governmental police power.
   (b) Any law, ordinance or governmental regulation relating to environmental protection.
   (c) Any law, ordinance or governmental regulation (including but not limited to building and zoning ordinances) restricting or regulating or prohibiting the occupancy, use or enjoyment of the land, or regulating the character, dimensions or location of any improvement now or hereafter erected on the land, or prohibiting a separation in ownership or a change in the dimensions or area of the land or any parcel of which the land is or was a part.
   (d) The effect of any violation of the matters excluded under (a), (b) or (c) above, unless notice of a defect, lien or encumbrance resulting from a violation has been recorded at Date of Policy in those records in which under state statutes deeds, mortgages, lis pendens, liens or other title encumbrances must be recorded in order to impart constructive notice to purchasers of the land for value and without knowledge; provided, however, that without limitation, such records shall not be construed to include records in any of the offices of federal, state or local environmental protection, zoning, building, health or public safety authorities.
2. Rights of eminent domain unless notice of the exercise of such rights appears in the public records at Date of Policy.
3. Defects, liens, encumbrances, adverse claims, or other matters (a) created, suffered, assumed or agreed to by the insured claimant; (b) not known to the Company and not shown by the public records but known to the insured claimant either at Date of Policy or at the date such claimant acquired an estate or interest insured by this policy and not disclosed in writing by the insured claimant to the Company prior to the date such insured claimant became an insured hereunder; (c) resulting in no loss or damage to the insured claimant; or (d) attaching or created subsequent to Date of Policy; or (e) resulting in loss or damage which would not have been sustained if the insured claimant had paid value for the estate or interest insured by this policy.

CONDITIONS AND STIPULATIONS

1. Definitions of Terms

The following terms when used in this policy mean:

(a) "insured": the insured named in Schedule A. The term "insured" also includes (i) the owner of the indebtedness secured by the insured mortgage and each successor in ownership of such indebtedness (reserving, however, all rights and defenses as to any such successor who acquires the indebtedness by operation of law as distinguished from purchase including, but not limited to, heirs, distributees, devisees, survivors, personal representatives, next of kin or corporate or fiduciary successors that the Company would have had against the successor's transferor), and further includes (ii) any governmental agency or instrumentality which is an insurer or guarantor under an insurance contract or guaranty insuring or guaranteeing said indebtedness, or any part thereof, whether named as an insured herein or not, and (iii) the parties designated in paragraph 2(a) of these Conditions and Stipulations.

(b) "insured claimant": an insured claiming loss or damage hereunder.

(c) "knowledge": actual knowledge, not constructive knowledge or notice which may be imputed to an insured by reason of any public records.

(d) "land": the land described, specifically or by reference in Schedule A, and improvements affixed thereto which by law constitute real property; provided, however, the term "land" does not include any property beyond the lines of the area specifically described or referred to in Schedule A, nor any right, title, interest, estate or easement in abutting streets, roads, avenues, alleys, lanes, ways or waterways, but nothing herein shall modify or limit the extent to which a right of access to and from the land is insured by this policy.

(e) "mortgage": mortgage, deed of trust, trust deed, or other security instrument.

(f) "public records": those records which by law impart constructive notice of matters relating to said land.

2. (a) Continuation of Insurance after Acquisition of Title

This policy shall continue in force as of Date of Policy in favor of an insured who acquires all or any part of the estate or interest in the land described in Schedule A by foreclosure, trustee's sale, conveyance in lieu of foreclosure, or other legal manner which discharges the lien of the insured mortgage, and if the insured is a corporation, its transferee of the estate or interest so acquired, provided the transferee is the parent or wholly owned subsidiary of the insured; and in favor of any governmental agency or

Title Insurance

CONDITIONS AND STIPULATIONS

1. Definition of Terms

The following terms when used in this policy mean:

(a) "insured": the insured named in Schedule A, and subject to any rights or defenses the Company may have had against the named insured, those who succeed to the interest of such insured by operation of law as distinguished from purchase including, but not limited to, heirs, distributees, devisees, survivors, personal representatives, next of kin, or corporate or fiduciary successors.

(b) "insured claimant": an insured claiming loss or damage hereunder.

(c) "knowledge": actual knowledge, not constructive knowledge or notice which may be imputed to an insured by reason of any public records.

(d) "land": the land described, specifically or by reference in Schedule A, and improvements affixed thereto which by law constitute real property; provided, however, the term "land" does not include any property beyond the lines of the area specifically described or referred to in Schedule A, nor any right, title, interest, estate or easement in abutting streets, roads, avenues, alleys, lanes, ways or waterways, but nothing herein shall modify or limit the extent to which a right of access to and from the land is insured by this policy.

(e) "mortgage": mortgage, deed of trust, trust deed, or other security instrument.

(f) "public records": those records which by law impart constructive notice of matters relating to said land.

instrumentality which acquires all or any part of the estate or interest pursuant to a contract of insurance or guaranty insuring or guaranteeing the indebtedness secured by the insured mortgage; provided that the amount of insurance hereunder after such acquisition, exclusive of costs, attorneys' fees and expenses which the Company may become obligated to pay, shall not exceed the least of:
- (i) the amount of insurance stated in Schedule A;
- (ii) the amount of the unpaid principal of the indebtedness as defined in paragraph 8 hereof, plus interest thereon, expenses of foreclosure and amounts advanced to protect the lien of the insured mortgage and secured by said insured mortgage at the time of acquisition of such estate or interest in the land; or
- (iii) the amount paid by any governmental agency or instrumentality, if such agency or instrumentality is the insured claimant, in the acquisition of such estate or interest in satisfaction of its insurance contract or guaranty.

(b) Continuation of Insurance after Conveyance of Title

The coverage of this policy shall continue in force as of Date of Policy in favor of an insured so long as such insured retains an estate or interest in the land, or holds an indebtedness secured by a purchase money mortgage given by a purchaser from such insured, and so long as such insured shall have liability by reason of covenants of warranty made by such insured in any transfer or conveyance of such estate or interest; provided, however, this policy shall not continue in force in favor of any purchaser from such insured of either said estate or interest or the indebtedness secured by a purchase money mortgage given to such insured.

3. Defense and Prosecution of Actions—Notice of Claim to be given by an Insured Claimant

(a) The Company, at its own cost and without undue delay, shall provide for the defense of an insured in all litigation consisting of actions or proceedings commenced against such insured, or defenses, restraining orders or injunctions interposed against a foreclosure of the insured mortgage or a defense interposed against an insured in an action to enforce a contract for a sale of the indebtedness secured by the insured mortgage, or a sale of the estate or interest in said land, to the extent that such litigation is founded upon an alleged defect, lien, encumbrance, or other matter insured against by this policy.

(b) The insured shall notify the Company promptly in writing (i) in case any action or proceeding is begun or defense or restraining order or injunction is interposed as set forth in (a) above, (ii) in case knowledge shall come to an insured hereunder of any claim of title or interest which is

Title Insurance 781

2. *Continuation of Insurance after Conveyance of Title*

The coverage of this policy shall continue in force as of Date of Policy in favor of an insured so long as such insured retains an estate or interest in the land, or holds an indebtedness secured by a purchase money mortgage given by a purchaser from such insured, or so long as such insured shall have liability by reason of covenants of warranty made by such insured in any transfer or conveyance of such estate or interest; provided, however, this policy shall not continue in force in favor of any purchaser from such insured of either said estate or interest or the indebtedness secured by a purchase money mortgage given to such insured.

3. *Defense and Prosecution of Actions—Notice of Claim to be given by an Insured Claimant*

(a) The Company, at its own cost and without undue delay, shall provide for the defense of an insured in all litigation consisting of actions or proceedings commenced against such insured, or a defense interposed against an insured in an action to enforce a contract for a sale of the estate or interest in said land, to the extent that such litigation is founded upon an alleged defect, lien, encumbrance, or other matter insured against by this policy.

(b) The insured shall notify the Company promptly in writing (i) in case any action or proceeding is begun or defense is interposed as set forth in (a) above, (ii) in case knowledge shall come to an insured hereunder of any claim of title or interest which is adverse to the title to the estate or interest, as insured, and which might cause loss or damage for which the Company may be liable by virtue of this policy, or (iii) if title to the estate or

adverse to the title to the estate or interest or the lien of the insured mortgage, as insured, and which might cause loss or damage for which the Company may be liable by virtue of this policy, or (iii) if title to the estate or interest or the lien of the insured mortgage, as insured, is rejected as unmarketable. If such prompt notice shall not be given to the Company, then as to such insured all liability of the Company shall cease and terminate in regard to the matter or matters for which such prompt notice is required; provided, however, that failure to notify shall in no case prejudice the rights of any such insured under this policy unless the Company shall be prejudiced by such failure and then only to the extent of such prejudice.

(c) The Company shall have the right at its own cost to institute and without undue delay prosecute any action or proceeding or to do any other act which in its opinion may be necessary or desirable to establish the title to the estate or interest or the lien of the insured mortgage, as insured, and the Company may take any appropriate action under the terms of this policy, whether or not it shall be liable thereunder, and shall not thereby concede liability or waive any provision of this policy.

(d) Whenever the Company shall have brought any action or interposed a defense as required or permitted by the provisions of this policy, the Company may pursue any such litigation to final determination by a court of competent jurisdiction and expressly reserves the right, in its sole discretion, to appeal from any adverse judgment or order.

(e) In all cases where this policy permits or requires the Company to prosecute or provide for the defense of any action or proceeding, the insured hereunder shall secure to the Company the right to so prosecute or provide defense in such action or proceeding, and all appeals therein, and permit the Company to use, at its option, the name of such insured for such purpose. Whenever requested by the Company, such insured shall give the Company all reasonable aid in any such action or proceeding, in effecting settlement, securing evidence, obtaining witnesses, or prosecuting or defending such action or proceeding, and the Company shall reimburse such insured for any expense so incurred.

4. *Notice of Loss—Limitation of Action*

In addition to the notices required under paragraph 3(b) of these Conditions and Stipulations, a statement in writing of any loss or damage for which it is claimed the Company is liable under this policy shall be furnished to the Company within 90 days after such loss or damage shall have been determined and no right of action shall accrue to an insured claimant until 30 days after such statement shall have been furnished. Failure to furnish such statement of loss or damage shall terminate any liability of the Company under this policy as to such loss or damage.

Title Insurance

interest, as insured, is rejected as unmarketable. If such prompt notice shall not be given to the Company, then as to such insured all liability of the Company shall cease and terminate in regard to the matter or matters for which such prompt notice is required; provided, however, that failure to notify shall in no case prejudice the rights of any such insured under this policy unless the Company shall be prejudiced by such failure and then only to the extent of such prejudice.

(c) The Company shall have the right at its own cost to institute and without undue delay prosecute any action or proceeding or to do any other act which in its opinion may be necessary or desirable to establish the title to the estate or interest as insured, and the Company may take any appropriate action under the terms of this policy, whether or not it shall be liable thereunder, and shall not thereby concede liability or waive any provision of this policy.

(d) Whenever the Company shall have brought any action or interposed a defense as required or permitted by the provisions of this policy, the Company may pursue any such litigation to final determination by a court of competent jurisdiction and expressly reserves the right, in its sole discretion, to appeal from any adverse judgment or order.

(e) In all cases where this policy permits or requires the Company to prosecute or provide for the defense of any action or proceeding, the insured hereunder shall secure to the Company the right to so prosecute or provide defense in such action or proceeding, and all appeals therein, and permit the Company to use, at its option, the name of such insured for such purpose. Whenever requested by the Company, such insured shall give the Company all reasonable aid in any such action or proceeding, in effecting settlement, securing evidence, obtaining witnesses, or prosecuting or defending such action or proceeding, and the Company shall reimburse such insured for any expense so incurred.

4. Notice of Loss—Limitation of Action

In addition to the notices required under paragraph 3(b) of these Conditions and Stipulations, a statement in writing of any loss or damage for which it is claimed the Company is liable under this policy shall be furnished to the Company within 90 days after such loss or damage shall have been determined and no right of action shall accrue to an insured claimant until 30 days after such statement shall have been furnished. Failure to furnish such statement of loss or damage shall terminate any liability of the Company under this policy as to such loss or damage.

5. *Options to Pay or Otherwise Settle Claims*

The Company shall have the option to pay or otherwise settle for or in the name of an insured claimant any claim insured against or to terminate all liability and obligations of the Company hereunder by paying or tendering payment of the amount of insurance under this policy together with any costs, attorneys' fees and expenses incurred up to the time of such payment or tender of payment by the insured claimant and authorized by the Company. In case loss or damage is claimed under this policy by an insured, the Company shall have the further option to purchase such indebtedness for the amount owing thereon together with all costs, attorneys' fees and expenses which the Company is obligated hereunder to pay. If the Company offers to purchase said indebtedness as herein provided, the owner of such indebtedness shall transfer and assign said indebtedness and the mortgage and any collateral securing the same to the Company upon payment therefor as herein provided.

6. *Determination and Payment of Loss*

(a) The liability of the Company under this policy shall in no case exceed the least of:
    (i) the actual loss of the insured claimant; or
    (ii) the amount of insurance stated in Schedule A, or, if applicable, the amount of insurance as defined in paragraph 2(a) hereof; or
    (iii) the amount of the indebtedness secured by the insured mortgage as determined under paragraph 8 hereof, at the time the loss or damage insured against hereunder occurs, together with interest thereon.

(b) The Company will pay, in addition to any loss insured against by this policy, all costs imposed upon an insured in litigation carried on by the Company for such insured, and all costs, attorneys' fees and expenses in litigation carried on by such insured with the written authorization of the Company.

(c) When liability has been definitely fixed in accordance with the conditions of this policy, the loss or damage shall be payable within 30 days thereafter.

7. *Limitation of Liability*

No claim shall arise or be maintainable under this policy (a) if the Company, after having received notice of an alleged defect, lien or encumbrance insured against hereunder, by litigation or otherwise, removes such defect, lien or encumbrance or establishes the title, or the lien of the insured mortgage, as insured, within a reasonable time after receipt of such notice; (b) in the event of litigation until there has been a final

Title Insurance

5. *Options to Pay or Otherwise Settle Claims*

The Company shall have the option to pay or otherwise settle for or in the name of an insured claimant any claim insured against or to terminate all liability and obligations of the Company hereunder by paying or tendering payment of the amount of insurance under this policy together with any costs, attorneys' fees and expenses incurred up to the time of such payment or tender of payment, by the insured claimant and authorized by the Company.

6. *Determination and Payment of Loss*

(a)   The liability of the Company under this policy shall in no case exceed the least of:
   (i)   the actual loss of the insured claimant; or
   (ii) the amount of insurance stated in Schedule A.

(b)   The Company will pay, in addition to any loss insured against by this policy, all costs imposed upon an insured in litigation carried on by the Company for such insured, and all costs, attorneys' fees and expenses in litigation carried on by such insured with the written authorization of the Company.
   (c)   When liability has been definitely fixed in accordance with the conditions of this policy, the loss or damage shall be payable within 30 days thereafter.

7. *Limitation of Liability*

No claim shall arise or be maintainable under this policy (a) if the Company, after having received notice of an alleged defect, lien or encumbrance insured against hereunder, by litigation or otherwise, removes such defect, lien or encumbrance or establishes the title, as insured, within a reasonable time after receipt of such notice; (b) in the event of litigation until there has been a final determination by a court of competent jurisdic-

determination by a court of competent jurisdiction, and disposition of all appeals therefrom, adverse to the title or to the lien of the insured mortgage, as insured, as provided in paragraph 3 hereof; or (c) for liability voluntarily assumed by an insured in settling any claim or suit without prior written consent of the Company.

8. *Reduction of Liability*

(a)   All payments under this policy, except payments made for costs, attorneys' fees and expenses, shall reduce the amount of the insurance pro tanto; provided, however, such payments, prior to the acquisition of title to said estate or interest as provided in paragraph 2(a) of these Conditions and Stipulations, shall not reduce pro tanto the amount of the insurance afforded hereunder except to the extent that such payments reduce the amount of the indebtedness secured by the insured mortgage.

Payment in full by any person or voluntary satisfaction or release of the insured mortgage shall terminate all liability of the Company except as provided in paragraph 2(a) hereof.

(b)   The liability of the Company shall not be increased by additional principal indebtedness created subsequent to Date of Policy, except as to amounts advanced to protect the lien of the insured mortgage and secured thereby.

No payment shall be made without producing this policy for endorsement of such payment unless the policy be lost or destroyed, in which case proof of loss or destruction shall be furnished to the satisfaction of the Company.

9. *Liability Noncumulative*

If the insured acquires title to the estate or interest in satisfaction of the indebtedness secured by the insured mortgage, or any part thereof, it is expressly understood that the amount of insurance under this policy shall be reduced by any amount the Company may pay under any policy insuring a mortgage hereafter executed by an insured which is a charge or lien on the estate or interest described or referred to in Schedule A, and the amount so paid shall be deemed a payment under this policy.

tion, and disposition of all appeals therefrom, adverse to the title, as insured, as provided in paragraph 3 hereof; or (c) for liability voluntarily assumed by an insured in settling any claim or suit without prior written consent of the Company.

8. *Reduction of Liability*

All payments under this policy, except payments made for costs, attorneys' fees and expenses, shall reduce the amount of the insurance pro tanto. No payment shall be made without producing this policy for endorsement of such payment unless the policy be lost or destroyed, in which case proof of such loss or destruction shall be furnished to the satisfaction of the Company.

9. *Liability Noncumulative*

It is expressly understood that the amount of insurance under this policy shall be reduced by any amount the Company may pay under any policy insuring either (a) a mortgage shown or referred to in Schedule B hereof which is a lien on the estate or interest covered by this policy, or (b) a mortgage hereafter executed by an insured which is a charge or lien on the estate or interest described or referred to in Schedule A, and the amount so paid shall be deemed a payment under this policy. The Company shall have the option to apply to the payment of any such mortgages any amount that otherwise would be payable hereunder to the insured owner of the estate or interest covered by this policy and the amount so paid shall be deemed a payment under this policy to said insured owner.

10. *Apportionment*

If the land described in Schedule A consists of two or more parcels which are not used as a single site, and a loss is established affecting one or more

10. Subrogation Upon Payment or Settlement

Whenever the Company shall have settled a claim under this policy, all right of subrogation shall vest in the Company unaffected by any act of the insured claimant, except that the owner of the indebtedness secured by the insured mortgage may release or substitute the personal liability of any debtor or guarantor, or extend or otherwise modify the terms of payment, or release a portion of the estate or interest from the lien of the insured mortgage, or release any collateral security for the indebtedness, provided such act occurs prior to receipt by the insured of notice of any claim of title or interest adverse to the title to the estate or interest or the priority of the lien of the insured mortgage and does not result in any loss of priority of the lien of the insured mortgage. The Company shall be subrogated to and be entitled to all rights and remedies which such insured claimant would have had against any person or property in respect to such claim had this policy not been issued, and if requested by the Company, such insured claimant shall transfer to the Company all rights and remedies against any person or property necessary in order to perfect such right of subrogation and shall permit the Company to use the name of such insured claimant in any transaction or litigation involving such rights or remedies. If the payment does not cover the loss of such insured claimant, the Company shall be subrogated to such rights and remedies in the proportion which said payment bears to the amount of said loss, but such subrogation shall be in subordination to the insured mortgage. If loss of priority should result from any act of such insured claimant, such act shall not void this policy, but the Company, in that event, shall be required to pay only that part of any losses insured against hereunder which shall exceed the amount, if any, lost to the Company by reason of the impairment of the right of subrogation.

11. Liability Limited to this Policy

This instrument together with all endorsements and other instruments, if any, attached hereto by the Company is the entire policy and contract between the insured and the Company.

Any claim of loss or damage. whether or not based on negligence, and

Title Insurance

of said parcels but not all, the loss shall be computed and settled on a pro rata basis as if the amount of insurance under this policy was divided pro rata as to the value on Date of Policy of each separate parcel to the whole, exclusive of any improvements made subsequent to Date of Policy, unless a liability or value has otherwise been agreed upon as to each such parcel by the Company and the insured at the time of the issuance of this policy and shown by an express statement herein or by an endorsement attached hereto.

11. *Subrogation Upon Payment or Settlement*

Whenever the Company shall have settled a claim under this policy, all right of subrogation shall vest in the Company unaffected by any act of the insured claimant. The Company shall be subrogated to and be entitled to all rights and remedies which such insured claimant would have had against any person or property in respect to such claim had this policy not been issued, and if requested by the Company, such insured claimant shall transfer to the Company all rights and remedies against any person or property necessary in order to perfect such right of subrogation and shall permit the Company to use the name of such insured claimant in any transaction or litigation involving such rights or remedies. If the payment does not cover the loss of such insured claimant, the Company shall be subrogated to such rights and remedies in the proportion which said payment bears to the amount of said loss. If loss should result from any act of such insured claimant, such act shall not void this policy, but the Company, in that event, shall be required to pay only that part of any losses insured against hereunder which shall exceed the amount, if any, lost to the Company by reason of the impairment of the right of subrogation.

12. *Liability Limited to this Policy*

This instrument together with all endorsements and other instruments, if any, attached hereto by the Company is the entire policy and contract between the insured and the Company.

Any claim of loss or damage, whether or not based on negligence, and which arises out of the status of the lien of the insured mortgage or of the title to the estate or interest covered hereby or any action asserting such claim, shall be restricted to the provisions and conditions and stipulations of this policy.

No amendment of or endorsement to this policy can be made except by writing endorsed hereon or attached hereto signed by either the President, a Vice President, the Secretary, an Assistant Secretary, or validating officer or authorized signatory of the Company.

12. *Notices, Where Sent*

All notices required to be given the Company, and any statement in writing required to be furnished the Company shall be addressed to it at the issuing office or to Chicago Title Insurance Company, Claims Department, 111 West Washington Street, Chicago, Illinois 60602.

which arises out of the status of the title to the estate or interest covered hereby or any action asserting such claim, shall be restricted to the provisions and conditions and stipulations of this policy.

No amendment of or endorsement to this policy can be made except by writing endorsed hereon or attached hereto signed by either the President, a Vice President, the Secretary, an Assistant Secretary, or validating officer or authorized signatory of the Company.

13. Notices, Where Sent

All notices required to be given the Company and any statement in writing required to be furnished the Company shall be addressed to its principal office at 111 West Washington Street, Chicago, Illinois 60602, or at any branch office of the Company.

ALTA 1970 LOAN REV. FORM

SCHEDULE A

FORM 3584

| Number | Date of Policy | Amount of Insurance |

1. Name of Insured:

2. The estate or interest referred to herein is at Date of Policy vested in:

3. The estate or interest in the land described in this Schedule and which is encumbered by the insured mortgage is:

4. The mortgage, herein referred to as the insured mortgage, and the assignments thereof, if any, are described as follows:

5. The land referred to in this policy is described as on the description sheet annexed.

SCHEDULE B

This policy does not insure against loss or damage by reason of the following:

Countersigned

_____
Authorized Signatory

NOTE: ATTACHED HERETO   ADDED PAGES.

ALTA 1970 OWNER'S FORM

SCHEDULE A

FORM 3583

Number   Date of Policy   Amount of Insurance

1. Name of Insured:

2. The estate or interest in the land described herein and which is covered by this policy is:

3. The estate or interest referred to herein is at Date of Policy vested in the insured.

4. The land herein described is encumbered by the following mortgage or trust deed, and assignments:

SCHEDULE B

This policy does not insure against loss or damage by reason of the following:

other mortgages

easements

leases

Countersigned

_____
Authorized Signatory

NOTE: ATTACHED HERETO   ADDED PAGES.

normally can be done by paying an added premium. If the owner substantially improves the property after he insures, some policies make him a coinsurer, providing he does not adequately increase the amount of coverage. As a coinsurer, he must bear some of the risk of loss.

In addition to protecting against title deficiencies, title insurance policies commonly provide certain benefits in case of litigation. These benefits usually include a commitment by the insurer, at its cost, to defend the insured in litigation over the title based on any claim not excepted by the policy. Failure of the insurer to defend can result in it being obligated to pay defense counsel retained by the insured.

As is true of other kinds of insurance, the scope of title insurance coverage is determined in large part by standard provisions in the insurers' policies. All companies use printed policy forms and their terms are often borrowed from state or national trade association approved documents. Of special importance have been the title policy forms developed and approved by the American Land Title Association, a national association of commercial title insurance companies, abstracters, and title lawyers, including counsel for large lending institutions. This association's forms, particularly its standard mortgagee's policies, have been widely adopted by title insurers.

NOTE

What are the major differences between the two preceding policies, and why do you think the differences exist?

Smith and Lubell, Real Estate Financing: Protecting the Lender with Title Insurance
5 Real Est. Rev. No. 1, at 14 (1975)[23]

THE NATURE OF TITLE INSURANCE

It may be of some interest and value to consider briefly just what title insurance is. Certainly, it bears little resemblance to other types of insurance, such as life or casualty insurance.

Life insurance insures a risk which is certain to occur in the future, that is, the death of the insured, although with term insurance the risk may not necessarily occur within the period insured. Possibly this form of insurance should more appropriately be categorized as "death" insurance. The pre-

---

23. Charles C. Smith is Associate General Counsel and Harold A. Lubell is Assistant General Counsel, New York Life Insurance Company. Both are members of the New York Bar. The views expressed are solely those of the authors and do not necessarily represent those of any institution with which they are associated.

Title Insurance

mium is usually paid in periodic installments, but the insurance may be purchased with a single lump-sum premium.

Casualty or hazard insurance protects against loss due to a future contingency, such as fire, windstorm, flood, personal injury, or the like, which may or may not occur. It is almost always in the nature of term insurance.

Unlike the foregoing two forms of insurance, title insurance protects against the risk of a state of facts that may exist at the time the insurance is obtained. That risk is the possibility of a defect in title. Title insurance much resembles a warranty, since it protects against possible defects in the product. In this case the product is title to a particular parcel of real property. Title insurance is invariably single-premium insurance. The protection which it affords is available so long as the party who is insured has any interest in the particular real estate, either directly or under a contingent liability, such as that of the grantor (seller) under a warranty deed.

Title insurance also differs from other forms of insurance in that an extremely high percentage of the "premium" for title insurance is attributable to the cost of examination of the title to be insured. The expense thus covers risk avoidance rather than risk assumption. While it is true that with virtually all forms of insurance a part of the premium covers the assessment of a particular underwriting risk (e.g., medical or fire underwriting), the percentage of the premium used to determine the existence of risks is much greater in the case of title insurance than in any other form of insurance.

SELECTION OF A TITLE INSURER

A mortgagee who is lending large sums of money, frequently in the millions, upon the security of a first lien upon a parcel of real estate is naturally concerned with the ability of the title insurer to respond to a claim in the event that the lien on the property or title to the security is defective. Most, if not all, national lenders have compiled lists of the title insurance companies whose policies they will accept. As a practical matter, the performance of the title insurance industry as a whole is very high and there are few if any title companies whose policies are not generally acceptable to all lenders. These lists also indicate the maximum amount of insurance which the lender is willing to accept from a particular title insurer on any single title risk. The following are some of the matters which lenders look at in determining the acceptability of title insurers and the maximum amount of insurance which is appropriate from any one title company on any one risk:

- Paramount in any such consideration is the financial ability of the insurer to respond to a claim. Factors which the lender considers are the net worth of the insurer, the nature of its investments, and the liquidity of its assets.

- Possibly more than in some other business endeavors, people make the company in title insurance. Before agreeing to accept a title policy from a particular insurer, a lender wants to be satisfied as to the abilities and experience of the title officers and other employees of the company. Lenders want to have title insurance which has been written by qualified personnel on a sound basis after proper searches. They do not want title insurance which has been issued after inadequate searches on a casualty rather than a risk-avoidance basis.

- All other things being equal, and given the high caliber of the title industry as a whole, approval of a title insurance company for a particular transaction is often made on the basis of the quality of service (promptness, attention to detail, courtesy, cooperation, and the like) which the insurer, by experience or reputation, is known to render. This is, of course, but another example of the ways in which people are important.

The Borrower Pays

In real estate financing, it is customary for the borrower to pay all costs and expenses in connection with the closing of the loan. Therefore, it is not surprising that title insurance premiums and charges are almost universally paid by the mortgagor rather than the mortgagee. Since the mortgagor is paying for title insurance for the benefit of the lender, it is appropriate to allow the mortgagor to select the title insurer for the loan transaction. The mortgagor makes his selection subject to the lender's requirements that the insurer be acceptable to the lender and that the amount of the risk not exceed that which the lender is willing to accept from the specific title insurer. If the amount of the insurance required by the lender exceeds the amount which the lender is willing to accept from the primary insurer, it is not necessary that a different insurer be selected. However, it is then customary to obtain reinsurance from qualified insurers. Generally, these reinsuring title companies are selected by the primary title insurance company, subject to the lender's approval, but upon occasion the lender will designate the reinsurer. In practice, it is unusual for the borrower to choose title reinsurers for the risk.

The Scope of Coverage

The institutional lender financing a shopping center, residential development, or office or industrial complex requires title insurance for two basic reasons.

Primarily, he wishes to be assured that the security for his loan is a valid first lien on the real property. Secondly, he wants to know that there are no easements, restrictions, leases, or other encumbrances that can impair the value of the security for his loan and therefore materially reduce the appraised value upon which the lender is relying for underwriting purposes.

Title Insurance

The title insurance policy insures the title to the property as it appears in the required local recording offices. Consequently, it insures both the validity and priority of the lien of the lender's mortgage or deed of trust as it appears of record. The policy of title insurance also affords protection against

- Forgeries;
- Defects in execution of documents;
- Defects in legal proceedings; and
- Defective legal process.

This protection is not available on the basis of an abstract and attorney's opinion, when used as an alternative to title insurance. The attorney for a national lender who has wrestled with the difficulties presented by a missing heir appearing fifty years ago in the chain of title can appreciate the assistance and comfort which a title insurance binder affords by virtue of its coverage of this gap in the chain of title. It is this acceptance by title insurers of minor title defects on the basis of local experience that has influenced national lenders, as much as almost anything else, to require title insurance in preference to other title evidence.

National lenders lack familiarity with purely local problems and practices. Therefore, they must rely on title insurance with respect to purely local matters, such as those relating to surveys (e.g., encroachments) and matters which are revealed by an inspection of the property. More recently, lenders are coming to look to title companies for protection in connection with possible zoning violations, a problem which certainly goes directly to the value of the security. Some title insurers still assert that this coverage, which is only available at a substantial premium, is not an appropriate subject for title insurance. The writers feel that where compliance with zoning can be insured on the basis of an examination of the applicable local ordinances, a survey, and an on-site inspection of the property, the coverage is as much a proper subject of title insurance as coverage based upon an examination of recording data plus a survey and inspection. Obviously, an appropriate additional premium should be charged for any policy endorsement covering zoning.

Lenders are now also concerned with the risks relating to environmental law requirements, which risks are a possible area for additional title insurance coverage.

While hopefully a matter of only temporary concern by reason of current high interest rates, the question of possible inadvertent violation of usury laws is a matter of consideration by permanent lenders in certain loans, particularly where the loan is being purchased by the permanent lender from the interim lender. In these cases, affirmative insurance against usury by title policy endorsement (based on affidavits, indemnities, and other assurances) can afford the permanent lender protection against a risk that it would not otherwise be willing to accept.

There is an increasing trend toward furnishing a variety of affirmative insurances of title risks by endorsement, in each case for an appropriate additional premium. Where such additional insurance is a proper matter for title insurance coverage, the benefit of such insurance is one which should be made available to the national lender who is otherwise not in a position to assess the risk involved because of a lack of familiarity with local conditions. The California Land Title Association has for many years taken the lead in making a number of types of "additional" coverage available by endorsement on a standardized basis. Some of these forms of endorsement

- Insure contiguity of multiple parcels of land;
- Provide limited zoning coverage;
- Provide coverage in appropriate situations that the right of rescission under the federal Truth-in-Lending Act does not apply to a transaction;
- Insure that an easement furnishes ingress and egress to and from a public street; and
- Provide coverage with respect to priority of the mortgage over mechanics' liens. . . .

The complexity and risks of a real estate venture are frequently eased by the presence of an astute title insurer who intelligently abstracts the title which is the lender's security for its loan and takes a measured view of the risks incumbent upon insuring the lender that its loan is secure.

NOTES

1. The coverage of title insurance policies is discussed in Burke, Law of Title Insurance cc. 2-4, 13 and 14 (1986); Rooney, A Primer for Attorneys, reprinted in American Bar Association, Section of Real Property, Probate and Trust Law, Title Insurance and You: What Every Lawyer Should Know 3 (1979); and Beasley, Special Forms of Coverage, id. at 19.

2. Beasley, Standard Endorsements for Extra Coverage, in Practicing Law Institute, Real Estate Law and Practice Course Handbook Series No. 251, at 135 (1984), describes such extra coverage as follows:

> Although the title policy gives extensive coverage for title-related matters, many situations occur where coverage must be tailored or extended to cover a specific problem. It is possible to tailor the title policy to meet an insured's specific problem in what could be termed various standard categories through endorsements. An endorsement gives specific affirmative insurance against loss or damage arising by reason of an incident occurring or perhaps, in some circumstances, an incident not occurring. The endorsement adds

coverage to the policy or, in some limited circumstances, the endorsement does not actually add coverage as much as it affirms the existence of coverage. . . .

Some endorsements, zoning as an example, affirmatively assure the insured that the property can be used for a specific purpose and that the improvements meet the requirements of the zone planning or building codes. Endorsements have been created for use with the ALTA policy form which was created and adopted by the American Land Title Association. Other states, through various title organizations, have created endorsements either for use with the ALTA policies or for use with specific policies issued in the state, such as the Oregon Land Title Association, California Land Title Association, New York Board of Title Underwriters, or others.

Among endorsements available throughout most of the United States are those protecting against loss from special assessments, mechanics' liens that may have priority over mortgage loans under certain circumstances, encroaching easements, covenants that may impair a mortgage loan, and zoning restrictions. An added premium may be required for these endorsements. Endorsements are also available to protect homeowners against inflation. Maximum policy coverage is increased periodically under such endorsements to reflect inflation according to a designated cost index. Inflation endorsements may set a ceiling of 150 percent, or some other amount, by which the coverage may be increased. Sample policy endorsements appear in Practicing Law Institute, Real Estate Law and Practice Handbook Series No. 236, at 251-260 (1983).

Note, Iowa's Prohibition of Title Insurance — Leadership or Folly?[24]

33 Drake L. Rev. 683, 695-701 (1983-1984)

The complexities of today's real estate transactions have made it necessary for buyers, sellers, and lenders to seek as much reassurance as possible that their title expectations will be met and that their interests will be protected. Subsequent loss of property due to title defects can wipe out a family's entire capital and savings, or cause huge losses to a commercial development. To avoid such costly losses, the title insurance industry was created over one hundred years ago and American consumers now pay more than one billion dollars in title insurance premiums every year. Title insurance provides an option for the real estate purchaser or lending institution to pay a relatively small one-time premium to insure their newly acquired interest in the property against the possibility of losing title to the property because of a title defect which was not discovered at the time of the purchase.

24. Footnotes omitted.

Title insurance has become an essential requirement in many real estate transactions. Many "[p]rivate institutional lenders and governmental organizations such as the Federal Home Loan Mortgage Corporation and Federal Mortgage Association automatically require title policies today." In many areas, lenders require potential mortgagors to obtain title insurance prior to granting the mortgage. Title insurance is almost universally purchased for large commercial transactions. Often it is the availability of title insurance that convinces a purchaser to accept a title he might have otherwise refused. Title insurance also helps to ease some of the worries associated with the single-state orientation of real property law by filling the gaps between local laws and customs and the requirements of national or nonlocal lenders, developers, lessees, and/or owners. . . .

IV. Criticisms of Title Insurance

Title insurance policies traditionally appeared "to be intentionally worded so as to obfuscate [their] true meaning and to confuse all but the select few truly knowledgeable insurance gurus in existence." Although the forms have been greatly simplified, and the language made more understandable, most consumers still do not understand their policies. They purchase the policy wanting the protection they believe it affords them, but are totally unaware of its dimensions and limitations. The typical title insurance purchaser not only does not understand the policy he purchases, but he is also totally without knowledge about available sellers and the services they offer.

Since real estate transactions are a rare occurrence in a typical property purchaser's life, there is no incentive for him to develop even a basic knowledge of title insurance. A basic lack of interest, and a desire not to slow down the transfer process usually lead the purchaser to delegate the selection of a title insurer to his attorney, banker, or real estate broker. Being unfamiliar with property law, and trusting the real estate professional's judgment, the purchaser usually accepts his recommendations without ever seeking out alternatives.

Due to the purchaser's nonparticipation in the selection of a title insurer, the market is an ineffective control on the industry, and the demand for owner's title insurance does not change significantly with changes in policy prices. When the purchase of title insurance becomes an integral step in real estate transactions, as it has in most states, consumer demand becomes highly inelastic, and the effectiveness of price competitiveness between sellers diminishes entirely.

The commercial title insurance industry operates as an oligopoly. There are only about ninety title insurers writing title insurance policies today, and over one-half of the title insurance written in this country is written by the nation's four largest title insurers. Although competition between title insurance companies is fierce, this competition does not manifest itself in premium rates which differ significantly within a geographic market. In many states, this lack of rate competition is forced upon the title insurance companies by state regulations setting the premium rates. In other areas, title insurers have formed state-sanctioned rating bureaus to gather industry loss data, and set uniform statewide rates.

As a result of the purchaser's lack of participation in the purchase of title insurance and the general unavailability of price competition, companies that have wished to increase their market share have been unable to do so by reducing prices or by improving coverage or services. Instead, the companies' competitive efforts have been channeled toward those individuals or institutions who would be advising the purchaser at the closing stages of the transaction: the brokers, the bankers, and the attorneys. The result is a system of "reverse competition," whereby the insurance companies compete for the recommendations of real estate professionals rather than for the business of the actual consumer. "Reverse competition" has often taken the form of payments to the real estate professional, in the form of rebates, commissions, fees, or kickbacks, and are *far in excess* of the payment justified by the work performed. As a result, the consumer pays a much higher premium than he would pay in a purely competitive situation.

These real estate professionals are, at least theoretically, in the best possible position to seek out the best policy at the best price, since they are constantly in the market for title insurance and have the business knowledge and facilities to investigate available policies. But because the title insurance companies solicit the real estate professional's referrals by providing him with more benefits or compensation than their competitors, "reverse competition" raises rather than lowers the premium price. The concern of the real estate professional is shifted thereby from looking after the best interests of the real estate purchaser he is advising to finding the title insurance company who will provide him the best return for his referral. When lenders receive a commission for referring a customer to a title insurance company, the incentive is strong to recommend its purchase even in cases where no title defect is suspected. Eventually, title insurance becomes a virtual requirement to obtaining a mortgage. In many parts of the country, lending institutions will no longer rely on the title opinions of local attorneys, and title insurance has become a necessity.

Perhaps the biggest controversy with regard to title insurance centers on the premium charged. The premium is typically derived by estimating the allowance needed by the company to cover the costs of operation, the required statutory reserves, the insured risks, and the property needs of the insurer. Title insurance rate structures, however, lack uniformity, and make evaluation and comparison difficult. . . . An overwhelming portion of premium costs is expended by the title insurance companies for expenses, overhead and commissions. The agent, for example, may retain as much as fifty percent of the premium as his commission for soliciting and processing the order and issuing the policy. The costs of the title search and examination, if done by the title insurer, also make up a large part of the company's operating expenses.

Only a small portion of the premium is actually used to pay for losses due to risks insured by the policy. Estimates of this "loss ratio" industry-wide are generally between five and ten percent. . . .

The face amount of a title insurance policy is the maximum amount payable under the policy. Whenever a claim is paid under a title insurance policy, the amount paid is deducted from the face amount of the policy, thereby reducing the amount of future coverage available to the insured. Legal expenses, however, are not deducted. The payment of a claim on a loan policy may be made to the lender without consent from or notice to the property owner. When the policy's face value has been decreased, an additional premium must be paid by the insured in order to maintain full coverage.

A similar problem occurs because of the effects of inflation. With property values increasing, the size of possible losses caused by title defects increase, but since few title insurance policies have built-in inflation clauses, the coverage under the policy does not keep pace, and the amount of coverage erodes. Consequently, to counter inflation, additional premiums must be purchased periodically. This is a trap that an unwary homeowner could easily fall into.

Another common criticism of the title insurance industry is that a lender's policy does not protect the interests of the purchaser/borrower, even though in most areas he is the party who is required to pay the premium. "While a lender's title insurance policy relates both to the lien of the mortgage and to the quality of the landowner's title, it does not do so for the benefit of the landowner. . . ."

Title insurance seeks to insure against only a limited number of title risks. The extensive exclusions and exceptions dilute considerably the coverage actually received. . . .

V. The Benefits of Title Insurance

Despite the problems caused by the inadequacies of title insurance coverage, however, the industry continues to expand because it does provide a very useful service to consumers. For a one-time premium, which is nominal when compared with the loss that the insured *could* sustain, the insured purchases "peace of mind". Since public records have become more complex, and the frequency of property transfers has greatly increased, the possibilities that the title search might overlook a cloud on the title, or that hidden defects might exist, have increased dramatically. Recovery against the title searcher, abstract company, or the attorney who gave the title opinion for loss of title due to defects is possible only when negligence can be proven, and even then, is limited by the financial situation of the negligent party. Title insurance provides "greater and longer economic accountability than the individual lawyer . . . and covers a number of risks which a search does not disclose and which therefore are excluded from the attorney's liability." Immediate or remote grantors also may desire protection since recovery may be sought from them based on the covenants of title contained in the purchaser's warranty deed, although such recovery may be barred, or may be subject to severe limitations.

The cost of the policy would be easily recaptured by the insured if the company defends him in a single title challenge action, and if the defense is unsuccessful, the title insurance company, not the insured, must suffer the loss, if it is covered under the policy. Without title insurance protection, the property owner must pay the expenses for defending his title whether he is successful or not, and additionally, must sustain the financial loss caused by the loss of title. . . .

Title insurance companies also tend to give the consumer a break when it appears that charging a full premium would be a windfall for the company. Discounted rates are often available when the company issues a new policy after an interest has been transferred or refinanced, and also when an abstract of the title has been previously compiled. Also, the problem caused by underinsurance tends to be greatly mitigated by the fact that "title losses rarely amount to more than a fraction of the coverage."

Sattler v. Philadelphia Title Insurance Co.
192 Pa. Super. 337, 162 A.2d 22 (1960)

WRIGHT, Judge. We are here concerned with an action in assumpsit for breach of a policy of title insurance. The case was tried before Honorable Emanuel W. Beloff without a jury. Plaintiff claimed damages in amount of $3,500, which was the policy limit. The trial judge found that there had been a breach of the policy, but assessed only nominal damages in amount of six cents. Plaintiff's motions for judgment n.o.v. and for a new trial were subsequently dismissed. This appeal followed. We then remitted the record for the entry of judgment.

On September 3, 1941, Florence Plawa Adams purchased from Hyman Hoffman premises situated at 825 North Marshall Street in the City of Philadelphia. On December 28, 1955, Florence Plawa Adams Zaronka and Alexander J. Zaronka, her then husband, conveyed the premises to Benjamin E. Sattler for the purchase price of $3,500. On January 11, 1956, the Philadelphia Title Insurance Company, hereinafter referred to as the Company, issued and delivered to Sattler its Title Insurance Policy No. 104985 in the sum of $3,500, which policy recited that, in consideration of the premium paid, the Company "does hereby insure . . . that the title of the Assured to the estate, mortgage or interest described in Schedule A hereto annexed, is good and marketable, and clear of all liens and incumbrances charging the same at the date of this Policy; saving such estates, defects, objections, liens, and incumbrances as may be set forth in

Schedule B . . . and any loss shall be payable upon compliance by the Assured with the Conditions hereto attached and not otherwise." Policy conditions 2 and 9 are set forth in the footnote.[1]

The record discloses that, on the date the policy was issued, there were two alleged encumbrances which were not excepted in Schedule B. One arose by virtue of a judgment entered on April 1, 1938, by William Lipshutz against Anthony Plawa, father of Florence Adams. This judgment was revived by a series of writs of scire facias issued against Plawa prior to his death on March 8, 1945. On December 19, 1946, a scire facias was issued wherein Florence Adams was named as a terre tenant, and judgment was entered thereon on January 24, 1947. This judgment was revived by a writ of scire facias issued January 21, 1952, again naming Florence Adams as terre tenant. On April 10, 1952, judgment was entered thereon. On April 10, 1956, damages were assessed on this judgment in the sum of $11,944.44. On the same date, a writ of fieri facias was issued by virtue of which the sheriff advertised the premises at 825 North Marshall Street for sale. At the instance of the Company, this sale was stayed by order of court. It is unnecessary to detail the subsequent proceedings, including an abortive motion to strike,[2] other than to note that, on April 1, 1959, the purported lien of this judgment was released as to the premises at 825 North Marshall Street.

The other encumbrance arose by virtue of a bill in equity, filed May 9, 1947, in which it was alleged that the conveyance from Hoffman to Florence Adams was made with the intent to defraud the rights of William Lipshutz, and that, although title was taken in the name of Florence Adams, the actual purchase was made by Anthony Plawa. No further steps were taken in the equity case until April 11, 1956, when judgment was entered for failure to file an answer. On May 4, 1956, at the instance of the Company, a rule was granted to show cause why Sattler should not be joined as a party defendant and let into a defense. On November 14, 1958, the rule was made absolute. On March 31, 1959, this case was settled, discontinued and ended as to Sattler.

The instant complaint sets forth the purchase of the premises at 825

---

1. "2. The company will at its own costs, defend the Assured in all actions of ejectment or other proceedings founded upon a claim of title, lien or incumbrance prior in date to this Policy and not excepted therein. In case any person having an interest in this Policy shall receive notice or have knowledge of any such action or proceeding, it shall be the duty of such person at once to notify the Company thereof in writing, and secure it the right to defend the action. Unless the Company shall be so notified within fifteen days, the insurance shall be void as to such person.

"9. If claim be made because of unmarketability or defect of title, or of liens or incumbrances not excepted in the Policy, the Company shall have the right to take the estate or interest insured at its then market value, irrespective of the alleged defect, lien or incumbrance, shall be entitled to a conveyance or assignment thereof, with proper allowance for all defects, liens or incumbrances not insured against by the Policy. And no action shall be brought against the Company for any claim under this Policy until thirty days after notice in writing of such claim."

2. See Lipshutz v. Plawa, 393 Pa. 268, 141 A.2d 226.

North Marshall Street, the issuance of the title insurance, and the subsequent disclosure of the judgment entered against Florence Adams as terre tenant. The complaint further alleges that, at the time Sattler acquired title and at the time of the issuance of the policy, his title "was not good and marketable and clear of all liens and encumbrances," that the market value of his title was worthless, and that he had suffered a loss in the sum of $3,500. The Company answered that the judgment against Florence Adams as terre tenant was not a lien on the premises for the reason that she "was not a terre tenant in fact." The answer further alleged that the Company "was ready at all times to insure the title to any conveyance of said premises by the plaintiff," that Sattler had "enjoyed uninterrupted possession and maintained control of said premises," and that he had suffered no loss. At the trial the material facts were stipulated. Sattler then offered the testimony of a realtor who stated that, at the time of purchase on December 28, 1955, the property had a market value of $3,500. In reply to a hypothetical question as to the market value of the property in May, 1956, assuming that it was subject to the record judgment, the witness stated, over objection, that the property would have no value. After mature deliberation, the hearing judge filed his decision, June 11, 1959, finding that the alleged encumbrances had no legal validity, and "that the plaintiff herein, although harassed and annoyed, got what he purchased."

Appellant contends that the Company cannot assert the invalidity of the lien of the judgment, and of the lis pendens arising from the equity action, as a defense to avoid liability on the policy. He argues "that a title insurance agreement is a guarantee that the title is good and marketable and that when this insurance agreement was written, at the moment that it is written, and there was a defect in the title which is not separated or excepted from the policy, the title agreement is breached." His position is that the obligation of the insurance contract was not merely against valid liens, but against liens charging the property insured, and that the title would be clouded and unmarketable as a result of any lien against the same, whether the lien was valid or not. To accept this proposition would mean that the insured could recover on the policy merely by showing an unexcepted claim, whether or not the claim was meritorious, and whether or not the insured suffered any loss resulting therefrom.

The correct rule, as laid down by our Supreme Court, is that a contract of title insurance is an agreement to indemnify against loss through defects of title. Foehrenbach v. German-American Title & Trust Co., 217 Pa. 331, 66 A. 561, 563, 12 L.R.A., N.S., 465. See also Pennsylvania Laundry Co. v. Land Title & Trust Co., 74 Pa. Super. 329. In the *Foehrenbach* case it was pointed out that the purpose of title insurance is to "indemnify those who actually suffer the loss." In the case at bar, it was incumbent upon appellant to establish a loss covered by the provisions of the contract. Fox Chase Bank v. Wayne Junction Trust Co., 258 Pa. 272, 101 A. 979. This simply means that the insured must show a loss resulting from the unexcepted encumbrances. In other words, a title insurance policy is a contract of indemnity and not of guaranty. Unless and until a loss occurs, there is no liability. See Narberth Building & Loan Assn. v. Bryn Mawr Trust Co., 126 Pa. Super. 74, 190 A. 149.

In the case at bar the court below determined that the alleged encumbrances were actually not valid. Indeed, appellant makes no assertion to the contrary. It is true that the judgment and the lis pendens were clouds on the title. Octoraro Water Co. v. Garrison, 271 Pa. 421, 114 A. 638; Onorato v. Carlini, 272 Pa. 489, 116 A. 387. Consequently, a right of action for technical breach of the policy inured to appellant. However, a second issue remains, namely, what was the amount of appellant's loss. He is entitled to recover only for loss which arose by reason of the defects or encumbrances against which the Company covenanted to indemnify. See Whiteman v. Merion Title & Trust Co., 25 Pa. Super. 320. Appellant argues that, in Fifth Mutual Building Society of Manayunk's Appeal, 317 Pa. 161, 176 A. 494, the measure of damages in such a case was stated to be the difference in the market value of the property subject to the encumbrance and what the market value of the property would have been had it not been subject to the encumbrance. But this measure of damages necessarily presupposes the validity of the encumbrance. Without proof of actual loss there can be no damage. Appellant attempted, by means of expert testimony, to prove the extent of his damage, but he failed to establish that he had actually sustained a loss. As stated by Judge Beloff in his well-considered opinion:

"We agree with the contention of the plaintiff at bar and it is perfectly obvious that the Title Insurance Company failed to reveal and disclose to the plaintiff the encumbrances existing on the face of the record against the property. Indeed, we are of the opinion that the plaintiff was annoyed and harassed thereby and perhaps incurred legal expenses. If there were a formula in the evidence before us upon which to predicate a finding to compensate the plaintiff for these items, we would be glad to do so. The plaintiff does not and cannot on the record before us support a claim for the damages he seeks, namely, the face amount of the policy. For, having disposed of the validity and effect of the bill in equity and the lis pendens in the proceedings in the Common Pleas Court, we are of the opinion that Florence Adams, in the eyes of the law, was never a terre tenant, and that the judgment, lien and assessment of damages against her property had no effect or validity in law."

Judgment affirmed.

NOTES

1. Do you think the result would have been different if this case had been decided prior to March 31, 1959? Why do you think plaintiff contin-

ued to press his appeal after the lien was released on April 1, 1959, and the settlement a day earlier?

2. How much the insured will recover if there is a loss covered by a title insurance policy may depend on the property's valuation date. The most common position, apparently, is to measure the insured's loss based on the property's value when the title defect was discovered, although there is authority for using the date of purchase by the insured, the date on which the insured contracted to sell the property, or the date on which the title actually failed. A case holding the appropriate valuation date to be the date of defect discovery is Hartman v. Shambaugh, 96 N.M. 359, 630 P.2d 758 (1981), noted in 12 N.M.L. Rev. 833 (1982), in which Note cases following other valuation theories are discussed. Which theory of valuation do you consider preferable and why?

3. Although title insurance losses are small compared to most other types of insurance losses, title insurers' losses as a percentage of their current operating costs have been increasing, and this has been causing concern to the title insurance industry. Major types of losses are plant searching and abstract procedure; examination and opinion errors; basic covered risks, with fraud and forgery being particularly high; closing or escrow procedure errors; and special risk coverage, with mechanics' lien losses being a substantial but declining cause of loss. See Little et al., Claims — A Crisis — What We Can Do About It, 62 Title News No. 6, at 7 (1983); and Jensen and McCarthy, Title Industry Reports Record Losses, 61 Title News No. 12, at 6 (1982). Earlier loss data appear in American Land Title Association, The Title Industry, White Papers vol. 1, c. 4 (1976), reprinted in 56 Title News No. 6, at 9 (1977).

4. If a title insurer indemnifies an insured, the insurer is subrogated to the rights of the insured against third persons. For a case in which such subrogation rights were held to exist, see Commonwealth to Use of Willow Highlands Co. v. Maryland Casualty Co., 373 Pa. 602, 97 A.2d 46 (1953). There a notary public had falsely certified to acknowledgement of a mortgage when signatures of the borrowers were forgeries. Insured paid the mortgagee for its loss under a title policy, and the insurer was then held subrogated to the insured's rights against the notary and his surety.

First National Bank & Trust Co. of Port Chester v. New York Title Insurance Co.
171 Misc. 854, 12 N.Y.S.2d 703 (Sup. Ct. 1939)

ALDRICH, J. The plaintiff brings this action to recover under a policy of title insurance issued by the defendant, covering the interest of the plaintiff as mortgagee upon certain real property to the extent of $8,400. The defendant pleads various defenses and a counterclaim for the cancellation or reformation of the policy. Many of the important facts of the case are not disputed.

In September, 1935, Max Karnowsky and Abe Karnowsky were, and had been for some thirty years, copartners engaged in the plumbing and heating business under the name of Karnowsky Brothers. They were indebted to the bank upon firm notes, indorsed by the partners individually, to the extent of $4,575. These notes were overdue. Prior to that time the partners had been the owners of certain real property known as 358 Willett avenue, in the village of Port Chester. Some time in August, 1935, the Karnowskys transferred the Willett avenue property to one Ike Nathan, a relative by marriage. This transfer came to the attention of the officers of the bank. The notes were turned over to the attorneys for the bank and an action commenced thereon. Conferences developed between the bank and its attorneys and the Karnowskys and their attorney. The Willett avenue property was subject to a first mortgage of $2,800 held by a third party. After some negotiations the Karnowskys agreed with the bank that the Willett avenue property should be reconveyed by Nathan to the Karnowskys, that the bank would take an assignment of the existing first mortgage for $2,800, that the Karnowskys would give an additional mortgage for $5,600, and that such two mortgages would be consolidated as one, the time of payment extended, etc. Out of the new mortgage there was to be paid all pending taxes and interest on the property; the balance was to be used in payment of the notes held by the bank. The plaintiff, having in mind the consummation of this arrangement, applied to the defendant for a policy of title insurance upon its interest as proposed mortgagee. The title was examined by the defendant and approved subject to certain exceptions not now material and the defendant company indicated its willingness to insure the title of the plaintiff accordingly.

The transfer of the title was consummated on September 30, 1935. The closing took several hours. The preparation of the papers and the handling of the closing was attended to by an attorney representing the title company, who later took care of recording the documents. By the transaction the property was conveyed back to the Karnowskys. The first mortgage of $2,800 was assigned to the bank. The new mortgage of $5,600 was executed and delivered to the bank. The consolidation agreement between the Karnowskys and the bank was duly executed. The papers were promptly recorded. The proceeds of the new mortgage were used for the payment of the notes and the other purposes indicated. The notes were surrendered and the action then pending on the notes was discontinued.

In accordance with its arrangement the title company issued its policy of title insurance, dated September 30, 1935, whereby it insured the plaintiff against all loss or damage not exceeding $8,400 "which the insured shall sustain by reason of any defect in the title of the insured to the estate or interest described in Schedule A hereto annexed, affecting the premises described in said schedule, or by reason of the unmarketability of the title of the insured described in said schedule to, or in said premises, or because

Title Insurance

of liens or incumbrances against the same at the date of this policy," subject to certain exceptions mentioned in Schedule "B," or excepted by the conditions of the policy. By Schedule "A," subdivision 1, the estate or interest insured by the policy was stated to be "Interest as mortgagee." By Schedule "A," subdivision 2, the description of the property the title to, or an interest in which was thereby insured, was the Willett avenue property. By Schedule "A," subdivision 3, the deed or other instrument by which the title or the interest thereby insured was vested in the insured was stated to be the assignment of the $2,800 mortgage, the new mortgage for $5,600 and the consolidation agreement. The excepted objections to title, etc., contained in Schedule "B," did not include any specification of any possible invalidity of the mortgage because in violation of the Bankruptcy Act against preferences.

On January 20, 1936, a petition in involuntary bankruptcy was filed against Max Karnowsky and Abraham Karnowsky, individually and as copartners doing business as Karnowsky Brothers. On February 5, 1936, they were duly adjudicated bankrupts accordingly by the District Court in the Southern District of New York. A trustee in bankruptcy was thereafter duly appointed. The trustee instituted an action in the District Court to set aside the $5,600 mortgage held by the bank on the ground that it was a preference. Issue was joined by the bank by the service of an answer containing a general denial. The bank gave notice to the title company of the institution of the action and demanded that the title company defend the suit. It appears that the title company, through the attorneys for the bank, defended the action under a disclaimer and subsequently paid the expenses of defending the case, without prejudice to the disclaimer. The case came on for trial in the District Court. On July 27, 1937, the court made its formal decision, containing findings of fact and conclusions of law, as a result of which judgment was directed setting aside the $5,600 mortgage upon the ground that it constituted a preference in violation of the Bankruptcy Law. Judgment was entered upon that decision on July 27, 1937, cancelling the $5,600 mortgage and the consolidation and extension agreement made thereunder. The first mortgage of $2,800 held by the plaintiff was validated to the extent of the full amount, with interest from August 1, 1937. No appeal was taken from that judgment. The plaintiff brings this action to recover the loss which it claims to have sustained under the policy. The amount demanded by the plaintiff in the complaint was $4,884.08. Upon the trial it was conceded that a final dividend to the plaintiff upon its claim as a general creditor for the amount by which it had been deprived of the benefits of the mortgage, amounting to $577.43, had been paid to the plaintiff through the bankruptcy court. The amount which the plaintiff claims is, therefore, $4,306.65. The bookkeeping statements presented on behalf of the plaintiff establish this amount as the paper loss. The defendant raises various objections to any recovery by the plaintiff.

First. The defendant contends that the policy cannot, in any event, be construed to cover the hazard of a loss sustained by the plaintiff by reason of the fact that the mortgage of $5,600 was declared invalid under the Bankruptcy Law. With this contention the court cannot agree. The title company knew that a new mortgage of $5,600 was to be given. It knew that the proceeds of that loan were to be used to pay the notes. It was fully acquainted with the general nature of the proposed transaction. It never indicated in the negotiations any intention not to cover this risk. There was never any oral agreement between the bank and the title company that the risk should not be covered by the policy. The policy insured the bank as mortgagee. The $5,600 mortgage was specifically included under Schedule "A." This particular risk was not excluded under Schedule "B." The policy, by its terms, insured against any loss or damage by reason "of any defect in the title of the insured to the estate or interest described." On the face of the policy it includes this particular defect in the title to the $5,600 mortgage. In accordance with the general rule, doubts and ambiguities, if any, contained in a policy of title insurance are to be resolved in favor of the insured, where the contract is drawn up by the insurer. (62 C.J. 1056 §18; Marandino v. Lawyers T.I. Corp., 156 Va. 696; 159 S.E. 181; Broadway Realty Co. v. Lawyers T. Ins. & T. Co., 226 N.Y. 335, 337.) The policy, by its foregoing terms, certainly does not exclude the hazard of an attack on the mortgage under the Bankruptcy Law. There is no ambiguity on the face of the policy with respect to those provisions. But if there were such an ambiguity it would have to be resolved against the defendant which drew the contract. Subdivision 13 of the condition of the policy provides as follows: "Defects and incumbrances . . . created, suffered, assumed or agreed to by the insured . . . are not to be deemed covered by it." The invalidity of the mortgage because of preference was certainly a defect in the title of the bank to the mortgage insured. The words "assumed or agreed to" had reference to some particular defect or incumbrance assumed or agreed to by the bank by the title conveyance to it or by some collateral agreement made by the bank with reference to that specific subject-matter. Such words do not apply here. The word "created" had reference to some affirmative act on the part of the bank itself. The bank took the mortgage but it did not create the defect. That was created by operation of law. Such a clause does not protect the defendant from the very act insured against, which was the taking of the mortgage. . . .

Third. The defendant argues that the insured has not sustained any loss or damage within the meaning of the policy. The reasoning seems to be that because the plaintiff held certain notes before the mortgage was given, the adjudication by a decree of the Federal court did nothing more than put the plaintiff where it had been previously. This contention also must be overruled. What the defendant insured was the validity of the mortgage. By the policy (Conditions, subd. 2) a claim for damages arose: "(IV.) When the insurance is upon the interest of a mortgagee, and the mortgage has been adjudged by a final determination in a court of competent jurisdiction to be invalid, or ineffectual to charge the premises described in this policy." That is exactly the situation which has arisen here. The policy insured a first lien to the extent of $8,400. By the decree of a competent court that lien was limited to the amount of $2,800. The word "loss" is a relative term. Failure to keep what a man has or thinks he has is a loss. To avoid a possible claim against him; to obviate the need and expense of professional advice, and the uncertainty that sometimes results even after it has been obtained, is the very purpose for which the owner seeks insurance. To say that when a defect subsequently develops he has lost nothing and, therefore, can recover nothing, is to misinterpret the intention both of the insured and the insurer. (Empire Development Co. v. Title G. & T. Co., 225 N.Y. 53, 59, 60.) Under such a policy the insurer is liable for the actual loss sustained. (Montemarano v. Home Title Ins. Co., 258 N.Y. 478.) A leading case on the precise point is Foehrenbach v. German American T. & T. Co. (217 Penn. St. 331; 66 A. 561). In that case the plaintiff supposed that he was the owner of the entire interest in certain real property. He applied to the defendant for title insurance. The policy was issued. Subsequently others claimed an interest in the premises. They brought an action in which it was held that the plaintiff possessed only a half interest and not the whole of the property. The trial court dismissed his complaint against the title company, upon the ground that he had lost nothing. Upon appeal the plaintiff was awarded judgment in his favor. It was said that "failure to keep that which one has is loss." Also, "the estate or interest of the insured which was covered by the policy was that of owner in fee of the entire property, and any defect in title which reduced his interest below that point was, it seems to us, just that much loss, or damage, for which he was entitled to be indemnified." That decision is directly applicable here. Applying these principles, the plaintiff here certainly sustained a loss and damage within the meaning of the policy. The following figures, conclusively established by the plaintiff, show the bookkeeping loss:

Original total of both mortgages		$8,400.00
Less payments through amortization		426.88
Unpaid principal of mortgages at date of decree		$7,973.12
Credits chargeable against bank		
Balance in escrow account	$29.20	
Due from trustee on accounting as per decree	106.37	
Received from agent's rent account	153.47	
By mortgage validated by decree	2,800.00	
		−3,089.04
Loss or damage to date of decree		$4,884.08
Less bankruptcy dividend on claim of $4,884.08		577.43
Net loss and damage		$4,306.65

The foregoing figure would not necessarily be the amount of a recovery to which the plaintiff would be entitled. The title company did not guarantee the payment of the debt. It did not insure the adequacy of the security. We must, therefore, consider the value of the property which stood as security for the $8,400 mortgages. That property after recovery by the trustee in bankruptcy was sold for $5,900. That, however, was obviously a forced sale. The bankruptcy proceeding had to be closed up. The evidence shows that the trustee was pressing the agent to get some customer at some price. The defendant offered testimony upon this trial that the fair value in July, 1937, was $5,650 but that testimony is not convincing, when considered in connection with the income and other pertinent factors. The witness for the plaintiff gave a value of $9,000. In order to cover the entire loss of the plaintiff, the property, even allowing $500 for the expenses of a possible foreclosure, needed only a value of $8,473.12. The court is satisfied, and it will be found as a fact, that the actual value of the property prior to and at the time of the decree was $9,000. As a matter of fact, the property was more than paying its way when the mortgage of $5,600 was declared invalid. It has more than paid its way since that time. Under the circumstances, to say there would have been a foreclosure is purely speculation. The value of the underlying property is not the sole index of the worth of a mortgage. The ascertainment of such value is a matter of the exercise of reasonable judgment after an intelligent and honest canvass of all factors relevant to the particular security. (Matter of New York Title & Mortgage Co., 277 N.Y. 66.) So considered, the mortgage was reasonably worth the face thereof. If the plaintiff is entitled to recover anything, it is entitled to a judgment for $4,306.65, with interest from the date the invalidity was adjudged. . . .

Fifth. The defendant pleads as a defense that provision of the policy which reads as follows (Conditions, subd. 5): "Any untrue statement made by the insured, or the agent of the insured, with respect to any material fact; any suppression of or failure to disclose any material fact; any untrue answer, by the insured, or the agent of the insured, to material inquiries before the issuing of this policy, shall void this policy."

It is upon the facts of the case, in the light of these provisions of the policy, that the litigation must be finally determined. The general principles applicable to such a subject-matter are substantially well settled. A title policy is one of insurance, so that it is governed for purposes of construction by the rules applicable to other insurance contracts. (62 C.J. 1056, §14; De Carli v. O'Brien, 150 Ore. 35; 41 P.[2d] 411.) In accordance with the general rule, an innocent misrepresentation of a fact material to the risk will avoid a policy of title insurance. (62 C.J. 1058, §25; Union Trust Co. v. Real Estate T. Co., 27 Pa. Co. Ct. 187.) Where a title insurance policy so provides, the suppression of a material fact will void the policy. (62 C.J. 1058, §27; Rosenblatt v. Louisville Title Co., 218 Ky. 714; 292 S.W. 333.) A failure by the insured to disclose conditions affecting the risk, of which he is aware, makes the contract voidable at the option of the company. (Stipcich v. Metropolitan Life Ins. Co., 277 U.S. 311.) Concealment of material facts by the insured is a defense. (Vaughan v. United States T.G. & I. Co., 137 App. Div. 623.) The same rule is laid down in other cases. (Phillips v. U.S.F. & G. Co., 200 App. Div. 208; *affd.*, 234 N.Y. 618; Town of Hamden v. American Surety Co., 93 F.[2d] 482; Raebeck v. Title Guarantee & T. Co., 229 App. Div. 727; Sebring v. Fidelity-Phoenix Fire Ins. Co., 255 N.Y. 382.) What is material under such circumstances has been the subject of judicial consideration. In Geer v. Union M.L. Ins. Co. (273 N.Y. 261) the court said (p. 266) that the question in such case is not whether the insurance company might perhaps have decided to issue the policy even if it had been apprised of the truth; the question is whether failure to state the truth where there was duty to speak prevented the insurance company from exercising its choice of whether to accept or reject the application upon a disclosure of all the facts which might reasonably affect its choice, and (p. 269) the question in such case is not whether the company might have issued the policy even if the information had been furnished; the question in each case is whether the company has been induced to accept an application which it might otherwise have refused, as any misrepresentation which defeats or seriously interferes with the exercise of such a right cannot truly be said to be an immaterial one. Materiality is a matter of degree and a misrepresentation through concealment of a fact is material where it appears that a reasonable insurer would be induced thereby to take action which he might not have taken if the truth had been disclosed (p. 272).

Tested by these rules, the disposition of this case seems clear. Without considering controverted matters, the undisputed proof with respect to certain of the subject-matter shows both an affirmative misrepresentation and a misrepresentation through non-disclosure on the part of the plaintiff. There was a specific misrepresentation with respect to one material fact. It is undisputed that the financial condition of Karnowsky Brothers was substantially the same at the time of the adjudication in bankruptcy as at the time when the mortgage was given. The officers of the plaintiff, upon the trial, claimed a thorough understanding on their part of the underlying facts with reference to the financial situation of the debtors. The claims allowed in bankruptcy aggregated $13,313.86. Of this total $4,884.08 was the claim of the plaintiff arising through the invalidity of the mortgage; $3,341.44 was the claim of Mutual Trust Company, concerning which both the plaintiff and the defendant were informed at or before the time of the closing, $1,490 was a claim on a second mortgage which covered certain real property of the bankrupts at 26-28 Rollhaus place, such mortgagees having disclaimed the security and having elected to stand as general creditors. This item was not considered as an unsecured claim by either plaintiff or defendant. Technically it was not an unsecured claim at that time. These three items aggregate $9,715.52. The balance of

$3,598.34 represented unsecured claims of general creditors. It appears that the attorney for Karnowsky Brothers in the discussion with an officer of the bank stated that the merchandise creditors totaled about $3,000. The attorney for the bank in his conference with the attorney for the title company does not appear to have stated the figures on such claims. He told them about the plaintiff bank and Mutual Trust Company claims and testified that with these exceptions he told the attorney for the title company "the general creditors were very small, very few." At the closing the attorney for the title company was given to understand by those present that the general creditors were very few and the amount inconsequential or negligible. Three thousand dollars is a substantial sum of money. There was a misstatement on that material subject.

There was a non-disclosure of various material matters. The bank failed to disclose the fact that it had in its files two credit statements from Karnowsky Brothers, one under date of October 18, 1933, and one under date of October 2, 1934. Referring, for a moment, to the second one, it appears that this statement was returned to Karnowsky Brothers when originally received by the bank "due to the irregularity appearing on the face of the same." The Karnowskys sent it back without correction. Neither the fact of the existence of the statement or its return by the bank with the expression quoted were made known to the title company. That there was at least one irregularity appearing on the face of the statement is certain. Under notes payable to banks the debtors listed $3,800. The claims of the bank itself, without considering the Mutual Trust Company, were in excess of that amount. The statement also discloses a gross overvaluation, among others, of the Willett avenue property. It was estimated at $25,000, when not even the officers, who claimed to be familiar with real estate values, have suggested any value in excess of $9,000. In connection with other circumstances, this statement had additional importance. By the statement certain premises at 407 North Main street were given an estimated value of $35,000, with mortgages of $10,850. In March, 1935, there came to the attention of the bank the fact that this property had been conveyed to one Markel. An estimated equity of some $24,000 thereby disappeared from the assets of the debtors. The fact of the conveyance known to the bank was not disclosed to the defendant. At the time of the mortgage the four months' period in which to attack the conveyance of March had expired under the Bankruptcy Law. The bank officers were fully familiar with the fact that the debtors were crowded for lack of cash. There was no disclosure to the defendant that a $24,000 unexplained departure of assets had occurred. If the explanation be that the value as estimated was grossly overstated, then the fact that the debtors had overstated was material to the defendant. If the explanation be that the property was conveyed without consideration, then it indicated a willingness on the part of the debtors to dispose of their property in such fashion and such willingness was a material matter from the standpoint of the defendant. If the explanation be that an additional consideration was paid and devoted to other purposes, then the disposition thereof was unknown. That also was material. If there be no explanation, and the record gives none, then the fact of the conveyance itself, in the light of the preceding statement, was of the utmost importance from the standpoint of the defendant. The bank knew that the deposit account of Karnowsky Brothers in the bank had been closed many months previously. The fact of the closing was not communicated to the defendant. The bank also knew that prior to the closing that account had been repeatedly overdrawn for a period of at least a year. That fact was not disclosed. On the contrary, the representation was made to the title company that Karnowsky Brothers had been customers of the bank for many years and that the bank thought very well of them. A comparison of the two financial statements also shows that the incumbrances upon 407 North Main street had increased from $7,500 on October 18, 1933, to $10,850 on October 2, 1934, and that the incumbrances upon 26-28 Rollhaus place had increased from $10,500 on the first date to $15,000 on the second date. The statements afford no adequate explanation of such increases aggregating $7,850. Nor does it appear what became of the money. This information was not disclosed by the bank. From the various facts above referred to various other inferences of the same nature might very well be drawn. It is sufficient to say that the record shows conclusively that there was not a full and frank disclosure by the bank to the defendant of all of the material information in the possession of the bank with respect to the risk to be insured against. For that reason, the complaint must be dismissed upon the merits. It will be so adjudged.

Sixth. The defendant pleads also a counterclaim for cancellation or reformation of the policy. This amounts to nothing more than a repetition of the various matters pleaded as a defense, and to which a reference has been made. The policy has an independent status so far as it applies to the $2,800 mortgage still in existence. The defendant is not entitled to rescission on the theory of a material misrepresentation, etc. It has neither repaid, tendered or offered to return the premium paid for the policy. Nor is there any basis for a reformation. There is nothing to indicate that by mutual mistake of both parties, or by a mistake of the defendant and fraud of the plaintiff, etc., the policy was drawn to cover a risk which the defendant did not intend to insure. So far as appears, the policy was drawn in the form that both parties intended it to be. There is nothing about it to be reformed. The counterclaim is dismissed upon the merits. . . .

NOTES

1. Can a large bank be expected to coordinate the activities of its personnel so as to avoid the risk of unintended misrepresentation and

concealment concerning the financial affairs of its mortgagors? To what extent should bank employees who negotiate and close mortgages covered by title insurance be expected to acquire information about mortgagors from bank files and other bank employees, and turn over this information to the title insurer?

2. The usual black letter requirement for valid insurance is that the insured must have an insurable interest in the thing insured; otherwise, the transaction is an illegal wager. Does and should title insurance meet this insurable interest requirement? Suppose at the time a title policy is issued the insured and insurer both incorrectly believe that the insured has a valid interest in a parcel of land. Can the insurer successfully refuse to pay out when it is later discovered that the insured never had any interest in the parcel and seeks to recover for a total loss under his policy? On insurable interest in property, see generally Keeton, Insurance Law — Basic Text 94-128 (1971); and 4 Appleman, Insurance Law and Practice cc. 109 and 110 (1941).

3. It is commonly stated in title insurance cases, as in insurance cases generally, that ambiguities and uncertainties are construed against the insurer. Should this be done if, as is commonly the case, the insured is a knowledgeable institutional lender, such as a bank or a life insurance company?

4. A title policy clause excluding from coverage "defects known to the insured claimant" was held not to apply to assignees of the original insured mortgagee when assignees took without notice of the defects, although the defects apparently were known by the original insured when it took out the policy. Southern Title Insurance Co. v. Crow, 278 So. 2d 294 (Fla. Dist. Ct. App. 1973).

5. A recorded easement, not discoverable by a chain of title examination, was excluded from coverage under a title policy provision excluding "easements . . . not shown by the public records." Ryczkowski v. Chelsea Title and Guaranty Co., 85 Nev. 37, 449 P.2d 261 (1969).

L. Smirlock Realty Corp. v. Title Guarantee Company
52 N.Y.2d 179, 418 N.E.2d 650 (1981)

JASEN, J. This appeal presents a question of first impression for our court. At issue is whether a policy of title insurance will be rendered void pursuant to a standard misrepresentation clause found therein as a result of the insured's failure to disclose a material fact which was a matter of public record at the time the policy was issued.

In November, 1967, the Town of Hempstead condemned and thereby acquired title to certain property on and adjacent to the premises known as 31-39 Carvel Place, which is located in Inwood, Long Island. At that time, the premises were owned by Bass Rock Holding, Inc. (Bass Rock), a corporation controlled by Helen and Anthony De Giulio. The Bass Rock property was improved by a warehouse and access to and from the property was over three public streets: Carvel Place to the north of the premises and St. George Street and Jeanette Avenue to its east. The principal loading docks for the warehouse were located at the easterly end of the building with direct access from St. George Street and Jeanette Avenue. In addition, there was an alleyway along the northern side of the warehouse connecting the Carvel Place entrance to these loading docks. However, clearance along this passageway was quite limited and trucks would often strike the warehouse building when attempting to maneuver down this alleyway. Because of this, the Carvel Street entrance was of little value as an access route for the warehouse facility.

The Bass Rock property was heavily indebted and in 1968 there was a default in mortgage payments. A foreclosure proceeding was instituted in the early part of 1969. It was at about this time that Gerald Tucker, general counsel for one of the mortgagees in the foreclosure proceeding, indicated an interest in the property and negotiations were commenced with the De Giulios with a view toward the eventual purchase of the Bass Rock property. Soon thereafter, the plaintiff corporation was formed by Tucker and a group of associated investors.

It was also around this time, according to the testimony of Abraham Lee, Special Counsel for the Town of Hempstead, that Lee telephoned Tucker to inform him that a portion of the Bass Rock property had been condemned by the town and should be excluded from the foreclosure proceeding. Lee testified that he identified the condemned parcel as "abutting on Carvel Place," but that Tucker stated that he was not interested and would proceed with the foreclosure action anyway. The parcel in question subsequently was identified in the record as the town's damage parcel 8-6, taken for street alignment purposes.

Sometime after Tucker spoke with Lee, Tucker and Joseph Tiefenbrun, the attorney retained by plaintiff, met with the Bass Rock attorney to discuss the details of the sales contract. At this meeting, Tucker was informed that, although the exact location of the property involved was uncertain, Bass Rock was entitled to a $5,000 to $6,000 condemnation award from the Town of Hempstead. As a result of this discussion, the contract was amended to include a clause assigning "any condemnation award affecting the premises then due or to be due in the future" to the plaintiff. It was agreed that the necessary information concerning this condemnation would be provided at the title closing. On April 25, 1969, the sales contract was executed by Bass Rock and the plaintiff. The purchase price was set at $600,000.

On May 14, 1969, title was closed. During the closing, and in the presence of defendant's title closer, Tucker and Mrs. De Giulio discussed the condemnation award referred to in the sales contract. In fact, Mrs. De Giulio sketched an outline of the condemned property on the Bass Rock title survey. The parcel marked by Mrs. De Giulio was adjacent to the southwest corner of the Bass Rock property, but it was not part of nor did it affect any access routes to the warehouse.

After title closed, defendant issued plaintiff a title policy covering the warehouse property. The policy contained the following clause insuring access to public streets: "Notwithstanding any provisions in this paragraph to the contrary, this policy, unless otherwise excepted, insures the ordinary rights of access and egress belonging to abutting owners." It should be noted that no exception was listed in the policy for any condemnation affecting Carvel Place, St. George Street or Jeanette Avenue.

At the time the property was purchased, plaintiff leased the entire premises to Pan American World Airways, Inc. In addition, plaintiff had spent an additional $95,000 above the purchase price in order to improve the premises for its new tenant. Unfortunately, it was soon discovered that the title search had failed to reveal that the roadbeds of St. George Street and Jeanette Avenue and a portion of the property along Carvel Place had been condemned by the Town of Hempstead two years prior to plaintiff's acquisition of the property. It was apparent that the defendant's title searchers simply failed to check the master card on file at the Nassau County Clerk's office covering the applicable section and block which would have revealed these condemnations.

By 1971, plans for urban development in the Town of Hempstead required the closing down of the warehouse access routes at St. George Street and Jeanette Avenue, thereby rendering the property valueless. As a result, Pan American quit the premises and plaintiff eventually lost 31-39 Carvel Place in a foreclosure sale. Plaintiff then commenced the present action against the defendant seeking to recover $600,000 in damages pursuant to its title insurance policy based on the defendant's failure to discover the condemned roadbed property.*

In its answer, defendant pleaded an affirmative defense based on the following standard provision in its policy:

"MISREPRESENTATION

"Any untrue statement made by the insured, with respect to any material fact, or any suppression of or failure to disclose any material fact, or any untrue answer by the insured, to material inquiries before the issuance of this policy, shall void this policy." According to defendant, plaintiff, through its agent Tucker, had knowledge prior to the closing of the town's condemnation as a result of his conversation with Lee. Defendant asserted

---

*As a second cause of action, plaintiff alleged that defendant was negligent in conducting its title search by failing to discover the public records of the condemnations. The Appellate Division held that this second cause of action properly was dismissed because any claim of negligence in the title search merged into the subsequently issued title policy pursuant to the express terms of the certificate of title. Inasmuch as no appeal was taken by plaintiff from this determination, we do not concern ourselves here with plaintiff's second cause of action in negligence.

Title Insurance

that plaintiff's failure to divulge this knowledge to the defendant was a "failure to disclose [a] material fact" which rendered the title policy void.

At the end of a nonjury trial, Trial Term dismissed plaintiff's claim. Finding that plaintiff, through Tucker, had knowledge of the condemnations prior to the issuance of the policy which it failed to disclose to the defendant, Trial Term concluded that the policy was nullified.

On appeal, a unanimous Appellate Division, 70 A.D.2d 455, 421 N.Y.S.2d 232, affirmed, but for reasons somewhat different than those expressed at Trial Term. The Appellate Division determined that although Tucker had been alerted by Lee as to the taking along Carvel Place of damage parcel 8-6, this fact offered no basis for the further inference, one apparently drawn by Trial Term, that Tucker also had knowledge of the condemnation of the roadbeds at St. George Street and Jeanette Avenue. Thus, the Appellate Division found that Tucker only had knowledge prior to the closing of the Carvel Place taking and of the condemnation of the small adjacent parcel at the southwest corner of the property which was identified at the closing by Mrs. De Giulio. According to the Appellate Division, the crucial issue of the case was whether "this knowledge concerned a material fact, the concealment of which was tantamount to a misrepresentation sufficient to permit defendant to void its title policy" (70 A.D.2d, at p. 461, 421 N.Y.S.2d 232).

In addressing this issue, the court below defined materiality in terms of "whether the suppression deprived the insurer of its freedom of choice in determining whether to accept or reject the risk upon full disclosure of all the facts which might reasonably affect that choice." (70 A.D.2d at p. 462, 421 N.Y.S.2d 232). The court went on to state (at p. 463, 421 N.Y.S.2d 232) that materiality "extends to any information that might have been revealed had further inquiry followed the initial disclosure of the suppressed facts." The court found that information regarding the condemnation of damage parcel 8-6 at Carvel Place was not itself material in that that taking had little, if any, effect on the value of the property. However, because disclosure of the Carvel Place taking, revealed to Tucker prior to closing, would have caused the defendant to check the appropriate public records and inevitably led to the discovery of the St. George Street and Jeanette Avenue condemnations, the Appellate Division concluded (70 A.D.2d, at p. 463, 421 N.Y.S.2d 232) that "no title insurance company with knowledge of [these] facts would have insured ingress and egress over streets already condemned for an urban renewal project." Therefore, inasmuch as Tucker's failure to disclose the information acquired in his conversation with Lee deprived the defendant of its "freedom of choice in determining the nature, scope and extent of the risk it would assume," the Appellate Division held (at p. 464, 421 N.Y.S.2d 232) that the suppression of the information regarding the Carvel Place condemnation was "material as a matter of law and would preclude recovery on the policy." We reverse.

At the outset, we note our agreement with the court below that information concerning the condemnations of damage parcel 8-6 adjacent to Carvel Place and the St. George Street and Jeanette Avenue roadbeds was material. It is manifest that revelation of this information certainly would have affected defendant's choice of insuring the risk covered by the policy issued to plaintiff. (See Vander Veer v. Continental Cas. Co., 34 N.Y.2d 50, 356 N.Y.S.2d 13, 312 N.E.2d 156; Geer v. Union Mut. Life Ins. Co., 273 N.Y. 261, 7 N.E.2d 125; Travelers Ins. Co. v. Pomerantz, 246 N.Y. 63, 158 N.E. 21; see, generally, 5A Warren's Weed New York Real Property, Title Insurance, §2.08.) However, contrary to the view expressed by the Appellate Division, the mere existence of knowledge of a material fact on plaintiff's part does not end the analysis. Rather, in order to ascertain whether the policy has been voided, a further determination must be made as to whether plaintiff was under a duty to disclose this information to defendant. (Geer v. Union Mut. Life Ins. Co., 273 N.Y. 261, 7 N.E.2d 125, supra; Sebring v. Fidelity-Phoenix Fire Ins. Co. of N.Y., 255 N.Y. 382, 174 N.E. 761.) In order to make that determination, we first must examine the nature of the agreement entered into by the parties and the respective expectations and obligations of the insured and insurer which arise out of a policy of title insurance.

By definition, title insurance involves "insuring the owners of real property . . . against loss by reason of defective titles and encumbrances thereon and insuring the correctness of searches for all instruments, liens or charges affecting the title to such property." (Insurance Law, §46, subd. 18; see also, §438.) Or, as one lower court has expressed it, "[a] policy of title insurance means the opinion of the company which issues it, as to the validity of the title, backed by an agreement to make that opinion good, in case it should prove to be mistaken and loss should result in consequence to the insured." (First Nat. Bank & Trust Co. of Port Chester v. New York Tit. Ins. Co., 171 Misc. 854, 859, 12 N.Y.S.2d 703.) Essentially, therefore, a policy of title insurance is a contract by which the title insurer agrees to indemnify its insured for loss occasioned by a defect in title. (See 9 Appleman, Insurance Law and Practice, §5201; 13 Couch, Insurance [2d ed.], §48:108.)

Beyond its purely contractual aspects, however, the unique nature of a title insurance transaction was quickly recognized by the courts. In Empire Dev. Co. v. Title Guar. & Trust Co., 225 N.Y. 53, 59-60, 121 N.E. 468, this court noted: "To a layman a search is a mystery and the various pitfalls that may beset his title are dreaded but unknown. To avoid a possible claim against him; to obviate the need and expense of professional advice, and the uncertainty that sometimes results even after it has been obtained is the very purpose for which the owner seeks insurance." Rather than being treated merely as a contract of indemnity, title insurance was viewed as being more in the nature of a covenant of warranty against encumbrances under which "mere knowledge of a defect [in title] by the insuring owner would not constitute a defense." (Empire Dev. Co. v. Title Guar. & Trust

Title Insurance 821

Co., supra, at p. 61, 121 N.E. 468; Maggio v. Abstract Tit. & Mtge. Corp., 277 App. Div. 940, 98 N.Y.S.2d 1011.)

Interestingly, in response to the decision in the *Empire Dev. Co.* case, title companies adopted as a standard provision in their policies the very misrepresentation clause at issue on this appeal. (See 5A Warren's Weed New York Real Property, Title Insurance, §2.08.) To date, however, this court has not been presented with an opportunity to examine the effect to be given to this clause in terms of imposing an obligation on the insured to disclose information to the insurer. Moreover, although at least one lower court has recognized the validity of this misrepresentation clause based on the insured's failure to divulge information to its insurer (Glickman v. Home Tit. Guar. Co., 15 Misc. 2d 167, 178 N.Y.S.2d 281, *affd.*, 8 A.D.2d 629, 185 N.Y.S.2d 756), other courts of this State which have addressed the issue of an insured's obligation to reveal information to its title insurer have held that the policy was voided by the insured's failure to disclose only in instances where there was evidence of intentional concealment on the part of the insured and the undisclosed information concerned a matter not of public record. (Vaughan v. United States Tit. Guar. & Ind. Co., 137 App. Div. 623, 122 N.Y.S. 393; First Nat. Bank & Trust Co. of Port Chester v. New York Tit. Ins. Co., 171 Misc. 854, 12 N.Y.S.2d 703, supra; cf. Sullivan v. Tomgil Bldg. Corp., 46 Misc. 2d 613, 260 N.Y.S.2d 465.)

One Federal court, addressing a provision identical to that found in the defendant's policy, stated that the clause "must be given a common sense application and, considering the nature of title insurance transactions, a duty to speak could be found only if the insurance applicant had actual knowledge of certain defects or encumbrances. Further, misrepresentation could be found only if one charged with such a duty to speak intentionally failed to disclose the information." (Lawyers Tit. Ins. Corp. v. Research Loan & Inv. Corp., 361 F.2d 764, 768.) In a like manner, other jurisdictions which have addressed similar clauses have required a showing that the insured had actual knowledge of the title defect which was intentionally concealed from the insurer. Moreover, these cases indicated, either expressly or by implication, that the title policy would only be voided in instances where the undisclosed information was not discoverable by the insurer by reference to publicly filed records. (Collins v. Pioneer Tit. Ins. Co., 629 F.2d 429; Rosenblatt v. Louisville Tit. Co., 218 Ky. 714, 292 S.W. 333; Fohn v. Title Ins. Corp. of St. Louis, 529 S.W.2d 1 [Mo.]; Pioneer Nat. Tit. Ins. Co. v. Lucas, 155 N.J. Super. 332, 382 A.2d 933, *affd.*, 78 N.J. 320, 394 A.2d 360; Laabs v. Chicago Tit. Ins. Co., 72 Wis. 2d 503, 241 N.W.2d 434; Bush v. Coult, 594 P.2d 865 [Utah]; see 9 Appleman, Insurance Law and Practice, §5205; 7 Powell, Real Property, Title Insurance, par. 1037.)

We agree with the view expressed by these cases. Therefore, we hold that a policy of title insurance will not be rendered void pursuant to a misrepresentation clause absent some showing of intentional concealment on the part of the insured tantamount to fraud. Moreover, because record information of a title defect is available to the title insurer and because the title insurer is presumed to have made itself aware of such information, we hold that an insured under a policy of title insurance such as is involved herein is under no duty to disclose to the insurer a fact which is readily ascertainable by reference to the public records. Thus, even an intentional failure to disclose a matter of public record will not result in a loss of title insurance protection.

In so holding, we merely recognize the practical realities of the transaction involved. As mentioned earlier, title insurance is procured in order to protect against the risk that the property purchased may have some defect in title. The emphasis in securing these policies is on the expertise of the title company to search the public records and discover possible defects in title. Thus, unlike other types of insurance, the insured under a title policy provides little, if any, information to the title company other than the lot and block of the premises and the name of the prospective grantor. Armed with this information, the title company then can search the various indices and maps to ascertain the state of title to the property. Indeed, it is because title insurance companies combine their search and disclosure expertise with insurance protection that an implied duty arises out of the title insurance agreement that the insurer has conducted a reasonably diligent search. (McLaughlin v. Attorneys' Tit. Guar. Fund, 61 Ill. App. 3d 911, 18 Ill. Dec. 891, 378 N.E.2d 355; Shotwell v. Transamerica Tit. Ins. Co., 16 Wash. App. 627, 628-631, 558 P.2d 1359, *affd.*, 91 Wash. 2d 161, 588 P.2d 208; see 9 Appleman, Insurance Law and Practice, §5213.) This duty may not be abrogated through a standard policy clause which would, if given the effect urged by defendant, place the onus of the title company's failure adequately to search the records on the party who secured the insurance protection for that very purpose. (See Empire Dev. Co. v. Title Guar. & Trust Co., 225 N.Y. 53, 121 N.E. 468, supra.)

Of course, an intentional failure by the insured to disclose material information not readily discernible from the public records will render the policy void. For instance, where the insured secures title insurance with knowledge that there exists some hidden defect in title, such as a forged deed, incapacity of the grantor, or the existence of an unrecorded easement (see, generally, 5A Warren's Weed New York Real Property, Title Insurance, §2.04) and the insured conceals that information from the title insurer, then such a failure to disclose will result in nullification of the policy.

In this case, there was no showing that plaintiff's agent, Tucker, intentionally failed to disclose the information concerning the Carvel Place condemnation. In fact, it would appear that defendant was at least put on notice as to the existence of condemnations affecting the Bass Rock property by the recital in the sales contract assigning all condemnation awards to plaintiff and by the discussion of the condemnation of the small southwest parcel which took place at the closing. In any event, it is undisputed that the existence of the St. George Street and Jeanette Avenue condemnations was readily ascertainable from the public records available at the Nassau County Clerk's office. Defendant, having failed to avail itself of this information, now attempts to avoid its obligation under the policy by claiming that plaintiff failed to disclose material information concerning title to the property. However, because plaintiff was under no duty to disclose this publicly available information to defendant, the policy will not be rendered void pursuant to the misrepresentation provision found therein.

Finally, defendant's answer contained a counterclaim premised upon an agreement entered into between the parties whereby the defendant advanced certain moneys in plaintiff's behalf for taxes and expenses attributable to plaintiff's attempt to secure a condemnation award from the Town of Hempstead. Pursuant to that agreement, plaintiff was to repay defendant the amounts so advanced subject to a setoff of any sums found due to plaintiff under its title policy. Inasmuch as plaintiff offers no basis for overturning the judgment rendered in defendant's behalf on this counterclaim, we do not disturb that award. Of course, payment of the amounts owing under this counterclaim must await a determination of the amount due plaintiff as damages under its title policy.

Accordingly, the order of the Appellate Division should be modified, with costs to plaintiff, to the extent of reversing the dismissal of plaintiff's first cause of action and remitting the case to Supreme Court, Nassau County, for a trial on the issue of plaintiff's damages. As so modified, the order should be affirmed.

Cooke, C.J., and Gabrielli, Jones, Wachtler and Fuchsberg, JJ., concur. Meyer, J., taking no part.

Order modified, with costs to plaintiff, and the case remitted to Supreme Court, Nassau County, for a trial on the issue of plaintiff's damages in accordance with the opinion herein and, as so modified, order affirmed.

NOTE

In subsequent proceedings on the issue of damages, plaintiff was awarded $593,850, plus interest, and also compensation for counsel fees and maintenance expenditures. L. Smirlock Realty Corp. v. Title Guarantee Co., 97 A.D.2d 208, 469 N.Y.S.2d 415 (1983), *aff'd*, 63 N.Y.2d 955, 473 N.E.2d 234 (1984).

Anderson v. Title Insurance Company
103 Idaho 875, 655 P.2d 82 (1982)

McFADDEN, Justice Pro Tem. Glenn A. Anderson and Ruth L. Anderson, appellants, purchased a parcel of real property in Fremont County on July 15, 1966, by a warranty deed for $1,250.00. The deed was recorded July

29, 1966. A title insurance policy was purchased on the land through defendants-respondents Fremont Title and Trust Company as an agent for The Title Insurance Company. Prior to the issuance of the policy, a preliminary report was given to appellant's counsel. In 1978, representatives of the Idaho Fish and Game Department apprised appellants of the existence of a prior conveyance to the State of Idaho in 1920 which granted to the State fee title to land on either side of the stream which passed through the property in question. It was conceded for purposes of the summary judgment that the conveyance to the state was genuine and had been properly recorded but that it had not been excepted from the title insurance policy upon which this suit was founded.

Respondents tendered to appellants the amount of the policy, $1,250.00, and deposited this amount to the court, but this was refused by appellants. Appellants filed a complaint in January, 1979, against the Title Insurance Company and Fremont Title Company, respondents, alleging breach of policy terms; negligence on part of Fremont; negligence on the part of The Title Insurance Company by reason of negligence of its agent for failure to report the lien of the State. Motions for summary judgment were filed by defendants.

Summary judgment was granted in favor of respondents. In effect the court held that the insurer, The Title Insurance Company's liability to the insured was limited to the loss of the value of the property within the limits of the policy. Defendants had also raised the statute of limitations in their motions for summary judgment but the court did not reach this issue. From the grant of summary judgment in favor of respondents, appellants appeal. We affirm.

Appellants contend that a title insurance company is liable in tort for failure to discover the conveyance of a portion of purchasers' land to the State of Idaho. Appellants argue that the practice in Idaho is that parties generally buy title insurance and rely on the insurance rather than an abstract of title. Before a purchaser buys property he orders a preliminary title report which tells him that the policy will insure against all encumbrances except those specifically listed in the report. Appellants argue that the purchaser is relying on the title insurer in the same manner in which he would rely on an abstractor of title and therefore the insurer has the same obligation as an abstractor and is liable in tort for errors or omissions. For this proposition appellants rely on Ford v. Guarantee Abstract and Title Company, Inc., 220 Kan. 244, 553 P.2d 254 (1976); Hillock v. Idaho Title and Trust, 22 Idaho 440, 126 P. 612 (1912), and Merrill v. Fremont Abstract Co., 39 Idaho 238, 227 P. 34 (1924).[1]

In *Ford* the Kansas Supreme Court stated

---

1. We decline to address what effect, if any, the enactment of I.C. §41-2708(1)(a), (b) has upon the duties of a title insurance company because that statute was enacted in 1973, and the acts complained of occurred in 1966.

Title Insurance

> Where a title insurer presents a *buyer* with both a preliminary title report and a policy of title insurance two distinct responsibilities are assumed; in rendering the first service, the insurer serves as an abstractor of title and must list all matters of public record regarding the subject property in its preliminary report. When a title insurer breaches its duty to abstract title accurately it may be liable in tort for all the damages proximately caused by such breach. 553 P.2d 254, 265.

That case arose from the title company's disbursement of plaintiffs' moneys to eliminate clouds on the title to the land without taking adequate steps to insure the money would be correctly applied to that purpose. Although the court makes the above statement it appears the court held that the title company was not being held liable for its negligent failure to discover a defect in the title but rather its gross negligence in disbursing the purchaser's money without clear title. That Kansas court imposed a fiduciary duty upon the insurance company by adopting the rule that:

> A corporation organized for the purpose among others, of examining and guaranteeing titles to real estate and which in all matters relating to conveyance and searching titles holds itself out to the public and assumes to discharge the same duties as an individual conveyancer or attorney, has the same responsibilities and its duty to its employer is governed by the principles applicable to attorney and client, 553 P.2d 254, 265, citing Mezzaluna v. Jersey Mortgage, 109 N.J.L. 340, 162 A. 743 (1932).

The court held:

> On the facts in this case Chicago Title Insurance Company, acting through Guarantee Abstract and Title Co., Inc., as agent, *was organized for the purpose of examining and guaranteeing titles to real estate and in all matters relating to conveyancing and searching titles held itself out to the public and assumed to discharge the same duties as an individual conveyancer or attorney.* It therefore had the same responsibilities and its duties to the Fords are governed by the principles applicable to attorney and client. It became responsible for due care in the process of disbursing the funds in representing the purchase price for the real property in question. Id. at 267. (Emphasis in original.)

Ford is distinguishable from the instant case in that Chicago Title Insurance Company was holding itself out to the public and assumed the same duties as an individual conveyancer or attorney. From this the court imposed a fiduciary duty and held the insurance company liable for its *negligent disbursement of funds,* not for failure to detect the defect. In the instant case the insurance company does not purport to act as anything other than a title insurance company. Chicago Title in the *Ford* case had assumed additional duties by acting as an escrow agent. The assumption of duties other than the issuing of an insurance policy is not present in our case.

Appellant also relies on the case of Banville v. Schmidt, 37 Cal. App. 3d 92, 112 Cal. Rptr. 126 (1974). In *Banville* the title insurance company argued that it had no duty to search title; that it acted in the transaction not as an abstractor but as an insurer; and that it was requested only to issue a policy of title insurance, which it did. The court rejected this argument noting that the policy recites that the premium of $113.60 was imposed as the "Total Fee for *Title Search, Examination*, and Title Insurance." (Emphasis in original.) The court stated:

> It is . . . clear that a portion of the total fee of $113.60 is attributable to a title search and examination. In other words, FIRST AMERICAN received a fee for a title search and examination, and the beneficiaries of said title search and examination, as stated in the insurance policy itself, are the (plaintiffs). It, therefore, appears unconscionable to say that FIRST AMERICAN did not owe a duty to the (plaintiffs) to reasonably and carefully perform their search and examination.

The court also discussed the title insurance company's duty as an escrow holder.

Banville was distinguished in Walters v. Marler, 83 Cal. App. 3d 1, 147 Cal. Rptr. 655 (1978). The *Walters* court stated: "[t]he title insurer's liability for negligence in *Banville* was based upon its performance as an abstractor of title. The liabilities of an abstractor differ from those of a title insurer." 147 Cal. Rptr. 655, 665. Appellant also relies on the case of Shotwell v. Transamerica Title Ins. Co., 16 Wash. App. 627, 558 P.2d 1359 (1976). However, on appeal the Washington Supreme Court, while acknowledging that there may be a duty to search title, decided the issue on narrower grounds and declined to impose a negligence cause of action against the insurer. Since the Washington Supreme Court refused to adopt the court of appeals' opinion, we find the opinion to have little precedential value.

The other two cases relied upon by appellant, Merrill v. Fremont Abstract Co., 39 Idaho 238, 227 P. 34 (1924), and Hillock v. Idaho Title and Trust Co., 22 Idaho 440, 126 P. 612 (1912), both dealt with abstractors of title and are therefore not applicable. Nowhere in this policy does it appear that it is anything other than what it purports to be, an insurance policy.[2]

---

2. The title insurance policy reads as follows:
"THE TITLE INSURANCE COMPANY, a corporation (incorporated under the laws of the State of Idaho), hereinafter called the Company, for a valuable consideration paid for this policy of title insurance,
DOES HEREBY INSURE
GLENN A. ANDERSON and
RUTH J. ANDERSON
husband and wife
together with the persons and corporations included in the definition of 'the insured' as set forth in the stipulations of this policy, against loss or damage not exceeding ONE THOU-

The fee charged was for an insurance policy, it does not appear to be for examination of title. Where title to a portion of insured property fails the insured is entitled to recover upon the loss up to the amount of insurance coverage under the policy. Hartman v. Shambaugh, 96 N.M. 359, 630 P.2d 758 (1981); Overholtzer v. Northern Counties Title Ins. Co., 116 Cal. App. 2d 113, 253 P.2d 116 (1953); J. Appleman, Insurance Law and Practice, Vol. 9, §§5201, 5216; 15 Couch on Insurance 57:179. The full amount of the policy, $1,200, has been tendered to the insureds and deposited to the court.

An insurance policy is a contract and must be construed the same way as other contracts. Title insurance policies are governed by the same general rules and principles of interpretation and construction as other insurance policies. Walters v. Marler, supra. J. Appleman, Insurance Law and Practice, Vol. 9, §5201.

This court stated in Thomas v. Farm Bureau Mutual Insurance Co. of Idaho, Inc., 82 Idaho 314, 318, 353 P.2d 776, 778 (1960), quoting with approval Miller v. World Insurance Co., 76 Idaho 355, 357, 283 P.2d 581, 582 (1955):

> Policies of insurance, as other contracts, are to be construed in their ordinary meaning and where the language employed is clear and unambiguous, there is no occasion to construe a policy other than the meaning as determined from the plain wording therein.
>
> It is the function of the Court to construe a contract of insurance as it is written, and the Court by construction cannot create a liability not assumed by the insurer nor make a new contract for the parties, or one different from that plainly intended, nor add words to the contract of insurance to either create or avoid liability.

Therefore, we decline to hold that the title insurance company was impliedly acting as an abstractor and we refuse to impose the liabilities of an abstractor upon a title insurance company merely because it issued a pre-

---

SAND TWO HUNDRED FIFTY DOLLARS & NO/100 . . . . . dollars, which the insured shall sustain by reason of:

1. Title to the land described in Schedule A being vested, at the date hereof, otherwise than as herein stated; or
2. Any defect in, or lien or encumbrance on, said title existing at the date hereof, not shown or referred to in Schedule B; or
3. Any defect in the execution of any mortgage or deed of trust shown in Schedule B securing an indebtedness, the owner of which is insured by this policy, but only insofar as such defect affects the lien or charge of such mortgage or deed of trust upon said land; or
4. Priority over any such mortgage or deed of trust of any lien or encumbrance upon said land existing at the date hereof, except as shown in Schedule B, such mortgage or deed of trust being shown in the order of its priority;

all subject, however, to SCHEDULES A and B, and the STIPULATIONS herein, all of which schedules and stipulations are hereby made a part of this policy."

liminary title report. Since this case is disposed on this ground we do not address the statute of limitations issue raised by respondent. We find no error by the trial court. The summary judgment of the trial court is affirmed.

Costs to respondent. Respondents have not shown themselves entitled to attorney fees on appeal. The money previously tendered to court, if not paid shall be paid to appellant.

Bakes, C.J., and Bistline, Donaldson and Shepard, JJ., concur.

NOTES

1. What tortious damage might plaintiffs have claimed in the *Anderson* case?

2. For a title insurer to be liable in negligence for failure to locate and report title defects, should it be necessary for the insurer to assume such liability explicitly in its contract with the insured? Or should the agreement to insure impliedly carry with it this further obligation to search and report carefully?

3. The supreme court of a neighboring state decided a case similar to Anderson v. Title Insurance Company at almost the same time and with the same insurer as one of the defendants. Lipinski v. The Title Insurance Company, 655 P.2d 970 (Mont. 1982). The *Lipinski* opinion, with three judges in dissent, states at page 974:

> Although title insurance applicants are interested in obtaining insurance coverage, their primary interest is in what the examination discloses. For this they rely on the title companies to tell them of any risks. Risks usually covered by title insurance policies include errors in the title examination, including the negligent failure to note a title defect. A title company, as insurer, owes its clients the duty of conducting a title search with reasonable care.

The Montana Supreme Court, in another split decision, reiterated its position that a title insurer has a duty to conduct a diligent search for title defects, as distinct from merely insuring the title, and may be liable for negligent failure to locate and notify the insured of title defects that are reasonably ascertainable. Malinak v. Safeco Title Insurance Company, 661 P.2d 12 (Mont. 1983).

The Supreme Court of Nebraska had this to say in its opinion in Heyd v. Chicago Title Insurance Company, 218 Neb. 296, 303, 354 N.W.2d 154, 158 (1984), an action charging an insurer with negligence in title searching and examination:

> We now hold that a title insurance company which renders a title report and also issues a policy of title insurance has assumed two distinct duties. In

rendering the title report the title insurance company serves as an abstractor of title and must list all matters of public record adversely affecting title to the real estate which is the subject of the title report. When a title insurance company fails to perform its duty to abstract title accurately, the title insurance company may be liable in tort for all damages proximately caused by such breach of duty. A title insurance company's responsibility for its tortious conduct is distinct from the insurance company's responsibility existing on account of its policy of insurance. Different duties and responsibilities imposed on the title insurance company, therefore, can be the basis for separate causes of action—one cause of action in tort and another in contract.

4. For liability beyond that provided for in the title insurance policy, see Beasley, Claims Outside the Title Policy, Practicing Law Institute, Real Estate Law and Practice Handbook Series No. 251, at 597 (1984). See also Note, Does a Title Insurer *Qua* Title Insurer Owe a Duty to Any But Its Insured?, 7 Okla. City U.L. Rev. 293 (1982).

Jarchow v. Transamerica Title Insurance Company
48 Cal. App. 3d 917, 122 Cal. Rptr. 470 (1975)

. . . In early June 1970, real estate broker Melvin A. Jarchow and building contractor William A. Canavier and their wives ("Plaintiffs") became interested in a three-acre parcel of real property located in the city of Placentia owned by Mr. and Mrs. LaBorde. Although the property was improved with a single family residence, plaintiffs felt it could be developed into a boat, trailer, and camper storage facility. They contacted Transamerica Title Insurance Company ("Defendant") and requested the title officer in the Fullerton branch to search the state of the record title and furnish them with a preliminary report. In searching the title, defendant's employees discovered an easement from Frank F. Hill and Kate L. Hill (the LaBordes' predecessors in interest) to Pete J. Perez and Annie Perez ("Perez Easement"), which had been recorded on November 28, 1960. The deed purported to convey to the Perezes a 20-foot easement for ingress and egress purposes across the northern boundary of the subject property. But for some inexplicable reason, reference to the recorded Perez Easement was omitted from the Preliminary Title Report furnished the plaintiffs. However, the report did indicate that in 1958, when the Hills conveyed the subject property to LaBordes, they had reserved a 20 x 395 foot easement for ingress and egress ("Hill Easement") across the northern boundary of the subject property.

After receiving the preliminary report, there were discussions between plaintiffs and Transamerica as to whether defendant would eliminate the Hill Easement as an exception to coverage and proceed to insure plaintiffs against the Hill Easement in the event the plaintiffs purchased the property. The escrow/title officer consulted with her superiors and obtained authorization to do so.

As a result of the title search and the conversations with the defendant, plaintiffs promptly entered escrow with the LaBordes. Transamerica acted as escrow holder and also acted as title insurer with the understanding it would provide a standard form title insurance policy insuring title in the name of the buyers and insuring the LaBordes' security interests as holders of the first trust deed.

On August 27, 1970, the escrow closed and Transamerica issued the title policy.[1] The policy did *not* list the Hill Easement as one of the items excluded from coverage. Nor was the Perez Easement mentioned.

Within a few days after they took possession of the property, plaintiffs were informed that Perez claimed an easement for ingress and egress across their property. The Perezes owned the land immediately to the north of the subject parcel and Perez claimed that he has been using the 20-foot strip for access to his duplex residence since 1954; he also claimed that he had a deed from Hill which he acquired in 1960 which gave him easement rights over the northern strip of plaintiffs' property — a strip 20 feet wide and variously described as being from 132 feet to 263 feet long.[2]

Upon being advised of Perez' claims, plaintiffs contacted Transamerica and requested the company to take action to establish plaintiffs' title against the threat presented by the Perez Easement. Transamerica refused to initiate any action upon the plaintiffs' behalf, taking the fatuous position that it had no obligation to plaintiffs under the title policy since the Perez Deed had been excluded from coverage — notwithstanding the fact that the Perez Easement was not even mentioned in the exclusionary provisions of the policy.

After receiving the negative response from Transamerica, plaintiffs filed their initial complaint wherein they sought quiet title and injunctive relief against the Perezes and damages and attorney fees against Transamerica. Transamerica filed a cross-complaint to reform the policy, claiming that a mistake had been committed by the escrow/title officer in preparing the typing instructions in that the Hill Easement should have been excepted from coverage.

---

1. The policy issued to the plaintiffs was prepared on a California Land Title Association Standard Coverage Policy Form; in essence, it provided that Transamerica insured the plaintiffs and the LaBordes against loss or damage in the sum of $72,000, together with any costs, attorney fees and expenses which the company may be obligated to pay and which the insureds sustain by reason of any defect in or lien or encumbrance on the title of the subject land as disclosed by the public records; excluded from coverage were all interests, claims, liens or easement which were not disclosed by the public records.

2. Both the Hill Easement and the Perez Easement were 20 feet wide and each overlapped the other so far as they affected the plaintiffs' land. However, at one time, the Hills owned all or most of the tract of which the Perez parcel and plaintiffs' parcel were a part. Consequently, the Hills had reserved a long strip to provide access to their other parcels to the west of Perez.

Pending the trial of the first action, plaintiffs applied for and obtained approval of their proposed Site Development Plan for the storage facility from the city of Placentia. However, development of the property was conditional; Perez had notified the city that he had a deed which he claimed gave him a right to use the strip; plaintiffs' proposed plan would have blocked the access to the Perez property with a building; one of the conditions imposed by the city because of the Perez Deed was to keep that access open. Although they received approval of their plan, plaintiffs decided not to proceed with it because of the clouds on the title.

While the trial on the complaint and cross-complaint was pending, plaintiffs filed the supplemental complaint seeking general and punitive damages on the basis of the aforesaid tort theories. It was stipulated that the material allegations thereof would be deemed denied without the necessity of Transamerica filing a formal answer thereto. It was also agreed that a bifurcation occur, with the action on the complaint and cross-complaint having priority.

The Court Trial

The first trial went on intermittently over a period of three months. At the conclusion thereof, the court handed down a Memorandum Decision and Findings of Fact and Conclusions of Law. Before entering judgment, the court amended the findings on two or three occasions. The material findings follow: The Perezes had no right, title or interest in the subject property by virtue of the deed from Hill or otherwise; in 1958, the Hills conveyed the subject parcel to the LaBordes and reserved the 20-foot strip for purposes of ingress and egress for the benefit of some other land they then owned; the deed containing the reserved easement was recorded; the use of the strip by Perez was with the consent of LaBordes, plaintiffs' predecessor in interest; said consent was subject to revocation by LaBordes and the plaintiffs; the consent had been revoked by the LaBordes' sale of the real property to the plaintiffs and by the plaintiffs' action in serving a notice of revocation upon Perez when they acquired the property; at the time Transamerica conducted its title search preparatory to the issuance of the preliminary report and at the time the plaintiffs' escrow closed on August 27, 1970, the Perez Deed of November 1960 and the Hill Easement of 1958 were both of record; the Perez Deed, being a void conveyance, was excluded from coverage under the Transamerica policy; however, Transamerica was negligent in preparing the preliminary report; Transamerica knew or should have known that plaintiffs would rely on the title search as evidenced by the preliminary report; the escrow/title officer discovered the existence of the Perez Deed before the preliminary report was prepared; Transamerica negligently failed to disclose the existence of the Perez Easement in the preliminary report; as a result of the negligence of Transamerica, plaintiffs temporarily lost the use of the strip from August 27, 1970 to May 1, 1973 and were entitled to $172 damages as a result thereof; plaintiffs also retained counsel and were entitled to attorney's fees in the sum of $7,184 to quiet title to the Perez Deed; however, Transamerica was *not* obligated to take legal action upon the plaintiffs' behalf to eliminate the Perez Easement;[3] as to the Hill Easement, it constituted a cloud on the title until May 1, 1973 (Transamerica obtained a quitclaim deed from Hills' successor-in-interest during the course of the first trial) and was insured against under the terms of the title policy; consequently, there was until May 1, 1973 a cloud or defect on the title insured against under the Transamerica policy; the Hill Easement, being a cloud on the title, resulted in *substantial damages*[4] to plaintiffs until removed in 1973; however, the property sustained no compensable detriment (e.g., from loss of use) despite the cloud created by the Hill Easement for two reasons: (1) Transamerica removed the cloud by obtaining a quitclaim deed from the Hills' successor-in-interest during the trial, and (2) plaintiffs failed to mitigate their damages since they did not develop the property pending the trial, although they could have done so; and finally, Transamerica was not entitled to reformation of the policy inasmuch as it had knowledge of the Hill Easement and agreed to insure against it.

The Jury Trial

In October 1973, the jury trial commenced. The testimony on the liability issue was understandably repetitive of that introduced in the first trial. However, extensive testimony was presented on the proximate cause and damage issues, particularly with reference to the distress and anguish experienced by plaintiffs from the time they learned of the clouds on the title until the time the same were extinguished—a period in excess of two and one-half years.

Canavier, age 53, suffered from a prior heart condition; he experienced tension and nervousness in being required to engage in court litigation for a period in excess of two and one-half years; his doctor prescribed Valium; the worry from tension created by the litigation caused him extreme stress; he worried over his wife's condition and her reaction to the litigation; and Transamerica's refusal to proceed against Perez caused him great emotional anguish.

Mrs. Canavier testified to the following effect: After discovering the existence of the Perez Deed and after determining that Transamerica intended to do nothing about it, she became extremely nervous; she was

3. This finding is wrong as a matter of law. (See Discussion, infra.)
4. In his initial findings, the trial judge inadvertently found the plaintiffs suffered *no damages* as a result of the defect in the title resulting from the Hill Easement; however, prior to instructing the jury and prior to entry of judgment, the trial judge modified or corrected the findings and found plaintiffs suffered *substantial damages* as a result of the cloud created by the Hill Easement.

unable to sleep and worried constantly over the litigation, the money situation, and what they would do with the property; she was also worried about the effect the litigation would have on her husband's heart condition; her observations of her husband's distress posed a worry to her over possible loss of security for herself and her daughter in the event her husband died; she was in constant turmoil over Transamerica's refusal to clear title to the property; she was worried about the coplaintiffs (the Jarchows) who put most of their savings into the project; she was constantly concerned about the paying of attorney fees and litigation costs; they had to continue payments on the property although its status and future remained clouded due to the litigation; she was shocked when she learned Transamerica refused to clear title and she was greatly disturbed about the mistake Transamerica made because she felt when you employ an expert in title matters you should receive a clear title; the litigation was long and costly; it took over two and one-half years to clear the title and their financial resources were being depleted in payments; the prospect of going to court disturbed her greatly; she was humiliated and embarrassed by having to discuss in public her private feelings and all the problems encountered with the property during the course of the litigation.

Jarchow, age 61, testified to the following effect: He was unable to sleep during the pendency of the litigation; he and his wife had put all of their reserve savings in the property; his wife was required to return to work after discovery of the Perez Easement; the burden of continuing to make payments on the subject property and the financial hardship imposed by litigation expenses was a constant source of worry; he was constantly concerned about the outcome of the litigation inasmuch as he had invested everything he had in the property and he was not at all certain as to whether the title would ever be straightened out; he was shocked about Transamerica's failure to honor the title policy and its failure to report the clouds on the title; he was humiliated by his wife having to go back to work and being compelled to go to a psychiatrist; his wife would awake at night and sob and moan and worry over the pending litigation; his emotional distress resulted, at least in part, from Transamerica's failure to sue Perez or otherwise eliminate the easement.

Mrs. Jarchow testified that since the litigation had commenced she suffered from loss of sleep and had to go back to work; their finances were declining; the worry over the attorney's fees was constant; she felt their security was gone as a result of the continued litigation; her blood pressure rose and she did not feel well; inasmuch as they had invested most of their savings in the property, she had been required to neglect her teeth; she was worried over her husband's health and the attorney's fees and court costs; she was amazed to learn of Transamerica's mistake and shocked when it refused to correct its error; she could not believe they purchased an insurance policy for the purpose of protecting them and then received no protection from the insurer.

A court appointed psychiatrist testified to the following effect: While the plaintiffs were deeply concerned about their investment being impaired and their supposed inability to develop the property because of the litigation, he was of the opinion that the litigation aggravated the symptoms, as did Transamerica's failure to honor its contractual commitments; in short, many of the plaintiffs' symptoms were directly attributable to the litigation and Transamerica's blatant refusal to clear the title.

After both sides rested, the court read its Findings of Fact and Conclusions of Law (as amended) to the jury and the jury was instructed it was bound thereby.

Special interrogatories were propounded to the jury. The jury answered that Transamerica did *not* act maliciously towards plaintiffs, did *not* defraud plaintiffs, and did *not* act outrageously towards the plaintiffs. Consequently, no punitive damages were awarded. However, the jury did expressly find, in answering the special interrogatories, that the plaintiffs' emotional distress was legally caused by defendant's negligence in failing to disclose the Perez Deed in the preliminary report and by defendant's conduct with regard to the cloud created by the Hill Easement. The jury also found that *not* all of the emotional distress suffered by the plaintiffs was caused by failure to proceed with the planned development of the real property; in other words, the jury impliedly found that the emotional distress suffered by the plaintiffs was caused by the defendant's negligence and bad faith and the resultant worry and anguish flowing from Transamerica's utter failure to provide a good title or to do anything to correct its errors in connection with the search it made, the preliminary report it prepared, and the policy it issued.

EMOTIONAL DISTRESS

. . . Transamerica asserts that California law tracks the majority common law rule: Damages for emotional distress will not be awarded in an action for negligence unless that distress resulted directly from, or manifested itself in, physical injury. The rule requires physical "impact or injury," thus limiting the number of situations in which mental distress damages, occasioned by "merely negligent" behavior, may be recovered. (2 Harper & James, The Law of Torts (1956) §18.4, pp. 1031-1032; 4 Witkin, Summary of Cal. Law (8th ed. 1974) §548, pp. 2815-2816.) But American jurisdictions have been far from uniform in their application of the foregoing rule.

Those courts which have strictly applied the "impact or injury" standard have offered a variety of reasons for doing so. Four have received particular attention: (1) Emotional distress not so severe as to result in physical injury is too trivial a harm to merit recognition and remedy. (2) Mental distress is an injury which may easily be feigned and, without the impact or injury requisite, courts would be inundated with fraudulent claims. (3) Such injuries are too difficult to measure in dollar amounts, and courts should refrain from imposing speculative judgments on defendants. (4) In most cases where physical impact and injury are absent, the casual link between a defendant's negligent act and a plaintiff's distress is sufficiently attenuated so that courts should refuse to adjudicate negligence actions alleging only mental distress damages; in other words, the proximate cause problem makes it nearly impossible for courts to place articulable limits on defendants' liability. (Rest. 2d Torts, §436A, com.; 2 Harper & James, The Law of Torts (1956) §18.4, pp. 1032-1034; Prosser, Law of Torts (4th ed. 1971) §54, pp. 327-328.)

But application of the "impact or injury" rule — which denies court access to arguably injured parties — has resulted in a jurisprudential conflict of no small proportions. A fundamental principle of our system of justice is that for every wrong there is a remedy (e.g., an injured party should be compensated for all damage proximately caused by a wrongdoer); and departure from this principle may be justified only by the most compelling considerations. (Crisci v. Security Ins. Co., 66 Cal. 2d 425, 433, 58 Cal. Rptr. 13, 426 P.2d 173.) Since application of the "impact of injury" requirement constitutes a significant departure from the aforestated maxim, it has been the object of much criticism by both jurists and scholars.

The argument that emotional distress is a trivial injury is an antiquated concept which the advance of modern psychology has repudiated; research has shown that mental trauma can be just as debilitating as physical paralysis. (Pound, Interpretations of Legal History (1923) p. 120.) Fraudulent claims are not likely to be eliminated by application of the rule, since the slightest impact, or the most attenuated of physical injuries have been found sufficient to satisfy the rule's requirement. (Battalla v. State, 10 N.Y.2d 237, 219 N.Y.S.2d 34, 176 N.E.2d 729.) Further, the California Supreme Court has observed that "the possibility that fraudulent assertions may prompt recovery in isolated cases does not justify a wholesale rejection of the entire class of claims in which that potentiality arises." (Dillon v. Legg, 68 Cal. 2d 728, 736, 69 Cal. Rptr. 72, 77, 441 P. 2d 912, 917.) Nor does the problem of speculative damages (given the current sophistication of the medical profession) present any greater problem in mental distress cases than it does, for example, in personal injury cases involving pain and suffering. (See Battalla v. State, supra, 10 N.Y.2d 237, 219 N.Y.S.2d 34, 176 N.E.2d 729; 59 Geo. L.J. 1237.) And, finally, the proximate cause problems raised by mental distress cases are really no greater than those which arise in many negligence actions involving physical injury. (See Prosser, Law of Torts (4th ed. 1971) §54, pp. 327-328.)[8] But the fact that this causation problem has so often been used as a justifi-

---

8. It should be noted that a number of states specifically have rejected the "impact or injury" rule and have permitted recovery for negligently inflicted emotional distress. (Rodriques v. State, 52 Hawaii 156, 472 P. 2d 509; Battalla v. State, supra, 10 N.Y.2d 237, 219 N.Y.S.2d 34, 176 N.E.2d 729; see also 59 Geo. L.J. 1237.)

cation for the "impact or injury" requirement merely serves to point up the fundamental concern which underlies the reluctance of many courts to recognize a cause of action in negligence for emotional distress. . . .

. . . From the preceding discussion, it necessarily follows that the only valid objection against recovery for mental distress is the danger of fraudulent claims. This problem should be confronted and resolved by rules of proof rather than by imposition of limits on the negligence action itself. (See Prosser, Law of Torts (4th ed. 1971) §54, p. 328.) . . .

In 1967, in Crisci v. Security Ins. Co., supra, 66 Cal. 2d 425, 58 Cal. Rptr. 13, 426 P.2d 173, the court expressly rejected strict application of the common law "impact or injury" requirement and suggested a new standard when it stated: "[I]t is settled in this state that mental suffering [including nervousness, grief, anxiety and worry] constitutes an aggravation of damages when it naturally ensues from the act complained of" and that "[s]uch awards are not confined to cases when the mental suffering award was in addition to an award for personal injuries," but may be recovered in cases where tortious conduct constituted an interference with property interests alone. In so holding, the court reasoned that where an actionable claim has resulted in substantial damages, apart from emotional distress, the danger of fictitious claims is greatly reduced: "other damages," be they to the plaintiff's person or to his property, provide the court with a sufficient guarantee of genuineness of the claim to accord redress for the emotional injury. (P. 433, 58 Cal. Rptr. 13, 426 P.2d 173.)[10] . . .

We conclude that the "impact or injury" rule is no longer strictly applied in California, and that courts may adjudicate negligence claims for mental distress when sufficient guarantees of genuineness are found in the facts of the case — e.g., when the plaintiff has suffered *substantial damage* apart from the alleged emotional injury.[11] . . .

Applying the aforestated standard, we have concluded that Transamerica's negligent act — its failure to list the Perez Deed on plaintiffs' preliminary title report — substantially damaged plaintiffs' financial and property interests in the amount of $7,270 ($170 for loss of use and $7,100 in attorney's fees). Such damages provide sufficient guarantees of the genuineness of plaintiffs' emotional distress claim to satisfy the *Crisci* standard. Having determined that plaintiffs' cause of action is not deficient for its failure to meet the common law "impact or injury" test, we

---

10. In *Crisci*, plaintiff suffered $91,000 in financial injury (presumably, in part, the property interest interfered with was the right to use these funds) when defendant-insurer failed to accept a reasonable settlement offer from an injured third party and exposed plaintiff to liability well beyond the limits of her insurance policy. The court found this substantial injury justified an accompanying award of $25,000 for emotional distress.

11. We note that the Supreme Court has yet to permit recovery for negligently inflicted emotional distress where the mental injury was the only damage caused by the defendant's wrongful conduct. Though endorsement of such an action seems to be the logical end product of the decisional trends in this area, we set forth no such rule in this case. As discussed, infra, the instant case involves substantial financial injury and thus resolution of this case may be had based upon the specific standard articulated in *Crisci*.

next must measure plaintiffs' case against traditional negligence analysis to insure that a cause of action in negligence was adequately set forth.

Actionable negligence involves three elements: (1) a legal duty to use due care; (2) breach of that duty; and (3) the breach as proximate (legal) cause of the resulting injury. (4 Witkin, Summary of Cal. Law (8th ed. 1974) §488, p. 2749.)

When a title insurer presents a buyer with both a preliminary title report and a policy of title insurance, two distinct responsibilities are assumed. In rendering the first service, the insurer serves as an abstractor of title — and must list *all* matters of public record regarding the subject property in its preliminary report. . . . The duty imposed upon an abstractor of title is a rigorous one: "An abstractor of title is hired because of his professional skill, and when searching the public records on behalf of a client he must use the degree of care commensurate with that professional skill . . . the abstractor must report all matters which affect his client's interests and which are readily discoverable from those public records ordinarily examined when a reasonably diligent title search is made." . . . Similarly, a title insurer is liable for his negligent failure to list recorded encumbrances in preliminary title reports. . . .

It is undisputed that Transamerica breached its duty. The Perez Deed was a recorded instrument; Transamerica had actual knowledge of it at the time the preliminary title report was issued. Transamerica was duty-bound to report all matters which could affect plaintiffs' interest in the subject property. Defendant failed to list an encumbrance of record and, in doing so, breached its duty to plaintiffs.

Turning to the causation issue a defendant's conduct is the proximate legal cause of a plaintiff's injury if it is a substantial factor in bringing about the harm suffered . . . ; but the proximate cause attributed to defendant's act *need not* be the sole cause of the harm. (Prosser, Proximate Cause in California, 38 Cal. L. Rev. 369, 379-380.) But for Transamerica's failure to report the Perez Deed, plaintiffs would not have suffered distress when they learned of its existence. It was entirely foreseeable that plaintiffs would suffer mental anguish and distress when they were apprised of defendant's negligence since they relied on the preliminary report before purchasing the property.

When a title insurer breaches its duty to abstract title accurately, it is liable, in tort, for all the damages proximately caused by said breach. (Civ. Code, §3333.) Since the "impact or injury" requirement presents no bar to plaintiffs' complaint — and the elements of an action for negligence have successfully been set forth — the trial court acted with propriety in determining that a cause of action for negligently inflicted emotional distress was pleaded and proved.[13]

---

13. Plaintiffs might have also stated an action herein for negligent misrepresentation. (See Hawkins v. Oakland Title Ins. & Guar. Co., supra, 165 Cal. App. 2d 116, 126, 331 P.2d 742; Williams v. Polgar, 391 Mich. 6, 215 N.W.2d 149; cf. Hale v. George A. Hormel & Co., . . . 121 Cal. Rptr. 144.)

Bad Faith

Transamerica next contends that plaintiffs' supplemental complaint failed to state a cause of action for breach of the title insurance policy's implied covenant of good faith and fair dealing, and argues that the trial court erred in denying its motion for judgment on the pleadings. Defendant maintains that it withheld none of the policy's benefits from plaintiffs; it had no duty to quiet title with regard to the Perez Deed and it fulfilled its policy obligations regarding the Hill Reserved Easement when it obtained a quitclaim deed during the course of the trial.

Every contract contains an implied in law covenant of good faith and fair dealing; this covenant provides that neither party will interfere with the rights of the other to receive the benefits of the agreement. . . . Breach of the covenant provides the injured party with a tort action for "bad faith," notwithstanding that the acts complained of may also constitute a breach of contract. . . . The cause of action is applicable to all insurance contracts, including policies of title insurance. . . .

Since a primary consideration in purchasing insurance is the peace of mind and security it will provide when the contingency insured against arises . . . , an insured may recover for any emotional distress suffered as a result of an insurer's bad faith, as well as any other detriment proximately resulting from the breach. . . .[14]

The gravamen of the supplemental complaint is that defendant failed to take affirmative action to remove the clouds cast upon plaintiffs' title by the Perez Deed and Hill Reserved Easement. We conclude that Transamerica's refusals to attempt to remove these encumbrances were acts of bad faith which breached the policy's implied covenant of good faith and fair dealing.

In determining what benefits or duties an insurer owes his insured pursuant to a contract of title insurance, the court may not look to the words of the policy alone, but must also consider the reasonable expectations of the public and the insured as to the type of service which the insurance entity holds itself out as ready to offer. . . .

Transamerica issued plaintiffs a standard form title policy (California Land Title Assn. Standard Coverage Policy #4000—1963, amended 1969). Paragraph four (4) of the policy's conditions and stipulations provides, in pertinent part, as follows: "The Company, at its own cost and *without undue delay* shall provide (1) for the defense of the Insured in all litigation consisting of actions . . . commenced against the Insured . . . ; *or* (2) *for such action as may be appropriate to establish the title . . . as insured*, which litigation . . . is founded upon an alleged de-

---

14. To recover for mental distress injuries an insured need not show that defendant's conduct was outrageous or otherwise intentional; mere indefensible unfair treatment is enough to justify recovery (Gruenberg v. Aetna Ins. Co., supra, 9 Cal. 3d 566, 580, 108 Cal. Rptr. 480, 510 P.2d 1032.)

fect, lien or encumbrance insured against by this policy. . . ." (Emphasis added.)

This provision of the title policy sets forth two obligations of the insurer: (1) To defend the insured's title if a third party claims, in a judicial proceeding, an interest insured against by the policy, and (2) in the event that a third party claimant chooses not to litigate his claim, to take affirmative action (by filing an action to quiet title or by offering to compromise the third party's claim) to provide the insured with title as stated in the policy. . . .

The case law regarding a title insurer's bifurcated obligation to seek judicial determination of insured-against title defects deals almost exclusively with the duty to defend.[15] Here, however, we have a third party claimant who did not find it necessary to sue the insureds to exercise his claimed right—he instead persuaded the city planning commission to impose restrictions on plaintiffs' development which would insure that he would continue to enjoy his asserted easement. . . .

In determining whether the insurer's duty to defend has matured, courts, after looking at the nature and kind of risk covered by the policy, must decide whether a *potential* of liability for indemnity under the title insurance policy is raised at the time the defense is requested. If possible liability exists, the title company is duty bound to defend the insured in a quiet title action. Failure to provide a defense under such circumstances gives rise to a cause of action in tort for bad faith. . . .[16] The rule regarding an insurer's duty to defend really can take no other form; otherwise the insured would be required to finance his own defense and then, only if he is successful, hold the insurer to its promise by means of a second suit for reimbursement. If this construction were followed, a basic reason for the purchase of insurance would be defeated: instead of having purchased insurance against the trauma and financial hardship of litigation, the insured will have found that he has purchased nothing more than a lawsuit. . . .

In applying the aforestated rules to the instant case, we must conclude that defendant breached its duty to take affirmative action to provide plaintiffs with a clear title as to both the Perez Deed and the Hill Reserved Easement.

The trial court erred in its findings of fact and conclusions of law (in the first trial) when it ruled that Transamerica owed plaintiffs no duty to quiet title in regard to the cloud created by the Perez Deed. The trial court

---

15. This is not surprising, since an insured is almost always in possession of the subject property and a third party encumbrancer must seek adjudication of his claimed right if it is to be exercised at all.
16. It should be noted that the insurer has an alternative to assuming the defense of its insured when the issue of coverage is unclear; it may file a declaratory relief action to test its duty. (State Farm Mut. Auto. Ins. Co. v. Allstate Ins. Co., 9 Cal. App. 3d 508, 527, 88 Cal. Rptr. 246.)

reasoned that since the Perez Deed was void ab initio, and not covered by the indemnity provisions of the policy, Transamerica's duty to quiet title on plaintiffs' behalf in regard to the Perez Easement never matured. But this reasoning erroneously assesses defendant's duty retrospectively.

It is the rule that "the duty to defend [the obverse of defendant's duty in the present case] . . . does not turn upon the ultimate adjudication of coverage but upon facts known to the insurer at the inception of the third party's suit against its insured." . . .[18]

. . . When plaintiffs requested that defendant remove the cloud created by the Perez Deed, they reasonably expected that Transamerica would honor their request by filing a quiet title action, pursuant to the obligation the company had assumed under paragraph four (4) of the policy's conditions and stipulations. When Transamerica refused it acted in bad faith and breached the policy's implied covenant of good faith and fair dealing.

In the course of determining whether Transamerica acted in bad faith in failing to take affirmative action in regard to the Hill Easement, two questions are raised: (1) Did plaintiffs give defendant sufficient notice of the existence of that encumbrance to give rise to a duty to quiet title; and (2) did plaintiffs suffer substantial enough injury as a result of the breach to justify an emotional distress award?

A duty to defend (or quiet title) arises when the insurer is notified of the existence of a defect. . . . And the duty to defend is fixed by the facts which the insurer learns, not only from the insured, but from the complaint and other sources as well. . . .

Transamerica conceded it had actual knowledge of the existence of the Hill Reserved Easement at the time it issued its preliminary title report. When plaintiffs requested that Transamerica quiet title in regard to the Perez Deed, defendant further admits that there was some confusion as to the relationship between the Perez and Hill interests and that, at one point, both were thought to be the same easement interest. When plaintiffs apprised the insurer that title to the strip of land claimed pursuant to the Perez Deed was in dispute (since defendant knew that the Hill Reserved

---

18. It is an oversimplification to assert that the duties to defend and to quiet title are precisely equivalent. The duty to defend arises only after a third party claimant has filed an action against the insured; in such circumstances it is plain that the insured's title is subject to a real cloud. However, the kindred duty to quiet title does not, and should not, arise in every situation in which the insured requests his insurer to act: there must be present in the facts and circumstances of the case some indicia that the encumbrance with which the policy holder is concerned is a genuine cloud upon his title. (Note, however, that should the insurer decide that the alleged cloud is illusory, it must bear the risk of its decision, and may, subsequently, be found to have acted in bad faith. (Comunale v. Traders & General Ins. Co., supra, 50 Cal. 2d 654, 660, 328 P.2d 198.)

In the present case such indicia were present: The Perez claim was recognized by the city planning commission (to the extent that they imposed certain restrictions on plaintiffs' development); hence, Perez' claim, in fact, encumbered plaintiffs' property and constituted an actual cloud on their title.

Easement also concerned at least a part of that same strip), Transamerica was effectively notified that the Hill Easement constituted a potential cloud on plaintiffs' title-as-insured. Hence, when Transamerica refused to take any action to remove the cloud, it breached its covenant of good faith and fair dealing.

A number of California decisions have suggested that the bad faith breach of an insurance agreement must result in "substantial damages" apart from those due to mental distress before an award for the emotional injury may be made. . . . Here, Transamerica maintains that plaintiffs did not suffer substantial damage because of the Hill Easement and, that therefore, a cause of action for bad faith infliction of emotional distress could not be stated.

But the Hill Easement was inextricably tied to the Perez Easement dispute and as such constituted a substantial cloud upon plaintiffs' property (and thus did substantial damage) until it was removed.

It appears that Hill reserved an easement interest in the plaintiffs' parcel (when initially conveyed in 1958) for the benefit of other of his parcels in the same tract (these did not include the Perez parcel). Several years after the aforementioned conveyance, Hill gave a deed to Perez which purported to convey an easement interest in the Hill Reserved Easement. When litigation commenced concerning the validity of the Perez Deed, the question of to what extent the Hill Easement still encumbered the subject property was inevitably raised. Thus, the legal fees paid by plaintiffs in prosecution of their quiet title action against Perez were, secondarily but necessarily, incurred to determine the effect of the Hill Easement upon their title. In addition, the pendency of the lawsuit constituted demands upon plaintiffs' time, energies and financial resources. These various burdens are sufficient evidence of real and substantial injury to satisfy the substantial damage standard set forth in *Crisci*. Defendant's contention that substantial damages were not incurred in regard to the Hill reservation because the injury suffered was not compensated by the trial court in the first proceeding is of no moment in light of our preceding discussion: substantial damages in this context need not be compensable. Consequently, plaintiffs were properly awarded damages for emotional distress for Transamerica's bad faith breach of the title policy.

Transamerica claims that it neither breached the covenant of good faith, nor substantially injured plaintiffs, because during the course of the first trial (to quiet title) it obtained a quitclaim deed of the Hill Easement. This argument has no merit. Defendant consistently refused to quiet title on plaintiffs' behalf in regard to a claim admittedly covered by the policy —forcing plaintiffs to bring suit and endure the trauma and financial hardship of litigation—and then sought to avoid bad faith liability for their delay by finally delivering to the insureds the benefit of their policy. This argument lacks integrity; if such a course of conduct were endorsed, an insurer's duty to clear title would not exist in fact, but only in form.

Defendant knew of the existence of the Hill reservation, its close connection with the Perez Deed, and admitted that the Hill Easement was covered by the policy—yet still refused to assume its duty to quiet title. This court must conclude that plaintiffs' supplemental complaint adequately set forth an emotional distress claim for bad faith breach of the title insurance agreement, and that the trial court's denial of defendant's motion for judgment on the pleadings was proper. . . .

SUFFICIENCY OF THE EVIDENCE

Defendant argues that its motion for judgment notwithstanding the verdict (Code Civ. Proc. §629), should have been granted by the trial court since the jury's awards of $50,000 to each of the plaintiffs were not supported by substantial evidence. Transamerica contends that the primary cause of plaintiffs' mental distress was their unreasonably perceived inability to develop the property. At the first trial the court found that the property could have, in fact, been developed in spite of the problems created by defendant's negligence and bad faith. The court therefore concluded that Transamerica was not liable for damages flowing from the failure to develop, and defendant contends that the record is silent as to emotional distress experienced for any other reason. We disagree. . . .

The record is replete with evidence that much of plaintiffs' distress was attributable to causes other than the delay in the development of their property. Each of the plaintiffs testified that he had experienced emotional distress (e.g., loss of sleep, anxiety, worry, tension and nervousness) because of concern over the litigation necessitated by Transamerica's negligence and bad faith, and the attorney's fees incurred therein. Both Canavier and Jarchow testified they were distressed and frustrated over defendant's refusal to fulfill its contractual obligations. Mrs. Jarchow was upset because the title insurance policy the plaintiffs had purchased appeared to be worthless. In addition, two psychiatrists testified that each of the plaintiffs was under emotional stress which had been engendered (at least secondarily) by the traumas attendant to the bringing of the present lawsuit. This sound, solid evidence satisfies the substantial evidence rule. . . .

EXCESSIVE DAMAGES

Where a jury award is so grossly disproportionate as to raise a presumption of passion or prejudice an appellate court is duty-bound to modify the award. . . . However, in searching the record for evidence of passion or prejudice, the reviewing court must be mindful that the trial court's determination should be accorded great weight. . . .

Transamerica argues that since the amount awarded plaintiffs for their property and financial injuries ($170 and $7,100) was small relative to the amount awarded for emotional distress, the latter award was excessive. However, in light of the tortious acts committed by Transamerica (notably the repeated acts of bad faith), it is likely that the greatest portion of plaintiffs' injuries would take the form of emotional distress (e.g., vexation, tension, frustration, and worry). As this court has previously noted, "there is no fixed or absolute standard by which to compute the monetary value of emotional distress." . . . Plaintiffs were required to suffer through years of litigation and frustration because of defendant's tortious acts. An award of $50,000 per plaintiff for over three years of anxiety and mental discomfort does not strike this court as being excessive nor motivated by passion or prejudice.

Finally, plaintiffs contend that they are entitled to attorney's fees on appeal. Contrary to their contention, the subject title insurance policy *does not* contain an attorney's fees provision for the benefit of the insurer, and, therefore cannot contain a reciprocal provision for the insureds' benefit. Consequently, plaintiffs are not entitled to an award of fees on appeal.

The judgment is affirmed.

Gardner, P.J., and Tamura, J., concur.

NOTES

1. Most title insurance policies contain provisions to the effect that the insurer shall provide for the defense of the insured in litigation challenging the title which has been insured. Such a covenant to defend may even create an obligation on the insurer to initiate proceedings to protect the insured's title if the insured may otherwise lose his asserted interest. For example, in Lawyers Title Insurance Corp. v. McKee, 354 S.W.2d 401 (Tex. Civ. App. 1962), a covenant to defend was construed as obligating the insurer to bring proceedings adjudicating the insured's title when the insured was out of possession and in peril of losing his asserted interest through adverse possession by a third party claimant. If the insurer breaches its duty to defend, the insured may retain his own counsel to handle the litigation and the insured's reasonable litigation expenses so incurred must be paid by the insurer. For the insurer to become obligated under its covenant to defend, the insured must promptly notify the insurer of any claim against the title, including litigation alleging a defect in the title.

If the insured elects to take over his own title defense, however, assuming no prior breach of the covenant to defend by the insurer, the insured waives his rights under the policy to have litigation expenses paid for by the insurer. Thus, in Buquo v. Title Guarantee and Trust Co., 20 Tenn. App. 479, 482, 100 S.W.2d 997, 998 (1936), the Tennessee Court of Appeals, Eastern Section, stated:

With respect to the right and duty of defendant to defend actions brought against complainant, the insured, the certificate provides as follows:

"The Title Guaranty & Trust Company of Chattanooga will, and shall have the right, at its own cost, to defend the party guaranteed in all actions of ejectment or other proceedings founded upon a claim of title or encumbrance prior in date to this certificate and not excepted therein. In case any person having an interest in this certificate shall receive notice or have knowledge of any such action or proceedings, it shall be the duty of such person at once to notify the company thereof in writing, and secure to it the right to defend the action. Unless the company shall be so notified within ten days, then all liability of this company in regard to the subject matter of such action or proceeding shall cease and be determined."

We think this clause of the certificate is to be construed as requiring the company, upon notice in writing, to defend such action. However, we think the party guaranteed, in the absence of any notice from the company that it insists upon its right to defend the action, could waive this benefit under the certificate and assume the defense of the action, employing attorneys of his own selection. While the company is interested in the defense of such an action to the extent of the amount of its liability to its insured, the insured might have, and often would have, as much or more at stake than the company. For this reason insured might, in some cases, prefer to conduct the defense himself even though entitled to this benefit under the terms of the certificate.

On the insurer's defense duty, see Pedowitz, The Title Insurer's Obligation to Defend the Insured, reprinted in Practicing Law Institute, Real Estate Law and Practice Course Handbook Series No. 251, at 587 (1984).

2. Differences of opinion can exist as to whether or not a title policy covers a particular claim of loss. What should a title insurer do to protect itself against contract and tort liability if an insured notifies it of a claim against the title, and the insurer believes in good faith that the title is not insured against such a claim? Does it make a difference if suit has been brought against the insured on the claim? What should the insurer do if it believes the policy insures against the alleged defect but that the claim is frivolous and cannot be proven? In the *Jarchow* case, would a declaratory relief action by the insurer to determine the issue of its liability have protected it adequately against emotional distress damage suffered by the insureds because of insurer's delay in defending or perfecting title?

3. Should title insurance companies, by contracts with their customers, be permitted to exculpate themselves from negligence liability in relation to title search and examination? And assuming that they are liable for negligence, should title insurers be permitted contractually to limit their liability to the face amount of the policy?

4. With or without the impact requirement, is negligent infliction of emotional distress a form of injury readily feigned? If such injuries can be readily feigned, do adequate legal protections exist to prevent unjustified recoveries for emotional distress in defective title cases?

5. A Missouri statute, Mo. Ann. Stat. §375.420 (Supp. 1985), provides as follows:

> In any action against any insurance company to recover the amount of any loss under a policy of automobile, fire, cyclone, lightning, life, health, accident, employers' liability, burglary, theft, embezzlement, fidelity, indemnity, marine or other insurance except automobile liability insurance, if it appears from the evidence that such company has refused to pay such loss without reasonable cause or excuse, the court or jury may, in addition to the amount thereof and interest, allow the plaintiff damages not to exceed twenty percent of the first fifteen hundred dollars of the loss, and ten percent of the amount of the loss in excess of fifteen hundred dollars and a reasonable attorney's fee; and the court shall enter judgment for the aggregate sum found in the verdict.

In Missouri, on facts similar to those in the *Jarchow* case, what do you think the insured parties would have recovered? Would this result be preferable to that in *Jarchow*?

3. Regulation of Title Insurers[25]

Title insurers are less rigorously regulated by the state than most other kinds of insurers. Their relatively low loss ratios no doubt are an important reason for this. Nonetheless, state statutes and regulations do impose some meaningful organizational and financial restrictions on title insurers similar to those applicable to insurers generally. There are, for example, provisions prohibiting title insurance firms from engaging in many kinds of businesses;[26] financial standards in the form of capital, reserves, and deposits that they must meet;[27] and limits on single risks that they may assume without sharing the risks with other companies.[28] Some kind of rate regulation is provided for by many states, commonly a requirement that title insurers file their rate schedules with a government agency that has power to disapprove proposed charges.[29] A variety of other insurer-type controls have been imposed by state legislatures and administrative agencies. In their substantive restrictions and enforcement efforts, New York and

---

25. On regulation of title insurers, see Burke, Law of Title Insurance cc. 5-7 (1986); Roberts, Holahan, Painter and Giannella, Public Regulation of Title Insurance Companies and Abstracters (1961); Roberts, Title Insurance: State Regulation and the Public Perspective, 39 Ind. L.J. 1 (1963); and Note, The Title Insurance Industry and Governmental Regulation, 53 Va. L. Rev. 1523 (1967). On title insurance rate regulation generally, see Practicing Law Institute, Rate Regulation, Real Estate Law and Practice Course Handbook Series No. 236, at 417 (1983).
26. E.g., Cal. Ins. Code §12360 (West 1972) (other classes of insurance cannot be written).
27. E.g., Cal. Ins. Code §§12370, 12380 to 12388 (West 1972).
28. E.g., Pa. Stat. Ann. tit. 40, §§910-19 to 910-21 (1971).
29. E.g., Pa. Stat. Ann. tit. 40, §§910-37 to 910-40 (1971).

Texas have been unusually strict in regulating title insurers.[30] Other kinds of government controls that have had an impact on the functions or operations of title insurers include antitrust legislation and restrictions on unauthorized practice of law. Efforts initiated by bar associations to enforce unauthorized practice of law restrictions have narrowed somewhat the range of services offered by title insurers, particularly the drafting of customers' security and conveyancing instruments.[31]

Quiner, Title Insurance and the Title Insurance Industry
22 Drake L. Rev. 711, 723-725 (1973)

Assuming one accepts the tenet that insurance should be publicly regulated, emphasis falls upon the insurer's solvency and rates. Measuring the financial condition of an insurance company at a given point in time is not an easy task, and this can be particularly true for title insurance companies. For example, it is difficult to match revenue with appropriate cash outlays since it is generally unknown when the cash must be disbursed. The accounting procedures used by the various companies are, in most cases, determined by the various state insurance departments.

Most of the present regulation seems to be primarily concerned with the solvency aspect. Many states place limitations on the size of the risk that can be assumed. In the valuation of the title plant, companies often have to value it at the cost of acquisition. Investment restrictions are usually stringent, perhaps more so than with other property and casualty companies. One of the most unique aspects of solvency of title insurance is the existence of the unearned premium reserve. With more typical lines, the premium can be earned over time as the policy period progresses. Since the life of the title insurance policy could conceivably be infinite, some type of system has to be devised for determining the unearned premium. Most states, on the basis of statistical data, arbitrarily set the policy life between

---

30. N.Y. Ins. Law §§430 to 442 (McKinney 1966, Supp. 1984-85); and Tex. Ins. Code Ann. c. 9 (Vernon 1981, Supp. 1985). On title insurance regulation in New York, see Fosket, Role of the State Regulator, reprinted in Practicing Law Institute, Real Estate Law and Practice Handbook Series No. 144, at 133 (1978). For arguments by two academic economists that title insurers in Texas are overregulated, especially as to policy rates, see Phillips and Butler, The Law and Economics of Residential Real Estate Markets in Texas: Regulation and Antitrust Implications, 36 Baylor L. Rev. 623 (1984).

In 1981, Utah enacted a comprehensive new statute regulating title insurers and their agents. Utah Code Ann. §§31-25-1 to 31-25-38 (Supp. 1983).

31. On title insurers and the unauthorized practice of law, see Payne, Title Insurers, the Legislatures and the Constitution, 21 Ala. L. Rev. 25 (1968); Payne, Title Insurance and the Unauthorized Practice of Law Controversy, 53 Minn. L. Rev. 423 (1969); and Brossman and Rosenberg, Title Companies and the Unauthorized Practice Rules: The Exclusive Domain Reexamined, 83 Dick. L. Rev. 437 (1979). See also Massey, Abstracts and Unauthorized Practice, 62 Title News No. 7, at 10 (1983).

fifteen and twenty-five years. A small portion of the premium, perhaps 10%, is then assigned to the unearned premium reserve. Then this portion is reduced yearly, starting at some determined point in time, by perhaps 2-5% per year and crediting it back into earnings until the entire fund is reduced to zero. Since title losses tend to occur without regularity, the existence of the unearned premium makes a valid financial evaluation more difficult, particularly when comparing companies operating under different formulas.

While it might be said that regulation of solvency is adequate, rate regulation seems to be lacking in quantity and quality. This problem was delved into by a questionnaire composed by this writer and distributed to the insurance commissioners of 49 states and Washington, D.C. Aided by a cover letter and follow-up letter by Commissioner William Huff III of the Iowa Department of Insurance, 46 states and the District of Columbia responded to this questionnaire.

Systems of rate regulation can be broken down into basically three groups: (1) prior approval, (2) file and use, and (3) open competition. A prior approval system is probably the most stringent since the rate structures must be filed with the appropriate state insurance department and approved before insurance can be sold. A file and use system is less effective since a company can proceed to write insurance even before the rate structure is approved.[34] The least stringent method of regulation is open competition, where insurance prices are left solely to the interacting forces in the market place. In terms of regulation systems, seventeen of the responding states utilized the prior approval system; three reported open competition; five reported file and use; and seventeen reported no regulation at all. In two cases, Florida and Texas, rates are actually promulgated in some manner by the state insurance department. Regarding the degree of regulation, sixteen of the respondents said that title insurance rates were regulated on the same basis with property and casualty rates. Twenty-five states claim that title insurance rates were watched less closely, and three states reported that they were regulated more closely. A majority of the state insurance commissioners seemed to believe that price competition was not extremely effective.[38]

The lack of price competition is logical, because it does not seem unreasonable to assume that there is a gross lack of knowledge on the part of consumers in this area. Real estate transactions are probably very baffling to the majority of people and knowledge of title insurance companies and their rates is probably scant. This view seems to be borne out by another question asked on the questionnaire regarding market structure. In a vast

---

34. There are indications that rate filings are seldom disapproved. . . .

38. Of the respondents, thirteen claimed that price competition was effective in keeping title insurance rates reasonable, non-discriminatory, and non-excessive. Nine states reported that price competition was ineffective in accomplishing this, and seventeen states reported that price competition does not exist.

majority of states, at least 50% of the business is controlled by the largest three companies in terms of written premium. The range of percentages for the amount of business controlled by the largest three companies varies from 45% in Texas (where rates are actually promulgated by a three member board), to 100% in Alaska. An unweighted arithmetic mean of these values falls around the 78% mark. This seems to bear out the view that title insurance companies are operating predominantly in oligopolies. The result is that the consumer is paying a higher price than he would in a purely competitive situation.

There is substantial evidence to indicate that in many states title insurance is in fact regulated less closely than other lines of insurance, and that price competition does not play a significant role in consumer protection. The question relating to market structure is a matter of public record, verified by a cross-check of several annual insurance reports prepared by various insurance departments, so that response must be considered fairly valid.

Part of the reason that regulation is so lacking is due to a feeling of ignorance on the part of various state insurance departments regarding title insurance and title insurance rates. Actuarial data and claim experience are lacking in many states, and the result is confusion on the part of state officials.

NOTES

1. What purposes are served by each of the statutory sections below, and why do you think they were passed?

> Every such [title insurance] company, domestic or foreign, . . . [qualified to do business in the state] shall deposit with the [State] Department of Financial Institutions, hereinafter called the Department, for the benefit of the creditors of the company who may become such by reason of any policy issued by it, the sum of $50,000, in bonds of the United States, or of this State, or of any body politic of this State. . . . So long as the company so depositing such securities shall remain solvent, such company shall be permitted to receive from the Director the interest on the deposit; provided that any such corporation as a condition precedent to guaranteeing or insuring titles and issuing policies on real estate located in more than one county of this State shall deposit with the Department further sums of $5,000 in securities as aforesaid for each additional county in which the real estate upon which such policies are issued is located until the deposits of the corporation amount to $500,000 in securities as aforesaid; and provided further, that any such corporation guaranteeing or insuring titles to real estate in counties having a population of 500,000 or more persons shall deposit with the Department the sum of $500,000 in securities as aforesaid. Any such corporation having deposited said sum of $500,000 in securities as aforesaid shall be entitled to guarantee or insure titles to real estate in any or all counties of the

State. . . . [Ill. Ann. Stat. c. 73, §479 (Smith-Hurd 1965, Supp. 1984-1985).]

[Title insurance companies] shall not be permitted to write any new contracts guaranteeing payment of principal and interest of bonds and mortgages. . . . [N.J. Stat. Ann. §17:24-7 (West 1985).]

(1) No title insurance policy or guarantee of title shall be issued upon a casualty basis.

(2) The term "casualty basis" as used in this section means the issuance of a title insurance policy or guarantee of title with disregard to the possible existence of adverse matters or defects of title. [Fla. Stat. Ann. §627.784 (West 1984).]

2. Iowa is the only state that prohibits title insurance. Iowa Code Ann. §515.48 (1949), provides:

"Any company organized under this chapter [domestic insurance companies] or authorized to do business in this state may: . . . 10. Insure any additional risk . . . except title insurance or insurance against loss or damage by reason of defective title, encumbrances or otherwise. . . ."

The constitutionality of this statutory prohibition of title insurance was upheld in Chicago Title Ins. Co. v. Huff, 256 N.W.2d 17 (Iowa 1977). Arguments for and against title insurance in Iowa are discussed in Note, Iowa's Prohibition of Title Insurance — Leadership or Folly?, 33 Drake L. Rev. 683 (1983-1984), at page 799 supra.

In your opinion, does the Iowa statute prevent title insurance from lawfully being written on Iowa land?

3. The McCarran-Ferguson Act, 15 U.S.C. §§1011 et seq., exempts insurers from the federal antitrust laws to the extent their activities are the business of insurance, are regulated by state law, and do not constitute a boycott, coercion, or intimidation. All states impose regulations on insurers. Title insurance is the business of insurance within the meaning of the McCarran-Ferguson Act. Commander Leasing Co. v. Transamerica Title Insurance Co., 477 F.2d 77 (10th Cir. 1973). However, the provision of escrow services by title insurance companies has been held not to fall within the business of insurance exemption of the federal antitrust laws. United States v. Title Insurance Rating Bureau of Arizona, Inc., 700 F.2d 1247 (9th Cir. 1983). On the McCarran-Ferguson Act, see Anderson, Insurance and Antitrust Law: the McCarran-Ferguson Act and Beyond, 25 Wm. and Mary L. Rev. 1 (1983); Grassley, Outlook: McCarran-Ferguson, 63 Title News No. 6, at 10 (1984); Mascari et al., Antitrust Exemption and Risk, 62 Title News No. 7, at 11 (1983); Comment, The McCarran Act's Antitrust Exemption for "The Business of Insurance": A Shrinking Umbrella, 43 Tenn. L. Rev. 329 (1976); and Note, the McCarran-Ferguson Act: A Time for Procompetitive Reform, 29 Vand. L. Rev. 1271 (1976).

4. In Land Title Company of Alabama v. State ex rel. Porter, 292 Ala. 691, 299 So. 2d 289 (1974), it was charged that title examinations and

commitments for title insurance by a title insurer constitute the unauthorized practice of law. The court held that the conduct in question was not the unauthorized practice of law, that a title insurer must be permitted to review public records in determining whether or not to insure, and that the commitments were not title opinions but binders to issue title policies. However, it has been held that title companies may not draft deeds and other conveyancing instruments, nor may they conduct real estate closings at which title company employees give legal advice or express opinions as to the effect of legal documents. See, e.g., Coffee County Abstract and Title Co. v. State ex rel. Norwood, 445 So. 2d 852 (Ala. 1984). Contra on title company drafting of deeds and legal instruments, Bar Assn. of Tenn. v. Union Planters Title Guarantee Co., 46 Tenn. App. 100, 326 S.W.2d 767 (1959).

Christie, Antitrust Update
62 Title News No. 7, at 21 (1983)

There are, of course, in this industry [title insurance] and others many cooperative or joint activities that are beneficial and without antitrust risk as long as properly structured and conducted. In addition . . . I would refer to some other longstanding and promising new activities which fall in this category. One is the joint title plant which has for many years been utilized in various locations around the country. Another would be the cooperative development of computer systems for use in the title insurance industry. The benefit to the public in terms of an improved product and the potential for cost-saving through the avoidance and duplicate facilities and efforts has led antitrust law enforcers to give general blessing to these kinds of activities. Nevertheless, in each case care must be taken to assure that the joint effort is not undertaken or conducted for the purpose of eliminating competition and the arrangement must contain no restrictions on the activities of the participants which unreasonably restrain competition or create unreasonable barriers to entry for other competitors. The precise legal requirements demanded by the antitrust laws would depend, of course, on the specifics of the project involved and the market setting in which it occurs, but these possibilities need not necessarily be foreclosed by the legal requirements of the antitrust laws.

Another form of permissible joint activity is, of course, participation in industry trade associations at the ALTA, state or local level. These associations serve legitimate and useful functions not only for the members but for the public as well. As a result, involvement in such organizations is not only permissible but should be encouraged. However, those who are involved and do attend should constantly have in mind that the context in which they are operating calls for some discretion in connection with association business as well as in a purely social context. . . .

Because of the changing rules in antitrust doctrines applicable to the title insurance business and the increasing costs associated with any involvement in antitrust litigation — not to mention the more stringent penalties for any violation — the development of increased corporate sensitivity concerning possible antitrust problems will be beneficial to the underwriters concerned as well as to the industry as a whole. That development might take the form of improving the channels of communication between operating people and the company's law department. Seeing the potential for a problem and discussing it in advance with company counsel will tend to avoid lots of down-the-road difficulty.

How do you do that? The best approach might well vary from company to company but I would offer some suggestions. Consider the development of a company compliance manual which would discuss the law, speak in practical terms of dos and don'ts and spell out the appropriate source within the company for the resolution of any questions. Such a manual ought to be comprehensible to operating people rather than a theoretical exercise and ought to address rather specifically the kinds of situations that may give rise to antitrust problems as might be encountered during the ordinary course of business. Consider occasional meetings in the field between company lawyers and operating people to discuss issues as they arise in a practical everyday sense. Consider an occasional antitrust audit by company counsel designed to isolate areas of concern before they become litigation problems. . . .

C. REFORMING THE SYSTEM

The American system of land title protection, particularly in large urban areas, is cumbersome and inefficient. Private title plants and private title insurance coverage have helped make it more workable but there still is considerable dissatisfaction with the costs and uncertainties of the system. Sporadic demands for reform have been made, of which mandatory land registration, adopted throughout much of the world, calls for what are very drastic modifications in the prevailing American system. Marketable title acts, a more limited but significant reform, have been passed in a number of American states and enhance the system's efficiency by reducing the scope of title searches. Other efforts to achieve comprehensive reforms in American land title protection through legislation have been much less successful. Torrens registration, providing for voluntary registration, was adopted many years ago in some states but has had no appreciable impact except in a few metropolitan areas. More recently, a carefully drafted uniform act pertaining to land title protection, the Uniform Simplification of Land Transfers Act, has been approved by the National

Conference of Commissioners on Uniform State Laws. However, neither this act nor its companion proposal, the Uniform Land Transactions Act, likewise approved by the National Conference, has been adopted by any state. Legislative ineffectiveness is also apparent at the federal level. A promising federal legislative reform designed principally to hold down title protection and other land transfer costs, the Real Estate Settlement Procedures Act, was enacted by Congress in 1974 but seriously weakened by amendments adopted the following year. This legislative record is indicative of strong vested interests favorable to perpetuating the status quo in American land title protection.

Among the troublesome policy issues bearing on reforms in the land title protection system are what kinds of land rights, if any, should be sacrificed to more efficient title search and examination; who should bear the out-of-pocket costs of reform in the land title protection system and, if the system is to be subsidized by the government, which level of government should do the subsidizing; what degree of state or national uniformity in title protection procedure and coverage is desirable; and whether integrated public land record systems — data banks — should be set up with stored information usable for many different purposes, of which title examination would be but one.

1. *Marketable Title Acts*

In recent years there has been considerable legislative interest in reforming land title record keeping and examination by means of so-called marketable title acts. The push for these acts has come largely from the practicing bar in states where private practitioners still do considerable title work. In 1919, Iowa adopted the first act generally called a marketable title act.[32] A number of other states,[33] mostly in the Midwest, have since passed similar legislation, and the number will probably grow. Marketable title acts rather drastically reform the impact of recording under the recording acts by extinguishing most interests in land not put of record during a set number of years, commonly forty years. They borrow elements of both statutes of limitations and curative acts, but they ordinarily apply more broadly than these other acts. Recording or re-recording are the usual means of preserving old interests under marketable title acts, rather than bringing suit. Constitutional objections have been encountered in some states when judicial proceedings were made mandatory to protect title claims.

---

32. 1919 Iowa Acts c. 270.
33. Connecticut, Florida, Illinois, Indiana, Kansas, Michigan, Minnesota, Nebraska, North Carolina, North Dakota, Ohio, Oklahoma, South Dakota, Utah, Vermont, Wisconsin, and Wyoming.

Basye, Trends and Progress — the Marketable Title Acts[34]

47 Iowa L. Rev. 261, 261-267 (1962)

I. PERSPECTIVE

"For avoiding all fraudulent conveyances, and that every man may know what estate or interest other men may have in any houses, lands, or other hereditaments they are to deale in. . . ." In so reciting, the first recording act adopted in America[1] suggested the duality in purpose and effect, and the unattained goal, that characterize the recording system to this day.

The colonists clearly understood that they were requiring every person acquiring an interest in land to record his conveyance. And, as the penalty for noncompliance, they were willing to impose loss of the interest intended to be acquired. But under the recording acts, as they have persisted to our time, the prospective purchaser of a piece of land need only take a deed from the seller and record it. That deed, if in proper form, will operate as an effective transfer, and the timely recording of it will preserve the interest received. But the purchaser is not interested merely in receiving an instrument of conveyance. He also wishes to be certain that the seller owns the interest purportedly transferred to him. He also wants to know that by the conveyance he will fully succeed to the seller's former ownership and thereby become able to market it himself later on. He can ascertain this only by examining the recorded evidence of all transfers up to and including the one by which his seller acquired title from his predecessor. Thus the recording system serves in dual capacities: (1) it performs a conveyance function; and (2) it preserves the written evidence by which we are enabled to appraise titles. Our entire system of conveyancing and title security, rooted in the American tradition, is predicated upon the assumption that a prospective purchaser can determine whether a seller has a good title by examining its history from the public records. Actually this is not completely possible, but the assumption is one upon which we must necessarily rely if we are to deal in land at all.

Mere statement of this dual function of recordation points unerringly to the shortcomings of the recording system in fulfilling its larger purposes in our time. Any modern system of land transfer must achieve economy, expediency, and security. Titles must be maintained in a sufficiently marketable condition to coincide with our current conception of land as a commodity that moves freely and easily in commerce. Certainly they cannot be permitted to become impaired and impeded by the functioning of the conveyancing machinery itself. That these objectives are not attained

---

34. Some footnotes omitted.
1. An act of the Massachusetts Bay Colony of 1640. See 4 American Law of Property §17.4 (Casner ed. 1952); Haskins, The Beginnings of the Recording System in Massachusetts, 21 B.U.L. Rev. 281 (1941).

by any of the conveyancing and title assurance methods founded upon the recording system has become apparent to all thoughtful observers.[2] Instead, for over half a century there has been ever increasing dissatisfaction with our system of transferring land. On a mounting scale real estate transactions have grown unnecessarily slow, unduly expensive, and needlessly uncertain. With the passage of years and the lengthening of chains of title, the process of appraising marketability has become progressively more cumbersome. The machinery employed for these purposes has become altogether inadequate for the needs of our time.

The inefficiency of this institution which has served us for 300 years might suggest that we throw the system overboard immediately and start afresh. Until twenty years ago we heard earnest advocation that we adopt the Torrens system of title registration. Even if we grant that this system has merit, it does not now appear to be acceptable in this country. In fact its use has been abolished in some states after an extended period of trial. Our one hope of bringing about simplicity would appear to be in a thorough overhauling and renovating of our present system. It has become increasingly clear that this can be accomplished only through enactment of systematic, comprehensive legislation.

In very recent years several states, striving to achieve the benefits of a simpler system for conveyancing procedure, have thoughtfully worked out one or more pieces of legislation which are the heart of any such legislative program. The measures are appropriately called marketable title legislation. So far ten states have adopted marketable title acts and many others are giving serious consideration to them. This type of legislation is rapidly gaining favor and proving to be highly effective. In fact, it bids fair to be the most successful expedient for promoting simplicity in land transfers in this country since the introduction of the Torrens system.

It is the thesis of this Article that the basic ideas involved in the acts, as improved upon and adapted to local conditions, should become, and promise to become, a permanent and universal feature of our recording systems.

Brief analyses are offered of the generic problems and the acts' general approach to their solution. The particular statutes and the several interesting decisions that have arisen under them are discussed. And lastly, the precise terms and application of such legislation are considered in connection with the provisions of the model act prepared under the auspices of

---

2. For recent articles detailing the aptly described "crisis in conveyancing," see Aigler, Clearance of Land Titles—A Statutory Step, 44 Mich. L. Rev. 45 (1945); Aigler, Title Problems in Land Transfers, 24 Mich. B.J. 202, 213 (1945); Basye, Streamlining Conveyancing Procedure (pts. 1, 3), 47 Mich. L. Rev. 935, 1097 (1949); Cribbet, Conveyancing Reform, 35 N.Y.U. L. Rev. 1291 (1960); Marshall, Reforming Conveyancing Procedure, 44 Iowa L. Rev. 75 (1958); Nelson, Conveyancing in New York, 43 Cornell L.Q. 617 (1958); Payne, The Crisis in Conveyancing, 19 Mo. L. Rev. 214 (1954); Spies, A Critique of Conveyancing, 38 Va. L. Rev. 245 (1952).

the Section of Real Property, Probate and Trust Law of the American Bar Association.

II. THE PROBLEMS STATED

A. GENERALLY

Ever since the establishment of a recording system in America we have assumed that the recording of an instrument disclosing an interest in A would give constructive notice of A's interest to all the world and, moreover, that it would continue to do so for all eternity unless that interest were sooner transferred or extinguished. That assumption is still basic to our recording system today.

So long as transfers of land remained few, so long as the history of a title was confined to a short expanse of time, examinations and appraisals of titles were relatively simple. But each successive transfer, whether by private instrument, by judicial proceedings or by operation of law, not only extends the length and scope of search but also requires a more intricate appraisal in order to ascertain the present status of land ownership. One may estimate the mounting proportion with which the labor and difficulty in examining a title varies with the number of transfers. Considering the number of long descriptions and the number and length of judicial proceedings, perhaps it would be fairly accurate to say that the task increases according to the square of the number of transfers.

A solution must be found. One can be found if we scrutinize with all possible openness of mind the actual performance of our conveyancing system as we find it today.

The essential reasons for the present inefficiency are fairly obvious. They may be enumerated as follows: (1) the increased burden of search; (2) the economic waste in repetitive examinations; (3) the development of overmeticulous title examination inherent in the system itself; (4) the failure of statutes of limitations to accomplish their intended purpose; and (5) the lack of effective legislation to redefine and promote marketability in reasonable ways.

B. BURDEN OF SEARCH

As ownership of land passes from one person to another, not only does the period of title search become greater but the number of instruments and proceedings which constitute the chain of title also increases. Both factors add progressively to the burden of search; both factors increase the possibility of error which results in unmarketable titles. Each transfer in the chain of title tends to make the job of the conveyancer more difficult and burdensome. We see the recording system slowly but inevitably bogging down of its own weight.

C. REPETITIVE EXAMINATIONS

Probably none of the pioneers who had a hand in originating our recording system envisaged the monumental task that title examiners would face after the passage of just one century of transfers. Every time that land is bought and sold, it becomes the burdensome task of some examiner to trace the title back to its origin and pass judgment anew upon each link in the chain. How much longer can we continue to justify this practice? How insurmountable will be the complications half a century hence, or even a quarter of a century hence!

Our recording system from its very beginning contemplated that a person having a permanent or long-term interest in land should be able to preserve that interest by merely recording proper notice of it. In addition to complete ownership, interests of this kind include easements, leases, mortgages, and also all kinds of future interests. Purchasers of land normally understand that they must take subject to these outstanding interests because they appear somewhere in the record history of the title. But we must not lose sight of the fact that their present existence can only be determined by a search of the whole title throughout the entire period of its history. We have previously felt that owners of interests of this kind should be able to protect themselves by one recording, especially if the interest is of a non-possessory kind. Repeated examinations thus become endlessly necessary under our existing systems.[8]

D. OVER-METICULOUS TITLE EXAMINATION

Every title examiner owes a duty to his client to advise him truly and conscientiously as to whether he believes the title which he intends to buy is a marketable one. On the subject of marketability an individual examiner is likely to advise the purchaser not only as to what he believes concerning its freedom from attack as a practical matter but also as to what a future examiner may say concerning it. He cannot justifiably ignore defects of which another might demand correction. Each appraisal of title tends to err on the side of caution and conservatism, with the result that trivialities are overemphasized. Thus the entire process tends to become dominated by overabundant caution and ultrameticulous judgments. "Unlike water, all conveyances seek the highest level," is the picturesque way one writer

---

8. The Massachusetts Judicial Council recently drew and precisely stated the contrary conclusion: "Today, after 300 years the need of re-recording of evidence to bring the document within the reach of a reasonable period of search is like the original need of recording." See Report of Judicial Council of Massachusetts, Improving Our Land Title Recording System 20, 22 (32d Rep. 1956).

has described this legal phenomenon. Title examiners are not to be unduly criticized for their punctilious observance of minutiae. The basic difficulty lies in the mechanical operation of the system itself. Its very nature demands satisfaction of whatever doubtful questions appear in titles.

Until a few years ago no attempt had ever been made to set up any standards to be followed by title examiners. Gradually it was felt that if certain standards could be laid down in advance, they could accomplish much to dispel fears that opinions of future examiners would be at variance with present appraisals. Knowledge as to how others will treat certain recurring problems will increase the confidence with which present opinions can be rendered. Thus far real estate title standards have been adopted in twenty-two states on a statewide basis and in several other communities on a county or city level. Lawyers in these states unhesitatingly attest their value. Title Standards committees in most states have been actively engaged in improving or extending their standards to make them function ever more efficiently to accomplish a job that has long needed to be done. A by-product of these title standards is that committees working with them become alert to the need for legislation to bring about needed improvements in local property law, and they have become increasingly instrumental in supporting needed statutory changes. Iowa has, for example, long been a leader in both movements.

E. SHORTCOMINGS OF STATUTES OF LIMITATIONS

Statutes of limitations have long occupied an essential and important place in property law. They express a policy that is designed to promote repose and give security to possession of land coupled with acts of ownership. They operate in two ways: first, by punishing an owner who fails to assert his right within a prescribed period of time; and, second, by quieting the title of one who consistently asserts his rights during a prescribed period of time. It is true that land is occasionally acquired by wrongful dispossession followed by adverse possession for the requisite length of time to confer title. But the vast majority of cases of adverse possession have their origin in an intended transfer of title which is ineffective merely for failure to comply with some formality of conveyancing.

Despite the beneficial effects produced by the application of statutes of limitations in individual cases, the importance of these statutes for providing a good record title is not so great as might be supposed. First, there is no device for registering a title acquired by adverse possession. Second, statutes of limitations do not ordinarily operate against owners of future interests, persons under disabilities, the state or other governmental units. Hence, conventional statutes of limitations do not and cannot achieve their full usefulness as a means of providing a record marketable title.

Notwithstanding the foregoing observations on the limited effects of statutes of limitations, they do in some respects have certain virtues in promoting marketable titles. Limitations apply not alone to cases of adverse possession; they can be made to apply equally well to all manner of nonpossessory rights. Judgments, mechanics' liens, mortgages, deeds of trust, land contracts, options, notices of lis pendens are all cases in point. How should statutes of limitations affect these interests?

We have long been accustomed to the rule which declares that a judgment shall cease to be a lien after the expiration of a fixed number of years. In other words the mere passage of time extinguishes the interest and does so absolutely, irrespective of disabilities or other factors which might ordinarily suspend or extend the running of the statute. We know that the same principle applies in the case of mechanics' liens. If notice of a mechanic's lien is filed but no suit is commenced within the statutory period thereafter, the notice of lien ceases to have any significance. It is extinguished as an interest, either actual or potential. To determine marketability, one need only examine the record with a calendar before him. That treatment should be extended to as many kinds of interests as possible without unduly prejudicing the rights of others.

F. REDEFINING MARKETABILITY BY LEGISLATION

The orthodox definition of marketable title is one free of all reasonable doubt, one which a reasonably prudent person would be willing to accept. Stated another way, a marketable title is one which does *not* contain a defect, outstanding interest or claim which may conceivably operate to defeat or impair the owner's title. This negative concept of marketability has become an implied invitation for courts to declare a title unmarketable if an examiner has entertained any doubt whatever in his mind with respect to it. A moment's reflection will convince us that we have been more concerned in the past with unmarketability of titles than with marketability. And too often unmarketability may depend upon some technical error or irregularity in an instrument many years old giving rise only to an apparent claim or interest that no court in the world would sustain.

We have long needed to replace this negative approach by a positive one which will make marketability of a title depend upon its condition during a recent interval of time rather than upon technical defects which may have occurred in the distant past. So long as we continue to rely on our recording system to perform its function in the conveyancing process, some such method is fundamental to the maintenance of any degree of simplicity.

THE MODEL MARKETABLE TITLE ACT

As part of the work product of a joint research undertaking on conveyancing reform by the American Bar Association's Section of Real Prop-

Reforming the System 859

erty, Probate and Trust Law, and the University of Michigan Law School, a Model Marketable Title Act has been developed. It is based in considerable part on the Michigan Marketable Title Act[35] and to some extent on an Ontario act,[36] and has substantially influenced the form of marketable title acts in a number of states. As drafted by Professor Lewis M. Simes and his assistant, Clarence B. Taylor, the Model Act provides as follows.

Model Marketable Title Act[37]

Section 1. *Marketable Record Title.* Any person having the legal capacity to own land in this state, who has an unbroken chain of title of record to any interest in land for forty years or more, shall be deemed to have a marketable record title to such interest as defined in Section 8, subject only to the matters stated in Section 2 hereof. A person shall be deemed to have such an unbroken chain of title when the official public records disclose a conveyance or other title transaction, of record not less than forty years at the time the marketability is to be determined, which said conveyance or other title transaction purports to create such interest, either in (a) the person claiming such interest, or (b) some other person from whom, by one or more conveyances or other title transactions of record, such purported interest has become vested in the person claiming such interest; with nothing appearing of record, in either case, purporting to divest such claimant of such purported interest.

Section 2. *Matters to Which Marketable Title Is Subject.* Such marketable record title shall be subject to:

(a) All interests and defects which are inherent in the muniments of which such chain of record title is formed; *provided,* however, that a general reference in such muniments, or any of them, to easements, use restrictions or other interests created prior to the root of title shall not be sufficient to preserve them, unless specific identification be made therein of a recorded title transaction which creates such easement, use restriction or other interest.

(b) All interests preserved by the filing of proper notice or by possession by the same owner continuously for a period of forty years or more, in accordance with Section 4 hereof.

(c) The rights of any person arising from a period of adverse posses-

---

35. 1945 Mich. Pub. Acts No. 200.
36. Ontario Investigation of Titles Act, Ont. Rev. Stat. c. 186 (1950).
37. The Model Act, with commentary, appears in Simes and Taylor, The Improvement of Conveyancing by Legislation 6-16 (1960). On marketable title acts, see also Conine and Morgan, The Wyoming Marketable Title Act — A Revision of Real Property Law, 16 Land and Water L. Rev. 181 (1981); Barnett, Marketable Title Acts — Panacea or Pandemonium, 53 Cornell L. Rev. 45 (1967); and Note, the Marketable Record Title Act and the Recording Act: Is Harmonic Co-existence Possible?, 29 U. Fla. L. Rev. 916 (1977).

sion or user, which was in whole or in part subsequent to the effective date of the root of title.

(d) Any interest arising out of a title transaction which has been recorded subsequent to the effective date of the root of title from which the unbroken chain of title of record is started; *provided*, however, that such recording shall not revive or give validity to any interest which has been extinguished prior to the time of the recording by the operation of Section 3 hereof.

(e) The exceptions stated in Section 6 hereof as to rights of reversioners in leases, as to apparent easements and interests in the nature of easements, and as to interests of the United States.

Section 3. *Interests Extinguished by Marketable Title.* Subject to the matters stated in Section 2 hereof, such marketable record title shall be held by its owner and shall be taken by any person dealing with the land free and clear of all interests, claims or charges whatsoever, the existence of which depends upon any act, transaction, event or omission that occurred prior to the effective date of the root of title. All such interests, claims or charges, however denominated, whether legal or equitable, present or future, whether such interests, claims or charges are asserted by a person sui juris or under a disability, whether such person is within or without the state, whether such person is natural or corporate, or is private or governmental, are hereby declared to be null and void.

Section 4. *Effect of Filing Notice or the Equivalent.*

(a) Any person claiming an interest in land may preserve and keep effective such interest by filing for record during the forty-year period immediately following the effective date of the root of title of the person whose record title would otherwise be marketable, a notice in writing, duly verified by oath, setting forth the nature of the claim. No disability or lack of knowledge of any kind on the part of anyone shall suspend the running of said forty-year period. Such notice may be filed for record by the claimant or by any other person acting on behalf of any claimant who is (1) under a disability, (2) unable to assert a claim on his own behalf, or (3) one of a class, but whose identity cannot be established or is uncertain at the time of filing such notice of claim for record.

(b) If the same record owner of any possessory interest in land has been in possession of such land continuously for a period of forty years or more, during which period no title transaction with respect to such interest appears of record in his chain of title, and no notice has been filed by him or on his behalf as provided in Subsection (a), and such possession continues to the time when marketability is being determined, such period of possession shall be deemed equivalent to the filing of the notice immediately preceding the termination of the forty-year period described in Subsection (a).

Section 5. *Contents of Notice; Recording and Indexing.* To be effective and to be entitled to record the notice above referred to shall contain an accurate and full description of all land affected by such notice which description shall be set forth in particular terms and not by general inclusions; but if said claim is founded upon a recorded instrument, then the description in such notice may be the same as that contained in such recorded instrument. Such notice shall be filed for record in the registry of deeds of the county or counties where the land described therein is situated. The recorder of each county shall accept all such notices presented to him which describe land located in the county in which he serves and shall enter and record full copies thereof in the same way that deeds and other instruments are recorded and each recorder shall be entitled to charge the same fees for the recording thereof as are charged for recording deeds. In indexing such notices in his office each recorder shall enter such notices under the grantee indexes of deeds under the names of the claimants appearing in such notices. Such notices shall also be indexed under the description of the real estate involved in a book set apart for that purpose to be known as the "Notice Index."

Section 6. *Interests Not Barred by Act.* This Act shall not be applied to bar any lessor or his successor as a reversioner of his right to possession on the expiration of any lease; or to bar or extinguish any easement or interest in the nature of an easement, the existence of which is clearly observable by physical evidence of its use; or to bar any right, title or interest of the United States, by reason of failure to file the notice herein required.

Section 7. *Limitations of Actions and Recording Acts.* Nothing contained in this Act shall be construed to extend the period for the bringing of an action or for the doing of any other required act under any statutes of limitations, nor, except as herein specifically provided, to affect the operation of any statutes governing the effect of the recording or the failure to record any instrument affecting land.

Section 8. *Definitions.* As used in this Act:

(a) "Marketable record title" means a title of record, as indicated in Section 1 hereof, which operates to extinguish such interests and claims, existing prior to the effective date of the root of title, as are stated in Section 3 hereof.

(b) "Records" includes probate and other official public records, as well as records in the registry of deeds.

(c) "Recording," when applied to the official public records of a probate, or other court, includes filing.

(d) "Person dealing with land" includes a purchaser of any estate or interest therein, a mortgagee, a levying or attaching creditor, a land contract vendee, or any other person seeking to acquire an estate or interest therein, or impose a lien thereon.

(e) "Root of title" means that conveyance or other title transaction in the chain of title of a person, purporting to create the interest claimed by such person, upon which he relies as a basis for the marketability of his title, and which was the most recent to be recorded as of a date forty years prior to the time when marketability is being determined. The effective date of the "root of title" is the date on which it is recorded.

(f) "Title transaction" means any transaction affecting title to any interest in land, including title by will or descent, title by tax deed, or by trustee's, referee's, guardian's, executor's, administrator's, master in chancery's, or sheriff's deed, or decree of any court, as well as warranty deed, quitclaim deed, or mortgage.

Section 9. *Act to Be Liberally Construed.* This Act shall be liberally construed to effect the legislative purpose of simplifying and facilitating land title transactions by allowing persons to rely on a record chain of title as described in Section 1 of this Act, subject only to such limitations as appear in Section 2 of this Act.

Section 10. *Two-Year Extension of Forty-Year Period.* If the forty-year period specified in this Act shall have expired prior to two years after the effective date of this Act, such period shall be extended two years after the effective date of this Act.

NOTES

1. Would the Model Act be constitutional if the exceptions section, §6, were omitted?

2. Marketable record title provisions, derived from the Model Marketable Title Act, are included as part of the Uniform Simplification of Land Transfers Act, an act approved in 1976 by the National Conference of Commissioners on Uniform State Laws. No dramatic new innovative proposals are contained in the act, but it does include in one concise and well-drafted document many provisions that would, if adopted, improve the conveyancing, recording, and lien laws of the average state. The prefatory note to the act describes in the following words what the act is trying to accomplish:

> The purposes of the Act include the furtherance of the security and certainty of land titles, the reduction of the costs of land transfers, the balancing of the interests of all parties in the construction lien area, and the creation of a more efficient system of public land records. . . .
>
> The high cost of real estate transfers has been seen by many analysts in recent years as being a substantial cause of the pricing of housing out of the reach of a large segment of the American public and of discouraging new investment in construction. This Act embodies a number of reforms designed to limit these costs. The required period of title search has been shortened through the adoption of marketable record title provisions similar to those which have proved successful in over a dozen states. The scope of the search has been further reduced by almost entirely eliminating those interests which can be asserted to those stated on the official record or of which a purchaser has actual knowledge. Wasteful formalities have been made unnecessary.

Considerable attention is paid to the mechanics of the recording system and to the division of functions among the various participants in the process. Persons presenting documents for recording are required to give detailed information to enable the recording officer to index the documents correctly. The recording officer is given discretion in the development of systems for modernization and automation of recording operations and is given the responsibility for moving toward a system of at least limited geographic indexing. At the same time, in anticipation of the eventual computerization of the recording system, the recording office is relieved of all responsibility for making conclusions about the legal effects of documents submitted for recording. The office of state recorder is created to allow for coordination and sharing of experience in the modernization of recording practices.

Lane and Edson, Land Title Recordation Systems: Legal Restraints and Reforms[38]

II-53 to II-60 (1978)

. . . Marketable title acts have spawned considerable commentary, most of it favorable, but some highly critical. What follows is a summary of the principal issues and concerns that have been expressed about marketable title acts.

1. Constitutionality—The principal constitutional problem (principally under state constitutions) arises out of the retroactive aspect of a marketable title act. This is the problem: The parties to interests in land created and recorded prior to the enactment of the marketable title act have formed a reasonable expectation that the interests will have the characteristics attributable to them under the then operative laws, of which one characteristic is an indefinite duration, subject only to the then applicable statutes of limitations. Then along comes the marketable title act which can cut off these interests through the passage of time, unless the holder of the interest makes a new recording, a factor he never counted on and, as a practical matter, may never even learn about. Because their interests have been diminished through legislation, the holders of these interests can claim a deprivation of their property by government action, a substantive due process violation, and under some circumstances, an impairment of the obligation of their contract rights.

Constitutional challenges on legislation of this nature are generally resolved by balancing the injury to the person against the public purposes sought to be achieved. The greater the injury, the more immediate and important the public purpose must be, although only rarely will a public purpose be admitted to justify a total deprivation of personal property rights.

---

38. A report prepared for the U.S. Department of Housing and Urban Development, pursuant to a contract with Booz, Allen & Hamilton, Inc.

Since the drafters of the marketable title acts were fully aware that courts take this approach to the constitutional issues presented by retroactive legislation, they sought to reduce the injury to persons by providing them with an opportunity of preserving their interests through a second recording. By this device, the effect of the marketable title act on the individual claiming an interest subject to being extinguished by the act could be said to be only that of imposing one additional requirement, that of recording a notice of his claim. This is similar to the requirements of the recording acts that have always been upheld by the courts. Those persons whose interests on the date that the marketable title act was passed were as old or older than the time period adopted by the act, were given two years or so to record their notices. Others had longer periods of time in which to record since their interests would be extinguished only after the 30 or 40 year period adopted by the act. With the individual injury reduced in this manner, and given the unquestionable public benefit from having shorter title searches and more secure titles, one court has specifically upheld the marketable title act enacted in its state, and a number of other decisions have been handed down applying the marketable title acts without questioning their validity.

Nevertheless, some commentators have expressed a concern for the constitutionality of these acts. Professor Payne believes that there is a risk that the means by which the older interests are extinguished, without even an attempt to provide notice to the holders of the interests, could be held by a court to deprive them of their procedural due process rights. . . .

2. Fairness—Consideration of the constitutionality of marketable title acts raises into focus the fairness of these laws, notwithstanding their apparent constitutionality. The critics of marketable title acts have stressed these problems.

Take, for example, the problem of future interests. Suppose a grantor conveys land to A for his life, with the remainder to B. Under this conveyance, B or his heirs will automatically acquire title upon A's death. After a couple of years, A conveys to C with a deed purporting to convey the full fee simple title. The 30 or 40 years of the marketable title act now pass so that the conveyance from A to C becomes the root of title. The remainder interest in B and his heirs is extinguished unless B and his heirs record their remainder interest sometime after the root of title. How really practical is that? B and his heirs have never heard of the marketable title act, and do not likewise know about A's conveyance to C. A probably intended to cut off B's interest when he used a deed purporting to convey a fee simple interest to C, so neither A nor C can be counted on to tell B of his jeopardy. . . .

Even without fraud on anyone's part, so-called "wild deeds," deeds outside the chain of title, do happen from time to time and a marketable title act can cause title to be awarded to the party with the less good claim if . . . respective claims were to be evaluated on the merits. Take a simple example: A grantor conveys a fee simple interest to A in 1930, and he conveys the same fee simple interest to B in 1931. Each deed is recorded at the time of its conveyance. In a dispute between A and B in 1940, A would prevail under the recording acts. In 1972, however, B would prevail under the marketable title act because his 1931 deed will have ripened into a mature root of title. . . .

When all is said and done, it seems that, despite our best efforts, some instances of gross unfairness can and will happen under marketable title acts. But given the infrequency with which instances of unfairness have actually occurred in states with marketable title acts for many years, the risk of unfairness can be fairly viewed as far less important than the immediate and substantial public benefits arising out of the marketable title acts.

3. Term of years in the act — The designated time period in enacted marketable title acts ranges from 20 to 50 years. If the period is too long, the principal benefits of the act will not be achieved. For example, a 50-year statute accomplishes little by way of shortening the period of title searching in an area where the customary period of searching is 60 years. On the other hand, if the period is too short, too many outstanding legal interests will have to be re-recorded, and the possibility of unfairness to those who neglect to re-record their interests and the inducement for fraud will increase. A short period would also strengthen the case of proponents for exceptions when the act is being considered by the legislature.

The Model Marketable Title Act prepared by Professor Simes elected a 40-year period, while USLTA shortens this to a 30-year period. Professor Payne supports the 30-year period with the interesting observation that it would eliminate most Depression-period conveyancing documents that were "awash with defective tax sales, foreclosures and the like." However, he also noted that any shorter period would be unacceptable to the mortgage lending industry.

4. Who benefits and what interests are protected by the act? — The original Iowa marketable title act and the Minnesota act by judicial interpretation were limited to owners claiming a fee simple title. Neither the Model Act nor USLTA contains this limitation, but both apply to all interests in land, whether total or partial. However, the drafters of the Model Act anticipated that it would be primarily holders of fee simple interests who would claim the benefits of the act.

Unlike the recording statutes, the benefits of the marketable title acts are not limited to bona fide purchasers for value. The acts are available to all persons holding or claiming protected interests in land, although, as discussed immediately below, some acts require the claimant to be in possession. However, the benefits of the marketable title act drafted by the Alabama Law Institute under the guidance of Professor Payne (but not yet enacted) would be limited to bona fide purchasers for value on the rationale that, by casting the statute in the same mold as a recording act, its constitutionality becomes unassailable.

5. Possession as a condition to claiming benefits of the act — A couple

of the enacted marketable title acts permit only title holders in actual possession of the property to claim the benefits of the act. The purpose of this requirement is to provide a means for resolving the "wild deed" problem where each of two claimants can demonstrate a chain of title beginning in an unrelated, but matured root of title. As between these two claimants, the marketable title act will operate to extinguish the interest of the party not in possession, without regard to whose root of title is more recent.

There are several objections to requiring the prerequisite of possession. One is that the act becomes inapplicable to unoccupied land where no one can be said to be in possession. This could be the case with timber holdings and unfenced rangeland. Professor Simes also rejected possession as a condition to the availability of the benefits of the Model Marketable Title Act, first, because it violated his basic [tenet] that all title disputes should be resolved on the basis of what appears in the public records, without inquiry into facts and circumstances existing beyond the record, and second because he believed that two independent chains of title would occur too infrequently to justify much concern.

6. Exclusions from the act — Commentators on marketable title acts have identified the number of interests in land exempted from the operation of the acts as a principal deficiency. An analysis of each of these exemptions from the act needs to be made to evaluate the justification for the exclusion, to measure the extent to which that exempted interest could, if successfully asserted against the owner, interfere with his use and enjoyment of his property and security of his title, and to determine whether assurance of the non-existence of the exempted interest can be formed only by extending the title search back in time beyond the root of title.

The Model Marketable Title Act drafted by Simes includes four exceptions. They are:

— any easement on the property that is observable by inspection.

> This exemption refers primarily to utility lines and railroads that pass over the surface of property. No one who visits a site can fail to observe these easements or be misled by the absence of a recorded notice within the time period of the act; yet, to deny an exception to the utility companies and railroads would impose a major burden on them of recording and re-recording notices. In the case of overhead wires, this could apply to every land parcel in a city. It is less clear whether the exception would include an access easement. It may depend on the extent of traffic over the easement or whether, even in the absence of traffic, there are readily observable tell-tale marks of an easement such as a worn path or a paved walkway.

Reforming the System

— any interest acquired by adverse possession in which some part of the period of possession was subsequent to the root of title.

This exemption is necessary because the marketable title acts are not intended to adversely affect the rights of persons claiming title by adverse possession unless the entire period of adverse possession preceded the root of title. This exception does not affect title searching anyway, since adverse possession cannot be discovered from the records.

— any interest of the United States.

Only the federal government can effectively cut off an interest it has in property, and Congress has not seen fit to do so. Making explicit this exception only restates what the law would be anyway, but it has the advantage of warning people of the risk.

— the interests of a lessor upon the termination of a lease.

This is intended to protect the lessor of a lease extending over the period of time of the marketable title act from the risk that his lessee might convey a fee simple interest to a third party. Alone among Simes' recommended exceptions, this one is probably not necessary since it is unlikely that a long-term lessee would try to convey a fee simple interest, or that his grantee would accept it when the record shows the lessor as owning the property. Further, the lessor would probably receive notice in plenty of time to take corrective action from the cessation of his rental payments or other events affecting the use or condition of the property.

In actuality, most of the enacted marketable title acts have lengthened the list of exceptions to include one or more of the following interests:

— the interests of the state, county, city or other political subdivision.
— all easements and other interests held by utilities and railroads.
— mineral interests and water rights.
— possibilities of reverter, rights of entry for conditions broken, and restrictive covenants.
— mortgages and other security interests.
— remainders and reversions.

NOTES

1. Which, if any, of the marketable title act exceptions referred to in the report immediately above, other than those appearing in the Model Act, do you consider desirable? Why?

2. Exceptions can seriously hamper the effectiveness of marketable title acts. As a commentator on the North Carolina act has said: "Unfortunately, the quest to assure victory for the marketable title legislation resulted in the loss of major battles to vested interests and the concession of numerous and broad exceptions to the thirty-year limitation." Note, 52 N.C.L. Rev. 211, at 221 (1973). The North Carolina exceptions even include "deeds of trust, mortgages and security instruments or security agreements duly recorded and not otherwise unenforceable," and certain covenants restricting property to residential use. N.C. Gen. Stat. §47B-3(11) (1984).

Wichelman v. Messner
250 Minn. 88, 83 N.W.2d 800 (1957)

Murphy, Justice. Action to determine adverse claims and to obtain possession of certain realty by Melvin Wichelman against Fred Messner, Independent Consolidated School District No. 81 of Sibley County, Victor Glaeser, and John Glaeser. The Glaesers have interests identical to plaintiff but, having refused to join plaintiff's action, they were joined as defendants. The trial court determined the fee simple interests to be an undivided $627/648$ in plaintiff, an undivided $14/648$ in John Glaeser, and an undivided $7/648$ in Victor Glaeser. From the judgment, defendants Fred Messner and Independent Consolidated School District No. 81 appeal.

On July 6, 1897, H. F. Hoppenstedt conveyed a parcel out of Lot 4 of his farm in Sibley County, 10 rods by 16 rods, to defendant school district's predecessor by a warranty deed, regular in form except for the following provisions:

". . . provided nevertheless and on condition however, that said premises shall be used and occupied as and for a school house site and school grounds and that whenever such occupancy and use of the same shall cease and terminate said premises shall revert to said parties of the first part, their heirs and assigns and again become a part of and belong to Lot No. 4 above described. And the said H. F. Hoppenstedt one of the parties of the first part for himself and his heirs, executors and administrators. . . ."

The defendant school board closed the school on the site on August 16, 1946, and since that date had not used the premises for school purposes. Following a vote on May 20, 1952, by the members of the school district to sell the school land, bids were solicited. Plaintiff, on September 24, 1952, submitted a bid of $1,356 which was not accepted. Subsequently, the school district by warranty deed sold and conveyed the premises to defendant Messner, the present owner of the original Hoppenstedt farm, for $1,650.

Plaintiff then solicited the Hoppenstedt heirs and received from them releases and quitclaim deeds for which he paid each various amounts from a minimum of $1 to a maximum of $10. Prior to the commencement of this action, no form of reentry had been attempted, nor had there been any notice filed pursuant to M.S.A. §541.023. The school district remained in possession until the sale to Messner.

At the trial the defendants contended that the original conveyance from Hoppenstedt to the school district was a fee simple on condition subsequent, while the plaintiff contended that the deed expressed a determinable fee which would vest title automatically without the necessity of reentry upon discontinued use of the property for school purposes. The distinctions between these two estates are discussed at length in Consolidated School District No. 102, Washington County v. Walter, 243 Minn. 159, 66 N.W.2d 881. Since we hold that §541.023 applies with equal force to both a determinable fee and a fee upon condition subsequent, further discussion of that issue is unnecessary.

We think this case is controlled by §541.023 which specifically relates to conditions and restrictions contained in old documents.

As to the operative provisions of this act, subd. 1 states: "As against a claim of title based upon a source of title, which source has then been of record at least 40 years, no action affecting the possession or title of any real estate shall be commenced by a person, . . . after January 1, 1948, to enforce any right, claim, interest, incumbrance or lien founded upon any instrument, event or transaction which was executed or occurred more than 40 years prior to the commencement of such action, unless within 40 years after such execution or occurrence there has been recorded in the office of the register of deeds [the required notice]. . . ."

In the same subdivision the statute discusses generally the kind of interest which might be extinguished by failure to file the required notice. It states: ". . . If such notice relates to *vested or contingent rights* claimed under a *condition subsequent or restriction* it shall affirmatively show why such *condition or restriction* is not, or has not become nominal so that it may be disregarded under the provisions of Minnesota Statutes 1945, Section 500.20(1)." (Italics supplied.)

Subd. 2, with reference to application of the act, states: "This section shall apply to every right, claim, interest, incumbrance or lien founded upon any instrument, event or transaction 40 years old at the date hereof, or which will be 40 years old prior to January 1, 1948, except those under which the claimant thereunder shall file a notice as herein provided prior to January 1, 1948."

Subd. 4 provides for the manner of filing and recording the notices with the register of deeds and registrar of titles.

Subd. 5 states that any claimant under any instrument, event, or transaction barred by the provisions of: ". . . this section shall be conclusively presumed to have abandoned all right, claim, interest, incumbrance or lien based upon such instrument, event or transaction; and the title in the name of any adverse claimant to the real estate which would otherwise be affected thereby shall not be deemed unmarketable by reason of the existence of such instrument, event or transaction. . . ."

The plaintiff contends that this statute was intended to eliminate "purely technical grounds of objection to the title" and was not intended to affect a substantial interest in real property. Counsel amici curiae for the plaintiff have by able arguments and briefs contended that the act by its own terms may properly be invoked "only by one who owns a separate and complete source of title which has been of record at least 40 years and for that period not subject to the adverse claim to be barred." They argue further that "The fundamental purpose and intent of this statute and its predecessors was and is to make secure and marketable those titles whose claims have been of record a substantial period of time, i.e., at least 40 years, as against *adverse claims* not asserted or otherwise preserved by the notice of claim." Stating the same proposition and amplifying it so as to include the precise situation involved in this suit, they argue that:

". . . the 40-year recorded source of title which is to be protected and stabilized is a *separate* source of title of record for at least 40 years and during all of that time free of the defect or adverse claim which is asserted —not a title predicated wholly upon the instrument which contains the right or condition to be barred or extinguished."

They argue that the title of the school district was not a source of title within the protection of the statute, asserting that for 40 years its interest was subject to the condition stipulated in the deed and consequently not a source of title adverse for 40 years, but only during the period from the time the school board decided not to use the property for school purposes, until this action was brought.

The defendants assert that the limiting conditions set forth in the conveyance express a condition subsequent or restriction within the meaning of subd. 1 of the act and that the interest is conclusively presumed to have been abandoned by reason of the failure to record notice of interest as provided by subds. 4 and 5 of the act.

As will appear from the discussion to follow, much of what we say goes beyond the immediate issues raised by the appeal. This is explained by the fact that counsel amici curiae have voiced concern as to the impact of the Marketable Title Act, §541.023. In deference to them and the considerable segment of the bar for whom they speak, we have attempted to express our views as to all the points raised. Consequently, the opinion is necessarily extended.

1. In construing the 40-year statute we are required by §645.16 to "ascertain and effectuate the intention of the legislature" and among other matters are to consider the occasion and necessity for the law; the circumstances under which it was enacted; the mischief to be remedied; and the object to be attained, as well as the consequences of a particular interpretation. We are required by §645.17 to keep in mind that the legislature does not intend a result that is absurd, impossible of execution,

or unreasonable; that the legislature does not intend to violate the Constitution of the United States or of this state; and that the legislature intends to favor the public interest as against any private interest.

We must further keep in mind that this particular statute is an amendment of the so-called 50-year statute enacted in 1943, later amended in 1945, and again amended by L. 1947, c. 118, which is now §541.023. The act must be construed in light of the significant fact that the legislature referred to the type of interest with which we are here concerned by making it applicable to "vested or contingent rights claimed under a condition subsequent or restriction." 17 Dunnell, Dig. (3 ed.) §8936(b), et seq.

2. Moreover, the expressed policy of the legislature that "ancient records shall not fetter the marketability of real estate" is itself a source of law which "should not only be construed and applied liberally, but . . . should be accepted as a new point of departure for the process of judicial reasoning." 17 Dunnell, Dig. (3 ed.) §8959, notes 47 and 48. "The Legislature has the power to decide what the policy of the law shall be, and if it has intimated its will, however indirectly, that will should be recognized and obeyed."

3. We are asked to define the term "claim of title based upon a source of title, which source has been of record at least 40 years" and to identify the particular estate in land which the legislature intended to protect by the provisions of the act. In doing so we may consider the relation of §541.023 to kindred statutes governing the subject of estates in land. 82 C.J.S., Statutes, §365.

4. It is plain from the wording of the statute itself that the legislature intended to relieve a title from the servitude of provisions contained in ancient records which "fetter the marketability of real estate." It is also clear from the plain wording of the act that it intended the provisions to benefit a title so as to relieve it from the restriction of "vested or contingent rights" derived from events or documents granting a "condition subsequent or restriction" which occurred more than 40 years prior to the commencement of the action.

5. Applying this language to estates in real property, as defined by §§500.01 and 500.02, the obvious conclusion is that the legislature intended this act to apply to a fee simple ownership. In Minnesota, estates in lands are divided into estates of inheritance, estates for life, estates for years, and estates at will and by sufferance. §500.01. Under the definition of §500.02, "Every estate of inheritance shall continue to be termed a fee simple, or fee; and every such estate, *when not defeasible or conditional,* shall be a fee simple absolute or an absolute fee." (Italics supplied.) Since a fee simple ownership is an estate of inheritance which may be defeasible or conditional, it is the estate which benefits by the sanctions of the act. It is clear that the act was intended to relieve the fee from old conditions and restrictions which §500.02 by definition recognizes. See, 41 Minn. L. Rev. 232. The Iowa Marketable Title Act (Iowa Code 1950, §614.17, I.C.A.),

uses the phrase "record title" to describe the title benefited. While it is uncertain what interpretation will be given to the term "title" in that act, it has been suggested that the meaning of this term is fee simple title. See, Comment, 2 Drake L. Rev. 76, 81.

6. It is important for us to note here that the statute expressly includes "vested or contingent rights claimed under a condition subsequent or restriction" among the interests which will be barred if the statutory notice is not filed. It must therefore follow that the word "title" includes not only the fee simple absolute but also the defeasible fees (§§500.02 and 500.07).

7. It is manifest from the express policy stated by the legislature that "ancient records shall not fetter the marketability of real estate," that by specific reference to conditions subsequent or restrictions, whether mature or immature, the legislature intended to bar these lesser interests which conflict with the fee, it being the expressed intention of the legislature that those interests which have substantial value may be preserved by recordation.

8. The fee simple defeasible is defined in Restatement, Property, §16, as follows: "An estate in fee simple defeasible is an estate in fee simple which is subject to a special limitation (defined in §23), a condition subsequent (defined in §24), an executory limitation (defined in §25) or a combination of such restrictions." By interpreting the phrase "a claim of title based upon a source of title" as a recorded fee simple ownership as defined by §500.02, a reasonable result follows. The fee simple estate is exempted from the clogs which impair its marketability. If such outstanding interests are not considered important enough to register, no action may be commenced upon them. Under this interpretation as pointed out by 41 Minn. L. Rev. 232, 234, ". . . lessors, remaindermen and owners of defeasible fees will not be barred by owners of lesser interests who would lack the fee simple title necessary to invoke the act."

9. As was observed with reference to the Iowa act (McClain, General Limitation of Real Estate Actions, 6 Iowa L. Bull. 77, 88), this measure is limited in its applications to cases in which the proper showing is or can be made and its application to each particular state of facts is to be determined as those facts arise. We may assume that the legislature has provided in general terms the conditions to which the act applies, leaving to the court the problem of determining the precise situations which come within its general provisions. Aside from the observations set forth hereafter which relate to continuing estates discussed in the briefs and arguments, we do not undertake to announce a general interpretation which might be understood to apply to each precise situation which might arise with reference to the myriad problems which grow out of transactions relating to real estate. In this decision we are limiting our holding to the question of whether the Minnesota Marketable Title Act permits the record owner of a fee simple title, as defined by §500.02, to be relieved from the burdens and restrictions outstanding against such fee, where the fee title itself is

predicated upon the instrument which contains the right or condition to be extinguished.

10. Counsel amici curiae for the plaintiff assert that the act raises serious questions as to the status of the relative rights of parties on all instruments of record more than 40 years and makes specific reference to certain continuing interests in real estate. In considering this objection we must continue to keep in mind that the statute should be given a reasonable construction in light of its stated purpose that "ancient records shall not fetter the marketability of real estate." Although the language of the statute is general, it may be limited in its operation to cases which may be said to fall within the mischief intended to be remedied.

50 Am. Jur., Statutes, §307, states: ". . . Such general words and phrases must be construed as limited to the immediate objects of the act, however wide and comprehensive they may be in their literal sense. These rules are particularly applicable where they are necessary to prevent absurd or futile results."

There are cases in which we may imply exceptions to the general provisions of the statute without being subject to the criticism of having entered the legislative field. This is particularly true where the exceptions are necessary to give effect to legislative intent.

". . . In this connection, it has been declared that where the whole context and the circumstances surrounding the adoption of an act show a legislative intention to make an exception to the general terms of the act, the exception will be recognized by the courts." 50 Am. Jur., Statutes, §432.

These principles will be applied in the following interpretation of the statute as it may relate to the various interests which counsel amici curiae for plaintiff feel might be extinguished by the interpretation for which the defendants contend. . . .

Mortgages: Recorded mortgages (securing monetary obligations payable over a term of at least 40 years), which are not barred by other statutes and which the fee owner has assumed or taken "subject to," are exempt from the requirement of filing notice under certain circumstances. Mortgages which are represented by a current active relationship with the fee owner are implicitly exempt from the requirement of filing notice. The mortgagor's affirmative act of making periodic payments to the mortgagee, when coupled with the terms of the recorded mortgage, is conclusive notice and recognition of the mortgagee's "living interest." Such an interest should be contrasted with possibilities of reverter and conditions subsequent which are of indefinite duration. The legislature may have properly assumed that these latter interests, having generally outlived the reasons for their creation, may be for the benefit of persons now deceased or successors who are disinterested in the observance of restrictions and conditions and that the interests consequently impede the full economic use of property and are contrary to public policy. As to such interests the filing of a written notice is essential to establish why the "condition or restriction is not, or has not become nominal" and that it has not been abandoned. Mortgages, on the other hand, are of definite duration; are an active relationship between persons currently interested in the performance of the mortgage agreement; facilitate the use and development of property; and are not against public policy. Current active mortgages are not "ancient records" which "fetter the marketability of real estate." Notice and recognition of the recorded mortgage as a valid living interest is inherent in the active relationship between the fee owner and the mortgagee. The filing of notice within the 40-year period after the creation of the mortgage, however, would provide more security to the mortgagee since he would not have to rely on having a sufficiently current and active relationship (a fact question) to preserve his right.

Leases: The fear that leasehold interests might ripen into ownership by reason of the Marketable Title Act is likewise unwarranted. See, §504.03. Since under the interpretation we have given to the term "claim of title based upon a source of title," as meaning recorded fee simple ownership, owners of lesser interests in real estate lack the fee simple title necessary to invoke the protection of the act. 41 Minn. L. Rev. 232.

Remainder interests: The plaintiff argues that the interpretation contended for by the defendants would operate to defeat the interests of remaindermen and in support of his argument proposes this hypothetical situation: "By decree or conveyance, a life interest is vested in A in 1910 with remainder to B upon expiration of such life estate. A goes into and retains possession for more than 40 years. In 1955 he decides to claim adversely to B or his heirs and assigns on the basis of this case and so notifies B. B sues to determine adverse claims, although he is not yet in possession." On this state of facts they suggest A would prevail because he owned an adequate source of title and B's only basis of claim is a document which was of record for more than 40 years.

It seems clear to us that it would be unreasonable and inconsistent with the statute's purpose to include within the meaning of the word "title" the term for years and the life estate and thus compel the reversioner or remainderman to file the statutory notice or be barred. It cannot be seriously argued that the holder of the life estate or his tenant would have an estate of inheritance which would permit him to invoke the protection of the act. "Only those who possess a title which complies with the conditions of the statute are qualified to invoke its aid." Lytle v. Guilliams, 241 Iowa 523, 529, 41 N.W.2d 668, 672, 16 A.L.R.2d 1377. The legislature does not intend a result that is unreasonable; and it does not intend to violate the Minnesota or United States Constitutions. §645.17 (1, 3).

11. We conclude that, taking §541.023 as a whole and construing the language used in it in light of the object and purpose which the legislature intended to accomplish, the term "source of title" must refer to *recorded fee simple ownership,* an estate which under §500.02 may be "defeasible or

conditional." It is the latter type of ownership, particularly, which may be impaired by stale conditions and restrictions which affect its marketability, and it is clear that the legislature intended to require those owning interests in old conditions and restrictions which burden such ownership to record notice of the continued existence of such rights or permit extinguishment of them.

12. The Marketable Title Act is a comprehensive plan for reform in conveyancing procedures and encompasses within its provisions the collective sanctions of (a) a curative act, (b) a recording act, and (c) a statute of limitations. It is a curative act in that it may operate to correct certain defects which have arisen in the execution of instruments in the chain of title. It is a recording act in that it requires notice to be given to the public of the existence of conditions and restrictions, which may be vested or contingent, growing out of ancient records which fetter the marketability of title (see, Klasen v. Thompson, 189 Minn. 254, 248 N.W. 817). It is as well a statute of limitations in that the filing of a notice is a prerequisite to preserve a right of action to enforce any right, claim, or interest in real estate founded upon any instrument, event, or transaction which was executed or occurred more than 40 years prior to the commencement of the action, whether such claim or interest is mature or immature and whether it is vested or contingent.

13. Curative statutes are a form of retrospective legislation which reach back on past events to correct errors or irregularities and to render valid and effective attempted acts which would be otherwise ineffective for the purpose the parties intended, particularly irregularities in conveyancing requirements. They operate to complete a transaction which the parties intended to accomplish but carried out imperfectly. Basye, Clearing Land Titles, §§201, 204. Such curative acts do not impair the obligation of contract. Ross v. Worthington, 11 Minn. 438, Gil. 323. Retrospective legislation in general, however, will not be allowed to impair rights which are vested and which constitute property rights. Seese v. Bethlehem Steel Co., D.C., D. Md., 74 F. Supp. 412, 417, *affirmed*, 4 Cir., 168 F.2d 58; Fuller v. Mohawk Fire Ins. Co., 187 Minn. 447, 450, 245 N.W. 617, 618.

14. Statutes of limitations are based on the theory that it is reasonable to require that stale demands be asserted within a reasonable time after a cause of action has accrued. See Basye, Clearing Land Titles, §52. In Baker v. Kelley, 11 Minn. 480 at page 493, Gil. 358 at page 371, we said: ". . . Statutes of limitation . . . prescribe a period within which a right may be enforced, afterward withholding a remedy for reasons of private justice and public policy. It would encourage fraud, oppression and interminable litigation, to permit a party to delay a contest until it is probable that papers may be lost, facts forgotten, or witnesses dead. A limitation law is intended to prevent this, and such a law is uniformly held valid." See, also, Bachertz v. Hayes-Lucas Lumber Co., 201 Minn. 171, 275 N.W. 694.

The constitutional prohibitions against retrospective legislation do not apply to statutes of limitation, "for such a statute will bar any right, however high the source from which it may be deduced, provided that a reasonable time is given a party to enforce his right." Meigs v. Roberts, 162 N.Y. 371, 378, 56 N.E. 838, 840; Day, Curative Acts and Limitations Acts, 9 U. of Fla. L. Rev. 145, 152; Basye, Clearing Land Titles, §206; Opinion of the Justices, N.H., 131 A.2d 49. This requirement of a reasonable time within which to assert the right, however, means that the holder of a future interest ordinarily cannot be barred by the operation of statutes of limitation until a reasonable time after he acquires the right to maintain an action to acquire possession. Simes and Smith, Law of Future Interests, §§1962; 1963; Basye, Clearing Land Titles, §55.

15. What may be a reasonable time depends upon the sound discretion of the legislature in the light of the nature of the subject and purpose of the enactment, and we have said that "the courts will not inquire into the wisdom of the exercise of this discretion by the legislature in fixing the period of legal bar, unless the time allowed is manifestly so short as to amount to a practical denial of justice." Hill v. Townley, 45 Minn. 167, 169, 47 N.W. 653, 654; Note, 33 Minn. L. Rev. 54.

16. It is apparent from the recordation provisions of the 40-year statute which we are considering that the legislature did not intend to arbitrarily wipe out old claims and interests without affording a means of preserving them and giving a reasonable period of time within which to take the necessary steps to accomplish that purpose. The recordation provisions of the act provide for a simple and easy method by which the owner of an existing old interest may preserve it. If he fails to take the step of filing the notice as provided, he has only himself to blame if his interest is extinguished. "The constitutionality of imposing this duty would seem to have been settled beyond question by the decisions sustaining retroactive recording statutes." Scurlock, Retroactive Legislation Affecting Interests in Land, Mich. Legal Studies, p. 82; Klasen v. Thompson, supra. . . .

17. A period of nine months was provided to file the required notice. Lesser periods than this have been held reasonable. . . .

Moreover it should be kept in mind that the Bar of Minnesota had knowledge of the enactment of this legislation. See, Reprint of Program Talks from Annual Meetings, 1947, 1948, Section of Real Property Law, Minnesota State Bar Association. It was aimed at an important legal reform. See Maloney, Comments on Minnesota Laws, 30 Minn. L. Rev. 32; Brehmer, Limitations of Actions, 30 Minn. L. Rev. 23; 32 M.S.A. p. 388. . . .

18. It has been argued that §541.023 is unconstitutional by reason of the fact that in the first sentence of subd. 1 the clause: "As against a claim of title based upon a source of title, which source has then been of record at least 40 years" is so vague and ambiguous as to render it meaningless. . . .

. . . It is a cardinal rule of construction that, rather than pronounce a statute unconstitutional and void, the court will draw inferences from the evident intent of the legislature. State ex rel. Foot v. Bazille, 97 Minn. 11, 106 N.W. 93, 6 L.R.A., N.S., 732. Extreme caution should be exercised by courts before declaring a statute void and it should be upheld unless it is so uncertain and indefinite that, after exhausting all rules of construction, it is impossible to ascertain the legislative intent. See, Anderson v. Burnquist, 216 Minn. 49, 11 N.W.2d 776.

19. The policy expressly stated by the act itself that ancient records shall not fetter the marketability of real estate must be a rule and guide in determining the meaning of the term "source of title" as used in the statute. Applying this rule so as to determine the kind of "title" whose marketability the legislature desires to promote, we conclude that by use of the term "claim of title based upon a source of title," the marketability of which might be impaired by a condition subsequent or restriction, the legislature had in mind the recorded fee simple title which may be a defeasible or conditional estate as defined by §500.02.

20-21. The plaintiff has contended that the term "source of title" is susceptible of so many varying and conflicting definitions that it is meaningless. Citing B.W. & Leo Harris Co. v. City of Hastings, 240 Minn. 44, 59 N.W.2d 813, he asserts that the grantee in a stray or interloping deed might become "the absolute owner" of property. We do not think the statute lends itself to an interpretation to the effect that title may be founded on a stray, accidental, or interloping conveyance. Its object is to provide, for the recorded fee simple ownership, an *exemption* from the burdens of old conditions and restrictions which at each transfer of the property interfere with its marketability. The statute does not operate to provide a foundation for a new title. But, in view of the persuasive arguments of the counsel amici curiae, it may be of benefit to examine more closely the objects which the statute seeks to accomplish.

For §541.023 to operate in a particular case to extinguish any interest, two basic requirements are necessary. First, the party desiring to invoke the statute for his own benefit must have a requisite "claim of title based upon a source of title, which source has then been of record at least 40 years," (i.e., a recorded fee simple title). Secondly, the person against whom the act is invoked must be one who is "conclusively presumed to have abandoned all right, claim, interest . . ." in the property (subd. 5).

There are three classes of persons against whom no one can invoke the act. They are (1) those persons who seek to enforce any right, claim, interest, encumbrance, or lien founded upon any instrument, event, or transaction which was executed or occurred *within* 40 years prior to the commencement of the action; (2) those persons who seek to enforce a claim founded on any such instrument or event which was executed or occurred *over* 40 years prior to the commencement of the action, *if they have filed proper notice* within 40 years of the execution or occurrence of the instrument, event, or transaction upon which it is founded; and (3) those excepted by subd. 6 of the act, which includes persons in possession. . . .

22. We must reject the construction suggested by counsel amici curiae for plaintiff that the 40-year period does not begin to run in favor of a determinable fee or a fee subject to a condition subsequent until after a breach of the restriction. Applying that construction to the facts of the instant case, where the restrictions were created in 1897 and broken in 1946, the 40-year period would not expire until 1986; and if a restriction were created in 1800 and not breached until 2000, the 40-year period would not expire until the year 2040. Some other statute of limitations, or adverse possession, or laches would probably operate within 40 years after breach and §541.023 would be unnecessary. The economic reason for which the original grantor imposed the restriction in either of these cases would probably have ceased long before its breach; yet unless it is breached the restriction has an indefinite duration. We may assume that in enacting this statute the legislature adopted the view that such a restriction on the fee is probably so scattered among numerous heirs and assignees that it is almost impossible to locate them. In the case before us the plaintiff who purchased quitclaims from the heirs was himself unable to acquire the total interest. Outstanding interests of this nature are likely to have merely nuisance value 40 years after their creation. They are the type of clogs at which the provisions of the act are aimed. Obviously the policy of preventing ancient records from fettering the marketability of the fee is frustrated by the construction contended for by the plaintiff.

23. Plaintiff asserts that Messner did not have a sufficient "source of title" to invoke the act. The term "source of title" must be interpreted in light of the stated policy of the act that "ancient records shall not fetter the marketability of real estate." We cannot agree with the argument of the plaintiff that the act can only be invoked by one who owns "a separate and complete source of title which has been of record at least 40 years and for that period is not subject to the adverse claim to be barred." If the Minnesota Marketable Title Act contained the same provision as the Indiana Law (Burns' Ind. Stat. Ann. §2-632) there would be some force to his contention. That statute provides: ". . . This section shall mean that the record title owner shall have a marketable title of that interest in the real property which the muniments of his title purport to convey to him." One writer has said that this provision expressly excepts interests created by provisions of limitations contained in the muniments of title of the record owner. The Minnesota act (M.S.A. §541.023, subd. 1) is entirely different in that it specifically refers to "vested or contingent rights claimed under a condition subsequent or restriction" as evils intended to be eliminated in attaining the goal of free alienability of land. The plaintiff fails to point out, under the construction he suggests how the statute would be of any real value in fostering the marketability of a fee title. It seems to us that the provision in the Indiana act defeats in large measure the very purpose of this type of legislation which is intended to relieve a chain of title from the

Reforming the System

accumulated burdens of old conditions and restrictions set forth in provisions contained in instruments making up the chain of title. . . .

26. It appears further that the constitutionality of the Minnesota statute is preserved by the provisions exempting persons in "possession of real estate" from the requirement of filing notice and allowing persons not in possession a reasonable time to file statutory notice. See, Aigler, Constitutionality of Marketable Title Acts, 50 Mich. L. Rev. 185; 38 Minn. L. Rev. 285; Hammon v. Hatfield, 192 Minn. 259, 256 N.W. 94. . . .

30. An examination of the various marketable title acts indicates that they were intended to operate as statutes of limitation to bar all interests, including vested future interests, if proper notice is not filed, as well as to correct irregularities that can be reached by pure curative statutes. The language of our statute itself supports this view. Basye, Clearing Land Titles, §171, et seq.

Yielding to the demand to solve the problems created by restrictions unlimited in time, a number of marketable title acts have been passed by various states. Such limiting statutes are considered vital to all who are engaged in or concerned with the conveyance of real property. They proceed upon the theory that the economic advantages of being able to pass uncluttered title to land far outweigh any value which the outdated restrictions may have for the person in whose favor they operate. These statutes reflect the appraisal of state legislatures of the "actual economic significance of these interests, weighed against the inconvenience and expense caused by their continued existence for unlimited periods of time without regard to altered circumstances." Trustees of Schools of Township No. 1 v. Batdorf, 6 Ill. 2d 486, 492, 130 N.E.2d 111, 115; see, 43 Ill. L. Rev. 90. They must be construed in the light of the public good in terms of more secure land transactions which outweighs the burden and risk imposed upon owners of old outstanding rights to record their interests.

Reversed.

The opinion filed herein August 10, 1956, is hereby withdrawn and the foregoing opinion is substituted in lieu thereof.

NOTES

1. Is the court's argument convincing that a stray deed may not be a source of title within the meaning of the Minnesota Act? What would be the result if there are two independent chains of title going back of record over forty years? How does the Model Marketable Title Act dispose of the stray deed and multiple chain of title problems?

2. In 1959, subsequent to the *Wichelman* decision, an additional subsection was added to the Minnesota Marketable Title Act. As amended, Minn. Stat. Ann. §541.023 (West 1947, Supp. 1985), provides as follows:

Subd. 7. *Source of title.* For the purposes of this section, the words "source of title" as used in subdivision 1 hereof shall mean any deed, judgment, decree, sheriff's certificate, or other instrument which transfers or confirms, or purports to transfer or confirm, a fee simple title to real estate, including any such instrument which purports to transfer, or to confirm the transfer of a fee simple title from a person who was not the record owner of the real estate. However, any such instrument which purports to transfer, or to confirm the transfer of, a fee simple title from a person who was not the record owner of the real estate to the grantee or transferee named in such instrument shall be deemed a source of title "of record at least 40 years" within the meaning of subdivision 1 only if, during the period of 40 years after it was recorded, the following two conditions are fulfilled: (1) another instrument was recorded which purports to transfer a fee simple title from said grantee or transferee to another person and (2) no instrument was recorded which purports to be or confirm a transfer of any interest in the real estate by or from whoever was the record owner in fee simple immediately before the commencement of said period of 40 years. The purpose of the next preceding sentence is to limit the effect of erroneous descriptions or accidental conveyances. Insofar as this subdivision 7 may bar any claim not otherwise barred or extinguished by this section or by some other statute, it shall not be effective until June 1, 1960, and it shall not then apply to any such claim with respect to which a notice has been filed under the provisions of this section prior to that date. This subdivision 7 shall not affect any action or proceeding which is now, or on or before June 1, 1960, shall be, pending in any court.

What weaknesses in the act do you think this section was intended to correct?

3. For a recommendation that Minnesota repeal its Marketable Title Act and adopt the Model Act, see Note, 53 Minn. L. Rev. 1004 (1969).

4. The Iowa Marketable Title Act was held constitutional in Presbytery of Southeast Iowa v. Harris, 226 N.W.2d 232 (Iowa 1975). A dissent to that opinion, at page 244, declares:

Because §614.24 does far more than simply bar claims, and in effect divests persons of their existing property interests, it cannot in the end be justified as a mere statute of limitations. Accordingly, the question must be whether the statutory procedure designed to forestall divestiture comports with constitutional guarantees of due process. The statute contains no provision for notice. Statutory enactment alone was evidently deemed sufficient notice for those persons whose interests in property would be affected. I am not persuaded that manner of notice is "such as one desirous of actually informing . . . might reasonably adopt to accomplish it" (the constitutional standard for due process). Mullane v. Central Hanover Bank & Trust Co., 339 U.S. 306, 315. . . . Moreover, I am frankly unable to reconcile recent decisions broadening the due process rights of persons possessing interests in personalty with the procedural burdens placed on persons under §614.24 to take affirmative action to protect their interests in realty. [Citing Snaidach

v. Family Finance Corp., 395 U.S. 337 (1969), and Fuentes v. Shevin, 407 U.S. 67 (1972), among other cases.]

5. In Marshall v. Hollywood, Inc., 236 So. 2d 114 (1970), the Florida Supreme Court said at page 120: "The certified question involved in this cause was, in effect, whether the Marketable Record Titles to Real Property Act, Ch. 712, F.S. confers marketability to a chain of title arising out of a forged or wild deed, so long as the strict requirements of the Act are met. The question is answered in the affirmative." Is this a desirable result? In accord with Marshall v. Hollywood, Inc. is a later Florida Supreme Court case, City of Miami v. St. Joe Paper Co., 364 So. 2d 439 (1978).

6. A void tax deed has been held to be a valid root of title under a statute patterned after the Model Marketable Title Act, and such a deed has been held effective, under the act, against a city. Mobbs v. City of Lehigh, 655 P.2d 547 (Okla. 1982). In dictum, the court in the *Mobbs* case stated that a forged deed, however, is a complete nullity and ineffective as a muniment of title for any purpose. See also Annot., Construction and Effect of "Marketable Record Title" Statutes, 31 A.L.R.4th 11 (1984).

2. *Torrens Registration*

In much of the world outside the United States, including England and a number of Commonwealth countries, land title registration is the prevailing form of title protection and the registered title the principal source of title data.[39] Registered titles, often referred to as Torrens titles,[40] are

39. On land registration in the United States, see American Land Title Association, The Title Industry: White Papers vol. 1, c. 5 (1976); 6A Powell, The Law of Real Property c. 83 (1984); 4 American Law of Property §§17.37 to 17.48 (1952); Burke, American Conveyancing Patterns c. 5 (1978); Lane & Edson, Improving Land Title Registration Systems (1978), a report prepared for the U.S. Department of Housing and Urban Development, pursuant to a contract with Booz, Allen & Hamilton; Shick and Plotkin, Torrens in the United States (1978); Lobel, A Proposal for a Title Registration System for Realty, 11 U. Rich. L. Rev. 501 (1977); Patton and Patton, Land Titles c. 14 (2d ed. 1957); McDougal and Brabner-Smith, Land Title Transfer: A Regression, 48 Yale L.J. 1125 (1939); and Comment, The Torrens System of Title Registration: A New Proposal for Effective Implementation, 29 U.C.L.A. L. Rev. 661 (1982).

There is vast literature on land registration in other countries. Selective examples are Burke, American Conveyancing Patterns, app. 6A (1978) (Great Britain); DiCastri, Thom's Canadian Torrens System (2d ed. 1962); Hayton, Registered Land (3rd ed. 1981) (England); Mapp, Torrens' Elusive Title, Alberta Law Review Book Series vol. 1 (1978) (comparative but special reference to Alberta); Ruoff and Roper, The Law and Practice of Registered Conveyancing (1979) (England); Simpson, Land Law and Registration (1976) (comparative with emphasis on Commonwealth countries); Whalen, The Torrens System in Australia (1982); Fiflis, Security and Economy in Land Transactions: Some Suggestions from Scotland and England, 20 Hastings L.J. 171 (1968); Fiflis, English Registered Conveyancing: A Study in Effective Land Transfer, 59 Nw. L. Rev. 468 (1964); and Risk, The Records of Title to Land: A Plea for Reform, 21 U. Toronto L.J. 465 (1971) (comparative).

40. In the United States, the term Torrens commonly is used to designate any land title registration system in which a binding title determination of each registered title is made by a

provided for by statute in eleven American states,[41] but in no state is registration compulsory, and no community has a majority of its parcels registered. Registration apparently is heaviest in the Honolulu area, with about 40 percent of the island of Oahu in Torrens; and it is fairly substantial in and around Chicago, Minneapolis-St. Paul, and Boston, although little used elsewhere. The period of greatest support for Torrens registration in the United States was earlier in this century, but interest faded and nine of the states that had Torrens statutes repealed them or let them expire.[42] As the accumulations of American land title records become ever more massive, and as revolutionary new ways of dealing with storage and retrieval of such accumulations continue to be made, a shift over to Torrens or some derivative of it may become necessary and desirable. The successful use of land title registration in many countries with problems similar to our own conceivably is a portent of what the United States too may find is the most effective title system for its needs. Support for an expanded use of Torrens by American states keeps surfacing, and title insurers obviously are concerned about this threat to their business.

a. Administration

Under land title registration systems, the title is registered, rather than possible evidences of title being recorded or registered. Registration involves periodic determinations by public officials as to the state of the title, and these determinations are generally binding. So, with certain exceptions, the various interests in a particular parcel of land may be ascertained by examining the registration certificate that has been issued for that parcel. In the United States, where Torrens statutes are in effect, land title registration is a county responsibility and the counties employ title examiners to make the requisite determinations. However, when a title is first being brought within the Torrens system in the United States, a judicial proceeding similar to a suit to quiet title must be brought; hence, initial registration is a judicial function. Appeal to the courts from the decisions of title examiners also may be available. Advantages commonly claimed

---

public official. However, some commentators, particularly in England, consider Torrens as but one of several registration systems differing in detail from one another, and they classify the English system as separate from the Torrens system followed in Australia, the United States, and most of Canada. For an analysis consistent with this latter usage and one that compares the English and Torrens systems, see Simpson, Land Law and Registration 76-80 (1976). Different types of land registration systems are also discussed in Burke, American Conveyancing Patterns 103-107 (1978).

41. Colorado, Georgia, Hawaii, Illinois, Massachusetts, Minnesota, New York, North Carolina, Ohio, Virginia, and Washington. See Comment, 29 U.C.L.A. L. Rev. 661, 677 n.85 (1982).

42. California, Mississippi, Nebraska, North Dakota, Oregon, South Carolina, South Dakota, Tennessee, and Utah.

for registration are that it is potentially a less cumbersome system and hence potentially a faster, cheaper, and more certain means of title protection. Needless to say, the American title insurance companies, and to some extent the practicing bar, challenge the claims of superiority made for Torrens over the American recording system with its supplemental protective devices that have been developed to implement recording.

Patton, Evolution of Legislation on Proof of Title to Land[43]

30 Wash. L. Rev. 224, 228-235 (1955)

Apparently the earliest method of proving title to land was by actual occupancy — not necessarily a complete or exclusive occupancy but nevertheless that form which precluded other use of the land. This was the basis, and the extent, of land ownership by the American Indians, both as tribes and as families. It has been the criterion among all nomadic people. It has a preferential status in the establishment of private ownership when the nomads changed their way of life and effected permanent settlements.

Some of the earliest legislation of the United States provided for the survey and sale of its public lands, and restricted the private acquisition of land from the government in other than the surveyed rectangular subdivisions of the survey. However it was necessary to recognize the possessory titles of pioneers who had settled on public land in advance of the making of the surveys. This was done by the enactment of numerous townsite acts which provided a legal procedure for proof of rights thus acquired and the issuance of patents to the respective settlers. Thus their possessory titles were changed to documentary or legal titles.

Possessory titles are recognized by the courts when they protect a first trespassing squatter against acts of a subsequent trespasser. They are given priority over the claims of the conventional title holder when the latter has lost his right to judicial assistance by reason of acts which raise an estoppel or for failure to act within a period of time which the courts or the legislature have fixed as a limitation of action. In these cases the holder of the possessory title may by court action secure a documentary title in the form of a judgment which confirms a title acquired by estoppel or by adverse possession. . . .

Just as experience has improved our methods of locating and marking the boundaries of any particular parcel of land and the terms by which it may be accurately described, it is reasonable to assume that experience may have also produced an improved method of indicating to anyone interested therein the ownership of that parcel of land and particularly of

---

43. Footnotes have been omitted.

enabling the owner to furnish ready proof of his title and the exact items of encumbrance thereon. The purchaser of an automobile or a lender taking automobile paper as security encounters no hazards of title requiring risk insurance: the auto license amounts to a certificate of ownership. The same is true of a passbook issued by a savings bank or a certificate of stock issued by a corporation. Sir Richard Torrens, then plain Richard Torrens, could have well obtained from the latter a suggestion of the applicability of the certificate system to land ownership. Not being a banker, but instead having spent much of his life as a customs officer before being appointed Registrar General of South Australia (and thus in charge of the registration of all instruments affecting title to real estate in the province), his earlier experience with the ship registry system led him to wonder why the title to a tract of land could not be registered the same as the title to a ship. The system with which he was comparing the land records which had come under his supervision was that provided by the English Merchants Shipping Law. Under it, a page in the registry is given to each ship, and on it appears the name and description of the ship, the name of the owner, and from time to time liens or encumbrances and releases. A duplicate of the page in the form of a certificate is given to the owner, and that is the evidence of his ownership in any part of the world. If ownership is divided, each owner is given a certificate for his share. To make a transfer, the certificate holder executes an assignment of a part or all of his interest, the assignment and the certificate are sent to the registry office, whereupon the certificate is cancelled, the page closed, and a new page is opened for the new owner or owners, and new certificates are issued. At no time is there outstanding more than one certificate for the same interest and it is not necessary to go back of any outstanding certificate nor to examine any page other than that currently in force. In view of its success as applied to such valuable property as ships, not only in England but in other ship registries, why might not the system be applied to real estate? The new Registrar General set about the drafting of legislation to that effect and had the satisfaction of seeing it enacted, not only locally but in many jurisdictions of the British Empire. During the twentieth century the system has been incorporated into the legal system of several American states, Hawaii, the Philippines and the Dominican Republic, and the name of Mr. Torrens has come into the language both as a verb (to torrens a title) and as an adjective (a torrens title).

Proof of title from the original title deeds served very well in England for several centuries; but at a time when land transfers other than by succession at death were very few. Then instrument registration served fairly well in the United States as well as in Australia and other British possessions so long as settled communities were small enough that questions of notice and bona fides were infrequent. But with the present increases in property values, number of transactions, and volume of records, something better is needed than a mere registration of instruments under

Reforming the System

which every transaction is at the risk of the investor — buyer, mortgagee or lessee, as the case may be, — and where any interest is acquired subject to all defects in the entire chain of title which have not been barred by limitation. What is needed is not a mere registration of instruments but a registration of title. That a "torrens title" is of this character has been well stated in the following quoted paragraphs:

"The basic principle of this system is the registration of the title to land instead of registering, as the old system requires, the evidence of such title. In the one case, only the ultimate fact or conclusion that a certain named party has title to a particular tract of land is registered, and certificate thereof delivered to him. In the other case, the entire evidence from which the proposed purchasers must, at their peril, draw such conclusion is registered."

"The official certificate will always show the state of the title and the person in whom it is vested. The basic principle of the system is the registration of the title to the land, instead of registering, as under the old system, the evidence of such title."

"That registration of title is in the abstract to be preferred to registration of assurances may at once be conceded, for the former aims at presenting the intending purchaser or mortgagee with the net result of former dealings with the property, while the latter places the dealings themselves before him, and leaves him to investigate them for himself. In one case he finds, so to speak, the sum worked out for him; in the other, he has the figures given him, and has to work out the sum for himself."

Like the metric system in comparison with our current non-decimal system of weights and measures, there can be no doubt that a certificate system of evidencing land titles would have been vastly superior to the recording system, and would have obviated much litigation and much of the unfairness and financial loss reflected in title decisions. Had it been inaugurated at the inception of colonial and proprietary titles, or even at the time of patenting of the public lands of the states and of the United States to settlers and purchasers, the patents could have been exchanged for certificates of title as is done in the provinces of Western Canada. But where instead the title to a tract of land has first been the subject of recording, as is the case in Eastern Canada and in the United States, there necessarily exists the hazard as to ownership and encumbrance which has already been mentioned as incident to titles covered by most of the recording acts, greater or less depending upon the type of the act. Without going into detail as to these hazards, the fact that they exist, and that the public is fully aware of the fact, is amply demonstrated by the size of various title insurance companies and the large percentage of the titles in many communities for which the owners consider insurance to be necessary. In order therefore to adapt a certificate system to proof of title in the United States, the most important feature of the authorizing statutes are those sections which outline a method for a conclusive determination as to ownership and encumbrance so that these items may be reflected in the first certificate of title. After issuance of that first certificate the matter is as simple as transferring or mortgaging corporation stock or a ship, the usual deed of conveyance serving the same purpose as an assignment or a bill of sale respectively. For issuance of that first certificate the status of a title cannot here be determined by an administrative office. Both in the original proceeding and in any subsequent proceeding in relation to a registered or "torrensed" title, any question which is exclusively judicial in character must be determined by the court. However this is an advantage rather than otherwise in that the title is thus kept at all times in the form of an adjudicated title rather than one merely presumptively good.

Accordingly in the United States the transfer of a title from the recording-act system to the certificate system must be by a judicial proceeding affirmative in character but nevertheless resembling a suit to quiet title — an action in which the court will be given judisdiction of all parties, both known and unknown, who could by any possibility assert an adverse right or claim, and in which the court can determine the holder of the fee title, the holder of all subordinate titles or interests with their conditions and limitations, and all existing liens upon or rights in the land.

The proceeding is conducted under the close supervision of an officer of the court, designated in the acts as an Examiner of Titles, but clothed with all the powers of a referee. The initial application of the claimant must be checked by him as to form and must receive his endorsed approval before it be filed. He must then examine the title records with the aid of an abstract or search furnished by the applicant; the premises must be inspected or surveyed for the purpose of determining all occupancies; the examiner-referee files a report showing all deviations from a direct chain of title in the applicant free of encumbrance and free from occupancy by other than the applicant (i.e., a report showing the record ownership of all interests in the land, all liens thereon, all possible claimants of interest or liens as shown by the records, the occupancies, or the admissions found in the application). The report further recommends (requires) certain parties as defendants, being all the parties necessary to an adjudication, on proper evidence at the subsequent hearing, that the applicant or applicants, as the case may be, hold the fee title to the premises, and as to exactly what interests, claims or liens are subsisting against the property.

This done, the burden then shifts to the attorney for the applicant. He prepares a petition for summons in which he must list under appropriate subdivisions all defendants named by the Examiner; or as to any found to be deceased, the parties who, per evidence to be produced by him at the hearing for a finding of fact in the courts' decree, have succeeded as heirs or devisees to ownership of the interest or claim of the decedent. On the basis of the petition, and any evidence required by the judge or the Examiner, there is entered an order for summons pursuant to which the clerk of court issues a summons addressed to said parties and to "parties unknown claiming any right, title or interest" in the land there described. The attorney attends to securing service of the summons on each and every defendant in the manner prescribed by statute as to the particular types of defendants (resident, non-resident, those who cannot be located), and upon the "parties unknown" by publication. All of the acts are meticulous in the matter of observing due process of law and in the main they conform, in this respect, to the "burnt record acts."

If an answer is filed, the issue is tried in the same manner as in any other land title case, in some states by a special land court and in others by the general trial court. In case of a default of appearance by the defendants, no decree is entered "pro confesso" but evidence must be produced to substantiate every claim of the applicant which is not affirmatively corroborated by the earlier report of the Examiner. Whether the hearing is conducted by the Examiner as referee or by the judge, it appears to be the usual practice to receive in evidence the Examiner's report and incidental thereto, by reference, all the records upon which it is based.

If it is found that the applicant lacks title to the land involved or to any portion thereof, the court must dismiss the application in toto or as to the portion to which the applicant is unable to prove title from the records or otherwise. As to the portion of the land to which the applicant proves title, usually the entire tract described in his application, the court enters a decree with appropriate findings of fact upon which to base paragraphs adjudicating that the title is in the applicant, either free from encumbrance or subject to specified items including rights of dower or courtesy or a statutory substitute and ordering that the Registrar of Titles enter a certificate of title in line with the adjudication upon the forthwith filing with him of a certified copy of the decree. The form of the certificate is prescribed by statute; and the latter also provides for issuance of a copy which is no different except for endorsement across its face of the words "Owner's Duplicate." A mortgagee's or a lessee's duplicate may be had also at a slight charge. The original certificate is retained by the Registrar and is bound with others in numerical order in a book designated as a register.

After entry of the first certificate, the matter of filing mortgages, judgments, attachments, mechanics' lien claims, notices of lis pendens and the like is substantially the same as for filing similar claims against a certificate of stock. The instrument is given a document number, retained by the Registrar and noted in considerable detail on the certificate of title in his register. Instruments discharging such claims are similarly filed and memorialized.

Voluntary transfers of title are effected in substantially the same manner as transfers of corporate stock: the Owner's Duplicate and the deed are filed with the Registrar; he makes appropriate entries in his indices and reception book and endorses a cancellation across the face of both the duplicate and the certificate in the register; if the deed is for all the land covered by the certificate, he enters a new certificate to the grantee (and issues a new Owner's Duplicate) for that land; if the deed is for a part only of the land described in the certificate, he enters a new certificate and an Owner's Duplicate to the grantee for the part described in the deed, and a residue certificate and duplicate for the unconveyed portion in favor of the registered owner named in the cancelled certificate.

In case of an involuntary transfer—devise, descent, execution sale, mortgage foreclosure, etc.—there arises a purely judicial question which the Registrar as a member of the administrative division of the tri-partite state government may not determine. The matter must be presented to the court by petition in a "proceeding subsequent to registration." If an issue can be made as to the granting of the order requested, notice must be given to all parties adversely interested. The notice may be by summons, order to show cause or other written notice depending upon the applicable statute. But if the issue is one which the court may properly determine without notice of the hearing, no notice need be given and an order to the Registrar is entered pro forma.

Conclusiveness of the certificates of title is safeguarded not only by expiration of the periods within which to reopen a proceeding or to appeal from an order or decree but also by a limitation statute as to any contest, six months under most of the torrens statutes. No one appears to have suffered from the shortness of the period and it obviates all necessity of examining the original proceeding six months after entry of the decree or registration. Not but that, as in the case of any judgment, a decree may be set aside for fraud. However this ground of attack need not concern a purchaser or mortgagee in that it is not available as against a bona fide purchaser without notice. In fact, the conclusiveness of the certificate is so strong that the certificate prevails when issued to a bona fide purchaser on the basis of a forged deed. So long however as the registered owner takes proper care of his duplicate there is no danger from this source in that a deed, or a purported deed, from him is inoperative and cannot be filed with the Registrar unless accompanied by the Owner's Duplicate. In case of loss or destruction of that instrument, the situation is the same as when a bond or a stock certificate is lost—no transaction regarding it is possible until there is a replacement. In the case of a title certificate this is accomplished by an order of court addressed to the Registrar, and entered only after ample testimony to establish the loss or destruction.

The superiority of the certificate system of evidencing title to land has been ably summarized in decisions of the courts among which are the following:

"The purpose of the judgment is to create a judgment in rem perpetually conclusive. Other proceedings in rem may determine the status of a ship or other chattel that is transient; this legislation provides for a decree that shall conclude the title to an interest that is as lasting as the land itself."

"The purpose of the Torrens law is to establish an indefeasible title free from any and all rights or claims not registered with the Register of Titles, with certain unimportant exceptions, to the end that any one may deal with such property with the assurance that the only rights or claims of which he need take notice are those so registered."

And these statements are particularly significant in contrast with one found in a case antedating the Torrens statutes and necessarily involving a title based upon the recording act, that "it is impossible in the nature of things that there should be a mathematical certainty of good title."

Barnett, Marketable Title Acts — Panacea or Pandemonium
53 Cornell L. Rev. 45, 92-94 (1967)

When a lawyer examines title to a piece of land, his title opinion is usually meant to reflect fully and accurately the present state of the complete record title. If he is both competent and careful, it will. And if all his requirements are satisfied, there seems to be little reason for any other expert handling a subsequent transaction involving the same land to cover the same ground again. He should simply pick up at the point in time when the first examiner left off. But since the bar has steadfastly refused to set up standards of competence for specialties within the law, and both examiners operate separately, with independent liabilities, the one dares not trust the other. Of course, within the same firm, whether it be a firm of lawyers or a title insurance company, no examiner ever retraces the steps of another, except perhaps unwittingly. The writer understands that in Florida, where a high percentage of the conveyancing bar participates in the same bar-related title insuring organization,[128] it is becoming the practice for participating lawyers to rely on the prior opinions of other participants. But until the liabilities of *all* examining experts are backed by the financial resources of the same organization, the waste resulting from repeated re-examinations of the same title will never be eliminated completely.

It may seem old hat to say so, but the writer does not see how the problem can be solved completely without resort to some type of official registration of the present state of the title — a sort of official title opinion that is constantly kept up to date. In other words, the need is for some type

---

128. The organization, Lawyers Title Guaranty Fund, has its own technique for assuring competence. This technique, which one might call the fraternity principle, probably leaves something to be desired in theory, though doubtless it works pretty well as a practical matter. Title examinations submitted to the Fund by an applicant lawyer are simply re-examined by a fully-participating member of the Fund until the latter is willing to certify to the Fund that the applicant has reached a safe level of proficiency. Thereupon the applicant is admitted to the fraternity. Since the Fund is out to corral all competent members of the conveyancing bar, and thereby keep lawyers' title services competitive with (or even preferable to) those of commercial title companies, there has been no problem of exclusiveness on the part of the fraternity.

of Torrens system. Such a system is not really such a radical departure from the recording system, except that the initial title examination results in an opinion that has official sanction, and each subsequent transaction is ineffective until officially noted on that "opinion." Thus, there is no need to retain for future examiners the records of all those past transactions on which the opinion is based. Under a Torrens system, of course, the initial title examination must be accompanied by an action in rem. But there are many land titles on which a quiet title action must be brought at some time or other, and, unlike the registration suit under a Torrens system, such an action does not have the advantage of being a "once-for-all" affair; an action of the same type may again become necessary to cleanse the records of accumulated "debris." Moreover, since many laymen are already familiar with a Torrens-type system in the motor vehicle registration laws, it should be much less likely to defeat their natural expectations than a marketable title act.

From the lawyers' point of view, there are two possible objections to a soundly-conceived, efficient title registration system. First, there will be an official check of their work product each time they handle a title transaction under a registered title. But a similar check exists under the recording system, namely, that provided by a subsequent title examiner. To have such a check provided immediately, rather than at the time of some subsequent title transaction, may, of course, be more embarrassing for the lawyer, but it is certainly better for the system. And the standards used in making the check are likely to be more uniform under a Torrens system. Second, a Torrens system may deprive lawyers of fees. But this fear is surely groundless. Lawyers would have to bring the initial registration suits under a Torrens system; many members of the conveyancing bar could be employed as special masters to examine titles for initial registration and, more permanently, as registrars, and lawyers will still have to handle all subsequent title transactions up to the point at which the executed instrument is sent to be registered. Lawyers should not find it difficult to justify charging the same fees for handling transactions under a Torrens system that they charge under the recording system.[129]

The writer is not necessarily suggesting that any particular Torrens act now on the books of any state or country is completely satisfactory; but surely it is possible to devise one that will operate just as quickly in effecting transfers as the recording system. While keeping titles far more reliable, a Torrens system can eliminate the tremendous waste and inefficiency of the recording acts. It is a baffling fact that the United States is rapidly becoming virtually the only country in the world whose land title system is not founded upon Torrens-type principles. The writer finds it incredible that

---

129. In most transactions today, the fee a lawyer can conscientiously charge is barely enough to compensate him for the time spent in preparing for and handling the closing. If he also prepares the contract of sale, he is over the limit. Thus, examining an abstract, let alone making a search through the records themselves, is rapidly becoming a profitless, as well as distasteful, chore.

a system which seems to work quite well almost everywhere else cannot be satisfactorily adapted to the United States. If all the brainpower expended by law professors and by the property-law sections of local, state, and national bar associations on marketable title acts were expended instead on devising a model Torrens act, surely a satisfactory adaptation could be found.[130]

With the opposition of the legal profession out of the way, only the abstractors and title insurance companies would be left. Their opposition is inveterate, because, as a Torrens system increases, they must decrease. Yet as long as these parasites that make their living off the inadequacies of the recording system succeed in enlisting the conveyancing bar in support of the proposition that "a little title examination is a good thing" (though all agree that too much is pure hell), legislatures are likely to continue to pass and courts to uphold, halfway measures like the marketable title acts, hoping to keep the whole present absurd system from collapsing under its own weight.

American Land Title Association, The Title Industry: White Papers
Vol. 1, pt. 5, 5-20 (1976)

THE PROBLEMS AND DRAWBACKS OF THE TORRENS SYSTEM

A. THERE ARE SUBSTANTIAL COSTS AND INCONVENIENCES IN THE INITIAL REGISTRATION OF A PARCEL IN THE TORRENS SYSTEM.

... The judicial proceeding that is needed to register a parcel in Torrens — a proceeding that may become quite complex and invariably

---

130. Professor Simes acknowledges that, in undertaking the research project initiated by the ABA Section on Real Property, Probate and Trust Law, which culminated in the publication of Simes & Taylor, he "disregarded as useless any investigation of the so-called Torrens Title Registration System." The reason given seems to be that in most American states where such legislation has existed, it hasn't been very successful—which is hardly the sort of reasoning to be anticipated in a project the very object of which is a general reform of inadequate statutory frameworks. He also says, addressing lawyers, that "whether we like it or not," the recording system will continue to be the heart of conveyancing. Simes, supra note 6, at 2358. Why this must be so, *whether the bar likes it or not*, the writer cannot fathom. Has the influence of lawyers and the organized bar in state legislatures atrophied to such an extent that they can do nothing without the support of the abstractors and title insurance companies? The writer feels that, unless lawyers resort to some co-operative plan such as the Florida Lawyers' Title Guaranty Fund, their role in land transactions will, sooner or later, be completely eliminated by the competition of title companies: "If you can't lick 'em, join 'em." A Torrens system, on the other hand, might well serve to rescue the conveyancing bar from such a fate, by eliminating every service title companies presently provide that cannot be considered the practice of law. Of course, there are those who fail to see any reason why the title companies should not be allowed to supplant lawyers completely in land transactions, but the writer is definitely not one of them.

will involve the services of an attorney experienced in Torrens matters—is necessary in order to ensure that the rights of parties with interests in the property are not arbitrarily cut off by the registration process. But fulfilling this requirement that all those with pre-existing interests be afforded due process of law through such a proceeding can involve a substantial amount of time and money. For example, in Suffolk County, Massachusetts, it is estimated that it takes between one and two years to register a parcel with the land court; in Hennepin County, Minnesota, which has a large staff of deputy examiners to process applications, an uncontested registration takes approximately six months, and a contested registration may take up to three years. Even in London, which is often cited as an excellent example of the feasibility of the Torrens system, registration invariably takes at least six to eight weeks, and frequently longer. A home owner may find that once he has initiated the registration process, he is unable to sell the property until the title certificate is actually issued. This is because a potential buyer may be unwilling to go ahead with the purchase while the registration litigation is pending.

The costs to the home owner of registering a parcel in Torrens are also substantially higher than the costs of transferring title under a recordation system. For example:

— In Suffolk County, Massachusetts, the average cost is approximately $1,500.
— In Cook County, Illinois, the costs of registering a $50,000 parcel averages about $500 to $600.
— In Hennepin County, Minnesota, the average cost for an uncontested registration is between $500 and $750.

The costs of trying to register all of the parcels in a given county under the Torrens system would involve astronomical sums. (As will be discussed shortly, to date only a relatively small proportion of the total parcels in the counties that have adopted Torrens have actually been registered.) For instance, the costs of registering all of the 280,000 assessed parcels of real estate in Hennepin County—a country with a population of less than 1 million—would be $140 million, and it has been estimated that the costs of registering all of the parcels in Pennsylvania would exceed $2 billion!

Three additional points should be noted in connection with the high initial costs of Torrens registration. First, contrary to the belief that the high initial costs are justified because of the savings that may be realized on subsequent transfers of the property, the fact is that the costs of subsequent transfers (for reasons that will be discussed below) may not be reduced substantially. Moreover, it is little comfort to a present owner of real property that he may have to incur very substantial expense, time and inconvenience in registering a parcel so that subsequent purchasers may realize some minor savings in title transfer costs.

Second, it has been argued by some that the government can "solve" the problem of the high initial registration costs of the Torrens system by subsidizing these costs. Apart from the many reasons why subsidizing uneconomic or undesirable ventures, such as a wholesale conversion to a Torrens system, makes little economic or political sense, there is a serious question of whether it is fair or equitable to ask taxpayers in general — many of whom may be in low or middle income brackets and who may never purchase a piece of real estate or who may only purchase a single home in their lifetime — to subsidize the costs of a real estate transfer system that will benefit primarily only a comparatively small number of people or corporations that are frequent sellers or purchasers of real estate.

Finally, an owner of a parcel of land registered in the Torrens system may not be finished with the courts after the initial registration. In some states, an owner of a lost certificate must petition the courts to have the Registrar of Titles issue an owner's duplicate certificate. Similarly, because of the conclusive nature of the Torrens certificate the Registrar may be unwilling to run the risk of issuing a new certificate to the heirs or devisees of a deceased registered owner, or to a person who may acquire the property by involuntary transfer, without the specific direction (and protection) of a court order. In fact, transfers by executors, trustees, guardians and attorneys-in-fact generally require court approval. All of these transfers involve additional time and costs beyond those that would be incurred in the transfer of the property under a recordation system.

B. THE PROBLEMS AND COSTS OF TRANSFERRING PROPERTY REGISTERED UNDER THE TORRENS SYSTEM ARE SUBSTANTIALLY GREATER THAN MAY BE COMMONLY UNDERSTOOD.

Proponents of the Torrens system frequently claim that while the costs of initial registration may be high, once a parcel of real estate is registered the owner can easily transfer the property by delivering the Torrens certificate to the buyer, that there is no need for any search of title records prior to the transfer, that the services of an attorney or title company can be dispensed with, and that the new owner can quickly and easily obtain a new Torrens certificate from the Registrar of Titles. Each of these claims warrants close scrutiny.

1. *A Search of Various Title Records Is Still Required before Registered Property Can Be Transferred.*

No Torrens system purports to require that *all* interests or rights in registered property be reflected in the Torrens certificate. As a result, any time registered property is sought to be transferred a determination must be made — which generally involves a search of various title-related records — of what other rights or claims must be taken into account by the buyer. . . .

To determine whether any of these potential claims may exist, a search and examination of tax, probate and court records is still required even under the Torrens system.

2. The Services of an Attorney or Title Company Will Still Be Required in the Transfer of Registered Property.

While the scope of the title search required in the subsequent transfer of registered property may be narrower than under a recordation system, the buyer's need for professional assistance in examining and evaluating the title information contained in a title certificate — and the attendant costs — will remain. A title certificate, after all, merely embodies in one document the various claims that have been registered against the property; the determination of the scope and effect of the various liens and claims memorialized in the title certificate — and the extent to which such liens and claims will affect the buyer's interest — will continue to be borne by the purchaser. Few purchasers of real estate, when presented with a title certificate by the seller indicating that various other persons (e.g., mortgagees, judgment creditors or other lienors, adjacent landowners claiming rights of way, government authorities, etc.) have registered claims against the property, are competent to interpret the significance of those claims. Consequently, most purchasers will not be willing to proceed with the purchase until they obtain professional assistance to determine the nature, scope and validity of these other claims or interests.

Moreover, the Torrens system does not eliminate the need for the drafting of documents, the handling of the closing or settlement, the proper disbursement of settlement funds and the filing with appropriate public authorities the various title documents — services that will continue to have to be performed by skilled professionals, whether private attorneys or title company personnel.

3. The Difficulties and Costs Incurred in the Registration of Interests That Have Been Transferred Are Greater Than May Be Popularly Assumed.

Under a recordation system, personnel in the Recorder of Deeds office do not have to make any substantive evaluation of documents presented to them for recording. As a result, relatively untrained personnel can be used, the number of employees needed can be kept to reasonable levels and generally there is little or no delay between the time a document is presented for recording and the time notice of the recorded document is given to the public.

Under a Torrens system, on the other hand, personnel in the Registrar of Title's office cannot simply register all documents presented to them, since the registration of a particular document — whether it be a deed, mortgage lien or other claim or encumbrance — has virtually conclusive legal effect. (In fact, the registration of a forged deed may wipe out the interest of the previous owner whose signature on the deed was forged.) Because of the important consequences that derive from the registration of a document, Torrens personnel must be highly trained in title matters (and therefore paid significantly higher salaries than clerical personnel in a Recorder of Deeds office), the number of Torrens personnel needed to handle a particular number of transactions is substantially greater than the number of employees that are needed under a recordation system,* and the delays and problems experienced in having a document or claim registered or in obtaining the transfer of a Torrens certificate are substantially greater than the recording of documents under a recordation system. In Suffolk County, Massachusetts, for example, it can take anywhere from two weeks to two months (depending on the complexity of the certificate and the other searches that are needed) from the time a request for a new certificate is made until the settlement can be held.

While the registration of a simple document or the transfer of a simple certificate may not involve major delays, the Registrar's office is naturally cautious — and, as a consequence, slow — in reviewing and evaluating all documents presented for registration. The Registrar's office must make sure that the document has the intended effect and that property rights are not mistakenly cut-off by the registration of incorrect or invalid documents. Titles that come through an estate, complex documents or documents that are not in absolute conformity with the rules of the Torrens office or with the outstanding Torrens certificate are frequently rejected for registration. In many cases, a court order must be obtained directing the Registrar to accept the document for registration. . . .

C. THE TORRENS SYSTEM OFFERS SUBSTANTIALLY LESS PROTECTION TO OWNERS AND OTHERS WHO HAVE INTERESTS IN REAL PROPERTY THAN IS OFFERED BY TITLE INSURANCE UNDER A RECORDATION SYSTEM.

Rights in real property have always enjoyed a unique place in American society; the encouragement and protection of home ownership has been a cornerstone of our laws and the growth of our economy. A fundamental aspect of the Torrens system, however, is directly contrary to these princi-

---

* In 1975, for example, while only 14% of real estate transfers in Cook County fell under the Torrens system, the expense to the county of running the Torrens Department was $1,574,000, compared to $868,000 for running the Recorder's Department, which handled 86% of the transfers of real property in the county. In 1976, the county budget calls for the employment of 134 people in the Torrens Department and 81 in the Recorder's Department.

ples. To ensure that the Torrens certificate represents a conclusive determination of the state of the title, the Torrens system provides that an administrative mistake or oversight in the registration of an interest or lien, or the registration of an interest in property acquired by fraud, may have the effect of summarily taking away a right in real property and substituting for it a right to financial compensation from the Torrens assurance fund. As Mr. Justice Oliver Wendell Holmes concluded in Eliason v. Welborn, 281 U.S. 457 (1930), when one deals with the Torrens system, all constitutional rights of due process are considered voluntarily waived.

But even assuming that financial indemnity can be an adequate substitute for the secure ownership of one's property, the protection offered by the Torrens assurance fund is significantly less than the protection afforded by title insurance. This Torrens assurance fund is generally established within each county by taking a portion of the registration and filing fees and setting them aside in a guaranty fund. In general, to recover from this fund, a person who has been deprived of an interest in land other than by the wrongful act or omission of an employee in the Registrar's office, must first attempt to recover against the person liable (e.g., the forger who has conveyed the real owner's interest). Only if the injured party cannot recover damages in this matter is he entitled to recover against the Torrens assurance fund. To do this he must bring suit against the fund.

The registered owner who must defend his title against challenges by parties whose rights are not cut-off by the registration process also has less protection than the owner who is protected by a title insurance policy. One of the most distinctive aspects of a title insurance policy is that the title insurer will pay for the costs of any legal defense against all claims to the title as insured, whether or not the claim is successful or unfounded. An owner of a Torrens certificate, on the other hand, must defend *at his own expense* his rights against all claims made against his title. Even if he is successful in this defense, he will have suffered expenses of litigation that are not reimbursable from the Torrens assurance fund.

An owner covered by a title insurance policy who suffers a title loss can recover up to the full face amount of the policy and can voluntarily increase his policy coverage to cover the increased value of his property. Under many Torrens systems, however, a person who has a valid claim against the Torrens fund can recover only up to the value of the property at the time the last payment into the Torrens fund was made with respect to the property.

Finally, the balances of most Torrens assurance funds are woefully small in relationship to the potential claims that may be made against the fund. Sloppy administration of a Torrens system can result in claims against the fund that are far in excess of the fund's resources — which is precisely what happened in California in the early 1950's, producing failure of the Torrens fund and the subsequent repeal of the California Torrens Act in 1955. Moreover, the total amount in the Hennepin County

Torrens Guaranty Fund as of December 31, 1975, was only $148,000, even though the fund has been in existence since 1901 and approximately one-third of the land in Hennepin County is under the Torrens system.

D. BECAUSE OF THE DIFFICULTIES, INCONVENIENCES AND COSTS ASSOCIATED WITH THE TORRENS SYSTEM, ITS USE IN AREAS WHERE IT HAS BEEN ADOPTED HAS BEEN LIMITED.

. . . Even in [the states with Torrens], in spite of the fact that the Torrens system may have been adopted 75 years ago or more, the overwhelming majority of transactions still take place under the recordation system.

For example, only 20-25% of all the tax parcels in Cook County have been registered in Torrens, and in 1975 only 14% of all real estate transfers in the county fell under that system. (Only nine applications for Torrens registration were filed during the year.) In Suffolk County, Massachusetts, less than 10% of the deeds recorded in the county in 1975 fell within the Torrens system, and in Ramsey and Hennepin Counties in Minnesota, only approximately one-third of the parcels are registered. . . .

Conclusion

The United States presently has a workable, effective system for the recordation and transfer of interests in land. While there may be certain shortcomings in this system, efforts to modernize and simplify the ways in which title records are maintained, indexed and retrieved are currently being pursued. Moreover, the goal of minimizing the costs and complexities of transferring title to real estate is a desirable one that is shared by the members of the American Land Title Association.

The belief, however, that broader use of the Torrens system can achieve the goals of simplifying land transfers or reducing the costs of such transfers, while at the same time maintaining the high level of protection and security that our society demands with respect to interests in real estate, is not supported by experience under the Torrens system. From a distance, the Torrens system appears to be an "easy" solution; but any examination of how the system really works, the costs and problems associated with it, and its lack of success in those areas where it has been tried, inevitably leads to the conclusion that home owners, home buyers and all who have interests in real property would not be well served by wider use of the Torrens system.

NOTE

The above evaluation of land title registration as it has operated in the United States is from a source, the American Land Title Association, which is strongly opposed to Torrens because Torrens is perceived as a threat to the Association's predominately title insurer and abstracter membership. To what extent are the problems and drawbacks of Torrens, as described by the American Land Title Association, legally and politically capable of being resolved in the United States? Why do you think that the White Paper did not give comparative conveyancing cost data for transactions in which title insurance has been obtained?

Anderson v. Shepard
285 Ill. 544, 121 N.E. 215 (1918)

CARTWRIGHT, J. Section 7 of an act entitled "An act to amend sections seven (7) and eighteen (18) of an act entitled, 'An act concerning land titles,' approved and in force May 1, 1897," contains the following provisions:

"It shall be the duty of all executors and administrators, appointed after the adoption of this act and trustees holding title or power of sale under wills admitted to probate after that date, to apply within six months after their appointment, to have registered the titles to all nonregistered estates and interests in land (situated in any county in which this act at the time is in force), which the several decedents they represent might have registered in their lifetime in their own right. Such application shall set forth the names and addresses of the persons entitled to the estate or interest sought to be registered, and any such person, not joining in the application, shall be made a defendant. The court, in its final decree, in addition to what is provided in the subsequent sections of this act, shall determine the several titles and interests of the persons claiming under the decedent, and declare the same, and decree in whom registration shall be made. Land so registered shall be subject to be sold for the debts of the estate of the decedent, as now provided by law: Provided, that the court of probate jurisdiction of the county in which the land is situated, in cases where registration may appear to be a hardship, may, by an order entered of record, excuse such application for registration as to the whole, or any part of the land." Laws of 1903, p. 121.

The act was only to be in force when adopted at an election, and after an abortive attempt to submit it for adoption in Cook county (Harvey v. Cook County, 221 Ill. 76, 77 N.E. 424) it was finally adopted at an election in November, 1910. The question to be decided is whether the provisions in question violate rights guaranteed by the Constitution, and that question arose in two cases under the following facts:

William Louis Shepard, the owner of lot 3 in block 3 in E.M. Condit's subdivision in section 29, town 38, range 14, died intestate on April 16, 1914, leaving Eleanor B. Shepard, his widow, and Katherine H. Shepard,

George P. Shepard, and William L. Shepard, his heirs at law. Katherine H. Shepard was appointed administratrix of his estate. The widow and all the heirs on November 20, 1917, conveyed the lot to William L. Anderson and Olga E. Anderson as joint tenants. On February 28, 1918, Katherine H. Shepard, as administratrix, applied to the probate court of Cook county for an order excusing her from registering title to the real estate, but the probate court denied her petition. William L. Anderson and Olga E. Anderson, owners of the property by the conveyance from the heirs at law, objected to the registration of their title by the administratrix on the ground that the provisions of the amendatory act were unconstitutional. The administratrix was proceeding to have the title registered when William L. Anderson and Olga E. Anderson filed their bill in the circuit court of Cook county to restrain the administratrix from proceeding to register the title. The administratrix demurred to the bill, and the demurrer was sustained and the bill dismissed.

Margaret Loranger, the owner of lots 8, 9, 10, and 11 in block 25 in Keeney's subdivision in Chicago Heights, died on February 19, 1916, leaving Louis Loranger, her husband, surviving her. On April 2, 1916, letters of administration were granted to Charles T. Mason, and he filed his petition in the probate court to be excused from making application to register the title to the lots and his petition was dismissed. He died before the estate was settled, and letters of administration de bonis non were granted to Shelby L. Mason on January 18, 1917. On October 16, 1917, Shelby L. Mason, as administrator de bonis non, filed his application in the circuit court to have registered the title to the real estate, and made Louis Loranger, the surviving husband, and the unknown heirs at law, if any, of Margaret Loranger, defendants. Louis Loranger answered, assailing the constitutionality of the provision in question, and alleged that he was sole heir at law of the deceased and objected to having his title registered. The court found that Louis Loranger was the sole owner in fee simple of the real estate and directed the title to be registered in his name, subject to certain charges and claims specified in the decree. Appeals were taken in each of the two cases and were consolidated in this court. The state's attorney of Cook county asked and obtained leave to intervene in the Loranger case as a representative of the public interest and of Joseph F. Haas, registrar of titles.

That section 7 as amended is arbitrary, offensive, and against common right cannot be doubted, and it invades rights guaranteed by the Constitution. On the death of an owner of real estate, the title vests at once in his heirs at law under the statute of descent, and, in case administration is granted, the personal estate vests in the executor or administrator upon the granting of letters testamentary or of administration. An executor has no estate in or power over the real estate of the testator by virtue of the law and has only such estate or power as is granted by the will. An administrator takes no title to real estate, either legal or equitable, but it descends to and vests in the heirs at once upon the death of the ancestor. The administrator has neither control over nor concern with the real estate, but becomes invested by the statute only with a mere naked power to apply to a court for and obtain leave to sell the same in case the personal estate is insufficient to pay debts. The heirs hold title in their own right, subject only to the payment of the debts of their ancestor in the particular mode prescribed by law and for the purpose prescribed and may sell and convey their title without hindrance. [Citations omitted.] Section 7 attempts to authorize executors and administrators, although they have no title to or control over real estate of the decedent, to apply for registering the title of the heirs and to make any heir who does not choose to join in the application a defendant and compel the registration of his title against his will. While an administrator has the title to the personal estate, he has only a right to apply to it the payment of debts and expenses of administration, and the residue belongs to the heirs at law; but the act permits an administrator or executor to expend personal estate belonging to the heirs for the employment of an attorney and payment of the costs of the proceeding, which are to be paid by the applicant. The proceeding is in equity, and there may be a void tax, claims, or other invalid charges against the land, and against them an owner may rest in security because they cannot be enforced against his property; but upon an application to register title the applicant must offer to, and the court will compel him to, reimburse the claimant. Gage v. Consumers' Electric Light Co., 194 Ill. 30, 64 N.E. 653; Harts v. Glos, 279 Ill. 485, 117 N.E. 68. The act would permit an administrator or executor to compel the heir at law to pay claims against which he would have a perfect legal defense. By the act money belonging to an heir at law may be taken from him and he made a defendant and subjected to trouble and expense for registering his title against his will.

It is not essential to the title of an heir at law that there should be any administration of the estate of the ancestor, and the act discriminates, without any reason, between heirs at law where there is administration and where there is not. Such a classification has no rational or reasonable relation to any conceivable purpose of the act. If the registration of the title of heirs at law is required in the public interest, the requirement applies equally to all heirs, and not to those, alone, where there is administration of the estate of the ancestor.

The act requires trustees holding title or power of sales under wills to apply for registration adversely to the beneficial owner, while trustees holding title or power of sale under conveyances, settlements, or any other instrument by which a trust may be created are exempt from the obligation, and there is no reason why an act should apply to one and not to the other.

The act provides that the probate court may excuse registration if it shall appear to be a hardship, and, whether such authority can be given to a probate court by which a law is to be enforced as to one person and not as to another, the act furnishes no standard for determining what shall be a hardship. There can be no hardship, in a financial sense, to an administrator, executor, or trustee if he has money belonging to the heirs above the payment of debts and expenses of administration of the estate or the trust; and, if the act contemplates an excuse where a hardship is on the owner of the land, the applicant to the probate court does not represent him, and he has no hearing, but is condemned without any opportunity to be heard.

It was said in People v. Simon, 176 Ill. 165, 52 N.E. 910, 44 L.R.A. 801, 68 Am. St. Rep. 175, which did not involve the question in any way, that the court saw no reason why the law might not make it compulsory to transfer real estate in the way contemplated by the act which was amended; but, if that is true, the General Assembly has made no provision that the title to real estate cannot be transferred except where it is first registered and then transferred in accordance with the act, but by this act an attempt is made to compel registration as to some owners and not as to others and without any regard whatever to alienation by the owner. The right or privilege of acquiring property by descent or devise is conferred by the statute, and inheritance taxes are sustained on the ground that the General Assembly may either deny the privilege entirely or prescribe the terms of its exercise. But this act does not prescribe the terms upon which property may be acquired by descent or devise, and, if it did, the act would still be invalid because it discriminates between different persons acquiring title by descent or devise and imposes the burden only in cases where there is administration.

The act is in violation of rights secured to the citizen by section 2 of article 2 of the Constitution, which provides that no person shall be deprived of life, liberty, or property without due process of law. Under that section of the Bill of Rights, neither the person nor property of an individual can be subjected to any liability or burden except by a law which operates equally upon all other persons in the same situation. Every one has a right to demand that he be governed by general rules, and a special statute which without his consent singles him or his property out to be regulated by a different law than that which is applied in all similar cases is prohibited by the Constitution. [Citations omitted.]

By what process a court, on an application by an administrator, executor, or trustee to register title, can compel an objecting defendant to reimburse the holders of stale and void claims against which he has a perfect defense, is not apparent; but, if the applicant is to make such an offer and to be required to reimburse the claimant, it must be for money belonging to the owner, and the Constitution does not permit such an invasion of private right. If the administrator seeks to be excused so that the law may not apply to him, the real party in interest has no hearing and is deprived of his property without process of law. For every reason specified above, the act is unconstitutional and void.

The decree in the case of Anderson v. Shepard is reversed, and the cause remanded, with directions to grant the relief prayed for in the bill, and the decree in the case of Mason v. Loranger is reversed.

Decrees reversed.

NOTES

1. Do you think that a compulsory system of Torrens registration could be worked out that would be constitutional in the United States? Is it likely that courts generally would today uphold the constitutionality of the statute struck down in Anderson v. Shepard? If so, why?

2. American Torrens statutes now in effect all provide that initial registration is voluntary; but once land has been registered, in some states it cannot be withdrawn from registration. For a statute providing for judicial proceedings to withdraw land from registration, see Ill. Ann. Stat. c. 30, §§96.1 to 96.7 (Smith-Hurd Supp. 1985).

b. Protection Provided

One of the most obvious advantages of a land registration system is the greater ease it provides for ascertaining the state of a title, as so much can be told just by examining the registration certificate. But in no jurisdiction is this advantage carried to its logical extreme and the certificate made the exclusive indicium of title. Wherever land registration is permitted, there are exceptions to what appears on the certificate necessarily being the sole or conclusive indication of legally protected rights in the registered land parcel. Valid off-certificate interests may exist and registered interests may even be invalid, the number and character of these possible exceptions to the binding effect of the certificate varying somewhat among jurisdictions with registration systems. This problem of off-certificate risks is analogous to that of off-record risks under the recording acts, and similar reasons apply in each of the two systems for making exceptions to a centralized public record of the state of the title. To some extent, off-certificate risks can be protected against by examining the premises, questioning knowledgeable parties or searching other public records, as is true of off-record risks under the recording acts. This ancillary checking is often done by lawyers in private practice representing land owners, claimants, prospective buyers or lenders. Such lawyers also bring initial registration proceedings and make registration submissions to the public examiners. Land title registration tends to reduce but not eliminate the title work of lawyers in private practice. Built into land registration systems are state administered insurance schemes applicable to all registered land parcels. These schemes provide compensation to some categories of persons who suffer losses in dealing with registered titles. The scope of coverage varies

Reforming the System   903

in different places but in some jurisdictions is more restrictive than the usual title insurance coverage offered by private insurers in the United States to those with recorded interests in land. Private title companies also will insure Torrens titles, and in the Chicago area, for example, such coverage is rather common.

NOTES

1. Express off-certificate exceptions are characteristic of Torrens statutes in the United States, although the statutes differ in the number and kind of exceptions. Typical of the exception statutes is Minn. Stat. §508.25(6) (Supp. 1985):

> Every person receiving a certificate of title pursuant to a decree of registration and every subsequent purchaser of registered land who receives a certificate of title in good faith and for a valuable consideration shall hold it free from all encumbrances and adverse claims, excepting only the estates, mortgages, liens, charges, and interests as may be noted in the last certificate of title in the office of the registrar, and also excepting any of the following rights or encumbrances subsisting against the same, if any:
> (1) Liens, claims, or rights arising or existing under the laws or the Constitution of the United States, which this state cannot require to appear of record;
> (2) The lien of any real property tax or special assessment for which the land has not been sold at the date of the certificate of title;
> (3) Any lease for a period not exceeding three years when there is actual occupation of the premises thereunder;
> (4) All rights in public highways upon the land;
> (5) The right of appeal, or right to appear and contest the application, as is allowed by this chapter;
> (6) The rights of any person in possession under deed or contract for deed from the owner of the certificate of title.
> (7) Any outstanding mechanics' lien rights which may exist under sections 514.01 to 514.17.

Why do you think the legislature included the exceptions listed in this section of the Minnesota statutes? Would any of them be valid encumbrances on Torrens titles even though not registered and not made exceptions by statute? How can a title examiner ascertain if a particular Minnesota land title is burdened with encumbrances of the kind listed in §508.25?

Some of the other American Torrens act exception sections are Hawaii Rev. Stat. §501.82 (1976); Ill. Ann. Stat. c. 30, §84.1 (Smith-Hurd Supp. 1985); and Mass. Ann. Laws c. 185, §46 (1977 and Supp. 1982).

2. American Torrens statutes generally provide that an owner of a registered land title may not lose his title by the adverse possession of

another. See, e.g., Minn. Stat. Ann. §508.02 (West 1946). What rationale is there for such a provision?

Eliason v. Wilborn
281 U.S. 457, 50 S. Ct. 382, 74 L. Ed. 962 (1930)

MR. JUSTICE HOLMES delivered the opinion of the Court. The appellants had been holders of a certificate of title under the Torrens Act of Illinois. As a result of negotiations they entrusted this certificate to one Napletone, who is alleged to have presented it together with a forged conveyance to himself to the Registrar and by those means to have obtained from the Registrar a new certificate of title in Napletone, on May 19, 1926. Napletone a few days later sold and conveyed to the Wilborns, appellees, whose good faith is not questioned. After the Wilborns had bought but before a new certificate was issued to them, they had notice of appellants' claim and the appellants notified the Registrar of the forgery and demanded a cancellation of the deeds and certificates to Napletone and the Wilborns and the issue of a certificate to themselves. The Registrar refused and this petition is brought to compel him to do what the appellants demand. It was dismissed on demurrer by the Circuit Court of the State, and the judgment was affirmed by the Supreme Court. 355 Ill. 352. The Supreme Court construed the statutes as giving title to the Wilborns, who purchased in reliance upon the certificate held by Napletone. Whether we are bound to or not we accept that construction and its result. The petitioners appealed to this Court on the ground that the statute, construed as it was construed below, deprived the appellants of their property without due process of law contrary to the Constitution of the United States, by making the certificate of title issued by the Registrar upon a forged deed without notice to them conclusive against them.

The sections objected to are appended. They are as in the original Act of 1897, except §40, amended by the laws of 1925, p. 250.*

---

* Section 40: "The registered owner of any estate or interest in land brought under this Act shall, except in cases of fraud of which he is a party, or of the person through whom he claims without valuable consideration paid in good faith, hold the same subject to the charges hereinabove set forth and also only to such estate, mortgages, liens, charges and interests as may be noted in the last certificate of title in the registrar's office and free from all others except:

(1) Any subsisting lease or agreement for a lease for a period not exceeding five years, where there is actual occupation of the land under the lease. The term lease shall include a verbal letting.

(2) General taxes for the calendar year in which the certificate of title is issued, and special taxes or assessments which have not been confirmed.

(3) Such right of appeal, writ of error, right to appear and contest the application, and action to make counterclaim as is allowed by this Act."

Section 42: "Except in case of fraud, and except as herein otherwise provided, no person taking a transfer of registered land, or any estate or interest therein, or of any charge upon

The appellants seem to claim a constitutional right to buy land that has been brought under the Torrens Act free from the restrictions that that Act imposes. But they have no right of any kind to buy it unless the present owner assents, and if, as in this case, the owner from whom the appellants bought, offered and sold nothing except a Torrens title we do not perceive how they can complain that that is all that they got. Even if the restrictions were of a kind that was open to constitutional objection, the appellants bought knowing them and got what they paid for, and knew that they were liable to lose their title without having parted with it and without being heard. Even if they had been the original holders under the Torrens Act and had attempted to save their supposed rights by protest the answer would be that they were under no compulsion when they came into the system, that an elaborate plan was offered of which the provisions objected to were an important part, and that they could take it as it was or let it

---

the same, from the registered owner shall be held to inquire into the circumstances under which or the consideration for which such owner or any previous registered owner was registered, or be affected with notice, actual or constructive, of any unregistered trust, lien, claim, demand or interest; and the knowledge that an unregistered trust, lien, claim, demand or interest is in existence shall not of itself be imputed as fraud."

Section 46: "The bringing of land under this act shall imply an agreement which shall run with the land that the same shall be subject to the terms of the act and all amendments and alterations thereof. And all dealings with land or any estate or interest therein, after the same has been brought under this act, and all liens, incumbrances and charges upon the same, subsequent to the first registration thereof, shall be deemed to be subject to the terms of this act."

Section 47: "A registered owner of land desiring to transfer his whole estate or interest therein, or some distinct part or parcel thereof, or some undivided interest therein, or to grant out of his estate an estate for life or for a term of not less than ten years, may execute to the intended transferee a deed or instrument of conveyance in any form authorized by law for that purpose. And upon filing such deed or other instrument in the registrar's office and surrendering to the registrar the duplicate certificate of title, and upon its being made to appear to the registrar that the transferee [sic] has the title or interest proposed to be transferred and is entitled to make the conveyance, and that the transferee has the right to have such estate or interest transferred to him, he shall make out and register as hereinbefore provided a new certificate and also an owner's duplicate certifying the title to the estate or interest in the land desired to be conveyed to be in the transferee, and shall note upon the original and duplicate certificate the date of the transfer, the name of the transferee and the volume and folium in which the new certificate is registered, and shall stamp across the original and surrendered duplicate certificate the word 'canceled.' "

Section 54: "A deed, mortgage, lease or other instrument purporting to convey, transfer, mortgage, lease, charge or otherwise deal with registered land, or any estate or interest therein, or charge upon the same, other than a will or a lease not exceeding five years where the land is in actual possession of the lessee or his assigns, shall take effect only by way of contract between the parties thereto, and as authority to the registrar to register the transfer, mortgage, lease, charge or other dealing upon compliance with the terms of this act. On the completion of such registration, the land, estate, interest or charge shall become transferred, mortgaged, leased, charged or dealt with according to the purport and terms of the deed, mortgage, lease or other instrument."

Section 58 (omitting immaterial parts): "In the event of a duplicate certificate of title being lost, mislaid or destroyed, the owner . . . may make affidavit . . . and the registrar, if satisfied as to the truth of such affidavit and the bona fides of the transaction, shall issue to the owner a certified copy of the original certificate . . . and such certified copy shall stand in the place of and have like effect as the missing duplicate certificate."

alone. There are plenty of cases in which a man may lose his title when he does not mean to. If he entrusts a check indorsed in blank to a servant or friend he takes his chance. So when he entrusts goods to a bailee under some factors' acts that are well known. So, more analogous to the present case, a man may be deprived of a title by one who has none; as when an owner who has conveyed his property by a deed not yet recorded executes a second deed to another person who takes and records the later deed without notice of the former. There are a few constitutional rights that may not be waived.

But there is a narrower ground on which the appellants must be denied their demand. The statute requires the production of the outstanding certificate, as a condition to the issue of a new one. The appellants saw fit to entrust it to Napletone and they took the risk. They say that according to the construction of the act adopted the Registrar's certificate would have had the same effect even if the old certificate had not been produced. But that, if correct, is no answer. Presumably the Registrar will do his duty, and if he does he will require the old certificate to be handed in. It does not justify the omission of a precaution that probably would be sufficient, to point out that a dishonest official could get around it. There is not the slightest reason to suppose that Napletone would have got a certificate on which the Wilborns could rely without the delivery of the old one by the appellants. As between two innocent persons one of whom must suffer the consequence of a breach of trust the one who made it possible by his act of confidence must bear the loss.

Decree affirmed.

NOTES

1. Do you think the result in the principal case would have been different if the facts had been the same except that Napletone had stolen the certificate from appellants?

In Fialkowski v. Fialkowski, 1 W.W.R. 216 (Alta. 1911), plaintiff owned registered lands, his certificate of title was stolen, the thief forged a transfer of the lands from plaintiff to himself, and upon submission of the certificate and transfer to the registrar secured a certificate in his, the thief's, name. The new certificate was then turned over to defendant bank as security for a loan. In an action seeking cancellation of the stolen certificate and issuance of a new certificate to plaintiff, the court held for defendant. Deposit of the certificate constituted an equitable mortgage, the court said, and in order to avoid this mortgage plaintiff would have to show that the bank participated in the fraud or at least had notice of it before obtaining the mortgage.

2. Note that in Eliason v. Wilborn, even if appellants were in possession when the Wilborns bought, the Wilborns presumably would still prevail. Under the Illinois Torrens Act a person acquiring a registered title

takes clear of the unregistered rights of a party in possession. Fraud by the transferee is an exception to this, but mere knowledge of the unregistered right or claim is not fraud. Bjornberg v. Myers, 212 Ill. App. 257 (1918).

On the *Eliason* facts, what would have been the result in Minnesota, considering particularly Minn. Stat. §508.25(6) (Supp. 1985), page 903 supra?

3. Mass. Ann. Laws c. 185, §46 (Supp. 1982), provides in part: "Every plaintiff receiving a certificate of title in pursuance of a judgment of registration, and every subsequent purchaser of registered land taking a certificate of title for value and in good faith, shall hold the same free from all encumbrances except those noted on the certificate, and any of the following encumbrances which may be existing. . . ."

The Massachusetts Supreme Judicial Court has held that purchasers of registered land take subject to unregistered interests of which they had actual knowledge when they took. "Any other construction would ignore the wording of section 46 which provides that one acquires registered land free from unregistered encumbrances if he is a purchaser for value and in 'good faith.'" Killam v. March, 316 Mass. 646, at 651, 55 N.E.2d 945, at 948 (1944). The *Killam* case was followed in Butler v. Haley Greystone Corp., 347 Mass. 478, 198 N.E.2d 635 (1964).

4. Basic to each Torrens system is a government-administered assurance fund available to compensate those suffering losses from operation of the system. In American Torrens states the fund is financed by payments from persons initially registering land and generally also from certain classes of transferors or transferees of registered titles. The amount of the payment, under most statutes, is one-tenth of one percent of the value of the property, valuation determined either by the registrar, a court, or from the last general property tax assessment. If the land subsequently increases in value, additional payments need not be made.

Most American Torrens funds apparently are safely solvent; the one for Cook County, Illinois, for example, apparently is further backed by the credit of the county. In some states, Massachusetts and Hawaii for example, funds are set up on a statewide basis, one fund for the entire state. In other states, such as Colorado, separate funds are provided for in each county, substantially increasing the chance of fund insolvency, especially in smaller counties. California's fund, however, which was statewide, only amounted to $39,000 in 1937 and became insolvent as the result of a $48,000 judgment in the case of Gill v. Johnson, 21 Cal. App. 2d 649, 69 P.2d 1016 (1937). 6A Powell, The Law of Real Property §908(3)(b), n.37 (1984). California's Torrens Act provided only for payments into the assurance fund at the time of original registration, the conventional rate of one-tenth of one percent of the land's value being charged. Cal. Gen. Laws Ann. act 8589, §100 (Deering 1944). No provision existed for making any governmental instrumentality responsible for making up losses if the fund became exhausted. For a statute requiring the state to make up deficiencies under such circumstances, see Mass. Ann. Laws c. 185, §104 (1977).

Each Torrens state has restrictions on when and under what circumstances those suffering losses may recover from the fund. Typical of such restrictions are those provided for in Mass. Ann. Laws c. 185, §101 (1977):

"A person who, without negligence on his part, sustains loss or damage, or is deprived of land or of any estate or interest therein after the original registration of land, by the registration of another person as owner of such land or of any estate or interest therein, through fraud or in consequence of any error, omission, mistake or misdescription in any certificate of title or in any entry or memorandum in the registration book, may recover in contract in the superior court compensation for such loss or damage or for such land or estate or interest therein from the assurance fund; but a person so deprived of land or of any estate or interest therein, having a right of action or other remedy for the recovery of such land, estate or interest, shall exhaust such remedy before resorting to the action of contract herein provided. This section shall not deprive the plaintiff of any action of tort which he may have against any person for such loss or damage or deprivation of land or of any estate or interest therein. But if the plaintiff elects to pursue his remedy in tort, and also brings an action of contract under this chapter, the action of contract shall be continued to await the result of the action of tort."

Overly solvent Torrens funds are subject to criticism, as these comments by an Australian lawyer indicate:

"One of the principal criticisms of the administration of the Australian Torrens acts, which all provide similar procedures for initial registration, has been that registrars have been far too finicky in scrutinizing applications for registration. There is criticism both of the reluctance of the registrars to register titles where there is merely a slight possibility of a defect and of the great wastage of manhours resulting from the minute and painstaking investigation of title that the registrars require. The fact that the registrars insist upon over-stringent requirements of initial registration has been amply demonstrated by reference to the state of the various Australian assurance funds. In New South Wales, contributions to the assurance fund were abolished in 1941 after some $A1,500,000 had been paid into the fund and about $A12,000 paid out. South Australia as of 1957 had a fund of about $A600,000, having paid out about $A7,000 in 45 years. The Victorian fund in 1957 stood at over $A300,000, but much more than that previously had been transferred from the fund to consolidated revenue — 93 claims on the fund had been admitted totaling less than $A25,000. . . ." Sackville, Some Aspects of the Torrens System in Victoria: A Comparison 37 (1966), an unpublished manuscript in the Yale Law Library collection.

"These failures on the part of the administrators of the Torrens scheme do not reveal a fundamental inefficiency or incompetence on their part, but simply a lack of imagination in seeking the most effective means of implementing the goals of the scheme. They have not been able to appreciate that their duty does not lie in protecting the assurance fund at all costs, but also in broadening the reach of the scheme, and that their real duty lies in achieving a sensible accommodation between these two aims." Id. at 30.

5. The English registration system, which is gradually becoming obligatory for that entire country, differs in important respects from the usual American Torrens system as set forth in American Torrens statutes. If interest in Torrens revives substantially in the United States, some features of the English system are likely to be enacted in American Torrens statutes to reduce the cost of initial registration and enhance general efficiency of operation. Among aspects of the English system that American states conceivably may borrow are these:

(1) initial registration by an administrative official, the registrar, rather than a court, with the registrar having considerable discretion in determining whether or not titles are adequate to merit registration;

(2) compulsory registration in certain counties and boroughs, eventually to include all sections of the country, whenever a freehold is conveyed or a long term lease is executed or transferred;

(3) parties in possession may have their titles registered "as is" at the time of registration, with subsequent transactions subject to the act and a possibility of the "as is" title becoming absolute with the passage of time;[44]

(4) land may be, and often is, registered with the exact boundaries left undetermined, the so-called general boundaries rule that reduces expenses and the prospect of dispute associated with registration; and

(5) registration is centralized in ten district land registries, each serving a sizable geographic area, and most public contact with the registrar's office is by mail.

Lane and Edson, Improving Land Title Registration Systems[45]

III-16 and 17 (1978)

Despite the serious problems revealed by the history of land title registration laws in the United States, the concept of state guaranteed land titles

---

44. These are known as possessory titles in England and may be registered by persons in actual possession of the land or by those receiving rents and profits from it. Applicants provide the registrar with whatever title documents they have, and make declarations of how long they have been in possession and of any encumbrances on the title of which they are aware. Registration of a possessory title does not prejudice the rights of any interest holders of whose rights the registrar was unaware at the time of initial registration. After fifteen years, however, an applicant in possession may have his possessory title converted to an absolute title. Curtis and Ruoff, The Law and Practice of Registered Conveyancing 92-94 (2d ed. 1965). It has been suggested that the English registered possessory title, in combination with a marketable title act or ten-year statute of limitations, might be worth adopting in the United States as one means of initially registering land and overcoming objections to Torrens. 6A Powell, The Law of Real Property §908(3)(b) (1984); and Fiflis, Land Transfer Improvement: The Basic Facts and Two Hypotheses for Reform, 38 U. Colo. L. Rev. 431, 474 (1966).

45. A report prepared for the U.S. Department of Housing and Urban Development, by Lane and Edson, pursuant to a contract with Booz, Allen and Hamilton.

has logical appeal and practical advantages and deserves consideration in any review of ways to achieve land title reform. However, the historical record demonstrates that there will be no future for the title registration system in this country unless the cost of initial registration can be cut substantially and unless the security provided by a certificate of title can be made equivalent to the protection now provided by title insurance. Cost reductions can be achieved by streamlining the initial registration procedure to remove those procedural requirements that can be eliminated without denying due process or sacrificing substantial accuracy of the registration decree. Acceptable security will inevitably follow if the coverage of a certificate of title is broad, if the registration procedure is well administered, if a readily accessible and ample assurance fund is maintained to compensate for errors, and if the system is designed to assure that registrations occur with sufficient frequency to familiarize the real estate industry and the public with the system.

Several factors have appeared that could contribute substantially to the revival and strengthening of a title registration approach.

First, the courts are likely to be more receptive to expedited—and hence faster and less costly—procedures for initial registration of land titles than might have been acceptable when the first Torrens statutes were enacted in the United States over 75 years ago. Although the courts have adhered to and frequently strengthened the fundamental protections of individuals guaranteed by federal and state constitutions, they have also become more flexible in sanctioning the procedures by which government actions are taken as long as fundamental rights are preserved. Thus, for example, the courts would now most likely approve a properly drafted title registration procedure conducted entirely by an administrative agency, subject only to judicial review for errors of law.

Second, the federal government has demonstrated an increased interest in urban development and a willingness to work with municipal and county governments for the improvement of American urban life. Through the contracts issued under the Real Estate Settlement Procedures Act and still broader federal planning programs, the federal government can stimulate much needed reform in land title records. Moreover, the federal government may be willing to contribute to the success of any land title registration system through its varied roles as purchaser, lienholder, lender and insurer of loans, although no willingness to do so has yet been demonstrated by the Department of Justice, the Internal Revenue Service, or the Federal National Mortgage Association. . . .

Third, dissatisfaction with present land transfer mechanisms and costs has increased to the point where lawyers and landowners may be receptive once again to experimenting with an effective title registration system.

A fourth factor referred to by recent writers as facilitating the implementation of a title registration system is the recent enormous advances in the processing, storage and retrieval of large amounts of data. However, while these technological advances permit a more rapid, economical consolidation of and access to records, and so must be taken into account, they do not address the principal problems faced by a title registration system.

3. Other Reforms and Reform Proposals

In addition to marketable title acts and title registration, a number of other reforms in the American system of land title protection have been proposed. Some of these ostensibly improved ways of doing things are operational already in some places, and their principal objective commonly is to enhance the efficiency of land title data storage and retrieval. Automation, using computers, is a means frequently suggested for increasing this efficiency. Reform efforts are often directed at the public sector, especially local government record keeping offices, as it is there that inefficiencies are most obvious.

This subsection highlights some of the more important modern proposals for land title reform in the United States other than marketable title acts and land title registration. Excerpts are included from background studies on land title systems made for the U.S. Department of Housing and Urban Development by Booz, Allen and Hamilton, and Lane and Edson, followed by an IBM official's statement on title data mechanization. Also included are commentaries on the Uniform Simplification of Land Transfers Act and the Real Estate Settlement Procedures Act. The reforms considered in this subsection are indicative of some of the important respects in which American land title protection systems may change over the next few decades, and the significant points at which resistance to change may prevail.

Booz, Allen and Hamilton, State-of-the-Art Report[46]
123-125, 139-141, 144-145, 155-156, 159-160, 163-164 (1978)

RECOMMENDED IMPROVEMENTS TO LAND TITLE RECORDATION SYSTEMS

The existing legal, political, economic, and technological framework in the United States allows for substantial improvement in local government land title operations. Most local government land title recordation operations can benefit from operational and procedural enhancements. These enhancements should be directed to improving the timeliness and efficiency of local government land title operations. . . .

Each of the six enhancements discussed in this chapter can, and should

---

46. A report prepared for the U.S. Department of Housing and Urban Development, pursuant to a contract with Booz, Allen and Hamilton.

be, developed according to the unique specifications of each local government land title recordation operation. . . . The designs of the enhancements discussed in this chapter are directed at representative land title recordation operations in jurisdictions across the country. In fact, many of the enhancements have been successfully utilized by both the private sector title services industry and select public jurisdictions.

The innovative features discussed in this chapter do not present complex technological solutions to operational problems. Rather, these enhancements are a consolidation of proven file management, document storage, information indexing, and management control procedures. These features are representative of newly developed information resource management industry techniques. . . .

1. PARCEL INDEXING WILL SIMPLIFY LAND TITLE RECORDS STORAGE, RETRIEVAL, MAINTENANCE, AND EXAMINATION

The concept of parcel indexing is neither new nor unproven in the land title records management field. The title services industry has, for many years, successfully utilized parcel identification numbers to relate land title documents to specific parcels of real property. By establishing geographic indexes to land title documents, private sector title service firms have simplified the maintenance storage access and retrieval of those records. The management and use of land title data is more logically served by assigning unique numeric identifiers to a parcel and labelling all documents referring to that property with that identifier.

The utility of parcel indexes transcends all uses of real property related information. Numeric parcel identifiers allow related real property data to be linked together to form a central source of parcel level information. For example, information from the tax assessor's office pertaining to property, description value and ownership can be linked to ownership transfer and sale price data from recorded land title documents by a unique parcel identifier. Similarly, planning and zoning information can also be linked to land title data by a unique parcel identifier thus allowing a review of possible use restrictions prior to a property transfer. . . .

2. GRANTOR/GRANTEE OR ALPHABETIC NAME INDEXES SHOULD BE CONSOLIDATED INTO A SINGLE INDEX AND AUTOMATED IF FEASIBLE AND PRACTICABLE

The maintenance of alphabetic name indexes to land title documents is required by law in all 50 states. The specific format and number of different indexes varies from state-to-state. While the requirement for and use of these indexes will be greatly reduced if land title recordation jurisdictions maintain parcel indexes, it will still be necessary to maintain alphabetic name indexes. Name indexes will be required to index those documents affecting the assets of individuals without specifically identifying the parcels [of] real property owned by that individual. Documents that fall into this category are primarily judgment and tax liens.

Modifications to the statutes governing the use and maintenance of alphabetic name indexes must be made to improve their utility. A single, general alphabetic name index should be maintained by a recording jurisdiction rather than the current practice of maintaining separate grantee/grantor indexes for deeds, mortgages, judgments, and other documents. Some jurisdictions are currently maintaining as many as seven separate grantor/grantee indexes. By eliminating multiple indexes and requiring a single consolidated alphabetic name index, the title search and examination process should be facilitated.

There is no need, for the most part, to modify existing manual name indexes in most jurisdictions beyond consolidation. There is little that can be done to enhance a manual name index and improve its use or ease of maintenance. Thus, in those jurisdictions with low recording volumes and no access to data processing support, the existing approach to indexing documents by name is sufficient once consolidated into a central alphabetic index. This approach, when supplemented with parcel indexing capabilities, should prove to be sufficient to meet most name indexing requirements.

Alphabetic name indexes do, however, lend themselves easily to automation. Those jurisdictions with access to data processing capabilities and sufficient recording volume may merit automated support of their name indexing function. Most jurisdictions can easily support both automated parcel indexing and automated, consolidated, alphabetic name indexing. . . .

3. MICROGRAPHICS SUPPORT FOR RECORDS MANAGEMENT IS A MANDATORY FEATURE OF A MODERN LAND TITLE SYSTEM

Land title records retention and storage is an ongoing function that increases in scope and volume in each succeeding year. Costs associated with records retention and storage may be well-defined for individual jurisdictions in terms of necessary clerical support and physical space storage requirements. These costs have risen steadily in the past and according to current indications, will continue to rise in the future. Only the use of micrographics can stem increasing records retention and storage requirements costs for land title operations.

The cost of micrographic technology has decreased rapidly over the past two decades. Now it is possible for even small, low-volume recording jurisdictions to utilize some form of micrographics support. . . . Of the current approaches to micrographics that are available, microfilm roll or cartridge, microfiche, and microfilm jacket systems are all acceptable micrographic media. . . .

4. RAPID INSTRUMENT PROCESSING CAN LOWER DOCUMENT PROCESSING COSTS AND IMPROVE CONSUMER SERVICES WITHOUT SUBSTANTIAL COST INCREMENTS AND WITHOUT THE NEED FOR COMPLEX TECHNOLOGICAL SUPPORT

Land title records must be recorded, indexed and, in most cases, a facsimile of the original document must be copied and stored by public sector recording jurisdictions. The original land title documents recorded belong to the citizens who filed them, thus forcing jurisdictions to develop techniques to copy the documents. . . .

Recordation jurisdictions can eliminate several steps involved in processing original land title documents. By installing reproduction (copying) equipment at the initial stages of the land title document recording process, local jurisdictions can eliminate most of the clerical processing of original land title documents. The original document can be returned to the consumer or delegated agent at the time of recording. This process, entitled rapid instrument processing (RIP), also allows jurisdictions to avoid the expenses associated with returning the original documents to their rightful owners. These expenses, clerical processing, envelopes, postages, etc., are fixed and if not eliminated, will continue to increase over time. . . .

5. STANDARD LAND TITLE DOCUMENT FORMS SHOULD BE DEVELOPED AT A STATE OR LOCAL LEVEL AND THEIR USE SHOULD BE MANDATED IN REAL PROPERTY CONVEYANCING

Land title recordation operations must, in addition to fulfilling legal recordation requirements, process land title documents to facilitate the title search and examination functions performed by the title services industry. The title search process which precedes the land title document examination process can be significantly simplified by placing variable instrument data in uniform and consistent location [within] the document. Standardized data locations can allow simplified document review and verification activities. Specific information such as grantor, grantee, property legal description and parcel identifier, recording date, and other information should be consistently placed in the same location on every land title document.

In a similar fashion, standard land title documents can improve the efficiency of title examinations. By placing all relevant variable data in a single location on a standard form, title examiners can quickly identify non-standard conditions affecting a property which are documented on a land title instrument. Standard land title documents should prove extremely valuable for most residential real estate transactions which are not

Reforming the System   915

contested and involve simple transfers. Since these transactions make up the largest volume of real estate transactions processed by most recording jurisdictions, standard forms should have a measurable impact on recordation, search, and examination functions. Instruments which should be considered for standardization include:

- Deeds
- Mortgages
- Leases
- Mechanic's liens
- Releases
- Satisfactions
- Reconveyances
- Consignments
- Tax liens (Federal, state, and local)
- Judgments (or abstracts thereof). . . .

6. ALL LEGAL DOCUMENTS AFFECTING THE CONVEYANCING OF REAL PROPERTY SHOULD BE RECORDED IN A COMMON RECORDING OFFICE

The most effective way to reduce title search and examination time and costs is to centrally process and locate all records impacting real property conveyancing. By centrally locating and maintaining all land title records in a single local government agency, consumers and the title services industry can receive improved services and efficiency of operations. Title recordation and maintenance functions may currently be performed by a combination of local government agencies, including clerks, recorders, clerks of courts, auditors, registrars of deeds, treasurers, and other officials. While it is not the intent to create a large bureaucratic land record agency, it is desirable, from a land title perspective, to consolidate land title recordation and maintenance functions in a single agency.

The proposed consolidation of title-related information in a single office would easily support the goal of effective land title recordation operations. A central land title records office should facilitate the development and use of a single parcel index and a single alphabetic name index to identify all interests in a specific parcel of real property. Central indexes will eliminate the need to access the records of several local government offices when attempting to establish a chain of title. A single recording office will also facilitate and enhance the title examination process. Finally, the central recording office concept provides for a single series of maintenance procedures, eliminating redundant indexes, duplicate storage systems, and redundant data sources. . . .

Lane and Edson, Land Title Recordation Systems: Legal Constraints and Reforms[47]

V-10 to 13 (1978)

The automation of land title records utilizing advanced computerized techniques for recording, storing and retrieving large volumes of data holds considerable promise for increasing the efficiency of recording offices, both internally and for its users. . . .

The legal constraints on automating land title records will vary depending upon the coverage of the automated system. Policy makers considering the desirability of automating the land title records will have to make an initial set of decisions among the following:

1. *Automate only selected functions in the recording office.* For example, it might be found most economical for a moderately busy recording office with extensive microfilming equipment already in place to automate only their grantor-grantee indexes, but retain the microfilm system for copying and storing documents. A number of private title plants combine automated functions with manual functions.

2. *Automate all title records in the recording office.* This option would establish a single automated system for all indexes and records maintained in the recording office.

3. *Automate all title records in the county or state.* This would be a far more ambitious undertaking and can be achieved in one of two ways. One way would be to enact legislation to force all land title information presently existing outside of the recording office to be recorded in the recording office where it would be placed in the recording office's automated system. The principal changes here would involve judgment liens, real estate tax liens and assessments, transfers by will or intestate succession, and federal and state income tax liens. . . .

The other way to achieve a fully automated state-wide title information system would be to automate the data existing in these other government offices — the tax assessor's and collector's office, the courts, the bureaus of vital statistics, and so forth — and then interconnect the data information systems so they may all be accessed from the terminals serving the recording office. This program would be a very expensive undertaking and probably politically infeasible because of the extent of interjurisdictional coordination required.

Any policy decision to automate the land title records must also address whether the automation should be prospective only or retroactive as well. While it would be clearly desirable to achieve a completely automated system as rapidly as possible, budgetary limitations might limit the extent to which back records can be read into the automated system. . . .

---

47. A report prepared for the U.S. Department of Housing and Urban Development, pursuant to a contract with Booz, Allen and Hamilton. Footnotes omitted.

Reforming the System

Assuming for present purposes that it is practical to consider automating only the recording office, as it presently functions, the minimum legal requirements are not many. They are:

1. *Eliminate all restrictive statutory specifications governing how land title records should be maintained.* Laws in those states that require that indexes and copies of recorded documents be maintained in bound volumes must be repealed. So too must those laws requiring the use of microfilming techniques. The authorizing legislation should impose the duty to maintain records on the recording office, but should leave it to that office to determine how best to accomplish it. . . .

2. *Eliminate the requirement that grantor-grantee indexes be maintained and substitute some form of parcel or geographic index.* Although a grantor-grantee index can be computerized, an entire automated record-keeping system must be organized around the individual parcel, and the parcel or geographic index is the key access point to the system. This should be the legal index on which purchasers are legally entitled to rely.

3. *Establish a system of parcel identifiers and require that every conveyancing document include its unique parcel identifier.* The problem is that the metes and bounds method of parcel description is too lengthy for practical use by a computer. . . . [T]he parcel identifier should be a number, but the number does not have to be related to the geographic location of the parcel. The parcel identifier number can be arbitrary and random as long as only one number is assigned to each parcel and that number is never reassigned to any other parcel in the jurisdiction.

In addition to these three requirements, there are a number of other statutory provisions that would be desirable to have to establish and operate an efficient automated title records system. Some of these are listed without regard to their relative importance. Other desirable provisions could probably be added to this list.

1. *Establish a system of personal identifiers and require that every conveyancing document identify the parties with their personal identifiers.* An automated system can function without personal identifiers, and automated private title plants do not now have personal identifiers. But the efficiency of the system is reduced. Because of the duplication of names, and because of the possibility of variant and sound-alike names, the automated system will have to retrieve a considerable amount of unnecessary information that the title searcher must then sort through manually. Complex systems have been developed by which computers will search through judgment information to identify all identical, variant and like-sounding names, but individual judgments are ultimately necessary to determine whether any of these names relate to the owner of the parcel in issue. These complexities can be eliminated with a universal system of unique personal identifiers. Then the computer would be able to limit its search to a single unique identifier, whether a number or a combination of words and numbers.

As discussed earlier in Part II-A, given the problems with using social security numbers, the best approach to a unique personal identifier might be to use the person's full name followed by numerals representing his birth date. . . .

2. *Place the risk of indexing errors on the recording party.* In a manual system . . . it seemed to be the better, but minority view to place the burden of loss from indexing errors on the party submitting the document for recordation since he can later check to be sure that the document has been indexed correctly. In an automated system, the recording office is able to return a copy of the indexing entry to the recording party much faster than in a manual system. Such a legal requirement would provide a helpful verification of the correctness of the entries made into the computerized data system.

3. *Reduce the length of title histories through marketable title acts.* By reducing the necessary length of title histories, the transitional period to a completely automated recording office system can be shortened without having to transcribe existing recorded information to the data processing system.

4. *Establish a state review and coordination function.* The operation of computers are not widely understood by non-specialists, and experience with computerized operations is probably lacking in most county recording offices. Effective computer hardware and software salesmen could have an undue influence in the local decision-making process. Further, it would be desirable to have the computerized system throughout the state as nearly uniform and compatible as possible, both for the convenience of the conveyancing professionals who will be dealing with recording offices and their requirements in more than one county, and to permit an eventual linkage of the county title records with the pertinent state-maintained records and with information in other counties. A state office, staffed with experienced persons, would seem vitally important to provide technical assistance to the county offices seeking to establish automated offices and to assure state-wide compatibility. North Carolina has established such an office as a part of its state land records management program. . . .

5. *Establish standard form legal instruments.* The efficiency of a computerized operation would be enhanced if standard legal forms were prepared for those real estate transactions that are capable of standardization. This should include most single family residential transactions. . . .

There are other measures that would help an efficient automated operation that may not require legislation if there is authority to adopt them by regulation or administrative implementation. These would include:

1. *Machine readable documents.* Optical scanners are now available to read and record written documents using special type faces which nevertheless are also readable by persons. This type can be easily inserted into most ball-type standard typewriters. Thus, it would seem to be feasible to require that all conveyancing documents being recorded be typed with machine readable type.

2. *Require summary information to accompany conveyancing documents being recorded.* As a condition for recording, certain summary information should be provided on a special form which includes the names of the parties, their personal identifiers, a description of the property and its parcel identifier, the type of conveyancing document being recorded, and the date. This information will facilitate the entry of the data into the computerized system, whether done manually or by machine-readable type....

3. *Establishment of multiple computer terminals.* Once the recording office information has been fully automated, there is no reason why arrangements cannot be made for title attorneys and abstractors and title insurance companies to have computer terminals in their own offices, to be used 24 hours a day at their convenience.

Bruce, An Overview of the Uniform Land Transactions Act and the Uniform Simplification of Land Transfers Act
10 Stetson L. Rev. 1-2, 13-19 (1980)

I. HISTORICAL BACKGROUND

A historical note is initially in order. The Commissioners began work in this area in 1969 by appointing a special committee to draft an act that would revolutionize and standardize real property law in the way the Uniform Commercial Code (UCC) accomplished that task for personal property law. The special committee responded with an original draft entitled ULTA, which covered the gamut of real property issues including contracts, conveyances, mortgages, condominiums, recording, priorities, mechanics' liens and land records. After considerable deliberation the Commissioners decided in 1975 that the original draft was unwieldy and should be broken into three separate acts. The material dealing with contracts, conveyances, and mortgages was retained and approved in 1975 under the ULTA label. The portion of the original draft dealing with recording, priorities, mechanics' liens, and land records was separated for further consideration. It was redrafted as USLTA and approved by the Commissioners in 1976. The portion of the original draft dealing with condominiums was also separated for further consideration. It was redrafted as the Uniform Condominium Act and approved by the Commissioners in 1977. Because the Uniform Condominium Act deals with a highly specialized area and approaches that area in a manner that is significantly different from the ULTA and USLTA approach, it is not treated in this article.

State legislatures did not immediately react to the Commissioners' approval of ULTA in 1975 and USLTA in 1976. One reason for this legislative reticence was that the American Bar Association withheld its approval of the acts pending a thorough review of each of them. Committees appointed by the Real Property Division of the Section of Real Property, Probate and Trust Law of the ABA studied ULTA and USLTA and suggested numerous drafting changes to each act. The Commissioners met with the ABA committees and as a result formally amended ULTA and USLTA in 1977. The ABA in turn approved both acts as amended in February, 1978. . . .

III. Uniform Simplification of Land Transfers Act (USLTA)

. . . USLTA is designed to complement ULTA. Thus, it serves many of the same purposes. Both acts are intended to promote the interstate flow of funds for real estate transactions and to protect consumer buyers and borrowers. In addition, USLTA was drafted to further the security and certainty of land titles, to reduce the costs of land transfers, to balance the interests of all parties in the mechanics' lien area, and to create a more efficient system of public land records. . . .

ARTICLE 2 — CONVEYANCING AND RECORDING

The portion of Article 2 dealing with recording represents an additional significant change in prior law. Virtually all restrictions on the eligibility of documents for recordation are abolished. Even the lack of an acknowledgment or witnesses does not prevent recordation. Although this approach promotes the efficient operation of the recorder's office, the elimination of the requirement for an acknowledgment or witnesses has been criticized on the ground that USLTA makes it simpler for dishonest persons to deal with real estate. Nevertheless, the Commissioners' position is that the existing requirements are anachronisms and that the recording problems they create outweigh benefits resulting from their possible prevention of fraud. . . .

ARTICLE 3 — PRIORITIES, MARKETABLE RECORD TITLES, AND EXTINGUISHMENT OF CLAIMS

. . . Article 3 also includes a complete marketable title act[97] and related curative provisions and limitations.[98] The purpose of the marketable title

---

97. Id. §§3-301 to 3-309. USLTA's marketable record title provisions are derived from the Model Marketable Title Act. Florida has already adopted legislation based on the Model Act. See id. Art. 3, Part 3, Introductory Comment; Fla. Stat. §§712.01 to .10 (1979).

98. USLTA §§3-401 to 3-411 (1977 version).

act is to limit title search to thirty years and extinguish any interests that antedate the root of title. The curative provisions and limitations are designed to automatically correct various title defects after the defects have been on record for a specified period and to resolve other questions of title, such as adverse possession, as quickly as is reasonably possible. Thus, this portion of the Act greatly simplifies title examination and should thereby reduce associated costs. . . .

ARTICLE 5 — CONSTRUCTION LIENS

This Article deals with the knotty problem of mechanics' liens. It is titled "Construction Liens" because the Commissioners believed that the title "Mechanics' Liens" would improperly imply that laborers were the primary beneficiaries of the law.[105]

One is at first tempted to say that an effort to bring uniformity to this area of the law is merely an exercise in futility because two virtually insurmountable obstacles stand in the way of reform. First, the variation among state mechanics' lien laws is greater than in any other statutory area.[106] Thus, the USLTA approach will be totally unfamiliar to the legislatures of most states. Florida is a notable exception, because the basic structure of Article 5 was borrowed from the existing Florida mechanics' lien law.[107] Second, numerous groups — owners, construction lenders, general contractors, subcontractors, and material suppliers — have conflicting interests in the contest for priority. The Commissioners were forced to strike a compromise that left all parties somewhat unsatisfied.[108] Hence, there are numerous potential opponents of Article 3 in each state.

Notwithstanding these obstacles, there is some possibility that Article 5 will gain favor. The present variety of mechanics' lien laws has made the activities of national lenders, suppliers, and builders more costly. The Act's effort to indirectly reduce building costs by achieving uniformity among the states in this area is sure to attract some proponents. Further, the Florida experience can be used as an example of how Article 5 will work in practice. . . .

Under USLTA any person who furnishes materials or services for construction is allowed a lien no matter how far he is removed from the contracting owner.[110] This approach is considerably more liberal than that taken by many state statutes which do not protect sub-subcontractors.[111]

---

105. USLTA, Art. 5, Introductory Comment (1977 version).
106. Id.
107. Fla. Stat. §§713.01 to .37 (1979).
108. . . . The organizations representing subcontractors and material supplies have expressed the most dissatisfaction.
110. Id. §5-201.
111. Id. Art. 5, Introductory Comment.

The Act also takes a liberal stance in its provision that a supplier obtains a lien whenever there is specific evidence that the supplier believed that the goods would be used on a particular site.[112] Unlike many existing statutes, Article 5 does not require delivery to the construction site as a precondition to the creation of a lien.[113]

The second area of mechanics' lien law affected by USLTA is priority of lien claimants over third parties. Article 5 rejects the popular view that claimants' liens date from the time construction actually commenced.[114] Because the visible commencement of construction is often an ambiguous event,[115] the Act adopts a notice recording system, similar to that used in Florida, under which the owner records a "notice of commencement" to make third parties aware that construction liens may be claimed against the property.[116] Under this system, construction lien claimants take priority over third parties whose encumbrances attach to the property after the notice of commencement is recorded.[117] Thus, the integrity of the recording system is promoted and the secret lien problem is avoided.[118]

The third area of impact of Article 5 is its effect on the liability of the owner to a lien claimant when the owner has paid the general contractor in full, but the general contractor has failed to pay the lien claimant.[119] At present some states protect the owner from double payment, others do not. USLTA offers each alternative, but the Commissioners state a preference for the provision eliminating liability for double payment.[121] . . .

---

112. Id. §5-204(a). The materials, of course, actually must be used in the construction.
113. The delivery of materials to the site, however, is still important. Under Article 5 it creates a presumption that the materials in fact were used in the course of construction. Id. §5-204(b).
114. Id. §5-301.
115. . . . Courts disagree as to whether such things as piling lumber on the land or clearing the land constitutes visible commencement of construction. . . .
116. USLTA, Art. 5, Introductory Comment (1977 version); id. §5-301. The Act does not totally abandon the visible commencement view. If a notice of commencement is not recorded, liens date from visible commencement of construction. Id.; see also id. §5-207(c).
117. Id. §5-209. The construction lien even has priority over all future advances made under a prior recorded security interest unless the advance is made under a construction security agreement and is for payment of the improvements, protection of the security interest or payment of a prior lien. Id.; see Note, Future Advances Under the ULTA and the USLTA: The Construction Lender Receives a New Status, 34 Wash. & Lee L. Rev. 1027 (1977).
118. . . . Among themselves, construction lien claimants on a particular site have equal priority. USLTA §5-208.
119. USLTA Art. 5, Introductory Comment (1977 version).
121. USLTA §5-206, Alternative A (1977 version) (The owner is protected from double payment); id. §5-206, Alternative B (The owner, if not a protected party, is liable for double payment).

ARTICLE 6 — LAND RECORDS

Article 6 applies to land records, the duties of local recording officers, and the duties of the state recording officer.[123] It envisions the continuation of the present recording system with two basic modifications: (1) the addition of a limited geographic or tract index system and (2) the creation of a state recording officer.[124]

The use of a geographic or tract index would certainly ease record examination. Under such a system all documents dealing with a particular parcel of land are listed together in the index. This is in stark contrast to the grantor-grantee index system where the title examiner must often examine several different indices.[126] Article 6, however, does not mandate the immediate elimination of the grantor-grantee index system.[127] Instead, a dual system of indexing is contemplated.[128] The main obstacle to a dual indexing system is a financial one. The expense of establishing and maintaining a separate tract index may cause many state legislatures to shy away from this portion of USLTA.

The Act's other basic modification of the existing land record system — the creation of a state recording officer — should be more readily accepted.[130] The cost of such a modification is minimal and the need for coordination of state recording procedures is great. Hence, the various state legislatures should have little hesitancy in adopting a provision of this type.

NOTES

1. Neither the Uniform Simplification of Land Transfers Act nor the Uniform Land Transactions Act has been adopted by any state. Given the time, effort, and money that go into the preparation of uniform acts, can such ventures be justified if the acts are never adopted, and if early on in preparation it is obvious that few if any adoptions are likely? Highly knowledgeable and able legal scholars and practitioners did the drafting and evaluation of both the USLTA and ULTA. Were they wasting their time?

2. On the Uniform Simplification of Land Transfers Act, see also

---

123. USLTA §6-101 (1977 version).
124. Id. §6-101, Comment.
126. Id. at 280-81.
127. USLTA §6-207, Comment (1977 version).
128. The Commissioners' adoption of a limited geographic index to be used in conjunction with the existing method of indexing has been criticized as being too modest a reform. . . .
130. USLTA §6-302 (1977 version).

Curtis, Simplifying Land Transfers: The Recordation and Marketable Title Provisions of the Uniform Simplification of Land Transfers Act, 62 Or. L. Rev. 363 (1983); Maggs, Land Records of the Uniform Simplification of Land Transfers Act, 1981 So. Ill. U. L.J. 491 (1981); Mattis, The Uniform Simplification of Land Transfers Act: Article 2 — Conveyancing and Recording, 1981 So. Ill. U. L.J. 511 (1981); and Comment, The Uniform Simplification of Land Transfers Act: Areas of Departure from State Law, 73 Nw. U.L. Rev. 359 (1978).

3. One purpose behind the USLTA and ULTA is to reduce land transfer costs, of which title examinations and evaluations are significant elements. Reducing or holding down so-called settlement or closing costs is an issue of popular concern that periodically surfaces in the political arena. In the early 1970s, Congress and relevant federal agencies explored the need for federal regulation of settlement costs in the transfer and financing of residential properties. In 1974, Congress passed the Real Estate Settlement Procedures Act of 1974 (RESPA), substantially revising it in a 1975 enactment, 12 U.S.C.A. §§2601 et seq. (West 1980 and Supp. 1985). The act, as revised, stresses lowering costs by making buyers more informed; this is to be achieved by requiring that those providing settlement services, lenders particularly, provide buyers with designated settlement cost information. The act also prohibits referral fees and fee splitting among providers of settlement services; requires that in home loan closings covered by the act a standard settlement statement form be used; and authorizes HUD to research land title operations and set up a few model systems. The act applies to most transactions that involve first mortgage loans on real estate. More specifically, for the act to apply, the loan must be federally related, and this means it must be federally assisted; made by a federally regulated or insured lender; a loan that the originating lender intends to sell to FNMA, GNMA, or FHLMC; or made by creditors who each make or invest more than $1,000,000 annually in real estate loans. 12 U.S.C.A. §2602 (1980 and Supp. 1985). The reaction to RESPA in some quarters has been negative, as is reflected in the following excerpt from a long article on RESPA by Diana Stoppello.

Stoppello, Federal Regulation of Home Mortgage Settlement Costs: RESPA and Its Alternatives
63 Minn. L. Rev. 367, 368-369, 423, 425-426 (1979)

When the Real Estate Settlement Procedures Act[1] (RESPA) was enacted in 1974, some hailed it as a law that would "ensure that the costs to the

---

1. Real Estate Settlement Procedures Act of 1974, Pub. L. No. 93-533, 88 Stat. 1724 (codified at 12 U.S.C. §§2601-2617 (1976)).

American home buying public will not be unreasonably or unnecessarily inflated by abusive practices."[2] Others condemned it as "a major defeat for consumers and a stunning victory for the real estate settlement lobby."[3] Realistically, RESPA merited neither high praise nor condemnation. RESPA's requirements of distribution of information booklets to homebuyers and at least twelve days advance disclosure of the settlement costs payable upon transfer of title were only a modest effort by the federal government to make the oftentimes bewildering process of buying and selling a home somewhat less mysterious for the parties to the transaction.

Little more than six months after its effective date, however, even that modest effort was undone. Following an intensive lobbying campaign by mortgage lenders, real estate brokers, and title insurance companies,[4] Congress passed the Real Estate Settlement Procedures Act Amendments of 1975,[5] which repealed the heart of RESPA. In its place, Congress substituted a regulatory scheme that requires mortgage lenders to estimate settlement costs and to disclose these costs to homebuyers in a form that is of little value and that denies homebuyers the right to know all of their actual settlement costs until the date of settlement. . . .

RESPA entitles a homebuyer to four different disclosures: (1) a special information booklet; (2) good faith estimates of charges for specific settlement services; (3) actual settlement costs known on the business day immediately preceding settlement; and (4) settlement costs actually paid.

The lender must provide the first two disclosures—the special information booklet and the good faith estimates—within three business days after the homebuyer submits an application for a federally related mortgage loan. The special information booklet, entitled Settlement Costs, was prepared by HUD. Part I of the booklet describes the settlement process and the nature of settlement charges and suggests questions for the homebuyer to ask the various settlement services providers. It also contains information about the homebuyer's rights—such as the right to good faith estimates—and remedies under RESPA, and alerts the homebuyer to unfair or illegal practices. Part II of the booklet is an item-by-item explanation of settlement services and costs, with sample forms and worksheets to assist the homebuyer in making cost comparisons. . . .

When measured against the purposes that a properly drawn scheme of federal regulation of settlement costs based upon the concept of disclosure should serve, the RESPA disclosures are inadequate for two reasons: they

---

2. H.R. Rep. No. 1177, 93d Cong., 2d Sess. 4 (1974); S. Rep. No. 866, 93d Cong., 2d Sess. 3 (hereinafter cited as S. Rep. No. 886), reprinted in (1974) U.S. Code Cong. & Ad. News 6546, 6548.

3. S. Rep. No. 866, supra note 2, at 13 (additional views of Mr. Proxmire), reprinted in (1974) U.S. Code Cong. & Ad. News 6546, 6557.

4. This lobbying campaign is described in J. Berry, The Power of Letters from Home (May 18, 1976) (unpublished newsletter of the Alicia Patterson Foundation).

5. Pub. L. No. 94-205, 89 Stat. 1157 (1976) (codified at 12 U.S.C. §§2602-2604, 2607, 2609, 2616-2617 (1976)).

come too late in the settlement process and they are too incomplete to be of significant assistance to the homebuyer.

From the standpoint of the homebuyer, the settlement process begins when he first thinks about purchasing a home. One of the first decisions he must make is whether he can afford to buy a home with the amount of cash he has available. If he has not purchased a home previously and is not otherwise familiar with the settlement process, he is likely to calculate his initial cash requirements by reference to the amount of down payment he would have to make at the prevailing loan-to-value ratio, without taking into account any loan origination and settlement costs. Although undoubtedly many real estate brokers give prospective homebuyers some information about the initial costs involved in purchasing a home, a real estate broker who is eager to consummate a sale might well fail to volunteer information about the magnitude of the total costs until the prospective homebuyer has entered into a contract of sale. The special information booklet and the good faith estimates now required by RESPA would enable the prospective homebuyer to calculate some of the front-end costs, but RESPA does not require that this information be made available until after the homebuyer has signed the contract of sale and applied for a mortgage loan.

Even if RESPA required these disclosures to be made at the precontract stage, they still would be inadequate because the good faith estimates do not include all items that the homebuyer will have to pay in cash at settlement. The items as to which good faith estimates are not required, such as hazard insurance premiums, reserves required to be deposited with the lender for future hazard and mortgage insurance premiums, property taxes and special assessments, adjustments between buyer and seller for property taxes and special assessments paid by the seller in advance, and legal fees for independent representation of the buyer, easily could total in excess of a thousand dollars.

Although the special information booklet does not contain descriptions of the items not required to be disclosed and instructions on how to calculate them, RESPA puts the task of obtaining the figures and making the calculations on the homebuyer. This allocation of responsibility is inconsistent with the concept of disclosure regulation. RESPA is, therefore, wholly inadequate to serve the first purpose of disclosure regulation: It does not enable a prospective homebuyer, prior to the time he becomes contractually bound, to determine whether he can afford to buy a particular home with the amount of cash he has available.

NOTES

1. On RESPA, see also Burke, American Conveyancing Patterns c. 6 (1978); and Whitman, The Real Estate Settlement Procedures Act: How

to Comply — Problems and Prospects, 4 Real Est. L.J. 223 (1976). HUD contracted out to Booz, Allen and Hamilton much of the research work authorized under the act, and some of this work was then subcontracted to Lane and Edson, P.C., a Washington, D.C. law firm, with David Falk of that firm the principal researcher. The research study reports prepared under the Booz, Allen and Hamilton contract are available in draft form from HUD. These reports are: Lane and Edson, Legal Bibliography on Title Recordation and Title Registration Systems (April 28, 1978); Lane and Edson, Proposals for Eliminating Repetitive Title Searches (May 12, 1978); Lane and Edson, Improving Land Title Registration Systems (May 19, 1978); Lane and Edson, Land Title Recordation Systems: Legal Constraints and Reforms (June 1, 1978); Booz, Allen and Hamilton, State-of-the-Art Research Bibliography on Land Title Systems (July 20, 1978); Booz, Allen and Hamilton, State-of-the-Art Report (October 16, 1978); and Booz, Allen and Hamilton, RESPA 13 HUD-Funded Demonstration Sites (November 7, 1978).

2. HUD's approach to its model title systems mandate under RESPA was to fund a small number of local governments in developing innovative model systems, with stress on indexing, reforms of public recording laws, and reforms of real property conveyancing laws. Jurisdictions that developed title system demonstration projects pursuant to HUD grants were St. Louis, Missouri; Warren County, Ohio; Pinal County, Arizona; Orange, Chowan, and Cherokee Counties, North Carolina; Southern Middlesex Registry, Massachusetts; Hennepin County, Minnesota; and Summit County, Colorado. On these demonstration projects, see Smith, Status of HUD-Funded Model Title System Projects, 61 Title News No. 5, at 9 (1982).

3. Another conveyancing-related sphere in which Congress has intervened is the interstate sale of land, supplementing state regulation of such transactions with the Interstate Land Sales Full Disclosure Act, 15 U.S.C. §§1701 et seq. (1983), initially passed in 1968 and amended at various times since. The act attempts to prevent fraudulent and misleading interstate sales of subdivision lots by requiring that specified information concerning land and sales proposals be made available to purchasers before they contract to buy. An informational statement on lots proposed to be sold also must be filed with HUD, and HUD may block interstate sales efforts if it finds the statement unsatisfactory. The act also applies to leases. A major objective of this federal statute has been elimination of unscrupulous practices in the interstate marketing of undeveloped subdivision lots for retirement and recreational purposes, particularly in parts of the Southwest where abuses have been prevalent.

Interstate land sale regulation by federal and state governments has been criticized as imposing duplicative and overly burdensome registration requirements on developers. Note, Regulation of Interstate Land Sales, 25 Stan. L. Rev. 605 (1973).

Cotesworth, Mechanized Processing of Title Data[48]

... In the future, nearly all title company files — including the property index, general index, tax status, old policy, and open order files — may be filed in direct access devices. This information may even be available to company searchers and title examiners through remote typewriter units and visual display terminals (similar to television tubes) connected to the system. By making a request on a terminal, title information may then be made available to any authorized requester. With an integrated system it may not be necessary to issue numerous requests for information concerning property and parties as is done today. When the request is properly identified, the data processing system can search from file to file and extract all associated information. In many cases it may even be possible for the system to go from order entry to report preparation with no manual intervention. The terminal operator conceivably will initiate the order by keying in the essential information, such as transaction type, property description, policy type, alleged owner, and buyer. The system will then search the property index and retrieve both the chain of title and essential elements of the old policy. At the same time the system will take each name in the chain of title, search the general index file, and check the tax status of the property. At this point, the system can automatically perform the title examination and the report preparation. By referring to the old policy and the chain of title and using the same logical process of the title examiner, the system can isolate the encumbrances and other matters needed for a title report. It can select a standard paragraph stored in the computer files to match each exception and add specific variable information, then format these paragraphs and prepare the title report on a high-speed printer. The title report can be maintained in an open-order file in the computer until it is time for the title policy to be prepared. If there is a delay before the policy is written, another search may be necessary to cover the period between the report and policy preparation. When this is done, the title examiner will have the policy prepared on a high-speed printer. The essential elements of the policy will then be retained in the old policy files.

If the title is so complex that the system cannot examine it automatically, the title examiner can receive from the system, for his perusal, such items as current chain of title, print-out of old policy, results of the general index search, and results of the tax search. The examiner then can physically examine the title evidence by viewing it on a visual display terminal connected to a micro-storage device through the computer system. When he

---

48. This article was prepared in 1970 especially for this casebook and is printed by courtesy of the International Business Machines Corporation and Mr. H. A. Cotesworth, an official of that company. The technology discussed by Cotesworth has developed rapidly but the future automated title system he discusses is slow in coming. On automation of land title records, see also A Symposium on Title Recordation, 22 Am. U.L. Rev. 239-406 (1973); and Symposium, Computerization of Land Title Records, 43 U. Cin. L. Rev. 465-555 (1974).

Reforming the System

determines the title defects that will appear on the title report, he can select the appropriate standard notations and supply information that is specific to the particular order. This data can be keyed into the system via the terminal, and the system can then format the title report by selecting the paragraph called for by the examiner and inserting the variable information.

Today, public land title files and records are physically scattered, with different local government instrumentalities responsible for preparing and keeping different kinds of records. Some consolidations, however, often exist. The property index, as maintained in many counties, merges the assessor's files and the recorder's files, and shows for each parcel a chain of ownership covering many years. The general index is a composite of court records and dispositions, as well as corporate personal property records. In an integrated system, all relevant files may be maintained in direct access storage devices for viewing through a terminal device by anyone authorized. Recording office personnel within seconds can retrieve, view, and copy stored documents and can furnish chains of title for a reasonable period of time. Most inquiries are for periods only five to ten years back. It may be unnecessary under an integrated system ever to printout grantor-grantee indices stored in direct access files when available for viewing on terminals. And when such indices are more than 10 or 15 years old and inquiry volume as to them has dropped, the most efficient procedure may be to have them transferred to magnetic tapes for long-term storage.

Eventually, the recorder will probably not have his own computer, but will inquire through terminals into a massive property file located at a central local government computer facility. Other local government personnel, such as planners, assessors, engineers, and welfare case workers, will also have access to the central computer file through their own terminals, receiving only that information authorized. The recorder will still create the records for which he is responsible but he will create them through his own terminal devices and they will be stored in a central computer. Will title companies always have their own computers? This is difficult to answer. It is conceivable, however, that the central local government facility with its extensive files may also be used by title companies through their own terminal equipment. Companies may still maintain their own files of issued policies, but rely on the central facility for most of the data needed for determining insurable risks and preparing title policies.

NOTES

1. What would be the effect on the private title insurance industry of an integrated public land record system with data stored in government maintained direct access storage devices? Would this make private title

plants obsolete? Would it encourage replacement of private title insurance by Torrens registration? Is there any likelihood that such an integrated and fully automated system will be developed and operated by title insurers or other private businesses?

2. Is there a risk that an integrated public land record system will collect and distribute some kinds of data that should remain confidential and not be accessible through public records? If so, what kinds of data might be subject to such abuse? And could the system be controlled so that if confidential information were stored, it would be released only to authorized personnel?

CHAPTER SIX

Shared Facilities Ownership: Co-ops, Condos, and Homes Associations

A quiet revolution has overtaken the housing scene. Not so long ago, in a legal if not social sense, most homeowners had little entanglement with their neighbors. The single-family detached structure resting securely upon its own lot dominated the market. Homeownership for most Americans meant a fee simple title to that lot, and one should not underestimate the symbolism that this evoked. There were, of course, occasional exceptions. Row-housing, with its party wall arrangements, was quite abundant in a few older urban neighborhoods; and in parts of New York City and Chicago, high-rise cooperatives offered almost the only option for those seeking shelter equity. And residential subdivisions, bound together by a declaration of covenants and restrictions regulating land use, have been around for more than a century.

What has changed dramatically, however, both in volume and complexity has been the spread of shared facilities developments. These are developments in which the housing unit itself is only part of the physical package that the owner acquires. Coupled thereto is an interest, variously defined, in common areas that the unit owner must share with his fellow residents. These common facilities may include only the land, hallways, and structural elements of the building itself, as in high-rise apartments, but today's homebuyers may also be getting much in the way of recreational and social amenities: swimming pools, tennis courts, community centers, nature trails, open space, etc. While hard figures are elusive, we estimate that nearly half of all currently built, "for sale" housing units are linked to a shared facilities complex.

There has occurred, in addition, a related development: time-sharing ownership. Geared to the leisure industry, time-sharing permits one to acquire ownership of a vacation unit for a fixed period (e.g., the month of July) every year.

The first part of this chapter looks closely at several law-related problems that have emerged as American homebuyers relinquish some of their sturdy independence in favor of "membership" in a shared facilities development, whether stock-cooperative, condominium, or homes association—the latter two by far the more usual. The second part of this chapter then explores some of the issues that a time-sharing scheme must try to solve.

PROBLEM

You are the attorney for a residential developer. She owns a tract of land that she wishes to develop into a 200-unit housing subdivision. The proposed venture will include extensive common recreational facilities, such as tennis courts, an artificial lake, and a community center; these will be available to all families within the subdivision. To help preserve first-growth woodland, the developer intends to rely upon the "cluster" provisions of the local zoning ordinance. In addition, all of the units will share party walls, so that the proposed layout will consist of 50 structures, each having four "town-house" units.

Your task is to create the legal structure that will implement your client's physical design in a form most likely to appeal to a mélange of potential "homebuyers," lenders, local officials, and, of course, your client. The materials in this chapter should help you consider the legal design, which, as you should assume, can take one of three forms:

1. The development would be divided into 200 parcels, one per unit, to be sold individually in fee simple absolute. An association of home owners would also be formed, in which membership would be compulsory. The developer then would either retain title to the recreational areas, which she would lease to the association, or transfer title to the association.

2. The developer would create a cooperative corporation, to which she would transfer title to the entire subdivision. Homebuyers would acquire stock in the corporation and a long-term proprietary lease in their individual units. The lease would also entitle stockholders to use the recreational facilities.

3. The developer would create a condominium association, which would manage all common areas. The developer would transfer to each homebuyer a fee simple interest in the interior living space of his or her unit and a co-tenancy interest in all the remaining real estate, including the recreational facilities.

As you consider the materials in this chapter, what do you see as the principal attractions and disadvantages of each legal arrangement?

A. CHOOSING A SHARED FACILITIES ARRANGEMENT

1. Introduction to the Stock-cooperative

Berger, Land Ownership and Use
226-227 (3d ed. 1982)

The cooperative apartment (co-op) occupies a small, localized corner in the housing market. Found chiefly in a few urban centers, the co-op remains heavily dependent upon either income tax advantage (for luxury units) or government subsidy.

The co-op appeals especially to those persons who wish to combine apartment occupancy and the advantages of home ownership. The Internal Revenue Code offers a major monetary advantage to the home-owning taxpayer: He may take itemized deductions for property tax payments and financing charges; yet he is not required, as reformers have urged, to impute as income the rental value of his dwelling. The home owner, furthermore, has an equity he may devise, alienate, or borrow against, and the value of his equity is likely to increase over the years in our land-scarce and inflationary economy. (To be sure, he also shoulders the risk of a short-term decline.) Residential leaseholds, on the other hand, seldom generate increments of value for the lessee. And finally, in our status-conscious society, home ownership for many consumers connotes social arrival and, as such, is a significant factor in their selection of housing.

We cannot date or place the origin of the co-op, but an 1886 lawsuit involving a co-op, Barrington Apartment Assn. v. Watson, 45 S. Ct. (38 Hun.) 545 (1886), suggests Manhattan in the decades after the Civil War as a possibility. In the years preceding the Great Depression, the luxury co-op began to abound in Chicago and New York — two cities where the well-to-do practiced the apartment habit, and, in 1927, the first middle-income co-op, Amalgamated Houses, rose in the Bronx. The Depression struck hard at all forms of real estate; because of their financial interdependence (see page 935 infra), co-ops were especially vulnerable. Nine of every ten co-ops went broke. When World War II began, the co-op movement was in near collapse.

In the postwar era, the co-op has managed a comeback. Several factors explain this recovery. Congress, in 1942, passed the forerunner of Internal Revenue Code §216, creating near-parity (regarding deductions for interest and property taxes) between homeowner and cooperator. The war-occasioned rise in tax rates gave the upper-income apartment dweller further incentive to reduce his tax burden by switching from a rental to a cooperative unit. The tenant's desire, in this rare instance, paralleled his landlord's, for the latter, faced with the wearying prospect of rent control, often wanted to sell out; his easiest (and most profitable) chance of doing so lay in conversion to cooperative and the giving of first option to his present tenants—a procedure rent control allowed, at least in New York. Congress, in 1950, once again spurred co-op activity when it added Section 213 to the National Housing Act, authorizing the FHA to insure the co-op mortgage. And middle-income co-ops received a major stimulus from the New York legislature in 1956, when it enacted the Mitchell-Lama Law (Private Housing Finance Law §§10-37) with its twin inducements of long-term, low-interest loans and property tax abatement. More recently, *lower-income* co-ops have received a slight boost from federal subsidy programs, especially the Section 8 program, whose rent supplement payments cannot be used for condominium units. Joselow, Making Cooperative Unit Mortgages More Liquid, Real Est. Rev. 103, 104 (Fall 1983).

Legal Arrangement. Title to the land and building is held by a single entity—usually a corporation, although a trust is sometimes used. Only those who are to become apartment "owners," the cooperators, may obtain a corporate (trust) interest; each cooperator acquires shares based on the value of his apartment. The right to occupy the apartment is embodied in a "proprietary" lease between the corporation (trust), as landlord, and the cooperator, as tenant. Under the lease provisions, the cooperator pays a periodic rental or assessment; this charge covers the cooperator's prorata share of the project's expenses, including debt service, maintenance, taxes, insurance, capital improvements, and reserves. Ordinarily the lease is for an initial three-to-five-year term, but is automatically renewable for like terms at the tenant's election.

Management of the cooperative is performed by a board of directors, elected by the project members in accordance with the governing by-laws. The directors fix the amount of the periodic assessment and enforce the lease against delinquent stockholder-tenants. Default may result in a member's eviction and in the forced sale of his stock and lease.

2. Introduction to the Condominium

Berger, Condominium: Shelter on a Statutory Foundation[1]

63 Colum. L. Rev. 987 (1963)

Mrs. Sullivan: "I am glad to hear about this [condominium] type of ownership. It is the first time I heard of it."

---

1. Adapted by the author for use in this case book. New footnotes supplied.

Mr. Addonizio: "This is a new concept, as far as I am concerned, but it is very interesting."
Senator Sparkman: "I must say I am intrigued by it. . . ."

Seldom have hard-nosed lawmakers greeted innovation more cordially than they have greeted the condominium. For whatever reason— whether the persuasiveness of its Puerto Rican proponents, the allure of a concept whose origins are said to predate Caesar, the inattention of its natural enemies, or simply its inherent merit—Congress was quick to bring condominium apartments within the Federal Housing Administration's (FHA) mortgage insurance powers by adding Section 234 to the National Housing Act.[2] There has followed an astonishing burst of activity among legal writers, bar committees, state assemblies, and members of the real estate profession. Today, familiarity with condominium is widespread; yet only three years ago Congress's housing experts were hearing of it for the first time.

What is this condominium that has aroused such sudden interest? According to its Latin meaning, condominium is co-ownership; however, co-ownership is not today its primary feature. The most common modern instance of condominium is a multi-unit dwelling each of whose residents enjoys exclusive ownership of his individual apartment. With "title" to an apartment goes a cotenant's undivided interest in the common facilities— the land, the hallways, the heating plant, etc. Remarkably flexible, condominium is susceptible of an endless variety of legal formulations and can be adapted to a multiplicity of land uses or project designs. But in all of its forms its principal goal remains constant: to enable occupants of a multi-unit project to achieve more concomitants of ownership than are now available either to renters or to cooperators. . . .

A still greater disadvantage (of the cooperative) is that, for purposes of mortgage financing and property taxation, the cooperator's stock-lease "estate" lacks sufficient personality to support an individual obligation. As a result the entire cooperative structure is burdened by a blanket mortgage and a single tax assessment. By saddling the venture with overall liens, the stock-cooperative imposes upon the tenants the duty of meeting collectively the tax and debt service obligations as they fall due; frequently the two items exceed two-thirds of the monthly assessment. Stipulate a vigorous economy, modest inflation, housing undersupply, healthy reserves, a competitive location, and no problems of disrepair or obsolescence, and the concern over this financial interdependence is academic. If a tenant defaults, the cooperative may quickly terminate his status and find a re-

---

2. Curiously, §234, which started it all, delivered fewer than 2000 units of condominium dwellings in the first five years after its enactment. U.S. Department of Housing and Urban Development, 1966 Statistical Report.

placement able to discharge the delinquent's pro rata obligation. There is no assurance, however, of the permanence of satisfactory conditions. Unsatisfactory conditions, moreover, breed further delinquency by stepping up the need for new cooperators at a time when their supply is shrinking. Since the blanket tax and financing burden remains fairly constant, any additional charges upon the surviving cooperators may affect adversely both their ability to pay and their desire to remain current. The calamitous experience of stock-cooperatives during the early 1930s reveals the risks inherent in the snowballing of individual defaults. Higher standards for the selection of tenants, larger down payment requirements, and the immediate funding of reserves would be forms of prophylaxis, but they would also discourage the wider use of cooperatives among lower- and middle-income families.

Even if the risk of financial interdependence has been overdrawn, the blanket mortgage scheme imposes serious disadvantages upon the cooperator. He lacks the flexibility with regard to debt reduction, refinancing, or resale that the home owner enjoys. He cannot shift his assets or take advantage of earnings peaks or asset increments to reduce or eliminate the mortgage affecting his unit. Refinancing, which is often needed to effect modernization, modify debt service charges, "borrow against one's equity," or facilitate resale, is not possible unless the cooperator can persuade his fellow stockholders to refinance the blanket debt. This disadvantage is especially significant at the time of resale if the unit has an enhanced equity value and if the venture permits the cooperator to realize the gain, for the seller is more likely to deal with a buyer who must borrow in order to arrange the purchase.[3] If the seller himself takes back the financing, he must defer the conversion into cash of his equity value. The new stockholder-tenant, who carries the heavier costs of a secondary loan whatever its source, may pose an added hazard for his fellow interdependent cooperators.

By enabling the unit owner to undertake an individual financing program, the condominium offers a major and perhaps critical advantage over the present-day cooperative. Yet the condominium relinquishes none of the ownership benefits afforded by stock-cooperatives—voice in its management, permanence of tenure, avoidance of profit to the landlord, and tax savings. . . .

---

3. Recent changes in state and federal law may facilitate financing of the *equity* portion of the cooperative stock-lease interest. New York State now allows lenders to make loans "secured" by the stock-lease equity. For example, savings banks may now loan on such security up to its full appraised value. N.Y. Banking Law §103(5) (McKinney Supp. 1985). And Congress, in 1974, gave the FHA authority to insure a mortgage on the equity in a cooperative dwelling unit. National Housing Act §203(n). HUD did not issue §203(n) regulations until 1977. Note, however, that the equity mortgage is necessarily a subordinate lien wherever a blanket mortgage encumbers the project.

II. The Need for a Statutory Foundation

In considering whether condominium is a feasible form of ownership under the common law or whether it requires special statutory provision, as it has in Latin America and Europe, one might note that England and Scotland have assimilated flat-ownership without benefit of statute, and, in the United States, there are instances of condominium that predate legislative recognition. In 1947, twelve ex-servicemen who wanted to buy jointly a building on Manhattan's East 84th Street containing a dozen units were unable to get a Veterans' Administration guarantee on a blanket mortgage. Therefore they created an entity resembling a condominium whereby each received a deed describing his respective apartment space and an undivided interest in the common premises. For each unit they were able to obtain a separate loan and persuade the VA to guarantee the mortgage. Quite recently interest in condominium has sparked more than fifty ventures, principally in Florida, Utah, and the San Francisco Bay area, where investors relied, temporarily at least, upon the compatibility of existing state law. Probably the area with the most extensive experience in common law condominium is southern California. There, separate ownership and financing, but not taxation, of apartment units, have become commonplace under a plan bearing the jaunty label — "Own-Your-Own Apartments." During the four-year period ending in 1961, the Real Estate Commissioner gave preliminary approval for nearly two hundred own-your-own projects in the Los Angeles area.

Condominium, it appears, can exist under the common law, but whether it will flourish without statutory provision is doubtful. Although the Manhattan venture has enjoyed fifteen successful years, it has not seeded similar projects in New York, and the California own-your-own plan has failed to attract the major institutional lenders. Moreover, the recent growth of condominiums in Florida, California, and Utah was probably based in part on a belief that each state statutory provision was imminent. Furthermore, the real estate community's pressure for enabling statutes undoubtedly reflects a feeling that legislation is badly needed.

What kind of legislation does condominium in its embryonic stage require? There is immediate need for an official imprimatur — an enabling statute that blesses the condominium concept and erases any doubts that our legal system can tolerate ownership estates in airspace lots. This alone should stimulate the interest and elicit the confidence of lenders, consumers, and suppliers. The statute would ensure that unit ownership is recognized as an interest in real property — a status denied by some courts to the stock-lease arrangement for a cooperative — and that unit mortgages, whether insured or conventional, qualify for institutional investment.

But the major burdens of such a statute are threefold: (1) to provide a procedure for the establishment and dissolution of a condominium and to secure a uniform pattern of legal documentation; (2) to accommodate existing legislation dealing with taxation, recording procedures, liens, land-use control, and security regulatory techniques to the special needs of the condominium; and (3) to anticipate possible judicial antagonism involving such matters as bars on partition and covenants real. . . .

III. Creation of the Condominium

To inform interested parties of the nature of the enterprise and its internal organization two important documents must be executed and recorded — the declaration and the operating by-laws.

The declaration serves roughly the same function for the condominium as the subdivision map and restrictive covenants serve in a tract development. It includes a legal description of the underlying land, a description in layman's terms of the building, apartment units, and common facilities, and a statement in fractions of each owner's share of rights and duties with respect to the common premises. This fraction fixes permanently the unit owner's pro rata burden of the common expenses and his share in any profit or distribution of capital. It is also the measure of his voice in the management. Because taxing officials will need a formula for apportioning a project's total value among the separate units, the fraction may be used to compute each apartment's assessment. And finally, the fraction may provide a basis for limiting the unit owner's individual liability for liens and for the claims of the project's creditors.[4]

Beyond these essential features, the content of the declarations may vary in accordance with the requirements of individual statutes. Nevertheless, most declarations will contain provisions regarding the establishment of an entity to manage the condominium's day-to-day affairs, measures to be taken against delinquent owners — such as the power to lien an individual unit, designation of persons upon whom process may be served, arrangements for blanket casualty and liability insurance, and procedures to be followed in the event of project destruction or obsolescence. The statutes may mandate some of these provisions, for example, the designation of persons to receive process; they will legitimize others, such as the power to impose assessment liens. For the internal administration of a condominium, by-laws are needed to regulate matters such as building maintenance, budgeting, assessment and collection, capital improvements, and occupant control. . . .

Either the declaration or the by-laws will also include various restraints

---

4. Management of the condominium by an unincorporated association makes each unit owner liable for any unpaid contract claim against the association. The liability is joint and several, which means that the creditor may recover against any unit owner, who, in turn, must then seek contribution from his fellow owners. Berger, Condominium: Shelter on a Statutory Foundation, supra at page 1007. What steps might the condominium take to insulate the unit owner against this risk?

upon the unit owner's freedom to alienate. Two involve the physical and legal integrity of the project: a restraint against partition of the common areas while the structure remains intact and subject to the condominium regime, and a bar against transfers that would divide ownership of a unit from ownership of the corresponding share of the common areas. Generally the unit owner's freedom to choose a vendee or tenant will also be restricted. . . .

Finally, the declaration will normally include the condominium plans and either a subdivision map or a statement of metes and bounds describing each of the units. These descriptions . . . are later incorporated in the deed of conveyance that the condominium member receives when he acquires his interest.

Heretofore the most common form of condominium management has been the unincorporated "Association of Owners." Unit ownership automatically bestows the status of association membership, which carries the privileges of voting for a board of directors and taking part in the association's business meetings. In turn, the board elects the association officers and, together with these and perhaps a manager, it directs the condominium's daily operations. . . .

3. Introduction to the Homes Association

Hyatt, Condominium and Home Owner Associations: Formation and Development

24 Emory L.J. 977, 980-983 (1975)

A housing development utilizing a homes association[14] may take many forms. The project might be a conventional subdivision,[15] attached housing,[16] cluster housing,[17] or a variety of other construction forms, including combinations of the possible forms. The first essential difference between the homes association and the condominium is that the individual purchaser acquires title to a dwelling unit. The owner's title includes the exterior of the unit and may also include a portion of the land adjacent to the unit. The second major difference is that the property not owned

---

14. The terms "landed homes association," "automatic homes association," and "homeowners association" refer to the same concept. For simplicity's sake, the term "homes association" will be used as inclusive of all; it should be noted that the landed association holds title to common areas, while in other possible forms of homes associations, this might not be the case.

15. See Krasnowiecki, Townhouse Condominiums Compared to Conventional Subdivision with Homes Association, 1 Real Estate L.J. 323 (1973), in which the author found the condominium development preferable because of zoning and "the luxury connotation."

16. Urban Land Institute, The Homes Association Handbook 18-19 (1964) (hereinafter cited as Handbook).

17. Id. at 55 and 73.

individually as dwelling units is owned by an association composed of the unit owners,[18] rather than by the unit owners in common.

The condominium and homes association developments have a common feature which is crucial to an appreciation of the many legal complexities involved: membership in the association is mandatory. Each purchaser, by accepting a deed, becomes an association member and submits to the authority of the association and the restrictions upon the use of the property contained in the Declaration of Condominium or in the Declaration of Covenants, Conditions, and Restrictions.

The role and function of the condominium association and the homeowners association in the homes association context are essentially identical. Therefore, having established the definitional framework, this article will refer to the "association" as including both except where the context necessitates separate treatment.

Basic to the development of an association is an appreciation of its role and function. First, the association provides a vehicle for the individual unit owners to work together. An "important aspect of the [community association] lies in its basic nature as a privately owned and operated vehicle of service to a specific community."[19] However, because all owners automatically become members of the association upon taking title and because the association is empowered to levy and collect assessments, to make and enforce rules, and to permit or deny certain uses of the property, it can exert tremendous influence upon the individual's property rights which are normally enjoyed as a concomitant part of fee simple ownership. It is this degree of control that raises the association to a level approaching that of a municipal government.

This dual role as a service oriented business and regulatory authority is a direct result of the powers conferred upon the association by the declaration[20] which created it. Filed before the sale of the first unit, the declaration immediately brings the association into existence;[21] the complacent assumption by some developers that the association does not exist until control is surrendered to the homeowners not only is incorrect but also is a miscalculation of the developer's own responsibility and hence his potential liability for failure to discharge the duties of and to protect the interests of the association.

18. See Handbook, supra note 16, at 4-5.
19. Urban Land Institute/Community Associations Institute, Managing a Successful Community Association 3 (1974) (hereinafter cited as ULI/CAI).
20. In the condominium context, this is the Declaration of Condominium; in the home owners association context, it is the Declaration of Covenants, Conditions, and Restrictions, often called the CCRs.
21. See Handbook, supra note 16, at 208-09. Three sound reasons are provided for the association to exist prior to a sale: (1) acknowledgment of the covenant requiring assessments; (2) establishment of a method of rule enforcement; and (3) good will. This latter point is most important: "Indeed the experience has been that where the developer merely holds out vague promises of an association, the homeowners will go out of their way to press him on every aspect of his development." Id. at 209.

Whether developer- or homeowner-controlled, the association must be operated in accordance with the declaration, by-laws, and governing statute, if any, in full recognition of the rights and responsibilities of the owners individually and of the association. The officers and directors must concern themselves, as would the officers and directors of any corporation, with business details such as finances, asset and property management, taxation,[22] insurance, employee relations, and many other considerations inherent in operating a substantial business.[23] The need to observe scrupulously the declaration and by-laws and to consider carefully the long-range effects of these provisions when originally drafting them is best illustrated by the association's regulatory role as a "minigovernment." [24]

In the condominium context, state law ordains the creation of the association; in both forms of development, moreover, the creating documents are filed with and enforced through the state courts. In most cases, the association provides for its members' utility services, road maintenance, street and common area lighting, and refuse removal; in many cases, it also provides security services and various forms of communication within the community. There exists, therefore, a clear analogy to the municipality's police and public safety functions;[25] moreover, these functions are financed through assessments, or taxes, levied upon the members of the community association. The governmental role which creates a special concern for strict observance of the dictates of due process of law is made more acute by the power of the association through its rule-making authority[26] and through its assessment authority[27] to regulate the use and enjoyment of property. This "power of levy" is a distinctive characteristic of the association[28] and removes it from a mere voluntary neighborhood civic group. The declaration, which must be strictly construed and

---

22. The impact of Rev. Rul. 74-14, 1974-1 Cum. Bull. 125 and Rev. Rul. 74-99, 1974-1 Cum. Bull. 131, will be discussed in more detail. . . .

23. It is not unusual for an average size association in the Atlanta area to have a budget well in excess of $100,000 a year. Associations maintaining relatively low assessments average approximately $250,000.

24. ULI/CAI, supra note 19, at 2.

25. Id.

26. In Johnson v. Keith, — Mass. — , 331 N.E.2d 879 (1975), while the court based its decision on another ground, it clearly stated that rules made by a condominium association are more like municipal by-laws than private deed restrictions. Therefore the court stated that statutory restrictions on private deed covenants would not be applied to condominium rules. See, e.g., Ga. Code Ann. §85-1606b (Supp. 1974): "Each apartment owner shall comply strictly with the bylaws *and with the administrative rules and regulations adopted pursuant thereto.* . . . Failure to comply with any of the same shall be ground for an action . . . for damages or injunctive relief or both maintainable by the manager or board of directors on behalf of the association. . . ." (emphasis added). See also Ga. Code Ann. §85-1625b (Supp. 1974).

27. E.g., Ga. Code Ann. §85-1621b (Supp. 1974) (creating a lien right).

28. Urban Land Institute/Community Associations Institute, Financial Management of Condominium and Home Owner Associations 1 (1975).

obeyed,[29] establishes a variety of use restrictions including, for example, restrictions upon sale and leasing,[30] exterior alterations, use of the common area, parking, and even limitations upon the nature of uses to which the interior of the unit may be placed. In addition, a typical declaration will empower the board of directors to make rules and to establish penalties for violations thereof. The imposition of penalties, whether fines collected as a lien upon the property or a denial of the use of facilities enforced by injunction, certainly represents a quasi-judicial power to affect an individual's property rights.

NOTES AND QUESTIONS

1. In addition to the unit owner's exposure in contract for any claims against the governing board, see page 938 supra, note 4, the condominium member may face several other forms of individual liability that the co-op member does not usually have. The various liabilities are grounded in tort, mortgage debt, and real estate tax debt (rarely). Explain. Cf. Berger, Condominium: Shelter on a Statutory Foundation, 63 Colum. L. Rev. 987, 1019 (1963). Which of these liabilities would follow the unit owner in a homes association?

2. Most buildings as they age require major capital improvements. Would it be easier in a co-op or a condominium to finance a substantial renovation? Similarly, for expansion of the recreational facilities? Also compare a condominium and a homes association.

3. By 1968, condominium enabling laws had appeared in all 50 states, the District of Columbia and Puerto Rico. These early statutes drew heavily from an FHA Model Statute. After working with their laws for nearly a decade, several states have written second-generation statutes that deal more successfully with matters barely anticipated in the first years of condominium: the spread of townhouse and detached dwelling projects; nonresidential adaptation; the need for consumer protection. For examples of new-look enabling laws, see Va. Code Ann. §§55-79-39 et seq. (Supp. 1976); Fla. Stat. Ann. §§718.101-718.508 (Supp. 1984).

4. In an effort that began in the early 1970s, the National Conference of Commissioners on Uniform State Laws has sought to offer comprehensive legislation that would apply, insofar as possible, to all three

---

29. Hoover Morris Development Co., Inc. v. Mayfield, 233 Ga. 593, 212 S.E.2d 778 (1975).

30. The author finds so-called "right of first refusal" clauses a vestige of an era he would like to believe has, and should have, passed. Developers say that they must include such provisions in order to satisfy the buyers who generally do not know or care whether or not the provision exists. The new Georgia Condominium Act, however, specifically continues the practice and modifies existing law only by imposing a time-notice limitation.

forms of common ownership. This effort has led to a series of Uniform Acts, to wit:
Uniform Condominium Act, adopted 1977;
Uniform Planned Community Act, adopted 1980;
Uniform Condominium Act (amended), adopted 1980;
Model Real Estate Cooperative Act, adopted 1981;
Uniform Common Interest Ownership Act (UCIOA), adopted 1982.

As of early 1984, only Connecticut had enacted UCIOA, although Maine, Minnesota, Missouri, New Mexico, Pennsylvania, Rhode Island, and West Virginia have borrowed from the earlier acts.

B. SELECTED PROBLEMS

1. The Cooperative Apartment: Realty, Personalty, or Hybrid?

State Tax Commission v. Shor
43 N.Y.2d 151, 371 N.E.2d 523, 400 N.Y.S.2d 805 (1977)

BREITEL, Chief Judge. This is a proceeding to enforce a money judgment, under CPLR article 52 on behalf of three creditors and lienors of the debtor Shor. They sought an order for the distribution of proceeds from the sale of Shor's interest in his co-operative apartment. Fidelity National Bank, a judgment creditor of Shor interpleaded as a respondent, opposed the motion, asserting a prior lien on the proceeds. Special Term granted the motion, and a unanimous Appellate Division affirmed. Fidelity appeals.

The issue is whether the debtor's interest in his co-operative apartment, that is, a stock certificate in the co-operative corporation and a "proprietary" leasehold granted by the corporation, is a "chattel real," and hence, real property under CPLR 5203, thereby entitling a judgment creditor to a lien on the property merely upon docketing his judgment.

The order of the Appellate Division should be affirmed.

The ownership interest of a tenant-shareholder in a co-operative apartment is sui generis. It reflects only an ownership of a proprietary lease, and therefore arguably an interest in a chattel real, conditional however upon his shareholder interest in the co-operative corporation, an interest always treated as personal property. The leasehold and the shareholding are inseparable. For some special purposes, the real property aspect may predominate (see Grenader v. Spitz, 2 Cir., 537 F.2d 612, 617-620, *cert. den.* 429 U.S. 1009, 97 S. Ct. 541, 50 L. Ed. 2d 619; cf. United Housing

Foundation v. Forman, 421 U.S. 837, esp. 854-860, 95 S. Ct. 2051, 44 L. Ed. 2d 621, *reh. den.* 423 U.S. 884, 96 S. Ct. 157, 46 L. Ed. 2d 115). But, where priorities of judgment creditors are involved, the stock certificate and lease involved in the typical co-operative apartment transaction fit better, legally and pragmatically, although with imperfect linguistic formulation, into the statutory framework governing personal property. Since a co-operative apartment leasehold, inseparable from co-operative shares, is not a chattel real for purposes of CPLR 5203, Fidelity did not obtain a lien merely upon docketing its judgment.

In 1951, Shor purchased 1,400 shares in 480 Park Avenue Corp., a co-operative apartment corporation. He received a stock certificate and a proprietary lease on a duplex apartment. The lease provided the lessor with a "first lien" on Shor's shares of stock for all monetary obligations arising under the lease. Eventually, on February 23, 1973, Shor was evicted for nonpayment of maintenance charges, dating from 1971, and 480 Park Avenue Corp. claims a first lien of $63,908.22 for back maintenance, with interest, expenses, and attorneys' fees.

Well before Shor's eviction, in July, 1967, Shor, as guarantor of a loan made by Chase to a corporate borrower, had granted Chase "a security interest in [and] a general lien upon . . . all money, instruments, securities, documents, chattel paper . . . and any other property, rights and interests of the undersigned, which at any time shall come into the possession or custody or under the control of the Bank." Chase had previously obtained possession of Shor's stock certificate and proprietary lease as collateral. Following various defaults, Chase, on April 28, 1972, obtained a judgment against Shor for $44,222.67. Based on the judgment with added interest and expenses, Chase asserts a first lien of $67,800.17 plus attorneys' fees in this proceeding.

On April 9, 1971, the State Tax Commission filed its first tax warrant against Shor. The commission levied execution on Chase on December 22, 1971, restraining Chase from making any transfer of the collateral. A similar levy was made on 480 Park Avenue Corp. on December 15, 1972. The Tax Commission's lien is for an amount greater than the total of the proceeds from the eventual sale of the apartment.

On August 9, 1973, on motion of Chase, and upon stipulation among Chase, the Tax Commission, and 480 Park Avenue Corp., Special Term authorized the sale of the collateral. All other creditors of Shor consented to the sale reserving any liens and priorities they might have in the proceeds. Appellant Fidelity insisted on payment of $5,000 in return for its consent. On April 24, 1974, the sale realized $141,000. Chase now holds that sum in escrow at interest pending the outcome of this proceeding.

Not in dispute are the priorities among Chase, the Tax Commission, and 480 Park Avenue Corp. Those three subject to court approval, stipulated, on July 24, 1974, to divide the sale proceeds thus: $56,000 to 480 Park Avenue Corp., $64,000 to Chase, and the balance, plus accrued

Selected Problems

interest, to the Tax Commission. Then, on January 9, 1975, Chase interpleaded other creditors of Shor, seeking to distribute the fund according to the July 24 stipulation, and to be discharged from liability to the interpleaded respondents. All of the interpleaded respondents, save Fidelity, defaulted.

Fidelity had obtained and docketed a judgment against Shor, for $152,589, on February 6, 1970, before Chase obtained any judgment against Shor, before Shor fell behind in his payments to 480 Park Avenue Corp., and before the State Tax Commission filed its warrants. Fidelity, however, never executed on the property. Although $40,000 of Fidelity's judgment was paid, the remainder, plus interest, exceeds the fund in escrow. Fidelity's contention is simple: Shor's interest in his co-operative is a chattel real, and hence treatable as real property (CPLR 105, subd. [r]). Therefore, docketing of the 1970 judgment gave Fidelity a lien on the property (CPLR 5203, subd. [a]), and hence priority over all other creditors, none of whom, Fidelity asserts, obtained liens until after 1970.

The growth of co-operative ownership of apartment buildings, throughout the Nation, but especially in New York City, has created legal problems not resolved by uncritical resort either to the rubrics governing real property or those governing personal property (see Silverman v. Alcoa Plaza Assoc., 37 A.D.2d 166, 173, 323 N.Y.S.2d 39, 45 [Steuer, J., dissenting]). The co-operative corporation owns the land and the building. Shares in the corporation are sold to each apartment "owner," who receives a stock certificate, not a deed to real property. The shares entitle the shareholder to a long-term apartment "proprietary" lease. (See 4B Powell, Real Property [Rohan-rev. ed.], par. 633.4.) One has, therefore, a mixed concept and terminology, superficially resembling the traditional rental apartment lease, except, for example, that the lessee pays monthly maintenance charges and is subject to assessments instead of rent. For some purposes it is a lease; for others it is a compact between co-operative corporation and co-operative tenant. In any case the rights of the tenant are initiated by the capital investment made in the shares of the co-operative corporation. (On the paradoxes with respect to co-operative apartment buildings and the desirability of legislative clarification see 4B Powell, Real Property, pars. 633.51-633.52.)

By viewing the shares of stock as the dominant aspect of the co-operative transaction, as respondents do, one could easily conclude linguistically that the co-operative "owners" hold only personal property, little different from the shareholders in a commercial real estate corporation. By focusing instead on the proprietary lease, as does appellant Fidelity, one could equally well conclude linguistically that the interest of the cooperative "owner" is real property, or at least a chattel real, which is treated as real property under the applicable CPLR provisions. Both approaches are overly facile. Neither the stock certificate nor the lease, inseparably joined, can appropriately be viewed or valued in isolation from the other. Nor may a dynamic jurisprudence ignore the manner in which economic affairs are conducted or the perception that the members of society have in conducting their affairs (see Cardozo, Nature of the Judicial Process, pp. 60-64).

CPLR 5203, governing priorities and liens upon real property, provides, in part: "No transfer of an interest of the judgment debtor in real property, against which property a money judgment may be enforced, is effective against the judgment creditor . . . from the time of the docketing of the judgment with the clerk of the county in which the property is located." CPLR 105 (subd. [r]) provides that, for purposes of the CPLR, real property includes chattels real. Thus, if Shor's interest in his co-operative apartment were a chattel real, Fidelity would have priority over all creditors with liens created after February 6, 1970, the date its judgment was docketed in New York County.

By contrast, CPLR 5202 and 5234, governing rights and priorities of judgment creditors in personal property, require delivery of execution to the Sheriff before a creditor may obtain priority in the property. Since Fidelity has never delivered an execution, if the lease and stock certificate are treated as personal property, Fidelity's interest must be subordinated to those of the other creditors.

Persuasive in this case are the 1971 amendments to the Banking Law which indicate strongly that priorities in the stock certificate and proprietary lease of a co-operative apartment corporation are to be treated under principles governing personal property (Banking Law, §235, subd. 8-a; §380, subd. 2-a). Both sections, dealing with permissible investments for various financial institutions, permit loans to finance purchase of ownership interests in co-operative apartments, provided the investment "is secured within ninety days from the making of the loan by an assignment or transfer of the stock or other evidence of an ownership interest of the borrower and a proprietary lease." (See, also, Banking Law §103, subd. 5.) No recording is required, as it would be in the case of a mortgage on real property (see, e.g., Banking Law, §235, subd. 8, par. [1]; see, also, 4B Powell, Real Property [Rohan-rev. ed.], par. 633.51[3]).

These provisions indicate a legislative intention that lenders in possession of the relevant documents of title be secure from claims of subsequent creditors without any filing or recording of the security interest. Thus, a possessory security interest in co-operative apartment stock and lease would be much like a possessory security interest in ordinary chattel paper, which requires no filing for perfection (see Uniform Commercial Code, §9-305). By contrast, if the "ownership" interest in a co-operative apartment were to be treated as real property, mere possession without recording would subordinate the lender's security interest to claims of other classes of creditors (see Real Property Law, §291; Lien Law, §13). Such a result could not have been intended by the Legislature seeking to protect the interests of banking depositors. . . .

Lastly, but cogent to the point of controlling, short of violation of public policy or positive law, co-operative tenants, co-operative corporations, and third parties dealing with them do not now, if they ever did, treat co-operative tenancies as chattels real. Indeed, the legislative response in the 1971 amendments to the Banking Law confirm this perception of the nature of the relationship in co-operative apartments and the quality of the property interest involved. The common-law process does not drag unwillingly the people it serves into a rigidly fenced corral, kicking, but reflects the fair conduct and expectations of fair, reasonable persons (see Gray, Nature and Sources of the Law, p. 282). . . .

Accordingly, the order of the Appellate Division should be affirmed, without costs.

Jasen, Gabrielli, Jones, Wachtler, Fuchsberg and Cooke, JJ., concur.

Order affirmed.

NOTES AND QUESTIONS

1. Silverman v. Alcoa Plaza Assn., 37 A.D.2d 166, 323 N.Y.S.2d 39 (1971), which the *Shor* opinion cites, illustrates the personalty versus realty issue in yet another context. There plaintiff had defaulted on his contract to purchase a co-op apartment and later sued to recover his $15,400 deposit after learning that the owner had sold the unit to another for the same price. At issue was whether the Uniform Commercial Code covered this transaction. If the stock-lease could be characterized as "goods," the defendant would be limited to its actual damages from plaintiff's breach. If the stock-lease was deemed "realty," the defendant could retain the deposit by way of forfeiture, without proof of damages. In holding for the plaintiff, the divided court wrote:

> A proprietary lease is no different from any other type of lease. It is personal property. Co-operative apartment stock is nevertheless stock, like any other stock in a corporation owning real estate. It does not appear that the pairing of the two together does anything to create a new classification of real estate. Important too, to the consideration herein, is the fact that the law frowns upon forfeiture or penalty. True as stated there are specific instances where the law mandates forfeiture as well as penalty. These situations are however limited in kind and scope and should not be unduly expanded except when clearly mandated. [323 N.Y.S.2d at 45.]

At page 46-47 of his dissenting opinion, Justice Steuer reasoned:

> Concepts of what is realty and what personalty are not static and are no exception to the proposition that the law accommodates to new developments as they occur. Co-operative apartments made their appearance long after classic distinctions between realty and personalty were formulated, and the guidelines to classification should be established by the inherent nature

of the property right rather than mere superficial resemblances to other forms. This is no new idea. For instance, while a lease for 99 years is still a lease, it is nevertheless realty, because, despite the form, in actuality the leaseholder has all the attributes of ownership.

Applying the principle to the co-operative shares, it is at once apparent that the dominant characteristic of such shares is the right to a proprietary lease, which is the essential and particularizing aspect of such shares (Penthouse Props. v. 1158 Fifth Ave., 256 App. Div. 685, 692) distinguishing them from the ordinary evidences of corporate stock ownership. While the owner does not acquire a fee in the apartment, he does possess so many of the rights and obligations peculiar to fee ownership that the status is for practical purposes indistinguishable. To name a few of these which have received statutory or decisional recognition: The shareholder has been authorized to bring summary eviction proceedings to obtain possession (Curtis v. Le May, 186 Misc. 853). The Statute of Frauds applicable to real estate transactions applies to sales of co-operative stock (Frank v. Rubin, 59 Misc. 2d 796). . . . Federal and New York State income tax laws give the same privileges to co-operative share owners as they do to fee owners in many respects (see U.S. Code, tit. 26, §121, subd. [d], par. [3]; §§216, 1034, and New York Tax Law §360, subd. 12). In addition, alienability, liability for maintenance and repairs, as well as the privileges of making interior alterations, give a popular recognition to the status of realty quite in accord with the decisional law which treats this type of property as realty.

2. In 1971, President Nixon invoked his statutory power to declare a temporary price freeze on real estate sales. While the freeze was on, plaintiff bought a cooperative apartment at a price greater than the apartment's value when the freeze began. In dismissing plaintiff's action for a statutory refund, the court held that the buyer's right to a proprietary lease did not convert what was essentially stock ownership into real estate. Stockton v. Lucas, 482 F.2d 979 (Temp. Emer. Ct. App. 1973).

3. Ordinarily, the public sale of shares of stock is subject to federal securities regulation, yet there is widespread agreement that the denomination of the purchaser's interest in a cooperative corporation as "stock" does not, by itself, create a security under the federal acts. Cf. United Housing Foundation, Inc. v. Forman, page 974 infra.

4. Note, Legal Characterization of the Individual's Interest in a Cooperative Apartment: Realty or Personalty?, 73 Colum. L. Rev. 250-288 (1973), mentions still other problem areas where the real versus personal classification may make a difference. These include:

a. The taxability of the transfer; for example, the New York sales tax applies to the retail sale of "tangible personal property";

b. The spousal co-ownership of the cooperative interest; for example, New York permits the creation of a tenancy by the entirety in real property only;

c. Estate administration; for example, does the cooperative interest pass to the devisee of "all real estate owned by me"? Cf. Matter of Miller,

205 Misc. 770, 130 N.Y.S.2d 295 (Sur. Ct. 1954); Matter of Turner, 36 Misc. 2d 684, 233 N.Y.S.2d 108 (Sur. Ct. 1962).

5. The Model Real Estate Cooperative Act, page 943 supra, note 4, contains the following provision:

> Unless the declaration provides that the cooperative interests are real estate for all purposes, the cooperative interests are personal property. [The cooperative interests are subject to the provisions of (insert reference to State Homestead Exemptions), even if they are personal property.]

In explaining this choice, the commissioners comment:

> 1. The classification of the cooperative interests as real property or as personal property is significant for purposes of such matters as tenure, sales, recordation, transfer taxes, property taxes, estate and inheritance taxes, testate and intestate succession, mortgage lending, perfection, priority and enforcement of liens, and rights of redemption.
> 2. The section deals with an important theoretical and practical issue which pervades the cooperative field: whether a tenant-stockholder holds an interest in real or in personal property. The section resolves that question by permitting the declarant [sponsor] to decide that issue for each cooperative on a project-by-project basis. By so doing, the section seeks to avoid changing traditional practice in the various states.

The editors of this casebook have seen little evidence that courts decide the classification question on a "project-by-project" basis, rather than as a general rule, as in the *Shor* decision. Nor have courts adopted a single rule — i.e., realty or personalty, instead of a rule tailored to the issue at hand.

Would it not be preferable for a legislature to indicate, as to each of the matters listed in the above comment, whether the cooperative interest is to be treated as personalty or realty?

2. Liability in Tort

White v. Cox
17 Cal. App. 3d 826, 95 Cal. Rptr. 259 (1971)

FLEMING, Associate Justice. Plaintiff White owns a condominium in the Merrywood condominium project and is a member of Merrywood Apartments, a non-profit unincorporated association which maintains the common areas of Merrywood. In his complaint against Merrywood Apartments for damages for personal injuries White avers he tripped and fell over a water sprinkler negligently maintained by Merrywood Apartments in the common area of Merrywood. The trial court sustained Merrywood's demurrer without leave to amend and entered judgment of dismissal. White appeals.

The question here is whether a member of an unincorporated association of condominium owners may bring an action against the association for damages caused by negligent maintenance of the common areas in the condominium project. In contesting the propriety of such an action defendant association argues that because it is a joint enterprise each member is both principal and agent for every other member, and consequently the negligence of each member must be imputed to every other member. Hence, its argument goes, a member may not maintain an action for negligence against the association because the member himself shares responsibility as a principal for the negligence of which he complains. (6 Am. Jur. 2d, Associations and Clubs, §31.)

We first consider the present status of an unincorporated association's liability in tort to its members. . . .

Since 1962 the trend of case law has flowed toward full recognition of the unincorporated association as a separate legal entity. A member of an unincorporated association does not incur liability for acts of the association or acts of its members which he did not authorize or perform. (Orser v. George, 252 Cal. App. 2d 660, 670-671, 60 Cal. Rptr. 708.) A partner in a business partnership has been allowed to maintain an action against the partnership for the loss of his truck as a result of partnership negligence. (Smith v. Hensley (Ky.), 354 S.W.2d 744, 98 A.L.R.2d 340.) In the latter case the court declared that the doctrine of imputed negligence, which would normally bar a partner's recovery against the partnership, was an artificial rule of law which should yield to reason and practical considerations; since the partnership would have been liable for damages to the property of a stranger, no just reason existed for denying recovery for damages to the property of a partner. In affirming a judgment for plaintiff the court said: ". . . under a realistic approach, seeking to achieve substantial justice, the plaintiff should be held entitled to maintain the action."

In view of these developments over the past decade we conclude that unincorporated associations are now entitled to general recognition as separate legal entities and that as a consequence a member of an unincorporated association may maintain a tort action against his association.

Does this general rule of tort liability of an unincorporated association to its members apply in the specific instance of a condominium? A brief review of the statutory provisions which sanction and regulate the condominium form of ownership will clarify the nature of what we are dealing with. A *condominium* is an estate in real property consisting of an undivided interest in common in a portion of a parcel of real property together with a separate interest in another portion of the same parcel. (Civ. Code, §783.) A *project* is the entire parcel of property, a *unit* is the separate interest, and the *common areas* are the entire project except for the units. (Civ. Code, §1350.) Transfer of a unit, unless otherwise provided, is presumed to transfer the entire condominium. (Civ. Code, §1352.) Ownership is usually limited to the interior surfaces of the unit, a cotenancy in the common areas, and nonexclusive easements for ingress, egress, and support. (Civ. Code, §1353.) Typically, a condominium consists of an apartment house in which the units consist of individual apartments and the common areas consist of the remainder of the building and the grounds. Individual owners maintain their own apartments, and an association of apartment owners maintains the common areas. The association obtains funds for the care of the common areas by charging dues and levying assessments on each apartment owner.

The original project owner must record a condominium *plan* (Civ. Code, §1351), and restrictions in the plan become enforcible as equitable servitudes (Civ. Code, §1355). The plan may provide for management of the project by the condominium owners, by a board of governors elected by the owners, or by an elected or appointed agent. Management may acquire property, enforce restrictions, maintain the common areas, insure the owners, and make reasonable assessments. (Civ. Code, §§1355, 1358.) Only under exceptional circumstances may the condominium project be partitioned. (Civ. Code, §1354; Code Civ. Proc., §752b.) Zoning ordinances must be construed to treat condominiums in like manner as similar structures, lots, or parcels. (Civ. Code, §1370.) Condominium projects with five or more condominiums are subject to rules regulating subdivided lands and subdivisions. (Bus. & Prof. Code, §§11004.5, 11535.1.) Individual condominiums are separately assessed and taxed. (Rev. & Tax. Code, §2188.3.) Savings and loan associations may lend money on the security of condominium real property. (Fin. Code, §7153.1.)

California's condominium legislation parallels that of other jurisdictions (see Law of Condominium, Ferrer & Stecher (1957)), and a review of this legislation brings out the two different aspects of the typical condominium scheme. (1) Operations. These are normally conducted by a management association created to run the common affairs of the condominium owners. The association functions in a manner comparable to other unincorporated associations in that it is controlled by a governing body, acts through designated agents, and functions under the authority of bylaws, etc. (the plan). In this aspect of the condominium scheme the management association of condominium owners functions as a distinct and separate personality from the owners themselves. (2) Ownership. In its system of tenure for real property the condominium draws elements both from tenancy in common and from separate ownership. Tenancy in common has also been brought into the structure of the management association, for under Civil Code section 1358 the management association holds personal property in common for the benefit of the condominium owners.

In a formal sense, therefore, the condominium owners are tenants in common of the common areas and the personal property held by the management association, and they are owners in fee of separate units, which are not separate in fact. It is apparent that in its legal structure the condominium first combines elements from several concepts—unincorporated association, separate property, and tenancy in common—and then seeks to delineate separate privileges and responsibilities on the one hand from common privileges and responsibilities on the other. At this juncture we . . . pose two questions. Does the condominium association possess a separate existence from its members? Do the members retain direct control over the operations of the association?

Our answer to the first question derives from the nature of the condominium and its employment of the concept of separateness. Were separateness not clearly embodied within the condominium project the unit owners would become tenants in common of an estate in real property and remain exposed to all the consequences which flow from such a status. We think the concept of separateness in the condominium project carries over to any management body or association formed to handle the common affairs of the project, and that both the condominium project and the condominium association must be considered separate legal entities from its unit owners and association members.

For answer to our second question we turn to the statutory scheme, whence it clearly appears that in ordinary course a unit owner does not directly control the activities of the management body set up to handle the common affairs of the condominium project. To illustrate from the facts at bench: White owns his individual unit and a one-sixtieth interest in the common areas of Merrywood. An administrator controls the common affairs of Merrywood and maintains the common area where White tripped over the sprinkler. The administrator is appointed by and responsible to a board of governors. The board of governors is elected by the unit owners in an election in which each owner has one vote, owners vote by proxy, and cumulative voting is allowed. White is not a member of the board of governors. The Merrywood condominium plan succinctly warns, "In case management is not to your satisfaction, you may have no recourse.". . . [W]e would be sacrificing reality to theoretical formalism to rule that White had any effective control over the operation of the common areas of Merrywood, for in fact he had no more control over operations than he would have had as a stockholder in a corporation which owned and operated the project.

. . . We conclude, therefore, that a condominium possesses sufficient aspects of an unincorporated association to make it liable in tort to its members. The condominium and the condominium association may be sued in the condominium name under authority of section 388 of the Code of Civil Procedure. The condominium and the condominium association may be served in the statutory manner provided for service on an unincorporated association (Corp. Code, §§24003-24007), and individual unit owners need not be named or served as parties in a negligence action against the condominium and the condominium association.³

We conclude (1) the condominium association may be sued for negligence in its common name, (2) by a member of the association, (3) who may obtain a judgment against the condominium and the condominium association.

The judgment of dismissal is reversed.

Compton, J., concurs.

ROTH, Presiding Justice (concurring).

I concur.

I agree that a member of an unincorporated association of condominium owners may sue the association in tort. (Code Civ. Proc., §388.) However, the majority opinion fails to define or distinguish the extent to which individual unit owners in a condominium project may become liable to another unit owner or to a third person for tortious conduct arising in the common areas of the condominium project. In footnote 3, the majority declines to hold on "what property execution may be levied to satisfy a judgment against the condominium and the condominium association."

When as at bench a judgment of dismissal entered after a demurrer without leave to amend has been sustained the question of a levy of execution may not be properly before this court. However, the question of the identities of the parties liable is not settled in this case¹ nor is the basis of the

---

3. We express no opinion on what property execution may be levied to satisfy a judgment against the condominium and the condominium association. With reference to liens for labor, services, or materials, the last sentence of Civil Code section 1357 reads:

The owner of any condominium may remove his condominium from a lien against two or more condominiums or any part thereof by payment to the holder of the lien of the fraction of the total sum secured by such lien which is attributable to his condominium.

It could be implied from the sense of the section that a condominium owner may satisfy his portion of any liability arising out of the operation of the condominium project by the payment of his proportionate share of the liability. Such a conclusion would conform to what has been written on the subject by text writers (Rohan and Reskin, Condominium Law and Practice (1970), Chapter 10A, and 4 Powell on Real Property, section 633.25), and parallels what has been achieved by statute in other states. Alaska, Massachusetts, and Washington provide that a cause of action in tort relating to the common areas may be maintained only against the association of apartment owners. A judgment lien becomes a common expense and is removed from an individual condominium upon payment by the individual owner of his proportionate share. (Alaska Stat., Title 34, §34.07.260; Annot. Laws of Massachusetts, Chap. 183A, §13; Rev. Code of Washington Annot., §64.32.240.) District of Columbia, Idaho, and Maryland provide more generally that any judgment lien against two or more condominium owners may be removed from an individual condominium upon payment by the condominium owner of his proportionate share. (Dist. of Columbia Code Encyclopedia, §5-924(c); Idaho Code, §55-1515; Annot. Code of Maryland, Art. 21, §138.) In contrast is Mississippi, whose code declares that individual owners have no personal liability for damages caused by the governing body or connected with use of the common area. (Miss. Code Annot., §896-15.)

1. In addition to Merrywood Apartments, the complaint named Does I through X as defendants.

liability of parties other than the association, to wit, Merrywood Apartments.

The ownership of the common areas in a condominium project is vested in the individual unit owners as tenants in common. (Civ. Code, §1353(b).) Thus, even though, as the majority holds, the association may be sued in its separate name, it is apparent that the legal owners of the common areas are not immunized from liability by virtue of the mere existence of the association.

A comparative study of California condominium legislation with that in other states shows that the question of the individual unit owner's tort liability in cases arising in the common areas has not been regulated by statute. The majority's suggestion that section 1357 of the Civil Code, in providing for the aliquot satisfaction of liens for labor, services, or materials, also provides for the distribution of tort liability among the owners is too great a strain on the expressly limited wording of that code section. This suggestion has been questioned by at least one commentator (Comment, 77 Harv. L. Rev. 777, 780, fn. 24) and it does not square with the fact that California has followed the lead of most states and has failed to provide adequate regulation or protection of the individual owner's interests in the case of torts arising from the common areas. (See Rohan, Perfecting the Condominium as a Housing Tool: Innovations in Tort Liability and Insurance (1967), 32 Law and Contemporary Problems 305, 308; Kerr, Condominium—Statutory Implementation (1963), 28 St. John's L. Rev. 1, 42-43; Comment, supra, 77 Harv. L. Rev. 777, 780.) The absence of an express statutory scheme for the re-distribution of tort liability, such as those found in the Alaska, Massachusetts and Washington legislation, is ample warning that the problem of protecting the individual unit owner from tort liability which, it should be noted, may exceed the value of his unit[2] (whether it be to another unit owner or to a third person) is yet an open question in California.

One practical answer is, of course, insurance taken out by the association to cover liability in respect of the common areas. (See Kerr, supra, at 43.)[3] It might then be argued depending on the terms of the written declaration between unit owners that, at least as between suing and defendant unit owners, the maximum amount of liability of defendant unit owners has been contractually limited to the maximum of the insurance taken out by the association.

At bench we have the declaration upon which the project at bench is grounded before us *only* insofar as its terms are reflected by the permit of the Commissioner of Corporations.

---

2. Thus, in California, the co-owners may have to respond for injuries arising out of the common areas in terms of the *personal* tort liability of tenants in common, which according to the common law and our statutory law results in joint and several liability. (Code Civ. Proc., §384; 86 C.J.S. Tenancy in Common §143.)

3. In California, the governing body of a condominium project may obtain insurance on behalf of, and for the benefit of condominium owners. (Civ. Code, §1355(b)(2).)

The permit, after setting forth the plan of management and powers of the Board of Governors, sets forth in pertinent part that the Board of Governors shall have the power to: "Contract and/or pay for fire, casualty, liability and other insurance and bonding of its members, maintenance, gardening, utilities, materials, supplies, services and personnel necessary for the operation of the project, taxes and assessments which may become a lien on the entire project or the common area, and reconstruction of portions of the project which are to be rebuilt after damage or destruction."

The above excerpt or summary (in the Permit) from the declaration is substantially similar to the powers set forth in section 1355, subdivision (b)(2) of the Civil Code, which empowers the Board of Governors to obtain ". . . fire, casualty, liability, workmen's compensation and other insurance insuring condominium owners, and for bonding of the members of any management body."

It occurs to me, therefore, on the limited record before this court that each unit holder of the project has *by contract* delegated to the Board of Governors which operates the project the power and responsibility to obtain adequate liability insurance for the project to cover claims of third persons and also adequate insurance to cover negligence actions of unit owners against the association and actions which any unit owner might bring against other unit owners because of the negligence of the association.

It seems to me therefore that any failure by management to obtain adequate insurance or any insurance leaves a unit holder injured by negligence of management (as distinguished from independent negligence of a fellow unit owner) with the right to proceed against the association to the extent of its insurance if any and with no right to proceed against other unit owners. A suit by one other than a unit owner is a question not raised by the litigation at bench, and cannot be similarly circumscribed. Generally, tenants in common may be joined as defendants and their liability is joint and several (Code Civ. Proc., §384), and the apportionment of liability as between unit owners is, of course, a difficult and vexing question. (See generally, 86 C.J.S. Tenancy in Common §143.)

3. The Delinquent Owner

1915 16th St. Co-Operative Assn. v. Pinkett

85 A.2d 58 (D.C. 1951)

CAYTON, Chief Judge. A co-operatively owned apartment house sued one of its member-tenants for possession of an apartment, charging that he owed three months rent under his lease. He denied the charge and the trial court ruled in his favor. Plaintiff brings this appeal. No brief has been filed by counsel for appellee, hence we do not know what position he takes on this appeal. But the issues are revealed in the pleadings, evidence, and documentary exhibits, and in a memorandum of the trial judge on which the decision was based.

Defendant John R. Pinkett, Jr., on July 17, 1950, entered into a "contract to purchase co-operative apartment" from plaintiff at an agreed price of $7950. Under the terms of the contract he made an initial deposit of $90 and agreed to pay $410 more to make up a $500 settlement figure. The agreement provided for payments of $90 per month, made up as follows: $54.50 on account of the deferred purchase money, $25 for maintenance, and $10.50 on a note of $386.50 which Pinkett gave to complete the settlement. The purchase agreement recited that at settlement Pinkett was to receive a certificate of ownership and a "proprietary lease" under which he was to have the right to "own and use" the apartment "as long as he remains a member of the association and abides by all the terms of this contract." On the same day a "proprietary lease" was signed by the parties running in favor of Pinkett for 99 years. Among the provisions of the lease was one authorizing the termination thereof "in case the Lessee shall default in the payment of any obligation required hereunder, or of any installment thereof." The same article of the lease also provided that upon termination the lessor would have the right "to reenter the demised premises and to remove all persons and personal property therefrom, either by summary dispossess proceedings or by any suitable action or proceeding at law . . . and to repossess the demised premises in its former state as if this lease had not been made."

Mr. Pinkett took possession and made two monthly payments of $90 each for July and August 1950. He has paid no more but has continued in default and in possession of the apartment.

In December 1950, plaintiff-owner brought this suit for possession in the Municipal Court alleging that Pinkett was in possession under a leasehold and was in default of payment of rent for the three months from September 17 to December 16. In his answer defendant denied that he was a tenant of plaintiff and denied being in default. The trial court in a written memorandum found that there was no intent on the part of plaintiff and defendant to create the relationship of landlord and tenant, that the contract was one for the purchase of an apartment and that the monthly sums payable by defendant were not rent but were payments on account of the purchase. The judge also ruled that there was in form a landlord-tenant relationship but that in substance defendant was the owner of the apartment with the "exclusive right to personal, perpetual use thereof as a dwelling," and that as between defendant and the other occupants in the building the relationship was in effect a partnership for their mutual benefit.

In testing the correctness of these rulings we must look to the transaction as a whole, to the writings between the parties, to the circumstances under which they were made, and to the matters with which they deal, and thereby determine the intent of the parties and the status they created.

The evidence discloses that defendant's right to possession was based initially on his purchase agreement, but more directly on his "proprietary lease." Undoubtedly the purchase agreement vested in him some of the attributes of an owner or landlord. This has been recognized in this jurisdiction, the courts holding that a member of a co-operative apartment house corporation may, when he desires possession for his own use, sue as a "landlord" under the local Rent Act and maintain a possessory action against a tenant who refused to yield an apartment to him. Abbot v. Bralove, D.D.C., 81 F. Supp. 532, *affirmed* 85 U.S. App. D.C. 189, 176 F.2d 64; Glennon v. Butler, D.C. Mun. App., 66 A.2d 519; Hicks v. Bigelow, D.C. Mun. App. 55 A.2d 924. But none of these cases held that the "landlord" status of such a co-operative member was his only legal status. On the contrary, they all were confined to a situation where a co-operative member was suing a tenant in possession.

What then is the status of a purchaser-lessee like this one who has defaulted in his payments to his co-operative corporation? We think the answer is clearly to be found in the lease between them. There it is provided, as we have already seen, that the lessee's right to possession is lost if he defaults in the payment of any installments due and that the lessor is expressly given the right of reentry. As applied to the facts of this case, we can think of no practical difference between this and conventional lease agreements. What it amounts to is that the lessee is given the right of occupancy so long as he does not default in his monthly payments, but that when default occurs the co-operative corporation has the right to terminate the lease. This right of termination has been recognized even in New York where some courts have treated such a relationship as in effect a partnership. Tompkins v. Hale, 172 Misc. 1071, 15 N.Y.S.2d 854, *affirmed* 259 App. Div. 860, 20 N.Y.S.2d 398.

We have concluded that the plaintiff had a right to maintain the suit, that defendant's right to possession derived from the lease, and that by his default under the lease such right has been lost. Accordingly, the Municipal Court is instructed to enter judgment for plaintiff for possession. . . .

Defendant may still wish to redeem his lost rights by bringing his payments up-to-date. If so we assume that the trial court would entertain an appropriate motion filed by him, accompanied by a tender of all payments in arrears together with interest and costs. See Trans-Lux Radio City Corp. v. Service Parking Corp., D.C. Mun. App., 54 A.2d 144.

Reversed.

On Motion for Rehearing

Before Cayton, Chief Judge, and Hood and Quinn, Associate Judges.

CAYTON, Chief Judge. Appellee filed a motion for rehearing and pursuant to our order oral argument has been had thereon. . . .

We must adhere to our previous ruling that there was a default under the lease and that by reason of such default the co-operative had a right to sue for and recover possession. . . .

HOOD, Associate Judge (dissenting). I joined in the original opinion in this case, but on further study I have concluded that such opinion was erroneous. I am now convinced that the Landlord and Tenant Branch of the Municipal Court had no jurisdiction to render a judgment for possession of the apartment.

The statute, Code 1940, §11-735, provides summary remedy for possession of real estate in a definitely limited class of cases. Aside from cases arising after sale under deed of trust or foreclosure of mortgage and cases of forcible entry and detainer (and obviously the present case falls in neither of those classes), the trial court may entertain suits for possession of real estate only in those cases where the conventional relation of landlord and tenant exists.

Whatever may be the exact relation between a corporation holding title to a co-operative apartment house and one to whom it has sold one of the apartment units, the relationship is far more than the conventional relationship of landlord and tenant. One who holds stock or other certificate entitling him to use of a cooperative apartment is generally said to have "purchased" the apartment, Wardman Const. Co. v. Flynn, 60 App. D.C. 357, 54 F.2d 831, and in effect is regarded as the owner of it. 542 Morris Park Ave. Corporation v. Wilkins, 120 Misc. 48, 197 N.Y.S. 625. It has been said that although the corporation holds legal title the entire equitable estate is distributed proportionately among the owners of the apartments and that ownership of an apartment constitutes an interest in real property. In re Pitts' Estate, 218 Cal. 184, 22 P.2d 694. This court has said that the purchaser of a cooperative apartment "is more than a mere tenant or lessee" and "has most of the attributes of an owner." Hicks v. Bigelow, D.C. Mun. App., 55 A.2d 924.

The parties recognized this in their dealings. Appellee contracted to purchase a "Certificate of Ownership" which would "entitle him to the perpetual use and occupancy" of the apartment. Appellant agreed "to cause to be conveyed to the purchaser a right of perpetual use as evidenced by a Proprietary Lease." The contract, the certificate of ownership and the proprietary lease are not severable. They must be considered together. Appellant would have the court disregard everything but the lease and consider the case as nothing more than an ordinary landlord and tenant proceeding. The complaint alleges appellee has defaulted in payment of rent, but in fact appellee agreed to pay no rent. The transaction is not one of leasing property in exchange for payment of rent but in essence is a purchase or capital investment.

In my opinion the corporation may not bring an action in the landlord and tenant court to oust the owner from possession, treating him as a mere tenant and ignoring his rights under his contract of purchase and certificate of ownership. His right to possession was what he purchased and if such right is to be terminated then all the rights and obligations between the parties ought to be adjusted. This proceeding would leave the rights and obligations under the contract of purchase unsettled and unadjusted. . . .

In short, I think that before the corporation can take back that which it sold, all rights and obligations between the parties under the contract of purchase and the proprietary lease must be settled and that this cannot be done in a summary landlord and tenant proceeding.

NOTES AND QUESTIONS

1. Accord Earl W. Jimerson Housing Co., Inc. v. Butler, 102 Misc. 2d 423, 425 N.Y.S.2d 925 (App. Term 1979); Model Real Estate Cooperative Act §3-115(a) (1981). Contra Plaza Road Co-op., Inc. v. Finn, 201 N.J. Super. 174, 492 A.2d 1072 (App. Div. 1985) (relationship between association and a cooperator-shareholder not that of landlord-tenant for the purpose of a summary dispossession action).

2. Compare a condominium or homes association. A unit owner fails to pay her assessment on the common areas. What is "management's" remedy? Cf. Rohan and Reskin, Condominium Law and Practice 6-25 through 6-31 (1985).

3. Compare a condominium or homes association. A unit owner breaks the project rules. What is "management's" remedy?

4. The condominium statutes in Alaska and Washington authorize the association, upon obtaining the approval of a majority of unit owners and upon serving a 10-day's notice, to sever all utility service to a delinquent owner. Alaska Stat. §34.07.230 (Supp. 1975); Wash. Rev. Code Ann. §64.32.200 (1983). Discuss the pros and cons of this approach to non-payment of assessments. Cf. Rohan and Reskin, Condominium Law and Practice 6-25 (1985).

5. The cooperative tenant loses his lease for nonpayment of rent. Does he also lose his "equity" in the apartment? Suppose that the corporation can resell the apartment for $100,000. To whom does the $100,000 belong? What analogies apply: default by installment land vendee; by mortgagor on power of sale mortgage; by lessee who has installed costly improvements? Cf. also Model Real Estate Cooperative Act §3-115(a) (if cooperative interest is personal property, lien for unpaid assessments may be foreclosed in like manner as a security interest under UCC Article 9; if cooperative interest is real estate, lien may be foreclosed by judicial sale or, where provided by statute and agreement, by power of sale).

6. A related issue is whether statutes protective of "tenants" would extend to the owners of cooperative apartments. Examples are:

a) Warranty of habitability: Suarez v. Rivercross Tenants' Corp., 107 Misc. 2d 135, 438 N.Y.S.2d 164 (App. Term 1981) (warranty applies to proprietary lessees);

b) Rights regarding household pets: Linden Hill No. 1 Cooperative Corp. v. Kleiner, 124 Misc. 2d 1001, 478 N.Y.S.2d 519 (Civ. Ct. 1984) (proprietary lessees enjoy similar rights).

4. Restraints on Alienation

Penthouse Properties, Inc. v. 1158 Fifth Ave., Inc.
256 A.D. 685, 11 N.Y.S.2d 417 (1939)

UNTERMYER, Justice. This submitted controversy concerns the validity of certain restrictions upon the right to transfer stock and upon the assignment of a proprietary lease in a co-operative apartment house.

The plaintiff and the corporate defendant are organized under the Stock Corporation Law of the State of New York. The corporate defendant was caused to be organized in 1924 by Houston Properties Corporation (referred to as Houston). Since then it has been the owner of real property at the southeast corner of Fifth Avenue and 97th Street, New York City, and the improvement erected there in that year. The building, a fifteen-story apartment house, was erected by Houston. In payment of the contract price for the construction of the building and the cost of the land, the defendant corporation issued its entire capital stock to Houston.

On September 24, 1925, Richard T. Harriss, the husband of the defendant Belle C. Harriss, entered into a subscription agreement with Houston, whereby he agreed to purchase 309 shares of the defendant corporation and became entitled to a proprietary lease for a term ending 99 years from October 23, 1924, of apartment 6-B, a ten-room apartment on the sixth floor. Pursuant to the subscription agreement, and on October 27, 1925, Mr. Harriss entered into a proprietary lease for the apartment and took possession thereof. On January 24, 1929, he executed an amended lease, in form similar to the lease subsequently executed by his wife.

About August 24, 1931, Mr. Harriss transferred his stock, together with his rights in the proprietary lease of apartment 6-B, to his wife, the defendant Belle C. Harriss, and on September 10, 1931, Mrs. Harriss became a stockholder of record of the defendant corporation. A new certificate was issued to her and a new proprietary lease was made in her name. The new certificate was in all respects similar to the certificate previously held by Mrs. Harriss.

In August, 1934, Mrs. Harriss exchanged her apartment for the duplex

Selected Problems

apartment known as 16-C, consisting of eleven rooms, theretofore occupied by a Mrs. Smith under a similar proprietary lease in connection with which Mrs. Smith had held 750 shares of stock. In consideration of this exchange, Mrs. Harriss, in addition to a cash payment, assigned to Mrs. Smith her 309 shares of stock and her rights in the proprietary lease of apartment 6-B. About the same time, Mrs. Harriss also purchased from Mrs. Smith 15 shares of stock including the right to a proprietary lease of maid's room No. 12 and an additional 12 shares which included the right to a proprietary lease of maid's room No. 4 in the building. The corporate defendant thereupon issued to Mrs. Harriss three new certificates, representing her ownership of 777 shares, and three new proprietary leases of apartment 16-C and the two maid's rooms.

About March 17, 1938, Mrs. Harriss wrote to the defendant corporation stating that she intended to dispose of her stock and leases, but that before making any other disposition she would sell to the corporate defendant at a substantial sacrifice. That offer was refused. About a week thereafter Mr. Harriss formed the plaintiff. Its entire capital stock was issued to him and is still owned by him. Mrs. Harriss then sold to the plaintiff her 777 shares of stock and all rights in the three proprietary leases. On March 28, 1938, she wrote to the corporate defendant to that effect. On the following day, the plaintiff demanded the transfer to it of the 777 shares of stock upon the corporate books and execution of three new proprietary leases in place of those previously held by Mrs. Harriss. The plaintiff also tendered to the defendant corporation the three certificates of stock in the name of Mrs. Harriss, duly endorsed for transfer with the necessary documentary stamps attached, and demanded that new certificates be issued in its name.

The defendant corporation notified the plaintiff of its refusal to recognize the transfer of the stock on account of non-compliance by the holder of the lease and stock with Articles X and XVII (d) of the proprietary lease under which the apartment was rented and the stock held. The defendant corporation also refused to accept checks tendered by the plaintiff in payment of monthly assessments and other charges for operating expenses, the bills for which had been sent to Mrs. Harriss. The monthly assessments for April to November, 1938, inclusive, amount to $5,184.27, for which the corporate defendant claims, among other things, to be entitled to judgment against Mrs. Harriss. . . .

It has been stipulated that the plaintiff was organized for the purpose of acquiring 777 shares of stock from Mrs. Harriss and to procure from the defendant corporation in connection therewith proprietary leases to the apartments. The plaintiff's certificate of incorporation provides that said apartments are to be used for private residential purposes only and by an individual or individuals approved by its board of directors.

It is conceded that the stock was acquired by Mrs. Harriss, as well as by the plaintiff from her, with full knowledge of the provisions contained in the leases and on the stock certificate, with respect to the transfer of the stock and leases.

These provisions are as follows:

"X. That Lessee shall not cause or permit any of his stock and/or this lease, or any right of Lessee arising therefrom, to be assigned or subjected to any lien or encumbrance, except as in Article XVII, subdivision (d), hereof, specifically provided; and shall not sublet the demised premises or any part thereof without the prior written consent of Lessor. . . .

"XVII. That this lease shall be terminated, otherwise than by expiration, as follows: . . .

"(d) By and upon a sale, assignment or transfer of the stock owned by Lessee, together with Lessee's right to a lease of the demised premises for the remainder of the term hereof, with the consent of Lessor in writing, and the assumption, in writing, by the assignee, of obligations identical with those of Lessee under this lease, for the remainder of the term hereof, either upon acceptance by the assignee of an assignment of this lease or of a new lease; the consent of Lessor to be by authority of the Board of Directors or, upon refusal thereof by said Board, by authority of the holders of two-thirds of the capital stock; provided, that the failure of the Board of Directors to authorize such consent within thirty days after application therefor shall be equivalent to a refusal thereof and that the vote of the members of the Board of Directors and of stockholders on such authorization may be expressed in writing or by telegram without a formal meeting. When this lease has been so terminated and Lessee has discharged all accrued obligations under this lease, he shall have no further liability hereunder and Lessor shall execute, acknowledge and deliver to Lessee a written release of Lessee from all further liability under this lease."

These are the provisions referred to in the endorsement on the stock certificate, with which, it is asserted, Mrs. Harriss failed to comply in undertaking to assign the stock and leases. It is these provisions which the plaintiff and Mrs. Harriss contend are invalid and unenforceable as in restraint of alienation.

Accordingly the plaintiff requests judgment, as does also Mrs. Harriss, that the following relief be granted: That the defendant corporation be required to recognize as valid the sale by Mrs. Harriss to the plaintiff of 777 shares of stock of the defendant corporation, and that the plaintiff be accorded all the rights of a stockholder therein, including the right to new certificates and new proprietary leases of the apartments allocated thereto.

In addition to a money judgment against Mrs. Harriss for $5,184.27 with interest, the defendant corporation demands a declaratory judgment that Mrs. Harriss is not entitled to assign her leases and stock without written consent of the Board of Directors of the corporate defendant or two-thirds of the stockholders, that her assignment to the plaintiff be declared ineffective, and for judgment dismissing the plaintiff's claim for transfer of the stock and the execution of new leases.

The question now presented, apparently never decided in this State, is the validity of the restrictive plan under which co-operative apartment houses have been constructed and the stock sold. The validity of such a plan is challenged by the plaintiff and by Mrs. Harriss on the ground that restraints against the alienation of the corporate stock imposed by the limitations contained in the lease, prohibiting any sale without the consent of the directors or two-thirds of the stockholders, are against public policy and therefore unenforceable.

The general rule that ownership of property cannot exist in one person and the right of alienation in another (De Peyster v. Michael, 6 N.Y. 467, 493, 57 Am. Dec. 470) has in this State been frequently applied to shares of corporate stock. [Citations omitted.] Cognizance has been taken of the principle that "the right of transfer is a right of property, and if another has the arbitrary power to forbid a transfer of property by the owner, that amounts to an annihilation of property" (Fisher v. Bush, 35 Hun. 641). The same rule has been applied in other States. [Citations omitted.] But restrictions against the sale of shares of stock unless other stockholders or the corporation have first been accorded an opportunity to buy, are not repugnant to that principle. [Citations omitted.] The weight of authority elsewhere is to the same effect. See Annotations on Validity of Restrictions, 65 A.L.R., pp. 1168-1171. Likewise, restrictions against the assignment by the tenant of a leasehold, or against subletting, without the consent of the landlord first obtained, have frequently been sustained. Ogden v. Riverview Holding Corporation, 134 Misc. 149, 234 N.Y.S. 678, *affirmed* 226 App. Div. 882, 235 N.Y.S. 850; Proctor Troy Properties Co., Inc., v. Dugan Store, Inc., 191 App. Div. 685, 181 N.Y.S. 786; Barrington Apartment Assn. v. Watson, 38 Hun. 545.

We are now required to decide within which of these divergent principles the co-operative apartment house restrictive plan is to be classified. In the consideration of that question the residential nature of the enterprise, the privilege of selecting neighbors and the needs of the community are not to be ignored. The tenant stockholders in a co-operative apartment building are concerned in the purchase of a home. Necessarily, therefore, the permanency of the individual occupants as tenant owners is an essential element in the general plan and their financial responsibility an inducement to the corporation in accepting them as stockholders. Under the "Plan of Organization" each stockholder is entitled to vote upon the choice of neighbors and their financial responsibility. The latter consideration becomes important when it is remembered that the failure of any tenant to pay his proportion of operating expenses increases the liability of other tenant stockholders. Thus, in a very real sense the tenant stockholders enter into a relation not unlike a partnership, though expressed in corporate form. . . .

From all these considerations it follows that if restraint on alienation of the stock may be said to be imposed at all, it is a restraint which in every respect is reasonable and appropriate to the lawful purposes to be attained. Compare Sacks v. Neptune Meter Co., 144 Misc. 70, 258 N.Y.S. 254, *affirmed* 238 App. Div. 82, 263 N.Y.S. 462. We are unwilling to declare that arrangement to be illegal and unenforceable, particularly since such a declaration would invalidate a form of enterprise to which the Legislature has accorded implied recognition. Civil Practice Act, Section 1410, Subdivision 1-a. We conclude, therefore, that the special nature of the ownership of co-operative apartment houses by tenant owners requires that they be not included in the general rule against restraint on the sale of stock in corporations organized for profit. 68 Beacon Street, Inc. v. Sohier, 289 Mass. 354, 194 N.E. 303.

It is proper to add that we have not considered nor do we decide whether the consent of the directors or stockholders may be, or has been, arbitrarily withheld. Justification for refusing to consent to a transfer, if justification is required, ordinarily presents an issue of fact (Feist et al. v. Fifth Avenue Bank of New York, 280 N.Y. 189, 20 N.E.2d 388 decided April 11, 1939), which is not presented by the agreed statement of facts nor argued in the briefs.

Judgment should accordingly be granted in favor of the defendant corporation, as prayed for in the submission, against the plaintiff, and in favor of the defendant corporation against the co-defendant Belle C. Harriss for the sum of $5,184.27 with interest, but without costs.

Judgment unanimously granted in favor of the defendant corporation, as prayed for in the submission, against the plaintiff, and in favor of the defendant corporation against the co-defendant Belle C. Harriss for the sum of $5,184.27 with interest, but without costs. Settle order on notice. All concur.

Chianese v. Culley

397 F. Supp. 1344 (S.D. Fla. 1975)

FULTON, Chief Judge. The plaintiffs in this lawsuit allege in a two count complaint that Article XII F of the Declaration of Condominium of the defendant San Remo, Inc. constitutes an illegal restraint on alienation of property, and that the defendants have discriminated against them on the basis of their religion or national origin. The parties to this cause have stipulated that the issue raised in count one, being a purely legal issue, may be resolved by the Court based on memoranda of law submitted by each side. These memoranda have now been received, and the issue to be resolved by the Court in this Order is whether Article XII F of the Declaration of Condominium of San Remo, Inc. (hereinafter, Article XII F) constitutes an illegal restraint on alienation of property. Neither count two of the complaint, which alleges that the defendants have discriminated against the plaintiffs on the basis of their religion or national origin, nor the counterclaim or crossclaim, is before the Court at this time.

The facts of this case are not complicated. The defendants Culley are husband and wife and were the owners of apartment number 548, Villa Raphael in the San Remo Condominium. The plaintiffs contracted to purchase this condominium unit from the defendants Culley, but said defendants refused to close the transaction because San Remo, Inc. and its directors asserted its rights under Article XII F of the Declaration of Condominium, and provided an alternate purchaser for the unit in question. At that point, the plaintiffs filed this lawsuit, alleging that Article XII F constituted an illegal restraint against alienation of property and that the defendants were discriminating against the plaintiffs on the basis of their religion or national origin. After this lawsuit was filed, the defendants Culley issued a warranty deed to the plaintiffs Chianese, but the defendants San Remo continue to refuse to recognize the consummation of the transaction between the Culleys and the Chianeses. The issue before the Court at this point is thus whether Article XII F of the San Remo Declaration of Condominium constitutes an illegal restraint on alienation of property.

Article XII F provides in pertinent part as follows:

"F. Conveyances — In order to secure a community of congenial residents and thus protect the value of the apartments, the sale, leasing and mortgaging of apartments by any owner other than the Developer shall be subject to the following provisions so long as the apartment building in useful condition exists upon the land:

"1. Sale or lease — No apartment owner may dispose of an apartment or any interest therein by sale or by lease without approval of the Association, except to another apartment owner. If the purchaser or lessee is a corporation that approval may be conditioned upon the approval of those individuals who will be occupants of the apartment. The approval of the Association shall be obtained as follows:

"(a) Notice to Association. An apartment owner intending to make a bona fide sale or a bona fide lease of his apartment or any interest therein shall give notice to the Association of such intention, together with the name and address of the proposed purchaser or lessee, together with such other information as the Association may require.

"(b) Election of Association. Within sixty (60) days after receipt of such notice, the Association must approve the transaction or furnish a purchaser or lessee approved by the Association who will accept terms as favorable to the seller as the terms stated in the notice. Such purchaser or lessee furnished by the Association may have not less than sixty (60) days subsequent to the date of approval within which to close the transaction. The approval of the Association shall be in recordable form and delivered to the purchaser or lessee. . . ."

The general rule is that the right to convey property is one of the incidents of ownership, and the law will not permit the rights of ownership to be fettered by the imposition of restraints by grantors who both seek to convey their properties and at the same time maintain control over them. 61 Am. Jur. 2d Perpetuities and Restraints on Alienation §93. This right to convey hearkens back to the Statute of Quia Emptores in the year 1290, and the right to alienate one's property has been accepted as an incident of an estate in fee simple ever since. Thus, if Article XII F is found to constitute an absolute restraint against alienation of property, that article is void. Davis v. Geyer, 151 Fla. 362, 9 So. 2d 727 (1942); Holiday Out in America at St. Lucie, Inc. v. Bowes, 285 So. 2d 63 (Fla. App. 4th Dist. 1973).

Florida Statutes Chapter 711.04(1) provides that "A condominium parcel is a separate parcel of real property, the ownership of which may be in fee simple, or any other estate in real property recognized by law." The complaint alleges, and the defendants have not contested, that the condominium parcel in question was owned by the Culleys in fee simple.

The plaintiffs cite Davis v. Geyer, 151 Fla. 362, 9 So. 2d 727 (1942) as being dispositive of the issue at bar. That case held that a provision in an agreement to convey property reading "No sale of the said property is to be made by the party of the first part until the same is approved by the party of the second part" was invalid since it constituted an unlimited restraint on alienation of property.

Article XII F provides that the condominium association upon notice must, within sixty days, either approve the proposed purchaser or furnish another purchaser who will accept terms equally favorable to the seller. This provision is distinguishable from that in Davis v. Geyer. That case involved an absolute restriction against sale without the permission of the second party: should that party withhold permission, for whatever reason, the property could never be sold. Article XII F does not contain such an absolute restriction. By its terms, within sixty days, the association must either provide another purchaser or approve the proposed purchaser. Thus, at the close of the sixty day period, the property can be sold, whether to the seller's purchaser or to one provided by the association. Article XII F is thus not an absolute restraint, such as was found in the Davis v. Geyer case, but rather grants instead a "pre-emptive option" or "right of first refusal" to the condominium association.

The Restatement of Property, Vol. 4 §413(1) takes the position that a provision that the owner shall not sell his property without giving a designated person the opportunity to meet any offer received does not constitute an invalid restraint on alienation, provided that such provision does not violate the rule against perpetuities. Plaintiffs in their memo stipulate that the rule against perpetuities is not applicable to condominiums under Florida Statute 711.08(2). The Florida courts have followed the Restatement position, and have upheld provisions similar to that contained in Article XII F. . . .

While covenants which restrict the use of land are not favored, they will be enforced if they are confined to lawful purposes, are within reasonable bounds, and are expressed in clear language. Zoda v. Zoda, 292 So. 2d 412 (Fla. App. 2d Dist. 1974). Article XII F complies with these requirements. The stated purpose of Section XII F is to insure "a community of congenial residents." "The very nature of the condominium concept of ownership requires a degree of control in the management" thereof. Holiday Out in America at St. Lucie, Inc. v. Bowes, 285 So. 2d 63 (Fla. App. 4th Dist. 1973). Chapter 711.08(1)(*l*) of the Florida Statutes states that the declaration of condominium shall provide for "such other provisions not inconsistent with this law as may be desired, including but not limited to those relating to . . . use restrictions, limitation upon conveyance, sale, leasing, purchase, ownership and occupancy of units. . . ." Chapter 711.08(1)(*l*) thus clearly provides for and anticipates limitations on the sale of condominium units, providing that such restrictions are valid under the law. This Court has previously held herein that Article XII F does not constitute an illegal restraint against alienation, but is instead a valid and enforceable pre-emptive right granted to the condominium association. Likewise, the provision under Article XII F that the association must, upon notice, either approve the seller's purchaser or provide another purchaser for the same price is reasonable. . . .

Pursuant to the foregoing discussion, the Court finds that Article XII F of the San Remo declaration of condominium does not constitute an illegal restraint on the alienation of property, but that Article XII F grants instead a valid and enforceable right of first refusal to the condominium association. Accordingly, the Court finds in favor of the defendants as to the issue raised in Count One of the complaint.

NOTES AND QUESTIONS

1. Contrast the restraint in *Penthouse Properties* with that in *Chianese*. These typify the arrangements one finds, respectively, in a cooperative and condominium. Would *Chianese's* first count have succeeded if the San Remo condominium had barred him under a *Penthouse Properties*-type restriction? In weighing a restraint on sale, should courts treat co-ops and condos differently because one gets stock and lease in the cooperative and a fee interest (usually) in the condominium? What factors should the courts consider? What is the status of title if a co-op or condo unit were transferred without complying with the "approval" procedures?

2. The unit owner wants to rent her unit out. As to whether a restraint is reasonable, are the considerations different in a rental and a sales situation? In a short-term rental (less than 3 months) and a long-term rental (more than one year)? Consider Seagate Condominium Assn. v. Duffy, 330 So. 2d 484 (Fla. Dist. Ct. App. 1976), where the declaration barred leasing "as a regular practice for business, speculative, [or] investment . . . purposes"; the Board could grant, however, a short-term exception "to meet

special situations or avoid undue hardship." The court upheld the restraint. See also Kroop v. Caravelle Condominium, 323 So. 2d 307 (Fla. Dist. Ct. App. 1975) (owner could not lease unit more than once).

3. Weisner v. 791 Park Avenue Corp., 6 N.Y.2d 426, 160 N.E.2d 720 (1959) is in accord with the *Penthouse Properties* decision. The court of appeals reversed the court below. Justice Bastow, writing for the appellate division, doubted that landlord and tenant law should apply to the relationship between the cooperative and proprietary tenant:

> The defendants herein rely upon the general rule applicable to a provision against subletting contained in a lease. In such case it has been held that the landlord is under no duty to give consent and may even arbitrarily and unreasonably withhold such consent. Cf. Ogden v. Riverview Holding Corp., 134 Misc. 149, 150, 234 N.Y.S. 678, 679, *affirmed* 226 App. Div. 882, 235 N.Y.S. 850. We do not agree that such a legal principle is applicable when considering the rights of a proprietary lessee and the owner of a co-operative apartment. It is unnecessary to here set forth the factual and legal distinctions of the relationship between a landlord and tenant, on the one hand, and of a proprietary lessee and the owner of a co-operative apartment on the other. These differences were set forth in Penthouse Properties, Inc. v. 1158 Fifth Avenue, Inc., supra. See also Gilligan v. Tishman Realty & Construction Co., 283 App. Div. 157, 126 N.Y.S.2d 813, *affirmed* 306 N.Y. 974, 120 N.E.2d 230. It is unnecessary to explore in detail the rights in such circumstances of a proprietary lessee. It is sufficient to state that we do not embrace in its entirety the rule that the owner under any and all circumstances may arbitrarily refuse consent to a proprietary lessee to the sale of his lease and stock. As suggested in the *Penthouse* case, supra, justification for such action would ordinarily present a factual issue. [7 A.D.2d 75, 80-81, 180 N.Y.S.2d 734, 739-740 (1958).]

4. If a cooperative were required to treat assignment requests reasonably, which of the objections below would seem reasonable?

(a) The proposed assignee is an Arab prince. The cooperative fears that his presence in the building might invite angry protests (or even a bombing) from activist Jewish groups;
(b) The proposed assignees are a homosexual couple;
(c) The proposed assignees are an unmarried couple;
(d) The proposed assignee is giving his seller a purchase money mortgage for 90 percent of the contract price.

5. Note that *Chianese's* second count claimed religious and ethnic discrimination. Fair housing laws, including the federal Civil Rights Act of 1968, would generally cover shared facilities development. However, the federal statute allows the owner of a single-family house to avoid compliance if he does not engage a broker. 42 U.S.C. §3603(b)(1)(1970). Should that grace apply (the statute is unclear) to a unit owner in a condo or homes association if his unit is a one-family detached structure?

5. *Protecting the Consumer*

The age of consumerism has arrived. This has led, quite predictably, to growing governmental oversight of the housing developer who undertakes a multi-unit, shared facilities project. Where everything the homebuyer acquires lies within the four corners of his lot and where title passes via a one-page deed, the consumer, aided by his lawyer, can reasonably fend for himself. Where, however, the buyer is paying also for the right to enjoy amenities that he must share with others (and that still others may own) and where the title papers cover dozens of pages, the consumer and even his lawyer might welcome a wary, tough-minded regulator. As the project becomes ever more ambitious, so, too, does the prospect of overreaching, under-financing, and plain, downright crookedness.

In the section following we will look at three aspects of consumer protection; (a) regulating the offering statement; (b) efforts to redress the uneven bargain; (c) the special problem of the rental conversion.

a. Regulating the Offering Statement

Securities Act of 1933 — Release No. 5347
January 4, 1973

GUIDELINES AS TO THE APPLICABILITY OF THE FEDERAL SECURITIES LAWS TO OFFERS AND SALES OF CONDOMINIUMS OR UNITS IN A REAL ESTATE DEVELOPMENT

The Securities and Exchange Commission today called attention to the applicability of the federal securities laws to the offer and sale of condominium units, or other units in a real estate development, coupled with an offer or agreement to perform or arrange certain rental or other services for the purchaser. The Commission noted that such offerings may involve the offering of a security in the form of an investment contract or a participation in a profit sharing arrangement within the meaning of the Securities Act of 1933 and the Securities Exchange Act of 1934.[1] Where this is the case any offering of any such securities must comply with the registration and prospectus delivery requirements of the Securities Act, unless an exemption therefrom is available, and must comply with the anti-fraud provisions of the Securities Act and the Securities Exchange Act and the regulations thereunder. In addition, persons engaged in the business of buying or selling investment contracts or participations in profit sharing agreements of this type as agents for others, or as principal for their own account, may be brokers or dealers within the meaning of the

---

1. It should be noted that where an investment contract is present, it consists of the agreement offered and the condominium itself.

Securities Exchange Act, and therefore may be required to be registered as such with the Commission under the provisions of Section 15 of that Act.

The Commission is aware that there is uncertainty about when offerings of condominiums and other types of similar units may be considered to be offerings of securities that should be registered pursuant to the Securities Act. The purpose of this release is to alert persons engaged in the business of building and selling condominiums and similar types of real estate developments to their responsibilities under the Securities Act and to provide guidelines for a determination of when an offering of condominiums or other units may be viewed as an offering of securities. Resort condominiums are one of the more common interests in real estate the offer of which may involve an offering of securities. However, other types of units that are part of a development or project present analogous questions under the federal securities laws. Although this release speaks in terms of condominiums, it applies to offerings of all types of units in real estate developments which have characteristics similar to those described herein.

The offer of real estate as such, without any collateral arrangements with the seller or others, does not involve the offer of a security. When the real estate is offered in conjunction with certain services, a security, in the form of an investment contract, may be present. The Supreme Court in Securities and Exchange Commission v. W. J. Howey Co., 328 U.S. 293 (1946) set forth what has become a generally accepted definition of an investment contract: "a contract, transaction or scheme whereby a person invests his money in a common enterprise and is led to expect profits solely from the efforts of the promoter or a third party, it being immaterial whether the shares in the enterprise are evidenced by formal certificates or by nominal interests in the physical assets employed in the enterprise." (298) The *Howey* case involved the sale and operation of orange groves. The reasoning, however, is applicable to condominiums.

As the Court noted in *Howey,* substance should not be disregarded for form, and the fundamental statutory policy of affording broad protection to investors should be heeded. Recent interpretations have indicated that the expected return need not be *solely* from the efforts of others, as the holding in *Howey* appears to indicate.[2] For this reason, an investment contract may be present in situations where an investor is not wholly inactive, but even participates to a limited degree in the operations of the business. The "profits" that the purchaser is led to expect may consist of revenues received from rental of the unit; these revenues and any tax

---

2. SEC v. Glenn W. Turner Enterprises, Inc. CCH Fed. Sec. L. Rep. 893,605 (D.C. Ore. No. 72-390, May 25, 1972). See also State v. Hawaii Market Center, Inc., 485 P.2d 105 (1971) (cited in Securities Act Release No. 5211 (1971)); and Securities Act Release No. 5018 (1969) regarding the applicability of the federal securities laws to the sale and distribution of whiskey warehouse receipts.

Selected Problems 971

benefits resulting from rental of the unit are the economic inducements held out to the purchaser.

The existence of various kinds of collateral arrangements may cause an offering of condominium units to involve an offering of investment contracts or interests in a profit sharing agreement. The presence of such arrangements indicates that the offeror is offering an opportunity through which the purchaser may earn a return on his investment through the managerial efforts of the promoters or a third party in their operation of the enterprise.

For example, some public offerings of condominium units involve rental pool arrangements. Typically, the rental pool is a device whereby the promoter or a third party undertakes to rent the unit on behalf of the actual owner during that period of time when the unit is not in use by the owner. The rents received and the expenses attributable to rental of all units in the project are combined and the individual owner receives a ratable share of the rental proceeds regardless of whether his individual unit was actually rented. The offer of the unit together with the offer of an opportunity to participate in such a rental pool involves the offer of investment contracts which must be registered unless an exemption is available.

Also, the condominium units may be offered with a contract or agreement that places restrictions, such as required use of an exclusive rental agent or limitations on the period of time the owner may occupy the unit, on the purchaser's occupancy or rental of the property purchased. Such restrictions suggest that the purchaser is in fact investing in a business enterprise, the return from which will be substantially dependent on the success of the managerial efforts of other persons. In such cases, registration of the resulting investment contract would be required.

In any situation where collateral arrangements are coupled with the offering of condominiums, whether or not specifically of the types discussed above, the manner of offering and economic inducements held out to the prospective purchaser play an important role in determining whether the offerings involve securities. In this connection, see Securities and Exchange Commission v. C. M. Joiner Leasing Corp., 320 U.S. 344 (1943). In *Joiner,* the Supreme Court also noted that: "In enforcement of [the Securities Act], it is not inappropriate that promoters' offerings be judged as being what they were represented to be." (353) In other words, condominiums, coupled with a rental arrangement, will be deemed to be securities if they are offered and sold through advertising, sales literature, promotional schemes or oral representations which emphasize the economic benefits to the purchaser to be derived from the managerial efforts of the promoter, or a third party designated or arranged for by the promoter, in renting the units.

In summary, the offering of condominium units in conjunction with any one of the following will cause the offering to be viewed as an offering of securities in the form of investment contracts:

1. The condominiums, with any rental arrangement or other similar service, are offered and sold with emphasis on the economic benefits to the purchaser to be derived from the managerial efforts of the promoter, or a third party designated or arranged for by the promoter, from rental of the units;

2. The offering of participation in a rental pool arrangement; and

3. The offering of a rental or similar arrangement whereby the purchaser must hold his unit available for rental for any part of the year, must use an exclusive rental agent or is otherwise materially restricted in his occupancy or rental of his unit.

In all of the above situations, investor protection requires the application of the federal securities laws.

If the condominiums are not offered and sold with emphasis on the economic benefits to the purchaser to be derived from the managerial efforts of others, and assuming that no plan to avoid the registration requirements of the Securities Act is involved, an owner of a condominium unit may, after purchasing his unit, enter into a non-pooled rental arrangement with an agent not designated or required to be used as a condition to the purchase, whether or not such agent is affiliated with the offeror, without causing a sale of a security to be involved in the sale of the unit. Further a continuing affiliation between the developers or promoters of a project and the project by reason of maintenance arrangements does not make the unit a security.

In situations where commercial facilities are a part of the common elements of a residential project, no registration would be required under the investment contract theory where (a) the income from such facilities is used only to offset common area expenses and (b) the operation of such facilities is incidental to the project as a whole and are not established as a primary income source for the individual owners of a condominium or cooperative unit.

The Commission recognizes the need for a degree of certainty in the real estate offering area and believes that the above guidelines will be helpful in assisting persons to comply with the securities laws. It is difficult, however, to anticipate the variety of arrangements that may accompany the offering of condominium projects. The Commission, therefore, would like to remind those engaged in the offering of condominiums or other interests in real estate with similar features that there may be situations, not referred to in this release, in which the offering of the interests constitutes an offering of securities. Whether an offering of securities is involved necessarily depends on the facts and circumstances of each particular case. The staff of the Commission will be available to respond to written inquiries on such matters.

By the Commission.

Ronald F. Hunt
Secretary

Selected Problems

NOTES AND QUESTIONS

1. Securities Act of 1933—Release No. 5347, has been the key SEC statement to date regarding condominiums and "all types of units within real estate developments." Suppose your client wishes to develop a resort condominium whose units may be rented out to transients when the owner is not present. Can your client avoid registration without meeting one of the Act's exemptions? As a practical matter, what do you see as the advantage and disadvantage to the developer of an SEC registration?

2. In their comment on Release No. 5347, two SEC specialists lent the following advice to rental pool developers seeking to avoid SEC registration. As a minimum, the offering statement should provide that: the unit owner may use his own rental agent; the unit owner may choose *not* to rent out his unit; and net rental proceeds are to be sent directly to the owner. In addition, the authors warned the developer's salespeople against recommending only one rental agent, or discussing income or tax benefits deriving from rental activity, or estimating rental income. A fortiori, the offering statement must also be silent as to these matters. Dickey and Cutler, Apartment Construction News, Sept. 1973; cf. SEC, No Action Letter, Re: Big Sky of Montana, Inc., March 14, 1973. Is it possible, without becoming subject to SEC registration, to give the rental pool purchaser some idea of what to expect?

3. Rohan and Reskin, Condominium Law and Practice (1985), contains two illustrative SEC prospectuses for rental pool condominiums. The prospectus for Gentle Winds, a 250-unit condominium in the Virgin Islands, contains 100 pages of close print, financial schedules, legal documents, and room layouts. Id. at §18.07(1). The "short form" prospectus for Inn of the Seventh Mountain, an 84-unit resort hotel condominium in Oregon, runs only 23 pages but contains no legal documents. Id. at §18.07[2]. Each contains in boldface the legend appearing on all SEC prospectuses:

These Securities Have Not Been Approved or Disapproved by the Securities and Exchange Commission, Nor Has the Commissioner Passed Upon the Accuracy or Adequacy of the Prospectus. Any Representation to the Contrary Is a Criminal Offense.

This legend exemplifies the controlling spirit of the Securities Act of 1933, which relies upon full disclosure to protect the offeree and not upon a prior regulatory decision as to whether the offering is sound or not. Some states, by contrast, give their securities' officials the power to approve or disapprove a proposed offering. See page 976 infra. In the present context, which attitude better serves the prospective purchaser of a resort condominium?

Section 5(a) of the Securities Act of 1933 makes it unlawful, absent an exemption, to sell a security using the means or instruments of interstate commerce or the mails unless a registration statement is in effect as to that security. However, the SEC does allow a developer to feel the market pulse before filing his registration statement provided he does not accept downpayments, purchase commitments, or "indications of interest." Securities Act of 1933, Release No. 5382, April 9, 1973. How might the developer pre-market without crossing the divide?

4. Section 3(a)(11) of the Securities Act of 1933 grants an exemption for so-called intrastate offerings. For real estate offerings, this requires that the property, the offerees, and the issuer all be located within the same state. For the issuer, this means his principal place of business; for the offerees, this means their permanent home. Securities Act of 1933, Rule 147, Release No. 5450, January 7, 1974.

Section 4(2) of the act exempts transactions that do not involve a public offering. Congress has not defined "public offering," but the SEC, in a series of rulings culminating in Securities Act of 1933, Release No. 5912, March 3, 1978, has sought to give some guidance to issuers. Rule 146 is the operative statement; it now contains a "safe harbor" provision that limits to thirty-five the number of purchasers in any offering, exclusive of near relatives or persons investing $150,000 or more in cash. Further requirements deal with the offeree's ability to bear the economic risk, as well as his capacity (alone or with assistance) to evaluate the merits and risks of the proposed investment.

5. Even if the sponsor qualifies for a registration exemption, the Securities Act of 1933 provides civil remedies *whenever* the transaction involves a security. Section 12(2) enables the buyer to recover damages for material misstatements or omissions in the registration statement (if one exists) and in all written and oral sales materials. Two other provisions deal only with offerings that require registration. Section 12(1) allows the buyer to rescind and recover his down payment whenever the sponsor sells unregistered securities in violation of the Act. (Suit must be brought within one year from the violation. If the buyer has already resold his securities, he may sue for damages.) Where registration has occurred, §11 allows the buyer to recover damages for material misstatements or omissions of material fact in either the registration statement or prospectus. Section 11 is more sweeping than 12(2); it subjects to liability not only the seller but also all underwriters, experts named in the statement as having helped prepare it, and persons signing the statement; §12(2) exposes only the seller himself. Moreover, §11 does not allow an "innocent mistake" defense on the seller's behalf.

6. The United States Supreme Court has held that the marketing of cooperative interests is not *per se* the offering of "securities" within the purview of the Securities Act of 1933 and the Securities Exchange Act of 1934. United Housing Foundation Inc. v. Forman, 421 U.S. 837 (1975). Writing for the Court, Justice Powell declared:

We reject at the outset any suggestion that the present transaction, evidenced by the sale of shares called "stock" must be considered a security transaction simply because the statutory definition of a security includes the words "any . . . stock." Rather we adhere to the basic principle that has guided all the Court's decisions in this area: "[I]n searching for the meaning and scope of the word 'security' in the Act[s], form should be disregarded for substance and the emphasis should be on economic reality" . . . Common sense suggests that people who intend to acquire only a residential apartment in a state-subsidized cooperative, for their personal use, are not likely to believe that in reality they are purchasing investment securities simply because the transaction is evidenced by something called a share of stock.

. . . The Court of Appeals, as an alternative ground for its decision, concluded that a share in Riverbay was also an "investment contract" as defined by the Securities Acts. . . . We perceive no distinction, for present purposes, between an "investment contract" and an "instrument commonly known as a security." In either case, the basic test for distinguishing the transaction from other commercial dealings is "whether the scheme involves an investment of money in a common enterprise with profits to come solely from the efforts of others." *Howey*, 328 U.S., at 301 . . .

There is no doubt that purchasers in this housing cooperative sought to obtain a decent home at an attractive price. But that type of economic interest characterizes every form of commercial dealing. What distinguishes a security transaction—and what is absent here—is an investment where one parts with his money in the hope of receiving profits from the efforts of others, and not where he purchases a commodity for personal consumption or living quarters for personal use. [421 U.S. at 858.]

7. The tenant-stockholders of Co-op City (Riverbay), the development involved in the *Forman* case, enjoyed a state subsidy; they could not, under the New York law, resell their shares at a profit. Nonsubsidized (or so-called luxury) co-operatives place no limit on their members' profit opportunity. As a result, persons buying such co-op apartments usually consider the investment aspects of their purchase. The Court's opinion in *Forman* kept alive the possibility that the sponsors of nonsubsidized projects would be required to register their offering as an investment contract.

Faced directly with that issue, the Second Circuit held that the securities acts did not apply. Grenader v. Spitz, 537 F.2d 612 (2d Cir. 1976), *cert. denied*, 429 U.S. 1009 (1976). The lawsuit involved the conversion of a 60-unit rental building into a *wholly* residential cooperative. The sponsors had filed an offering plan with state officials but had not registered with the SEC. Tenant-stockholders sued for damages alleging that the offering plan contained misleading statements or omissions of material facts.

The court's opinion stressed that the building had no commercial tenants and insignificant income from coin-operated laundry and cable TV, and that the shareholder-tenants were not to receive any distribution from the earnings and profits of the Corporation. There still remained the distinguishing feature of possible *resale* profit, but this did not convince the court:

> We note initially that the *Howey* test first requires that the investor be led to expect profits! There is nothing in the record before us to support the contention that the investor here was attracted by the prospect of realizing a profit on his investment. . . . The offering plan . . . is barren of any representation or intimation of anticipated profits. Unlike the hawking siren song of the promoter, the plan here is a prosaic recitation of the financial facts underlying their transaction with an *exhaustive* [sic] recitation of the physical properties and condition of the Building and the apartments offered as well as the terms of the tenancy and the obligations of the lessee. There is no reference to the possibility or probability of profits. . . . There is a further flaw in [tenants'] argument. *Howey* requires that the profits arise "solely from the efforts of the promoter or a third party." . . . Realistically [appreciation in value] will depend upon the general housing market, the status of the neighborhood and the availability of credit. See Berman and Stone, Federal Securities Law and the Sale of Condominiums, Homes and Homesites, 30 Bus. Law. 411, 422-24 (1975). [537 F.2d at 618-619.]

8. After *Forman* and *Grenader,* do any situations remain where *residential* co-ops (or condominiums) might still be subject to federal regulation? Suppose that the sponsor *has* retained a long-term management contract? Or that the sponsor has retained title to the recreational facilities which he leases to the project? Or that the tenant-stockholders can prove that they relied upon commercial rentals to decrease carrying charges and increase share values?

9. The cooperative offering in Grenader v. Spitz was first submitted to the state Attorney-General, who has the power to regulate "any public offering or sale in or from the State of New York of participation interests in real estate ventures including cooperative interests in realty." N.Y. Gen. Bus. Law §352-e (McKinney 1984). This power extends to planned unit developments and condominiums. SEC registration would not have obviated the need to follow state procedure.

The New York procedures are quite elaborate. Documentation worthy of a full-dressed SEC registration must accompany the request for state approval. Levine, Registering a Condominium Offering in New York, 19 N.Y.L.F. 493 (1974).

New York is one of several states (the number grows) that systematically regulate co-op and condominium ventures. In many other states, offerings may sometimes be subject to blue-sky control; for example, the Uniform Securities Act (adopted in nearly 40 states) defines securities to include "investment contracts."

What are the arguments for entrusting states with primary authority over the marketing of shared facilities developments? What are the arguments against?

10. The Interstate Land Sales Full Disclosure Act, 15 U.S.C. §§1701

Selected Problems

et seq. (1982), may also apply to some shared facilities developments. Passed by Congress in 1968 to control mail order promotions of undeveloped lots, the law contains broad exemptions which will excuse smaller projects (fewer than 100 units) and projects where the unit is either completed before it is sold or must contractually be finished within two years of sale. To gain this latter exemption, the sponsor must complete not only the housing unit but also all recreational and other common facilities that are included in the purchase.

The Office of Interstate Land Sales Registration, a division of the Department of Housing and Urban Development, administers the program. Before offering lots in a nonexempt subdivision, the promoter must obtain a HUD-approved Property Report. The Report is a full disclosure of detail such as the promoters' financial and criminal background, topography, climate, nuisances(!), deed restrictions, road access, utilities, municipal services, taxes. For a sample subdivision filing, see [1977] Hous. and Dev. Rep. (BNA) §150:0351.

b. Reaching the Overreaching Developer

Point East Management Corporation v. Point East One Condominium Corporation, Inc.

282 So. 2d 628 (Fla. 1973)

ADKINS, Justice. By petition and cross-petition for writ of certiorari, we have for review a decision of the District Court of Appeal, Third District (258 So. 2d 322), which allegedly conflicts with a prior decision of this Court (Lake Mabel Development Corporation v. Bird, 99 Fla. 253, 126 So. 356 (1930)) on the same point of law. We have determined that we have jurisdiction pursuant to Fla. Const., art. V. §3(b)(3), F.S.A.

Petitioners are the original developers of the Point East condominium project, a management corporation contracted to manage the project for a period of 25 years, and lessors of a recreation facility to the condominium association on a 99-year lease. The various identities of petitioner simply represent different stages of the developers' involvement with the project. Petitioner developed the condominium project and, subsequent to the formation of the condominium associations, contracted with itself for management of the condominiums and for the lease.

Respondents are the condominium associations—as presently constituted by individual condominium unit owners—who brought suit for rescission of the lease and management contract, for damages in fraud, for damages for breach of a fiduciary duty, and for damages for breach of contract. All relief sought was denied by the trial court except for invalidation of the management contract, and the District Court of Appeal, Third District, affirmed.

Petitioner seeks a reversal of the District Court of Appeal on the invalidation of the management contract, and respondents, by cross-petition, seek reversals of the District Court of Appeal on the affirmance of all other holdings of the trial court.

We have carefully reviewed those issues raised by the cross-petition and find them to be without merit. However, we have determined that the point raised by petitioner is meritorious, and the District Court of Appeal must be reversed on its invalidation of the management contract.

The District Court of Appeal recognized that rescission of the management contract would not lie merely because it arose from the dealings of the developers with themselves while they constituted all of the members of the condominium associations and of the management corporation. Lake Mabel Development Corporation v. Bird, supra.

However, the District Court of Appeal held that the 25-year management contract is void because it violates the provisions of the Condominium Act in wresting the control of the management of the condominiums away from the associations. This interpretation is based on three sections of the Condominium Act.

First, Fla. Stat. §711.03(2), F.S.A., defines the association as "the entity responsible for the operation of a condominium." Fla Stat. §711.03(12), F.S.A., then defines operation of the condominium as including "the administration and management" of the property. Finally, the District Court of Appeal relies upon Fla. Stat. §711.12(1), F.S.A., which provides: "The operation of the condominium shall be by the association, the name of which shall be stated in the declaration."

The District Court of Appeal then, in effect, rescinded the contracts complained of, holding them to be invalid because they "[D]ivest from the association in a material or substantial degree the power and privilege granted it by the statute to operate the condominium. . . ." Point East Management Corporation v. Point East One Condominium Corporation, 258 So. 2d 322, p. 325.

We cannot agree with the District Court of Appeal that the Legislature, by placing in the condominium associations the power and duty to manage the condominium properties, intended to restrict the ability of the associations to contract for the management of the associations. The fact that the contract is of long duration does not make the contract any more objectionable, and as pointed out in Lake Mabel Development Corporation v. Bird, supra, the fact that the developers of the condominiums contracted with themselves for the management contract does not invalidate it.

The Legislature has chosen, through the adoption of Fla. Stat. §711.13(4), F.S.A., which became effective January 1, 1971, to allow the owners of condominium units to cancel initial management contracts by a vote of 75 percent of the owners of the individual units. Accordingly, it must be assumed that the Legislature recognized the existence of and chose not to abolish such contracts. It is impossible, therefore, to discover a legislative prohibition against a management contract.

The fact of the contract and its terms were made known — or at least available — to all who bought or considered buying condominium units, and the contracts of sale included affirmation of the management contract. Admittedly, a prospective purchaser had no option as to the management contract, but he knew or should have known that the contract was part of the purchase price of his condominium unit. Considered in that light, enforcement of the contract cannot be said to work a hardship on the present condominium owners.

Accordingly, that portion of the decision of the District Court of Appeal, Third District, which sought to invalidate the management contract between petitioner and respondents is quashed, and the remainder of the decision is approved. The case is remanded to the District Court of Appeal, Third District, for further proceedings not inconsistent herewith.

It is so ordered.

Carlton, C.J., McCain and Dekle, JJ., and Mager, District Court Judge, concur.

Ervin, J., dissents with opinion.

Boyd, J., dissents and agrees with Ervin, J.

ERVIN, Justice (dissenting): We are clearly without jurisdiction to decide the merits of petitioner's cause under Article V, Section 3(b)(3), Florida Constitution, F.S.A. The decision under review does not conflict with Lake Mabel Development Corporation v. Bird, 99 Fla. 253, 126 So. 356 (1930), and the writ of certiorari should now be discharged as having been improvidently issued. . . .

Having mistakenly reached the merits of petitioner's claim, the majority have proceeded to misconstrue the Condominium Act (F.S., Chapter 711, F.S.A.). The four similar management contracts between the condominium associations and the management corporation, which the trial court and the District Court of Appeal, Third District, have found to be invalid, contain provisions inimical to F.S., Sections 711.03(12), 711.03(12), and 711.12(1), F.S.A.

As is stated in the majority opinion, the petitioner, as developer of the condominium, contracted with itself for management of the condominium and for the lease. Thus, the management contracts were executed by the developers while they controlled the condominium associations prior to their present makeup of individual condominium apartment owners. The resulting lopsided character of these "agreements" are best evidence by an examination of the provisions contained therein. The contracts extend for periods of up to twenty-five years with no right of termination by the condominium associations except for cause after sixty days notice of default. The manager [petitioner], "to the exclusion of all persons including the Association [respondent] and its members [presently, the apartment owners]" is given *in part,* the following powers:

(1) The right to hire, supervise, and fire, "*in its absolute* discretion" such persons as are required to fulfill its duties under the management agreement.

(2) The power to collect *all assessments* from the associations' members and to take such action in the name of the associations as is needed to collect payment — to include "foreclosing the association's lien therefore, or by way of other legal process as may be required. . . ."

(3) The power to carry on "normal" maintenance and repair work except that no one item of repair is to exceed *$30,000.00* unless authorized by the associations.

(4) The right to purchase "equipment, tools, vehicles, appliances," etc., as are "reasonably necessary" to perform its duties.

(5) The right to maintain all books and records subject only to the right of the associations to conduct an independent audit at their own expense.

(6) The right to deposit funds collected from the associations either in a special bank account or to commingle the monies with similar funds "as the Manager shall determine."

(7) The right to "retain and employ attorneys-at-law, tax consultants, certified public accountants, health consultants and such other experts and professionals whose services the Manager may reasonably require. . . ." (The result of this provision is that the apartment owners are paying the costs sustained by both parties in the present suit.)

(8) The power to insure that payments received from assessments or other revenue are sufficient to pay the costs of all services and to adequately fund reserves. Failure of the associations to increase the monthly assessments as requested by the manager "within a reasonable time may, at the option of the manager, be construed as a breach of this agreement."

The above provisions are only a sampling of the terms of the "Management Agreement" that was before the trial court together with voluminous testimony attesting to the impotency of the associations to have the benefits and to function autonomously under the Condominium Act when saddled by the terms of what amount to adhesion contracts together with details of the resultant excessive and overreaching extractions mulched from the unit owners. These provisions led the trial court to conclude: "The Management Agreements in this case, considered in light of their specific provisions and the length of their terms, completely and effectively delegate and abdicate the responsibility and control of the plaintiff, Condominium Associations, to the defendant. This delegation and abdication of responsibility and control exceeds the bounds of statutory authority and defeats the purposes of the Condominium Act." Point East Management Corp. v. Point East One Condominium Corp., 258 So. 2d 322, at 324 (Fla. App. 1972).

F.S., Section 711.03(2), F.S.A., defines the association as "the entity responsible for the operation of a condominium" and Section 711.03(12) defines operation of a condominium as including "the administration and management of the condominium property." The unmistakable intent of the Legislature as reflected in that language is further reinforced by the following statement appearing further in the Condominium Act: "The operation of the condominium shall be by the association, the name of which shall be stated in the declaration." F.S., Section 711.12(1), F.S.A.

This language does not mean that the associations cannot enter into management contracts so long as they are ultimately responsible as a self-autonomous group for the administration of the property and maintain supervision and control over the managing party. The long duration of the contracts herein makes them statutorily objectionable because it serves to undercut the legislative mandate of autonomy for the unit owners. That problem is further compounded in the present case because the associations (i.e., the developers) were of an entirely different composition when the contracts were negotiated. As is stated in petitioner's brief and may be taken as an admission against interest: "At the time the Management Agreements and the Community Facilities Lease were made, no interests of any purchasers or other third parties were involved. No apartment units had been sold. The developer . . . was the sole owner of all apartment units and the entire condominium property, and *the developer was the only member of the associations.* No interests of anyone other than the developer were in anywise affected by the Management Agreements and the Community Facilities Leases." Petitioner then asserts, as does the majority, that no harm resulted from this blatant attempt to circumvent the intent and mandate of the Condominium Act because "the apartments were sold and purchased with full disclosure and complete knowledge of the contents of the Management Agreements and Community Facilities Leases. . . ." Such rationalization not only ignores the statutory provision for association autonomy, but completely ignores the reality of unequal bargaining positions between individual apartment purchasers and a multi-million dollar corporation intent on foisting long-term management contracts of adhesion upon them, contrary to regulatory law.

The fact that the Legislature has more recently taken further steps to insure that such unconscionable contracts can be terminated by a vote of seventy-five percent of the apartment unit owners does not have the secondary effect of rendering Respondents remediless in this litigation because the subject contracts were entered into prior to the effective date of that legislation. See, F.S., Section 711.13(4), F.S.A. The fact that the Legislature became more acutely aware of this problem and further acted three years ago to bolster remedies against future injustice, does not mean that the courts are powerless to strike down an illegal contract that is clearly violative of other provisions of, F.S., Chapter 711, F.S.A., in effect at the time the contracts were signed.

Having accepted jurisdiction in this cause, the majority would do better to focus their attention on Respondent's crosspetition as it pertains to its original suit brought against the management corporation seeking damages in excess of $500,000 for fraud, breach of a fiduciary duty, and breach of contract. In affirming the trial court's refusal to grant the associations an accounting by the management corporation and damages, the District Court of Appeal, Third District, held that "the findings of the trial court in that regard are not without support in the evidence." Point East Management Corp. v. Point East One Condominium Corp., 258 So. 2d 322, at 325 (Fla. App. 1972). It also accepted the trial court's finding that the Community Facility Lease was valid and binding by virtue of estoppel although "the lease in question contains provisions which *appear to be of a kind that might be expected to motivate a court of equity to grant relief* therefrom to the associations upon which the lease was thus imposed." Id. at 326. (Emphasis supplied.)

The doctrine of estoppel should not serve as a refuge for a party whose apparent fraud, as reflected in the record, effected the imposition of a 99-year lease at what would appear to be an exorbitant net rental of $222,000 per year, upon the apartment owners. An examination of the record indicates that the lease in question should be declared void as not complying with F.S., Sections 711.08(1)(e) and 711.12, F.S.A. . . .

NOTES AND QUESTIONS

1. *The 99-year lease of the recreational facilities.* By retaining title to the recreational facilities, which it then leases to the condominium association, the developer can inflate (and effectively conceal) the purchase price of the individual units. The Florida statute, at issue in the instant case, contains no stricture against this practice other than the general obligation — as to all leases and contracts made by an association prior to assumption of association control by the unit owners — that the arrangements be "fair and reasonable." Fla. Stat. Ann. §718.302(1) (West 1979).

In the instant case, the trial court, while disturbed by the terms of the recreational lease, invoked an estoppel to bar rescission of the lease, the execution of which preceded the effective date of the remedial statute:

> The evidence establishes that the Community Facility leases are valid and binding by virtue of estoppel; that the defendants made full disclosure concerning the facilities described therein, and that the plaintiffs and their respective members had appropriate knowledge and information concerning the facilities at the time of purchase of the condominium units, and the Community Facility leases were duly ratified and confirmed. [258 So. 2d at 325.]

In a later action involving a different project but the same developers and a similar 99-year lease, the plaintiff association also sued to invalidate the lease. The court dismissed one claim based on Florida's antitrust statute (holding that the condition that unit purchasers also sign the recreational lease was not an illegal tying arrangement), but sustained, as stating a cause of action, an unconscionability claim, which did not depend upon the "fair and reasonable" provisions of the not-yet applicable statute.

Where the recreational facilities are subject to a long-term lease, how should the unit purchaser calculate the additional (hidden) costs of his unit? How would a rental escalation clause geared to increases in the consumer price index affect that calculation?

2. The Uniform Condominium Act §3-105 (1977), provides:

> If entered into before the executive board elected by the unit owners [after the developer relinquishes control] takes office, (1) any management contract, employment contract, or lease of recreational or parking areas or facilities, (2) any other contract or lease to which [the developer is a party], or (3) any contract or lease which is not bona fide or which was unconscionable to the unit owners at the time entered into under the circumstances then prevailing, may be terminated without penalty by the association at any time . . . upon not less than [90] days notice to the other party.

The Uniform Common Interest Ownership Act §3-105 (1982), contains identical language.

c. Regulating the Conversion of Rental Units

Comment, the Condominium Conversion Problem: Causes and Solutions
1980 Duke L.J. 306

In many major urban and suburban areas, condominiums[1] and co-operatives[2] are becoming a significant element of the housing market.[3] A pri-

---

1. A condominium has been described as follows:

   In a condominium, an individual has fee title to his own unit and, with the owners of other units, has an undivided interest in the common elements and facilities that serve the development.

   The common elements typically include such things as land, roofs, floors, main walls, stairways, lobbies, halls, parking space, and community and commercial facilities. These common elements and facilities are usually maintained by an association of owners (which in some jurisdictions is referred to as a Council of Co-owners or similar name). Each unit owner makes a monthly contribution to the association covering his share of the costs of maintaining and operating the common elements.

   Taxes and special assessments are levied against individual units, not against the whole project or building. Also, each unit bears its own mortgage. Thus, the owner is not liable for the mortgage or real estate taxes of the others. All states, and the District of Columbia, Puerto Rico, and the Virgin Islands, have enacted some form of legislation recognizing condominium ownership.

   [Reference File 2] Hous. & Dev. Rep. (BNA) 25:0011 (1978).

2. A cooperative may be described as follows:

   A cooperative is a member-owned corporation. A member of a cooperative does not directly own his dwelling unit, as in a condominium. Rather, the member has a membership certificate or stock in a corporation which owns the property. Membership in the cooperative carries with it the exclusive right to occupy a dwelling unit in the development and to participate in the operation of the cooperative corporation either as a member of the Board of Directors or as a voter in the same manner as a shareholder in any other corporation. Id.

3. For the purposes of this Comment the distinctions between condominiums and cooperatives are not important. The term "condominium" will be used to refer to both types of housing unless otherwise specified.

mary feature of the condominium boom, accounting for the largest share of new condominium units on the market, is the conversion of rental apartments to condominiums. One survey estimates that conversions have doubled from approximately 50,000 units in 1977 to 100,000 units in 1978. Approximately seventy-five percent of these conversions took place in seven major markets: New York, Chicago, Houston, Seattle, Denver, Los Angeles, and Washington, D.C. When the data are compiled, it is likely that 130,000 units will have been converted in 1979.

The surge in condominium conversions is attributable to a number of factors. Demand for condominiums is strong, particularly for converted units, which are generally priced lower than newly constructed units. At the same time, conversion provides an opportunity for landlords with ever decreasing profits to sell their properties for substantial gains.

Condominium conversion has many benefits. Conversion meets the strong demand for condominium ownership and offers one of the best long-range solutions for urban decay. There are, however, many negative effects associated with the process. Conversion displaces existing tenants who do not want or cannot afford to buy units in the converted building. Each conversion also reduces available rental housing, making it difficult for displaced tenants to find suitable alternative housing. The burden of the conversion boom clearly falls most heavily on the poor and the elderly, groups that can least afford to purchase the converted units. . . .

I. Explanations of the Conversion Phenomenon

A. Demand for Condominium Ownership

Several factors explain the increasing demand for new and converted condominiums. First, the coming of age of the "baby boom generation" has brought an increase in the number of persons in the house-buying age bracket, an effect expected to continue at least until the mid-1980s.

A second factor is the increase in smaller households searching for units designed to accommodate their size. Later marriages and the postponement of having children account for a significant increase in one- and two-person households.[14] In addition, single females are becoming significant wage earners and home buyers, contributing further to this increase.

Third, for young professionals making increasingly higher salaries, homeownership in the form of a condominium offers many tax advantages over rental living. When a buyer invests in a condominium he purchases real property, entitling him to the same deductions allowed any owner of

---

14. One authority estimates that approximately 60-70% of those in today's condominium market are married and have no children. The approximate size of the average condominium household is 2.5 persons. Schwab, Factors to Be Considered, in Condominium and Cooperative Conversions 13 (1979).

conventional residential property.[16] The condominium owner may deduct state and local real property taxes assessed against the unit, as well as interest paid on mortgage liabilities. Along with these benefits, the condominium owner may also deduct any amounts lost on the condominium unit due to "fire, storm . . . or other casualty" that are uncompensated by insurance. In contrast, renters cannot take advantage of any of these benefits, for no purchase of real property is involved. Furthermore, additional tax benefits may be realized on a subsequent sale of the property. The Internal Revenue Code allows the condominium owner to deduct from gross income sixty percent of any gain realized on the subsequent sale of the condominium unit. The owner thus pays taxes on only forty percent of the realized gain. The seller obtains a further advantage if the gain realized on the sale is used for acquisition of a new residence: if the condominium sold was the taxpayer's principal residence and he applies the gain from the sale to the purchase of a new principal residence within eighteen months, the taxpayer may defer the tax liability until the subsequent sale of the acquired unit. This provision gives the taxpayer an opportunity to make a profit on money effectively borrowed from the federal treasury without interest.

Probably the two greatest advantages of condominium ownership over rental arrangements are the acquisition of equity and the appreciation in property value. As the condominium owner makes each mortgage payment, he acquires equity in the property that may be recaptured in a subsequent sale of the condominium unit. Renters do not enjoy this advantage, since rental payments can never be recovered. Condominiums are also desirable because their value appreciates rapidly. In most markets condominiums appreciate a minimum of twenty percent in the first year after conversion; in some markets the units have appreciated as much as fifty percent in the first year. Thereafter, aside from units in downtown areas, the appreciation rate is roughly equivalent to that for single family homes. Clearly, investment in converted units offers one of the best hedges against inflation.

Finally, as American lifestyles become increasingly oriented toward leisure, the demand for onsite amenities and recreational facilities grows. Condominiums offer homeowners the use of facilities such as swimming pools, tennis courts, and elevators at a significantly lower cost than would be possible in a single family dwelling. Since the condominium owner is a tenant in common with regard to recreational facilities, he pays only his pro rata share of the cost and maintenance. Furthermore, since maintenance is overseen by a board of managers, who generally hire full-time employees, the condominium owner avoids all the maintenance responsi-

---

16. The same advantages would, of course, be gained upon purchase of traditional single-family dwellings. Many buyers may, however, find the cost of such property prohibitively high. Condominiums provide the same tax advantages without the high capital costs.

bilities that normally accompany ownership of these facilities while enjoying all the benefits.

While the factors discussed thus far explain the current demand for condominium units generally, there are additional factors that explain the even greater demand for converted condominium units. One factor accounting for this increased demand is the lower price of converted units compared to new units. As costs of materials, labor, financing, and marketing increase, the price of newly built condominium units cannot remain competitive with the price of converted units. In addition, when rental buildings are converted into condominiums, most renting tenants are given the chance to purchase their units at substantial discounts.

A further advantage of conversion over new condominium construction is that conversion allows the relatively inexpensive use of the choice central city locations of older buildings. Demand for housing in close proximity to business district employment is growing, especially with higher costs of commuting due to increased fuel prices. New downtown construction either must be on expensive and increasingly rare vacant land or else include the cost of demolition in the already higher prices.

B. SUPPLY: INCENTIVES FOR LANDLORDS AND DEVELOPERS TO CONVERT

Strong demand for condominium units is only half of the explanation for the current conversion phenomenon. There are also strong economic and practical incentives inducing many landlords either to convert their buildings into condominiums themselves, or to sell to developers who will then convert. In a nutshell, landlords convert because profit margins for rental property are decreasing while substantial profits can be made by selling either individual units to homebuyers or entire buildings to developers.

For landlords, conversion is an effective alternative to dealing with the rapidly rising costs and slowly rising rents that result in eroding profits. Between 1972 and 1977, the consumer price index rose more than forty-one percent. At the same time, building costs increased at an even faster rate of fifty percent. Rapidly rising energy and utility prices increased the cost of maintaining rental buildings even further. If rents kept up with these increased costs, there would be no incentive to convert. However, landlords in all but the highest rent districts have been unable to raise rents rapidly enough to keep pace with inflation. The major impediment to meeting costs is rent control, or the fear of it. It is no coincidence that many cities facing the most serious conversion problems are rent control cities, and as the rent control movement spreads, condominium conversion problems are likely to follow.

The ever decreasing profitability of maintaining rental housing contrasts with the increased profitability of conversion, either by the landlord himself or by sale to a developer. "Individually marketed units provide a significantly higher return in comparison with the amount that could be realized on a single sale of the entire complex." One authority advises that condominium conversion should yield a *minimum* profit on the total sales price of each individual unit of twenty percent. Profits may, in fact, be substantially higher.

In addition to the pure cost-return factors inducing landlords to convert or sell, tax laws also encourage conversion rather than maintenance of buildings as rental properties. Many owners of older rental buildings sell because they have used up their depreciation allowances. Without depreciation deductions to offset income, rental apartment buildings lose any tax advantage they may have previously held for their owners. As interest rates soar, refinancing of rental property becomes more and more difficult, thus precluding another tax advantage, the deduction of interest. Finally, the Tax Reform Act of 1976 limited the tax shelter under which owners of rental buildings could deduct accelerated depreciation on used residential rental property against other income. Since the amount of accelerated depreciation an owner may deduct is decreased, maintaining a rental building is no longer a tax shelter. The tax laws also encourage sale by providing favorable capital gains treatment for high profits the owner may realize on the sale. As a result, landlords generally prefer to sell the whole building to condominium developers for the advantage of capital gains treatment.

Profits from sale to a developer will exceed profits from sale to an investor wishing to maintain the property for rental purposes because the building is worth more to a developer due to the profitability of condominium development. Admittedly, a developer will not be entitled to capital gains treatment on profits realized from the sale of the units since the property is most certainly "held by the taxpayer primarily for sale . . . in the ordinary course of . . . business." Nevertheless, by purchasing the building on borrowed money and a small personal equity investment, he can turn quick sales into substantial profits on a small investment.

Developers wishing to capitalize on the high demand for condominiums see conversion as an attractive alternative to new construction, since the quick profits on small equity investments in conversions compare favorably to those offered in time-consuming and expensive construction. In summary, in a market of strong demand, conversion allows investors and developers to make available rapidly a substantial supply of condominium units with a relatively small short-term, low-risk investment.

II. Effects of Conversion: A Public Policy Perspective

A. Advantages to Individuals Seeking Homeownership

Most of the benefits of conversion for those desiring to own their own homes have been discussed. Principally, conversion satisfies a strong demand for condominium ownership. If conversion were restricted, this demand would not be satisfied, and prices of existing units would rise and thus force many buyers out of the market. Furthermore, converted units provide an inexpensive housing alternative in or around major urban areas, offering the benefits of homeownership to persons who might otherwise be unable to afford a home. When combined with the discounts available to prior rental tenants, the appreciation factor on converted condominium units provides a tremendous hedge against inflation for a homeowner and an excellent investment.

B. ADVANTAGES OF CONVERSION FOR URBAN AREAS

Conversion has several important beneficial effects that militate against its restriction. One of the primary benefits of conversion is that it aids in reversing the detrimental decentralization process. Decentralization is the process by which middle and upper socio-economic groups are encouraged to move from the city to the suburbs. One important incentive fostering such movement is the tax benefits that accompany the purchase of owner-occupied housing. As long as most inner city housing is rental property, middle or upper income people seeking to own housing must move to the suburbs or the urban fringe to obtain these tax advantages.

The detrimental effects of such decentralization are numerous:

> [D]ecentralization can and often does cause a relative decline in the ability of the central cities to pay for the provision of public facilities. If, as has been the case in the U.S., families leaving the central city are younger, better educated, better trained and have higher incomes than the remaining population, the central cities will usually suffer as a consequence of this outmigration. It will become more difficult for these cities to pay for public services with declining revenues. The remaining elderly, low income population may also create additional service demands. Property values may fall and maintenance investment decline. As a result, urban blight and inner city decay spreads and further encourages the income and racial segregation which typifies many U.S. cities.

It is often stated that condominium conversions have "sparked a back-to-the-city movement among families," aiding in the reversal of decentralization. Thirty percent or more of converted condominium dwellers are estimated to have moved to their city homes from the suburbs. As middle and upper income households return to the city to live in converted condominium units, revenues increase, cities stabilize, and the city's ability to provide essential services improves. . . .

Another significant benefit of the condominium conversion process is its rehabilitative effect on the city's physical housing stock. Many physical improvements are made on older rental buildings during conversion. Members of the condominium development profession argue that "new capital investment effectively recycles these properties for another 10 to 20 years. This replenishment of the existing housing stock is essential because high construction costs and the fear of controls have chilled new apartment construction. . . ." Rehabilitation in the form of condominium conversions could save many dwelling units that would otherwise be lost to abandonment or demolition.

Condominium conversions also help revitalize blighted and decaying neighborhoods. Three interrelated factors are blamed for deterioration of many residential rental areas and publicly-assisted rental housing projects: "the physical deterioration of the property, a lack of commitment on the part of the residents because they are not owners, and no structure for self governance." Condominium conversions affect all three areas of concern: "The immediate neighborhood benefits, because residency in a condominium is no longer transient in nature. The interests of homeowners and condominium owners are relatively identical. New resident apartment owners have a vested, long-term interest in the social and political fabric of *their* neighborhood."

A single restoration can often result in the revitalization of an entire neighborhood and even surrounding neighborhoods. Many small development firms become attracted to such areas because the conversions create new business opportunities. Noted examples of such revitalization include the Quincy Market and Waterfront area in Boston, Oldtown Mall in Baltimore, and Society Hill in Philadelphia.

In summary, condominium conversions benefit urban areas by revitalizing the deteriorating housing stock, reversing decentralization, increasing cities' tax bases, and adding stability to decaying neighborhoods. As stated by condominium authority Professor Patrick Rohan, "[T]here is today a strong . . . interest in encouraging such conversions: it is increasingly apparent that occupier-ownership in the form of . . . condominiums offers the best long-range solution to the problem of urban decay."

C. DISADVANTAGES OF CONVERSION

Although condominium conversions offer clear benefits, they also create difficulties. Foremost among these difficulties is tenant displacement, a hardship that falls most heavily upon the poor and elderly. In addition, each conversion removes more rental units from the market, with the result that more displaced tenants are searching for fewer rental opportunities. This reduction in rental units also creates problems for transient residents such as students. Furthermore, as older buildings are renovated and neighborhoods are generally improved, dwelling unit prices increase, thus removing an important source of low-cost housing for lower income households.

While conversion of rental units to condominiums does obviously decrease the number of rental units, conversion is not the primary cause of the severe shrinkage of the rental market. The growing unprofitability of maintaining rental units is a significant reason for the reduction in supply. Unprofitability leads not only to conversion, but also to abandonment and demolition. Conversion, like abandonment and demolition, is a symptom of the ailing rental market.

The dwindling supply of rental units caused by abandonments, demolition, decay, and conversions is exacerbated by the decrease in private construction of new rental units. Factors behind this decline in new construction include soaring construction costs and skyrocketing interest rates. . . .

The most serious and most widely publicized adverse effect of condominium conversion is the displacement of tenants who either cannot afford to buy, or choose not to buy. This problem is particularly acute for the poor and elderly, who often live in the well-located old, but substantial, buildings that are prime targets for conversion. Many of these people cannot make the down-payments necessary to purchase their apartments. This is particularly true of the elderly, who often have sufficient incomes to pay controlled rents, but who cannot provide the large cash outlays necessary for a purchase.

Studies indicate that most displaced tenants are able to find alternative housing within a reasonable amount of time after conversion, sometimes only a short distance from the converted property. The availability of housing should not, however, obscure the very real problems caused by displacement. Displacement poses economic hardships for poor and elderly tenants, since the rents for alternative housing may be far higher than for the converted property. Each new conversion compounds the problem, as it decreases the rental unit supply, already reduced by abandonment and demolition. Increasing numbers of displaced tenants then compete for dwindling numbers of rental units, pushing rents even higher. Furthermore, displacement may cause significant psychological difficulties, particularly for elderly persons forced to leave buildings or neighborhoods where they have lived for long periods. Cites and states considering the conversion phenomenon should be aware of the difficulties faced by poor and elderly tenants and should design legislative responses that address these problems.

III. Alternative Approaches to Conversion Regulation

A. PRESENT RESPONSES

In response to the recent increase in condominium conversions, and the effects that accompany the conversions, several states and cities have enacted provisions regulating condominium construction. This portion of the Comment will discuss some of the regulatory schemes enacted to deal

Selected Problems 991

with the conversion phenomenon. The regulations discussed are by no means exclusive; they do, however, represent the mainstream in conversion regulation and illustrate the manner in which most states and cities have chosen to deal with conversions.

1. *Prohibitions.* Many state and local governments are enacting moratoriums on condominium conversions. These moratoriums are imposed in response to perceived emergency situations, and are generally effective for periods of 30 to 120 days. Although most conversion moratoriums are too recent to have been tested in the courts, at least one decision, by Judge McGarr in the Federal District Court for the Northern District of Illinois, held that a total moratorium on conversions amounts to a taking of property without due process of law.[90] Judge McGarr overturned the Chicago moratorium, stating that the buying and selling of property is a fundamental constitutional right.[91] While the government has a duty to balance the rights of the public against a property owner's right to do with his property as he wishes, in view of some courts, a moratorium simply goes too far.

Even if moratoriums are permissible, they may not be wise. Prohibitions against conversions reduce the supply of condominium units on the market. If demand remains strong, prices of existing units rise. The result is that many who could own homes only through condominium conversions are forced into the already strained rental market. Finally, an absolute prohibition against condominium conversions prevents society from enjoying the benefits of conversion.

2. *Eviction Regulations.* Some state and local governments have dealt with tenant displacement by regulating the eviction of tenants from converted apartment buildings. In May 1979, the town of Brookline, Massachusetts, passed an amendment to an existing ordinance giving tenants in a converted apartment building the right to remain in the apartment virtually indefinitely unless they commit specified violations. The 1979 amendment eliminated provisions that allowed a landlord to recover possession for his own personal use or the use of a close relative, subject to a six-month grace period for the tenant in hardship cases. The unamended ordinance regulated eviction by the landlord only; thus, a landlord could sell a unit as a condominium to a purchaser, who, as the new landlord, could then sue to evict the tenant and recover possession for his own personal use, subject to the six-month grace period.[96]

In Grace v. Town of Brookline,[97] the Supreme Court of Massachusetts recently rebuffed due process and equal protection attacks on the pre-amendment ordinance. Although the amended ordinance has not yet

---

90. Chicago Real Estate Bd. v. City of Chicago, No. 79-C1284 (N.D. Ill. Apr. 3, 1979).
91. Id. Judge McGarr also stated that the fact that conversions can be and are being regulated, does not mean they can be prohibited entirely, even for a short period of time. Id. . . .
96. See Grace v. Town of Brookline, — Mass. —, 399 N.E.2d 1038 (1979).
97. Id.

been tested, language in *Grace* indicates that the Massachusetts Supreme Court would uphold it. It should be noted that the Brookline ordinance applies only to rent-controlled units.

It is clear that the Brookline ordinance will drastically reduce, if not stop, condominium conversions. Thus, the ordinance has the same practical effect as a moratorium. In addition, the ordinance may have the unintended effect of encouraging landlords to give large settlements to tenants in order to induce them to leave. Such settlements could result in unjust enrichment for stubborn tenants for whom moving poses no serious burdens. The ordinance could also become a prime source of friction between such tenants and landlords, or between those tenants who wish to buy and thus favor the conversion and those who do not wish to buy yet refuse to move. Finally, like the moratorium, the eviction regulation ignores the positive aspects of conversion.

3. Tenant Purchase Requirements: The New York Approach. New York City is the prime example of a city suffering from deficiencies in the urban housing market. With costs constantly increasing, and rent control or stabilization in effect for most units, landlords have turned to large-scale demolition, abandonment, and conversion. In response to these obvious problems, the state has enacted one of the most restrictive condominium conversion regulations short of a moratorium.[106] Under the New York regulations, a landlord may not proceed with a plan to evict tenants unless a minimum of thirty-five percent of the tenants occupying rental units at the time the conversion plan is accepted for filing agree to purchase units. In addition, new regulations prohibit the eviction of any elderly person with an annual income under $30,000 who has lived in the building for at least two years as a primary resident. The purpose of this tenant purchase requirement is to protect tenants "against excessive pricing and unfair terms. . . . [T]he requirement of sales to at least 35% of the existing tenants within one year to make the plan effective enables the tenants to organize into a strong bargaining unit. A well organized group of tenants can . . . make counter offers and . . . either negotiate acceptable terms or defeat the sponsor's plan." . . . The practical effect of the tenant purchase requirement is to make conversion much easier for landlords of luxury buildings than for landlords of rent-controlled buildings. In buildings in which rent control is keeping rent prices substantially below market prices, tenants will most often be unable or unwilling either to purchase or to move and pay substantially higher rents, thus making conversion difficult, if not impossible.

Under the present restrictive conversion regulations, many landlords in New York will allow their rental buildings to deteriorate, or else simply

---

106. N.Y. Gen. Bus. Law §352-eeee (McKinney Cum. Supp. 1979) (effective July 5, 1979; to expire July 1, 1981). . . .

abandon them. Furthermore, like eviction regulations, purchase requirements can become a prime source of friction between landlords and tenants, and between tenant factions. The additional restrictions, giving virtual life tenancies to elderly tenants, may also have the ironic effect of making rental housing less available for the elderly, since landlords with long term conversion plans may be unwilling to rent to elderly persons.

Finally, any government agency that deals with restrictions on property rights should be sensitive to striking the proper balance between a landlord's property rights and the legitimate necessity of protecting tenants, and should avoid unnecessarily tipping the balance to one side. Unlike the Brookline ordinance, which regulates eviction and *indirectly* affects the landlord's right to convert his property, the New York regulations *directly* affect a landlord's right to convert, subjecting the decision to approval of the tenants. Such regulation is of questionable constitutionality. In Rothman v. Borough of Fort Lee,[117] a New Jersey superior court overturned a similar purchase percentage requirement as unconstitutionally vague and unjustified when applied to luxury apartments in a rent emergency situation. However, in Renier-Kaiser Associates v. McConnachie,[119] a state court recently upheld the New York regulations in the face of an equal protection attack.

   4. *Tenant Consent and Vacancy Rate Formulas.* The District of Columbia law concerning condominium conversions, when not preempted by a moratorium, presents a more thoughtful approach to regulating conversion, but still includes some shortsighted responses to the problem.[120] The regulation allows unrestricted conversion of units if the "accommodation is a high rent housing accommodation or if that rental unit is located in a high rent housing accommodation." For those buildings not in the high rent category, conversion is tied to a vacancy rate and consent formula, with conversion allowed as long as the vacancy rate is above three percent. If the vacancy rate is three percent or below, conversion is permitted only when "a majority of the heads of households actually residing in such housing accommodation, as of the first day of the month in which the application . . . is filed, have signed a written agreement consenting to such conversion." The District of Columbia regulation also allows tenants the right of first refusal to purchase their individual units or the whole property, and requires relocation and housing assistance for eligible tenants.

The District of Columbia approach has at least two major problems. First, the tenant consent provision is likely to inhibit condominium conversions much like the tenant purchase requirements of the New York regulations. Like New York City, Washington is a rent-controlled city.

---

117. No. L21679-73 P.W. (Super. Ct. Bergen County, N.J. June 14, 1974).
119. N.Y.L.J., Aug. 27, 1979 at 13, col. 1 (Queens County Civ. Ct.).
120. D.C. Code Encycl. §§5-1281 to 1282 (West Cum. Supp. 1978).

Tenants unwilling or unable to purchase their units are unlikely to consent to conversion and thus subject themselves to the discomforts and problems of moving and the likelihood of paying an increased rent after the move. Second, as a practical matter, the vacancy rate formulas, computed continuously, could be very costly and difficult to administer. In addition, such formulas fail to deal with the actual causes of low vacancy rates. Like conversion restrictions, low vacancy rates reflect severe problems in the rental housing sector. Effective legislation should be aimed at finding a solution to these low rates, not using them as a basis to restrict conversions.

5. *The Conversion Tax: The Gilchrist Proposal.* In order to deal with conversion problems in Montgomery County, Maryland, Montgomery County Executive Charles Gilchrist recently proposed a conversion tax scheme designed to retard the rate of conversion without prohibiting conversions altogether. Under the Gilchrist proposal, the initial seller of a condominium unit would be required to pay a one-time transfer tax of four percent. Units selling for under $35,000 would be exempt from the tax.

The Gilchrist proposal reflects an attempt to find a more practical solution to the conversion problem and offers many advantages. Gilchrist proposes that part of the money that would be raised by the tax — an estimated $4.8 million in 1980 — be used to expand the county's rent subsidy program. He also suggests that the county supplement the tax revenue with $500,000 of county funds for emergency lump sum payments to displaced elderly and handicapped tenants. The proposal would go a long way toward alleviating the "desperate hardships" faced by displaced tenants. The revenues collected could also supply a source of funds for providing low-interest loans and downpayment assistance. In addition to other tenant protections, such as rights of first refusal and limited eviction grace periods, the Gilchrist proposal could offer one of the best long-range solutions to the conversion problem.

6. *Notice and Right of First Refusal: The Model Code and Uniform Act Approaches, with Local Variations.* Two model acts respond to many of the problems associated with condominium development, including conversion: the Model Condominium Code and the Uniform Condominium Act. The Uniform Condominium Act requires the developer to give the tenants notice of the conversion no later than 120 days before they may be required to vacate, subject to eviction on grounds of nonpayment of rent, waste, or conduct disturbing to neighbors. For a period of sixty days after notice is given, the developer must offer each tenant the first opportunity to purchase the unit on terms at least as good as those offered to the public for the following 180 days. The Act expressly allows a tenant to remain in possession of the unit if his or her written lease exceeds the 120-day notice period.

The Model Condominium Code is very similar to the Uniform Condominium Act. Under the Code, however, tenants have a ninety-day right to purchase. In addition, the Code imposes a three-year limit on eviction of nonpurchasers, measured from the date the conversion plan is first presented to the tenants. Most importantly, however, the Model Code prohibits local legislation, restricting regulation to the state level. This restriction is to insure that local governments do not subvert the state's policy of encouraging conversion whenever tenant rights are adequately protected, a policy clearly recognized by the framers of the Uniform Act.

Some jurisdictions have enacted provisions similar to the model acts. A recent Montgomery County, Maryland, ordinance contains an interesting variation of the right of first refusal concept.[145] The tenants, through a tenants' organization or similar body, must be offered first right to buy the entire property. They are then allowed 120 days to complete the deal. This requirement may give tenants significant benefits without unduly burdening the rights of property owners.

Other local variations of the model acts require that the landlord provide displaced tenants with relocation assistance. In addition, an Evanston, Illinois, condominium conversion regulation provides for correction of all building and fire code violations by the developer.[150] To assure completion of any required corrections, the developer must establish escrow accounts and may not convey title until violations are corrected. The requirement that developers bring all buildings into compliance with building code regulations is necessary to protect tenants from hidden expenses if they choose to purchase; it also provides for physical rehabilitation of buildings.

In addition, the Evanston ordinance requires the developer to guarantee expressly the common areas and systems of the condominium for two years from the date he conveys the first unit of the building. The developer also must expressly warrant the individual unit's "mechanical equipment" for a year from the date the unit is sold. The developer is required to set up escrow accounts to secure compliance with these requirements. Like the building code correction requirements, warranties insure that developers will provide at least minimal rehabilitation to the physical housing stock.

Despite their dissimilarities, the regulations discussed above have the common distinction of being short term, politically motivated solutions to the condominium conversion problem. Each regulation attempts to reduce current political animosity without giving sufficient attention to the need for an effective, long term solution. Conversion is the symptom of a diseased housing market; it is not the disease itself. Even if conversions are inhibited, the disease in the housing market will manifest itself in other

---

145. Montgomery County, Md., Montgomery County Code §§11A-8, 11A-9 (May 26, 1980).

150. Evanston, Ill., Ordinance 12-0-79 §2-105(A) (Mar. 6, 1979). . . .

forms such as decay, demolition, and abandonment. In order to remedy defects inherent in the housing market, regulations must do more than merely attempt to stamp out the symptoms.

B. AN ALTERNATIVE APPROACH

To be truly effective, any long term solution must address the source of the housing sector's difficulties. Preservation of the rental market as a source of low and moderate cost housing should be a primary goal. Prohibitions and inhibitions of the conversion process are not effective methods for attaining this goal. Rather, increased construction and maintenance of the current rental housing market should be encouraged through a system of incentives. This is not to say that all forms of tenant protection are unnecessary, for while the number of persons seriously burdened by displacement is not great, displacement does pose a significant problem for many poor and elderly tenants. Regulations should focus on protecting these people from the hardships of displacement rather than discouraging conversion per se.

 1. *State Preemption.* Condominium conversions should not be discouraged without ample justification. As has been previously noted, local ordinances in particular tend to restrict conversions. For this reason, condominium legislation should be limited to the state level where local political pressures may be less oppressive. In addition, state regulations should preempt local ordinances that indirectly prevent or inhibit conversion, such as zoning restrictions based on condominium status rather than physical characteristics.

 2. *Tenant Protection.* Regulations that directly affect condominium conversion should focus on protecting tenants, not on restricting conversion, and special attention should be given to protecting the poor and the elderly. The Model Condominium Code and the Uniform Condominium Act both provide good foundations for regulatory schemes, but other minimum tenant protection provisions should also be included.

 (a) *Notice and eviction grace period.* A landlord should be required to give tenants sufficient notice of conversion before he can force them to vacate. This notice period should be no shorter than 120 days and no longer than one year, although additional time might be considered necessary for elderly and handicapped persons. . . .

 (b) *Relocation assistance.* Unplanned and unanticipated moves are often expensive and time-consuming. When tenants are forced to vacate their homes to accommodate a developer, they should be compensated for their expenses. At a minimum, regulations should require developers to reimburse displaced tenants for reasonable moving expenses, including an allowance for costs incurred in searching for new housing. . . .

 (c) *Purchase options.* Tenants should be given first option to purchase their individual units. . . .

Selected Problems

(d) *Warranty requirements and correction of building code violations.* Since rehabilitation is a major benefit associated with the conversion process, property improvement should be encouraged. A minimum improvement is guaranteed if developers are required to correct all building and fire code violations. Accordingly, all units should be certified by the city before the developer is allowed to convey title. . . .

3. *Incentives to Increase Construction and Maintenance of Rental Housing.* If reasonably priced rental units were available, condominium conversions would pose fewer problems. Further, if rental housing maintenance were made more attractive, fewer conversions would occur. Rather than attempting to restrict conversions, thus leaving the existing housing problems to manifest themselves in other forms, legislatures should enact provisions encouraging growth in the rental sector. In addition, regulations should be considered that would facilitate unit purchases for those tenants who wish to purchase. A brief overview of some potential solutions follows.

(a) *Facilitating tenant purchases.* Many displaced low and moderate income tenants would purchase their units if they could afford to do so. Federal and local government subsidies should be developed to facilitate such purchases. . . .

(b) *Improving the attractiveness of the rental housing sector for investors.* One of the primary aims of any regulation should be to encourage growth in the rental market by making the rental market more attractive for investment. The essential action that should be considered is decontrol of rents. If rents were allowed to return to their normal market level, maintenance of rental housing would again become profitable. Profitability would, in turn, stimulate new investment, which would ease the current shortage of rental housing.

There are, however, political and practical realities that must be faced when considering rent decontrol. It is extremely difficult politically to advocate decontrol: "Rent controls represent one of those economic policies which, once implemented, is difficult to repeal. The beneficiaries are numerous and the benefits to them are substantial. With the passage of time, the expected shock of decontrol to household living expenses gets progressively worse, making it difficult for elected officials to favor decontrol publicly."

In order to deal with the political realities of decontrol, rent subsidies could be employed to make rental housing affordable for the poor and the elderly. This shift of the subsidization burden from landlords to government should help attract investment to the rental housing sector. State legislatures should consider rent subsidy programs such as those currently undertaken by the federal government. Subsidization would avoid the political difficulties of decontrol as well as the undue hardship on lower income groups forced to pay an unrealistic portion of their incomes for rent.

IV. Conclusion

The current condominium conversion phenomenon is the result of many supply and demand factors at work in the housing market. Conversion can provide numerous advantages to society, but these advantages are accompanied by significant disadvantages for displaced tenants, the poor, and the elderly. Thus, regulators face the difficult task of trying to encourage the conversion process while affording tenants the protection they deserve. Many of the current regulatory schemes severely restrict conversion in an attempt to protect tenants. Such regulations are shortsighted and will probably prove ineffective as a means of preserving the ever decreasing rental market.

The Uniform Condominium Act and the Model Condominium Code provide solid foundations for model tenant protection schemes. State regulators should augment this foundation by imposing conversion taxes and insuring that tenants have rights of first refusal. Further, regulators should remove disincentives to investment in the rental sector. Only this two-pronged approach of encouraging housing development while protecting tenants can provide a truly equitable, long term solution to the housing crisis manifested by the condominium conversion phenomenon.

Flynn v. City of Cambridge
383 Mass. 152, 418 N.E.2d 335 (1981)

HENNESSEY, Chief Justice. The plaintiffs contest the legal power and authority of the Cambridge city council to enact c. 23 of the Code of the city of Cambridge, Ordinance 926 (ordinance), an ordinance regulating eviction from and condominium conversion of housing subject to rent control (controlled rental units). They contend that even if the ordinance was properly enacted, it so restricts the uses for which their units may be utilized as to amount to an unconstitutional taking of their property. We uphold the validity of the ordinance. . . .

The pertinent facts stipulated are as follows. Prior to the enactment of the ordinance on August 13, 1979, rents and evictions in Cambridge were controlled pursuant to c. 842 of the Acts of 1970 (c. 842).[3] Chapter 842

---

3. Chapter 842 of the Acts of 1970 was passed by the Legislature following our decision in Marshal House, Inc. v. Rent Review & Grievance Bd. of Brookline, 357 Mass. 709, 260 N.E.2d 200 (1970). In *Marshal House* we held that Brookline could not enact a rent control by-law under its home rule powers because the challenged by-law was a civil law affecting a civil relationship, id. at 716-717, 260 N.E.2d 200, and rent control was not incident to an independent municipal power, id. at 717-718, 260 N.E.2d 200. After c. 842 (a general enabling act), subsequently conferred the power to regulate rents and evictions, Brookline then restricted condominium conversions by regulations promulgated by its rent control board. We held that the Brookline rent control board was without authority to enact such regulations, because the regulations contradicted the policy of c. 842 to encourage home

Selected Problems   999

was a Statewide general enabling act allowing the regulation of rents and evictions in a substantial number of rental housing units in Cambridge. After being extended for one year by c. 851 of the Acts of 1975, it expired on April 1, 1976. This general enabling act was supplanted by c. 36 of the Acts of 1976 (c. 36). Chapter 36 is a special act entitled "An Act enabling the city of Cambridge to continue to control rents and evictions." The ordinance whose validity is challenged here is entitled "Regulations pertaining to controlled rental housing units." Following an emergency preamble, the ordinance states that "[i]n order to carry out the purposes of [c. 36] . . . it is necessary for the Cambridge City Council, in the exercise of its powers under section 6 of the Home Rule Amendment and under section 5(c) of [c. 36], to regulate the removal of controlled rental housing units from the market." Thus the ordinance claims legitimacy from at least two sources, and the judge below found that both c. 36 and the Home Rule Amendment provided authority for the enactment of the ordinance. We do not examine the Home Rule Amendment since we find implicit authority in c. 36 which empowers Cambridge to enact the ordinance.

The plaintiffs claim that the ordinance amounts to a taking of their property since in some circumstances an owner of a condominium will be prohibited from occupying his unit. The ordinance prohibits the removal of any controlled rental unit unless the city rent control board issues a permit. The permit requirements and related provisions of the ordinance are set forth in the margin.[4] "Removal from the market" is defined in

---

ownership. Zussman v. Rent Control Bd. of Brookline, 367 Mass. 561, 566-567, 569, 326 N.E.2d 876 (1975). A special rent control statute, St. 1970, c. 843, was thereafter interpreted by Brookline as authorizing the implementation of rent and eviction controls. The special authority conferred on Brookline by c. 843, was not limited by the policy of encouraging home ownership which we found in the general act, c. 842. This special authority was used by the town to regulate condominium conversion by by-law amendments. These amendments were upheld in Grace v. Brookline, — Mass. — (Mass. Adv. Sh. [1979] 2257), 399 N.E.2d 1038 (1979). In *Grace* we observed that c. 843 evidenced the Legislature's realization that a unique problem existed in Brookline, and that the policy of encouraging home ownership that we found in c. 842 was absent from c. 843, id. at ——— (Mass. Adv. Sh. [1979] at 2265-2266), 399 N.E.2d 1038. We note here that this policy is also missing from, or at most secondary in, the legislation challenged in this case. St. 1976, c. 36, §9(a)(10). See generally Schlein, Government Regulation of Condominium Conversion, 8 B.C. Env. Af. L. Rev. 919, 925-937 (1980).

4. "(d) *Considerations.* In deciding whether to grant a permit under this section, the board shall consider:

"(1) the benefits to the persons sought to be protected by the Act and by this section;
"(2) the hardships imposed on the tenants residing in the unit proposed to be removed, including any mitigating provisions made by the applicant; and
"(3) any aggravation of the shortage of decent rental housing accommodations, especially for families of low and moderate income and elderly people on fixed incomes, which may result from the removal.

"(4) *Effectiveness.* This section shall take effect immediately, but shall cease to be effective if the board files its certificate with the city clerk that:

§1(b)(4)(i) of the ordinance as including occupation by an owner of a controlled rental unit which is a condominium, if the last previous occupant was a tenant. However, if the "last previous occupant" purchases the condominium, the ordinance then permits him to occupy his unit. In addition, the ordinance does not apply if a purchase and sale agreement was entered into or a unit deed recorded prior to August 10, 1979. In essence, what the ordinance does is require that any unit which is a controlled rental unit on August 10, 1979, remain part of the rental housing stock of the city of Cambridge. It does not prevent an owner from converting his controlled rental units into condominiums, but it does prohibit those condominiums from being used for purposes other than rental housing.

I. THE AUTHORITY OF THE CITY COUNCIL TO ENACT ORDINANCE 926

The declaration of emergency in §1(a) of the ordinance states: "[a] serious public emergency continues to exist in the City of Cambridge with respect to the housing of a substantial number of its citizens, as declared by Chapter 36 of the Acts of 1976, for the reasons stated in the Act. The emergency has worsened since 1976 because of the removal of a substantial number of rental housing units from the market by condominium conversion, demolition, and other causes." The plaintiffs do not contest that the city council could reasonably have made these findings, and they likewise do not contest that the city council could reasonably have concluded that the challenged provisions of the ordinance would alleviate these conditions. In the declaration of emergency in §1 of c. 36, the Legislature found that "unless residential rents and eviction of tenants are regulated and

---

"(1) the vacancy rate in the total supply of controlled rental [housing] exceeds four percent, or
"(2) the total number of rental units in the city excluding public housing units, exceeds that number as of January 1, 1970.
"If such a certificate ceases to be correct, the board shall withdraw it by filing a new certificate, and this section shall then again be effective until one of the above conditions again prevails.

"(f) *Penalty.* Any person who violates this section shall be punished by a fine of not more than five hundred dollars. The removal of each unit shall constitute a separate violation."

The board has promulgated regulations in order to implement these and other provisions in the ordinance. The plaintiffs have referred at length to these regulations, suggesting that they seek a judgment regarding the validity of the regulations. Having challenged only the facial validity of the ordinance, however, they are not entitled to such a ruling. Moreover, any attack on the validity of the regulations would have to be brought in the District Court, rather than the Superior Court where the plaintiffs commenced this action. Marshal House, Inc. v. Rent Control Bd. of Brookline, 358 Mass. 686, 707-709, 266 N.E.2d 876 (1971). Section 10 of c. 36 of the Acts of 1976.

controlled, such emergency and the further inflationary pressures resulting therefrom will produce serious threats to the public health, safety and general welfare of the citizens of Cambridge. . . ." Chapter 36 itself provides restrictions on evictions from controlled rental units, and it expressly states that "[r]ecovery of possession in order to convert an apartment unit to a condominium unit shall not be a valid reason to recover possession of a controlled rental unit." §9(a)(10). The ordinance provides additional restrictions, all consistent with c. 36. The plaintiffs' contention, though, is that the city council lacked authority to enact the ordinance.

It is beyond question that c. 36 enables Cambridge to control rents and evictions. In addition to the express powers conferred by c. 36, however, certain powers are implied. When analyzing a grant of power to a municipal government we must keep in mind that "a grant of an express power carries with it all unexpressed, incidental powers necessary to carry it into effect." . . .

In order to determine whether the city council was empowered by c. 36 to enact the ordinance, we must decide whether the city's ability to regulate the removal of rental housing stock from the market is an "unexpressed, incidental power necessary to carry [c. 36] into effect." We conclude that it is.

If the power to control rents is to be anything more than an interim measure effective for only the short period needed to convert the entire rental housing stock, it must include by implication the power to make reasonable regulations governing removals from the rental housing market. "It is no coincidence that many cities facing the most serious conversion problems are rent control cities, and as the rent control movement spreads, condominium conversion problems are likely to follow." Comment, The Condominium Conversion Problem: Causes and Solutions, 1980 Duke L.J. 306, 312. In 1979 there were 20,115 controlled rental units in Cambridge. In the seven-year period 1970 to 1976, inclusive, condominium master deeds were filed with respect to a total of 445 residential rental units. The conversion rate escalated, however, from January 1, 1977, to August 13, 1979, the effective date of the ordinance. In this thirty-one month period condominium master deeds were filed with respect to 1,554 residential units: 80.6 per cent of these units were subject to rent control. Thus, immediately prior to the passage of the ordinance, conversion of controlled rental housing was sharply reducing the supply of affordable rental housing in Cambridge, housing which c. 36 was expressly designed to conserve. Even if the conversion rate did no more than level off, the power conferred by c. 36 to control rents would steadily and irreversibly be transformed into the power to control nothing. The power to control rents and evictions is not so illusory that it does not comprehend the right and responsibility of preventing removals from its reach. We conclude that the power to control removals from the rental housing market is essential to the operation of c. 36, and is therefore conferred by implication in the rent control statute.

II. THE CONSTITUTIONALITY OF THE ORDINANCE

The plaintiffs contend that the ordinance is unconstitutional because it eliminates an owner's right to possess his condominium unit, and the owner is not compensated for this deprivation. Such a deprivation, claim the plaintiffs, is unduly oppressive and arbitrary in its allocation of rights of possession to persons other than the owner. We do not agree.

The ordinance does deny a condominium owner the right to occupy his unit if it was used for rental housing on and not converted before the effective date of the ordinance. There are two classes of owners who are affected. The first class, those owners who purchase their condominium units after the effective date of the ordinance, are on notice that they have no right to use their property as owner-occupied housing. They are fairly warned that they are purchasing property which may be used for rental housing only, and presumably the purchase price reflects this use restriction. Since these owners were notified that they had no right to occupy their unit, they were not denied a right to which they had a legitimate expectation. Clearly the government is not required to compensate an individual for denying him the right to use that which he has never owned.

The second class of owners is comprised of those owners whose units were purchased prior to, and which were being used for rental housing on, the effective date of the ordinance. These owners, under prior law, did have a right to occupy their unit. That right is now denied them. However, "the submission that [plaintiffs] may establish a 'taking' simply by showing that they have been denied the ability to exploit a property interest that they heretofore had believed was available for development is quite simply untenable. . . . 'Taking' jurisprudence does not divide a single parcel into discrete segments and attempt to determine whether rights in a particular segment have been entirely abrogated. In deciding whether a particular governmental action has effected a taking, [the focus is] rather both on the character of the action and on the nature and extent of the interference with rights *in the parcel as a whole*" (emphasis added). Penn Central Transp. Co. v. New York City, 438 U.S. 104, 130-131, 98 S. Ct. 2646, 2662-63, 57 L. Ed. 2d 631 (1978). In *Penn Central* two factors persuaded the Court that no taking had occurred: the governmental action did not interfere with the owner's primary expectation concerning the use of the property, and the owner was still able to obtain a reasonable return on its investment. Id. at 136, 98 S. Ct. at 2665. The presence of these two factors in this case likewise convinces us that no taking has occurred. By definition, any owner in the second class of owners was using his unit for rental housing on the effective date of the ordinance, so his primary expectation has not been frustrated. While the use restrictions subsequently enacted undeniably diminish the value of the property, this alone does not establish a taking. See Euclid v. Ambler Realty Co., 272 U.S. 365, 47 S. Ct. 114, 71 L. Ed. 303 (1926); Hadacheck v. Sebastian, 239 U.S. 394, 36 S. Ct. 143, 60 L. Ed. 348 (1915). "Government hardly could go on if to some extent values incident to property could not be diminished without paying for every such change in the general law." Pennsylvania Coal Co. v. Mahon, 260 U.S. 393, 413, 43 S. Ct. 158, 159, 67 L. Ed. 322 (1922). In addition, the owner of a controlled rental unit is *assured* by §7(*a*) of c. 36, of the right to receive a fair net operating income for his unit. It is not disputed that the ordinance serves a legitimate public purpose. We conclude that there has been no taking. In similar cases, analysis of the factors that we have considered herein has led to identical conclusions. See, e.g., Agins v. Tiburon, 447 U.S. 255, 261, 100 S. Ct. 2138, 2142, 65 L. Ed. 2d 106 (1980); Andrus v. Allard, 444 U.S. 51, 64-68, 100 S. Ct. 318, 326-328, 62 L. Ed. 2d 210 (1979); Penn Central Transp. Co. v. New York City, 438 U.S. 104, 136, 98 S. Ct. 2643, 2665, 57 L. Ed. 2d 631 (1978).

Judgment affirmed.

NOTES AND QUESTIONS

1. The Uniform Common Interest Ownership Act (UCIOA) (1982), offers existing renters minimal rights in the event of conversion. The sponsor would be required to give each residential tenant or subtenant in possession notice of the conversion and a copy of the offering statement no later than [120] days before such persons would be required to vacate their units. Upon receipt of the offering statement, the renter would then have [60] days to decide whether to acquire the unit or not. Should the renter decide against purchase, the sponsor would be disabled during the next [180] days from offering the unit to outsiders at a price or upon terms more favorable than those available to the party in possession. Id. at §4-112. This arrangement is taken, verbatim, from the Uniform Condominium Act.

2. In New York State at present (as of the summer of 1985), most conversions are so-called noneviction plans, under which nonpurchasing residents may continue their occupancy as rent-stabilized (or rent-controlled) tenants even after the building becomes a cooperative or condominium. The law allows conversion to become effective upon the sale of 15 percent of the units; this may result in the seeming anomaly of a cooperative or condominium whose occupants, mainly, have no ownership interest in their units. Consider what problems might arise to trouble a condominium project if, for example, twenty units are owned by their occupants and the remaining eighty units are owned either by the sponsor or by outside

investors (who, under New York law, may not evict a stabilized or rent-controlled tenant except for nonpayment of rent or other leasehold violations).

6. Income Taxation

a. The Residential Owner

The association homeowner and the condominium unit owner enjoy in all respects the taxable status of a conventional homeowner. The itemizing taxpayer may deduct mortgage interest[5] and real estate tax outlays.[6] Rev. Rul. 64-31, 1964-1 C.B. 300. Such person may also write off casualty losses in excess of $100 which exceed 10 percent of the individual's adjusted gross income. Resale profits are taxable as capital gains but, if the unit serves as the taxpayer's principal residence, the roll-over provisions of I.R.C. §1034 apply; similarly, where the taxpayer has reached the age of 55 and during the preceding five-year period has used the unit as principal residence for at least three years, §121 would exclude the first $125,000 of gain. (Each of these sales gain provisions apply as well to those taxpayers owning or acquiring "qualifying" cooperative units. I.R.C. §§121(d)(3), 1034(f).) If the taxpayer rents the unit out, he or she gains full cost recovery and other trade or business deductions (viz., insurance, repairs, etc.) unless the venture is seen as a "not-for-profit" activity, §183, page 357 supra, or involves excessive personal use, §280A, page 355 supra. Finally, the taxpayer would report any commercial income generated by taxpayer's pro rata share of the common areas, offset by the usual cost recovery and expense deductions.

This taxable identity for conventional ownership does not automatically extend to the residential cooperator who, after all, is a tenant in the unit, rather than the fee owner. Since direct liability for the debt is a prerequisite for the deductibility of mortgage interest[7] and real estate tax payments, and ownership of the underlying real estate is a condition for the deductibility of cost recovery, cooperative tenants cannot avail themselves of §§163 and 164, where it is the cooperative landlord who incurs

---

5. President Reagan's 1985 Tax Reform proposal would subject to the investment interest limitation of §163(d) all interest not incurred in connection with a trade or business other than interest on debt secured by the taxpayer's principal residence. Federal Taxes, The President's Tax Proposals to the Congress for Fairness, Growth, and Simplicity c. 13.01 (P-H, May 1985). If adopted, this proposal would greatly curtail the deductibility of interest on other than the taxpayer's principal residence.

6. Similarly, the President's proposal would entirely eliminate the deductibility of state and local taxes, including the real estate tax. Id. at c. 3.09.

7. To the degree that the cooperator has borrowed to finance the "equity" portion of the purchase price, cooperator is liable for the debt directly and may avail himself of the provisions of §163.

the blanket mortgage and suffers the property tax assessments; nor can the tenants (who rent their apartment out) proceed under §§167 and 168, where, again, the landlord owns the improvements.

In 1942, in the interest of offering cooperators homeownership equivalence, Congress enacted §216. This provision allows "tenant-stockholders" to deduct their pro rata share of the housing corporation's real estate tax and interest payments. Additionally, cooperators may depreciate their investments to the extent that they use their proprietary leases in a trade or business or for the production of income.

Section 216 has not resulted, however, in exact equivalence between the cooperator and a homeowner (or unit owner in a homes association or condominium). This disparity results from Congress's decision to limit the availability of §216 to those taxpayers holding stock-and-lease in a qualifying "cooperative housing corporation." Section 216(b) states four conditions that the cooperative must satisfy before its members may gain the deductions. Trickiest of these conditions is the so-called Eighty-Twenty rule, §216(b)(1)(D), which requires that at least 80 percent of the cooperative's gross income for the taxable year be derived from tenant-stockholders — i.e., those individuals who, by reason of their stock-ownership, are entitled to occupy the underlying unit for dwelling purposes. Where the cooperative falls short of that requirement, each member loses his or her *entire* deduction for project expenses during that year.

Eckstein v. United States, 452 F.2d 1036 (Cl. Ct. 1971), demonstrates that the Eighty-Twenty rule can be a mine field, especially for mixed-use cooperatives where some of the corporation's gross income derives from commercial or professional tenants who, ordinarily, will not be entitled to occupy their units for dwelling purposes and, therefore, will not satisfy the Code's definition of "tenant-stockholder"; any rental income that the corporation receives from such persons would work to prevent qualification. In the *Eckstein* case, the cooperative failed to qualify; in addition to the commercial income, which alone would not have been disqualifying, the corporation was not able to include as qualifying "income" that part of the cooperative's rental payments used to reduce the mortgage *principal* on the project's blanket mortgage. The Commissioner viewed mortgage amortization not as "income" properly included in the numerator and denominator for purposes of fixing the percentage, but as a contribution to the corporation's "paid-in surplus," properly excluded from both the numerator and denominator for purposes of fixing the percentage.[8] The *Eckstein* opinion suggests how a bookkeeping treatment of mortgage amortization different from the one used by the corporation would have changed the result; presumably, cooperative accountants have now been

---

8. To illustrate how this treatment of mortgage amortization might be decisive, if we assume mortgage amortization of 10, and inclusion of amortization within income, a cooperative qualifies if the ratio is 80/100. If amortization is excluded from the cooperative's income, the ratio drops to 70/90, which is less than 80 percent, and thus nonqualifying.

properly educated so that the "amortization" problem is unlikely to resurface. But the tainting effect of nonresidential income has remained a serious issue for mixed-use cooperatives and continues strongly to influence their design.

NOTES AND QUESTIONS

1. Associations and condominiums are free of the Eighty-Twenty rule. Regardless of the sources of the project income, unit owners may, by itemizing their deductions, enjoy tax parity with homeowners. This permits, inter alia, far more flexibility in planning mixed-use projects than can be ventured in the cooperative. What policies argue for (or against) treating cooperatives differently?

2. The loss of the entire deduction is a stiff penalty for the cooperative member in a nonqualifying project. Are there less drastic alternatives that Congress might have considered? Cowan, Tax Reform on the Home Front: Cooperative Housing Corporations, Condominiums, and Homeowners Associations, 5 J. Real Est. Taxn. 101-112 (1978), examines the origins of the Eighty-Twenty rule and some of the qualification problems.

3. The requirement of *individual* tenant-stockholders once posed a deductibility problem for any institutional lender that obtained an apartment after a mortgage default upon the stock-lease. Moreover, assessments paid by the lender did not apply toward the qualifying 80 percent, although the use of an individual nominee to acquire the stock-and-lease might have been an acceptable arrangement. Section 216(b)(5) now addresses the problem by treating the foreclosing lender as a tenant-stockholder for a period not to exceed three years from the date of acquisition. In a similar vein, §216(b)(6) gives tenant-stockholder status to any units held by an "original seller" who acquires the unit via foreclosure or, within one year after the transfer of real estate title to the cooperative corporation, acquires the unit from the corporation (to wit, any unsold units). The same three-year grace period applies.

4. X cooperative contains residential and commercial space. In 1978, the cooperative earns $100,000 in commercial rental income for space that costs $50,000 to operate. This allows a $50,000 reduction in the assessments levied against the residential tenants. Discuss the possible tax consequences of the "bargain rental." Consider also a mixed-use P.U.D. or condominium. Cf. Anaheim Union Water Co. v. Commissioner, 321 F.2d 253 (9th Cir. 1963).

b. The Central Body

When we turn to the central body, other tax issues appear. The cooperative corporation and the homes or condominium association are separate entities which must file returns and, when there is income, pay taxes.

In Park Place, Inc., 57 T.C. 767 (1972), the Tax Court considered whether a cooperative should report all the income it receives from tenant-stockholders (against which it would deduct outlays for interest, taxes, and operation), or only any excess assessments that might occur. The court held that any assessments actually devoted to project expenditures should be excluded from the corporation's income, on the somewhat questionable theory that the corporation — as to these items — was a mere conduit for the assessments.[9] But any excess assessments, the court continued, must be included.[10]

The major problem with respect to overassessments lies in the taxability of replacement reserves. Typically, the central body builds these reserves to handle sudden obsolescence, or the inevitable wearing out of major building components, or a decision to expand the common facilities. Often these reserves also provide a cushion against any future shortfall due to unpaid assessments. The reserves accumulate through regular assessments of the project members' and the reserve's investment earnings.

These earnings, except when derived from tax-exempt sources, are routinely taxable.[11] Less clear, however, has been the taxability of the members' payments into the reserve. Despite the Tax Court holding that overassessments *were* taxable, tax scholars argued that reserve payments could be excluded on analogy to the capital contribution analysis which appears in the *Eckstein* opinion. Do you see the analogy? Some experts also asserted — in the case of homes and condominium associations — that these bodies enjoyed tax-exempt status under either §501(c)(4) (nonprofit civic organizations operated exclusively for social welfare) or §501(c)(7) (club operated exclusively for pleasure, recreation, and other nonprofitable purposes, no part of its net earnings to benefit any private shareholder). In a series of rulings, the Service rejected the §501(c)(4) claim. Rev. Rul. 74-17, 1974-1 C.B. 130; Rev. Rul. 74-99, 1974-1 C.B. 131.[12] Nor did the §501(c)(7) analogy seem more promising. Levine, Real Estate Transactions, Tax Planning 229 (1976).

The Service offered some basis for tax exemption, however, by ruling that an assessment collected from condominium owners for a specified purpose (for example, the construction of a parking lot) would be treated as contribution to capital if the funds were segregated in a special account. Rev. Rul. 74-563, 1974-2 C.B. 38. Subsequent rulings brought more

---

9. The court's logic ought to prevent "mere conduit" receipts from being treated as *income* from tenant-stockholders for the purpose of satisfying the Eighty-Twenty rule. Anticipating this objection, the court said that the calculation should include such receipts. 57 T.C. 767, 779 (1972).

10. Excess amounts are not taxable if the proceeds are used in the following year or, in the alternative, returned to the members. Cf. Rev. Rul. 70-604, 1970-2 C.B. 9 (condominium).

11. This assumes, of course, that the central body's overall return shows taxable income.

12. Earlier the courts had rejected a §501(c)(4) claim made on behalf of a housing cooperative. Commr. v. Lake Forest Inc., 305 F.2d 814 (4th Cir. 1962). And the Service had ruled against exempting a cooperative under §501(c)(12) ("mutual or cooperative telephone companies, or like organizations"). Rev. Rul. 65-201, 1965-2 C.B. 170.

relief. By forming a separate corporation to maintain the common areas, the condominium could exempt special assessments raised to replace common elements such as the roof or elevators,[13] Rev. Rul. 75-370, 1975-2 C.B. 25, or personalty such as poolside furniture which the corporation itself owned but provided for the unit owners.[14] Rev. Rul. 75-371, 1875-2 C.B. 52. Although the rulings dealt only with a condominium, the legal analysis would seem to apply a fortiori to a homes association.

The Tax Reform Act of 1976 brought further relief to homes and condominium associations. Since nothing in tax law is any longer simple, the relief provision, §528, is quite lengthy, as is the Senate Committee Report. In essence, §528 would give tax exemption to a qualifying homeowners association[15] for so-called exempt function income. This would include membership dues, fees, or assessments received from the residential owners within the homes association or condominium. This would not include, however, the investment earnings of the reserve funds, or fees received for use of the association facilities from nonmembers, or special use fees received from association members in their capacity as customers —for example, payments for maid service, secretarial service, etc. (Nor does §528 provide any tax relief either for housing cooperatives[16] or nonresidential condominiums.) As to any nonexempt-function income, the qualifying homeowners association would be subject to corporate tax

---

13. The Treasury viewed the corporation as a fiduciary that held the special assessments as an agent for the benefit of the "unit owners," the corporation's sole stockholders. This reasoning approaches the "conduit" theory of the *Park Place* decision discussed in the text.

14. In this ruling, the Treasury returned to the capital contribution theory of Rev. Rul. 74-563, 1974-2 C.B. 38. The special assessments levied against the unit-owner stockholders were a nontaxable (§118) capital contribution enabling the corporation to acquire the poolside furniture. Note the difference, however, between the factual content of the two rulings. In the earlier case, the unit owners are adding directly to their own equity since the unincorporated association has no assets (other than the reserve funds) and does not issue shares as would a corporation. Thus the 1974 ruling does not rest on §118 but on analogy, perhaps, to partnership tax principles.

15. To qualify, the homeowners association must derive 60 percent or more of its gross income from membership dues, fees, or assessments paid by its residential members and must apply 90 percent or more of its expenditures for the "acquisition, construction, management, maintenance, and care of association property." Association property will usually mean the common elements, whether owned by the association or its members in common. But §528 also allows for association expenditures on privately owned elements which affect the overall appearance and structure of the project. For example, "the condominium association may enforce covenants with regard to the appearance . . . of the exterior walls and roof of the individual units." P-H Tax Reform Act of 1976, p. 853 (Sen. Comm. Rpt.).

The 60 percent gross income test raises at least one uncertainty in view of the Treasury rulings that preceded §528. The Senate Committee Report states that assessments for capital improvements which would otherwise be treated as capital contributions do not qualify for the 60 percent test. Id. This is the very situation discussed in Rev. Rul. 75-371, 1975-2 C.B. 52, and parallels the facts of Rev. Rul. 74-563, 1974-2 C.B. 38, which both resulted in tax exemption on a capital contributions theory. While these assessments would keep their exempt status under §528, removing them from the forms of gross income that satisfy the 60 percent test might unintendedly result in the association losing its exemption as to all other income.

16. The Senate Report explains the failure to bring housing cooperatives within section 528: "They have a long history of being treated as taxable organizations." Id. at 854. Is this a convincing reason?

levies, whether or not it took the corporate form. A later amendment to §528(b) fixed the tax as equal to 30 percent of the association's taxable income.[17]

Although §528 failed to offer housing cooperatives a tax-exempt election for their reserve funds, the 1976 statute benefited them in another way which may ultimately prove even more valuable. At stake was the right of a cooperative corporation to depreciate the building improvements. One would expect a clear right to do so: the cooperative holds legal title to the structure; the cooperative, qua landlord, operates a trade or business. Yet the tax court had upheld the commissioner's refusal to allow depreciation, except for any units not leased to tenant-stockholders. Park Place, Inc., 57 T.C. 767 (1972). The court reasoned that only the tenant-stockholders enjoyed an economic interest in the apartments and that the corporation was merely a custodian of the bare legal title for the convenience of its tenant-stockholders.

In amending §216(c), Congress has impliedly overruled the *Park Place* holding. The Code would now allow the cooperative to depreciate the property it leases to a tenant-stockholder even though the latter might himself be entitled to depreciate his stock to the extent that he uses the unit in a trade or business or for the production of income.[18] It follows, necessarily, that the cooperative may depreciate the leased property when the tenant-stockholder makes no business use of the unit.

Most cooperatives should now have sufficient depreciation to absorb any excess assessments which they receive from tenant-stockholders. Recalling the *Eckstein* case again, do you see how the cooperative's right to take depreciation may relate to the accounting decision whether to treat "mortgage reduction" as income or capital contribution?

c. The Converter of Rental Apartments

Problem: X owns a 100-unit rental building, which he acquired five years ago. X, who has utilized straight-line depreciation, has an adjusted basis of $4,000,000 in the property (land = $1,000,000, improvements = $3,000,000). X sees profit in converting the apartments into condominium units and believes that the apartments, if sold as condominiums, will realize $10,000,000. X is uncertain whether to undertake the conversion himself directly, to sell the building to an independent condominium developer—who would pay about $7,000,000 for the property—or to explore some intermediate arrangement which might maximize his aftertax profit. What advice can you give him?

---

17. The association is permitted, however, to offset taxable income with deductions for directly connected expenses. There is also permitted a specific deduction of $100.
18. Congress seemed unconcerned about the tax avoidance possibility of a cooperative and the tenant-stockholders both depreciating the same affect. This confidence rests on §277, which would prevent the cooperative from offsetting its income from nonmember sources with spillover losses (via depreciation) from its membership activity.

If X undertakes the conversion directly, he will almost certainly be deemed a "dealer," §1221(1), and except for the possibility of some limited relief under §1237 (which requires a five-year minimum holding period for other than real property acquired by inheritance or devise, and bars the making of substantial improvements prior to sale),[19] X's gain will be taxable as ordinary income. If X's $10,000,000 estimate of resale value is correct, he would net, after taxes, about $7,000,000 from the conversion[20] if we also assume that the applicable tax rate is 50 percent. If X takes back any part of the financing, the installment sale provisions of §453 would permit some deferral of the tax.

If X sells the building to an independent converter, he will realize after taxes only $6,400,000, although X is spared, of course, the headache of overseeing the conversion. A $600,000 headache suggests considerable anxiety, but X is prepared to accept the burdens of conversion if, somehow, he can net significantly more than $600,000 from the added responsibility.

Prior to the 1984 amendments, professionals believed that one could follow a path through the Code which would achieve a more favorable aftertax outcome than either of the above alternatives. This path required a multiple transaction strategy, to wit:

1. X would form the controlled X Corporation, to which he would transfer the rental property. Qualifying under §351, the transfer would be nontaxable. The Corporation would have a $4,000,000 carryover basis in the property;
2. The Corporation would hold the property for a sufficient period, let us say one year, so that its corporate activity would be substantively respected;
3. The Corporation would market 40 units at an aggregate price of $4,000,000. Its gain on these sales, taxable as ordinary income, would be $2,400,000. If we assume an effective 44 percent rate, the Corporation would net approximately $3,000,000 after taxes;
4. The Corporation would liquidate, distributing to X $3,000,000 cash and the 60 remaining units. Under §336, the Corporation would recognize no gain from distributing its assets directly to X in return for his stock as part of a complete liquidation. Under the

---

19. The commissioner has ruled that §1237 does not apply to the conversion of rental units into condominiums. Rev. Rul. 80-216, 1980-32 I.R.B. 10. Bolling and Carper, Capital Gains in Condominium Conversions? Internal Revenue Code Section 1237, 13 Real Est. L.J. 45 (1984), argues that the ruling is unsupported by the section's legislative history.

20. The taxpayer might claim that the entire gain should be treated as a long-term capital gain on the "liquidation of investment" theory, but two fairly recent decisions seriously undermine the claim: Commissioner v. Parkside, Inc., 571 F.2d 1092 (9th Cir. 1977); Biederharn Realty Co. v. United States, 526 F.2d 409 (5th Cir. 1976). See also Kaster, Residential Co-ops and Condominiums Development Projects and Conversions Promoter's Tax Techniques, 38th N.Y.U. Ann. Inst. Fed. Taxn. 13-1, 15-16 (1980).

general rules of §331(a)(1), X would treat the complete liquidation of the X Corporation as a sale of his stock. Through this liquidating sale, in which X would receive assets valued at $9,000,000 (cash = $3,000,000, unsold units = $6,000,000), X would suffer a tax of approximately $1,320,000 on his long-term capital gain ($9,000,000 − $2,400,000 × .20);

5. X would sell the 60 remaining units for $6,000,000. Having a $6,000,000 stepped-up basis for the units, he would incur no further tax. Accordingly, X would net $7,680,000 from the conversion, more than would have resulted from the earlier alternatives.

What the 1984 amendments have changed, so as greatly to inhibit the above arrangement, is the treatment of collapsibility. Previously, one could avoid §341, the collapsible corporation provision, whenever the corporation had realized a "substantial" part of the potential net income from the transaction before making a liquidating distribution of the remaining assets. A series of decisions, culminating in Commissioner v. Kelley, 293 F.2d 904 (5th Cir. 1961), ruled that recognition at the corporate level of one-third of the corporation's potential income satisfied the "substantiality" requirement. See Rev. Rul. 72-48, 1972-1 C.B. 102. In the example above, we provided for the sale of 40 percent of the assets before the corporate liquidation, a safety move given our uncertainty as to the ultimate net income which the venture would realize. But Congress, in 1984, believing that the *Kelley* rule was overly generous to developers and other tax avoiders, amended §341(b) so as to require that the corporation realize two-thirds of the taxable income prior to liquidation. This tougher requirement does not negative entirely the use of a corporate intermediary, but any potential benefit is much diminished. Moreover, taxes are essentially prepaid under the above scheme, inasmuch as X would suffer the tax with respect to the unsold units at the time of liquidation rather than upon the units' eventual sale. Therefore, X must gamble upon a rapid resale and, in calculating whether to use the corporate intermediary, must apply some discount to reflect the interval between liquidation and resale.

Other possibilities exist for an owner who wishes to participate in the conversion profits, but wishes also to maximize that part of the gain likely to be treated as long-term capital. Consider, for example, a "joint venture" with Y, in which X and Y share equally the conversion potential. The transaction might take the following form.

Step 1: X and Y form the X-Y Partnership.

Step 2: Y contributes $3,500,000 to the Partnership; X contributes a one-half interest in the building (fair value = $3,500,000) to the Partnership. The contribution under §721 is nontaxable. The Partnership's basis in the property under §723 is $2,000,000.

Step 3: X sells his remaining one-half interest in the building to the Partnership for $3,500,000.[21] The sale under §707(a) is taxable. X suffers a long-term capital gain of $1,500,000, on which he pays a $300,000 tax. X nets $3,200,000 from the sale. The Partnership's basis in the property under §1012 is $3,500,000.

Step 4: The X-Y Partnership carries out the conversion, selling all 100 units for $10,000,000. The Partnership reports a taxable gain of $4,500,000 ($10,000,000 − $5,600,000). As a dealer in real property, the Partnership gain will be ordinary income. X's share of the gain, $2,250,000, will be taxed to him personally; assuming a 50 percent individual rate, he will suffer a $1,125,000 tax.

Step 5: The X-Y Partnership completes a liquidation distribution. X will receive his one-half share of the sales proceeds, or $5,000,000. The distribution under §731 is nontaxable.

As a result of the above events, X enjoys an aftertax net slightly in excess of $7,000,000, roughly his return if he were to undertake the conversion directly. By taking in a partner, however, X benefits from both the joint responsibility (particularly if Y is an experienced converter) and from an accelerated partial return on his investment (the first $3,500,000).

Much writing exists on the tax aspects of cooperative and condominium conversion. Citations include: Kaster, Residential Co-ops and Condominium Development Projects and Conversions Promoter's Tax Techniques, 38 N.Y.U. Ann. Inst. Fed. Taxn. 13-1 (1980); Limberg, *Bradshaw* Provides Support and Guidelines for Capital Gains in Condominium Conversions, J. Real. Est. Taxn. 328 (1984).

C. TIME-SHARING OWNERSHIP

Vogel, The Tax Consequences of Time-Sharing
10 J. Real Est. Taxn. No. 3, at 323 (Spring 1983)

An intriguing concept that has generated much debate among land developers, prospective purchasers, and lending institutions is the time-sharing of property ownership. . . .

. . . Time-sharing is the term used to describe the diverse ways of buying or utilizing resort vacation condominiums, homes, ship cabins, and hotel and motel accommodations for a specific period each year. This is

---

21. In forming the Partnership, X should be aware of the limitations of §707(b)(2), which would subject his gain to treatment as ordinary income if X owns, directly or indirectly, more than 80 percent of either the capital interest or the profits interest in the partnership.

Time-sharing Ownership

achieved through an array of legal structures, ranging from a simple license or right-to-use agreement to an actual conveyance of the time period by means of a warranty deed coupled with title insurance. The latter concept is implemented through the use of either "timespan" or "interval" land ownership.

Time-share ownership is a method of acquiring an equity interest in a vacation-type resort for just that part of the year during which the purchaser plans to occupy the resort. The buyer saves by purchasing the property for only the time he will use the facility. His purchase price and yearly maintenance costs are less because they are shared with others. In most cases, one can even make a down payment with a credit card. The possibility also exists of enjoying continued vacation savings each year a time-sharer returns to a resort. Considering the constant rise of vacation costs at hotels and motels, this represents a substantial benefit. . . .

Most time-share customers hesitate about investing in a single resort location for a vacation for an extended period. There is, however, a resolution to this dilemma: Should the buyer tire of one location, he can exchange his time-share segment for another of similar value through two international networks. One network operates like a bank. When the owner makes a deposit of his time segment, he may make a withdrawal of an equal time. The other exchange method attempts to match each unit owner's preference with that of another's through the use of computers. Though both systems are not perfect, they do increase the marketability of time-sharing. . . .

. . . Though some observers held that time-sharing was a product of hard times and would disappear with the recovery of the real estate market, they proved to be wrong. Today nothing seems to be inhibiting the growth of time-sharing. Resorts built completely around the concept of time-sharing flourish from Florida to Hawaii and along both coasts. Wherever a vacation can be enjoyed, there is likely to be a developer considering the use of time-sharing.

The rapid growth of this creative idea has been impressive. In 1973, only three time-share projects were in existence in the United States. Within the following six-year period, an estimated 3,509 world-wide resorts were in operation. Carl Burlingame, a publisher of the industry newsletter Resort Time-Sharing Today and a recognized authority on the growth and history of time-sharing, commented on this phenomenon: "All the growth has really occurred since 1976, literally doubling in each of those years until sales totaled about $300 million by the end of 1978. Sales for 1979 totaled $650 million and are expected to reach $1.2 to $1.5 billion in 1980."

Some of the reasons for this growth are obvious. Time-sharing allows the buyer to fight inflation by purchasing future vacations with present dollars. Other contributing factors are the increase in leisure time and mobility of various segments of the population; lower- and middle-class segments of the population have more time on their hands. In addition, automobiles available for leisure-time use and the growing popularity of recreational activities have led to more frequent "long weekends" and a concerted effort to implement the four-day work week. Today buyers will drive 100 to 150 miles from urban centers on express highways for a mini-vacation.

Initially, this increase in leisure time and vacation mobility led to the marketing of resort condominiums. The high costs of ownership and year-round maintenance were dealt with through the use of "rental pools." When the Securities Exchange Commission and various state security bureaus determined these arrangements to be "securities" and required disclosure and the licensing of the salespeople, the resort housing developers sought a less costly, less regulated means of marketing their product. Time-sharing is a viable alternative. Although there are increased marketing costs using the time-sharing approach, by applying the principle of subdivision economics (the parts can be sold for more than the whole), the time-share industry has developed a profitable product.

Types of Time-Sharing

Vacation License, Vacation Lease, or Condominium Club

One way marketing resort condominiums arose was through the vacation license, vacation lease, or condominium club. All three employ the same basic concept. These time-share methods allow the purchaser the mere right to use or occupy a condominium unit for a specific length of time each year for a specified number of years. One type of program is the Holiday Club International, which offers the right to use a certain class of units at designated locations. But under no circumstances do the purchaser and seller of these right-to-use programs intend that this approach will give rise to what is commonly considered the ownership of land. The developer or sales firm always retains the fee interest.

From the consumer's viewpoint, because he has paid for the right in advance, a potential problem of this arrangement is whether the resort will even be a functioning operation in the future. This potential hazard is also a concern to many federal, state, and local agencies. If the time arrangement suggests investment potential, this may also give rise to federal and state securities law problems. In addition, since the licensee has no interest in the underlying fee, he remains unprotected against encumbrances by the fee owner or the owner's creditors. This could even mean the imposition of a federal tax lien on the property.[21]

---

21. Prior to purchase, the land records of the resort project should be examined for any federal tax liens. The IRS can impose a general tax lien on the underlying resort property if the owner-operator after demand refuses or neglects to pay his federal taxes. I.R.C. §6321. A time-share lessee is considered a "purchaser" and is afforded priority if he acquired the interest *before* the taxman. I.R.C. §6323(h)(6); see W. Plumb & L. Wright, Federal Tax Liens 49 (2d ed. A.L.I., 1967).

OWNERSHIP "TIMESPAN" AND "INTERVAL" OWNERSHIP

"Timespan" and "interval" ownership are two popular types of time-share ownership that assure buyers dual protection of title to the property and title insurance. They both allow the owners to will, lease, or sell their interests, including their time periods, as long as no restrictions to the contrary were imposed by the developer. The owners pay the property taxes and are able to deduct interest and taxes pro rata.

Timespan Ownership

"Timespan" ownership is a legal structure developed to enable vacation homes or condominium resorts to be owned in fee. A tenancy in common is formed among the various time-period owners and an occupancy agreement is executed. This agreement gives each tenant in common the exclusive right to occupy the premises (usually a specified unit) during a particular time each year. In addition, each time-share purchaser receives possessory rights in the project's commonly owned areas. The length of this occupancy agreement is usually for the estimated useful life of the building.

This arrangement has appeal because it is based on property concepts that are familiar to lending institutions and title companies. But it does possess several drawbacks that may necessitate statutory assistance to effectively eliminate possible flaws.

One possible drawback is that general property-law principles require that all co-tenants share a single right to possess the premises. Obviously, this concept is not possible with time-sharing because each owner desires exclusive possession of his unit for his particular time apportionment. By drafting supplemental declarations of covenants, conditions, and restrictions that are added to the resort project's master condominium deed, the parties can agree among themselves to forfeit the possessory rights for the major part of the year. This occupancy agreement should have a limited term.

Another problem inherent with the tenancy-in-common method is the right to judicial partition of the time-share unit. This is a basic common-law right that arises out of any co-tenancy interest. Without enforceable waivers or statutory assistance, any discontented co-owner could force a partition of the time-share unit. But to divide up the unit and common areas with so many parties involved would present an unworkable situation. In all likelihood, the unit would be sold and the co-owners would divide up the proceeds.

This type of time-sharing must also face the possibility that a federal tax lien will be imposed on the co-tenancy.[31] It is well established that the government has the power to foreclose on this lien against one co-tenant,

---

31. I.R.C. §6321 places a general tax lien on all property or rights to property in favor of the United States for the party's unpaid amount of federal taxes.

sell the entire property, and divide the proceeds to pay off the tax debt.[32] Luckily, this hard-line approach can be nullified through the use of the court's equitable powers and at least one court of appeals has taken this approach.[33] . . .

Interval Ownership

"Interval" ownership is another legal structure developed to make it possible for vacation homes or resort condominium units to be owned in fee.

The interval purchaser receives a deed that brings about a revolving or recurring estate for years (generally for a two-week period in a specified unit) and a vested remainder as a tenant in common with his fellow interval owners at the finish of his estate for years. The duration of the estate for years is usually the estimated future use of the project's structure.

The difference between interval and timespan time-sharing goes to the root of the conveyance. In the former, the owner's right of occupancy and ownership are represented in the one instrument of deed. In the latter, the owner's claim to right of possession rests on the covenants contained in the resort condominium declarations of rights and duties.

One possible problem with the interval's estate-for-years approach is that it resembles a lease and may give rise to a landlord-tenant relationship. Such a classification would be disastrous to the interval time-share developer. In order to avoid this appearance of a lease, the developer conveys with the estate for years any fee simple remainder interest.

A related question is the common-law rule of merger[:] where a greater estate and a lesser estate join in the same conveyance to one party, the lesser estate will be extinguished. Interval owners hold a fee simple remainder interest as tenants in common. Since a fee simple estate is the largest form of property ownership, the operation of this rule would require that a lesser estate, like the estate for years, be merged or disappear. Thus, the interval method of time-sharing would be eliminated.

This would occur if the doctrine of merger operated automatically and inexorably. The majority of jurisdictions, however, proceed from an equitable standpoint and look to find the intent of the parties before they will enforce the rule of merger. This appears to be a more sensible approach and adaptable to the time-sharing setup.

---

32. United States v. Overman, 424 F.2d 1142 (9th Cir. 1970) (community property); Washington v. United States, 402 F.2d 23 (4th Cir. 1968) (wife's inchoate dower interest); I.R.C. §7403(a); see United States v. Trilling, 328 F.2d 699 (7th Cir. 1964) (land held jointly by husband and wife).

33. In United States v. Hershberger, 475 F.2d 677 (10th Cir. 1970), and United States v. Eaves, 499 F.2d 869 (10th Cir. 1974), the Tenth Circuit ruled that a court could, in its discretion refuse to order the sale of the co-tenancy where the burden on the co-owners outweighs the gain to the government. Also, the *Trilling* line of cases involved the enforcement of liens involving a husband and wife. They can be distinguished from time-share owners who are usually unrelated and many in number. . . .

In summary, interval ownership offers another alternative to the time-share developer that is founded in familiar property concepts to facilitate its acceptance by the public and by traditional financial institutions. With some statutory assistance, it is a practical way to market vacation resorts.

State v. Carriage House Associates
94 Nev. 707, 585 P.2d 1337 (1978)

OPINION

PER CURIAM. Respondent sought to enjoin and restrain the Real Estate Division of the Nevada Department of Commerce from exercising jurisdiction over and regulating respondent's marketing of "vacation licenses." Appellant opposed the injunction contending respondent's sale of "vacation licenses" was subject to the licensing requirements of NRS ch. 119 and NRS ch. 645.[1] After a hearing on the matter the district court granted a permanent injunction concluding the "vacation licenses" neither constitute nor convey an interest in real property and, thus, persons engaged in the marketing of "vacation licenses" do not have to comply with the licensing requirements of NRS ch. 119 and NRS ch. 645.

The thrust of appellant's argument in this appeal is that a "vacation license" is both (1) a leasehold interest in "real estate," as defined by NRS 645.020, and therefore, persons selling such interest must be licensed in accordance with NRS 645.230; and (2) an interest in a "subdivision," as defined by NRS 119.110, and therefore, persons who sell such interests must be licensed in accordance with NRS 119.130.[2] We disagree.

---

1. NRS ch. 119 and NRS ch. 645 provide basic jurisdiction for regulation of the sale of real property.

2. NRS 645.020 provides:
"As used in this chapter, 'real estate' means every interest or estate in real property including but not limited to freeholds, leaseholds and interests in condominiums, townhouses or planned unit developments, whether corporeal or incorporeal, and whether the real property is situated in this state or elsewhere."

NRS 645.230 provides, in pertinent part:
"1. After June 1, 1947, it shall be unlawful for any person, copartnership, association or corporation to engage in the business of, act in the capacity of, advertise or assume to act as, a real estate broker or real estate salesman within the State of Nevada without first obtaining a license as a real estate broker or real estate salesman from the real estate division as provided for in this chapter."

NRS 119.110 provides:
"'Subdivision' means any land or tract of land in another state, in this state or in a foreign country from which a sale is attempted, which is divided or proposed to be divided over any period into 35 or more lots, parcels, units or interests, including but not limited to undivided interests, which are offered, known, designated or advertised as a common unit by a common name or as a part of a common promotional plan of advertising and sale."

NRS 119.130 provides, in pertinent part:
"Except as provided in NRS 119.120, no subdivision or lot, parcel, unit or interest in any subdivision shall in any way be offered or sold in this state by any person or broker until: . . .

"2. Such person or broker has received a license under NRS 119.160."

Respondent owns and operates a 192-unit resort complex in Las Vegas, Nevada, known as the Carriage House. In July, 1975, respondent commenced its marketing of "vacation licenses" in Las Vegas. The "vacation license" is a form of time-sharing which divides the occupancy rights to resort units among multiple parties. Under the Carriage House program, the purchaser acquires the contractual right to reserve for occupancy at the Carriage House, for an aggregate of seven days each year, a suite of a designated type and location during a designated season of the year. This right extends for the useful life of the Carriage House, which is stated to be not less than 40 years nor more than 60 years from January 1, 1976. Purchasers of the "vacation licenses" are not entitled to make reservations for any particular date or any specific suite. The "vacation licenses" are irrevocable and may be transferred by gift or devise or with the written approval of Carriage House Associates. However, the purchasers may neither rent nor sub-license their accommodations and receive no deed or other indicia of title or interest in the property.

In consideration of the purchase price, respondent agrees to operate and maintain the property as a luxury resort condominium and to provide regular hotel maid service, towels, linens and kitchenware for the resort units.

Under these circumstances, we are constrained to agree with the district court's conclusion that a "vacation license" is a mere contractual right which fails to achieve the status of an interest in real property. Indeed, it is not a license, as defined by the law of real property, because it is irrevocable and transferrable. See Fisher v. General Petroleum Corp., 123 Cal. App. 2d 770, 267 P.2d 841 (1954); Lehman v. Williamson, 35 Colo. App. 372, 533 P.2d 63 (1975). Nor is it a lease because it is not definite as to its duration or description of the property involved. Beckett v. City of Paris Dry Goods Co., 14 Cal. 2d 633, 96 P.2d 122 (1939). See Club v. Investment Co., 64 Nev. 312, 182 P.2d 1011 (1947).

We are persuaded by the district court's analysis of this case:

> It's really an anomaly. It doesn't fit neatly into any nice legal terminology. But I cannot reach the conclusion that an individual entering into the contract with [Carriage House] acquires an interest in real estate. He just simply does not acquire an interest in real property and accordingly I feel that if the Legislature wishes to regulate this kind of business, they're going to have to either amend Chapter 119 or they're going to have to create a new chapter.
>
> I don't think that it was the intent of the Legislature looking at the land sales act to regulate the kind of "vacation license" that is presented in this case.

We perceive no error in the district court judgment and, accordingly, it is affirmed.

Cal-Am Corp. v. Department of Real Estate
104 Cal. App. 3d 453, 163 Cal. Rptr. 729 (1980)

STEPHENS, Acting Presiding Justice. This is an appeal from the denial of a petition for a peremptory writ of mandamus. It concerns the jurisdictional authority of the Department of Real Estate (hereinafter Department) to regulate, in the State of California, the sale of time-share interests in resort condominiums. In order to be subject to Department regulations requiring permits and public reports, the sale by appellant of membership interests in the Royal Hawaiian Adventure Club must constitute the sale or lease of lots or parcels in a subdivision. (Bus. & Prof. Code, §§10249.1, 11000, 11004.5.) We affirm the finding of the superior court that the Department acted within its authority in issuing an order requiring appellant to desist and refrain from selling or leasing or offering for sale or lease, membership interests in the Royal Hawaiian Adventure Club, until such time as it has obtained from the commissioner of real estate a permit and public report. The desist and refrain order was properly issued pursuant to Business and Professions Code, section 11019.

I

Cal-Am Corporation (hereinafter Cal-Am) is in the business of selling membership interests which entitle members to the use of one-bedroom condominium units for one or more weeks each year until December 31, 2041, in the Royal Kuhio Building, Honolulu, Hawaii. The resort contains 385 condominium units of which Cal-Am owns and leases approximately 154 units. Appellant has established a time-sharing program consisting of 52 one-week time share interests, of which it retains 7 one-week periods as partial consideration for management services.

Members of the Royal Hawaiian Adventure Club may purchase up to 4 one-week time share interests in the resort condominiums, but they are not entitled to reserve any particular units. The assignment of units is left to the discretion of the RHAC board of directors. RHAC obligates itself only to make a unit available on confirmation of reservations made at least 60 days in advance of the selected period and on a first come, first served, basis. Members may permit others the use of their membership, may transfer all rights under the membership agreement with the consent of RHAC, and may bequeath their time share interests without consent.

Appellant does not question these findings of the administrative law judge. The basic contention of appellant is that the membership interests being sold do not constitute the sale or lease of interests in a subdivision or subdivided lands as defined in sections 10249.1, 11000, and 11004.5, subdivision (f)(1), of the Business and Professions Code. Section 10249.1

defines the term subdivision for out of state land promotions as "improved or unimproved land or lands divided or proposed to be divided for the purpose of sale or lease, whether immediate or future, into five or more lots or parcels."

Section 11000 of the Business and Professions Code defines subdivision and subdivided lands as "improved or unimproved land or lands divided or proposed to be divided for the purpose of sale or lease or financing, whether immediate or future, into five or more lots or parcels . . ." and section 11004.5, subdivision (c), of said code adds to the provisions of section 11000, "Any condominium project containing two or more condominiums as defined in Section 783 of the Civil Code." Added by amendment in 1979, Business and Professions Code section 11004.5, subdivision (f)(1), provides that the following interests are subject to the subdivision laws and the regulations of the Department:

> Any accompanying memberships or other rights or privileges created in, or in connection with, any of the forms of development referred to in subdivisions (a), (b), (c), or (d) above by any deeds, conveyances, leases, subleases, assignments, declarations of restrictions, articles of incorporation, bylaws or contracts applicable thereto.

Thus, section 11004.5, subdivision (f)(1), of said code includes in the definition of subdivision any membership rights in condominium projects (subdivision (c)) created by leases or contracts applicable thereto.

The membership interests sold by appellant constitute interests in real property. While it is unnecessary for purposes of this appeal to classify the interest in real property thus created, the nature of the interest is that of a lease. The test for determining whether an agreement for the use of real property is a license or a lease is whether the contract gives exclusive possession of the premises against all the world, including the owner, in which case it is a lease, or whether it merely confers a privilege to occupy under the owner, in which case it is a license. (Von Goerlitz v. Turner (1944) 65 Cal. App. 2d 425, 429, 150 P.2d 278.) Membership in RHAC grants the right to exclusively possess a resort condominium unit during the member's annual period. Despite appellant's contentions, the fact that RHAC retains the right to specify which unit will be occupied and to provide maintenance and maid services to each unit does not derogate the exclusive possessory interests of the members during their annual periods of one to four weeks. The membership agreement itself guarantees to members the right to occupy, during their annual periods, one of the club's condominiums. One who buys exclusive occupancy, even for only a portion of each year, in a condominium, occupies a special position with relation to a portion of the condominium premises. Regardless of the term used to describe the purchaser's rights of exclusive occupancy, it is an estate or interest or possessory interest in the property itself. "It is unnecessary to assign a name to the interest thus created." (Estate of Pitts (1933) 218 Cal. 184, 191, 22 P.2d 694, 697.)

We do not find persuasive the holding of the Nevada Supreme Court in State Department of Commerce, Division of Real Estate v. Carriage House Associates (1978) 585 P.2d 1337, wherein that court found, on facts very similar to those in the case at bar, that a membership interest in a resort condominium constitutes neither a license nor a lease. (Id. at p. 1339.) The court held that there was no leasehold interest in the property because the lease was not definite as to its duration or description of the property involved. *Carriage House* is distinguishable from this case in the element of specificity of time — members in that case held their interests only for the useful life of the building, *estimated* as being between 40 and 60 years. Members of the Royal Hawaiian Adventure Club hold their interests until *precisely* December 31, 2041.

Beckett v. City of Paris Dry Goods Co. (1939) 14 Cal. 2d 633, 96 P.2d 122, cited by the Nevada court as authority for the definition of a lease, involved an optometrist who entered into an agreement with a local department store to run an optical department for three years out of a space to be designated by the store. Upon early removal of the optometrist from defendant's store, he sued for breach of contract, alleging unlawful eviction. Defendant asserted that it had granted a mere license to use any space which it chose to designate, and that it could withdraw that license at any time. The California Supreme Court found that the requirement of specificity, both as to duration and description of the property involved, was met in *Beckett*. That the defendant could freely move the optometrist to any place in the store that it chose was insufficient to render the lease void for lack of specificity. (Id. at p. 635, 96 P.2d 122.) Likewise, the fact that RHAC members are assigned to particular units on a year by year basis does not negative the specificity of the property involved. Members have the right to occupy one of 154 substantially identical one-bedroom condominium units in the Royal Kuhio Building, Kuhio Avenue, Honolulu, Hawaii. That right is defined and specific. That the particular unit to be occupied during the annual period is not designated until shortly before the annual period is unimportant in determining whether there is a right to use one of the condominiums in that building for a period certain each year until and including the year 2041.

Appellant has engaged in the sale or lease of interests in 5 or more lots or parcels of real property, thereby invoking the authority of the Department to require by regulation both real property securities permits and subdivision public reports. Since it is unchallenged that appellant has not obtained a permit or public report, respondent acted properly, pursuant to Business and Professions Code section 11019 in ordering appellant to cease and desist from violating sections 10238.3, 10249, 11010 and 11018.2 of the Business and Professions Code. . . .

The judgment is affirmed.

In re Sombrero Reef Club, Inc.

18 Bankr. 612 (1982)

Partial Findings and Conclusions

JOSEPH A. GASSEN, Bankruptcy Judge. The principal asset of the debtor, Sombrero Reef Club, Inc., is a resort-marina complex in the Florida Keys. Prior to the bankruptcy reorganization, it unsuccessfully attempted to turn the property into a time-share operation, and approximately 200 valid time-share purchase agreements exist as a result of that effort. It now wishes to sell the real property and this adversary proceeding is part of the litigation it has brought to clarify the rights of all parties claiming an interest in the real property.

In the main bankruptcy proceeding, the debtor, Sombrero Reef Club, Inc., filed a motion to reject executory contracts (Case No. 80-01266-BKC-JAG, C.P. No. 101) in conjunction with its motion for leave to sell real property. At approximately the same time, it filed its complaint for declaratory judgment (Adversary Case No. 81-0583-BKC-JAG-A, C.P. No. 1) against the debtor's time-share purchasers, seeking a declaratory judgment that the time-share contracts were not unexpired leases or executory contracts for the sale of real property and that upon rejection of those contracts, the defendants would have no further rights in the underlying real property. . . .

There were at least two versions of the time-share purchase agreements which Sombrero used, but they differed only slightly. A prototype, titled "Latitude 24° Vacation Club Membership Agreement" was admitted as debtor's Exhibit No. 2. Purchasers would pay an initial price ranging from under $1,000 to over $3,000 for the right to use the chosen type of accommodation for one week in a year with that right extending for a period of thirty years. In addition, each member was required to pay annual dues, with the initial rates varying from $42 to $84. The annual dues charge could be adjusted for inflation. The original price and annual dues rate varied according to the type of accommodation selected and which of three seasons the purchaser's vacation week would fall within. Each year members could reserve their particular vacation week not less than sixty days prior to the desired date nor more than one year prior to the date. Reservations were on an "as available" basis, and members could not designate specific rooms or accommodations. Sombrero Reef was responsible for all obligations of maintaining and operating the facility, including maintenance of insurance, provision of utilities and furnishing the rooms as well as providing maid service and activities programmed.

The basic purchase price could be paid in full initially or on installment terms. Some defendants had fully paid and others had not completed making their installments on the purchase price. Installment payments continued to be collected following the filing of the chapter 11 petition in bankruptcy, but the debtor-in-possession did not collect, and instructed its collecting agent, the Bank of California, not to collect any further installments once the motion to reject the contracts was filed. Some of the contract holders paid their annual dues during this period, but Sombrero Reef made no effort to collect them. Likewise, some persons utilized their vacation weeks but others were unable to. The debtor-in-possession maintained that the only persons turned away were so treated because reservations were full, but the quality of accommodations and services provided during the reorganization period has been below the level originally anticipated by all parties.

Some of the time-share contract accounts receivable were assigned as security for loans obtained by Sombrero Reef from individuals. Those individuals not only object to the rejection of the contracts, but request that, if the contracts comprising their collateral are rejected, they be given adequate protection.

Sombrero Reef has made previous attempts to sell the property and has entered into several previous contracts for sale, none of which was consummated in a closing. On April 21, 1981, an order authorizing sale to one of these earlier proposed purchasers was entered (Case No. 80-01266-BKC-JAG, C.P. No. 72). That purchaser wished to assume the contracts and the order authorized such assumption. Now, however, the debtor-in-possession believes it is necessary to reject the time-share contracts in order to sell the real property. . . .

 . . . 11 U.S.C. §365 permits the rejection of an executory contract by a trustee or debtor-in-possession and sets forth the effect of and the rights of parties upon rejection. That section specifically controls the primary issues in this case. . . .

. . . Defendants' next position is that the contracts for which the purchase price has been paid in full are no longer executory and therefore cannot be rejected. The court concludes that these time-share contracts are all executory, including the ones for which the "purchase price" has been paid in full.

The legislative history for §365 provides: "Though there is no precise definition of what contracts are executory, it generally includes contracts on which performance remains due to some extent on both sides." H.R. Rep. No. 95-595, 95th Cong., 1st Sess. 347 (1977), [1978] U.S. Code Cong. & Ad. News 5787, 6303; S. Rep. No. 95-989, 95th Cong., 2nd Sess. 58 (1978), [1978] U.S. Code Cong. & Ad. News 5844. A more exacting standard was set by Professor Countryman who defined an executory contract (in discussing the term under the former Bankruptcy Act) as one "under which the obligation of both the bankrupt and the other party to the contract are so far unperformed that the failure of either to complete performance would constitute a material breach excusing the performance of the other." Countryman, Executory Contracts in Bankruptcy, 57 Minn. L.R. 439, 460 (1973). . . .

It is true that the contract holders in this case who have paid the initial fee in full have purchased something (just what that "something" is will be discussed further below,) but the completion of that purchase does not preclude a finding that the overall contract is executory. In fact, substantial obligations remain to be performed on both sides. The debtor-in-possession must maintain the property and provide accommodations and services for one or more weeks per contract holder for at least twenty-five years from now. Defendants downplay the obligations still due from the contract holders, but in contrast to the contracts in the cases cited above, the annual dues requirement from each defendant here is not a de minimis obligation. If each contract were to run its course, the total of the annual dues would be substantially more than the initial "purchase price" even without any cost of living increases. By entering into the contracts, the buyers obligated themselves to pay these annual fees *whether or not* they utilized the accommodations (paragraph 14). And, if the annual dues are not paid, the membership may be cancelled without any reimbursement (paragraph 20). This militates against a conclusion that something of value separate and apart from the ongoing yearly obligations has been purchased upon payment of the purchase price. And, the failure of either party to complete its yearly performance would constitute a material breach excusing the performance of the other. Therefore, all the contracts are deemed to be executory. . . .

The court having approved the rejection of the time-share contracts, plaintiff seeks a determination that the contracts are not leases and not contracts for the sale of real property because, under certain circumstances, special protections are given to the rejected parties for these types of contracts. All parties agree that the contracts give some type of time-share interest to the purchasers of these contracts, but there is no agreement about the nature of that interest. For purposes of this case, it need only be decided whether or not the interests fall into either of the above two categories. Section 365(h)(1) covers leases:

> If the trustee rejects an unexpired lease of real property of the debtor under which the debtor is the lessor, the lessee under such lease may treat the lease as terminated by such rejection, or, in the alternative, may remain in possession for the balance of the term of such lease and any renewal or extension of such term that is enforceable by such lessee under applicable nonbankruptcy law.

and §(i)(1) deals with sales of real property:

> If the trustee rejects an executory contract of the debtor for the sale of real property under which the purchaser is in possession, such purchaser may treat such contract as terminated, or, in the alternative, may remain in possession of such real property.

Time-sharing Ownership

Turning to the contract itself (the memorialization of the entire agreement between the parties), the title is "Latitude 24° Vacation Club *Membership* Agreement" (emphasis added). The drafters appear to have been unwilling to describe or limit the contract to a more definite or conventional category of real property interest.

Paragraph 15, "Assignment of Benefits and Sale of Membership," covers all possibilities with the restriction: "You may not rent your accommodations or enter into any sub-lease or sub-license agreement. We will not make rental, sub-lease or sub-license arrangements for you."

Therefore the court must make a determination of the nature of the contract from an analysis of its terms. Paragraph 3, "What You Are Buying," provides: "The type of club membership you are purchasing at the Resort gives you and us various rights, privileges and obligations. The primary ones follow." The separate paragraphs following this introductory paragraph cover type of membership, type of accommodations and time period, amount of use, choice of accommodations, seasons, time periods, purchase price, finance charge, reserving accommodations, annual dues and so on. Paragraph 11 provides that, in addition to the "purchase price," "annual dues" are to be paid "for the privilege of utilizing the accommodations selected and other membership privileges." Paragraphs 12 and 13 provide in part, "Your privilege is to use a type of accommodations [sic] and not a specific unit," and that use is "on an 'as available' reservation basis." In paragraph 15, it is stated explicitly: "You understand that you will not have any interest in the properties or operations of the Resort, or any of its rooms or other facilities, or in the revenues therefrom, except the right to reserve and occupy accommodations and use certain facilities upon the terms and conditions contained in this Agreement."

Based on these provisions, the court concludes that the time-share contracts here do not fall under either subsection (h) or subsection (i) of §365. Subsection (i) does not refer to an "interest" in real property or an "estate" in real property; it refers only to a "sale of real property." The legislative history refers to "a purchaser of real property under a land installment sales contract," H.R. Rep. No. 95-595, 95th Cong., 1st Sess. 349-50 (1977); S. Rep. No. 95-989, 95th Cong., 2d Sess. 60 (1978), U.S. Code Cong. & Admin. News pp. 5846, 6306. See 2 Collier on Bankruptcy, 15th ed. ¶356.10. Under the time-share contracts in question, no delivery of title of any kind was contemplated. Nothing more was given or to be given than a right to use the property on certain agreed terms. It was specifically set forth that the contract purchasers would have no interest in the properties except the right to reserve and occupy accommodations. This does not amount to a sale of property under §365(i).

Neither do the Florida statutes identify or limit the nature of time-share agreements, although in the 1981 legislative session, the Florida legislature enacted the Real Estate Time Sharing Act, Ch. 721, Fla. Stats. In

§721.05(14), Fla. Stats., a "time-sharing plan" is defined to include all possible types of legal interests:

> "Time sharing plan" means any arrangement, plan, scheme, or similar device, but not including exchange programs, whether by membership, agreement, tenancy in common, sale, lease, deed, rental agreement, license, right to use agreement, or by any other means, whereby a purchaser, in exchange for consideration, receives a right to use accommodations or facilities, or both, for a specific period of time less than a full year during any given year, but not necessarily for consecutive years, and which extends for a period of more than 3 years.

It is also more specifically recognized that sale of a time-share does not necessarily require the conveyance of any interest in real property. Among items which must be included in a contract for sale is "[a] description of the nature and duration of the time share period being sold, including *whether any interest in real* property is being conveyed . . . ," §721.06(5), Fla. Stats.

Although a more difficult question, the court also concludes that the contracts are not leases protected under §365(h). Section 365(i) makes a distinction between sales of real property where the purchaser is in possession and where the purchaser is not. Section 365(h) does not make a distinction between leases where the lessee is in possession and where he is not, but implies the necessity of possession by referring to a lessee *remaining* in possession. Possession is not defined. If these time-share contracts were leases, it might be that they would be denied protection under subsection (h) because the defendants were not "in possession." However, given the concepts of constructive possession and possession by agents which might be encompassed in §365(h), the court does not rule on that basis. Instead, the lack of physical possession here is one of the indicia that the agreements were not leases.

No intention of the parties to consider the contract a lease appears on the face of the prototype contract, and there is not sufficient basis for the court to construe it to be a lease. It is labeled a "membership agreement," not a lease, and the terms "landlord" and "tenant" or "lessor" and "lessee" are not used anywhere. The term "sublease" appears only in a negative and disjunctive form in paragraph 15, quoted above. The executed agreements do not conform with the witnessing requirements for leases of a term of more than one year. Members had no rights to use any particular rooms, or to use them at any specific time. In fact, they were not guaranteed a right to use them at all unless they were willing to use them at a time which was available. They did not purchase a right to occupy and use certain real estate for a certain period—a lease—but rather, purchased a qualified right to obtain accommodations of a certain quality within certain time periods. The "membership" which each purchased is more akin to an option to make reservations at a hotel on stated terms. Despite various theoretical arguments, the right to possess *or* use was a very small part of what the purchasers bargained for and got. The rooms alone would be of very little value to the members without the accompanying services provided by Sombrero. Although leases vary as to the degree of services provided by the landlord, the services and facilities here were such a substantial part of each contract that they appear to be something *other* than leases of real property. . . .

The contracts having been rejected, the defendants are entitled to damages and have claims for such damages. The amount of damages as to each defendant will be determined at a hearing to be set by the court. The counterclaims seeking damages will likewise be concluded at that hearing. . . .

CHAPTER SEVEN

Complex Forms of Land Finance

A. THE SHOPPING CENTER DEVELOPMENT

Post-World War II America has seen the shopping center replace the commercial strip as the dominant retail market. Beginning as compact neighborhood clusters, usually built around a supermarket as principal tenant and offering such day-to-day conveniences as a dry cleaner, restaurant, and drugstore, shopping centers have evolved through two further growth stages: community centers and regional centers. The community center has for its anchor a variety store or junior department store, and offers a broader range of convenience outlets than the neighborhood center can support. The regional center almost certainly will feature at least one full-line department store; the center's depth and variety of merchant both requires and can attract a market population the size of a small city.

Whatever its scope, the shopping center development calls upon the developer's lawyer to exercise his full array of real estate skills. He will face problems of land acquisition, zoning, contracting, financing, tax assessment, lease negotiation; he will have to deal with architects, builders, government officials, rental agents, corporate vice-presidents, many other lawyers; often bitter dispute will arise between landlord and tenant that will engage the lawyer's best instincts for conflict resolution. One could easily build a casebook or a law school course around the problems of shopping center development and operation.

In this brief section, we will examine three recurring aspects of the shopping center lease: the use of restrictive covenants, the percentage rental provision, and the landlord's duty to maintain the common areas.

1. Restrictive Covenants

Problem: X owns a neighborhood shopping complex containing ten stores. X leases the grocery to A. X covenants not to lease any other store for the sale of gourmet foods. A covenants not to sell housewares. X leases a hardware to B and a candy shop to C. In violation of his lease, A opens a houseware department. In violation of her lease, C opens a gourmet food department. What are B's rights against X and A? What are A's rights against X and C? Would your analysis change if B and C had made their leases before A had made his? If C's lease did not expressly bar the sale of gourmet foods?

Note, Restrictive Covenants in Shopping Center Leases
34 N.Y.U. L. Rev. 940 (1959)

Leases of business property frequently contain a covenant by the lessor restricting the use of other premises owned by him to activities which do not compete with the lessee's business. This type of restrictive covenant, which has long been common in leases of store premises from the owner of a large building or block of stores, is becoming increasingly important with the mushrooming growth of suburban shopping centers in which a common landlord allocates business sites among a variety of business tenants.

Pervading the various problems involved in construing this type of covenant are conflicting judicial attitudes towards its social utility. The courts have traditionally been hostile to enforcing such covenants because they tend to limit business opportunities and retard the transfer of land by encumbering its permissible use. Thus, although such covenants are seldom held void as unreasonable restraint of trade, courts generally state that such covenants must be construed strictly against the party seeking to enforce them and that any doubts as to their meaning should be resolved against enforcement. Furthermore, such a covenant will not be found by implication, but must be clearly set forth.

On the other hand, it is recognized that parties are entitled to a degree of freedom in contracting to protect their own economic interests and that controlled development of a given business center may be desirable in attracting established business enterprise to that locale. Thus the courts will abide by the manifested intent of the parties in enforcing such covenants and will admit evidence of collateral circumstances which show that an ambiguously worded covenant was intended to afford the protection claimed by the lessee. The rule of strict construction is also tempered by the equitable nature of most enforcement proceedings, and the courts will sometimes go beyond the literal wording of the covenant to enforce it against apparent efforts to avoid obligations for formalistic subterfuge.

Although such covenants raise problems involving property, contract and equity principles, the great majority of cases present problems of construction, many of which could have been avoided by careful draftsmanship. This note will survey and analyze the legal problems which have arisen under this type of provision primarily from the point of view of aiding the draftsman in avoiding the pitfalls which have befallen such covenants.

I. Effect of Restrictive Covenants on Those Not Parties to the Lease

The protection afforded by the restrictive covenant would frequently be of minimal value if its burdens and benefits were enforceable only between the original parties to the lease. The tenant generally desires to protect himself against competition not only from the lessor but from other tenants and purchasers from the lessor. He also wishes to protect the market value of his lease by making sure that the covenant's benefits will inure to the benefit of his assignees.

The extent to which this protection may be afforded has been complicated by the vagaries of the law governing real covenants. At early common law, only those who were parties to the covenant could be bound by its terms. This rigid rule was first modified by statute, to allow the successors in interest of both parties to a lease to sue thereon. The statute was narrowly construed in the famous Spencer's case so that, inter alia, only those covenants which "touch or concern the demised premises" could run with the land to bind successors in interest of the original parties. The controversy over what covenants "touch or concern the demised premises" has continued to the present time without the development of any firmly established rule. The authorities as to whether restrictive covenants against competing business uses "touch or concern the demised premises" are sparse, old and conflicting. Equity, on the other hand, developed the doctrine of equitable servitudes holding that such covenants are enforceable by and against successors in interest to the original parties provided that the original parties intended that they be bound and that the party to be charged with the burden had notice of the covenant. As a result of the greater clarity and liberality of the equity rule (and because equitable relief is generally more effective), protection sought by or against one not a party to the lease is almost always sought on the equity side of the court and courts generally refuse to consider whether such covenants do run with the land. The present status of the law and equity protection afforded may be summarized as follows:

Assignee of the tenant-covenantee.—Although a conflict of authority exists as to whether, at law, the benefit of a restrictive covenant can run with the leasehold to the tenant's assignee, the better view seems to be that it can. . . . The right of the assignee of the tenant to equitable relief seems well established.

It is also necessary, if the covenant is to run, in both law and equity that the parties have intended the covenant to inure to the benefit of the assignee. While the inclusion of the word "assigns" is not absolutely necessary and the requisite intent has been supplied from the circumstances surrounding the execution of the lease where no express words occur, good draftsmanship requires that the lease be drafted expressly for the benefit of the tenant *and his assigns.*

Purchasers from the lessor. — At law it appears that the burden of the restrictive covenant cannot run with the other property so restricted by the covenant. In equity, however, the purchaser of the other property with notice of the restriction is bound to abide by it under the doctrine of equitable servitudes. Various reasons have been advanced for imposing this duty. Most courts have been content to base their decision on the principle that "equity will not allow one who has knowledge of the just rights of another to defeat them." More elaborate rationalizations have been developed, either considering the restriction as a property interest of the lessee in the lessor's other property analogous to an easement, or enforcing the restriction as a necessary protection of the covenantee's equitable right to specific performance of a contract concerning land from encroachment by third persons. . . .

Other competing tenants. — The position of the tenant of property which the lessor has restricted by covenant is substantially the same as that of the purchaser from the lessor. While probably not bound at law, he is bound in equity if he had notice of the restrictive covenant at the time he entered into the lease. Where he had no notice at the time of execution, he cannot be enjoined from competing during the term of the lease, and the covenantee or his assigns are remitted to an action for damages against the lessor. . . .

Notice. — Notice of the restriction, either actual or constructive, is essential to the equitable enforcement of covenants not to compete. Where the lease has not been recorded, constructive notice has been found from provisions in the competing tenant's lease in some manner referring to the lease containing the covenant. Moreover, where the competing tenant had knowledge of a prior lease which had been renewed on substantially similar terms, he has been charged with knowledge of the terms carrying over from the old lease but not of the terms modified. . . .

The effect of recording the lease containing the restrictive covenant as constructive notice to subsequent purchasers and tenants varies with the different recording statutes and conflicting interpretations of the scope of their application. The inputation of notice based on recordation of an instrument arises only as to those instruments which are recordable under the applicable statute. Short term leases are often excluded from the recording statutes,[43] and the recording of such leases does not constitute constructive notice of covenants contained therein.

Even if the lease is recordable, however, its recordation may not constitute constructive notice. It is well established that, for most purposes, a purchaser will be charged with constructive notice only of those recorded instruments which lie in his direct chain of title. A restriction contained in a deed or lease of land other than that purchased or rented by the person sought to be charged with constructive notice has been held not to lie in his chain of title. Thus, in a leading New York case,[46] the owner of a large parcel of land conveyed certain lots therein to gasoline distributors and covenanted in the deed that he would not permit other lots in the larger parcel of land to be used for the same purpose. The deed was recorded. Other lots were later conveyed to the plaintiff without restriction. Buyer from plaintiff objected to marketability of title because of the restriction in the deed to the gasoline distributor. The court of appeals held the title marketable, stating that the recorded deed was not in the vendor's chain of title and therefore not constructive notice of its contents.[47]

Other jurisdictions have taken a contrary view, requiring that the purchaser or tenant examine the contents of all the deeds given by his grantor (and presumably of all his predecessors in title) to determine whether such restrictions exist.[48] The latter point of view imposes an unrealistic burden in searching titles, especially upon a tenant, and would unduly extend the effect of such restrictions contrary to the policy against perpetuating competitive restraints. . . .

FTC and Shopping Centers — Dos and Don'ts for Major Tenants

3 Real Est. L. Rep. No. 11 (April 1974)

In May 1972 the Federal Trade Commission instituted a proceeding against Gimbel Brothers, Inc., a department store chain, alleging that 20

---

43. In some states, however, all leases are recordable. See, e.g., Tex. Rev. Civ. Stat. art. 6627 (Vernon 1948); Va. Code Ann. §§55-96 (1950).

46. Buffalo Academy of the Sacred Heart v. Boehm Bros., 267 N.Y. 242, 196 N.E. 42 (1935).

47. Accord, Hancock v. Gumm, 151 Ga. 667, 107 S.E. 872 (1921); Glorieux v. Lighthipe, 88 N.J.L. 199, 96 A. 94 (Ct. Err. & App. 1915); King v. James, 88 Ohio App. 213, 97 N.E.2d 235 (1950) (dictum). Plaintiff in the Buffalo Academy case could pass marketable title free of the restriction, despite *actual* notice to his vendee, because plaintiff took without notice, either actual or constructive, and conveyance to a bona fide purchaser cuts off an equitable servitude, as to such purchaser or his successors in interest. See Restatement, Property §539, comment 1 (1944).

48. Dick v. Sears-Roebuck & Co., 115 Conn. 122, 160 A. 432 (1932); Slice v. Carozza Properties, Inc., 215 Md. 357, 137 A.2d 687 (1957); Finley v. Glenn, 303 Pa. 131, 154 A. 299 (1931). . . .

of its 24 shopping center leases contained provisions illegally restraining competition within the 20 centers in question. The Commission and Gimbels have agreed on a consent order significantly reducing the control that a major retail tenant may exercise over other retailers in a shopping center. This is important not only to the major tenant but to the smaller tenants, as well, who now have a wider field when negotiating their own leases. The developer is no longer in a position to say to the smaller tenants that his hands are tied because the major tenants insist upon certain controls.

The following is a list of the prohibited and approved lease provisions according to the consent order.

Prohibited Clauses

As a tenant in a shopping center, Gimbels must cease and desist from making or enforcing, directly or indirectly, an agreement which:

(1) Grants Gimbels the right to disapprove the entry into a shopping center of any other retailer;

(2) Grants Gimbels the right to disapprove the floor space that any other retailer may lease or purchase in a shopping center;

(3) Prohibits the admission into a shopping center of any particular retailer or class of retailers, including other department stores, junior department stores, discount stores, or catalogue stores;

(4) Limits the types or brands of merchandise or services which any other retailer in a shopping center may offer;

(5) Specifies that any other retailer in a shopping center shall or shall not sell its merchandise or services at any particular price or range;

(6) Grants Gimbels the right to disapprove the location in a shopping center of any other retailer;

(7) Prohibits any type of advertising by other retailers, other than advertising within a shopping center;

(8) Prohibits or controls price advertising within a center by retailers so as to make it difficult for customers to discern advertised prices from the common area of the shopping center, or

(9) Prevents expansion of a shopping center.

As a tenant in a shopping center, Gimbels may not enter into or carry out any arrangement with any other tenant to exclude any tenants from a shopping center.

Approved Clauses

Gimbels may include in its leases, clauses such as the following:

(1) When Gimbels is the first major tenant to agree to become a tenant of a shopping center, the agreement may provide for its termination by Gimbels if the developer or landlord does not also obtain one other major tenant acceptable to Gimbels to operate a store in the center.

(2) Gimbels may negotiate an agreement with a developer or a landlord of a shopping center (or if Gimbels owns its store in a shopping center, then with the owners of other buildings and land in such shopping center) which:

(a) Permits Gimbels to establish reasonable categories of retailers from which the developer or the landlord may select tenants to be located in the area immediately proximate to Gimbels' store, provided that such categories shall not specify price ranges or lines, trade or store names, trademarks, brands, or lines of merchandise of retailers, or identity of particular retailers;

(b) Requires the developer or the landlord to maintain reasonable standards of appearance, signs, and maintenance in the shopping center;

(c) Prohibits occupancy of space in the shopping center by clearly objectionable types of tenants, e.g., pornography shops;

(d) Gives Gimbels the right to approve an initial layout of the shopping center, which layout may designate Gimbels' store, set forth the location, size, and height of all buildings, locate parking areas, roadways, utilities, and common areas, and establish a proposed layout for future expansion;

(e) Requires that any expansion of the shopping center not provided for in the initial layout:

(i) Shall not interfere with efficient traffic flow between Gimbels' store and access roads, parking areas, malls, and other common areas;

(ii) Shall not interfere with the efficient operation of Gimbels' store, including its visibility from within the shopping center and adjacent highways;

(iii) Shall not result in a change of the shopping center's parking ratio; the location of a number of parking spaces reasonably accessible to Gimbels' store; and the entrances and exits to and from Gimbels' store and any malls; and

(iv) Shall be accomplished only after any and all covenants, obligations, and standards (construction, architecture, operation, maintenance, repair, alteration, restoration, parking ratio, and easements) of the shopping center shall be made applicable to the expansion area, and shall be made prior in right to any and all liens, encumbrances, and all other covenants, obligations, and standards applicable to the expansion area.

(Gimbel Brothers, Inc., FTC Dkt. 8885, Consent Order announced Nov. 29, 1973, 39 Fed. Reg. 7164 (1974), Final Order, Jan. 30, 1974.)

Comment

On the same day in 1972 that the FTC commenced its proceedings against Gimbels it began a similar proceeding against Tysons Corner Regional Shopping Center, located in a suburb of Washington, D.C., and three of the center's major retail tenants.

Tysons Corner and two of the tenants have agreed to a consent order. The tenants were May Department Stores Company, and Woodward and

Lothrop, Inc. The consent order rendered the anticompetition clauses of the leases unenforceable, and among other determinations provided:

(1) The stores may not fix prices;
(2) Advertising by the center or by other tenants cannot be controlled by the two stores;
(3) Discount selling in the center cannot be prohibited; and
(4) The amount of space leased to other tenants cannot be limited by the two stores.

(Tysons Corner Regional Shopping Center, FTC Dkt. 8886, Consent Order announced March 5, 1974.)

NOTES AND QUESTIONS

1. The third major department chain, City Stores, refused, however, to join in the *Tysons Corner* consent agreement. The City Stores lease gave it the unfettered right to approve any tenant located within 125 feet of its store or occupying more than 30,000 square feet anywhere within the center, and the qualified right, to be exercised reasonably, to approve all other tenants. Adjudication led to an FTC final order barring tenant from enforcing its right to exclude other businesses or to specify types or brands of merchandise, price ranges, or floor space for other tenants. FTC Dkt. 8886, Final Order, June 10, 1975, CCH Trade Reg. Rep. ¶20,933. The agency found that the lease was a per se violation under §5 of the Clayton Act, which makes unlawful "unfair methods of competition in commerce." 15 U.S.C. §45(a)(1) (1983). The lease might also be an illegal restraint of trade under §1 of the Sherman Act or an unlawful attempt to monopolize under §2 of that Act. 15 U.S.C. §§1, 2 (1983).

2. It is usually the anchor tenants in a community or regional center who can demand control over the entry of other tenants into the complex. Other than sheer bigness, what is the source of the anchor's bargaining power? Or putting the question differently, why should the developer agree to share his power over tenant selection? Cf. Note, The Antitrust Implications of Restrictive Covenants in Shopping Center Leases, 86 Harv. L. Rev. 1201, 1205-1207, 1218-1238 (1973).

3. A Clayton Act violation requires a finding that the challenged practices are "in [interstate] commerce." The Tysons Corner Center is located in Virginia, nine miles from the center of the District of Columbia, on an interstate beltway a short drive from Maryland. Would the FTC have ruled differently if the shopping center had been located in Phoenix, Arizona or Columbus, Ohio? Cf. Harold Friedman, Inc. v. Thorofare Markets, Inc., 587 F.2d 127 (3d Cir. 1978).

4. The most common restrictive covenants found in shopping center leases take one of four forms:

a. *"Tenant" Approval Clauses:* the right of major tenants to approve other tenants in the Center;
b. *"Quality of Goods" Approval Clauses:* the right of major tenants or the developer to control the quality and the price of goods to be offered by the Center lessees;
c. *"Exclusive" Clauses:* the duty of landlords not to lease to the tenant's competitors;
d. *"Radius" Clauses:* the duty of tenants not to open another retail operation within a specified distance from the Center. [Marsh, The Federal Antitrust Laws and Radius Clauses in Shopping Center Leases, 32 Hastings L.J. 839, 840 (1981).]

Relying upon its Clayton Act authority, the FTC has obtained a consent decree against Sears, Roebuck and Co. wherein respondent agreed, in its role as both tenant and developer, not to impose radius restrictions upon other merchants. 59 F.T.C. 240 (1977).

2. The Percentage Lease

For many retail businesses, a favorable location is the key to success. But a location that is new and untested, especially if it is to be rented for a long term, presents serious risks to the businessman. If the site later disappoints him, the businessman-tenant does not want too heavy a rental burden. On the other hand, the landlord wants to be amply paid if the site should fulfill his tenant's expectations. The carefully drawn percentage lease attempts to reconcile these contradictory desires. Today, its use for shopping center stores is almost universal and its use for retail shops elsewhere is rather common.

In its report, The Percentage Lease, A Complete Manual of Principles and Practices, the Building Managers Association of Chicago lists four types of percentage leases:

(a) The tenant pays as rental a specified percentage of gross sales with a guaranteed minimum.

(b) The tenant pays as rental a specified percentage of gross sales with no guaranteed minimum.

(c) Initially, same as (b) supra, but after a stated interval, a guaranteed minimum is established, based on the average rentals already paid.

(d) The tenant pays as rental a specified percentage of profits.

The first arrangement is most common. Tenants might prefer not to pay a guaranteed minimum and might even agree to pay a somewhat higher percentage to eliminate the minimum, but such leases are not easy to finance. Can you explain why? Percentages based on profits rather than gross sales can cause serious accounting disputes and are usually avoided. See, e.g., Mileage Realty Co. v. Miami Parking Garage, Inc., 146 So. 2d

403 (Fla. 1962). Would the "sharing" of profits create a partnership between the landlord and the tenant? Cf. Friedman, Leases ¶6.101 (1974).

a. Definition of the Percentage Rental Base

Hempstead Theatre Corp. v. Metropolitan Playhouses, Inc.

6 N.Y.2d 311, 160 N.E.2d 604 (1959)

FROESSEL, Judge. This is an action for rent claimed to be due under written leases of four motion picture theatres. The leases provide for a fixed minimum rental and a graduated percentage rental on "gross receipts." The question presented is what the parties meant by their definition of "gross receipts" as related to the sale of candy and refreshments.

In 1948, the subtenant, Skouras Theatres Corporation, formed Circuit Vendors, Inc., for the purpose of conducting a candy and refreshment concession in said theatres. We are all agreed that upon this record Circuit Vendors was the alter ego of Skouras and may be treated as though Skouras itself operated the concession. Accordingly, we are called upon to decide whether plaintiffs-landlords are entitled to 20% of the total gross receipts of the concession without deduction of any kind, or 20% of the income derived therefrom.

It is not disputed that if the concession had been leased to a third party the percentage rental payable to the landlords thereon would be computed only on the amount paid by the third party to Skouras for the privilege of the concession.

In our judgment, the provisions of the lease, as related to the issue here presented, are clear. "Gross receipts" are first defined generally and broadly. There then follow specific provisions that such receipts "shall include: (1) all box office *receipts* excluding taxes on admissions; (2) all *rentals* and/or *income* derived from apartments, stores, offices or rentable space contained in said theatres, and all *income* derived from concessions and advertising." (Emphasis supplied.) In other words, while box office *receipts* (excluding admission taxes) and *rentals* are the basis upon which the landlords are entitled to 20%, only the *income,* and *not the receipts,* from concessions may form the basis of the landlord's percentage rental. In differentiating between "receipts" on the one hand and "income" on the other, we must assume the parties had a purpose, and it seems to us that no belabored analysis is necessary to discover such purpose. Had they intended that all *receipts* from the candy and refreshment concession should be the basis on which to calculate the 20% additional rental, it would have been exceedingly simple to say so, as they did with regard to the box office. Not having done so, it would seem to follow that the "income" should be computed by deducting from the "receipts" of the candy and refreshments sold the cost thereof.

This construction seems to be the only reasonable one for, at a 20% rental in addition to the fixed rental, it could not have been within the contemplation of the parties that the tenant would have to pay this percentage upon the cost of the candy and refreshments sold. It concededly would not have to do so if it permitted an outsider to operate the concession, as was the case when People's Candy Company had the concession. It should not be penalized if it operates the concession directly, after having paid a substantial consideration in 1949 to eliminate People's Candy Company, and particularly so where, as here, the landlord has been benefited thereby.

Inasmuch as the record contains no evidence as to the cost of the candy and refreshments, it will be necessary for Special Term to take proof thereof and recalculate the amount due plaintiffs. The judgment appealed from should accordingly be reversed, with costs and the matter remitted to Trial Term for further proceedings not inconsistent with this opinion.

FULD, Judge (dissenting). My disagreement with the decision is basic, for, in my judgment, the majority has, under the guise of construction, rewritten the agreement which the parties made. Both the trial court and the Appellate Division found in favor of the plaintiffs on each of the issues presented and it seems to me that the facts in the record before us compel an affirmance.

The plaintiffs, owners of four motion picture theatres located in Nassau County, brought this action to collect rent claimed to be due under written leases. The defendant Metropolitan Playhouses is the tenant which signed the leases, the defendant Skouras Theatres Corporation is the subtenant operating the theatres and the defendant Circuit Vendors, a wholly owned subsidiary organized by Skouras to handle the selling of candy and refreshments in the theatres. Since Metropolitan and Skouras are equally liable, I refer to these defendants interchangeably as Skouras.

The leases in question call for a fixed minimum rent plus a graduated percentage rental based on "gross receipts," and the litigation revolves about the meaning to be ascribed to that term insofar as it relates to the sale of candy and refreshments in the theatres. Plaintiffs claim that the percentage rent is to be figured on gross receipts, that is, on the basis of all proceeds from such sales, while the defendants urge, first, that the percentage is to be calculated only on the basis of an alleged concession fee [of $20,000] paid by Vendors to Skouras and, second, that, if such fee be disregarded and Skouras itself treated as the seller of such candy, then, the percentage should be figured on the basis of net income, not gross receipts. . . .

It was in 1948 that Skouras initiated the sale of candy in the theatres. For about a year, Skouras granted a concession therefor to People's Candy Company. In June of 1949, however, concluding that it was more profitable for a theatre operator to run its own refreshment stands and itself sell candy, Skouras eliminated People's and undertook the operation through its 100%-owned subsidiary Vendors. As the trial court found, although Skouras acted through Vendors, the latter "exists only in name . . . [and] has no independent corporate life." In short, as the trial court put it, "there was no concession in fact from Skouras to Vendors," for it was Skouras which received for itself every penny realized from the sale of the candy and refreshments. . . .

We need not become involved in any discussion of independent entities or of piercing the corporate veil. The simple fact is that Vendors was nothing more or less than the alter ego of Skouras or, in a term more earthy, its dummy. We are, therefore, all agreed that the receipts of Vendors are the receipts of Skouras, and its percentage rental must be figured on the basis of such an amount.

We come, therefore, to the question of whether the lease agreement provides that the stipulated percentage is to be computed on gross receipts, as both Special Term and the Appellate Division concluded, or on gross receipts *less* the cost of the candy and refreshments sold, as the court is now holding.

The contract, it is plain, provides that the base on which the percentage rental is to be computed is "gross receipts," as that term is ordinarily and reasonably understood. As here applicable, the lease agreement, after declaring that the tenant was to pay [in addition to the fixed rent] a sum of money equal to 20% "of all . . . yearly gross receipts in excess of" $1,000,000 for each year, goes on to define that term as follows:

"V. (A) 'Gross Receipts,' as used in this agreement, shall be deemed to include *all income and revenue* arising from the operation of each of the demised premises, less such gross receipts taxes as may be levied, imposed or assessed against such gross receipts, *including* all receipts of whatsoever kind derived from each of said demised premises, *and without limiting* the generality of the foregoing, *shall include:* (1) all box office receipts excluding taxes on admissions; (2) all rentals and/or income derived from apartments, stores, offices or rentable space contained in said theatres, and all income derived from concessions and advertising; (3) all net receipts derived from the sale of admission or coupons outside of the box office." (Italics supplied.)

And then, dealing expressly with the subject of "deduction," the agreement continues: "The Tenant shall be allowed no deductions whatsoever from the gross receipts, as hereinabove defined, excepting, only, that the Tenant shall be allowed to deduct therefrom the amount of assessments paid by the Tenant . . . the additional rent arising from and payable . . . pursuant to . . . lease . . . relating to the Calderone Theatre . . . [and] the additional expense incurred for actual salaries paid to vaudeville performers or stage performers, stage hands and musicians . . . and any and all other expenses incidental thereto."

The agreement could hardly have been phrased more broadly. The yardstick is "gross receipts," and this term, by the contract's own definition, includes "all income and revenue" arising from the operation of the premises, "less such gross receipt taxes as may be levied . . . against such gross receipts, including all receipts of whatsoever kind" derived from the premises. Indeed, the clause goes on to recite that, "without limiting the generality of the foregoing," gross receipts "shall include" (1) all box office receipts excluding only taxes on admissions; (2) all rentals from apartments, stores or rentable space in the theatres and all income from concessions and advertising; and (3) all net receipts from the sale of tickets outside of the box office.

In short, every bit of income — "all income and revenue" — is to be the base for the computation of the percentage rental excepting only the items specified, that is, excepting only gross receipts taxes; taxes on admissions; amount of assessments; adjustment for the building costs of the Calderone Theatre and expenses incurred for salaries paid to vaudeville performers, stage hands and musicians. In fact, the only reference in the agreement to a figure other than a "gross" amount is in clause (3) — that gross receipts include "all *net* receipts" derived from the sale of admissions or coupons outside of the box office — and its use therein unequivocally demonstrates that, if the parties had intended that the percentage rent should be computed on the basis of "net" income or of receipts "less cost," they would have so provided.

As is apparent, the provision defining gross receipts was designed to give it the broadest possible scope. This is plainly reflected by the phrasing; gross receipts, as used in this agreement, it is written, "shall be deemed to *include*" the items enumerated. And what are these items? The answer, supplied by the agreement, is clear: "all income and revenue" arising from the operation of the demised premises. And almost as significant as the language just remarked is the use of the word "such." Gross receipts, we have seen, shall include "all" income and revenue, less "*such* gross receipts taxes" as may be levied or assessed against "such gross receipts." The "such" in the latter phrase is a reference back to the term "all income and revenue," and the use of the phrase "*such* gross receipts" serves to accentuate the exceedingly broad reach of the term "all income and revenue." In brief, as the writing makes plain, gross receipts were to include all revenue received by the tenant excepting only the several items listed and, as is equally patent, no provision was made for the deduction of the cost of candy or, for that matter, the cost of any other revenue-producing operation.

That this was the understanding of Skouras itself is, indeed, confirmed by its conduct before any controversy developed. The theatres had other operations, besides the sale of candy, from which the tenant realized revenue and, in connection with each of these operations, the tenant, in figuring and reporting the sum of which the percentage rental was to be calculated, listed the "full," the "whole," amount of income received without deducting a penny of cost or expense incurred in producing such gross income. Here we have practical construction, of the term gross receipts, of a most impressive and persuasive character.

How, then, does the court seek to avoid the compulsion of language, logic and practical construction and reach the conclusion that, insofar as the candy operation is concerned, the percentage rental is to be figured not on the entire gross receipts from the candy sales, but on such gross receipts *less* the cost of such merchandise? It argues that, "*if* the concession had been leased to a third party the percentage rental payable to the landlords thereon would be computed only on the amount paid by the third party to Skouras for the privilege of the concession" (opinion, 6 N.Y.2d at page 313, 189 N.Y.S.2d 838, 160 N.E.2d 605). This is, of course, so, but I fail to perceive what it has to do with the case before us. There was here no *grant of a privilege to sell* candy, the prerequisite to the existence of a concession. The business of selling candy and refreshments was a self-operation, the very antithesis of a concession. Since, then, there was no concession, the agreement makes it unequivocally clear that the percentage rental is to be calculated on "all income and revenue" arising from the operation of the theatres — without deduction of any kind "from the gross receipts — and not, under clause (2), on the basis of "income derived from concessions." . . .

Finally — and this might well have been our point of beginning — if the base be not gross receipts, then, the agreement supplies no method or predicate for figuring the percentage rental on the sales from candy. If gross receipts from such sales are not to be accounted for, if the computation is not on the basis of gross receipts, there would be no measure for determining the amount to be paid on these sales and, as the trial court recognized, Skouras "would have had a source of income 'from the operation of each of the demised premises' without paying anything for it." The agreement carefully lists "gross receipts taxes," "taxes on admissions" and "the amount of assessments" as the items "allowed" to be deducted from gross receipts, but it makes no mention of any item of cost or expense incurred in the sale of candy or other merchandise. A court should not rewrite the agreement either to provide for their deduction or to specify the particular item of "cost" or "expense" to be deducted. The very impossibility of arriving at a figure representing net income from the candy operation further confirms the construction which has been accorded by the courts below to the term "gross receipts."

In brief, then, the lease agreement requires Skouras to pay a percentage rental on the sales of candy and refreshments, not on the alleged license fee of $20,000 from its wholly owned subsidiary Vendors, and that percentage is to be computed on the basis of gross receipts, not gross receipts less the cost of the merchandise or any other base.

The judgment of the Appellate Division should be affirmed.

Conway, C.J., and Dye and Van Voorhis, JJ., concur with Froessel, J. Fuld, J., dissents in an opinion in which Desmond and Burke, JJ., concur.

Judgment reversed and a new trial granted in accordance with the opinion herein, with costs to appellants in all courts.

Mutual Life Insurance Co. of New York v. Tailored Woman, Inc.
309 N.Y. 248, 128 N.E.2d 401 (1955)

DESMOND, Judge. The facts of this controversy, and the issues, are set forth and discussed in the Appellate Division opinion. We will limit ourselves to a statement of our views on the principal questions of law.

Since plaintiff is suing for additional percentage rental under the 1939 ten-year lease of the three lower floors of 742 Fifth Avenue, New York City, it must base its claim on the covenants of that lease. Two only of those covenants are pertinent. We take them up in turn. The 4% percentage rental was to be paid on all sales made "on, in, and from the demised premises." After, by separate leases, made in 1945, defendant had taken over from plaintiff part of the fifth floor (and the eighth floor, not involved here), defendant made it a practice to pay commissions, on fur sales made on the fifth floor, to salespeople on the lower floor who sent customers to the fifth floor fur department. We think it not unreasonable to hold, with the Appellate Division, that such sales were, within the lease's intent, made "from" the main store and so subject to percentage rent. Such sales may be considered "main store" sales, as if a clerk in response to a telephone call took merchandise to a customer's home, and there effected a sale. It would be going too far, though, to hold that all fur sales were made "from" the lower store simply because, as hereinafter more fully explained, the fur department was moved up to the fifth floor after that floor had been "integrated" with the main store.

By the other language (of the 1939 percentage lease) which we find pertinent, the tenant promised that the store it would conduct in the lower three floors would "at all times contain a stock of first class merchandise" and would "be conducted and maintained in a manner substantially similar to the Tenant's present store at 729 Fifth Avenue" (that is, the store across the street from which defendant was moving). That verbiage is to be read with the purpose clause (of that same 1939 lease) which prescribed the sale of all kinds of women's apparel and accessories. Here, again, we agree with the Appellate Division that no more was intended than an agreement that there should be conducted, on the three lower floors of 742 Fifth Avenue, under the percentage lease, a woman's clothing shop of the same general character as defendant's store across the street. If plaintiff had desired further restrictions as to kinds of merchandise, etc., it should have insisted on them. Absent fraud and trickery (and the findings properly say there was none), defendant could carry on its business in the way that suited it so long as it did not deviate from those very broad and general lease specifications.

In 1945, defendant, needing more space, bought out a custom-made dress business which had been conducted in part of the fifth floor by another concern and made with plaintiff a new lease of that space at a flat no-percentage rent. Again, the lease terms went no further as to purpose than to state that the added space was to be used for the sale of female wearing apparel and accessories and for workrooms. The fifth floor custom-made dress department was not successful and was soon discontinued. Defendant then made such physical changes in the building that two elevators, which had theretofore served the first three floors from inside the main store, now could be, and were, used to carry passengers inside the store not only to and from the first three floors but to and from the fifth floor, also (and the eighth floor, although that is not important here). The result was that the first, second, third and fifth floors were, as the phrase goes, "integrated" into one store fronting on Fifth Avenue and served by elevators reached through the main store from the Fifth Avenue entrances. Formerly, the fifth floor could be reached by the use of two other elevators only, to which elevators entrance was from the side street lobby on the 57th Street side of the building. Then defendant moved its fur department to the fifth floor, and thereafter paid no percentage rent on fur sales.

Trial Term held that plaintiff did not acquiesce in these changes. The Appellate Division held that it did. The question of fact is a close one but, acquiescence or not, we think the undisputed facts forbade a recovery here by plaintiff of more than the percentage on certain fur sales, hereinbefore described as made on the fifth floor, but "from" the lower floors. There is nothing in the main lease to forbid the moving of the fur department and when plaintiff made the second, or fifth floor, lease, it again failed to include any restrictions as to particular kinds of merchandise to be sold in one or the other part of the building. It is clear enough that plaintiff did not contemplate, when it leased the fifth and eighth floors for a flat rental, that the fifth floor would be "integrated" with the lower floors into one store but such lack of foresight does not create rights or obligations. True, the second lease said that it would "not have any effect" on the earlier lease but the effect of the two leases, read together and enforcing both, was that defendant had the right to sell all kinds of women's apparel, etc., in any part of the four floors, so long as no other use was made of the premises. As we see it, defendant merely exercised that right when it moved the fur department. As to changing the elevator doors, if that were a violation of any implied covenants (certainly not of an express covenant) redress could be had by injunction or, perhaps, by the landlord putting the elevator doors back as they had been and charging the expense to the tenant. But such violations (if they were violations) could not result in a liability for additional rent not promised in the lease. Except as to the fur sales to customers sent upstairs, there were no additional sales, "on, in or from" the premises covered by the percentage lease, even though certain activities with respect to furs continued to be carried on in the lower store.

In the view we take of the case, it is unnecessary to engage in interesting but unproductive computations or speculations as to whether or not the new "integrated" store actually produced more percentage rent for plaintiff than if the fur department and the elevators had not been changed. It is the fact, though, that plaintiff proved no loss in that respect.

In deciding this case as we do, we are not moving away from the good old rule that there is in every contract an implied covenant of fair dealing. Kirke La Shelle Co. v. Paul Armstrong Co., 263 N.Y. 79, 188 N.E. 163. Defendant, as we see it, was merely exercising its rights. Nor do we reject such authorities as Cissna Loan Co. v. Baron, 149 Wash. 386, 270 P. 1022, which penalize unconscionable diversion of business from percentage-lease premises to others. The present case does not fit into that pattern.

The judgment should be affirmed, without costs.

BURKE, Judge (dissenting). The defendant is liable for additional percentage rental under the 1939 ten-year lease of the premises 742 Fifth Avenue, New York City, for sales of furs made on the fifth floor, as they were sales made on, in and from the main premises.

This appeal involves conflicting constructions of two leases entered into between the plaintiff and defendant.

The defendant was the lessee under a 1939 lease of three floors with the exclusive use of a Fifth Avenue entrance, an entrance on 57th Street and two passenger elevators. Those premises, known as 742 Fifth Avenue, were leased at a fixed rental, plus 4% of the gross receipts in excess of $1,200,000. "Gross receipts" is defined in the lease as including "all sales . . . on, in or from the demised premises." In the spring of 1945, the proprietor of a retail custom dress business, the tenant of half of the fifth floor at 1 West 57th Street, offered her business for sale. The defendant purchased the custom dress business and thereafter, under a fixed rental lease commencing June 1, 1945, the defendant rented the same space on the fifth floor in the premises known as 1 West 57th Street, New York City, "for the sale, display of all types of wearing apparel accessories, worn or carried by women or misses, and as workrooms, and for no other purpose." Such lease provided (1) that the space on the fifth floor in 1 West 57th Street was to be serviced by the elevators in the 57th Street lobby at the landlord's expense "on business days from 8 A.M. to 6 P.M. except on Saturdays when the hours shall be from 8 A.M. to 1 P.M."; (2) that no alterations could be made without the written consent of the landlord; (3) that failure to require strict performance was not to be deemed a waiver, and (4) that the receipt of the rent with the knowledge of a breach was not to be deemed a waiver. The defendant in a short time altered the fifth floor of 1 West 57th Street, so as to give access through the private elevators of 742 Fifth Avenue.

The plaintiff alleges two causes of action. The first cause of action is based upon the theory that the fur sales were made "on, in or from" the main premises. All of the activities of the defendant from the initiation of the alterations to the actual sales were designed to hold out to the public that the fur department was part of the premises 742 Fifth Avenue. The physical layout, the advertising, the window displays, the storage of the furs, and the use of the main store personnel characterized the fur department as an integral part of the main store operations. The second cause of action seeks damages upon the theory that if fur sales were not made "on, in or from" the main premises, nevertheless, the defendant, in removing the fur department from the main premises, violated express and implied covenants of the main lease against diversion of sales. It is implicit in every percentage rental agreement that the tenant has an obligation to conduct its business with regard for the landlord's interest in the tenant's gross receipts. "A promise may be lacking, and yet the whole writing may be 'instinct with an obligation,' imperfectly expressed." Wood v. Lucy, Lady Duff-Gordon, 222 N.Y. 88, 91, 118 N.E. 214; Alexander v. Equitable Life Assur. Soc. of United States, 233 N.Y. 300, 306, 135 N.E. 509, 511. Unless a percentage rental agreement is so interpreted, the percentage requirement would have no meaning.

The question to be resolved is whether under the terms of the leases and the proof adduced at the trial, the plaintiff is entitled to recover on one or both causes of action. Both causes of action are well founded.

There is no doubt that the sales were made "on, in or from" the main premises. The evidence shows that the furs were delivered to the basement of the main store, prepared for display there, stored in the basement of the main store, packed and shipped out from the main store premises. The entire fur business was administered and conducted in the Fifth Avenue premises, yet the defendant would have us construe the leases so as to permit it to operate a fur department as part of a main store in a space with an address different from the address set forth in the lease of that space, doing a business with average annual gross receipts of over $600,000, for a fixed rental of $3,800 a year free from the percentage provisions of the main store lease. The leases fail to disclose such an authorization. The 742 Fifth Avenue lease limited the exclusive use of the entrances and elevators to three floors and basement. The 1 West 57th Street lease prohibited alterations without consent, and also prohibited any interference with the premises of 742 Fifth Avenue.

We can perceive no distinction between the customer who was sent to the fifth floor fur department by salespeople on the lower floors, and the customers who responded to the advertisements or displays that proclaimed that the defendant's fur department was located at 742 Fifth Avenue. All these customers were patrons of the Fifth Avenue Tailored

Woman store, and were attracted to that store by the advertisements and window displays using the Fifth Avenue address. Therefore, it necessarily follows that the terms of the lease of 742 Fifth Avenue must apply to all transactions taking place at that address.

Moreover in every contract there is an implied covenant that neither party shall do anything which shall have the effect of injuring or destroying the right of the other party to receive the fruits of the contract. Kirke La Shelle Co. v. Paul Armstrong Co., 263 N.Y. 79, 188 N.E. 163. The defendant cannot make a virtue of a violation of the lease. It made alterations without the written consent of the landlord of 1 West 57th Street. It violated the prohibition in paragraph 36 of the 1945 lease that the said lease was not to have any effect on the lease dated June 29, 1939, between the Mutual Life Insurance Co. of New York and the Tailored Woman, Inc. (1) by moving its fur department to the fifth-floor space from a lower floor, and (2) by advertising that the fifth-floor space described in the lease as space in the building known as 1 West 57th Street was located at 742 Fifth Avenue. The consequence of these violations was to bring about the condition wherein the defendant was using a Fifth Avenue address and sales space for the sale of furs as a rental rate of a side-street office salesroom.

Furthermore, under the terms of the 742 Fifth Avenue lease, the defendant agreed to maintain a business substantially similar to that which it had maintained at 729 Fifth Avenue, where the defendant had a fur department. As a result of the removal of the fur department to the fifth floor, the plaintiff was deprived of a substantial portion of the fruits of the contract. By excluding the fur sales from the calculations required by the percentage terms of the lease, the defendant excluded almost 20% of the average gross receipts collected at the premises 742 Fifth Avenue. Such an act constitutes an unreasonable diversion of business from a percentage leased premises to a fixed rental premises.

The intent of the parties as expressed in the two leases was that the fifth-floor space at 1 West 57th Street would be operated independently of the main premises. For example, the landlord by lease restricted the use of the elevators in 1 West 57th Street by providing that they would operate only until 1:00 P.M. on Saturdays and 6:00 P.M. on business days, whereas the elevators in 742 Fifth Avenue were within the absolute control of the defendant and could operate until 6:00 P.M. or later on Saturdays, business days and legal holidays only to the third floor.

The rent fixed for the fifth-floor space reflects the restrictions imposed on doing business in an off-street office salesroom space which is not serviced on Saturday afternoons or on legal holidays. Such restrictions are not incompatible with the use permitted by the 1 West 57th Street lease, i.e., the sale and display of women's wearing apparel. Such uses are commonly so restricted. In this very case the former tenant on the fifth floor was engaged in the women's wearing apparel business.

The limitation of the use of the elevators to five and one-half days as well as the necessity of sharing the use of the elevators with the other tenants in 1 West 57th Street make it clear that any permitted diversion of business from the main store was intended to be confined to a five and one-half day operation with all the inconvenience of sharing public elevators. Naturally these conditions in themselves forbid the transfer of a major department from the main store to the off-street office salesroom.

Since the defendant, in order to avoid the restrictions of the 1 West 57th Street lease, elected, in violation of the provisions of the leases, to operate part of the fifth floor as an integral part of the main premises and to make the fur sales on, in and from the main premises, it has subjected the gross receipts collected from these operations to the percentage rental terms of the main store lease. Such a conclusion is supported by the evidence, by a common-sense interpretation of the leases, and by the prevailing law in other jurisdictions. Cissna Loan Co. v. Baron, 149 Wash. 386, 270 P. 1022; Gamble-Skogmo, Inc., v. McNair Realty Co., D.C., 98 F. Supp. 440, *affirmed* 193 F.2d 876; Dunham & Co. v. 26 East St. State Realty Co., 134 N.J. Eq. 237, 35 A.2d 40.

The judgment of the Appellate Division should be reversed and the judgment of the Trial Term reinstated.

Dye, Fuld, Froessel and Van Voorhis, JJ., concur with Desmond, J.

Burke, J., dissents in opinion in which Conway, C.J., concurs.

Judgment affirmed.

NOTES AND QUESTIONS

1. Draft leasehold language that would have strengthened the landlord's claim in the two principal cases. Would you ascribe the landlord's rental loss to bad lawyering or bad judging? If bad lawyering, was it a lawyer's failure to anticipate the dispute, or was it a lawyer's failure to prepare suitable leasehold language?

2. In a gross sales percentage lease, some items of receipt are often excluded from the base or are handled at a lower percentage. Consider why this might be true of these department store receipts:

(a) goods returned or exchanged;
(b) sales taxes;
(c) customer conveniences, including pay toilets, pay phones, stamp machines;
(d) employee conveniences, including cafeteria sales, discounts on goods.

Should credit sales be included when the customer defaults?

Should receipts from the sale of loss leaders, i.e., goods sold below cost as a sales promotion, be excluded? Receipts from the sale of goods made by telephone? See generally Halpern, Shopping Center and Store Leases 74-87 (1979).

3. Much litigation, similar to that in the *Hempstead* case supra, arises over the application of a percentage clause to the business of a subtenant or concessionaire. Although in general the lessor expects that the percentage formula governing the lessee will also apply to the subtenant or concessionaire, a poorly drafted lease might eliminate or greatly reduce this source of rental. Can you construct a clause that serves the landlord badly? See, e.g., Town of Islip v. Smith, 3 A.D.2d 726, 159 N.Y.S.2d 763 (1957) (landlord's judgment for $24,538.98 reduced to $484.66). Conversely, a tenant is apt to feel the pinch if he continues to pay a percentage based on the sales of a subtenant while collecting a fixed rental from the subtenant. See, e.g., G. R. Kenney, Inc. v. White, 48 So. 2d 733 (Fla. 1950).

The landlord must also consider the probable volume of the subtenant's business in comparison with that of the prime tenant. Where the landlord has agreed (or is required by law) to act reasonably in passing upon a sublease proposal, may he reject a subtenant whose business activity is likely to cause a lower percentage return? Cf. Rowe v. Great Atlantic & Pacific Tea Co., 42 N.Y.2d 62 (1978) (in absence of express restriction, percentage lessee may assign lease to lower volume merchant). Rather than reject the prospective subtenant, how might the landlord make acceptance possible without giving away rental income?

What if the principal tenant is a large department store having many concession outlets. Does business prudence demand that the tenant be free to modify his concession arrangements without getting the landlord's prior approval in each instance?

4. Often more troublesome than reaching agreement on the percentage rate is the bargaining over the guaranteed minimum. What factors should each of the parties weigh in setting the fixed rental? See, e.g., McMichael and O'Keefe, Leases, Percentage, Short and Long Term 40-42 (5th ed. 1959).

5. In collecting a percentage rental, the landlord must rely upon gross sales figures given him by the tenant. Yet, not all is left to the tenant's inborn honesty. What are the minimum reporting and policing features that a landlord would need to better insure a fair count? What control can a tenant accept before he becomes overburdened or too divulgent? See, e.g., McMichael and O'Keefe, note 4 above, at 48-55; Pollack, Clauses in a Shopping Center Lease, 20 Prac. Law. 63 (Dec. 1974); Colbourn, A Guide to Problems in Shopping Center Leases, 29 Brooklyn L. Rev. 56, 59-61 (1962).

6. The magazine, Buildings, The Facilities Construction and Management Magazine, publishes an annual seven-city survey of percentage lease rates arranged by type of store. The December 1984 survey includes the following data:

Type of Store	Range in % Rate (seven cities)
Bakeries	4 to 8
Barber shops	5 to 10
Bowling lanes	6 to 10
Department stores	0 to 3
Discount stores (over 75,000 square feet)	0 to 4
Gas stations (cents per gallon)	0 to 2
Grocery stores (chains)	½ to 2
Grocery stores (convenience)	1 to 3½
Hardware	2 to 6
Motion picture theaters	4 to 15
Parking lots and garages (attended)	40 to 80
Women's shoes	4 to 10

b. Percentage Tenant's Duties

Kauder, Klotz & Venitt v. Rose's Stores, Inc.
359 F. Supp. 1280 (E.D.N.C. 1973)

LARKINS, District Judge. On June 3, 1953, defendant Rose's entered into a 25-year lease agreement with Marion Investment Company for four lots and a building in Morehead City, North Carolina. In 1961 plaintiff acquired the property subject to the original lease. The lease provides for a $15,000 per year minimum guaranteed rental which covered the 15,000 square foot building. In addition the lease provides for a 5% of gross sales override over $300,000 per year as additional rental. The store covered by the lease in question is at the corner of Arendell and 8th Streets in downtown Morehead City and is Rose's Store #59. It has been continuously operated since 1953, having produced sales in every year which returned additional rental to the owners from the percentage of sales override.

On or about August 1, 1971, Rose's opened a 50,000 square foot store (#200) in the Plaza Shopping Center approximately 1.9 miles west of downtown Morehead City. During the next year, gross sales in Store #59 dropped substantially resulting in the instant suit.

The plaintiff alleges in the complaint that the opening of Store #200 in the immediate vicinity of the demised premises diverted business from the demised premises and thereby substantially diminished sales and income at the demised premises, resulting in a drop in plaintiff's rental income based on gross sales. Plaintiff contends that these actions of the defendant violated express and implied conditions, covenants, and promises contained in the lease. The plaintiff further contends that the defendant's actions were done willfully with the intention of diverting business from Store #59 and thus reducing the amount of rent attributable to gross sales. Plaintiff prays for an accounting, compensatory and punitive damages, interest, and costs. Plaintiff also prays for the Court to enjoin the defendants from diverting business from the demised premises and maintaining a store in competition therewith.

The defendant admits the terms of the lease entered into in 1953 and the opening of the new store, #200, in the Plaza Shopping Center in 1971. However, defendant denies that it has violated any express or implied covenants, conditions, or terms of the lease and denies that it willfully opened the new store to intentionally divert business from the plaintiff's store.

Specifically, the defendant contends (1) that in the late 1960's Morehead City had expanded westward and that Carteret County was losing customers to other localities because of poor product selection, noncompetitive pricing, poor parking facilities, and a lack of modern stores; (2) that the opening of the new 50,000 square foot store would offer a wider selection of items at a lower cost to the consumer in a modern shopping center with ample parking; (3) that the defendant has at all times operated Store #59 as a profitable business and continues to do so; and (4) that the guaranteed minimum of $15,000 is a reasonable rental value of the property with 5% additional rent on gross income over $300,000 being a bonus to the plaintiffs in that Store #59 has done considerably better than anticipated by the parties making the lease.

This cause is now before this Court on a Rule 12(b)(6) motion to dismiss filed by the defendant and motions for summary judgment filed by both parties. A hearing was held in Trenton, North Carolina on May 23, 1973.

There is no express condition in the lease in question which prohibits the defendant from opening another store in any given area. Nor is there any term or condition of the lease which specifically prohibits competition in any fashion by the defendant. The key provision upon which the plaintiff relies is:

>   1. The Tenant shall use and occupy the entire building on the demised premises for the sales by Tenant at retail of merchandise and for no other purpose.
>   Tenant shall diligently and continuously operate and conduct its retail business throughout the entire term and shall use all proper and reasonable efforts consistent with good business practice to the end that the gross sales of such business shall throughout the entire term be as large as possible.

The plaintiff claims that the above quoted provision places the burden upon the defendant to diligently and continuously operate its business and to use all proper and reasonable efforts to make gross sales as large as possible. Plaintiff further claims that the provision obligates the defendant to do nothing inconsistent with the production of maximum rent.

These allegations are sufficient to raise the issue that the defendant violated certain terms and conditions of the lease. Therefore, a valid cause of action has been stated and defendant's motion to dismiss under Rule 12(b)(6) must be denied.

Therefore, both parties having moved for summary judgment under Rule 56, and it appearing that there is no genuine issue as to any material fact, the Court, having carefully studied the pleadings, affidavits, answers to interrogatories, and other material in the record, will next consider the cross motions for summary judgment.

The language of the lease provides that the defendant has an obligation to diligently and continuously operate its business in Store #59 and to use all proper and reasonable efforts to make gross sales as large as possible. Therefore, the issue is whether, by opening Store #200 in the Plaza Shopping Center, the defendant has breached its obligation. This Court feels that it has not.

The basic law in this area is found in 52 C.J.S. Landlord and Tenant §502(2), pp. 454 and 455:

> Where there is an implied obligation on the part of the lessee to occupy and use the demised property for the purpose expressed in the lease, he cannot, by ceasing to operate, or by changing the nature of his business, or by transferring operations to other locations, as by diverting his business to another store which he owns, or by moving some departments of the business to other premises, avoid liability for the percentage rent and pay merely the minimum amount provided for or guaranteed.
>
> In this connection it has been stated that the unconscionable diversion of business by the lessee from percentage-lease premises should be penalized, and, thus, where a lessee opens a like business in the immediate vicinity, resulting in loss of business on the leased property, the income from the new place may be treated as belonging to the old. *Whether a lessee under a percentage lease or rental agreement is prohibited from engaging in a competing business in the vicinity depends on the facts and circumstances of the particular case.* (emphasis added)

First of all, the Court notes that Rose's did not open Store #200 in the "immediate vicinity" of Store #59. Store #200 is 1.9 miles from Store #59 and is in a suburban shopping center as opposed to Store #59's downtown location.

Next, the Court notes that in most cases which arise under similar circumstances the defendant has vacated the demised premises, changed the nature of the business, transferred operations to another location, or diverted his business. All of this is done in an attempt to diminish the rent

The Shopping Center Development

paid the lessor on a percentage basis. Looking at the facts and circumstances in the instant case, it is noteworthy that Rose's is continuing to operate Store #59, has not changed the nature of the business, and is still paying a percentage on gross sales over $300,000 per year. The fact that some operations may have been transferred to Store #200 and that business may have been diverted from Store #59 does not appear to be the result of an attempt to diminish the rent payable to the plaintiffs on a percentage basis.

The Court has carefully studied the Retail Consumer Survey of Carteret County tabulated in 1970. The report found that a substantial percentage of apparel, general merchandise, and furniture sales were lost to the county. The reasons given were that the stores in the county could not offer the large volume, narrow profit margin competitive pricing available in other areas. The report concluded, "Carteret stores are not modern, do not have satisfactory parking facilities, and have an inadequate variety of merhandise that is not competitively priced."

The defendant, faced with the accurate details of the above report, had an opportunity to locate in the new Plaza Shopping Center in the rapidly growing western part of Morehead City. They had a chance to lease a 50,000 square foot store which would enable them to offer large volume, narrow profit margin items which the public demands and which Store #59, with its space limitations, could not handle. Store #200 would offer a wide variety of competitively priced items in a modern facility with ample parking. L. H. Harvin, Jr., President of Rose's, stated in his affidavit, "The Rose's management felt that if we did not exercise our opportunity to continue to be the lead mercantile store in the area that one of our many competitors would exercise the opportunity and we would be relegated to a secondary sales position in our old store and would be faced with materially decreasing sales and the possibility of an unprofitable operation."

It is the opinion of this Court that the opening of Store #200 was not an attempt to diminish the rent payable to the plaintiffs but was merely a sound business venture. The defendant is engaged in a highly competitive business in a rapidly growing community. There is nothing unusual in chain stores adding to their number.

The original lease was entered into in 1953. Our country has changed greatly in the last 20 years with regard to consumer demand, the effects of inflation, and mobilization away from the city. Downtown area stores now have branches in suburban shopping centers. People do not want to fight the traffic, parking problems, and added distance to shop downtown when a one stop shopping center can meet their needs. The trend has always been to shop for convenience and economy. Today, a modern suburban shopping center fulfills this demand.

There has been a definite decrease in gross sales in Store #59 since the opening of Store #200. The first year gross sales dropped from over

$1,000,000 to just over $500,000, a loss of $695,673.79 to be exact. This would be a rental loss of $34,783.69. This loss can be partially attributable to the trend away from downtown shopping. It is also logically attributable to the opening of Store #200. However, with the trend toward shopping center patronage, had defendant not opened the new store, a competitor would probably have done so, and business in Store #59 would likewise be hurt. Thus the Court concludes that the opening of Store #200, even if it did diminish gross sales in #59, was not done willfully with intention of diverting business from Store #59.

The Court, in reaching this decision, has studied Food Fair v. Blumberg, 234 Md. 521, 200 A.2d 166, which analysed the extent of restrictions imposed upon chain store lessees. This Court, like the Maryland court, is unable to conclude that the lessees could not expand their business to the area of the new store.

This Court is also of the opinion that the minimum rent stipulation is, in itself, a fair and adequate rent and that the percentage override is more in the nature of a bonus. See 170 A.L.R. pp. 1117, 1118. Mr. Harvin states in his affidavit, ". . . in 1953 such a guaranteed minimum rental was reasonable and realistic and was designed to provide a realistic return on the investment in such a store, . . . that sales volume in this store has, over the years of its operation since 1953, been considerably greater than was anticipated at the time of the entry into this lease. . . ."

This statement seems feasible when it is seen that the plaintiffs paid $265,071.00 for the property in 1961.

It has been held that where the percentage lease provides no minimum guaranteed rental or a purely nominal guarantee, the tenant is under an implied obligation to conduct the business in good faith. (cites omitted). It has also been held that if the guaranteed rental provides the landlord an adequate return on his investment and the percentage rental feature is in the nature of a bonus, there is no obligation upon the tenant as to the manner of conducting the business not expressed in the lease. (cites omitted). See *Food Fair,* supra at 173.

The $15,000 annual guarantee is more than a purely nominal rental figure. But even if it were not so, the defendant has made a good faith effort to conduct the business in a proper and reasonable manner. The lease obligates the defendant to try to insure that gross sales will be as great as possible, and this is being done under the circumstances in this case. The fact plaintiffs are not receiving an extremely high rent is no reason to say the defendant has breached the lease. Should the defendant vacate the premises, a different conclusion might be reached.

The leading case in North Carolina is Jenkins v. Rose's 5, 10 and 25¢ Stores, Inc., 213 N.C. 606, 197 S.E. 174 (1938), which held: "In the absence of specific provision in the lease contract that lessee should occupy and use the demised premises, lessee is not bound so to do, and lessors are entitled only to the minimum rent stipulated in the contract for the year in question." In most cases of this sort, the defendant has either vacated the demised premises or opened a competing store adjacent to or close by the old store. That is not the case here. To say that by opening a new store nearly 2 miles from the demised premises is a failure to diligently use all proper and reasonable efforts consistent with good business practice to the end that gross sales be as large as possible and is a breach of the lease is to try to write a restrictive covenant against competition into the lease when none exists. . . .

It is the conclusion of this Court that the defendant has breached no obligation imposed by the lease. Rose's is continuously operating the plaintiffs' store and is making a good faith effort to use all proper and reasonable methods to make gross sales as great as possible. The opening of Store #200 was consistent with good business practice, and to hold Rose's liable for breaching the lease by opening this store would unduly restrict a modern chain store in an era in which the public demands cannot be met by the once popular downtown store.

Now therefore, in accordance with the foregoing, it is. . . .

Further ordered, that the defendant's motion for summary judgment be, and the same is, hereby allowed. . . .

B. THE GROUND LEASE

1. Introduction

Hecht, Long Term Lease Planning and Drafting
1-2, 13-16 (1974)

Rockefeller Plaza, Madison Square Garden, the Pan Am Building, the Waldorf-Astoria, the New York Hilton, the Washbridge apartment development, and numerous cooperative, residential and office buildings are modern monuments to the vitality, flexibility and utility of the long term ground lease.

The long term ground lease is primarily an urban financing and investment vehicle that enables a lessor to convey land or air rights to a lessee who undertakes to develop the property through new construction or substantial improvements. As such, this device comprises relationships that embrace the criteria of time and function. In terms of time, common usage in the real estate industry treats twenty-one years, exclusive of renewal options, as the shortest period for the long term ground lease. Yet, length of time alone does not adequately distinguish such a lease from a thirty-year lease of office space. The additional criterion of function is the distinguishing feature of a long term ground lease, since it is more than a temporary transfer of possession in exchange for rent. Invariably it is a net lease,[3] with the lessor enjoying carefree ground rental income and the lessee assuming the managerial roles of developing and operating the property. Indeed, it is this phenomenon of separating ownership from operation that makes the net lease such a flexible commercial device.

Varieties of Lessors

Who are the leading landholders in today's major ground lease transactions and what are their objectives? Common experience verifies the Biblical observation that "the poor shall not cease." Casting one's eyes over today's great cities and burrowing beneath corporate facades and holding companies, one might unhesitatingly add: "Nor shall the landed aristocracy diminish." For the fact is that, aside from occasional dispositions for estate tax purposes, the landed aristocracy generally do not sell their heritage. The Astors, Rhinelanders, Goelets, Beekmans and Phippses are landlords even to their more recent aristocratic entrepreneurial cousins, the duPonts and Rockefellers. Although these "traditional family" landowners normally do not sell, they are receptive to opportunities to convey an interest in their land by way of a net long term ground lease enabling others to improve and operate the properties while they, as lessors, benefit from increased property values and obtain higher returns generated by fully developed land, without risking additional capital. Accordingly, these private landowners constitute a major group of long term ground lessors.

Equally anxious to acquire and retain land for purposes of long term leasing are institutional investors. Members of this group are not pressed to dispose of their acquisitions by estate tax considerations and, therefore, are in an ideal position to become long term lessors. Trinity Church; the Roman Catholic Church; the Dutch Reformed Church; Sailor's Snug Harbor; Columbia University; John Hancock Mutual Life Insurance Company; New York Life Insurance Company; The Equitable Life Assurance Society of the United States; the Penn Central Company; unions; pension funds; however divergent their primary service or product may be, their common denominator is vast land holdings. Municipalities, the third major group of lessors, increasingly are resorting to the lease device as a community planning aid and a source of new revenue.

---

3. See Howard, The Essential Elements of a Net Lease, 8 Prac. Law. 15 (Feb. 1962).
   We often hear people refer to a "Net Lease," a "Net, Net Lease," a "Net, Net, Net Lease," or an "Absolutely Net Lease," as though some distinction exists among the different designations. It is submitted that a lease is either "Net" or it is not "Net." The use of more than one "Net," or the addition of a descriptive adjective is mere surplusage.

The Ground Lease

Goals of the Lessor

1. INVESTMENT OBJECTIVES

The lessor's primary objective is to maintain his underlying investment in the land while having it generate secure, carefree, long term rental income. Normally, a lessor's investment in real estate will increase in market value over a period of years. By employing variable rental devices, he can share in the enhanced value of his property without personally supplying any managerial skill or additional capital outlay. Moreover, a lessor's ability to benefit from the potential value of his land by means of a net long term ground lease obviates his exposure to entrepreneurial risks, which are invariably encountered in land development. This lease device also enables a lessor to receive rental income without being subjected to the harrassing details of daily business decisions required in the operation and management of the improved property.

2. TAX ADVANTAGES

The lessee's development of the land under a long term lease also enables a lessor to retain fee ownership while obtaining substantial mortgage funds without tax consequences. Since the underlying value of the land will have increased as a result of the lessee's improvements and operations (with the attendant substantial ground rental income being capitalized to establish a high loan-to-value ratio), the ground landlord is able to mortgage the improved property for a much higher figure than could be obtained for a fee mortgage on the raw land. Although the proceeds of such a mortgage must be repaid with interest, the interest charges are tax deductible expenses. In addition, the lessor achieves three benefits. First, he has immediate access to substantial cash proceeds. Second, in the case of a taxable entity, he avoids a diminution of his net worth that would have resulted from a sale and consequent payment of a capital gains tax. Third, in the case of an individual lessor, he generally assures his heirs or devisees a stepped-up basis for the property.

PROBLEM

X owns a commercially zoned midtown parcel that he acquired years ago for $1.0 million. The parcel's present market value is $5.0 million. If X sells the parcel, he will pay $1.0 million combined federal-state income tax (capital gains and minimum tax), which would leave X with $4.0 million for reinvestment. If X enters into a long-term ground lease, D will pay X an annual net ground rental of $450,000 (based upon 9 percent of the parcel's market value) for an initial ten-year term and will pay upward adjustments thereafter to reflect any increased market value. Armed with D's leasehold obligations, X may now borrow $4.0 million (X receives the proceeds tax free), pledging the rental stream or mortgaging the fee as security. X's debt service on his $4.0 million loan comes only to $436,400 yearly (10 percent interest, level payment debt service, 25 year maturity).

Do you see any fallacy in this analysis? Or by leasing rather than selling, can X have his cake while also eating it?

2. Leasehold Revaluation

Hecht, Long Term Lease Planning and Drafting
19 (1974)

Retention of the land as a hedge against inflation is another prime objective of the lessor. Although realty has traditionally been considered an excellent investment during inflationary periods, there is little basis for this general assumption. Urban land economists have demonstrated that realty values do not necessarily vary directly with the dollar's decreasing value since particular market factors, such as location, may determine an increase or decrease in the value of the land. Moreover, when long term lease rentals are payable at a fixed rate, the lessor is not protected against inflation and is, in fact, greatly handicapped. By appropriate negotiation and careful draftsmanship, however, variable rental provisions (e.g., step-up linkage, percentage rental and revaluation clauses) can be created to protect the lessor against inflation. When provisions of this type are incorporated into a net long term ground lease, the leasehold device should provide the lessor with an effective hedge against inflation.

Eltinge and Graziadio Development Co. v. Childs
49 Cal. App. 3d 294, 122 Cal. Rptr. 369 (1975)

ROTH, Presiding Justice. Appellants, Eltinge and Graziadio Development Co., a partnership, George Eltinge and George L. Graziadio, the partners, appeal from a judgment interpreting the rental provisions of a ground lease entered against them in their action for declaratory relief against respondents, Kenneth and Margaret Childs.

On May 1, 1964, appellants (lessees) executed a ground lease on real property for a fixed period of 60 years, commencing May 1, 1964, in Palm Desert, with respondents (lessors) and terminating on October 31, 2025, with an option to lessees to extend the term for an additional 30 years.

Rental on a "net, net, net" basis was fixed for the first five years and was defined as "basic ground rent." Thereafter at the expiration of each five year period "additional ground rent shall be authorized by which 6% of . . . appraisal value[1] exceeds the annual basic ground rent. . . ." (Emphasis added.)

The lease in Article II thereof contains warranties by lessees which in pertinent part recite that "their *purpose*" (emphasis added) is for the development of a shopping center; class A buildings will be constructed to accommodate the purpose and that no space will be subleased by lessees which shall at any time be used for sale of alcoholic beverages, pool or dance hall, distressed business; new or used vehicles or gambling or lottery activities or any unlawful activities.

Lessees contend that appraised value means value of the land based upon its use as a shopping center. Lessors assert it means fair market value.

The parties stipulated that: the only issue to be tried was the interpretation of the provisions of the lease contained in sections 3 and 4 of lease; such interpretation was to be made "only upon an examination of the 'four corners' of . . . lease, and such indisputable facts . . . supplied to the Court upon mutual agreement of the parties, in the event of a specific request from the Court for any such facts." The Court made no request and no additional facts were supplied.

The court made its determination based upon the four corners of the lease without any qualifying testimony. Its construction thereof is a matter of law to be settled in accordance with the applicable principles governing the construction of contracts. (Bates v. Industrial Property Holding Co. (1957) 155 Cal. App. 2d 697, 318 P.2d 741.) Since the trial court's interpretation did not depend upon the credibility of extrinsic evidence, we are not bound by its determination. (Parsons v. Bristol Development Co. (1965) 62 Cal. 2d 861, 44 Cal. Rptr. 767, 402 P.2d 839.) Whenever possible the whole of a contract is to be read so that each clause helps to interpret the other and give effect to every part thereof. (Civil Code, §1641.) It has also been held that a covenant in a lease to use property for a particular purpose does not necessarily mean that lessee may only use the leased property for that purpose. (Lippman v. Sears Roebuck & Co. (1955) 44 Cal. 2d 136, 280 P.2d 775.) A lease, too, should be so interpreted as to make it reasonable without violating the intent of the parties. (Civil Code, §1643.) Finally, it is not our function, nor do we have the power, to make a contract for the parties other than the one that they themselves have entered into. (Addiego v. Hill (1965) 238 Cal. App. 2d 842, 48 Cal. Rptr. 240.)

Although the lease was unquestionably executed by the parties in the expectation that a shopping center would be initially built thereon, none of

---

1. "There shall be periodic appraisals made of the demised premises (exclusive of any improvements) beginning five years from the effective date of this lease and, at the option of lessors, on every fifth anniversary thereafter during the term of this lease." Appraisal was to be conducted by members of the Masters Appraisers Institute. Provision was made for settlement of any dispute as to the evaluation.

its terms required the maintenance of a shopping center for any fixed portion of the original 60 year period or during the option period of 30 years, should the option be exercised, nor do any of its terms exclude the use of the premises for a purpose other than those activities which are by its terms specifically excluded.

The judgment in pertinent part provided: "The term that 'there shall be periodic appraisals made of the demised premises (exclusive of any improvements)' in Article IV, Section 3, of the subject ground lease, shall for all purposes throughout the term of the subject ground lease, and any extension thereof, means appraisals of the fair market value of the demised premises in accordance with its highest and best use as if vacant and without regard to the terms and conditions of the subject ground lease." We agree.

Lessees argue that in determining the appraised value the appraisers must take into account the fact that the premises are being used as a shopping center. This contention was decided adversely to the position of lessees by this court in Bullock's, Inc. v. Security-First Nat. Bank (1958) 160 Cal. App. 2d 277, 325 P.2d 185.) In *Bullock's* which involved a similar situation, we held that value in the lease meant fair market value since the lease showed that the parties had not stated "value in use" but merely value.

In *Bullock's* we said at p. 283, 325 P.2d at 189:

"It is obvious from the rental provisions that the parties were contracting for the lessors to receive as rent a fixed percentage return on the value of the land, such value to be redetermined every ten years. They might have agreed on four percent or six percent, but they chose five instead. Moreover, it must be remembered that this is a 'net' lease — i.e., the lessee pays *all* taxes and other expenses in connection with the property. From the method of calculation which the parties agreed upon it may reasonably be inferred that they were thinking in terms of interest rate on a capital investment. They fixed the net rate of return on the lessor's investment at five percent, but they also provided for fluctuation in the value of such investment. They realized that this capital asset might fluctuate in value from time to time and therefore provided for periodic reevaluation in order that the lessors might continue to receive a five percent return on the value of their investment. When the parties referred to the 'value' of the land in question they meant its monetary worth or marketable price — i.e., its *market value*.

"Appellants argue that 'if the parties had intended market value, they would have said market value.' However, we have already pointed out that using merely the word 'value' in the lease indicates that the parties meant market value. In fact, it seems clear that if the parties had intended anything *other than* market value, they would have said so expressly."

Lessees in reply to *Bullock's* assert that courts have never made a fetish out of the term "market value" and cite as illustrations condemnation

The Ground Lease

cases in which there may not be any market value, or when the market value may not be the true indication of property taken. (See e.g. Citizens Utilities Co. v. Superior Court (1963) 59 Cal. 2d 805, 31 Cal. Rptr. 316, 382 P.2d 356; City of Pleasant Hill v. First Baptist Church (1969) 1 Cal. App. 3d 384, 397 n.1, 82 Cal. Rptr. 1.) However, these cases are inapplicable since the rationale behind them is that when market value is not a true indication of the property involved, then the courts will use some other method of valuation in order to establish reasonable compensation. Such is not the situation at bench.

As an adjunct to the same argument lessees urge upon us the rationale adopted by the New York courts and other states in cases such as Plaza Hotel Associates v. Wellington Associates (1967) 55 Misc. 2d 483, 285 N.Y.S.2d 941, *affd.* (1968) 22 N.Y.2d 846, 293 N.Y.S.2d 108, 239 N.E.2d 736, which hold that in cases such as the one at bench the term "value" means "value in use" not "market value." However, we see no reason to depart from our holding in *Bullock's* and thus cause confusion in the law of leases. If the parties desire some other form of valuation they are free to spell it out in the lease. Absent a provision indicating some other form of valuation *Bullock's* clearly indicates, and has for some 15 years, that the "value" means "market value."

The judgment is affirmed.

Fleming and Compton, JJ., concur.

Plaza Hotel Associates v. Willington Associates

55 Misc. 2d 483, 285 N.Y.S.2d 941 (1967), aff'd without opinion, 28 A.D.2d 1209 (1967), aff'd, 22 N.Y.2d 846, 239 N.E.2d 736, 293 N.Y.S.2d 108 (1968)

ABRAHAM J. GELLINOFF, J. Plaintiffs move for summary judgment (1) declaring invalid an appraisal conducted for the purpose of determining the rent payable to defendant by Plaza Hotel Associates (hereinafter referred to as "Associates"), (2) directing a new appraisal, and (3) directing an accounting of excess rental payments claimed to have been made to defendant.

On October 1, 1953 Hilton Hotel Corporation (hereinafter "Hilton"), the owner of the land and the buildings thereon known as the Plaza Hotel, sold the hotel property to Park—59th Street Corporation (hereinafter "Park"). As part of the transaction, Hilton received an agreement entitling it to an option, exercisable between October 1, 1965 and March 31, 1966, to repurchase an undivided one-half interest in the land only, for (1) $400,000 and (2) an assumption of one half the mortgage indebtedness and one half the real estate taxes applicable to the land itself. The option agreement provided that, upon exercise of the option, Hilton (or its assignee) would grant to the then owner of the other undivided one-half interest in the land a lease of Hilton's one-half interest in the land for a term of 20 years with an option to the lessee to extend the term for an additional 30 years. If, however, the property was no longer used primarily for hotel purposes at the time of the exercise of Hilton's option, Hilton (or its assignee), was not to be required to enter into such a lease and was to have all the rights of a tenant in common of the land. Annexed to the option agreement of October 1, 1953 was the form of the lease to be executed in the event that the option was exercised.

Article Two of the lease form provides that "Lessee shall pay as rent for the interest in the land hereby demised an annual ground rental equal to 3% of the value of all of the land (wherever permitted by the context the word 'land' as herein used is intended to mean the land only, exclusive of the buildings and improvements thereon) as of the date of the commencement of the term of this lease." The same article provides for an appraisal of the land value if the parties fail to agree as to the value within 60 days from the commencement of the term of the lease.

Article Nine of the lease form provides that the lessee shall have the right to alter, reconstruct, and demolish any and all buildings and improvements and erect new buildings and structures "provided that if any such renovation, reconstruction, demolition or new building or structure is designed to be used primarily for purposes other than hotel purposes, the prior written consent of the *Lessee* [sic] shall be required." (Italics supplied.) The italicized word "lessee" is obviously a typographical error and must be read as "lessor." Otherwise the article is wholly meaningless.

Article Eleven provides that "if at any time the land and the buildings and improvements thereon shall cease to be used primarily for hotel purposes, the Lessor shall have the right to terminate this lease by written notice given . . . within six months from the date of the cessation of such use."

Article Nineteenth provides that upon the expiration or other termination of the lease for any reason whatever, the lessor and the owners of any other interest in the land or buildings shall thereupon have such "rights, privileges and obligations as by law such ownership bestows or entails in the absence of any agreement."

In the Fall of 1965, Hilton sold its option rights to Chatham Associates, Inc. (hereinafter "Chatham") which thereupon exercised the option and acquired a 50% interest in the land underlying the Plaza Hotel structure. As required by the option agreement, Chatham granted a lease, in the form annexed to the agreement, to a subsidiary of plaintiff Associates. The subsidiary subleased the leasehold interest to Hotel Corporation of America (hereinafter "HCA"), the coplaintiff herein, and assigned the interest retained by it to Associates. Chatham transferred its half interest in the land to defendant Wellington Associates, Inc. At the present time, therefore, Associates and Wellington each own an undivided half interest in the land. Associates owns the entire building and is the lessee of Wellington's interest in the land. HCA is sublessee of Wellington's interest in the land and is the present operator of the hotel.

As the parties were unable to agree as to the value of the land for the purpose of determining the rental to be paid to defendant, an appraiser was selected by Associates and another by Wellington. Since the appraisers could not agree, a third appraiser was selected. He and the appraiser selected by Wellington appraised the value of the land at $28,000,000.

Concededly, all three appraisers valued the land as if it were unencumbered by the lease and by the restrictions to hotel use imposed by the lease. The third appraiser's appraisal states that the purpose of the appraisal is to establish the market value of the land "as though free and clear of any encumbrances, *vacant and ready to be devoted to the highest and best use*" and concludes "Employing all available guides to value giving consideration to location, size of plot *and highest and best use* . . . the market value of the land is Twenty-Eight Million Dollars." The appraisal of the appraiser selected by defendant also states that the land was to be appraised "as if vacant and unimproved" and that he considered, inter alia, the "highest and best use to which the land may be put." The appraisal by the appraiser selected by Associates states that it values the land "as if vacant and unimproved" and also declares that "in our determination of value, we have projected a hypothetical office building improvement" for the land. The valuation is based, in part, on "earnings and residual land value which would be achieved if a multistory office building were erected on the commercially zoned land."

All three appraisers have thus ignored the fact that the land is encumbered by a lease for 20 years, extendable at the lessee's option for an additional 30 years, under which the property may be used only for hotel purposes. Admittedly the appraisers all were of the opinion that such a use was not the highest and best use to which the property could be put and fixed values materially in excess of those which they would have found if they had to take into account that the property was restricted to use as a hotel.

Plaintiffs urge that the lease provision for fixation of the value of the land does not provide that the land was to be valued as if it were unencumbered by the lease restricting the use of the property to hotel purposes. They urge that the purpose of using the words value of "the land only, exclusive of the buildings and improvements thereon" was merely to make it clear that the value was not to include the value of the building on the land, no part of which was owned by Hilton or its assignee. They point out that, when the parties wished to state that an interest should be free of encumbrances they did so, giving as an example a provision of paragraph 4 of the option agreement that Hilton's interest in the "land (exclusive of the buildings and improvements thereon)" was to be "free of all encumbrances except as hereinafter stated."

In the court's opinion, the points made by plaintiff are well taken.

There is no suggestion in the language of article Two that, in valuing the land, the restrictions to hotel use imposed by the lease were to be disregarded and the land valued as if it were vacant and available for the highest and best use. In United Equities v. Mardordic Realty Co. (16 Misc. 2d 996, *mod.* 8 A.D.2d 398) the lease provided for rent for the renewal term equivalent to 6% of the value of the land. The Special Term had held that restrictions imposed by the lease as to the use of the property had to be taken into account by the appraisers. The Appellate Division agreed with this reasoning, but disagreed with the lower court's findings that there were such restrictions. It said (p. 400): "This case is unlike Ruth v. S.Z.B. Corp. (2 Misc. 2d 631, 634, *affd.* 2 A.D.2d 970) wherein provision was made for basing the rental upon the fair value of the land 'free of lease and unencumbered.' Hence, there is no language in the lease or modification thereof which excludes them in the determination of the fair market value of the land. The fair market value of the land is therefore to be determined by reference to the term of and the renewal options contained in the lease and modifications thereof, and, in addition, the restrictions, if any, therein affecting the land."

That valuations of land must take into consideration all encumbrances thereon, including restrictions as to its use, unless there is a clear provision to the contrary, is well settled (Kernochan v. Manhattan Ry. Co., 161 N.Y. 339; Livingston v. Sage, 95 N.Y. 289, 294-95; United Equities v. Mardordic Realty Co., supra). . . .

For the reasons indicated, the motion is granted to the extent of granting judgment declaring the appraisal invalid and directing a new appraisal. Until such new appraisal and a proper determination of the rent to be paid, it is impossible to determine whether and to what extent plaintiffs have paid excessive rent. That branch of the motion which seeks an accounting for excess rental is therefore held in abeyance pending a determination of the rent to be paid, for which purpose this court retains jurisdiction in the matter.

NOTES AND QUESTIONS

1. The *Plaza Hotel* dispute was a meal-ticket for lawyers and appraisers. After the appellate division and court of appeals both had affirmed Judge Gellinoff's decision setting aside the original appraisal, a referee was appointed to take new testimony and issue a report. This led Judge Gellinoff to fix value at $18.5 million. Tenant appealed. The appellate division modified the value downward to $11.5 million. 46 A.D.2d 642, 360 N.Y.S.2d 433 (1974). The court of appeals affirmed. 37 N.Y.2d 273, 333 N.E.2d 168, 372 N.Y.S.2d 35 (1975).

In rejecting the $18.5 million figure, the appellate division gave "controlling significance" to the contemporaneous (1965) arm's length sale, in which Chatham paid nearly $5.0 million to acquire Hilton's one-half interest in the property. Since Hilton and Chatham both were sophisticated real estate operators, the court believed that their agreed upon price must have approximated the value of that interest. Thus the full land value could not have exceeded $11.5 million. On this "reasoning," the court of appeals affirmed.

While concurring with the result, Chief Judge Breitel refused to treat the above price as having "controlling significance." He argued that the two one-half interests in the land were not of equal value. Why not?

Under the ground rent formula, the original appraisal would have yielded $840,000 yearly. With land value finally set at $11.5 million, tenant would pay only $345,000 yearly. Such are the stakes of careful draftsmanship.

The *Plaza Hotel* litigation had one more chapter. Having paid its rental conditionally under the first appraisal, tenant was entitled to a $4.4 million refund. To recover this sum, tenant had to invoke extraordinary remedies. 84 Misc. 2d 777, 378 N.Y.S.2d 859 (Sup. Ct. 1975).

2. The facts in Ruth v. S.Z.B. Corp., 2 Misc. 2d 631, 153 N.Y.S.2d 163 (Sup. Ct. 1956), on which the landlord in the *Plaza Hotel* case vainly relied, were these: Parties in December 1935 entered into a 40-year lease for a mid-Manhattan block front. A two story store-front and three small brownstones occupied the site. The lease called for reappraisal after 20 years, the new rent to be 6 percent of "the full and fair value of the land . . . which the same would sell for as one parcel considered as vacant and unimproved, in fee simple, by private contract, free of lease and unencumbered."

By 1955, the blockfront had become enormously more valuable because of the removal of the adjoining elevated railway. The parcel had been rezoned to permit high-rise apartments, which were becoming common in the neighborhood.

Tenant sought to restrict the appraisal to reflect various leasehold restrictions that would obligate tenant to maintain the existing buildings, by then an underdevelopment for the site. In holding for the landlord, the court stressed the phrase "free of lease":

> If the phrase "free of lease" is given its plain and natural meaning, the lease in its entirety must be eliminated from consideration, whether its provisions spell good or ill fortune for one party or the other. The restriction on use, which, according to the defendant's contention, impairs the value of the land, if imposed at all, is imposed solely by the underlying lease. The broad question whether a restrictive covenant in a deed or like instrument, affecting the value of the land, may be considered is not before the court. The precise question is whether the asserted limitation on use, created by the lease before the court may be taken into account in applying a formula which prescribes that the land is to be valued "free of lease." In my opinion it would be repugnant to the language employed to hold that the limitation on use

springing exclusively from the lease itself may be treated by the arbitrators as an element of value. Whatever else the parties may have had in mind, it is inconceivable that when they declared explicitly that the land be valued "free of lease," they intended that the arbitrators might give heed to the very lease which so declared. Such a ruling would delete the phrase "free of lease" from the formula. [2 Misc. 2d at 636, 153 N.Y.S.2d at 167-168]

3. The ninety-nine year lease in Funder v. Maizels, 377 A.2d 70 (D.C. 1977), stated: "Said appraisal shall be made . . . as if the leased land were vacant, unencumbered, unimproved, and not under lease." At issue was whether the appraisal might consider any enhancement in value because of "assemblage potential." The court held for the landlord.

4. What steps should the long-term tenant take to be sure he or she isn't "caught between a rock and a hard place" when appraisal results in a significant increase in the ground rent?

5. Other devices exist to protect the dollar worth of the lessor's return. These include step-up provisions, linkage clauses, and percentage rental. Step-up provisions, known also as "graded" leases, "crescendo" clauses, or "escalator" clauses, detail in advance the exact amount and dates of future rental increases. Linkage clauses permit rental adjustments by linking the base rental to some independent item or index that reflects changes in the purchasing power of money. Sometimes a ground lease will contain two or more adjustment devices. Cf., e.g., Ruth v. S.Z.B. Corp., note 2 above. From the parties' standpoint, what are the strengths and weaknesses of each device? Cf. generally Hecht, Long Term Lease Planning and Drafting 57-110 (1974).

3. Taxation of the Leasehold Interest

The ground-tenant, as the owner of investment property, is entitled to deduct all ordinary and necessary expenses, which will include, of course, ground rental, real estate taxes, operating costs, repairs, and mortgage interest. Two other categories of expenditure will concern the tax-wise ground-tenant: his leasehold acquisition costs and, more importantly, his investment in building improvements.

Acquisition costs may involve brokerage fees, closing expenses, and any premium paid to the prior tenant for a leasehold assignment. The cost of building improvements may involve not only the expenditure on a new structure but also tenant removal and demolition costs on the previous structure.

The ground-tenant must capitalize and then write off the acquisition and improvement costs. What must be determined is the appropriate write-off period. Most ground leases contain one or more renewal clauses, which give the tenant the privilege of extending the term for many years.

The Ground Lease

Prior to 1981, when Congress enacted TEFRA and created a fifteen-year recovery period for real property improvements — a term shorter than the initial term of most ground leases — the existence of options complicated the calculation of amortization and depreciation allowances. To illustrate the pre-1981 problem (and the post-1981 problem as to improvements subject to the pre-TEFRA provisions), assume tenant builds an office building having a 45-year estimated useful life. The tenant holds a 30-year ground lease with two 20-year renewal options. How should tenant write off tenant's outlay: Amortize on a 30-year schedule? Amortize on a 50-year or 70-year schedule? Depreciate on a 45-year schedule?

With the recovery term for real property likely, under proposed legislation, to rise from its current level (nineteen years except for low-income housing (fifteen years)), option periods will again become more relevant in calculating write-off allowances for tenant-built improvements. And as to the amortization of leasehold acquisition costs, which is not geared to "recovery" periods, the situation did not change in 1981.

Congress, seeking to provide tenants with "easily followed" guidelines, enacted the following code provision.

Internal Revenue Code of 1954

§178. *Depreciation or Amortization of Improvements Made by Lessee on Lessor's Property.* (a) General Rule. — Except as provided in subsection (b), in determining the amount allowable to a lessee as a deduction for any taxable year for exhaustion, wear and tear, obsolescence, or amortization — (1) in respect of any building erected (or other improvement made) on the leased property, if the portion of the term of the lease (excluding any period for which the lease may subsequently be renewed, extended, or continued pursuant to an option exercisable by the lessee) remaining upon the completion of such building or other improvement is less than 60 percent of the useful life of such building or other improvement, or (2) in respect of any cost of acquiring the lease, if less than 75 percent of such cost is attributable to the portion of the term of the lease (excluding any period for which the lease may subsequently be renewed, extended, or continued pursuant to an option exercisable by the lessee) remaining on the date of its acquisition, the term of the lease shall be treated as including any period for which the lease may be renewed, extended, or continued pursuant to an option exercisable by the lessee, unless the lessee establishes that (as of the close of the taxable year) it is more probable that the lease will not be renewed, extended, or continued for such period than that the lease will be so renewed, extended, or continued.

    (b)   *Related Lessee and Lessor* — . . .

    (c)   *Reasonable Certainty Test.* — In any case in which neither subsection (a) nor subsection (b) applies, the determination as to the amount allowable to a lessee as a deduction for any taxable year for exhaustion, wear and tear, obsolescence, or amortization — (1) in respect of any building erected (or other improvement made) on the leased property, or (2) in respect of any cost of acquiring the lease, shall be made with reference to the term of the lease (excluding any period for which the lease may subsequently be renewed, extended, or continued pursuant to an option exercisable by the lessee), unless the lease has been renewed, extended, or continued or the facts show with reasonable certainty that the lease will be renewed, extended, or continued.

NOTES AND QUESTIONS

1. Note carefully how the Code operates. Section 178(a)(1) contains a 60 percent rule for depreciation and §178(a)(2) contains a 75 percent rule for amortization. Unless these percentages are reached, the Code creates a presumption that the taxpayer will renew his lease. For the taxpayer, who seeks a shorter write-off period, the Code requires him to overcome the presumption of renewability by a showing that "it is more probable that the lease will not be renewed." By contrast, if the taxpayer achieves the subsection (a) percentages, the Code creates a presumption that the taxpayer will not renew his lease. For the commissioner, who seeks a longer write-off period, the Code requires him to overcome the presumption of nonrenewability by a showing of "reasonable certainty that the lease will be renewed."

The probability tests are applied to each renewal period. Thus the taxpayer might not achieve the requisite percentages for the first renewal term but might satisfy them for the second renewal term. In that event, unless either party overcomes the presumptions, the leasehold term would be deemed to include one renewal. Treas. Reg. §1.178-1(b)(2).

Note, especially, that the 60 percent rule relates leasehold term to the improvement's *useful life*. The 75 percent rule speaks, instead, of leasehold term and the leasehold's *cost*.

2. How might either the taxpayer or the Commissioner use the following factors to overcome the presumption of renewability [§178(a)] or of nonrenewability [§178(c)]: the suitability of the leased premises for tenant's business; the vitality of the neighborhood; the amount of leasehold rent; the cost of the improvements?

3. A tenant pays $50,000 to acquire a lease for 20 years, with two options to renew for periods of 5 years each. If the contract of assignment allocates the $50,000 cost between the original and renewal terms, should the allocation bind either the Commissioner or the taxpayer? Suppose that tenant and his assignor have made no allocation: What method exists for making an after-the-fact allocation? Cf. Treas. Reg. §1.178-1(b)(5).

4. Self-evidently, tenant may only depreciate improvements for which

he has paid. Conversely, landlord may not write off lessee-built improvements during the leasehold term. When the lease terminates, possession and ownership of the improvements then pass to the fee owner. The lease may require landlord to pay tenant a sum based on the improvement's current value, or some fraction thereof, on the termination date. What tax consequences would flow, for example, if landlord paid the terminating tenant $2.0 million for the tenant-built improvements?

Suppose, instead, that the fee owner pays nothing at leasehold termination for improvements having a current $2.0 million value: What tax consequences would flow from that event? See I.R.C. §§109, 1017.

5. *The interplay of §178 and depreciation recapture.* If a tenant receives payment for selling or canceling the lease, he must treat as "excess depreciation" the difference between the amortization he has already taken and the amortization he would have taken had he included the renewal period. (However, the addition of the renewal period cannot extend the amortization period by more than two-thirds.) I.R.C. §1250(b)(2).

Illustration: Tenant signs a 20-year lease plus one 15-year renewal term. He amortizes costs over the initial term (i.e., at the rate of 5 percent per year). He sells the lease before the end of 20 years. He must recalculate his amortization to include the renewal term (but without extending the original term more than two-thirds); the reconstituted term becomes $33\frac{1}{3}$ years; the revised amortization rate becomes 3 percent. The excess depreciation (2 percent a year) is applied to the tenant's sales proceeds to determine the allocation between ordinary income and capital gains. See The Mortgage and Real Estate Executives Report, June 1, 1977, pp. 6-8.

6. Consider the converse. Taxpayer purchases a fee interest subject to a ground lease expiring in ten years. Taxpayer pays $5.0 million. She allocates $4.0 million to the land and $1.0 million to the present value of the tenant-built improvements that she will acquire when the lease expires. On what basis may taxpayer write off the $1.0 million outlay? Cf. Geneva Drive-In Theatre, Inc., 67 T.C. No. 57 (1977); World Publishing Co. v. Commissioner, 299 F.2d 614 (8th Cir. 1962), *rev'g* 35 T.C. 7 (1960).

4. The Leasehold Mortgage

Mark, Leasehold Mortgages — Some Practical Considerations
14 Bus. Law. 609-620 (1959)

Although real estate financing through the medium of leasehold mortgages is far from a recent innovation, it has taken on an increasingly important role in the post-war building boom and in many metropolitan areas it has become an almost standard method for providing funds for the construction of large commercial and residential structures. The leasehold mortgage, when based on a properly drawn lease, can in many cases act as a catalyst in bringing together the conflicting interests of a property owner who does not want to incur the expense of constructing an adequate improvement on his land but desires an adequate return, an operator who sees an opportunity to improve the same property but does not want to buy it, and a lending institution seeking a safe investment for a large sum of money with a minimum of servicing expense. In the field of residential financing the leasehold mortgage offers the opportunity of creating on the same property two mortgages, each of which might be considered a legal investment for savings banks, insurance companies and fiduciaries. The first of such mortgages would be a leasehold mortgage insured under the provisions of the National Housing Act. The second would be a mortgage on the fee estate underlying the leasehold. It is rumored that the provisions of the National Housing Act permitting the insurance of leasehold mortgages were originally intended to apply only to ground leases in areas such as Baltimore, Maryland, and elsewhere in which a ground lease is practically the equivalent of a fee estate, and were not intended to apply to conventional leasehold financing. These provisions, however, have been widely used for the insurance of mortgages on leasehold estates created specifically for the purpose of financing a project and leaving the fee estate available as security for a conventional mortgage. Parenthetically, interesting problems of appraisal are raised in determining the value of such a fee estate for the purpose of ascertaining the maximum amount which may be loaned thereon under statutory provisions limiting the loan-to-value ratios available to various supervised lenders. The question of appraisal, however, is not within the scope of this paper.

It is readily apparent that a leasehold mortgage loan, being based on an estate subject to defeasance, presents problems which do not exist where a mortgage is based on a fee estate. Since the security behind a leasehold loan is the leasehold estate, and since the leasehold estate is created by the lease, the place to deal with these problems is the lease itself. If the lease does not contain adequate protection for the leasehold mortgagee, no amount of tinkering with special mortgage provisions can be of any avail, since no mortgage can in any way impose or alter the estate on which it creates a lien. The purpose of this paper is to discuss some of the basic problems inherent in leasehold financing and to suggest solutions which it is hoped will be found useful and practical.

1. Preparation of the Lease

Rare indeed is the lease which counsel for a leasehold mortgagee would approve unless it has been drawn with the basic requirements of such a lender in mind. Some years ago the writer had the privilege of reviewing for a lender a long term lease on a New York City property. Lessor and

The Ground Lease

Lessee had been represented by brilliant counsel, learned in the law and skilled in the use of the English language. From the point of view of draftsmanship, and as a protection for the rights of their respective clients, the lease was a masterpiece, but it was completely devoid of any provisions which would make it acceptable to a leasehold mortgagee. Since the lease had not been drawn with leasehold mortgage financing in mind, it took almost a year to revise it in such a way as to afford to a leasehold lender the protection to which it was entitled. Such a vast expenditure of time (and the borrower's money) could have been avoided had the proper protective provisions been inserted in the first place. It is therefore apparent that where there is even a reasonable chance that a leasehold estate may be mortgaged at some time in the future, it is well to insert in the lease provisions for protection of prospective mortgagees. A fortiori, in a case where it is known that a project will be financed by a leasehold mortgage, participation by the lender's counsel in the preparation of the lease will be in the best interest of all concerned.

2. Length of Initial Term

Some statutes authorizing investment in leasehold mortgages provide that the term of the lease shall be for not less than a given number of years, including enforceable options of renewal.[1] Such a statutory provision raises two questions.

The first is what is meant by "an enforceable option of renewal" or more accurately, in whose hands is the option of renewal enforceable. It is submitted that it is not sufficient that the option be enforceable by the Lessee, for in such case the Lessee, by failing to exercise the option, would be in a position to permit the mortgagee's security to disappear by allowing the leasehold estate to lapse. Nor would the mortgagee be protected by a mortgage clause providing for a default if the Lessee failed to exercise the option, since the event which constituted the default would be the same event which destroyed the security. It is believed that such statutory provisions should be construed so as to require that the option of renewal should be enforceable by the leasehold mortgagee. Therefore, for proper protection of the mortgagee, the lease should provide that so long as the mortgage is a lien on the leasehold estate, the mortgagee shall have the right, as attorney-in-fact for the Lessee, to exercise the option of renewal on behalf of the Lessee. The mortgagee is then in a position to insure that regardless

---

1. See, e.g., N.Y. Ins. Law §81-6(a) (McKinney 1966) (leasehold estates having an unexpired term of not less than twenty-one years, inclusive of the terms provided by enforceable options of renewal; annual debt service must be at the rate sufficient to amortize the loan completely at the end of four-fifths of the unexpired term of the lease). The state's banking law contains similar authority for mutual savings banks, specifying, however, that any option of renewal whose term is relied upon must be "enforceable at the *exclusive discretion* of the savings bank." N.Y. Banking Law §2356(i) (McKinney Supp. 1968-1969). — Eds.

of the failure of the Lessee to exercise the renewal option, the lease will be in existence for as long as the mortgage remains a lien on it.

The second question concerning the length of the term is of equal importance. This relates to the possible bankruptcy of a Lessor who has granted a lease containing an option to renew. Under Section 70(b) of the Bankruptcy Act a trustee in bankruptcy is authorized to reject executory contracts of the bankrupt "including unexpired leases of real property." The section further provides that "unless a lease of such property shall expressly otherwise provide, a rejection of such lease or of any covenant therein by the trustee of the lessor shall not deprive the lessee of his estate." It is thus clear that at least during the initial term of a lease, the leasehold estate would be unaffected by a rejection of the lease by the trustee of a bankrupt Lessor, unless the lease provided otherwise. It has been held, however, that the trustee of a bankrupt Lessor may reject an option of renewal. Coy v. Title Guarantee & Trust Co. 198 F. 275 (D.C. Ore. 1912). Thus, if the entire term of a leasehold mortgage exceeded the initial term of the lease, and the mortgagee relied on an option of renewal to extend the term so as to expire not earlier than the maturity of the mortgage, the mortgagee would be at the mercy of the trustee of a bankrupt Lessor, and this would be so whether or not the lease granted to the mortgagee the right to exercise the option of renewal as attorney-in-fact for the Lessee.

It is quite possible to argue that part of the Lessee's estate is the right of renewal and that therefore the rejection of the renewal option by the trustee of a bankrupt Lessor would not be effective. Indeed there is authority to the effect that upon the exercise of a renewal option there is an extension of the original term of the lease as an original demise for the original and renewal terms. Orr v. Doubleday, Page & Co., 223 N.Y. 334 (1918); Erickson v. Boothe, 79 Cal. App. 2d 266 (1947); Ackerman v. Loforese, 111 Conn. 700 (1930). However, as mentioned in Orr v. Doubleday, Page & Co., there is a considerable body of authority to the contrary. The contrary view is stated in the *Orr* case at page 340 as follows:

"This conclusion is not in accord with the view of a considerable and weighty body of judicial opinion, which is, that the interest of a lessee exercising the privilege of renewal is purely equitable. That view rests upon a distinction made between a privilege or covenant of a renewal and a privilege or covenant of an extension. It holds that the former is a right to the grant of an estate, the latter a present demise operative immediately upon the exercise of the privilege. (Sutherland v. Goodnow, 108 Ill. 528; Leavitt v. Maykel, 203 Mass. 506; Quinn v. Valiquette, 80 Vt. 434; Fergen v. Lyons, 162 Wis. 131; Luthey v. Joyce, 132 Minn. 451; Grant v. Collins, 157 Ky. 36; Miller v. Albany Lodge, 168 Ky. 755; Steen v. Scheel, 46 Neb. 252."

In view of the division of authority on this subject, it would appear safe to assume that a trustee of a bankrupt Lessor did not have the power to reject a renewal option in a lease.

The Ground Lease

The practical protection against a rejection of an option of renewal by the trustee of a bankrupt Lessor is to exclude terms available under renewal options when fixing the term of the lease for the purposes of the mortgage. Under no circumstances should the initial term of the lease expire prior to the maturity of the mortgage, and in states where the mortgage is required to mature prior to the expiration of the lease term, the initial term should be long enough so that in computing the maximum permitted maturity of the mortgage, reliance need not be placed on renewal options to make certain that the term of the lease will expire sufficiently long after the maturity of the mortgage.

Of course, where a renewal option can be exercised at any time during the initial term, a mortgagee would be protected by requiring that the renewal option be exercised at the time of the closing of the loan.[2]

3. Assignability of the Lessee's Estate

One of the most cherished possessions of any Lessor, the right to control the identity of his Lessee through control of the right to assign the Lessee's estate, becomes a casualty in a properly drawn lease securing a leasehold mortgage. A prime condition precedent to the acceptability of a lease for mortgage purposes is the unrestricted right of the Lessee to transfer the leasehold estate by assignment, without any need for the consent of the Lessor, and indeed, a lease is not acceptable for such purposes unless it so provides.

This matter of assignability has two aspects. The first relates to the question whether a covenant against assignment is violated by the making of a mortgage on the lease, or by the sale of the lease following the foreclosure of a mortgage thereon. In some states it is the rule that a covenant against assignment is violated by the making of a mortgage on the lease, or by the sale of the lease following foreclosure, or both. In other states the rule is directly to the contrary.[3] It is well, therefore, from this aspect of the problem of assignability, to have the lease provide express permission for the Lessee to mortgage the lease and for the leasehold mortgagee to take the lease by assignment in lieu of foreclosure and to sell it either after foreclosure or after taking an assignment, all without the consent of the Lessor.[4]

The other aspect of the problem of assignability is of equal, if not greater, importance and relates to the ability of a mortgagee to realize on

---

2. Would the lessee find this an acceptable arrangement? Another writer recommends that the original and renewal term be combined into a single term, but that the lessee be given the option to cancel the "renewal" period, presumably before it begins. Thomas, The Mortgaging of Long-Term Leases, 39 Dicta 363, 366 (1962). What tax advantage might this procedure cause the lessee? What further safeguard would the leasehold mortgagee demand if the lessee were to have a cancellation power? — EDS.

3. See, e.g., Great Southern Aircraft Corp. v. Kraus, page 1098 infra. — EDS.

4. *Query:* If the lease is otherwise silent respecting assignment, is an express permission to mortgage even necessary? — EDS.

its security following the acquisition of the lease either by foreclosure or assignment in lieu thereof or following the obtaining of a new lease from the Lessor under the circumstances discussed in Part 4 of this paper. As a fee mortgagee is free to sell an acquired fee without restriction of any kind, so a leasehold mortgagee must be in a position to dispose of the leasehold estate without let or hindrance. It follows that a leasehold mortgagee cannot allow itself to be put in the position of being required to seek the Lessor's permission in order to liquidate its security. Accordingly, a lease acceptable to a leasehold lender must provide absolute and unrestricted assignability of the Lessee's estate, free and clear of any control of the Lessor.

In dealing with this problem, Lessors sometimes suggest that their consent will not be required for any mortgage, or for any assignment to the mortgagee or to the immediate assignee of the mortgagee. Although at first blush this might appear adequate, a second look quickly reveals the flaw in the suggestion. A lease with such a provision is unmarketable as a practical matter, for the purchaser who buys the lease from the mortgagee could not thereafter dispose of it without the Lessor's consent, and therefore in the exercise of prudent judgment would decline to purchase from the mortgagee in the first place.

Another Lessor's suggestion to be avoided is an offer of a covenant by the Lessor not unreasonably to withhold its consent to an assignment of the lease. Although a covenant not unreasonably to withhold consent is in most states not without meaning, there are many bases on which a lessor may rely in withholding consent without being unreasonable, such as a poor credit rating of the assignee to maintain or manage the property. Furthermore, to determine whether the Lessor is reasonable or unreasonable in withholding consent is readily capable of being the subject of litigation. Such litigation would either take the form of an action for a declaratory judgment or a summary proceeding based upon assignment without consent in which the defense is raised that consent was unreasonably withheld. The possible necessity of any such litigation, plus the possibility that it might be unsuccessful from the Lessee's point of view, would in all probability make a lease containing such a covenant entirely unacceptable to a prospective lender. Such a covenant should therefore be excluded from the lease.

It is not uncommon for a lease to provide the Lessee's estate may be assigned provided the assignee assumes the obligations of the lease, or that the acceptance of an assignment constitutes an assumption of the Lessee's obligations thereunder.[5] Such a provision is not unacceptable to a leasehold mortgage if it is further provided that following an assignment of the

---

5. Query: In the absence of an assumption agreement, what are the limits of the assignee's personal obligation for the performance of the leasehold duties? See Berger, Cases and Materials on Land Ownership and Use 456-463 (2d ed. 1975). — EDS.

lease, the assignor is relieved of all obligations under the lease except those which accrued during the period when the assignor was the Lessee under the lease. In this connection the lease should specifically provide that the leasehold mortgagee shall not be liable for the Lessee's obligations under the lease until it becomes the owner of the lease either by foreclosure or assignment in lieu thereof,[6] or has acquired a new lease as discussed in Part 4 of this paper.

To conclude on the question of assignability, the lease should provide for complete and unrestricted assignability of the lease without the necessity for consent of the Lessor of any kind.[7]

4. NOTICE OF DEFAULT AND NEW LEASE

As stated in the earlier portion of this paper, a basic distinction between a fee mortgage and a leasehold mortgage is that the latter is based on an estate subject to defeasance, whereas the former is not. It is therefore of paramount importance that the lease protect the leasehold mortgagee against the consequences of those events which may give to the Lessor the right to terminate the Lessee's estate. Of all the problems faced in dealing with leasehold mortgages it can be accurately said that this is the most crucial. Unless a lease provides adequate protection against defeasance of the Lessee's estate it is wholly inadequate as security for a leasehold mortgage.[8]

Except through the operation of the power of eminent domain there is no way that the Lessee's estate can be terminated without a default on the part of the Lessee in the performance of its obligations under the lease. All properly drawn leases provide that before a Lessor can terminate a Lessee's estate because of a default, notice or default must be given to the Lessee, who then has an opportunity to cure the default within a specified

---

6. In some states, this exoneration is absolutely essential. See, e.g., Williams v. Safe Deposit & Trust Co., page 1103 infra. — EDS.

7. One writer suggests a plan that would allow the lessor to control the identity of the lessee after a leasehold mortgage default without making the security less valuable for the mortgagee. The mortgagee's freedom to assign, etc., would continue, but the lessor would be given the right, after notice by the mortgagee, either to cure the mortgage default or to purchase the mortgage from the mortgagee, so as to prevent a sale on foreclosure. See Thomas, The Mortgaging of Long-Term Leases, 39 Dicta 363, 376 (1962).

Should unrestricted assignability of the lease also include unrestricted subletting of the premises? Why or why not?

As attorney for the leasehold mortgagee, would you accept a lease provision limiting the use of a building to a high class hotel or office building, or to a concert hall? Would you find acceptable a requirement that the building be managed by persons experienced in managing a high class hotel, office building, etc.? — EDS.

8. More than prudence is involved. Statutes usually require that the leasehold mortgagee be given an adequate chance to take remedial action before the leasehold estate can be forfeited. See, e.g., N.Y. Ins. Law §81-6(a) (McKinney 1966): ". . . provided there is no condition or right of reentry or forfeiture not insured against . . . under which, in the case of leaseholds, the [mortgagee] is unable to continue the lease in force for the duration of the loan." — EDS.

time or at least to commence to cure the default. Unless, however, a leasehold mortgagee has notice that a default has been called on the Lessee, the failure of the Lessee to cure the default and the consequent termination of the Lessee's estate could occur before the leasehold mortgagee was even aware of the existence of the default. It is therefore necessary for the essential protection of the mortgagee, that the mortgagee also receive from the Lessor a notice of any Lessee's default. A lease properly drawn from the mortgagee's point of view will provide that no notice of default given by a Lessor to a Lessee shall be valid for any purpose unless simultaneously with the notice to the Lessee similar notice is given to the mortgagee.

Vital as notice of default undoubtedly is to the mortgagee, it is of little use unless the mortgagee is in a position to cure the default. The lease should therefore provide that the mortgagee is given time in which to cure the default for the account of the Lessee,[9] and that when the mortgagee has performed the obligation, the non-performance of which was the subject of the notice of default, the default shall be deemed cured. This last provision is desirable to forestall an allegation by the Lessor that although action to cure the default was taken, it was not taken by the Lessee who therefore remains in default. Appropriate covenants in the mortgage would provide that all expenses incurred by the mortgagee in curing the Lessee's defaults would be added to the mortgage debt and be secured by the lien of the mortgage.

The right of a leasehold mortgagee to receive notice of default and to cure the default is adequate to protect the leasehold mortgagee against defaults which can be cured by the payment of money or the performance of work, such as repairs, alterations, construction and the like. It is not adequate to protect against defaults which cannot be cured by the payment of money or the performance of work. Many leases provide that the Lessee shall be deemed to be in default if the Lessee becomes a bankrupt, or confesses an inability to pay its debts, or if a receiver is appointed for the Lessee or if any one of a number of similar events shall occur. Against the destruction of the Lessee's estate following such a default the leasehold mortgagee is not protected by a provision for receipt of notice of default and a right to cure, since such a default cannot be cured by payment of money or performance of work or any other act of the mortgagee. It is the view of some counsel for lending institutions that a lease is unacceptable for mortgage lending purposes if it is subject to termination for defaults of

---

9. How much time would the mortgagee need? Consider, for example, the lessee's failure to make repairs or to comply with local building and housing codes. How must the mortgagee proceed before he can begin to perform these and similar lessee's duties?

The following language appears in a lease: "In the event of a default, and the mortgagee's prompt and continuous effort to cure the default, lessor shall not terminate the lease provided all other covenants are performed when due." As the leasehold mortgagee's attorney, what are your objections to this clause? As the lessor's lawyer? — EDS.

the character above mentioned.[10] On the other hand it seems unreasonable to preclude a Lessor from terminating a lease with a bankrupt Lessee and becoming thereby involved in the bankruptcy proceeding through no fault of the Lessor. It has been suggested that one solution to the problem of uncurable defaults is to be found in a lease provision to the effect that despite the bankruptcy of the Lessee the lease cannot be terminated as long as the rent is paid and the other terms of the lease are complied with. Such a provision is acceptable from the point of view of the leasehold mortgagee, as it restores the protection afforded by notice of default and the right to cure. It would appear to be somewhat less satisfactory to the Lessor as it would not free the Lessor from participating in the bankruptcy proceeding.

A generally used device for protecting a leasehold mortgagee against these uncurable defaults is a provision that upon the termination of the Lessee's estate following such a default, the Lessor will enter into a new lease in which the mortgagee or its nominee shall be the lessee. Such a new lease would be for the unexpired portion of the initial or renewal term as the case might be, and would be on the same terms and conditions, including rentals and renewals, as the original lease. Under the operation of such a provision, the mortgagee would be in the same position as if it had foreclosed its mortgage or had acquired the lease by assignment in lieu of foreclosure. Assuming the lease contained appropriate provisions for assignability discussed in Part 3 above, it would be able to realize on the security to the same extent as it could following a mortgage default. It would seem that such a provision would provide adequate protection for the mortgagee and at the same time would be more satisfactory to the Lessor.[11] Obviously, either method of dealing with uncurable defaults is a matter of indifference to the Lessee.

5. SUBORDINATION TO FEE MORTGAGES

Some statutes authorizing leasehold mortgage investments specifically require that the fee estate be not subject to prior liens. Others require that the leasehold estate shall be unencumbered. However, regardless of statu-

---

10. See, e.g., Thomas, The Mortgaging of Long-Term Leases, 39 Dicta 363, 368 (1962). A portion of this article appears at page 1088 infra. — EDS.
11. "The right to obtain a new lease is a fine second string to the bow in case of a slip. [It is not] a proper substitute for the right to prevent the lease from being terminated. There is some doubt as to whether the ability to obtain a new lease is the equivalent of the ability 'to continue the lease in force,' within the meaning of the New York Insurance Law. There are two substantive objections to the mortgagee agreeing in advance to rely for protection solely on a new lease. In the first place, it substitutes for an existing lease a right of action for specific performance of an agreement to give a lease. And the right to enforce such a covenant in the event of bankruptcy of the land is subject to at least the same risk, if not a greater one, as is the right of a tenant to enforce a right to renew the term. . . . Furthermore, we cannot be positive that the new lease will not be subject to liens attaching to the fee subsequent to the original lease." Id.— EDS.

tory provisions, it would appear clear that prudence on the part of the leasehold mortgagee requires either that the fee estate be unencumbered or that any encumbrances thereon be subordinated to the estate created by the lease.

It is certainly arguable that a fee mortgage is not an encumbrance on a leasehold estate, even where the lease is subordinated to the lien of the fee mortgage. However, regardless of the technical validity of this argument, the fact remains that where a fee mortgage is prior in lien to the leasehold estate, the latter can be cut off by a foreclosure of the former, and no provision of the lease or the leasehold mortgage can protect the leasehold mortgagee from the complete destruction of its security under such circumstances.

It is therefore of prime importance that the lease should in fact be prior to any fee mortgage on the premises at the time of the making of the lease or thereafter placed upon the premises. It is good practice for the lease to provide for such superiority in haec verba, thus giving notice to all subsequent encumbrancers and lienors. In this connection it seems superfluous to state that in all cases involving leasehold mortgages the lease should be recorded in the appropriate recording office.[12]

Many leases are submitted which contain provisions directly to the contrary of the foregoing. They provide for the complete subordination of the lease to any and all fee mortgages now or hereafter placed against the premises. Such leases are wholly unacceptable from the point of view of the leasehold mortgagee for the reasons stated above.

A variation of the complete subordination to fee mortgages discussed in the immediately preceding paragraph is the so-called "nondisturbance clause," pursuant to which a fee mortgagee agrees that so long as the Lessee is not in default under the lease the Lessee's possession will not be disturbed in the event of a foreclosure of the fee mortgage. On the surface this might seem an answer to the problems raised by a complete subordination of the lease to fee mortgages. Upon reflection, however, it is obvious that it deals solely with the question of possession, and leaves the Lessee in all other respects in a position inferior to the fee mortgagee. For instance, such a position would leave the Lessee and its leasehold mortgagee in a subordinate position in relation to the proceeds of fire insurance and condemnation awards, to give only two important examples of the inadequacy of such a provision from the point of view of the leasehold mortgagee.

In conclusion, regardless of statutory requirements, prudence requires that a lease securing a leasehold mortgage be superior in all respects to all fee mortgages placed upon the premises at any time, and to all other title conditions pursuant to which the leasehold estate could

---

12. Should a leasehold mortgage be recorded as a real property or a chattel mortgage? See, e.g., Harbel Oil Co. v. Steele, 83 Ariz. 181, 318 P.2d 359 (1957), page 262 supra. — EDS.

be cut off in any way, by reverter, reversion, termination of a life estate or otherwise.[13]

6. INSURANCE

Except for the question of disposition of condemnation awards, there is probably no subject more discussed in the negotiation of a lease than the question of disposition of hazard insurance proceeds. However, the basic needs of the leasehold mortgagee are simple. It wants to be a named insured on the hazard insurance policies pursuant to a standard mortgagee clause, to have all losses payable to it and to have the option to apply the insurance proceeds on the mortgage debt or to the restoration of the premises. However, insistence on having all these rights will undoubtedly result in a collapse of the proposed transaction, as parts of such provisions are entirely unacceptable to the Lessor and the Lessee. Both Lessor and Lessee desire to make certain that the proceeds of insurance are available for the restoration of the premises and can be readily obtained as the work of restoration progresses. The possibility that the insurance proceeds would be applied on the mortgage debt would be wholly unacceptable to the Lessor and in all probability, only slightly less unacceptable to the Lessee.

From the point of view of the leasehold mortgagee, adequate protection is afforded under lease provisions requiring that the mortgagee be insured under a standard mortgagee clause, with loss payable to the mortgagee so long as the mortgage is held by a lending institution, otherwise to an insurance trustee such as a bank or trust company, the loss proceeds to be paid out as the work of restoration progresses upon production of appropriate architects' certificates, with such provisions for hold-backs before final disbursement as the parties might agree upon. The lease should also provide that the mortgagee has the right to participate in the adjustment of losses.

7. CONDEMNATION

Another fruitful source of protracted negotiation is the subject of the taking of all or a part of the demised premises as a result of the exercise of eminent domain. Here we deal with three situations: a total taking, a partial taking and a use taking.[14]

The last mentioned, a taking of the use of the premises without vesting

---

13. Sometimes an existing fee mortgage must be subordinated to a subsequently executed lease. In that event, the mortgagee may be able to drive a bargain. What should he ask for? See American Bar Association Committee on Leases, Ground Leases and Their Financing, 4 Real Prop. Prob. & Tr. J. 437, 440 (1969). — EDS.

14. For an instance of a use taking that caused a landlord and tenant row, see Leonard v. Autocar Sales & Service Co., 392 Ill. 182, 64 N.E.2d 477 (1945), *cert. denied,* 327 U.S. 804 (1946). — EDS.

of title in the condemning authority, ordinarily would present no problem to a leasehold mortgagee. Presumably the condemnor would pay the condemnation award in installments similar to rent, the debt service would be met from these payments and the mortgagee would be unaffected.

On the other hand, a leasehold mortgagee will be vitally interested in being protected against a total or partial taking which vests title in the condemnor. In the case of a total taking, or a partial taking which leaves the premises so damaged that it cannot be restored, a proper lease will provide that the leasehold mortgagee is the first to be paid out of that portion of the award which represents the value of the improvements erected on the premises. Such a provision is adequate in a situation where the Lessee has constructed the improvement, as is often the case, but it is somewhat less than realistic when the lease relates to an existing building owned in fee by the Lessor. In such a case that portion of the award representing the value of the Lessee's estate should be made available for payment of the leasehold mortgage and provision should be made for methods of determining the value of the Lessee's estate in the event that the award is silent on this subject.

Where a lease is not terminated by a partial taking, it is apparent that all parties (except perhaps the leasehold mortgagee) will wish to have the condemnation proceeds applied to the restoration of the premises. Lease provisions for this purpose resemble those discussed above relating to the use of proceeds of hazard insurance under analogous circumstances.

To assure the mortgagee of proper protection in the condemnation proceedings, the lease should provide that the leasehold mortgagee is expressly authorized to participate in the condemnation proceeding.

8. Sub-Leases

Except in the unusual circumstance of a Lessee being itself the sole occupant of the demised premises and paying the debt service as an expense of its business, the funds for payment of principal and interest on the leasehold mortgage will be derived from rentals paid by sub-tenants occupying space in the demised premises pursuant to sub-leases in which the Lessee is the landlord. The leasehold mortgagee, as would a fee mortgagee in an analogous situation, will insist upon the sub-tenant's being of good credit rating and in all respects suitable occupants of the property. It will also insist that all sub-leases be approved by the mortgagee as to rent, term and the provisions of the lease.

Since the source of funds for the liquidation of its investment will be rentals under the sub-lease, the mortgagee will wish to be certain that the covenants of the sub-lease will not be changed, that the term of the sub-lease will not be reduced, that there will be no prepayment of rent nor a surrender of the sub-lease without the consent of the leasehold mortgagee. Some counsel for lenders are of the opinion that protection against these contingencies is obtained by the assignment to the leasehold mortgagee of the Lessee's interest as landlord under the sub-lease. It is the opinion of the writer, however, that unless following such an assignment the subrentals are paid directly to the mortgagee prior to default, the assignment is not effective to protect the mortgagee against sub-lease modifications and similar transactions between the Lessee and its sub-tenants.

It is the opinion of the writer that in order to protect a leasehold mortgagee against the modification of sub-leases without the lender's consent, the ground lease should contain a covenant to the effect that all sub-leases will specifically provide that they cannot, without the consent of the leasehold mortgagee, be modified so as to reduce the rent, change renewal privileges, shorten the term or provide for pre-payment of rent, and that any such modification without the consent of the mortgagee shall be void as against the mortgagee. It is believed that such a provision will go far to assure the mortgagee that when it takes over the property following default, it will find in effect the same sub-leases on which it relied in making the loan in the first place.

Another problem in connection with sub-leases relates to attornment by sub-tenants in the event of a termination of the ground lease for a noncurable default and the issuance to the lender of a new lease under the circumstance discussed in Part 4 above. Since the estate created by the sub-lease stems from the leasehold estate of the Lessee under the ground lease, it is apparent that following a termination of the ground lease the estates created by sub-leases would be cut off, and the obligations of the sub-tenants to stay in possession and pay rent would cease. In order that the leasehold mortgagee may be protected against a loss of rental income after it has signed its new lease, the ground lease should contain a covenant requiring that all sub-leases must contain an agreement by the sub-tenant to attorn to the leasehold mortgagee if it becomes the holder of a new ground lease. Proper protection for the sub-tenants would be provided by a reciprocal clause to the effect that the leasehold mortgagee would accept the attornment and recognize the continued existence of the sub-lease.

American Bar Association Committee on Leases, Ground Leases and Their Financing[15]

4 Real Prop. Prob. and Tr. J. 437, 440-449 (1969)

II. Right of Tenant to Mortgage Fee; Subordination of Landlord's Fee Title to Mortgage Executed by Tenant

Securing a loan on a leasehold is much more difficult than where the property is owned in fee simple by the tenant who plans to erect improvements on the property. At the time the lease is executed, the tenant has

---

15. Some footnotes have been omitted.

little or no equity on which to borrow. Presumably the rental agreed upon is of such an amount, as capitalized, as equals the value of the leased land. Only after a lapse of time, during which the land may increase in value, can the tenant hope to have an equity in the property.

Assuming that the tenant contemplates a needed and logical real estate development and his primary motive is not pure speculation, landlords frequently will agree to subordinate their fee title to a mortgage to be secured by the tenant.

A. ADVANTAGES TO TENANT

. . . Advantages to the tenant that may result from the landlord subordinating his fee to a mortgage are: (1) the greatly increased amount of financing available for a project based on the fact that the underwriting approach by the mortgage is almost the same as to a fee mortgage;[16] (2) the amount of equity capital required for the project is greatly reduced and possibly eliminated as a result of the increased financing available;[17] . . .

C. DISADVANTAGES TO LANDLORD

The disadvantages to the landlord of subordinating his fee are numerous and certainly entitle him to a higher rent than if he did not subordinate. A close evaluation of the situation would normally lead the well informed landlord to demand either an equity participation in the profits or the cash flow of the project in return for his agreement to subordinate his fee, or a percentage rental feature of some type. In today's economy with a rapid state of inflation, the landlord is shortsighted to execute a long term lease at a flat rental which includes the subordination of his fee to a mortgage. Even the inclusion of periodic readjustments of the rent on a ten or 15-year basis today appears to be inadequate protection against inflation.

While the normal standards of the rental of a net lease still are 6 percent to 8 percent of market value, the landlord, like the mortgagee of today,[23] should demand and receive an equity participation in return for subordination. The risk of losing his fee far outweighs the 1 percent or 2 percent additional per year that he will receive for a subordinated lease over an

---

16. Hopkins, Investing in Leasehold Mortgages, XIX Proc. Assn. Life Ins. Counsel 493 (1964); Johnson, Security in Subordination, Nat'l Assn. Real Estate Brokers 16 (1965); see Matthews v. Hinton, 234 Cal. App. 2d 736, 741, 44 Cal. Rptr. 692 (1965).

17. For example, let it be assumed that the leased land is worth $200,000, for which the tenant pays a rental of $16,000 annually, which is on an 8 percent basis. Plans are made for the erection of a $300,000 building on the land, but the tenant only has $75,000 to put into the erection of the building. It is necessary that the tenant secure a loan of not less than $225,000, which can be obtained because the combined land, valued at $200,000, and the building, to cost $300,000, have a total value of $500,000.

23. Gunning and Roegge, Contemporary Real Estate Financing Techniques, 3 Real Prop. Prob. & Tr. J. 325, 327 (1968).

unsubordinated lease. He is pledging his interest in the land as security for a tenant's mortgage and certainly must protect himself in a lease against any diversion of the loan proceeds. The lease is usually made after the proposed tenant has presented a project and a planned specific use. Certainly it would be carelessness on the part of the landlord to agree to subordinate his fee without knowing in great detail the type of project being undertaken.

An exception to this requirement would perhaps lie in the case of a financially strong tenant. However, such a tenant would probably be able to obtain sufficient financing without the necessity of subordination of the fee. The landlord should be satisfied that the lease contains specific requirements for the amount of the loan, purpose of the loan, terms of the loan and exact use of the proceeds.[24] Failure of the tenant to complete the project leaves the landlord in a difficult position, as he will then be required to step in and complete it himself in order to save his reversionary interest.

The landlord may not wish to be placed in the position of having to proceed with the completion of construction, especially if there has been a change in the economic outlook between the time of the execution of the lease and the time when the problem arises. A partially finished building may also lead to problems in regard to mechanics' liens.

D. REQUIREMENTS IN LEASES

A clause in a lease providing for subordination of the fee has been rare, but since the post-World War II building boom, people have awakened to the potentialities of such a financing device; hence its increased use. In spite of the disadvantages to the landlord fee owner, a great number of landlords, for a variety of reasons, find it to their advantage to grant their tenants the power to mortgage the fee. This may be done to obtain higher rental, participation in the tenant's cash flow, concessions in other lease clauses or benefits to adjoining property owned by the landlord.

Two basic types of lease clauses can be used to subordinate the fee — a covenant by the landlord to join in a mortgage of the fee[26] or a power of attorney to the tenant to execute a mortgage on the fee. In addition, where the tenant demands subordination of the landlord's fee title to an existing mortgage of the leasehold estate, a subordination agreement similar to

---

24. In the absence of a restriction on the use of the loan proceeds by the tenant, the landlord has no legal complaint if the loan proceeds are not used to improve the property. Matthews v. Hinton, 234 Cal. App. 2d 736, 44 Cal. Rptr. 692 (1965).

26. . . . It has been stated that this is "the only way in which the result can be accomplished." Schurch, Subordination Agreements and Partial Release Clauses, California Land Security and Development §5.22, p. 140 (1960). However, in Cambridge Accept. Corp. v. American Nat'l Motor Inns, 96 N.J. Super. 183, 232 A.2d 692 (1967), *aff'd sub nom.* Cambridge Accept. Corp. v. Hockstein, 102 N.J. Super. 426, 246 A.2d 138 (App. Div. 1968), the court recognized an automatic subordination contained in the lease.

those used to subordinate one mortgage to another may be executed by the landlord. If the covenant to join is used, it is contemplated that the landlord will himself execute the mortgage to the mortgagee. The landlord need not sign the note and thus subject himself to personal liability on the obligation. If the power of attorney is used, it is contemplated that the tenant shall have full power to mortgage the fee without execution by the landlord.

Regardless of which type of clause is used, several legal difficulties must be considered by a prudent tenant and a prudent landlord:

1. Tenant's Considerations

It is essential that the clause satisfy the requirements for effective execution of both the state in which the land is located and the state in which the lease is executed. No particular difficulty is presented with the execution of a joinder clause; it will be a valid covenant if executed in the manner required for the execution of the lease as a whole — that is, in writing and signed by the parties.[28]

The clause should be certain with respect to the amount of the loan, interest rate, points, term, manner of repayment, source of the loan funds and ultimate use of the proceeds of the loan.[29]

If the clause is sufficiently certain that the landlord is bound to join in the execution of the mortgage on the fee, such clause will bind the heirs, divisees and assigns of the landlord if it is a real covenant which runs with the land rather than a purely personal covenant on the part of the landlord. No direct authority has been found to the effect that such a covenant is real and runs with the land; however, covenants to execute a mortgage have been enforced against successors with notice.[30]

A well drafted subordination agreement should apply to any interim or temporary construction financing, one or more so-called permanent loans and any refinancing. This, of course, favors the tenant, and it is possible that the parties would agree that there be subordination only to one long-

---

28. Care must be taken to see that statutory or other requirements for a valid power of attorney are complied with. In California, for example, a power of attorney to execute a mortgage must be in writing, subscribed, acknowledged, or proved, certified, and recorded. Cal. Civ. Code §§1213, 1215, 2933 (1872).

29. . . . An agreement by the landlord to subordinate his fee title to permit the tenant "to obtain financing" is too uncertain for enforcement. Lahaina-Mani Corporation v. Tau Tet Hew, 362 F.2d 449 (9th Cir. 1966). The court held that since the lease might be executed at an early state and prior to the negotiation of the proposed loan, the clause necessarily cannot specify all the details of the proposed loan, but the clause should specify at least the maximum amount of the proposed loan and the maximum rate of interest.

30. 4 Pomeroy, Equity Jurisdiction §1235 (5th ed. Symons). For a discussion of the problem without citation of authority, see Johnson, op. cit. supra note 16, at 17. It is suggested that the covenant does affect the title and interest of both the covenantor and covenantee as to enable the latter to offer more attractive security to a prospective mortgagee. In Sacramento S.F.L. Co. v. Whaley, 50 Cal. App. 125, 194 P. 1054 (1920), for example, a provision in a mortgage providing for partial releases of parcels was held to run with the land.

term permanent loan, leaving the tenant to obtain the interim construction loan on the strength of either his own credit or that of his subtenants. Refinancing may involve a recasting of the leasehold mortgage, or may apply to financing done subsequent to the repayment of the original long-term mortgage, and it may be a replacement of this long-term mortgage, a renewal of it or may apply to subsequent construction.

For example: a 99-year lease may have three 30-year long-term loans covering perhaps even three structures, the second and third replacing the first improvements made to the property. The tenant taking a long-term lease needs great flexibility because he really cannot determine at the time of the execution of the lease the best use to which the property can be put for the entire term of the lease and any renewal periods. The landlord may not wish to agree to an unlimited time and number of mortgages. There is great difficulty in trying to project the possible uses to which property may be best put and the cost of such a use in the future. Thus it would be most difficult to circumscribe the limits and terms of any refinancing. There is also the reasonable view that by the time the first mortgage has been retired, the value of the land should have increased to the point that subordination of the fee is not necessary to secure adequate refinancing.

2. *Landlord's Considerations*

A lease is usually subordinated to a mortgage in the case of undeveloped land where the tenant plans to make substantial improvements and probably lease the then transformed and improved property to one or more subtenants . . .

In order to minimize the danger of losing his fee through a foreclosure of a leasehold mortgage, the prudent landlord wishes to protect himself and to see that the proceeds of any leasehold mortgage will be used for construction purposes or the purposes for which they were intended. With so many mortgage loans today relying solely on the value of the land, improvements and leases as collateral, and not requiring any personal liability on the part of the mortgagor, the danger of foreclosure can be real, especially when one adds to the situation the possibility or probability that the tenant is a dummy or shell corporation or a similar type nominee.[32]

The lease, or more specifically the clause therein relating to the agreement by the landlord to subordinate his fee, should be very precise in its discussion of the type and amount of loan and mortgage to which the landlord is willing to subordinate. Such things as maximum principal, interest rate and term (minimum and maximum) and mode of repayment

---

32. This was the case in Cambridge Accept. Corp. v. American Nat'l Motor Inns, 96 N.J. Super. 183, 232 A.2d 692 (1967), *aff'd sub nom.* Cambridge Accept. Corp. v. Hockstein, 102 N.J. Super. 426, 246 A.2d 138 (App. Div. 1968), which involved an example of the type of financing and arrangements proposed for a motel lease where the property was never improved and the tenant became bankrupt.

and the amount of fees permitted are usually covered. The amount of the loan obviously should relate to the improvements planned to be created and should not provide for over-financing, leaving the tenant with tax free cash in hand and possibly the landlord with a burdensome obligation, which he must either meet or suffer the loss of his equity.[34]

It is obvious that the landlord should look realistically at the economics of the planned improvements and determine to his own satisfaction that the amount of the loan relates to the cost of improvements and that such improvements will generate enough cash flow in the hands of the tenant to meet the rental payments under the lease, the debt service of the mortgage, taxes, insurance, maintenance and a reasonable return to the tenant. [Since landlords have been held bound by their subordination agreements even if the proceeds of a construction loan have been used for purposes other than the cost of construction],[36] his documentation should be very specific as to the proposed use of the loan proceeds and, if possible, he should require and try to obtain from the interim lender at least (if he is agreeing to subordinate to such a loan) an agreement as to how and when the funds will be disbursed.

The type of mortgage permitted may also be of importance to the landlord. An institutional lender such as a bank or insurance company might be slower to foreclose such a mortgage then another type of lender. The old definition of an institutional lender which customarily included banks and insurance companies should be broadened here to cover union and management pension and welfare funds as well as charitable foundations, as these lenders are becoming increasingly active in this type of loan.

The prudent landlord should also insist upon a provision in the lease that, if the tenant is not able to obtain a commitment for interim financing and permanent financing within a specified period of time, the lease shall terminate unless the tenant is financially responsible. The exposure of the landlord should thus be kept to a minimum. . . .

Among the title problems to be faced are the desire on the part of any lender to know that he has a first mortgage on the fee as well as the leasehold and to have it insured as a first mortgage, and the fear on the part

---

34. Joanaco Projects, Inc. v. Nixon & Tierney Constr. Co., 248 Cal. App. 2d 821, 57 Cal. Rptr. 48 (1967).

36. Matthews v. Hinton, 234 Cal. App. 2d 736, 44 Cal. Rptr. 692 (1965); Gill v. Mission Sav. & Loan Assn., 236 Cal. App. 2d 753, 46 Cal. Rptr. 456 (1965). In the absence of language impliedly or expressly restricting the use of loan proceeds, the landlord has no cause of complaint if the proceeds are used for something other than the improvement of the property. Matthews v. Hinton, supra. . . .

If an interim or construction mortgagee fails to administer the loan in the conventional manner of a construction loan . . . or fails to comply with the conditions of the subordination agreement, the mortgagee will lose his priority. Collins v. Home Sav. & Loan Ass'n, 205 Cal. App. 2d 86, 22 Cal. Rptr. 817 (1962); Miller v. Citizens Sav. & Loan Ass'n, 248 Cal. App. 2d 655, 56 Cal. Rptr. 844 (1967), where the mortgagee lost its priority for that portion of the loan not used for construction purposes. See 2 Miller & Starr, Current Law of California Real Estate 103 (1968).

of the lender's attorney or title insurer that perhaps the courts will upset the validity of the first mortgage on the fee and in effect revoke the subordination agreement because of a failure on the part of the borrower to comply with the stated intent of the loan.[41]

F. MANNER OF SUBORDINATION; EXAMPLES OF EACH

Once the landlord has agreed to subordinate, the question arises as to the type of clause or documentation necessary to effect such subordination. Obviously the joinder by the landlord in the execution of the note and mortgage is the simplest and most effective. Needless to say, the joinder by the landlord in any note and mortgage should, by his request, be limited to the mortgaging of his fee and eliminating any personal liability on his part for any deficiency and for any violations of the mortgage causing a default. One way of handling the problem is for the landlord to execute a separate agreement in recordable form, subordinating his fee to the mortgage. Another manner of effecting the subordination is by means of a power of attorney granted to the tenant by the landlord, giving him the authority and power to execute a mortgage on the fee. This method requires exact compliance with the local formalities for the valid execution of a power of attorney and serious questions can still be raised as to whether or not such a power is valid in the event of the death, disability, bankruptcy, etc., of the landlord between the time of the execution of the power and the execution of the mortgage. Title under exercise of powers may not be sufficiently clear of record for the lender's attorney or title insurer to be willing to accept it without joinder by the landlord in the mortgage.

The power of attorney executed by the landlord should state that it is irrevocable and would be so declared only if it can be considered as one coupled with an interest.[46] There are those who believe that the interest of a tenant in a long term lease is a sufficient interest to render a power to mortgage a fee irrevocable during the term of the lease.[47] Nevertheless, the loan will not be made unless the lender's attorney or title insurer is sufficiently satisfied with the record evidence of valid exercise of the power.

Most of the litigation concerning subordination provisions and whether or not the self-executing provision is valid has involved not leasehold mortgages, but cases where a seller retained a purchase money mortgage and further agreed to subordinate to a construction loan. This manner of financing is quite common in California. Self-executing clauses do not

---

41. Cambridge Accept. Corp. v. American Nat'l Motor Inns, Inc., 96 N.J. Super. 183, 232 A.2d 692 (1967), *aff'd sub nom.* Cambridge Accept. Corp. v. Hockstein, 102 N.J. Super, 426, 246 A.2d 138 (App. Div. 1968). The practical aspects of a transaction are shown in Butcher v. Dauz, 257 Cal. App. 2d 524, 65 Cal. Rptr. 166 (1967).
46. 2 C.J.S. Agency §86, p. 1175.
47. Johnson, op. cit. supra note 16.

appear to be in favor with either lenders or title companies. It must be remembered, however, in considering the California situations that subordination agreements in that state are now regulated, at least in part, by statute.[50]

One of the biggest problems that can arise is the situation where the lease contains an agreement on the part of the landlord to subordinate and where the landlord subsequently refuses to join in either the note, mortgage or other agreement. The question is then whether or not the tenant can obtain specific performance of that agreement. It is submitted that if the subordination agreement contained in the lease is specific in its requirements as to those items of the loan such as interest rate, term, manner of payment, source and use of proceeds and if the proposed loan complies with these requirements, specific performance would probably be ordered and against successors with notice. The discussion of this question has been concerned for the most part with the subordination agreements on the part of a seller in regard to subordinating his purchase money mortgage to a loan made for construction purposes on the property.[54] In order for the tenant to obtain specific performance it is clear that the terms and conditions of the proposed loan must be specified with exceptional certainty.[55]

Thomas, The Mortgaging of Long-Term Leases[16]
39 Dicta 363, 379-382 (1962)

III. THE MORTGAGE

Once the provisions of the lease have been satisfactorily resolved, the drafting of the mortgage will be comparatively easy, almost anti-climactic. Speaking generally, most of the standard provisions of a fee mortgage should be found in a leasehold mortgage with little or no change. There are, however, a number of provisions which must be added to a leasehold mortgage. Most of them will be fairly obvious. Few should cause much argument by borrower's counsel. The landlord, of course, has no direct concern with the terms of the mortgage — unless he has agreed to join it. It is considered prudent practice, however, to require the landlord to agree to recognize any authorization granted by the tenant mortgagor to the mortgagee to exercise tenant's rights under the lease. The more common of the distinctive leasehold mortgage provisions in addition to the difference in description, are summarized in the following paragraphs.

---

50. Cal. Civ. Code §§2953.1, 2953.2.
54. Subordination of Purchase Money Security, 52 Calif. L. Rev. 157 (1964).
55. Miller, Starr & Regalia, Subordination Agreements in California, 13 U.C.L.A. L. Rev. 1298, 1302 (1966). . . .
16. Footnotes have been omitted. — EDS.

The Ground Lease

A. *Conformity with Lease Requirements.* — The mortgage itself may not contain provisions inconsistent with those of the lease. Of frequent consideration in this area are the use of proceeds of fire insurance or of an award for a taking in condemnation. However, the mortgage may impose additional obligations on the borrower-tenant if the lease seems inadequate. An example would be a requirement that the tenant furnish additional insurance policies with a standard mortgagee clause, if the lease did not permit one on policies to be furnished the landlord. If the age of the building is such that ordinary insurance might be substantially inadequate to effect the restoration required by the lease, the mortgage should require the tenant to carry insurance on a replacement basis to cover physical depreciation. If the lease does not provide for a rental abatement while damage is being restored, the ability of the tenant to continue to pay the rent and other lease charges should be assured by the mortgage requiring the tenant to maintain rent insurance or business interruption insurance.

B. *Tenant to Comply with Lease.* — The mortgage will require the tenant to agree expressly to perform or comply with all of the covenants of the tenant to be performed under the lease. The lease will have provided for a notice by the landlord to the mortgagee of any default under the lease which could form a basis for termination. If there are other possible notices from the landlord of which the mortgagee wishes to learn, the mortgage may provide that copies be sent by the tenant to the mortgagee. In addition, if the lease clauses are considered inadequate, the mortgage may require the tenant to furnish evidence of payment of ground rent, taxes, etc., before any grace period given in the lease has expired. The mortgage should expressly provide that the failure of the tenant to perform and subsequent performance by the mortgagee will not remove the default as between tenant and mortgagee but that until the tenant shall have reimbursed the mortgagee for the cost of performance, the mortgagee will have the right to accelerate and add the cost to the mortgage debt.

C. *Shortening of Tenant's Grace Period under the Lease.* — Depending upon the provisions in the lease which require the landlord to give the mortgagee notice of the tenant's defaults and the opportunity to cure them, the mortgage may require the tenant to cure any such defaults within a shorter period than that permitted the mortgagee, so that the mortgagee will have time within which to cure if the tenant does not.

D. *Prohibition of Lease Modification or Termination.* — The mortgage will, of course, prohibit the tenant from agreeing to any modification or termination or surrender of the lease without the mortgagee's consent. Notifying the landlord of the existence of the mortgage may be sufficient to prevent the landlord from agreeing to any such modification, termination or surrender, but an express agreement by the landlord is more satisfactory. Incidentally, the lease will probably require the tenant to notify the landlord of any leasehold mortgage and the mortgage will require the tenant to give such notice. The mortgagee should nevertheless be satisfied beyond question that the notice has been given.

E. *Control of Arbitration.* — If the lease provides for arbitration in any particular aspect, the mortgagee may require the tenant to authorize the mortgagee to represent the tenant in certain areas of arbitration or in certain circumstances. Again, it would be well to have the landlord agree to recognize such authorization.

F. *Control of Renewal of Term.* — If the tenant has the right to renew the lease, the mortgagee should be authorized to renew on behalf of, and in the name of, the tenant if the tenant fails to renew at any time when the security of the mortgage would be jeopardized by such failure. Again, the landlord should recognize such authorization or it should be clear, as a matter of law, that the landlord cannot refuse to recognize the authorization.

G. *Fee Interest Acquired by Tenant to Be Subject to Mortgage.* — Any purchase option in the tenant should be covered by the mortgage expressly and although it would be an unusual situation in which the mortgagee would be justified in insisting that the tenant exercise such an option, it should continue with the lease in the event of foreclosure. In any event, the mortgage should provide that if the tenant should acquire the fee of all or any portion of the leased property whether by exercise of a purchase option or otherwise, the fee would immediately become subject to the mortgage and the mortgagor would execute whatever confirmatory instrument might be required. However, provision should be made to prevent a merger of the lease in the fee if, under state law, the consequent disappearance of the lease would permit valued subtenants to effectively claim that the sublease falls with the disappearance of the primary lease.

H. *Subleases.* — In a majority of large real estate financings the terms of occupancy and the financial responsibility of the occupying tenants are of primary importance, whether the property be an office building, a shopping center, a department store or a post office. We are here concerned, however, only with the aspects of such leasing as may peculiarly relate to leasehold financing. In this context, the occupancy leases are subleases.

First, it should be apparent that the subleases must be integrated with the primary lease and that no rights can be granted the subtenants more extensive than those granted under the primary lease. Indeed, it is not uncommon for the sublease to contain an express stipulation to that effect.

In the second place, if the primary lease provides for a new lease to the mortgagee in the event of termination of the primary lease, . . . any sublease considered valuable by the mortgagee must contain a covenant by the subtenant to attorn to the lessee under any such new lease. Otherwise the subtenant may effectively claim that the sublease and his obligations thereunder fall with the termination of the primary lease. As a matter of fact, a subtenant of a large amount of space may well require the overlandlord to agree that if the lease is terminated and the mortgagee does not obtain a new lease, either the subtenant may obtain a new lease on the same terms as the primary lease or the overlandlord will recognize the continu-

The Ground Lease

ance of the sublease as a direct lease from the overlandlord. Careful drafting will provide for such recognition by the overlandlord during the period in which the mortgagee is making up his mind whether or not to take a new lease.

An ABA group, the Subcommittee on Leasehold Encumbrances, of the Committee on Leasing, Real Property Division, has issued a Report that contains "model" leasehold encumbrance protective provisions for use in long-term leases. The Report at page 399 speaks of these provisions as reflecting an attempt "to fine tune the balancing of the interests of the landlord and of the leasehold lender."

The Subcommittee devoted special attention to the matter of the tenant's non-curable default:

> In addition to the many areas considered, special consideration was given to the desirability of "New Lease" provisions which require a fee owner to enter into a New Lease with the leasehold mortgagee at such mortgagee's request in the event of a termination of the leasehold. The use of the New Lease provisions which have been added as subsection (h) to these model provisions is elective. The use of such provisions is sufficiently well established in practice to warrant their use although dependence by the mortgagee upon the availability of a New Lease may be dangerous. One must consider the possibility of intervening third party rights and of whether the obligation to enter into the New Lease would be effected by proceedings under the Bankruptcy Code involving the lessor. . . . The tenant should seek to modify the renewal provisions of the lease to permit the leasehold mortgagee to exercise renewal options if the lessee fails to do so. . . .
>
> **(h) New Lease,** *(Optional Provision)*
> In the event of the termination of this Lease as a result of Tenant's default Landlord shall, in addition to providing the notices of default and termination as required by subsections (e) and (f) above of this section [Insert section number of lease], provide each Leasehold Mortgagee with written notice that the Lease has been terminated, together with a statement of all sums which would at that time be due under this Lease but for such termination, and of all other defaults, if any, then known to Landlord. Landlord agrees to enter into a new lease ("New Lease") of the Demised Premises with such Leasehold Mortgagee or its designee for the remainder of the term of this Lease, effective as of the date of termination, at the rent and additional rent, and upon the terms, covenants and conditions (including all options to renew but excluding requirements which are not applicable or which have already been fulfilled) of this Lease, provided:
>
> (i) Such Leasehold Mortgagee shall make written request upon Landlord for such New Lease within 60 days after the date such Leasehold Mortgagee receives Landlord's Notice of Termination of this Lease given pursuant to this subsection (h).
>
> (ii) Such Leasehold Mortgagee or its designee shall pay or cause to be paid to Landlord at the time of the execution and delivery of such New

Lease, any and all sums which would at the time of execution and delivery thereof be due pursuant to this Lease but for such termination and, in addition thereto, all reasonable expenses, including reasonable attorney's fees, which Landlord shall have incurred by reason of such termination and the execution and delivery of the New Lease and which have not otherwise been received by Landlord from Tenant or other party in interest under Tenant. Upon the execution of such New Lease, Landlord shall allow to the Tenant named therein as an offset against the sums otherwise due under this subsection (h)(ii) or under the New Lease, an amount equal to the net income derived by Landlord from the Demised Premises during the period from the date of termination of this Lease to the date of the beginning of the Lease term of such New Lease. In the event of a controversy as to the amount to be paid to Landlord pursuant to this subsection (h)(ii), the payment obligation shall be satisfied if Landlord shall be paid the amount not in controversy, and the Leasehold Mortgagee or its designee shall agree to pay any additional sum ultimately determined to be due plus interest [at the rate of 8 percent per annum] and such obligation shall be adequately secured.

(iii) Such Leasehold Mortgagee or its designee shall agree to remedy any of Tenant's defaults of which said Leasehold Mortgagee was notified by Landlord's Notice of Termination and which are reasonably susceptible of being so cured by Leasehold Mortgagee or its designee.

(iv) Any New Lease made pursuant to this subsection (h) and any renewal Lease entered into with a Leasehold Mortgagee pursuant to section [Insert section number of lease], hereof shall be prior to any mortgage or other lien, charge or encumbrance on the fee of the Demised Premises and the Tenant under such New Lease shall have the same right, title and interest in and to the Demised Premises and the buildings and improvements thereon as Tenant had under this Lease.

(v) The Tenant under any such New Lease shall be liable to perform the obligations imposed on the Tenant by such New Lease only during the period such person has ownership of such Leasehold Estate.

15 Real Prop. Prob. and Tr. J. 395, 399, 406-408 (1980).

Levitan, Leasehold Mortgage Financing: Reliance on the "New Lease" Provision
15 Real Prop. Prob. and Tr. J. 413 (1980)

I. INTRODUCTION

In discussing the difference between a fee mortgage and a leasehold mortgage,[1] one respected authority has stated that:

> 1. For purposes of this article, the leasehold mortgage considered would involve a ground lease to the borrower as lessee, with the leasehold mortgagee providing the permanent loan for the improvements which are made to the leasehold estate. The interests of the ground landlord are prior to the leasehold mortgage, and thus a termination of the ground lease for any reason would destroy the security for the leasehold mortgage.

The Ground Lease

A mortgage on a lease, on the other hand, is like a mortgage on a balloon. Prick it and it's gone.[2]

The basic problem in protecting the leasehold mortgagee is to keep the mortgaged lease in existence so that the lender may at all times be assured of the security for its loan.[3] The result of this effort is a ground lease with sufficient leasehold mortgage protective provisions to give the leasehold mortgagee the ability to cure defaults under the lease in all instances thereby making the lease virtually nonterminable by the landlord (the fee owner).[4] The preceding committee report in this volume provides an in-depth analysis of those provisions that are needed in a ground lease to make it "financeable," not only at the origin of the transaction, but, as importantly, when the parties desire a refinancing.[5] The committee report contains revised Model Leasehold Provisions[6] which now contain a "New Lease Provision" for use on an elective basis.[7] The committee report goes on to warn that although such a provision is commonly included in drafting the "financeable" ground lease, dependence on its enforceability "may be dangerous."[8]

The purpose of this article is to explore in greater detail the nature of the New Lease provision in a ground lease in terms of its reliability as a method of protecting the leasehold mortgagee. The conclusion reached is that, unfortunately, once the "balloon" has been pricked it is not likely that it can be resuscitated. . . .

The New Lease provision on its face appears to provide a simple and absolute solution for the leasehold mortgagee's legitimate security needs.[21] However, this solution is deceptive in its simplicity, and, as we will show, is basically an unreliable method of protecting the leasehold mortgagee.[22] The problems created by this provision stem from the difficulty of characterizing the nature of this "right" granted to the leasehold mortgagee, and, further, of the legal consequences both in terms of enforceability and basic validity, which would flow from each of the different characterizations.

---

2. Friedman, Friedman on Leases 262 (2d ed. 1978).
3. Id.
4. Shea, Leasehold Mortgage Financing, II ALI-ABA Resource Materials: Modern Real Estate Transactions 629, 630 (2d ed. 1976).
5. Subcommittee on Leasehold Encumbrances, Committee on Leasing, ABA Real Property, Probate & Trust Law Section, Model Leasehold Encumbrance Provisions, 15 Real Prop., Prob. & Tr. J. 395 (1980) (hereinafter cited as Committee Report).
6. Id. at 399 et seq., note 9.
7. Id. at 406-08.
8. Id. at 399 and 406, note 26.
21. Friedman, supra note 2, at 269.
22. Id. at 269, see also Committee Report at 406, note 26.

III. VALIDITY OF THE NEW LEASE PROVISION

A. TREATMENT AS AN EXECUTORY CONTRACT

The first concern of the draftsman in anticipating the potential problems which could jeopardize the lender's security is how the New Lease provision would be treated under the federal Bankruptcy Code.[23] The answer will also turn on which party to the ground lease is involved in the bankruptcy proceeding.

The specific problem stems from the power of the trustee in bankruptcy to reject any executory contract or unexpired lease of the debtor.[24] In a case where the lessee (borrower) goes into bankruptcy, the critical question is whether the trustee's rejection of the lease would also have the effect of terminating the rights of the leasehold mortgagee to obtain a New Lease from the lessor.[25] The natural argument in such a case would be that the New Lease Provision was a right that ran not to the lessee but to a third party, and, in essence, was a separate contractual commitment on the part of the lessor supported by the consideration of the lessee entering into the lease. While this puts the leasehold mortgage into the role of a third party beneficiary of the right to a new lease (which may impact upon its enforceability) it is submitted that the "right" should be deemed separable from the lease itself, and would thus survive the rejection of the lease by the lessee's trustee in bankruptcy.[26]

A more difficult problem arises when the lessor is the bankrupt party. Here, the trustee in bankruptcy would likely have the power to reject not

---

23. 11 U.S.C. §101 (1978).

24. 11 U.S.C. §365(a) (1978).

25. Committee Report at 406, note 26. Assuming that the bankruptcy of the lessee is one such noncurable default situation, the leasehold mortgagee needs sufficient time to protect its interests in the bankruptcy proceeding by either being granted relief from the automatic stay (see Federal Bankruptcy Code, supra note 23, at §362) so that it can proceed to foreclose its leasehold mortgage or to submit a plan of reorganization which would protect the relative interest of both the ground lessor and the leasehold mortgagee who would then stand in the shoes of the lessee.

26. See Creedon & Zinman, Landlords Bankruptcy: Laissez Les Lessees, 26-5 Bus. L. 1391 (1970) for a discussion of the problems arising under §70(b) of the prior Federal Bankruptcy Act in the event of a landlord's bankruptcy. The cases under §70(b) cited in the article made a distinction between the contractual rights and obligations under the lease which could be rejected by a trustee in bankruptcy and the lessee's possessory interests in the property which would remain. The separation of contract rights and property interests would tend to support the conclusion that the rejection of the lease by the lessee's trustee would only cause a termination of lessee's possessory interest and contractual obligations, but not those interests of third parties. Some caution must be noted in that the consideration for the lessor's agreement to provide a new lease is supported by the lease, which if terminated may destroy the consideration and thus the obligation. See 49 Am. Jur. 2d Landlord and Tenant §367 (1970). However, the leasehold mortgage also provided the funds for the permanent financing of the improvements to the property, thus enhancing the reversionary interest of lessor, and this in itself may provide separate and continuing consideration for the lessor's agreement to provide a New Lease.

only the lease, but also the "right" to a New Lease.[27] The Bankruptcy Code does provide some protection in that the lessee of the rejected lease may remain in possession for the balance of the term including enforceable renewals or extensions.[28] However, it would appear that the right to a New Lease would be subject to rejection on its own part as an executory contract.[29] This does not immediately affect the lender's security, but it would destroy any right to a New Lease in the event that, for some reason, the lessee's right to possession is later terminated due to subsequent default on its part.[30] This scenario has the effect of making the New Lease provision itself unreliable as an "absolute" protection of the lender's security. . . .

C. THE RULE AGAINST PERPETUITIES

While normally one would not consider the rule against perpetuities[45] as having significant impact in the area of commercial transactions, there are several modern cases which deal with the applicability of the rule to situations involving options to purchase and agreements to lease real estate which are analogous to an option for a New Lease.[46]

In United Virginia Bank v. Union Oil Company,[47] the dispute arose over the validity of an option agreement to purchase land located at the corner of two proposed highways, which option was granted for a period of 120 days after the rights of way to the highways were acquired by the municipal authorities. The court held that the option violated the rule because of the possibility, however remote, that the option could be exercised beyond the period of the rule, in this case 21 years.[48]

---

27. 11 U.S.C. §365(a) (1978). The legislative history included what might be viewed as a definition of an executory contract: "Though there is no precise definition of what contracts are executory, it generally includes contracts on which performance remains due to some extent on both sides." H.R. Rep. No. 95-595, 95th Cong. 1st Sess 344 (1977).
  28. 11 U.S.C. §365(h)(1) (1978).
  29. Id. §365(a).
  30. Under the Bankruptcy Code, in the event that the lessor is bankrupt, the lessee has the right to remain in possession for the remaining lease term plus enforceable extensions. While unstated, it is presumed that the lessee must still comply with all the terms and covenants in the lease, but may offset rent to cover the costs of those obligations of the lessor which are not being performed, see 11 U.S.C. §365(h) (1978). Also, in the event of a default thereafter by lessee, the trustee or its assigns would have the right to terminate even this possessory interest, thus putting the leasehold mortgagee in jeopardy.
  45. See, e.g., Mass. Gen. Laws Ann. ch. 184A, §1-4 as an example of the modern-day rule of perpetuities. The rule against perpetuities (hereinafter the Rule) is defined as follows: "No interest is good unless it must vest if at all not later than 21 years after some life in being at the creation of the interest." Gray, Rule Against Perpetuities 191 (4th ed. 1942).
  The determinative period for purposes of analyzing this type of transaction is 21 years without reference to a life in being. See cases cited at note 49 infra and the annotation cited at note 48, at 1302.
  46. Leach, Perpetuities: New Absurdity, Judicial and Statutory Correctives, 73 Harv. L. Rev. 1318, 1322 (1960).
  47. 214 Va. 48, 197 S.E.2d 174 (1973).
  48. Id., see also Annot., 66 A.L.R.3d 1294 (1975).

In the area of agreements to lease real property, the courts have taken several different approaches to uphold their validity in the face of a challenge under the rule.[49] The fact situations involved agreements which provided that a lease would commence upon the completion of construction of a building on the property.[50] In one of the cases, the court, applying the rule as in effect in Virginia, held that the lessee's interest in the property subject to the agreement vested when there existed a present right to possession either at a present or future time, and thus the agreement was not subject to the rule.[51] In a California case,[52] facing a similar situation, the court held that while the lease would vest only upon completion of the building, there was a presumption that the completion would only occur within a reasonable time, and thus the lease would not violate the rule.[53]

Faced with these decisions, all of which utilized 21 years as the determinative period, the applicability of the rule to the New Lease provision must be considered in terms of the provision's validity and ultimate enforceability. The option clearly might not be exercised within the 21-year period, since the condition precedent (termination of the lease) may not occur until late in the life of a normally long-term lease. The presumption of "reasonable time" does not apply since the contingency may occur beyond any "reasonable length of time" and may in fact never occur. Applying the concept of present vesting also seems inapplicable, since the nature of the provision as an option does not involve any interest in the underlying property until the option itself is exercised.[54] In a more favorable direction, there seems to be general authority for the conclusion that options to purchase property and renewal options when contained in a lease are excluded from the application of the rule.[55] However, it is still open to question as to whether or not the rights of someone other than the lessee under the lease would fall within such an exception irrespective of whether the right is contained in the lease.[56] In conclusion, it must be again stated that the New Lease provision may be subject to attack under the rule, and this increases the risk to the lender of it being unreliable.

---

49. See Haggerty v. City of Oakland, 161 Cal. App. 2d 407, 326 P.2d 957 (1958); Isen v. Giant Food, Inc., 295 F.2d 136 (Ct. App. D.C., 1961); Wong v. DiGrazia, 386 P.2d 817 (Cal. 1963); In re Wonderfair Stores, Inc. of Arizona, 511 F.2d 1206 (9th Cir. 1975).

50. This is a quite normal clause in a lease which involves a building to be constructed. See, Wong v. DiGrazia, 386 P.2d 17.

51. Isen v. Giant Food, Inc., 295 F.2d 136 (D.C. Cir. 1961).

52. Wong v. DiGrazia, 386 P.2d at 824.

53. Id. at 825-29. Accord In re Wonderfair Stores, Inc., 511 F.2d 1206 (9th Cir., 1975).

55. Restatement of Property §395 (1936). See also, Gray, supra note 45, at §230.2; Annot., 66 A.L.R.2d 733, 735 (1959); 3 Simes & Smith, Future Interests §1242 (2d ed. 1956).

56. This exception facilitates the necessary commercial transaction of extending or renewing leases, and recognizes that these events should not be subject to the Rule. See also, Annot., 66 A.L.R.3d 1294 (1975).

D. THE CONCEPT OF LEASE IN REVERSION

One possible solution to the problems mentioned above involves the utilization of an actual lease in reversion as opposed to relying on the New Lease provision. A lease in reversion is simply a lease which becomes effective only at the expiration of the term of a prior lease.[57] The interest of the lessee under such a lease is referred to as an interesse termini (i.e. right to enter).[58] In this context, the lessor would grant an independent lease to the leasehold mortgagee which would allow the leasehold mortgagee to take possession of the property immediately upon the termination of the prior lease.[59] There is some authority which supports the conclusion that this would result in an immediately vested interest which would take this type of lease out of the application of the rule against perpetuities.[60] Further, since the lease would be a bilateral, mutually binding agreement, the problems as to enforceability as an option would not arise. While the leasehold mortgagee does lose the flexibility to walk away from the transaction which is provided in the context of the option feature of the New Lease provision, it is submitted that, on a practical basis, the leasehold mortgagee would in most cases elect the New Lease provision.[61] Faced with the choice of a New Lease provision which may be unreliable, the concept of a lease in reversion may provide a more enforceable method of protecting the interests of the lender. . . .

V. CONCLUSION

Based on the problems faced, the New Lease provision should be recognized as an unreliable method of protecting the leasehold mortgagee's interests. While no provisions in the ground lease will provide absolute protection, the essential concept is that the ground lease must provide that no default by the lessee thereunder will cause a termination of the lease without sufficient opportunity being given the leasehold mortgagee to curve. In this context, the New Lease provision could provide an optional alternative to resolve the problem of a termination assuming that no dispute arose over its enforceability at the time of its election. If the lender

---

57. 49 Am. Jur. 2d Landlord and Tenant §100 (1970).

58. Id., §100. See also, Casner, American Law of Property §3.22 (1952).

59. It also may be suggested that the lease in reversion in any event could cover a specific period of time at the end of the prior lease term thereby avoiding the argument that it might never "vest" any possessory interest. In the event, at that point, that the lease in reversion actually commenced, an appropriate assignment to the lessee subject to the mortgage could put the parties back in the intended positions.

60. Casner, supra note 58, at §3.22, but see, contra, Simes & Smith, supra note 55, at §1242. A recent Florida statute provides that a lease to commence in futuro is exempt from the Rule but invalid unless the term commences within 40 years, Fla. Stat. §689.22 (1979).

61. In either case, the lease could provide for an exculpation of the leasehold mortgagee against any corporate liability beyond its interest in the property or at least a limitation that liability would be assumed only for the period when the lender is the owner.

determines that more "insurance" is needed, the concept of a lease in reversion may provide a higher degree of security and enforceability.

In the final analysis, it is submitted that the lender and its counsel must carefully consider the various alternatives presented in determining the amount of acceptable risk that the transaction should involve.

a. Real or Chattel Mortgage?

Harbel Oil Company v. Steele
83 Ariz. 181, 318 P.2d 359 (1957) (page 262 supra)

b. Some Risks of the Leasehold Mortgagee

Great Southern Aircraft Corp. v. Kraus
132 So. 2d 608 (Fla. Dist. Ct. App. 1961)

BARKDULL, Judge. This is an interlocutory appeal from an order granting a writ of possession, subsequent to a foreclosure sale of a leasehold estate.

The principal question for determination is whether the lessor of the leasehold estate was an indispensable party to the proceedings. It appears, under the facts revealed by this record, that it was not.

The lease involved was given by the Dade County Port Authority, as lessor, and contained the following provision:

"This lease shall not be sold or assigned or the premises or rights granted hereunder, sublet in whole or in part without the written consent of the Lessor; provided, however, that the Lessee may assign this lease without such consent to any corporation with which the Lessee may merge or consolidate or which may succeed to the business of the Lessee."

Thereafter, the lessee executed a note to the appellee, Kraus, and secured the payment of the note with a mortgage on the leasehold. After a default in the note and mortgage, a foreclosure suit was commenced by Kraus and a lis pendens was filed. While the foreclosure proceeding was pending, the leasehold estate was assigned to the appellant, Great Southern Aircraft Corporation, who had constructive notice of the foreclosure proceeding by the lis pendens and actual notice, as the assignment contained the following provision: ". . . that the lease is free from all encumbrances except a possible mortgage on the buildings payable to Philip & Anna Kraus; . . ." After the assignment to the appellant, a partial final decree of foreclosure against the leasehold estate was entered by the chancellor. The leasehold estate was sold thereunder and purchased by the appellee, Kraus, who then assigned it to the appellee, Tamiami Aviation, Inc. The appellees then sought a writ of assistance to obtain possession of the leasehold estate, and the writ which is the subject matter of this appeal was issued, reading in part as follows:

"That the petitioners are entitled to the possession of the leased premises as described in the lease, dated July 15, 1956, entered into between the Board of County Commissioners of Dade County, Florida, as Lessors, and the Liberty School of Aviation, Inc., as Lessee, and subject to the terms of said lease."

Appellant urges that no writ could have been issued without joining lessor, as it was an *indispensable party* to the proceedings, it being conceded that the Port Authority did not consent in writing to the execution of the mortgage. The propriety of proceedings without joinder of an indispensable party may be raised at any stage of the proceedings, although a different rule would apply as to proper or necessary parties. Martinez v. Balbin, Fla. 1954, 76 So. 2d 488. An indispensable party has been defined as one who has ". . . an interest of such a nature that a final decree cannot be rendered between other parties to the suit. . . ." 24 Fla. Jur., Parties, §3.

A non-assignable clause does not prevent a mortgage of the lessee's interest in the leasehold estate. Provisions restricting the power of the lessee to transfer his term are traditionally construed very strictly and in favor of alienation to the greatest extent possible. Boyer, Florida Real Estate Transactions, 1219. Further, such a restriction is solely for the benefit of the lessor and his assigns and may be waived by those for whose benefit it was included. Farmers' Bank & Trust Co. v. Palms Publishing Co., 86 Fla. 371, 98 So. 143; Baker v. Clifford-Matthew Investment Co., 99 Fla. 1229, 128 So. 827. Since a mortgage in Florida is not a transfer of title to this leasehold, but merely a lien upon it, §697.02 Fla. Stat., F.S.A., the voluntary action of a lessee in mortgaging the leasehold is not such a transfer as would violate a non-assignable provision. Even if such a mortgage did violate the covenant against assignment, the fact would not have any effect on a case such as the one at bar, since a violation of a covenant against assignment without consent is nevertheless a binding assignment between the lessee and his assigns which passes the leasehold estate, subject to the option of the lessor to forfeit the lease for breach of the covenant. Chapman v. Great Western Gypsum Co., 216 Cal. 420, 14 P.2d 758, 85 A.L.R. 917. Nor would any transfer that may be occasioned by a default in the mortgage fall within the confines of a non-assignable clause, since this would be involuntary transfer by operation of law. Similar provisions in cases arising in other jurisdictions have been held not to be violated by actions or proceedings in the nature of *execution*, Hockman v. Sunhew Petroleum, 92 Mont. 174, 11 P.2d 778; *bankruptcy*, Miller v. Fredeking, 101 W. Va. 643, 133 S.E. 375, 46 A.L.R. 842; *mortgage foreclosure*, Riggs v. Pursell, 66 N.Y. 193, approved in Dunlop v. Mulry, 85 App. Div. 498, 83 N.Y. 477, 1104 [sic]; or *assignment as security for an indebtedness*, Crouse et al. v. Michell et al., 130 Mich. 347, 90 N.W. 32.

This litigation is between the appellant as the successor to the original lessee-mortgagor, and the mortgagee and his successor through foreclosure sale and assignment. The rights between the parties are separate and distinct from any rights which the lessor may hav[e] which would be an issue between the lessor and its tenant under the lease, and we do not here decide any of the rights of the lessor under this lease, the chancellor having specifically recognized the paramount interest of the lessor in the leasehold estate on the issuance of the writ of possession, it is clear that the Dade County Port Authority, as the lessor, was not an indispensable party to these proceedings. Therefore, the issuance of the writ of possession is affirmed.

Affirmed.

Jacob Hoffman Brewing Co. v. Wuttge
234 N.Y. 469, 138 N.E. 411 (1923)

CRANE, J. On June 1, 1913, the defendant John L. Klages made a lease to the defendant Frank Wuttge of premises known as 422 Jackson avenue, borough and county of Queens in the city of New York, for a term of 21 years, at a rental for the first five years of $3,000 per year, the next five years $3,500 per year, the next five years $4,000 per year, and for the remaining six years $4,500 per year. The lessee covenanted to pay the rent in advance in equal quarterly payments to be made the 1st day of each September, December, March, and June. He also covenanted in the lease as follows:

"7. In case of default in any of the covenants or conditions, or in case the whole or any part of said premises shall become vacant, the landlord may resume possession of the premises, either by force or otherwise, without being liable to any prosecution therefor, and re-let the same during the remainder of the term, at the best rent that he can obtain for the account of the tenant, who will make good any deficiency."

The tenant entered into possession of the premises under this lease. On the 1st day of February, 1920, there was due the landlord $978.09 for rent and water rates. Personal demand was made upon the tenant, but he failed to pay. On February 16, 1920, dispossess proceedings were commenced by the landlord in the Municipal Court in the city of New York, which resulted in a final order on the 20th of February, 1920, awarding possession to the landlord. The tenant did not appear. A warrant was issued to the sheriff, directing him to remove the tenant. This warrant was not served. The tenant voluntarily surrendered possession to the landlord and gave him the key to the place. Thereafter and on the 28th of February, 1920, the owner made a new lease at an increased rental to one Samuel Horowitz.

On the 12th of March, 1920, Frank Wuttge, the tenant, confirming his

The Ground Lease 1101

surrender, executed a writing duly acknowledged on the last page of the defendant Klages' copy of the lease, surrendering and yielding up to the lessor the lease and the lands and the premises therein mentioned, and all the term yet to come. Thereafter, on application to the Municipal Court in which the dispossess proceedings had been had, an order was made on the 4th of June, 1920, vacating and setting aside and discontinuing all such proceedings.

The Jacob Hoffmann Brewing Company, the plaintiff herein, held a mortgage of $10,000 on this lease made by Klages to Wuttge. It was dated January 19, 1914, and was given to secure a bond in that amount dated the same day. In it the mortgagor covenanted with the brewing company as follows:

"Fourth. The mortgagor will pay the rent and other charges mentioned in and made payable by said lease or of any renewal thereof, or any new lease, within ten days after said rent or charges are payable, and if not paid, the company may pay the same and add the amount thereof to the indebtedness hereby secured, and the mortgagor hereby authorizes the company to pay such rent and charges if not so paid by the mortgagor."

This mortgage was duly recorded and was in existence at the time of the dispossess proceedings above mentioned and the surrender by the mortgagor-lessee to the owner.

Learning of the proceedings, the brewing company filed in the Municipal Court a notice of its intention to redeem the premises in the manner provided by sections 2257, 2258, and 2259 of the Code of Civil Procedure. As the warrant to the sheriff had not been executed, these provisions of the Code gave to the mortgagee no right to redeem. This notice was not followed up by any payment or tender of payment of all rent in arrears with interest thereon and with costs and charges incurred by the landlord. The brewing company and its counsel must have understood that it had no right to redeem under these sections of the Code.

This action was commenced on the 14th of November, 1921, to foreclose this mortgage which the plaintiff had on Wuttge's lease, and prayed judgment that the lease and the leasehold interest be sold according to law and the plaintiff paid the amount owing to it on its bond. At the opening of the case counsel for the plaintiff claimed his position to be that as the lessor had not proceeded with his dispossess proceedings and executed a warrant so as to give the mortgagee a chance to redeem, the lessor had waived the default of the lessee in the nonpayment of rent; that the lease was therefore still in existence subject to the plaintiff's mortgage which it was foreclosing. The action was tried upon this theory. The Appellate Division has also adopted this view, for it said in its opinion that the defendant Wuttge having granted to the brewing company an interest in the leasehold by way of mortgage, had no right or power to destroy the interest by surrendering the lease to the landlord. This is contrary to our decision in Cornwell v. Sanford, 222 N.Y. 248, 118 N.E. 620, where we held that the moving of the tenant from the leased premises thereby enabling the landlord to take peaceable possession of them after the issuance and service of a precept in summary proceedings, cancels the lease, and annuls the relation of landlord and tenant as of the time of removal. The removal, we said, was the precise act and effect the landlord sought through the service of the precept and that it was entirely immaterial whether it was produced through the warrant or the conduct of the tenant in obedience to the precept. Surely the mortgage given by the tenant to this plaintiff could not reduce the lessor's rights under the lease or prevent him from pursuing any and all of his remedies for the nonperformance of the covenants. When Wuttge failed to pay his rent, the owner was not called upon to consult the tenant's assignees, mortgagees, or subtenants before taking action. Neither was he compelled to resort to legal proceedings. He could accept the voluntary surrender of the premises and enter into possession and re-let them according to the terms and conditions of his lease. Wuttge had covenanted in his lease that if he failed to pay his rent at the times specified, the owner could re-enter and re-let the premises. What was there in the act of mortgaging the leasehold which prevented the landlord from doing this? If the lessor and lessee had entered into any new arrangement not a part of the lease and the surrender by the tenant was either in bad faith or under such new arrangement or contrary to the provisions of the lease, then in such case a mortgage on the leasehold would not be affected or cut off. Such was the case in Eten v. Luyster, 60 N.Y. 252, which distinctly recognized, however, that the termination of the leasehold according to the provisions of the lease would cause all rights dependent upon the lease to fall with it.

The plaintiff brewing company when it took its mortgage must have known the terms of this lease. It knew that the tenant had covenanted to pay the rent at a certain time and that in default thereof the landlord could regain possession. Its duty, therefore, in accordance with its privilege reserved in the mortgage, was to pay the rent itself if it desired to keep alive the lease. Dunlop v. James, 174 N.Y. 411, 414, 67 N.E. 60.

We therefore are of the opinion that the lease between Klages and Wuttge was terminated by the surrender of the tenant, and that the mortgage of the plaintiff thereupon ceased to exist as a lien.

We do not mean to intimate that under the conditions here existing the brewing company would not have had a right to redeem in equity, although technically under the provisions of the Code it had no such right. Where possession has been obtained without a warrant and the unexpired term exceeds five years, equity might in a proper case permit redemption. Howard v. Fanshawe, L.R. 1895, 2 Ch. 581.

No doubt if such relief were granted equity would follow the statute by requiring the payment or tender of payment of the rent within the time prescribed by the statute, i.e., a year and a day. Coit v. Campbell, 82 N.Y. 509, 514. However, we need not now determine what the plaintiff's rights would have been in equity, as this action is not brought for redemption or upon any such theory and the plaintiff has never paid or offered to pay the rent due from Wuttge under the lease.

For the reasons here stated, the judgments of the Appellate Division and the Special Term must be reversed and the complaint dismissed, with costs in all courts.

Hiscock, C.J., and Hogan, Cardozo, Pound, McLaughlin, and Andrews, JJ., concur.

Judgments reversed, etc.

Williams v. Safe Deposit & Trust Co.
167 Md. 499, 175 A. 331 (1934)

Parke, J., delivered the opinion of the Court.

Nathalie Thomas Whiting devised the reversion in and to an improved lot of ground in Baltimore City unto the Safe Deposit & Trust Company of Baltimore under trusts which still continue. The ground rent was created by a lease dated May 4th, 1867, whereby the lot of ground and premises were demised for the term of ninety-nine years, renewable forever, and the annual ground rent of $480 issuing out of the lot was reserved, payable in equal semi-annual installments on the fourth days of every May and November. By the lease, the lessee, for himself, his personal representatives and assigns, covenanted and agreed to pay the installments of rent as each should become due and payable, and to pay all taxes levied upon said lot and improvements when and as such taxes should become payable.

After mesne assignments, the title to the leasehold estate became vested in Louis Hurwitz and Benjamin Voloshen, who mortgaged their leasehold estate in said property to Charles J. Bonaparte as security for a mortgage indebtedness of $12,000, and covenanted by the mortgage to pay the ground rent and taxes on the demised property. After the death of Benjamin Voloshen, his undivided one-half interest in the leasehold estate was assigned to Sarah Voloshen. The mortgage and mortgage indebtedness to Charles J. Bonaparte were duly assigned to Mary W. Williams, who acquired her title on February 19th, 1925, and who thenceforth held the mortgage debt and mortgage until December 29th, 1932, when she released the mortgage debt and lien.

The mortgage debt became in default, and thereupon the right under the covenant in the mortgage that entitled the mortgagors to remain in possession until default terminated, and Mary W. Williams, the assignee, became entitled to the right of immediate possession of the leasehold estate in the year 1930; and, although she never actually took possession, she constantly remained, by reason of a continuous default, so entitled to possession, until the mortgage was released by her on December 29th, 1932.

During this period of default, the ground rent for May and November, 1932, amounting to $480, and the state and city taxes for the years 1931 and 1932, and a special paving tax of 1932, aggregating $1,010.59, were not paid. By reason of the failure to pay these taxes, interest and penalties accrued, which the owner of the reversion was compelled to pay in the amount of $144.41 in order to prevent the property from being sold for the nonpayment of the taxes. The owner of the reversion thereupon demanded of the assignee of the mortgage that she refund the amount so paid. Before an action at law in covenant had been instituted against the assignee for her failure to pay, the assignee released the mortgage of the leasehold estate, and then a suit in equity was begun by the owner of the reversion against the assignee.

The cause was heard on the facts, and the chancellor entered a decree in favor of the Safe Deposit & Trust Company of Baltimore, as trustee under the will of Nathalie Thomas Whiting, and against Mary W. Williams for the sum of $1,585.02, with interest from the date of the decree and costs.

The questions presented by the appeal are (1) whether the mortgagee of a leasehold estate, who has not entered in possession of the mortgaged property, although so entitled, under the terms of the mortgage, by the default of the mortgagor, is bound by the covenant of the lessee, his personal representatives and assigns, to pay the rent and taxes accruing due on the leasehold property, during the default and before the assignee released the deed of mortgage. . . .

At common law, a defeasible legal estate vested in the mortgage, that became absolute upon default. The mortgagee is entitled to immediate possession upon the execution of a mortgage unless there is some other agreement of the parties. . . .

Equity, however, has assumed jurisdiction to relieve the mortgagor against an absolute forfeiture upon his default in performing the condition subsequent, and, recognizing that the purpose of the mortgage is merely a pledge to secure a debt, and that it is unreasonable that the mortgagee should, on the failure of the debtor to meet his obligation to pay on the day specified, be entitled to acquire, as his own property, what was intended as a security for its payment, has allowed the mortgagor to reclaim the property upon the payment of the mortgage debt with interest. . . . Mizen v. Thomas, 156 Md. 313, 318, 319, 144 A. 479.

Accordingly, there is usually incorporated in a mortgage of a leasehold estate, as was incorporated in the mortgage at bar, a provision whereby the mortgagors, their personal representatives and assigns, may continue to hold and possess the mortgaged premises, and to receive the rents and profits thereof, upon paying in the meantime the ground rent, and all taxes levied or assessed on the mortgaged property, with a covenant on the part of the mortgagors, their personal representatives and assigns, to pay the ground rent and taxes. The effect of this agreement on the part of the mortgagee, which is known as a redemise, is to make of the mortgagor, in most respects, a tenant to the mortgagee. . . .

Through the right of possession until default under the mortgage, and the equity of redemption, the mortgagor is now regarded as the real and beneficial owner of the mortgaged premises as to all persons except the mortgagee and those claiming under him, yet to create the mortgage as security for the mortgage debt there must be a transfer of the mortgagor's estate in the property pledged to the mortgagee. So, in Maryland, a mortgage conveys the whole legal estate to the mortgagee, subject, generally, to the condition subsequent that, upon due payment of the mortgage debt and a performance of all the covenants by the mortgagor, the mortgage deed is avoided. . . .

Since the legal title is transferred by the deed of mortgage, the mortgage of the whole interest in the original lease operates as an assignment of the lease; and the mortgagee thereby becomes the assignee of the leasehold interest, and, as such assignee, he is liable on the covenants of the lease, which arise from privity of estate, either from the date of the assignment, if there is no provision for the mortgagor to retain possession until default, or from the time of the mortgagor's default in the performance of the covenants he has made in the mortgage, if there is a provision in the mortgage agreeing that the mortgagor shall remain in possession until such default. . . .

It is a principle of law that an assignee of a lease is subject to the performance of all the covenants that arise from privity of estate, such as covenants to pay rent, taxes, or assessments. Kent's Com. 144: Lester v. Hardesty, 29 Md. 50, 54; Worthington v. Cooke, 52 Md. 297, 309. Nor can the assignee escape this liability on his lessee's covenants that run with the estate in land on the ground of the lessee's ignorance of their existence, since the lessee is bound to take notice of the obligations and conditions of the instrument of lease. Abrahams v. Tappe, 60 Md. 317, 322; Washington Natural Gas Co. v. Johnson, 123 Pa. 576, 16 A. 799, 801. Neither does the liability of the assignee on the covenant depend, according to the weight of authority, upon his actual entry or taking possession. It is sufficient if the right of possession exist, as was determined in the case of Mayhew v. Hardesty, 8 Md. 479, 494, 495. This case has been cited with approval in Commercial Bldg. etc. Assn. v. Robinson, 90 Md. 615, 618, 45 A. 449, and in Gibbs v. Didier, 125 Md. 486, 94 A. 100, where the court stated: "The rule is well established that after forfeiture a mortgagee is regarded as the assignee of the term, and hence is liable on the real covenants." Page 492 of 125 Md., 94 A. 100, 101, Tiffany on Real Property (2nd Ed.) sec. 56, subsecs. c, d, pp. 179-181. . . .

The assignee, however, is not liable on covenants running with the land which are broken before assignment to him of the term. Consumers' Ice Co. v. Bixler, 84 Md. 437, 446, 447, 35 A. 1086. When the assignment is by way of a mortgage which does not give the mortgagee the right of immediate possession, but provides for the possession of the mortgaged property by the mortgagor until his default under the mortgage, the redemise to the mortgagor, assuring a tenancy to the mortgagor on condition subsequent, prevents the whole interest in the leasehold estate being in the mortgagee until a default by the mortgagor on the covenants of the mortgage, but upon the happening of the default, the redemise is terminated, and the whole interest in the leasehold estate is vested in the mortgagee, with a right of immediate possession, and, therefore, the liability of the mortgagee, qua assignee, to the holder of the reversion for the covenants running with the estate in land begins with such default of the mortgagee. Supra. Similarly, the assignee is not liable for breaches of covenant which are committed after he has assigned all his interest in the demised premises, unless he has so expressly agreed; when the privity of estate ends, the basis for the liability of an assignee on covenants that run with the estate in land is gone. Reid v. Wiessner Brewing Co., 88 Md. 234, 236, 237, 40 A. 877. Consequently, the assignee by way of mortgage of a leasehold interest, who is liable by reason of the fact that the mortgage transfers the legal title, may free himself of future liability by determining his title to the mortgage and thus end the privity of estate, by a release or discharge of the mortgage. 1 Tiffany on Landlord and Tenant, vol. 1, sec. 158, pp. 976, 977. . . .

It follows that the decree of the chancellor was in accordance with principles of law that have long been recognized and enforced in this jurisdiction. In reply to the argument that established rules be ignored on the ground of the hardship ascribed to their effect upon the assignee of the term by way of mortgage in the pending case, it is sufficient to say that she had the opportunity to avoid her present liability at the time of the assignment of the mortgage. If, in the words of an ancient authority, she was "ill-advised to take an assignment of the whole term" (Coote on Mortgages, 119, 18 Law Lib., 51), she must abide the consequences, since it is a primary function of the court to maintain and enforce rules of property. In Myers v. Silljacks, 58 Md. 319, at page 330, Alvey, J., speaking for the court with reference to reversionary freehold and leasehold estates, declared: "It is of the utmost importance, therefore, that the tenure be maintained with entire certainty; that the true relation of the parties to the property be at all times fully recognized, so that their exact rights may be known and enforced, and that third parties may know how to deal with respect to those rights." The liability of the assignee grows out of, not only her right of possession, but also her interest in the leasehold estate. Since it was a beneficial interest that she acquired, there is no sound basis in law or in equity why she should not be liable to its burdens.

Decree affirmed, with costs to the appellee.

Ash v. Egar[17]

25 Ariz. App. 72, 541 P.2d 398 (1975)

HOWARD, Chief Judge. This case involves the interpretation of two 99-year leases on two parcels of land upon which apartment buildings were constructed by appellants. Appellees are the owners-lessors of the land.

The dispute revolves around paragraph 13 of the lease agreements. Paragraph 13(f) provides: "(f) Landlord's interest in the demised premises shall not be subordinated to any loan or loans secured by a mortgage where such loan is to replace original mortgage financing or to refinance original mortgage financing other than interim construction financing, UNLESS: (1) The other provisions of this Article are complied with, (2) Such new loan is procured for the purpose of refinancing or replacing the original loan, (3) Such new loan is procured to provide funds for remodeling or new improvements, or (4) Unless such new loan is procured to construct improvements after such time as original improvements become obsolete, or original improvements are demolished and new improvements erected, but in no event shall original improvements be demolished before June 1, 1988."

The trial court in deciding in appellees' favor made findings of fact among which were the following:

"8. Paragraph 13 of the lease agreements listed the only purposes for which the loans, to be secured by mortgages to which defendants would be required to subordinate their interests, could be used.

"9. Paragraph 13 of the lease agreements was intended to provide and did provide that any loan secured by a mortgage to which defendants would be required to subordinate their interests would both (a) meet the requirements of subparagraphs (a) and (b) of Paragraph 13, and (b) be for one of the three purposes defined in subparagraphs (2), (3) and (4) of subparagraph (f) of Paragraph 13.

"10. The purposes for which a loan could be used if it were to be secured by a mortgage to which defendants would be required to subordinate their interests were those purposes listed in subparagraphs (2), (3) and (4) of subparagraph (f) of Paragraph 13, and no others.

"11. The purposes for which the loans to be secured by the mortgages to which plaintiffs demanded that defendants subordinate their interests were to be used included purposes not listed or permitted in Paragraph 13."

In January of 1970, appellants procured an original mortgage on the properties and improvements for $800,000. This money was used to construct the apartments. In the spring of 1973, there was $780,000 remaining to be paid on the mortgage. Pursuant to the lease which allowed a mortgage to be placed on the property in a sum not to exceed 70% of the

---

17. Footnotes omitted.

then-appraised value, appellants had the properties reappraised and secured a commitment from a lending institution to lend the sum of $1,000,000 which was somewhat less than the 70% of the then-appraised value of the properties.

The purpose of the new loan and mortgage was to release capital to appellants' investors. The $1,000,000 was to be applied as follows: $780,000 to pay off the original mortgage and the balance of $220,000 less $4,400 in "points" to be distributed to the original investors who had originally invested $265,000 in the properties. A very small sum was to be kept on hand for remodeling.

Appellants wrote a letter to appellees requesting them to subordinate their interest in the property, pursuant to Article 13(f) of the lease, to the new mortgage. When they refused to do so, appellants filed this action for declaratory judgment and damages.

Both parties agreed at trial that subparagraphs 2, 3 and 4 of Paragraph 13(f) are to be read in the disjunctive and not the conjunctive. Their disagreement centers on Paragraph 13(f)(2), which requires subordination only if "Such new loan is procured for the *purpose of refinancing* or replacing the original loan." (Emphasis added)

It is appellants' contention that the term "refinancing the original mortgage" means that a new mortgage can be placed on the properties in an amount based upon the current appraised value of the properties and not limited by the amount of the original loan.

Appellees' position is that when Paragraph 13(f) is read as a whole, it is evident that under Paragraph 13(f)(2) the new mortgage can either be in an amount which does not exceed the original loan (refinancing) or in the amount of the balance of the original loan (replacing).

To aid the court in interpreting the disputed provision, extrinsic evidence was introduced. Appellants produced the testimony of two persons who were "experts" in the mortgage loan field to explain the term "refinancing." The one deduction that can be made from their testimony is that the term has no special meaning, custom or usage, and is not a word of art. As one of the witnesses said, "I would expect anybody to comprehend the word 'refinancing.'" Both witnesses testified that the term "refinancing" did not imply any limitation on the amount of the loan. At this point we observe that the issue is not what the term "refinancing" means but rather what does that term mean in the context of the lease agreement?

Mr. Sonenblick testified as to conversations with Mr. Schorr, the attorney for Mr. Brodsky, who subsequently acquiesced and with Mr. Brodsky himself. After testifying that the drafts of the lease were composed by both Schorr and himself, he stated:

A. I told Mr. Schorr that I objected to the provision [on subordination] because it provided that at some later time when the tenants ground lease if he were to refinance, as I recall the testimony, provided we could not refinance, beyond the then original balance. If it had been reduced from $800,000 to $400,000, we could only go out and get a new $400,000 loan. We couldn't even build it back up to $800,000 and I said, "This is intolerable." So, I left his office and I talked to Mrs. Ash and I said to him —

Q. Not here your testimony about the conversation with Ash. Did you then have a conversation with Schorr again or with Brodsky about that?
A. I then had a conversation with Mr. Brodsky.
Q. How long after the Schorr conversation?
A. Probably within a week....
Q. Would you relate that conversation?
A. I told Mr. Brodsky, I said, "Mr. Schorr is taking a very inflexible position. You are a developer of property Irving, and you understand the position of a developer." He said, "Yes." and I said "Irving, you know what we have to do from time to time. From time to time, as is normal, you have to refinance property mortgaging up properties go up," and he said, "Jerry, I will talk to Mr. Schorr and straighten it out." He said, "You know there is two protections I have to have. The first protection is I will not allow the interest rate to go over 8 and ¾ percent. I don't want you placing a 10 or 11 or 12 percent mortgage on the property. That is too high and excessive, and it can hurt our security." I said, "Well, Irving, that is fine. As you know, we are talking about an 8 and ½ percent loan now." I said — he said he understood that. "What else," he said, "I must have that protection that you don't get over 70 percent to market value ratio. I must have that 30 percent gap to protect our lease hold position." And I said, "Both of those Irving are very reasonable and unfortunately, it just doesn't stand up. He is taking an overprotective position," and Irving said, "Look, I understand." And he said, "I will go back and see Sy and work it out."
Q. Did you have any subsequent conversation with either Mr. Brodsky or Sy Schorr about that point?
A. Yes.
Q. Who was the next person?
A. The next meeting was with Mr. Schorr, I believe it was in his office again shortly thereafter.
Q. Were the two of you alone?
A. Yes. The two of us were alone....
A. (By the witness): I [Mr. Schorr] am against it but if this is what you and Mr. Brodsky worked out, then I will go along with it and we subsequently drafted Article 13 as you now know it.

Mr. Sonenblick also explained to the trial court the desirability of having a subordination provision in a long term lease which would allow the tenant to secure a new mortgage subject to subordination with a lower interest rate. He also stated that it would be difficult to sell a leasehold interest in a situation such as this if the refinancing was limited to the balance due on the original mortgage.

Both parties at trial maintained that the provisions in question were clear and unambiguous. The purpose of appellants' extrinsic evidence was ostensibly to show that there was no ambiguity. It is clear to us, however, that the contract is ambiguous in that subparagraphs (3) and (4) of Paragraph 13(f) have no meaning or purpose if subparagraph (2) is literally interpreted. In other words, why have the limitations in subparagraphs (3) and (4) if one can refinance based upon the current appraisal value of the property?

Interpretation of a contract is a question of law for the court when its terms are unambiguous on its face; but if there are ambiguities and it is necessary to consider the circumstances in determining its meaning, it is a question for the trier of fact to determine what those circumstances were. Ridara Livestock Co. v. Agricultural Products Co., 61 Ariz. 473, 150 P.2d 761 (1944).

The previously quoted testimony of Mr. Sonenblick shows that at one time the refinancing provision was very restrictive and only allowed refinancing based upon the current balance of the mortgage. Sonenblick objected to this and it was changed. Sonenblick's testimony is, however, consistent with appellees' contention that the refinancing is limited to the original total amount of the old mortgage. . . .

In interpreting the meaning of the words in subparagraph (2), they should not be considered apart from other provisions which may throw light upon their meaning. Tevis v. Ryan, 13 Ariz. 120, 108 P. 461 (1910). The lease must be construed as a whole and the intentions of the parties thereto must be collected from the entire instrument and not from detached portions. O'Malley Investment & Realty Co. v. Trimble, 5 Ariz. App. 10, 422 P.2d 740 (1967); Hiett v. Howard, 17 Ariz. App. 1, 494 P.2d 1347 (1972). . . .

When subparagraphs (2), (3) and (4) of Paragraph 13(f) are read together, it is clear the parties intended that there be no subordination by the appellees unless the funds from the mortgage were used on the properties themselves, or, unless the mortgage did not exceed the total amount of the original mortgage. . . .

Judgment affirmed.

Krucker and Hathaway, JJ., concur.

Dugan v. First National Bank in Wichita
227 Kan. 201, 606 P.2d 1009 (1980)

MILLER, Justice. The plaintiff, Mrs. Nancy Dugan, appeals from the order of the trial court granting summary judgment to all defendants. Mrs. Dugan brought this action for damages and for reformation or cancellation of two mortgages and two subordination agreements against defendants First National Bank in Wichita, K & B Development Corporation, and

The Ground Lease 1111

Harry D. Bledsoe. The Bank impleaded defendants Emmet A. Blaes, William D. Shirk, Claire E. Shirk, and Dolores J. Engels, as interested parties.

The primary issue is the propriety of the entry of summary judgment. Other of the numerous issues raised will be stated and discussed later in this opinion. The facts are somewhat lengthy and complex, but a statement of the background facts is necessary to an understanding of the issues presented.

Mrs. Dugan is a widow in her seventies. She has some infirmities and suffers from Parkinson's disease and coronary disease. She owns a large tract of farm land located in the west part of Wichita, adjoining or near the municipal airport. Parts of the land, and particularly that along Kellogg, have been extensively developed through various arrangements, often including long-term leases of parcels to commercial developers. Most of the development occurred prior to the death of her husband in 1971.

Mrs. Dugan, as lessor, entered into an 87-year lease with defendant Bledsoe, as lessee, in 1972. The lease covers slightly over one acre of land. The provisions of an earlier recorded lease are included by reference. Of interest here is the following special provision:

> a) If the Lessee in financing new construction on the leased premises encounters a requirement requiring Lessors to subordinate in favor of a first mortgage, Lessors agree to cooperate with Lessee in said financial arrangements and subordinate their leasehold interests thereto.

Bledsoe, in 1973, assigned his interest in the 1972 lease to K & B Development Corporation, of which Bledsoe was the principal (51%) stockholder. K & B then secured a construction loan of $275,000 and executed a note and mortgage to the Bank. Mrs. Dugan, on August 8, 1973, executed a subordination agreement, whereby she subordinated her fee simple interest in the leased land to the lien of the Bank's mortgage. The subordination agreement executed by Mrs. Dugan and also by corporate officers on behalf of K & B and the Bank contained the following provision:

> WHEREAS, in order to induce Lessors to execute this Subordination Agreement, Lessee does hereby covenant, warrant and represent that the actual costs of new construction of improvements on the leased premises described in exhibit "A" shall exceed the sum of $275,000.00.

This document was prepared by an attorney for the Bank.

Mrs. Dugan and her late husband were customers of the First National Bank in Wichita from the 1930's up until the time of the events giving rise to this litigation, and during the same period they were clients of the Wichita law firm of Jochems, Sargent & Blaes. In later years Mr. Robert

Braden of that firm handled their affairs. Mrs. Dugan sought Mr. Braden's advice before signing the $275,000 subordination agreement; thereafter she signed it, the mortgage and subordination agreement were placed of record, and the loan was dispersed to K & B.

The leased land included a building which was operated as a restaurant by Mr. Wong. Mrs. Dugan was aware that K & B was buying his business, including furniture and fixtures, at a cost of $40,000. K & B utilized the old building or at least portions of it, remodeled extensively, built an extensive new addition, installed all new furniture and fixtures, and opened the new club and restaurant for business in late 1973. At that time K & B had outstanding debts in addition to the bank loan, and when the financial picture did not improve in 1974, K & B sought unsuccessfully to increase the bank loan. Mr. Bledsoe consulted his attorney, Mr. Blaes, and eventually Blaes and the other impleaded defendants agreed to loan K & B the sum of $100,000, conditioned upon Mrs. Dugan again subordinating her fee interest.

K & B agreed to execute a mortgage to the First National Bank in Wichita. The Bank, as escrow agent and the named mortgagee, was to handle the loan. Mr. Blaes and his associates, William S. Shirk, Claire E. Shirk and Dolores J. Engels, were to advance the money; the Bank was to receive all loan payments and remit to the actual lenders in their appropriate proportionate shares. Documents to accomplish these ends were prepared and executed.

Meanwhile, Mr. Blaes prepared a subordination agreement for Mrs. Dugan's signature, and this was presented to her at her home one evening in April, 1975, by Mr. Bledsoe. Mrs. Dugan was not informed as to the actual parties involved in the loan or as to the intended use of the money. According to her deposition testimony, Mr. Bledsoe told her that it had taken more for construction and equipment than had been anticipated; and he told her or led her to believe that he would take the document to Mr. Braden so that he might look it over for her. With that understanding, she signed the second subordination agreement. Bledsoe did not present the document to Braden for review. Instead, the second subordination agreement and the new mortgage were placed of record and the loan proceeds were delivered to K & B.

When the original subordination agreement was executed in 1973, construction was nearing completion. Bledsoe informed Mrs. Dugan that the loan proceeds of $275,000 would be used for building construction costs and equipment. The loan proceeds were disbursed by the Bank under the following authorizations:

Working Capital	$ 10,000.00
Architect	$ 5,946.28
Equipment and Fixtures	$ 82,131.82
Contractor	$176,171.90
Engineering	$ 750.00

Mrs. Dugan complains of the "working capital" disbursement. In 1976, Mrs. Dugan discovered that Bledsoe had not taken the second subordination agreement to Braden; that Braden had not examined and approved it on her behalf; that the $100,000 loan proceeds had not gone into building and construction costs but instead had gone to pay debts of K & B; and that Mr. Blaes and other persons, and not the Bank, had made the second loan. Soon thereafter this action was filed.

The plaintiff claims that a portion of the funds from the 1973 mortgage was not used for the construction of improvements and to that extent the mortgage and the subordination agreement are void:

(1) for failure of consideration. . . .

She asks that the 1973 mortgage be reformed. As to the 1975 mortgage and subordination agreement, she claims that these instruments are void:

(1) for failure of consideration. . . .

After the completion of discovery, motions for summary judgment were sustained. The trial court made findings of fact (some of which are disputed) and conclusions of law, and entered judgment for the defendants. In substance, its conclusions of law were: . . .

(7) that the consideration for the original lease is sufficient consideration for the subsequent subordination agreements. . . .

Plaintiff contends that there was a failure of consideration to the extent that mortgage proceeds were not used to improve the real estate. She strictly construes the provision of the lease, and seeks to have the mortgage construed to secure only that portion of the funds which is directly traceable into construction. The appellees, on the other hand, would not measure the required subordination against the disbursements, but against the value of the improvements, and the total cost to K & B. In G. Credit Co. v. Mid-West Land Development, Inc., 207 Kan. 325, 485 P.2d 205 (1971), we considered the phrase "for purposes of financing the improvements to be placed upon said property" to include the cost of incidental and preliminary expenses prior to actual construction. We mentioned fees for engineering and architectural plans and specifications, lease rental, and interest during construction, as examples of such preliminary expenses. From the record before us, it appears that in excess of the $275,000 mortgage proceeds were used for actual construction or for items allowable under *Mid-West* rule. Bledsoe and K & B contend that much more than $375,000 was spent on the improvements, including construction, architect's fees, equipment, and fixtures; and they claim that the present value of the improvements exceeds $500,000. The latter we regard as immaterial. It is undisputed that very substantial improvements were made on the property. It is not necessary that every mortgage dollar be traceable directly into the project; K & B may well have spent some funds directly for improvements while the original loan papers were being prepared, but prior to receipt of the loan proceeds. Substantial improvements were made, and we conclude that there was ample consideration to support the 1973 subordination agreement.

The second or 1975 subordination agreement, however, is a different kettle of fish. Mrs. Dugan claims that *none* of the proceeds from the 1975 loan was spent for improvements of any kind to her property. She was obligated under the lease to subordinate her fee interest only "in financing new construction on the leased premises." Nothing in the lease requires her to subordinate her fee interest in order to bail the lessee out of a financial predicament. The lease contemplates improvement to the land in exchange for subordination. A promise of improvement is the consideration; here plaintiff alleges in effect that no improvements to the land were contemplated or intended by K & B and none were made. Ordinarily, where there is some consideration, a valid contract may result; but where there is a complete lack of consideration, there can be no contract. Every contract, to be legally enforceable, must be supported by a consideration. [Citations omitted.] We conclude that the trial court, on the facts before it, was correct in holding that there was consideration for the 1973 agreement, but that the court erred in holding as a matter of law that there was consideration for the 1975 subordination agreement. Consideration for the original lease is not consideration for a subsequent subordination agreement, at least where the latter is one not required by the terms of the lease. . . .

HERD, J., dissenting.

. . . Here, Mrs. Dugan was required by the lease to subordinate to loans for new construction. Misrepresentation is irrelevant when one has an obligation to perform a task. She signed the subordination agreement without relying on any statements made by Bledsoe. She complied with her prior contractual obligation and she can not now complain of her bargain. The facts are uncontroverted that K & B expended in excess of $390,000 for new construction of the club and restaurant, which was appraised at $500,000. The appraisal evidence is material in corroborating the evidence of the amount of the cost of new construction. Mrs. Dugan has subordinated her fee interest in the total amount of $375,000 in the two agreements to obtain improvements worth $500,000. She has gained $125,000 in security by virtue of K & B's new construction and at this date the loans have been reduced in excess of $90,000. The thrust of appellant's argument appears to be that she was defrauded because the proceeds of the second loan went to pay the temporary financing rather than the contractor. That reasoning is faulty. The construction was completed in late 1973 and the club and restaurant opened for business. Mrs. Dugan was aware of this. She visited there five or six times, during construction and afterward. The contractor had to be paid upon completion of the work or risk the filing of a mechanic's lien. The second subordination agreement was obtained on April 14, 1975, and the loan proceeds used to repay those who had paid the contractor for K & B. I find nothing irregular, surprising or suspicious about such arrangement. However, I find it material to know the improvements were made and that they enhanced the value of the realty. This was shown by the unrefuted testimony of Bledsoe and Schultz, Bledsoe's bookkeeper, detailed by invoices of purchases admitted in evidence.

Viewing the evidence in the light most favorable to the appellant, I find no material issue of fact remaining, making summary judgment a proper remedy. The judgment of the trial court should be affirmed.

ETHICAL CONSIDERATION

According to the opinion, the same Witchita law firm handled the affairs of Mrs. Dugan, the plaintiff-lessor, and Mr. Bledsoe, the defendant-lessee; additionally, Mr. Blaes, one of the 1975 lenders, was a principal of the firm. Discuss the ethical considerations that arise from this multiple representation.

C. NEW MODES OF CAPITAL ASSEMBLY

1. The Sale and Leaseback

The sale and leaseback has become a fixture on the American commercial scene. Endlessly versatile, this financing device is well known both to real estate *and* corporate specialists, and has become routine in our capital centers *and* smaller cities. To complete this course without a thorough understanding of the sale and leaseback is to bathe without water.

The sale and leaseback transactions, as this term denotes, comprises two simultaneous events: the sale of property to an investor or institutional lender and the long-term lease of the property back to the seller, generally a developer, operator, or user. The sale and leaseback of tangible property occurs widely: airplanes, tankers, and construction equipment are typical subject matter. But real estate transactions remain the concern of this course, so we will examine the sale and leaseback as it involves land, or land and buildings, or, sometimes, even a building alone.

a. The Sale versus Mortgage Issue

Lifton, Practical Real Estate in the '80s
497-499 (2d ed. 1982)

HISTORY

The sale and leaseback form was first introduced in 1936 by Safeway Stores. By the early 1940's it became fashionable to use a tax favored entity, like a charitable institution, as the investor-lessor. In the late 1940's, the elimination of statutory prohibitions against ownership of real estate by banks and insurance companies opened the door for such institutions to become investors-lessors. Although insurance companies first found the sale and leaseback a particularly advantageous transaction (because of their then low effective tax rate), with the elimination of their tax advantage, they have, for the most part, dropped out of the market. In the 1950's, pension funds and noninstitutional investors including income-oriented syndicates joined the fold of investor-lessors and continue today to be a major source of funds.

Sale vs. Mortgage

Patently, the sale and leaseback transaction has many of the elements of mortgage financing: the property is used as collateral to raise money, and the party receiving the money enters into an obligation, in the case of a user-lessee supported by its credit, to make regular payments sufficient to return the funds advanced plus pay an interest factor for the use of the money. The form of transaction is flexible enough to accommodate a real sale or a financing transaction, depending on the parties' aims. At one end of the spectrum is the true sale and leaseback. The property is sold at an arm's length price, based on its fair market value, and leased back to the seller at a fair rental that would be arrived at in an arm's length negotiation between a landlord and a tenant. At the end of the initial term of the lease, there may be renewal options that are based on the then market value of the property or tied to the realistic rentals for the earlier term. When the last renewal option expires, the tenant has no further interest in the property. If the tenant has an option to purchase, it is at the fair market value at the time of exercise or at a presently determined price which stands up as a reasonable estimate of the future fair market value.

At the other end of the spectrum is a transaction that has the characteristics of a secured loan. The property is sold at a price lower or higher than the true value of the property, related solely to the capitalized value of the rent to be paid under the lease. The rent will be lower or higher than a realistic rent for that property because the rent represents a return of the funds advanced for the purchase and a charge for the use of the money. After some specified period, the purchaser-lessor may have the right to "put" the property to the lessee, which is obligated to buy it, at a price which pays the seller back for the property and, taken together with the lease rents, provides a return on its funds outstanding to that date. Alternatively, the lessee may have an option at the end of the lease to extend the term at an unrealistically low rent or to buy the property back for an unrealistically low price.

As we shall see, substantially different tax and legal consequences flow from the characterization of the transaction as a mortgage loan rather than as a sale and leaseback. In the tax realm, whether the transaction is a "true" sale and leaseback, rather than a secured loan, has perplexed even (or especially) the Supreme Court. See Frank Lyon Co. v. United States, page 1120 infra.

Del Cotto, Sale and Leaseback: A Hollow Sound When Tapped?
37 Tax L. Rev. 1, 3-9 (1981)

COMMERCIAL AND TAX ATTRIBUTES OF THE SALE AND LEASEBACK

Although the sale and leaseback can serve what many view as legitimate commercial and business needs, parties to the transaction understand that this form may also provide mutual tax advantages. For the seller, the primary tax advantage is full deductibility of rental payments as ordinary and necessary business expenses, despite the fact that under a loan theory these payments include an interest portion and the amortized sale price of the property. Thus, over the lease term the seller-lessee will deduct rental payments equal to the full fair market value of the property, whereas with conventional mortgage financing only the interest portion of the payment would be deductible and no deduction would be allowed for amortized principal payments.

Of course, with conventional financing, as owner the seller-lessee would be able to take depreciation deductions, but only with respect to depreciable items, thus excluding land from the depreciation base. Hence, the rental deduction under the sale and leaseback is usually preferable to a depreciation deduction in that in effect it allows for depreciation of land. This feature is particularly attractive if the ratio of land cost to improvement cost is high. Or, if the property has appreciated in value, through rental deductions a sale and leaseback in effect allows depreciation of full market value, rather than of only the cost of the property. Similarly, if the property has been fully depreciated, sale and leaseback generates deductions otherwise unavailable. Furthermore, a sale and leaseback obviates determination of the property's salvage value and exclusion of it from the depreciable amount.

Even on property that has not been depreciated to any great extent, sale and leaseback provides the advantage of what is essentially accelerated depreciation. The rental deductions not only represent the full value of the property, they are deducted over the term of the lease, the length of which may be for a shorter period than the useful life of the property. Of course, amendments to the Code since the inception of the sale and leaseback device which allow acceleration depreciation have diminished the comparative utility of the sale and leaseback as a means of achieving the same end.

With respect to deductions, then, by financing with a sale and leaseback rather than conventional borrowing, the seller hopes to acquire rental deductions and is willing to forego deductions for depreciation and interest. The advantage gained by a rental deduction is offset somewhat by loss of a remainder interest in the property at the end of the lease term, unless the seller is also given a repurchase option, which in turn would invite recharacterization of the transaction as a financing rather than as a sale.

Assuming the transaction is respected as a sale, an additional tax consequence of a sale and leaseback is current recognition of the seller's gain or loss. By timing the transaction under section 1231, the seller may recognize ordinary losses, and capital gains, while retaining use and possession of property which is needed for business operations. If the adjusted basis of the asset is higher than its fair market value, a loss may be recognized, reducing tax liability or perhaps permitting a refund of a prior year's taxes. If, however, the adjusted basis of the asset is less than its fair market value, the taxpayer can utilize a sale and leaseback to recognize gain in order to take advantage of offsetting losses which could otherwise be wasted. Gain on the sale of a section 1231 asset, however, may be subject to depreciation recapture and taxed as ordinary income rather than as long-term capital gain.

Turning to the buyer-lessor, the sale and leaseback offers an investment on which at least part of the rentals received will not be taxed due to an offsetting depreciation deduction. Although the buyer must include the full rental payments in gross income, deductions for depreciation and interest on any mortgage debt are allowed. As owner, the investor can claim a depreciation deduction based on cost, including any mortgage debt, which, in an arm's length transaction, would be the full market value of the property.

On the other hand, if the buyer were treated as a conventional lender rather than a buyer-lessor, only the interest portion of the payments received would be includable in gross income. The remainder would be a return of capital. For tax-exempt organizations, this difference between the two transactions is irrelevant if the organization can pay cash. If, however, the sale and leaseback is debt-financed by the organization, all or some portion of the rental payments would be subject to taxation under sections 511 and 514 as "unrelated business income." Though the nonexempt buyer is in a less advantageous position, there are advantages it can, and will, pursue. The buyer can leverage its investment, borrowing at a lower rate than the rate at which the interest portion of the rental payment is calculated. With newly constructed, highly leveraged real estate, the sale and leaseback can be structured so that interest and accelerated depreciation deductions exceed rental payments, thus sheltering nonrental income from taxation. In addition, if the property is newly constructed, the buyer may be eligible for an investment tax credit.

A variety of nontax considerations recommend utilizing the sale and leaseback device. "[E]ven were there no tax inducements whatsoever some corporations today would enter into these transactions for the business and legal advantages they may afford."[31] A primary advantage of the sale and leaseback from the seller's perspective is that the seller receives the proceeds from the sale of a nonliquid asset yet retains for a term the use and possession of the asset. This retained use may be important in a variety of situations in which the seller plans eventually to terminate its relationship with the property. . . .

. . . Even sellers who do not wish ultimately to dispose of property may use a sale and leaseback where the combination of the retained possessory term and other advantages override loss of the remainder. This situation often arises in the use of a sale and leaseback as a financing device in order to provide the seller with working capital. Given the earning potential of working capital, taxpayers may prefer not to tie it up in nonliquid assets. Indeed, some contend that from the seller's perspective the principal purpose of a sale and leaseback is to increase or conserve working capital. In this respect, the sale and leaseback form of financing is particularly advantageous in that it often provides the seller with 100 percent of the fair market value of the property sold. In contrast, other financing arrangements — mortgage loans or corporate bonds — may yield only 75 to 80 percent of the value of the property. Hence, the sale and leaseback enables a company to obtain greater aggregate capital than through other forms of financing, while retaining for a term the use and possession of the asset sold.

These advantages of the sale and leaseback recommend its use in a variety of business situations. Builders and developers can effectively use the sale and leaseback device as a financing tool for construction purposes. By selling undeveloped or partially improved land for cash and leasing it back, the builder acquires capital for construction. The sale and leaseback serves a similar function in providing expansion opportunities for businesses needing to enlarge existing facilities or build new ones. A company can build or enlarge its plant or store to meet its specifications, sell it to an investor to recoup its cash investment, and then lease it back. If the company is unable to obtain the initial construction financing, a buyer can be found and the sales proceeds used to finance the costs of construction. Hence, the company can have the use and possession of a physical facility tailored to its needs without sacrificing working capital for fixed assets. This consideration is especially important for businesses like retail stores which require large amounts of working capital for inventory and operating expenses. For these businesses, the sale and leaseback also affords the advantage of piecemeal financing. The sale and leaseback of one or more units can be timed to coincide with the need for funds to finance new units.

31. Cary, Tax Aspects of the Sale and Leaseback of Corporate Property, 7 N.Y.U. Inst. Taxn. 599, 601 (1949).

Thus, funds are acquired as needed, in contrast to debt financing through the sale of a company's securities, where funds may be received over a short period. . . .

There are other commercial and business reasons why a sale and leaseback may or must be used in lieu of conventional financing.[51] Suffice it to say here that although the desire to avoid taxes does not contaminate a commercially sound sale and leaseback, such desires have led to substantial litigation in a continuing struggle to determine whether tax consequences should literally follow form.

Frank Lyon Company v. United States
435 U.S. 561, 98 S. Ct. 1291, 55 L. Ed. 2d 550 (1978)

Mr. Justice BLACKMUN delivered the opinion of the Court.

This case concerns the federal income tax consequences of a sale-and-leaseback in which petitioner Frank Lyon Company (Lyon) took title to a building under construction by Worthen Bank & Trust Company (Worthen) of Little Rock, Ark., and simultaneously leased the building back to Worthen for long-term use as its headquarters and principal banking facility.

I

The underlying pertinent facts are undisputed. They are established by stipulations, App. 9, 14, the trial testimony, and the documentary evidence, and are reflected in the District Court's findings.

Lyon is a closely held Arkansas corporation engaged in the distribution of home furnishings, primarily Whirlpool and RCA electrical products. Worthen in 1965 was an Arkansas-chartered bank and a member of the Federal Reserve System. Frank Lyon was Lyon's majority shareholder and board chairman; he also served on Worthen's board. Worthen at that time began to plan the construction of a multistory bank and office building to replace its existing facility in Little Rock. About the same time Worthen's competitor, Union National Bank of Little Rock, also began to plan a new bank and office building. Adjacent sites on Capitol Avenue, separated only by Spring Street, were acquired by the two banks. It became a matter of competition, for both banking business and tenants, and prestige as to which bank would start and complete its building first.

Worthen initially hoped to finance, to build, and to own the proposed facility at a total cost of $9 million for the site, building, and adjoining parking deck. This was to be accomplished by selling $4 million in deben-

---

51. Accounting considerations are summarized in Cook, Sales and Leasebacks, BNA Tax Mgmt. Portfolio 36-3d, at A-5 through A-35 (1981).

New Modes of Capital Assembly

tures and using the proceeds in the acquisition of the capital stock of a wholly owned real estate subsidiary. This subsidiary would have formal title and would raise the remaining $5 million by a conventional mortgage loan on the new premises. Worthen's plan, however, had to be abandoned for two significant reasons:

1. As a bank chartered under Arkansas law, Worthen legally could not pay more interest on any debentures it might issue than that then specified by Arkansas law. But the proposed obligations would not be marketable at that rate.

2. Applicable statutes or regulations of the Arkansas State Bank Department and the Federal Reserve System required Worthen, as a state bank subject to their supervision, to obtain prior permission for the investment in banking premises of any amount (including that placed in a real estate subsidiary) in excess of the bank's capital stock or of 40% of its capital stock and surplus. See Ark. Stat. Ann. §67-547.1 (Supp. 1977); 12 U.S.C. §371d (1976 ed.) [12 U.S.C.S. §371d]; 12 C.F.R. §265.2(f)(7)(1977). Worthen, accordingly, was advised by staff employees of the Federal Reserve System that they would not recommend approval of the plan by the System's Board of Governors.

Worthen therefore was forced to seek an alternative solution that would provide it with the use of the building, satisfy the state and federal regulators, and attract the necessary capital. In September 1967 it proposed a sale-and-leaseback arrangement. The State Bank Department and the Federal Reserve System approved this approach, but the Department required that Worthen possess an option to purchase the leased property at the end of the 15th year of the lease at a set price, and the federal regulator required that the building be owned by an independent third party.

Detailed negotiations ensued with investors that had indicated interest, namely, Goldman, Sachs & Company; White, Weld & Co.; Eastman Dillon, Union Securities & Company; and Stephens, Inc. Certain of these firms made specific proposals.

Worthen then obtained a commitment from New York Life Insurance Company to provide $7,140,000 in permanent mortgage financing on the building, conditioned upon its approval of the titleholder. At this point Lyon entered the negotiations and it, too, made a proposal.

. . . Lyon in November 1967 was approved as an acceptable borrower by First National City Bank for the construction financing, and by New York Life, as the permanent lender. In April 1968 the approvals of the state and federal regulators were received.

In the meantime, . . . Worthen itself began construction.

In May 1968 Worthen, Lyon, City Bank, and New York Life executed complementary and interlocking agreements under which the building was sold by Worthen to Lyon as it was constructed, and Worthen leased the completed building back from Lyon:

1. Agreements between Worthen and Lyon. Worthen and Lyon executed a ground lease, a sales agreement, and a building lease.

Under the ground lease dated May 1, 1968, . . . Worthen leased the site to Lyon for 76 years and 7 months through November 30, 2044. The first 19 months were the estimated construction period. The ground rents payable by Lyon to Worthen were $50 for the first 26 years and 7 months and thereafter in quarterly payments:

12/1/94 through 11/30/99 (5 years)—$100,000 annually
12/1/99 through 11/30/04 (5 years)—$150,000 annually
12/1/04 through 11/30/09 (5 years)—$200,000 annually
12/1/09 through 11/30/34 (25 years)—$250,000 annually
12/1/34 through 11/30/44 (10 years)—$10,000 annually.

Under the sales agreement dated May 19, 1968, . . . Worthen agreed to sell the building to Lyon, and Lyon agreed to buy it, piece by piece as it was constructed, for a total price not to exceed $7,640,000, in reimbursements to Worthen for its expenditures for the construction of the building.

Under the building lease dated May 1, 1968, . . . Lyon leased the building back to Worthen for a primary term of 25 years from December 1, 1969, with options in Worthen to extend the lease for eight additional 5-year terms, a total of 65 years. During the period between the expiration of the building lease (at the latest, November 30, 2034, if fully extended) and the end of the ground lease on November 30, 2044, full ownership, use, and control of the building were Lyon's, unless, of course, the building had been repurchased by Worthen. . . . Worthen was not obligated to pay rent under the building lease until completion of the building. For the first 11 years of the lease, that is, until November 30, 1980, the stated quarterly rent was $145,581.03 ($582,324.12 for the year). For the next 14 years, the quarterly rent was $153,289.32 ($613,157.28 for the year), and for the option periods the rent was $300,000 a year, payable quarterly. . . . The total rent for the building over the 25-year primary term of the lease thus was $14,989,767.24. That rent equaled the principal and interest payments that would amortize the $7,140,000 New York Life mortgage loan over the same period. When the mortgage was paid off at the end of the primary term, the annual building rent, if Worthen extended the lease, came down to the stated $300,000. Lyon's net rentals from the building would be further reduced by the increase in ground rent Worthen would receive from Lyon during the extension.

The building lease was a "net lease," under which Worthen was responsible for all expenses usually associated with the maintenance of an office building, including repairs, taxes, utility charges, and insurance, and was to keep the premises in good condition, excluding, however, reasonable wear and tear.

Finally, under the lease, Worthen had the option to repurchase the building at the following times and prices:

> 11/30/80 (after 11 years) — $6,325,169.85
> 11/30/84 (after 15 years) — $5,432,607.32
> 11/30/89 (after 20 years) — $4,187,328.04
> 11/30/94 (after 25 years) — $2,145,935.00.

These repurchase option prices were the sum of the unpaid balance of the New York Life mortgage, Lyon's $500,000 investment, and 6% interest compounded on that investment.

2. Construction financing agreement. By agreement dated May 14, 1968, . . . City Bank agreed to lend Lyon $7,000,000 for the construction of the building. This loan was secured by a mortgage on the building and the parking deck, executed by Worthen as well as by Lyon, and as assignment by Lyon of its interests in the building lease and in the ground lease.

3. Permanent financing agreement. By Note Purchase Agreement dated May 1, 1968, . . . New York Life agreed to purchase Lyon's $7,140,000 6¾% 25-year secured note to be issued upon completion of the building. Under this agreement Lyon warranted that it would lease the building to Worthen for a noncancelable term of at least 25 years under a net lease at a rent at least equal to the mortgage payments on the note. Lyon agreed to make quarterly payments of principal and interest equal to the rentals payable by Worthen during the corresponding primary term of the lease. . . . The security for the note were a first deed of trust and Lyon's assignment of its interests in the building lease and in the ground lease. . . . Worthen joined in the deed of trust as the owner of the fee and the parking deck.

In December 1969 the building was completed and Worthen took possession. At that time Lyon received the permanent loan from New York Life, and it discharged the interim loan from City Bank. The actual cost of constructing the office building and parking complex (excluding the cost of the land) exceeded $10,000,000.

Lyon filed its federal income tax returns on the accrual and calendar year basis. On its 1969 return, Lyon accrued rent from Worthen for December. It asserted as deductions one month's interest to New York Life; one month's depreciation on the building; interest on the construction loan from City Bank; and sums for legal and other expenses incurred in connection with the transaction.

On audit of Lyon's 1969 return, the Commissioner of Internal Revenue determined that Lyon was "not the owner for tax purposes of any portion of the Worthen Building," and ruled that "the income and expenses related to this building are not allowable . . . for Federal income tax purposes." . . . He also added $2,298.15 to Lyon's 1969 income as "accrued interest income." This was the computed 1969 portion of a gain, considered the equivalent of interest income, the realization of which was based on the assumption that Worthen would exercise its option to buy the building after 11 years, on November 30, 1980, at the price stated in the lease, and on the additional determination that Lyon had "loaned" $500,000 to Worthen. In other words, the Commissioner determined that the sale-and-leaseback arrangement was a financing transaction in which Lyon loaned Worthen $500,000 and acted as a conduit for the transmission of principal and interest from Worthen to New York Life.

All this resulted in a total increase of $497,219.18 over Lyon's reported income for 1969, and a deficiency in Lyon's federal income tax for that year in the amount of $236,596.36. The Commissioner assessed that amount, together with interest of $43,790.84, for a total of $280,387.20.

Lyon paid the assessment and filed a timely claim for its refund. The claim was denied, and this suit, to recover the amount so paid, was instituted in the United States District Court for the Eastern District of Arkansas within the time allowed by 26 U.S.C. §6532(a)(1) (26 U.S.C.S. §6532(a)(1)).

After trial without a jury, the District Court, in a memorandum letter-opinion setting forth findings and conclusions, ruled in Lyon's favor and held that its claimed deductions were allowable. 75-2 U.S.T.C. ¶9545 (1975); 36 A.F.T.R. 2d ¶75-5059 (1975). It concluded that the legal intent of the parties had been to create a bona fide sale-and-leaseback in accordance with the form and language of the documents evidencing the transactions. It rejected the argument that Worthen was acquiring an equity in the building through its rental payments. It found that the rents were unchallenged and were reasonable throughout the period of the lease, and that the option prices, negotiated at arm's length between the parties, represented fair estimates of market value on the applicable dates. It rejected any negative inference from the fact that the rentals, combined with the options, were sufficient to amortize the New York Life loan and to pay Lyon a 6% return on its equity investment. It found that Worthen would acquire an equity in the building only if it exercised one of its options to purchase, and that it was highly unlikely, as a practical matter, that any purchase option would ever be exercised. It rejected any inference to be drawn from the fact that the lease was a "net lease." It found that Lyon had mixed motivations for entering into the transaction, including the need to diversify as well as the desire to have the benefits of a "tax shelter." . . .

The United States Court of Appeals for the Eighth Circuit reversed. 536 F.2d 746 (1976). It held that the Commissioner correctly determined that Lyon was not the true owner of the building and therefore was not entitled to the claimed deductions. It likened ownership for tax purposes to a "bundle of sticks" and undertook its own evaluation of the facts. It concluded, in agreement with the Government's contention, that Lyon "totes an empty bundle" of ownership sticks. Id., at 751. It stressed the following: (a) The lease agreements circumscribed Lyon's right to profit from its investment in the building by giving Worthen the option to purchase for an amount equal to Lyon's $500,000 equity plus 6% compound interest and the assumption of the unpaid balance of the New York Life mortgage. (b) The option prices did not take into account possible appreciation of the value of the building or inflation. (c) Any award realized as a result of destruction or condemnation of the building in excess of the mortgage balance and the $500,000 would be paid to Worthen and not Lyon. (d) The building rental payments during the primary term were exactly equal to the mortgage payments. (e) Worthen retained control over the ultimate disposition of the building through its various options to repurchase and to renew the lease plus its ownership of the site. (f) Worthen enjoyed all benefits and bore all burdens incident to the operation and ownership of the building so that, in the Court of Appeals' view, the only economic advantages accruing to Lyon, in the event it were considered to be the true owner of the property, were income tax savings of approximately $1.5 million during the first 11 years of the arrangement. Id., at 752-753. The court concluded, id., at 753, that the transaction was "closely akin" to that in Helvering v Lazarus & Co., 308 U.S. 252, 84 L. Ed. 226, 60 S. Ct. 209 (1939). "In sum, the benefits, risks, and burdens which (Lyon) has incurred with respect to the Worthen building are simply too insubstantial to establish a claim to the status of owner for tax purposes. . . . The vice of the present lease is that all of (its) features have been employed in the same transaction with the cumulative effect of depriving (Lyon) of any significant ownership interest." 536 F.2d, at 754.

We granted certiorari, 429 U.S. 1089, 51 L. Ed. 2d 534, 97 S. Ct. 1097 (1977), because of an indicated conflict with American Realty Trust v United States, 498 F.2d 1194 (CA4 1974).

II

This Court, almost 50 years ago, observed that "taxation is not so much concerned with the refinements of title as it is with actual command over the property taxed — the actual benefit for which the tax is paid." Corliss v Bowers, 281 U.S. 376, 378, 74 L. Ed. 916, 50 S. Ct. 336 (1930). In a number of cases, the Court has refused to permit the transfer of formal legal title to shift the incidence of taxation attributable to ownership of property where the transferor continues to retain significant control over the property transferred. E.g., Commissioner v Sunnen, 333 U.S. 591, 92 L. Ed. 898, 68 S. Ct. 715 (1948); Helvering v Clifford, 309 U.S. 331, 84 L. Ed. 788, 60 S. Ct. 554 (1940). In applying this doctrine of substance over form, the Court has looked to the objective economic realities of a transaction rather than to the particular form the parties employed. The Court has never regarded "the simple expedient of drawing up papers," Commissioner v Tower, 327 U.S. 280, 291, 90 L. Ed. 670, 66 S. Ct. 532, 164 A.L.R. 1135 (1946), as controlling for tax purposes when the objective economic realities are to the contrary. "In the field of taxation, administrators of the laws, and the courts, are concerned with substance and realities, and formal written documents are not rigidly binding." Helvering v Lazarus & Co., 308 U.S., at 255, 84 L. Ed. 226, 60 S. Ct. 209. See also Commissioner v P.G. Lake, Inc., 356 U.S. 260, 266-267, 2 L. Ed. 2d 743, 78 S. Ct. 691 (1958); Commissioner v. Court Holding Co., 324 U.S. 331, 334, 89 L. Ed. 981, 65 S. Ct. 707 (1945). Nor is the parties' desire to achieve a particular tax result necessarily relevant. Commissioner v Duberstein, 363 U.S. 278, 286, 4 L. Ed. 2d 1218, 80 S. Ct. 1190 (1960).

In the light of these general and established principles, the Government takes the position that the Worthen-Lyon transaction in its entirety should be regarded as a sham. The agreement as a whole, it is said, was only an elaborate financing scheme designed to provide economic benefits to Worthen and a guaranteed return to Lyon. The latter was but a conduit used to forward the mortgage payments, made under the guise of rent paid by Worthen to Lyon, on to New York Life as mortgagee. This, the Government claims, is the true substance of the transaction as viewed under the microscope of the tax laws. Although the arrangement was cast in sale-and-leaseback form, in substance it was only a financing transaction, and the terms of the repurchase options and lease renewals so indicate. It is said that Worthen could reacquire the building simply by satisfying the mortgage debt and paying Lyon its $500,000 advance plus interest, regardless of the fair market value of the building at the time; similarly, when the mortgage was paid off, Worthen could extend the lease at drastically reduced bargain rentals that likewise bore no relation to fair rental value but were simply calculated to pay Lyon its $500,000 plus interest over the extended term. Lyon's return on the arrangement in no event could exceed 6% compound interest (although the Government conceded it might well be less. . . . Furthermore, the favorable option and lease renewal terms made it highly unlikely that Worthen would abandon the building after it in effect had "paid off" the mortgage. The Government implies that the arrangement was one of convenience which, if accepted on its face, would enable Worthen to deduct its payments to Lyon as rent and would allow Lyon to claim a deduction for depreciation, based on the cost of construction ultimately borne by Worthen, which Lyon could offset against other income, and to deduct mortgage interest that roughly would offset the inclusion of Worthen's rental payments in Lyon's income. If, however, the Government argues, the arrangement was only a financing transaction under which Worthen was the owner of the building, Worthen's payments would be deductible only to the extent to claim depreciation; Lyon would not be entitled to deductions for either mortgage interest or depreciation and it would not have to include Worthen's "rent" payments in its income because its function with respect to those payments was that of a conduit between Worthen and New York Life. . . .

III

There is no simple device available to peel away the form of this transaction and to reveal its substance. The effects of the transaction on all the parties were obviously different from those that would have resulted had Worthen been able simply to make a mortgage agreement with New York Life and to receive a $500,000 loan from Lyon. Then *Lazarus* would apply. Here, however, and most significantly, it was Lyon alone, and not Worthen, who was liable on the notes, first to City Bank, and then to New York Life. Despite the facts that Worthen had agreed to pay rent and that this rent equaled the amounts due from Lyon to New York Life, should anything go awry in the later years of the lease, Lyon was primarily liable. No matter how the transaction could have been devised otherwise, it remains a fact that as the agreements were placed in final form, the obligation on the notes fell squarely on Lyon. Lyon, an ongoing enterprise, exposed its very business well-being to this real and substantial risk.

The effect of this liability on Lyon is not just the abstract possibility that something will go wrong and that Worthen will not be able to make its payments. Lyon has disclosed this liability on its balance sheet for all the world to see. Its financial position was affected substantially by the presence of this longterm debt, despite the offsetting presence of the building as an asset. To the extent that Lyon has used its capital in this transaction, it is less able to obtain financing for other business needs. . . .

The Court of Appeals acknowledged that the rents alone, due after the primary term of the lease and after the mortgage has been paid, do not provide the simple 6% return which, the Government urges, Lyon is guaranteed, 536 F.2d, at 752. Thus, if Worthen chooses not to exercise its options, Lyon is gambling that the rental value of the building during the last 10 years of the ground lease, during which the ground rent is minimal, will be sufficient to recoup its investment before it must negotiate again with Worthen regarding the ground lease. There are simply too many contingencies, including variations in the value of real estate, in the cost of money, and in the capital structure of Worthen, to permit the conclusion that the parties intended to enter into the transaction as structured in the audit and according to which the Government now urges they be taxed. It is not inappropriate to note that the Government is likely to lose little revenue, if any, as a result of the shape given the transaction by the parties. No deduction was created that is not either matched by an item of income or that would not have been available to one of the parties if the transaction had been arranged differently. While it is true that Worthen paid Lyon less to induce it to enter into the transaction because Lyon anticipated the benefit of the depreciation deduction it would have as the owner of the building, those deductions would have been equally available to Worthen had it retained title to the building. The Government so concedes. Tr. of Oral. Arg. 22-23. The fact that favorable tax consequences were taken into account by Lyon on entering into the transaction is no reason for disallowing those consequences. We cannot ignore the reality that the tax laws affect the shape of nearly every business transaction. See Commissioner v Brown, 380 U.S. 563, 579-580, 14 L. Ed. 2d 75, 85 S. Ct. 1162 (1965) (Harlan, J., concurring). Lyon is not a corporation with no purpose other than to hold title to the bank building. It was not created by Worthen or even financed to any degree by Worthen.

The conclusion that the transaction is not a simple sham to be ignored does not, of course, automatically compel the further conclusion that Lyon is entitled to the items claimed as deductions. Nevertheless, on the facts, this readily follows. As has been noted, the obligations on which Lyon paid interest were its obligations alone, and it is entitled to claim deductions therefor under §163(a) of the 1954 Code, 26 U.S.C. §163(a) (26 U.S.C.S. §163(a)).

As is clear from the facts, none of the parties to this sale-and-leaseback was the owner of the building in any simple sense. But it is equally clear that the facts focus upon Lyon as the one whose capital was committed to the building and as the party, therefore, that was entitled to claim depreciation for the consumption of that capital. The Government has based its contention that Worthen should be treated as the owner on the assumption that throughout the term of the lease Worthen was acquiring an equity in the property. In order to establish the presence of that growing equity, however, the Government is forced to speculate that one of the options will be exercised and that, if it is not, this is only because the rentals for the extended term are a bargain. We cannot indulge in such speculation in view of the District Court's clear finding to the contrary. We therefore conclude that it is Lyon's capital that is invested in the building according to the agreement of the parties, and it is Lyon that is entitled to depreciation deductions, under §167 of the 1954 Code, 26 U.S.C. §167 (26 U.S.C.S. §167). Cf. United States v Chicago B. & Q. R. Co., 412 U.S. 401, 37 L. Ed. 2d 30, 93 S. Ct. 2169 (1973).

IV

We recognize that the Government's position, and that taken by the Court of Appeals, is not without superficial appeal. One, indeed, may theorize that Frank Lyon's presence on the Worthen board of directors; Lyon's departure from its principal corporate activity into this unusual venture; the parallel between the payments under the building lease and the amounts due from Lyon on the New York Life mortgage; the provisions relating to condemnation or destruction of the property; the nature and presence of the several options available to Worthen; and the tax benefits, such as the use of double declining balance depreciation, that accrue to Lyon during the initial years of the arrangement, form the basis of an argument that Worthen should be regarded as the owner of the building and as the recipient of nothing more from Lyon than a $500,000 loan.

We, however, as did the District Court, find this theorizing incompatible with the substance and economic realities of the transaction: the competitive situation as it existed between Worthen and Union National Bank in 1965 and the years immediately following; Worthen's undercapitalization; Worthen's consequent inability, as a matter of legal restraint, to carry its building plans into effect by a conventional mortgage and other borrowing; the additional barriers imposed by the state and federal regulators; the suggestion, forthcoming from the state regulator, that Worthen possess an option to purchase; the requirement, from the federal regulator, that the building be owned by an independent third party; the presence of several finance organizations seriously interested in participating in the transaction and in the resolution of Worthen's problem; the submission of formal proposals by several of those organizations; the bargaining process and period that ensued; the competitiveness of the bidding; the bona fide character of the negotiations; the three-party aspect of the transaction; Lyon's substantiality and its independence from Worthen; the fact that diversification was Lyon's principal motivation; Lyon's being liable alone on the successive notes to City Bank and New York Life; the reasonableness, as the District Court found, of the rentals and of the option prices; the substantiality of the purchase prices; Lyon's not being engaged generally in the business of financing; the presence of all building depreciation risks on Lyon; the risk, borne by Lyon, that Worthen might default or fail, as other banks have failed; the facts that Worthen could "walk away" from the relationship at the end of the 25-year primary term, and probably would do so if the option price were more than the then-current worth of the building to Worthen; the inescapable fact that if the building lease were not extended, Lyon would be the full owner of the building, free to do with it as it chose; Lyon's liability for the substantial ground rent if Worthen decides not to exercise any of its options to extend; the absence of any understanding between Lyon and Worthen that Worthen would exercise any of the purchase options; the nonfamily and nonprivate nature of the entire transaction; and the absence of any differential in tax rates and of special tax circumstances for one of the parties—all convince us that Lyon has far the better of the case.

In so concluding, we emphasize that we are not condoning manipulation by a taxpayer through arbitrary labels and dealings that have no economic significance. Such, however, has not happened in this case.

In short, we hold that where, as here, there is a genuine multiple-party transaction with economic substance which is compelled or encouraged by business or regulatory realities, is imbued with tax-independent considerations, and is not shaped solely by tax-avoidance features that have meaningless labels attached, the Government should honor the allocation of rights and duties effectuated by the parties. Expressed another way, so long as the lessor retains significant and genuine attributes of the traditional lessor status, the form of the transaction adopted by the parties governs for tax purposes. What those attributes are in any particular case will necessarily depend upon its facts. It suffices to say that, as here, a sale-and-leaseback, in and of itself, does not necessarily operate to deny a taxpayer's claim for deductions.

The judgment of the Court of Appeals, accordingly, is reversed.

It is so ordered.

Mr. Justice White dissents and would affirm the judgment substantially for the reasons stated in the opinion in the Court of Appeals for the Eighth Circuit. 536 F.2d 746 (1976).

SEPARATE OPINION

Mr. Justice STEVENS, dissenting. In my judgment the controlling issue in this case is the economic relationship between Worthen and petitioner, and matters such as the number of parties, their reasons for structuring the transaction in a particular way, and the tax benefits which may result, are largely irrelevant. The question whether a leasehold has been created should be answered by examining the character and value of the purported lessor's reversionary estate.

For a 25-year period Worthen has the power to acquire full ownership of the bank building by simply repaying the amounts, plus interest, advanced by the New York Life Insurance Company and petitioner. During that period, the economic relationship among the parties parallels exactly the normal relationship between an owner and two lenders, one secured by a first mortgage and the other by a second mortgage. If Worthen repays both loans, it will have unencumbered ownership of the property. What the character of this relationship suggests is confirmed by the economic value that the parties themselves have placed on the reversionary interest.

All rental payments made during the original 25-year term are credited against the option repurchase price, which is exactly equal to the unamortized cost of the financing. The value of the repurchase option is thus limited to the cost of the financing, and Worthen's power to exercise the option is cost-free. Conversely, petitioner, the nominal owner of the reversionary estate, is not entitled to receive *any* value for the surrender of its supposed rights of ownership. Nor does it have any power to control Worthen's exercise of the option.

"It is fundamental that 'depreciation is not predicated upon ownership of property *but rather upon an investment in property.*' No such investment exists when payments of the purchase price in accordance with the design of the parties yield no equity to the purchaser." Estate of Franklin v Commissioner, 544 F.2d 1045, 1049 (CA9 1976) (citations omitted; emphasis in original). Here, the petitioner has, in effect, been guaranteed that it will receive its original $500,000 plus accrued interest. But that is all. It incurs neither the risk of depreciation, nor the benefit of possible appreciation. Under the terms of the sale-leaseback, it will stand in no better or worse position after the 11th year of the lease—when Worthen can first exercise its option to repurchase—whether the property has appreciated or depreciated. And this remains true throughout the rest of the 25-year period.

Petitioner has assumed only two significant risks. First, like any other lender, it assumed the risk of Worthen's insolvency. Second, it assumed the risk that Worthen might *not* exercise its option to purchase at or before the end of the original 25-year term. If Worthen should exercise that right *not* to repay, perhaps it would *then* be appropriate to characterize petitioner as the owner and Worthen as the lessee. But speculation as to what might happen in 25 years cannot justify the *present* characterization of petitioner as the owner of the building. Until Worthen has made a commitment either to exercise or not to exercise its option, I think the Government is correct in its view that petitioner is not the owner of the building for tax purposes. At present, since Worthen has the unrestricted right to control the residual value of the property for a price which does not exceed the cost of its unamortized financing, I would hold, as a matter of law, that it is the owner.

I therefore respectfully dissent.

NOTES AND QUESTIONS

1. "We cannot ignore the reality that the tax laws affect the shape of nearly every business transaction." Frank Lyon Co. v. United States, at 1128 supra.

The departure point in your understanding of the sale and leaseback is to consider why it matters to the taxpayers that the transaction not be recast as a mortgage, and, also, why Justice Blackmun almost certainly is mistaken when he asserts that "the Government is likely to lose little revenue, if any, as a result of the shape given the transaction by the parties." Id. at 1127.

To help understand the tax stakes, consider first with the mindset of a buyer-lessor the treatment of both a sale and leaseback and an equivalent mortgage. To use a simple illustration: B acquires property from A for $1,000,000, which he leases back to A at a $100,000 yearly rental. Cost recovery in the first year is $70,000. If B were to lend A $1,000,000 on an equivalent basis, debt service would be $100,000 yearly; the first year's interest component would be $90,000.

Sale and Leaseback:		
	Rental Income	$100,000
	Less Cost Recovery	70,000
	Taxable Income	$ 30,000
Secured Loan:		
	Interest Income	$ 90,000

Although B's cash flow is the same in either case, B's taxable income in year one, reduced by the cost recovery deduction, is lower under a sale and leaseback than it would be had B made an equivalent $1,000,000 loan. On the other hand, A would suffer a reciprocal disadvantage.

Sale and Leaseback:		
	Rental Expense	$100,000
Secured Loan:		
	Interest Expense	$ 90,000
	Cost Recovery	$ 70,000
	Deductible Expenses	$160,000

Although A would incur a $100,000 outlay, whether in rent or debt service, his relevant deductions in year one would be $60,000 less in the event of a sale and leaseback. A would be reluctant to structure this transaction as a sale and leaseback unless (a) the extra deductions were worth more to B than to A, and (b) B was prepared, in some fashion, to share with A these tax benefits — for example, by paying a somewhat inflated price for the property.

This analysis suggests that a common scenario for a sale and leaseback is one which involves an investor "suffering" higher marginal rates than those applicable to the user-lessee. Despite Justice Blackmun's belief that the outcome of the *Frank Lyon* case would be tax neutral, it seems that as a commercial bank Worthen was able to shelter income even without the cost recovery deduction, and that cost recovery in this case was, indeed, more useful to Lyon than to the bank. Wolfman, The Supreme Court in the *Lyon's* Den: A Failure of Judicial Process, 66 Cornell L. Rev. 1075, 1094-1098 (1981).

2. As you are aware, the relative advantage which the buyer-lessor enjoys over the mortgagee in the early years stems from the excess of cost recovery over that part of the rental payment which is a surrogate for "mortgage amortization." Alluding again to our illustration, B's $60,000 "decrease" in taxable income is simply the difference between the $70,000 in cost recovery and the $10,000 of amortization which A would

pay (and B would not report) had the transaction been cast as a mortgage. But some years later the relative advantage shifts away from the buyer-lessor as his cost recovery deductions drop, and — on a level payment mortgage — the amortization component rises. To illustrate the fifteenth year, once again from B's vantage:

> Sale and Leaseback:
> Rental Income $100,000
> *Less* Cost Recovery   40,000
> Taxable Income $ 60,000
>
> Secured Loan:
> Interest Income $ 30,000

The shoe is now on the other foot, and B — as the buyer-lessor — will suffer more taxable income from this transaction than he would incur as a straight mortgagee. Reciprocally, A — as the seller-lessee — will now be better off:

> Sale and Leaseback:
> Rental Expense $100,000
>
> Secured Loan:
> Interest Expense $ 30,000
> Cost Recovery $ 40,000
> Deductible Expenses $ 70,000

These shifting tax fortunes reflect a fundamental difference in the treatment of "cost recovery" by an owner of depreciable property and by a mortgage holder. Present law allows the owner to recover his cost on an accelerated basis, whereas the lender recovers its capital tax-free only as the principal of its investment, the loan, is repaid. Lenders, in effect, amortize their loan for tax purposes on a sinking fund theory of capital recovery. Wolfman, note 1 supra, at 1089.

3. Turning your attention to the Court's rationale, how persuaded are you that Justice Blackmun has given lawyers and judges useful guidelines for distinguishing between a good and "bad" sale and leaseback. Among the factors that to the Court seemed to "reveal the substance" of this transaction were that:

a. Lyon was primarily liable on the permanent loan to New York Life;
b. Lyon had committed $500,000 of its own capital to this transaction;
c. If Worthen chose not to exercise its repurchase option, Lyon would be gambling that the rental value of the building during the last 10 years of the ground lease, at a time when the ground rental was minimal, would be sufficient to recoup its investment;
d. Here there was a "genuine multiple-party transaction with eco-

nomic substance compelled or encouraged by business or regulatory realities";

e. One felt the cumulative impact of the twenty-six factors set forth under Part IV of the opinion.

As its title implies, Wolfman, The Supreme Court in the *Lyon's* Den: A Failure of Judicial Process, 66 Cornell L. Rev. 1075 (1981), takes strong exception to the Court's decision. The author also reports that early in 1981 Worthen repurchased the bank building from Lyon — in accordance with the lease repurchase option terms. For each of the eleven years during which the lease remained in effect (1969-1980), Lyon's depreciation and interest deductions exceeded its rental income. Had Lyon remained the owner after 1981, its rental income would have exceeded the relevant deductions. Id. at 1101.

4. The Court in *Lyon* refused to apply Helvering v. Lazarus & Co., 308 U.S. 252 (1939). There the department store taxpayer sold its property to a bank and immediately leased it back for ninety-nine years, obtaining in the same transaction successive purchase options. Although the Supreme Court opinion in *Lazarus* does not disclose the option prices, these were based on the unamortized balance of the moneys which the bank had provided the taxpayer. 32 B.T.A. 633 (1935). The *Lazarus* Court disregarded the sale and leaseback form and, over the Commissioner's (!) objection, recast the transaction as a mortgage.

In *Lyon*, how convincing is Justice Blackmun when he writes:

> The effects of the transaction on all the parties were obviously different from those that would have resulted had Worthen been able simply to make a mortgage agreement with New York Life and to receive a $500,000 loan from Lyon. Then *Lazarus* would apply. Here, however, and most significantly, it was Lyon alone, and not Worthen, who was liable on the notes, first to City Bank, and then to New York Life. [435 U.S. at 576.]

What if the New York Life loan had been nonrecourse?

Alternatively, what if New York Life had purchased the property directly and then had leased it back to Worthen?

5. In applying *Frank Lyon*, the Tax Court has quoted from that part of the opinion which speaks of the Worthen deal as being "a genuine multiple party transaction with economic substance which is compelled or encouraged by business or regulatory realities, is imbued with tax-independent considerations, and is not shaped solely by the tax-avoidance features that have meaningless labels attached. . . ." 435 U.S. at 583-584. Two cases, decided quite differently, develop this theme:

(a) In Hilton v. Commissioner, 74 T.C. 305 (1980), decided for the Commissioner, the salient facts were these: A newly constructed department store was sold to a financing corporation and leased back under a long-term lease. The corporation financed the purchase by selling its notes, secured by a mortgage and lease assignment, to several insurance companies. The taxpayers, members of a syndicate, then acquired the fee subject to the lease and mortgage. The annual lease rental for the initial thirty-year term was set at 6.33 percent of the purchase price; the lessee had options to renew the leases for additional terms of twenty-three years, twenty-three years, and twenty-two years at annual rentals of 1½, 1, and 1 percent, respectively, of such purchase price. The rentals were calculated without regard to a fair rental value, but were enough to service the underlying debt, which would result in a 10 percent balloon payment at the end of the initial thirty-year term. The tenant had full control over the use of the leased premises and could terminate the lease in the event the property was condemned or destroyed.

The Tax Court's discussion continues at pages 346-359:

> Notwithstanding the intricacies of the above-described tier partnership labyrinth, the central issue in this case is the bona fides of the sale-leaseback. This is essentially an exercise in substance versus form, and as earlier stated by the Supreme Court, "In the field of taxation, administrators of the law, and the courts, are concerned with substance and realities, and formal written documents are not rigidly binding." Helvering v. Lazarus & Co., 308 U.S. 252, 255 (1939). Notwithstanding the approval of the sale-leaseback in the *Frank Lyon* case, we do not understand the teaching of the Supreme Court's decision in that case to be that we are to accept *every* putative sale-leaseback transaction at face value, but rather that our precept is to determine whether there is, in the words of the Supreme Court, "a genuine multiple-party transaction with economic substance which is compelled or encouraged by business or regulatory realities, is imbued with tax-independent considerations, and is not shaped solely by tax-avoidance features that have meaningless labels attached." Frank Lyon Co. v. United States, 435 U.S. 561, 583-584. . . .
>
> One key element of the above test is the phrase "genuinely multiple-party" for obviously, when looked at only from the viewpoint of Broadway, as seller-lessee, the transaction had economic substance and was encouraged by business realities. Petitioners have claimed in their brief and we have no reason to gainsay them that, had conventional mortgage financing been used, the insurance companies would have lent only 75 percent of the value of the property. The insurance companies, furthermore, had limitations on the total amounts and proportions of their funds that could be committed to direct real estate mortgages. Under the sale-leaseback approach Broadway was, in effect, able to finance 100 percent of the acquisition cost of the property. In addition, the purchase of corporate notes, which were secured by a lease between the corporation and a well-rated tenant, avoided certain other insurance company lending restrictions.
>
> Similarly, Broadway had limitations in its loan and credit agreements with its banks which put a ceiling on the total amount of debt it could incur and also limited the total value of its property which could be mortgaged. At the same time, Broadway expected to be able to deduct as rent, during the initial 30-year term of the lease, an amount equal to 90 percent of the principal

amortization and 100 percent of the interest costs of the underlying mortgage on the property. The mortgage contained a 10-percent balloon at the end of the 30-year term.

It is thus apparent that, viewed broadly from the vantage point of Broadway and the insurance companies, the sale-leaseback transaction followed what is essentially a widely used and acceptable business practice embracing substantial business as well as tax purposes and which had significant economic, nontaxable substance. In this context, we do not deem the existence of a net lease, a nonrecourse mortgage or rent during the initial lease term geared to the cost of interest and mortgage amortization to be, in and of themselves, much more than neutral commercial realities. Furthermore, the fact that the transaction was put together by an "orchestrator" (to use petitioner's term) would not alone prove fatal to the buyer-lessor's cause provided the result is economically meaningful on both sides of the equation. For even before the enactment of the at-risk rules of section 465, equipment-leveraged leases, often "packaged" by brokers, were acceptable to the Commissioner where substantial nontax economic interests were acquired by the buyer-lessor. Rev. Proc. 75-21, 1975-1 C.B. 715.

Overall, considering the involvement of Broadway and the insurance companies, there was at least a two-party aspect to the transaction. We explore subsequently herein, whether the facts, as they did in *Frank Lyon*, disclose a genuine *three*-party aspect.

But what Broadway sees is a reflection from only one polygon of the prism. In the *Frank Lyon* case, the Supreme Court appraised not only the substance of the seller-lessee's interest, but also that of the buyer-lessor and the legal and economic substance of the contractual relationship between the two.

We, therefore, turn now to a consideration of the substance of the buyer-lessor's (i.e., the petitioners') interest, and here the substantiality of that interest, aside from tax considerations, is far less apparent. We must thus inquire: does the buyer-lessor's interest have substantial legal and economic significance aside from tax considerations, or is that interest simply the purchased tax byproduct of Broadway's economically impelled arrangement with the insurance companies? . . .

Under the *Frank Lyon* test, petitioners must show not only that their participation in the sale-leaseback was not motivated or shaped solely by tax avoidance features that have meaningless labels attached, but also that there is economic substance to the transaction independent of the apparent tax shelter potential. Another way of stating the test is suggested by the Ninth Circuit's opinion in Estate of Franklin v. Commissioner, 544 F.2d 1045 (9th Cir. 1976), *affg.* 64 T.C. 752 (1975), to wit: Could the buyer-lessor's method of payment for the property be expected at the outset to rather quickly yield an equity which buyer-lessor could not prudently abandon? An affirmative answer would produce, in the words of the Circuit Court, "the stuff of substance. It meshes with the form of the transaction and constitutes a sale." (544 F.2d at 1098.) Consequently, if the test is not met, the buyer-lessor will not have made an investment in the property, regardless of the form of ownership. And it is fundamental that depreciation is not predicated upon ownership of property but rather upon an investment in property. Estate of Franklin v. Commissioner, supra at 1049; Mayerson v. Commissioner, 47 T.C. 340, 350 (1966). . . .

Petitioners and respondent each relied substantially upon the testimony of expert witnesses to show the presence or absence of economic motivation on the part of petitioners. . . .

The knowledge and experience of Steichen (respondent's expert witness) in real estate development and investment generally, and especially with regard to retail properties, were impressive. We find his analyses, opinions, and conclusions to be generally persuasive. His report and testimony, unlike that of petitioners' expert, were based upon a thorough investigation of the property and the details of the actual transaction before us, and we find the underlying premises of his analysis to be valid.

Steichen examined the 1965 agreement between Sears and Broadway and took it into account in his analysis. He made two trips to Bakersfield to familiarize himself with the physical aspects of the store and the shopping center, the general neighborhood surrounding the shopping center, and the city of Bakersfield as a whole. He examined the structure of the store and its merchandising layout. He examined the building permits for the store. He tried, but was unable, to examine or obtain copies of the tax assessor's records for the property. He did consider the impact of increasing interest rates.

Based upon the investigations he made in the field and personal observations he made by driving through the area surrounding the store, Steichen concluded that the property was located in the fastest growing suburban neighborhood in the city of Bakersfield, and that the shopping center was located there in order to serve the growing suburban market. . . .

In Steichen's opinion, it is highly unlikely that a department store would go into a location with the expectation of occupying a building at that location for only 30 years. Since Broadway found there was economic justification to enter this market area, Steichen expressed the belief that Broadway's expectation would run through the normal life expectancy of the viability of the market area the store was designed to serve. Consequently, Steichen believed that in 1967 and 1969, the petitioners had every reason to expect Broadway would exercise its right to extend the lease through the first-option period of 23 years. . . .

. . . [D]ue to the highly speculative nature of any predictions concerning the future of the property, and the fact that the value of the economic returns produced by an extension of the lease past 2021 would be relatively small on a discounted basis, Steichen concluded that the value of those returns should not be considered in determining the fair market value of the property in 1980 or 1998.

Steichen analyzed the potential sources of economic gain for the petitioners under the following categories:

(1) Net income or losses;
(2) Net proceeds resulting from : (a) mortgage refinancing; (b) condemnation; or (c) sale.

Following Steichen's approach, of which we approve, we first address the following question: At what point, at what time, and under what conditions could it be presumed there would be net income to distribute, and in what amounts? Under the lease and deed of trust, all rent payments due under the lease for the first 30 years are to be used to service the mortgage notes, so no cash flow will be available to petitioners during the 30-year period. The lease rental is sufficient to amortize 90 percent of the principal amount of the mortgage notes, leaving $313,750 due in 1998.

At the end of the initial term of the lease, petitioners will have the option of either making capital contributions to cover the balloon payment or refinancing the balloon. Since there would be little incentive to do the former, in light of the rent provisions in the lease for subsequent option periods and the probability (as discussed supra) that Broadway would continue its occupancy for 23 years (at least beyond 1998), it must be assumed that, if possible, refinancing will be sought.

Assuming refinancing at 5⅛-percent interest (the rate in the original mortgage) over the 23-year period of the first lease extension, the annual financing cost would be approximately $23,000, to be paid out of the fixed rental of $47,062.50; thus leaving a total pre-tax cash flow for division among and distribution to all of the petitioners of approximately $23,000 per annum. It goes without saying that the opportunity to earn $23,000 annually, commencing 30 years from the inception of the transaction, would not in and of itself appear to justify the $334,000 original investment by the petitioners in the 14th P.A. and 37th P.A. partnerships.

The foregoing analysis assumes, of course, that Broadway would exercise its renewal option for the first 23-year period. Given the extremely favorable terms on which Broadway could renew, however, the only conceivable reason why it (or any corporate successor) would not renew would be that the property had lost its economic viability, in which event the property would also be worthless to the petitioners. . . .

In concluding the part of his report dealing with cash flow, Steichen stated that "an analysis of the cash flow from the rentals to be received when adjusted to reflect the financing costs indicates that there would be no cash available for distribution to the partners until the 31st year of the lease term and that where tax considerations are not taken into account the return at that time is too small to justify the wait." We agree.

The other possibilities for economic gain foreseeable at the inception of the transaction were sale, condemnation, or destruction or mortgage refinancing of the property. Section 21 of the lease deals with a sale or transfer of the property, and provides, in effect, that if the lessor receives a bona fide offer for the purchase of the property and decides to accept such offer, the lessee would have the right to purchase the interest of the lessor for $50,000. The property would still remain subject to the nonrecourse debt. Of this purchase price, the limited partners of both partnerships would be entitled to receive, as a group, 49 percent or $24,500. The limited partners of 14th Property Associates would thus suffer a loss of $155,500, and the limited partners of 37th Property Associates would lose $130,500. If the offering price were greater than $50,000, Broadway, as lessee, would merely exercise its option and pocket the gain. . . .

Regardless of section 21, however, petitioners' opportunity for gain on any sale will be limited to any then-present value of the rental income flow and the residual, the combined total of which, as we have shown, is minimal and in any event less than petitioners investment. The reason for this is that section 26(a) of the lease (also quoted in our findings) gives Broadway carte blanche to sublet the property or assign its leasehold interest after the original term of the lease. Since Broadway will thereby continue to have virtually total control of the property for an additional 68-plus years after the expiration of the original term, and since petitioners' interest will be strictly limited for all those years, Broadway, and not petitioners, will be in a position to realize the true economic value of the property by the simple expedient of using the property, itself, at nominal cost or subletting or assigning it to another for the then-going rate of property of this type in Bakersfield, Calif. In other words, Broadway's purchase option was essentially surplusage. . . .

Another possible source of economic gain would be through receipt of the proceeds of condemnation. However, since the act of condemnation lies wholly beyond the control of the owner or the lessee of property, and since the amounts of awards cannot even be speculated in advance, a prospective investor would not ordinarily look to condemnation as a likely source of economic gain. . . .

A final potential source of economic gain is through mortgage refinancing. Under the mortgage notes, a total prepayment is permitted in any calendar year beginning with 1978, subject to prepayment penalties beginning with 3 percent of the then-outstanding principal and reducing gradually to 0.15 percent in 1997. Taking into consideration the premium to be paid for prepayment and the fixed rental terms which generate no net cash flow during the initial lease term, the only opportunity for economic gain would occur in the event of a substantial decrease in interest rates below the 5⅛ percent provided for in the financing.

Respondent's expert, Steichen, testified at the trial that since the stated rate of interest of the mortgage notes was below the prevailing commercial lending rates at the time the financing was obtained, and since there was already in evidence continuing upward pressure on interest rates in general, the likelihood of a substantial reduction in interest payments which would lead to an economic gain through mortgage refinancing was quite remote. We find Steichen's testimony on this point convincing.

(b) The facts in Dunlap v. Commissioner, 74 T.C. 1377 (1980), where the taxpayers prevailed, offer an interesting comparison. Safeway Stores sold a regional office facility to a single-purpose finance corporation for $8.8 million, and leased the property back for an original twenty-five-year term. The corporation financed the purchase by placing its secured notes with institutional lenders, then transferred title to the taxpayers, subject to the lease and financing, for $387,000. The rental during the initial term was adequate to self-amortize the financing at the end of the twenty-five years. Safeway Stores held, in addition, the option to extend the lease for six additional periods of five years each at an annual rent of $264,000. In holding for the taxpayers, the court stressed that:

i. If the lease were renewed, the taxpayers' yield would be a high percentage of their initial investment;

ii. If the lease were not renewed, the evidence indicated that the property, by then situated in a densely populated area, could be put to another use better suited to its increased value.

6. A thoughtful, systematic effort to set specific guidelines for determining the validity of real estate sale and leaseback transactions appears in Harmelink and Shurtz, Sale-Leaseback Transactions Involving Real Estate: A Proposal for Defined Tax Rules, 55 S. Cal. L. Rev. 833 (1982). The authors name eight general criteria indicating that the transaction involves a lease, not a mortgage:

    a. Title does not pass to the lessee by the end of the lease term;

    b. The lessee is under no economic compulsion (i.e., bargain option price) to exercise the purchase option;

    c. The lease term plus renewals does not exceed 75 percent of the estimated useful life of the property;

    d. The selling price for the property is comparable to the fair market value of the property;

    e. The rentals are reasonable;

    f. A present value test favorably compares the lessee's interest with the lessor's interest. Ownership is indicated in the taxpayer who has the more substantial interest;

    g. The lessee does not bear any significant risks, such as those of obsolescence or major capital improvements;

    h. The lessee qua seller does not guarantee any loans necessary for the purchase of the property.

In addition, if the sale and leaseback involves nonrecourse financing, the selling price of the property (whether or not it is inflated), the lessor's initial investment (whether or not it is nominal), and the profitability of the transaction, would also be examined, using a *Hilton*-like cash flow analysis. Id. at 886-894.

The authors fail to indicate, however, the weight to be given to the enumerated factors and whether an absence of any one or more would be disqualifying per se.

b. The Sale versus Exchange Issue

Another tax aspect of the sale and leaseback involves the treatment of losses, should any result from the first step of the transaction. Ideally, the seller would like to obtain ordinary loss recognition. Several pitfalls lie in the way. The first hazard, already mentioned, is that the sale will be treated as a loan. The second hazard, since the purchase price is not always related to market values, is that the commissioner, relying upon §482, will rewrite the transaction to rectify artificial distortions of income; to date, the commissioner has not seized this power. The final hazard, the nonrecognition feature of §1031, is considered in the following case.

Leslie Co. v. Commissioner
64 T.C. 247 (1975), aff'd, 539 F.2d 943 (3d Cir. 1976)

IRWIN, Judge. Respondent determined deficiencies in petitioner's income tax as follows:

Year	Deficiency
1965	$176,551.77
1966	50,700.90
1968	155,770.75

The issues presented for our determination are (1) whether the sale and leaseback of property by petitioner in 1968 constituted an exchange of property of a like kind within the meaning of section 1031(a) and, if so, (2) whether petitioner should be entitled to depreciate the property under any of the methods specified in section 167(b) and to avail itself of investment credits pursuant to section 38.

The deficiencies in 1965 and 1966 result from the disallowance of net operating loss carrybacks and investment credit carrybacks based on a claimed net operating loss in 1968 and are completely dependent upon our determination of whether the sale and leaseback comes within the purview of section 1031.

FINDINGS OF FACT

Some of the facts have been stipulated and the stipulation of facts, together with the exhibits attached thereto, are found accordingly.

Petitioner Leslie Co. (hereinafter referred to as Leslie or petitioner) is a New Jersey corporation primarily engaged in the design, manufacture, and industrial distribution of pressure and temperature regulators and automatic instantaneous water heaters. . . .

For many years prior to 1966 Leslie operated its entire business, plant, and office in Lyndhurst, N.J. In 1966 Leslie determined that the Lyndhurst plant would be inadequate for future use and decided to construct a new facility in Parsippany. Upon completion of the new plant the Lyndhurst property was to be sold. Pursuant to the decision to move, Leslie acquired land in Parsippany in March 1967.

On October 30, 1967, after having explored other financing possibilities without success, Leslie agreed to a sale and leaseback of the land with improvements to the Prudential Insurance Co. of America (hereinafter referred to as Prudential). The agreement provided that Prudential would enter into a contract for the purchase and leaseback of the Parsippany property, subject, inter alia, to the following requirements and conditions:

1. The sale price shall not exceed $2,400,000 or the actual cost of land, building and other improvements erected thereon, whichever is the lower. . . .

2. Leslie Co. shall have erected and completed on the above premises a one story, 100% sprinklered, masonry and steel industrial building containing approximately 185,000 square feet. . . . The building is to be constructed and improvements made according to detailed plans and specifications which have been approved by The Prudential. Any changes to the plans . . . must be approved by Prudential prior to commencement of construction. . . .

4. Prudential will be furnished with the following prior to closing:

(a) A lease with Leslie Co. satisfactory in form and substance to Prudential and Leslie Co. for a term of 30 years at an absolute net rental of $190,560, or 7.94% of purchase price if less than $2,400,000 to be paid monthly, in advance, in equal monthly installments. The lease shall include two (2) renewal options of 10 years each with an absolute net annual rental of $72,000, or 3% of purchase price if less than $2,400,000. The lease shall further include a rejectable offer to purchase at the end of the fifteenth, twentieth, twenty-fifth or thirtieth year based on the following schedule:

at the end of the 15th year	$1,798,000
at the end of the 20th year	$1,592,000
at the end of the 25th year	$1,386,000
at the end of the 30th year	$1,180,000

On December 16, 1968, after completion of the plant as approved by Prudential, Leslie delivered the deed to the Parsippany property to Prudential for $2.4 million. The fair market value of the property at the time of sale was in the neighborhood of $2.4 million. Contemporaneously with the transfer of title to Prudential, Leslie and Prudential entered into the lease as specified in the above agreement. The annual net rental of $190,560 was comparable to the fair rental value of similar types of property in the northern New Jersey area. The lease also provided that all condemnation proceeds, net of any damages suffered by Leslie with respect to its trade fixtures and certain structural improvements, would become the property of Prudential without deduction for the leasehold interest of petitioner.

Leslie's total cost in purchasing the land and constructing the plant was $3.187 million, consisting of the following:

Land	$ 225,000
Building	2,410,000
Paving and landscaping	72,000
Boiler (including special features)	140,000
Special electrical wiring	138,000
Miscellaneous personal property (including certain special items)	140,000
Interim finance costs	20,000
Selling costs	12,000
Total cost	$3,187,000

Leslie would not have entered into the sales part of the transaction without the guarantee of the leaseback.

The Parsippany plant was not in operation on December 16, 1968, the date of closing, and did not become fully operational until mid-January 1969. The useful life of the new plant was stipulated to be 30 years. Leslie sold the Lyndhurst plant for $600,000 when it moved into the Parsippany facilities.

Leslie is not a dealer in real estate.

On its 1968 corporate income tax return Leslie reported the disposition of the Parsippany property as a sale with a gross sale price of $2.4 million and a cost of $3,187,414 with a loss thereon of $787,414. The claimed loss resulted in a net operating loss of $366,907, which was carried back to 1965. In addition, an investment credit of $436.41, not utilizable in 1968 on account of the claimed net operating loss was carried back to 1965. An investment credit of $50,700, likewise not utilizable in 1968 on account of the claimed net operating loss, was carried back to 1966. Respondent, in disallowing the claimed loss, thereby disallowed all of the claimed carrybacks. Respondent would allow the loss as a cost of obtaining the 30-year lease and permit it to be amortized over the period of the lease.

Leslie treated the claimed loss as an unrecovered cost of plant construction on its books to be amortized over 30 years.

Prudential treated the rental receipts as rental income and depreciated the property on its corporate income tax returns.

Opinion

Respondent, relying upon section 1.1031(a)-(1c), Income Tax Regs.,[4] and *Century Electric Co.* [Dec. 17,912], 15 T.C. 581 (1950), *affd.*, 192 F.2d 155 (8th Cir. 1951), *cert. denied*, 342 U.S. 954 (1952), submits that the sale and leaseback between petitioner and Prudential falls within the nonrecognition provisions of section 1031, and that, therefore, petitioner's claimed loss is not allowable. In the same breath, respondent would allow the claimed loss as a "cost" of acquiring the leasehold and amortize it over the 30-year term. Petitioner, on the other hand, submits that there was no "exchange" within the meaning of section 1031, and that, therefore, the claimed loss must be recognized. We agree with petitioner that section 1031 is inapplicable and that the loss must be recognized. The amount is not in dispute.

---

4. "(c) No gain or loss is recognized if (1) a taxpayer exchanges property held for productive use in his trade or business, together with cash, for other property of like kind for the same use, such as a truck for a new truck or a passenger automobile for a new passenger automobile to be used for a like purpose; or (2) a taxpayer who is not a dealer in real estate exchanges city real estate for a ranch or farm, or exchanges a leasehold of a fee with 30 years or more to run for real estate, or exchanges improved real estate for unimproved real estate; or (3) a taxpayer exchanges investment property and cash for investment property of a like kind."

As an exception to the general rule requiring the recognition of all gains and losses, section 1031 must be strictly construed. See sec. 1002 and the regulations thereunder, particularly sec. 1.1002-1(b), Income Tax Regs. In order for this nonrecognition provision to come into play it must first be established that an exchange occurred. An exchange is defined in the regulations as a transaction involving the reciprocal transfer of property, as distinguished from a transfer of property for a money consideration. Sec. 1.1002-1(d), Income Tax Regs. See also *Vernon Molbreak*, 61 T.C. 382, 390-392 (1973), *affd. per curiam*, 509 F.2d 616 (7th Cir. 1975).

In the instant situation petitioner executed a sale and leaseback agreement with respect to the Parsippany property. It is clear that the sale and leaseback were merely successive steps of a single integrated transaction. It is also equally clear that petitioner, unable to obtain financing to construct a new plant, employed the sale and leaseback mechanism to obtain the needed new facilities. These factors, however, do not dispose of the issue.

While the leaseback arrangement was a necessary condition to the sale, we are of the opinion that, based on the record before us, the leasehold herein did not have any separate capital value which could be properly viewed as a portion of the consideration paid or exchanged. Petitioner received $2.4 million on the sale of the property. The sale and leaseback agreement, executed prior to construction of the new facility, provided that the sale price was to be actual cost to petitioner or $2.4 million, whichever was less. This was based on Prudential's appraisal of the worth of the property after improvements. As it turned out, the actual cost to construct the new facilities (including purchase of the land) totaled $3.187 million. Although we are troubled by the disparity between $2.4 million and $3.187 million, the only evidence in the record (and this presented by respondent) indicated that the fair market value of the property as improved at the date of sale was in the neighborhood of $2.4 million, not $3.187 million. Respondent has also not objected to petitioner's proposed finding of fact that the property as improved had a fair market value of $2.4 million at the date of sale.[7] We also note that the evidence presented indicated that this valuation was comparable to the fair market value of similar types of property in the area. The annual net rental was also comparable to the fair rental value of similar types of property in the area. Based on the record before us, we have no choice but to find that the fair market value of the property was within the $2.4 million range. In our judgment, therefore, the sole consideration paid for the property was the $2.4 million in cash. The leasehold, while integral to the transaction, had no separate

---

7. We hypothesize that respondent's willingness to accept petitioner's proposed finding of fair market value was due to his desire to ensure that the transaction would not be characterized as merely financial with title in substance remaining with petitioner. At the same time, relying upon *Century Electric Co.* [Dec. 17,912], 15 T.C. 581 (1950), he must have assumed that this Court would disregard the fair market values in finding sec. 1031 applicable. What he has failed to take into account is that it must first be determined that an "exchange" occurred for sec. 1031 to apply.

capital value and was not a part of the consideration. See *City Investing Co.*, 38 T.C. 1, 9 (1962). In support of our finding that the leasehold had no capital value in and of itself at the time of the sale, we also note that in addition to the fact of the sale price and net rentals being for fair value, the condemnation clause in the lease agreement provided (with certain exceptions not material herein) that in the event of condemnation all proceeds would be paid to Prudential without deduction for the leasehold interest. This clause, while clearly not conclusive on the issue, is further evidence of a lack of capital value.

Respondent, however, in the body of his reply brief, argues that since petitioner's cost exceeded the contract price, the difference must be equal to the capital value of the lease. We find this unsupported by the evidence presented. In essence, it would appear that respondent is arguing that although the leasehold had no capital value, it had a premium value to petitioner. The excess expenditures over $2.4 million would not be a loss as such to petitioner since it would be able to utilize the improvements as lessee and thus would be willing to spend more than $2.4 million. Although this argument seems to comport to economic realities, it does not give the leasehold value. The difference between $2.4 million and $3.187 million is clearly attributable to the cost of building the plant (including the purchase of land); it is not attributable to the leasehold. While it may be true that it was only because of the leasehold that petitioner was willing to spend $3.187 million, it does not follow that the leasehold had a value equal to the difference between $2.4 million and $3.187 million. To reach such a result, it must be shown that the fair market value of the improved property was $3.187 million, not $2.4 million. This was not done.

From an accounting standpoint it is true that the loss, being an extraordinary item, may cause a distortion of income. That is probably why petitioner amortized the unrecovered costs over the 30-year term in its financial statements. Petitioner's treatment of the item on the books, however, is not dispositive of the issue for tax purposes. It is not at all uncommon to find that the book and tax treatment of a given transaction differ. Although losses may be amortized for book purposes, nothing in the Code permits such amortization for tax purposes.

When all the cards are on the table, the fact remains that petitioner had a cost basis of $3.187 million in the improved property and realized $2.4 million on the sale. The bonafideness of the sale was not questioned by respondent. As stated previously, since the evidence indicates that petitioner would be paying a net rent comparable to the fair rental value, the leasehold could have no value at the time of sale, and thus could not be a part of the consideration paid. It was merely a condition precedent to the sale; no more and no less. The fact that petitioner was willing to sell the property "only with some kind of leaseback arrangement included does not of itself detract from the reality of the sale." Cf. *City Investing Co.*, supra.

We, therefore, include that there was a bona fide sale of the property and not an "exchange" within the meaning of section 1031. See Jordan March Co. v. Commissioner, 269 F.2d 453 (2d Cir. 1959), *nonacq.* Rev. Rul. 60-43, 1960-1 C.B. 687, *rev'g.* a Memorandum Opinion of this Court. We need not consider *Century Electric Co.,* supra, and its possible conflict with *Jordan Marsh Co.* since we have found that there was no "exchange" within the meaning of section 1031. We do note, though, that if an "exchange" had been found, then, assuming "like kind" property, the fair market value of such property would appear not to be relevant.

Since the nonrecognition provisions of section 1031 are not applicable, the general rule of recognition under 1002 applies.

Because of our holding in the above issue we need not consider the other issue presented.

Reviewed by the Court.

Decision will be entered for the petitioner.

TANNENWALD, J., dissenting. If I understand the majority opinion correctly, its rationale is (1) the sale and leaseback constituted "integral parts of a single transaction" but this factor is not dispositive of the issue of whether there was an exchange under section 1031, and (2) since the sales price and the lease rental were "for fair value," the lease lacked "capital value" and "the transaction must be classified as a bona fide sale and not as an exchange." I think this rationale is erroneous.

I start from the premise that the record supports a finding that the price Prudential paid for the property was equal to its fair market value and that the lease rental was "fair" (as to which the record, to put it mildly, is sparse). But the fact of the matter is that although the lease in the instant case may not have had a "capital value" in the normal sense of that term, it did have a value beyond the fair rental value to the petitioner herein.

Whatever the respective values of the lease and the fee, it is clear from the record herein that petitioner entered into the transaction with its eyes wide open. It knew at the outset that Prudential would acquire the full benefit (in the form of title to the fee) of all of its expenditures with regard to the property. It committed itself to expend whatever sums it took to construct the building with those improvements required by its own special needs and to pay the legal fees and other costs required to consummate the transaction with Prudential. The record herein contains insufficient evidence to support a finding that the petitioner did not contemplate or should not have reasonably contemplated the possibility of a cost overrun; indeed, the record tends to indicate that the opposite was the case. The reason for petitioner's willingness to run the risk of this financial exposure is obvious; in order to operate its business, it needed and was entitled to obtain the lease from Prudential. Thus, the lease had a value *to this petitioner* beyond the rental value, namely, any excess cost that it might incur. In this respect, the situations of the taxpayers in both Jordan Marsh Co. v. Commissioner, 269 F.2d 453 (2d Cir. 1959), *rev'g.* T.C. Memo. 1957-237, and Century Electric Co. v. Commissioner, 192 F.2d 155 (8th Cir. 1951), *aff'g.* 15 T.C. 581 (1950), are clearly distinguishable. In both those cases, the costs in excess of the fair market value of the fee and/or the fair value of the lease were incurred long before the transaction under scrutiny (in one case, 12 years, and in the other, 13 years). It could not possibly be said that those costs were undertaken in order to consummate the transaction. Here, by way of contrast, petitioner incurred the excess costs for the express purpose of engaging in the transaction with Prudential. Under these circumstances, petitioner, unlike the taxpayer in *Jordan Marsh,* was not "clos[ing] out a losing venture" (see 269 F.2d at 456), i.e., a venture that did not start out on a predetermined course.

Under my reasoning, it is unnecessary for me to decide the extent to which the decision or rationale of the Second Circuit Court of Appeals in *Jordan Marsh* is in conflict with *Century Electric.* See *City Investing Co.,* 38 T.C. 1, 7 (1962). I have no hesitancy, however, in holding that, even though there was a sale and not an exchange under section 1031, the excess expended by petitioner over the cash received from Prudential, as far as the petitioner is concerned, should be considered as akin to a bonus paid for the lease and amortized over its term. University Properties, Inc., 45 T.C. 416 (1966), *aff'd,* 378 F.2d 83 (9th Cir. 1967), and cases cited therein.

Raum, Drennen, Quealy, and Hall, JJ., agree with this dissent.

[Dissenting opinion of WILBUR, J., omitted.]

NOTES AND QUESTIONS

1. Accord Crowley, Milner and Co. v. Commissioner, 76 T.C. 1030 (1981), *aff'd,* 689 F.2d 635 (6th Cir. 1982).

2. Before trial, Leslie Co. amended its petition to argue, in the alternative, that the transaction, if not a sale, should be viewed as a mortgage financing arrangement, entitling Leslie Co. to the depreciation deductions and the investment tax credit. 539 F.2d at 945 n.6. In view of the court's holding, this issue was not reached. Had this been necessary, what outcome would you have foreseen?

3. The *Leslie Co.* opinion mentions two circuit court decisions, Century Electric Co. v. Commissioner, 192 F.2d 155 (8th Cir. 1951), *cert. denied,* 342 U.S. 954 (1952), which the government had cited, and Jordan Marsh Co. v. Commissioner, 269 F.2d 453 (2d Cir. 1959), on which taxpayer had relied. Refusing to find any kind of exchange, the Tax Court concluded (incorrectly!) that neither decision controlled the outcome; but the two cases stand as the leading — and somewhat contradictory — authority as to when a leaseback might result in a nontaxable exchange.

The facts in *Century Electric* first: Taxpayer owned business property carried on its books at $531,000. A small college purchased the property for $150,000 and immediately leased it back for 95 years at an aggregate rental of $367,000 for the first 25 years and $11,400 per year thereafter. In refusing to allow taxpayer the benefit of a $381,000 loss deduction, the court simply cited the Treasury Regulation that equates a lease of at least 30 years and "real estate" as property of like kind. Treas. Reg. §1.1031(a)-1(c)(2).

Now the facts in *Jordan Marsh:* A department store owned business property with a book value of $4,770,000. It sold the property for $2,300,000 on a leaseback for 30 years and 3 days, with renewal options for another 30 years. The annual lease rental during the initial term was $138,000, concededly the full rental value, and full rental value was also to be paid during any renewal. The seller was given no repurchase option. The commissioner disallowed the tax loss on the basis of *Century Electric* and the Treasury Regulations. The Tax Court upheld him. 29 T.C. 1281 (1957). Despite the apparent similarity between this and the *Century Electric* case, the Second Circuit reversed the commissioner, holding — as did the court in *Leslie Co.* — that the *Jordan Marsh* transaction was a sale and not an exchange; by taking this position, the Second Circuit did not reach the issue of "likeness" between a 30-year lease and a fee simple:

". . . By the transaction its capital invested in the real estate involved had been completely liquidated for cash to an amount fully equal to the value of the fee. This, we hold, was a sale — not an exchange within the purview of §112(b).

"The Tax Court apparently thought it of controlling importance that the transaction in question involved no change in the petitioner's possession of the premises; it felt that the decision in Century Electric Co. v. Commissioner of Internal Rev., supra, controlled the situation here. We think, however, that the case was distinguishable on the facts. For notwithstanding the lengthy findings made with meticulous care by the Tax Court in that case, 15 T.C. 581, there was no finding that the cash received by the taxpayer was the full equivalent of the value of the fee which the taxpayer had conveyed to the vendee-lessor, and no finding that the leaseback called for a rent which was fully equal to the rental value of the premises. . . ." 269 F.2d 453, 456-457 (2d Cir. 1959).

Although the Second Circuit's reasons are sound for treating the *Jordan Marsh* transaction as a sale, its effort to distinguish *Century Electric* is, at best, unconvincing. The Eighth Circuit certainly seemed satisfied (or, at least, kept any doubts to itself) that the sales price measured the market. With such equivalence, the leaseback has no independent *monetary* value, the transfer of a fee for cash *is* a sale, and the Eighth Circuit erred in believing that it had to decide whether the "exchange" was of like kind.

By distinguishing, rather than repudiating, the *Century Electric* precedent, the Second Circuit stresses an imaginary conflict between itself and the Eighth Circuit over nontaxable exchanges, whereas a real conflict was brewing over the distinction between sale and exchange. The commissioner has refused to follow *Jordan Marsh.* Rev. Rul. 60-43, 1960-1 Cum. Bull. 687.

A loss that is disallowed, as in *Century Electric,* will be treated as an acquisition cost of the leaseback and amortized over the leasehold term. 192 F.2d 155, 160; cf. Int. Rev. Code of 1954, §162. The leaseback term in *Century Electric* was 95 years, far longer than the estimated useful life of the undepreciated improvements that were the subject of the transaction. The court, in rejecting taxpayer's contention that the loss should be apportioned between the land and improvements in proportion to their respective bases, argued that the taxpayer had "invested" in a leasehold and not in its constituent properties.

4. If a sale and leaseback transaction should result in gain instead of loss, which side of the sale versus exchange argument would taxpayer and the commissioner each be most likely to advance?

5. *Transactions between related parties.* Taxpayers who might be tempted to push a close family or business relationship into an advantageous sale and leaseback will find the Code a minefield. For example, the Code does not recognize any loss incurred on a sale between members of a family (brothers and sisters, spouses, ancestors, and lineal descendants), between an individual and a "controlled" corporation, between the grantor and fiduciary of a trust, and between the fiduciary and beneficiary of a trust. Int. Rev. Code of 1954, §267. For a detailed treatment of sale and leasebacks between related parties, see Anderson, Tax Factors in Real Estate Operations 303-310 (2d ed. 1965); Burke, Why Some Sale and Leaseback Arrangements Succeed While Others Fail, 26 J. Taxn. 130, 132-133 (1967).

c. The Issue of Genuineness

Estate of Franklin v. Commissioner
544 F.2d 1045 (9th Cir. 1976)

SNEED, Circuit Judge. This case involves another effort on the part of the Commissioner to curb the use of real estate tax shelters.[1] In this instance he

---

1. An early skirmish in this particular effort appears in Manuel D. Mayerson, 47 T.C. 340 (1966), which the Commissioner lost. The Commissioner attacked the substance of a nonrecourse sale, but based his attack on the nonrecourse and long-term nature of the purchase money note, without focusing on whether the sale was made at an unrealistically high price. In his acquiescence to *Mayerson,* 1969-2 Cum. Bull. xxiv, the Commissioner recognized that the fundamental issue in these cases generally will be whether the property has been "acquired" at an artifically high price, having little relation to its fair market value. "The Service emphasizes that its acquiescence in *Mayerson* is based on the particular facts in the case and will not be relied upon in the disposition of other cases except where it is clear that the property has been acquired at its fair market value in an arm's length transaction creating a bona fide purchase and a bona fide debt obligation." Rev. Rul. 69-77, 1969-1 Cum. Bull. 59.

seeks to disallow deductions for the taxpayers' distributive share of losses reported by a limited partnership with respect to its acquisition of a motel and related property. These "losses" have their origin in deductions for depreciation and interest claimed with respect to the motel and related property. These deductions were disallowed by the Commissioner on the ground either that the acquisition was a sham or that the entire acquisition transaction was in substance the purchase by the partnership of an option to acquire the motel and related property on January 15, 1979. The Tax Court held that the transaction constituted an option exercisable in 1979 and disallowed the taxpayers' deductions. Estate of Charles T. Franklin, 64 T.C. 752 (1975). We affirm this disallowance although our approach differs somewhat from that of the Tax Court.

The interest and depreciation deductions were taken by Twenty-Fourth Property Associates (hereinafter referred to as Associates), a California limited partnership of which Charles T. Franklin and seven other doctors were the limited partners. The deductions flowed from the purported "purchase" by Associates of the Thunderbird Inn, an Arizona motel, from Wayne L. Romney and Joan E. Romney (hereinafter referred to as the Romneys) on November 15, 1968.

Under a document entitled "Sales Agreement," the Romneys agreed to "sell" the Thunderbird Inn to Associates for $1,224,000. The property would be paid for over a period of ten years, with interest on any unpaid balance of seven and one-half percent per annum. "Prepaid interest" in the amount of $75,000 was payable immediately; monthly principal and interest installments of $9,045.36 would be paid for approximately the first ten years, with Associates required to make a ballon payment at the end of the ten years of the difference between the remaining purchase price, forecast as $975,000, and any mortgages then outstanding against the property.

The purchase obligation of Associates to the Romneys was nonrecourse; the Romneys' only remedy in the event of default would be forfeiture of the partnership's interest. The sales agreement was recorded in the local county. A warranty deed was placed in an escrow account, along with a quitclaim deed from Associates to the Romneys, both documents to be delivered either to Associates upon full payment of the purchase price, or to the Romneys upon default.

The sale was combined with a leaseback of the property by Associates to the Romneys; Associates therefore never took physical possession. The lease payments were designed to approximate closely the principal and interest payments with the consequence that with the exception of the $75,000 prepaid interest payment no cash would cross between Associates and Romneys until the ballon payment. The lease was on a net basis; thus, the Romneys were responsible for all of the typical expenses of owning the motel property including all utility costs, taxes, assessments, rents, charges, and levies of "every name, nature and kind whatsoever." The

Romneys also were to continue to be responsible for the first and second mortgages until the final purchase installment was made; the Romneys could, and indeed did, place additional mortgages on the property without the permission of Associates. Finally, the Romneys were allowed to propose new capital improvements which Associates would be required to either build themselves or allow the Romneys to construct with compensating modifications in rent or purchase price.

In holding that the transaction between Associates and the Romneys more nearly resembled an option than a sale, the Tax Court emphasized that Associates had the power at the end of ten years to walk away from the transaction and merely lose its $75,000 "prepaid interest payment." It also pointed out that a *deed* was never recorded and that the "benefits and burdens of ownership" appeared to remain with the Romneys. Thus, the sale was combined with a leaseback in which no cash would pass; the Romneys remained responsible under the mortgages, which they could increase; and the Romneys could make capital improvements.[2] The Tax Court further justified its "option" characterization by reference to the nonrecourse nature of the purchase money debt and the nice balance between the rental and purchase money payments.

Our emphasis is different from that of the Tax Court. We believe the characteristics set out above can exist in a situation in which the sale imposes upon the purchaser a genuine indebtedness within the meaning of section 167(a), Internal Revenue Code of 1954, which will support both interest and depreciation deductions. They substantially so existed in Hudspeth v. Commissioner, 509 F.2d 1224 (9th Cir. 1975), in which parents entered into sale-leaseback transactions with their children. The children paid for the property by executing nonnegotiable notes and mortgages equal to the fair market value of the property; state law proscribed deficiency judgments in case of default, limiting the parents' remedy to foreclosure of the property. The children had no funds with which to make mortgage payments; instead, the payments were offset in part by the rental payments, with the difference met by gifts from the parents to their children. Despite these characteristics this court held that there was a bona fide indebtedness on which the children, to the extent of the rental payments, could base interest deductions. See also American Realty Trust v. United States, 498 F.2d 1194 (4th Cir. 1974); Manuel D. Mayerson, 47 T.C. 340 (1966).

In none of these case, however, did the taxpayer fail to demonstrate that the purchase price was at least approximately equivalent to the fair market value of the property. Just such a failure occurred here. The Tax Court explicitly found that on the basis of the facts before it the value of the

---

2. There was evidence that not all of the benefits and burdens of ownership remained with the Romneys. Thus, for example, the leaseback agreement appears to provide that any condemnation award will go to Associates. Exhibit 6-F, at p. 5.

property could not be estimated. 64 T.C. at 767-768.[4] In our view this defect in the taxpayers' proof is fatal.

Reason supports our perception. An acquisition such as that of Associates if at a price approximately equal to the fair market value of the property under ordinary circumstances would rather quickly yield an equity in the property which the purchaser could not prudently abandon. This is the stuff of substance. It meshes with the form of the transaction and constitutes a sale.

No such meshing occurs when the purchase price exceeds a demonstrably reasonable estimate of the fair market value. Payments on the principal of the purchase price yield no equity so long as the unpaid balance of the purchase price exceeds the then existing fair market value. Under these circumstances the purchaser by abandoning the transaction can lose no more than a mere chance to acquire an equity in the future should the value of the acquired property increase. While this chance undoubtedly influenced the Tax Court's determination that the transaction before us constitutes an option, we need only point out that its existence fails to supply the substance necessary to justify treating the transaction as a sale ab initio. It is not necessary to the disposition of this case to decide the tax consequences of a transaction such as that before us if in a subsequent year the fair market value of the property increases to an extent that permits the purchaser to acquire an equity.[5]

Authority also supports our perception. It is fundamental that "depreciation is not predicated upon ownership of property *but rather upon an investment in property.* Gladding Dry Goods Co., 2 B.T.A. 336 (1925)." *Mayerson,* supra at 350 (italics added). No such investment exists when payments of the purchase price in accordance with the design of the parties yield no equity to the purchaser. Cf. Decon Corp., 65 T.C. 829 (1976); David F. Bolger, 59 T.C. 760 (1973); Edna Morris, 59 T.C. 21 (1972). In the transaction before us and during the taxable years in question the purchase price payments by Associates have not been shown to constitute an *investment in the property.* Depreciation was properly disallowed. Only the Romneys had an investment in the property.

Authority also supports disallowance of the interest deductions. This is

---

4. The Tax Court found that appellants had "not shown that the purported sales price of $1,224,000 (or any other price) had any relationship to the actual market value of the motel property. . . ." 64 T.C. at 767.

Petitioners spent a substantial amount of time at trial attempting to establish that, whatever the actual market value of the property, Associates acted in the good faith *belief* that the market value of the property approximated the selling price. However, this evidence only goes to the issue of sham and does not supply substance to this transaction. "Save in those instances where the statute itself turns on intent, a matter so real as taxation must depend on objective realities, not on the varying subjective beliefs of individual taxpayers." Lynch v. Commissioner, 273 F.2d 867, 872 (2d Cir. 1959). See also Bornstein v. Commissioner, 334 F.2d 779 (1st Cir. 1964); MacRae v. Commissioner, 294 F.2d 56 (9th Cir. 1961). . . .

5. These consequences would include a determination of the proper basis of the acquired property at the date the increments to the purchaser's equity commenced.

said even though it has long been recognized that the absence of personal liability for the purchase money debt secured by a mortgage on the acquired property does not deprive the debt of its character as a bona fide debt obligation able to support an interest deduction. *Mayerson,* supra at 352. However, this is no longer true when it appears that the debt has economic significance only if the property substantially appreciates in value prior to the date at which a very large portion of the purchase price is to be discharged. Under these circumstances the purchaser has not secured "the use or forbearance of money." See Norton v. Commissioner, 474 F.2d 608, 610 (9th Cir. 1973). Nor has the seller advanced money or forborne its use. See Bornstein v. Commissioner, 334 F.2d 779, 780 (1st Cir. 1964); Lynch v. Commissioner, 273 F.2d 867, 871-872 (2d Cir. 1959). Prior to the date at which the balloon payment on the purchase price is required, and assuming no substantial increase in the fair market value of the property, the absence of personal liability on the debt reduces the transaction in economic terms to a mere chance that a genuine debt obligation may arise. This is not enough to justify an interest deduction. To justify the deduction the debt must exist; potential existence will not do. For debt to exist, the purchaser, in the absence of personal liability, must confront a situation in which it is presently reasonable from an economic point of view for him to make a capital investment in the amount of the unpaid purchase price. See *Mayerson,* supra at 352.[6] Associates, during the taxable years in question, confronted no such situation. Compare Crane v. Commissioner, 331 U.S. 1, 11-12, 67 S. Ct. 1047, 91 L. Ed. 1301 (1947).

Our focus on the relationship of the fair market value of the property to the unpaid purchase price should not be read as premised upon the belief that a sale is not a sale if the purchaser pays too much. Bad bargains from the buyer's point of view — as well as sensible bargains from buyer's, but exceptionally good from the seller's point of view — do not thereby cease to be sales. See Commissioner v. Brown, 380 U.S. 563, 67 S. Ct. 1047, 91 L. Ed. 1301 (1965); Union Bank v. United States, 285 F.2d 126, 128, 152 Ct. Cl. 126 (1961). We intend our holding and explanation thereof to be understood as limited to transactions substantially similar to that now before us.

Affirmed.

NOTES ON SALE AND LEASEBACK VARIANTS

1. In lieu of a second mortgage, X built a 408-unit garden apartment project costing $5.25 million. He obtained a $4.65 million mortgage at

---

[6]. Emphasis on the fair market value of the property in relation to the apparent purchase price animates the spirit, it not the letter, of Rev. Rul. 69-77, 1969-1 Cum. Bull. 59.

10.7 percent constant. This left X with a $600,000 equity and a net cash flow after debt service of $102,000 yearly (17 percent).

X then sold the land (only) to a pension fund for $625,000. Simultaneously, X leased back the land for ninety-nine years at an annual ground rental of $75,000. Net result: X had an annual cash flow of $27,000 on zero cash investment, retained all depreciation deductions, and would be able to refinance the first mortgage since the pension fund agreed to subordinate the fee for the entire ninety-nine year term of the lease. Cf. Mortgage & Real Estate Executive's Report, pp. 2-3 (May 21, 1971).

2. As the key to a real estate exchange, X owned a 165-acre farm valued at $1.5 million, subject to a $1.275 million mortgage. X wanted to realize a return on his equity investment without paying a capital gains tax on the sale of the farm, which he had owned for thirty years.

Y owned an apartment house valued at $1.6 million, subject to a $1.185 million mortgage. Y had no incentive to sell the property, which was in top condition. But Y would happily convert some or all of its equity into cash.

An exchange was worked out that imaginatively met both X's and Y's objectives. Y obtained the farm at the $1.5 million figure (which it then sold). X obtained the apartment house at the "reduced" price of $1.41 million. Simultaneously, X leased back the apartment house to Y; the ground rental gave X a satisfactory return on his equity. The key provision was a repurchase option (at $1.41 million), permitting Y to recover the fee interest in the apartment house should it ever wish to. Cf. Mortgage & Real Estate Executive's Report, pp. 4-5 (May 21, 1971).

3. *Lease-layering*. Once the seller becomes the tenant under a net lease in a sale-leaseback transaction, he can take the further step of selling the lease and *sub*leasing back. The practice is described below:

"William Zeckendorf, the dynamic president of Webb & Knapp, may have been the originator of this type of transaction. He conceived of various layers of leases analogous to the varying types of securities (common stock, preferred stock, first-mortgage bonds, second-mortgage bonds, and debenture bonds) issued by a corporation, each carrying a return related to the risk involved. Applying this graduated-risk system to real estate, the sale-leaseback of property by an insurance company would be the first step, entailing the company assuming a modest risk as fee owner, analogous to the risk in a high-credit, low-interest bond.

"The lease could then be sold by the lessee to an investor, with a sublease back to the seller who would operate the property. The main lease (often called a "sandwich lease") would produce a fixed return to its holder represented by the difference between the rent payable by the sublessee to the main lessee and the rent payable by the main lessee to the fee owner. This main lease would involve somewhat more risk than ownership of the fee since the holder of the main lease has a fixed rental obligation to the fee owner that would continue even if the sublessee defaulted. It is possible to add another layer to the "sandwich" by creating an intermediate sublease, which would make the operating lease a sub-sublease.

"The value of the main and intermediate leaseholds would be determined by capitalizing the returns received by the respective lessees in their landlord capacities. The sub-sublease (the operating position) has a real estate value, since the tenant operates the property and therefore receives space rents, provides management and building servies, and has all the other incidents of ownership. In addition, leasehold mortgages can be placed on each lease. And, of course, the fee may be mortgaged if the purchaser is capable of mortgaging it and desires to do so.

"If the holder of a "sandwich lease" insists on participating in the fruits of the operation of the property, the lease can provide that the holder (lessor) will receive a percentage of the income that the operating subtenant derives from the property over and above the fixed sublease rental.[3] This adds to the value of the "sandwich" lessee's position. A provision of this type can also be used in a straight sale-leaseback, where the seller-lessee retains the operating portion.

"Lease-layering can also be used in a sale-leaseback deal that separates the land from the building. In one actual transaction, a corporation with nationwide operations proposed to construct a new building for its home office through sale-leaseback financing. Initially, the corporation sold the land to an investor and leased it back, with the investor agreeing in the lease to construct the building for the corporation. The investor sold the land, subject to the corporation's leasehold, to a REIT which, in this particular instance, had no need for depreciation deductions. The investor-seller then leased the land back from the REIT, retaining in the lease its obligation to construct the building as provided in the initial lease to the corporate seller. This second gound lease also provided that the investor, as the intermediate tenant, would retain ownership of the building to be constructed. The rent on this second "sandwich lease" was, of course, less than the rent to be paid by the original corporate seller under its leaseback. The intermediate lease also provided for the joinder by the REIT landlord in a mortgage to be obtained by the investor, for proceeds of which were used to construct the building. The REIT then provided a leasehold mortgage loan on such lease. As a result of this multilayered transaction, 100 percent financing was provided to construct the new building." Sillcocks, Financial Sense in Sale and Real Estate Leasebacks, 5 Real Est. Rev. 89, 94-95 (Spring 1975).

2. *The Real Estate Syndication*

Real estate syndication involves the pooling of resources to enable a group of investors to develop or acquire property. This might define

---

[3]. If the landlord is a REIT or a pension or profit-sharing trust, the additional rent must be based on *gross* income only and the tenant must be restricted from making subleases providing for rent in any way based on net income. The Internal Revenue Code specifically bars these tax-favored trusts from directly or indirectly participating in a tenant's net income.

several relatives or close friends who have formed a joint venture, taking title, quite possibly, as tenants in common or as a closely held corporation and making collectively the ownership decisions. But the syndications that concern us here tend to have many more members, generally unrelated and often unknown to each other; management power is concentrated in a promoter who has "found the deal" or who seeks development funds; and tax shelter advantage overshadows equity buildup as the primary incentive that attracts the syndicate member.

In this section, we will examine two typical real estate syndications. The first illustrates a vehicle which enjoyed great popularity during the late 1950s and early 1960s; the second represents the dominant mode of the 1970s. Either or both deserve careful study; they permit us to see how tax advantage is packaged and sold to high-bracket investors while the promoters usually retain the equity build-up and leveraging potential for themselves.

Berger, Real Estate Syndication: Property, Promotion, and the Need for Protection[18]
69 Yale L.J. 725 (1960)

Readers of the June 29, 1958, edition of the New York Times may have puzzled over a sixteen-page advertising supplement urging them to buy units in a syndicate that would soon acquire the leasehold on one of Manhattan's prominent office buildings. For many, this was their first glimpse of syndication—a technique that has become the vogue in real estate investment. Syndication—the pooling of the resources of a group of individual investors to acquire or develop an agreed-upon real asset—presently covers property worth upwards of three billion dollars. . . . Although a syndicate may consist of a handful of wealthy investors, well known to one another, and each personally concerned with the operation of the enterprise, the major focus of this Article will be directed towards the widely held venture, whose participants are dependent upon the integrity, judgment, and ability of a syndicate manager for their investment rewards. Often the investor is getting his first taste of real estate investment, and brings to the venture the hopes, fears, and confusion of the dabbler. By contrast, the syndicator usually has "been around"; he has lived in a world where "balloon," "prime tenant," and "leaseback" are terms of everyday speech. . . .

The promoter has many sources of profit in a typical syndication. He may receive a brokerage fee from the seller of the property; a profit on the transfer of the property or assignment of the executory sales contract to the syndicate; and promotional underwriting discounts and commissions.

18. Footnotes omitted.

Should he be an attorney, his office may receive legal fees for handling the transaction, as well as an annual retainer. Promoters generally share in the property's revenues, either as the operating tenant or as the owner of a participating interest in the syndicate. Realtor promoters may undertake management of the property; thereby earning a management fee. Finally, the promoter usually reserves the right to a disproportionate share of any gains from a resale or refinancing of syndicate property. . . .

The syndicate seldom retains the direct management responsibility—the "operating position"—in the property which it owns. Rather, it usually leases its property on a long-term net rental basis, the amount of the rent being tailored to produce an annual distribution to the investors at the yield advertised in the offering. The syndicate promoter, his wholly owned affiliate, or a second syndicate group also under his control quite frequently takes the operating position by becoming the tenant or subtenant of the syndicate entity. Because the lease or sublease is ordinarily a long-term, net-rental instrument, effective control or management of the property rests with the tenant. In its practical effect, the position of the syndicate investor can be analogized to that of the tenant's bondholders. . . .

When the promoter wishes to retain the operating position, he rarely assumes personal liability for the rental payment. Should the property fail to produce sufficient income, the promoter-lessee ordinarily reserves the right either to reduce the net rental payment or to terminate the lease unilaterally. In the event the lease is so terminated, the investors may be confronted with the unexpected burden of undertaking new arrangements for the property's management, presumably at a time when the going is rough. . . .

In part, the (limited) degree of investor control derives from the legal form of the syndicate entity. If a limited partnership has been created, the rights of a limited partner are circumscribed by the particular jurisdiction's version of section 10 of the Uniform Limited Partnership Act. He may examine the company's books, count his profits, obtain an accounting, and seek dissolution; the exercise of greater rights may transform his status to that of a general partner and expose him to unlimited liability.

The corporate form of syndicate venture does not appreciably increase investor control. Typically, the corporate investor acquires a combination of debentures and nonvoting preferred stock. All of the voting power rests in the few shares of common stock held solely by the syndicate promoter. Only in the event of a protracted default in the payment of debenture interest and preferred stock dividends do the voting rights, and thereby control, shift to the investor.

The use of the general partnership, in which the general partner divides his interest among the syndicate investors who then participate with him as joint venturers, can offer the investor a somewhat higher level of control. Investor control, however, is usually limited by the partnership agreement, which delegates the unlimited decisionmaking power to the promoter partner *as agent* for the investor partners. In this capacity, the promoter needs investor consent only for stated major decisions, such as lease or mortgage modification or the sale, transfer, and mortgaging of the property. Furthermore, this semblance of residual investor control over major policy is rendered somewhat illusory; for if most of the partners approve the proposal the promoter usually has the right to reacquire the interests of the nonconsenting investors. And the "buy-out" price, normally original cost less previous capital distributions, does not reflect any increment in the equity value of the investment interest. Thus, the pressure of a forced sale upon potentially undesirable terms undercuts the likelihood that an investor will assert himself.

Where does this leave the syndicate promoter? Except for the minimal limitations to which he may agree, he retains almost exclusive power, regardless of the syndicate form, to make all major investment decisions.

Syndication Prospectus

$10,470,000 OF PARTICIPATIONS IN PARTNERSHIP INTERESTS IN GARMENT CAPITAL ASSOCIATES

I. GENERAL NATURE OF THE OFFERING

GARMENT CAPITOL ASSOCIATES ("Associates") is a partnership consisting of Lawrence A. Wien, William F. Purcell and Alvin Silverman.

Associates proposes to purchase the land and building located at 498 Seventh Avenue, New York City, at a total cost of $10,500,000. This is to be paid all in cash and the property will be owned by Associates free and clear of any mortgages. A deposit of $1,000,000 already has been made on account of the purchase price. . . .

Associates will not operate the property. Simultaneously with the purchase, it will execute a 25-year net lease of the entire premises, renewable for two like terms, to 498 Seventh Avenue Associates, a partnership comprised of Harry B. Helmsley, Messrs. Wien, Purcell and Silverman and ten other persons. . . .

The lessee will pay an annual net rent of $1,090,000 to Associates. The lessee also will pay all operating and maintenance expenses.

The partners in the lessee group will be personally liable on the lease for the first three years of its term. Thereafter, it can be surrendered or assigned by the lessee, without further liability, upon sixty day's notice to Associates.

Each of the three partners in Associates will contribute at least $10,000 to the capital of the partnership. In addition, by this Prospectus, each partner is offering $3,490,000 of Participations in his partnership interest in Associates. Thus, upon completion of the offering the partnership capital will be $10,500,000.

The proceeds from the sale of Participations will be used to pay the balance of the cash required in order to acquire title and to reimburse the partners for $970,000 of the deposit advanced. The lessee will pay $50,000 to be used to defray the costs of this offering.

Purchasers of Participations will share proportionately in the ownership of the partnership interests in Associates under Participating Agreements with the partners.

The rent to be received by Associates under the net lease has been set at a sum sufficient to enable Associates to defray administrative costs and to make a monthly cash distribution to each participant equal to 10% per year of his original cash Participation. . . .

II. TERMS OF THE OFFERING

1. The offering is being made by the partners in Associates.
2. Offers to purchase Participations will be accepted only from individuals of full age.
3. Each offer to purchase shall be for $10,000 or a multiple thereof. . . .
4. The title closing is expected to take place on April 1, 1957, with rights of adjournment to May 1 or June 1, 1957. However deposits will be repaid, without interest, if offers totalling $9,500,000 have not been accepted by June 1, 1957. This is the minimum sum required to make the final cash payment pursuant to the purchase arrangements. . . .
5. After the required minimum amount of offers has been accepted, the partners may sell the remainder of the Participations ($970,000) covered by this Prospectus, so that they may be reimbursed for a portion of the deposit advanced in connection with the purchaser.

III. 498 SEVENTH AVENUE

1. *Description.* 498 Seventh Avenue is located in the heart of New York's "Garment District," occupying a plot of approximately 38,800 square feet. . . .

Erected in 1921, the building is of fireproof, steel construction, and contains 24 floors, penthouse and basement. It has a volume of approximately 10,388,000 cubic feet with a rentable floor area of 826,221 square feet. The premises are in excellent condition and require no unusual repairs. Major improvements to the building within the past ten years include new roof, new lighting fixtures, new freight elevator cabs, new plumbing lines and sanitary facilities throughout the premises, new ceilings and terrazza floors in most corridors, and installation of 1000-ton cooling tower with circulating equipment.

Approximately 40% of the building is air-conditioned. About half of the air-conditioning equipment is owned by the landlord and the balance by tenants. All such equipment utilizes permanent electric power and water facilities installed by the landlord. There are 11 Otis passenger and 10 Otis freight elevators in the building. The 1956-57 assessed valuation of the property is $6,250,000, of which $2,070,000 is allocated to the land and $4,180,000 to the building.

The building contains office, showroom and loft space which is used by manufacturers of ladies wearing apparel. Many of the leaders in this industry are included among the tenants. Up to the present time, persons in this industry have concentrated their places of business in the area between 34th and 40th Streets and Ninth Avenue and Broadway, which is known as the "Garment District." 498 Seventh Avenue competes with a number of other buildings in the Garment District. In that area, the only recent construction consists of one building erected over six years ago (912,000 square feet) which has a mixed tenancy and is reported to be virtually 100% occupied. Associates has no knowledge of any other pending new construction for the Garment District.

2. *Rental Statistics.* At present, the building is 100% rented, which has been virtually true for the past six years. The average rate per square foot is $2.14 and the total annual rent roll is $1,767,150.

The following lease expiration schedule applies as of the date of this prospectus:

Year	No. of Leases Expiring	% of Total No. of Leases	Area in Sq. Ft.	Gross Rent	% of Gross Rental Value
Statutory	3	2.89	6,400	13,000	.74
1958	20	19.23	104,953	226,900	12.84
1959	23	22.12	228,015	432,000	24.45
1960	22	21.15	198,165	409,500	23.17
1961	17	16.35	129,243	288,750	16.33
1962	12	11.54	123,145	265,000	15.00
1964	1	.96	3,600	10,000	.57
1966	2	1.92	18,900	37,000	2.09
1968	1	.96	7,200	15,000	.85
1970	1	.96	7,800	40,000	2.26
1971	2	1.92	6,000	30,000	1.70
	104	100.00	826,221	$1,767,150	100.00

3. *Operations.* Associates does not have access to complete operating figures of the prior owner for 498 Seventh Avenue. The prior owner, which is not affiliated with Associates in any way, has stated that the

building has been operated by it in conjunction with other properties, and has not made available any separate expense figures for this building. However, the prior owner has furnished Associates with a certified Summary of Gross Receipts for 498 Seventh Avenue for the past five years. This Summary . . . shows gross rentals received as follows: 1956—$1,703,435.14; 1955—$1,631,418.10; 1954—$1,598,023.87; 1953—$1,577,175.07; and 1952—$1,535,579.14. In addition to rents, other income received for electricity and sundry items, such as water, steam, air-conditioning and the like, increased the total gross receipts for the building to the following: 1956—$1,970,926.34; 1955—$1,852,980.43; 1954—$1,814,919.60; 1953—$1,791,931.09; 1952—$1,748,380.12.

Since Associates does not have access to separate operating expense figures for 498 Seventh Avenue, and the operating costs of its net lessee will depend on future events, no definitive statement can be made at this time as to the actual net operating profit before rent which will be realized by the lessee, or as to how such profit will compare with the rent payable under the net lease. . . .

However, the individual members of the lessee partnership are experienced in operating similar properties, have evaluated the operation of 498 Seventh Avenue, and are of the opinion that, barring a substantial change in present economic and rental conditions, the net operating income will be sufficient to pay the minimum fixed rental under the net lease. Based upon an analysis of the prior owner's consolidated statements for the various properties which it operated, it is doubtful that the operating results in previous years for 498 Seventh Avenue alone would have been sufficient to cover such proposed minimum fixed rental. However, the net lessee believes it can operate the building in a different manner than the prior owner. Furthermore, existing leases and tenancies provide a rental of $1,769,316 for the year to commence April 1, 1957, as compared with $1,703,435 for the calendar year 1956. Obviously, the renewal rates on future leases will depend upon economic conditions at the time and there is, therefore, no assurance that renewals of existing leases in 1958 and subsequent years will be effected at increased rates.

Although there is no assurance that the foregoing opinions of the lessee will necessarily materialize, the members of the lessee partnership have personally obligated themselves to pay the rent under the net lease for the first three years of its term. More than half of the existing leases will be subject to renewal during that period. . . .

IV. FORMATION OF ASSOCIATES

1. Associates was formed in New York, by a written agreement, dated January 10, 1957, for the purpose of purchasing the land and building at 498 Seventh Avenue, New York City.

2. Lawrence A. Wien, has assigned to Associates his right to purchase this property under a contract, executed on January 7, 1957, between him, as purchaser, and Garment Center Capitol, Inc., as seller. The important terms of the purchase contract and of the assignment are stated below. As there shown, the purchase contract also covers the purchase of certain other buildings, in addition to 498 Seventh Avenue. Mr. Wien's assignment to Associates, however, relates to the acquisition of 498 Seventh Avenue only. Title to the other buildings will be taken by a different purchaser, as hereinafter described.

3. Under the partnership agreement, the partners will share equally in the profits and losses of the partnership.

4. The partnership will continue until it has disposed of all of its assets. The partnership is not to be interrupted for any other cause, including the death of a partner or assignment of his interest. Provision is made for succession to the interest of a deceased partner by a designee or through the purchase of his interest by the remaining partners.

5. The consent of all partners is required for any sale, mortgage, or any other transfer of the property, the modification of any mortgage thereon, or the making or revision of any lease of the property by the partnership, or the disposal of any partnership asset.

6. Associates will only own and lease the property. Upon the acquisition of title, it will immediately execute a net lease thereof to 498 Seventh Avenue Associates. The rent received by Associates from its lessee, after payment of administrative expenses, will be distributed monthly to the participants.

V. PROPOSED ACQUISITION OF 498 SEVENTH AVENUE BY ASSOCIATES

1. *Arrangement made by Lawrence A. Wien for the Purchase of 498 Seventh Avenue and Certain Other Buildings.* (a) Under a single contract with Garment Center Capitol, Inc., seller, Mr. Wien has agreed to purchase the following four buildings: 498 Seventh Avenue, 500 Seventh Avenue, 512 Seventh Avenue and 228 West 38th Street, all in New York City.

(b) The contract provides for one indivisible purchase price of $24,245,250 for the four properties, payable as follows:

$1,000,000 deposit, which was paid on execution of the contract;

$17,762,750 in cash to be paid upon the closing of title;

$5,482,500 by taking subject to a consolidated first mortgage in that amount, which is now a lien on all of said buildings.

The contract price is net to the seller, so that the purchaser is responsible for the payment of all brokerage commissions in connection with the sale.

(c) Title closing date is April 1, 1957. By giving appropriate notice, the purchaser can adjourn the closing date to May 1 or June 1, 1957, upon payment of an additional deposit of $250,000 for each one month period of adjournment. Any such additional deposit will be applied toward the cash payment due on closing.

(d) In addition to the contract price as aforesaid, Associates is advised that costs aggregating $804,750 will be incurred in connection with the acquisition of title to the various properties (such as brokerage commissions, legal and accounting fees, surveys, building inspection and appraisal costs and recording fees). Thus, the total aggregate cost of acquiring title to the four properties covered by the contract, including the purchase price and all acquisition expenses, will be $25,050,000.

(e) As previously stated, of the properties covered by the contract, only 498 Seventh Avenue is to be acquired by Associates under the assignment from Mr. Wien. The remaining properties will be conveyed at the closing to a major national insurance company at Mr. Wien's direction. The contract specifically permits Mr. Wien to make such disposition of his purchase rights, provided that deeds to all four parcels are delivered and accepted on the closing date.

(f) Mr. Wien has informed Associates that the over all acquisition costs of $25,050,000, required in order to consummate the contract, will be met on the closing date in the following manner:

$10,500,000 will be contributed by Associates in return for which it will receive title to 498 Seventh Avenue;

$12,500,000 will be contributed by the insurance company which will obtain title to the remaining buildings and will immediately lease them to a lessee group;

$2,050,000 will contributed by such lessee group in consideration of the value of their lease.

At the closing the present consolidated first mortgage, now a lien on all of the properties covered by the contract, will be discharged with a portion of the aforesaid funds.

2. *Assignment to Associates of Mr. Wien's Purchase Rights Relating to 498 Seventh Avenue.* (a) On January 11, 1957, Mr. Wien assigned to Associates his rights and Associates has assumed his obligations under the above-described contract insofar as they relate to the purchase of 498 Seventh Avenue. Mr. Wien also assigned to Associates his right in the $1,000,000 deposit made by him under the contract.

(b) The assignment agreement provides that in payment for this property Associates will contribute $10,500,000 toward the total cost of acquiring the several properties under the contract. This sum will be paid as follows:

$1,000,000 deposit, for which Associates has been credited as a result of the assignment to them of the deposit made by Mr. Wien under contract;

$9,500,000 in cash upon the closing of title.

(c) It is a condition of the transaction that on the closing date Mr. Wien will cause the lien to the present consolidated first mortgage, noted under 1(b) above, to be discharged.

(d) If there is any adjournment of the date for closing of title under the purchase contract, Associates will not be required to advance any part of the additional deposit called for by the purchase contract.

(e) As previously noted, Mr. Wien's purchase contract with the seller provides for a single, indivisible price for the four buildings covered thereby. Associates' determination as to the portion thereof that should constitute the purchase price for 498 Seventh Avenue was based on their consideration of real estate values in general and a comparison of the rent rolls and estimated income possibilities of the various buildings.

Of the buildings, other than 498 Seventh Avenue, which are covered by the purchase contract, and which are to be conveyed to an insurance company for $12,500,000, the largest is 500 Seventh Avenue. It is 36 years old, contains 18 stories, 621,915 square feet of rentable space and has a current rent roll of $1,086,705. 512 Seventh Avenue, erected in 1929, has 44 stories, 536,431 square feet of rentable space and a rent roll of $1,243,050. 228 West 38th Street is a five-story light-protector for 500 Seventh Avenue, and has a rent roll of $8500.

When the insurance company obtains title to these properties, it will lease them to a lessee corporation in which Lawrence A. Wien, Harry B. Helmsley and Samuel Kronsky (a priminent New York realtor and mortgage broker) will be the sole stockholders. This lease will be for an initial term of 25 years at an annual net rent of $937,500, and will provide for three renewal terms of 21 years each at an annual net rent of $437,500. As previously stated, in consideration of the value of the lease, this lessee corporation has agreed with Mr. Wien to contribute $2,050,000 toward the total sum required in order to conclude his contract with Garment Center Capitol, Inc. Associates will have no interest in the ownership or operation of 500 or 512 Seventh Avenue or 228 West 38th Street.

VI. OPERATION OF 498 SEVENTH AVENUE UNDER NET LEASE

1. *Provisions of the Net Lease.* To obtain the lease, the lessee will pay $50,000 which will be used to defray costs of this offering. Important provisions of the lease are:

(a) A term of 25 years from the date of title closing with renewal privileges for two additional 25 year terms at the same rental.

(b) An annual net rent of $1,090,000 in equal monthly installments.

(c) The lessee will pay all operating and maintenance expenses, all real estate taxes, will make necessary repairs and replacements, and will keep the property adequately insured against fire and accident.

(d) The partners in the lessee will be personally liable on the lease for the first three years of the term. Thereafter, the lessee may surrender the lease at its option upon 60 days written notice without further liability after the effective date of surrender. If the lease is so surrendered, Associates will undertake to effect a new lease on the most favorable terms possible.

(e) The lessee may assign the lease provided its assignee assumes in writing all obligations as lessee. If any such assignments is made during the first three years of the lease, the members of the lessee partnership will remain personally liable for all lessee obligations accruing during the three year period.

(f) If the lessee's net income from operation of the property, after payment of the rent and expenses as aforesaid, but before amortization of the cost of the lease and before income taxes, exceeds $200,000 in any one year, it shall pay 50% of such excess to Associates as additional rent.

2. *The Lessee.* 498 Seventh Avenue Associates is a partnership consisting of Lawrence A. Wien, Harry B. Helmsley [and twelve others—members of the Wien Law Firm or of the Helmsley Real Estate Management Firm].

Associates is satisfied that the lessee partnership is financially responsible and capable of fulfilling the terms of the lease. However, since the lessee has the right to surrender or assign the lease after three years, without further obligations, the investment should be appraised on the basis of the present status and future income potential of the building. Of course, the income may vary from time to time depending upon general economic conditions and the rentability of space in the building.

VII. STATUS OF PURCHASERS OF PARTICIPATIONS

1. *Participating Agreements.* Each of the three partners in Associates will enter into a Participating Agreement with investors contributing $3,490,000 towards the $10,500,000 total required to acquire the property. Each partner also will contribute $10,000 toward the partnership capital.

Each Participating Agreement will create a joint venture among the parties thereto, who will own the particular partner's one-third interest in Associates, in proportion to their respective contributions to its total cost. The Agreements will contain the following provisions:

(a) The partner will act as "Agent" for the participants in his one-third partnership interest.

(b) The participants will share proportionately in all profits or losses realized by the Agent as a partner in Associates. Under New York law, one participant may be liable to a person outside the venture for the full amount of any obligation of the Agent as a partner in Associates. However, he would be entitled to demand and receive pro rata contributions from his co-participants.

(c) The Agent may not agree to sell, mortgage or transfer the partnership interest or the property owned by Associates, to modify any mortgages on the property, to make or modify and lease thereon, or to dispose of any partnership asset without the consent of all his participants. However, if participants owning ninety percent of the Agent's interest consent to any such action, the Agent or his designee shall have the right to purchase the interest of any non-consenting participant at its original cost, less any capital repaid thereon.

(d) The Agent will incur no personal liability for any action taken by him, except for wilful misconduct, gross negligence or any liabilities under the Securities Act of 1933.

(e) Except as above limited, the Agent may bind his participants, and the participants will agree to indemnify him proportionately against any liability arising by reason of his acting as Agent.

(f) The Agent may resign upon accounting to his successor for all funds he has received. He may be removed by the written direction of participants owning at least three-fourths of the Agent's interest.

(g) If the Agent dies, is removed, resigns or is unable to act, he will be succeeded by one of five persons named as successors in each agreement. If no such designee qualifies, the owner of at least three-fourths of the interest shall select the new Agent.

(h) Each joint venture shall continue until it has disposed of the entire interest which it owns in Associates. It will not be interrupted for any other cause, including the death of a participant or transfer of his interest.

(i) A participant may transfer his interest in the joint venture to any individual of full age. The transferee must accept the transfer in writing, and duplicate originals of the transfer instruments must be filed with the Agent, before the transfer shall be effective.

(j) Upon the death of a participant, any individual of full age designated in the decedent's will or by his executor or administrator may succeed to his interest. If no such individual qualifies within eight months after date of death, the surviving parties to the joint venture may purchase proportionately the interest of the decedent, at its original cost, less any capital repaid thereon.

(k) The Agent shall receive no compensation for acting in that capacity.

2. *Tax Status.* The status for Federal income tax purposes of Associates and the joint ventures described in this Prospectus has been passed upon by Roswell Magill, Esq. of Cravath, Swaine & Moore, 15 Broad Street, New York City and by the firm of Paul, Weiss, Rifkind, Wharton & Garrison, 1614 Eye Street, N.W., Washington, D.C., tax counsel.

Both such counsel have furnished Associates with separate opinions that the members of Associates and of the joint ventures to be formed under the Participating Agreements will qualify as partners for Federal income tax purposes. Therefore, the individual members of Associates and each participant will be taxed on his distributive share of the net income, but the net income of Associates and the joint ventures will not be taxable as such.

Both opinions note that the Treasury Regulations contain provisions under which partnerships or joint ventures may be taxed on their net income in the same manner as corporations and the members thereof may be taxed as shareholders. Each opinion, however, concludes that Associates and the joint ventures involved herein do not fall within the said provisions, and therefore should not be taxable as corporations.[19]

3. *Projected Statement of Income and Expenses of Associates—Cash Distribution to Participants.* The following schedule, which assumes that Associates and the joint ventures will be taxable to partnerships, estimates the aggregate cash income to Associates annually over the term of the lease. It also shows the portion of such income distributable to participants under the Participating Agreements.

The rent income shown is based upon the minimum annual net rent provided for in the net lease with 498 Seventh Avenue Associates. The schedule assumes that the net lease will continue in accordance with its terms over this period. There is no assurance that the foregoing assumptions necessarily will hold true but if such rent is paid and Associates and the joint ventures are taxable as partnerships, the following schedule will apply:

	Per Year
Rent Income	$1,090,000.00
Less Legal and Accounting Expenses	40,000.00
Net Profit before Depreciation	$1,050,000.00
Depreciation on Building, 30-year Life, 3⅓% of $8,000,000*	266,666.67
Net Profit allocable to Participants for income tax purposes	$ 783,333.33

* This depreciation base was determined by allocation to the building of that portion of the total cost of acquiring the property which Associates believes represents fair value of the building alone.

Cash Available for Distribution

Total (Net Profit before depreciation)	$1,050,000.00
Per $10,000 Participation	$ 1,000.00

The cash available for distribution, shown immediately above, will represent both income and, to the extent of annual depreciation, a return of capital. That portion which represents a return of capital investment will not be reportable as income for federal income tax purposes. There follows a table breaking down the annual cash distribution on the foregoing basis to the holder of a $10,000 Participation.

Portion constituting income	$ 746.03
Portion representing return of capital and not reportable as income	253.97
Cash distribution per $10,000 Participation	$1,000.00

19. Cf. I.R.C. of 1954, §7701; Treas. Reg. §301.7701-2; *Morrissey v. Commissioner,* 296 U.S. 244 (1935). — EDS.

Assuming the renewal of the lease at the end of the initial term, the foregoing analysis will continue to apply through the 30th year. Thereafter, the full amount will be reportable as income since the building then will be fully depreciated.

Congressional Budget Office, Real Estate Tax Shelter Subsidies and Direct Subsidy Alternatives
(May 1977)

REAL ESTATE TAX SHELTERS

The primary function of real estate tax shelters is to provide developers and builders of rental property with part of the money they need "up front" to finance new building construction. Tax shelters provide a 10- to 20-year stream of tax savings which the builder/developer can sell to wealthy outside investors. The money they pay him is used, along with a mortgage loan, to finance construction of the building. In effect, therefore, real estate tax shelters are simply a device to provide a government subsidy for building construction.

WHO DOES WHAT IN A REAL ESTATE TAX SHELTER

The real estate tax shelter subsidy system requires the involvement of people in four different roles. Frequently, as in the case of a builder/developer, one individual will play more than one role. But the roles are separate ones, and they involve different risks, rewards, and incentives.

The Developer. The developer pulls together the land, financing, local clearances, and subsidies from HUD and other sources. He handles the planning, brings together the other participants, and oversees most phases of the development process. The developer is the "prime mover" in the project, and the one who bears most of the risks in the early stages of the process. His rewards may come in part from various fees and charges in the development stage of the project, but his primary reward comes from the sale of interests in the project and its future tax benefits and rents to outside investors. If he retains an ownership share (as he was assumed to do in the sample project), there are also potential future returns to him from tax benefits and rents and from sale or refinancing of the project if it increases in value.

The Builder. The developer is often also the builder, but the builder's role is a separate one. The builder's main interest is in building the project, getting his payment for it, and then getting out so that he can invest his capital and resources in another project. His main risk is that cost overruns and delays will eat up his profit on the project. The builder, along with the developer, plays a central role in the project. It could not be built without their efforts.

The Syndicator. The developer may also handle the syndication, but this too is a separate role. The syndicator gets his return from the syndication fees he receives from the developer and/or from outside investors. His main interest is in continuing and expanding his syndication business. This requires that he bring in outside equity capital for the developer quickly and efficiently, and that the outside investors he brings in get the financial return they expect. His main risk is that he will be unable to satisfy the expectations of the developer or the outside investors, and thereby lose future syndication business. The syndicator may well perform a useful screening role by providing a sophisticated analysis of the economic viability of the project, and an evaluation of the reputation and ability of the developer and builder. The syndicator can only do this adequately, however, if he is acting solely as an agent of the outside investors. If he has ties to the builder/developer, as is often the case, the syndicator's analysis and evaluation will be less useful to the outside investors. Even syndicators who are independent of the builder/developer may not do an adequate job of screening projects and builder/developers. Some syndicators are better than others. Syndicators are also not the only ones who could perform this screening role. It could also be done by private lenders, state housing agencies, or HUD.

Outside Investors. The outside investors contribute a relatively small but important share of the total capital needed for the project, ranging from 10 percent or less in some projects, up to as much as 30 percent or more in others. They are interested primarily in getting as large and as early a return on their investment as they can. In a low- and moderate-income rental housing project, they expect their main return to come from the tax benefits; little or no return is expected from rents or from appreciation in the value of the property. Investors in upper-income rental housing, by contrast, expect more of their return to come from rents and appreciation, with less coming from the tax benefits.

One of the outside investors' main risks, especially in low- and moderate-income projects with high tax benefits, is that the project will go into foreclosure before the tax savings are fully realized, or while they are still subject to "recapture" under the tax laws. The outside investors may therefore apply some pressure for good management and maintenance of the completed project—at least management and maintenance good enough to keep the project from going into foreclosure.

Since outside investors may have a degree of knowledge and sophistication about real estate investment which can be useful for screening purposes. This is more likely if the syndication is a small one (5-10 outside investors) in which the syndicator, developer, and investors know each other and live in the same area. More frequently, however, the outside investors are doctors, lawyers, dentists, or other professionals with little knowledge of or background in real estate. They are simply buying tax losses. Often they live in another part of the country, and are in no position to judge the ability of the developer and builder, or the potential viability of the project. They are wholly dependent on the syndicator for these judgments.

A Simplified Real Estate Tax Shelter in Operation

Assumptions for Sample Real Estate Tax Shelter Project

Development
Property Acquisition … $75,000
Construction Cost
(including architectural and engineering) … 750,000

Carrying Charges (12 months)
Interest at 9% on ½ mtge	$41,000	
Financing Fee	9,000	
Taxes	10,000	
Legal & Organizational	10,000	
Miscellaneous	15,000	
Total		$ 85,000

Developer's Profit (10% ± of above) … 90,000
Total Development Cost … $1,000,000
Mortgage Amount (90%) … $ 900,000

Operating
Gross Effective Income … $ 180,000
Operating Expenses … (60,000)
Real Estate Taxes (20% of income) … (36,000)

Net Income … $ 84,000
Debt Service (7½% + ½%, 40 Years = 8.4 constant) … (75,600)
Cash Flow … $ 8,400

Tax Treatment
Non-depreciable … $ 75,000

Depreciable[a]
Construction	$750,000	
Legal and Miscellaneous	25,000	
Developer's Net Profit (syndication + fee less equity)	130,000	
Total		$ 905,000

Expensed
Interest	$ 41,000	
Financing Fee	9,000	
Real Estate Taxes	10,000	
Total		$ 60,000

Total (mortgage + syndication) … $1,040,000

Syndication
Investment: $140,000 in three equal annual installments
Allocation: 95 percent of tax and cash benefits to investors
Sale Conditions: $1 over mortgage in year 20

[a] SYD depreciation method; 200 month phaseout of recapture. Depreciable components:

building shell	$724,000 at 40 years
roof, equipment, etc.	90,500 at 20 years
appliances, finishes, cabinetry, etc.	90,500 at 10 years
Total	$905,000

Financing a Rental Housing Project

The project to be built is an apartment building. The total cost of development, including land and construction costs, is $1,000,000. [Refer to Tables 7-1 and 7-2.] The builder/developer[4] is able to obtain a 40-year loan for 90 percent of that cost ($900,000) from a private lender (bank, savings and loan association, insurance company, etc.) or from a state housing agency.[5] The builder/developer must come up with the additional $100,000 on his own. If possible, he would like to raise more than that in order to increase his profit.

In order to obtain the $900,000 loan plus the additional $100,000-plus he needs, the builder/developer has the following potential sources of income which he can borrow against or sell interests in:

Cash return from rents on the completed project. In a middle- or upper-income rental housing project, the potential return from rents is a major inducement for potential lenders and investors. In a project intended for low- and moderate-income renters, however, the rents tenants can afford to pay will be low. In addition, HUD and state housing agencies frequently limit the cash distribution from rents in subsidized low- and moderate-income projects. Some additional inducements are therefore necessary.

Possible increase in the project's value. If the project increases in value over time, it can be sold or refinanced at a profit. This is another major inducement for potential lenders and investors. In the past, investors tended to discount the possibility that low- and moderate-income projects would increase in value, since locations were often less desirable, amenities fewer, and rent increases harder to obtain. In recent years, subsidized projects have been built in better locations with competitive amenities, and subsidy programs have been designed to make it easier to obtain rent increases. Whether investor perceptions have changed accordingly is not certain.

Subsidies from HUD and state or local housing agencies. Low- and moderate-income rental housing construction is subsidized by a wide variety of federal, state, and local programs. These subsidies, many of which are often combined in a single project, include contracts for future rent payments on behalf of lower-income tenants, interest subsidies, reductions in local real estate taxes, and direct and guaranteed loans. In the case of low- and moderate-income rental housing, however, these subsidies may not be enough to make up fully for the lower return on rents and the smaller likelihood of future increases in the project's value.

Special tax advantages that, in combination, will permit income to be sheltered and tax payments avoided or deferred. These tax advantages can

---

4. While the builder and the developer of a real estate project are often different people, the roles are combined frequently enough that it is customary to refer to them together. The custom will be followed in this report unless there is some reason to make a distinction.

5. FHA mortgage insurance would be needed to obtain these terms from a private lender. The 7½ percent interest rate which is assumed is based on current FNMA/GNMA Tandem Plan Financing or State Housing Agency Financing using tax-exempt bonds.

[TABLE 7-1]
Complete 20-Year Projection, in Dollars
Income and Expenses

Year	Project Income	Construction Expenses	Operating Expenses	Interest and MIP	Depreciation	Total Deductions	Loss (Income)	95 Percent Allocation
0	0	60,000	0	0	0	60,000	60,000	57,000
1	180,000	0	96,000	71,900	60,400	228,300	48,300	45,900
2	180,000	0	96,000	71,600	57,400	225,000	45,000	42,800
3	180,000	0	96,000	71,300	54,600	221,900	41,900	39,800
4	180,000	0	96,000	70,800	51,500	218,300	38,300	36,400
5	180,000	0	96,000	70,500	48,600	215,100	35,100	33,300
6	180,000	0	96,000	70,100	45,600	211,700	31,700	30,100
7	180,000	0	96,000	69,700	42,600	208,300	28,300	26,900
8	180,000	0	96,000	69,100	39,600	204,700	24,700	23,500
9	180,000	0	96,000	68,600	36,800	201,400	21,400	20,300
10	180,000	0	96,000	68,100	33,700	197,800	17,800	16,900
11	180,000	0	96,000	67,400	30,800	194,200	14,200	13,500
12	180,000	0	96,000	66,800	29,500	192,300	12,300	11,700
13	180,000	0	96,000	66,100	28,100	190,200	10,200	9,700
14	180,000	0	96,000	65,400	26,800	188,200	8,200	7,800
15	180,000	0	96,000	64,500	25,600	186,100	6,100	5,800
16	180,000	0	96,000	63,700	24,300	184,000	4,000	3,800
17	180,000	0	96,000	62,700	22,900	181,600	1,600	1,500
18	180,000	0	96,000	61,700	21,600	179,300	(700)	(700)
19	180,000	0	96,000	60,600	20,300	176,900	(3,100)	(2,900)
20	180,000	0	96,000	59,400	18,900	174,300	(5,700)	(5,400)
Total	3,600,000	60,000	1,920,000	1,340,000	719,600	4,039,600	439,600	417,700

[TABLE 7-2]
Cash Flow

Year	Total Income	Operating Expenses	Interest and MIP	Amortization	Surplus (Deficit)	Total Applications	Cash Distributions	95 Percent Allocation
0	0	0	0	0	0	0	0	0
1	180,000	96,000	71,900	3,700	0	171,600	8,400	8,000
2	180,000	96,000	71,600	4,000	0	171,600	8,400	8,000
3	180,000	96,000	71,300	4,300	0	171,600	8,400	8,000
4	180,000	96,000	70,800	4,700	100	171,500	8,400	8,000
5	180,000	96,000	70,500	5,000	100	171,500	8,400	8,000
6	180,000	96,000	70,100	5,400	100	171,500	8,400	8,000
7	180,000	96,000	69,700	5,800	100	171,500	8,400	8,000
8	180,000	96,000	69,100	6,300	200	171,400	8,400	8,000
9	180,000	96,000	68,600	6,800	200	171,400	8,400	8,000
10	180,000	96,000	68,100	7,300	200	171,400	8,400	8,000
11	180,000	96,000	67,400	7,900	300	171,300	8,400	8,000
12	180,000	96,000	66,800	8,500	300	171,300	8,400	8,000
13	180,000	96,000	66,100	9,100	400	171,200	8,400	8,000
14	180,000	96,000	65,400	9,800	400	171,200	8,400	8,000
15	180,000	96,000	64,500	10,600	500	171,100	8,400	8,000
16	180,000	96,000	63,700	11,400	500	171,100	8,400	8,000
17	180,000	96,000	62,700	12,300	600	171,000	8,400	8,000
18	180,000	96,000	61,700	13,300	600	171,000	8,400	8,000
19	180,000	96,000	60,600	14,300	700	170,900	8,400	8,000
20	180,000	96,000	59,400	15,400	800	170,800	8,400	8,000
Total	3,600,000	1,920,000	1,340,000	165,900	6,100	3,425,900	168,000	160,000

be quite valuable, but the builder/developer is rarely able to use them himself. The main reason is that the tax advantages take the form of tax losses which can be used to offset or shelter other income, and the builder/developer usually does not have enough outside income to use the losses. In addition, the tax losses are spread out over time, and the builder/developer needs the money right away. He therefore sells interests in the project and the right to these losses to wealthy outside investors. The money the builder/developer receives from selling the right to these tax losses is what provides him with the remainder of the capital he needs to make the project a viable one. In low- and moderate-income projects, a large share of the total return comes from the sale of tax losses and from the various government subsidies. In higher-income projects, a greater share comes from rents and future increases in the project's value.

Selling the Tax Benefits

The tax benefits from real estate tax shelters are spread out over a period of years. While many of the benefits are concentrated in the first five or ten years of the project's life, the stream of benefits continues to flow over a period of 15 to 20 years.

In trying to determine how much he can sell the tax shelter benefits for, the builder/developer tries to calculate what this stream of tax benefits would be worth to an outside investor if he had to pay for all of them today. He asks, in other words, what the "present value" of a 20-year stream of tax shelter benefits would be to a potential outside investor. To determine this, he must discount the tax benefits to be received in each year according to a formula that takes account of the fact that $100 received in year 20 is much less valuable to an investor than $100 received in year five.

The discount rate used in this calculation will take into account the rate of return the outside investor could earn on alternative investments, and the risk that the project might not be as successful or the tax benefits as great as expected. Taking these factors together, a builder/developer will commonly assume that the average outside investor's discount rate is about 20 percent.

But an additional factor must also be taken into account. The losses or deductions from the tax shelter will be worth more to an investor in the top 70 percent marginal tax bracket than to one in the 50 percent marginal bracket. Eact $1,000 in annual losses or deductions from the tax shelter will save a 70 percent bracket taxpayer $700 a year in taxes, while it will save the 50 percent bracket taxpayer only $500 a year in taxes. If the builder/developer could sell all the tax losses to 70 percent bracket taxpayers, he could get more for them, since they are worth more in tax savings to these top-bracket investors. But there are usually not enough 70 percent bracket investors to go around. In most cases, the builder/developer will have to sell the tax losses at a price low enough to attract a 50

New Modes of Capital Assembly

percent bracket taxpayer.[6] This means that the builder/developer will get less for his tax losses, and that any investors with marginal tax brackets over 50 percent will get a windfall benefit that increases in size as their top marginal tax bracket increases.

The top left portion of [Table 7-3] shows the present value of the 20-year stream of total benefits in this sample project to outside investors with marginal tax brackets of 50, 60, and 70 percent. Column (1), entitled "Tax Shelter Savings," separates out the tax savings that result from the special advantages of tax shelters.[7] As indicated, the builder/developer probably will not be able to sell this future stream of tax savings for much more than $71,800, the amount they are worth to a 50 percent bracket taxpayer.

In this sample project, however, he has other benefits he can also sell to outside investors. There are the additional tax savings resulting from straight-line depreciation, reduced by whatever capital gains tax must be paid when the project is sold in year 20. As shown in column (2), the net value of these "Other Tax Savings" is $29,200 to an investor in the 50 percent bracket. There are also the after-tax "Cash Distributions from Rents" over 20 years, which have a present value of $39,000 for investors in all tax brackets (column (3)).

Taking all these benefits into account, outside investors in real estate tax shelter projects are usually willing to pay from 15 to 20 percent of the mortgage amount ($900,000 in this project) for a 95 percent interest in the project and its tax and cash benefits. In this sample project, it is assumed that the outside investors are willing to pay $140,000 or 15.6 percent of the mortgage. As column (4) shows, the present value of the anticipated 20-year stream of benefits to outside investors with marginal tax brackets above 50 percent is much greater than the $140,000 they are required to

---

6. Tax shelters are rarely, if ever, a profitable investment for taxpayers with marginal brackets below 50 percent. The following table shows the number of taxpayers with top marginal tax brackets of 50 percent or higher for 1973, the latest year for which these statistics are available. The total number of returns filed in that year was 64,673,050.
Source: U.S. Internal Revenue Service, *Statistics of Income, 1973, Income Tax Returns* (November 1976), Publication 79 (11-76), Table 3.14, p. 111.

Top Marginal Bracket	Number of Returns	Percent of Total returns filed
50%	205,918	0.32%
51-59%	247,459	0.38
60%	29,501	0.05
61-69%	68,480	0.11
70%	17,491	0.03
Total	568,849	0.88%

7. These special tax shelter savings include those which result from (1) using accelerated rather than straight-line depreciation, (2) deducting construction period interest and taxes immediately rather than writing them off over the life of the building, and (3) paying tax on the gain on the sale in year 20 at capital gain rates (no recapture of depreciation) rather than ordinary income rates (full recapture).

[TABLE 7-3]
Discounted Present Value of 20 Years of Project Benefits

Sample Project Benefits Over 20 Years Present Value Discounted at 20 Percent

Investor Tax Bracket	Present Value to Outside Investors (95 Percent Share)				Present Value to Builder/Developer[d] (5 Percent Share)			
	Tax Shelter Savings[a] (1)	Other Tax Savings[b] (2)	Cash Distributions from Rents[c] (3)	Total (4)	Tax Shelter Savings[a] (5)	Other Tax Savings[b] (6)	Cash Distributions from Rents[c] (7)	Total (8)
50%	$71,800	$29,200	$39,000	$140,000	$3,800	$1,500	$2,100	$7,400
60%	86,200	35,800	39,000	161,000	4,500	1,900	2,100	8,500
70%	100,600	42,100	39,000	181,700	5,300	2,200	2,100	9,600

[a] Includes tax savings from (1) using accelerated rather than straight-line depreciation, (2) deducting construction period interest and taxes immediately rather than writing them off over the life of the building, and (3) paying tax on the gain on sale in year 20 at capital gain rates (no recapture of depreciation) rather than ordinary income rates (full recapture).

[b] Tax savings from deductions for straight-line depreciation, reduced by the present value of the tax paid on the gain on sale at capital gain rates. A small adjustment has been made in this column to reconcile the 20.4 percent return used for syndication pricing purposes with the 20 percent present value discount rate used in this table.

[c] These are after-tax or "tax-free" benefits. They have been internally sheltered from tax by losses which would otherwise be reflected above as "Other Tax Savings" (columns (2) and (6)).

[d] The builder/developer is assumed to be in the same tax bracket as the investors.

put into the project. They may therefore receive substantial extra benefits solely because of their higher tax bracket.

NOTES AND QUESTIONS

1. The above excerpts appear in a background paper which the Congressional Budget Office submitted to the House and Senate banking committees and the House budget committee. The study analyzed the revenue losses which flowed from the illustrative shelter; these were placed at $121,400 (using a 7.5 percent discount rate) for 50 percent taxpayers and $170,000 for 70 percent taxpayers. Roughly half of this tax "subsidy" reaches the outside investors; the rest is split between the syndicator and builder/developer, the syndicator keeping about 7.5 percent.

The study also examined the overall impact of tax shelters on both the treasury and real estate construction. Using fiscal year 1978 for its projection (which would reflect the 1976 reforms), the study anticipated a $1.3 billion revenue loss; of this amount, $0.3 billion would stem from new construction in the current year, the balance from older projects. Significantly, only 11.5 percent of the tax subsidy would help to provide low-income rental housing. Commercial properties (34.6 percent) and middle- or upper-income rental projects (53.8 percent) would enjoy most of the benefit. Id. at 37-39.

2. Without making specific recommendations, the background paper offers several alternative means for subsidizing the construction of low-income rental housing. These include:

(a) *Direct HUD construction grants to builder/developers.* These would equal a percentage of the initial project cost. For example, on the illustrative project, the developer would have received $64,800 of his $1.0 million project cost in the form of "tax shelter savings." A direct $64,800 "tax free" construction grant could replace the tax shelter (id. at 67-72);

(b) *Refundable investment tax credit for builder/developers.* This would substitute for the HUD-administered grant and use the tax system to administer the benefit. The developer would be offered a refundable tax credit (i.e., he would receive a Treasury check if the credit exceeded his tax liability) for a specified percentage of the initial project cost (id. at 72-76);

(c) *Nonrefundable investment tax credit for builder/developers.* This would work much like the present system of investment tax credits. (I.R.C. §§46-48.) Unused credits would receive carryover treatment (id. at 76-80); and

(d) *Interest subsidies for builder/developers.* A 3.0 percent interest reduction (from 7.5 to 4.5 percent) in the illustrative project mortgage would increase the yearly after-tax cash flow by $15,500. The developer could sell this added income stream to outside investors for approximately the same sum that he would now get for the sale of tax shelter savings (id. at 80-85).

The report then compares the present system and each of these possibilities against the following criteria:

a) cost;
b) efficiency — i.e., the percentage of subsidy reaching the builder/developer;
c) ease of administration;
d) incentives for good management and maintenance;
e) tax equity and neutrality;
f) visibility and controllability (id. at 102-103).

3. All that you have read assumes that the project fares well, that the builder completes it within the cost limits, that rent-up proceeds smoothly, and that the revenue and expense projections remain on target. For some investors, however, project failure may become a grim reality. In the very short run, this may increase their tax benefit (as losses rise); in the longer run, however, unless the investors are prepared to contribute added funds, mortgage default may occur, followed by mortgage foreclosure. Taxwise, that can be calamitous. Even though the investors' "equity" will be wiped out, they will be deemed to have realized a gain measured by the excess of mortgage balance over adjusted basis. Where the investors have "suffered" heavy tax losses, the gain may be sizable. Cf. Tufts v. Commissioner, 461 U.S. 300 (1983). Moreover, some of it will be recapturable as ordinary income if the project has utilized accelerated cost recovery.

D. CHOICE OF ENTITY FOR REAL ESTATE OWNERSHIP

Madden, Taxation of Real Estate Transactions — An Overview
Portfolio 480 Tax Mgmt. (BNA) A-101, A-134 to 140 (1984)

III. CHOICE OF ENTITY FOR REAL ESTATE OWNERSHIP

If the decision is made to invest in real estate for business or investment purposes, the question that typically occurs first is in what form the real estate investment should be held. Should title be taken in the individual's name alone or in some form of joint ownership with another individual, such as a spouse, or should the title to the property be held by either a general or limited partnership, a corporation or an S corporation? This Part will review the major factors which affect the choice of entity for real estate ownership in the business or investment context. The choices of the form of ownership for a parcel of real estate held for personal use, such as a residence, although theoretically as broad as those in a business context, are typically less complex. Most personal residences are held in the name of individuals or as tenants by the entirety (for married couples) unless estate planning considerations dictate otherwise. Only in the rarest of circumstances will a personal residence be held in some other form of ownership. . . .

A. SOLE PROPRIETORSHIPS

The ownership of real estate in a sole proprietorship means that the business or investment in that real estate is not maintained in a separate legal entity. The title to the property is held in the name of the owner of the business and it is operated for legal and tax purposes as his or her own. No other individuals share the ownership.

1. Taxation

If real estate is operated as a sole proprietorship, it is not a separate taxpayer. The effect of holding business property as an individual is quite similar to the operation of a partnership or S corporation in that losses from the operation of the property are deducted from that individual's income and profits are added to it. Thus, there is no double taxation as there is in a regular corporation. If a business is operated as a sole proprietorship, the profits and losses are reported by the individual owner on Schedule C of Form 1040. As such, the losses from the business, if any, can be used to offset other income and the profits, if any, are added to the proprietor's income so as to increase his taxable income. Consequently, the profits from the operation may be taxed at the maximum individual income tax rate. If the individual proprietor is already in a high income bracket and if the particular real property produces a considerable amount of taxable income, it may be best to separate the ownership from that individual's personal tax situation and have this income taxed in corporate form. On the other hand, if the accelerated depreciation deductions from the real estate mean that they create tax losses, a sole proprietorship may be a preferable means of ownership for a relatively small real estate investment.

2. Non-Tax Considerations

Perhaps the greatest advantage of the sole proprietorship is its simplicity. Holding property in a sole proprietorship simply means placing title to that property in the individual owner's name. There is no need to establish a separate legal entity of any type, and thus the cost and recordkeeping requirements associated with a separate entity are eliminated. The business owner is still required to maintain records on his particular investment property, but the recordkeeping requirements and cost of a separate entity are avoided.

Because the sole proprietorship does not involve a separate legal entity and is owned by one individual, there is also a great deal of flexibility accorded to that individual in his operation and dealing with the real estate. For example, the individual may buy, sell or transfer the property without the consent of others, and may devise the property owned by him to those of his choosing in a last will and testament. But since the property is individually owned, the capital to acquire and operate the property is limited to the individual owner's resources — that is, his equity capital and sources for borrowing funds. Sole proprietorship, by definition, means that the capital of others is not involved in the ownership and operation of the entity.

Sole proprietorship also creates unlimited personal liability for the owner of the property. Since the property is titled in his or her own name, the owner has personal liability for debts arising out of its operation and for any potential tort liability associated with the ownership and operation of the property. Because of this unlimited personal liability, most business or investment real estate held in an individual's name as a sole proprietorship is typically protected by liability insurance.

B. PARTNERSHIPS — GENERAL AND LIMITED

Real estate owned and operated by a partnership may be held in one of two forms. The general partnership essentially has one type of partner — an individual who has unlimited joint and several liability for partnership obligations. Partners in a general partnership have unlimited personal liability and also have a mutual agency relationship between them, so that they have an equal ability to bind the partnership and to participate in its management. A limited partnership,[1770] on the other hand, has two classes of partners. The general partner in a limited partnership has the same unlimited personal liability for partnership debts as the partner in the general partnership, and similarly has joint management abilities and responsibilities with the other general partners, if any. The limited partners, however, have liability for the partnership's debts, in most circumstances, limited to their agreed-upon capital contribution. In other words, if a limited partner agrees to contribute the sum of $10,000 to a limited partnership as his share of capital, his liability for partnership debts and, hence, his potential losses from the operation generally cannot exceed $10,000. A limited partner may not, however, participate in the manage-

---

1770. Throughout this discussion it is assumed that a limited partnership has qualified for that status under the appropriate legislation in the state in which it was formed.

ment of the partnership. In order to maintain his limited liability, he must remain a passive investor who has turned over the management responsibilities of the partnership to the general partners.

1. Taxation

Both general and limited partnerships are pass-through entities, with tax consequences being passed through to each of the individual partners.[1771] This means that all items of income, deduction, loss and credit will be allocated to the partners in proportion to their interests in the partnership.[1772] Most notably in the context of real estate, losses from the operation of the partnership, such as those created by depreciation or cost recovery on the property, may be passed through to the partners and used to offset personal income from other sources. This, perhaps, is the major reason that many real estate investments and indeed most syndicated real estate offerings are organized in partnership form. The same characteristic also means that taxable income from the real estate will be added to the partners' other income and increase their potential personal tax liability. Thus, real estate operations that are producing non-sheltered income, such as a management company or brokerage firm, are perhaps best organized in other forms.

Other major tax characteristics of a partnership that impact upon its potential use in the ownership and operation of real estate should also be briefly noted. Partnerships may have many classes of partners with different rights to cash flow, liquidation proceeds and profits and losses. Consequently, the partnership entity offers a good deal of flexibility in making special allocations to coincide with these differing class structures. Generally speaking, §704(a) permits a partner's distributive share of income, gain, loss, deduction or credit to be determined by the partnership agreement. Section 704(b) then provides that a partner's distributive share of these various items will be determined by taking the partner's interest in the partnership into account if the partnership agreement does not provide as to the partner's distributive share of income, loss deduction or credit or if the allocation in the agreement does not have substantial economic effect. . . . In general, a partnership does provide flexibility in allocating profits and losses and other items among various partners with differing interests and rights. This too is a reason that partnerships, both limited and general, tend to be favored investment vehicles for real estate ownership. . . .

A further advantage of partnership operation is that the partnership

---

1771. If a limited partnership possesses too many corporate characteristics, in some circumstances it will be taxed as a corporation. . . .

1772. If the allocations of losses and other items in the partnership agreement do not have substantial economic effect, the Commissioner does have authority to reallocate them. See generally §704(b). . . .

may be liquidated tax free to the individual partners. Under §731(a)(1), gain is recognized to a partner in a liquidating distribution by a partnership only to the extent that the cash distributed exceeds the adjusted basis of the partner's partnership interest immediately prior to the distribution. Thus, no gain will be recognized if cash is not distributed. Consequently, it is possible to distribute real properties held by a partnership to the individual partners without the recognition of taxable gain. In contrast, if appreciated real property was distributed by a corporation, gain would be recognized by the corporate shareholder to the extent that the value of the property received exceeded his adjusted basis in the stock.

One other major factor to consider in the taxation of a partnership is that a sale or exchange of 50 percent or more of the total interest in the partnership capital and profits within a twelve (12) month period will cause the partnership to terminate for tax purposes.[1778] This could result in an inadvertent termination of the partnership, thereby causing a possible recognition of gain or loss on distribution of the assets if the partnership is reconstituted,[1779] basis adjustments,[1780] a loss of tax elections,[1781] or the closing of the partnership year with resultant bunching of income.[1782] There may also be a recapture of investment credit[1783] and premature distributions from a Keogh plan[1784] as a result of this inadvertent termination.

2. Non-Tax Considerations

As noted earlier, one of the major characteristics of a general partnership is the unlimited personal liability to which a partner is subject. A partner in a general partnership is jointly and severally liable for all of the partnership's obligations, as well as the wrongful acts of his or her partners. A general partner in a limited partnership has the same unlimited personal liability. In contrast, limited partners are not liable for the partnership's obligations except to the extent of their agreed-upon capital contribution. In order to achieve this limited liability, the various statutory formalities, such as the filing of a proper certificate of limited partnership, must be adhered to. The limited partner must also refrain from participation in the management of the partnership in order to continue his status as a limited partner. It is only the general partner who has the management responsibilities in a limited partnership.

1778. §708(b)(1)(B). The partnership will also terminate if no part of any business financial operations, or venture of the partnership continues to be carried on by any of the partners in a partnership. §708(b)(1)(A).
1779. §731(a).
1780. §§733, 722.
1781. §703(b).
1782. See §706(c)(1).
1783. §47.
1784. §72(m)(5).

Choice of Entity for Real Estate Ownership

One unfavorable characteristic of a partnership is that the death or withdrawal of a partner results in the dissolution of the partnership unless the partners agree otherwise in the governing instrument. Accordingly, the draftsman of the partnership agreement must take care to provide for the continuation of the business if a partner dies or terminates his relationship with the partnership. Absent such terms and conditions, the partnership may be forced to terminate and liquidate upon the withdrawal of one of its members. Similarly, the death or withdrawal of all general partners or the sole general partner terminates a limited partnership. The death or withdrawal of fewer than all of the general partners will not cause the dissolution of a limited partnership if the business is continued by the remaining general partners under a right to do so contained in the certificate of limited partnership or with the consent of the other members.[1785]

Partnerships generally do not possess the ease of interest transferability that is present with respect to a corporation. First, there is the potential dissolution problem referred to above. In addition, a partner in a partnership or a general partner in a limited partnership must obtain the consent of all partners to transfer his partnership interest and substitute the transferee for himself. A limited partner may freely assign his limited partnership interest, but the transferee will have only the transferor's right to share in the profits and will not be a substitute limited partner.[1786] Both of these characteristics may be modified by agreement, however. Typically, the partnership will wish to restrict the transferability of its interests — particularly among general partners, inasmuch as the investors in a particular partnership typically do not want their interests being managed by a complete stranger. Similarly, since free transferability of interests is a corporate characteristic, a limited partnership may wish to restrict transferability of limited partnership interests so as to help assure its partnership status for tax purposes. Although corporations might place similar restrictions on transferability of stockholders' interests, these restrictions are not of the type that are inherent in the nature of the organization as is the case with the partnership.

C. CORPORATIONS

A corporation is a separate legal entity formed in accordance with the requisite formalities required by state law. This involves filing of articles of incorporation which conform to the specific state requirements, and the payment of the required fees of the particular jurisdiction. The corporation must then conform to the requirements of that jurisdiction in order to maintain its status as a legal entity. Typically, this involves the filing of an annual report with the appropriate governmental body, the conduct of

---

1785. Uniform Limited Partnership Act, §21.
1786. Uniform Limited Partnership Act, §19.

1. Taxation

A corporation is a separate legal entity and is taxed as such. Corporations are subject to the corporate income tax, which is imposed by §11 of the Code at rates which range from 15 percent to 46 percent.[1788] Consequently, the profits and losses achieved by a corporation will not be passed through to its owners, but rather will be taxed separately according to this rate structure. Because of this, the corporation is not a favored entity for the types of real estate investments which are anticipated to produce tax losses to the investors. Thus, most syndications are organized in the form of a limited partnership rather than a corporation. The corporation may be more useful in the real estate context for those types of ventures which achieve considerable taxable income. In these cases, the corporation will segregate this income, and submit to taxation under a separate rate structure, with a cap at 46 percent (as opposed to the personal income tax rate which maximizes at 50 percent).

If corporate profits are distributed to the shareholders of the corporation, it usually is a taxable event to the shareholders. This so-called double taxation in the case of corporations arises because the distribution of dividends is taxable to the shareholders to the extent of earnings and profits of that corporation.[1789] If, however, the payments being made to the shareholders represent reasonable compensation for services performed, they will be deductible by the corporation (as opposed to dividends, which are not deductible) and will be taken into income by the recipient employee. By way of contrast, partnerships are subject to only one level of taxation. The partners are taxed on the income that is earned by the partnership, whether or not it is distributed. The distribution of cash by a partnership to its partners in the ordinary course of business is typically a non-taxable event unless the payments represent guaranteed payments under §707(c).

If the corporation retains its earnings so as to avoid the double taxation, it may unintentionally be subject to the accumulated earnings tax imposed on corporations. This penalty tax, which is imposed in addition to the corporate income tax, is levied on improper accumulations of earnings.[1790]

1788. §11(b). The rates that are currently in effect are 15 percent of the first $25,000 of taxable income, 18 percent on the next $25,000, 30 percent on the next $25,000, 40 percent on the next $25,000, and 46 percent on the taxable income in excess of $100,000. For tax years beginning after 1983, the 1984 Act amends this section and imposes an additional corporate tax equal to the lesser of $20,250 or 5 percent of taxable income in excess of $1 million. This change has the effect of phasing out the graduated corporate tax rate for high income corporations. P.L. 98-369, §66.

1789. §§301, 316. The dividends are not deductible to the corporation, either.

1790. §531.

Choice of Entity for Real Estate Ownership 1185

This tax is essentially imposed on amounts accumulated in excess of $250,000 for most corporations and $150,000 for certain service corporations.[1791] This tax will not be applied to the extent that funds are accumulated for the reasonable needs of the business.[1792] There is no equivalent penalty imposed upon partnerships. The "penalty" paid by partners of a partnership for accumulation of earnings is that they are taxed upon earnings of the partnership whether or not these earnings are distributed. Consequently, the partners individually pay tax on the earnings of the partnership whether or not a distribution is made.

If a shareholder in a corporation sells his or her interest in that corporation, capital gain will generally be realized on this transaction. There are three major exceptions to this rule. First, if the capital gain holding period requirement for the stock has not been met, the sale will be treated as a short term capital gain and taxed at ordinary income rates. Secondly, if for some reason the shareholder is a dealer in securities, the shares will be considered to be properties held primarily for sale to customers in the ordinary course of trade or business under §1221(1), and the sale will result in recognition of ordinary income. Finally, if the corporation is a collapsible corporation, the transaction which otherwise would result in a capital gain will result in the realization of ordinary income. Essentially, a collapsible corporation is one that is formed principally for the manufacture, construction, or production of property or for the purchase of property[1795] with a view to the sale, liquidation, or distribution before the corporation has realized a substantial part of the taxable income to be derived from such property and the shareholders have realized gain attributable to the property.

Similarly, the redemption of a shareholder's shares may also produce capital gain under §302. Such redemption will not create a deduction for the corporation but will result in capital gain treatment to the shareholder if the corporation is not collapsible, the holding period requirements have been met, and the shares are capital assets in the shareholder's hands. A redemption will qualify for capital gain treatment rather than as a dividend under the following circumstances:

(1) The redemption completely terminates the shareholder's interest in the corporation.[1797]

1791. §535(c)(2). The types of service corporations subject to the $150,000 limit are those in the fields of health, law, engineering, architecture, accounting, actuarial science, performing arts or consulting. §535(c)(2)(B).

1792. §535(c)(1). The term reasonable needs of the business includes the reasonably anticipated needs of the business, the §303 redemption needs of the business, and the excess business holdings redemption needs of the business. §537(a).

1795. §341(b). Section 341 assets are essentially stock in trade of the corporation, property held for sale to customers in the ordinary course of trade or business, unrealized receivables or fees, and some §1231(b) property—any of which has been held for a period of less than three years. §341(b)(3).

1797. §302(b)(3).

(2) A redemption is substantially disproportionate with respect to this shareholder.[1798]

(3) The redemption is not essentially equivalent to a dividend.[1799]

A redemption of the shareholder's stock, unlike the partnership situation, will not cause a termination of the corporation for tax purposes. . . . A liquidation of the corporation will also, in most circumstances, be a capital gain transaction under §331. In contrast, a liquidation of a partnership is not a taxable event unless cash is distributed in excess of the partner's basis.

The most notable aspect of corporate taxation which impacts upon the choice of entity in the real estate situation is the fact that the corporation is itself a taxable, rather than a pass-through, entity. This means that the corporation is typically not utilized in those real estate transactions, such as syndications, in which the depreciation or cost recovery under §168 from the real estate produces substantial tax losses. If, however, the real estate project is creating taxable income, the corporation may be an appropriate vehicle to shield all or a portion of income from taxation at individual income rates. The distribution of appreciated property from a corporation is also typically a taxable transaction to the shareholders. Consequently, the distribution of an appreciated real estate project to an individual shareholder would be taxable whereas a similar transaction in a partnership would not be taxable in many circumstances. If there is a plan to transfer properties to an owner as they appreciate in value, the partnership again may be the most appropriate vehicle.

2. Non-Tax Considerations

. . . [C]orporations have four major non-tax characteristics: continuity of life, centralization of management, limited liability, and free transferability of interests. All of these characteristics are important attributes which must be weighed when considering the advantages or disadvantages of the corporate form. A corporation has continuous life to the extent provided under the articles of incorporation or state statute. Frequently, this duration is perpetual. Thus, a corporation will not be dissolved by the sale of the interest of one of its members or a transfer of such interest among members. Every time a portion of the business changes hands, the corporation does not have to be reconstituted. This can be a significant advantage for ongoing projects which are expected to be of considerable duration. The corporation is in place and will remain in place for an unlimited period of time.

1798. §302(b)(2). A redemption is substantially disporportionate if the ratio which the voting stock of the corporation owned by the shareholder immediately after the redemption bears to all the voting stock of the corporation at such time is less than 80 percent of the ratio which the voting stock of the corporation owned by the shareholder immediately before the redemption bears to all of the voting stock of the corporation at such time. §302(b)(2)(C).
1799. §302(b)(1).

Choice of Entity for Real Estate Ownership

Similarly, the centralized management provided in the corporate form allows for a chosen few people to manage the particular real estate investment while others remain in a passive role. This can be a significant advantage where a large real estate project requires many investors but the management expertise of just a few. It must be pointed out, however, that the same type of management centralization can be achieved in a limited partnership where the limited partners are passive investors whose equity interests are being managed by the general partner. This characteristic does not exist in the general partnership where all of the partners have equivalent management authority. Again, however, even a general partnership agreement can contain provisions which would allocate these responsibilities among one or more of the partners.

Perhaps the corporate characteristic which is most frequently considered to be significant is that of limited liability. The corporate shareholders can limit their liability to the amount of their agreed-upon capital contribution to the corporation. Upon the occurrence of an event creating tort or contractual liability, the individual shareholders do not have to be concerned with unlimited personal liability. As such, the role of the shareholders is similar to that of the limited partners in a limited partnership. (In a limited partnership, however, at least one individual or a corporation with significant assets must serve as the general partner and consequently have the unlimited personal liability.)

It must be noted, however, that there are two major factors which tend to reduce the distinction between corporations and partnerships in regard to this characteristic. First, the purchase of liability insurance by a partnership will largely protect the partners against their fears of tort liability. Consequently, unless the amount of insurance purchased is insufficient or a particular incident is not covered by the partnership's insurance policy, the partners can achieve a good deal of comfort simply by the purchase of liability insurance. In addition, lenders to a corporation frequently demand the personal guarantees of its major stockholders in order to make a loan to the entity. Banks simply do not make loans to a shell corporation without this type of guarantee in the absence of considerable security furnished by the corporation. Accordingly, once such guarantees are demanded by the lending institution, the liability may not be as limited as appears in the corporate statutes.

The final corporate characteristic of free transferability of interests is also of significance. When one owner of a corporation desires to sell his or her interest, it can be accomplished, consistent with whatever restrictions are placed on it by the corporation documents, in a relatively easy manner. The transfer of corporate stock does not involve the technical dissolution of the entity and thus may be somewhat easier to accomplish than in the partnership, which must be reconstituted after each transfer. A corporation does require somewhat more in the way of formalities than a partnership in that the corporate filings must be made and frequently annual reports must be filed with the appropriate state authorities. These particular requirements are not unduly burdensome or expensive, and should not dissuade a potential investor from utilizing the corporate form except in very small ventures.

D. S CORPORATIONS

The final type of organization to be weighed and considered for real estate holdings is the S corporation. The S corporation is a corporation organized under the laws of a particular jurisdiction which makes an election to be taxed under Subchapter S[1802] of the Internal Revenue Code. . . .

1. Taxation

An S corporation which has a valid election in effect passes through its tax losses and profits to its shareholders in a manner similar to a partnership. Typically, there is no income tax imposed on the S corporation; rather, the shareholders are taxed on the corporation's earnings in proportion to their holdings. Thus, the S corporation avoids the corporate problem of double taxation upon its earnings and also permits the pass-through of losses from the depreciation of real estate, for example, to its shareholders. The major exception to this rule is provided by §1374 which imposes a tax on capital gain realized by an S corporation if the net capital gain exceeds $25,000 and 50 percent of its taxable income for the year, and the taxable income of the corporation exceeds $25,000.[1803] This capital gains tax is not imposed if the S corporation election which is in effect with respect to the corporation has been in effect for the three immediately preceding taxable years.[1804] The capital gains tax will also not be imposed on an S corporation if it has been in existence for less than four taxable years and the S corporation election has been in effect with respect to the corporation for each of its taxable years.[1805] Other than the aforementioned exceptions, each shareholder in the S corporation takes into account his pro rata share of items of income, loss, deduction, or credit of the corporation.[1806]

In order for a corporation to qualify for the S corporation election, the entity must be a domestic corporation which is not an ineligible corporation[1807] and which does not have (1) more than thrity-five shareholders, (2)

1802. §§1361-1379. The time and manner for making the election is set forth in §1362(a).
1803. §1374(a).
1804. §1374(c)(1).
1805. §1374(c)(2).
1806. §1366(a).
1807. An ineligible corporation is a corporation which is a member of an affiliated group determined under §1504 without regard to the exceptions in §1504(b), a financial institution to which §585 or §593 applies, an insurance company subject to tax under subchapter L, a corporation to which an election under §936 applies, or a DISC or a former DISC. §1361(b)(2).

a shareholder who is not an individual (other than an estate or trust described in §1361(c)(2)), (3) a nonresident alien shareholder, or (4) more than one class of stock.[1808] Consequently, the S corporation cannot be used in those transactions which have more than thirty-five equity owners or in which differing classes of ownership with different rights and responsibilities are desired. In addition, the S corporation cannot be used when there is a non-resident alien shareholder or in the multiple-tiered corporation situation. These factors, in and of themselves, tend to limit the use of the S corporation in many real estate transactions.

If a corporation qualifies under the above criteria, S corporation status does hold an attraction in real estate transactions since it permits a pass-through of tax attributes to its equity owners and yet offers the advantages of limited liability that derive from the corporate form. There are, however, a number of limiting factors which tend to restrict the use of S corporations in the real estate context.[1809] The major such factor is that the losses that can be deducted by an S corporation shareholder are limited to that shareholder's basis in the entity.[1810] The basis of a shareholder in an S corporation equals the adjusted basis of his stock[1811] plus the amount of indebtedness of the S corporation to the shareholder.[1812] Thus, mortgage liabilities on real property owned by an S corporation cannot be added to the shareholder's basis. In contrast, such mortgage liabilities can frequently be added to the basis of partners in a partnership. The net result of this is that the amount of losses that can be passed through to the shareholder in an S corporation is more restricted than in a partnership. Accordingly, for those entities such as syndications which are designed to pass through considerable losses in excess of capital investment to investors,[1813] the S corporation may be an inappropriate vehicle.

In addition, the S corporation may realize gain if appreciated property is distributed to its shareholders,[1814] whereas this is not the case with respect to a partnership. Also, as noted above, the limitation of the S corporation to one class of stock and the requirements that tax items be allocated proportionately to stock ownership restrict the ability of a real estate owner to use an S corporation where special allocations of income and/or loss are desired. Finally, the fact that an increase in the mortgage loans on real property will not increase the stockholders' basis in their S

1808. §1361(b)(1).
1809. These limiting factors are discussed more extensively in II, F, 2 [omitted—Eds.].
1810. §1366(d)(1).
1811. The basis of the shareholder's stock generally consists of the price paid for such stock increased by income of the corporation and decreased by losses and distributions made by the corporation. §1367(a).
1812. §1366(d)(1).
1813. Of course, the "at risk" rules of §465 restrict the ability to pass through such losses in transactions which do not involve the holding of real property (other than mineral property).
1814. §1363(d). This does not apply in the case of complete liquidation or a reorganization where stock is received tax free pursuant to §§354, 355 or 356. §1363(e).

corporation stock limits the ability of the S corporation to distribute tax-free refinancing proceeds, as frequently can be accomplished by a partnership. Although the S corporation acts in a manner similar to a partnership in the pass-through of tax losses, there are several limiting factors. Consequently, the S corporation is probably not appropriate for use in a heavily leveraged transaction designed to produce considerable tax shelter. In other types of situations it may be a useful vehicle since it avoids the double taxation associated with the subchapter C corporation and permits the pass-through of losses in the early years of operation. If the entity can be organized so as to meet the S corporation requirements and its shareholders can otherwise live with the limitations discussed herein, the S corporation should be considered for many real estate transactions. Like a partnership, the S corporation is probably not appropriate for an investment designed to accumulate funds since the shareholder will be taxed on income whether or not it is distributed. If accumulation is desired, a subchapter C corporation may be more appropriate.

2. *Non-Tax Considerations*

The non-tax considerations involved in an S corporation are essentially identical to those of a subchapter C corporation. The S corporation is formed like any other corporation, under state law, which usually imposes no additional requirements simply because the corporation subsequently elects to be taxed as an S corporation. Thus, the S corporation also provides the corporate characteristics of centralization of management, free transferability of interests, limited liability, and continuity of life.

E. HOW TO DETERMINE REAL ESTATE RETURN ON INVESTMENT

The Mortgage and Real Estate Executive's Report
5-7 (June 16, 1985)

How to Determine Real Estate Return on Investment

Return on investment (ROI) analysis has come a long way since buy and sell decisions were made strictly on the basis of the first year cash-on-cash return. (Some would argue that the original method remains the best.)

All of the more recent ROI techniques seek to estimate annual returns over a fairly long period — five or 10 years in most cases. The trend to long-range projections reflects the fundamental change in the source of equity capital for real estate. Formerly, equity came mostly from sophisticated real estate professionals who put up their own money and relied on their judgment in making investments. For them, the current profit and loss statement was all they needed. (It was also true that returns were often much higher than today, affording a cushion against mistakes.)

Now, however, equity capital comes primarily from large institutional investors (pension funds and equity-sharing lenders) and from the public (via syndicates and real estate investment trusts). For these investors, detailed projections substitute for the "intuitive" sense of the professional.

A projected ROI will be worth looking at only if two conditions are met: (1) the projected figures (rentals, expenses, resale prices, etc.) have been carefully and conservatively arrived at; and (2) the method of estimating the return on investment is clearly understood by the investor. This second condition is the subject of this article. (The examples used in the article were prepared by Robert A Stanger & Co., and appear in the current issue of *The Stanger Report*.)

COMPOUNDED GROWTH RATE IS KEY MEASURE

The most popular technique for measuring ROI is the internal rate of return (IRR). The workings (and limitations) of IRR are detailed below, and it is then compared with the adjusted rate of return (ARR) method. Before doing this, however, some comments should be made about compound interest and the concept of compounded growth rate.

Compound interest, as everyone knows, is interest on interest. If $100 is deposited in a five-year certificate of deposit with a guaranteed annual rate of 10 percent, the sum will grow to $161.05 at the end of the term. The original $100 grows to $150 ($10 interest per year for five years). The additional $11.05 represents compound interest—the interest earned each year on the prior accumulated interest.

The special feature of a certificate of deposit with a guaranteed yield, as with a zero coupon bond, is that no reinvestment risk exists. That is, the accumulated interest will earn the same return as the original deposit. Thus, we can say with certainty that the above investment will have a compounded growth rate of 10 percent over its five-year term. In virtually all other types of investments, however, there *is* a reinvestment risk and it is this factor that leads to confusion about the meaning of the internal rate of return.

CALCULATING INTERNAL RATE OF RETURN

We have just seen that when (1) the annual rate of return on an initial investment is known and (2) each year's gain will itself earn the same rate of return (compounded return), it is a simple matter to calculate the future value of the initial investment.

Now suppose the future value (total of future economic benefits) is known and the investor wants to determine the annual rate of com-

TABLE [7-4]
12% IRR

Beginning of Year	(1) Investment	(2) Annual Economic Benefits	(3) Present Value Factor	(4) Present Value
1	$10,000	—	—	—
2	—	$ 5,000	.893	$ 4,465
3	—	3,000	.797	2,391
4	—	1,800	.712	1,282
5	—	1,500	.636	954
6	—	900	.567	510
7	—	500	.506	253
8	—	330	.453	149
Totals	$10,000	$13,030		$10,004
Reinvestment Earnings		$ 4,008		
New Worth in Year 8*		$17,038		

* Assumes reinvested benefits earn 6% after tax per annum.

pounded return. He must reverse the process just described. This in essence is the internal rate of return technique.

Table [7-4] illustrates how IRR works. An initial investment of $10,000 will produce a value of $13,030 as a result of seven annual repayments or tax benefits. By using a present value table, we can determine the compounded interest rate that will permit an initial $10,000 sum to grow to $13,030 as indicated in column 2. That compounded interest rate is 12 percent.

This may be more clearly understood if the initial investment of $10,000 is viewed as a number of separate investments, each equal to the present value of each future payment (i.e., the present values listed in column 4). For example, $4,465 of the initial investment is treated as repaid to the investor at the beginning of Year 2 together with $535 of interest (or a total of $5,000). This represents an annual return of 12 percent. The second segment of the initial investment, $2,391, is repaid at the beginning of the third year together with $609 of interest. This also represents a compounded return of 12 percent, and so on for the remaining five payments.

REINVESTMENT EARNINGS ARE IGNORED

The important point to note about the process just described is that IRR *does not show the compound annual growth on the entire initial investment,* but only for the period of time each segment is invested. Thus, when compar-

COMPARING INVESTMENTS

To show the importance of including a reinvestment factor when comparing the total return from different investments, compare Tables [7-4] and [7-5]. Table [7-5] shows the annual returns (including return of principal in the final year) from an investment of $10,000 in a tax-free bond yielding 8.5 percent. The total value of the annual payments is $15,950, $2,920 more than the total payments in Table [7-4]. However, the IRR of the tax-free bond investment is only 8.5 percent, 3.5 percent less than the IRR in Table [7-4]. The reason is obvious. Most of the annual returns in Table [7-4] come in the earlier years, while the opposite is true in Table [7-5]. (That is, the average holding period is shorter in Table [7-4].) Thus, when the reinvestment of annual returns is ignored, Table [7-4] shows the higher return.

However, the conclusion may change depending on the assumption one makes about reinvestments. The lower portions of Tables [7-4] and [7-5] compare the two investments when it is assumed that annual benefits are reinvested at a 6 percent after-tax rate of return until the end of the overall holding period of seven years. It then turns out that the tax-free bond shows the higher return. The reason is that the real estate investment,

TABLE [7-5]
8.5% IRR

Beginning of Year	(1) Investment	(2) Annual Economic Benefits	(3) Present Value Factor	(4) Present Value
1	$10,000	—	—	—
2	—	850	.921	$ 783
3	—	850	.849	722
4	—	850	.783	666
5	—	850	.722	614
6	—	850	.665	565
7	—	850	.612	520
8	—	10,850	.565	6,130
Totals	$10,000	$15,950		$10,000
Reinvestment Earnings		$ 1,184		
Net Worth in Year 8*		$17,134		

* Assumes reinvested benefits earn 6% after tax per annum.

TABLE [7-6]
Adjusted Rate of Return

	"12% IRR Partners"			Bond Yielding 8.5% After Tax		
Year	Investment	Annual Economic Benefits	Earnings from Reinvestment of Benefits*	Investment	Annual Economic Benefits	Earnings from Reinvestment of Benefits*
1	$10,000	—	—	$10,000	—	—
2	—	$ 5,000	—	—	850	—
3	—	3,000	$ 300	—	850	$ 51
4	—	1,800	498	—	850	105
5	—	1,500	636	—	850	162
6	—	900	764	—	850	223
7	—	500	864	—	850	287
8	—	330	946	—	850	356
Totals	$10,000	$13,030	$4,008	$10,000	$15,950	$1,184

Total Return** $17,038 $17,134
Adjusted Rate of Return   7.9%   8.0%

* Assumes reinvested benefits earn 6% after tax per annum.
** Total annual economic benefits plus total earnings from reinvestment.
Source: The Stanger Report.

which returns most of the initial investment in the early years, subjects more of the initial investment to a lower reinvestment rate of only six percent. In the case of the tax-free bond, although the initial rate is only 8.5 percent, a larger proportion of the initial investment earns that rate for a longer period of time; consequently, less of the initial investment must be reinvested at the 6 percent rate.

WHAT IRR REALLY TELLS THE INVESTOR

As can be seen from the tables, the internal rate of return tells an investor what the compounded interest rate is on equity remaining in the particular investment at any given point. It does *not* represent the compounded return on the total initial investment over the entire holding period. Therefore, it is essential for the investor to make some assumption about a reinvestment rate.

In the example shown in Table [7-4], if annual returns could be reinvested at the same 12 percent rate the initial investment earns, then it could be said that the $10,000 put up in year 1 earns 12 percent compounded annually through the end of year 8. If the reinvestment rate is more or less than 12 percent, then the total return on the investment over the holding period will be different from 12 percent.

USING THE ADJUSTED RATE OF RETURN

The adjusted rate of return (ARR) is a better way of comparing investments because it specifically identifies a reinvestment rate to be applied to amounts repaid to the investor during the holding period. Table [7-6] combines the information contained in Tables [7-4] and [7-5] to show how an ARR is calculated. When reinvestment of benefits is assumed at 6 percent after tax, the tax-free bond shows an ARR of 8 percent, versus 7.9 percent for the real estate investment.

Observation: Of course, even the ARR cannot determine precisely the future return, since the reinvestment rate can only be assumed. Nevertheless, it provides a much sounder comparison between alternative investments than does the IRR. Note that in the case of a zero coupon bond or certificate of deposit, the ARR and the IRR are identical, since in these investments the reinvestment rate is guaranteed to be the same as the rate on the original investment.

APPENDIX A
Glossary of Real Estate Terms

Madway, A Mortgage Foreclosure Primer
8 Clearinghouse Rev. 146, 178-181 (July 1974)

Abstract of Title — A summary of conveyances, transfers, *mortgages* and any other factual evidence which may confirm or impair the validity of title to real property.

Acceleration Clause — A clause in a *note*, a *deed of trust* or *mortgage* providing that if the *mortgagor* fails to pay any of his payments when due or breaches any of the other convenants in the *mortgage* instrument, the balance of the obligation becomes immediately due and owing.

Accrued Interest — *Interest* that has been earned but not collected.

Amortization — The process of repaying a loan by equal periodic installments calculated to retire the principal at the end of a fixed period and to pay *accrued interest* on the outstanding balance.

Appraisal — The act of placing an estimate of the real or *market value* on real estate.

Assessed Valuation — The valuation placed by a local governmental unit upon real property for purposes of real estate taxation. Usually, it is less than the *market value* of the property. The relationship between *assessed* and *market value* varies widely from place to place.

Assessment — Usually a charge made against property by a state, county, city or other authorized taxing jurisdiction.

Assignee — The party to whom a *note* and the *mortgage* or *deed of trust* it secures have been transferred, usually for consideration.

Assignor — The party who assigns or transfers the *note* and the *mortgage*.

Assumption of Mortgage — The act of taking title to real estate and assuming payment of the outstanding indebtedness on it.

Balloon Mortgage — A type of *mortgage* loan which involves regular monthly payments for *interest* plus either no or partial *amortization* of the loan principal, so that at the end of the *term* of the *mortgage* there is a lump sum payment, commonly called a balloon payment, of the remaining principal due.

Beneficiary—The person designated to receive the payment from the borrower *(trustor)* under a *deed of trust,* usually the lender or its *assignee.*

Closing—Meeting of parties to adjust final sale figures, taxes, etc., and to sign and deliver *mortgage* and property title transfer documents.

Cloud on Title—An instrument, such as deed, *deed of trust, mortgage,* tax or *assessment,* judgment, or decree, that, if valid, would impair the title to land.

Collateral—The specific real property the borrower pledges as security for a loan.

Commitment—A promise by a lender to make a specific loan to a prospective borrower.

Compound Interest—Interest computed on both the original principal and its *accrued interest.*

Conventional Mortgage—In modern mortgage parlance, a *mortgage* that is not insured, guaranteed and/or subsidized by any governmental or quasi-governmental agency. It should be noted that conventional mortgages are often insured by private mortgage insurers.

Conveyance—The transfer of the title to land from one person, or class of persons, to another.

Correspondent—A mortgage loan correspondent; a mortgage banker who *services* mortgage loans as agent for the owner of the mortgage. Also applied to the mortgage banker in his role as originator of mortgage loans for the investor.

Deed of Trust—Essentially a three-party *mortgage;* the owner, as *trustor,* conveys the property to a *trustee* to hold for the benefit of a *beneficiary,* the lender, to secure payment of a debt or obligation owed to the *beneficiary.* The deed of trust invariably gives the *trustee* the power to sell the property upon demand of the beneficiary in the event of a default.

Debt Service—The regular payments that are made to pay off the principal of a mortgage loan, plus *interest* on the unpaid balance of the principal.

Debt Service Constant—A factor that, multiplied by the total loan amount, or total principal, yields the annual *debt-service* payment (principal plus interest) required to amortize a loan.

Decree of Foreclosure and Sale—In judicial foreclosure jurisdiction, the court decree or judgment that establishes the amount of the *mortgage* debt and orders the property sold to satisfy the debt.

Default—The nonperformance of a duty arising under a *note, mortgage* or *deed of trust or installment land sale contract.*

Deficiency—The difference between the amount of the mortgage indebtedness and any lesser amount recovered by the mortgagee from the foreclosure sale.

Deficiency Judgment—A personal judgment created by a court decree for the amount of the deficiency against any person liable for the mortgage debt.

Glossary of Real Estate Terms

Downpayment — The amount of cash that a buyer is required to put up in order to purchase a piece of property; it is equal to the purchase price minus the amount of any mortgage loans used to finance the purchase.

Direct-Reduction Mortgage — A *mortgage* directing that all payments must be used for reduction of the outstanding balance of the principal.

Discount Points — Amount paid by the borrower to the lender to secure a mortgage loan. One point is equal to one percent of the loan.

Due-on-Sale or Encumbrance — A clause in a *mortgage* or *deed of trust* providing that if the mortgagor or trustor sells, transfers or in any way encumbers the property, (e.g., gives a *second mortgage* or *deed of trust*, permits a lien to attach) the *acceleration clause* is triggered and the balance of the obligation becomes due.

Encumbrance — A claim or *lien* attached to a piece of property, limiting in some way the owner's rights to the property.

Escrow Account — An account in which the borrower's monthly payments for taxes and insurance are placed and held in trust by the lender.

Equity of Redemption — The right of a *mortgagor* to redeem his property after he has breached some convenant of the *mortgage*, usually by failing to make a payment when due, and the *mortgagee* has elected to accelerate the balance of the obligation. Redemption is accomplished by payment of the entire debt, plus accrued interest and costs. The equity of redemption must be distinguished from the *statutory right of redemption*. The former is a creature of equity, while the latter, of statute. The equity of redemption is cut off when the foreclosure sale takes place. In jurisdictions which provide a statutory right of redemption, that right usually accrues upon the foreclosure sale and remains available to the mortgagor for a specified period of time, in some places, up to two years. In effect, it permits him to oust the party who purchased the property at the foreclosure sale and regain possession by paying the foreclosure sale price or the amount of the outstanding obligation, plus accrued interest and costs, depending on the statute.

Execution — A writ issued by a judicial officer and directed to a sheriff, constable, marshal or commissioner appointed by the court to enforce a judgment against the property or person of a judgment debtor.

Federal Home Loan Banks — A national system of eleven regional banks established by the Home Loan Bank Act of 1932 to provide facilities for savings and loan associations and similar institutions, mutual savings banks, and life insurance companies, in connection with their home-mortgage lending activities, on condition that they become members of the system.

Federal National Mortgage Association ("FNMA" or "Fannie Mae") — An association organized February 10, 1938 under the provisions of the National Housing Act. During its earlier years, it was grouped under a series of federal departments and agencies and was authorized to purchase, or commit for purchase, FHA insured and Veterans' Administration guaranteed mortgage loans. Funds for those mortgage purchases were obtained by FNMA by borrowing from the Treasury. In 1954, Congress rechartered FNMA into a mixed private-public ownership corporation. Under the Housing and Urban Development Act of 1968, FNMA was spun off from the federal government as a government sponsored but privately owned corporation. By purchasing mortgages, the FNMA provides a "secondary market" for mortgages, thus permitting home mortgage lenders to increase their liquidity and make more money available for new loans.

First Mortgage—A type of *mortgage* where the property which secures it has no other mortgages with prior or greater rights to the property; a *mortgage* that is a first lien on the property pledged as security.

Forbearance—The act of refraining from taking legal action despite the fact that a *mortgage* is in *default*—usually granted only when the *mortgagor* makes a satisfactory arrangement by which the *default* will be cured at a future date.

Foreclosure—The legal process by which a *mortgagor* is deprived of his interest in the property. Usually, property is sold, either pursuant to a court *decree of foreclosure* or pursuant to a *power of sale* provision. The proceeds of the sale are customarily applied to pay off the amount still owed on the *note* which the *mortgage* secured, plus the expenses of the foreclosure proceeding and/or the sale.

Fully Amortized Mortgage—A method of repaying a mortgage loan which involves regular payments for *interest* plus *amortization* of the loan principal so that at the end of the term the principal has been entirely repaid.

Garnishment—An attachment of assets in the possession of a third person.

General National Mortgage Association ("GNMA" or "Ginnie Mae")—Created by the Housing and Urban Development Act of 1968, GNMA is part of the U.S. Department of Housing and Urban Development. GNMA operates a number of "special assistance" programs under which it buys certain categories of FHA and VA mortgages at prices above the *market price,* thus encouraging lenders to make loans falling in these categories. Many of these "special assistance" programs are conducted pursuant to the "tandem plan," under which GNMA buys mortgages at prices more favorable than the *market price* and then sells them to *FNMA* or other investors at prevailing market prices, absorbing the difference between the GNMA price and the higher *market price* as a subsidy.

Grant—A generic term applicable to all transfers of an interest in real property.

Grantee—A person to whom a *grant* is made.

Grantor—The person by whom the *grant* is made.

Holder—The current owner of an indebtedness secured by a *mortgage* or *deed of trust.*

Homestead Estate—The rights of record, belonging to a family or head of a household in real estate owned and occupied as a home, that are exempt from seizure by creditors.

Glossary of Real Estate Terms 1201

Hypothecate— To pledge a thing without delivering the title or possession of it to the pledgee.

Installment Land Sales Contract— An agreement whereby a seller agrees to convey title to real property to a buyer when the buyer has paid the seller the purchase price of the property, with *interest* at a specified rate, and with the payment schedule spread over a number of years. Depending upon the jurisdiction, this type of financing arrangement places the buyer in the position of the tenant except that, after the pay-out period, the seller conveys his interest in the land to the buyer. The buyer receives no deed until he pays the seller the entire purchase price, and the seller may have all of the remedies of a landlord against the defaulting buyer.

Income Limits— Family income limits established for admission to FHA, and FmHA homeownership programs. Limits are based on family size, type of dwelling and cost of living in the area.

Interest Rate— The rate at which the amount charged for use of money is computed.

Interest Reduction Programs— Programs operated by FHA and FmHA which subsidize the market *interest rate* on mortgage loans for low and moderate-income housing, thus lowering the cost to the buyer.

Interim Financing— Loans covering land and construction costs, current real estate taxes, and other incidental expenses during the construction period.

Institutional Lender— A mortgage lender that invests its own funds in *mortgages* and carries a majority of such loans in its own portfolio, e.g., mutual savings banks, life insurance companies, commercial banks, savings and loan associations. Although individuals or mortgage companies may hold and service mortgage loans, they are not generally classified as institutional lenders.

Junior Mortgage— A type of *mortgage* where the property which it secures already has one or more *mortgages* on it with prior or greater rights.

Late Charge— A penalty permitted by FHA covering any monthly payment not made by the 15th of the month in which the payment is due. The FHA usually permits 2% of the monthly payment as a late charge. Many lenders exact a late charge for delinquency on *conventional mortgage* loan installments.

Lender— Any mortgage lender, e.g., mutual savings bank, commercial bank, savings and loan association, etc., that invests its own funds in *mortgages*. Also, the *holder* of the *mortgage*, the permanent lender for which the mortgage banker services the loan.

Level-Payment Mortgage— A *mortgage* that provides for the payment of like sums at periodic intervals during its term. Part of the payment is credited to the *interest* for the time involved, and the balance is used to amortize the principal.

Lien— A hold or claim one person has upon the property of another as security for a debt. In many states, a *mortgage* is regarded as a lien.

Loan Trust Funds— In FHA loans, the funds accumulated to take care of taxes, fire insurance, mortgage insurance and premiums as they become due and payable.

Loan-Value Ratio — The relationship between the amount of the loan and the appraised value of the property, usually expressed as a percentage.

Market Value — The price at which a property could be sold on the open market, free of the pressures created by a forced sale.

Maturity — Termination of the period a note or obligation has to run.

Mechanic's Lien — A claim created by statute in most states, in favor of mechanics or other persons who have performed work or furnished materials in and for the erection or repair of a building.

Moratorium — A period during which a borrower has a legal right to delay payment obligations. Especially, a period granted in an emergency or generally by a moratory law.

Mortgage — A contract by which specific property is *hypothecated* as security for the performance of an act or the payment of a debt.

Mortgage Insurance Premium — The price paid by the borrower for insurance under FHA and VA loans. The insurance is furnished by the federal government in favor of the lender, and insures payment of the loan in event that the proceeds of a foreclosure sale fail to cover the outstanding balance of the obligation.

Mortgage Note — A promissory note secured by a mortgage on specific real property.

Mortgage Portfolio — The aggregate of mortgage loans held by a mortgage lender.

Mortgage Risk — A hazard of loss of principal and/or interest in the lending of funds secured by a mortgage.

Mortgagee — The lending party under the terms of a *mortgage*.

Mortgagor — The borrowing party who pledges property to secure the loan.

Note — See *mortgage note,* supra.

Open-End Mortgage — A *mortgage* or *deed of trust* so written as to secure and permit additional advances on the original loan.

Package Mortgage — See *open-end mortgage,* supra.

Plat — A map showing the dimensions of a piece of real estate based upon the legal descriptions.

Power of Sale — A provision in a *mortgage* or *deed of trust* which empowers a *mortgagee* or *trustee,* without resort to any judicial procedures, to sell the property in the event of *default* by the *mortgagor* and apply the proceeds of the sale to satisfy the obligation, the costs of invoking the procedure (e.g., attorneys' fees, recordation fees, etc.), and the expenses of sale.

Points — The percentage deduction from the nominal amount of a discounted loan. On a $1000 loan discounted two points, the borrower receives $980.

Prepayment Penalty — A penalty exacted from the borrower for the right to repay a debt before it actually becomes due.

Glossary of Real Estate Terms

Purchase Money Mortgage — A *mortgage* given to the seller by the buyer to secure in whole or in part the purchase price of real property.

Quiet Title — An action to judicially determine the rights and interests to specific real property.

Reinstatement — The curing of all defaults by a borrower; the restoration of a loan to current status through payment of arrearages.

Refinancing — The process of obtaining a new *mortgage* loan when the old note has been partially repaid. The proceeds of the new loan are customarily used to repay the outstanding balance of the old.

Refunding — The process of refinancing a debt that cannot be paid conveniently when due.

Right of Redemption — See *equity of redemption,* supra.

Risk Rating — A process by which risks are divided and evaluated, as to neighborhood, property, the *mortgagor,* and the *mortgage* pattern.

Satisfaction — A written instrument evidencing the full payment of a *mortgage* debt and extinguishing the *mortgage lien.*

Second Mortgage — A type of *junior mortgage* where the property is encumbered by only one other *mortgage,* the first *mortgage,* that has prior or greater right to the property.

Secondary Financing — A loan secured by a second *mortgage* or *deed of trust.*

Servicing — The collection of payments of *interest* and principal and *trust-fund* items such as fire insurance, taxes, and others on a note. Servicing by the lender also consists of operational procedures covering accounting, bookkeeping, insurance, tax records, loan-payment-follow-up, delinquent loan-follow-up, and loan analysis. Servicing may be performed either by the *holder* of a *mortgage note* or by its agent appointed for that purpose.

Standing Mortgage — A method of repaying a mortgage loan which involves a regular payment for interest but no *amortization* of the loan principal.

Straw — A person or firm named as the owner of a piece of property, when in fact it is in reality a front for the real owner.

Strict Foreclosure — A type of foreclosure proceeding used in a few states in which title is vested directly in the mortgagee by court degree without holding a foreclosure sale.

Subordination — The written acknowledgment of the creditor that the debt due to him by the debtor is inferior to a debt due another creditor by the same debtor.

Tandem Plan — See General National Mortgage Association supra.

Term — The time period in which a loan must be repaid.

Term Mortgage — A *mortgage* having a specific *term,* usually not over five years, during which interest is paid but the principal is not reduced.

Title Insurance — Insurance to protect a property owner from loss if a title proves imperfect.

Trust Deed — See *Deed of Trust,* supra.

Trustee — A person in whom property is vested for the purpose of securing performance of an obligation.

Trustor — The borrower under a *deed of trust.*

Usury — Taking, or contracting for, a rate of interest in excess of that permitted by law.

Waiver of Lien — A written evidence in many states from a contractor or materialman surrendering his right of lien to enforce collection of a debt against property.

Waste — Damage to property by willful neglect, abuse, misuse, etc.

Yield — Effective return on a *mortgage* based upon the face rate of interest and the price paid for the *mortgage.*

APPENDIX B

Exclusive Listing Agreement*

In consideration of the services of _____, herein called Broker, I hereby employ Broker, exclusively and irrevocably, for the period beginning _____, 19__ and ending at midnight _____, 19__, to sell the property situated in _____, County of _____, California, described as follows: _____
and I hereby grant Broker the exclusive and irrevocable right to sell said property within said time for _____ dollars ($_____) and to accept a deposit thereon _____.
Terms: _____

    I hereby agree to pay Broker as commission _____ percent _____ of the selling price if said property is sold during the term hereof or any extension thereof by Broker or by me or by another broker or through any other source. If said property is withdrawn from sale, transferred, or leased during the term hereof or any extension thereof, I agree to pay Broker said percent of the above listed price.

    If a sale, lease or other transfer of said property is made within three (3) months after this authorization or any extension thereof terminates to parties with whom Broker negotiates during the term hereof or any extension thereof and Broker notifies me in writing of such negotiations, personally or by mail, during the term hereof or any extension thereof, then I agree to pay said commission to Broker.

    Evidence of title shall be a California Land Title Association standard coverage form policy of title insurance to be paid for by _____.

    If deposits or amounts paid on account of purchase price are forfeited, Broker shall be entitled to one-half thereof, but not to exceed the amount of the commission.

* California Real Estate Association.

Exclusive Listing Agreement

I hereby acknowledge receipt of a copy hereof.

Dated _____, 19___.

_____, California

_____
(Address of Owner)

_____(City)_____ _____(Zone)_____ _____(Phone)_____

_____
_____
_____

Owner

In consideration of the execution of the foregoing, the undersigned Broker agrees to use diligence in procuring a purchaser.

_____
(Address of Broker)

_____(City)_____ _____(Zone)_____ _____(Phone)_____

Broker

By _____

APPENDIX C
Contract of Sale*

1. Sale. _____ (Purchaser) agrees to purchase at a price of $_____ on the terms set forth herein, the following described real estate in _____ County, Illinois: [*If legal description is not included herein at time of execution,* _____ *is authorized to insert it thereafter.*] commonly known as _____, and with approximate lot dimensions of _____ × _____, together with the following personal property presently located thereon: (strike items not applicable) (a) storm and screen doors and windows; (b) awnings; (c) outdoor television antenna; (d) wall-to-wall, hallway and stair carpeting; (e) window shades and draperies and supporting fixtures; (f) venetian blinds; (g) electric, plumbing and other attached fixtures as installed; (h) water softener; (i) refrigerator(s); (j) _____ stove(s). . . .

2. Encumbrances. _____
(Insert names of all owners and their respective spouses)
(Seller) agrees to sell the real estate and the personal property described above at the price and terms set forth herein, and to convey or cause to be conveyed to Purchaser or nominee a good title thereto (in joint tenancy) by a recordable _____ deed, with release of dower and homestead rights, and a proper bill of sale, subject only to: (a) covenants, conditions and restrictions of record; (b) private, public and utility easements and roads and highways, if any; (c) party wall rights and agreements, if any; (d) existing leases and tenancies; (e) special taxes or assessments for improvements not yet completed; (f) installments not due at the date hereof of any special tax or assessment for improvements heretofore completed; (g) mortgage or trust deed specified below, if any; (h) general taxes for the year _____ and subsequent years; and to _____.

3. Payments. Purchaser has paid $_____ (and will pay within _____ days the additional sum of $_____) as earnest money to be applied on the purchase price, and agrees to pay or satisfy the balance of the purchase price, plus or minus prorations, at the time of closing as follows: *(strike subparagraph not applicable)*
    (a)   The payment of $_____

---

* Chicago Title and Trust Company Revised 1968 Form.

(b) The acceptance of the title to the real estate by Purchaser subject to a mortgage (trust deed) of record securing a principal indebtedness (which the Purchaser [does] [does not] agree to assume) aggregating $_____ bearing interest at the rate of _____% a year, and the payments of a sum which represents the difference between the amount due on the indebtedness at the time of closing and the balance of the purchase price.

4. Loan Commitment. This contract is subject to the condition that Purchaser be able to procure within _____ days a firm commitment for a loan to be secured by a mortgage or trust deed on the real estate in the amount of $_____, or such lesser sum as Purchaser accepts, with interest not to exceed _____% a year to be amortized over _____ years, the service charges for such loan not to exceed _____%. If, after making every reasonable effort, Purchaser is unable to procure such commitment within the time specified herein and so notifies Seller thereof within that time, and if seller within a like period of time following the Purchaser's notice does not procure for Purchaser such a commitment or notify Purchaser that Seller will accept a purchase money mortgage upon the same terms, this contract shall become null and void and all earnest money shall be refunded to Purchaser. [*strike paragraph if inapplicable*]

5. Closing. The time of closing shall be on _____, or 20 days after notice that financing has been procured if paragraph 4 is operative (whichever date is later), unless subsequently mutually agreed otherwise, at the office of _____ or of the mortgage lender, if any, provided title is shown to be good or is accepted by Purchaser.

6. Possession. Seller shall deliver possession to Purchaser on or before _____ days after the sale has been closed. Seller agrees to pay Purchaser the sum of $_____ for each day Seller remains in possession between the time of closing and the time possession is delivered.

7. Broker's Commission. Seller agrees to pay a broker's commission to _____ in the amount recommended in the present schedule of commissions of the _____ Real Estate Board applicable to this sale.

8. Depositary. The earnest money shall be held by _____ for the mutual benefit of the parties.

9. Representation. If the building or structure located on the real estate is subject to the provisions of "An Act relating to contracts to sell multiple dwelling units," passed by the General Assembly of the State of Illinois and approved August 11, 1967, Seller warrants that no notice from any city, village or other governmental authority of a dwelling code violation which existed prior to the execution of this contract has been issued and received by Seller or his agent.

Contract of Sale   1209

10. Delivery of Contract.   A duplicate original of this contract, duly executed by the Seller and his spouse, if any, shall be delivered to the Purchaser within _____ days from the date hereof, otherwise, at the Purchaser's option, this contract shall become null and void and the earnest money refunded to the Purchaser.

This contract is subject to the Conditions set forth on the back page hereof, which Conditions are made a part of this contract.

Dated _____

Purchaser _____	(Address) _____
Purchaser _____	(Address) _____
Seller _____	(Address) _____
Seller _____	(Address) _____

CONDITIONS

1. Title Insurance Policy.   Seller shall deliver or cause to be delivered to Purchaser or Purchaser's agent, not less than 5 days prior to the time of closing, a title commitment for an owner's title insurance policy issued by the Chicago Title and Trust Company in the amount of the purchase price, covering title to the real estate on or after the date hereof, showing title in the intended grantor subject only to (a) the general exceptions contained in the policy, (b) the title exceptions set forth above, and (c) title exceptions which may be removed by the payment of money at the time of closing and which the Seller may so remove at that time by using the funds to be paid upon the delivery of the deed. The title commitment shall be conclusive evidence of good title as therein shown, subject only to the exceptions as therein stated. Seller also shall furnish Purchaser an affidavit of title covering the time of closing, subject only to the title exceptions permitted by this contract.

2. Defects in Title.   If the title commitment discloses exceptions relating to title other than those referred to in the preceding paragraph, Seller shall have 30 days from the date of the delivery thereof to have these exceptions removed from the commitment. If Seller fails to have these exceptions removed within this time, Purchaser may terminate this contract or may elect, upon notice to Seller within 10 days after the expiration of the 30-day period, to take title as it then is with the right to deduct from the purchase price liens or encumbrances of a definite or ascertainable amount. If Purchaser does not so elect, this contract shall become null and void without further action of the parties.

3. Adjustments at Closing.   Rents, premiums under assignable insurance policies, water and other utility charges, fuels, prepaid service contracts, general taxes, accrued interest on mortgage indebtedness, if any, and other similar items shall be adjusted ratably as of the time of closing. If the amount of the current general taxes is not then ascertainable, the adjustment <u>thereof shall be on the basis of the amount of the most recent ascertainable taxes.</u> Existing leases and assignable insurance policies, if any, shall then be assigned to Purchaser. Seller shall pay the amount of any stamp tax imposed by law on the transfer of the title, and shall furnish a completed Real Estate Transfer Declaration signed by the Seller or the Seller's agent in the form required pursuant to the Real Estate Transfer Tax Act of the State of Illinois.

[margin note: seller's sentence only true if no increase]

4. Destruction of Improvements. If prior to closing, the improvements on said real estate shall be destroyed or materially damaged by fire or other casualty, this contract, at the option of the Purchaser, shall become null and void and the earnest money shall be returned to the Purchaser.

5. Application of Earnest Money on Termination. If this contract is terminated without Purchaser's fault, the earnest money shall be returned to the Purchaser, but if the termination is caused by the Purchaser's fault, then at the option of the Seller and upon notice to the Purchaser, the earnest money shall be forfeited to the Seller and applied first to the payment of Seller's expenses and then to payment of broker's commission; the balance, if any, to be retained by the Seller as liquidated damages.

6. Option for Escrow. At the election of Seller on Purchaser upon notice to the other party not less than 5 days prior to the time of closing, this sale shall be closed through an escrow with Chicago Title and Trust Company, in accordance with the general provisions of the usual form of Deed and Money Escrow Agreement then in use by Chicago Title and Trust Company, with such special provisions inserted in the escrow agreement as may be required to conform with this contract. Upon the creation of such an escrow, anything herein to the contrary notwithstanding, payment of purchase price and delivery of deed shall be made through the escrow and this contract and the earnest money shall be deposited in the escrow. The cost of the escrow shall be divided equally between seller and purchaser. *(strike paragraph if inapplicable)*

7. Time of the Essence. Time is of the essence of this contract.

8. Notices. All notices herein required shall be in writing and shall be served on the parties at the addresses following their signatures. The mailing of a notice by registered or certified mail, return receipt requested, shall be sufficient service.

APPENDIX D

Mortgage Note (Family Home)

_____, 19___   _____, <u>NEW JERSEY</u>
                 [City]   [State]

[Property Address]

1. **BORROWER'S PROMISE TO PAY**

   In return for a loan that I have received, I promise to pay U.S. $_____ (this amount is called "principal"), plus interest, to the order of the Lender. The lender is <u>BERKELEY FEDERAL SAVINGS AND LOAN ASSOCIATION OF NEW JERSEY</u>
   I understand that the Lender may transfer this Note. The Lender or anyone who takes this Note by transfer and who is entitled to receive payments under this Note is called the "Note Holder."

2. **INTEREST**

   Interest will be charged on unpaid principal until the full amount of principal has been paid. I will pay interest at a yearly rate of _____%.
   The interest rate required by this Section 2 is the rate I will pay both before and after any default described in Section 6(B) of this Note.

3. **PAYMENTS**

   (A) **Time and Place of Payments**
   I will pay principal and interest by making payments every month.
   I will make my monthly payments on the <u>FIRST</u> day of each month beginning on _____, 19___ I will make these payments every month until I have paid all of the principal and interest and any other charges described below that I may owe under this Note. My monthly payments will be applied to interest before principal. If, on _____, _____, I still owe amounts under this Note, I will pay those amounts in full on that date, which is called the "maturity date."

1211

I will make my monthly payments at <u>21 BLEEKER STREET   MILLBURN NEW JERSEY 07041</u> or at a different place if required by the Note Holder.

(B) Amount of Monthly Payments

My monthly payment will be in the amount of U.S. $_____

4. BORROWER'S RIGHT TO PREPAY

I have the right to make payments of principal at any time before they are due. A payment of principal only is known as a "prepayment." When I make a prepayment, I will tell the Note Holder in writing that I am doing so.

I may make a full prepayment or partial prepayments without paying any prepayment charge. The Note Holder will use all of my prepayments to reduce the amount of principal that I owe under this Note. If I make a partial prepayment, there will be no changes in the due date or in the amount of monthly payment unless the Note Holder agrees in writing to those changes.

5. LOAN CHARGES

If a law, which applies to this loan and which sets maximum loan charges, is finally interpreted so that the interest or other loan charges collected or to be collected in connection with this loan exceed the permitted limits, then: (i) any such loan charge shall be reduced by the amount necessary to reduce the charge to the permitted limit; and (ii) any sums already collected from me which exceeded permitted limits will be refunded to me. The Note Holder may choose to make this refund by reducing the principal I owe under this Note or by making a direct payment to me. If a refund reduces principal, the reduction will be treated as a partial prepayment.

6. BORROWER'S FAILURE TO PAY AS REQUIRED

(A) Late Charge for Overdue Payments

If the Note Holder has not received the full amount of any monthly payment by the end of __15__ calendar days after the date it is due, I will pay a late charge to the Note Holder. The amount of the charge will be __5__% of my overdue payment of principal and interest. I will pay this late charge promptly but only once on each late payment.

(B) Default

If I do not pay the full amount of each monthly payment on the date it is due, I will be in default.

(C) Notice of Default

If I am in default, the Note Holder may send me a written notice telling me that if I do not pay the overdue amount by a certain date, the Note

Mortgage Note (Family Home) 1213

Holder may require me to pay immediately the full amount of principal which has not been paid and all the interest that I owe on that amount. That date must be at least 30 days after the date on which the notice is delivered or mailed to me.

(D) No Waiver By Note Holder

Even if, at a time when I am in default, the Note Holder does not require me to pay immediately in full as described above, the Note Holder will still have the right to do so if I am in default at a later time.

(E) Payment of Note Holder's Costs and Expenses

If the Note Holder has required me to pay immediately in full as described above, the Note Holder will have the right to be paid back by me for all of its costs and expenses in enforcing this Note to the extent not prohibited by applicable law. Those expenses include, for example, reasonable attorneys' fees.

7. GIVING OF NOTICES

Unless applicable law requires a different method, any notice that must be given to me under this Note will be given by delivering it or by mailing it by first class mail to me at the Property Address above or at a different address if I give the Note Holder a notice of my different address.

Any notice that must be given to the Note Holder under this Note will be given by mailing it by first class mail to the Note Holder at the address stated in Section 3(A) above or at a different address if I am given a notice of that different address.

8. OBLIGATIONS OF PERSONS UNDER THIS NOTE

If more than one person signs this Note, each person is fully and personally obligated to keep all of the promises made in this Note, including the promise to pay the full amount owed. Any person who is a guarantor, surety or endorser of this Note is also obligated to do these things. Any person who takes over these obligations, including the obligations of a guarantor, surety or endorser of this Note, is also obligated to keep all of the promises made in this Note. The Note Holder may enforce its rights under this Note against each person individually or against all of us together. This means that any one of us may be required to pay all of the amounts owed under this Note.

9. WAIVERS

I and any other person who has obligations under this Note waive the rights of presentment and notice of dishonor. "Presentment" means the right to require the Note Holder to demand payment of amounts due. "Notice of dishonor" means the right to require the Note Holder to give notice to other persons that amounts due have not been paid.

10. UNIFORM SECURED NOTE

This Note is a uniform instrument with limited variations in some jurisdictions. In addition to the protections given to the Note Holder under this Note, a Mortgage, Deed of Trust or Security Deed (the "Security Instrument"), dated the same date as this Note, protects the Note Holder from possible losses which might result if I do not keep the promises which I make in this Note. That Security Instrument describes how and under what conditions I may be required to make immediate payment in full of all amounts I owe under this Note. Some of those conditions are described as follows:

Transfer of the Property or a Beneficial Interest in Borrower. If all or any part of the Property or any interest in it is sold or transferred (or if a beneficial interest in Borrower is sold or transferred and Borrower is not a natural person) without Lender's prior written consent, Lender may, at its option, require immediate payment in full of all sums secured by this Security Instrument. However, this option shall not be exercised by Lender if exercise is prohibited by federal law as of the date of this Security Instrument.

If Lender exercises this option, Lender shall give Borrower notice of acceleration. The notice shall provide a period of not less than 30 days from the date the notice is delivered or mailed within which Borrower must pay all sums secured by this Security Instrument. If Borrower fails to pay these sums prior to the expiration of this period, Lender may invoke any remedies permitted by this Security Instrument without further notice or demand on Borrower.

WITNESS THE HAND(S) AND SEAL(S) OF THE UNDERSIGNED.

_____ _____(Seal)
Witness: Borrower

_____ _____(Seal)
Witness: Borrower

                                   _____(Seal)
                                                                     Borrower

[*Sign Original Only*]

APPENDIX E

Mortgage (Family Home)

THIS MORTGAGE ("Security Instrument") is given on _____ 19____. The mortgagor is _____ _____ ("Borrower"). This Security Instrument is given to _____ **BERKELEY FEDERAL SAVINGS AND LOAN ASSOCIATION OF NEW JERSEY**, which is organized and existing under the laws of <u>THE UNITED STATES OF AMERICA</u> and whose principal office and mailing address is <u>21 Bleeker Street, Millburn, N.J. 07041</u> ("Lender"). Borrower owes Lender the principal sum of _____ Dollars (U.S. $_____). This debt is evidenced by Borrower's note dated the same date as this Security Instrument ("Note"), which provides for monthly payments, with the full debt, if not paid earlier, due and payable on _____. This Security Instrument secures to Lender: (a) the repayment of the debt evidenced by the Note, with interest, and all renewals, extensions and modifications; (b) the payment of all other sums, with interest, advanced under paragraph 7 to protect the security of this Security Instrument; and (c) the performance of Borrower's covenants and agreements under this Security Instrument and the Note. For this purpose, Borrower does hereby mortgage, grant and convey to Lender the following described property located in _____ County, New Jersey:

which has the address of _____, _____,
                                                    [Street]   [City]
New Jersey _____ ("Property Address");
              [Zip Code]

TOGETHER WITH all the improvements now or hereafter erected on the property, and all easements, rights, appurtenances, rents, royalties, mineral, oil and gas rights and profits, water rights and stock and all fixtures now or hereafter a part of the property. All replacements and additions shall also be covered by this Security Instrument. All of the foregoing is referred to in this Security Instrument as the "Property."

BORROWER COVENANTS that Borrower is lawfully seised of the estate hereby conveyed and has the right to mortgage, grant and convey the Property and that the Property is unencumbered, except for encumbrances of record. Borrower warrants and will defend generally the title to the Property against all claims and demands, subject to any encumbrances of record.

THIS SECURITY INSTRUMENT combines uniform covenants for national use and non-uniform covenants with limited variations by jurisdiction to constitute a uniform security instrument covering real property.

UNIFORM COVENANTS. Borrower and Lender covenant and agree as follows:

1. Payment of Principal and Interest; Prepayment and Late Charges. Borrower shall promptly pay when due the principal of and interest on the debt evidenced by the Note and any prepayment and late charges due under the Note.

2. Funds for Taxes and Insurance. Subject to applicable law or to a written waiver by Lender, Borrower shall pay to Lender on the day monthly payments are due under the Note, until the Note is paid in full, a sum ("Funds") equal to one-twelfth of: (a) yearly taxes and assessments which may attain priority over this Security Instrument; (b) yearly leasehold payments or ground rents on the Property, if any; (c) yearly hazard insurance premiums; and (d) yearly mortgage insurance premiums, if any. These items are called "escrow items." Lender may estimate the Funds due on the basis of current data and reasonable estimates of future escrow items.

The Funds shall be held in an institution the deposits or accounts of which are insured or guaranteed by a federal or state agency (including Lender if Lender is such an institution). Lender shall apply the Funds to pay the escrow items. Lender may not charge for holding and applying the Funds, analyzing the account or verifying the escrow items, unless Lender pays Borrower interest on the Funds and applicable law permits Lender to make such a charge. Borrower and Lender may agree in writing that interest shall be paid on the Funds. Unless an agreement is made or applicable law requires interest to be paid, Lender shall not be required to pay Borrower any interest or earnings on the Funds. Lender shall give to Borrower, without charge, an annual accounting of the Funds showing credits and debits to the Funds and the purpose for which each debit to the Funds was made. The Funds are pledged as additional security for the sums secured by this Security Instrument.

If the amount of the Funds held by Lender, together with the future monthly payments of Funds payable prior to the due dates of the escrow items, shall exceed the amount required to pay the escrow items when due, the excess shall be, at Borrower's option, either promptly repaid to Borrower or credited to Borrower on monthly payments of Funds. If the amount of the Funds held by Lender is not sufficient to pay the escrow items when due, Borrower shall pay to Lender any amount necessary to make up the deficiency in one or more payments as required by Lender.

Upon payment in full of all sums secured by this Security Instrument, Lender shall promptly refund to Borrower any Funds held by Lender. If under paragraph 19 the Property is sold or acquired by Lender, Lender shall apply, no later than immediately prior to the sale of the Property or its acquisition by Lender, any Funds held by Lender at the time of application as a credit against the sums secured by this Security Instrument.

3. **Application of Payments.** Unless applicable law provides otherwise, all payments received by Lender under paragraphs 1 and 2 shall be applied: first, to late charges due under the Note; second, to prepayment charges due under the Note; third, to amounts payable under paragraph 2; fourth, to interest due; and last, to principal due.

4. **Charges; Liens.** Borrower shall pay all taxes, assessments, charges, fines and impositions attributable to the Property which may attain priority over this Security Instrument, and leasehold payments or ground rents, if any. Borrower shall pay these obligations in the manner provided in paragraph 2, or if not paid in that manner, Borrower shall pay them on time directly to the person owed payment. Borrower shall promptly furnish to Lender all notices of amounts to be paid under this paragraph. If Borrower makes these payments directly, Borrower shall promptly furnish to Lender receipts evidencing the payments.

Borrower shall promptly discharge any lien which has priority over this Security Instrument unless Borrower: (a) agrees in writing to the payment of the obligation secured by the lien in a manner acceptable to Lender; (b) contests in good faith the lien by, or defends against enforcement of the lien in, legal proceedings which in the Lender's opinion operate to prevent the enforcement of the lien or forfeiture of any part of the Property; or (c) secures from the holder of the lien an agreement satisfactory to Lender subordinating the lien to this Security Instrument. If Lender determines that any part of the Property is subject to a lien which may attain priority over this Security Instrument, Lender may give Borrower a notice identifying the lien. Borrower shall satisfy the lien or take one or more of the actions set forth above within 10 days of the giving of notice.

5. **Hazard Insurance.** Borrower shall keep the improvements now existing or hereafter erected on the Property insured against loss by fire, hazards included within the term "extended coverage" and any other

hazards for which Lender requires insurance. This insurance shall be maintained in the amounts and for the periods that Lender requires. The insurance carrier providing the insurance shall be chosen by Borrower subject to Lender's approval which shall not be unreasonably withheld.

All insurance policies and renewals shall be acceptable to Lender and shall include a standard mortgage clause. Lender shall have the right to hold the policies and renewals. If Lender requires, Borrower shall promptly give to Lender all receipts of paid premiums and renewal notices. In the event of loss, Borrower shall give prompt notice to the insurance carrier and Lender. Lender may make proof of loss if not made promptly by Borrower.

Unless Lender and Borrower otherwise agree in writing, insurance proceeds shall be applied to restoration or repair of the Property damaged, if the restoration or repair is economically feasible and Lender's security is not lessened. If the restoration or repair is not economically feasible or Lender's security would be lessened, the insurance proceeds shall be applied to the sums secured by this Security Instrument, whether or not then due, with any excess paid to Borrower. If Borrower abandons the Property, or does not answer within 30 days a notice from the Lender that the insurance carrier has offered to settle a claim, then Lender may collect the insurance proceeds. Lender may use the proceeds to repair or restore the Property or to pay sums secured by this Security Instrument, whether or not then due. The 30-day period will begin when the notice is given.

Unless Lender and Borrower otherwise agree in writing, any application of proceeds to principal shall not extend or postpone the due date of the monthly payments referred to in paragraphs 1 and 2 or change the amount of the payments. If under paragraph 19 the Property is acquired by Lender, Borrower's right to any insurance policies and proceeds resulting from damage to the Property prior to the acquisition shall pass to Lender to the extent of the sums secured by this Security Instrument immediately prior to the acquisition.

6. Preservation and Maintenance of Property; Leaseholds. Borrower shall not destroy, damage or substantially change the Property, allow the Property to deteriorate or commit waste. If this Security Instrument is on a leasehold, Borrower shall comply with the provisions of the lease, and if Borrower acquires fee title to the Property, the leasehold and fee title shall not merge unless Lender agrees to the merger in writing.

7. Protection of Lender's Rights in the Property; Mortgage Insurance. If Borrower fails to perform the covenants and agreements contained in this Security Instrument, or there is a legal proceeding that may significantly affect Lender's rights in the Property (such as a proceeding in bankruptcy, probate, for condemnation or to enforce laws or regulations), then Lender may do and pay for whatever is necessary to protect the value of the Property and Lender's rights in the Property. Lender's actions may include paying any sums secured by a lien which has priority over this

Mortgage (Family Home)

Security Instrument, appearing in court, paying reasonable attorneys' fees and entering on the Property to make repairs. Although Lender may take action under this paragraph 7, Lender does not have to do so.

Any amounts disbursed by Lender under this paragraph 7 shall become additional debt of Borrower secured by this Security Instrument. Unless Borrower and Lender agree to other terms of payment, these amounts shall bear interest from the date of disbursement at the Note rate and shall be payable, with interest, upon notice from Lender to Borrower requesting payment.

If Lender required mortgage insurance as a condition of making the loan secured by this Security Instrument, Borrower shall pay the premiums required to maintain the insurance in effect until such time as the requirement for the insurance terminates in accordance with Borrower's and Lender's written agreement or applicable law.

8. **Inspection.** Lender or its agent may make reasonable entries upon and inspections of the Property. Lender shall give Borrower notice at the time of or prior to an inspection specifying reasonable cause for the inspection.

9. **Condemnation.** The proceeds of any award or claim for damages, direct or consequential, in connection with any condemnation or other taking of any part of the Property, or for conveyance in lieu of condemnation, are hereby assigned and shall be paid to Lender.

In the event of a total taking of the Property, the proceeds shall be applied to the sums secured by this Security Instrument, whether or not then due, with any excess paid to Borrower. In the event of a partial taking of the Property, unless Borrower and Lender otherwise agree in writing, the sums secured by this Security Instrument shall be reduced by the amount of the proceeds multiplied by the following fraction: (a) the total amount of the sums secured immediately before the taking, divided by (b) the fair market value of the Property immediately before the taking. Any balance shall be paid to Borrower.

If the Property is abandoned by Borrower, or if, after notice by Lender to Borrower that the condemnor offers to make an award or settle a claim for damages, Borrower fails to respond to Lender within 30 days after the date the notice is given, Lender is authorized to collect and apply the proceeds, at its option, either to restoration or repair of the Property or to the sums secured by this Security Instrument, whether or not then due.

Unless Lender and Borrower otherwise agree in writing, any application of proceeds to principal shall not extend or postpone the due date of the monthly payments referred to in paragraphs 1 and 2 or change the amount of such payments.

10. **Borrower Not Released; Forbearance By Lender Not a Waiver.** Extension of the time for payment or modification of amortization of the sums secured by this Security Instrument granted by Lender to any successor in interest of Borrower shall not operate to release the liability of the original Borrower or Borrower's successors in interest.

Lender shall not be required to commence proceedings against any successor in interest or refuse to extend time for payment or otherwise modify amortization of the sums secured by this Security Instrument by reason of any demand made by the original Borrower or Borrower's successors in interest. Any forbearance by Lender in exercising any right or remedy shall not be a waiver of or preclude the exercise of any right or remedy.

11. Successors and Assigns Bound; Joint and Several Liability; Co-signers. The covenants and agreements of this Security Instrument shall bind and benefit the successors and assigns of Lender and Borrower, subject to the provisions of paragraph 17. Borrower's covenants and agreements shall be joint and several. Any Borrower who co-signs this Security Instrument but does not execute the Note: (a) is co-signing this Security Instrument only to mortgage, grant and convey that Borrower's interest in the Property under the terms of this Security Instrument; (b) is not personally obligated to pay the sums secured by this Security Instrument; and (c) agrees that Lender and any other Borrower may agree to extend, modify, forbear or make any accommodations with regard to the terms of this Security Instrument or the Note without that Borrower's consent.

12. Loan Charges. If the loan secured by this Security Instrument is subject to a law which sets maximum loan charges, and that law is finally interpreted so that the interest or other loan charges collected or to be collected in connection with the loan exceed the permitted limits, then: (a) any such loan charge shall be reduced by the amount necessary to reduce the charge to the permitted limit; and (b) any sums already collected from Borrower which exceeded permitted limits will be refunded to Borrower. Lender may choose to make this refund by reducing the principal owed under the Note or by making a direct payment to Borrower. If a refund reduces principal, the reduction will be treated as a partial prepayment without any prepayment charge under the Note.

13. Legislation Affecting Lender's Rights. If enactment or expiration of applicable laws has the effect of rendering any provision of the Note or this Security Instrument unenforceable according to its terms, Lender, at its option, may require immediate payment in full of all sums secured by this Security Instrument and may invoke any remedies permitted by paragraph 19. If Lender exercises this option, Lender shall take the steps specified in the second paragraph of paragraph 17.

14. Notices. Any notice to Borrower provided for in this Security Instrument shall be given by delivering it or by mailing it by first class mail unless applicable law requires use of another method. The notice shall be directed to the Property Address or any other address Borrower designates by notice to Lender. Any notice to Lender shall be given by first class mail to Lender's address stated herein or any other address Lender designates by notice to Borrower. Any notice provided for in this Security

Mortgage (Family Home)

Instrument shall be deemed to have been given to Borrower or Lender when given as provided in this paragraph.

15. Governing Law; Severability. This Security Instrument shall be governed by federal law and the law of the jurisdiction in which the Property is located. In the event that any provision or clause of this Security Instrument or the Note conflicts with applicable law, such conflict shall not affect other provisions of this Security Instrument or the Note which can be given effect without the conflicting provision. To this end the provisions of this Security Instrument and the Note are declared to be severable.

16. Borrower's Copy. Borrower shall be given one conformed copy of the Note and of this Security Instrument.

17. Transfer of the Property or a Beneficial Interest in Borrower. If all or any part of the Property or any interest in it is sold or transferred (or if a beneficial interest in Borrower is sold or transferred and Borrower is not a natural person) without Lender's prior written consent, Lender may, at its option, require immediate payment in full of all sums secured by this Security Instrument. However, this option shall not be exercised by Lender if exercise is prohibited by federal law as of the date of this Security Instrument.

If Lender exercises this option, Lender shall give Borrower notice of acceleration. The notice shall provide a period of not less than 30 days from the date the notice is delivered or mailed within which Borrower must pay all sums secured by this Security Instrument. If Borrower fails to pay these sums prior to the expiration of this period, Lender may invoke any remedies permitted by this Security Instrument without further notice or demand on Borrower.

18. Borrower's Right to Reinstate. If Borrower meets certain conditions, Borrower shall have the right to have enforcement of this Security Instrument discontinued at any time prior to the earlier of: (a) 5 days (or such other period as applicable law may specify for reinstatement) before sale of the Property pursuant to any power of sale contained in this Security Instrument; or (b) entry of a judgment enforcing this Security Instrument. Those conditions are that Borrower: (a) pays Lender all sums which then would be due under this Security Instrument and the Note had no acceleration occurred; (b) cures any default of any other covenants or agreements; (c) pays all expenses incurred in enforcing this Security Instrument, including, but not limited to, reasonable attorneys' fees; and (d) takes such action as Lender may reasonably require to assure that the lien of this Security Instrument, Lender's rights in the Property and Borrower's obligation to pay the sums secured by this Security Instrument shall continue unchanged. Upon reinstatement by Borrower, this Security Instrument and the obligations secured hereby shall remain fully effective as if no acceleration had occurred. However, this right to reinstate shall not apply in the case of acceleration under paragraphs 13 or 17.

NON-UNIFORM COVENANTS. Borrower and Lender further covenant and agree as follows:

19. **Acceleration; Remedies.** Lender shall give notice to Borrower prior to acceleration following Borrower's breach of any covenant or agreement in this Security Instrument (but not prior to acceleration under paragraphs 13 and 17 unless applicable law provides otherwise). The notice shall specify: (a) the default; (b) the action required to cure the default; (c) a date, not less than 30 days from the date the notice is given to Borrower, by which the default must be cured; and (d) that failure to cure the default on or before the date specified in the notice may result in acceleration of the sums secured by this Security Instrument, foreclosure by judicial proceeding and sale of the Property. The notice shall further inform Borrower of the right to reinstate after acceleration and the right to assert in the foreclosure proceeding the nonexistence of a default or any other defense of Borrower to acceleration and foreclosure. If the default is not cured on or before the date specified in the notice, Lender at its option may require immediate payment in full of all sums secured by this Security Instrument without further demand and may foreclose this Security Instrument by judicial proceeding. Lender shall be entitled to collect all expenses incurred in pursuing the remedies provided in this paragraph 19, including, but not limited to, attorneys' fees and costs of title evidence permitted by Rules of Court.

20. **Lender in Possession.** Upon acceleration under paragraph 19 or abandonment of the Property, Lender (in person, by agent or by judicially appointed receiver) shall be entitled to enter upon, take possession of and manage the Property and to collect the rents of the Property including those past due. Any rents collected by Lender or the receiver shall be applied first to payment of the costs of management of the Property and collection of rents, including, but not limited to, receiver's fees, premiums on receiver's bonds and reasonable attorneys' fees, and then to the sums secured by this Security Instrument.

21. **Release.** Upon payment of all sums secured by this Security Instrument, Lender shall cancel this Security Instrument without charge to Borrower. Borrower shall pay any recordation costs.

22. **No Claim of Credit for Taxes.** Borrower will not make deduction from or claim credit on the principal or interest secured by this Security Instrument by reason of any governmental taxes, assessments or charges. Borrower will not claim any deduction from the taxable value of the Property by reason of this Security Instrument.

23. **Riders to this Security Instrument.** If one or more riders are executed by Borrower and recorded together with this Security Instrument, the covenants and agreements of each such rider shall be incorporated into and shall amend and supplement the covenants and agreements

Mortgage (Family Home)

of this Security Instrument as if the rider(s) were a part of this Security Instrument. [Check applicable box(es)]

☐ Adjustable Rate Rider ☐ Condominium Rider ☐ 2-4 Family Rider
☐ Graduated Payment Rider ☐ Planned Unit Development Rider
☐ Other(s) [specify]

By Signing Below, Borrower accepts and agrees to the terms and covenants contained in this Security Instrument and in any rider(s) executed by Borrower and recorded with it.

Signed, sealed and delivered in the presence of:

_____ _____(Seal)
                                                                Borrower

_____ _____(Seal)
                                                                Borrower

_____ [Space Below This Line For Acknowledgment] _____

State of New Jersey _____ County ss:

On this _____ day of _____, 19____, before me, the subscriber, personally appeared _____ who, I am satisfied, _____ the person(s) named in and who executed the within instrument, and thereupon _____ acknowledged that _____ signed, sealed and delivered the same as _____ _____ act and deed, for the purposes therein expressed.

_____
Notary Public

This instrument was prepared by:

Receipt of a true copy of this instrument, provided without charge, is hereby acknowledged.
Witness:

_____ _____(Seal)
                                                                Borrower

_____ _____(Seal)
                                                                Borrower

APPENDIX F
Warranty Deed

This indenture, made the _____ day of _____, nineteen hundred and _____, between _____, party of the first part, and _____, party of the second part,

Witnesseth, that the party of the first part, in consideration of Ten Dollars and other valuable consideration paid by the party of the second part, does hereby grant and release unto the party of the second part, the heirs or successors and assigns of the party of the second part forever,

All that certain plot, piece or parcel of land, with the buildings and improvements thereon erected, situate, lying and being in the _____.

Together with all right, title and interest, if any, of the party of the first part of, in and to any streets and roads abutting the above-described premises to the center lines thereof; Together with the appurtenances and all the estate and rights of the party of the first part in and to said premises; To Have and To Hold the premises herein granted unto the party of the second part, the heirs or successors and assigns of the party of the second part forever.

And the party of the first part, in compliance with Section 13 of the Lien Law, covenants that the party of the first part will receive the consideration for this conveyance and will hold the right to receive such consideration as a trust fund to be applied first for the purpose of paying the costs of the improvement and will apply the same first to the payment of the cost of the improvement before using any part of the total of the same for any other purpose.

And the party of the first part covenants as follows: that said party of the first part is seized of the said premises in fee simple, and has good right to convey the same; that the party of the second part shall quietly enjoy the said premises; that the said premises are free from incumbrances, except as aforesaid; that the party of the first part will execute or procure any further necessary assurance of the title to said premises; and that said party of the first part will forever warrant the title to said premises.

The word "party" shall be construed as if it read "parties" whenever the sense of this indenture so requires.

In witness whereof, the party of the first part has duly executed this deed the day and year first above written.

Warranty Deed

In presence of: _____

State of New York⎫
County of   ⎬ ss.
                  ⎭

On the _____ day of _____, 19__, before me personally came _____, to be known to be the individual _____ described in and who executed the foregoing instrument, and acknowledged that _____ executed the same.

State of New York   ⎫
County of _____ ⎬ ss.
                          ⎭

On the _____ day of _____, 19__, before me personally came _____, to me known, who, being by me duly sworn, did depose and say that __ he resides at No. _____; that __ he is the _____ of _____, the corporation described in and which executed the foregoing instrument; that __ he knows the seal of said corporation; that the seal affixed to said instrument is such corporate seal; that it was so affixed by order of the board of directors of said corporation, and that __ he signed h__ name thereto by like order.

State of New York   ⎫
County of _____ ⎬ ss.
                          ⎭

On the _____ day of _____, 19__, before me personally came _____, the subscribing witness to the foregoing instrument, with whom I am personally acquainted, who, being by me duly sworn, did depose and say that __ he resides at No. _____; that __ he knows _____ to be the individual described in and who executed the foregoing instrument; that __ he, said subscribing witness, was present and saw _____ execute the same; and that __ he, said witness, at the same time subscribed h__ name as witness thereto.

APPENDIX G

Settlement Statement

HUD-1 Rev. 5/76

Form Approved
OMB NO. 63-R-1501

A.

U.S. DEPARTMENT OF HOUSING AND URBAN DEVELOPMENT

SETTLEMENT STATEMENT

B. TYPE OF LOAN

1. ☐ FHA 2. ☐ FmHA 3. ☐ CONV. UNINS.
4. ☐ VA   5. ☐ CONV. INS.

6. File Number: 7. Loan Number:

8. Mortgage Insurance Case Number:

C. NOTE: *This form is furnished to give you a statement of actual settlement costs. Amounts paid to and by the settlement agent are shown. Items marked "(p.o.c.)" were paid outside the closing; they are shown here for informational purposes and are not included in the totals.*

D. NAME OF BORROWER:

E. NAME OF SELLER:

F. NAME OF LENDER:

G. PROPERTY LOCATION:

H. SETTLEMENT AGENT:

PLACE OF SETTLEMENT:

I. SETTLEMENT DATE:

J. SUMMARY OF BORROWER'S TRANSACTION		**K. SUMMARY OF SELLER'S TRANSACTION**	
100. GROSS AMOUNT DUE FROM BORROWER:		**400. GROSS AMOUNT DUE TO SELLER:**	
101. Contract sales price		401. Contract sales price	
102. Personal property		402. Personal property	
103. Settlement charges to borrower (line 1400)		403.	
104.		404.	
105.		405.	
Adjustments for items paid by seller in advance		*Adjustments for items paid by seller in advance*	
106. City/town taxes to		406. City/town taxes to	
107. County taxes to		407. County taxes to	
108. Assessments to		408. Assessments to	

(Form Continues on Next Page)

109.	
110.	
111.	
112.	
120.	*GROSS AMOUNT DUE FROM BORROWER*
200.	**AMOUNTS PAID BY OR IN BEHALF OF BORROWER:**
201.	Deposit or earnest money
202.	Principal amount of new loan(s)
203.	Existing loan(s) taken subject to
204.	
205.	
206.	
207.	
208.	
209.	
	Adjustments for items unpaid by seller
210.	City/town taxes to
211.	County taxes to
212.	Assessments to
213.	
214.	
215.	
216.	
217.	
218.	
219.	
220.	*TOTAL PAID BY/FOR BORROWER*
300.	**CASH AT SETTLEMENT FROM/TO BORROWER**
301.	Gross amount due from borrower (line 120)
302.	Less amounts paid by/for borrower (line 220) ( )
303.	*CASH (☐ FROM) (☐ TO) BORROWER*
409.	
410.	
411.	
412.	
420.	*GROSS AMOUNT DUE TO SELLER*
500.	**REDUCTIONS IN AMOUNT DUE TO SELLER:**
501.	Excess deposit *(see instructions)*
502.	Settlement charges to seller *(line 1400)*
503.	Existing loan(s) taken subject to
504.	Payoff of first mortgage loan
505.	Payoff of second mortgage loan
506.	
507.	
508.	
509.	
	Adjustments for items unpaid by seller
510.	City/town taxes to
511.	County taxes to
512.	Assessments to
513.	
514.	
515.	
516.	
517.	
518.	
519.	
520.	*TOTAL REDUCTION AMOUNT DUE SELLER*
600.	**CASH AT SETTLEMENT TO/FROM SELLER**
601.	Gross amount due to seller (line 420)
602.	Less reductions in amount due seller (line 520) ( )
603.	*CASH (☐ TO) (☐ FROM) SELLER*

(Back of Form Continued on Next Page)

L. SETTLEMENT CHARGES

	PAID FROM BORROWER'S FUNDS AT SETTLEMENT	PAID FROM SELLER'S FUNDS AT SETTLEMENT
700. TOTAL SALES/BROKER'S COMMISSION based on price $ @ % =		
Division of Commission (line 700) as follows:		
701. $ to		
702. $ to		
703. Commission paid at Settlement		
704.		
800. ITEMS PAYABLE IN CONNECTION WITH LOAN		
801. Loan Origination Fee %		
802. Loan Discount %		
803. Appraisal Fee to		
804. Credit Report to		
805. Lender's Inspection Fee		
806. Mortgage Insurance Application Fee to		
807. Assumption Fee		
808.		
809.		
810.		
811.		
900. ITEMS REQUIRED BY LENDER TO BE PAID IN ADVANCE		
901. Interest from to @ $ /day		
902. Mortgage Insurance Premium for months to		
903. Hazard Insurance Premium for years to		
904. years to		
905.		
1000. RESERVES DEPOSITED WITH LENDER		
1001. Hazard insurance months @ $ per month		
1002. Mortgage insurance months @ $ per month		
1003. City property taxes months @ $ per month		
1004. County property taxes months @ $ per month		
1005. Annual assessments months @ $ per month		
1006. months @ $ per month		
1007. months @ $ per month		

(Form Continues on Next Page)

1008.	months @ $ per month	
1100. TITLE CHARGES		
1101.	Settlement or closing fee	to
1102.	Abstract or title search	to
1103.	Title examination	to
1104.	Title insurance binder	to
1105.	Document preparation	to
1106.	Notary fees	to
1107.	Attorney's fees	to
	(includes above items numbers:)	
1108.	Title insurance	to
	(includes above items numbers:)	
1109.	Lender's coverage $	
1110.	Owner's coverage $	
1111.		
1112.		
1113.		
1200. GOVERNMENT RECORDING AND TRANSFER CHARGES		
1201.	Recording fees: Deed $; Mortgage $; Releases $	
1202.	City/county tax/stamps: Deed $; Mortgage $	
1203.	State tax/stamps: Deed $; Mortgage $	
1204.		
1205.		
1300. ADDITIONAL SETTLEMENT CHARGES		
1301.	Survey to	
1302.	Pest inspection to	
1303.		
1304.		
1305.		
1400. TOTAL SETTLEMENT CHARGES (enter on lines 103, Section J and 502, Section K)		

HUD-1 Rev. 5/76

APPENDIX H

Mortgage Commitment (Construction Loan)

_____
[Date]

_____
_____

Re: Construction Loan for _____
         _____
                   (the "subject development")

Gentlemen:

We are pleased to advise you that _____ has approved construction financing for the subject development on the following terms:

1. **LOAN AMOUNT AND PURPOSE:** $_____ to be used to finance construction of _____
_____
_____
located at _____, _____, on land owned by you.

2. **INTEREST:** _____% over the Bank's prime rate, to move with such prime rate, computed on a 360-day basis and the actual number of days elapsed.

3. **TERM:** _____ months, but not later than _____.

Mortgage Commitment (Construction Loan)

4. LOAN FEE: Nonrefundable loan fee of $_____ payable upon loan closing.*

5. LOAN TO VALUE RATIO: Not to exceed _____ % of appraised value of the real property security for the loan as determined by the Bank.

6. PAYMENTS: The loan will be evidenced by a promissory note satisfactory to the Bank. Interest will be payable monthly on funds disbursed. Principal will be due and payable at the earlier to occur of loan maturity or date of funding of your long-term loan.

7. SECURITY: The Bank will require as security for its loan:

    a. First Deed of Trust, Assignment of Rents and Security Agreement covering the proposed improvements and appurtenant lands. You will provide the Bank with a legal description of the subject real property satisfactory to the Bank.

    b. First-lien security interest on personal property owned by you and related to the operation of the subject development or used in connection with construction of the subject improvements, or other collateral satisfactory to the Bank.

    c. Assignment to the Bank of all leases or occupancy agreements affecting the real property security covered by the Bank's deed of trust.

    d. Any other collateral or security required by your long-term lender.

8. CONDITIONS OF FUNDING: Funding of the loan will be subject to your fulfilling the following conditions to the satisfaction of the Bank:†

    a. [You must obtain and be in compliance with an institutional permanent loan commitment acceptable to us

---

* *Note:* As written, this provision probably makes payment of the loan fee contingent upon closing. If this is not the desired result, rephrase this condition along the following lines: "Nonrefundable commitment fee of $_____ payable to the Bank as follows: _____. Said fee is consideration for the issuance of this commitment by the Bank and the substantial services which the Bank has rendered and will render and incur in preparation for the closing of the loan. It is nonrefundable under any circumstances whether or not the loan closes, except only if the failure to close the loan is due solely to the Bank's default."

† *Note:* For a subdivision or condominium project, add the following condition: "You must obtain Bank approval of all subdivision, condominium, or planned development maps, agreements, restrictions and constituent documents."

which will repay our loan within _____ months from the date of funding but not later than _____. You and the institutional lender must enter into a satisfactory buy-sell agreement with the Bank, and the Bank's loan will be funded pursuant to satisfactory joint documentation with the permanent lender.]* You must satisfy all conditions of your permanent loan commitment that in the Bank's judgment can reasonably be fulfilled prior to the closing of the Bank's loan.

  b. All loan documentation must be satisfactory to the Bank and our special counsel for this loan, Morrison & Forster. Whether or not the loan closes, you agree to pay the legal fees and disbursements of our special counsel incident to preparation and review of loan documentation and closing of the loan. You will deliver such evidence of your authority to execute and carry out the terms of the loan documents as our counsel may require, including an opinion of counsel satisfactory to the Bank. [Bank must receive a satisfactory opinion from Bank's counsel in the State of _____ attesting to the validity and enforceability of the subject loan and the loan documents.] [You must obtain the Bank's approval of your partnership agreement, including but not limited to the conditions under which any partnership profits or contributions can be distributed to partners during the term of the Bank's loan, and you must deliver satisfactory evidence to the Bank of the due formation of the partnership and its compliance with all applicable laws relating to transacting business in the State of California.]

  c. You must obtain Bank approval of the plans and specifications for the subject development, the costs of construction of the subject development, a survey of the property and soils report, the contractor for the subject development and the terms of his contract, and insurance coverage with respect to the subject development.

  d. You must obtain and deliver to Bank executed copies of a Contractor Agreement and Architect Agreement in form and substance satisfactory to Bank.

  e. Loan funds will be disbursed under the Bank's disbursement control program and in accordance with a Construction Loan Agreement satisfactory to the Bank. At the option of Bank, you and the contractor must provide a performance bond plus labor and material payment bond in dual obligee form satisfactory to the Bank and naming the Bank as lender.

---

 * *Note:* Alternative for loans on residential properties: "You must obtain and be in compliance with an institutional permanent loan commitment acceptable to us for FHA, VA and conventional loans to buyers of the subject residential units which must be kept available and in full force and effect at all times during the term of our loan. Sales of units must be sufficient to repay our loan in full on or before its maturity. At the option of the Bank, the Bank may require that your permanent loan commitment be assigned to the Bank prior to the closing of the Bank's loan."

Mortgage Commitment (Construction Loan)

f. The Bank will use a consulting architect/engineer of its choice to review plans and specifications and for inspection services during the course of construction, to be paid for by you.

g. You will obtain at your expense title insurance coverage for the Bank's deed of trust acceptable to the Bank and the permanent lender as to insurer, form, coverage and exceptions, and showing the Bank's deed of trust in a first-lien position. The condition of title to all property taken as security must be approved by the Bank. The Bank may require that the title policy be brought current with each loan disbursement by issuance of indorsements satisfactory to the Bank to be paid for by you.

h. All funds in excess of the Bank's loan required to complete the subject development, as determined by the Bank, must be made available by you to the satisfaction of the Bank at the time of loan closing. In addition, the loan documentation will require you to provide, in a manner satisfactory to the Bank, all funds needed to cover any subsequent cost increases of any nature for construction of the subject development.

i. You must submit to the Bank satisfactory evidence that all applicable laws, ordinances, regulations (including environmental regulations) and recorded covenants, conditions and restrictions have been complied with to permit the lawful construction of the subject development, and that all required governmental approvals and permits have been obtained.

j. You must obtain Bank approval of all operating agreements, utility agreements, access rights, easements, and other arrangements necessary in the judgment of the Bank or the permanent lender for the uninterrupted and orderly operation of the subject development.

k. You must deliver to Bank a satisfactory Tenant Estoppel Certificate and Subordination Agreement from any tenant or proposed occupant of preleased space, if requested by Bank.

l. The Bank reserves the right not to fund the loan if prior to loan closing there is a material adverse change in your financial condition [or in the financial condition of the permanent lender].

m. Whether or not the loan closes, you agree to pay all costs and expenses in connection with the funding of the Bank's loan and the fulfillment of any conditions of this commitment, including but not limited to title insurance premium, recording charges and taxes, appraisal and inspection fees, and brokerage fees or commissions, and the Bank will have no liability therefor.*

---

* *Note:* As written, this provision probably makes payment of these expenses contingent upon loan closing. If a different result is desired, add language along the following lines:

n. The Bank's customary loan opening conditions for this type of financing will be applicable.*

This commitment is not assignable by you without the Bank's written consent.

This commitment must be accepted by you no later than _____, 19___, or it will expire. The loan must be recorded by _____, 19___, or this commitment will terminate at the option of the Bank. Any extensions will be at the sole option of the Bank and must be in writing.

We are pleased to be able to provide you with this commitment and look forward to working with you in the development of your facility.

Sincerely,

_____,
a national banking association

By _____

Accepted and agreed to on the above terms and conditions.

_____,
a _____

By _____
Its _____
Date _____

"You agree to pay such costs and expenses whether or not the loan closes, except only if the failure to close the loan is due solely to the Bank's default."

* *Note:* Certain other conditions to loan funding should be specifically stated, including requirements for guarantees, terms of partial releases, additional security requirements, pre-sale requirements, opening or maintenance of deposits with the Bank, and the like.

APPENDIX I

Purchase Agreement (Investment Property)

PURCHASE AGREEMENT

Table of Contents

		Page
1.	Property Included in Sale	1236
2.	Purchase Price	1237
3.	Title to the Property	1238
4.	Conditions to Closing	1238
5.	The Closing	1240
6.	Representations and Warranties of Seller	1242
7.	Representations and Warranties of Buyer	1244
8.	Indemnification	1244
9.	Loss by Fire or Other Casualty; Condemnation	1244
10.	Possession	1245
11.	Maintenance of the Property	1245
12.	Buyer's Consent to New Contracts Affecting the Property	1245
13.	Miscellaneous	1245
	(a) Notices	1245
	(b) Brokers and Finders	1246
	(c) Successors and Assigns	1246
	(d) Amendments	1246
	(e) Continuation and Survival of Representations and Warranties	1246
	(f) Governing Law	1246
	(g) Merger of Prior Agreements	1246
	(h) Enforcement	1246
	(i) Time of the Essence	1247
	[(j) Short Form]	1247
14.	Acceptance of Agreement by Seller	1247

List of Exhibits

Exhibit A — Description of Real Property
Exhibit B — Schedule of Personal Property
Exhibit C — Form of Warranty Bill of Sale
Exhibit D — Form of Tenant's Estoppel Certificate
Exhibit E — Form of Assignment of Leases
Exhibit F — Form of Assignment of Service Contracts, Warranties and Guaranties and Other Intangible Property
Exhibit G — Form of Notice of Lease Assignment
[Exhibit H — Form of Memorandum of Agreement]

PURCHASE AGREEMENT

THIS AGREEMENT is dated as of _____, 19__, by and between _____, a _____ (the "Seller"), and _____, a _____ (the "Buyer").

IN CONSIDERATION of the respective agreements hereinafter set forth, Seller and Buyer agree as follows:

1. Property Included in Sale. Seller hereby agrees to sell and convey to Buyer, and Buyer hereby agrees to purchase from Seller, subject to the terms and conditions set forth herein, the following:

(a) that certain real property [consisting of/commonly known as _____ and] more particularly described in *Exhibit A* attached hereto (the "Real Property");

(b) all rights, privileges and easements appurtenant to the Real Property, including, without limitation, all minerals, oil, gas and other hydrocarbon substances on and under the Real Property, as well as all development rights, air rights, water, water rights and water stock relating to the Real Property and any other easements, rights-of-way or appurtenances used in connection with the beneficial use and enjoyment of the Real Property (all of which are collectively referred to as the "Appurtenances");

(c) all improvements and fixtures located on the Real Property, including, without limitation, that certain _____, as well as all other buildings and structures presently located on the Real Property, all apparatus, equipment and appliances used in connection with the operation or occupancy of the Real Property, such as heating and air conditioning systems and facilities used to provide any utility services, refrigeration, ventilation, garbage disposal, recreation or other services

Purchase Agreement (Investment Property)

on the Real Property (all of which are collectively referred to as the "Improvements");

    (d) all personal property of Seller located on or in or used in connection with the Real Property and Improvements, and described in *Exhibit B* attached hereto (the "Personal Property"); and

    (e) all of the interest of Seller in any intangible personal property now or hereafter owned by Seller and used in the ownership, use and operation of the Real Property, Improvements and Personal Property, including, without limitation, the right to use any trade name now used in connection with the Real Property and, to the extent that the same are approved by Buyer pursuant to the provisions of this Agreement, any contract or lease rights, agreements, utility contracts or other rights relating to the ownership, use and operation of the Property, as defined below.

All of the items referred to in subparagraphs (a), (b), (c), (d) and (e) above are hereinafter collectively referred to as the "Property."

2. Purchase Price.

    (a) The purchase price of the Property is _____ Dollars ($_____) (the "Purchase Price").

    (b) The Purchase Price shall be paid as follows:

    (i) Within ___ (___) days after the execution of this Agreement by both Buyer and Seller, Buyer shall deposit in escrow with _____ ("Title Company"), a deposit in the amount of $_____ (the "Deposit"). [Upon the satisfaction of the conditions contained in paragraph 4 hereof, Buyer shall increase the Deposit to $_____.] All sums comprising the deposit shall be held in an interest-bearing account and interest accruing thereon shall be held for the account of Buyer. In the event the sale of the Property as contemplated hereunder is consummated, the Deposit plus interest accrued therein shall be credited against the Purchase Price. In the event the sale of the Property is not consummated because of the failure of any condition or any other reason except a default under this Agreement solely on the part of Buyer, the Deposit plus interest accrued thereon shall immediately be returned to Buyer. If said sale is not consummated because of a default under this Agreement solely on the part of Buyer, the Deposit but not the interest accrued thereon shall be paid to and retained by Seller as liquidated damages. The parties have agreed that Seller's actual damages, in the event of a default by Buyer, would be extremely difficult or impracticable to determine. Therefore, by placing their initials below, the parties acknowledge that the Deposit has been agreed upon, after negotiation, as the parties' reasonable estimate of Seller's damages and as Seller's exclusive remedy against Buyer, at law or in equity, in the event of a default under this Agreement solely on the part of Buyer.

    INITIALS: Seller _____   Buyer _____

(ii) At the closing of the sale contemplated hereunder (the "Closing"), Buyer shall take title to the Property subject to the first mortgage loan (the "Loan") of _____ ("Lender"). The Loan bears an interest rate of _____ %, payable in equal monthly installments of $_____ with the final payment due on _____, and will have a balance as of the Closing Date (as defined in paragraph 5 below) of approximately $_____.

(iii) The balance of the Purchase Price, over and above the amount owing on the Loan as of the Closing Date, shall be paid to Seller in cash at the Closing. Said cash sum shall include the Deposit plus accrued interest thereon but shall be reduced by any credits due Buyer hereunder.

3. Title to the Property.

(a) At the Closing, Seller shall convey to Buyer marketable and insurable fee simple title to the Real Property, the Appurtenances and the Improvements, by duly executed and acknowledged [grant] deed in a form acceptable to Buyer. Evidence of delivery of marketable and insurable fee simple title shall be the issuance by Title Company of an ALTA Owner's Policy of Title Insurance (Form B, rev. 10/17/77), in the full amount of the Purchase Price, insuring fee simple title to the Real Property, the Appurtenances and the Improvements, in Buyer, subject only to such exceptions as Buyer shall approve pursuant to paragraph 4(a) below. Said policy shall provide full coverage against mechanics' or materialmen's liens arising out of the construction, repair or alteration of any of the Improvements or any tenant improvements and shall contain such special endorsements as Buyer may reasonably require. [Consider whether reinsurance is necessary or appropriate.]

(b) At the Closing, Seller shall transfer title to the Personal Property by a bill of sale in the form attached hereto as *Exhibit C* such title to be free of any liens, encumbrances or interests of third parties.

4. Conditions to Closing. The following conditions are conditions precedent to Buyer's obligation to purchase the Property:

(a) Buyer's review and approval of title to the Property, as follows. Seller shall as soon as possible after executing this Agreement deliver to Buyer:

(i) a current extended coverage preliminary title report on the Real Property, accompanied by copies of all documents referred to in the report;

(ii) copies of all existing and proposed easements, covenants, restrictions, agreements or other documents which affect the Property and which are not disclosed by the preliminary title report, or, if no such documents exist, a certification of Seller to that effect;

(iii) an "as-built" survey of the Real Property and Improvements by a licensed surveyor or civil engineer. Said survey shall be acceptable to, and certified to, Buyer and in sufficient detail to provide

Purchase Agreement (Investment Property)

the basis for an ALTA Owner's Policy of Title Insurance without boundary, encroachment or survey exceptions, and shall show the location of all easements and Improvements (including underground improvements) and any and all other pertinent information with respect to the Property. The survey shall also indicate any encroachments of Improvements onto easements or onto adjacent properties or certify to their absence and shall indicate the presence of improvements and easements on property adjoining the Real Property if located within 5 feet of the boundaries of the Real Property; and

(iv) copies of the most recent property tax bills for the Property.

Buyer shall advise the Seller within fifteen (15) business days after actual receipt of all such materials, what exceptions to title, if any, will be accepted by Buyer. Seller shall have 30 days after receipt of Buyer's objections to remove any objectionable exceptions from title and to provide Buyer with evidence satisfactory to Buyer of such removal or to provide Buyer with evidence satisfactory to Buyer that said exceptions will be removed on or before the Closing.

(b) Buyer's review and approval, within fifteen (15) business days from actual receipt from Seller, of all service contracts, maintenance contracts, management contracts, mortgage documents, certificates of occupancy, warranties, soils reports, insurance policies, and other contracts or documents of significance to the Property.

[(c) Buyer's review and approval of the terms and conditions of the proposed long-term mortgage financing of the Property within five (5) business days from the actual receipt from Seller of the loan commitment and pertinent documentation relating to such mortgage financing.]

[(d) Seller obtaining the consent of Lender to the proposed sale of the Property to Buyer subject to the Loan with no change in interest or amortization payments under the Loan, with no new charges or fees payable by Buyer, and subject to no events of default under the Loan.]

(e) Buyer's review and approval, within fifteen (15) business days from the actual receipt thereof from Seller, of: (i) all existing and pending leases (and any amendments thereto) affecting the Property; (ii) a current rent roll for the Property, listing for each tenant the name, rent, percentage rent, if any, sales volume break point, offsets or credits to percentage rent, if any, obligation for reimbursement for expenses, amount of deposit and prepaid rent, if any, lease commencement date, lease termination date, lease options, option rent, and cost of living or other rent escalation clauses; and (iii) a schedule of any employees employed by Seller or the present owner of the Property or contractors retained by Seller or the present owner of the Property in the operation of the Property, setting forth names, salaries, other compensation, and other pertinent information concerning such employees or contractors, including the terms of any contracts with them.

(f) Buyer's review and approval of the structural, mechanical, electrical and other physical characteristics of the Property within fifteen (15) business days from the actual receipt from Seller of a copy of the as-built plans and specifications for the Property.

(g) Buyer's review and approval, within fifteen (15) business days from the date of Seller's execution of this Agreement, of all zoning, land-use, subdivision, environmental, building and construction laws and regulations restricting or regulating or otherwise affecting the use, occupancy or enjoyment of the Property.

(h) Seller obtaining and delivering to Buyer tenant estoppel certificates in form and substance satisfactory to Buyer from any and all tenants occupying any portion of the Property. Said certificates shall be substantially in the form attached hereto as *Exhibit D* and shall be dated no earlier than thirty (30) days prior to the Closing Date.

The foregoing conditions contained in items (a) through (h) are intended solely for the benefit of Buyer. If any of the foregoing conditions are not satisfied, Buyer shall have the right at its sole election either to waive the condition in question and proceed with the purchase or, in the alternative, terminate this Agreement and obtain refund of the Deposit plus accrued interest thereon. [The Closing Date may be extended, at Buyer's option, a reasonable period of time if required to allow said conditions to be satisfied, subject to Buyer's further right to terminate this Agreement and obtain a refund of the Deposit plus accrued interest thereon upon the expiration of the period of any such extension if all said conditions have not been satisfied.] In the event Buyer elects to terminate this Agreement, Seller shall pay any title and escrow charges, and neither party shall have any further rights or obligations under this Agreement.

5. The Closing.

(a) The Closing hereunder shall be held and delivery of all items to be made at the Closing under the terms of this agreement shall be made at the offices of _____ on _____, 19__, or such other date prior thereto as Buyer and Seller may mutually agree in writing (the "Closing Date"). Such date may not be extended without the prior written approval of both Seller and Buyer, except as otherwise expressly provided in this Agreement. In the event the Closing does not occur on or before the Closing Date, the escrow holder shall, unless it is notified by both parties to the contrary within five (5) days after the Closing Date, return to the depositor thereof items which may have been deposited hereunder. Any such return shall not, however, relieve either party hereto of any liability it may have for its wrongful failure to close.

(b) At or before the Closing, Seller shall deliver to Buyer the following:

(i) a duly executed and acknowledged [grant] deed conveying to the Buyer the Real Property, the Appurtenances and the Improvements and all rights, privileges and easements appurtenant thereto as required by paragraph 3(a) above;

(ii) a duly executed Bill of Sale covering the Personal Property and any apparatus, fixtures, equipment or appliances which are a part of the Improvements in the form attached hereto as *Exhibit C;*

(iii) a Certificate from the Secretary of State or other appropriate government official of the state in which the Property is located indicating that, as of the Closing Date, there are no filings against Seller in the office of the Secretary of State or other government official under the California Uniform Commercial Code of such state which would be a lien on any of the items specified in the Bill of Sale referred to in paragraph 5(b)(ii) above (other than such filings, if any, as are being released at the time of the Closing);

(iv) originals of all leases (and amendments thereto, if any, and all records and correspondence relating thereto) covering any portion of the Property, any security deposits relating thereto, and a duly executed and acknowledged Assignment of Leases in the form attached hereto as *Exhibit E;*

(v) duly executed tenant estoppel certificates as required pursuant to paragraph 4(h) above.

(vi) originals or copies of all service contracts, maintenance contracts and management contracts affecting the Property (collectively, the "Service Contracts") to be continued by Buyer after the Closing, and any warranties or guaranties received by Seller from any contractors, subcontractors, suppliers or materialmen in connection with any construction, repairs or alterations of the Improvements or any tenant improvements;

(vii) a duly executed assignment of Service Contracts and any warranties and guaranties in the form attached hereto as *Exhibit F;*

(viii) originals or copies of building permits and certificates of occupancy for the Improvements and all tenant-occupied space included within the Improvements;

(ix) one complete set of the final as-built plans and specifications for the Improvements, certified by Seller and the architect and engineer for the design and construction of the Improvements;

(x) notices to the tenants at the Property in the form attached as *Exhibit G,* duly executed by Seller;

[(xi) a beneficiary statement from the Lender in form and substance satisfactory to Buyer with respect to the Loan, confirming the outstanding balance of principal and accrued and unpaid interest on the Loan as of the Closing Date, the interest rate of the Loan, the maturity date of the Loan, and that the Loan is not in default, and containing such other information as Buyer may reasonably require;]

[(xii) originals, or copies certified by Seller as being true and complete copies, of the documents evidencing and securing the Loan;]

[(xii)] closing statement in form and content satisfactory to Buyer and Seller; and

[(xiii) any other documents, instruments, records, correspondence or agreements called for hereunder which have not previously been delivered. Buyer may waive compliance on Seller's part under any of the foregoing items by an instrument in writing].

(c) Seller and Buyer shall each deposit such other instruments as are reasonably required by the escrow holder or otherwise required to close the escrow and consummate the purchase of the Property in accordance with the terms hereof.

(d) Rents actually collected (whether such collection occurs prior to, on or after the Closing), real property taxes, interest on the Loan, water, sewer and utility charges, amounts payable under the Service Contracts, annual permits and/or inspection fees (calculated on the basis of the period covered), insurance premiums (as to those policies, if any, that Buyer determines will be continued after the Closing), and other expenses normal to the operation and maintenance of the Property shall be prorated as of 12:01 a.m. on the date the [grant] deed is recorded on the basis of a 365-day year. Seller and Buyer hereby agree that if any of the aforesaid prorations cannot be calculated accurately on the Closing Date, then the same shall be calculated within thirty (30) days after the Closing Date and either party owing the other party a sum of money based on such subsequent proration(s) shall promptly pay said sum to the other party, together with interest thereon at the rate of _____ percent (_____ %) per annum from the Closing Date to the date of payment if payment is not made within ten (10) days after delivery of a bill therefor.

(e) Seller shall pay the amount of any assessments or bonds on the Property. [Buyer] [Seller] shall pay the premium for the policy of title insurance. Seller shall pay the cost of any transfer taxes applicable to the sale and all other costs and charges of the escrow for the sale. Seller shall pay all leasing commissions and tenant improvement costs accrued in connection with any lease executed on or before the Closing. Buyer shall be entitled to a credit against the Purchase Price for the total sum of all security deposits paid to Seller by tenants under any leases affecting the Property.

6. Representations and Warranties of Seller. Seller hereby represents and warrants to Buyer as follows:

(a) There are now, and at the time of Closing will be, no material physical or mechanical defects of the Property, including, without limitation, the plumbing, heating, air conditioning and electrical systems and, to the best of Seller's knowledge, all such items are in good operating condition and repair and in compliance with all applicable governmental laws or regulations.

Purchase Agreement (Investment Property)   1243

(b) The use and operation of the Property now is, and at the time of Closing will be, in full compliance with applicable building codes, environmental, zoning and land use laws, and other applicable local, state and federal laws and regulations, to the best of Seller's knowledge.

(c) The survey, mechanical and structural plans and specifications, soil reports, leases, certificates of occupancy, warranties, operating statements, rent roll and income and expense reports, and all other books and records relating to the Property and all other contracts or documents delivered to Buyer pursuant to this Agreement or in connection with the execution hereof are and at the time of Closing will be true and correct copies, and are and at the time of Closing will be in full force and effect, without default by (or notice of default to) any party.

(d) Except as disclosed to Buyer in writing, Seller does not have knowledge of any condemnation, environmental, zoning or other land-use regulation proceedings, either instituted or planned to be instituted, which would detrimentally affect the use and operation of the Property for its intended purpose or the value of the Property, nor has Seller received notice of any special assessment proceedings affecting the Property.

(e) All water, sewer, gas, electric, telephone, and drainage facilities and all other utilities required by law or by the normal use and operation of the Property are and at the time of Closing will be installed to the property lines of the Real Property, are and at the time of Closing will be all connected pursuant to valid permits, and are and at the time of Closing will be adequate to service the Property and to permit full compliance with all requirements of law and normal usage of the Property by the tenants thereof and their licensees and invitees.

(f) Seller has obtained all licenses, permits, easements and rights of way, including proof of dedication, required from all governmental authorities having jurisdiction over the Property or from private parties for the normal use and operation of the Property and to insure vehicular and pedestrian ingress to and egress from the Property.

(g) Seller is a [type of entity] duly organized and validly existing and in good standing under the laws of the State of _____ and is in good standing under the laws of the State of _____; this Agreement and all documents executed by Seller which are to be delivered to Buyer at the Closing are or at the time of Closing will be duly authorized, executed, and delivered by Seller, are or at the time of Closing will be legal, valid, and binding obligations of Seller, are and at the time of Closing will be sufficient to convey title (if they purport to do so), and do not and at the time of Closing will not violate any provisions of any agreement or judicial order to which Seller is a party or to which Seller or the Property is subject.

(h) At the time of Closing there will be no outstanding contracts made by Seller for any improvements to the Property which have not been fully paid for and Seller shall cause to be discharged all mechanics' or materialmen's liens arising from any labor or materials furnished to the Property prior to the time of Closing.

(i) Seller knows of no facts nor has Seller failed to disclose any fact which would prevent Buyer from using and operating the Property after Closing in the normal manner in which similar properties in the area are operated.

7. **Representations and Warranties of Buyer.** Buyer hereby represents and warrants to Seller as follows: Buyer is a [type of entity] duly organized and validly existing under the laws of the State of _____ _____ and is in good standing under the laws of the State of _____; this Agreement and all documents executed by Buyer which are to be delivered to Seller at the Closing are or at the time of Closing will be duly authorized, executed, and delivered by Buyer, and are or at the Closing will be legal, valid, and binding obligations of Buyer, and do not and at the time of Closing will not violate any provisions of any agreement or judicial order to which Buyer is a party or to which it is subject.

8. **Indemnification.** Each party hereby agrees to indemnify the other party and hold it harmless from and against any and all claims, demands, liabilities, costs, expenses, penalties, damages and losses, including, without limitation, reasonable attorneys' fees, resulting from any misrepresentations or breach of warranty or breach of covenant made by such party in this Agreement or in any document, certificate, or exhibit given or delivered to the other pursuant to or in connection with this Agreement. The indemnification provisions of this paragraph 8 shall survive beyond the delivery of the [grant] deed and transfer of title, or, if title is not transferred pursuant to this Agreement, beyond any termination of this Agreement.

9. **Loss by Fire or Other Casualty; Condemnation.** In the event that, prior to Closing, the Property, or any part thereof, is destroyed or materially damaged, or if condemnation proceedings are commenced against the Property, Buyer shall have the right, exercisable by giving notice of such decision to Seller within fifteen (15) days after receiving written notice of such damage, destruction or condemnation proceedings, to terminate this Agreement, in which case, except as provided in paragraph 8, neither party shall have any further rights or obligations hereunder and the Deposit plus accrued interest thereon shall be refunded to Buyer. If Buyer elects to accept the Property in its then condition, all proceeds of insurance or condemnation awards payable to Seller by reason of such damage, destruction or condemnation shall be paid or assigned to Buyer. In the event of non-material damage to the Property, which damage Seller is unwilling to repair or replace, Buyer shall have the right, exercisable by giving notice within fifteen (15) days after receiving written

Purchase Agreement (Investment Property)

notice of such damage, either (a) to terminate this Agreement as hereinabove in this paragraph provided, or (b) to accept the Property in its then condition and proceed with the purchase, in which case Buyer shall be entitled to a reasonable reduction of the Purchase Price to the extent of the cost of repairing or replacing such damage. For purposes of any repairs or replacements under this paragraph, the Closing Date may be extended, at Buyer's election, for a reasonable time to allow such repairs or replacements to be made.

10. Possession. Possession of the Property shall be delivered to Buyer on the Closing Date, provided, however, that Seller shall afford authorized representatives of Buyer reasonable access to the Property for the purposes of satisfying Buyer with respect to the representations, warranties, and covenants of Seller contained herein and with respect to satisfaction of any conditions precedent to the Closing contained herein.

11. Maintenance of the Property. Between the Seller's execution of this Agreement and the Closing, Seller shall maintain the Property in good order, condition and repair, reasonable wear and tear excepted, shall perform all work required to be done by the landlord under the terms of any lease affecting the Property, and shall make all repairs, maintenance and replacements of the Improvements and any Personal Property and otherwise operate the Property in the same manner as before the making of this Agreement, the same as though Seller were retaining the Property.

12. Buyer's Consent to New Contracts Affecting the Property. Seller shall not, after the date of Seller's execution of this Agreement, enter into any lease, amendment of lease, contract or agreement or permit any tenant of the Property to enter into any sublease, assignment of lease, contract or agreement pertaining to the Property, or modify any lease, contract or agreement pertaining to the Property or waive any rights of Seller thereunder, without in each case obtaining Buyer's prior written consent thereto, which consent Buyer agrees shall not be unreasonably withheld.

13. Miscellaneous.

(a) *Notices.* Any notice required or permitted to be given under this Agreement shall be in writing and shall be deemed to have been given when deposited in the United States mail, registered or certified mail, postage prepaid, return receipt required, and addressed as follows:

If to Seller: _____
_____
_____

Att'n: _____

If to Buyer: _____
_____
_____

Att'n: _____

or such other address as either party may from time to time specify in writing to the other.

(b) *Brokers and Finders.* Neither party has had any contact or dealings regarding the Property, or any communication in connection with the subject matter of this transaction, through any licensed real estate broker or other person who can claim a right to a commission or finder's fee as a procuring cause of the sale contemplated herein, except for _____ whose commission shall be paid by Seller. In the event that any other broker or finder perfects a claim for a commission or finder's fee based upon any such contract, dealings or communication, the party through whom the broker or finder makes his claim shall be responsible for said commission or fee and all costs and expenses (including reasonable attorneys' fees) incurred by the other party in defending against the same.

(c) *Successors and Assigns.* This Agreement shall be binding upon, and inure to the benefit of, the parties hereto and their respective successors, heirs, administrators and assigns. Without being relieved of any liability under this Agreement, Buyer reserves the right to take title to the Property in a name or assignee other than Buyer.

(d) *Amendments.* Except as otherwise provided herein, this Agreement may be amended or modified only by a written instrument executed by Seller and Buyer.

(e) *Continuation and Survival of Representations and Warranties.* All representations and warranties by the respective parties contained herein or made in writing pursuant to this Agreement are intended to and shall remain true and correct as of the time of Closing, shall be deemed to be material, and shall survive the execution and delivery of this Agreement and the delivery of the grant deed and transfer of title. All statements contained in any certificate or other instrument delivered at any time by or on behalf of Seller in connection with the transaction contemplated hereby shall constitute representations and warranties hereunder.

(f) *Governing Law.* This Agreement shall be governed by and construed in accordance with the laws of the State of _____.

(g) *Merger of Prior Agreements.* This Agreement and the exhibits hereto constitute the entire agreement between the parties with respect to the purchase and sale of the Property and supersedes all prior agreements and understandings between the parties hereto relating to the subject matter hereof.

(h) *Enforcement.* In the event either party hereto fails to perform any of its obligations under this Agreement or in the event a dispute arises concerning the meaning or interpretation of any provision of this Agreement, the defaulting party or the party not prevailing in such dispute, as the case may be, shall pay any and all costs and

Purchase Agreement (Investment Property) 1247

expenses incurred by the other party in enforcing or establishing its rights hereunder, including, without limitation, court costs and reasonable attorneys' fees.

(i) *Time of the Essence.* Time is of the essence of this Agreement.

[(j) *Short Form.* Upon the execution of this Agreement by Buyer and Seller, a short form hereof, in the form attached as Exhibit H, will be recorded in the Official Records of the County in which the Real Property is located.]

14. **Acceptance of Agreement By Seller.** This Agreement shall be null and void unless it is accepted by Seller and two fully executed copies hereof are returned to Buyer on or before 5:00 p.m. on _____, 19__.

IN WITNESS WHEREOF, the parties hereto have executed this Agreement as of the date first above written.

Buyer: _____,
a _____

By _____
Its _____

Seller: _____,
a _____

By _____
Its _____

APPENDIX J
Mortgage (Investment Property)

RECITAL

The Mortgagee has loaned to the Mortgagor the Mortgage Amount which is evidenced by a note (the Note) of the Mortgagor of even date herewith in that amount and the Mortgagor, in order to secure the payment thereof, has duly authorized the execution and delivery of this Mortgage.

CERTAIN DEFINITIONS

The Mortgagor and the Mortgagee agree that, unless the context otherwise specifies or requires the following terms shall have the meanings herein specified, such definitions to be applicable equally to the singular and the plural forms of such terms.

"Chattels" means all fixtures, fittings, appliances, apparatus, equipment, machinery and articles of personal property and replacements thereof, other than those owned by lessees, now or at any time hereafter affixed to, attached to, placed upon, or used in any way in connection with the complete and comfortable use, enjoyment, occupancy or operation of the Improvements on the Premises.

"Events of Default" means the events and circumstances described as such in Section 2.01 hereof.

"Improvements" means all structures or buildings now or hereafter located upon the Premises or on any part thereof, including all plant equipment, apparatus, machinery and fixtures of every kind and nature whatsoever forming part of said structures or buildings.

"Premises" means the premises described in Schedule A hereto including all of the easements, rights, privileges and appurtenances thereunto belonging or in anywise appertaining, and all of the estate, right, title, interest, claim or demand whatsoever of the Mortgagor therein and in the streets and ways adjacent thereto, either in law or in equity, in possession or expectancy, now or hereafter acquired.

"Involuntary Rate" means the rate of interest per annum provided in

Mortgage (Investment Property)

the Note plus 1½% but in no event to exceed the maximum rate allowed by law.

All terms of this Mortgage which are not defined above have the meaning set forth in this Mortgage.

Granting Clause

Now, Therefore, the Mortgagor, in consideration of the premises and in order to secure the payment of both the principal of, and the interest and any other sums payable on, the Note or this Mortgage and the performance and observance of all the provisions hereof and of the Note, hereby gives, grants, bargains, sells, warrants, aliens, remises, releases, conveys, assigns, transfers, mortgages, hypothecates, deposits, pledges, sets over and confirms unto the Mortgagee, all its estate, right, title and interest in, to and under any and all of the following described property (the Mortgaged Property) whether now owned or held or hereafter acquired:

 (i)   the Premises;
 (ii) the Improvements;
 (iii) the Chattels;
 (iv) all proceeds of the conversion, voluntary or involuntary, of any of the foregoing into cash or liquidated claims, including, without limitation, proceeds of insurance and condemnation awards; and
 (v) all leases of the Premises now or hereafter entered into and all right, title and interest of the Mortgagor thereunder, including, without limitation, cash or securities deposited thereunder to secure performance by the lessees of their obligations thereunder, whether such cash or securities are to be held until the expiration of the terms of such leases or applied to one or more of the instalments of rent coming due immediately prior to the expiration of such terms, including, further, the right upon the happening of an Event of Default, to receive and collect the rents thereunder.

To Have and to Hold unto the Mortgagee, its successors and assigns forever.

ARTICLE I

Particular Covenants of the Mortgagor

The Mortgagor covenants and agrees as follows:

Section 1.01. The Mortgagor warrants that it has a good and marketable title to an indefeasible fee estate in the Premises subject to no lien, charge or encumbrance except such as are listed as exceptions to title in the title policy insuring the lien of this Mortgage; that it will own the Chattels free and clear of liens and claims; and that this Mortgage is and will remain a valid and enforceable first lien on the Mortgaged Property subject only to the exceptions referred to above. The Mortgagor has full power and lawful authority to mortgage the Mortgaged Property in the manner and form herein done or intended hereafter to be done. The Mortgagor will preserve such title, and will forever warrant and defend the same to the Mortgagee and will forever warrant and defend the validity and priority of the lien hereof against the claims of all persons and parties whomsoever.

SECTION 1.02. The Mortgagor will, at the cost of the Mortgagor, and without expense to the Mortgagee, do, execute, acknowledge and deliver all and every such further acts, deeds, conveyances, mortgages, assignments, notices of assignment, transfers and assurances as the Mortgagee shall from time to time require, for the better assuring, conveying, assigning, transferring and confirming unto the Mortgagee the property and rights hereby conveyed or assigned or intended now or hereafter so to be, or which the Mortgagor may be or may hereafter become bound to convey or assign to the Mortgagee, or for carrying out the intention of facilitating the performance of the terms of this Mortgage, or for filing, registering or recording this Mortgage and, on demand, will execute and deliver, and hereby authorizes the Mortgagee to execute in the name of the Mortgagor to the extent it may lawfully do so, one or more financing statements, chattel mortgages or comparable security instruments, to evidence more effectively the lien hereof upon the Chattels.

SECTION 1.03. (a) The Mortgagor forthwith upon the execution and delivery of this Mortgage, and thereafter from time to time, will cause this Mortgage and any security instrument creating a lien or evidencing the lien hereof upon the Chattels and each instrument of further assurance to be filed, registered or recorded in such manner and in such places as many be required by any present or future law in order to publish notice of and fully to protect the lien hereof upon, and the interest of the Mortgagee in, the Mortgaged Property.

(b) The Mortgagor will pay all filing, registration or recording fees, and all expenses incident to the execution and acknowledgment of this Mortgage, any mortgage supplemental hereto, any security instrument with respect to the Chattels, and any instrument of further assurance, and all federal, state, county and municipal stamp taxes and other taxes, duties, imposts, assessments and charges arising out of or in connection with the execution and delivery of the Note, this Mortgage, any mortgage supplemental hereto, any security instrument with respect to the Chattels or any instrument of further assurance.

SECTION 1.04. The Mortgagor will punctually pay the principal and interest and all other sums to become due in respect of the Note at the time

Mortgage (Investment Property) 1251

and place and in the manner specified in the Note, according to the true intent and meaning thereof, all in any coin or currency of the United States of America which at the time of such payment shall be legal tender for the payment of public and private debts.

SECTION 1.05. The Mortgagor, if a corporation, will, so long as it is owner of the Mortgaged Property, do all things necessary to preserve and keep in full force and effect its existence, franchises, rights and privileges as a business or stock corporation under the laws of the state of its incorporation and will comply with all regulations, rules, ordinances, statutes, orders and decrees of any governmental authority or court applicable to the Mortgagor or to the Mortgaged Property or any part thereof.

SECTION 1.06. All right, title and interest of the Mortgagor in and to all extensions, improvements, betterments, renewals, substitutes and replacements of, and all additions and appurtenances to, the Mortgaged Property, hereafter acquired by, or released to, the Mortgagor or constructed, assembled or placed by the Mortgagor on the Premises, and all conversions of the security constituted thereby, immediately upon such acquisition, release, construction, assembling, placement or conversion, as the case may be, and in each such case, without any further mortgage, conveyance, assignment or other act by the Mortgagor, shall become subject to the lien of this Mortgage as fully and completely, and with the same effect, as though now owned by the Mortgagor and specifically described in the granting clause hereof, but at any and all times the Mortgagor will execute and deliver to the Mortgagee any and all such further assurances, mortgages, conveyances or assignments thereof as the Mortgagee may reasonably require for the purpose of expressly and specifically subjecting the same to the lien of this Mortgage.

SECTION 1.07. (a) The Mortgagor, from time to time when the same shall become due, will pay and discharge all taxes of every kind and nature, all general and special assessments, levies, permits, inspection and license fees, all water and sewer rents and charges, and all other public charges whether of a like or different nature, imposed upon or assessed against the Mortgaged Property or any part thereof or upon the revenues, rents, issues, income and profits of the Mortgaged Property or arising in respect of the occupancy, use or possession thereof. The Mortgagor will, upon the request of the Mortgagee, deliver to the Mortgagee receipts evidencing the payment of all such taxes, assessment, levies, fees, rents and other public charges imposed upon or assessed against the Mortgaged Property or the revenues, rents, issues, income or profits thereof.

The Mortgagee may, at its option, to be exercised by thirty (30) days' written notice to the Mortgagor, at the time of each payment of an instalment of interest or principal under the Note, [demand] an additional amount sufficient to discharge the obligations under this subsection (a) when they become due. The determination of the amount so payable and of the fractional part thereof to be deposited with the Mortgagee, so that the aggregate of such deposit shall be sufficient for this purpose, shall be made by the Mortgagee in its sole discretion. Such amounts shall be held by the Mortgagee without interest and applied to the payment of the obligations in respect to which such amounts were deposited or, at the option of the Mortgagee, to the payment of said obligations in such order or priority as the Mortgagee shall determine, on or before the respective dates on which the same or any of them would become delinquent. If one month prior to the due date of any of the aforementioned obligations the amounts then on deposit therefor shall be insufficient for the payment of such obligation in full, the Mortgagor within ten (10) days after demand shall deposit the amount of the deficiency with the Mortgagee. Nothing herein contained shall be deemed to affect any right or remedy of the Mortgagee under any provisions of this Mortgage or of any statute or rule of law to pay any such amount and to add the amount so paid together with interest at the legal rate to the indebtedness hereby secured.

(b) The Mortgagor will pay, from time to time when the same shall become due, all lawful claims and demands of mechanics, materialmen, laborers, and others which, if unpaid, might result in, or permit the creation of, a lien on the Mortgaged Property or any part thereof, or on the revenues, rents, issues, income and profits arising therefrom and in general will do or cause to be done everything necessary so that the lien hereof shall be fully preserved, at the cost of the Mortgagor, without expense to the Mortgagee.

(c) Nothing in this Section 1.07 shall require the payment or discharge of any obligation imposed upon the Mortgagor by this Section so long as the Mortgagor shall in good faith and at its own expense contest the same or the validity thereof by appropriate legal proceedings which shall operate to prevent the collection thereof or other realization thereon and the sale or forfeiture of the Premises or any part thereof to satisfy the same; provided that during such contest the Mortgagor shall, at the option of the Mortgagee, provide security satisfactory to the Mortgagee, assuring the discharge of the Mortgagor's obligation hereunder and of any additional charge, penalty or expense arising from or incurred as a result of such contest; and provided further, that if at any time payment of any obligation imposed upon the Mortgagor by subsection (a) of this Section shall become necessary to prevent the delivery of a tax deed conveying the Mortgaged Property or any portion thereof because of non-payment, then Mortgagor shall pay the same in sufficient time to prevent the delivery of such tax deed.

SECTION 1.08. The Mortgagor will pay any taxes except income taxes imposed on the Mortgagee by reason of its ownership of the Note or this Mortgage.

Mortgage (Investment Property)

SECTION 1.09. (a) The Mortgagor will keep the Improvements and Chattels insured against loss by fire, casualty and such other hazards as may be specified by the Mortgagee for the benefit of the Mortgagee. Such insurance shall be written in forms, amounts, and by companies, satisfactory to the Mortgagee, and losses thereunder shall be payable to the Mortgagee pursuant to a standard first mortgage endorsement substantially equivalent to the New York standard mortgagee endorsement. The policy or policies of such insurance shall be delivered to the Mortgagee. The Mortgagor shall give the Mortgagee prompt notice of any loss covered by such insurance and the Mortgagee shall have the right to join the Mortgagor in adjusting any loss in excess of $50,000. Any moneys received as payment for any loss under any such insurance shall be paid over to the Mortgagee to be applied at the option of the Mortgagee either to the prepayment of the Note, without premium, or to the reimbursement of the Mortgagor for expenses incurred by it in the restoration of the Improvements.

(b) The Mortgagor shall not take out separate insurance concurrent in form or contributing in the event of loss with that required to be maintained under this Section 1.09, unless the Mortgagee is included thereon as a named insured with loss payable to the Mortgagee under a standard mortgage endorsement of the character above described. The Mortgagor shall immediately notify the Mortgagee whenever any such separate insurance is taken out and shall promptly deliver to the Mortgagee the policy or policies of such insurance.

(c) If the Premises are located in an area which has been identified by the Secretary of Housing and Urban Development as a flood hazard area, the Mortgagor will keep the Improvements covered for the term of the Note by flood insurance in an amount at least equal to the full amount of the Note or the maximum limit of coverage available for the Premises under the National Flood Insurance Act of 1968, whichever is less.

SECTION 1.10. If the Mortgagor shall fail to perform any of the covenants contained in Section 1.01, 1.03, 1.07, 1.08, 1.09 or 1.12, the Mortgagee may make advances to perform the same in its behalf, and all sums so advanced shall be a lien upon the Mortgaged Property and shall be secured hereby. The Mortgagor will repay on demand all sums so advanced on its behalf with interest at the Involuntary Rate. The provisions of this Section 1.10 shall not prevent any default in the observance of any covenant contained in said Section 1.01, 1.03, 1.07, 1.08, 1.09 or 1.12 from constituting an Event of Default.

SECTION 1.11. (a) The Mortgagor will keep adequate records and books of accounts in accordance with generally accepted accounting principles and will permit the Mortgagee, by its agents, accountants and attorneys, to visit and inspect the Premises and examine its records and books of account and to discuss its affairs, finances and accounts with the officers of the Mortgagor, at such reasonable times as may be requested by the Mortgagee.

(b) The Mortgagor will deliver to the Mortgagee with reasonable promptness after the close of its fiscal year a balance sheet and statement of profit and loss setting forth, in comparative form, figures for the preceding year. Throughout the term of this Mortgage, the Mortgagor, with reasonable promptness, will deliver to the Mortgagee such other information with respect to the Mortgagor as the Mortgagee may reasonably request from time to time. All financial statements of the Mortgagor shall be prepared in accordance with generally accepted accounting practice, shall be delivered in duplicate, and, shall be accompanied by the certificate of a principal financial or accounting officer of the Mortgagor, dated within five (5) days of the delivery of such statements to the Mortgagee, stating that he knows of no Event of Default, nor of any default which after notice or lapse of time or both would constitute an Event of Default, which has occurred and is continuing, or, if any such default or Event of Default has occurred and is continuing, specifying the nature and period of existence thereof and what action the Mortgagor has taken or proposes to take with respect thereto, and, except as otherwise specified, stating that the Mortgagor has fulfilled all its obligations under this Mortgage which are required to be fulfilled on or prior to the date of such certificate.

(c) The Mortgagor, within three (3) days upon request in person or within five (5) days upon request by mail, will furnish a written statement duly acknowledged of the amount due whether for principal or interest on this Mortgage and whether any offsets or defenses exist against the Mortgage indebtedness.

SECTION 1.12. The Mortgagor will not commit any waste on the Premises or make any change in the use of the Premises which will in any way [increase the premiums for any] ordinary fire or other hazard [insurance upon the premises]. The Mortgagor will, at all times, maintain the Improvements in good operating order and condition and will promptly make, from time to time, all repairs, renewals, replacements, additions and improvements in connection therewith which are needful or desirable to such end. The Improvements shall not be removed, demolished or substantially altered, nor shall any Chattels be removed without the prior written consent of the Mortgagee, except where appropriate replacements free of superior title, liens and claims are immediately made of value at least equal to the value of the Chattels removed.

SECTION 1.13. The Mortgagor, immediately upon obtaining knowledge of the institution of any proceedings for the condemnation of the Premises or any portion thereof, will notify the Mortgagee of the pendency of such proceedings. The Mortgagee may participate in any such

Mortgage (Investment Property) 1255

proceedings and the Mortgagor from time to time will deliver to the Mortgagee all instruments requested by it to permit such participation. In the event of such condemnation proceedings, the award or compensation payable is hereby assigned to and shall be paid to the Mortgagee. The Mortgagee shall be under no obligation to question the amount of any such award or compensation and may accept the same in the amount in which the same shall be paid. In any such condemnation proceedings the Mortgagee may be represented by counsel selected by the Mortgagee. The proceeds of any award or compensation so received shall, at the option of the Mortgagee, either be applied, without premium, to the prepayment of the Note and at the rate of interest provided therein regardless of the rate of interest payable on the award by the condemning authority, or be paid over to the Mortgagor for restoration of the Improvements.

Section 1.14. (a) The Mortgagor will not (i) execute an assignment of the rents or any part thereof from the Premises unless such assignment shall provide that it is subordinate to the assignment contained in this Mortgage and any assignment executed pursuant hereto, or (ii) except where the lessee is in default thereunder, terminate or consent to the cancellation or surrender of any lease of the Premises or of any part thereof, now existing or hereafter to be made, having an unexpired term of two (2) years or more, except that any lease may be cancelled provided that promptly after the cancellation or surrender thereof a new lease is entered into with a new lessee having a credit standing, in the judgment of the Mortgagee, at least equivalent to that of the lessee whose lease was cancelled, on substantially the same terms as the terminated or cancelled lease, or (iii) modify any such lease so as to shorten the unexpired term thereof or so as to decrease the amount of the rents payable thereunder, or (iv) accept prepayments of any instalments of rents to become due under such leases, except prepayments in the nature of security for the performance of the lessees thereunder, or (v) in any other manner impair the value of the Mortgaged Property or the security of the Mortgage.

(b) The Mortgagor will not execute any lease of all or a substantial portion of the Premises except for actual occupancy by the lessee thereunder, and will at all times promptly and faithfully perform, or cause to be performed, all of the covenants, conditions and agreements contained in all leases of the Premises now or hereafter existing, on the part of the lessor thereunder to be kept and performed and will at all times do all things necessary to compel performance by the lessee under each lease of all obligations, covenants and agreements by such lessee to be performed thereunder. If any of such leases provide for the giving by the lessee of certificates with respect to the status of such leases, the Mortgagor shall exercise its right to request such certificates within five (5) days of any demand therefor by the Mortgagee.

(c) The Mortgagor shall furnish to the Mortgagee, within thirty (30) days after a request by the Mortgagee to do so, a written statement containing the names of all lessees of the Premises, the terms of their respective leases, the space occupied and the rentals payable thereunder.

Section 1.15. To the extent not so provided by applicable law each lease of the Premises, or of any part thereof, shall provide that, in the event of the enforcement by the Mortgagee of the remedies provided for by law or by this Mortgage, the lessee thereunder will, upon request of any person succeeding to the interest of the Mortgagor as a result of such enforcement, automatically become the lessee of said successor in interest, without change in the terms or other provisions of such lease, provided, however, that said successor in interest shall not be bound by (i) any payment of rent or additional rent for more than one month in advance, except prepayments in the nature of security for the performance by said lessee of its obligations under said lease, or (ii) any amendment or modification of the lease made without the consent of the Mortgagee or such successor in interest. Each lease shall also provide that, upon request by said successor in interest, such lessee shall execute and deliver an instrument or instruments confirming such attornment.

Section 1.16. Subject to the conditions specified in the next paragraph of this Section, the Mortgagee will, upon request of the Mortgagor, execute nondisturbance and attornment agreements with lessees of the Premises which shall provide that in the event the Mortgagee or any purchaser at foreclosure shall succeed to the Mortgagor's interest in the Premises, the leases of such lessees will remain in full force and effect and be binding upon the Mortgagee or such purchaser and such lessee as though each were the original parties thereto.

The Mortgagee's obligation to execute such agreements shall be subject to conditions as follows: (i) the credit of the lessee and the terms of the lease shall be satisfactory to Mortgagee, (ii) the Mortgagee shall have been provided with a standard form of lease to be used in connection with the leasing of the Premises and shall have approved the same, (iii) upon each request for such an agreement the Mortgagee shall receive a counterpart of the executed lease in which all changes from the standard form shall be indicated by appropriate markings, such markings to be certified to be true and complete by the responsible officer of the Mortgagor or by its counsel, and (vi) the Mortgagee shall receive a letter, signed by the Mortgagor and addressed to the lessee, to be forwarded to the lessee by the Mortgagee, giving notice of the assignment of each lease provided for herein.

ARTICLE II

Events of Default and Remedies

Section 2.01. If one or more of the following Events of Default shall happen, that is to say:

(a) if (i) default shall be made in the payment of any interest on the Note, or in the payment of any instalment of principal, in either such case, when and as the same shall become due and payable, and such default shall have continued for a period of ten (10) days or (ii) default shall be made in any other payment of the principal of the Note, when and as the same shall become due and payable, whether at maturity or by acceleration or as part of any prepayment or otherwise, in each case, as in the Note and this Mortgage provided and such default shall have continued for a period of ten (10) days or (iii) default shall be made in the payment of any tax required by Section 1.07 to be paid and said default shall have continued for a period of twenty (20) days; or

(b) if default shall be made in the due observance or performance of any covenant or agreement on the part of the Mortgagor contained in Section 1.01, 1.03, 1.08, 1.09, and such default shall have continued for a period of twenty (20) days after written notice thereof shall have been given to the Mortgagor by the Mortgagee; or

(c) if default shall be made in the due observance or performance of any other covenant or condition on the part of the Mortgagor in the Note or in this Mortgage contained, and such default shall have continued for a period of thirty (30) days after written notice specifying such default and demanding that the same be remedied shall have been given to the Mortgagor by the Mortgagee; or

(d) if by the order of a court of competent jurisdiction, a trustee, receiver or liquidator of the Mortgaged Property or any part thereof, or of the Mortgagor shall be appointed and such order shall not be discharged or dismissed within sixty (60) days after such appointment; or

(e) if the Mortgagor shall file a petition in bankruptcy or for an arrangement or for reorganization pursuant to the Federal Bankruptcy Act or any similar law, federal or state, or if, by decree of a court of competent jurisdiction, the Mortgagor shall be adjudicated a bankrupt, or be declared insolvent, or shall make an assignment for the benefit of creditors, or shall admit in writing its inability to pay its debts generally as they become due, or shall consent to the appointment of a receiver or receivers of all or any part of the Mortgaged Property; or

(f) if any of the creditors of the Mortgagor shall file a petition in bankruptcy against the Mortgagor or for reorganization of the Mortgagor pursuant to the Federal Bankruptcy Act or any similar law, federal or state, and if such petition shall not be discharged or dismissed within sixty (60) days after the date on which such petition was filed; or

(g) if final judgment for the payment of money shall be rendered against the Mortgagor and the Mortgagor shall not discharge the same or cause it to be discharged within sixty (60) days from the entry thereof, or shall not appeal therefrom or from the order, decree or process upon which or pursuant to which said judgment was granted, based or entered, and secure a stay of execution pending such appeal; or

(h) if it shall be illegal for the Mortgagor to pay any tax referred to in Section 1.08 hereof or if the payment of such tax by the Mortgagor would result in the violation of the usury laws of the state in which the Premises are located;

then and in every such case:

I. During the continuance of any such Event of Default, the Mortgagee, by written notice given to the Mortgagor, may declare the entire principal of the Note then outstanding (if not then due and payable), and all accrued and unpaid interest thereon, to be due and payable immediately, and upon any such declaration the principal of the Note and said accrued and unpaid interest shall become and be immediately due and payable, anything in the Note or in this Mortgage to the contrary notwithstanding;

II. During the continuance of any such Event of Default, the Mortgagee personally, or by its agents or attorneys, may enter into and upon all or any part of the Premises, and each and every part thereof, and may exclude the Mortgagor, its agents and servants wholly therefrom; and having and holding the same, may use, operate, manage and control the Premises and conduct the business thereof, either personally or by its superintendents, managers, agents, servants, attorneys or receivers; and upon every such entry, the Mortgagee, at the expense of the Mortgaged Property, from time to time, either by purchase, repairs or construction, may maintain and restore the Mortgaged Property, whereof it shall become possessed as aforesaid; and likewise, from time to time, at the expense of the Mortgaged Property, the Mortgagee may make all necessary or proper repairs, renewals and replacements and such useful alternations, additions, betterments and improvements thereto and thereon as to it may seem advisable; and in every such case the Mortgagee shall have the right to manage and operate the Mortgaged Property and to carry on the business thereof and exercise all rights and powers of the Mortgagor with respect thereto either in the name of the Mortgagor or otherwise as it shall deem best; and the Mortgagee shall be entitled to collect and receive all earnings, revenues, rents, issues, profits and income of the Mortgaged Property and every part thereof, all of which shall for all purposes constitute property of the Mortgagor; and after deducting the expenses of conducting the business thereof and of all maintenance, repairs, renewals, replacements, alternations, additions, betterments and improvements and amounts necessary to pay for taxes, assessments, insurance and prior or other proper charges upon the Mortgaged Property or any part thereof, as well as just and reasonable compensation for the services of the Mortgagee and for all attorneys, counsel, agents, clerks, servants and other employees by it properly engaged and employed, the Mortgagee shall apply the moneys arising as aforesaid, first, to the payment of the principal of the Note and the interest thereon, when and as the same shall

Mortgage (Investment Property) 1259

become payable and second, to the payment of any other sums required to be paid by the Mortgagor under this Mortgage.

III. The Mortgagee, with or without entry, personally or by its agents or attorneys, insofar as applicable, may:

(1) sell the Mortgaged Property to the extent permitted and pursuant to the procedures provided by law, and all estate, right, title and interest claim and demand therein, and right of redemption thereof, at one or more sales as an entity or in parcels, and at such time' and place upon such terms and after such notice thereof as may be required or permitted by law;

(2) institute proceedings for the complete or partial foreclosure of this Mortgage; or

(3) take such steps to protect and enforce its rights whether by action, suit or proceeding in equity or at law for the specific performance of any covenant, condition or agreement in the Note or in this Mortgage, or in aid of the execution of any power herein granted, or for any foreclosure hereunder, or for the enforcement of any other appropriate legal or equitable remedy or otherwise as the Mortgagee shall elect.

SECTION 2.02. (a) The Mortgagee may adjourn from time to time any sale by it to be made under or by virtue of this Mortgage by announcement at the time and place appointed for such sale or for such adjourned sale or sales; and, except as otherwise provided by any applicable provision of law, the Mortgagee, without further notice or publication, may make such sale at the time and place to which the same shall be so adjourned.

(b) Upon the completion of any sale or sales made by the Mortgagee under or by virtue of this Article II, the Mortgagee, or an officer of any court empowered to do so, shall execute and deliver to the accepted purchaser or purchasers a good and sufficient instrument, or good and sufficient instruments, conveying, assigning and transferring all estate, right, title and interest in and to the property and rights sold. The Mortgagee is hereby appointed the true and lawful attorney irrevocable of the Mortgagor in its name and stead, to make all necessary conveyances, assignments, transfers and deliveries of the Mortgaged Property and rights so sold and for that purpose the Mortgagee may execute all necessary instruments of conveyance, assignment and transfer, and may substitute one or more persons with like power, the Mortgagor hereby ratifying and confirming all that its said attorney or such substitute or substitutes shall lawfully do by virtue hereof. Nevertheless, the Mortgagor, if so requested by the Mortgagee, shall ratify and confirm any such sale or sales by executing and delivering to the Mortgagee or to such purchaser or purchasers all such instruments as may be advisable, in the judgment of the Mortgagee, for the purpose, and as may be designated in such request. Any such sale or sales made under or by virtue of this Article II, whether made under the power of sale herein granted or under or by virtue of judicial proceedings or of a judgment or decree of foreclosure and sale, shall operate to divest all the estate, right, title, interest, claim and demand whatsoever, whether at law or in equity, of the Mortgagor in and to the properties and rights so sold, and shall be a perpetual bar both at law and in equity against the Mortgagor and against any and all persons claiming or who may claim the same, or any part thereof from, through or under the Mortgagor.

(c) In the event of any sale made under or by virtue of this Article II (whether made under the power of sale herein granted or under or by virtue of judicial proceedings or of a judgment or decree of foreclosure and sale), the entire principal of, and interest on, the Note, if not previously due and payable, and all other sums required to be paid by the Mortgagor pursuant to this Mortgage, immediately thereupon shall, anything in the Note or in this Mortgage to the contrary notwithstanding, become due and payable.

(d) The purchase money, proceeds or avails of any sale made under or by virtue of this Article II, together with any other sums which then may be held by the Mortgagee under this Mortgage, whether under the provisions of this Article II or otherwise, shall be applied as follows:

First: To the payment of the costs and expenses of such sale, including reasonable compensation to the Mortgagee, its agents and counsel, and of any judicial proceedings wherein the same may be made, and of all expenses, liabilities and advances made or incurred by the Mortgagee under this Mortgage, together with interest at the Involuntary Rate on all advances made by the Mortgagee and all taxes of assessments, except any taxes, assessments or other charges subject to which the Mortgaged Property shall have been sold.

Second: To the payment of the whole amount then due, owing or unpaid principal at the Involuntary Rate from and after the happening of any Event of Default described in clause (a) of Section 2.01 from the due date of any such payment of principal until the same is paid.

Third: To the payment of any other sums required to be paid by the Mortgagor pursuant to any provision of this Mortgage or of the Note.

Fourth: To the payment of the surplus, if any, to whosoever may be lawfully entitled to receive the same.

(e) Upon any sale made under or by virtue of this Article II, whether made under the power of sale herein granted or under or by virtue of this Article II, whether made under the power of sale herein granted or under or by virtue of judicial proceedings or of a judgment or decree of foreclosure and sale, the Mortgagee may bid for and acquire the Mortgaged Property or any part thereof and in lieu of paying cash therefor may make settlement for the purchase price by crediting upon the indebtedness of the Mortgagor secured by this Mortgage the net sales price after deducting therefrom the expenses of the sale and the costs of the action and any other sums which the Mortgagee is authorized to deduct under this Mortgage.

Mortgage (Investment Property)

SECTION 2.03. (a) In case an Event of Default described in clause (a) of Section 2.01 shall have happened and be continuing, then, upon written demand of the Mortgagee, the Mortgagor will pay to the Mortgagee the whole amount which then shall have become due and payable on the Note, for principal or interest or both, as the case may be, and after the happening of said Event of Default will also pay to the Mortgagee interest at the Involuntary Rate on the then unpaid principal of the Note, and the sums required to be paid by the Mortgagor pursuant to any provision of this Mortgage, and in addition thereto such further amount as shall be sufficient to cover the costs and expenses of collection, including reasonable compensation to the Mortgagee, its agents, and counsel and any expenses incurred by the Mortgagee hereunder. In the event the Mortgagor shall fail forthwith to pay such amounts upon such demand, the Mortgagee shall be entitled and empowered to institute such action or proceedings at law or in equity as may be advised by its counsel for the collection of the sums so due and unpaid, and may prosecute any such action or proceedings to judgment or final decree, and may enforce any such judgment or final decree against the Mortgagor and collect, out of the property of the Mortgagor wherever situated, as well as out of the Mortgaged Property, in any manner provided by law, moneys adjudged or decreed to be payable.

(b) The Mortgagee shall be entitled to recover judgment as aforesaid either before or after or during the pendency of any proceedings for the enforcement of the provisions of this Mortgage; and the right of the Mortgagee to recover such judgment shall not be affected by any entry or sale hereunder, or by the exercise of any other right, power or remedy for the enforcement of the provisions of this Mortgage, or the foreclosure of the lien hereof; and in the event of a sale of the Mortgaged Property, and of the application of the proceeds of sale, as in this Mortgage provided, to the payment of the debt hereby secured, the Mortgagee shall be entitled to enforce payment of, and to receive all amounts then remaining due and unpaid upon, the Note, and to enforce payment of all other charges, payments and costs due under this Mortgage, and shall be entitled to recover judgment for any portion of the debt remaining unpaid, with interest. In case of proceedings against the Mortgagor in insolvency or bankruptcy or any proceedings for its reorganization or involving the liquidation of its assets, then the Mortgagee shall be entitled to prove the whole amount of principal and interest due upon the Note to the full amount thereof, and all other payments, charges and costs due under this Mortgage, without deducting therefrom any proceeds obtained from the sale of the whole or any part of the Premises, provided, however, that in no case shall the Mortgagee receive a greater amount than such principal and interest and such other payments, charges and costs from the aggregate amount of the proceeds of the sale of the Mortgaged and Property and the distribution from the estate of the Mortgagor.

(c) No recovery of any judgment by the Mortgagee and no levy of an execution under any judgment upon the Mortgaged Property or upon any other property of the Mortgagor shall affect in any manner or to any extent, the lien of this Mortgage upon the Mortgaged Property or any part thereof, or any liens, rights, powers or remedies of the Mortgagee hereunder, but such liens, rights, powers and remedies of the Mortgagee shall continue unimpaired as before.

(d) Any moneys thus collected by the Mortgagee under this Section 2.03 shall be applied by the Mortgagee in accordance with the provisions of paragraph (d) of Section 2.02.

SECTION 2.04. After the happening of any Event of Default and immediately upon the commencement of any action, suit or other legal proceedings by the Mortgagee to obtain judgment for the principal of, or interest on, the Note and other sums required to be paid by the Mortgagor pursuant to any provision of this Mortgage, or of any other nature in aid of the enforcement of the Note or of this Mortgage, the Mortgagor will (a) waive the issuance and service of process and enter its voluntary appearance in such action, suit or proceeding, and (b) if required by the Mortgagee, consent to the appointment of a receiver or receivers of the Premises and of all the earnings, revenues, rents, issues, profits and income thereof. After the happening of any Event of Default and during its continuance, or upon the commencement of any proceedings to foreclose this Mortgage or to enforce the specific performance hereof or in aid thereof or upon the commencement of any other judicial proceeding to enforce any right of the Mortgagee, the Mortgagee shall be entitled, as a matter of right, if it shall so elect, without the giving of notice to any other party and without regard to the adequacy or inadequacy of any security for the Mortgage indebtedness, forthwith either before or after declaring the unpaid principal of the Note to be due and payable, to the appointment of such a receiver or receivers.

SECTION 2.05. Notwithstanding the appointment of any receiver, liquidator or trustee of the Mortgagor, or of any of its property, or of the Mortgaged Property or any part thereof, the Mortgagee shall be entitled to retain possession and control of all property now or hereafter held under this Mortgage.

SECTION 2.06. No remedy herein conferred upon or reserved to the Mortgagee is intended to be exclusive of any other remedy or remedies, and each and every such remedy shall be cumulative, and shall be in addition to every other remedy given hereunder or now or hereafter existing at law or in equity or by statute. No delay or omission of the Mortgagee to exercise any right or power accruing upon any Event of Default shall impair any such right or power, or shall be construed to be a waiver of any such Event of Default or any acquiescence therein; and every power and remedy given by this Mortgage to the Mortgagee may be exercised from time to time as often as may be deemed expedient by the

Mortgage (Investment Property)

Mortgagee. Nothing in this Mortgage or in the Note shall affect the obligation of the Mortgagor to pay the principal of, and interest on, the Note in the manner and at the time and place therein respectively expressed.

SECTION 2.07. The Mortgagor will not at any time insist upon, or plead, or in any manner whatever claim or take any benefit or advantage of any stay or extension or moratorium law, any exemption from execution or sale of the Mortgaged Property or any part thereof, wherever enacted, now or at any time hereafter in force, which may affect the covenants and terms of performance of this Mortgage, now claim, take or insist upon any benefit or advantage of any law now or hereafter in force providing for the valuation or appraisal of the Mortgaged Property, or any part thereof, prior to any sale or sales thereof which may be made pursuant to any provision herein, or pursuant to the decree, judgment or order of any court of competent jurisdiction; nor, after any such sale or sales, claim or exercise any right under any statute heretofore or hereafter enacted to redeem the property so sold or any part thereof and the Mortgagor hereby expressly waives all benefit or advantage of any such law or laws, and covenants not to hinder, delay or impede the execution of any power herein granted or delegated to the Mortgagee, but to suffer and permit the execution of every power as though no such law or laws had been made or enacted. The Mortgagor, for itself and all who may claim under it, waives, to the extent that it lawfully may, all right to have the Mortgaged Property marshalled upon any foreclosure hereof.

SECTION 2.08. During the continuance of any Event of Default and pending the exercise by the Mortgagee of its right to exclude the Mortgagor from all or any part of the Premises, Mortgagor agrees to pay the fair and reasonable rental value for the use and occupancy of the Premises or any portion thereof which are in its possession for such period and, upon default of any such payment, will vacate and surrender possession of the Premises to the Mortgagee or to a receiver, if any, and in default thereof may be evicted by any summary action or proceeding for the recovery or possession of premises for nonpayment of rent, however designated.

ARTICLE III

MISCELLANEOUS

SECTION 3.01. In the event any one or more of the provisions contained in this Mortgage or in the Note shall for any reason be held to be invalid, illegal or unenforceable in any respect, such invalidity, illegality or unenforceability shall, at the option of the Mortgagee, not effect any other provision of this Mortgage, but this Mortgage shall be construed as if such invalid, illegal or unenforceable provision had never been contained herein or therein.

SECTION 3.02. All notices hereunder shall be in writing and shall be deemed to have been sufficiently given or served for all purposes when presented personally or sent by registered mail to any party hereto at its address above stated (in the case of the Mortgagee, attention Real Estate and Mortgage Loan Department) or at such other address of which it shall have notified the party giving such notice in writing.

SECTION 3.03. Whenever in this Mortgage the giving of notice by mail or otherwise is required, the giving of such notice may be waived in writing by the person or persons entitled to receive such notice.

SECTION 3.04. All of the grants, covenants, terms, provisions and conditions herein shall run with the land and shall apply to, bind and inure to the benefit of, the successors and assigns of the Mortgagor and the successors and assigns of the Mortgagee.

SECTION 3.05. No provision in this Mortgage or in the Note shall require the payment or permit the collection of interest in excess of the maximum amount permitted by law in commercial construction or permanent mortgage loan transactions between parties of the character of the parties hereto. The Mortgagor shall not be obligated to pay any interest in excess of such maximum amount.

SECTION 3.06. This Mortgage may be executed in any number of counterparts and each of such counterparts shall for all purposes be deemed to be an original; and all such counterparts shall together constitute but one and the same mortgage.

SECTION 3.07. The information set forth on the cover hereof is hereby incorporated herein.

IN WITNESS WHEREOF, this Mortgage has been duly executed by the Mortgagor.

Attest: By _____

_____

Witnesses:

_____
_____

Table of Cases

Abstract Corp. v. Fernandez Co., 762
Adam, Robert L., 371
Alessi, Matter of, 95
Allen v. Commissioner, 410
Alsworth-Washburn Co. v. Helvering, 397
American Land Co. v. Zeiss, 741, 752
Anaheim Union Water Co. v. Commissioner, 1006
Anderson v. Barron, 710
Anderson v. Shepard, 898
Anderson v. Steinway & Sons, 552
Anderson v. Title Ins. Co., 823
Ash v. Egar, 1107

Bain v. Fothergill, 626
Ballentyne v. Smith, 318
Banner v. Elm, 526
Bar Assn. of Tenn. v. Union Planters Title Guar. Co., 850
Barnhardt v. Morrison, 721
Barr v. McGlothin, 469
Bartsas Realty v. Nash, 60
Bates v. State Bar of Ariz., 88
Bennion, Van Camp, Hagaen & Ruhl v. Kassler Escrow, 83
Berry v. Howard, 735
Best Fertilizers of Ariz. v. Burns, 240
B. F. Saul Co. v. West End Park N., 155, 161
Biggs v. Commissioner, 401
Biggs v. Steinway & Sons, 552
Bjornberg v. Myers, 907
Blakeney v. Home Owners' Loan Corp., 721
Blank v. Borden, 38
Bokser v. Lewis, 160
Booth v. Milliken, 472
Boyle Holding Corp. v. Medgreen Holding Corp., 527
Branden v. Driver, 315
Brett v. Cooney, 527
Bristol Lumber Co. v. Dery, 695
Bron v. Weintraub, 528
Brooks v. LaSalle Natl. Bank, 347
Brown v. Cardoza, 159
Brown v. Federal Natl. Mortgage Assn., 282

Brown v. Khoury, 720
Brown v. Mifflin, 660
Brown, Royce W., 372
Bryant v. Ellenburgh, 720
Buquo v. Title Guar. and Trust Co., 843
Butler v. Haley Greystone Corp., 907
Butts v. Samuels, 175
Byram v. Commissioner, 364

Calamari v. Grace, 762
Cal-Am Corp. v. Department of Real Estate, 1019
Carlson v. Hamilton, 347
Carolina Light & Power Co. v. Waters, 567
Centex Homes Corp. v. Boag, 508
Central Fin. Servs. v. Spears, 275
Central Holding Co. v. Bushman, 253
Century Elec. Co. v. Commissioner, 1147
C. Frederick Frick, 372
Chestnut Corp. v. Bankers Bond and Mortgage Co., 142
Chianese v. Culley, 964
Chicago Bar Assn. v. Quinlan and Tyson, Inc., 82
Chicago B. & Q.R. Co. v. Wasserman, 721
Chicago Title Ins. Co. v. Huff, 849
Cities Serv. Oil Co. v. Dunlap, 574
City of Miami v. St. Joe Paper Co., 881
Coffee County Abstract and Title Co. v. State ex rel. Norwood, 850
Cohen v. A.F.A. Realty Corp., 501
Commander Leasing Co. v. Transamerica Title Ins. Co., 849
Commissioner v. Kelley, 1011
Commissioner v. Stuart, 392
Commonwealth to Use of Willow Highlands Co. v. Maryland Casualty Co., 807
Conference Center v. TRC, 286
Connor v. Great Western Sav. and Loan Assn., 596
Conroy v. Conroy, 721
Continental Mortgage Investors v. Sailboat Key, 156, 161, 166
Conway-Bogue Realty Inv. Co. v. Denver Bar Assn., 83
Crocker v. Malley, 118

Crowley, Milner & Co. v. Commissioner, 1147
Cultum v. Heritage House Realtors, 73

Dail v. Campbell, 246
Daugharthy v. Monritt Assocs., 234
Dawn Inv. Co. v. Superior Ct. of Los Angeles County, 143
DeKalb County v. United Family Life Ins. Co., 142
Dennen v. Searle, 731
Dewey v. Allgire, 720
D & H Dev. Co. v. Sherwood & Roberts, 155
Dixon v. Kaufman, 721
Dobbs, Ellsworth, Inc. v. Johnson, 53, 476
Doering v. Fields, 495
Dolan, Matter of, 96
Dry Dock Bank v. American Life Ins. & Trust Co., 171
Dugan v. First Natl. Bank in Wichita, 1110
Dugan v. Grzybowski, 141
Duke v. Garret, 635
Dunlap v. Commissioner, 1139
Durrett v. Washington Natl. Ins. Co., 339
Dworak v. Michals, 49

Earl W. Jimerson Housing Co. v. Butler, 959
Eckland v. Jankowski, 721
Eckstein v. United States, 1005
Eliason v. Wilborn, 904
Ellsworth Dobbs, Inc. v. Johnson, 53, 476
Eltinge and Graziadio Dev. Co. v. Childs, 1058
Erickson v. Bohne, 720
Estate of Franklin v. Commissioner, 1149
Estate of Josephine Clay Simpson, 371
Evelyn v. Raven Realty, 500

Federal Natl. Mortgage Assn. v. Howlett, 281
Feller v. Architects Display Bldg., 167
Fialkowski v. Fialkowski, 906
Fidelity Chem. Prods. v. Rubino, 629
Fidelity Sav. & Loan Assn. v. De La Cuesta, 144
First. Am. Title Ins. Co. v. First Title Serv. Co., 762
First Fed. Sav. & Loan Assn. of Gary v. Arena, 246
First Fed. Sav. & Loan Assn. of Miami v. Fisher, 695
First Natl. Bank & Trust Co. of Port Chester v. New York Title Ins. Co., 807
First Vt. Bank & Trust Co. v. Kalomiris, 297
First Wis. Natl. Bank of Oshkosh v. KSW Invs., 275
Fitzpatrick v. Federer, 275

Fleischer v. Cosgrove, 469
Flureau v. Thornhill, 626, 630
Flynn v. City of Cambridge, 998
Fohn v. Title Ins. Corp. of St. Louis, 710
Frank Lyon Co. v. United States, 1117, 1120
Franklin v. Jameson-Wohler, 299
Franklin, Estate of v. Commissioner, 1149
Franks v. Wood, 719
Freedman v. Rector, Wardens & Vestrymen of St. Mathias Parish, 477
Freeway Park Bldg. v. Western Wholesale Supply, 346
French v. Mortgage Guar. Co., 161
Frick, C. Frederick, 372
Friedman, Harold, Inc. v. Thorofare Mkts., 1036
Fuentes v. Shevin, 281, 722, 723
Fuller, Peter, Enters. v. Manchester Sav. Bank, 137
Funder v. Maizels, 1066

G. R. Kenny, Inc. v. White, 1049
Gabel v. Drewrys Ltd., 660
Gammon v. Hodges, 685
Garafano v. Wells, 84
Garriffa v. Taylor, 601
Gatlinburg Real Estate Co. v. Booth, 33
Gear v. Webster, 29
Gelfert v. National City Bank, 318
General Motors Acceptance Corp. v. Mackrill, 175
Geneva Drive-In Theatre, 1069
Gerruth Realty Co. v. Pire, 442, 466
Gilbert v. Ludtke, 61
Gill v. Johnson, 907
Goldfarb v. Virginia State Bar, 85
Goodman v. United States, 370, 371, 372
Grayson v. LaBlanche, 446
Great So. Aircraft Corp. v. Kraus, 1098
Greene v. Grievance Comm., 95
Gregory v. Alexander, 716
Grenader v. Spitz, 975
G-W-L, Inc. v. Robichaux, 596

Hadrup v. Sale, 716
Handy v. Gordon, 202
Harbel Oil v. Steele, 262, 1098
Harold Friedman, Inc. v. Thorofare Mkts., 1036
Harris v. Woodard, 569
Hartman v. Shambaugh, 807
Hauck v. Crawford, 721
Haymes v. Rogers, 29
Hecht v. Meller, 54
Heiman v. Bishop, 318
Helvering v. Lazarus & Co., 1134
Hempstead Theatre Corp. v. Metropolitan Playhouses, 1038

Table of Cases

Hersch v. Silberstein, 528
Heyd v. Chicago Title Ins. Co., 828
Higgins v. Loup River Pub. Power Dist., 527
Hilton v. Commissioner, 1134
Hoagland v. Celebrity Homes, 595
Hodge v. Blanton, 568
Hoffman, Jacob, Brewing Co. v. Wuttge, 1100
Home Sav. and Loan Assn. v. Bates, 161
Honeyman v. Jacobs, 318
Hoover v. Wukasch, 567
Horan v. Blowitz, 500
Horton v. Kyburz, 652
Hosier v. Great Notch Corp., 710
Houtz v. Hellman, 518

Indoe v. Dwyer, 448
In re Sombrero Reef Club, 1022
Insurance Co. of N. Am. v. Alberstadt, 550
Islip, Town of v. Smith, 1049

Jacob Hoffman Brewing Co. v. Wuttge, 1100
Jameson v. Warren, 159
Jarchow v. Transamerica Title Ins. Co., 763, 829, 844, 845
Jimerson, Earl W., Housing Co. v. Butler, 959
J. M. Realty Inv. Corp. v. Stern, 295
Johnson v. First Natl. Bank of Montevideo, Minn., 325
Johnson v. Jefferson Std. Life Ins. Co., 275
Johnson v. Watson, 567
Jones v. Commissioner, 398
Jones v. Jones, 695
Jordan v. Talbot, 346
Jordan Marsh Co. v. Commissioner, 1147

Kahn v. Sohmer, 171
Kasten Constr. Co. v. Maple Ridge Constr. Co., 492
Kauder, Klotz & Venitt v. Rose's Stores, 1050
Kemp v. Thurmond, 226
Kenny, G. R., Inc. v. White, 1049
Kentucky Coal & Timber Dev. Co. v. Conley, 685
Killam v. March, 907
Kirsen v. Barnes, 505
Kiser v. Clinchfield Coal Corp., 667
Koffler v. Joint Bar Assn., 88
Kovarik v. Vesely, 437
Kraemer v. Smith, 61
Kraft v. Michael, 474, 491
Kroop v. Caravelle Condominium, 968

Ladue v. Detroit, Milwaukee R. R., 230
Lady v. Realty Assocs., 60
Land Title Co. of Ala. v. State ex rel. Porter, 849
Lane v. Trenholm Bldg. Co., 594
Langel v. Betz, 523
La Sala v. American Sav. & Loan Assn., 143
Lawyers Title Ins. Corp. v. McKee, 843
Lenexa State Bank v. Dixon, 719
Leslie Co. v. Commissioner, 1141
Linden Hill No. 1 Coop. Corp. v. Kleiner, 960
Lipinski v. The Title Ins. Co., 828
L. Smirlock Realty Corp. v. Title Guar. Co., 816, 823
Luette v. Bank of Italy Natl. Trust & Sav. Assn., 631
Lyon, Frank, Co. v. United States, 1117, *1120*
Lyons v. National Sav. Bank, 160

Magneson v. Commissioner, 410
Major v. Christian County Livestock Mkt., 527
Malat v. Riddell, 362
Malinak v. Safeco Title Ins. Co., 828
Mandelino v. Fribourg, 171
Manoog v. Miele, 271
Manufacturers and Traders Trust Co. v. First Natl. Bank in Ft. Lauderdale, 660
Markman v. Hoefer, 595
Marlenee v. Brown, 721
Marsh v. Pike, 240
Marshall v. Hollywood, Inc., 881
Martin v. Carter, 721
Martin v. Seigel, 562
Martinique Realty Corp. v. Hull, 711
Masgai v. Masgai, 239
Matter of Alessi, 95
Matter of Dolan, 96
Matter of Miller, 948
Matter of Turner, 949
McCahill v. Travis Co., 672
McCue v. Deppert, 46
McDaniel v. Daves, 471
Melcer v. Zuck, 612
Mellos v. Silverman, 54
Mendes v. Johnson, 346
Miami, City of v. St. Joe Paper Co., 881
Middlebrook-Anderson Co. v. Southwest Sav. & Loan Assn., 468
Mileage Realty Co. v. Miami Parking Garage, 1037
Milholin v. Vorhies, 48
Miller v. Green, 705
Miller v. Pacific First Fed. Sav. & Loan Assn., 144
Miller, Matter of, 948
Mindlin v. Davis, 222

1268 Table of Cases

Mission Hill Dev. Corp. v. Western Small Business Inv. Co., 160
Mobbs v. City of Lehigh, 881
Mokar Properties Corp. v. Hall, 624
Moog v. Palmour, 447
Moran v. Kenai Towing and Salvage, 152
Morgan v. Lewis, 510
Morrissey v. Commissioner, 118
Mosley v. Magnolia Petroleum Co., 721
Mugaas v. Smith, 722
Mutual Fed. Sav. & Loan Assn. v. Wisconsin Wire Works, 144
Mutual Life Ins. Co. of N.Y. v. Tailored Woman, Inc., 1043
Myers-Macomber Engrs. v. M.L.W. Constr. Corp., 256

National Mut. Bldg. & Loan Assn. v. Retzman, 253
New Jersey State Bar Assn. v. New Jersey Assn. of Realtor Bds., 82
1915 16th St. Co-Operative Assn. v. Pinkett, 955
Norman Lumber Co. v. United States, 699

Oaks v. Weingartner, 229
Ohralik v. Ohio State Bar Assn., 88
Olszewski v. Sardynski, 512
1000 Grandview Assn. v. Mt. Wash. Assocs., 596
Osin v. Johnson, 661
Owen v. Neely, 561, 763

Paganelli v. Swendsen, 710
Page v. Frazier, 763
Park Place, Inc., 1007, 1009
P.B.R. Enters. v. Perren, 604
Penthouse Properties v. 1158 Fifth Ave., Inc., 960, 968
Perkins v. Spencer, 349
Peter Fuller Enters. v. Manchester Sav. Bank, 137
Phalen Park State Bank v. Reeves, 156
Plaza Hotel Assocs. v. Wellington Assocs., 1061
Plaza Rd. Co-op v. Finn, 959
Point E. Mgmt. Corp. v. Point E. One Condominium Corp., 977
Pope County Bar Assn. v. Suggs, 83
Prater v. Prater, 721
Pritchett, Richard, 371
Prudential Ins. Co. of Am. v. Holliday, 651

Ray v. Robben, 566
Real Estate Listing Serv. v. Connecticut Real Estate Commn., 21
Reid's Admr. v. Benge, 721

Reliance Ins. Co. v. Allstate Indem. Co., 551
Richard Pritchett, 371
Richards v. Powercraft Homes, 590
Ricker v. United States, 281
Riddell v. Scales, 371
Robert L. Adam, 371
Robertson Lumber Co. v. Stephen Farmer Coop. Elevator Co., 595
Rogers v. Williamsburgh Sav. Bank, 142
Rogers Carl Corp. v. Moran, 505
Ross Realty Co. v. First Citizens Bank & Trust Co., 319
Rothman Realty Co. v. Bereck, 476
Roundhouse Constr. Corp. v. Telesco Masons Supplies Co., 722, 723
Rowe v. Great Atl. & Pac. Tea Co., 1049
Royer v. Carter, 470
Rudd v. Lascelles, 629
Ruth v. S.Z.B. Corp., 1065, 1066
Ryczkowski v. Chelsea Title and Guar. Co., 816

Saak v. Hicks, 730
Salem v. Salem, 660
Sanders v. Stevens, 34
Sanford v. Alabama Power Co., 710
Sattler v. Philadelphia Title Ins. Co., 803
Saul, B. F., Co. v. West End Park N., 155, 161
Schaeffer v. Commissioner, 397
Schipper v. Levitt & Sons, Inc., 594
Schmid v. Whitten, 526
Schneider v. Ferrigno, 248
Schoenberg v. Benner, 33
Schultz v. Rudie, 581
Scribner v. O'Brien, Inc., 607
Seagate Condominium Assn. v. Duffy, 967
Seguin v. Maloney-Chambers Co., 661
Seventeenth and Locust Sts. Corp. v. Montcalm Corp., 239
79–83 Thirteenth Ave., Ltd. v. De Marco, 188
Shine Laundry v. Washington Loan & Banking Co., 252
Shockey v. Page, 252
Shurtleff v. Marcus Land & Inv. Co., 469
Sieverts v. White, 499
Silverman v. Alcoa Plaza Assn., 947
Silverstein v. Wakefield, 155
Silver Waters Corp. v. Murphy, 230
Simpson, Josephine Clay, Estate of, 371
Skelly Oil Co. v. Ashmore, 537
Smirlock, L., Realty Corp. v. Title Guar. Co., 816, 823
Smith v. Continental Bank, 596
Smith v. Mady, 488
Smith v. Prudential Property and Casualty Ins. Co., 551

Table of Cases

Smith, Wilbur, and Assocs. v. National Bank of S.C., 61
Snaidach v. Family Fin. Corp., 281, 722, 723
Snyder v. Schram, 60
Sombrero Reef Club, In re,* 1022
Southern Title Insurance Co. v. Crow, 816
Springer Corp. v. Kirkeby-Natus, 282
Stanford v. Owens, 607
Starek v. TKW, Inc., 719
Starfish Condominium Assn. v. Yorkridge Serv. Corp., 594
Starker v. United States, 410
State v. Carriage House Assocs., 1017
State v. Dinger, 83
State Bar of Ariz. v. Arizona Land Title & Trust Co., 83
State Tax Commn. v. Shor, 943
Steiber v. Palumbo, 589
Stenehjem v. Kyn Jin Cho, 454
Stevens v. Jayhawk Realty Co., 38
Stockton v. Lucas, 948
Storthz v. Arnold, 523
Suarez v. Rivercross Tenants' Corp., 960

Taft v. Rutherford, 561
Tague Holding Corp. v. Harris, 472
Tenco, Inc. v. Manning, 566
Thomassen v. Carr, 160
Tibbals v. United States, 371
Tobin v. Courshon, 83
Town of Islip v. Smith, 1049
Tramontozzi v. D'Amicis, 700
Trenta v. Gay, 453
Tripler v. MacDonald Lumber Co., 660
Tucker v. Lassen Sav. & Loan Assn., 143
Turner v. Blackburn, 282
Turner, Matter of, 949
Tysons Corner Regional Shopping Center, 1036

United Housing Found. v. Forman, 948, 974
United States v. Crain, 315
United States v. Ellis, 314
United States v. Haddon Haciendas Co., 315
United States v. MacKenzie, 315

United States v. Stadium Apartments, 299
United States v. Stewart, 315
United States v. Title Ins. Rating Bureau of Ariz., 849
United States v. Union Cent. Life Ins. Co., 700
United Surgical Steel Co. v. Commissioner, 397

Valley Assocs. Corp. v. Rogers, 627
Van Deven v. Harvey, 583
Vogel v. Northern Assurance Co., 547

Wagoner v. Brady, 252
Walker v. Valley Plumbing, 720
Wallach v. Riverside Bank, 609
Ward v. Taggart, 29
Warden v. Sabins, 719
Warren v. Government Natl. Mortgage Assn., 276
Watts v. Archer, 721
Weaver Hardware Co. v. Solomovitz, 174
Weeks v. Rumbaugh, 724
Weidner v. Hyland, 635
Weisner v. 791 Park Ave. Corp., 968
Wellenkamp v. Bank of Am., 143
Welling v. Crosland, 511
Westoak Realty & Inv. v. Hernandez, 271
Whalley v. Small, 684
White v. Cox, 949
Whitehurst v. Abbott, 688
Wichelman v. Messner, 868
Wilbur Smith and Assocs. v. National Bank of S.C., 61
Williams v. Fulton, 566
Williams v. Polgar, 754
Williams v. Safe Deposit & Trust Co., 1103
Wingfoot Cal. Homes Co. v. Valley Natl. Bank of Phoenix, 259
Winthrop v. Tomlinson, 371
Woodruff v. National City Bank of Evansville, 229
Woods v. Garnett, 670
World Publishing Co. v. Commissioner, 1069
Wright v. Schutt Constr. Co., 45

Zichlin v. Dill, 37

Index

Abstracters
　functions of, 646
　insurers' liabilities as, 823-829
　liability of, 754-763
　licensing of, 648-649
　public officials as, 649-650
Abstracts of title
　nature of, 646-648
　standardization of, 647-648
Adverse possession
　mineral interests, 670
　prior adverse possession, effect under the recording acts, 721-722
　title clearance, effect of, 730-731
　Torrens titles, effect on, 903-904
Affidavits, use of in clearing land titles, 752-754
Alternative mortgage instruments
　contingent interest mortgage, 185-186
　deferred interest mortgage, 184
　flexible loan insurance program, 184
　graduated payment mortgage, 180
　price level adjusted mortgage, 187
　renegotiable rate mortgage, 183-184
　shared appreciation mortgage, 186-187
　tenants in common keeping equity (TICKET), 184
　variable-rate mortgage, 182-183
Amortization of mortgages
　"balloon" mortgage, 180
　constant amortization, 180
　level payment debt service, 178-179
Antitrust, 849-851
Attorney and client. *See* Lawyers

Binders, 445-446
Boundary description. *See* Description of land
Brokerage commissions
　contract of sale provisions, 7
　listing agreements
　　duration of, 60-61
　　exclusive, 7, 18-19, 21-28, 46, 64, 1205-1206
　　multiple, 7-8, 17-19, 21-28, 85-87
　　net, 28

　　open, 19, 21-28, 46
　　withdrawal from sale, 38-46
　litigation concerning, 1-5
　local market uniformity, 86-87
　regulation of, 21-29, 85-87
　seller's payment of, 10
　when earned, 38-64
Brokers
　advertising and solicitation by, 87
　antitrust restrictions on, 84-87
　buyer's duties to, 46-48
　chains and franchises, 20
　conflicting interests, 15-17, 109
　contract for brokerage, 65-66
　customer security funds, 33-34
　defined, 5 n.2
　dual representation, 11-12, 15-17
　duties to buyer
　　as agent, 9-10, 12-14
　　disclosure, 12-13
　　false representation of seller's price, 34-36
　　honesty and good faith, 11, 37-38
　duties to seller
　　competence, 33
　　fiduciary character of, 8-9
　　honesty and good faith, 8-9, 29-33
　listing agreements. *See* Brokerage commissions
　misrepresentation by, 34-38
　monopoly of, 83-85
　National Assn. of Realtors, 28-29, 87
　number of, 20
　occupational regulation, 72-87
　organization of industry, 1-5, 86-87
　realtors defined, 6 n.6, 29
　role of, 5-17
　seller's duties to, 54-64
　unauthorized practice of law by, 73-84
Buyer's remedies
　contract for limited liability, 612-617, 624-627
　for misrepresentation, 589
　quality deficiencies, 545, 588-608
　title deficiencies
　　damages, 612-617, 624-627
　　specific performance, 545, 612-617, 627-630

1271

Choice of entity for real estate ownership
  corporations, 1183-1188
  partnerships, 1180-1181
  sole proprietorships, 1179-1180
  Subchapter S corporations, 1188-1190
Closing
  general characteristics, 71-72
Condominium
  comparison with stock-cooperative, 935-936
  condominium's rights against the delinquent owner, 959
  condominium's rights against the overreaching developer, 977-983
  conversion of rental units
    regulating the conversion process, 983-1004
    tax treatment, 1009-1012
  documents, 938-939
  FHA mortgage insurance (§234), 935
  income tax treatment, 352, 355, 357-358, 1004, 1006-1009
  legal arrangement, 935-939
  owner's liability in tort, 949-955
  regulation of the offering statement, 969-975
  specific performance of contract of sale, 508-510
  statutory foundation, 937-938, 942
  transfer of interests, 964-968
Construction loans, 116-117, 120-121, 446
Contract of sale
  assignability, 522-523
  attorney's approval, 448-453
  blank clauses, 446
  boundaries, 562-570
  brokerage provisions, 7
  buyer fails to close
    election of remedies, 500-502
    liquidated damages clause, 472-492
    rescission, 492-501
    retention of deposit, 472-492
    seller's damages, 468-472
    specific performance, 476-477, 508-516, 545, 629
    vendor's lien, 516-517
  contract provisions (form contract), 1207-1210, 1235-1247
  deed requirements, 609-611
  definiteness
    boundaries, 562-570
    financing provisions, 437-448
  executory period. *See* Executory interval
  financing conditions, 437-448, 513-516
  general characteristics, 67-68
  merger of contract into deed, 605, 609
  overreaching buyer, 523-535
  recordability, 503-504
  recording as slander of title, 504-508

  seller fails to close
    contract for limited liability, 612-617, 624-627
    for misrepresentation, 589
    quality deficiencies, 545, 588-608
    specific performance, 545, 612-617, 627-630
    title deficiencies, damages for, 612-617, 624-627
  subordination agreements, 453-468
  time and the essence, 492-508
Conveyancing procedures, 65-72
Cooperative apartments
  comparison with condominium, 935-936
  conversion of rental units
    regulating the conversion process, 983-1004
    tax treatment, 1009-1012
  cooperative's rights against the delinquent owner, 955-959
  FHA mortgage insurance (§213), 934
  history of, 933-934
  income tax treatment, 355, 1004-1009
  legal arrangement, 934
  Mitchell-Lama law, 934
  realty, personalty, or hybrid, 943-949
  regulation of the offering statement, 975-976
  transfer of interests, 960-964, 968
Corporations. *See* Choice of entity for real estate ownership
Covenants for title, 610-611
Credit quartet. *See* Mortgage terms
Curative acts, 724, 731-735, 875

Damages. *See* Buyer's remedies; Seller's remedies
Data storage and retrieval. *See* Mechanized processing of title data
Deed absolute as mortgage, 192-197
Deeds
  quitclaim, 609-610
  warranty, 609-611, 1224-1225
Depreciation. *See* Income taxation
Description of land
  apportionment of errors, 583-588
  canons of construction, 572-574
  causes of errors in, 581
  fractional part, 556-557
  government survey, 557-559
  informal, 562-570
  lawyers and, 560-561
  metes and bounds, 555-556, 570-572, 574-581
  monuments
    lost, 558
    noncalled, 582
  multiple description, 559

Index

plane coordinates, 560
plat reference, 559
quantity, 582-583
reformation of, 566, 569, 574-582
resolving errors and ambiguity, 554-555
street numbers, 562-568
streets as boundaries, 574-581
surveyors and, 561
Destruction of premises. *See* Executory interval
"Due-on" clauses, 143-146
Dummies. *See* Strawmen

Economic Recovery Tax Act, 372
Equitable conversion, 545-547
Executory interval
 eminent domain during, 552
 equitable conversion, 536-551
 insurance, 536-553
 proof of title during, 620
 rezoning during, 552
 risk of loss during, 535-553

Federal Home Loan Bank System, 115
Federal Hous. Admin. *See* FHA-insured mortgages
Federally chartered secondary market lenders
 Federal Home Loan Mortgage Corp. (Freddie Mac), 123-124
 Federal Natl. Mortgage Assn. (Fannie Mae), 122-123
 Government Natl. Mortgage Assn. (Ginnie Mae), 124-127
Federal Natl. Mortgage Assn. (Fannie Mae), 120-123
Federal Tax Lien Act of 1966, 704
Federal Sav. and Loan Ins. Corp., 115
FHA-insured mortgages, 113-114, 146
 §203, 133 n.15
 §213, 934
 §221(d)(3), 133 n.16
 §234, 935
 §235, 146
 §236, 146
 warranty of housing quality, 607-608
Financial Institutions Deregulation and Monetary Control Act of 1980, 176-178
Financing conditions, 437-448
Foreclosure of mortgages. *See* Mortgage default
Fraud. *See* Misrepresentation and concealment by insured; Misrepresentation by seller

Government Natl. Mortgage Assn. (Ginnie Mae)
 GNMA-guaranteed mortgage-backed securities programs, 125-127
 the tandem programs, 125
Ground lease
 description, 1055-1056
 goals of the lessor, 1057
 leasehold mortgages
  advantages, 1069-1070
  leasehold mortgage provisions, 1088-1092
  leasehold provisions (un)acceptable to the lender, 1070-1080, 1092-1098
  real or chattel mortgage, 1098
  risks of the leasehold mortgagee, 1098-1115
  subleasehold provisions (un)acceptable to the lender, 1080-1081
  subordination of fee to leasehold mortgage, 1081-1088
 leasehold revaluation, 1058-1066
 taxation of the leasehold interest, 1066-1069

Homes associations
 income tax treatment, 1004, 1006-1009
 legal arrangements, 939-942

Income taxation
 Accelerated Cost Recovery System. *See* depreciation
 classification of real property
  condominiums, 357-358
  cooperative apartments, 1004-1006
  home office, 355
  "not-for-profit" activity, 357-358
  personal residence, 352-355
  property held for the production of income (investment property), 355-358
  property held for use in trade or business, 358-360
  property held primarily for sale to customers, 360-372
 condominiums and homes associations, 352, 355, 357-358, 1004, 1006-1009
 conversion of rental apartments, 1009-1012
 cooperative apartments, 1004-1009
 deferred payment method of postponing taxes, 397-398
 depreciation
  Accelerated Cost Recovery System, 373-376
  collapse of tax shelter, 386-388
  depreciation methods, 376-378

1274   Index

Income taxation *(continued)*
    depreciation recapture, 378-381, 1069
    election to expense assets in lieu of
        depreciation, 384-385
    lessee-built improvements, 1066-1069
    Tax Reform Act of 1969, 380-382
    Tax Reform Act of 1976, 380
    Tax Reform Act of 1984, 410, 417
    tax shelter, 385-388
    installment land contracts, 198, 202-203,
        388-397
    installment sale, 388-397
    investment tax credit, 382-383
    like-kind exchanges, 398-417
    minimum tax, 381-382
    original issue discount, 417-435
    real estate investment trust, 119-120
    real estate syndication, 1166-1178
    rehabilitation tax credit, 383-384
    sale and leaseback, 1117-1149
    tax shelter, 385-388
    wrap-around mortgage, 225-226
Installment land contracts
    advantages to the seller, 197-200, 213
    defective title prior to conveyance date,
        630-635
    hazards to the purchaser, 200-203,
        630-635
    seller's remedies on default
        forfeiture of equity, 347-350, 477-488
        recovery of possession by self-help,
            199-200, 345-347
    tax treatment. *See* Income taxation,
        installment land contracts
    use in farm transactions, 204-205
    use in slum area transactions, 205-212
Insurable title. *See* Title insurance
Insurance, fire, 536-553
Interest rates
    usury, 149-178
    variable-rate mortgages, 146-148
Interstate Land Sales Full Disclosure Act,
    203, 927, 976-977

Land trust, 190-191
Lawyers
    advertising and solicitation by, 87-95
    antitrust restrictions on, 84-85
    approval of contract of sale, 448-453
    client security funds, 34
    conflict of interest in representing buyer
        and seller, 95-109
    curing title defects, 764
    liability for negligent title search or
        examination, 561, 762-763
    monopoly of, 73-84
    occupational regulation generally, 72
    overmeticulous title examiners, 622-623

    preventing description errors, 560-561
    role of in real estate transactions, 65-72
    title search and examination by, 646-647
Leasehold mortgage. *See* Ground lease
Leases
    ground lease. *See* Ground lease
    sale and leaseback. *See* Sale and leaseback
    shopping center lease
        percentage rental, 1037-1055
        restrictive covenants, 1030-1037
Leverage, 133-135
Lis pendens, 503, 688-695
Loan-to-value ratio, 131-135

Marketable title
    abatable title flaws, 545, 612-617, 629-630
    administrative problems, 620-621
    contract for limited liability, 612-617, 624-627
    defined, 858
    encumbrances, nature of, 617-618
    enhancing by suits to quiet title, 751-752
    insurable title, relation to, 613
    meanings of, 608, 617-620
    postcontract zoning change or eminent
        domain, 552
    proof of ownership required for, 619-620
Marketable title acts, 852-881, 918
Mechanized processing of title data, 645,
    770-771, 910-911, 913-914,
    916-919, 928-930
Misrepresentation and concealment by
    insured, 807-823
Misrepresentation by seller, 589, 590,
    601-604, 607
Model Real Estate Cooperative Act, 943, 949
Mortgage commitment, 1230-1234
Mortgage default
    "deed" in lieu of foreclosure, 262-265, 341
    equitable right of redemption, 266, 268, 285
    junior encumbrancer, risks of, 285-286,
        293-295
    mortgage foreclosure
        bankruptcy considerations, 324-339
        constitutionality of power of sale
            procedures, 276-282
        deficiency judgments, 316-324, 342
        effect on tenant's rights, 286-293
        general characteristics, 265
        omitted parties, 282-286
        postforeclosure redemption rights,
            296-315, 342
        receivers, 254-256, 259-262, 340-341
        reform proposals, 340-344

Index

sale price problems, 271-275
types of foreclosure, 188-190, 266-271, 342
wrap-around mortgage foreclosure, 295-296
nonmonetary defaults, 295
Mortgage lenders
  commercial banks, 116-117
  Federal Home Loan Mortgage Corp. (Freddie Mac), 123-124
  Federal Natl. Mortgage Assn. (Fannie Mae), 122-123
  Government Natl. Mortgage Assn. (Ginnie Mae), 124-127
  life insurance companies, 117
  mortgage companies (mortgage bankers), 117-118
  mutual savings banks, 113-115
  possession, rights and obligations when in, 253-259
  preforeclosure rights, 253-265
  real estate investment trusts, 118-121
  remedies of, 253-344
  savings and loan (building and loan) associations, 115
Mortgage market
  construction loans, 116-117, 120-121
  conventional mortgages, 112-113
  FHA-insured mortgages, 112-113
  mortgage lenders, 113-127
  primary market, 112
  secondary market, 112, 121-127
  second mortgages, 112
Mortgages
  alternative mortgage instruments, 181-187
  deed absolute, 192-197
  defined, 188-190
  equity of redemption, 189, 266, 268, 285
  glossary of mortgage terms, 1197-1204
  leasehold mortgage. *See* Ground lease
  "lien" vs. "title" theory, 188 n.20
  mortgage note or bond, 188, 1211-1214
  mortgage provisions (family home), 1215-1223
  mortgage provisions (investment property), 1248-1264
  mortgage with power of sale, 190
  second mortgage, 214-219
  statutory right to redeem, 189, 296-315, 342
  trust deed mortgage (deed of trust), 190-191
  wrap-around mortgage, 219-226
Mortgage terms
  "balloon" mortgage, 180
  credit quartet, 131-180
  down payment and loan-to-value ratio, 131-135
  "due-on" clauses, 143-146
  length of mortgage, 135-146
  level payment debt service, 178-179
  "leverage," 133-135
  method of amortization, 178-180
  mortgage prepayment, 137-143
  open-ended mortgages, 226-232
  rate of interest, 146-178
  self-amortization, 178
  usury, 149-178
  variable-rate mortgages, 146-148

National Assn. of Home Builders, 607
National Assn. of Realtors, 6 n.6, 11, 28-29, 84-87
Notice. *See* Recording acts

Occupational regulation, 72-109
Off-record risks. *See* Recording acts; Torrens registration
Open-ended mortgage
  obligatory future advances, 226-232
  optional future advances, 226-232
Options, 522-523, 527, 546

Partnerships. *See* Choice of entity for real estate ownership
Percentage leases. *See* Shopping centers
Privilege of prepayment, 137-143

Quality
  caveat emptor, 588-590, 605, 609
  express warranty, 600-608
  implied warranty, 590-600

Real estate investment return
  adjusted rate of return, 1194-1195
  internal rate of return, 1190-1195
Real estate investment trust, 118-121
Real Estate Settlement Procedures Act, 852, 924-927
Real estate syndication
  description, 1155-1156
  economic attributes, 1156-1158
  offering statement, 1158-1168
  tax shelter attributes, 1168-1178
Recording acts
  administration, 644-650
  bona fide purchasers. *See* classes of persons protected
  chain of title searches, 667-680
  classes of persons protected, 652-667
  defined, 639-640, 686 n.14
  defrauding of a grantor, effect of, 720-721

Recording acts *(continued)*
  destroyed or missing public records
      notice of, 684-685
    suits to quiet title following, 741-751
  errors in indexing, transcribing, filing,
      667, 675-677, 682-684
  estoppel by deed, 678-679
  examination of premises. *See* possession,
      constructive notice of parties in
  forged instruments, effect of, 721
  general characteristics of, 639-642,
      853-854
  grace periods for recording, 644
  history of, 640-641
  incapacity of grantor, 720
  indexes
    errors in, 667, 675-677, 682-684
    grantor-grantee index, 680-681,
        912-913, 917
    relation to recordation, 681-683
    rule of immateriality, 676-677
    tract index, 680-681, 912, 917
  judgments and other judicial records,
      constructive notice of, 695-699, 704
  liens
    federal tax liens, 700-704
    judgment liens, 698-699, 704
    local and state tax liens, 704
    location of records, 686-687, 915
    mechanic's and materialman's liens,
        704-705, 716-720, 722-723
  notice
    actual and constructive notice defined,
        697-698
    lis pendens, 688-695, 704
    off-record risks, constructive notice of,
        638, 640, 705-723, 902
    public records not required by the
        recording acts, constructive notice
        of, 686-705
    recitals in recorded or other instru-
        ments, constructive notice of,
        672-673
    recording, effect of, 667-686
  off-record risks. *See* notice
  original instruments on file, constructive
      notice of, 684
  possession, constructive notice of parties
      in, 667-670, 698, 705-716
  pretermitted after-born child, effect of,
      721
  prior adverse possession, 721-722
  recommended improvements, 851-930
  recordable instruments, 650-652
  statutes of limitations, adverse posses-
      sion, curative acts, 724-735
  subsequent probated will, effect of, 721
  types of acts: race, race-notice, notice,
      641-644, 670-672, 679-680

unacknowledged instrument, effect of,
    721
void instrument, effect of, 705, 721
weaknesses in, 638, 642, 687-688,
    853-858
Redlining
  Home Mortgage Disclosure Act of 1975
      (U.S.), 128-129
  Home Mortgage Disclosure Act of 1977
      (Conn.), 130-131
Registered titles. *See* Torrens registration
Risk of loss. *See* Executory interval

Sale and leaseback
  accounting treatment, 1120 n.51
  commercial and tax attributes, 1117-1120
  comparison with mortgage, 1116-1117
  description of, 1115-1116
  tax treatment
    bona fides of purchase money
        financing, 1149-1153
    comparison with mortgage,
        1116-1117, 1120-1140
    sale versus exchange, 1140-1149
  variants
    as part of like-kind exchange, 1154
    leaseback of land only, 1153-1154
    lease-layering, 1154-1155
Sale-buyback, 160
Second mortgages, 214-219
Security devices
  deed absolute as mortgage, 192-197
  installment land contract. *See* Installment
      land contracts
  lease. *See* Leases
  mortgage. *See* Mortgages
  sale and leaseback. *See* Sale and leaseback
  trust deed mortgage (deed of trust),
      190-191
Seller's election of remedies, 500-502
Seller's remedies
  election of remedies, 500-502
  liquidated damages clause, 472-492
  rescission, 492-501
  retention of deposit, 472-492
  seller's damages, 468-472
  specific performance, 545, 629
  vendor's lien, 516-517
Seller's title obligation, 608-621
Servicemen's Readjustment Act of 1944,
    113
Settlement statement, 1226-1229
Shopping centers
  percentage leases
    definition of percentage rental base,
        1038-1050
    tenant's duties, 1050-1055
    restrictive covenants, 1030-1037

Index

Slander of title, 504-508
Soldiers' and Sailors' Civil Relief Act of 1940, 318
Sole proprietorships. *See* Choice of entity for real estate ownership
Specific performance. *See* Buyer's remedies; Seller's remedies
Statute of frauds
  assumption of mortgages, requirement of, 239
  broker's listing agreement, requirements of, 4-5, 9 n.39, 46-48, 60-61
  contract of sale, 437-448, 562-570, 607, 617
Statutes of limitations, 724-730, 857-858, 875-876
Stock-cooperatives. *See* Cooperative apartments
Strawmen
  concealment of buyer's identity, 522-523
  liability avoidance
    contract of sale, 518-521
    mortgage, 521-522
Subchapter S corporations. *See* Choice of entity for real estate ownership
"Subject to financing." *See* Financing conditions
Subordination agreements
  fee to leasehold mortgage, 1081-1088
  purchase money mortgage to development financing, 453-468
Suits to quiet title, 735-754
  classification of statutes, 751-752
  due diligence in seeking claimants, 735-741
  following destruction of public records, 741-751
  for Torrens registration, 752
Surveyor liability, 561
Surveys, 69

Tax Reform Act of 1969, 380, 382
Tax Reform Act of 1976, 380
Tax Reform Act of 1984, 410, 417
Time-sharing
  bankruptcy treatment, 1022-1027
  regulation of sale of time-sharing interests, 1017-1021
  types of time-sharing
    interval ownership, 1016-1017
    timespan ownership, 1015-1016
    vacation club, 1014
Title companies. *See* Title insurers
Title insurance
  administration, 765-773
  benefits of, 802-803
  cost. *See* premiums
  coverage. *See* protection provided
  criticisms of, 800-802
  foreign land coverage, 764 n.20
  growth in, reasons for, 764-765
  history of, 764-765
  indemnity, nature of, 803-807
  insurable interest, 816
  litigation expense coverage, 794, 829-844
  loss, 765, 803-845
  misrepresentation and concealment, 807-823
  off-record risks, 705-723, 773
  operations, types of, 764
  policy forms, 774-793
  premiums, 765-766, 794-796, 799, 801-802
  prohibition of, in Iowa, 849
  protection provided, 69, 773-845
  regulation of, 845-851
  reliance on public records, 644-646, 686, 767
  Torrens titles, insured by private companies, 903
  valuation date, 807
Title insurers
  antitrust risks, 849-851
  bar-related insurers, 766, 889
  defense of claim obligations, 794, 829-844
  disclosure obligations, 823-829
  emotional distress liability, 829-844
  opposition to Torrens registration, 883, 891-898
  regulation of, 845-851
  search and examination functions, 646-647, 767-773
  search liability, 823-829
  subrogation rights of, 807
  title clearance obligations of, 829-845
  title plants, 686, 767-773, 850-851
  tort liability of, 823-844
  unauthorized practice of law by, 849-850
Title plants. *See* Title insurers
Title protection, general characteristics, 637-639
Title registration. *See* Torrens registration
Title search and examination
  automation of land title records. *See* Mechanized processing of title data
  chain of title searches, 667-680, 683
  forms of, 646-650
  liability of searchers and examiners, 754-763, 823-845
  occupations performing, 68, 754
  recommended improvements, 911-919
Title standards, 621-623, 857
Torrens registration
  administration, 882-902
  advantages of, 882-883, 889-891, 909-911
  certification procedure, 752, 885-890

Torrens registration *(continued)*
  constitutionality of compulsory registration, 898-902
  exceptions to coverage, 903-907
  extent of in United States, 851, 881-882
  foreign land registration, 881-882, 908-909
  fraud, forgery, theft, effect of, 904-907
  improvements recommended, 909-911
  insurance, 902-903, 907-909
  opposition to, 890-898
  origin of, 883-884
  protection provided, 902-911
Transfers of mortgaged property
  assumption of mortgage, 233-246
  defenses to mortgagee's suit on debt
    discharge of grantor as surety, 246-252
    failure to exhaust other remedies, 252
    subsequent change of the contract of assumption, 252
    usury in the original transaction, 253
  rights of grantor against the grantee, 239-240
  rights of the mortgagee against the grantee, 240-253
    break in the chain of assumption, 243-246
    theories of recovery, 240-242
  subject to mortgage, 233-234
Trust deed mortgage (deed of trust), 190-191

Unauthorized practice of law
  brokers, 73-84
  escrow agents, 83
  lawyers, 83-84
  title insurers, 849-850
Uniform Common Interest Ownership Act, 943, 983, 1003
Uniform Condominium Act, 943, 983
Uniform Federal Tax Lien Registration Act, 703-704
Uniform Land Transactions Act, 498-499, 852, 919-920, 923-924
Uniform Planned Community Act, 943
Uniform Simplification of Land Transfers Act, 851-852, 919-924
Uniform Vendor and Purchaser Risk Act, 537-545
Usury
  choice of laws, 161-167
  corporate-borrower exemption, 167-171
  defense in suit by mortgagee against assuming grantee, 253
  Financial Institutions Deregulation and Monetary Control Act of 1980, 176-178
  historical treatment, 149-152
  penalties, 175-176
  purchase money mortgage exception, 171-175
  what constitutes usury, 152-161
  wrap-around mortgage, 222-223

VA guaranteed mortgages, 113
Vendor's lien, 517-518

Warranty. *See* Quality
Wrap-around mortgage, 219-226, 295-296